W9-CPN-992

THE OXFORD ENCYCLOPEDIA OF
THE BIBLE AND GENDER STUDIES

THE OXFORD ENCYCLOPEDIA OF
THE BIBLE AND GENDER STUDIES
STUDIES

Julia M. O'Brien

EDITOR IN CHIEF

VOLUME 2

PAT–WOM

OXFORD

UNIVERSITY PRESS

OXFORD
UNIVERSITY PRESS

Oxford University Press is a department of the
University of Oxford. It furthers the University's objective
of excellence in research, scholarship, and education
by publishing worldwide.

Oxford   New York
Auckland   Cape Town   Dar es Salaam   Hong Kong   Karachi
Kuala Lumpur   Madrid   Melbourne   Mexico City   Nairobi
New Delhi   Shanghai   Taipei   Toronto

With offices in
Argentina   Austria   Brazil   Chile   Czech Republic   France   Greece
Guatemala   Hungary   Italy   Japan   Poland   Portugal   Singapore
South Korea   Switzerland   Thailand   Turkey   Ukraine   Vietnam

Oxford is a registered trademark of Oxford University Press
in the UK and certain other countries.

Published in the United States of America by
Oxford University Press
198 Madison Avenue, New York, NY 10016
www.oup.com

Library of Congress Cataloging-in-Publication Data
The Oxford encyclopedia of the Bible and gender studies / Julia O'Brien, editor in chief.
2 volumes   cm
Includes bibliographical references and index.
ISBN 978-0-19-020488-4 (v. 1 : alk. paper)—ISBN 978-0-19-020489-1 (v. 2 : alk. paper)—
ISBN 978-0-19-983699-4 (set : alk. paper)   1. Bible and feminism—Encyclopedias.
2. Women in the Bible—Encyclopedias.
I. O'Brien, Julia M., editor.
    BS680.W7O94   2014
    220.8'3053—dc23   2014028030

1 3 5 7 9 8 6 4 2

Printed in the United States of America on acid-free paper

Abbreviations Used in This Work

// or ‖	parallel passages
§	section
Acts	Acts of the Apostles
Add Dan	Additions to Daniel
Add Esth	Additions to Esther
Amos	Amos
ANE	ancient Near East
ASV	American Standard Version
b.	Babylonian Talmud
Bar	Baruch
2 Bar.	*2 Baruch*
Barn.	*Barnabas*
B.C.E.	Before the Common Era (= B.C.)
Bel	Bel and the Dragon
c.	century
ca.	circa
CAD	*The Assyrian Dictionary of the Oriental Institute of the University of Chicago* (Chicago, 1956)
CD	Cairo Genizah, *Damascus Document*
C.E.	Common Era (= A.D.)
cf.	*confer,* compare
ch./chs.	chapter/chapters
1–2 Chr	1–2 Chronicles
Col	Colossians
col./cols.	column/columns
cont.	continued

1–2 Cor	1–2 Corinthians
d.	died
Dan	Daniel
Deut	Deuteronomy
DH	Deuteronomistic History
Did.	*Didache*
DSS	Dead Sea Scrolls
Dtr	Deuteronomist
Eccl	Ecclesiastes
ed.	editor (pl., eds), edition
1 En.	*1 Enoch*
Eng.	English
Eph	Ephesians
Ep Jer	Letter of Jeremiah
1–2 Esd	1–2 Esdras
Esth	Esther
Exod	Exodus
Ezek	Ezekiel
Ezra	Ezra
4 Ezra	*4 Ezra*
f.	feminine
frag.	fragment
Gal	Galatians
Gen	Genesis
Gk.	Greek
Gos. Mary	*Gospel of Mary*
Gos. Phil.	*Gospel of Philip*
Gos. Thom.	*Gospel of Thomas*
Hab	Habakkuk
Hag	Haggai
HB	Hebrew Bible
Heb	Hebrews
Heb.	Hebrew (biblical citations and language)
Hos	Hosea
Isa	Isaiah

Jas	James
Jdt	Judith
Jer	Jeremiah
Job	Job
Joel	Joel
John	John
1–2–3 John	1–2–3 John
Jonah	Jonah
Jos. Asen.	*Joseph and Aseneth*
Josh	Joshua
Jub.	*Jubilees*
Jude	Jude
Judg	Judges
1–2 Kgs	1–2 Kings
KJV	King James Version
Lam	Lamentations
Lat.	Latin
LGBTQIA	Lesbian, gay, bisexual, transgender, queer, intersex, asexual (and/or ally)
Lev	Leviticus
lit.	literally
Luke	Luke
LXX	Septuagint
m.	masculine
m.	Mishnah
1–2 Macc	1–2 Maccabees
3–4 Macc	3–4 Maccabees
Mal	Malachi
Mark	Mark
Matt	Matthew
Mic	Micah
Midr.	*Midrash*
ms/mss	manuscript/manuscripts
MT	Masoretic Text
NA 27	*Novum Testamentum Graece,* Nestle-Aland, 27th ed.

NAB	New American Bible
Nah	Nahum
NAS	New American Standard Version
n.d.	no date
NEB	New English Bible
Neh	Nehemiah
neu.	neuter
NIV	New International Version
NJB	New Jerusalem Bible
NJPS	Tanakh: The Holy Scriptures: The New JPS Translation according to the Traditional Hebrew Text
NKJB	New King James Bible
n.p.	no place
NRSV	New Revised Standard Version
NT	New Testament
Num	Numbers
Obad	Obadiah
Odes	*Odes of Solomon*
OG	Old Greek
OL	Old Latin
OT	Old Testament
P.	Papyrus
p./pp.	page/pages
1–2 Pet	1–2 Peter
Phil	Philippians
Phlm	Philemon
PN	personal name
Pr Azar	Prayer of Azariah
Pr Man	Prayer of Manasseh
Prov	Proverbs
Ps(s)	Psalm(s)
Ps 151	Psalm 151
Pss. Sol.	*Psalms of Solomon*
Q	*Quelle*, a hypothetical source used by Matthew and Luke

Q (preceded by numeral)	Qumran
r.	reigned
Rev	Revelation
rev.	revised
Rom	Romans
RSV	Revised Standard Version
Ruth	Ruth
1–2 Sam	1–2 Samuel
Sg Three	Song of the Three Young Men
Sib. Or.	*Sibylline Oracles*
Sir	Sirach
Song	Song of Solomon
SP	Samaritan Pentateuch
supp.	Supplement
Sus	Susanna
Syr.	Syriac
t.	Tosefta
Tg(s).	Targum(s); Targumic
1–2 Thess	1–2 Thessalonians
1–2 Tim	1–2 Timothy
Titus	Titus
Tob	Tobit
v./vv.	verse/verses
vol./vols.	volume/volumes
Vulg.	Vulgate
Wis	Wisdom of Solomon
y.	Jerusalem Talmud
Zech	Zechariah
Zeph	Zephaniah

THE OXFORD ENCYCLOPEDIA OF
THE BIBLE AND GENDER STUDIES

P

Patriarchy/Kyriarchy

Early in January 2014, a U.K. press report highlighted a statistical imbalance in the ratio of male and female children among certain ethnic minority communities in Britain that suggested that female fetuses were being systematically aborted. Interviews that accompanied the report gave a picture of enormous social and cultural pressure on the women of these communities to produce sons rather than daughters (Connor, 2014). Whatever the truth behind the statistics, the pressure to produce male children instead of females is a disturbing manifestation of patriarchy, a state of affairs that is as widespread as it is pernicious. This article explores some of its ramifications.

Definition: What Is Patriarchy? There are a number of definitions of the term "patriarchy," some of which are more specific than others but not all of which are relevant to the modern enterprise of gender studies. In political thought "patriarchy" has traditionally denoted a hierarchical society in which power resides in the male property-owning father-figure both at the familial level and by extension or parallel at the state level. Thus, a man has legal power over his wife, his children, and his servants/slaves, who are regarded as his property alongside his land; the fathers of the state—that is, its governors and the head of state who are likewise free property-owning males—wield equivalent power over the rest of the state, which consists

not only of elite males but also of women and other subordinate classes including non-propertied males. This explains the origin of the term "patriarchy," which etymologically means the "rule of the father." Ancient Roman society is a good example of a patriarchal constitution, and the picture given in the Hebrew scriptures of society in Iron Age Israel is likewise patriarchal: the biblical legal codes are addressed to males throughout and conceive of men alone as the legal actors, even at one point listing women alongside house, oxen, asses, and servants as men's property (Exod 20:17). In addition, the sign of the covenant between God and Israel of which the laws are supposedly an expression is male circumcision (Gen 17:9–11), which excludes women.

In addition to this strictly political definition, however, patriarchy is also conceived of more widely to refer to a system in which males in general are privileged over women in general. Understood in this sense, the concept of patriarchy has been widely used in feminist writing, and feminists in many areas of study have made it their job to show how the workings of such patriarchy have blighted, and continue to blight, the lives of women. A helpful definition of patriarchy is given by the feminist theorist Sylvia Walby: it is "a system of social structures and practices in which men dominate, oppress and exploit women" (Walby, 1990, p. 20). This definition is sufficiently specific to capture the essence of patriarchy, but sufficiently general to be exemplified in a range of situations. Another definition, framed in terms of a description of what it means to be patriarchal, comes from Allan Johnson: "A society is patriarchal to the degree that it promotes male privilege by being *male dominated, male identified*, and *male centered.* It is also organized around an obsession with control and involves as one of its key aspects the oppression of women" (Johnson, 2005, p. 5; emphasis in original). The key characteristic of patriarchy, as Judith Bennett (2006, pp. 57–58) points out, is that it refers to a situation in which women *as women* are subordinated or disadvantaged in relation to men of the same class. It is not a claim that all women are subordinated to all men, which is clearly not the case; rather, it highlights the fact that women are routinely and systematically disadvantaged in comparison to their male peers. In this sense it is not simply a question of individual males' attitudes toward or treatment of women, nor a question of how individual men or women fare in relation to an absolute standard of power, wealth, or self-determination. Rather, it is about the overarching patterns of advantage and disadvantage that are produced by prevailing attitudes toward males and females and by expectations of how they ought to relate to each other and to wider society. These attitudes and expectations may or may not be explicitly enshrined in law, but they are often implicit in the way that laws are framed and are often more determinative than the law for how individuals behave.

Kyriarchy. In considering how patriarchy functions to disadvantage women, it is important to note that gender-based subordination frequently interacts with other systems of subordination or disadvantage such as those based on race, social class, or religion, thereby creating a range of oppressions that affect certain groups of women disproportionately. The system of disadvantage is therefore much more complex than simply being a question of binary opposition between men and women, since as Elisabeth Schüssler Fiorenza points out it has often been the case that women of color or of lower social status have experienced more oppression from privileged (white) women than from men of their own group,

such white women serving as the conduits for patriarchal values (Schüssler Fiorenza, 1992, pp. 114, 123). Hence, to highlight these other dimensions of oppression that are an integral part of patriarchy but are rendered invisible when focusing purely on gender-based oppressions, Schüssler Fiorenza coined the term "kyriarchy" as an alternative to "patriarchy." If patriarchy is the rule of the father, kyriarchy is the rule of the master (or *kyrios*). Like "patriarchy," the term "kyriarchy" refers to a system of dualistic oppositions that justifies the domination of certain groups by certain other groups, and it certainly includes the domination of females by males. However, it goes beyond gendered domination to refer to a hegemonic male's domination of men and women whom kyriarchal logic has constructed as inferior by definition on account of their racial or social or religious identity.

Moreover, the term recognizes that women who are members of the elite classes are equally capable of behaving in an oppressive manner toward women and men from those classes that are constructed as inferior. This is a critique that has become particularly pointed with the rise of postcolonial perspectives in scholarship, but that is also reflected in the development of womanism and *mujerista* theology, two modes of feminist activism that originated among women in the United States. Womanism is a critique of patriarchal/kyriarchal oppression from the perspective of women of color, and as well as highlighting gender-based oppression it addresses issues of race and class that are overlooked by white "elite" feminism. The term "womanist" was coined by African American writer and activist Alice Walker in 1983. Similarly, *mujerista* theology was established by Ada María Isazi-Díaz in 1987 as a liberational critique that speaks to the experiences of Hispanic women, who in a majority white society are also often oppressed economically and racially as well as on the grounds of their sex.

Androcentrism. A fundamental characteristic of patriarchy/kyriarchy is androcentrism, or male-centeredness. Schüssler Fiorenza defines androcentrism as "a linguistic structure and theoretical perspective in which man or male represents the human" (Schüssler Fiorenza, 2013, p. 102); according to her analysis, "androcentrism characterizes a 'mind-set'," whereas "patriarchy represents a socio-cultural system in which a few men have power over other men, women, children, slaves, and colonized people" (Schüssler Fiorenza, 2013, p. 60). Androcentrism results in the privileging of male interests because it takes the male as the default human being and arranges systems on that basis. As Bem puts it, "males and male experience are treated as a neutral standard or norm for the culture or the species as a whole, and females and female experience are treated as a sex-specific deviation from that allegedly universal standard" (Bem, 1993, p. 41).

Androcentrism is strongly disadvantageous to women in a host of different ways. For example, many career paths in Western capitalist economies assume a pattern of work whereby the employee works consistently long hours on a daily, weekly, and yearly basis, and the greatest rewards (salary and promotion) and securities (pension and other welfare benefits, job security) accrue to those who are able to fulfill such a commitment. But this is a pattern of employment and progress that is based on a male model, in that it makes no allowance for career breaks such as those that are required for childbearing or for the flexibility of working hours that is often needed to manage child-care responsibilities. It is true that in these days of increased awareness of women's rights and equal opportunities, in the United Kingdom employers are legally required to grant maternity leave to women and are not allowed to discriminate against women when recruiting. However, the fact remains that the basic pattern of work assumes a male employee who will not need accommodation for family matters because he has a female partner at home to take care of them. This means that women who do need such accommodation are of necessity disadvantaged in employment and often find themselves faring significantly worse than men in recruitment, in career progress, and in the consequent job-related securities. Indeed, even women who do not actually need accommodation for child care and family responsibilities can be disadvantaged because of an ingrained sense that careers are for men and women should not deprive men of what is rightfully theirs.

Some sense of the disadvantaging of women in career terms can be gained from a briefing paper for the British House of Commons dated 31 May 2013, which gives statistics about the representation of women in public life and the professions (Cracknell, 2013). Taking the university sector as an example, the statistics show that although the number of female academic staff has increased rapidly since 1994, in 2011–2012 women made up only 20 percent of full professors and 39 percent of all other academics. This is despite the fact that according to the statistics compiled by the Government's Higher Education Statistics Agency, 56.4 percent of all students in university-level education in the United Kingdom in 2011–2012 were female. In this as in other areas, therefore, women are disproportionately concentrated at the lower end of the career ladder.

Origins. One of the most vexing issues relating to patriarchy is how it originated. This is important, because if patriarchy and the abuses associated with it are not to be regarded as simply the inevitable result of human beings' essential gendered biological characteristics, there must have been a time when patriarchy did not exist; and this in turn means that it must have had a beginning in time. Gerda Lerner is not alone among feminist theorists in locating the origins of patriarchy—at least for Western civilization—in the move away from tribal societies (who sustained their existence by means of subsistence horticulture and hunting) toward statehood. She postulates a number of factors in the shift toward male dominance of women: (1) the development of animal husbandry, most probably by men, which would have resulted in surpluses of animal products such as pelts for the men who carried it out; (2) the development of agriculture, which was labor-intensive, required a larger workforce, involved activities such as ploughing that were unsuitable for women with children, and generated some surpluses for those (again, probably men) who carried it out; (3) intertribal warfare during times of scarcity, which would have resulted in increased status for the male combatants and their acquisition of surpluses as the result of conquest; and (4) the exchange of women between tribes, which would have served to stabilize intertribal relationships and also to facilitate generation of the larger workforce needed for agricultural subsistence but that contributed toward viewing women and/or their reproductive capacity as commodities. These developments eventually came together in the emergence of archaic states, in which kinship alliances were replaced by class divisions dependent on who owned what and who was in control of the distribution of surpluses. This would locate the beginnings of patriarchy around seven thousand years ago (Lerner, 1986, pp. 36–53; see also Gross, 2009, pp. 165–167; Johnson, 2005, pp. 70–75). Although this might seem an inordinately long period of time over which patriarchy has been operative, it is nevertheless relatively short in the context of the whole of human history and prehistory, suggesting that the development of patriarchy was a response to changes in external circumstances and environment rather than an expression of an innate aspect of human genetic makeup whereby men "naturally" dominate women.

Indeed, archaeological and anthropological studies have provided ample evidence for non-patriarchal societies in which complementary roles for males and females accompany an equitable distribution of power and resources among women and men. Richard Lee and Richard Daly cite the precolonial Native American Iroquois and the modern-day !Kung of Botswana as two examples of tribal hunter-gatherer societies in which men and women have separate roles but equal access to resources. Such societies function largely on the basis of kin groups and would be inoperable without the equal participation of men and women. In terms of food production, men are the hunters, while women gather and grow plants and vegetables, work that can be done along with children. However, the unpredictable nature of hunting means that it is impossible to survive simply on what the men catch, so that for the !Kung people meat is a supplement to the diet rather than its mainstay (Lee and Daly, 1987, pp. 34–35). In such societies, then, women with their horticultural food production play a major and active role in the survival and well-being of the community alongside the men. On the assumption that a similar lifestyle and division of labor would have existed in pre-patriarchal tribal societies, women would also probably have been responsible for a number of technical innovations related to their work of food production, such as basket-weaving and pottery, in order to create means of carrying and storing their produce. They would also have possessed significant knowledge in matters such as healing based on plant pharmaceutical products.

Two features of these societal models should be noted. First, they should not be regarded as matriarchal. Matriarchy is simply an inversion of patriarchal hierarchy that elevates women at the expense of men, whereas these societies are more accurately regarded as egalitarian or (somewhat less idealistically) as non-patriarchal. They do not evidence a privileging of women over and above men; rather, they demonstrate a collaboration between men and women in which both parties share in the tasks that are vital to the well-being of the community as a whole, assisting each other in their respective tasks where necessary and having equal access to the means and fruits of production.

To date, there is no known evidence for a matriarchal society in which women dominated men as men dominate women under patriarchy. Although theorists from the nineteenth-century such as the Swiss scholar Johann Jakob Bachofen (1815–1887) onward have argued for pre-patriarchal matriarchies (Bachofen's book *Das Mutterrecht* was published in 1861), this is not a widely accepted position even among feminist scholars. Indeed, Bachofen's ideas have been discredited because of the mistaken basis for his argument: he assumed that myths such as the Orestes cycle or the defeat of the Amazonian women in which female principles were subjected by males reflected some kind of historical reality: instead of the overthrow of a primordial matriarchy, they may instead be an expression of subliminal anxieties and conflicts in the present (Davies, 2005, pp. 505–506). Not even more recent theorists who are strongly pro-women in their interpretation of the archaeological and other evidence have argued for matriarchies in the full sense. Marija Gimbutas is a good example of a scholar whose controversial and expansively woman-friendly reconstructions of prehistoric society in Old Europe have nevertheless urged an egalitarian rather than a strictly matriarchal society (Gimbutas, 1991). Gimbutas has been criticized for her overly utopian and sweeping reconstructions and for reading too much into the available evidence (Gross, 2009, p. 162; Hogenson, 1991; Thornton, 1999), but even she eschews a matriarchy proper, arguing instead for a matrifocal and matrilineal society centered on worship of the Great Goddess, who was peaceful rather than aggressive and confrontational.

There is general agreement, then, that matriarchy proper has never existed. The precise contours of these non-patriarchal societies would of course have varied from context to context, but all would have operated on the basic principles of shared and cooperative labor and comparable access to skills and resources for both males and females. The fact that such societies have existed and do still exist in some areas indicates that patriarchy is not an inevitable result of the human genetic makeup, but that it is a contingent response to particular historical circumstances and so should be possible to terminate, given the appropriate circumstances.

Biological Factors: Is Patriarchy Natural? The preceding text has indicated that patriarchy should not be seen as biologically determined; it is not the result of immutable and fixed characteristics of men and women that compel humans to interact in ways that subordinate females to males. However, there remains a popular assumption—and indeed, some scientists continue to argue—that there is a biological element to patriarchy; that it is natural for women to be subordinate to men because men are naturally stronger, more dominant, more aggressive, and more intelligent, whereas women are naturally weaker, more passive, more self-effacing and nurturing, and less intelligent. Such assumptions have been common in the West for millennia, largely due to the mistaken and misogynistic speculations of the Greek philosopher Aristotle (384–322 B.C.E.), whose ideas about the physical and mental constitution of women pervaded the Greco-Roman society in which Christianity was born and nurtured and which were adopted by the exponents of this new religion in their dogmatic speculations. Perhaps most famously, Aristotle considered the female to be a "mutilated male" (*On*

the Generation of Animals II.3), a concept that was later repeated by the mediaeval Christian theologian Thomas Aquinas in his *Summa Theologia* 92.1. Aristotle also regarded the human female as inferior to the male, made to be ruled by the male (*Politics* I.5, 12, 13), and as having a smaller brain than the male (*On the Parts of Animals* II.7).

Even though Aristotle's ideas about the physiology of women have been refuted by modern science, the gender stereotypes and prejudices generated by Aristotelian thought have endured in Western society because of their incorporation into Christianity. As a result, even though there is enormous variety among both men as a class and women as a class in terms of their actual physical, emotional, and intellectual characteristics, and even though men and women as classes are emotionally and intellectually comparable and equally capable of undertaking strenuous physical activity, many modern paradigms distinguish emphatically between men and women and form the basis of human socialization from birth. These paradigms are patriarchal in that they conceive of men as physically, intellectually, and socially dominant and women as more delicate, less capable, and made for childbearing and supporting roles. Sadly, advances in biological knowledge have had little effect on deep-rooted, prejudicial ideas about women's basic inferiority to men, and it is this witting or unwitting refusal to accept the possibility of women's comparability to men that fuels the arguments to prove that patriarchy is biologically determined. Indeed, as Carmen Schifellite (1987) argues, such attitudes may well even influence the way that research is undertaken and how its results are interpreted.

Gender roles. As noted previously, patriarchy dictates appropriate behavior for males and females and depends on a strong fundamental differentiation between the two. Indeed, without the maintenance of hierarchical divisions between males and females, patriarchy could not function. While roles for men and women in patriarchal societies are often presented as natural accommodations to each sex's innate predispositions, more recent theorizing has distinguished biological sex from social gender, highlighting the constructed nature of gender as learned and inculcated by constant repetition from an early age. In British or American society, one only needs to think of rough-and-tumble girls being reprimanded for not being ladylike, or of boys being taunted as "girls" for crying or lacking in sporting prowess, to recognize the constant conditioning process for making male and female human beings conform to ideal constructions of masculinity and femininity. Gender-role socialization begins from birth with the toys and clothing colors that the newborn is given, and adults often treat male and female children differently in ways that affect the children's self-perception—for example, by playing more roughly with boys than with girls even at a very early age (see Bem, 1993, p. 34), and encouraging boys to be noisy and active but girls to be quiet and restrained. Because the gender socialization process is so pervasive, it is extremely difficult to determine how much gender-stereotypical behavior is the result of innate predisposition or of socialization. Some individuals may have the innate predispositions deemed appropriate to their sex, but the argument that sexually differentiated behavior emerges from such predispositions is unjustifiable. The realities that gender-role socialization must be learned and continually reinforced and that the standards of acceptable behavior for "men" and "women" differ from place to place clearly indicate how *un*natural gender norms are.

Like other systems of oppression such as slavery, patriarchy persists partly as a result of collusion of those who are oppressed with the system that oppresses them. It is certainly true that women internalize and perpetuate patriarchal values just as strongly as men. Supporters of patriarchal values often claim that women themselves reject feminist demands such as the right to work on an equal basis with men or claims for reproductive rights such as contraception and abortion. Stereotypical patriarchal values about female sexual purity are inculcated into daughters by their mothers, even to the extent that in some African, Asian, and Middle Eastern societies mothers perpetuate practices such as female genital mutilation in order to keep their daughters eligible for marriage (see WHO Fact Sheet No, 241, 2013). Such acceptance of patriarchal practices, however, is a survival mechanism, particularly in societies where women are entirely dependent on men for financial support; although women might wish to change or resist the structures, the very nature of the structures that leave them without power or independent access to resources prevents them from doing so.

Patriarchy and Sexuality. Not only is gender constructed along patriarchal lines; the duality of biological sex itself is likewise a patriarchal construct. Bodies are commonly identified as male or female on the basis of the reproductive organs they possess, but there are significant numbers of individuals who have indeterminate genitalia and cannot be readily identified as one sex or the other. In addition, some perceive themselves to be in the wrong body (i.e., men who perceive themselves as women, and vice versa) and some persons find that their bodies may fit one sex profile in terms of genital identity but another in terms of other characteristics such as height, strength, body hair, breast development, and so on. Biological sex is therefore much more accurately regarded as a continuum or spectrum than as a dichotomy between male (strong, superior) and female (weak, inferior). As is the case with gender, the constructedness of patriarchal dualistic sexuality can be seen from the enormous amounts of time and money that are spent by both men and women on physical training and medical and cosmetic procedures to make their bodies conform more closely to the supposed norms for their sex. Bodies of "men" and "women" do not just happen; they are painstakingly created and carefully maintained.

Homosexuality, prostitution, double standards. Given this painstaking cultivation of dualistic sexuality both in terms of gender roles and biological sex, it is understandable that patriarchy cannot tolerate deviations from the model, such as homosexuality or lesbianism, that destabilize it. Men whose sexual desire is for another man and women who desire another woman both undermine patriarchal constructions of hegemonic masculinity by highlighting the fragility of such constructions. Gay men threaten "real" men both by putting other men in the position of women—that is, under sexual scrutiny from someone of equal or possibly greater power—and by allowing themselves to be used as women (that is, as the receptive partner in sexual congress). Gay women threaten "real" men by being unreceptive to their sexual advances. Gays and lesbians blur the boundaries of sex and gender, and in patriarchal terms they embody a feminization of patriarchal heterosexual masculinity.

Patriarchal sexuality, then, is configured in exclusively heterosexual terms, in which males have the prerogative of sexual initiative and sexual dominance. Such norms create distinctive configurations of both male and female sexuality: female sexuality is regarded as belonging to males, and male virility is measured in the number of female conquests a male can achieve. It thus promotes a notorious double standard of patriarchal sexuality whereby males are entitled, even expected, to have free sexual access to multiple women while women are expected to maintain virginity before marriage and chastity within it; they can be severely punished for failing to do so, even when their supposed failure is the result of coercion. The tension between these incompatible expectations for male sexual access and female sexual seclusion is resolved to some extent by means of prostitution, which allows males to have sexual access to a wide range of women while their own women remain chaste. Because of her sexual availability the prostitute is thus a despised but necessary figure in the patriarchal construction of sexuality. The effect of this construction of male–female relationships is to separate the recreative, pleasurable aspects of female sexuality from its reproductive, mothering aspects, so that women are defined as either mothers or whores, and female sexual pleasure is associated with unchastity. The biblical story of the patriarch Judah and his daughter-in-law Tamar (Gen 38) is a good example of this double standard: Judah is perfectly happy to visit a prostitute himself, but when he hears that his widowed daughter-in-law Tamar is pregnant because of prostitution he orders her to be burnt.

Patriarchy and Religion. The discussion thus far has focused on social expressions of patriarchy and the human elements in it. However, the religious dimension of patriarchy is also noteworthy. It is fairly widely agreed that a society's religious systems will reflect and legitimize its social ideals, and so it is not surprising that patriarchal societies often have strong male divinities. Nonetheless, societies whose pantheons include female as well as male deities are not necessarily less patriarchal; female deities in a polytheistic pantheon can be allocated to quite subservient positions, and the chief deity can be a male with a consort, thus modeling patriarchal marriage notions. Even the presence of powerful female deities in a mixed pantheon does not in itself guarantee an egalitarian social structure; the religious systems of ancient Greece and Rome, for example, included powerful female as well as male deities, and yet both societies were highly patriarchal. However, on the positive side, the presence of goddesses creates an association between woman and the divine and gives space for women as religious actors. A good example of this is the festival known as the Thesmophoria celebrated by women (more precisely, the wives of citizens) in ancient Athens in honor of the earth mother goddess Demeter and her daughter Kore or Persephone. The rites appear to have involved sacrificing pigs, which symbolized female sexuality (Parker, 2007, p. 275), letting them rot in a pit together with imitation male genitals made of dough, and collecting some of the remains of the previous year's pig and dough offerings to spread on the fields at sowing time (pp. 272–273). According to Robert Parker, the festival, from which men were specifically excluded, gave its female participants the glory of being in charge of the rites on which the fertility of the fields depended—no small privilege—as well as relating to women's own fertility (pp. 279–280).

Monotheism. If polytheism provides some mitigation for women of patriarchal structures, however, there is a strong link between monotheism and the enforcement of patriarchal societal values. Indeed, monotheism itself is almost always patriarchal; until the emergence of the modern Western goddess movement in the late twentieth century, a female monotheistic deity was unknown. The three main monotheistic religions of the current era—Judaism, Christianity, and Islam—all have a lone male deity who embodies the principles of divinity and takes upon himself the functions of both male and female but who in his controlling and organizing function is most readily seen as male. This is highly significant, for in the famous words of Mary Daly, if God is male, then the male is god (Daly, 1973, p. 19). By having a male monotheistic deity, masculinity is associated with divinity, strength, control, and divine right, whereas femininity is associated with humanity, weakness, fallibility, and the need to be controlled and to obey. The idea of female inferiority is thereby given divine sanction, making it much harder to combat in environments where patriarchal monotheism is a significant factor.

Summary. Patriarchy is, then, a complex, multifaceted and all-encompassing phenomenon that permeates the fabric of many a modern society and has a strongly detrimental effect on the well-being of millions. Even though much progress has been made in Western societies such as the United Kingdom and the United States toward challenging patriarchal structures and correcting the balance of injustice, there is still a long way to go. Legal reforms are to be welcomed, but often they can only address the symptoms of patriarchy rather than treating its cause, which is in the deeply engrained attitudes of both men and women. Real change will come about only with a change of attitude, together with a commitment from those who wield political and especially economic power, to enable a more egalitarian state of affairs.

[*See also* Gender; Heteronormativity/Heterosexism; Intersectional Studies; Masculinity and Femininity, *subentries on* Early Church *and* Greek World; Mujerista Criticism; Religious Participation, *subentry* Greek World; Transgender/Third Gender/Transsexualism; *and* Womanist Criticism.]

BIBLIOGRAPHY

Bem, Sandra Lipsitz. *The Lenses of Gender: Transforming the Debate on Sexual Inequality.* New Haven, Conn., and London: Yale University Press, 1993.

Bennett, Judith M. *History Matters: Patriarchy and the Challenge of Feminism.* Manchester, U.K.: Manchester University Press, 2006.

Christ, Carol P. "'A Different World': The Challenge of the Work of Marija Gimbutas to the Dominant World-View of Western Cultures." *Journal of Feminist Studies in Religion* 12, no. 2 (1996): 53–66.

Connor, Steve. "The Lost Girls: Thousands of 'Missing' Girls Revealed by Analysis of UK 2011 Census Results." *The Independent* 14 January 2014. http://www.independent.co.uk/news/science/the-lost-girls-thousands-of-missing-girls-revealed-by-analysis-of-uks-2011-census-results-9059905.html

Cracknell, Richard. "Women in Public Life, the Professions and the Boardroom." House of Commons Library SN/SG/5170, last updated 31 May 2013. http://www.parliament.uk/business/publications/research/briefing-papers/SN05170/women-in-public-life-the-professions-and-the-boardroom

Daly, Mary. *Beyond God the Father: Towards a Philosophy of Women's Liberation.* Boston: Beacon, 1973.

Davies, Peter. "Myth and Maternalism in the Work of Johann Jakob Bachofen." *German Studies Review,* 28 (2005): 501–518.

Gimbutas, Marija. *The Civilization of the Goddess: The World of Old Europe.* Edited by Joan Marler. San Francisco: HarperCollins, 1991.

Goodison, Lucy, and Christine Morris, eds. *Ancient Goddesses: The Myths and the Evidence.* Madison: University of Wisconsin Press, 1998.

Gross, Rita M. "The Prepatriarchal Hypothesis: An Assessment." In *A Garland of Feminist Reflections: Forty Years of Religious Exploration,* pp. 156–170. Berkeley: University of California Press, 2009.

Hayden, Brian. "Old Europe: Sacred Matriarchy or Complementary Opposition?" In *Archaeology and Fertility Cult in the Ancient Mediterranean: Papers Presented at the First International Conference on Archaeology of the Ancient Mediterranean, the University of Malta, 2–5 September 1985,* edited by Anthony Bonanno, pp. 17–30. Amsterdam: B. R. Grüner, 1986.

Higher Education Statistics for the United Kingdom 2011/12. http://www.hesa.ac.uk/content/view/2993/393/

Hogenson, George B. "The Great Goddess Reconsidered." *San Francisco Jung Institute Library Journal* 10, no. 1 (1991): 5–24.

Isasi-Díaz, Ada María. *En la Lucha/In the Struggle: Elaborating a* Mujerista *Theology.* 2d ed. Minneapolis: Fortress, 2003.

Johnson, Allan G. *The Gender Knot: Unraveling Our Patriarchal Legacy.* Rev. ed. Philadelphia: Temple University Press, 2005.

Lee, Richard, and Richard Daly. "Man's Domination and Woman's Oppression: The Question of Origins." In *Beyond Patriarchy: Essays by Men on Pleasure, Power, and Change,* edited by Michale Kaufman, pp. 30–44. Toronto and New York: Oxford University Press, 1987.

Lerner, Gerda. *The Creation of Patriarchy.* New York: Oxford University Press, 1986.

Moghadam, Valentine M. *Patriarchy and Development: Women's Positions at the End of the Twentieth Century.* Oxford: Oxford University Press, 1996.

Nye, Andrea. *Feminist Theory and the Philosophies of Man.* London: Croom Helm, 1988.

Paper, Jordan. *The Deities Are Many: A Polytheistic Theology.* Albany: State University of New York Press, 2005.

Parker, Robert. *Polytheism and Society at Athens.* Oxford: Oxford University Press, 2007.

Schifellite, Carmen. "Beyond Tarzan and Jane Genes: Toward a Critique of Biological Determinism." In *Beyond Patriarchy: Essays by Men on Pleasure, Power, and Change*, edited by Michael Kaufman, pp. 45–63. Toronto and New York: Oxford University Press, 1987.

Schüssler Fiorenza, Elisabeth. *But She Said: Feminist Practices of Biblical Interpretation.* Boston: Beacon, 1992.

Schüssler Fiorenza, Elisabeth. *Changing Horizons: Explorations in Feminist Interpretation.* Minneapolis: Fortress, 2013.

Thornton, Bruce. "The False Goddess and Her Lost Paradise." *Arion*, 3d ser. 7, no. 1 (1999): 72–97.

Walby, Sylvia. *Theorizing Patriarchy.* Oxford: Blackwell, 1990.

Walker, Alice. *In Search of Our Mothers' Gardens: Womanist Prose.* New York: Harcourt Brace Jovanovich, 1983.

World Health Organization. Fact Sheet No. 241: Female Genital Mutilation, updated February 2013. http://www.who.int/mediacentre/factsheets/fs241/en/

Deborah W. Rooke

PAUL

There are not many explicit statements in the undisputed letters of Paul (to which this article is confined) concerning gender issues. But the interpretation of the few that can be found have had a significant impact in subsequent history, not only at the level of scriptural interpretation but also in communities and societies that were decisively shaped by interpretations and ethics derived from biblical traditions. Church and state authorities have referenced Pauline statements in declaring the legitimacy of gendered hierarchies and respective appropriate behavior. Perceptions and attitudes over against women, same-sex relations, and men who did not conform to the majority image of masculinity were sanctioned—with reference to Paul. The use of Paul and his letters in support of gender discrimination rendered him a problematic figure for emerging gender-sensitive approaches (i.e., feminist biblical interpretation). It is an uneasy relationship, burdened with a problematic reception history, with detrimental implications for all who did not cohere with certain standard perceptions of the "ideal" man.

Initial debates about Paul and gender concentrated on Paul's perception of women and their roles in the early Christ-movement, with positive and negative evaluations, depending on the respective hermeneutical presuppositions; these were complemented in a second stage by analyses that considered structural dimensions of Pauline discourses such as his rhetoric and its relevance in relation to gender issues; a further strand advocated that the relevance of gender issues could not be confined to women's issues but should include his theologizing in general. Broadly speaking, thematic and structural dimensions are the two major strands in all subsequent gender-sensitive studies on Paul, with numerous intersections, complemented by additional recent focal points in biblical interpretation, such as empire studies, postcolonialism, and more recently masculinity studies, as well as Paul's Judaism. This article will thus focus on the following: (1) Paul and women, (2) structure and gender, (3) intersections, and (4) particularity, universalism, and gender.

Paul and Women. Early examination of Paul and gender emerged with the arrival and growing recognition of feminist approaches in biblical studies with their focus on uncovering the hidden histories and voices of women. Although feminist interpretation found liberating dimensions in the Gospels, Paul provided difficulties in this respect. Earlier feminist interpreters struggled with the tensions between Paul's statements about women and his apparent cooperation with them (e.g., Rom 16). The explicit gender hierarchy advocated in 1 Corinthians 11:2–16, paired with the command that women should be silent in the assembly (1 Cor 14:33–35, if not considered an interpolation), was considered the main cause for the reintroduction of hierarchies generally, and of gender hierarchies in particular, into an originally egalitarian movement of equals. The reasons for this were variably attributed either to Paul's familiarity with Greek or Hellenistic thought

(Martin, 1995; Boyarin, 1994) or to his Jewish heritage generally or some specific rabbinic training (see discussion in Ehrensperger, 2004). However, it has been clearly demonstrated that claims that such statements were the result of Paul's supposed rabbinic training are completely unhistorical and anachronistic (Levine, 2006, p. 178).

Nevertheless, without such anachronistic presuppositions, Paul has still been seen as the one who distorted the original ethos of the Christ-movement through the introduction of hierarchical structures into the Christ-movement (Schüssler Fiorenza, 1983, p. 233, and 1999, pp. 149–173). This is considered particularly problematic since it is seen as having led to the oppression of other voices, particularly those of women (Kittredge, 1998; Wire, 1990). Paul is seen as a Hellenistic thinker who is shaped by concepts of essential hierarchical dualisms, which impact decisively on Paul's perception of gender (Castelli, 1991; Boyarin, 1994).

Rather than focusing on Paul's explicit statements about women, Schüssler Fiorenza and MacDonald have also concentrated on Paul's actual cooperation with women, which is considered quite remarkable given the first-century context of Paul's activities. MacDonald (1999) foregrounds Paul's actual recognition of women in leadership roles over against his explicit statements, which are seen as being of less relevance since they did not seem to have impinged on Paul's actual appreciation and recognition of the role of women in the Christ-movement. It seems evident that Paul's actual relation to women in the Christ-movement points to a more egalitarian practice than his actual statements would indicate. He certainly accepts women in leadership roles according to the list of Romans 16. Wire has questioned that this is also the case in Corinth, where she rather sees him as trying to diminish the influence and power of such leading women (Wire, 1990).

Some recent research into the status and role of women in Judaism has added further insights not only to women's leadership roles but also to some of Paul's explicit statements. Ilan (2006) has drawn attention to parallels between Paul's arguments about intermarriage between Christ-followers and outsiders in 1 Corinthians 7 and similar Pharisaic stances.

She found that this is affirmed in a discussion of whether Pharisee men or women could remain or get married to members of the *am-haaretz*, in that the status of the insider is seen as not affected by the status of the outsider. Moreover, Paul's inclusive practice of table fellowship is seen as rooted in Pharisaic inclusive table-fellowship traditions, as is his acceptance of women in leadership roles (Ilan, 2006; Brooten, 1982). Paul's guidance concerning women's active participation in community gatherings also shows analogies to general practice in synagogue assemblies. It is evident according to biblical texts (e.g., Ezra 2:65; Neh 7:67; Jdt 15:12–13) as well as Second Temple Literature (Philo, *Decal.* 32; *Mos.* 1.180; 2.256; Josephus, *Ant.* 14.258; 14.260) that women were part of the synagogue assemblies on a sabbath and were active participants through singing and praying as were men. The issue differs when it comes to reading and interpreting the scriptures; this is a role and task assigned to men of special knowledge (*Omn. Prob. Lib.* 81–82). Paul's stance in 1 Corinthians 11, which clearly assumes active participation of women in the assemblies, and in 1 Corinthians 14:33–35, which seems be in contradiction to the previous passage, may reflect this difference in gendered activities. 1 Corinthians 14:33–35 might be directed at some involvement in teaching and learning activities of women rather than being a general call to silencing women in the assemblies of Christ-followers (Ehrensperger, 2014). Rather than introducing new restrictive roles into the Christ-movement, Paul here could be seen as providing guidance to his gentile communities in analogy to community practice with which he was familiar.

The diverse ways in which Paul's explicit and implicit stances in relation to women have been approached demonstrate the significance of critical reflection on the hermeneutical presuppositions that frame interpretation as well as the significance of in-depth research into the first-century context of Paul's writing. In as much as Greek and Roman culture and practice are important and must be considered, Paul's Judaism has only just begun to be explored in this respect but is proving to be important for many aspects of Paul's dealings with women (Ehrensperger,

2014). However, the focus on Paul's explicit and implicit statements concerning women is not the only relevant field from a gender-sensitive perspective. There are aspects of Pauline discourses that are highly relevant in this respect, in terms of theological content as well as at a structural level (Schottroff, 1996; Sutter Rehmann, 2000; Ehrensperger, 2004).

Gendered Structures. Since gender permeates any discourse and shapes perceptions, perspectives, and evaluations, Pauline discourse has been recognized as a gendered discourse and analyzed as such. Structural aspects of Paul's way of arguing have been moved to center stage, particularly in approaches that highlight hierarchies and power in Pauline rhetoric. Thus Paul's call to imitation is interpreted as a request to mimicry or a discourse of sameness through which the apostle is perceived as having claimed superiority and established a dominating hierarchy over his communities. This interpretation is based on the presupposition that Paul's imitation language followed Greek perceptions of *mimesis*, including the notion that the achievement of sameness is the ideal of imitation. This attributes a superior and unattainable status to the model, that is, the apostle, because perfect sameness with him cannot be attained by any member of his communities (Castelli, 1991, pp. 86–89). According to this perception, a static, dominating hierarchy was advocated by Paul in the vein of the male elite ideology of Greco-Roman culture. Also presupposing predominantly Greco-Roman influence, Kittredge (1998) concludes that Paul's rhetoric of obedience replicates the obedience discourse of the dominating imperial male elite culture. This is clearly a discourse of subjugation and submission deriving from the ideology of conquest, and based on this presupposition, the conclusions in relation to Pauline discourse are plausible and have already been argued by Bultmann and Käsemann (see discussion in Ehrensperger, 2007, pp. 155–158).

In a similar although different vein, Marchal (2006) analyzes the letter to the Philippians structurally as a friendship letter, oriented on the Greco-Roman ideal of friendship, which, rather than being merely a relationship of equals, shared with explicit patron-client relationships hierarchical mechanisms of authority and control. The friendship rhetoric in this letter is seen as veiling conflict between Paul and the Philippians rather than expressing a special bond and thus was a means through which Paul tried to re-establish his authority and control over this community. Paul presents himself in the vein of the ideal man of the imperial elite who thereby imposes his power on the predominantly gentile community, which is thus in the position of the dominated female.

A replication of imperial structures of domination by Paul is also found in his rhetoric of community/*ekklesia* construction (Økland, 2004). Økland argues that Paul constructs the *ekklesia* as communal public space, thus replicating the gendered public (male)/private (female) space of the dominating culture. In her analysis of 1 Corinthians 11–14, real women are not in focus but "women" are seen as being used "to think with" in support of the construction of the public/male *ekklesia* space. Through the construction of *ekklesiai* as public/male spaces, Paul is seen as replicating dominating gender hierarchies. But since Paul seemed to have taken the unity of men and women in this male *ekklesia* space for granted, Økland concludes that the women through their presence could subvert this structure and create nevertheless some alternative "women's space" within the *ekklesia*.

Approaches that predominantly focus on the structure of Paul's way of arguing tend to contextualize his discourse as either embedded in, or influenced by, the dominating Greek and Roman elite ideology. Through the structural and linguistic parallels identified from within this context, it is concluded that Paul mainly replicates, or certainly contributes to the replication of, imperial male-dominated power structures. Thus, Pauline discourse is seen as gendered in accordance with the imperial ideology and practice with Paul in the assigned position of the subject in the dominating, male position. There can be no doubt that this gendered image of Paul has had a massive impact in reception history. Unlike in the approaches described above, this image, rather than being considered problematic, was considered the universally applicable or true image of Paul. What is evaluated in its problematic implications for gender perceptions in these recent approaches was advocated as the authoritative image of Paul in mainstream Christendom. Significantly, this male-dominated image of Paul was inherently intertwined with the image of Paul as a lonely hero whose theology had overcome the particularistic constraints of Judaism (Schottroff, 2004; Johnson-DeBaufre and Nasrallah, 2011). This image of Paul has sometimes been replicated by early feminist approaches in that the anachronistic perception of Judaism, in its role as a negative foil for Christian self-understanding, served to depict a law-free gospel advocated by Paul as liberating women from patriarchal Jewish constraints such as purity laws (for a discussion see Schottroff, 2004).

Intersections. As noted above, different hermeneutical presuppositions and contextualizations thus contribute significantly to the perception of Paul and gender. If structural aspects are rendered central and read as analogous to Greek and Roman dominating patterns, a male-gendered Pauline discourse is uncovered. It is thus not a surprise that if the presuppositions and contextualization of Paul are envisaged differently, this has also implications for the dimension of gender inherent to his discourse. As far as Paul's explicit statements concerning women are concerned, it has been demonstrated that they can well be placed within Jewish traditions of the time. But rather than seeing this as a fallback into pre-Christian traditions, which Paul should actually have overcome through the so-called law-free gospel he advocated, this contextualization demonstrates the diversity of roles and perceptions of women in Judaism. The knowledge and understanding of first-century Judaism is thus decisive for a sociohistorically informed understanding of Paul's statements and relation to women in the early Christ-movement.

Other aspects of Paul's theologizing also have been read without the presupposition of a separation of the early Christ-movement from Judaism, nor of a contextualization of the Pauline discourse primarily within Greek and Roman ideologies and patterns, nor in accordance with these. Empire studies have found aspects of Paul's language as resonating with imperial ideology but, rather than replicating it, explicitly or implicitly challenging it. Thus,

Elliott (2008) has advocated that Pauline discourse, although resonating with imperial ideology, claimed its key terminology for characteristics of life in Christ and thus challenged and subverted the imperial ideology and its totalizing claims. An alternative to the imperial ideology and domination is thus being formulated and, rather than replicating the domination system, Paul's discourse radically subverted it. Elliott's approach is part of an interpretive tradition indebted to scholars such as Georgi (1997). Paul's embeddedness in Judaism is recognized in such approaches; his theologizing is thus not perceived through the lens of the opposition between a particularistic and legalistic Judaism and a universal, law-free gospel. Rather, the antithesis is between imperial ideology and actual domination and the message of the gospel.

Although overcoming the interpretation of Paul in antithesis to Judaism is to be welcomed from a gender-sensitive perspective, the anti-imperial stance found in Paul has been critically questioned by feminist scholars in two aspects in particular. The inversion—or as Georgi had formulated it, the "turning upside down" of imperial terminology—does not amount to an actual change of the discourse per se. It just exchanges roles, but the rhetoric of domination and submission remains in place, albeit now in the service of the Christ-movement. Thus, imperial patterns of arguing and acting are reintroduced into the Christ-movement and could be and have been exploited to that effect as subsequent reception history demonstrates. This is the caveat highlighted by approaches such as Marchal's mentioned above. Intertwined with this critique is the note that the gendered dimension of the imperial discourse has not been addressed in most anti-imperial approaches to Paul.

In the wake of the recognition of the gendered dimensions of Greco-Roman ideology, interpretations began to focus on masculinity discourses in Paul's letters. Paul the man as well as Pauline rhetoric were the focus of analyses by Clines (2003), Larson (2004), Glancy (2004), and Lopez (2008), to mention only a few. Whereas Clines analyzes the man Paul according to set categories identified by him as clear indicators of manliness in biblical literature (strength, violence, powerful and persuasive speech, male bonding, womanlessness) and concludes that the image of Paul (in his letters and the book of Acts) coheres with these categories, Larson and Glancy have demonstrated that compared with the elite Greek and Roman ideal of masculinity, Paul fails to cohere with these at almost every level. His "boasting of beatings" renders him a figure of contempt, his self-declared foolishness (2 Cor 11) can hardly serve as an example of self-assertion, and his failure to deliver his message in impressive rhetorical performances disqualifies him from credentials expected of any orator, namely the ability of expressing the power of the words through respective masculine body language (Glancy). Paul's lack of the expected masculine credentials as evident in his beaten, weak body demonstrates clearly the gendered character of the power play at stake in the debates about his apostleship in the Corinthian correspondence. Paul enters the ring of competition reluctantly and presents as his credentials unmanly or effeminate characteristics.

The focus on the image of Paul the man draws attention to the fact the Roman imperial discourse was itself a gendered discourse par excellence. The claim to exercise power and domination over others was formulated in a gendered way: the ideal man of the Roman elite was depicted as the one who had the right and strength to force others into subjugation, whether these are competitors, women, slaves, children, or conquered peoples. Competition for dominating power was at the heart of this masculinity discourse, infusing society with an ethos of a fierce striving for male honor. The losers in this competition were degraded to femininity, to a servile status of shame and contempt. This also applied to conquered peoples, as Lopez (2008) has demonstrated, and was visualized in Roman imperial art of conquered nations as violently subjugated women. Paul was a member of such a subjugated people, and he proclaimed a message of someone who was tortured to death on a Roman cross. The accumulation of femininity according to the dominating imperial discourse could hardly be more explicit. In this contextualization, Paul is thus seen as a Jewish man, which as such disqualifies him from cohering to the ideal of masculinity of the dominating power. In

addition, he cannot present the bodily credentials required of a manly leader according to the dominating discourse; the recognition of one crucified accentuates the inversion of the dominating gendered discourse of Roman imperialism. According to Lopez this inversion happened for Paul at his "conversion," which she interprets as the conversion from identification with violent imperial imposition of control against those who differ, that is, from an ideal of impenetrable masculinity to embracing a "feminine" stance. Through this experience he places himself at the bottom of the imperial hierarchy, in solidarity with the defeated and colonized. One might question this interpretation of Paul's calling experience because Paul before and after his call was a member of a defeated and colonized nation, but the emphasis on the gendered dimension of the imperial discourse and the contextualization of Paul and of his activities among, and letters to, members of other conquered nations in relation to this discourse provide numerous valuable insights.

The dimension of Paul's Judaism is recognized by some of the approaches that draw attention to Paul's masculinity in the context of the gendered imperial discourse. However, the recognition of Paul's Judaism is relevant in light of the question of gender not only because Paul is acknowledged as a member of a conquered people, but also in a wider sense. This tradition had developed an alternative discourse of meaning and ethos of life based on its scriptural traditions over a long period of interaction with and distinction from dominating imperial powers (Rajak, 2009; Ehrensperger, 2013). The masculinity advocated by Roman and other imperial powers was not merely replicated in this tradition. The image of Paul, the feminized apostle as the man who does not cohere to the dominating ideal of imperial masculinity, resonates clearly with images of leaders in scriptural narratives who also do not conform to the latter. Leading male characters do not display any of the characteristics of the imperial ideal of masculinity. Leaders like Moses, David, or prophets are ambiguous, vulnerable, deceitful, and at times failing human beings (Ehrensperger, 2007). That this was the tradition of a conquered nation made it all the more prone to contempt from an imperial perspective, but it is most likely that Paul's understanding of his role, as well as his interpretation of the cross and of the Christ-event as such, was embedded in such Jewish traditions.

Particularity, Universalism, and Gender. Not only clearly identifiable notions of gender or gendered discourses in the Pauline letters are relevant in light of the question of gender. As noted above, there are trajectories in Paul's way of doing theology that merit further attention. A number of aspects highlighted in Pauline interpretation (although rarely recognized in relation to gender questions) deserve attention here: the fact that Paul's letters are actual letters, addressed to particular communities at a particular moment in time, indicates that they are examples of concrete theologizing. This coheres with emphases in feminist approaches that theologizing is a search for meaning in relation to the context of the concreteness of everyday life in all its aspects. The fact that Paul's letters are part of an ongoing conversation provides insight into "theologizing in process," although only in fragments. Both the emphasis on the necessity of theology to relate to concrete life in its particularity and the notion that theologizing and interpretation are ongoing processes, ideally in the form of conversations over meaning, are dimensions that have been emphasized by gender-sensitive approaches. The fact that the letters of Paul are communal, that is, sent by small groups of people to communities, provides glimpses of insights into collective rather than individual leadership (Ehrensperger, 2007; Kittredge, 2003; Johnson-DeBaufre and Nasrallah, 2011). The fragmentary character of the Pauline letters, their communal dimension (both on the part of the senders and on the part of the recipients), and their concrete particularity are highly relevant structural factors in light of gender-sensitive approaches.

Although all dimensions of Paul's (and his colleagues') theologizing require consideration in light of gender, the aspect of Paul's theologizing that will be highlighted here is the emphasis on the recognition of particularity of and in his letters. It is an aspect that is structurally, as well as in terms of the message Paul conveys, significant in light of the question of gender.

There is growing recognition that the Pauline letters are addressed to gentiles, or members of the non-Jewish nations, and thus are "particular" not only in that they are addressed to specific communities, but also in the sense that the communities addressed were founded by himself (apart from Romans) and thus were predominantly "gentile." Paul considered his call to have commissioned him to convey the *hypakoēn pisteōs* of the "nations" (Rom 1:5) and was careful not to go beyond the boundaries set to him (Rom 15:20). Paul's guidance and explanations are particular in the sense that they address Christ-followers from the nations and thus must consider their particular context of life and understanding. In contrast, the message Paul and his colleagues proclaim is part of the Jewish social and symbolic universe, as are the senders of the letters. The challenge the senders face is to convey a message out of a Jewish context of life and understanding to a gentile audience. Thus, they are involved in a process of cultural translation (Ehrensperger, 2013). Evidently Paul strongly defends the particular identity of Christ-followers from the nations over against any notions that to be part of this movement they would have to become Jews. But with the same clarity, Paul never argues or expects that Jews would cease to be Jews when joining the Christ-movement.

According to Paul, particularity, be it Jewish or gentile, is not considered a problem that needs to be overcome in Christ. Having identity, values, and commitment of a particular people, the Jews are not considered an obstacle for peace and reconciliation between people who are different, nor are the identity and values of Christ-followers from the nations a problem per se, except that they have to "turn away from idols" (1 Thess 1:9). Although the latter certainly had major implications at an everyday level for those from the nations, Paul consistently and repeatedly insists that Jews and gentiles retain their identity in Christ, that they remain in the calling in which they were called (1 Cor 7:17). The recognition of Jewish and gentile identity in Christ is the recognition of particularity and difference. At the heart of the earliest Christ-movement is thus not a hegemonic claim to sameness, but the recognition of unity and equality in difference. Neither Jew nor Greek must assimilate to the identity of the other for unity and reconciliation to be possible in Christ. "Never to put a stumbling block or hindrance in the way of another" (Rom 14:13), not to injure one another (Rom 14:15), but to accommodate to one another (Rom 15:2), and to welcome one another (Rom 15:7) are certainly not calls to assimilate to the identity of the other or to become the same. Recognition and respect for others in their difference is a prerequisite for understanding, reconciliation, and unity. It means to recognize that there is no such phenomenon as a universal human being in this earthly existence—there are only particular human beings in particular places at specific moments in time.

The recognition of particularity in Paul's theologizing is a decisive aspect for approaches that try to overcome any universalizing hegemonic tendencies in contemporary interpretation and for gender-critical approaches in particular. Feminist approaches have criticized universalizing interpretations of Paul (Castelli, 1991), although these were attributed to Paul rather than to his (male) interpreters. The so-called traditional image of Paul considered him the champion of universalism, understood as a hegemonic discourse of sameness with particularity being the problem that was overcome in Christ (for a discussion see Ehrensperger, 2004). Universalism and particularity tend to be considered mutually incompatible, just as diversity and particularity are considered the obstacle to unity—which could only be overcome through an eradication of difference and particularity. The notion of oneness in Christ (Gal 3:28) is interpreted as that which overcomes difference and particularity. Such universalizing tendencies in interpretation not only denied recognition to Jewish identity but also continued to legitimize androcentric gender perceptions in that the ideal generic human being was conceptualized according to the dominating elitist template of masculinity. Those who did not conform to this image, whether men or women, would not be granted equal respect because their difference was considered a hindrance to full humanity. The ideal Christian could be neither Jewish nor female. The image of the ideal elite (Roman) man dominated Western societies for centuries and Christendom integrated this

image into its value system. This universalization of a particular male ideal had detrimental effects for women, for Jews, and for peoples who eventually became subject to European colonization, as well as for men who did not conform to this image of masculinity.

The universalization of a particular image of men as representing humanity as such imposed assimilation on those who were different or exposed them to contempt and humiliation. Feminist theory and gender studies, from their beginnings, have used a variety of approaches on identity to critically reveal the flaws of universal definitions of human beings on one hand and of the "othering" of women and gay men in the wake of such definitions on the other. Although the difficulty with defining identity permeates gender studies as well as other disciplines trying to address such issues, it can be said with some confidence that there is a consensus in feminist theory and gender studies that inherent to the recognition of the contextuality of human existence is the omnipresence of gender in all social interactions and processes in the form of variations of a theme. Without resorting to essentialized or biologist notions of gender in terms of characteristics, roles, or sexuality, the social and contextual dimension of human existence includes the embodiment of gender in various ways. Gender is not an abstraction, but is always concrete and thus particular, embodied or "inhabited" by men and women in particular ways within the contexts of their societies.

An analogy can be drawn between the universalization of the image of the so-called ideal elite man as the template for being human and the universalization of the non-Torah-oriented way of life as the one and only way of life in Christ. Both are universalizations of particulars and thus are discourses of assimilating domination. To declare a particular embodiment or way of life universal means to ignore, eradicate, or otherwise delegitimize any other form or way of life, not only at the level of linguistic discourse but also in actual reality. The contempt and at times violent oppression of women, Jews, non-elite men, and homosexuals are expressions of similar efficacies of universalizing notions and practices.

The recognition of particularity as being at the center of the Pauline letters is thus an important step in light of gender-sensitive perspectives because it resonates with the latters' emphasis on embodiment and the particularity of human experiences, practices, and perceptions. Although the emphasis in the Pauline letters is on the recognition and respect of particularity and diversity as constitutive of unity in Christ of Jews and non-Jews, this emphasis in and of itself challenges the notion of an assimilating sameness discourse at the center of the early Christ-movement. Paul himself did not draw out these implications in relation to gender. However, in light of contemporary gender questions there is no reason not to draw implications of this emphasis by analogy. The passage often referred to in so many discussions, Galatians 3:28, has been interpreted as meaning that the identity of Jews and Greeks is rendered "obsolete," or given up in Christ. Only rarely has such an argument been advocated in relation to male and female (e.g., Boyarin, 1994). Gender diversity thus has not been considered a problem in Christ, and the question must be asked, then, why the particular forms of life of Jews or Greeks should be rendered obsolete. The issue is not the particularity of these diverse identities but discrimination against others based on them. The focus on particularity is a concern in gender studies as well as in the Pauline letters. This is thus an important, although certainly not the only, intersection, for Paul, Pauline studies, and the question of gender.

[*See also* Feminism, *subentry* Second-Wave Feminism; Gender; Historical-Critical Approaches; Imagery, Gendered, *subentry* Pauline Literature; Intersectional Studies; Legal Status, *subentry* New Testament; *and* Rhetorical-Hermeneutical Criticism.]

BIBLIOGRAPHY

Boyarin, Daniel. *A Radical Jew: Paul and the Politics of Identity.* Contraversions 1. Berkeley: University of California Press, 1994.

Brooten, Bernadette J. *Women Leaders in the Ancient Synagogue. Inscriptional Evidence and Background Issues.* Chico, Calif.: Scholars Press, 1982.

Castelli, Elisabeth A. *Imitating Paul: A Discourse of Power.* Literary Currents in Biblical Interpretation. Louisville, Ky.: Westminster John Knox, 1991.

Clines, David J. A. "Paul, the Invisible Man." In *New Testament Masculinities*, edited by Stephen D. Moore and Janice Capel Anderson, pp. 181–192. Semeia Studies 45. Leiden, The Netherlands: Brill, 2003.

Ehrensperger, Kathy. *That We May Be Mutually Encouraged: Feminism and the New Perspective on Paul.* New York: T&T Clark International, 2004.

Ehrensperger, Kathy. *Paul and the Dynamics of Power: Communication and Interaction in the Early Christ-Movement.* Library of New Testament Studies 325. New York: T&T Clark, 2007.

Ehrensperger, Kathy. *Paul at the Crossroads of Cultures: Theologizing in the Space-Between.* Library of New Testament Studies 456. New York: T&T Clark, 2013.

Ehrensperger, Kathy. "The Question of Gender: Relocating Paul in Relation to Judaism." In *Paul within Judaism: A Post-New Perspective Approach to the Apostle.* Edited by Mark D. Nanos and Magnus Zetterholm. Minneapolis: Fortress, 2014.

Elliott, Neil. *The Arrogance of Nations: Reading Romans in the Shadow of Empire.* Paul in Critical Contexts. Minneapolis: Fortress, 2008.

Georgi, Dieter. "God Turned Upside Down." In *Paul and Empire: Religion and Power in Roman Imperial Society*, edited by Richard A. Horsley, pp. 148–157. Harrisburg, Pa.: Trinity Press International, 1997.

Glancy, Jennifer A. "Boasting of Beatings (2 Corinthians 11:23–25)." *Journal of Biblical Literature* 123, no. 2 (2004): 99–135.

Ilan, Tal. *Silencing the Queen: The Literary History of Shelamzion and Other Jewish Women.* Texte und Studien zum antiken Judentum 115. Tübingen, Germany: Mohr Siebeck, 2006.

Johnson-deBaufre, Melanie, and Laura Nasrallah. "Beyond the Heroic Paul: Toward a Feminist and Decolonizing Approach." In *The Colonized Apostle: Paul Through Postcolonial Eyes*, edited by Christopher D. Stanley, pp. 161–174. Paul in Critical Contexts. Minneapolis: Fortress, 2011.

Kittredge, Cynthia Briggs. *Community and Authority: The Rhetoric of Obedience in the Pauline Tradition.* Harvard Theological Studies 45. Harrisburg, Pa.: Trinity Press International, 1998.

Kittredge, Cynthia Briggs. "Rethinking Authorship in the Letters of Paul: Elisabeth Schüssler Fiorenza's Model of Pauline Theology. In *Walk in the Ways of Wisdom: Essays in Honor of Elisabeth Schüssler Fiorenza*, edited by Shelley Matthews, Cynthia Briggs Kittredge, and Melanie Johnso-deBaufre, pp. 318–333. Harrisburg, Pa: Trinity Press International 2003.

Larson, Jennifer. "Paul's Masculinity." *Journal of Biblical Literature* 123, no. 2 (2004): 85–97.

Levine, Amy-Jill. *The Misunderstood Jew: The Church and the Scandal of the Jewish Jesus.* New York: Harper Collins, 2006.

Lopez, Davina C. *Apostle to the Conquered: Reimagining Paul's Mission.* Paul in Critical Contexts. Minneapolis: Fortress, 2008.

MacDonald, Margaret Y. "Reading Real Women through the Undisputed Letters of Paul." In *Women and Christian Origins*, edited by Ross Shepard Kraemer and Mary Rose D'Angelo, pp. 199–220. New York: Oxford University Press, 1999.

Marchal, Joseph A. *Hierarchy, Unity, and Imitation: A Feminist Rhetorical Analysis of Power Dynamics in Paul's Letter to the Philippians.* Academica Biblica 24. Atlanta: Society of Biblical Literature, 2006.

Martin, Dale B. *The Corinthian Body.* New Haven, Conn.: Yale University Press, 1995.

Økland, Jorunn. *Women in Their Place: Paul and the Corinthian Discourse of Gender and Sanctuary Space.* Journal for the Study of the New Testament Supplement Series 269. New York: T&T Clark, 2004.

Rajak, Tessa. *Translation and Survival: The Greek Bible of the Ancient Jewish Diaspora.* New York: Oxford University Press, 2009.

Schottroff, Luise. "Gesetzesfreies Heidenchristentum— und die Frauen? Feministische Analysen und Alternativen." In *Von der Wurzel getragen: Christlich-feministische Exegese in Auseinandersetzung mit Antijudaismus*, edited by Luise Schottroff and Marie-Therese Wacker, pp. 227–245. Biblical Interpretation Series 17. Leiden, The Netherlands: Brill, 1996.

Schottorff, Luise. "'Law-Free Gentile Christianity'— What about the Women? Feminist Analyses and Alternatives." In *A Feminist Companion to Paul,* edited by Amy-Jill Levine, pp. 183–194. Feminist Companion to the New Testament and Early Christian Writings 6. London and New York: T&T Clark 2004.

Schüssler Fiorenza, Elisabeth. *In Memory of Her: A Feminist Theological Reconstruction of Christian Origins.* New York: Crossroad, 1983.

Schüssler Fiorenza, Elisabeth. *Rhetoric and Ethic: The Politics of Biblical Studies.* Minneapolis: Fortress, 1999.

Sutter Rehmann, Luzia. "German-Language Feminist Exegesis of the Pauline Letters: A Survey." *Journal for the Study of the New Testament* 79 (2000): 5–18.

Wire, Antoinette C. *The Corinthian Women Prophets: A Reconstruction through Paul's Rhetoric.* Minneapolis: Fortress, 1990.

Kathy Ehrensperger

POLITICAL LEADERSHIP

This entry contains six subentries: Ancient Near East; Hebrew Bible; Greek World; Roman World; New Testament; *and* Early Church.

Ancient Near East

This article will discuss the role of gender in the political leadership of the first millennium B.C.E. Near East during the rule of the two large empires: the Neo-Assyrian Empire (934–612) and the Neo-Babylonian Empire (612–539). All dates in the article are B.C.E. Political leadership is here viewed on two levels: (1) social reality and the process of governmental and institutional decision making and (2) the construction of imagined reality regarding gender and kingship, in other words gender ideology and royal ideology.

There is an interesting discrepancy between imagined reality and what actually took place in the Neo-Assyrian court. Quantitatively speaking, arenas relating to writing were masculine spheres of action—the majority of persons appearing in the texts are men. However, there is little qualitative difference in the ways in which elite women and men acted in the palace administration. Ideologically, femininity was seen as silent and subservient, but when we look at the evidence from the palaces this is not at all the image we get.

Social rank influenced a person's responsibilities more than gender. Overall, it seems that the ties between political power and the construction of gender were fluid in first-millennium Mesopotamia. In other words, rules were different for elite women such as queens. Iconography portrayed them as politically powerful as well as feminine. This portrayal is unequivocally supported by the textual evidence describing the social reality.

The imagined reality of masculinity—vocal and martial—was closely linked to royal ideology. An important part of depicting the king was depicting him as a warrior, which in turn had a very clear connection to masculinity. How strong the connection was to the actual social reality (i.e., a king's actual actions) is, of course, difficult to assess. Certainly, on a more general level, such portrayals of idealized masculinity seem to have been in accord with the social reality.

Evidence. Regarding the Neo-Assyrian Empire, most of our textual evidence dates to the Sargonid dynasty (721–612). The palace archives from Nineveh (mostly published in the State Archives of Assyria series, hereafter SAA) include such genres as letters, treaties, loyalty oaths, oracular queries, legal transactions, administrative records, astrological reports, and literary texts. Royal inscriptions (most recently published in the Royal Inscriptions of the Neo-Assyrian Period series) as well as archives from the administrative centers of the provinces (e.g., Kalhu, published in the Cuneiform Texts from Nimrud series) are preserved as well. We have only a few private or temple archives.

Much of southern Mesopotamia was intermittently controlled by the Neo-Assyrian Empire in 747–626. Throughout this period, the male—and possibly even female—elite of certain long-established cities (e.g., Sippar, Babylon, Borsippa, and Nippur) enjoyed special privileges that apparently even the Neo-Assyrian monarch was expected to honor. A successful rebellion ended Assyrian control and by 626 Nabopolassar had secured the Babylonian throne. After a decade of fighting, in 616, he launched an attack against Assyria. Medes joined in and Nineveh, the capital city of Assyria, was sacked in 612. The last resistance was overcome in 608.

There is also a wealth of evidence from the Neo-Babylonian era (612–539). The majority of Neo-Babylonian archives have been recovered either from the temple of Šamaš in Sippar or from Ištar's temple in Uruk. Many texts come from private archives of the Babylonian elite, but a state archive has also been found. Babylonian royal inscriptions and the so-called Babylonian Chronicles (ca. 744–549) offer a glimpse of historical events. Babylonian archives often extend into the Achaemenid period in Mesopotamia (with the language form changing from Neo- to Late Babylonian), attesting to continuity in the area.

Most spheres of life that are documented were male dominated, which means that women appear rarely in the sources. Of approximately 50,000 names in Neo- and Late Babylonian texts, roughly 2 percent are feminine (approximately three quarters of these belong to slaves). Consequently, less than 5 percent (ca. 700) of Neo-Assyrian individuals known by name are female. Nonetheless, women do appear in most kinds of text genres and in many roles. There are few text genres that exist in both empires in sufficient quantities to enable direct comparison between Neo-Assyrian and Neo-Babylonian eras. Regarding financial transactions, there is some comparable evidence, but as far as political leadership is concerned, most of our first-millennium evidence is Neo-Assyrian.

Naturally, our evidence mostly documents the actions of the elite: the officials in palaces and temples and the members of wealthy families. Both men and women of the elite bought, sold, leased, borrowed, lent, and traded both land and other commodities during the Neo-Assyrian and Neo-Babylonian eras. Generally speaking, both men and women had full legal rights, although autonomy in the modern sense should not be posited. Individuals practically always acted for a family, which was usually headed by a male. However, there is no evidence that women would have needed explicit permission from a male guardian to engage in financial transactions. As was common throughout Mesopotamian history, sons inherited more of the family's assets, whereas daughters were given dowries by their family. In addition to financial transactions, both men and women could have official duties in the administration of the empire or the temples. As in texts describing financial transactions, men form the overwhelming majority in the evidence regarding administration and temple positions. At the same time, most married women had concerns that men did not: child care, organization of the household, and maintenance of domestic religious practices, as well as possible involvement in the production of goods for the family or the family business (e.g., textiles). A sphere of action that was particularly masculine was warfare. From a gender perspective, questions of why and how some women do enter male arenas are crucial and connect gender to other factors, such as status.

Neo-Assyrian and Neo-Babylonian Royal Families and High Dignitaries. Much of our evidence regarding Neo-Assyrian royal offspring relates to the crown prince. He needed to demonstrate ability as well as descent from the male line of royal family, although he did not need to be a direct descendant of the ruling king. In the "Succession Palace" he was schooled and prepared for his eventual kingship. The crown prince had his own staff and, depending on his age and experience, could lead armed forces and take care of varied administrative and cultic duties as well. He was still working under the supervision of the king, but (like the queen) he was an important asset for controlling the realm. The wife of the crown prince, designated "Lady of the House," had a household as well. She, the crown prince, and apparently other members of the royal family (both male and female) received at least a basic education in scribal arts.

Neo-Assyrian royal daughters and other female members of the royal family (not including the queens) are known from 30 texts, 19 of which mention daughters. The earliest of these is a dedication to Ištar of Kidmuri by the sister of Ashurnaṣirpal II (883–859). The most prominent figure among these royal daughters is Šeru'a-eṭirat, the daughter of Esarhaddon, best known for her letter to the wife of the crown prince (SAA 16 28). Royal daughters were involved in rituals and financial transactions and are mentioned in administrative texts and letters. If they remained in court, they could exert considerable influence, but their involvement in foreign policy was limited to marriages to foreign leaders.

More than seventy texts also attest to the existence of female administrative staff, some of whom—especially the female administrator of the queen (*šakintu*)—wielded considerable influence in the running of the palaces. However, women in administrative offices are heavily outnumbered by men and none of the "magnates," the most important officials of the realm, was female.

From the Neo-Assyrian period, there is also evidence regarding female tribal leaders. Numerous Chaldean, Aramaean, and Arabic tribes wielded considerable influence in Mesopotamia during the first millennium. Some of these tribes had female leaders (*šarratu*, literally "queen"). There are altogether nineteen references to them, most of which appear in the annals of Assyrian kings, citing their position as vassals or military opponents.

Compared with the Neo-Assyrian Empire, there is little information regarding the royal family and high officials in the political sphere of the Neo-Babylonian Empire, mainly because much of the material still remains unpublished and palace archives are rare. Three of the daughters of Nebuchadnezzar II (604–562) are known to us. The best-known is Kaššaya, whose name appears in six texts, whereas Innin-eṭirat and Ba'u-asitu are both attested only once each. Nebuchadnezzar's son ruled only for two years, after which he was supplanted by his brother-in-law, Neriglissar. Some circumstantial evidence suggests that Kaššaya was the daughter married to Neriglissar. This marriage alliance would have been important for Neriglissar, first as a way to gain support for his coup and later for legitimation of his rule.

Neriglissar's daughter Gigitu was in turn given in marriage by her father to a certain Nabû-šum-ukin, who belonged to the highest echelons of the priestly elite in the city of Borsippa. The urban elite of Babylonian cities had become important political players under the rule of the Neo-Assyrian kings. Therefore, the marriage constituted a beneficial alliance for both families. Since the marriage agreement (the only known document that mentions Gigitu) is dated to the first day of the first month of the reign of Neriglissar, one is even tempted to speculate that the marriage was a reward for aiding Neriglissar's coup.

The last Neo-Babylonian king, Nabonidus (555–539), had no blood ties with the previous royal families. In the second year of his reign, he installed his own daughter as the *ēntu* priestess in the temple of the moon-god Sîn in Ur. It seems possible that this nomination, an almost forgotten custom in the Neo-Babylonian period, was part of Nabonidus's effort to elevate the cult of the moon-god (as shown below, this objective is also evident in his mother's pseudo-biography), which was traditionally eclipsed in Babylonia by the cult of the national god Marduk. It was also a time-honored tradition in Mesopotamia to place relatives in positions of power to bolster the influence of the dynasty. Some archival texts from Sippar and one from Uruk refer to other daughters of Nabonidus, two of whom are known by name: Ina-Esagil-rimat and Akkubuzaba.

The royal daughters of the Neo-Babylonian period played similar roles to their Neo-Assyrian counterparts. They appear as landowners and as contributors to the temple of Ištar of Uruk, the goddess Nanaya, and the Ebabbar temple in Sippar. From the point of view of political leadership, their marriages served to cement strategic alliances. However, whereas the Neo-Assyrians married foreign kings, the Neo-Babylonian kings used their daughters to solidify internal alliances, perhaps because of the relative turbulence of the Neo-Babylonian period. The establishment of Nabonidus's daughter as the *ēntu* of Ur can be seen as part of the same trend.

Neo-Assyrian Queens and Mothers of Kings. The Neo-Assyrian Empire was led by the king, the vice regent of the national god Aššur. Ideologically at least, all political power flowed from the king and he was responsible for all aspects of cultic, military, and administrative activities. On practical terms, however, the highest officials of the country, the magnates, played a key role in managing the administration of Assyrian provinces and the army. Additionally, scholars receiving the patronage of the king offered him advice based on interpretation of divine signs, which indicated the will of the gods. A separate category was formed by the queen (literally "the woman of the palace," MÍ.É.GAL, *sēgallu*) and the crown prince (literally "the son of the king," *mār šarri*). Their households were closest to the king and highest in court hierarchy. Other members of the royal family could be influential as well, but these two are the only family members with a constant tradition of a full branch of administration working under their supervision.

The queen's household had extensive land holdings and offices throughout the empire, employing hundreds of people. This household was not the personal property of the woman herself; it was the title of queen that carried with it a large governmental office. Cited as the highest-ranking member of the court after the king, the queen supported the temple institutions, engaged in cultic activities, and was involved in making political decisions. After the rule of Sennacherib, the queen also came to have her own military units. Staff headed by a female administrator (*šakintu*) was employed by the queen. The queen's household resembled the households of the magnates as far as administrative and economical activities were concerned.

There are only a few depictions of Neo-Assyrian queens. Queens are portrayed with a mirror, which was a feminine symbol. A specifically Neo-Assyrian symbol carried by queens was the mural crown. This represented political dominion. Furthermore, queens are depicted in texts and iconography as enthroned, generally a sign of reverence in Mesopotamian imagery. This is a clear indication of their importance. The symbology of the throne and mural crown must be interpreted in context of texts that describe the social reality: Neo-Assyrian queens were deeply involved in the governing of the state, as can be seen from the wide economic and administrative reach of their households, the specific vocabulary related to them, and their involvement in political decisions. It would seem that the queens appropriated symbols of rulership that were usually used by males. Such symbols and actions expanded the sphere of political power, extending it into the queen's realm.

The queen is mentioned in about 120 texts. As a general rule, it seems that there was only one queen in the Neo-Assyrian realm at any given time, yet circumstantial evidence suggests that the queen may have continued as the head of the queen's household even after her spouse was replaced by a new king. The strongest evidence for this is seen with Queen Naqi'a, also known by her Akkadian name as Zakûtu. She was the head of the queen's household during the reigns of three consecutive kings: Sennacherib (704–681), Esarhaddon (680–669), and Ashurbanipal (668–ca. 630). During the reign of her son Esarhaddon, Ešarra-ḫammat (the spouse of Esarhaddon) assumed the title until her death in 672. After that, Naqi'a took over again and carried out the duties of the queen at least until the early part of her grandson Ashurbanipal's reign.

Naqi'a is perhaps best known from the text known as the "Treaty of Zakûtu." It states that Naqi'a/Zakûtu bound Ashurbanipal's brothers, the whole court, and even the whole nation in unswerving loyalty to the new king Ashurbanipal, who is called her "favorite grandson" in the text (SAA 2 8). This is unique in Mesopotamia and although it is not the only evidence we have regarding Naqi'a's important role in governmental decision making, it is certainly the clearest. Naqi'a's extraordinary authority in the Neo-Assyrian court might have been part of Esarhaddon's plan to bolster his mother's status to enable her to smooth the road for the kingship of Ashurbanipal. Although Naqi'a stands out from the body of Neo-Assyrian evidence, she is not alone. There is still debate whether Sammu-ramat, the mother of King Adad-Nirari III (810–783), was a co-regent with her son. In any case, however, she did go on a military campaign with him, and together they erected a monument to commemorate their victory.

The body of textual and iconographical evidence on the Neo-Assyrian queen suggests that her position was important throughout that era. Queens like Naqi'a and Sammu-ramat are easily highlighted as exceptions. Perhaps because of a specific historical situation or their own personalities, they were able to extend their influence further than other queens, but their activities were qualitatively the same as those of other, lesser-known, queens. For although Neo-Assyrian queens engaged in financial and administrative duties, both the vocabulary and the content of texts—as well as iconography—also associate them with political power.

Additionally, the queen, the mother of the king, and the crown prince were important for royal ideology. Hints of this can be observed especially in the portrayal of the queens in public monuments and rituals, as well as in their role as guarantors of legitimate succession (e.g., Treaty of Zakûtu). On the other hand, their absence from most royal inscriptions and narratives probably relates to the masculine nature of Mesopotamian kingship.

Adad-Guppi and the Legitimization of Kingship. The reverence of Neo-Babylonian King Nabonidus for the moon-god Sîn is emphasized in the pseudo-biography of his mother Adad-Guppi, which was composed after her death in 574 and inscribed on a

stele as part of the restoration project of the temple of Eḫulḫul, dedicated to the god Sîn, in the city of Harran. The text does not include any reference to the father of the king, although Nabonidus mentions him in his inscriptions.

All in all, the text exalts Adad-Guppi's piety in serving the moon-god in Harran. Sîn's decision to return to Harran and restore the Eḫulḫul temple is portrayed as a just reward for Adad-Guppi. She is described as a loyal worshipper of Sîn, for which the god selected her son for kingship and granted her the longevity of a centenarian. It seems that she was part of the Babylonian court, attending both Nebuchadnezzar and Neriglissar. The text also says that she introduced her son to these kings and that he served them well, although no specific position is mentioned. The funeral inscription further recounts how Nabonidus in turn promoted his mother in court and how Nebuchadnezzar and Neriglissar exalted her "as though [she] had been a daughter born of their loins" (Beaulieu, 1989, p. 69). Interestingly, immediately after this passage the text proceeds to recount the deaths of Nebuchadnezzar and Neriglissar, with nobody performing the proper offerings for the deceased until Adad-Guppi took charge. Since funerary offerings were traditionally the responsibility of the direct descendants of the deceased, it is possible that the author intended to present Adad-Guppi as the adopted daughter of the kings.

An age-old tradition in Mesopotamia was to legitimate kingship through blood relationship to previous kings. It seems clear that Nabonidus's father was not mentioned for a reason: Nabonidus's attempt to legitimize his claim for kingship was specifically through his mother, who was portrayed as a worthy king's mother on two counts, her daughter-like relationship to the previous kings and her piety.

The mother-son relationship between Nabonidus and Adad-Guppi has an explicit connection with Neo-Assyrian royal ideology. In the Neo-Assyrian tradition, mothers were portrayed as the guarantors of legitimate succession because of their great piety. The significant difference here, of course, is that Adad-Guppi is not presented as the queen of the previous king. Instead, she is portrayed as their adopted daughter. There are also other points of connection with Neo-Assyrian queens. Like Neo-Assyrian queens, Adad-Guppi appears in a literary genre usually reserved for kings and she acted in ways that were commonly the province of the king alone. In this context, it is not insignificant that Nabonidus himself apparently saw his rule as part of the great continuum of Mesopotamian rulers, including the last great Assyrian kings.

In the case of Sammu-ramat and Naqiʾa, in addition to the legitimization of their sons' rule, they played a part in the politics of the country. Whether Adad-Guppi also wielded power in the Neo-Babylonian social reality remains an unanswered question.

Assessment. Neo-Assyrian and Neo-Babylonian source materials differ, but there are some common trends that can be identified. In this essay, political leadership is viewed both from the perspective of social reality and from the ideological perspective. Contrasting "ideology" with "social reality" is too simplistic a methodological approach, but here it serves as a useful departure point since portrayals of kingship, femininity, and masculinity can hardly be accepted at face value.

The imagined masculine gender—militant and vocal—is well represented in the texts describing social reality. The majority of evidence relates to activities of individuals grammatically identified as male. Men form the bulk of office holders, are the sole holders of the highest administrative positions, and dominate military affairs.

This evidence on social reality supports the Assyrian ideological construction of femininity as timid, obedient, and silent. However, when examined more closely, it becomes apparent that women of high social rank acted in similar ways as men of high social rank. Their financial activities were similar and both could hold offices in palaces or temples. Female officials and female members of the royal family—most prominently the queen—could have an authoritative role in the making of political and institutional decisions.

Finally, a few words on the royal ideology are needed. Kingship was portrayed with strong ties to masculinity and warfare. The head of state was always male

and royal women are mostly absent from royal narratives of warfare and building endeavors. Nonetheless, occasionally women (especially the king's mother) could appear in the royal narratives as vocal and decisive agents, jarring the gender ideology. Most often this break in gender ideology related to legitimization of kingship; in other words, the actions of women were important to the legitimatizing narrative of kingship. Even the Babylonian Creation Epic can be interpreted from this point of view, as a cautionary tale of a queen (the deity Tiamat) who attempts to oust her children from kingship, introducing her spouse as the new king. In the social reality of the first millennium, queen as king-maker was a recurring trope. It was expected and appropriate to make one's son a king, but illegitimate and wrong to elevate one's spouse.

[*See also* Deity, *subentry* Ancient Near East; Education, *subentry* Ancient Near East; *and* Religious Leaders, *subentry* Ancient Near East.]

BIBLIOGRAPHY

Bahrani, Zainab. *Women of Babylon: Gender and Representation in Mesopotamia.* London: Routledge, 2001.

Beaulieu, Paul-Alain. *The Reign of Nabonidus King of Babylon 556–539 B.C.* New Haven, Conn., and London: Yale University Press, 1989.

Beaulieu, Paul-Alain. "Women in Neo-Babylonian Society." *Canadian Society for Mesopotamian Studies Bulletin* 26 (1993): 7–14.

Beaulieu, Paul-Alain. "Baʾu-asītu and Kaššaya, Daughters of Nebuchadnezzar II." *Orientalia* 64 (1998): 173–201.

Holloway, Steven, JoAnn Scurlock, and Richard Beal, eds. *In the Wake of Tikva Frymer-Kensky.* Piscataway, N.J.: Gorgias, 2009.

Macgregor, Sherry Lou. *Beyond Hearth and Home: Women in the Public Sphere in Neo-Assyrian Society.* Helsinki: Neo-Assyrian Text Corpus Project, 2012.

Melville, Sarah. *The Role of Naqia/Zakutu in Sargonid Politics.* Helsinki: Neo-Assyrian Text Corpus Project, 1999.

Parpola, Simo, and Robert Whiting, eds. *Sex and Gender in the Ancient Near East: Proceedings of the XLVIIe Rencontre Assyriologique Internationale.* Helsinki: Neo-Assyrian Text Corpus Project, 2002.

Radner, Karen. "Assyrian and Non-Assyrian Kingship in the First Millenium B.C." In *Concepts of Kingship in Antiquity: Proceedings of the European Science Foundation*

Exploratory Workshop, edited by Giovanni Lanfranchi and Robert Rollinger, pp. 25–34. Padua, Italy: Sargon Editrice e Libreria, 2010.

Roth, Martha. "Marriage and Matrimonial Prestations in First Millennium B.C. Babylonia." In *Women's Earliest Records: From Ancient Egypt and Western Asia*, edited by Barbara Lesko, pp. 245–344. Atlanta: Scholars Press, 1989.

Steele, Laura. "Women and Gender in Babylonia." In *The Babylonian World*, edited by Gwendolyn Leick, pp. 299–316. New York and London: Routledge, 2007.

Svärd, Saana. "Power and Women in the Neo-Assyrian Palaces." University of Helsinki, February 2012. https://helda.helsinki.fi/bitstream/handle/10138/29538/powerand.pdf?sequence=1

Wunsch, Cornelia. "Women's Property and the Law of Inheritance in the Neo-Babylonian Period." In *Women and Property in Ancient Near Eastern and Mediterranean Societies*, edited by Deborah Lyons and Raymond Westbrook. Cambridge, Mass.: Center for Hellenic Studies, Harvard University, 2003. http://chs.harvard.edu/wb/1/wo/b1gCdaKi6bfYMB17PLxJKo/0.1.

Saana Svärd

Hebrew Bible

The question of evidence troubles discussions of women's political roles in antiquity. What evidence of female political leadership do biblical texts provide? Does such evidence attest to female exclusion or to the biases of the writers? Should female figures such as prophetesses and queens be understood as representative of women in ancient history? Can we read between the lines or excavate countertraditions that suggest greater political autonomy for women prior to state formation and the consolidation of its justifying narrative? Does a female oral tradition at times interrupt the stories of male covenant and heroism? Is evidence itself a gendered concept?

Biblical evidence is of a textual nature. Although the texts are not attributed to authors and are arranged according to a loose plot of progress, decline, and revival, many biblical scholars are deeply committed to ideas of authorship and the notion of competing or, at least, different sources comprising the Hebrew Bible. Assuming such an approach, one can assess how specific sources treat the question of female political leadership.

Harold Bloom suggested that a woman wrote the J source and conferred considerable social authority to female characters. Although biblical scholars have questioned Bloom's literary analysis of the evidence, Carol Meyers, in a reading informed by the archaeological record, has shown how the early J source represents female participation and equality in labor and household leadership.

The Nation in Priestly Texts. In Priestly texts, women are expressly or tacitly addressed by purity laws, but it seems that the very definition of Israel as a nation is predicated on the effacement of the female. The category of the female is a component part of the Priestly creation story—"male and female He created them" (Gen 1:27 JPS) and women also contribute to the establishment of the Tabernacle, a sacred event long recognized as a reflex of creation.

The sacred space of the Tabernacle constitutes the center of the nation in the opening of the Priestly book of Numbers. Because the tribes are arranged in fixed positions along the circumference of the Tabernacle, they appear as constituent parts of a larger unified whole. The national configuration is clarified as Moses conducts a census, which, according to divine command, is to encompass all of Israel. The heads of everyone in the entire community of Israel are to be counted and situated according to clan, ancestral house, and individual (Num 1:2). The individual is singled out according to the male exclusive term *zakhar*, which lacks the female analog *neqevah* present at creation. This means that "the entire community of Israel" that becomes manifest through the census contains no women (Num 1:2).

The opening census of the book of Numbers is based on the effacement of women, but it is the encroachment of a woman that motivates the book's closing census. At Shittim on the East Bank of the Jordan a figure from well outside the Priestly schema is brought into the sphere of the Israelites at the entrance to the Tent of Meeting (Num 25:6). A Midianite woman named Cozbi daughter of Zur with a pedigree within the tribal structure of Midian is escorted to the Israelite zone at the entrance of the Tent of Meeting by Zimri son of Salu, who similarly is the son of a clan leader from the tribe of Simeon. As Claudia Camp has shown, the mixing of nations at work in this couple troubles the Priestly order at the same time that it brings it into relief (Camp, 2000, pp. 212–215). Women, who do not count within the national configuration of Israel, have no place in the Tabernacle environs. To make matters worse, Cozbi is a stranger who must be sacrificed because her presence contaminates the very sanctity of the entrance.

In the census following the illicit sacrifice of Cozbi, the foreign woman is contrasted with an acceptable category of women. Thus the second census names specific female characters and concedes to a scenario in which women might find themselves owners of land. Their potential ownership of land causes them to resemble Israelite men in having a public, political presence. The census of Numbers 26 is also concerned with the number of military men, yet the word emphasizing maleness, *zakhar*, is absent. It seems that the absence of this word makes way for the introduction of the acceptable category of women: daughters.

A hierarchy becomes apparent when the census names no "daughters of Israel" as counterparts to the "sons of Israel," but only daughters of particular tribal founders. The census names the five daughters of Zelophehad (Mahlah, Noah, Hoglah, Milcah, and Tirzah) (Num 26:33), Serach daughter of Asher (Num 26:46), and Yocheved daughter of Levi (Num 26:59). Such daughters, should they mind their place and marry within their tribe, can legitimately own land in the absence of brothers (Num 27:8).

The daughters of Zelophehad secure this right when they present their claim "before Moses, Eleazar the Priest, the chieftains and all of the community at the entrance of the Tent of Meeting" (Num 27:2). That the daughters approach the very place encroached upon by Cozbi illustrates the acceptability of their position. The possibility of land ownership that they secure entails a provision for participation in the political realm that constitutes "all Israel."

The Nation in Deuteronomistic Texts. As in the censuses of Numbers, texts ascribed to the Deuteronomistic source represent corporate Israel in mili-

tary terms. The image of fighting men bound by common purpose forms the basis of national public space. For example, the book of Deuteronomy applies military imagery to the image of collective assembly. The supportive presence of the divine replaces the opposition of an enemy, but the national collective still resembles the lineup of troops. According to Saul Olyan, the God of Israel who requires "that every Israelite male stand before YHWH three times a year with offerings (as in Deut 16:16)…as a vassal approaches a sovereign" commands supreme power (Olyan, 2010, p. 36). However, all Israel assembled for the jubilee includes "men, women, children, and the strangers at your gates" (Deut 31:11–12).

In dialogue with Olyan, Susan Ackerman counters that Deuteronomy's collective address does not "offer to women a place in ancient Israel's social order equivalent to (or even approaching) that available to men" (Ackerman, 2010, p. 16). Olyan is correct that women appear in the rank and file at some Jerusalem assemblies, and Ackerman's qualification identifies the power differential operative at the gatherings. Ackerman further shows how becoming a wife can signal the end of representation in most biblical texts.

Deborah the Prophetess, a "mother in Israel," has the role of military advisor and leader (Judg 5:7). The general Barak refuses to go to battle without her, so Deborah joins him in the field against a Canaanite army led by Sisera. Sisera is undone in the tent of Jael where Jael uses domestic tools to kill him in his sleep. This episode portraying female military prowess belongs to the collection of local, regional tales collected in the book of Judges. Where books like Numbers and Deuteronomy that depict Israel as nation largely suppress female political participation, local traditions reflect significant female influence in the realm of politics. It seems that women in ancient Israel were politically active at the same time that the narratives generated by centralizing governments sought to conceal or censure this fact.

The House. The site of sustained female political power is "the house." In societies where the household is "the fundamental unit of society" such as ancient Israel, "women have a strong role in decision making and consequently exercise considerable power"

(Meyers, 1998, pp. 127, 174). Deuteronomy 12, for example, summons "you and *the households* with which God has blessed you" to "the place where God chose from out of all your tribes to place His name" (12:5–7). The metonymic continuum of house and woman is not without its problems, but the institution of the household registers in national politics and bears traces of female power. When the text brings us into individual homes, we can see the strategic, political acts of women like Rahab, Achsah, Jael, Delilah, Michal, Abigail, and Bathsheba.

Mieke Bal's brilliant work on the book of Judges reveals the lethal dimension of the home for women. Jepthah's daughter (whom Bal names Bath), Samson's wife (Kallah), and the Levite's concubine (Beth) number among the women of marriageable age who are destroyed in and around the household. Because the house represents lineage—for example, the House of David—as well as position in a clan, fathers and husbands compete for their place as well as their future through the bodies of nubile women. In each case, the house cannot stand under the pressure. The young women die instead of giving birth and Israel splits into opposing armies as a result of the toppled houses (Judg 20).

The homes of Jael and Delilah, Bal shows, display a reverse dynamic in which women bring about the demise of men. As their homes enter the sphere of war, Jael and Delilah take part in public political maneuvering. This is likewise the case in the only home portrayed in the book of Joshua, that of Rahab the Canaanite. Prior to Israel's march into its promised land, Joshua sends two spies across the Jordan. The spies go to "the house of a woman" (Josh 2:1) positioned in the wall of Jericho (2:15). Rahab thwarts the king of Jericho's messengers when they appear at her home and narrates Israel's past in a manner that ensures its future in Canaan. Her home is a space traversed by opposing forces—the messengers of Joshua and the king of Jericho—where Rahab determines a sweeping political outcome.

Achsah establishes her household by renegotiating her patrimony with her father Caleb. Married to her kinsman Othniel as a prize for the conquering of Kiriyat-Sefer (Debir), Achsah returns to her father to recon-

figure the borders of her land. "You have given me away as Negev (desert) land, now give me springs of water" (Josh 15:19). Understanding that Achsah must run a household in the desert, Caleb redistributes a water system with upper and lower springs (Josh 15:16–19, Judg 1:12–15). As a consequence of the words of one of the few women depicted in the book of Joshua who speaks to a collective need, water rights are negotiated within a nonmilitary discourse. This dialog that pertains to water rather than war stands out in a book focused on battle. The text introduces a female speaker who is, therefore, not a soldier to depict a local sphere where women influence and sustain the community.

The word for "house" in Hebrew indicates both the local sphere of the extended family and a hereditary or royal line such as "the House of David." Women exercise power in both the local domain of the household and in the designation of hereditary power. The figure of Michal represents the rocky transition from the House of Saul, the first monarchy in Israel, to the House of David. In the beginning when Michal actively loves David, her father Saul tries to leverage the bride-price of 100 Philistine foreskins into David's demise (1 Sam 18:20–28). David survives and marries Michal as Saul absorbs the signs of David's predominance. When Saul begins his pursuit of David, Michal sides with her husband and employs classic trickster modes of subterfuge to protect him (1 Sam 19:11–17). God withdraws favor from Saul who, as if grasping for ways to reduce David, takes Michal from David's house and marries her to Paltiel (1 Sam 25:44).

As an act of constituting his monarchy, David demands the return of Michal, citing her dangerous bride-price (2 Sam 3:14). The transfer of Michal to David's house is intended to symbolize the transition from the House of Saul to the House of David. The tears of Michal's husband, Paltiel, as he follows her back to David indicate the emotional toll of the political transition (2 Sam 3:16). Michal articulates her bitterness about her change of status from beloved wife to symbol of a fallen house when she criticizes David's public behavior. She thereby loses the potential to advance the candidacy of her offspring (2 Sam 6:20–23).

Within royal households, women often used their authority or influence to secure the throne for their children. In many cases, there is a continuum of power between a queen and her son. The story of Bathsheba and Solomon dramatizes this dynamic. With a shivering David attended by the beautiful, young Abishag the Shunammite as he approaches death, his sons begin stirring. Adonijah, whom David had never disciplined (1 Kgs 1:6), gathers his allies excluding Solomon, Benaiah, and the prophet Nathan. A panicked Nathan turns to Bathsheba, going so far as to tell Bathsheba what to say and to follow her as live expositor.

If the book of Esther provides a parallel, then Bathsheba takes a risk by going into David's chamber without being invited. But David only asks, "What do you want?" (1 Kgs 1:16). Bathsheba recalls David's pledge that Solomon would succeed him, informs David of Adonijah's insurrection, reminds him "the eyes of all Israel are upon you," and describes the consequence of David's inaction for her and Solomon (1 Kgs 1:17–21). Nathan interrupts her to tell the same story with a particular emphasis on his own political future (1 Kgs 1:22–27). David halts Nathan with the demand that he "call Bathsheba." He pledges to her that Solomon her son will sit on the throne (1 Kgs 28–30). Bathsheba's continued influence during her son's rule is apparent both in the interloper Adonijah's request that she secure Abishag the Shunammite as his wife (1 Kgs 2:17) and in Solomon's placement of a throne for the queen mother on the right side of the king's (1 Kgs 2:19).

Queens. The foreign Queen of Sheba is an autonomous sovereign. Arriving in Jerusalem with her own impressive retinue, she comes not to bow to Solomon but to test his wisdom. Her riddles and extensive tour of the palace and temple reveal to her the nature of Solomon's power. The queen seems also to have a revelation of the God of Israel while in Jerusalem (1 Kgs 10:5, 7, 9). That she tells Solomon "everything in her heart" and he gives her "all that she desired" implies intimacy (10:3, 13). Yet, despite their mutual respect and matched generosity, the Queen of Sheba does not remain or become wife to Solomon. With the vision of Jerusalem, she returns to rule her own

land. True to the biblical motif of the foreign woman, the Queen of Sheba commands more authority than native queens of Israel.

Why do foreign women like the Queen of Sheba enjoy greater mobility and autonomy than Israelite women? Perhaps the foreign woman represents a kind of third gender that opens up possibilities beyond culturally proscribed gender codes. Perhaps ascribing action and initiative to a foreign woman is a less threatening way to present acts of female power to the native audience.

Foreign women are also subject to particularly vehement forms of demonization. Some biblical texts portray their participation in the public sphere as a form of contamination. The Sidonian queen Jezebel who establishes shrines to foreign gods (1 Kgs 16:30–33, 21:25), persecutes Israelite prophets (18:4), and has a man killed to expropriate his property (21:5–15) enacts the antithesis of the values advocated in the book of Kings. More pointedly, she is the stark opponent of miracle wielding Elijah the Prophet (1 Kgs 19:1–2, 2 Kgs 9:36–37).

Where Jezebel's influence spoils the already bad king Ahab, foreign women also have a deleterious effect on the golden king Solomon (1 Kgs 11:1–5). However, the question arises of whether the central problem with these women is their foreignness or their femininity. Is femininity in a public, political arena always represented as foreign? The charge of introducing the alien goddess Asherah is also leveled at the Judean queen Maacah. Only after her son, Asa, deposes her from her status as queen mother—a position likely established by Bathsheba—does his rule become secure (1 Kgs 15:13).

The theme of banishing women from the halls of royal power runs through the books of Kings. The removal of women from positions of influence often works in tandem with the elimination of practices and symbols deemed corrupting. Many scholars understand the correspondence as resulting from a process of centralization in which a state in formation outlaws popular practices and local forms of authority in the name of strengthening its rule. In such a scenario, local forms of female authority, along with regional traditions, become outlawed as heterodox.

The only woman to command sole rule is Athaliah. The daughter of Omri, king of Israel, Athaliah seizes power in Judah by having other claimants put to death (2 Kgs 11:1, 3). Not only does Athaliah fulfill the role of the wicked queen, but also her ouster enables Israel to reconstitute itself as a nation. Although another woman, Jehosheba daughter of King Joram, ultimately undoes Athaliah by hiding a male heir to the throne (11:2), the army and the priests find common purpose in opposing a woman's rule (11:4, 12). The putsch is portrayed as righting all that is wrong with Israel. The priest Jehoiada arms the guards with the weapons of King David stored in the Temple as if to renew David's age of loyalty and faith (2 Kgs 11:10). He orders guards to protect the sanctuary from a contaminating death by escorting Athaliah to a run for horses, where she is killed (11:15). Afterward, Jehoiada restores the covenant among God, king, and Israel and reconstitutes the "nation" through the confirmation that it is a male entity (11:17). No women are party to this covenant so ambivalence as to whether women can participate in the nation becomes matched with certainty that they cannot lead it.

A Book of One's Own. Later biblical texts, written in the Persian period, are more permissive toward female heroes. Women like Esther and Ruth have their own books in which they perform the roles of savior and founder. In these books, the inherent foreignness of women is shown to be an asset for Israel. Esther's indeterminate nationality lands her in the Persian palace, a queen among a harem of women, from whence she foils an extermination plot launched by an enemy of the Jews. Esther is a heroic precursor of Jewish political power in the diaspora.

Ruth is indeed an exceptional character but, all the same, she displays the very qualities that readers expect from a foreign Moabite woman. Recently arrived in Bethlehem, she goes out to work in the fields to sustain Naomi and herself. This shows that she gladly accepts the responsibility as the head of a family and feeds Naomi the food grown on her own land, something that Naomi's husband and sons failed to do.

There are plenty of clues that Naomi and Ruth are in the throes of a conspiracy to reclaim the land rightly due them. Ruth just "happens" to end up gathering barley in the field of Boaz, the overseer of Naomi's land (Ruth 2:3), and, with perfectly orchestrated timing, Ruth goes down to the threshing floor, where she seduces Boaz. Subsequently, when Boaz negotiates his marriage to Ruth with the elders of Bethlehem, the land in question becomes the heart of the matter. Boaz employs the ruse that Naomi wishes to sell her late husband's fields as a way to secure his ownership of the land and marriage to Ruth.

Although Boaz would imagine himself the master, he is more the instrument with which Ruth and Naomi secure land and an heir. Fulfilling the duty of levirate marriage, Boaz speaks to the need "to establish the name of the dead on his patrimony" (Ruth 4:10), but after the child is born, the women of Bethlehem name him Obed, "a son born to Naomi" (4:17). Ruth successfully gives birth to Naomi's child.

Ruth is a woman who presses a land claim and, to the degree that a woman can own land, is awarded it. Where Boaz would have her be satisfied with the occasional repast, gleanings, and the wages dispensed by God (Ruth 2:14, 12), Ruth expands the parameters of a woman's place in the nation. When Ruth—with praise and in public—joins the community of Bethlehem, engineers a female territorial claim, and founds the Davidic house, a woman makes it into the center of the Israelite power constellation of God, land, and heredity. The book of Ruth advocates not only for the stranger at the gates to be ushered in, but also for women's access to the central constellation of power.

[*See also* Imagery, Gendered, *subentry* Deuteronomistic History; *and* Legal Status, *subentry* Hebrew Bible.]

BIBLIOGRAPHY
Ackerman, Susan. *Warrior, Dancer, Seductress, Queen: Women in Judges and Biblical Israel*. Anchor Bible Reference Library. New York: Doubleday, 1998.
Ackerman, Susan. "Only Men Are Created Equal." *Journal of Hebrew Scriptures* 10, no. 9 (2010): 14–27.
Bal, Mieke. *Death and Dissymmetry: The Politics of Coherence in the Book of Judges*. Chicago: University of Chicago Press, 1988.
Berlin, Adele. "Characterization in Biblical Narrative: David's Wives. *Journal for the Study of the Old Testament* 23 (1982): 69–85.

Bird, Phyllis. "Harlot as Heroine." *Semeia* 46 (1989): 119–139.

Bloom, Harold. *The Book of J.* Translated by David Rosenberg. New York: Grove, 1990.

Camp, Claudia V. *Wise, Strange and Holy: The Strange Woman and the Making of the Bible.* Sheffield, U.K.: Sheffield Academic Press, 2000.

Caspi, Mishael Maswari, and Rachel Havrelock. *Women on the Biblical Road: Ruth, Naomi, and the Female Journey.* Lanham, Md.: University Press of America, 1996.

Fewell, Danna N. "Achsah and the (E)razed City of Writing." In *Judges and Method: New Approaches in Biblical Studies,* edited by Gale Yee, pp. 119–145. Minneapolis: Fortress, 2007.

Fleming, Daniel. *The Legacy of Israel in Judah's Bible: History, Politics, and the Reinscribing of Tradition.* New York: Cambridge University Press, 2012.

Havrelock, Rachel. "Outside the Lines: The Status of Women in Priestly Nationalism." In *Embroidered Garments: Priests and Gender in Biblical Israel,* edited by Deborah W. Rooke, pp. 89–101. Hebrew Bible Monographs 25. Sheffield, U.K.: Sheffield Phoenix, 2009.

Havrelock, Rachel. *River Jordan: The Mythology of a Dividing Line.* Chicago: University of Chicago Press, 2011.

Meyers, Carol. *Discovering Eve Ancient Israelite Women in Context.* New York: Oxford University Press, 1988.

Niditch, Susan. *Underdogs and Tricksters: A Prelude to Biblical Folklore.* San Francisco: Harper & Row, 1987.

Olyan, Saul. *Asherah and the Cult of Yahweh in Israel.* Atlanta: Scholars Press, 1988.

Olyan, Saul. "Equality and Inequality in the Socio-Political Visions of the Pentateuch's Sources." *Journal of Hebrew Scriptures* 10, no. 9 (2010): 35–41.

Pardes, Ilana. *Countertraditions in the Bible: A Feminist Approach.* Cambridge, Mass.: Harvard University Press, 1992.

Pardes, Ilana. *The Biography of Ancient Israel: National Narratives in the Bible.* Berkeley: University of California Press, 2000.

Stein, Dina, "A King, a Queen, and the Riddle Between: Riddles and Interpretation in a Late Midrashic Text." In *Untying the Knot: On Riddles and Other Enigmatic Modes,* edited by Galit Hasan-Roken and David Shulman, pp. 125–150. New York: Oxford University Press, 1996.

Stone, Ken. *Sex, Honor, and Power in the Deuteronomistic History.* Journal for the Study of the Old Testament Supplement Series 234. Sheffield, U.K.: Sheffield Academic Press, 1996.

Zlotnick, Helena. *Dinah's Daughters: Gender and Judaism from the Hebrew Bible to Late Antiquity.* Philadelphia: University of Pennsylvania Press, 2002.

Rachel Havrelock

Greek World

When Alexander the Great defeated Darius III in 330 (all dates B.C.E.) and took over the Persian Empire, he ushered in a new phase of political leadership in the Greek world, a period termed the "Hellenistic." His style of kingship involved a heroic masculinity and was imitated by the self-declared kings who divided up and fought over his empire (seen in the descriptions of Daniel 2:39–43; 7:6, 20–26; 8:21–25; 11:3ff.). Alexander and most of these successors were Hellenized Macedonians, not Greeks, and through their careers they witnessed other cultural modes of exercising power, notably from the Persians. As each successor dynasty established its own sphere of dominance, these other traditions influenced the Macedonian model of leadership, producing distinctive representations of power and the gendered expressions of royal identity. Their shared Macedonian background, extensive intermarrying, and similar methods for demonstrating rulership permit comparisons between the Hellenistic dynasties, while significant contrasts derived from cultural influences in the areas they controlled—especially Egyptian for the Ptolemies and Anatolian, Mesopotamian, and Iranian for the Seleucids—all of which played into gender constructions for men and women of each dynasty. Also important, but easily overlooked, are historical changes to dynastic characteristics resulting from political events, choices, and reactions (Carney, 2011). The major Hellenistic royal families exposed a successful route to sovereignty through their aggressive performances of Alexandrine kingship and dynastic politics, and so they set the tenor for power holding and political leadership among upwardly mobile elites, comprising new royal houses like the Attalids of Pergamum, Hasmonaeans in Judaea, and various kingdoms of eastern Anatolia and the Caucasus, as well as aristocrats based in the hundreds of cities around the eastern Mediterranean and Near East.

The Development of Hellenistic Royalty. Alexander died (in 323) too soon to fully formulate his own expression of postconquest kingship, but many of his successors had been present during his campaign through Asia and had a clear sense of Alexander's legacy as it worked for them, visible in posthumous portraits and historiography of him as well as developing iconographies for themselves. Alexandrine masculinity was rooted in physical vigor and demonstrated by courageous and successful warfare, enthusiasm for hunting, and bodily attractiveness—at least ideally, and Demetrius Poliorcetes ("the Besieger") and Demetrius Kalos ("the Fair") were famous for their handsome looks, and other successors copied Alexander's famous *anastolē* ("cowlick") hairstyle. This was matched by a charismatic heroic temperament schooled in magnanimity, justice, and honor. Alexander himself introduced two key iconographic elements for depicting kingship: youthful beardlessness and the diadem, a white band tied around the head with its ends left hanging behind. In 330 he added the diadem, probably derived from the Greek athletic victor's fillet, along with the Persian king's purple tunic, to his Macedonian costume of *kausia* (a soft hat) and purple *chlamys* (cavalryman's cloak), as a symbol of his victorious conquest to date (Smith, 1988; Stewart, 1993). Wearing the diadem became crucial to any claim of kingship, and its designation of royalty worked for both men and women, as is apparent in coin portraits of kings and queens. The early kings celebrated military prowess and successful conquest in their coins, often including in portraits of themselves and Alexander ram horns (for Zeus-Ammon), bull horns (ancient Near Eastern symbols of masculine leadership), lion-skin headdresses (reminiscent of the Greek hero Heracles), elephant-skin headdresses (allusions to Asian or African conquests), and Zeus's aegis.

The Greek word for queen, *basilissa*, appears early on in the evidence, contemporary with the first usages of "king," *basileus*, by the successor generals. The title did not describe a single, common, queenly role but was adopted as part of the process of asserting royal legitimacy, just as the title *basileus* was experimental, adopted by Alexander's successors, who still had to prove their fitness for rule by military victory. Macedonian tradition positioned women as possible inheritors of ruling power (*dynasteia*), and as a result succession was often a violent competition among several legitimate claimants. Among the fourth-century Argeads of Macedon and under Alexander's successors, women were construed as possessing the ability to confer legitimacy, making them sought-after as wives, either to enhance royal claims or to establish or strengthen alliances (Carney, 2011). This notion was not alien to Near Eastern thinking, since the Achaemenids had undertaken exogamous, endogamous, and polygynous marriages to establish legitimacy and alliances (Brosius, 1996). Although bearers of legitimacy and sometimes appearing on the field of battle to exhort their soldiers, Macedonian royal women were not accepted as sole rulers, and they came to the fore of political leadership during periods of disputed succession, as did Alexander's mother, Olympias; his sister Cleopatra; and his sister-in-law Eurydice after his death. In later centuries, as their dynasties' concepts for queenship developed, other women were more successful at ruling in their own right, particularly among the Ptolemies.

Marriage and Women's Power. Most of the attested events involving Hellenistic royal women concern succession politics and their connection to international affairs. A notable example is Arsinoe II (ca. 316–268), married three times, first in ca. 299 to Lysimachus (as his third wife), then to her half-brother Ptolemy Keraunos, then to her full brother Ptolemy II. She bore Lysimachus three sons and feuded with their main rival, Agathocles, her stepson and the husband of her paternal half-sister Lysandra, culminating in his execution for treason in 282. This came to naught in 281 when her second husband slew her children, forestalling any further agitation by her on their behalf against himself, whereupon she fled, arriving in Egypt and the court of Ptolemy II, whom she married and whose children from his previous marriage she adopted. After the failure to forge a dynastic link with Lysimachus and the vulnerability revealed by Ptolemy Keraunos's actions, redirecting Arsinoe's political capital inward proved the best option for the family, and she and Ptolemy generated new prestige by titling themselves the *theoi philadelphoi*, "sibling-loving gods," celebrated on coins and in official documents. This marriage successfully managed succession politics for the time being and confirmed Ptolemaic adherence to pharaonic practices. Later generations adopted the sibling marriage, linking it to co-rulership and expanding the royal titulature that celebrated filial affection. Problems still arose whenever there were multiple siblings competing for the throne, but the term "domestic" should be avoided in describing such conflicts, lest it be assumed that they were private or trifling matters. The familial concerns of the Hellenistic dynasties shaped administrative practices and diplomatic decisions, as a result making the activities and roles of the women crucial elements in this period's history.

Ptolemaic incest and joint rule was one strategy developed to limit succession problems. Seleucus I attempted a different form of incest in 292, marrying his second wife, Stratonice, to his son Antiochus I, at the same time making him co-ruler. With Demetrius Poliorcetes as her father and Antipater as maternal grandfather, Stratonice herself possessed a strong claim to rulership, and marriage to Antiochus prevented a conflict between him and the heirs she bore for his father. At least one other incestuous Seleucid marriage is known, between Antiochus and Laodice, eldest children of Antiochus III (r. 222–187) and Laodice III, echoing their parents' fictive titles of "brother" and "sister" (they were cross cousins) and intended to strengthen the appearance of dynastic solidarity. Seleucids normally handled succession by appointing the eldest sons as co-rulers after the pattern of Seleucus I and Antiochus I, but this failed with the sons of Antiochus II and later with the brothers Seleucus IV (r. 187–175) and Antiochus IV (r. 175–164), whose heirs fought for primacy until the end of Seleucid kingship in 64. Most Seleucid women married outside rulers to create or consolidate alliances and claims on foreign territory; Antiochus's half-sister Phila married her maternal uncle Antigonus Gonatas, and his daughters Apame and Stratonice married, respectively, Magas of Cyrene (her third maternal cousin) and Demetrius II (son of Phila and Antigonus). The wives of Seleucid princes are more difficult to identify, with most given the name "Laodice," but they probably originated from neighboring minor dynasties, as had Apame I of Sogdiana and Laodice III of Pontus. Similar marriages linked the Seleucids with the Ptolemaic, Attalid, Cappadocian, and Armenian royal houses.

Continued intermarriage among the dynasties meant that virtually every royal marriage was endogamous. This connectivity intensified the rivalries inherent in dynastic management, leading to and accelerating the political fragmentation, which advantaged the Parthians and Armenians in the east and Romans in the west. Throughout the Hellenistic period, territorial control as a political aim was tightly bound to the quest for dominance in dynastic politics, and women with multiple kinship ties were integral to diplomatic strategizing. Ptolemy II engineered a Seleucid succession crisis by marrying his daughter Berenice Syra in 253 as part of a peace treaty to Antiochus II (cf. Dan 11:6), who already had four children with his wife Laodice. The plan culminated in 246 when Laodice and her two sons became embroiled in war both with Ptolemy III and Berenice Syra (who was soon assassinated) and with each other until the 220s. Women's leadership during the later second century drove an explosive mix of internecine violence, serial incest, and war in Syria-Palestine. The female protagonists were Cleopatra II, married to her brothers Ptolemy VI and VIII; her daughter Cleopatra III (r. 116–101), married to Ptolemy VIII (alongside her mother); her sister Cleopatra Thea (r. 125–121), married to Seleucid kings Alexander Balas (r. 152–145), Demetrius II (r. 145–138), and his brother Antiochus VII (r. 138–129); Cleopatra Tryphana, married to Antiochus VIII (r. 125–96); her sister Cleopatra Selene, married to their brother Ptolemy IX, Antiochus VIII, Antiochus IX (r. 115–95), and his son Antiochus X (r. 95–93/2). These incestuous marriages were directly connected to contests for supremacy in the Ptolemaic and Seleucid kingdoms; two of the queens ruled jointly with their sons, and all of them established and undermined the kingship of their other male relatives. Congruently, the Hasmonaeans also practiced endogamy as a means to retain their hold on legitimate power and struggled with dynastic strife, giving significant power to the women of the family. John

Hyrcanus bequeathed rule to his wife, not his sons; Salome Alexandra dispatched Aristobulus I (r. 104–103), arranged her marriage to Alexander Jannaeus (r. 103–76), and later ruled alone (r. 76–67). That her two husbands are both credited as first to wear the diadem is most likely a reflection of her wifely role for generating royal legitimacy (Josephus, *Jewish Antiquities* 13.301; Strabo, 16.2.40). Similarly, Herod the Great married Mariamne, daughter of parallel cousins Alexandra and Alexander, and great-grandchild of Salome, as part of his preparation for a royal career (Jos., *AJ* 14.300, 467).

Succession crises were fruitful ground for new formulations of kingly and queenly identity. This had been the case as Alexander's first successors married each other's female relations, took up royal titles, and developed a royal iconography during the race to establish themselves in kingship. Similar processes occurred later, for example when Berenice of Cyrene, betrothed to Ptolemy III, resolved the tensions caused by her mother, Apame, in Cyrene and Berenice Syra's rivalry for queenship in Egypt with an assertive campaign to position herself as heir of Arsinoe II and paragon of divinely romantic and supportive consortship modeled after the goddess Hathor (Llewellyn-Jones and Winder, 2011). Ptolemaic portraiture from periods of heightened dynastic uncertainty shows new stylistic elements corresponding to the developing characters of the rulers; the complicated period of Ptolemy VIII; his two wives, Cleopatra II and III; and their children witnesses several parallel portrait series for each ruler, mirroring the sensuous, refined, loyal, and warlike aspects of their changing self-representations and political activities.

It is true that Hellenistic royal women experienced limitations of self-determination, generally regarding choice of spouse. These were not the impositions of men on women, but the results of a highly competitive dynastic milieu. There were many occasions when kings or queens employed offers of a princess's hand to leverage advantageous alliances or territorial dominance, but kings and princes were also limited in their marital choices. The constraints imposed on Ptolemaic kings by their family's tradition of sibling marriage produced a kingly gender

role distinct from that of other dynasties, and one which saw co-rule with a female relation, whether mother, wife, or sister, as a normal state of affairs. The prevalence of endogamy among the ruling members of the other Hellenistic dynasties indicates that the involvement of women with royal lineage was a criterion for legitimacy, as important as the enactment of Alexandrine masculinity. The visibility and political significance of queens set Hellenistic royal masculinity apart from traditional Greek constructions (Roy, 1998).

Other royal women. Daughters of the Hellenistic dynasties were not the only women active in the constellations of power holders at court: the courtesan (*hetaira*), concubine (*pallakis*), and wife of nonroyal background were important political agents, whose role overlapped that of royally born queens. These women typically had high status in their own right as members of regional or civic aristocracies. Outstanding is Apollonis of Cyzicus, the wife of Attalus I (r. 241–197) and mother of four sons, including two kings, Eumenes II (r. 197–159) and Attalus II (r. 159–138). She appears titled as *basilissa* in dedicatory, honorific, and administrative inscriptions from Pergamum. Married to Apollonis's son Athenaeus was Kallippa, the previous mistress of the Attalids' enemy Perseus, and she acted as kingmaker to the Macedonian pretender Andriscus around 150 while in Pergamum, supplying him with a diadem. Literary sources describe dozens of royal courtesans and mistresses, many of whom bore children who obtained prestigious marriages or political roles. Many, like Kallippa, became royal wives. There is some fluidity in the attributions of their precise marital status because during their careers many did advance to being considered royal spouses (Ogden, 1999, p. 231ff.).

It is possible to attribute the presence of royal concubines to the ostentatious masculinity of Hellenistic kingship, and view these women as accessories for displaying the kings' sexual prowess alongside other luxurious pursuits. This certainly was how classical Greeks critiqued the activity of women at the Achaemenid court in Persia (Brosius, 1996, pp. 1–2). Given the Hellenistic propensity for foregrounding women's roles in the legitimizing of royal power, however, it is problematic to emphasize such an orientalist cliché and downplay royal women's political agency. Negative views in the Greek literary sources of promiscuous, corrupt, or belligerent women at Hellenistic courts emerge from ancient propaganda battles and obscure these women's true status and power. Actual political errors among Hellenistic royal women do not indicate the lack of personal autonomy or a lapsed adherence to gender norms: power brought with it the capability for making poor decisions. While Hellenistic royal femininity prioritized kinship, sexual relationships with royal men, and succession matters, it did not exclude the potential for political leadership, handling of administrative duties or appearances on the battlefield. When they acted in this manner Macedonian women behaved royally and did not transgress their gender role or encroach on men's, and pejorative accounts of courtly life concerned the misdeeds of men as much as women. In an important cultural precedent, the Achaemenid evidence shows royal women present on campaign, in hunts, at feasts, and at royal audiences, where their presence was accepted as normal royal behavior, a practice inherited by Alexander, who (we must remember) captured Darius III's harem in 333 (Brosius, 1996, pp. 84–97).

Receptions of Royal Power. Reactions of Greek cities to royal women show recognition of their political status and proximity to ruling power, usually expressed by the institution of cult honors. In the 340s Philip II had already notified the Greeks that Macedonian hegemony was dynastic and therefore involved the women of his family when he included chryselephantine statues of his wife Olympias and mother, Eurydice, in the Philippeum at Olympia (Carney, 2000, pp. 25–26). Beginning with one of Alexander's officials and the early Antigonids was a long-lasting association of Aphrodite with prominent women in sexual relationships with kings. Harpalus established an Aphrodite cult for his *hetairai* Pythonice at Babylon and Glycera at Tarsus; both courtesans were reportedly honored as *basilissai*. The Athenians honored Phila, the wife of Demetrius Poliorcetes, as "Phila Aphrodite," ca. 307, in tandem

with cults for her husband and father-in-law, and Demetrius's *hetairai* Leaenea and Lamia were also honored with Aphrodite cults in their names at Athens and Thebes. Smyrna honored Phila's daughter as "Stratonice Aphrodite," and Antiochus I conflated her with the goddess Ishtar in his Babylonian propaganda, and she herself patronized the cult of the Syrian goddess Astarte at Hierapolis-Bambyce (Syria). Around 195 Iasos (Ionia) instituted a festival for Aphrodite Laodice, the wife of Antiochus III. Ptolemy II's famous mistress Bilistiche also enjoyed an Aphrodite cult in Alexandria at his behest. Cultic links to Aphrodite for the Ptolemaic queens generally appeared in conjunction with pharaonic associations to Hathor and Isis.

Subject cities of the dynasties, both old Greek poleis and new colonial foundations, developed methods for honoring royalty that suited the dynasties' preferences and still stayed roughly within their own democratic or oligarchic traditions. The favored method was to honor the divine and virtuous characteristics of kings and queens, partly an attempt to curry favor, partly in an effort to provide local traction to the dynasties' particular iconographies and modes of representing leadership. This resulted in a body of evidence, largely epigraphic, providing insight to how the roles of kings and queens and other royals were understood by their subjects. Of interest is how these newly represented royal roles proved influential for civic elites aspiring to greater status: Hellenistic royal power reconfigured for local conceptualizations of leadership. Greek inscriptions praise the beneficence, ability to dispense law and order, *eunoia* (kindness), *philotimia* (love of honor), *sebeia* (reverence), and *aretē* (excellence) of leaders, qualities attributable to nonroyal persons of authority and increasing influence without disrupting civic traditions. Certain honors were reserved for royalty: for women the Aphrodite cults described above, for men statues of kings and princes in the Alexandrine heroic nude likening them to gods. The religious context for many of these civic honors is noteworthy, the common meeting point for idiomatic cultural understandings of power. The dynasties patronized old cults, instituted new dynastic ones, appropriated divine titles, and used divine iconography in ways that suited themselves and their subjects, providing an opening for the latter to understand and honor the dynasties without compromising their traditions. This did not always work—the Hasmonaean rise to power was fuelled by hostile reactions to royal cultic impositions, but even that dynasty subsequently operated on a Hellenistic model.

Female models of leadership. Little is known about the wives of nonroyal political leaders beyond references to their names in funerary or dedicatory inscriptions. After the fourth century, however, portrait statues for these women began to be set up in cities, both by the women themselves and their male relatives, showing a new acceptance for their public roles. Often such statues were of priestesses, such as Nikeso, Timonassa, and Niko at Priene (Ionia), women already performing a public duty, now representing that role and their personal merits on the same stage as men (Dillon, 2010, p. 53). Women also appear honored as *euergetai*, "benefactors," receiving the same types of praise as men. An outstanding example is Archippe of Kyme, whose career produced a series of inscriptions detailing her own benefactions of a new council house and food rations, the city's honors of tax exemptions, and a gilded statue of her, as well as her negotiation of tax exemption in exchange for bequests to provide long-term revenues (van Bremen, 1996, pp. 13–18). These women emulated the beneficent donations of Hellenistic queens, who because of their dynastic roles enjoyed an independence and agency not normally available to Greek women. When faced with the favor of so-inclined women, the cities reacted as they would to queens, by decreeing public thanks and prestigious honors, thus confirming the new elevated status of their patronesses. This development grew substantially through the Roman period, to the point where women might be holders of public magistracies and political leaders in an official capacity.

Assessment. Hellenistic rulership operated in a paradigm of continual experimentation with legitimacy, which in its earliest Macedonian iterations had closely tied the identity and presence of women to political success. The movement of Alexander's successors toward royal status set precedents for subsequent successor dynasties to establish themselves while the rivalries of the major houses played out. Hellenistic royal masculinity and femininity were malleable, permitting changes to gender roles as cultural specifics, dynastic strategies, and political affairs required, and lending themselves to emulation by nonroyal elites. Strong traditions of representing kingship and queenship did remain throughout the period and across groups, reflective of the heightened integration among dynasties produced by the relationships of royal women.

[*See also* Marriage and Divorce, *subentry* Greek World; *and* Masculinity and Femininity, *subentry* Greek World.]

BIBLIOGRAPHY

Brosius, Maria. *Women in Ancient Persia, 559–331 B.C.* Oxford: Clarendon, 1996.

Carney, Elizabeth. "The Initiation of Cult for Royal Macedonian Women." *Classical Philology* 95, no. 1 (2000): 21–43.

Carney, Elizabeth. "Being Royal and Female in the Early Hellenistic Period." In *Creating a Hellenistic World*, edited by Andrew Erskine and Lloyd Llewellyn-Jones, pp. 195–220. Swansea, U.K.: Classical Press of Wales, 2011.

Dillon, Sheila. *The Female Portrait Statue in the Greek World.* New York: Cambridge University Press, 2010.

Llewellyn-Jones, Lloyd, and Stephanie Winder. "A Key to Berenike's Lock? The Hathoric Model of Queenship in Early Ptolemaic Egypt." In *Creating a Hellenistic World*, edited by Andrew Erskine and Lloyd Llewellyn-Jones, pp. 247–269. Swansea, U.K.: Classical Press of Wales, 2011.

Ogden, Daniel. *Polygamy, Prostitutes and Death: The Hellenistic Dynasties.* London: Duckworth, 1999.

Ogden, Daniel. "How to Marry a Courtesan in the Macedonian Courts." In *Creating a Hellenistic World*, edited by Andrew Erskine and Lloyd Llewellyn-Jones, pp. 221–246. Swansea, U.K.: Classical Press of Wales, 2011.

Ramsey, Gillian. "The Queen and the City: Royal Female Intervention and Patronage in Hellenistic Civic Communities." In *Special issue: Gender and the City before Modernity*, edited by Lin Foxhall and Gabriele Neher. *Gender and History* 23, no. 3 (2011): 510–527.

Roy, Jim. "The Masculinity of the Hellenistic King." In *When Men Were Men: Masculinity, Power, and Identity in Classical Antiquity*, edited by Lin Foxhall and John Salmon, pp. 111–135. London: Routledge, 1998.

Smith, R. R. R. *Hellenistic Royal Portraits*. Oxford: Clarendon, 1988.

Stanwick, Paul Edmund. *Portraits of the Ptolemies: Greek Kings as Egyptian Pharaohs*. Austin: University of Texas Press, 2002.

Stewart, Andrew. *Faces of Power: Alexander's Image and Hellenistic Politics*. Berkeley: University of California Press, 1993.

van Bremen, Riet. *The Limits of Participation: Women and Civic Life in the Greek East in the Hellenistic and Roman Periods*. Amsterdam: J. C. Gieben, 1996.

Gillian Ramsey

Roman World

Like many premodern societies, the Romans of the imperial period saw the world as divided into two spheres: the public, which belonged to men, and the private, which was the proper place for women. Men, especially elite men, were expected to excel in war and politics, and to put their mark on the historical record of the times; women, by contrast, were supposed to focus their attention on their homes, their families, and the work of the household. Funerary epitaphs are a good source for studying the normative values of a society, and there we commonly find men praised for their strength, glorious exploits, and political offices achieved; women's virtues tend to be modesty, chastity, obedience, and a commitment to wool working. The invisibility of women on the public stage was seen as an index of the well-being of Roman society, so that, for instance, Valerius Maximus sees the evil of the civic conflicts of the first century B.C.E. as reflected in the fact that women were called to give evidence in political assemblies: "What do women have to do with a public meeting? Nothing, if our ancestral customs were preserved: but where domestic quiet is stirred up by the turbulence of sedition, the authority of old habits is overturned, and what violence compels is stronger than what modesty urges and instructs" (*Memorable Words and Deeds* 3.8.6). Similarly, Cicero condemns Plato for suggesting that the ideal state would allow women to participate in government: "How great will be the misfortune of that city in which women assume the offices of men!" (*De re publica* 5).

At the same time, however, early Roman history is rife with stories in which women transgress this gendered boundary and make a mark not just on civic life but on the stories about it handed down to later generations. Thus, for instance, one of the most important and frequently repeated stories about early Roman politics concerns Lucretia, whose death is the pretext for Rome's transformation from a monarchy into a republic. During the days of early Rome, when the state was still ruled by kings, Lucretia was the daughter of a Roman nobleman and the wife of another, the two of whom were away from home on military campaign with the sons of Tarquin, the present king of Rome. While drinking together one night, the group proposes a contest to see who has the most virtuous wife; while the other women are discovered out at a dinner party, Lucretia is found weaving with her servants in her home, and is thus declared the winner. One of the princes, however, invades her house and rapes her, which causes her—after she discloses the crime to her husband and father—to commit suicide out of shame. This incident becomes the catalyst for the first major shift in Roman governance, as her male relatives (led by a family friend, Lucius Junius Brutus) rise up in anger and, displaying the bloodied knife with which Lucretia took her life in the Forum, whip up the sentiments of the Roman public against the monarchy. As a result, the kingship is overthrown, establishing the republican system that would govern Rome for the next five hundred years. Like the Sabine women, therefore, Lucretia has a significant effect on the masculine sphere of politics—not despite, but because of, her virtuous adherence to domestic virtues. The notionally impermeable boundary between the private sphere of women and the public one of men is thus transgressed in the name of political progress. Moreover, that transgression is celebrated as one of the great founding myths of the early Roman state. As Seneca the Younger would later put it, giving equal or greater credit to the female role in the political shift, "Lucretia and Brutus threw off the king from the heads of the Romans: we owe freedom to Brutus, Brutus to Lucretia": (*Ad Marciam* 16.2).

Although stories like that of Lucretia had long been part of the canon of Roman historical myth, it is not surprising that one place they are prominently presented is in the early imperial historian Livy's monumental history of the city of Rome. Livy lived and wrote under the emperor Augustus, who oversaw the formal transition of the Roman state from republic back to hereditary monarchy. The Roman republic had lasted slightly less than 500 years, from the death of Lucretia in 509 B.C.E. to the end of the civil wars and the "Augustan settlement" of 27 B.C.E. Governance by a single man, and dynastic passage of imperial power through the generations of a single family, would remain the norm in Rome until the fall of the empire in 476 C.E. Livy thus lived in a time in which the imperial "house," or family, was being transformed into one of the central institutions of the Roman state.

Women's Political Roles from Republic to Empire. With the advent of the imperial "house" as a locus of political influence, women's roles in governance were profoundly affected. One reason for this is that the wives, sisters, and daughters of emperors had direct and unmediated access to the central power, namely, the single man who was ruling the state; another was the fact that the dynastic succession could only be effected through women's production of male heirs. In the Julio-Claudian dynasty inaugurated by Augustus, we can see the particular difficulties that afflicted ruling families and the ways in which they allowed women to attain positions of considerable influence in imperial politics. Augustus himself married a woman who already had two sons from a previous husband, one of whom (Tiberius) would go on to become his successor. But Augustus left only one biological child, a daughter. Consequently all subsequent rulers, were they to trace their blood back to the original emperor, would have to do so through the female line. As the dynasty grew older, and male scions of the imperial house died young on the battlefield or because of political machinations, female members of the family continued to grow in importance, because very often it was they who lived long enough to produce and influence subsequent generations of the family.

This pattern under the Julio-Claudians began with the formidable wife of Augustus, Livia, who seems to have been instrumental not only in the conduct of her husband's rule but also in the succession and early policies of her son. Along with Augustus's sister Octavia, Livia enjoyed unprecedented honors such as *sacrosanctitas*, "inviolability" of her person under the law, a right that had before only been enjoyed by men holding the political office of tribune of the plebs. Octavia and Livia also both sponsored significant building projects in Rome under their own names, something that echoed a practice long used by male politicians under the republic to gain popular influence. Later historians apparently had remarkable access to information about Livia's influence on her husband, as Augustus insisted on communicating with her in writing and having copies of the documents placed in the public archives (the Acta Diurna). After Augustus's death and subsequent deification, she was made his chief priestess and given the title Julia Augusta. "Augusta" would continue to be a title adopted by imperial women—even those not related to the Julio-Claudian dynasty—to signify their authority and power. At the same time, however, it is clear that even Livia's power was to a certain extent grounded in her performance of traditional female roles. As one small but significant example, the historian Tacitus reports that, when Augustus lay on his deathbed, Livia sealed the imperial house to the outside while she sent for her son, thereby ensuring that Tiberius would be in the correct place to take the throne when his stepfather's death was announced. Her control over women's traditional sphere, the house, thus became the basis for her control over the future of the Roman state.

Although women's roles in the political life of Rome certainly underwent a transformation with the advent of Augustus, it would be a mistake to see imperial women's authority as arising ex nihilo with the advent of imperial rule. Indeed, we can see women moving into positions of significant influence under the late republic, not surprisingly affected by the social transformations that would eventually bring down the republican government.

With the growth of the empire and the concentration of power in the hands of fewer, extremely powerful men, women's "informal" power networks took on increasing importance. In particular, their responsibility to contract marriages meant that they were in a good position to create alliances to further their own, or their families', political ambitions: thus, for instance, the republican matron Fulvia, who would earn opprobrium for assisting her husband Mark Antony in the civil war against Octavian (later Augustus), was previously married to the great *popularis* leader P. Clodius Pulcher and the prominent politician C. Scribonius Curio. Curio, and subsequently Antony, seems to have married her not simply for her wit and beauty but because she would give them credibility with Clodius's numerous supporters. Moreover, the civil conflicts of the last hundred years of the Roman republic meant that men often found themselves in difficult political situations, so that they ended up relying on their female relatives to conduct business in the capital city. For example, Cicero reports on several meetings he took with Servilia, Brutus's mother, who took it upon herself to negotiate with her son's allies in Rome after his assassination of Julius Caesar forced him to flee to Greece. One of these meetings was also attended by Tertulla and Porcia, Brutus's half-sister and second wife, respectively. One of Servilia's reported comments during the meeting—that in order to prevent her son from going to Rome, she herself would see to the rewording of a senatorial decree—makes it clear that part of women's power lay in their ability to directly influence events in Rome while their male relatives whiled away their time in the provinces.

Thus, it is clear that the great matrons of the late Roman republic laid the groundwork for the women of the imperial house to assume positions, if not of formal leadership, at least of great visibility and importance. At the same time, scholars have often pointed out that the political roles that imperial women were called on to play were often assimilated to traditional ideals of female behavior. Livia's public acts, for instance, were understood as arising out of her domestic roles: one of her major building projects included a shrine to *concordia* (harmony), a virtue of both a good marriage and a stable state. She is also portrayed as exercising toward the Roman people the kind of benevolence befitting a nurturing mother. The historian Velleius Paterculus comments on her death that she was "a very eminent woman, whose power no one felt except for the alleviation of danger and the elevation of rank" (*Roman History* 2.130.5). Similarly, the Senatusconsultum de Cnaio Pisone Patre, a senatorial decree from the reign of Tiberius, makes explicit the connection between her role as mother in the emperor's household and her public benevolence. The inscription expresses the Senate's gratitude to her, "not only for the birth of our emperor, but also for her many and great kindnesses towards all ranks of men" (116–117). The inscription goes on to remark that it is pleased to accede to her request to spare Plancina, the wife of a man who plotted against the emperor, because "although she rightly and deservedly should be able to exercise the highest influence over what she requests from the Senate, she uses that right most sparingly" (117–118). This emphasis on restraint is echoed in the extensive praise of the imperial household—especially its female members—for the "moderation" (*moderatio*) of their grief over the death of Augustus's great-nephew Germanicus, supposedly assassinated in the conspiracy, as they waited for the Senate's verdict in the case and took no dramatic action. These imperial women's influence on public life is profound, but it is made rhetorically acceptable by an emphasis on their unwillingness to wield it.

Masculinity and Imperial Political Leadership. The advent of imperial rule did not only affect the ideas and ideals that governed women's public roles. Indeed, its effect on the performance of masculinity by elite citizens in particular was also profound. Under the republic, politics and warfare were the two primary arenas in which a Roman male could prove himself worthy of the name. On the battlefield, a man was expected to be a brave, loyal, and stalwart soldier; elite men were supposed to lead effectively without undue concern for their own, or their men's, lives. A particularly victorious general could expect to be honored with a triumph, in which he led a parade of captured spoils through Rome to the temple of Capitoline Jupiter and received the title of *imperator*. In politics, an elite male was expected to perform his manliness (*virtus*) by participating in the highly competitive games of civic life: running for office, jockeying for friends and influence, or performing oratorically in public assemblies or high-profile court cases. Whereas in the modern world, achievement may be measured in monetary terms, and finance is often coded as a sphere of masculine competition, traditional Roman mores barred men of the highest rank from participating in commerce. Thus the attainment of political rank was one of the few external measures of success, and gaining the consulship—the highest magistracy in the republic, elected yearly—was considered the summit of many an aristocratic man's life. Moreover, although Rome became a large empire, its political institutions were still anchored in the capital, so that it remained largely a face-to-face society. All behavior in public could be judged, and masculinity, particularly, was seen as much as a performance of self as the manifestation of an inherent quality: even the gestures that a man made while speaking in public were seen as an index of his adherence to correct gender norms.

The Emperor as Domestic Leader: Augustus and the Julio-Claudians. As noted, the transcendence of a single man and a single family under imperial rule created significant difficulties for Roman ideals of manliness. While Augustus formally restored the Senate, the consulship, and most of the rest of the political system in 27 B.C.E., it was also clear at that point that achievement in the political arena was never again going to mean what it had under the republic. A man might become consul, but he could not—without significant military and social upheaval—hope to become emperor unless he was related to the ruling family. And it was with the emperor that the real power in Rome lay. On the military front, it was still possible to gain a certain amount of glory from achievements on the battlefield, but Augustus and his successors understood that it was a mistake to let anyone gain purchase on the public imagination through holding a triumph: the last to be held by anyone who was not a member of the imperial family

was in 19 B.C.E. Aristocratic virtues, therefore, were forced to undergo a dramatic shift in meaning to accommodate the radical reduction in the sites where they could be displayed. Thus, for instance, rhetoric—which, under the republic, had been the central tool with which a man could make his way in public life—became under the empire merely ornamental, used for display in schools and in mock oratorical battles on set topics held among members of the elite. Moreover, it has been argued that traditional qualities associated with masculinity, even *virtus* itself, were gradually redefined to be philosophical or internal qualities rather than ones needing to be performed on a public stage. In this way, the empire made space for the display of manliness in contexts where it did not have any real effect on civic life.

However, the masculinity of the Julio-Claudian emperors was also complicated, both in fact and in representation. Augustus goes down in history as curiously "domesticated": perhaps in part in an effort to distance himself from his violent and bloody youth, when he assassinated or cowed huge numbers of Roman aristocrats, he seems to have made an effort in later years to be seen as humble, homely, and approachable. He made *pietas* (duty) and *clementia* (mercy) two of the standard imperial virtues, qualities that had resonance in both public and private life. Suetonius reports that his house was decorated in a notably simple and unadorned style, and that he slept in the same bed, winter and summer, for forty years. He only ever wore homespun clothing, made by his wife and daughter, whom he insisted must learn to weave (*Divus Augustus* 72). On a larger level, he famously adopted the title *pater patriae*, or "father of the country," assimilating his position to a male role, to be sure, but a domestic rather than a military or civic one. A quip of his is handed down to later generations in which he says that he had two troublesome daughters, Julia and the republic (Macrobius, *Saturnalia* 2.5.4). Augustus was thus understood as manifesting a certain kind of house-based masculinity, which is distinguished from that which had characterized leaders under the old republican system of governance.

Fortunately or unfortunately, his successors within his own dynasty seem not to have been able to maintain his legacy, and, in particular, as the women of the Julio-Claudian house are recorded as growing increasingly powerful, the emperors with whom they were associated were seen as increasingly weak. The dynasty culminated in the rule of Nero, whose theatrical pretensions, florid manner of dressing and acting, and luxurious tastes marked him as deeply unmasculine in the Roman mind. Part of this view of Nero, however, was his dependence on his mother, Agrippina, who was seen as dominating her son and insisting on a level of influence inappropriate for a woman. After her death, Nero himself is made to claim "that she had expected to share in the imperial power, to have the praetorians swear themselves to a woman, and create a like disgrace for the Senate and the people" (Tacitus, *Annals* 14.11). It is difficult to tell how much of this portrait of Agrippina is due to the hostility of our sources to her son, but she seems to have been a formidable woman in much the same way as her great-grandmother Livia: indeed, she is explicitly described as copying Livia's behavior in the way that she managed the accession of her son to the throne (Tacitus, *Annals* 12.69.2). Agrippina seems to have spent less time carefully crafting her public image, so that her influence was not disguised under the cloak of domestic virtues that had served Livia so well.

Gender and Political Leadership after Augustus. The women of the Flavian dynasty (69–96 C.E.) do not seem to have had nearly the same influence as their Julio-Claudian predecessors: they appear in the historical record mostly in a negative light, in clear attempts to discredit the men with whom they were associated. In part, the opprobrium accorded the women of the Flavians may have been a reaction against the influence that the female Julio-Claudians had enjoyed. Curiously, however, following the assassination of Domitian and the shift to a new dynasty of emperors, women reappear as influential players in the game of imperial politics. Plotina, wife of the emperor Trajan, and Sabina, wife to Hadrian, were depicted on coins with reverse images of Vesta, Fides, or Pietas, creating associations between them and the personifications and goddesses. Hadrian also conferred the title Augusta and deification not

only on Plotina but on Trajan's sister Marciana and her daughter Matidia—who were, not coincidentally, the grandmother and mother of Hadrian's own wife, Sabina. Again, we see women functioning as the connecting tissue between the reign of one emperor and the next. Indeed, it is worth noting that the "dynasty" founded by Nerva was one only loosely based on biology: although each successor (Trajan, Hadrian, Antoninus Pius, Lucius Verus, and Marcus Aurelius) was formally adopted by his predecessor, there was little or no genetic relationship between them. Each, however, married a female relative of the previous emperor. Hadrian's own successor, Antoninus Pius, married Faustina the Elder, who was the daughter of Sabina's half sister. Their daughter, in turn, was married to Marcus Aurelius, one of Antoninus Pius's designated successors, and in 174 C.E. was given the title *mater castrorum* ("mother of the military camps") to honor her role in accompanying her husband on his numerous foreign campaigns.

The very title *mater castrorum*, which continued to be awarded to imperial women through the end of the western empire, neatly sums up the position of imperial women as political leaders, as it blends a domestic role (mother) with an environment firmly associated with masculinity (military camps). Although Roman women could never fully escape their association with the private sphere, then, certain of them were able to make their presence strongly felt in the world of Roman politics.

[*See also* Family Structures, *subentry* Roman World; Gender Transgression, *subentry* Roman World; Legal Status, *subentry* Roman World; Masculinity and Femininity, *subentry* Roman World; *and* Political Leadership, *subentries on* Greek World *and* New Testament.]

BIBLIOGRAPHY

Alston, Richard. "Arms and the Man: Soldier, Masculinity and Power in Republican and Imperial Rome." In *When Men Were Men: Masculinity, Power, and Identity in Classical Antiquity*, edited by Lin Foxhall and John Salmon, pp. 205–223. London: Routledge, 1998.

Barton, Carlin. "All Things Beseem the Victor: Paradoxes of Masculinity in Early Imperial Rome." In *Gender Rhetorics: Postures of Dominance and Submission in History*, edited by Richard C. Trexler, pp. 83–92. Binghamton, N.Y.: Medieval and Renaissance Texts and Studies, 1994.

Connolly, Joy. "Mastering Corruption: Constructions of Identity in Roman Oratory." In *Women and Slaves in Greco-Roman Culture: Differential Equations*, edited by Sandra R. Joshel and Sheila Murnaghan, pp. 130–151. London: Routledge, 1998.

Corbier, Mireille. "Male Power and Legitimacy through Women: The Domus Augusta under the Julio-Claudians." In *Women in Antiquity: New Assessments*, edited by Richard Hawley and Barbara Levick, pp. 178–193. London: Routledge, 1995.

Fischler, Susan. "Social Stereotypes and Historical Analysis: The Case of Imperial Women at Rome." In *Women in Ancient Societies: An Illusion of the Night*, edited by Léonie J. Archer, Susan Fischler, and Maria Wyke, pp. 115–134. New York: Routledge, 1994.

Flory, Marleen Boudreau. "Sic Exempla Parantur: Livia's Shrine to Concordia and the Porticus Liviae." *Historia* 33 (1984): 309–330.

Gardner, Jane F. *Women in Roman Law and Society*. London: Croom Helm, 1986.

Ginsburg, Judith. *Representing Agrippina: Constructions of Female Power in the Early Roman Empire*. Oxford: Oxford University Press, 2006.

Hemelrijk, Emily A. *Matrona Docta: Educated Women in the Roman Elite from Cornelia to Julia Domna*. London: Routledge, 1999.

Hillard, Tom. "Republican Politics, Women, and the Evidence." *Helios* 16, no. 2 (1989): 165–182.

Milnor, Kristina. *Gender, Domesticity, and the Age of Augustus: Inventing Private Life*. Oxford: Oxford University Press, 2005.

Purcell, Nicholas. "Livia and the Womanhood of Rome." *Proceedings of the Cambridge Philological Society* 32 (1986): 78–105.

Richlin, Amy. "Gender and Rhetoric: Producing Manhood in the Schools." In *Roman Eloquence: Rhetoric in Society and Literature*, edited by William J. Dominik, pp. 90–110. London: Routledge, 1997.

Severy, Beth. "Family and State in the Early Imperial Monarchy: The *Senatus Consultum de Pisone Patre*, Tabula Siarensis, and Tabula Hebana." *Classical Philology* 95, no. 3 (2000): 318–337.

Kristina Milnor

New Testament

The New Testament writings envision political leadership as a masculine affair, as did the Greco-Roman culture at large. Men were widely assumed to be superior to women, and traits that were essential for leadership—mastery, courage, action, strength—were imagined as male attributes. However, the New Testament also reflects a broader cultural ambiguity regarding leadership and gender. Some women exercised leadership, and some men in leadership roles were described in feminized ways. The New Testament gives evidence both of sides of this tension. It affirms cultural norms of masculinity and dominance but also belies the presence of women whose political influence was taken for granted by their communities.

Addressing the intersection of political leadership and gender in the New Testament is complicated by four factors. First, the political sphere reflected in the New Testament writings was somewhat broader than the modern conception of politics. It was not limited to legislative, judicial, and military functions, but intersected with the religious and social spheres as well. Devotion to God or the gods was foundational for the well-being of the city and state, for divine beings were protectors who promoted the prosperity of their region and people. Social influence was also closely related to political power. In the imperial period, legislative and judicial decisions were concentrated in the hands of a few, yet many more people could effect change through patronage and social influence. Because of the broad scope of the political, this essay explores rulers with official titles, social influence in the political realm, and the political tenor of religious leadership.

A second issue regarding New Testament texts is the difficulty encountered in uncovering the ways women functioned in political decision making. Women only occasionally played legislative or judicial roles. In the New Testament, for example, the Candace of Ethiopia lends her social status to the description of her eunuch in Acts 8:27. More frequently, however, women intervened in politics through the exertion of social power. Social status was a function of a number of factors, including wealth, family of origin, gender, citizenship, and whether one was slave, freed, or freeborn. Because of this, the status of men and women was relative. Highborn women had greater social influence than poor men or noncitizens, for example. Women of high status exercised informal political leadership. To understand political leadership, then, one must look beyond heads of state for women and men who acted as patrons or exerted social influence over political events.

Third, the New Testament must be read alongside the gendered cultural norms and virtues of Greco-Roman culture. It draws on these norms to portray leaders, both positively and negatively. The ideal leader in the Greco-Roman world was the person who exhibited ideal masculine traits. Perhaps the foremost of these traits was mastery—over both oneself and others. The ideal ruler was not overly concerned with his own comfort or the satisfaction of his passions. He commanded others who obeyed his will. Other virtues like courage and strength—also conceived as masculine virtues—were required in exhibiting mastery over others. Men who were fearful or who exhibited other "womanish" qualities were by definition poor leaders. As the supreme leader, the emperor was imagined as the ideal male, and could be described as the head of a very large household. Like the *paterfamilias*, the *pater patrias* exercised authority over all of his subjects. In both cases, a thriving, well-ordered household was evidence of the excellent leadership at its head. The expression of political leadership in the New Testament often reflects shared cultural values and assumptions about leaders.

Fourth, the use of masculine and feminine traits as rhetorical tropes complicates what can be known about actual men and women within the scope of the New Testament writings. Masculine traits were automatically viewed as superior to feminine traits. Criticism of males as "womanish" or embodying traits defined as feminine cast aspersions on their character. Similarly, women could be praised for achieving masculine virtues or blamed for acting too masculine. The gendered rhetoric signifies the author's wish to praise or criticize, but does not give accurate information about the person described. Although the actions approved or condemned may be unreliably portrayed, the language reaffirms gendered assumptions that were widely agreed upon.

Roman Officials in the New Testament. The political leaders mentioned in the New Testament primarily appear as characters in the Gospels and Acts. The authors of these writings draw on conventions of leadership—including gendered virtues—in crafting their story. The officials are not the focal point of the story, but through them the reader may see a reflection of cultural values that the author shapes to communicate his point about Jesus or Paul.

Herod. Herod's execution of John the Baptist (Matt 14:1–11; Mark 6:17–28; Luke 3:19–20) reflects familiar patterns of gendered political leadership. On the one hand, Herod is portrayed as the decision maker. Mark, for example, attributes action to Herod: "Herod himself had sent men who arrested John, bound him, and put him in prison" (Mark 6:17). Herod also gives the command to behead John (6:27).

On the other hand, both Mark and Matthew also portray Herod being ensnared by his own desire and arrogance (Mark 6:17–29; Matt 14:1–12). Pleased by the dancing of his daughter (Mark 6:22) or stepdaughter (Matt 14:6), he promises her whatever she wishes before a crowd of local dignitaries. Prompted by her mother, she asks for John's head on a platter. Herod feels unable to refuse, though both writers convey his reluctance. Thus, Herod is a powerful decision maker, yet he is entrapped by his failure to control his desire. He makes extravagant promises he then feels obliged to keep. Drawing on the conventions of masculine leadership in this way, John's death is portrayed as a tragedy that results from Herod's failure to be master of himself and his situation. (See Herodias, below.)

Pilate. Pilate condemns Jesus to be crucified in all four Gospels (Matt 27:11–26; Mark 15:1–15; Luke 23:1–25; John 18:28—19:16). John's version sets up a dramatic contest between Pilate and the Jews in which both parties try to exert power over each other. Pilate emerges as the dominant male who outmaneuvers the Jews rhetorically to exert dominance. Their declaration "we have no king but the emperor" (John 19:15) is a rejection of Jesus that also validates Rome's power, even on the eve of Passover, the celebration of Israel's freedom from foreign domination. Pilate also imposes over Jesus's cross the words "Jesus of Nazareth,

King of the Jews" (19:19), against the objections of the Jews, who want clarification that this was merely a claim Jesus made (19:22). Thus Pilate emerges as one who can manipulate opponents, symbolically squelching Jewish hopes for self-rule.

Yet John's trial narrative is also a reminder of the ultimate ideal authority of the emperor, to whom even Pilate must defer. The claim that Jesus is "Son of God" frightens Pilate (John 19:7–8). Fear is an inappropriate quality in a leader, one that can appear "womanish." Pilate's attempts to release Jesus are stopped by the Jews' claim, "if you release this man, you are no friend of the emperor" (19:12). This suggests that Pilate also must acknowledge the authority of the emperor and not be seen to support rebellion.

Tribune, governor, king, emperor. A number of rulers who appear in Acts illustrate the overlap between social influence and political power. Paul is imprisoned and passed along a chain of command until he ends up in Rome, the seat of political power. The military tribune in Jerusalem, Claudius Lysias (Acts 21:31; 23:26–30) passes Paul along to the governor, Antonius Felix (procurator of Judea, 52–56 C.E.; Acts 24:1–27). Felix is succeeded by Porcius Festus (appointed procurator in 60 C.E.; Acts 24:27) who hands Paul over to Herod Agrippa II (53–93 C.E). Agrippa eventually sends Paul on to Rome (26:32).

Each of these leaders exercises power, but their power is limited both by those with greater authority and by those below them who exert social and political pressure. On the one hand, they protect Paul from plots of the Jews (e.g., 23:16–24) and allow Paul's friends access to him in prison (24:23). On the other hand, they detain Paul as a favor to the Jews (Acts 24:27; 25:3). Furthermore, each ruler shows deference to those higher up the chain of command. The tribune fears repercussion for having bound a Roman citizen (22:26–29) and Paul's appeal to the emperor (25:10; 26:32) begins a chain of events that takes Paul out of the control of these figures. Such officials rule through the negotiation of interests between competing demands of those above and below.

Social Influence and Political Change. People without official political roles exert social influence to change judicial outcomes or influence decisions.

This was the case with the Jewish leaders whom Luke describes influencing Paul's case. Another example from the New Testament is Joseph of Arimathea, who requests the body of Jesus from Pilate (Matt 27:57–61; Mark 15:42–46; Luke 23:50–53; John 19:38–42). Joseph is a man of stature: Matthew identifies him as a rich man; Mark and Luke say he is a member of the council. His social influence extends to the case of an executed criminal. Joseph's position gives him access to Pilate, who grants his request.

Herodias. Women of high social standing also are portrayed as shaping the course of events. Herodias, Herod's wife, acts decisively in the story about Herod. All three Synoptic Gospels cite a conflict with John the Baptist over the marriage of Herodias and Herod (Mark 6:17; Matt 14:4; Luke 3:19). Herodias, granddaughter of Herod the Great (who ruled from 37 to 4 B.C.E.), was married to her uncle Herod Philip but divorced him to marry Herod Antipas, tetrarch of Galilee (Josephus, *Ant.* 18.136). Such practices of divorce and remarriage were relatively common among the Roman elite and would have garnered little moral approbation in those circles, but this apparently went against John's understanding of proper behavior for Jews. John's religious objection creates enough of a political disturbance for Herod and Herodias that he has John imprisoned.

Mark describes Herodias as holding a grudge against John for his denunciation of her divorce and marriage (Mark 6:19). Herodias seizes an opportunity and acts decisively, pressing her daughter to ask for John's head (Mark 6:24; Matt 14:8). Herodias has no formal power to pass judgment on John but uses her social influence to achieve political goals.

Pilate's wife. Pilate's wife also plays a role in Matthew's trial of Jesus, for as Pilate sits on the judge's bench she sends word to him: "Have nothing to do with that innocent man, for today I have suffered a great deal because of a dream about him" (Matt 27:19). Pilate seems to have realized that the charges against Jesus are trumped up (27:18), and so his wife's message is not the only influence on his decisions. But it is evidence of the kind of day-to-day access to power that elite women had. Furthermore, dreams were often viewed as a form of divine communication, so

Pilate's wife assumes a role of religious leadership that has political implications. Matthew assumes his reader will not only find this story plausible, but will also see her dream as further confirmation of Jesus's innocence.

King Agrippa and Bernice [Berenice]. With Herodias, Bernice is one of few New Testament women known from outside sources. A daughter of King Agrippa I, she was married to her uncle Herod, king of Chalcis (Josephus, *Ant.* 19.277) and after his death to King Polemo of Cilicia. In the face of "unprecedented" brutality of the procurator Gessius Florus against the Jews, Josephus describes Berenice's protest (*War* 2.308; cf. 309–314). While unsuccessful, Josephus presents her as a person of high status whom Florus defies.

Luke gives few details about Bernice, but his inclusion of her suggests again that it was conventional for elite women to have access to the locus of power. As noted above, King Agrippa is invited by Festus to intervene in Paul's case in order to clarify the charges brought against Paul. Agrippa is the highest-ranking official to appear in Acts and is at the center of these events. His sister Bernice (Berenice) is noted as traveling with him (Acts 25:13) and ceremonially entering with him into the audience hall (25:23). She is present when Paul speaks and responds favorably, along with the others in the king's party (26:30).

Patronage. While elite women and men had access to influence at the highest levels of power, men and women of lower standing also used social influence to effect change in their lives. Patronage also functioned among the lower classes. They sought favors from wealthy patrons, offered hospitality, served as leaders, and donated money to associations, and owned and freed slaves.

Women and men who act as patrons of Jesus, Paul, or of local churches are examples of this phenomenon in the New Testament. One of the women who provided for Jesus's ministry was "Joanna, the wife of Herod's steward, Chuza" (Luke 8:3; cf. 24:10). Chuza was most likely a freedperson and former slave of Herod, for slaves could not form legal marriages. His proximity to Herod would have given him relative wealth and power. Joanna also has resources of her own that she uses to support the Jesus movement.

Other patrons include Lydia, another woman of relative wealth and social standing. She is identified as a "dealer in purple cloth" and head of her household (Acts 16:14–15). She offers hospitality to Paul and his party, an act of patronage. Paul's letters record emissaries like Timothy (1 Cor 16:10; 1 Thess 2:2) and Phoebe, who is a deacon and patron (Rom 16:1–2). Patrons like Aquila and Prisca (1 Cor 16:19; cf. Acts 18:1–3, 26; Rom 16:3–4) or Nympha (Col 4:15) also hosted churches in their homes. Their roles as hosts and emissaries put them in positions to wield influence among the churches.

The Political Nature of Religious Leadership. Religious leadership also had political dimensions, as seen in various ways in the New Testament.

Jesus as a political leader. The Gospel writers imagine Jesus's leadership in part as political leadership. He is hailed as a king (e.g., Matt 2:2; John 1:49; 6:15; 12:13) and is executed under the charge "the king of the Jews" (Matt 27:37; Mark 15:26; Luke 23:38; John 19:19). Many interpreters read elements of Jesus's ministry as making political claims. For example, Jesus's casting a "legion" into the sea in the story of the Gerasene demoniac is often viewed as a critique of the Roman government, whose armies were divided into "legions" (Mark 5:1–20). Many interpreters understand the claim that Jesus is the Son of God (e.g., John 20:31) as a political claim, for emperors were also referred to as sons of God.

To some extent, Jesus's leadership is described in ways that evoke the ideal ruler. For example, John's Jesus always appears to be in control. He has complete foreknowledge of his death (e.g., John 2:4; 7:33; 13:1). His active role in the arrest scene (18:5) and handing over his spirit on the cross (19:30) emphasize his ultimate control even over the events of his crucifixion (cf. John 10:17–18).

Like the ideal ruler, Jesus's speech is effective and persuasive. His voice halts a storm (Matt 14:32; Mark 4:39, 41; Luke 8:24) and commands the dead to walk (e.g., Mark 5:41; Luke 7:14). When tested by others, he silences his opponents with a clever response (e.g., Matt 21:23—22:46; Luke 20:1–26). In these ways Jesus embodies traits of the effective leader, traits that were gendered masculine in the Greco-Roman world.

However, Jesus's leadership is also "not of this world" and in some ways diverges from or subverts the dominant paradigm. For example, frequent sayings like "the least among all of you is the greatest" (Luke 9:48; cf. Matt 18:4; 23:11; Mark 9:35; Luke 22:26) or "the Son of Man came not to be served but to serve" (Matt 20:28; Mark 10:45) underscore an alternative view of the leader's role. In his trial and crucifixion, Jesus becomes subject to the will of others, as exemplified in the soldiers' treatment of him: they strip him, mock him, and spit upon him (e.g., Matt 27:27–31; Mark 15:16–20). Jesus's passivity and refusal to answer charges against him could be viewed as feminine. They go against the grain of usual expectations for effective (masculine) leadership.

In Revelation Jesus's leadership is often portrayed in political and masculine terms. He is a military leader whose speech is effective. He issues edicts and commands the churches to obey (Rev 2—3). While Jesus is also envisioned as a lamb, many of Revelation's images depend on masculine ideals. Rome's power is also at issue in Revelation. But Rome is depicted either as beastly (e.g., Rev 13) or feminine (Rev 17—18), both of which render it less than the masculine ideal. To some extent Revelation's critique of Rome embraces the masculine stereotypes of the culture and presents Christ as the one who meets that ideal.

Paul's leadership and gender. Paul's religious leadership also has political overtones. In Thessalonika, Paul and Silas are accused of "acting contrary to the decrees of the emperor, saying that there is another king named Jesus" (Acts 17:7; cf. 16:20–21). Paul's activity attracts the disapproval of the Jews, but also brings him into contact with the local authorities.

In his own leadership, Paul displays many of the same gendered virtues of leadership familiar from Roman culture. Luke portrays Paul as a powerful speaker (e.g., Acts 13:16–49; 14:1; 24:24–46; 26:1–32) and worker of miracles (Acts 14:3, 8–10; 19:11–12; 20:7–12). Paul's letters show his persuasive powers and his assumed authority over his churches (e.g., 1 Cor 9:1–2; 2 Cor 10:1–6).

Another of Paul's leadership qualities is self-mastery. He endures many hardships and persecution (e.g., 2 Cor 6:4; 11:23–28). He exercises control over his body and desires, using imagery of the athletic contest (1 Cor 9:24–27) and of warfare (Rom 13:12; 2 Cor 10:3–4).

As with Jesus, Paul's suffering at the hands of others could be viewed as feminine. Paul also characterizes himself in feminine terms, as mother or nurse caring for children (1 Thess 2:7; cf. 1 Cor 3:2). The gendered language expresses and reinforces the cultural notion that political leadership is imagined as masculine, and caretaking roles are imagined as feminine.

Leadership qualities in the New Testament. In a general sense, leadership envisioned by the New Testament reflects the ideals of masculine political leadership. For example, the leadership qualities identified in 1 Timothy 3:1–13 reflect many of the norms discussed earlier. Leaders should be heads of their household who govern well (1 Tim 3:4–5). They should exercise self-control (3:2, 8, 11).

Many interpreters have seen these qualifications of religious leaders as a reflection of a political agenda. Attempting to avoid persecution, early Christian communities adopted the norms and virtues of the Roman political order. From this viewpoint, the political implications of religious beliefs affected the forms of leadership the church developed. The church sought to adapt to the social order as a means of fitting in and avoiding political persecution.

Yet the Christian system of leadership described here not only reflects the household language of Roman political order but also the availability of roles for women. Women served less frequently than men in official roles, but nevertheless held civic and religious titles, especially in Asia Minor, the region around Ephesus, to which the letter is addressed (1 Tim 1:3). Women who served their communities in civic and religious roles were often praised as exemplars of virtue and self-control (e.g., Iunia Theodora, *SEG* 18.143).

Similarly, the church order prescribed by 1 Timothy includes women deacons (3:11) whose qualifications mirror those of male deacons (3:8–10). At the same time, expectations of modesty for women are also affirmed (1 Tim 2:8–15). Although many interpreters have understood the expectations of modesty to negate the possibility of women's leadership, the cultural parallels may suggest that praise for modest behavior existed alongside accepted practices of leadership by women.

Read from this perspective, the language of 1 Timothy affirms norms of modesty while acknowledging that virtuous women played formalized leadership roles in those communities.

The early church inhabited the same cultural paradox as the Greco-Roman culture at large. Leadership was gendered as male, and gender stereotypes were used to praise or blame one's allies or adversaries. Yet women also served as leaders and could be praised for doing so effectively. The cultural tension remains unresolved and is reproduced in early Christian writings like those of the New Testament.

[*See also* Masculinity and Femininity, *subentry* Roman World; Political Leadership, *subentry* Roman World; *and* Race, Class, and Ethnicity, *subentry* New Testament.]

BIBLIOGRAPHY

Clines, David J. A. "Paul, the Invisible Man." In *New Testament Masculinities,* edited by Stephen D. Moore and Janice Capel Anderson, pp. 181–192. Atlanta: Society of Biblical Literature, 2003.

Conway, Colleen M. "'Behold the Man!' Masculine Christology and the Fourth Gospel." In *New Testament Masculinities*, edited by Stephen D. Moore and Janice Capel Anderson, pp. 163–180. Atlanta: Society of Biblical Literature, 2003.

Conway, Colleen M. *Behold the Man: Jesus and Greco-Roman Masculinity.* Oxford: Oxford University Press, 2008.

Crook, Zeba. "Honor, Shame, and Social Status Revisited." *Journal of Biblical Literature* 128 (2009): 591–611.

Ilan, Tal. *Integrating Women into Second Temple History.* Tübingen, Germany: Mohr Siebeck, 1999.

Knust, Jennifer Wright. *Abandoned to Lust: Sexual Slander and Ancient Christianity.* New York: Columbia University Press, 2006.

Liew, Tat-siong Benny. "Re-Mark-able Masculinities: Jesus, the Son of Man, and the (Sad) Sum of Manhood?" In *New Testament Masculinities*, edited by Stephen D. Moore and Janice Capel Anderson, pp. 93–135. Atlanta: Society of Biblical Literature, 2003.

Meyers, Carol, Toni Craven, and Ross S. Kraemer, eds. *Women in Scripture: A Dictionary of Named and Unnamed Women in the Hebrew Bible, the Apocryphal/Deuterocanonical Books, and the New Testament.* Grand Rapids, Mich.: Eerdmans, 2000.

Osiek, Carolyn. "The Patronage of Women in Early Christianity." In *A Feminist Companion to Patristic Literature*, edited by Amy-Jill Levine, pp. 173–192. New York: T&T Clark, 2008.

Osiek, Carolyn, and Margaret Y. MacDonald. *A Woman's Place: House Churches in Earliest Christianity*. Minneapolis: Fortress, 2006.

Thurman, Eric. "Looking for a Few Good Men: Mark and Masculinity." In *New Testament Masculinities*, edited by Stephen D. Moore and Janice Capel Anderson, pp. 137–161. Atlanta: Society of Biblical Literature, 2003.

van Bremen, Riet. *The Limits of Participation: Women and Civic Life in the Greek East in the Hellenistic and Roman Periods*. Amsterdam: J. C. Gieben, 1996.

Susan E. Hylen

Early Judaism

See Religious Leadership, *subentry* Early Judaism.

Early Church

In modern terms, women did not have real political power in the early Church period. That is, they were not allowed to hold civic offices (with some Jewish exceptions noted below). But there were other ways of exercising power and influence through patronage. Women in both Jewish and Christian communities found some measure of equality and opportunities for leadership. While the focus here is on political leadership, leadership within the *ekklēsiai* ("churches") was political as well as religious. The conception of "religion" as a separate, private sphere of human activity is a modern notion and there was no separation of "church" and "state" in the Second Temple or Greco-Roman world. Indeed, leadership in the associations or institutions we now call "churches" was one of the few opportunities for women to exercise political leadership. While this continued throughout the period of early Christianity, forces of resistance to women's leadership found in many second-century texts increased through the third and fourth centuries C.E. As orthodox churches became increasingly dominated by social and imperial elites, and Christianity more reflective of the culture of Late Antiquity, women's leadership was greatly diminished by the fourth century.

To complicate matters, our sources are problematic for recovering women's roles and influence. Both

Jewish and Greco-Roman texts, perhaps all of which were written by men, are constrained by ancient views of gender. Josephus, or his source Nicolaus of Damascus, portrayed powerful women negatively. Roman writers such as Juvenal, Livy, Tacitus, or Valerius Maximus exhibited similar tendencies. Strong and politically powerful women such as Athaliah, Shelomzion, and Livia are often described negatively by male historians. Rather than always recovering lost women voices when reading these texts, we are often reading how male authors employed women characters for different ideological purposes. Inscriptions and other evidence from material culture have enriched the evidence for women's social-political activity in the Roman Empire.

Biblical and Jewish Traditions. Biblical women, although often mythological characters, provided important role models for early Christian women. Eve, the mother of humanity in Genesis 1—3, appears in gnostic literature. Rebekah shows initiative in choosing to go to Canaan to marry Isaac (Gen 24:58) and then manipulates Isaac on Jacob's behalf (Gen 26:5–17, 42–45), taking responsibility for her actions and protecting him from Esau, without any negative implications for her character. Her stories in Genesis could have been written to support the machinations of Bathsheba for the succession of Solomon (1 Kings 1—2). Rachel defies her father and protects Jacob as they flee from Laban (Gen 31:19, 32–34). Miriam, in contrast, who leads the Hebrew women in a victory song by the sea (Exod 15:20–21), is punished for exercising prophetic power (Num 12:1–15). The hypostasized figure of "Lady Wisdom" (*Hokma* [Heb], *Sophia* [Gk]) in Proverbs 8 plays an important role in the creation of the world and becomes a central figure in gnostic Christian traditions.

Biblical traditions include several women heroes. Judges 4—5 highlights the political and military leadership of Deborah, judge and prophet(ess). She singles out the role of women in battle (Judg 4:9), which is fulfilled when Jael kills Sisera (4:21). Naomi and Ruth do not exercise political leadership but work the ancient social welfare system with Boaz to ensure the line leading to David continues (Ruth). Esther skillfully gains power at the court of Ahasu-

erus as chief concubine and, with Mordecai's help, defeats the plans of Haman to exterminate the Jews (Esth). The wealthy and beautiful widow Judith acts as both strategist and assassin to save the Jews of Bethulia from Holofernes (Jdt). The mother of the seven brothers tortured and killed by Antiochus IV (175–164 B.C.E.) is described heroically in 2 Maccabees 7:24–42 and 4 Maccabees 14:11—17:6. These women are literary characters in texts almost certainly written by men, and therefore represent male constructions of the feminine in support of patriarchal ideologies, but nonetheless inscribe in scripture the important political idea that women can take initiative and exercise leadership.

Two ruling queens are recorded in biblical and Jewish texts: Athaliah in ancient Judah and Shelamzion in the Hasmonean period. Athaliah, granddaughter of the important Israelite king Omri, ruled for six years after the death of her son Ahaziah (1 Kings 11:1-20), who was killed after a one-year reign in Jerusalem at the hand of Jehu, king of Israel, as part of the civil war fostered by Elijah and Elisha. She killed the Davidic children of Ahaziah except for Joash, who was hidden and replaced her in a coup in which she was executed. As an Omride, she would be viewed negatively by the Deuteronomic editor so it is difficult to discern misogynism, but the absence of a formulaic summary for her in 1 Kings suggests that the editor did not view her reign as legitimate.

Queens feature prominently in Josephus's accounts of the Hasmonean household. Of these, the most significant queen was the Hasmonean Shelamzion (Salome) Alexandra, who ruled from 76–66 B.C.E. Sources include fragments in the Dead Sea Scrolls (4Q331, 4Q332) and possible encoded references in the *pesharim* on Nahum 3:1 and Hosea 2:11–12 (4Qp-Nahum ii, 4Q166). She was the widow of Alexander Jannaeus (Yannai) and succeeded him even though they had two sons. The books of Esther and Judith could have been written, and certainly read, to support her reign. Josephus describes her reign twice, more favorably in *J. W.* 1.107–119 and negatively in *Ant.* 13.398–432. Despite the rhetorical differences, there are several points of agreement in the two accounts. Achievements during her reign included raising an army, moving against Damascus, and making a peace treaty with Tigranes of Armenia. She also restored the Pharisees to positions of power after her husband's purge; Josephus claims she governed others while the Pharisees governed her. When she fell sick, her younger son Aristobulus II attempted a coup and her death led to civil war between him and his brother John Hyrcanus II, who was high priest, leading eventually to the Roman occupation under Pompey. Shelamzion receives favorable mention in early Tannaitic halakic midrash, *Sifre Deuteronomy* 42, because of her support of the Pharisees, but the Babylonian Talmud diminishes her importance. Herod the Great's execution of his second wife Mariamne shows the continued political influence of Hasmonean women. The Synoptic Gospels attribute the execution of John the Baptist to the influence of Herodias, the wife of Herod Antipas (Mark 6:17–28 and parallels).

Greco-Roman Models of Leadership. Throughout the ancient cultures in which Christianity developed, gender performance was central to political leadership. Sexual relationships were understood as between the dominant, or penetrator, and dominated, or penetrated, and this ideology was translated to the political realm. A ruler's strength and virility was an important political statement to those who were ruled. The Roman emperors inherited and built upon Hellenistic images of virility. Statues of emperors depict them primarily in military garb or naked, as a god. Augustus was also portrayed as *Pontifex Maximus*, high priest, and *Pater Patriae*, father of the homeland, as well as *Imperator*, Emperor, notably in the reliefs of the Ara Pacis. As Lopez has shown, the gendered images of Roman power and stability were often combined in imperial reliefs of the conquered nations, such as Claudius and Britannia in the Sebasteion relief, which were imaged as the opposite in every way of the Romans: as lawless, conquered, and colonized barbarians. These images of conquered nations were gendered as female, passive, and penetrated (2008).

Women in the Greek world were identified with domestic tasks in the *oikos* (household) from the archaic period onward (*Iliad, Odyssey*); the public space of political leadership in the *polis* (city-state) was, therefore, male space. Women were expected to be subservient daughters and wives; fertile mothers of legitimate children; and managers of the *oikos*. Roman women had more social freedom, particularly elite women, and could attend dinner parties and own property. But they could not vote, hold political office, or attend assemblies (cf. Valerius Maximus 3.8.6; (*Auct.*) *de viris illustribus* 73). Roman women could hold religious offices. The Vestal Virgins were the most prominent, with special rights from the Republican period onward, but the priests wives (*flaminicae*) of the priestly colleges *flamines Dialis* and *flamines Martialis* had status as well.

The most powerful women in politics were the Hellenistic queens and imperial wives. The public images of these women expressed the dominant "feminine" values of domesticity, faithfulness, loyalty, and subservience. But as with the Hasmonean queens, the Hellenistic queens exercised political influence privately and cultural influence publicly, such as Antiochos III's wife Laodike establishing a bridal cult and playing a role in the ruler cults. The Julio-Claudian women exercised even more significant political power. The *Domus Caesarum* or Household of the Caesars was a political entity in the empire that included the imperial women. Livia Augustana, the wife of the first Imperator, was one of the most powerful people in the empire during the *imperium* of Augustus and Tiberius. Such elite politics were fairly removed from the early Christian *ekklēsiai*, but the images of the imperial women were part of the imperial cult in Asia.

Patronage was the most diffuse area socially where women exercised power and influence. All Roman women could participate in business activities that included a range of profit-making activities, including trading, manufacturing, and owning real estate for rent. Such activities involved women in the public sphere more actively, particularly the legal system. Wealthy women protested against a tax instituted by the triumvirs Octavian, Antony, and Lepidus in 43 B.C.E. Wealth acquired through business or marriage gave women *patrona* influence in the political sphere. While they could not hold office, they could back family members and friends. Livia was a famous and powerful patron.

Women in the Early Church. The feminist project of recovering lost women's voices and roles has been successful at establishing the centrality of women in early Christianity. Women held important, even crucial, leadership positions in the Jesus movement and Pauline *ekklēsiai*. This claim holds even though women also appear as literary fictions in male-authored texts and therefore as figures of male-oriented gender performance. First-century texts consistently show women in leadership roles and second-century and later texts contain controversies over the role of women in the *ekklēsiai*. Women were buried at Qumran; were full members of the Pharasaic *havurah* (Ilan, 2001; 2006); and were both leaders and patrons of Jewish synagogues. There is no reason therefore that women would not have been both participants in and patrons of the Jesus movement.

The earliest gospels. All of the Christian gospels feature women leaders and actors, primarily Mary Magdalene. Of the earliest gospels, Mark has the most evidence for women in the movement. Mark minimizes the role of women patrons but their influence is clear in the text. The author introduces the central figure Mary Magdalene (of Magdala), along with Mary the mother of James and Joses and Salome, only when their presence is necessary for the passion narrative (15:40–41; 16:1–8), but her central role at the burial of Jesus and indeed the origin of what comes to be Christianity indicates a leadership role from the beginning of the movement (cf. Luke 8:2). Mark includes other women patrons. Jesus's ministry begins at the home of Peter's mother-in-law, who could have been an early patron of the healing movement (Mark 1:30–34). The Syrophoenician woman who requests a healing miracle would most likely have been a woman of stature and influence (Mark 7:24–30), although the story in the gospel focuses on a mission to the gentiles before the turning point at Caesarea Philippi. So too the unnamed woman in Mark 14:3–10, memorialized in Schüssler Fiorenza's seminal book (1983), was most likely a patron of Jesus. The reconstructed Q gospel does not mention any women leaders or followers with Jesus, but it references the feminine Wisdom in 11:49 and compares Jesus to a mother in 13:34. The references to women and gender in the *Gospel of Thomas* (15, 22, 46, 79, 96, 97) are primarily symbolic with regard to the unity or duality of the soul. Mary of Magdalene appears in logion 21 and, more ambivalently, 114. Read politically, this final logion, probably from the second century C.E., shows the continuing presence of and controversy over women's leadership in different Christian communities.

Paul and Pauline traditions. Women held important leadership positions in the Pauline *ekklēsiai*. This shows the influence of both the ideology of gender equality "in Christ" expressed in Galatians 3:28 and Paul's Pharasaic background, since women were part of the Pharasaic *havurah*. Notable leaders in the Corinthian community include Chloe (1 Cor 1:11), a patron whose clients report to Paul of divisions in the *ekklēsia*, and women prophets addressed in 1 Corinthians 11:2–17. Paul sends greetings from Prisca and Aquila (1 Cor 16:19; cf. Rom 16:3 and "Priscilla" in Acts 18:2, 18, 26). She and her partner were important co-workers of Paul who supported house *ekklēsiai* and Paul's ministries. Her name is listed first in Romans 16:3 and Acts 18:18, 26, highlighting her importance as equal to her husband Aquila. The greetings in Romans 16 include a number of important women leaders. These include Phoebe, a deacon at Cenchreae (16:1–2), whose role as patron (*prostatis*) is highlighted; Prisca; and Mary (16:6). The verb used for Mary here, *kopiaō*, to work or toil, is the same used in 1 Thessalonians 5:12 for the work of unnamed persons who have charge over the *ekklēsia*. Scribal and ecclesiastical traditions have attempted to hide their gender or erase their role in the Pauline communities.

Post-Pauline texts show considerable controversy and struggle over women's leadership in the Christian communities. The book of Revelation records an encounter between the author, John, and a women prophet, teacher, and leader in Thyatira slanderously called "Jezebel" (Rev 2:20–25). The graphic and violent female imagery in the visions, such as the harlot and city of Babylon, functions as a political statement against Rome as well as condemnations of women in the *ekklēsiai*. "Babylon's" destructions in Revelation 17:16 and 18:2–24 invoke Roman gendered political themes of rape and the domination of conquered peoples. Women play a more prominent role in Luke–Acts, which is probably a second-century text, than in the other Synoptic Gospels. In Luke 8:3, the role of the women patrons of the Jesus movement are highlighted early in the narrative whereas in Mark they are not mentioned until the crucifixion. Luke's Gospel features important women characters, such as Mary the mother of Jesus and the sisters Martha and Mary. Although these women are not political leaders and function as part of the authors focus on women as a literary trope, the author places a powerful political message in Mary's song, traditionally called the Magnificat, in Luke 1:51–53. Martha, who manages her own house, appears to be another patron of Jesus (Luke 10:38–42). So too the independent and wealthy merchant Lydia (Acts 16:14–15), who offers support to Paul and his traveling companions while traveling herself on business, manages a household. Women in leadership positions would not have appealed widely to Roman male society. Celsus includes the presence of women as part of his attack on Christianity (Origen, *Contra Celsum* 3.10, 44, 49, 55–57) and Pliny mentions, neutrally, two women *ministrae*, probably deacons, among the accused Christians he arrested (*Ep.* 10.96; cf. *Contra Celsum* 7.41). Luke–Acts probably accurately reflects the role of women as patrons and leaders, although Luke's emphasis on high-status women would have made the new movement more acceptable in Greco-Roman society (Acts 1:14; 13:50; 17:4).

The letters in the New Testament labeled deutero-Pauline and Pastoral Epistles present increasing strictures on women's leadership in the *ekklēsiai*. Colossians contains the first Christian *Haustafel*, or household code of duties (3:18—4:1), which stipulates subservient roles for women. Versions of the code appear in Ephesians 5:21—6:9, 1 Peter 2:12—3:7, and Titus 2:2–10. Both 1 Peter and 1 Timothy include more extended arguments against women's leadership in the *ekklēsiai*, such as scriptural examples of submission in 1 Peter 3:6 and outright bans on women's leadership in 1 Timothy 2:11–15, which also cites Eve as an example to follow. These texts are evidence of increasing patriarchalization within some Christian communities in the second century but are also indirect evidence of continued women's leadership. Hauptman has identified a parallel increase in restrictions on Jewish women in the Rabbinic text Mishnah, edited circa 200 C.E., when compared to the Tosefta, which was compiled in the third century (1999). Within both Jewish and Christian second- and third-century communities, there were power struggles over the political leadership of women.

Women in gnostic texts. A text from the same generation of Christianity as the Pastoral Epistles, the *Gospel of Mary*, shows that women's leadership continued to be celebrated. Mary Magdalene is the hero of this gospel. She comforts the other apostles at Jesus's departure and provides special knowledge about the ascent of the soul. Her leadership and teachings are directly challenged by Andrew and Peter at the end of the gospel, but Levi reaffirms her central role. This gospel was most likely written and transmitted by gnostic Christian communities that valued women leaders. Rather than reflecting the actual history of Jesus's first followers, this text functions to uphold women's authority in later Christian communities. Mary also plays an important role in the *Gospel of Phillip*, along with Jesus's mother Mary, as his constant companion whom he used to kiss often, which could suggest spiritual insight as well as possible sexual relations. The *Gospel of Phillip* refers to the enigmatic "bridal chamber," which is also referred to in the Flavia Sophē inscription from third-century Rome. While this inscription does not indicate political power, she was clearly an important member of this Christian community. Mary Magdalene also appears as an apostle of equal stature with Judas and Matthew in *The Dialogue of the Savior*, again affirming women leaders in some Christian communities. Read against the Pastoral Epistles, these gnostic texts imply a political struggle within Christian communities over the leadership of women.

In a social world where women had little tangible political power compared to men, symbolic expressions such as the *Gospel of Mary* were a means of expressing women's political power. Female characters such as Barbelo, Sophia, Zoe, and Eve and her daughter Norea appear in many Nag Hammadi texts along with historical women, such as Mary Magdalene. Many of these texts can be read politically as well as philosophically and theologically. Three of the more prominent expressions of women's power are *Hypostasis of the Archons*, the *Trimorphic Protennoia*, and *Thunder: Perfect Mind*. The term *archōn* ("ruler") is itself a political title. In this text, as with many gnostic myths, the hermaphroditic Archons, under the Chief Ruler Samael (=Ialdabaoth), are evil and benighted rulers of an inferior, material earth. They create Eve from Adam's side and rape her physical or carnal image. Cain is the product of this union. The rape of Eve suggests the Roman rape of the Sabines, a foundation story for Rome that appears in Livy, Pliny, and frequent statues and art work. Zoe and Norea also are powerful figures; Zoe elevates Sabaoth on the throne of God and Norea, after dialogue with the angel Eleleth, achieves the Pleroma. The *Trimorphic Protennoia* and *Thunder: A Perfect Mind* are powerful, often paradoxical, expressions of the Divine Feminine as Sophia/Christ, using "I am" statements. This tradition of the divine feminine goes at least as far back as Proverbs 8. *Thunder*, moreover, contains images of violence that can be read as political critique of the Romans and images of female subordination to male power that are ultimately subverted in the text's unified vision of the human and divine.

New Prophecy. The various gnostic texts from the second and third century were not the only expressions of women's leadership in early Christianity. One of the earliest renewal and reform movements, "New Prophecy," was led by Montanus (hence "Montanism") and three women prophets, Priscilla, Maximilla, and Quintilla (Eusebius, *Ecclesiastical History* 5.14). This was a charismatic, apocalyptic (and therefore political) movement that gained many adherents in the early church, with Tertullian being one of the most prominent. Rejection of marriage and opportunities for leadership attracted women for centuries. According to the heresiologist Epiphanius, there were women ministers in the fourth century who appealed to the biblical models of Eve, Miriam, and the four daughters of Philip (Acts 21:8–9; *Panairion*

49.2). *The Passion of Perpetua and Felicitas* highlights two women heroes of New Prophecy.

Assessment. Elite women such as Lucilla of Carthage, Marcella of Rome, and Melania the Elder and the Younger continued to exercise political power through patronage in the early church through the fourth century. But the ideology of gender equality that emerged from the Jesus movement and developed in the Pauline *ekklēsiai* lost significant ground over time. By the era of the imperial Orthodox Church, men continued to hold the vast majority of political power in the churches.

[*See also* Political Leadership, *subentries on* Hebrew Bible, New Testament, *and* Roman World; *and* Religious Leaders, *subentries on* Early Church, New Testament, *and* Roman World.]

BIBLIOGRAPHY

Bauman, Richard A. *Women and Politics in Ancient Rome.* London: Routledge, 1992.

Dixon, Suzanne. *Reading Roman Women: Sources, Genres, and Real Life.* London: Duckworth, 2001.

Hauptman, Judith. "Women and Inheritance in Rabbinic Texts: Identifying Elements of a Critical Feminist Impulse." In *Introducing Tosefta*, edited by Harry Fox and Tirza Meacham, pp. 221–240. Hoboken, N.J.: KTAV, 1999.

Ilan, Tal. *Integrating Women into Second Temple History.* Texts and Studies in Ancient Judaism 76 Peabody, Mass.: Hendrickson, 2001.

Ilan, Tal. *Silencing the Queen: The Literary Histories of Shelamzion and Other Jewish Women.* Texts and Studies in Ancient Judaism, 115. Tübingen, Germany: Mohr Siebeck, 2006.

King, Karen L. "Ridicule and Rape, Rule and Rebellion: The Hypostasis of the Archons." In *Gnosticism & the Early Christian World*, edited by James M. Robinson and James E. Goehring, pp. 3–24. Sonoma, Calif.: Polebridge, 1990.

Kraemer, Ross Shepard. *Unreliable Witnesses: Religion, Gender, and History in the Greco-Roman Mediterranean.* New York: Oxford University Press, 2011.

Lewis, Nicola Denzey. *Introduction to Gnosticism: Ancient Voices, Christian Worlds.* Oxford: Oxford University Press, 2013.

Lopez, Davina C. *Apostle to the Conquered: Reimagining Paul's Mission.* Paul in Critical Contexts. Minneapolis: Fortress, 2008.

Pippin, Tina. *Death and Desire: The Rhetoric of Gender in the Apocalypse of John.* Louisville, Ky.: Westminster John Knox, 1992.

Schüssler Fiorenza, Elisabeth. *In Memory of Her: A Feminist Theological Reconstruction of Christian Origins.* New York: Crossroad, 1983.

Torjesen, Karen Jo. *When Women Were Priests: Women's Leadership in the Early Church and the Scandal of Their Subordination in the Rise of Christianity.* San Francisco: HarperSanFrancisco, 1995.

Wire, Antoinette Clark. *The Corinthian Women Prophets: A Reconstruction through Paul's Rhetoric.* Minneapolis: Fortress, 1990.

Robert M. Royalty Jr.

POPULAR RELIGION AND MAGIC

This entry contains seven subentries: Ancient Near East; Hebrew Bible; Greek World; Roman World; New Testament; Early Judaism; *and* Early Church.

Ancient Near East

The stereotype of official state religion in stark contrast (if not open opposition) to popular religion and magic is not applicable to ancient Mesopotamia. Instead, there was a symbiosis between the official "religious" cult (*šangūtu*), designed to cater to the needs and wants of the divine world, and "magical" practices, designed to benefit individual human beings (*āšipūtu*). The official cult was meant to benefit the community as a whole and involved both passive and active public participation on festival days but did not extend to life-cycle rites, which were not matters of public performance. The official priestly establishment kept the divinity localized in his shrine or temple and generally in a good mood, allowing the great gods of the pantheon to serve as enforcers for legitimate private magical rites. Private rites served a wide variety of human needs, including healing from illness; avoiding misfortune; having success in business, love, and in courts of law; and resolving quarrels. The temple also provided expertise in the form of staff for the performance of private rites. Paid experts were available whenever needed, at minimal cost.

Hittite culture was similar but with a much larger pantheon (the "thousand gods of Hatti"), encompassing the religious and magical traditions not only of the Hittites themselves but also of Hattians, Luwians, and Hurrians. Both Hattians and Luwians seem to have relied on female magical experts. These women were highly respected by the Hittites and received employment even in the palace itself. Many of their names are recorded as the authors or transmitters of rituals.

Ancient Mesopotamian magical practices were, for the most part, ungendered. Magical rituals used to assist plant medicines in the healing of illness and disease were administered in or near the patient's house by *āšipus* (physicians/magical experts) associated with the temples of major gods of the pantheon. Exclusively for the benefit of women were rituals to protect expectant mothers from the baleful attentions of a fever notorious for causing miscarriages and killing young children. This fever was laid at the door of a demoness named Lamaštu, an ancestress of the Jewish Lilith, who did her evil not out of any malice or ill will but because she was herself a frustrated mother. Too ugly and unloved to ever be able to have children of her own, she stole other women's babies and attempted to suckle them with her poisonous milk. As with other diseases, magical and medical treatments were used together against Lamaštu.

Popular superstition was much concerned with lucky and unlucky days and with ill-omened events drawn from daily life. To help, the *āšipu* constructed hemerologies with recommendations for specific rituals to be performed and activities or foods that needed to be avoided on particular days. These seem generally to have served as much or more as an explanation for misfortune than as a guide for behavior.

Ill omens could be averted by ritual practices of the type known as NAM.BÚR.BIs. For example, one NAM.BÚR.BI ritual warded off the ill consequences of a man having had sex with a goat. The resulting bad luck was transferred from the goat to a beer merchant who was supposed to suffer a resulting decline in profits. A ritual in the *āšipu*'s arsenal to protect a house invaded by a *katarru* fungus (parallel to the biblical ritual for "leprosy" in houses—Lev 14.3–57) refers to household gods. The Mesopotamian assignment of divinities to specific parts of the house often reverses normal gender roles. While the Romans assigned the hearth, where the woman of the house spent much of her time, to a goddess (Vesta) and the doorposts, used by the man of the house to go about into the world, to a god (Janus), in Mesopotamia, the house itself and its grounds were under the protection of the goddess Gula. The hearth was the purview of Išum, a god, invoked to save the master of the household from harm. The grain storerooms, where the woman of the house kept her supplies, was overseen by the Pleiades, seven gods who were appeased to save the son and heir. Conversely, the doorposts were under the protection of Ištar, a goddess, who was understood to save the mistress of the household from harm.

On a more intimate scale, the libations poured at mealtimes benefited personal gods and goddesses, of which both men and women had one each. If these divinities became angry, ritual intervention could be initiated by the *āšipu*, who made up amulets and administered salves to control the stress of angina.

Women expected to give birth were attended exclusively by other women; with one exception, men were banned from the birth room in ancient Mesopotamia. In complicated births, a male doctor might assist in delivering the baby and/or saving the mother's life. The latter was the priority of ancient physicians, and they did not hesitate to administer abortifacients to ensure it. As evidenced in recitations designed to magically aid in difficult births, the soon-to-be mother was imagined as "creating" the baby and endowing it with a soul brought by her during labor from the "quay of death" to the "quay of life" using the umbilical cord as a mooring rope. A Middle Assyrian recitation compares her to a hero on the field of battle, and a very old recitation still in use in Neo-Assyrian times enlisted the help of the moon god (the divine patron of childbirth presumably by virtue of the ten lunar months of a normal pregnancy). This includes what is apparently a popular myth in which the moon god fell in love with a particularly well-endowed ("richly adorned with adornments") cow and subsequently had to intervene to ensure that the humanoid child that resulted was born safely.

In the Hurrian version of this myth ("The Sun God, the Cow, and the Fisherman"), the sun god became enamored of a sexy cow; the cow gave birth without a difficulty but was displeased by the two-legged offspring, a problem solved by giving the child to a childless fisherman. The fisherman promptly went home with his new son and instructed his wife to lie down on a bed and scream so that the neighbors would be fooled into thinking she had recently given birth and consequently would bring presents of bread and beer.

If all went well, the professional Mesopotamian midwife (*šabsūtu*) covered her head and girded her loins. Then, reciting blessings with a beaming, joyful face, she drew a circle of flour on which she laid an unbaked brick in commemoration of the first delivery of seven boys and seven girls from a giant oven/womb by the goddess Bēlet-ilī. Combining the information given in ancient Mesopotamian texts with similar customs observed in modern Iran, it is possible to reconstruct the birth-brick ritual. The baby was delivered onto the brick, followed by the afterbirth. Afterbirth and brick were left in the birth chamber for seven to nine days, and then both were buried (or otherwise disposed of) together by the midwife, thus giving the afterbirth a sort of baby analogue to keep it from molesting the real baby who had left it behind. The midwife was also responsible for cutting the umbilical cord with a knife or a sliver of cut reed and cleaning up both mother and baby. Cleaning the amniotic fluid out the baby's nose and mouth was a mini-ritual with its own recitation. The baby was also turned upside down and smacked.

Childbirth was supervised by a variety of holy women who performed the essential magical rites of birth, which no man, apart from an attending doctor, was allowed to witness. Most prominent among these was the *qadištu* (biblical *qadeshah*) who acted as a sort of magical midwife's assistant and arranged for wet-nursing. Forbidden from having children of her own by virtue of her dedication to a god, she cared for other women's children—the good version of Lamaštu (who is often called a *qadištu* in recitations). Financially independent, she belonged to a class of "women without men" who, in many societies, are frequently charged with life-cycle rites. Of particular interest in this regard is another holy woman, the *ištarītu*, whose job it was to prevent her goddess (Ištar) playing tricks on humans. According to the Šarrat-Nippuri hymn, the goddess had the power to "turn men into women" or vice versa; the *ištarītu*-woman prevented this gender switch by handing the newborn child toys appropriate to his/her gender—a weapon for a boy and a spindle and *kirissu* (or crucible) for a girl. (In Akkadian, "crucible" is used as a synonym for "womb".)

A variety of magical practices accompany weddings in all cultures. Hittite wedding jars were covered with figural representations depicting the wedding celebrations, the unveiling of the bride, and a curious magical rite consisting of a comical enactment of the wedding night by two male dancers—one of whom is dressed as a woman. The latter rite was designed to ensure that the groom was able to deflower the bride, a particularly pointed form of performance anxiety.

At Emar, the wedding of the *entu* priestess to the storm god outlines the basics of the local wedding ceremony, including the Emariot equivalent of throwing the bride's garter to a bridesmaid to ensure her speedy marriage. The washbasin in which the bride's sister washed her feet on her wedding night had a silver ring slipped into it, which she was allowed to keep as a good luck token for her future nuptials. Wedding rings were worn by women in Mesopotamia, allegedly in honor of Enkidu's preventing Gilgamesh from exercising the right of the first night with Urukean brides. From Mesopotamia also come what may be wedding songs in the form of Ištar-Dumuzi poems. This type of literature is designed to enable young girls to safely make the transition from virgin girl to mother of a family and to magically ensure that the participants in an arranged marriage will end up delighted with one another.

In case harmony did not ensue, the Hittites could turn to a ritual authored by Maštigga, an "old woman"

of Kizzuwatna. This directed a full-fledged magical attack on the tongues and hands of a quarreling duo, who could be father and son, husband and wife, or sister and brother, living or dead. In the course of the ritual, the quarrel was sucked off into fish, variously colored thread, wax, dough, and sunflowers. Figurines of tongues and hands were broken and thrown into the fire and pots were smashed, a universal folk magical rite designed to prevent the return of an unwelcome visitor. The couple was also encouraged to spit into the mouth of a variety of animals, which were then offered to the sun god. A white sheep was "lifted" over the couple and then killed and buried in a pit along with bread and wine. A black sheep was then "waved" over the couple and offered as a holocaust in a specially built hearth. As in Israel, the carcass of the holocaust sheep was dismembered and completely burnt, accompanied by offerings of oil, bread, and wine. In distinction to Israel, however, honey was included, and the bread was leavened. The addition of a piglet and a puppy to the buried "wave" offerings was also not kosher. To prevent escape, the Hittite "old woman" pegged these offerings into the earth with copper pegs. As at Yom Kippur in Israel, there was also a live sheep, which was designated as a scapegoat and consecrated to the sun god along with offerings of cheese, bread, and wine. This sheep was taken away with her by the "old woman" when she left, along with the rich garments worn by the participants. Most curiously, the "old woman" set up *huwaši* stones, the Hittite equivalent of *bethel* or *masseboth*, and the quarrelers were instructed to kick them over. Finally, the participants' wash water was sealed into a bull's horn that was to be opened only "when the ancient kings return to examine the land and customs."

The Mesopotamian *āšipu* also had rituals meant to be performed by a wife to calm a husband's anger. She had only to touch the mortal wound of a sheep with a magnet in the right hand and an iron boat in the left while reciting a prayer to Ištar. A man who found himself unable to perform sexually with his wife could choose from a variety of rituals to supplement medicines (including horse urine). In one ritual, the wife rubbed a salve on her husband's penis and her own vulva and recited sexually explicit poetry to her husband. Prayers were addressed to Ištar, with the occasional inclusion of Šazu, a manifestation of Marduk and presumably the functional equivalent of the Greek god Ares, the Seducer.

Women played a key role in funerals. In ancient Mesopotamia, a dying person was moved to a special deathbed and the soul was released from the body by the recitation of a ritual formula. The body was then washed, anointed with perfumed oil, and dressed for the wake. During this period, the dead was considered still present and was wailed over, praised, and fed with offerings left on a special chair lit by a lamp that served to contain the soul. Finally, the body, accompanied by its lamp, was carried to the grave site, which was often conveniently located in a family tomb under the floor of the house. Grave goods consisting of personal items were left with the corpse as the first installment of a series of funerary offerings provided by the family. Offerings consisted of bread, water, hot soup, and, if the family could afford it, ribs, and were accompanied by a simple ritual involving the invocation of the name of the deceased and the pouring out of a libation. Ghosts were among the potential causers of illness and were placated with special magical rituals designed around their wants and needs.

Ancient Mesopotamian kings had longer mourning periods and more splendid grave goods and funerary offerings than ordinary mortals, but otherwise the rituals were more or less the same. Among the Hittites, since the king and queen actually became gods after death, a special supplementary ritual had to be performed. This took a full fourteen days and involved cremation of the body. As with the funerals described in Homer, the pyre was extinguished with wine and the bones gathered up by the women. They took them up with silver tongs and dipped them into oil in silver vessels and finally wrapped them in cloth. At this point the "old woman" emancipated the dead king's soul from the body through means of a ritual, and the bones were then moved to a stone house, where they remained. Meanwhile the soul of the deceased took up residence in a statue that was transported in a seating chariot and seated on the silver throne (for a king) or gold bench (for a queen)

to receive several days' worth of offerings, part of which were imagined as a shared banquet with the sun goddess of the earth, the sun goddess of heaven, and the grandmothers and grandfathers (his ancestors). The dead king also received the livers and hearts of sacrificed animals in order to calm his anger and was magically sent by the "old woman" vast numbers of sheep and oxen, horses and mules, grapevines, and fruit trees full of birds. Finally, he was honored with a wish: "May thy kingdom be eternal down all generations!" All of this was accompanied by lamentations performed by mourning women accompanied by Ištar's *balag* instrument.

Women may have been prominently involved in the composition and performance of Mesopotamian funeral laments. Surviving texts include a heartfelt Neo-Assyrian lament in which a wife who died in childbirth speaks with her own voice to converse with the living:

> On the day I bore fruit, how happy I was! I was happy; happy my husband. On the day of my labor pains, my face was overcast; on the day I gave birth, my eyes were clouded. With my hands opened (in supplication), I prayed to Bēlet-ilī (saying): "You are the mother of those who give birth, save my life!" (But) when Bēlet-ilī heard me, she veiled her face (saying): "…Why do you keep praying to me?"…[In] those days (when) I was with my husband, (when) I lived with him who was my lover, death slunk stealthily into my bedroom. He made me leave my house; he separated me from my husband (and) set my feet to a land from which I will never return.

In ancient Mesopotamia, men were not forbidden to weep and beat their breasts, but more extreme mourning practices such as tearing out hair and clawing faces were only considered appropriate for women.

Another job of the *āšipu* was regulating magical practices considered borderline or illegal.

One class of quasi-legitimate magic was designed to help people get through legal troubles and to protect those appointed to high office by the king from slander. Although women could sue in court and men were well-known for their talents at slander, the texts envisage a masculine performer warding off sorcerous attack by a male opponent at law and/or magically incapacitating a female slanderer. Given the context, the female slanderer was likely to be the man's opponent in a court of law or that opponent's wife. In other words, it was men rather than women who were more typically suspected of using mechanical sorcery to harm other men.

Although either sex might practice sorcery, there were types of witchcraft only directed by women against other women. One type inflicted venereal disease on the victim. Another was designed to cause other women to have miscarriages or, conversely, to be bound fast so that the baby could not emerge. More violent sorcery was contemplated among the Hittites. A Luwio-Hittite birth ritual invokes the storm god to roar to the rescue of a mother and newborn under attack by a sorceress who has "brought the moon down from the sky" to produce hemorrhage and death, first of the mother and then of the child.

[*See also* Religious Participation, *subentry* Ancient Near East.]

BIBLIOGRAPHY

Abusch, Tzvi, and Daniel Schwemer. *Corpus of Mesopotamian Anti-Witchcraft Rituals.* Ancient Magic and Divination 8/1. Leiden, The Netherlands: Brill, 2011.

Beckman, Gary M. *Hittite Birth Rituals.* 2d ed. Studien zu den Boğazköy-Texten 29. Wiesbaden, Germany: Harrassowitz, 1983.

Biggs, Robert D. *ŠÀ.ZI.GA: Ancient Mesopotamian Potency Incantations.* Texts from Cuneiform Sources 2. Locust Valley, N.Y.: J. J. Augustin, 1967.

Friedrich, Johannes. "Churritische Märchen und Sagen in hethitischer Sprache." *Zeitschrift für Assyriologie* 49 (1949): 213–255.

Kassian, Alexei, Andrej Korolëv, and Andrej Sidel'tsev. *Hittite Funerary Ritual: Šalliš Waštaiš.* Alter Orient und Altes Testament 288. Münster, Germany: Ugarit-Verlag, 2002.

Labat, René. *Hémérologies et Ménologies d'Assur.* Paris: Librairie d'Amérique et d'Orient Adrien-Maisonneuve, 1939.

Livingstone, Alasdair, ed. *Court Poetry and Literary Miscellanea.* State Archives of Assyria 3. Helsinki: Helsinki University Press, 1989.

Maul, Stefan M. *Zukunftsbewältigung: Eine Untersuchung altorientalischen Denkens anhand der babylonisch-assyrischen Löserituale (Namburbi).* Mainz, Germany: Philipp von Zabern, 1994.

Miller, Jared L. *Studies in the Origins, Development, and Interpretation of the Kizzuwatna Rituals.* Studien zu den Boğazköy-Texten 46. Wiesbaden, Germany: Harrassowitz, 2004.

Scurlock, Jo-Ann. "Baby-Snatching Demons, Restless Souls, and the Dangers of Childbirth: Medico-magical Means of Dealing with Some of the Perils of Motherhood in Ancient Mesopotamia." *Incognita* 2 (1991): 135–183.

Scurlock, Jo-Ann. "Death and the Afterlife in Mesopotamian Thought." In *Civilizations of the Ancient Near East,* edited by Jack M. Sasson, pp. 1886–1993. New York: Scribner, 1995.

Scurlock, Jo-Ann. "Soul Emplacements in Ancient Mesopotamian Funerary Rituals." In *Magic and Divination in the Ancient World,* edited by Leda Ciraolo and Jonathan Seidel, pp. 1–6. Leiden, The Netherlands: Brill, 2002.

Scurlock, Jo-Ann. "Ancient Mesopotamian House Gods." *Journal of Ancient Near Eastern Religions* 3 (2003) 99–106.

Scurlock, Jo-Ann. "The Interplay of 'Magic,' 'Religion,' and 'Science' in Ancient Mesopotamian Medicine." In *A Companion to the Ancient Near East,* edited by Daniel C. Snell, 302–315. Malden, Mass.: Blackwell, 2005.

Scurlock, Jo-Ann. *Magico-Medical Means of Treating Ghost-Induced Illnesses in Ancient Mesopotamia.* Ancient Magic and Divination 3. Leiden, The Netherlands: Brill/Styx, 2006.

Scurlock, Jo-Ann. "Techniques of the Sacrifice of Animals in Ancient Israel and Ancient Mesopotamia: New Insights through Comparison." *Andrews University Seminary Studies* 44 (2006): 13–49, 241–264.

Stol, M. *Birth in Babylonia and the Bible: Its Mediterranean Setting.* Groningen, The Netherlands: Styx, 2000.

Jo-Ann Scurlock

Hebrew Bible

The place and function of women in ancient Israelite religion has been summed up by J. B. Segal as follows: "Women took no part in formal religious ceremonial in Israel; but in Israel, as elsewhere in the ancient world, they were supposed to have close relations with the realm of magic" (Segal, 1976, p. 6). This statement associates magic, rather than "traditional" religious practices, with women's popular religion. The association of women, popular religion, and magic is unfortunate and was later reevaluated. Feminist interpretation, noting a symbolic worldview controlled by patriarchal voices and shaped by male experiences, challenges the assumption that women's religious experiences can be subsumed under that of men. When we glimpse ancient Israelite women's religious practices, they are more often than not assessed negatively and viewed as outside "the norm." Phyllis Bird's view that "women's practice cannot simply be identified with magic or mediums or local cults because it transgresses their boundaries" (Bird, 1976, p. 103) is a plea to reconfigure the place of women's religious life and bring it from the margins to a more central position in ancient Israelite religion (p. 98).

General Overview of Gendered Dynamics of Popular Religion and Magic: Methodological Issues. Although there is textual evidence of the explicit participation of women in religious events (e.g., Lev 2:1, 5:1–2; Deut 16:11–14; 1 Sam 1:3–4), the capacity in which they were involved and the manner of their participation has not been fully recorded. In order to present a full picture one must tackle a number of methodological issues.

"Popular" versus "official" religion. The concept of "popular" religion has often been defined in terms of exclusion, that is, in contrast to "official" religion (Ackerman, 1992, p. 1; Zevit, 2003, p. 124; Albertz, 2008, p. 91). This negative definition has its origins in the polemic between Roman Catholic authorities and other forms of religions in medieval times (Zevit, 2003, p. 129) and carries with it notions of dominance. While there is no consensus as to what the definition, sources, nature, and terminology might be (Gomes, 2003, p. 32), it is becoming clear that the concept of "popular" religion needs to be reevaluated along more fluid lines. A more sociologically complex model based either on a three-tier system of national, tribal, and household/family piety (Albertz, 2008, p. 89) or a "nested" system (Zevit, 2003, p. 231) seems to be emerging. Francesca Stavrakopoulou calls for abandoning the traditional categories for a distinction between what is portrayed in the Bible and "the likely religious realities" of ancient life in Israel and Judah (Stavrakopoulou, 2010, p. 50).

"Foreign" versus "native" religious forms. This dichotomy also needs reassessment. Popular religion and magic are pitted against one another in the Hebrew Bible, with "magic" being seen as part of Canaanite practices. Both a critical assessment of the Bible and recourse to archaeology show that there is continuity between the two (Jeffers, 2007).

"Public" versus "private." The distinction between public and private spheres is rooted in eighteenth-century Western life and may not be useful when dealing with an ancient Near Eastern environment (Meyers, 2003, p. 434). One of the difficulties encountered by theoreticians of popular religion is that the boundaries between the use of "private" and "public" space are often blurred. Space is used by individuals and groups of both sexes. If we understand the household to be the main economic unit in ancient Israel, assessing the religious practices of its members as they interact throughout the seasons is a complex task. Distinguishing them along gender lines is also fraught with difficulties.

Time and space. Time and space also have to be taken into consideration. It is no longer satisfactory to say that there was a clear cutting point between the establishment of a normative, national Yahwism/monotheism and the heterodoxy, religious diversity, and pluralism that existed before (Edelman, 1995, p. 19). This has implications for women's religious practices: there may be stronger arguments for the continuity of women's involvement and leadership in religious life across historical periods. Apart from women's religious participation in rituals determined by the yearly seasons, there are rituals connected to the important phases in a woman's life. Space is also important insofar as religious practices are influenced by their occurring in the northern or southern kingdoms, urban or rural space, or in household compounds or other locations, such as the high places.

"Religion" and "magic." Approaches to the differentiation between religion and magic have shifted, from a clear demarcation and opposition between the two concepts (often following an evolutionary model that assigns "primitive" to magic and a more

"evolved" form to "religion" proper) to a more nuanced model that highlights the ideological nature of the distinction (Jeffers, 2007). The collapse of this distinction between magic and religion has powerful implications for women: it takes seriously the polemic nature of the Hebrew Bible, which condemns a range of diverse religious practices often labeled "magic" to distinguish them from the religious practices of a powerful male elite minority. As Carol Meyers observes, "Magic should be acknowledged as a valuable and important aspect of religious life. If women are particularly implicated in the use of practice that is deemed magic, then their practices must be understood as religious in nature and must be accordingly recognized and evaluated" (Meyers, 2005 p. 22). A reassessment of texts associating women with magic is essential to placing women at the center of religious life rather than in its margins.

Patriarchal bias. Finally, any methodological endeavor will have to take into account the patriarchal culture in which women's religious functions are embedded, as well as centuries of patriarchal interpretation. While patriarchal ideology is a serious impediment to a full recovery of women's practices, a number of attempts have been made using textual data from the Hebrew Bible (Bird, 1991; Meyers, 2001; Ackerman, 2003). Any reconstruction needs to acknowledge the "muted" nature of women's religious experiences (van Dijk-Hemmes, 1993, p. 27): the final form of the Hebrew Bible is the product of a dominant male voice, expressing a patriarchal worldview, driven by the Yahwist-alone movement whose aim is to establish an exclusive monotheism (Edelman, 1995; Smith, 2002). So when a number of texts record the presence of the people in the religious sphere, these may include women. The androcentric nature of the Hebrew language, which uses masculine pronouns when both males and females are concerned, complicates the issue. If we take a "maximalist" approach, however, the presence of women is assumed and the picture we get of women's participation in "mainstream" religion is more rounded than previously believed. The lack of reference to women's participation suggests that women's religious experiences may have been ignored (intentionally or not), distorted, or forgotten.

These problems of language and power have been studied by anthropologists who developed models of women's culture. The idea of a "muted culture" of women, with its double discourse of "dominant" and "muted," is a useful tool for uncovering women's religious culture (van Dijk-Hemmes, 1993, pp. 26–27). Although the task seems daunting, feminist scholarship suggests that we can get a glimpse of the religious practices of women. If we take seriously the collapse of dichotomies sketched above, and listen to the "double voice" behind women's narratives, their participation becomes manifest throughout social classes, "official" or "popular" cultic participation, and "public" and "private" spheres of religious activities. Archaeological and iconographic finds, as well as the use of comparative material, contribute to a fuller picture of women's religion.

Key Documents/Sources for Information. Along with the Hebrew Bible, archaeology has brought to light findings relevant to women's magico-religious life.

The Hebrew Bible. The material can be classified under a number of headings. First there are laws forbidding magical practices. Prohibitions can be found explicitly referring to women (Exod 22:17; Isa 57:3), to men and women (Lev 19:31; 20:6, 27), and to men but most likely inclusive of women (Deut 18:9–14). There are similar prohibitions in the narratives composed by Deuteronomistic historians in the context of Josiah's reform (2 Kgs 23:24). In the prophetic corpus, a number of texts denounce magico-religious practices among women. Some examples can be found in Isaiah 8:3, 57:3; Jeremiah 7:18; 44:15–19, 25; and Ezekiel 8:14, 13:17–23. The only other narrative describing divinatory practices is that of the woman of Endor in 1 Samuel 28:3–25.

If we take a maximalist view of religion and magic, that is, a view that takes an inclusive view of women's acting in the religious sphere, such texts as Genesis 31:19–35 (the case of Rachel's theft of the *tĕrāpîm*), Exodus 4:24–26 (Zipporah's apotropaic ritual of circumcision), and 1 Samuel 1–2 (Hannah's participation in yearly festivals, independent praying, and vow making) need to be considered. Further texts relating to the magico-religious involvement of women may be classified into narratives relating to (in)fertility (Gen 30:14–15; 1 Sam 1; Prov 31:2), birth and health care (Gen 35:17, 38:28; Ezek 13:17–23), naming (Gen 29:32–34, 30:6), blessing (1 Sam 2:1–10; Judg 17:2; Ruth 4:14–15), menarche (Judg 11:34–40), cursing (Judg 17:2), death and mourning (Ezek 8:14), and special occasions in times of crisis (Exod 4:24–26; 1 Sam 28:4–25). Women are seen "inquiring" (Gen 25:22), praying (1 Sam 1:10–12, 26–27; Ps 131), having a religious experience (Gen 16:7; Judg 13:7), or leading worship songs of thanksgiving in times of military victory (Exod 15:20–21).

Other women playing magico-cultic roles may include Micah's unnamed mother, who is associated with the ephod and *tĕrāpîm*, both used as mode of inquiry of the divine, in her son's household (Judg 17:2–4). In the Temple the role of the *qĕdēša* may need to be reassessed (Deut 23:17; Hos 4:14), as well as that of weavers for Asherah (2 Kgs 23:7) and women serving "at the entrance" of a sanctuary (Exod 38:8; 1 Sam 2:22). In political life, queen mothers (1 Kgs 15:13; 2 Chr 15:16), a female judge (Judg 4:4–5), and prophetesses (Exod 15:20; Judg 4:4; 2 Kgs 22:14; 2 Chr 34:22; Isa 8:3; Ezra 13:17; Neh 6:14) appear. These texts tell a "double voiced" story about the magico-religious life of women: all hint at specific functions, often hidden beneath intentional or unintentional patriarchal ideology.

Archaeological data. Archaeological data are of various kinds. Inscriptions yielded by the sites of Kuntillet Ajrud in the eastern Sinai Peninsula and Kirbet el-Qom in the southwest of Jerusalem (Dever, 2005) are putting the goddess Asherah at the center of religious life. Small terracotta pillar figurines often representing women holding their breasts, found throughout ancient Israel and Judah in both urban and rural contexts, also bear witness to women's religious life. Numerous amulets have been found in many places; they were understood to have apotropaic powers (Albertz, 2008, p. 101). Finally, other archaeological findings have brought to light anepigraphic evidence (Dever and Gitin, 2003, p. 282) in the form of portable altars, incense burners,

and lamps. The interpretation of this data is often difficult; but when combined with textual data, it fills in the complex picture of women's magico-religious life.

Pertinent Ancient Vocabulary. We take the maximalist view that many words used in connection to specific magical activities may include women (see Deut 18:9–11). However, it is noteworthy that the only feminine form of a word designating a woman magician (NRSV "sorceress") in Hebrew is *mĕkaššēpâ* (Exod 22:17). Because of the ideological distortion of the text concerning these women, it is difficult to know exactly what their religious functions were. However, they may have assumed a cultic role as religious intermediary. Their explicit condemnation in Exodus must mark a shift in their status, meaning their function is redundant; power now rests with the monotheists.

Others, "medium and wizards," can be either male or female (Lev 20:27). These words are also used in 1 Samuel 28:4–25, the story of the *baălāt-ôb*, literally, the mistress of a spirit, which can best be translated as "the voice of the ancestors" (Jeffers, 2013; see also Leviticus 19:31; 20:6, 27 where the same words are used). The seekers of the dead (*dōrēš el-hammētîm*) belong to the same category. In Isaiah 57:3, *ʿōnĕnāh* also translated as "sorceress," is closer to the function of oracle giver (Jeffers, 1996, p. 81), possibly pointing to a cultic role.

A term associated with prophecy, *nĕbîʾāh* ("prophetess") occurs only six times in the Hebrew Bible. The most interesting figures in this context are the prophesying women of Ezekiel 13:17. The actions described in this passage may be a distortion of midwives' apotropaic healthcare (Meyers, 2001, p. 34).

Another woman closely associated with the Temple is the *qĕdēša* (Deut 23:17; Hos 4:13–14), usually translated as "temple prostitute" but best understood as a cultic professional. *Gĕbîrâ* or "queen mother" seems to have cultic duties (see below). *Hăkāmôt* are "skilled women" or wise women (Jer 9:17).

The wide range of vocabulary used to designate female religious intermediaries suggests a complex network of practitioners, possibly organized in guilds whose roles have been downgraded by new power structures introduced by Josiah's reforms.

Religious Practices Not Sanctioned by Canonical Writers Illustrating "Women's Religion." There is a great variety of expressions of "women's religion" in all areas of women's lives, from birth to death. A number of topics may be highlighted.

Teraphim. The association of women with *tĕrāpîm* is shown in the stories of Rachel (Gen 31:19–34) and Michal (1 Sam 19:13). Karel van der Toorn's suggestion that they are "ancestor figurines" (van der Toorn, 1996, p. 206) has gained scholarly consensus. While their function is variously associated with divination (Ezek 21:21; Zech 10:2) and ancestral worship (or a combination of the two, as in the story of Micah and his mother's sanctuary in Judges 17—18), the mode of consultation might include consultation of dead ancestors (van der Toorn, 1996, p. 215). Their presence in the bedchamber makes their consultation accessible to the women of the house (Ackerman, 2008, p. 132).

Asherah. A classic case of distortion and mutedness is found in the numerous references to Asherah/ *asherah* (either as goddess or cultic object). Athirat is a well-known goddess from the Ugaritic pantheon, El's consort and mother of the gods. She has roles as a fertility goddess and wet-nurse and is often represented by a tree. Her identification with Asherah is undisputed (Day, 2000, p. 42). The goddess's presence is well-attested in the Bible, both positively (the *asherah* stood in the temple at Bethel [2 Kgs 23:15], Samaria [1 Kgs 16:33], and "on every high hill and under every green tree" [1 Kgs 14:23, 2 Kgs 17:10]; vessels were used for making offerings to Asherah's statue [2 Kgs 23:7]; women wove vestments for Asherah's statue [2 Kgs 23:7]) and negatively (associated with foreign practices [Judg 6:25–26, 28, 30] and apostasy [Exod 34:13; Deut 7:5, 12:3]).

The office of the queen mother provides another example of the importance of Asherah's cult in Israel. While Jezebel is the only queen mother in the North associated with Asherah (1 Kgs 18:19), the office appears more often in the South. In the story told in 1 King 15:13, Maacah, mother of Asa, was removed from her position because she made an abominable image of Asherah. Ackerman suggests that Asherah's position in the Canaanite pantheon

makes her a fitting symbol for women's lives (Ackerman, 2003, p. 460).

Archaeological discoveries underpin the importance of Asherah's cult. The evidence is threefold. Firstly, plaques found in Kuntillet Ajrud and Khirbet el-Qom show a close association between Yahweh and "His" Asherah (a relationship equivalent to that of El and Asherah, his consort in the West Semitic pantheon). Secondly, hundreds of pillar figurines, mostly of women, have been uncovered in urban and in rural households. These may be connected with Asherah's cult (Ackerman, 2003, p. 463). Thirdly, iconography attests the wide use of stylized trees (Keel and Uehlinger, 1998, p. 219). Clearly, worship of female deities or female representations of a deity does not necessarily imply an exclusively female following. However, the large-breasted figurines might point to a cultic function for women related to fertility and lactation (Bloch-Smith, 1992, p. 219).

Asherah's cult gives us insight into the continuity of cultic practices in the West Semitic world and provides us with an example of distortion and "whitewashing" (Edelman, 1995, p. 18). It is present in both "official" and "popular" settings, and its condemnation attests to the continuity of the cult throughout much of the Iron Age. It also gives credence to the theory of women's mutedness by tracing how the magico-religious practices of women became muted. By recovering women's beliefs in life-giving powers, beliefs that are scarcely recorded in the Hebrew Bible, we may catch a trace of women's "double voice."

Queen of Heaven. The consensus on the identification of the Queen of Heaven points to a syncretistic goddess with astral and fertility features from the Mesopotamian goddess Ishtar and the Ugaritic Astarte (Day, 2000, p. 148; Ackerman, 2008, p. 142). Its popularity among women is attested in Jeremiah 7:16–20 and 44:15–19, 25. The polemic tenor of the text must not blind us to the ritual actions performed by the whole family under the leadership of women. While Jeremiah 7:16–20 focuses on three main parts of the ritual, namely, making cakes, pouring out libations, and burning incense to the Queen of Heaven, the apotropaic nature of the ritual is articulated in

Jeremiah 44. These rituals give expression to survival strategies for the women's families and the land they inhabit.

As food production is connected with the activities of women in the household, it serves several functions, from the feeding of the family to ritual purposes, such as feeding the ancestors. The continuity between food production as mainly controlled by women and ritual is also illustrated by archaeological findings such as "cult corners" in rooms at Megiddo (Ackerman, 2008, pp. 142, 144).

Women weeping for Tammuz. The reference in Ezekiel 8:14 to women "weeping for Tammuz" is set in the context of Ezekiel's visionary denunciations of the people's behavior. It is the third of four "abominations" taking place in or near the Temple in Jerusalem (Ezek 4–11). The reference to "weeping for Tammuz" harks back to an Eastern Semitic myth celebrating the cycle of death and renewal of nature's fertility. As Kathryn Pfisterer Darr observes, this ritual "must be seen in context of rites practiced for millennia throughout the Ancient Near East as part of women's religious observances related to childbirth and fertility" (Darr, 2000, p. 335).

Ancestor worship. There is little doubt that rituals associated with the dead were familiar to ancient Israelites. Erecting burial stones (Gen 28:22, 35:20; 2 Sam 18:18), consulting the dead (Deut 18:11; 1 Sam 28:4–25; Isa 8:19, 29:4), feeding them (Gen 28:17–18, 22; Gen 31:53–54; Deut 26:14; Isa 57:8), and lamenting them (1 Kgs 13:20; Jer 22:18; Lev 19:28) were all common practices in ancient Israel. They are also attested by archaeological remains (Bloch-Smith, 1992, pp. 213–219). Van der Toorn's suggestion that the cult of the dead should be seen as a part of ancestral religion practiced in the family (van der Toorn, 1996, p. 233) needs to be extended to the wider community (Bloch-Smith, 1992, p. 222). Mourning and lamenting the dead is also an important way in which women participate in religious life as professionals (2 Sam 14:2; Jer 9:17) or as part of yearly rituals (Ezek 8:14).

The ancestral dead were also consulted, most famously in the story of the woman of Endor in 1 Samuel 28:4–25. While acknowledging necromancy, the final editors of the Hebrew Bible present it as part of forbidden practices. Women are not included in monotheism's new leadership, and consulting the deity is now only permitted through prophetic channels (Jeffers, 2013).

Finally, it is noteworthy that archaeology's discovery of bench tombs, food remains, and pillar figurines in tombs (Bloch-Smith, 1992, p. 218) seems to give credence to a wide and continuous practice.

Making vows. Vow making is another example of magico-religious action by women. While it is part of officially sanctioned religion (all women can make vows: Num 6:2–21, 30:3–15), it is striking that in the cases of Hannah (1 Sam 1:11), Lemuel's mother (Prov 31:2), and the women worshipping the Queen of Heaven (Jer 44:25), the aim of the vow is to remedy women's fertility. This practice collapses the distinction between "public" and "private," "official" and "popular," "magic" and "religion." While we do not have many examples of the mechanism of vow making, it pertains to the magico-religious sphere. It expresses a desire to communicate with the divine and to avail oneself of the bountiful forces of life. While there may not be an automatic connection between vow making and fertility, making vows in order to bear children was probably a practice prevalent among seemingly infertile women in Israel.

Assessment. The emerging picture of the religious/magical participation of women in ancient Israelite society is more complex than previously thought. As scholarship revises and reassesses its methodological presuppositions, taking into account the forgotten and the distorted, we can recover a female presence in these texts. Future research will need to work beyond Western dichotomies and adopt a more fluid model that takes seriously internal religious pluralisms.

[*See also* Deity, *subentry* Hebrew Bible; *and* Religious Participation, *subentry* Hebrew Bible.]

BIBLIOGRAPHY

Ackerman, Susan. *Under Every Green Tree: Popular Religion in Sixth-Century Judah.* Atlanta: Scholars Press, 1992.

Ackerman, Susan. "At Home with the Goddess." In *Symbiosis, Symbolism, and the Power of the Past: Canaan, Ancient Israel, and their Neighbors from the Bronze Age through Roman Palaestina*, edited by William G. Dever and Seymour Gitin, pp. 455–468. Winona Lake, Ind.: Eisenbrauns, 2003.

Ackerman, Susan. "Household Religion, Family Religion, and Women's Religion in Ancient Israel." In *Household and Family Religion in Antiquity*, edited by John Bodel and Saul M. Olyan, pp. 127–158. Malden, Mass.: Blackwell, 2008.

Albertz, Rainer. "Family Religion in Ancient Israel and Its Surroundings." In *Households and Family Religion in Antiquity*, edited by John Bodel and Saul M. Olyan, pp. 89–112. Malden, Mass.: Blackwell, 2008.

Berlinerblau, Jacques. *The Vow and the "Popular Religious Groups" of Ancient Israel: A Philological and Sociological Inquiry*. Sheffield, U.K.: Sheffield Academic Press, 1996.

Binger, Tilde. *Asherah: Goddesses in Ugarit, Israel and the Old Testament*. Sheffield, U.K.: Sheffield Academic Press, 1997.

Bird, Phyllis. "Israelite Religion and the Faith of Israel's Daughters. Reflections on Gender and Religious Definition." In *The Bible and the Politics of Exegesis: Essays in Honor of Norman K. Gottwald on His Sixty-Fifth Birthday*, edited by David Jobling, Peggy L. Day, and Gerald T. Sheppard, pp. 97–108. Cleveland, Ohio: Pilgrim, 1991.

Bloch-Smith, Elizabeth M. "The Cult of the Dead in Judah: Interpreting the Material Remains." *Journal of Biblical Literature* 111, no. 2 (1992): 113–124.

Brenner, Athalya. *The Israelite Woman: Social Role and Literary Type in Biblical Narrative*. Sheffield, U.K.: Journal for the Study of the Old Testament, 1985.

Brenner, Athalya, and Fokkelien van Dijk-Hemmes. *On Gendering Texts: Female and Male Voices in the Hebrew Bible*. Leiden, The Netherlands: Brill, 1993.

Darr, Kathryn Pfisterer. "Women Weeping for Tammuz." In *Women in Scripture: A Dictionary of Named and Unnamed Women in the Hebrew Bible, the Apocryphal/Deuterocanonical Books, and the New Testament*, edited by Carol Meyers, pp. 335–336. Boston: Houghton Mifflin, 2000.

Day, John. *Yahweh and the Gods and Goddesses of Canaan*. Sheffield, U.K.: Sheffield Academic Press, 2000.

Dever, William G. *Did God Have a Wife? Archaeology and Folk Religion in Ancient Israel* Grand Rapids, Mich.: Eerdmans, 2005.

Dever, William G., and Seymour Gitin, eds. *Symbiosis, Symbolism, and the Power of the Past: Canaan, Ancient Israel, and their Neighbors from the Bronze Age through Roman Palaestina*. Winona Lake, Ind.: Eisenbrauns, 2003.

Dijkstra, Meindert. "Women and Religion in the Old Testament." In *Only One God? Monotheism in Ancient Israel and the Veneration of the Goddess Asherah*, edited by Bob Becking, Meindert Dijkstra, Marjo C. A. Korpel, and Karel J. H. Vriezen, pp. 164–188. London: Sheffield Academic Press, 2001.

Edelman, Diana Vikander, ed. *The Triumph of Elohim: From Yahwisms to Judaisms* Grand Rapids, Mich.: Eerdmans, 1995.

Gomes, Jules. "Popular Religion in Old Testament Research: Past, Present, and Future." *Tyndale Bulletin* 54, no. 1 (2003): 31–50.

Jeffers, Ann. "Interpreting Magic and Divination in the Ancient Near East." *Religion Compass* 1, no. 6 (2007): 684–694.

Jeffers, Ann. "Wicked Witches of the West: Constructions of Space and Gender in Jezreel." In *Constructions of Space IV: Further Developments in Examining Ancient Israel's Social Space*, edited by Mark K. George, pp. 76–91. London: Bloomsbury T&T Clark, 2013.

Keel, Othmar, and Christoph Uehlinger. *Gods, Goddesses, and Images of God in Ancient Israel*. Translated by Thomas H. Trapp. Edinburgh: T&T Clark, 1998.

Marsman, Hennie J. *Women in Ugarit and Israel: Their Social and Religious Position in the Context of the Ancient Near East*. Leiden, The Netherlands: Brill, 2003.

Meyers, Carol. "From Household to House of Yahweh: Women's Religious Culture in Ancient Israel." In *Congress Volume Basel 2001*, edited by A. Lemaire, pp. 277–303. Leiden, The Netherlands: Brill, 2002.

Meyers, Carol. "Material Remains and Social Relations: Women's Culture in Agrarian Households of the Iron Age." In *Symbiosis, Symbolism, and the Power of the Past: Canaan, Ancient Israel, and their Neighbors from the Bronze Age through Roman Palaestina*, edited by William G. Dever and Seymour Gitin, pp. 425–445. Winona Lake, Ind.: Eisenbrauns, 2003.

Meyers, Carol. *Households and Holiness: The Religious Culture of Israelite Women*. Minneapolis Fortress, 2005.

Segal, J. B. "Popular Religion in Ancient Israel." *Journal of Jewish Studies* 27 (1976): 1–22.

Smith, Mark S. *The Early History of God: Yahweh and the Other Deities in Ancient Israel*. 2d ed. Grand Rapids, Mich.: Eerdmans, 2002.

Stavrakopoulou, Francesca. "'Popular Religion' and 'Official' Religion: Practice, Perception, Portrayal." In *Religious Diversity in Ancient Israel and Judah*, edited by Francesca Stavrakopoulou and John Barton, pp. 37–58. London: T&T Clark, 2010.

van der Toorn, Karel. *Family Religion in Babylonia, Syria and Israel: Continuity and Change in the Forms of Religious Life*. Leiden, The Netherlands: Brill, 1996.

Van Dijk-Hemmes, Fokkelein, and Athalya Brenner. *On Gendering Texts: Female and Male Voices in the Hebrew Bible*. Leiden, The Netherlands, and New York: Brill, 1993.

Zevit, Ziony. "False Dichotomies in Descriptions of Israelite Religion: A Problem, Its Origins, and a Proposed
Solution." In *Symbiosis, Symbolism, and the Power of
the Past: Canaan, Ancient Israel, and Their Neighbors
from the Bronze Age through Roman Palaestina*, edited
by William G. Dever and Seymour Gitin, pp. 223–235.
Winona Lake, Ind.: Eisenbrauns, 2003.

Ann Jeffers

Greek World

The fifth-century B.C.E. historian Thucydides begins
to close Pericles's funerary oration for the Athenian
war dead with the sentence, "The greatest honour of
a woman is to be least discussed amongst men,
whether for praise or blame" (*History of the Peloponnesian War* 2.45.2). Silent and unnoticed, with little to
no legal or political rights and utterly dependent on
male relatives: these are the markers of an ancient
Greek—or at least Athenian—woman. Furthermore,
if we turn to the fourth-century B.C.E. philosophers
Xenophon and Aristotle, we hear how women and
men are biologically different: Xenophon tells us how
the different sexes were created according to their
functions, women for a life indoors spent rearing
children and men for a life outdoors spent protecting
the household, city, and state (*Oeconomicus* 7.22–28),
whereas Aristotle talks of women—and boys—as un-
formed men whose physical states reflect their inability to produce semen (*On the Generation of Animals* I.728a). Indeed, for Aristotle it is these physical
differences that explain typical gender characteristics: the female of the species is passive, emotional,
and a departure from the norm, whereas the male of
the species is active, rational, and normal. These
views see a world that is genderized, genderized according to space (women/feminine: inside; men/
masculine: outside), according to activity (women/
feminine: rearing children; men/masculine: protection of the state), and according to psychology
(women/feminine: emotional; men/masculine: self-
controlled).

There was, however, one realm in which these
gendered cultural norms are said to be disrupted:
that of popular religion and magic. As Plato tells us
in his fourth-century B.C.E. philosophical treatise
Laws, women were especially active in traditional
religious activity (909e–910a). Through dedicatory
practices, acting as priestesses and their role in
ritual, ancient Greek women appeared to transcend
gendered spheres of activity so as to be vocal and
present in the traditionally male public realm. However, "appear" is the critical term. This entry will indicate how although male and female norms were
seemingly disrupted through religious and magical
activity, these so-called disruptions operated within
the traditional ancient constructs of masculinity
and femininity.

Religion, Genderization, and Gender Norms. First,
however, we must acknowledge that the genderization of space, activity, and psychology so ubiquitous
to Greek society was indeed reflected and reinforced through Greek religious activity. We only
need think, for the genderization of space, of the
Classical Athenian wedding rites. These rites see,
inter alia, the unveiling of the bride and the procession from the bridal home to that of the groom's, or
more particularly, to the groom's hearth, the center
of the home. It is this movement from natal to marital hearth, a movement ritually effected by male
relatives, that marks the marriage and the movement of the bride from her father's protection to
that of her husband's. Thus, through ritual movement and control, we are reminded of the feminine
space—the inner hearth—and a masculine motion
between spaces.

For the genderization of spheres of activity, we need
only consider rituals for the young. Let us take as examples the *Arrephoria* and *Brauronia* rituals. The
former sees select young girls serving the goddess
Athena on the Athenian Acropolis for a year during
their prepubescence. Debate rages as to the symbolic
purposes of the central *Arrephoria* rite, which com-
prises a ritual descent and testing (see Parker, 2005,
pp. 221–223); however, what can be agreed upon is that
these young girls commence the annual weaving of
the goddess's peplos. In the *Brauronia* we see young
girls chosen to "play the bear" at the sanctuary of Artemis at Brauron in Attica, during which time they partake in premarriage activities while ritually enacting,

and experiencing, a taming of feminine wildness (Parker, 2005, pp. 228–248). Hence, through ritual activity, young girls are immersed within, allocated to, and prepared for normative feminine spheres of activity (weaving, serving the house, and being a wife). Similarly, many of the rituals for young boys focus on their introduction and training into the normative male spheres of political and warrior activity. Consider the *Apatouria*, which included the ritual introduction of boys into their respective phratries (hereditary and social groups central to Athenian citizenship), or the *Ephebia*, which combined military and political training with religious observances. Not just for preparing young Athenians for their adult lives, these rituals, in the separation of genders and the corollary ritual enactment of gender identity, continually recreated and reinforced a genderization of activity and, ultimately, of ancient Greek society itself.

Of course, not all rituals were separated according to gender. However, when genders do intermix, they often do so according to this genderization of society. This can best be seen in the ubiquitous ritual activity of sacrifice. Ancient Greek sacrifice was the mode by which communication between mortals and nonmortals was opened; hence, it was central to Greek religious life. Both genders partook of sacrificial activity, although they often adopted different roles within this communal activity. The central sacrificial act—when presupposing normative animal sacrifice—of the killing of the sacrifice was traditionally performed by men (although there are exceptions: Connelly, 2007, pp. 182–184; Dillon, 2002, pp. 245–246). The role of women was to carry the basket in which the sacrificial accoutrements were placed, to prepare sacrificial offerings, and to raise the *ololyge*, the sacrificial cry. This cry, like the funerary lament that is also traditionally placed in the mouths of women, is particularly feminine in its supposed emotionality. That is, because of its central characteristic of lacking emotional control, it belongs to the feminine realm of emotion as opposed to the masculine realm of self-control (Clay, 2009). Hence, in sacrifice different genders perform different roles according with Greek preconceptions of masculine and feminine spheres of activity.

Religion and the Disruption of Gender Norms. It is, nevertheless, commonplace to note that it is through religious activity that women can physically and metaphorically transcend their normative modes of being and activity. By conducting their duties as priestesses, women are seen as active rather than passive, and by participation in dedicatory practices and communal rituals, women operate in the public, rather than the private, realm. However, when we examine these practices more closely we still find a genderization of activity.

Consider the role of priestesses in the ancient world. While acting as priestesses, citizen women were seen publicly through their roles in sacrifice and other acts. However, such women were still under the control of their male guardians and were still portrayed in a feminine manner. Dillon (2002, pp. 80–83) has explored representations of priests and priestesses on gravestones. He shows how priestesses were often depicted carrying keys or holding cult images, whereas priests were shown holding sacrificial knives: priestesses were associated with caring for the house and its occupants, in contrast to priests, who were associated with the central act of ritual communication. Consider also the act of dedication. Although we do see instances of women— often priestesses—dedicating temples and altars, it is more common to see dedications of smaller, domestic items such as spindles, clothing, mirrors, and other typically feminine gifts (Dillon, 2002, pp. 9–25). Furthermore, when we find dedications of larger items, like the famous *korai* (large, stylized female statues, approximately 10 percent of which were dedicated by women), attendant inscriptions betray the commonality of identifying female dedicators through male relatives. Take as an example the seventh-century B.C.E. dedication by Nikandre of Naxos now housed in the National Archaeological Museum at Athens (NM 1). The inscription on this *kore* reads, "Nikandre dedicated me to the far-shooter of arrows, excellent daughter of Deinodikes of Naxos, sister of Deinomenes, wife of Phraxos n(ow?)."

Hence, although public and so transcending one aspect of gender norms, the roles of priestess and dedicator still operated within ancient Greek gendered spheres of activity and gendered identities. The same can be said for the two key rituals in ancient Athens that are often used as examples for the disruption of gender norms: the *Adonia* and the *Thesmophoria*.

The *Adonia* was celebrated by all classes of women. It comprised a lamenting for the god Adonis and the growing of temporary gardens in his honor on the roofs of private houses. Often satirized for the loudness of its celebrations and for the spectacle it created, it was a time when women were seen in an ecstasy of grief. Note, however, the activities of lamenting and emotional grieving—activities that are attributed in the ancient Greek world to the feminine realm. Note also the location of the activities: as Morgan (2007, p. 300) argues, the roof remains within the boundary of the house. Therefore, although visible and audible, and therefore public, this disruption of the gender norm of "women: inside/passive" is still bounded physically in a normative feminine space and symbolically in normative feminine emotionality.

The *Thesmophoria* can similarly be seen as a disruption that takes place within bounded norms. This women-only festival consisted of a three-day celebration of the goddess Demeter Thesmophoros centering on the myth of Demeter's mourning for the loss of her daughter, Kore. This festival saw the movement of citizen women outside of their homes to a public space that, at this time, excluded men. We should note, however, the purpose of this rite, which was to promote fertility, human and agricultural, and to reinforce the community of citizen women (Morgan, 2007, pp. 304–305; Parker, 2005, pp. 275–283). We should also note the relationship between Demeter's epithet in this rite (Thesmophoros: Law-bringer) and its activities. Faraone (2011) has shown that the *Thesmophoria* provided a forum through which its female participants could raise accusations of injustice— traditionally the remit of men—both orally and then later through the use of curses/prayers for justice. This method of seeking justice was, however, peculiarly nonnormative. This is reflected in the fact that the day for such accusations of injustice coincided with the closing of the normal, male-dominated, courts. Hence, the *Thesmophoria* too sees a bounding of the disruption of gender norms through its concentration first on the traditional feminine realm of fertility and second through the highlighting of the nonnormative nature of its adaptation of the masculine realm of legal justice.

Therefore, although ancient Greek gender norms may appear to be transcended by female religious activity, we can see how this activity still operates within a genderization of society: priestesses are identified according to gender attributes, dedicatory practices reveal gendered spheres of activity and male control of female public life, and when ritual activities do push gender boundaries they do so while—paradoxically—remaining within, and reinforcing, the boundaries themselves. Significantly, when women are seen to break into a traditionally male sphere of activity—obtaining justice—they do so through curse tablets (thin metal tablets on which binding spells are inscribed). This use of the accoutrements of ancient Greek magic by women again reinforces gender stereotypes.

Magic, Gender Stereotypes, and Reality. Before discussing ancient Greek magic in detail, it should be stressed that the separation between religion and magic is artificial. Magic is an aspect of Greek religion, rather than separate to it, in that it is formed out of the same religious beliefs and practices as that of nonmagical ritual activity. Magic itself is said to have come into force as a concept in the fifth century B.C.E. as a paradigm of alterity; that is, it became a category of religion that was supposedly practiced by "others": nonmales, non-Greeks, noncitizens (Dickie, 2001, pp. 18–46; Stratton, 2007, pp. 39–70). This is best illustrated on the Athenian tragic stage. Here we find Deianeira, the wife of Heracles, accidentally killing her husband with what she thought was a love potion in Sophocles's mid-fifth-century B.C.E. production of the *Trachiniae*. Or we hear, in Euripides's *Hippolytus* of 428 B.C.E., how it is women who create incantations and words that charm (ll. 478–481). Or we are confronted with effeminate oriental magic-workers in the form of Dionysos in Euripides's *Bacchae* of 405 B.C.E. or the nameless Persian necromancers of Aeschylus's *Persae* of 472 B.C.E.

Further, we cannot deny that this is reflected somewhat in the nonliterary evidence. We find, for example, in a speech of Demosthenes against Aristogeiton of approximately 330 B.C.E. the mention of Theoris, who is named as a witch and who passed on drugs and incantations to her maid. Indeed, the presence of such women is reflected in a fictional legal speech by Antiphon in the late fifth century B.C.E. In this, we hear how, like Deianeira, the concubine of one Philoneos is tricked into killing her lover with what she believes is a love spell. However, the picture portrayed by literature—of the dominance of female and non-Greek magic-workers—cannot hold up to scrutiny. Many men too used magic (Dillon, 2002, pp. 46–76) and it is these that we find criticized by our ancient Greek philosophers and physicians. Consider Plato's censure in his fourth-century B.C.E. *Republic* of itinerant beggar priests (male) who claim a power over the gods by charms and bindings or Hippocrates's attacks, in the Classical *On the Sacred Disease*, on magic-workers and beggar priests who use purifications and incantations in the supposed healing of epilepsy. Indeed, as Gager (1992) has shown in his exploration of ancient curse tablets and binding spells, the physical remnants of magic reveal little gender (or ethnic) disjunction in its use. Hence, whereas Greek literature uses magic as a form of alterity and so others its practices onto marginalized figures, the practical use of magic, like the practical uses of religion, is for all.

We cannot ignore, however, the language used in relation to magic-workers. Female magic-workers tend to be called (in the plural) *pharmakeutriae* and *pharmakides*, whereas male magic-workers tend to be called (again in the plural) *epaoidoi, goetes,* and *magoi*. Although there is occasional overlap in these categorizations (Dillon, 2002, p. 12), the gender differentiation is significant enough to be called commonplace. *Pharmakeutriae* and *pharmakides* derive from the Greek noun *pharmakos*. This noun can be translated either as drugs or as spells, suggesting a drug/potion/herbal nature to the spells used by female magic-workers. *Epaoidoi* and *goetes*, however, stem from singing (*epoide*: song; *goetes*: wailer). Here then, at the linguistic level, we can see a gender disjunction between female magic-workers who are associated with nature and the passive application of spells (cf. the often secretive nature of potion/drug use) and male magic-workers whose magic is associated with their own strength of voice and the active application of spells (they wield the magic power in their own bodies). "*Magoi*" does not fit in this gendered language because it is based instead in an ethnic othering, derived as it is from the Persian *magos* (priest).

Gender, Love Magic, and Genderization. Such differentiation is also seen in the stereotypical allocation of female magic-workers to love magic. This can be detected in our examples above: Deianeira and Philoneos's concubine attempt love spells and Euripides in his *Hippolytus* is talking predominantly about love spells. This stereotype is best seen in the third-century B.C.E. idyll by the poet Theocritus (*Idyll* 2). This poem depicts a girl named Simaetha conducting a love spell aimed at Delphis, her neglectful lover. While calling upon the goddesses Artemis and Hecate, Simaetha attempts to draw Delphis back to her side. This is a powerful poem that shows a female lover attempting to gain dominance (physical and mental) over her male beloved. Such a love spell seems to contradict others that we hear of in the ancient world, which portray a male agent attempting physical and mental dominance over a female victim. These can be found in the Greek Magical Papyri (*PGM*), a collection of spell books dating from the fourth century B.C.E. to the fifth century C.E., and the corollary curse tablets.

Love spells and other spells concerning matters of the heart form a significant bulk of the *PGM* and curse tablets (1/4 curse tablets: Gager [1992, p. 78]; approximately 27 percent of the *PGM*). Faraone (2002) divides these into *eros* spells—violent spells used mainly by men to instill passion in women—and *philia* spells—gentle spells used mainly by women to instill affection in men. This differentiation suggests a genderization of love magic whereby violent active spells are masculine and mostly performed by men, whereas gentle, less active spells are feminine and performed by women or men in subservient roles.

However, the key word here is "mostly." Although the violent *eros* spells are mostly orientated toward male agents and female victims (83 percent; Faraone, 1999, p. 43), many are orientated elsewhere. Gager (1992, p. 80) highlights eight *PGM* spells and six tablets that contain alternative relationships: women in pursuit of women, men in pursuit of men, and women in pursuit of men. In actuality, we can go further in arguing that many of the so-called *eros* spells found in the *PGM* can be orientated to both a male and a female agent.

Our first inkling of this can be found in the fact that those spells and tablets that do suppose different gender relationships use the same language as the male-agent/female-victim spells. Consider the late oval-shape lead tablet from Hermoupolis Magna in Egypt (Brooten, 1996, pp. 81–90), which talks of inflaming the heart, liver, and spirit of one Gorgonia (female), of binding her and forcing her to "surrender like a slave" to a certain Sophia (female). Or consider *PGM* XVI.1–75, which talks of inflaming the heart and sucking out the blood of one Sarapion (male) so that he feels love, passion, and pain for a certain Dioskorous (female). These can be compared to the male-agent/female-victim type such as is found in *PGM* XIXa.1–54, which talks of inflaming one Karosa (female) and of causing her to yearn for Apalos (male), or *PGM* IV.1496–1595, which talks of inflaming the bodily organs and spirit of NN (female) and of sucking out her blood until she comes to NN (male). The similarity between these spells suggests that the users of the *PGM* are adapting the same spells no matter their gender or sexual orientation.

Furthermore, we must remember that many of the male-agent/female-victim type are generalized. Rather than being geared toward named individuals, they use pronouns that can be adapted for each user. See, for example, *PGM* VII.467–477, which demands "bring me NN (female) who NN bore." Although these spells use the masculine pronoun for the agent and the feminine for the victim, they do not assume the same gender differentiation in their practical application. This can be best witnessed through *PGM* XXXVI.69–101. This spell begins by claiming that "it attracts men to women and women to men" and yet the spell proper talks only of inflaming "the soul, the heart of her, NN, whom NN bore." This confusion between the gender of pronouns and the actual gender of users is not unique to the *PGM*. Consider the so-called Orphic Gold Tablets that were found in tombs scattered throughout the ancient world. These tablets detailed the deceased's journey through the underworld and guided them to a better afterlife. Let us take as an example the earliest extant tablet (ca. 400 B.C.E.), which was found in the grave of a woman in Hipponion in Southern Italy. This tablet talks not of its female user but instead uses the masculine pronoun when it tells the user to claim "I (masculine) am parched with thirst."

Why then is the feminine pronoun so ubiquitously used to designate the victim in the *PGM*'s nameless love spells? Here we must turn to language. The physical binding of the intended victims, the inflaming of their spirit and organs, and the metaphorical aligning of them to the status of slaves cannot but suggest a language of dominance and submission. Such a language is underlined in some of the rituals that accompany the spells that call for the piercing of poppets as a representation of the binding of the victims (e.g., *PGM* IV.296–246). Gager (1992, p. 81) suggests that this piercing is not indicative of intended harming but rather is therapeutic for the spell-doer. Brooten (1996, pp. 97–102) assumes instead that this piercing, and the accompanying slavery imagery, should be taken literally: the spells are expected to physically affect the victims and so effect the dominance of the agents. Brooten's argument gains credence when we turn to *PGM* CXXIV, which details a charm to inflict illness. This charm involves creating a poppet and piercing its eyes: the piercing is clearly supposed to result in the harming of the victim. One might argue, then, that the gendered language of the spells can be explained not by recourse to the intended gender of the user but rather by recourse to the genderization of society noted at the beginning of this entry that aligns the masculine to dominance and action and the feminine to submission and passivity.

Therefore, just as in Greek religion, we find that ancient Greek magic provides a forum within which men and women can operate outside their normative gender roles while, at the same time, ensuring operation within the traditional ancient constructs of masculine and feminine activity. It is in this way that popular religion and magic in the ancient Greek world can be said to both reflect and reinforce gender constructs and genderizations of society while allowing for a transcendence of gender norms.

Where Next? Of course, this entry has comprised quite a general overview of what is a hugely complex and broadly temporal, geographical, and cultural topic. We have been led by the extant evidence, which forces a focus on Classical Athens and Greco-Roman Egypt. Explorations of different cultures and times within ancient Greece would likely throw some interesting nuances on the tale. Much good work has been conducted in this area—especially in relation to Sparta—and these can be explored through the bibliography below.

[*See also* Gender Transgression, *subentry* Greek World; Popular Religion and Magic, *subentries on* Early Church, Early Judaism, New Testament, *and* Roman World; *and* Religious Participation, *subentry* Greek World.]

BIBLIOGRAPHY

Betz, Hans Dieter. *The Greek Magical Papyrii in Translation: Including the Demotic Spells: Texts.* Vol. 1. Chicago: University of Chicago Press, 1986.

Brooten, Bernadette J. *Love between Women: Early Christian Responses to Female Homoeroticism.* Chicago: University of Chicago Press, 1996.

Burkert, Walter. *Greek Religion: Archaic and Classical.* Cambridge, Mass.: Harvard University Press, 1985.

Clay, Christina A. "To Kneel or Not to Kneel: Gendered Nonverbal Behavior in Greek Ritual." In *Women, Gender and Religion*, edited by Susan Calef and Ronald A. Simkins, pp. 6–20. Omaha, Neb.: Kripke Center, 2009.

Connelly, Joan Breton. *Portrait of a Priestess: Women and Ritual in Ancient Greece.* Princeton, N.J.: Princeton University Press, 2007.

Dickie, Matthew W. *Magic and Magicians in the Greco-Roman World.* London: Routledge, 2001.

Dillon, Matthew. *Girls and Women in Classical Greek Religion.* London: Routledge, 2002.

Faraone, Christopher A. "Agents and Victims: Constructions of Gender and Desire in Ancient Greek Love Magic." In *The Sleep of Reason: Erotic Experience and Sexual Ethics in Ancient Greece and Rome*, edited by Martha C. Nussbaum and Juha Sihvola, pp. 400–426. Chicago: University of Chicago Press, 2002.

Faraone, Christopher A. "Curses, Crime Detection and Conflict Resolution at the Festival of Demeter Thesmophoros." *Journal of Hellenic Studies* 131 (2011): 25–44.

Gager, John G. *Curse Tablets and Binding Spells from the Ancient World.* Oxford: Oxford University Press, 1992.

Morgan, Janett. "Women, Religion, and the Home." In *A Companion to Greek Religion*, edited by Daniel Ogden, pp. 297–311. Malden, Mass., and Oxford: Blackwell, 2007.

Ogden, Daniel. *Magic, Witchcraft and Ghosts in the Greek and Roman Worlds. A Sourcebook.* Oxford: Oxford University Press, 2002.

Parker, Robert. *Polytheism and Society in Ancient Athens.* Oxford: Oxford University Press, 2005.

Stratton, Kimberly B. *Naming the Witch: Magic, Ideology and Stereotype in the Ancient World.* New York: Columbia University Press, 2007.

Pauline Hanesworth

Roman World

The term "popular religion" generally refers to the religious activities of ordinary people, especially those rituals, beliefs, and behaviors that are unsanctioned by religious authorities. The term popular religion as applied to the Roman world fits only imperfectly. It can be misleading, in that Roman religion was not generally "sanctioned." Those holding religious offices were not responsible for, and neither dictated nor authorized, the religious activities of ordinary people. Popular religion in the Roman world can be better understood, therefore, as "religion on the ground"—rites, actions, and beliefs that could be either traditional (i.e., passed down from generation to generation) or improvised to suit a particular situation. The forum for these rites, actions, or beliefs might be public (as in pilgrimages or the public celebration of festivals) or private (as in domestic or household religion). These sacred rites of individuals, the so-called *sacra privata*, were considered a fundamental, lawful, and crucial Roman right and responsibility (Cicero, *On the Laws* 2.22).

Popular religion has often been subjected to a two-tier system of evaluation, denigrated or dismissed as the unschooled, misdirected, superstitious activities of common people; hence the negative connotations of the associated term "folk religion." As such, popular religion has also been perceived as alternately quaint or threatening, charming or dangerously unauthorized and misguided. However, it should be emphasized that in the Roman world, informal or quotidian religious acts (or even beliefs) were not necessarily different for people of different social classes. Public religion was, for the most part during the first and second centuries C.E., driven by the demands and traditions of the Roman state; that is, it was primarily civic in nature. Although formal religious offices were restricted, in the main, to the elites (and almost exclusively to elite men), those of lower social status were not free to define the contours of their own religious experience but actively participated in public, civic ritual. These religious behaviors were frequently set out on public noticeboards (the *fasti*) and although "popular" on the one hand—in that they were the rites and practices "of the people"—they were also carefully controlled by Roman elites (Cicero, *On the Laws* 2.19). Whether it was the celebration of a local festival, the propitiation of a specific deity, or a pilgrimage to a sacred site, these forms of popular devotion tended to cross social hierarchies. The term "popular religion" here, therefore, is not meant to be synonymous with erroneous and outdated concepts such as the "religion of the masses."

"Magic" is no less problematic a term than popular religion. It too invites misconceptions and negative connotations, which are often unwarranted and which cannot be sustained from the ancient evidence. The term itself derives from the ancient Greek *mageia* or *magos* (Sophocles, *Oedipus Rex* 387–389; *On the Sacred Disease*, 2; Aeschylus, *Persians*, 317); the term *goës* ("sorcerer"), always pejorative, also appears in Greek literature of the Roman period. We find *magos* already as a term of abuse as early as Athenian sources from the 420s B.C.E. Common to modern understandings of the term is that magic tends to be driven by individual action,

seeks to manipulate powers or deities, can be improvised, and is generally unauthorized by established religious structures of power. Magic is "illicit" where religion—even popular religion—is licit. In the Roman world, however, magic and religion were never juxtaposed. Magic, at least in contemporary parlance, also often connotes the manipulation of forces and powers for malevolent purposes and ends; a prime case (and one well attested in Roman literary sources) is necromancy, the reanimation of corpses or their use for purposes of divining knowledge, or so-called aggressive magic such as curses and abjurations.

Contemporary scholarship recognizes the problematic and arbitrary use of the term "magic" to classify forms of social behavior that defy easy categorization. The subjectivity of such classification is evident when we consider behaviors often linked to magic, such as prayer, exorcism, healing, or medicine, which carry no such negative connotations. What Romans termed magic (specifically the practice of magic) was associated with liminal places, including thresholds, crossroads, or cemeteries—all places where, in the literature, we find mention of witches (Lat. *striga*). Noteworthy is the connection between Roman magic, a set of liminal practices, and women, as often socially liminal beings, all the more so when they are at significant thresholds of social status; hence, the consistently negative valence of elderly women or girls who die unmarried. Roman literature often draws upon the trope of women exercising power through illicit channels such as magic, given that other sanctioned forms of religious power were unavailable to them. However, critical studies of magic in the Roman world reveal no particular correlation between women and the practice of magic.

Ritual and Practice. In the public domain, Romans honored their gods in an extensive and expanding pantheon. The deities (and attendant practices) of colonized peoples were assimilated into Roman religion, which already built on the two central conceptual foundations of native Italic and Etruscan traditions on the one hand and on Greek religions on the other. According to the statesman and rhetor Cicero

(106–43 B.C.E.; *On the Nature of the Gods* 2.8), the very definition of Roman religion was the *cultus deorum*—the care and cultivation of the gods. Although animal sacrifices, sometimes enacted on an impressive scale, were the chief public ways to honor the gods, these were usually the impresario acts of priests and attendants who specialized in offering sacrifices. People participated through attending these sacrifices, performed outside the temples on the altars that formed the focal point of a god's cult, and through the public feasts that followed. Like the sacrifices, the temples were restricted, in the main, to priestly officials. Nevertheless, the gods were accessible to all people; they could be petitioned through private prayer and supplications; celebrated at parades (*pompa*), festivals, games (*ludi*), circuses, and theaters; and thanked with acts as grand as the staging of public events or as modest as an anatomical terracotta votive deposited in gratitude for a healing or successful delivery of a child. Religious devotion to the gods was both pragmatic and contractual, accessible, and omnipresent.

A separate class of gods, the *Lares* and *Penates*, was associated with the Roman home (*domus*) and honored with private rites and devotional acts generally directed by the *paterfamilias*. These were performed for the benefit of members of the extended household, including its slaves. These gods—figured as statuettes kept in painted shrines (*lararia*) in the house—received small gifts, including incense, wine, and garlands, in exchange for keeping the house and its inhabitants safe. These "bloodless" sacrifices were every bit as essential for the successful spiritual economy of the empire as a whole as large, staged public rituals directed to Rome's chief gods. Within the household, the *paterfamilias* also led rites associated with birth, marriage, and death. Outside the home but within the confines of a private property, the *paterfamilias* oversaw rites dedicated to various tutelary deities, including Silvanus, Mars, Diana, and Flora, the goddess of blossoming plants (Martial, *Epigram* 10.92). Although less common, women, too, could make offerings to any and all of these gods (Plautus, *Pot of God*, 23–25; *Merchant* 678–680).

Not all Roman deities had formal cults. Often not anthropomorphized, some were associated with woods, streams, and places within the physical environment. Others were associated with specific days or the turning of the year, like Anna Perenna. Still others were abstractions, like Fortuna or Concordia. They were nonetheless perceived as puissant forces that needed to be respected, appeased, avoided, or celebrated. Neither was Roman religion necessarily oriented solely around deities; there was a strong sense of things, days, places, and actions as auspicious or inauspicious. Things could be polluted or pure; figures or actions could be taboo. The fear of the evil eye or generalized *malum* was widespread and could be offset by ritual actions or by apotropaic objects.

Women, in particular, recognized, honored, or invoked a broad spectrum of minor deities involved with life-cycle rituals such as marriage and with pregnancy and childbirth. Iugatinus, Subigus, and Cinxia were symbolically present during the marriage ritual; Cinxia, whose name comes from a bride's *cingulum*, or belt, was also associated with various tying and untying rituals during labor. Mena (or Dea Mena) and Fluonia were both associated with menstrual flow and its retention during pregnancy. According to Augustine (*City of God* 7.2–3), Sentinus, Alemona, and Vitumnus nourished the embryo in the womb. Juno Lucina presided over childbirth; the triple Nixi Di oversaw elements of labor, and Egeria was propitiated by pregnant women to safely push out (*egerere*) newborns. Postverta and Prosa might prevent breech births. After birth, the newborn was carefully protected from the baleful influences of demons who specialized in infant mortality. The poet Ovid mentions, for instance, that people hung Rhamnus (buckthorn) branches in the doorway of their home to ward off *striges*, winged witches who lived on the blood of newborns (*Fast.* 6.101ff).

Since they were not officially regulated, funerals and commemoration of the dead also fall under the rubric of popular religion. The dead were honored with prayers and small gifts such as a sprinkling of grain, some violets, or bread soaked in wine (Cicero,

On the Laws 2.22; Ovid, *Fast.* 2.533–542); At the Parentalia and Feralia festivals (18–21 February), people brought gifts to the tombs of their family and ancestors and feasted in honor of the dead—practices that carried over into the early Christian era. People of all social classes participated in these rituals, although we can see in the accounts of Cicero and Ovid attempts by the Roman upper class to curtail displays and behaviors around funerals and commemoration that they found vulgar or ostentatious.

Changes in Popular Religion during the Roman Empire. Beyond the state system of priestly offices, the first century C.E. witnessed a growing corps of independent religious specialists who offered particular services, including various types of divination, astrology, and magic. Although attested as early as the second century B.C.E. (Plautus, *Braggart Soldier*, 692–694; Cicero, *De Div.* 1.132), the rise of these specialists in the first century C.E. marked both a type of "privatization" of Roman religion in the empire and a new entrepreneurial spirit that made novel religious options both available and attractive for the first time. These more improvised and unstructured religious specialists are not to be confused with the rise of other more organized religious options to emerge at the same time—notably Mithraism—but shared with these cults both audience and philosophy, that is, that certain kinds of privileged knowledge or experience could be accessed through innovative religious techniques that were hitherto restricted to a small number of elite practitioners.

These types of popular religious or magical practices that religious practitioners employed were often met by derision or ridicule in Latin literary sources. The Roman author Lucian (125–180 C.E.), for example, lampoons miracle-workers who claimed to heal people through what amounted to quackery, such as tying the tooth of a weasel picked up from the ground with the left hand to one's feet to cure rheumatism (*Lover of Lies* 7–8, 12, 16). In Lucian's *Life of Alexander of Abonoteichus*, the magician Alexander sets up shop in Bithynia to take advantage of gullible but wealthy women. Although these examples of religious behavior survive as satire, they reveal the widespread and essentially fungible nature of mag-

ical and popular religious practices in the Roman world.

Women could also find an audience as independent religious specialists, although again, an accurate picture needs to be read through the distorting lens of Latin literature. The Roman satirist Petronius writes of Quartilla, who presides over extravagant rites to the ithyphallic god Priapus, and the "priestess" Oenothea who cures another character's impotence (*Satyricon* 16–26; 131.1–7; 136–137). Although these women are fictional, there is no question that women could, and did, find roles as religious entrepreneurs.

Popular Religion and Magic in Roman Literature. In Roman literature, women are frequently the practitioners of magic, particularly as necromancers. In Latin literature, we find the first instances of the word *maga* in the first century B.C.E. (e.g., Aesop 117). The Roman author Lucan (39–65 C.E.) features the witch Erictho, who lives among tombs and violates human corpses (*Pharasalia* 6). Erictho's horrifying activities include necromancy, both for the purpose of gaining information about the outcome of a distant war and for sending information to the shades trapped in the underworld below. Erictho's most abominable crime is child sacrifice, where she tears a fetus from the womb and throws it on an altar (6.558–559). Seneca's tragedy *Medea* features the witch pouring her own blood on an altar as a libation to Hecate (797–810). Another popular writer, Horace (65–8 B.C.E.), gives a satirical account of two hags on Rome's Esquiline Hill who excavate corpses for necromantic purposes (*Satire* 1.8). Among Roman writers of the second century C.E., Lucius Apuleius (125–180 C.E.) includes in his satire *The Golden Ass* the character Pamphile, a witch who draws upon a stable of conventional objects drawn from corpses and cemeteries: crucifixion nails, body parts, even the pulsating entrails drawn from a still-living human being (3.15–18; cf. the witch Meroe in 1.8–10; 2.28–50). The witches of Horace's *Epode* 5 starve a boy to use his liver for a love potion.

Women witches in Latin literature have other specialties as well. Some employ magical potions that have the power to transform human bodies into animal bodies. In *The Golden Ass*, Pamphile transforms into a bird (*Golden Ass* 3.21); another witch turns her enemies into a frog and a beaver (1.8, 9; cf. Circe in *Odyssey* 10.212). In Ovid's *Fasti* 2.533–638, a repulsive hag appears in the home on a particular festival, making an odd ritual of closing a fish's mouth as an offering to the goddess Tacita: apparently this was a binding spell. Trimalchio in Petronius's *Satyricon* warns of nocturnal witches who "turn everything upside down" (63.9).

It must be remembered, in all these instances, that literature teaches us about attitudes, biases, and tendencies among Roman male elites, but not about gender and witchcraft in the Roman world. These cases of so-called witches and witchcraft point to the Roman devaluation of women through identifying them closely with sources of pollution, such as corpses or tombs, or through social marginalization. Simultaneously, Roman literature excises men from the domain of magical practices, where they ought not to be, since "real men" did not have to resort to magic to exercise influence (Graf, 1999).

Although Roman literature presents magic as the exclusive domain of women practitioners, modern scholarship suggests otherwise. Spell books and curse tablets (*defixiones*) reveal that men requested magical intervention more frequently than women (Dickie, 2000, pp. 563, 571). The strong erotic attractions of magical spells may have been necessary to sever women's ties from the close bonds of family in which they were locked in the Greek and Roman worlds; they may also have "excused" young women from behaving in ways that were socially unacceptable, such as engaging in sexual activity before marriage or prematurely leaving the familial unit (Gager, 1992). Love spells may have brought social advantage to both men and women by helping to secure advantageous marriage, thus playing a competitive, rather than strictly erotic, function (Graf, 1999). However, the specific and explicit language of erotic spells, along with the frequent demand that women remain faithful to only one lover, helps modern scholars to reconstruct a picture of sexual activity in the Roman world that showed women to be independent sexual beings rather than innocent virgins who were kept protected by their families (Dickie, 2000, p. 571).

Material Culture: Votives, Lamellae and Defixiones, and Amulets. The popular religion of the Roman world is most clearly perceived through substantial material deposits: votive offerings and inscriptions; "aggressive" magical objects including engraved sheets of metal (*lamellae*), curse tablets (*defixiones*), and other magical objects, the goal of which was to actively curse the recipient; apotropaic objects including amulets and other small finds of the same nature (i.e., *bullae* and *crepundia*); magical bowls; and occasionally biological material including animal and human bone or teeth or human fetuses.

Votives. Large numbers of anatomical votives gathered from cult sites in the Roman world reveal the widespread practice of fulfilling vows as thanks to various deities for healings. Some of these were associated with healing shrines such as those dedicated to Aesculapius; others, however, had no such universally recognized cult, such as the Ponte di Nona site nine miles east of Rome, which yielded over 8,000 votives in modern excavations, or the *Laghetto del Monsignore* in Latium, Italy, with 11,400 pieces of pottery, metal, or bone deposited in the lake over the course of at least four centuries. The nature of these votives indicates that both men and women engaged in this ritual practice.

Lamellae and defixiones. Lamellae are thin sheets of metal that are inscribed and then folded and placed inside a capsule to be worn, usually around the neck. The inscriptions were prayers or invocations, calling upon the protection of the wearer. In some cases, the *lamella* was not worn but deposited in graves or springs and contained curses (*defixiones*) drawing upon the power of maleficent forces to harm an opponent or enemy. Both men and women commissioned these objects.

Amulets. The Roman use of amulets was widespread and taken for granted. These were crafted from a variety of materials known to have magical or apotropaic powers, including amber, rock crystal, lead, and tin (Pliny, *Natural History* 37.9ff). Some amulets were connected to both gender and life stages; Roman boys wore *bullae* amulets around their necks; girls often carried small objects known as *crepundia* in pockets or pouches. Both types of amulets were used in life, but are also found in funerary contexts. Inscribed rings and other pieces of jewelry called for good luck for their wearers, who were almost always male. "Good luck" and "good health" formulae directed at the (male) wearer also appear on helmets, shoes, and textiles. These objects and their adjurations transcend pat categorization into "pagan," "Jewish," or "Christian," especially when their language (i.e., "Lord, help!") is general and found in a variety of possible contexts.

A number of amulets aimed to protect wearers from disease, particularly fevers, pains in the stomach, and digestive ailments. A large corpus of amulets is associated with female reproduction: to ensure fertility, retain pregnancies, or ensure a good birth. Many amulets feature depictions of uteri figured as large-mouth kettles and, on occasion, entreat the uterus to contract or the fetus to hasten downward (i.e., through the birth canal). However, many uterine amulets are concerned with its closing (i.e., the sealing during pregnancy, but also stopping a hemorrhage) or opening (bringing menstruation or miscarriage). Most amulets are crafted of hematite ("blood stone"), which was believed in antiquity to staunch or slow blood flow. These amulets demonstrate the interconnection of magic and medicine.

A third category of amulet was explicitly apotropaic. We find amulets against snakes, scorpions, and other creeping things or "evil eye" spells used to ward off demonic interest, especially interest in infants. A number of demons appear in the sources to be associated with child mortality: Gello (perhaps associated with the Hebrew Lilith), Abyzou, Petasia ("she who strikes"), and Paedopniktria ("child suffocator"). It is not clear, however, that women were the chief practitioners of magical healing or apotropaic spells or the principal commissioners of amulets.

Assessment. The ancient Romans engaged in a wide range of religious behaviors, both privately and publicly, directed both toward gods and toward non-anthropomorphic forces, both traditional and improvised. Popular religion cannot be simplistically drawn as the religion of the masses in contradistinction to religion of the elite; Romans participated in the *cultus deorum* together, feared unseen malevolent forces together, and attempted to control and

understand their world together, whether elite or subelite. Women fare worse than men in the negative pictures of witches and sorceresses drawn in Latin literature, but these negative evaluations of the female religious practitioner masked a social reality wherein men were as likely to participate in magic as women and where independent female experts could find an audience for their particular religious specialties, whatever these might have been.

[*See also* Popular Religion and Magic, *subentries on* Early Church, Greek World, *and* New Testament; Religious Leaders, *subentry* Roman World; *and* Religious Participation, *subentries on* New Testament *and* Roman World.]

BIBLIOGRAPHY

Beard, Mary, John North, and Simon Price. *Religions of Rome.* 2 vols. New York: Cambridge University Press, 1998.

Betz, Hans Dieter, ed. *The Greek Magical Papyri in Translation.* Vol. 1. Chicago: University of Chicago Press, 1986.

Bremmer, Jan N. "The Birth of the Term 'Magic.'" *Zeitschrift für Papyrologie und Epigraphik,* 126 (1999): 1–12.

Dickie, Matthew W. "Who Practised Love Magic in Classical Antiquity and the Late Roman World?" *Classical Quarterly* 50, no. 2 (2000): 563–583.

Faraone, Christopher. "A Greek Curse against a Thief from the Koutsongila Cemetery at Roman Kenchreai." *Zeitschrift für Papyrologie und Epigrafik* 160 (2007): 141–157.

Gager, John. *Curse Tablets and Binding Spells in the Ancient World.* New York: Oxford University Press, 1992.

Graf, Fritz. *Magic in the Ancient World.* Translated by Franklin Philip. Cambridge, Mass.: Harvard University Press, 1999.

Stratton, Kimberly. *Naming the Witch: Magic, Ideology, and Stereotype in the Ancient World.* New York: Columbia University Press, 2007.

Warrior, Valerie. M. *Roman Religion.* New York: Cambridge University Press, 2006.

Nicola Denzey Lewis

New Testament

As a concept, magic has been constructed and deconstructed so many times that, like a sandcastle recently submerged under a wave, its delineations can no longer be determined with the confidence of scholarship from a century ago. Some think the term should be ditched altogether, the binary oppositions between magic and religion, science, and modernity all being modern biases rather than ancient understandings. Others seek to explore its rhetorical usage, since its terminology is quite old even if its meanings have changed throughout time. A socially contextual approach, however, that demonstrates how the terminology developed, was deployed, and sometimes was claimed under particular social conditions is a prominent direction forward in current scholarship. So what does it mean when someone claims that Jesus—or another early Christian—was a magician? Is it a statement of fact? Is it a matter of perception and representation? Is it merely name-calling, applying stereotypes and literary tropes to fill in one's account; or, even if polemical, do such accusations have content?

In the preface to his 1978 study, *Jesus the Magician*, Morton Smith wrote, " 'Jesus the magician' was the figure seen by most ancient opponents of Jesus; 'Jesus the Son of God' was the figure seen by that party of his followers which eventually triumphed; the real Jesus was the man whose words and actions gave rise to these contradictory interpretations" (p. vii). Although Smith sought to determine whether Jesus was a magician by ancient definitions, these opening lines express the problem of magic in not only ancient discourse, but also medieval and modern. With some important exceptions in which people have claimed the title "magician," it has been a discourse of alterity applied to those on the margins who were perceived as a threat to social order—lower classes, women, foreigners, and colonial subjects—to regulate society according to the definers' norms and values.

Although Smith might have been correct that Jesus's words and actions often resemble those who were called magician in antiquity, the differences among magicians, sorcerers, witches, prophets, and miracle workers were in fact blurry. The question is not whether Jesus or any of his followers were magicians. Rather, one must situate Jesus's and his followers' activities into broader social frameworks and trajectories of reading to see how and why accusations of magic operated among early Christians as they were charged, eluded such charges, and charged others with magic.

Ancient Greek Terminology. Unlike many other problematic terms debated in modern biblical scholarship (e.g., religion, Gnosticism), the terms "magic" and "magician" circulated widely in ancient Mediterranean discourses. The terminology of magic (*mageia*) and magician (*magos, magoi*) originated among the Magi, the priestly tribe of Medo-Persians; nonetheless, starting in the fifth century B.C.E. in Greek sources the term had already been reappropriated in the Mediterranean world as one of denigration. Although occasionally used technically to refer to such a Median and sometimes as a self-designation, it was mostly employed as a polemical term.

A more common term used was *goës, goëtes, goëteia*—often translated as "sorcerer" and "sorcery." This term was not as ambivalent as *magos*, but had a decidedly more negative connotation to it. Women, additionally, were more often accused of *pharmakeia*, the mixing of herbs, which is often useful for medicinal healing, but also for harmful effects of potions for love and death.

In the weight of ancient evidence, Greeks, Romans, the Hebrew Bible, Second Temple Judaism, and Rabbinic Judaism all tended to charge women more often than men with magic, forms of which—through love and death—undermined male sexual privilege, although, significantly, the preponderant material evidence for surviving love spells instruct men how to attract a woman. Early Christians in the first centuries C.E., however, tended to portray magicians as men who victimized women.

The Charge of Magic in the New Testament and Beyond. There are no explicit charges of magic against Jesus and his disciples in the New Testament. Although *magos* and related terms appear, they never cling to members of the early Jesus movement. Famously, the Magi—positively represented—come from the East at Jesus's birth in Matthew 2:1–2. Acts and Revelation level the accusations against outsiders, competitors, and figures of traditional institutional authority.

Nonetheless, the Synoptic Gospel accounts portray a series of accusations that in its local context would have been understood as relating to magic even if they do not use the terminology. Whereas in Greek, Roman, and Rabbinic sources the charge of magic was primarily made against women, in the New Testament sources men are the primary objects, feminizing and exoticizing them by placing them in a series of conceptually overlapping alterities of illegitimate channels of numinous power.

Miracle workers, including Jesus and many of his early followers, drew indictments of magic and leveled such charges at others. The gospel narratives acknowledge such accusations and represent Jesus and his earlier disciples in the Gospels and Acts in such a way to elude them. Garrett (1989) argues, in fact, that on the surface there may be little difference in the activities of magicians and those of the emergent Jesus movement in Luke–Acts, that Luke–Acts may even rely upon the similarities, but the rhetoric of Luke–Acts demonstrates that Jesus's power comes from God rather than the devil; therefore, from its own perspective, Jesus was not a magician.

First let us look at the charges of magic in the New Testament and oppositional literature (e.g., Rabbinic literature) and then consider the broader social conditions that allow and disallow such a labeling to occur.

The charge of magic in the New Testament. Charges of magic relate to Jesus's miracles, particularly his exorcisms and his healings. But did Jesus have help? From where did he receive his power?

The first potential accusation is subtle. It is easy to miss in the Synoptic Gospel narratives. It circulates as rumor rather than a direct accusation, but its implications for perceptions of Jesus are significant. If one reads Mark 6:14–16 (par. Matt 14:1–2; cf. Luke 9:7–9), one notices it is not about Jesus's identity, but about the source of Jesus's power: "Some were saying, 'John the baptizer has been raised from the dead; and for this reason these powers are at work in him [Jesus]'" (Mark 6:14b). It never says Jesus is John the Baptist, except insofar as John may possess Jesus, but receives his power from John being raised from the dead. The charge is that Jesus was a necromancer;

John became his spirit helper. The disagreement is which spirit is helping him: John the Baptist, Elijah, one of the prophets of old, etc. Herod Antipas decides it must be John the Baptist getting his revenge for having his head cut off. The spirit of one who had an especially violent death like John—or Jesus for that matter—fits the broader view of possible sources of a spirit helper.

On a related note, in the Gospels and Acts people not immediately associated with Jesus's group exorcise demons in Jesus's name. In the Gospels (Mark 9:38–41; Luke 9:49–50; dropped by Matthew), this is encouraged by Jesus since "whoever is not against us is for us" (Mark 9:40). Yet, in Acts such an action is discouraged. There the seven sons of Sceva are itinerant exorcists who try and fail to cast out demons in Jesus's name (19:13–16). Why is this allowed in the Synoptic Gospels and not in Acts? One difference is that in the Gospels, Jesus is alive; in Acts, he had already experienced death but, having died a violent death, would be seen as useful for a magician to use him as a familiar spirit (Garrett, 1989, p. 3; Smith, 1978, pp. 35–36).

Better known is the pericope where scribes or Pharisees from Jerusalem (that is, those closer to traditional institutional power) charge Jesus directly (and not as rumor) of casting out demons by Beelzebul (Mark 3:22–30; cf. Matt 12:22–37; Luke 11:14–23), that is, the prince of demons. Jesus's power is acknowledged—even his enemies claim he can heal or exorcise demons—but it is a corrupt source. Jesus retorts that "if a house is divided against itself, that house will not be able to stand," indicating that the source of his power is, in fact, legitimate. He turns the tables on his accusers, claiming that they blaspheme the Holy Spirit by claiming that the Spirit's works are that of an unclean spirit. That is, Jesus's source is divine rather than demonic; his miracles, moreover, are evidence that Satan's kingdom is coming to an end (Mark 3:26).

Even as New Testament accounts present Jesus similar to magicians, but largely defend Jesus against accusations of magic, New Testament works also level such charges against others. Revelation employs such language occasionally. Conjuring the name of "Jezebel"

(Rev 2:20) as an emblem of a false prophetess, John of Patmos engages the overlapping stereotypes of foreign, female, and dangerous—and, from the Hebrew Bible, Jezebel practices "sorceries" (2 Kgs 9:22). Rome, moreover, is depicted as a whore who deceived by her sorcery (*pharmakeia*) (18:23). Although not a human woman, a feminized Rome stands accused of the magic most associated with women (*pharmakeia*).

Acts works through a series of comparisons and contrasts between proper miracles and magic, usually depicting any competitors among the apostles as practicing magic, derived from the devil, instead of miracles from God. Most famously, Simon "Magus" performed "magical works" (Acts 8:11; trans. author). After Philip converts him to Christianity, he attempts to purchase the power of the Holy Spirit. It is the portrayal of a buy-and-sell attitude that brings his activities into the stereotypes of ancient magicians as charlatans trying to make a buck. The charge of magic is also leveled at Elymas bar Jesus (Acts 13:4–12), the seven sons of Sceva (19:13–16), who "adjured" in Jesus's name and others, seeing their failures, gave up their magical books (19:19), and the female slave with the Pythian spirit (16:16–18).

The charge of magic against Jesus beyond the New Testament. In addition to the Gospel accounts, which favor Jesus, other sources also accuse Jesus of magic and sorcery. Justin Martyr, a second-century Christian, had to counter the charge of Jesus as magician, as did Origen in the third century against the previous accusations by Celsus (Justin, *Dial.* 69:6f; 108:2; *1 Apol.* 30; cf. Tertullian, *Spect.* 30; *Cels.* I.6, 26, 28, 38, 40, 66, 67, 58; II.1, 6, 7, 9–12, 44; III beginning; IV.75).

Schäfer (2007) reads the Talmudic traditions of Jesus learning magic in Egypt as inverting traditions from the Gospel of Matthew. In Matthew, Jesus goes to Egypt as a child to escape Herod's persecutions (Matt 2:13ff) after being visited by the Magi (Matt 2:2). The rabbis take these connections and the relationship between Egypt and magic in antiquity and invert them, aligning the story of Jesus with a preexisting story of Ben Stada. Whereas the book of Matthew positively relates Jesus to Egypt, the Magi, and healing powers, the Rabbis negatively associate

Egypt as the place where Jesus gained illicit magical powers to perform his miracles and healings—never doubting he performed them, but questioning the source of his power (cf. Smith, 1978, pp. 47–48).

Although there are Talmudic stories related to Jesus in the Babylonian versions that have nothing to do with Jesus in the Palestinian ones (*b. Sanh. 107b*; *b. Soṭah 47a*) and the Babylonian Talmud claims that Jesus was killed for his sorcery (*b. Sanh. 43a*), there is a greater tendency to ascribe magic to Jesus in Palestinian than in Babylonian Rabbinic sources (Schäfer, 2007, pp. 101–106, 114).

Like the Gospels and Acts, many Rabbinic sources report one's ability to heal in Jesus's name and assume that such an invocation of Jesus's name was effective (*T. Ḥul.* 2:22f; *y. 'Abod. Zar.* 2:2/12, fol. 40–41a; *y. Šabb.* 14:4/13, fol. 14d–15a; *Qoh. Rab.* 1:24; *b. 'Abod. Zar.* 27b) but that it was better to die than to be healed in Jesus's name. Jesus's name has recognized power, even from among his enemies, but its source is questionable. In another story, a healing is actually accomplished, but it is still better to die than be healed by a heretic (*y. 'Abod. Zar.* 2:2/7, fol. 40d; *y. Šabb.* 14:4/8, fol. 14d; *Qoh. Rab.* 10:5).

Overall, it is not what Jesus does that disturbs the Rabbis—and, indeed, although the Rabbis associated magic with idolatry, there is much evidence of many Jews practicing the very things the Rabbis condemn as Christian—but the competing source of power that disturbs (Schäfer, 2007, pp. 104–105). What activities, social conditions, or power relations, therefore, elicited or eluded the charges of magic?

The Social Conditions of the Charge of Magic. As anthropologists since Van Gennep, Turner, and Douglas have known, margins are places of power and danger. Those on the margins have the power to destabilize or reinforce existing social structures and hierarchies. The margin is a source of creativity and destruction. Societies seek to tap the power of the margin and, in a delicate balancing act, regulate it so that it will not destabilize.

Whether one calls them magicians, sorcerers, miracle workers, or holy people, marginal intermediary figures mediating between a superhuman source of power and the people will elicit suspicion from those already in authority within existing social institutions. That is, the charge of magic is relational, operating within multiple overlapping institutional systems and competing channels of power.

Reimer (2002) has sought to move beyond positivistic accounts, which ask whether Jesus really was a magician, and rhetorical accounts, which see magic as merely a charge, as something with some content, relying upon J. Z. Smith's "polythetic classification." Nonetheless, he never is able to escape the socially constructed nature of the category as a form of slander. Responding to a similar argument, Stratton (2013) writes, "I propose…that we define magic not according to a concrete set of practices, which are universally defined (even according to the broad polythetic model), but as culturally specific ideas about illegitimate and dangerous access to numinous power, whose local applications need to be considered on their own terms in order to understand the work they do in their respective societies" (p. 245). Reimer does get beyond an "empty" definition of polemic, but few scholars saw such slander as empty; rather, it had stereotypical attributes attached to it. As Stratton has argued, these stereotypes were developed and deployed in specific ways in local contexts. Certain activities, however, would more likely elicit a charge of magic and such a charge relies strongly upon one's local social situation.

Magic is a discourse of alterity, but one's actions or behaviors could open one up to such a charge under particular social circumstances, so it is a term that, although notoriously ambiguous, has a residue of stereotyped content. Magical accusations relate to power structures and threats to established order. The charge of magic solidifies structure against potential disorder. Thus a miracle worker who appears disruptive will be accused of magic. To rebuff the charge, one must demonstrate that such a person actually supports established social order or belongs to a higher, divine order. It is a means to regulate power relations. That is why perceived outsiders to established power are the most often accused: women, lower classes, and foreigners. The Median Magi still fit into this social discourse since, although they were centrally positioned within their own society, from the perspective of the overlapping Mediterranean discourses, they represented outsiders and foreign practices.

Both power and danger arise from the interstices and fringes of social systems. Based upon various charges against people as magicians and the "evidence" used, one can see the content of the rhetoric and how others will represent someone as either a magician or a miracle worker, whether or not they actually possessed such qualities.

First, one gains numinous power from withdrawal from society (Reimer, 2002, pp. 47–141). Jesus going into the desert fits this pattern, as do the great ascetics of Late Antiquity Native American dream seekers, or several cross-cultural accounts of the rites of passage. Subsequently, the power gained in the fringe spills over into regular society in the form of miraculous acts.

Marginal intermediaries remain untied to local forms of authority or power. That is, they will remain transient and mobile and will not seek other social forms of authority. This might be one reason why the Gospels and Acts portray Jesus and his disciples as itinerants. Magicians, however, are portrayed as resident and will use their power to access more authority. A mediator actually gains authority by appearing to be dead to human ambition (Brown, 1971). Telling the disciples not to accept money would also avoid such a charge, the inverse of the Simon Magus story.

When the inarticulate power of a holy man meets the articulated power in established society, then one finds a "sorcerer" (Reimer, 2002, pp. 142ff). Magic is not so much a given thing, but a relational term of power of the intermediary as it relates to the articulated power of society. To avoid the charge of magic, the outsider intermediary will attempt to locate himself within the legitimacy of existing traditional structures, passing off his activity or teaching as an extension of the preexisting beliefs and values of a local religious community (Reimer, 2002, p. 174).

Ultimately a miracle worker will have fringe status, be itinerant, have no concern for self, no personal ambitions, perform miracles, and deflect honor and status. These descriptions will be applied differently to friend or foe, embellishing the more rhetorical aspects of the charge of magic rather than overturning it. Thus, Jesus receives the charge of magic in the New Testament because, although a fringe, itinerant miracle worker who largely deflected status, he was often perceived to come into conflict with local forms of established religious authority (scribes, Pharisees, and priests), eliciting the charge of magic. Acts, however, overturns this model while relying upon it. Although in Acts there is an obvious prompt for the charge against the apostles' competitors as competitors, the social location of the charges is significant. Although Simon was primarily a competitor of similar marginal status as the earliest Christians or represented a form of Christianity that the author of Acts sought to marginalize with this story, the other figures represent traditional forms of authority. Elymas was an advisor to the proconsul, belonging to established civic authority; the sons of Sceva are related to the Hebrew priesthood in the story, representing established forms of mediation in Judaism; and even the female slave with the Pythian spirit represents traditional Greek forms of access to the divine, since she possesses the Pythia, the traditional source of oracular authority co-opted by Apollo at Delphi. John of Patmos, moreover, uses associations with sorcery via Jezebel for internal regulation of the churches in Asia Minor, while conjuring Rome—the established centralized authority par excellence—as a great whore and sorceress.

Although the discourse of magic is primarily seen as established authority to put marginal figures "in their place," Acts and Revelation turn these power relations on their heads, challenging broader social expectations of legitimate and illegitimate mediators of the divine. In it, marginal, liminal figures—the ones typically associated with magic—accuse established, institutional forms of authority, in their turn, as magical in the Roman government, portions at least of the Hebrew priesthood, and one of the most recognizable names of Greek oracular tradition. The fringe countered the discourse of magic and turned it back onto its disseminators, but ultimately remained enmeshed within it, adding to it the particular Jewish and Christian associations between magic and demonic forces.

Jesus as sorcerer in late antique Rabbinic documents demands further commentary. Christianity was no longer a fringe movement, but was gaining power in the Roman world. Significantly, the charge of magic was more common in Palestinian circles, where Christian power would have been greater than in Babylonian sources, where Christian political authority would have been weaker. As Christianity became less marginal during and after the fourth century, the charge of magic against Jesus and, *mutatis mutandis*, his followers increased in Jewish sources, which were, from the Christianized Roman perspective, marginal.

As the emergent Jesus movement received, deflected, and leveled charges of magic, they were participating in a broader polemicizing discourse of alterity used to stabilize central forms of authority; it was no mere empty rhetoric, no mere castles on clouds, but belonged to broader social frameworks that regulated the delicate balancing of the potentially chaotic reservoirs of numinous power. These social frameworks employed the discourse of magic to strengthen boundaries between self and other that operated upon the overlapping binaries between male and female, domestic and foreign/exotic, institutional and popular, and legitimate and illegitimate. As social groupings sought stability—often because they were themselves unstable, in a state of transition—they labeled aspects within their social networks as magic, marking them as illegitimate—yet effective!—forms of access to the numinous and allying them with connotations of foreign, female, and dangerous, attempting to assert their own place as authoritative agents of the holy.

[See also Popular Religion and Magic, *subentries on* Early Church, Early Judaism, *and* Roman World; Religious Leaders, *subentries on* Early Judaism *and* New Testament; *and* Social Interaction, *subentry* New Testament.]

BIBLIOGRAPHY

Brown, Peter. "The Rise and Function of the Holy Man in Late Antiquity." *Journal of Roman Studies* 61 (1971): 80–101.

Garrett, Susan. *Demise of the Devil: Magic and the Demonic in Luke's Writings.* Minneapolis: Fortress, 1989.

Reimer, Andy M. *Miracle and Magic: A Study in the Acts of the Apostles and the Life of Apollonius of Tyana.* Journal for the Study of the New Testament Supplement Series 235. London: Sheffield Academic Press, 2002.

Schäfer, Peter. *Jesus in the Talmud.* Princeton, N.J.: Princeton University Press, 2007.

Segal, Alan. "Hellenistic Magic: Some Questions of Definition." In *The Other Judaisms of Late Antiquity*, edited by Alan Segal, pp. 79–108. Atlanta: Scholars Press, 1987.

Smith, Morton. *Jesus the Magician.* San Francisco: Harper & Row, 1978.

Stratton, Kimberly. *Naming the Witch: Magic, Ideology, and Stereotype in the Ancient World.* New York: Columbia University Press, 2007.

Stratton, Kimberly. "Magic Discourse in the Ancient World." In *Defining Magic: A Reader*, edited by Bernd-Christian Otto and Michael Strausberg, pp. 243–254. Sheffield, U.K.: Equinox, 2013.

Styers, Randall. *Making Magic: Religion, Magic, and Science in the Modern World.* Oxford: Oxford University Press, 2004.

Taussig, Michael. *Mimesis and Alterity: A Particular History of the Senses.* New York: Routledge, 1993.

Jared C. Calaway

Early Judaism

Until recent times scholars of early Judaism neglected the study of magic. Yet ritual practices that can be characterized as magical were commonplace among the peoples of the Mediterranean, including ancient Jews.

The prohibitions on various kinds of ritual practitioners in Exodus 22:17 and Deuteronomy 18:10–11 were, of course, well known to Jewish interpreters of later periods, but so were the biblical stories of miraculous holy men like Moses, Elijah, and Elisha. Magical traditions gathered around David and Solomon as masters of demons and around charismatic Jewish figures like Honi the rainmaker (Josephus, *Ant.* 14.22; *m. Taʿan.* 3.8). Early Jewish traditions did not speak univocally against magic qua magic; those that address the topic only criticize certain kinds of practitioners (Bohak, 2008). Late antique interpreters, such as the rabbis, carried forward this complex approach to ritual practices and practitioners.

Among scholars of religion, the entire category of magic remains disputed and its delimitation has implications for the treatment of gender. Historians of religion tend to avoid the category of magic because they view it as a tool of polemical discourse, not specifying any particular activity but merely used to cast aspersions upon individuals perceived as threatening. This approach proves particularly relevant for the gendered nature of magical accusations in early Judaism. Jewish sources interpreting the laws of the Hebrew Bible or discussing the relative merits of different ritual specialists tend to speak particularly negatively about women or other outsiders.

However, using a more general term, such as "ritual practices," is problematic because it is too broad, making every religious ritual magical. Thus, scholars like Gideon Bohak (2009) have suggested defining magic in the context of early Judaism "as a separate and independent sphere of action within the wider Jewish cultural tradition…best represented by the large corpus of Jewish magical texts and objects, a corpus which is characterized by its specific technical-professional nature" (p. 111). This approach focuses on the wide variety of Jewish texts and objects that are recognizable by scholars as magical. According to this perspective, people involved in the production of magical texts were experts comparable to other skilled and learned men in late antique Jewish communities. The shortcoming of this approach is that when it is coupled with the presumption that only men in antiquity could become literate experts, the participation of women in magical production is precluded a priori. Paradoxically, contemporary scholars dismiss the possibility that ancient Jewish women produced magical texts while early Jewish sources insist all women engaged in magical practices.

Key Sources. Materials that fall in the scholarly category of Jewish magic may be divided into "insider" and "outsider" sources (Bohak, 2008, p. 70). Outsider evidence includes apocryphal and pseudepigraphic sources, the first-century C.E. writings of the Jewish philosopher Philo and the Jewish historian Josephus, and legal and narrative traditions in Rabbinic literature that discuss magic and its practitioners. Insider evidence includes such materials as the Hebrew and Aramaic amulets from Palestine, Jewish Aramaic incantation bowls from Babylonia, and the late antique Hebrew treatise *Sepher Ha-Razim*. Such materials become especially abundant after the fourth century C.E. Both insider and outsider evidence describe ritual practitioners as individuals who wield power over and against demons, other divine powers, and other practitioners. Outsider evidence casts women as witches particularly concerned with interpersonal matters and describes them as repellant to the divine. Their magic is portrayed as both dangerously efficacious and, at the same time, fraudulent.

Key Vocabulary. In early Jewish sources, the two relevant terms that remained in use from the Hebrew Bible are *keshafim* (witchcraft or magic) and *qesamim* (magical practices). The term *keshafim* (singular *kishuf*, cf. witch *mekhashef/a* of Exod 22:18) appears most often in Rabbinic sources applied to practices of suspect men or to women. Tal Ilan (2006) points out that in Rabbinic literature *kishuf* and its derivatives are "almost entirely reserved for women. In far more than 50% of the occurrences of this root in the two talmudim the context is that of the female witch" (p. 240).

Qesamim, meaning magical practices (*Qosem*, magician), still signaled suspect activity, but as a term it was more mild in connotation and could be applied by the sages to others sages as well (e.g., *y. Ma'aś.* 3:10, *51a*).

Further complicating matters is the fact that, in many rabbinic stories that describe the sages' interactions with other ritual practitioners, the words denoting incantations, spells or acts of inhuman power are utterly neutral: *milta* (literally a word or in certain context, a spell [*b. Ḥul.* 105b]), *ma'aseh* (literally "deed," "happening," "story" or in context, "a magical act" [*b. Pesaḥ.* 11b]), *amar de-amar* (literally "he said what he said"; in context, "he uttered an incantation" [*y. Sanh.* 7.13, *25d*]). This serves as a reminder of the complexity of the category of magic in Jewish antiquity; descriptions of ritual practices could be taken for granted among the sages, even elevating them, or serve to marginalize other practitioners.

Hellenistic and early Roman period (298 B.C.E.–70 C.E.). Already in the Second Temple period, Jewish writings speculated that the origin of magic secrets was with the fallen angels of Genesis 6:1–4 and their union with mortal women. Expansions of these tantalizing verses appeared in the Book of Watchers (200–150 B.C.E.), where the angels were said to have revealed divine secrets and mysteries, including sorcery, charms, and healing, to women (*1 En.* 7:1, 8:1–3).

Reflecting misogynist attitudes of the Greco-Roman period, the Testament of Reuben blames women for bewitching and seducing the angels with adornments: "my children, flee from sexual promiscuity, and order your wives and your daughters not to adorn their heads and their appearances so as to deceive men's sound minds. For every woman who schemes in these ways is destined for eternal punishment. For it was thus that they charmed the Watchers" (*T. Reu.* 5:5–6; trans. Charlesworth, 1983, p. 784).

Pseudo-Philo retells the biblical story of Saul's encounter with the necromancer of Endor (1 Sam 28:7–25). Its author is the only source to offer Saul's vanity as the reason for his expulsion of seers and witches from Israel (Charlesworth, 1983). Samuel, raised from the dead, is quick to point out that he did not come at the beckoning of the king or the woman, but only in keeping with divine orders that he continue to rebuke Saul for his sins against God (63:2).

Where the Testament of Solomon upholds the wise king as a master of magical lore, it names Queen Sheba as a witch, demoting her from the high status with which she is described in biblical sources (1 Kgs 1—10). Other Jewish traditions made Solomon the authoritative source on demonic lore and exorcism; exorcising demons in his name was apparently a common practice in the later Second Temple period (Josephus, *Ant.* 8.45–49).

Although some argue against the historicity of this event, there is evidence that a witch-hunt took place just beyond the borders of the Hasmonean kingdom in Ashkelon, perhaps during the reign of Queen Shelamzion (76–67 B.C.E.; Ilan, 2006). The Mishnah (ca. 200 C.E.) mentions that Shimon ben Shetah hung 80 women there (*tractate Sanh.* 6:4) and later commentary identifies these women as witches, sharing a fanciful account of Shimon ben

Shetah outsmarting these capable witches and executing them (*y. Sanh.* 6:8, *23c*).

The Jewish philosopher Philo (20 B.C.E. to 45 C.E.) is perhaps the earliest source to provide an emic definition of magic (Bohak, 2008). He distinguishes between true magic, the scientific study of nature pursued by kings and the famous Persian Magi, and its base counterpart "pursued by mendicant priests and altar-parasites and the basest of the women and slave population" who engage in erotic magic (*Spec. Laws* 3.101–102; LCL with minor changes).

Roman and Late Antique period (70 C.E.–636 C.E.). After the destruction of the Temple and especially in Late Antiquity the primary evidence for magical practices and secondary sources commenting about magicians becomes much more abundant. The Jewish historian Josephus (ca. 37/8–100 C.E.), who lived in Rome in the aftermath of the Jewish revolts in the late first century C.E., was especially proud of Jewish achievements in the field of exorcism. Not only did Judea possess the special plant needed for exorcisms, but also King David was an exorcist—ridding Saul of his demons—and Solomon was the master of demons par excellence (*J.W.* 7.180–185; *Ant.* 6.214; cf. 1 Sam 19.9–10).

Sepher haRazim. A handbook of magic spells called *Sepher HaRazim* (the Book of Mysteries, fourth century C.E.) declares itself to be the revelation of the angel Raziel given to Noah in the year of the Flood. Scholars suggest it was composed in Palestine, where it was aimed at a male Jewish elite that could read its lucid Hebrew prose. The treatise combines Hellenistic Jewish cosmology with magic recipes that reflect the broad spectrum of magic popular in the Greco-Roman Mediterranean, including spells for love, healing, wealth, and political success as well as more aggressive magic. Like other magical spells from the Greco-Roman Mediterranean, it is peppered with warnings to keep away from women, especially menstruating women, to ensure the efficacy of the ritual practices described therein. Still, some of its magical recipes employ the angels to guard and protect women.

If magic is defined broadly to include ancient medicine or chemistry, we may note the case of Maria the Jewish alchemist. An Alexandrian writer named Zosimus often quotes Maria the Jewess as an authority on many alchemical techniques in second-century C.E. Alexandria (Janowitz, 2001; Ilan, 2006).

Rabbinic literature. In general, the Babylonian Talmud is a much richer source for the study of magic and ritual practices than the Jerusalem Talmud (see especially *b. Sanh. 67b* ff.). As mentioned above, the Jewish sages inherited traditions that both proscribed magic and included authoritative figures that could enact supernatural feats. Hence, the rabbinic attitudes to magic are complex, ambivalent, and seemingly contradictory.

The Mishnah gives evidence of Jewish legal discussions of magic. The rabbis acknowledge the prevalence of illusions and trickery as well as real magical practice. It was the latter that really bothered them. *M. Sanhedrin* 7:11 states, "The magician that performs an act is liable to punishment and he that deceives the eyes is not [liable to punishment]." To be able to discern the difference and adjudicate accordingly, would-be judges ought to study magic. So one tradition states, "We do not seat anyone on the Sanhedrin unless they are masters of wisdom, masters of vision, masters of stature, masters of old age, masters of magic, and knowledgeable in seventy languages" (*b. Menaḥ. 65a*). Thus mastery of magic is mentioned among other positive attributes, but only for rabbinic men. Rabbinic discussions, then, distinguish between the lawful learning of magical techniques for the sake of judiciary matters and the unlawful learning of it for the sake of practicing it (*b. Sanh. 68a; b. Šabb.75a*).

Whereas the legal sources might suggest there were no magical practices among the rabbis, narrative sources reveal a much different picture of the rabbis in action. In one tradition, a man approaches the rabbis for help when demons residing in a certain sorb bush attack him and threaten his life. The first rabbi he consults accidentally writes him an amulet against only a single demon and it proves ineffective. The second rabbi he approaches writes him an amulet against sixty demons, and that one proves successful at provoking the demons to depart the bush (*b. Pesaḥ. 111b*).

The sage Abaye summarizes laws on magic as follows: "The laws of magicians are like those of the sabbath. Certain activities are punished by stoning, some are not liable to punishment but still forbidden, and others are entirely permitted. If one actually practices magic he is stoned; if he only creates an illusion he is exempt but the action is still forbidden. Entirely permitted are such deeds as those that were performed by Rav Hanina and Rav Oshia, who spent every eve of the sabbath studying the laws of creation, then created for themselves a one-third grown calf to eat" (*b. Sanh. 67b*).

Some traditions portray the sages reciting incantations and performing amazing feats to demonstrate that they are equal or superior to ill-intentioned ritual specialists, such as female witches or male heretics. One story portrays a witch confronting and trying to bind the Babylonian sages Rav Hisda and Rabbah. They in turn know the proper countercharms to thwart her (*b. Ḥul.105b*). Another famous story from the Jerusalem Talmud takes place at a bathhouse in Tiberias and depicts a heretic cursing and binding the sages Rabbi Eliezer, Rabbi Yehoshua, and Rabbi Akiva to the vault of the bathhouse. Rabbi Yehoshua manages to cast a binding spell, which traps the heretic to the door. Both parties agree to annul their spells but continue their magical duel. Going down to the sea, the heretic recites an incantation and splits the sea in two, proclaiming himself as great as Moses. The sages challenge him to walk through the sea as Moses did, and when he does, Rabbi Yehoshua calls on the angel of the sea to drown him. Thus, the dramatic competition ends and sages emerge victorious (*y. Sanh.7.19, 25d*).

As Jacob Neusner (1969) explains, Torah was the basis of the rabbis' supernatural power, the means to their magic that ultimately justified their ends: "The rabbis controlled the power of Torah because of their mastery of Torah quite independently of heavenly action. They could issue blessings and curses, create men and animals. They were masters of witchcraft, incantations, and amulets. They could communicate with heaven. Their Torah was sufficiently effective to thwart the action of demons" (p. 20). Because in Late Antiquity rabbinic Torah learning

and its public representation was strictly the privilege of men, this was a source of authority and power only rabbinic men could pursue.

This context might explain the general attitude toward women in connection with magic in rabbinic literature. Already in *m. 'Abot,* Hillel is quoted as saying, "the more women, the more witchcraft." Commenting on the prohibition against witches in Exodus 22:17, which specifically targets female witches, the Jerusalem Talmud states that "scripture teaches you about the way of the world in which the majority of women are witches" (*Sanh.* 7:13, *40b*). The Babylonian Talmud agrees, "most women engage in witchcraft" (*Sanh. 67a*). Furthermore, we find statements in the Jerusalem Talmud that not even pious women avoided magic: "even the best woman is an expert at magic" (*Qidd.* 4.11). The Babylonian Talmud similarly states, "Even if the majority [of the town] is Israelite, you do not say a blessing because the daughters of Israel burn incense for magic" (*Ber.53a*).

There are a few examples of rabbis turning to women for their special knowledge. According to a story in the Babylonian Talmud, a fourth-century C.E. sage named Amemar learned from "the head of the women who practice magic" an incantation to deflect a female practitioner should he chance to run into one (*Pesah. 110a*). Abaye shares traditions learned from his foster mother (or a woman named Em, as she is cited elsewhere without reference to Abaye) for healing incantations (*b. Šabb.66b*) as well as medical practices that border on the magical (*b. Šabb.134a*).

Amulets and Babylonian incantation bowls. Archaeological excavations from Palestine and Babylonia have unearthed many ritual objects from the fourth to seventh century C.E. (Naveh and Shaked, 1985, 1993). The most popular "magical" object was the amulet (Hebrew *Qamea*), an inscribed text rolled up and worn around the neck by men and women all over the ancient Mediterranean, including late antique Jewish Palestine. The Mishnah takes some popular practices like wearing apotropaic amulets for granted, but arrogates to the rabbis the authority to decide who is a qualified maker of amulets. The incantation bowls from Babylonia also refer to themselves as amulets. In the twentieth century dozens of Hebrew and Aramaic amulets were found in Palestine, and hundreds of incantation bowls in Jewish Babylonian Aramaic have come to light. The incantation bowls discovered in situ were excavated in present-day Iraq and Iran, but most are without provenance. About the size of cereal bowls, these bowls contain Hebrew and Aramaic incantations appealing to God, angels, and others, for all sorts of problems and aspirations; the script is generally written from the center of the bowl spiraling out to the edges.

In these artifacts gender issues emerge in several ways: Jewish men and women, singularly and together, are the clients of magical amulets, which seek protection from demons, illnesses, or the curses of others. In addition to generalized requests for protection, a few amulets show Jewish men seeking commercial success, seeking good standing in their communities, or pursuing the love of a woman. Apart from men, Jewish women seek maintenance of their pregnancies, healthy babies, and restored love in their marriages. Notably, there is a 60:40 ratio of male to female clients desiring aid in the Babylonian incantation bowls (Morony, 2003), which suggests that more men than women sought ritual assistance in this particular medium.

Interestingly, one oft-copied formula in the incantation bowls targets female in-laws because they are seen as the source of curses directed at the male client (Segal, 2000). In several incantation texts, including one of the few in Talmudic Aramaic, feminine subjects address demons or other antagonists (Müller-Kessler and Kwasman, 2000; Segal, 2000). It proves impossible to ascertain whether women actually authored or performed these incantations or whether their names were inserted into a prefabricated incantation text.

Modern Debates. As mentioned earlier, the usefulness of the category of magic for ancient Mediterranean religions continues to be debated. Gideon Bohak (2008) argues for a practical definition of magic that points to the corpus of magical texts from antiquity. Other scholars such as Naomi Janowitz (2001) place emphasis on the problematic discourse of magic and argue, "authorities cannot—by definition—engage in magic. They can, however, bless, curse, heal, exorcise, predict the future, and

put angels to work" (p. 99). As Tal Ilan (2006) puts it, echoing John Gager (1992), "what the rabbis did was considered religious practice, but when women did it, it was considered witchcraft" (p. 240).

Jewish women's involvement or lack thereof in the traditional category of ancient magic and witchcraft continues to be debated as well. The view of the rabbinic sources, which blamed outsiders for exposing ancient Jews to magic and Jewish women in particular for internalizing it, was carried forth by Jewish historians into the twentieth century.

Taking rabbinic stereotypes of women at their word, albeit sympathetically, Meir Bar-Ilan (1993) writes that "women were removed entirely from the social circle of the community. As a result, it appears that the tendency by women to indulge in witchcraft was a type of expression of their desire to rule" (p. 20). Similarly, Simcha Fishbane (1993) posits that in patriarchal Rabbinic Jewish communities, which excluded females from public religious activities, women developed their own ritual practices and formed their own groups, which in turn were condemned as witchcraft by the rabbis. Although both of these scholars situate magic outside the rabbinic movement, Bohak (2008) finds evidence of magical practices among the rabbis themselves and further notes that, on account of literacy patterns in antiquity, men are far more likely candidates for the composition of textual magic than women.

Melissa Aubin (1998) contributed the most sustained assault on scholarly readings of rabbinic sources that accept the description of women as witches, writing that "common to all of these views is the assumption that passages in Rabbinic literature demonizing women's involvement in so-called magic provide a window onto the mischief of the lower classes, resulting from either ignorance or subversive tendencies" (p. 51). She suggests that rabbinic sources on magic are much more fruitfully mined for ascertaining rabbinic ideology and "cultural constructions of gender" rather than the reality of ancient women.

Likewise, Rebecca Lesses (2001) highlights the way rabbinic rulings about magic served to construct gender differences in ancient Jewish society, excluding women from alternative sources of authority. Lesses contrasts Talmudic sources on magic with the incantation bowls, noting how the rabbis are primarily concerned with threats to themselves as men, whereas the incantation bowls show the concerns of both men and women (Lesses, 2001). She writes that the bowls demonstrate that "women (as well as men) employed incantations and other rituals (such as going to the roof to curse the demons) to protect themselves, to expel the demons, and to effect healing" (Lesses, 2001, p. 367).

Kimberley Stratton (2007) shows how accusations of witchcraft could be used to discredit women within the Rabbinic movement who dared to resist or challenge the development of Jewish law. She further traces accusations of women's involvement in magic to Rabbinic anxiety that their legal rulings could not be enforced in the kitchen, the area of food preparation managed by women, and the realm of Rabbinic law, which was most fundamental to the creation of the Jewish social body.

[*See also* Popular Religion and Magic, *subentries on* Greek World *and* Roman World; *and* Religious Participation, *subentry* Early Judaism.]

BIBLIOGRAPHY

Aubin, Melissa Margaret. "Gendering Magic in Late Antique Judaism." PhD. diss. Duke University, 1998.

Bar-Ilan, Meir. "Witches in Bible and Talmud." In *Approaches to Ancient Judaism*, Vol. 5: *Historical, Literary, and Religious Studies*, edited by Herbert Basser and Simcha Fishbane, pp. 7–32. Atlanta: Scholars Press, 1993.

Bohak, Gideon. "Prolegomena to the Study of the Jewish Magical Tradition." *Currents in Biblical Research* 8, no. 1 (2009): 107–150.

Bohak, Gideon. *Ancient Jewish Magic: A History*. Cambridge, U.K.: Cambridge University Press, 2008.

Charlesworth, James H. *The Old Testament Pseudepigrapha*. 2 vols. Garden City, N.Y.: Doubleday, 1983.

Fishbane, Simcha. "Most Women Engage in Sorcery." In *Approaches to Ancient Judaism*, Vol. 5: *Historical, Literary, and Religious Studies*, edited by Herbert Basser and Simcha Fishbane, pp. 143–165. Atlanta: Scholars Press, 1993.

Gager, John. *Curse Tablets and Binding Spells from the Ancient World*. Oxford: Oxford University Press, 1992.

Ilan, Tal. *Silencing the Queen: The Literary Histories of Shelamzion and Other Jewish Women*. Tübingen, Germany: Mohr Siebeck, 2006.

Janowitz, Naomi. *Magic in the Roman World: Pagans, Jews, and Christians*. New York: Routledge, 2001.

Lesses, Rebecca Macy. "Exe(o)rcising Power: Women as Sorceresses, Exorcists, and Demonesses in Babylonian Jewish Society of Late Antiquity." *Journal of the American Academy of Religion* 69, no. 2 (2001): 343–375.

Montgomery, James. *Aramaic Incantation Texts from Nippur*. Philadelphia: University Museum, 1913.

Morgan, Michael, trans. and ed. *Sepher Ha-Razim: The Book of Mysteries*. Chico, Calif.: Scholars Press, 1983.

Morony, Michael. "Magic and Society in Late Sasanian Iraq." In *Prayer, Magic, and the Stars in the Ancient and Late Antique World*. Edited by Scott B. Noegel, Joel Thomas Walker, and Brannon Wheeler. University Park: Pennsylvania State University Press, 2003.

Müller-Kessler, Christa, and Theodore Kwasman. "A Unique Talmudic Aramaic Incantation Bowl." *Journal of the American Oriental Society* 120, no. 2 (2000): 159–165.

Naveh, Joseph, and Shaul Shaked. *Amulets and Magic Bowls: Aramaic Incantations of Late Antiquity*. Jerusalem: Magnes, 1985; reprint 1998.

Naveh, Joseph, and Shaul Shaked. *Magic Spells and Formulae: Aramaic Incantations of Late Antiquity*. Jerusalem: Magnes, 1993.

Neusner, Jacob. "Phenomenon of the Rabbi in Late Antiquity." *Numen* 16, no. 1 (1969): 1–20.

Nickelsburg, George W. E., and James C. Vanderkam. *1 Enoch*. Minneapolis: Fortress, 2004.

Segal, J. B. *Catalogue of the Aramaic and Mandaic Incantation Bowls in the British Museum*. London: British Museum, 2000.

Seidel, Jonathan. "Charming Criminals: Classification of Magic in the Babylonian Talmud." In *Ancient Magic and Ritual Power*, edited by Marvin Meyer and Paul Mirecki, pp. 145–156. Boston: Brill, 2001.

Stratton, Kimberley. *Naming the Witch: Magic, Ideology, & Stereotype in the Ancient World*. New York: Columbia University Press, 2007.

Swartz, Michael. "Jewish Magic in Late Antiquity." In *Cambridge History of Judaism: The Late Roman Period*. Cambridge, U.K.: Cambridge University Press, 2006.

Mika Ahuvia

Early Church

The religious landscape of the Hellenistic and Roman Mediterranean was characterized not by doctrine, but effectiveness. Although it was popular among certain religious traditions to speculate about a future disembodied condition or passionless (*apatheia*) existence, the body was that piece of the real that constantly harked the wandering mind back to its materiality. Without knowledge of modern biology or pharmacology, the ailments that struck the body were perplexing and mysterious. The ancient Mediterranean was a world permeated with daimons, spirits, and gods; each influenced the body in different ways. Extreme conditions of poverty (malnutrition, mental disorder, high infant mortality rates, and disease) plaguing every segment of society required rituals that were effective. Hence, "what worked" triumphed over what was deemed "right." "Magic" was practiced by the emerging orthodox church as well as proto-heterodox groups. Indeed, the existence of magic in the early church demonstrates that ritual distinctions between orthodox and heterodox are artificial in the first centuries C.E.

"Popular religion," although difficult to define, concerns traditions and rituals that either depart from officially sanctioned cults or apply them in divergent or subversive ways. In official pre-Christian Roman cults, commoners usually did not compete with sanctioned cults in terms of doctrine or conscious subversion, but rather in terms of what worked. A person might bring his sick relative to the shrine or temple of a particular god with the hope of healing, but if this did not work, it would not be uncommon to then seek out a healer, exorcist, or some concoction or potion that could provide relief. This, again, was not conscious subversion of official cults in favor of popular religion, but a form of pragmatism. However, practitioners of these alternative ritual options did occasionally position themselves as rivals to official cults (e.g., John the Baptist, Jesus of Nazareth's reported healing campaign).

Popular religion is often associated with magic, which, with its pejorative connotations, was used to distinguish between sanctioned and prohibited ritual. Likewise, magic, in modern parlance, tends to operate in the domain of the prohibited. This is the result of the rhetoric of various early church theologians; but it is important to stress that second-century rhetoric should not be interpreted as reality. Magic was resisted by the emerging hierarchy of the early church not because it was a form of imaginative fancy, but because it was perceived as being effective.

Magic is often interpreted as spiritual power competing with sanctioned religion; that is, if a miracle occurs within a sanctioned cult, it is a miracle, but if it happens outside official limits, it is magic. This article uses the term neutrally to contextualize the early church's experience of the miraculous in dialogue with the cultic traditions that preceded and competed with it. Representations of Jesus in the Synoptic Gospels, the Johannine tradition, and subsequent early church tradition in the second century are undoubtedly in line with what could be defined as magic. Given the controversial nature of this term, there are two alternatives that may be used to alleviate this tension: "ritual" and "wondrous work." Ritual implies the use of symbolic formulae to influence events that are normally beyond the control of the individual or community concerned. Wondrous work derives from the Greek terms *thauma* ("wonder," "miracle") and *ergon* ("work"). Thus, one who works wonders or miracles (on behalf of a god) was a thaumaturge, and ritual was the means by which these wonders were enacted. For our purposes, "thaumaturge" and "magician" will be used interchangeably.

The gods of the Hellenistic Mediterranean world dwelt in sacred temples and shrines. The house of the god was the place of divine mysteries, miraculous healings, and social welfare. The last point highlights the socioeconomic function of shrines: priests, who were required to be wealthy, would present themselves as "lovers-of-the-city" by bequeathing such gifts as wine, oil, and money on the people. The house of the god was where the god could offer graces upon the people in the form of gifts or healings. An example of this can be drawn from a report of a healing at the temple of the god Asclepius: a woman named Cleo, it was reported, had been pregnant for five years. She was brought prostrate on a palette to the temple of Asclepius as a supplicant. "Immediately as she came from him and from the temple, she bore a boy…After she had accomplished this, she wrote about it in a votive offering…Five years Cleo bore the burden in her womb until she slept in the temple and she became healthy" (Cartlidge and Dungan, 1994, p. 151). Such narratives served to popularize different healing shrines wherein doctors often offered their services.

Asclepius, like Jesus, was son of male god (Apollo) and human mother (Coronis); he was also a universal god-man with healing or magic power. In the New Testament era, it was believed that one had to coax and entice a god into action. In the Jesus tradition, the "divine one" is not in a temple in the form of an image awaiting the appropriate ritual purity, invocations, and supplications, but an embodied person among the people.

There is no consensus on the question of whether the historical Jesus was himself a magician. Scholars are certain, however, that many of the early Jesus groups in the first century at least represented Jesus as a thaumaturge in their narratives.

Performativity and the Earliest Magic Stories in the Jesus Tradition. Critical scholarship approaches gospel literature as products not of historical memory, but of experimental performance and elaboration. The convention of using particular sayings or aphorisms (chreiae) for making new meaning was common among Greek writers. Greek rhetorical manuals (*progymnasmata*, preliminary exercises) of the first century C.E. outlined this process of elaborating sayings/chreiae into performative arguments.

One of the earliest and multiply attested thaumaturgic traditions in the Jesus literature that demonstrates this elaborative convention is the "beelzebul" controversy (Q/Luke 11:14–23//Matt 12:22–32//Mark 3:22–30). Herein the core saying is the charge that Jesus "drives out demons in the name of the head demon" and that he is able to do so because he "is under the control of Beelzebul." The Q and Mark traditions elaborate this core saying/charge in slightly different ways, but both follow the general elaborative conventions of the *progymnasmata*. This trajectory is important for the magic stories in the Jesus tradition because it shows that such performance trumps eyewitness accounts. Thus, scholarship might move beyond the question of the historicity of these accounts to see miracle (and sayings) traditions as part of performance, not merely reminiscence. The question of whether Jesus actually healed people shifts toward the conviction that one was healed by Jesus,

despite the possibility that the historical Jesus did not literally heal the person.

The performative aspects of acting as Jesus and healing others offer a variation on the performance of being a particular gender. Indeed, chreia elaboration was a mechanism by which the rhetorician would become—that is, perform as—another person. This goal of imitating and being another was known as *prosōpopoeia*. Given this performative dimension, magic traditions can be interpreted as derivative of certain people being a Jesus, taking on his role as healer. This is developed in the Acts of the Apostles, where followers of Jesus heal in the same manner as he did in the gospel narratives.

Sources for the Jesus Magic Tradition. Various ancient sources have been investigated for the ways in which they depict Jesus's magical activity and its gendered significance.

Pre-Markan miracle chains. A number of scholars have adapted P. Achtemeier's proposal that two sets of magic/miracle traditions were incorporated into the Gospel of Mark. Jesus, in these miracle chains, is presented as founding a new community of Israel as a composite form of a Moses-Elijah figure.

In pre-Markan magic and miracle chains, there is a mythological founding of a (new) people of Israel: as in the Exodus narrative, there is miraculous crossing of water (the stilling of the storm in Mark 4:35–41 and walking on water in Mark 6:45–51). Moreover, just as Yahweh fed the Israelites in the wilderness with manna, so do pre-Markan miracle chains end with a miraculous meal (five thousand people in Mark 6:34; 44, four thousand people in Mark 8:1–10).

Mack (1998) demonstrates how the period between the Crossing of the Red Sea and Yahweh's guidance in the Sinai wilderness presented a period of time in which the writers of the epic could "test" the people of Israel and set cultural boundaries. These boundaries are crossed in the six healings that stand between the beginning and end of the two pre-Markan miracle chains. This, then, was a literary mechanism that enacted a change in the social and ethnic makeup of the people of (this new) Israel.

There are a series of gender dynamics operating in pre-Markan sources for the thaumaturgic activity of

Jesus. The woman with the hemorrhages does not submit to Jesus's *exousia*, (masculine) authority, but takes initiative in taking power from him. This reversal is interpreted by Mark's Jesus as an act of faith. The story of the Syrophoenician woman is contextualized by a remark indicating that Mark's Jesus did not want to be seen in the "impure" gentile territory of Tyre. The woman presents herself in a submissive posture before Jesus and makes a request on behalf of her daughter. Mark's Jesus demeans her rhetorically with a quick-witted response: "[l]et the children be fed first, for it is not fair to take the children's food and throw it to the dogs" (Mark 7:27b). Yet, the Syrophoenician woman's aphoristic wit trumps Jesus's one-liner: "Sir, even the dogs under the table eat the children's crumbs" (v. 28). This wit evinces a performative false humility, which Mark's Jesus acknowledges. The woman performed as if she was submissive, yet uses these gender dynamics to unleash a comedic act that disrupts the symbolic place where Jesus had put her. Reading Jesus's response with a wink and grin, one can see the aphoristic style often attributed to the Cynic philosophic tradition (although this is not to equate the two).

The Johannine signs source. A series of scholars, led chiefly by Fortna (1970), have proposed that the first half of the Gospel of John was formed and elaborated around a set of seven "signs" or miracles. These can be outlined as follows:

Turning water into wine	John 2:1–11
Healing an official's son	John 4:46–54
Healing a paralytic near the pool	John 5:1–9
Feeding 5,000	John 6:1–15
Jesus walks on water	John 6:16–21
Healing a blind person	John 9:1–8
Raising of Lazarus	John 11:1–44

The author(s) of the Gospel of John elaborated the magic stories, presenting them as signs to precipitate and substantiate belief in Jesus's participation in the activity of the Father. The raising of Lazarus highlights this transformation of the miracle tradition into a signs tradition by making the Lazarus event a sign of Jesus's resurrection.

Crossan (1993) has proposed an alternative theory for the miracle tradition behind Mark and John. Taking the "Secret Gospel of Mark" (recovered from Mar Saba monastery by M. Smith) seriously as part of an early form of the Gospel of Mark, Crossan aligns the raising of Lazarus with the raising of the young person in Secret Mark, outlined as follows:

Healing a paralytic (Mark 2:1–12)	Healing a paralytic near the pool (John 5:1–9)
Feeding 5,000 (Mark 6:35–44)	Feeding 5,000 (John 6:1–15)
Jesus walks on water (Mark 6:45–52)	Jesus walks on water (John 6:16–21)
Healing a blind person (Mark 8:22–26)	Healing a blind person (John 9:1–8)
Raising a young person (Secret Mark)	Raising of Lazarus (John 11:1–44)

Although the veracity of Secret Mark as an actual source, referred to in a letter of Clement of Alexandria, remains debated, it demonstrates the sometimes tenuous condition of gender studies within biblical scholarship. Secret Mark portrays a young man Jesus loved who, like Lazarus, is raised from the dead. Yet, it is what follows in the narrative that has caused so much controversy: after being raised, the young man is inducted into the mysteries of the basileia of God in a ritual baptism. Because the young man approaches Jesus with a linen (baptismal) covering over his naked body and is described as "loving" Jesus, some have interpreted this as a homosexual relationship (and thus cannot be historical, or original to Mark). Although such a relationship is certainly possible, nothing in this story requires such an interpretive move because nakedness, devotion to Jesus, and a (presumably white) linen covering are consistent with ancient baptismal ritual in the early church.

The magic of Jesus in historical context. Cotter (1999) identifies three primary ways that miracles could be interpreted in Greco-Roman antiquity: (1) as the result of an intervention by a god, (2) as Nature's obedience to the intercessions of a holy person, or (3) as Nature's submission to a divinely appointed hero that has been given dominion over the earth (Cotter, 1999, p. 170). The Jesus tradition evinces each of these modes. Although there are parallels with the Rabbinic materials (Honi the Circle-Drawer and Hanina ben Dosa, among others), Jesus's miracles in the gospel traditions reflect the literary culture and activity of magicians in the broader Hellenistic world. With the advent of Rabbinic Judaism, there was a concerted move away from the thaumaturge and the scriptural paradigm of the charismatic intercessor toward a model that understood the study of Torah as the font of healing.

The Jesus presented as a magician is also singular in comparison with the "standard" Hellenistic magician. Jesus did not make use of incantations or spells, nor did he recommend the use of amulets; he also never exorcised entire households, but remained interested in individuals. However, Jesus's profile as magician adheres to the common Hellenistic image by performing many of the same wonders (curing blindness, resurrecting the dead, calming the seas, healing paralytics, exorcising demons, and curing skin diseases) and by assuming that disease was the result of sinful behavior (hence Jesus's refrain, "sin no more.") Moreover, the Jesus that is presented as a magician adheres to purity codes by commanding those whom he healed to show their cleanliness to the symbolic authorities (Mark 1:40–45).

Early christian magic scrolls. The belief that ritual—as expressed in symbolic formulae, incantations, potions, and charms—can influence the earthly realm and the divine or heavenly realm is that with which magic is concerned. Scholars have recovered a vast array of ritual and magic prayer scrolls that addressed a series of needs including requests for healings from disease, prayers for erotic pleasure, pleas for sexual potency, and direction in spiritual ascent, among others. Early Christian magic/ritual scrolls offer a perspective on alternative avenues for supplication and acknowledgment.

A pre-Christian example of the genre comes from "The Old Coptic Schmidt Papyrus," a first-century C.E. magic scroll that records a complaint by a woman named Esrmpe against a man named Hor, son of Tanesneou. Esrmpe appeals to Osiris to "render justice to me and Hor (son) of Tanesneou for the things

that I have done to him and the things that he has done to me." Esrmpe reveals that she is socially marginalized as a woman, acknowledging that she is "without power" and has "no champion son" to protect her or advocate on her behalf, as she is "a barren women." Her barren condition shows how biological women were defined in relation to men in the first century C.E. In this sense, she was not treated as a true subject on her own. In her symbolic universe, men defined women in relation to themselves; thus, she lost value in the economy of sexuality. Osiris serves as a last resort for her supplication. Esrmpe has been wronged by Hor and demonstrates the precarity of being a socially defined woman when she announces that "many are the things that he has done to me." Because there was no justice for the marginalized gender, she appeals to the gods in this scroll to "render" her "justice." This is one of the ways in which magic can subvert the sociosymbolic system in an effort to offer justice.

It is common to find a mix of appeals to Christ and other intercessors (angels and saints) juxtaposed with non-Christian divinities in the same magic scroll. One example comes from the Magical Papyrus of Paris (fourth century C.E.), requesting the exorcism of a demon. This papyrus includes a magical formula that was to be incanted over the head of the possessed individual by the magos: "[p]lace olive branches before him and stand behind him and say, 'Greetings, god of Abraham; greetings, god of Isaac; greetings, god of Jacob, Jesus the upright, the holy spirit, the son of the father, who is below the seven, who is within the seven'" (Meyer and Smith, 1999, p. 43). This is followed by a chain of partially meaningful divine titles that are transformed into meaningless incantations: "bring Yao Sabbath; may your power issue forth from [Name], until you drive away this unclean demon Satan, who is in him. I adjure you, demon, whoever you are, by this god, Sabarbarbathioth Sabarbarbathiouth Sabarbarbathioneth Sabarbaphai" (Meyer and Smith, 1999, p. 43).

Such chains of senseless words are common in ancient magic. In Hellenistic antiquity, magic worked not because it was understood, but precisely because it was not understood. Various scholars have sought after the meaning of the various magic formulae, but have often fallen short of cataloging the majority of them. A powerful sign or symbol functions because it lacks meaning. Its meaning is its effectiveness, its causal potency, not its imaginary associations: it works because it is not invested with normal meaning, but with a meaning that moves beyond the symbolic realm.

After an exorcism, it was common to acknowledge the authority responsible by adorning the body with an amulet, and the example that follows again demonstrates the use of meaningless chains that are endowed with meaning: "after driving out (the demon), hang around the [person] an amulet... with these things written on a tin metal leaf: 'BOR PHOR PHORBA PHOR PHORBA BES CHARIN BAUBO TE PHOR BORPHORBA PHORBABOR'" (Meyer and Smith, 1999, p. 44). These words sound exotic and are foreign to the magos. "Magikos" itself was a foreign (i.e., Persian, barbarian) term, and thus its exotic and at-first-meaningless nature may have been what was attractive about it in the first place.

Putting together the unknown term(s) with (perceived) effectiveness is what made magikos so compelling in the early Christian world. Theurgic activity is best understood within the context of appreciating the meaning and effectiveness of apparently meaningless symbols or words. These meaningless fragments, formulae, or *goetia* ("barbaric words") in various magical papyri make use of this. Gender, likewise, presents an artificial and symbolic reference for something that has little or no biological correlate. Biological sex does not overlap evenly with social or symbolic designations of gender. Magic and gender both make reference to terms (mystical words for magic and biological designations of sex) that lack correlates in the empirical realm.

Early Christian magic scrolls also shift perspective on some of the rhetoric surrounding what certain second-century C.E. theologians referred to as "Gnosticism." Theologians such as Irenaeus of Lyons and Tertullian charged that so-called Gnostics were proffering an elitist form of Christianity. However, the magic scrolls demonstrate that these different angelic intercessors or aeons were appealed to for rudimentary daily concerns such as love, sex, sick-ness, or success. In one example from the sixth century C.E., a man appeals to "the power of Yao Sabaoth," a divine being normally associated with Gnosticism, for the love of another man (Meyer and Smith, 1999, pp. 177–178). Yao Sabaoth is not appealed to as some sort of elitist "gnostic" divinity, but as a familiar intercessor in popular religion. Papapolo son of Noe declares that his love must seek him "from town to town, from city to city, from field to field, from region to region, until he comes to me and subjects himself under my feet."

Many of the erotic magic rituals in the early church describe love and gender dynamics in terms of a right to enjoy the other. Much of the love in these popular ritual texts is related to masturbatory satisfaction—the lover serves to satisfy the desire of the other. A magic incantation from the Berlin 8325 Papyrus (ninth century C.E.) captures this love-for-the-purpose-of-satisfaction dynamic: "you may give her desire for me, and she may desire me with endless desire and come to me in the place where I am, and I may lay my breast upon her and satisfy all my desire with her, and she may satisfy my desire, right now, right now, at once, at once!" (Meyer and Smith, 1999, p. 161). A sixth/seventh-century C.E. scroll also describes desire in masturbatory terms, such that the subject meets his own desire in the other, as if in a mirror: "With my desire may she desire me, with love may she love me. May my [desire] and my love dwell insider her, [Name], daughter of [Name], like an angel of god in her presence" (London Hay 10376; Meyer and Smith, 1999, p. 165). Although this scroll is a late example, the impressive continuity between the ancient Coptic/Greek scrolls and the modern Ethiopic (Ge'ez) scrolls (which use many of the same divine names) suggests that these later scrolls preserve an early church tradition.

Beyond requests for good fortune and sexual satisfaction, there are many examples of curses. Masculinity was defined in antiquity in terms of sexual potency and symbolic authority. One way to emasculate a socially defined "man" was to pray for his sexual impotency. An example from the Strasbourg Coptic manuscript 135 makes this dynamic clear: "It (?) must not have an erection, it must not become hard, it must not ejaculate. May he—Shinte son of Tenheu—be like a corpse left in a tomb and like an old rag left on a manure pile" (Meyer and Smith, 1999, p. 181).

Assessment. Examples of popular religion evinced in the early church indicate that much orthodox rhetoric was simply that: rhetoric. The popular religion of the Hellenistic age continued alongside the development of the early church and continues in "orthodox" countries (such as Ethiopia) today.

[*See also* Popular Religion and Magic, *subentries on* Greek World, New Testament, *and* Roman World; Religious Leaders, *subentry* Early Church; *and* Religious Participation, *subentries on* Early Church *and* New Testament.]

BIBLIOGRAPHY

Achtemeier, Paul. "The Origin and Function of the Pre-Markan Miracle Catenae." *Journal of Biblical Literature* 91, no. 2 (1972): 198–221.

Allison, Dale C., John Dominic Crossan, and Amy-Jill Levine, eds. *The Historical Jesus in Context*. Princeton Readings in Religions. Princeton, N.J.: Princeton University Press, 2006.

Cartlidge, David R., and David L. Dungan. *Documents for the Study of the Gospels*. Minneapolis: Fortress 1994.

Conner, Robert. *Jesus the Sorcerer*. New York: Mandrake, 2006.

Cotter, Wendy. *Miracles in Greco-Roman Antiquity: A Sourcebook for the Study of New Testament Miracle Stories*. New York: Routledge, 1999.

Cotter, Wendy. *The Christ of the Miracle Stories, Portrait through Encounter*. Grand Rapids, Mich.: Baker Academic Press, 2010.

Crossan, John Dominic. *The Historical Jesus: The Life of a Mediterranean Jewish Peasant*. San Francisco: Harper One, 1993.

Faraone, Christopher A., and Dirk Obbink, eds. *Magika Hiera: Ancient Greek Magic and Religion*. New York: Oxford University Press, 1997.

Fortna, Robert T. "Source and Redaction in the Fourth Gospel's Portrayal of Jesus' Signs." *Journal of Biblical Literature* 89, no. 2 (1970): 151–166.

Mack, Burton L. *A Myth of Innocence: Mark and Christian Origins. Foundations and Facets*. Minneapolis: Fortress, 1998.

Meyer, Marvin W., and Richard Smith. *Ancient Christian Magic: Coptic Texts of Ritual Power*. Princeton, N.J.: Princeton University Press, 1999.

Smith, Morton. *The Secret Gospel: The Discovery and Interpretation of the Secret Gospel According to Mark*. New York: Harper & Row, 1973.

Smith, Morton. *Jesus the Magician: Charlatan or Son of God?* New York: Harper & Row, 1978.

Twelftree, Graham H. *In the Name of Jesus: Exorcism among Early Christians*. Grand Rapids, Mich.: Baker Academic Press, 2007.

Wainwright, Elaine. *Women Healing/Healing Women: The Genderization of Healing in Early Christianity*. London: Acumen, 2006.

Justin Marc Lasser

POSTCOLONIAL APPROACHES

The adjective "postcolonial," like "gender," can be fluid and difficult to define. There are many discussions about what the prefix "post-" means, as well as who, when, and where is the postcolonial. Just as gender must be understood beyond binaries (male/female, masculine/feminine, heterosexuality/homosexuality), postcolonial studies must challenge its dualistic categories (colonizer/colonized, center/periphery, metropolis/colony). Both "gender" and "postcolonial studies" are also umbrella terms: each involves a variety of approaches and a range of emphases.

Gender and Postcolonial Studies. Gender and postcolonial studies share more than an analogical relationship. The terms "gender" and "postcolonial" are similarly slippery, and both fields function to resist domination—in terms of gender and empire, respectively. Rather than seeing gender and postcolonial studies as parallel but separate, studying gender is indispensable to postcolonial studies because colonial domination is often engendered through gender constructions.

White men (and women) saving brown women from brown men. Gayatri Chakravorty Spivak (1988) emphasizes how gender is used to justify colonialism with her catchy phrase, "white men saving brown women from brown men." While Spivak's example is the British attempt to abolish Indian widows' practice of *sati*, colonial men *and* colonial women have pointed to various practices concerning women (e.g., foot binding, veiling, genital mutilation) as evidence of a society's, religion's, or culture's deficiencies to justify colonial interventions. Read as objects of patriarchal oppression from within and benevolent salvation from without, colonized women are not known and their agency not acknowledged.

Saving self from and through other(ing) wo/men. Colonialism and its objectification of colonized women are engendered by colonial desire and fear. Anne McClintock (1995) begins her book on "race, gender and sexuality in the colonial context" with three vignettes—a bestseller about hidden treasure in Africa with a map that looks like a female body; Columbus's description of the world as a woman's breast with a nipple; and a painting of America as a naked woman being literally "dis-covered" by Amerigo Vespucci—to discuss "a long tradition of male travel as an erotics of ravishment" that she calls "porno-tropics," where women, often hypersexualized, "served as the boundary markers" in colonial contacts (22, 5). If this tradition reflects a colonial desire to rape, it also betrays colonial anxiety. Agency of the colonized, even colonized women, is not always unacknowledged. It can be amplified as threatening and brutal and embodied in female figures, like the Amazons in early writings of European colonialism (Loomba, 1998, p. 154). Representing foreign lands as dangerous female natives justifies colonialism as necessary for the colonizers' security. The allure and peril of a foreign people is seen by their hypersexualization. "Deviant" sexuality (and hence the awkward "wo/men" in the heading above) can be simultaneously menacing and enticing (Aldrich, 2003; Boone, 2014). The native or "other" wo/man functions in multiple ways in colonial imaginations as a boundary marker: it both projects colonial fantasy and anxiety to the outside and provides definitions for propriety and identity at home.

Saving white women from brown men and brown women from white men. Colonial identity is constructed through gender, race, and class. Gender is crucial in colonial space because (1) European citizenship is idealized as an "honorable" or "reputable" adult white male, (2) the domestic rather than the public sphere is key to forming the young into proper citizens, especially in colonial contact zones,

and (3) women are responsible for birthing and raising children for family, nation, and race. In order to make and maintain racial, class, and cultural differences between colonizers and colonized through a cult(ivation) of domesticity around "values of monogamy, thrift, order, accumulation" (McClintock, 1995, pp. 167–168), an empire needs white women to perform their service properly as transmitters of colonial culture. This justifies the management of women's activity and sexuality. White women in colonial spaces would not necessarily ally with colonized women to resist patriarchy, however, since doing so would risk losing advantages that come with their position as colonizers. White women may also use a colonial situation ("saving brown women from brown men") to negotiate and change the class and gender restrictions they face at home (Sharpe, 1993, pp. 27–55).

If colonial readings of gender function to justify imperialism, imperialism also functions to fashion European identity and justify disciplining gender. Alongside white women's need to perform national service as mothers, white boys, as tomorrow's citizens, must learn "essential dispositions of manliness, bourgeois morality, and racial attribute" (Stoler, 1995, p. 108). This both explains and engenders "the figure of the weak, irresolute, effeminate [native man as] a special target of contempt and ridicule" (Chatterjee, 1993, p. 69). White men must prove their identity and citizenship too; none can be polluted or corrupted by the colonized to go native.

The potential of pollution in colonial contexts justifies gender restrictions for colonial *and* anti-colonial reasons and turns Spivak's catchy phrase to "white men saving white women from brown men" and "brown men saving brown women from white men." This problematizes the simplistic "colonizer-as-male-and-colonized-as-female" metaphor. Franz Fanon talks about "the woman of color and the white man" and "the man of color and the white woman," showing how gender, sexuality, and racial purity also preoccupy colonized men (1967). His work on Algeria's veiled women shows how women become the battleground between colonialism and anti-colonial nationalism (1965; see also Yeğenoğlu, 1998). Women, as mothers who birth and raise children, become mothers of the nation or race. They are boundary markers for both colonizers and colonized and must be "protected" to ensure the nation's/race's purity. The complex relations between women and nation have generated numerous important studies (e.g., Yuval-Davis and Anthias, 1989; McClintock et al., 1997). Hypervisuality, like hypersexuality—for women, native, and particularly native women—does not necessarily signify inclusion or power (Chow, 1995, 2007).

Saving sex from culture or culture from sex. While postcolonial studies originates with Edward Said's use of Foucault in *Orientalism*, it has not fully engaged a field that Foucault's work also helped originate: queer studies, especially its critique of heteronomativity and gender categories. This might have something to do with Foucault's inattention to race and empire (Young, 1995), but it also has much to do with how queer sexuality and nonwhite culture are often presented as mutually exclusive (Aydemir, 2011). Queer sexuality is presented as being free from cultural constraints and an expression of autonomy, individuality, modernity, and westernization. Culture is understood as monolithic, unchanging, and constraining. Culture thus comes to differentiate those who are "enlightened" about sexuality from those who are not. Although the modern West is itself a culture, it is different because, as Wendy Brown explains, " 'We' have culture while culture has 'them,' or we *have* culture while they *are* a culture" (cited in Aydemir, 2011, p. 15). Sexual identity and cultural identity are, therefore, antagonistic. Both are presumed to be all-consuming: if you embrace one, you cannot embrace the other. This framework creates two seemingly opposing but ideologically linked figures: (1) the desirable queer asylum seeker from the Third World whose sexual individuality is threatened but deserves to be protected since it is, by definition, queer, modern, and Western and (2) the undesirable homophobic immigrant into the First World who remains bound by his or her culture's unenlightened sexual mores. What is seldom acknowledged is (1) how state policy, like relying on family reunification to maintain a low-wage workforce but

simultaneously refusing to provide a social safety net, may actually strengthen the heteropatriarchy of immigrant life; (2) how homophobia might become a form of resistance to safeguard some cultural, racial/ethnic, or religious particularity, since the demand to accept queer sexuality becomes a kind of forced assimilation; (3) how many will assume and fantasize that a Third World or immigrant person only has a repressed, unemancipated, perverse, and possibly excessive and exciting sexuality; and (4) how postcolonial studies and queer studies end up being embraced by different groups of people and develop along separate tracks. Fortunately, attempts are being made to break out of this framework and put queer and postcolonial studies into productive conversations (Hawley, 2001a, 2001b; Puar, 2007).

Gender and Postcolonial Biblical Interpretations. Postcolonial criticism appeared in biblical studies in the 1990s. Several mappings of postcolonial biblical criticism are available, including those by Stephen Moore (see also Sugirtharajah, 2013). Moore (2000) distinguishes postcolonial readings that view biblical texts as (1) subverting or resisting colonialism; (2) supporting colonialism; or (3) both subverting and supporting colonialism in ambivalent manners. Moore also discusses postcolonial approaches to the Bible that (1) emerge out of contextual hermeneutics and engage lightly with the larger field of postcolonial studies; (2) emphasize "empire" without engaging the larger field of postcolonial studies; and (3) engage the larger field of postcolonial studies heavily (2006, pp. 14–23). While Moore's two mappings share a three-pronged structure, they are not mirror images. Moore recognizes, for instance, that critics from different paths in his second mapping may share the view that biblical texts are ideologically supportive of colonialism.

Developed a decade or so after postcolonial studies emerged in the larger academic world, postcolonial biblical readings tend to be attentive to gender questions early on, though not across the board (e.g., Sugirtharajah 1998; Segovia, 2000). Elisabeth Schüssler Fiorenza's (1992) feminist concept of kyriarchy already recognizes that domination works at intersections. In her introduction to an early anthology on postcolonial biblical readings, Laura Donaldson insists that colonial and gender considerations not be isolated in biblical scholarship (1996; see also Donaldson, 2005; Kwok, 2005, pp. 77–99). Referring to Shakespeare's *The Tempest*—particularly how a colonized native called Caliban and a white woman named Miranda fail to support each other even though both are victims of the colonial patriarch—Donaldson identifies a "Miranda complex" in how white feminists read violence against the concubine in Judges 19 apart from violence against Gibeah's Benjaminites in Judges 20, when New England's settlers read both chapters together to legitimate massacring the Pequot people in 1637.

Scholars have read various New Testament books to scrutinize empire *and* gender dynamics, including how Roman colonial authority destabilizes gender in Mark's Gospel, especially its depiction of masculinity (Thurman, 2003); how Mark's narrative of a widow's offering in the Temple might signify colonized women's response to foreign imperialism or native patriarchy, or both (Kim, 2010; Liew, 2008); how John's Gospel is an anti-imperial but patriarchal nationalist discourse from a "woman-and-nation" framework (Kim, 2004); how Jesus's incarnation in John involves transgendering as well as racial/ethnic drag (as an *Ioudaios*) to put into crisis both Roman colonialism and anti-Roman nationalism that is built on patriarchy and purity (Liew, 2009); how Galatians shows Paul's transformation from internalizing the Roman ideology of masculinist conquest to identifying with the conquered and "effeminized" nations of the Roman Empire to become a "s/he" to birth a movement of solidarity and resistance (Lope, 2008); how Philippians inscribes imperial and patriarchal hierarchy (Marchal, 2008); how translation of 1 Peter is influenced by imperial and patriarchal assumptions of translators (Dube, 2009); how Revelation's Rome-Roma-Babylon motif betrays the author's ambivalence toward a sexualized empire (Moore, 2009); and how methodologically queer and postcolonial theory might inform New Testament interpretation (Punt, 2011).

There are similar readings of the Hebrew Bible, including the following examples.

Exodus. Donaldson authored a postcolonial biblical reading that examines Zora Neale Hurston's re-reading or rewriting of Moses and Exodus (1992, pp. 102–117), which Hurston describes as "look[ing] like a bloody rape to the Canaanites" (cited in Donaldson, 1992, p. 104). Citing Gloria Anzaldúa's work on the *mestiza* and Riane Eisler's on power as a circle of connections rather than a pyramid of hierarchical domination, Donaldson proposes that Hurston's novel, *Moses, Man of the Mountain*—published in 1939 during a time of German, British, and U.S. imperialism—hybridizes and destabilizes Moses's ethnicity and even God's gender to discourage a quest for freedom from turning into an ethnocentric, patriarchal, and militaristic nationalism.

For Musa Dube (2000), Exodus shares a colonial literary strategy with ancient texts like Virgil's *Aeneid* and modern ones like Joseph Conrad's *Heart of Darkness*: travel is encouraged for God, gold, and glory to dominate a foreign people or land. Using Mary Louise Pratt's work on "contact zone" and "autoethnography," Dube argues that the Exodus replicates empire-building strategies of Israel's colonizers by also using gender in its conquest narrative: (1) stories of women only move the plot toward the promise of conquest; (2) Israelite women suspend their gender roles to participate in Israel's struggle for freedom, but patriarchy (re)emerges with the giving of the law to Moses when women are identified as property of men (Exod 20:17) and sources of pollution (Exod 19:15); and (3) intermarriage is forbidden because women, both Israelite and non-Israelite, play crucial roles in Israel's future as wives and mothers.

Joshua and Judges: Rahab, Jael, and Samson. Linking Exodus with Joshua, Dube (2000) turns to Rahab, a prostitute known for hiding Israelite spies and facilitating their conquest of her town and people to secure her future among the Israelites. Like Pocahontas, she becomes a representative of her culture, people, or land to "feminize" what is "native" and indicate the natives' willingness to welcome, consent to, and collaborate with colonial advances. Dube is adamant, however, that Joshua's Rahab was written by her colonizers. With what she calls "Rahab's reading prism," Dube suggests a decolonizing feminist strategy that acknowledges layered dynamics of oppression and approaches biblical texts from various angles to resist both imperial and patriarchal ideologies, "resurrect" women who are doubly colonized in terms of gender and race to speak for themselves, and realize a different future of interdependence.

Focusing on references to Rahab as prostitute, Lori Rowlett (2000) stresses the tendency of colonizers to "feminize" a foreign land and people and accuse them of "excessive sensuality" and "heightened sexuality and infidelity" (pp. 67, 68). Juxtaposing Rahab and Pocahontas (Disney's cartoon version), Rowlett reads Rahab's collaboration with and conversion to Israel's God as "a symbol of…the transformation of the land from sexually lascivious paganism (in Hebrew eyes) to colonized docility" (p. 68). She notes the gender polarity that is found in Rahab: a female prostitute who proclaims the "machismo of the Hebrews' god" in Joshua 2:9–10 (p. 69). Since "colonizing powers telling the story have given [Rahab and Poncahontas] words to speak in praise of themselves as conquering heroes," Rowlett concludes that both are "cartoon figures" (p. 75).

Dube (2003) also compares Rahab with Judith, concluding that both figures are products of patriarchy and imperialism, though in contrasting ways. Unlike the Canaanite prostitute who betrays her people to side with Israelite invaders, Judith is a faithful Israelite widow who stands for land and people under threats of Assyria's imperial invasion. She is able to remain pure, resist, and rescue her people by posing as a traitor to kill the Assyrian general. Both women are reductive representations of their land or people by patriarchal Israelites for patriarchal Israelites, whether the purpose is colonial or anti-colonial.

In another, more affirmative reading of Rahab, Dube identifies her own situation in Africa with that of Rahab: she is caught in a (neo)colonial situation "where the powerful threaten to wipe out the cities" and a colonial-type conquest in the AIDS epidemic (2005b, p. 177). Rahab tying a crimson cord in her window becomes for Dube a choice for life after an honest assessment of reality. Dube does highlight a difference between herself and Rahab; instead of

waiting for the colonizers to knock down the walls that divide the world into powerful and less powerful, Dube's article is her red ribbon that invites the world to acknowledge the impact of imperialism and HIV/AIDS and "stand in solidarity with Africa and all other people…to save life" (p. 178).

Reading the 2004 U.S. presidential election by another triplet of G-s ("God, guns, and gays"), Pui-lan Kwok (2006) underscores connections among Bible, empire-building through militarism, and gender and sexual mores to interpret Rahab. Citing Foucault and postcolonial theorists like Said and Homi Bhabha, Kwok emphasizes that "sexuality is always embedded and inscribed in larger societal structures and political discourses": Rahab as a prostitute "symbolizes not only the availability of her female body and reproductive power, but also the domestication of the land, the licentious behavior of the Canaanites, and the unequal position between the colonizers and the conquered" (2006, pp. 29, 45). Rather than highlighting her agency positively as a heroine (as many white feminists do) or negatively as a sellout (as Dube does in her earlier work), Kwok compares Rahab with sex workers in Asia and focuses on social forces that limited Rahab's choices.

Erin Runions (2008) reads Rahab as a hybrid and queer figure. Building on the work of scholars like Randall Bailey and Ken Stone, Runions suggests that Rahab, as Canaanite and prostitute (thus not a mother, wife, or monogamous), embodies racialized nonheteronormativity. Arguing that this hybrid, queer figure has the potential to undercut the affective value of colonial heteronormativity, Runions refers to a wide assortment of resources. She appeals, for example, to Althea Spencer Miller's work on orality as corrective to colonial preferences for the literary and Spencer Miller's humorous but subversive story about a Jamaican nanny, who, to protect her rebel colleagues, bares her behind to distract British soldiers and nonfatally absorb their bullets. Runions also refers to historical-critical scholarship to argue that there was, behind the book of Joshua, an earlier indigenous story about Rahab that functions like the nanny story. Removing Rahab's confession of faith and negotiation with the spies, Runions suggests that the earlier tale consists of Joshua 2:1–8, 15–16, and 22–23. In this earlier tale, the spies are irresponsible (they visit a prostitute when told by Joshua to scout out the land), incompetent (their exact location is known to Jericho's king), and impotent (their desire for sexual conquest by visiting a prostitute is not only frustrated but reversed, as they become objects of Rahab's commands), and they thus come across as idiotic, silly, and laughable. The king of Jericho and his men do not look much better. Tricked by Rahab, they spend their time on a wild-goose chase. Rahab comes across in this tale as a nonheteronormative Canaanite trickster in control of her life and situation. For Runions, the reversal from the Israelites spying to invade the land and oust the Canaanites to Rahab becoming the subject who sends away the spies is both funny and disruptive of the Deuteronomistic redaction that turns Rahab into a turncoat collaborating with the colonization of her city/people. Humor is disruptive in Runions's view because it is also queer; it works by making odd connections.

Highlighting tropes from their experiences as Asian Americans, Kah-Jin Jeffrey Kuan and Mai-Anh Le Tran (2009) read Rahab as moving from a "hybrid subject" living epistemologically and physically in a liminal space between Canaanite and Israelite worlds, to a "model minority" but simultaneously objectified and "sexualized other" who betrays her people for her own survival, to finally a "perpetual foreigner" who is "figuratively and literally returned to Canaan"—Rahab and her kindred were all sent "outside the camp of Israel" after the conquest (Joshua 6:23). Rahab's story does not just use a native woman to represent the land and the complicity of the native people in their own colonization. It also keeps the native woman "outside" during the conquest and ousts her afterward.

Marcella Althaus-Reid's (2007) reading of a "postcolonial Rahab" makes two points about queer reading and postcolonial reading: (1) they share a commitment to challenge the "tyranny of custom" and (2) they have different understandings of "frontier"—the postcolonial frontier refers to the border that colonizers use to construct the imperial self, but

the queer frontier is transgenderism. Althaus-Reid notes how the text locates Rahab at the frontier; her house is not only in the wall that defines the boundary of the city but also between the public (as a business) and the private (as a domestic home). Reading Rahab's story alongside a novel by Lázaro Covadlo and a poem by Anzaldúa, Althaus-Reid suggests that Joshua's text asks Rahab to give up her frontier existence and independence to live by "a heterosexual, mono-loving, mentality of only one nation, one God and one faith" that "silenc[es]…the right to difference" by calling "the imperial destruction of trangressive [sic] women…salvation" (2007, pp. 134, 139, 140).

Recognizing that colonizers and colonized use a native woman figure for different purposes, Steed Davidson (2013) suggests that Rahab is presented as a woman with agency to "feminize" and shame native men. The inability of native men to control their women indicates their inability to protect their land. Besides bringing native men into this discussion, Davidson brings into the mix two other women: one native and one Israelite. Davidson points to similarities between Rahab and the Kenite woman Jael of Judges 4. Like Rahab, Jael is a native woman who betrays her own people to serve the interests of the invading Israelites: by killing Sisera (the military leader of Canaan's King Jabin)— even though Sisera is supposedly under the protection of Jael's husband—Jael facilitates Jabin's destruction and Israel's victory. Davidson then points to differences between Jael and Deborah. Jael is an extension of Deborah, an Israelite "prophetess" who gives Barak the plan to defeat Sisera and "arose as a mother in Israel" (Judg 4:4; 5:7). However, Jael performs the violent act of murder and remains a tent-dwelling Kenite. Jael is, in the language of Bhabha's exploration of colonial mimicry, "almost the same as Deborah but not quite" (Davidson, 2013, p. 85). The apparent agency of Jael, like that of Rahab, is thus only another manifestation of brown women being saved from brown men. These two native women not only subvert non-Israelite patriarchal authority but also reveal the weaknesses of all natives, men and women included.

Davidson is not interested in repudiating native women as pawns or focusing on their agency in colonial discourse. Citing Althaus-Reid's "queer epistemology," Davidson emphasizes reading these textual images of native women as already fractured because these images are almost the same as native women in flesh and blood but not quite. Similarly, Davidson questions the binary construction of native men and native women in these texts. A postcolonial approach to the Bible in general—and to native women in the Bible in particular—involves for Davidson a destabilization of the text and its constructed images into ambiguity. Finally, Davidson suggests that the hope of postcolonial biblical readings lies in the postcolonial reader. "Precisely in the tension between text and reality, between woman and Woman," Davidson writes, "the image shatters because real women read these texts" (2013, p. 90).

Instead of focusing on non-Israelite women, Uriah Kim (2014) looks at a male Israelite, Samson. Reading Judges within the framework of the Deuteronomistic history, Kim (1) stresses the imperial context of this corpus's writing, with Israel struggling to survive under three successive empires (Assyria, Babylon, and Persia), and (2) suggests that Samson could be read as a representative of, and a metaphor for, Israel, particularly its ruling elite males. If Samson's death represents Israel's victimization at imperial hands, his life might tell more about life in the shadow of empires. Pointing out how Samson's father is ignored and sidelined as his wife and the angel anticipate and plan for Samson's birth and future, as well as how Samson is humiliated or "feminized" by Delilah (she shaves his head) and other Philistines (they force him to do what is generally done by women and sexually suggestive: grinding at a mill and performing to entertain), Kim argues that this reflects what Israelite elite males were feeling during their exile: loss of male identity and patriarchal authority. In fact, Kim states that women in Judges "function as threats to [Israel's] identity, either as instruments or as causes," so male characters sacrifice, kill, and rape women characters (like Jephthah's daughter, the unnamed concubine, and the women of Shiloh) in the book to protect or reestablish their identity and authority as "sons of Israel" (2014, pp. 7–8).

Beyond lamenting this loss, Samson's story also protests against imperial cruelty. Kim suggests that throughout the "tit-for-tat" contest between Samson and the Philistines, Samson behaves with a sense of fairness and a "concept of proportionality" while the Philistines do not (2014, p. 14). For example, the Philistines solve Samson's riddle by blackmailing Samson's wife, while Samson's retirement to Etam after slaughtering the Philistines in revenge for their burning of his wife and her family indicates Samson's readiness to call it even. Considering the translation of Samson's request to God in Judges 16:28 as "so that I may be avenged upon the Philistines for one of my two eyes," Kim proposes that we see in the unevenness of this equation the colonized's protest against abuses they suffered at the hands of their colonizers.

Ruth. Another woman who attracts postcolonial readings is Ruth. Davidson observes that Ruth, a gentile like Rahab, becomes part of the Israelite lineage by separating herself from native land and culture (2013, p. 74). In her reading of Ruth, Donaldson (1999; see also McKinlay, 2004, pp. 37–56), noting that native women among the Quiché Mayan would prefer the tale of Judith to that of Moses and Exodus, highlights a reading process by the colonized that "actively selects and invents, rather than passively accepts" colonial texts through a persistent American Indian tradition or "Native 'survivance'" (1999, p. 22). Donaldson then (1) connects Ruth with Rahab and Pocahontas, (2) contests intermarriage that Ruth went through not once but twice as a strategy that Thomas Jefferson proposed to assimilate Native Americans, and (3) compares the different paths taken by Ruth and her Moabite sister-in-law, Orpah. While Ruth's assimilation leads to her own displacement (her child with Boaz is given to Naomi), Orpah, though only mentioned twice in the book, provides a counternarrative and a more important model than Ruth by returning to her "mother's house" and hence her own nonpatriarchal heritage and racial/ethnic identity. For Donaldson, Orpah's is "a courageous act of self and communal affirmation: the choosing of the indigenous mother's house over that of the alien Israelite Father" (1999, p. 36).

Agreeing with Donaldson about the need for postcolonial readings to be informed by a reader's cultural traditions, Dube (2005a) takes Donaldson's proposal for postcolonial inventive readings a step further by imagining four letters that Orpah wrote to Ruth after their tearful goodbye to each other. Dube literarily allows Orpah and Ruth to tell their own version of their story. In these letters, Dube imagines (1) an origin story regarding the Moabites that is different from Genesis 19, where, as Donaldson points out through Bailey's work, Moabites were hypersexualized as descendants of an incestuous affair between Lot and his eldest daughter (Donaldson, 1999, pp. 23–24), (2) Orpah and Ruth as sisters and princesses, (3) Orpah becoming a queen and priestess upon returning to her mother's house, and (4) Orpah encouraging Ruth to instill in her children a respect for the Moabites. In another article on Ruth, Dube (2001) reads the relationship between Ruth the Moabite and her Israelite mother-in-law, Naomi, as symptomatic of unequal relations between nations: (1) Ruth's pledge to Naomi is not reciprocated by Naomi, so it signifies not a mutually loving but a slave-to-master relationship; and (2) the land of Moab is associated with death (Naomi lost her husband and sons there), but its resources are used to benefit Naomi (Ruth's service as an obedient daughter-in-law, including bearing a son for Naomi). Ruth's story is thus for Dube "unusable as a model of liberating interdependence between nations" (2001, p. 194).

Gale Yee's (2009) reading of Ruth as "model minority" and "perpetual foreigner" notes that Ruth vanishes at the closing of her story and focuses on economic and class issues in the story. For Yee, readers must remember that Ruth is an impoverished woman whose actions are compelled by economic urgency. Like Dube, Yee reads Ruth's pledge to Naomi as "a verbal contract" between subordinate and superior (p. 130). This explains for Yee why Ruth does, and Naomi does not, go out to glean; why Ruth gleans "without resting even for a moment" (Ruth 2:7); why Ruth follows Naomi's instructions so readily; and why Naomi displaces Ruth as Obed's mother. Yee also discusses Boaz's economic exploitation of Ruth. Like Naomi, Boaz does not need to labor physically; he only gives commands. Boaz's desire to keep Ruth working in his field might have more to do with Ruth's tireless productivity, not to mention the piece of land that Boaz gains by taking Ruth as his wife. If Ruth's marriage strengthens Boaz's economic status as a landowner in Judah, Ruth's child preserves the lineage of Naomi's husband and hence secures Naomi's economic place in the community. Ruth's story, for Yee, "becomes an indictment of those…who live in the First World who exploit the cheap labor of developing countries and poor immigrants from these countries who come to the First World looking for jobs" (2009, p. 134).

Ezra-Nehemiah. Yee mentions the possibility that Ruth was written during the time of Ezra-Nehemiah, when marriage with foreign women was condemned for Israelite males. For Roland Boer (2013), the condemnation of foreign women in Ezra-Nehemiah is part of a collective political subjectivity construction, since the lists in these books indicate a desire and anxiety to separate people into identifiable groups, both *from* and *within* the inside (see also Boer, 2005). Beside emphasizing the importance of Marxist analysis in reading these books (since the lists divide people into groups that labor and those that do not), Boer argues that a "spiral of exclusion" (2013, p. 224) is necessary and endless for constructing a collective political subjectivity because boundary, whether between insider and outsider or between the process and product of subject construction, is always fluid and leaky.

Micah. While Runions is interested in the individual reader as subject, her reading of Micah (2001) shares many of the features found in Boer's reading above. Boer's interest in collective political subjectivity is close to Runions's interest in the question of nation in Micah. Like Boer, Runions investigates postcolonial, gender, and class concerns in a biblical text and highlights a text's instability or indeterminacy to question binary assumptions. Specifically, Runions argues that the scholarly tendency of reading in Micah "the nation as a punished, passive and suffering woman waiting for her divine male hero to lead her into a glorious future of dominion over other nations" results more from a reader's ideology about gender hierarchy and Israel's divinely ordained nationhood than the text of Micah itself. Pointing out that the text is incoherent in its depiction of the nation—especially how Micah 4:8–14 and Micah 5–6 portray the nation as both male and female, human and divine, colonizer and colonized—Runions suggests that, if read carefully, Micah's nation as a hybrid figure might sensitize a reader to his or her own ideology and subject position and hence carry the potential of shifting a reader's ideology and subject position.

Conclusion. The question of subjectivity returns us to the difficulty of defining who, when, where, and what is postcolonial as well as the instability of gender identity. Just as gender and postcolonial concerns might bring about a productive tension, the ambiguity of gender and the instability of the postcolonial can create a momentum to keep asking new questions and bringing new angles to old questions (Trinh, 1989). The intersection between postcolonial and gender concerns in biblical interpretation remains open-ended, which explains the diversity, elasticity, and intertextuality demonstrated in the illustrations above.

[*See also* Imagery, Gendered, *subentry* Deuteronomistic History; Intersectional Studies; Patriarchy/Kyriarchy; Queer Readings; *and* Reader-Oriented Criticism.]

BIBLIOGRAPHY

Aldrich, Robert. *Colonialism and Homosexuality.* London: Routledge, 2003.

Althaus-Reid, Marcella María. "Searching for a Queer Sophia-Wisdom: The Post-Colonial Rahab." In *Patriarchs, Prophets and Other Villains*, edited by Lisa Isherwood, pp. 128–140. London: Equinox, 2007.

Aydemir, Murat. "Introduction: Indiscretions at the Sex/Culture Divide." In *Indiscretions: At the Intersection of Queer and Postcolonial Theory*, edited by Murat Aydemir, pp. 9–30. Amsterdam: Rodopi, 2011.

Boer, Roland. "No Road: On the Absence of Feminist Criticism of Ezra-Nehemiah." In *Her Master's Tools: Feminist and Postcolonial Engagements of Historical-Critical Discourse*, edited by Caroline Vander Stichele and Todd Penner, pp. 233–252. Atlanta: Society of Biblical Literature, 2005.

Boer, Roland. "Then I Cleansed Them from Everything Foreign: The Search for Subjectivity in Ezra-Nehemiah." In *Postcolonialism and the Hebrew Bible: The Next Step*, edited by Roland Boer, pp. 221–237. Atlanta: Society of Biblical Literature, 2013.

Boone, Joseph Allen. *The Homoerotics of Orientalism.* New York: Columbia University Press, 2014.

Chatterjeee, Partha. *The Nation and Its Fragments: Colonial and Post-Colonial Histories.* Princeton, N.J.: Princeton University Press, 1993.

Chow, Rey. *Primitive Passions: Visuality, Sexuality, Ethnography, and Contemporary Chinese Cinema.* New York: Columbia University Press, 1995.

Chow, Rey. *Sentimental Fabulations, Contemporary Chinese Films: Attachment in the Age of Global Visibility.* New York: Columbia University Press, 2007.

Davidson, Steed Vernyl. "Gazing (at) Native Women: Rahab and Jael in Imperializing and Postcolonial Discourses." In *Postcolonialism and the Hebrew Bible: The Next Step*, edited by Roland Boer, pp. 69–92. Atlanta: Society of Biblical Literature, 2013.

Donaldson, Laura E. *Decolonizing Feminisms: Race, Gender, & Empire-Building.* Chapel Hill: University of North Carolina Press, 1992.

Donaldson, Laura E. "Postcolonialism and Biblical Reading: An Introduction." *Semeia* 75 (1996): 1–14.

Donaldson, Laura E. "The Sign of Orpah: Reading Ruth through Native Eyes." In *Vernacular Hermeneutics*, edited by R. S. Sugirtharajah, pp. 20–36. Sheffield, U.K.: Sheffield Academic, 1999.

Donaldson, Laura E. "Gospel Hauntings: The Postcolonial Demons of New Testament Criticism." In *Postcolonial Biblical Criticism: Interdisciplinary Intersections*, edited by Stephen D. Moore and Fernando F. Segovia, pp. 97–113. New York: T&T Clark International, 2005.

Dube, Musa W. "The Unpublished Letters of Orpah to Ruth." In *Ruth and Esther: A Feminist Companion to the Bible*, edited by Athalya Brenner, pp. 145–150. Sheffield, U.K.: Sheffield Academic, 1999.

Dube, Musa W. *Postcolonial Feminist Interpretation of the Bible.* Saint Louis, Mo.: Chalice, 2000.

Dube, Musa W. "Divining Ruth for International Relations." In *Postmodern Interpretations of the Bible: A Reader*, edited by A. K. M. Adam, pp. 67–80. Saint Louis, Mo.: Chalice, 2001.

Dube, Musa W. "Rahab Says Hello to Judith: A Decolonizing Feminist Reading." In *Toward a New Heaven and a New Earth: Essays in Honor of Elisabeth Schüssler Fiorenza*, edited by Fernando F. Segovia, pp. 54–72. Maryknoll, N.Y.: Orbis, 2003.

Dube, Musa W. "Circle Readings of the Bible/Scripturatures." In *Study of Religion in Southern Africa: Essays in*

Honor of G. C. Oosthuizen, edited by Johannes A. Smit, P. Pratap Kumar, and G. C. Oosthuizen, pp. 77–96. Leiden, The Netherlands: Brill, 2005a.

Dube, Musa W. "Rahab Is Hanging Out a Red Ribbon: One African Woman's Perspective on the Future of Feminist New Testament Scholarship." In *Feminist New Testament Studies: Global and Future Perspectives*, edited by Kathleen Wicker, pp. 177–202. Basingstoke, U.K.: Palgrave Macmillan, 2005b.

Dube, Musa W. "Towards Postcolonial Feminist Translations of the Bible." In *Reading Ideologies: Essays on the Bible & Interpretation in Honor of Mary Ann Tolbert*, edited by Tat-siong Benny Liew, pp. 215–239. Sheffield, U.K.: Sheffield Phoenix, 2009.

Fanon, Frantz. *A Dying Colonialism*. Translated by Haakon Chevalier. New York: Grove, 1965.

Fanon, Frantz. *Black Skin, White Masks*. Translated by Charles Lam Markmann. New York: Grove, 1967.

Hawley, John C. *Postcolonial and Queer Theories: Intersections and Essays*. Westport, Conn.: Greenwood, 2001b.

Hawley, John C., ed. *Postcolonial, Queer: Theoretical Intersections*. Albany: State University of New York Press, 2001a.

Kim, Jean Kyoung. *Woman and Nation: An Intercontextual Reading of the Gospel of John from a Postcolonial Feminist Perspective*. Leiden, The Netherlands: Brill, 2004.

Kim, Seong Hee. *Mark, Women and Empire: A Korean Postcolonial Perspective*. Sheffield, U.K.: Sheffield Phoenix, 2010.

Kim, Uriah Y. "More to the Eye than Meets the Eye: A Protest against Empire in Samson's Death?" *Biblical Interpretation* 22 (2014): 1–19.

Kuan, Kah-Jin Jeffrey, and Mai-Anh Le Tran. "Reading Race Reading Rahab: A 'Broad' Asian American Reading of a 'Broad' Other." In *Postcolonial Interventions: Essays in Honor of R. S. Sugirtharajah*, edited by Tat-siong Benny Liew, pp. 27–44. Sheffield, U.K.: Sheffield Phoenix, 2009.

Kwok, Pui-lan. *Postcolonial Imagination and Feminist Theology*. Louisville, Ky.: Westminster John Knox, 2005.

Kwok, Pui-lan. "Sexual Morality and National Politics: Reading Biblical 'Loose Women.'" In *Engaging the Bible: Critical Readings from Contemporary Women*, edited by Choi Hee An and Katheryn Pfisterer Darr, pp. 21–46. Minneapolis: Fortress, 2006.

Liew, Tat-siong Benny. "Postcolonial Criticism." In *Mark and Method: New Approaches in Biblical Studies*, 2d ed., edited by Janice Capel Anderson and Stephen D. Moore, pp. 211–231. Minneapolis: Fortress, 2008.

Liew, Tat-siong Benny. "Queering Closets and Perverting Desires: Cross-Examining John's Engendering and Transgendering Word across Different Worlds." In *They Were All Together in One Place? Toward Minority Biblical Criticism*, edited by Randall C. Bailey, Tat-siong Benny Liew, and Fernando F. Segovia, pp. 251–288. Atlanta: Society of Biblical Literature, 2009.

Loomba, Ania. *Colonialism/Postcolonialism*. New York: Routledge, 1998.

Lopez, Davina C. *Apostle to the Conquered: Reimagining Paul's Mission*. Minneapolis: Fortress, 2008.

Marchal, Joseph A. *The Politics of Heaven: Women, Gender, and Empire in the Study of Paul*. Minneapolis: Fortress, 2008.

McClintock, Anne. *Imperial Leather: Race, Gender, and Sexuality in the Colonial Conquest*. New York: Routledge, 1995.

McClintock, Anne, Aamir Mufti, and Ella Shohat, eds. *Dangerous Liaisons: Gender, Nation, and Postcolonial Perspectives*. Minneapolis: University of Minnesota Press, 1997.

McKinlay, Judith E. *Reframing Her: Biblical Women in Postcolonial Focus*. Sheffield, U.K.: Sheffield Phoenix, 2004.

Moore, Stephen D. "Colonialism/Postcolonialism." In *A Handbook for Postmodern Biblical Interpretation*, edited by A. K. M. Adam, pp. 182–188. Saint Louis, Mo.: Chalice, 2000.

Moore, Stephen D. *Empire and Apocalypse: Postcolonialism and the New Testament*. Sheffield, U.K.: Sheffield Phoenix, 2006.

Moore, Stephen D. "Metonymies of Empire: Sexual Humiliation and Gender Masquerade in the Book of Revelation." In *Postcolonial Interventions: Essays in Honor of R. S. Sugirtharajah*, edited by Tat-siong Benny Liew, pp. 71–97. Sheffield, U.K.: Sheffield Phoenix, 2009.

Puar, Jasbir K. *Terrorist Assemblages: Homonationalism in Queer Times*. Durham, N.C.: Duke University Press, 2007.

Punt, Jeremy. "Queer Theory, Postcolonial Theory, and Biblical Interpretation: A Preliminary Exploration of Some Intersections." In *Bible Trouble: Queer Reading at the Boundaries of Biblical Scholarship*, edited by Teresa J. Hornsby and Ken Stone, pp. 321–342. Atlanta: Society of Biblical Literature, 2011.

Rowlett, Lori. "Disney's Pocahontas and Joshua's Rahab in Postcolonial Perspective." In *Culture, Entertainment and the Bible*, edited by George Aichele, pp. 66–75. Sheffield, U.K.: Sheffield Academic, 2000.

Runions, Erin. *Changing Subjects: Gender, Nation and Future in Micah*. Sheffield, U.K.: Sheffield Academic, 2001.

Runions, Erin. "From Disgust to Humor: Rahab's Queer Affect." *Postscripts* 4 (2008): 41–69.

Schüssler Fiorenza, Elisabeth. *But She Said: Feminist Practices of Biblical Interpretation*. Boston: Beacon, 1992.

Segovia, Fernando F. *Decolonizing Biblical Studies: A View from the Margins*. Maryknoll, N.Y.: Orbis, 2000.

Sharpe, Jenny. *Allegories of Empire: The Figure of Woman in the Colonial Text*. Minneapolis: University of Minnesota Press, 1993.

Spivak, Gayatri Chakravorty. "Can the Subaltern Speak?" In *Marxism and the Interpretation of Culture*, edited by Cary Nelson and Lawrence Grossberg, pp. 271–313. Urbana: University of Illinois Press, 1988.

Stoler, Ann Laura. *Race and the Education of Desire: Foucault's History of Sexuality and the Colonial Order of Things*. Durham, N.C.: Duke University Press, 1995.

Stoler, Ann Laura. *Carnal Knowledge and Imperial Power: Race and the Intimate in Colonial Rule*. Berkeley: University of California Press, 2002.

Sugirtharajah, R. S. *Asian Biblical Hermeneutics and Postcolonialism: Contesting the Interpretations*. Maryknoll, N.Y.: Orbis, 1998.

Sugirtharajah, R. S. "Postcolonial Biblical Interpretation." In *The Oxford Encyclopedia of Biblical Interpretation*.

Vol. 2: *Metaphor Theory and Biblical Texts—Womanist Interpretation*, edited by Steven McKenzie, pp. 123–132. New York: Oxford University Press, 2013.

Thurman, Eric. "Looking for a Few Good Men: Mark and Masculinity." In *New Testament Masculinities*, edited by Janice Capel Anderson and Stephen D. Moore, pp. 137–161. Atlanta: Society of Biblical Literature, 2003.

Trinh, T. Minh-ha. *Woman, Native, Other: Writing Postcoloniality and Feminism*. Bloomington: Indiana University Press, 1989.

Yee, Gale A. "'She Stood in Tears amid the Alien Corn': Ruth, the Perpetual Foreigner and Model Minority." In *They Were All Together in One Place? Toward Minority Biblical Criticism*, edited by Randall C. Bailey, Tat-siong Benny Liew, and Fernando F. Segovia, pp. 119–140. Atlanta: Society of Biblical Literature, 2009.

Yeğenoğlu, Meyda. *Colonial Fantasies: Towards a Feminist Reading of Orientalism*. New York: Cambridge University Press, 1998.

Young, Robert J. C. "Foucault on Race and Colonialism." *New Formations* 25 (1995): 57–65.

Yuval-Davis, Nira, and Floya Anthias, eds. *Woman-Nation-State*. New York: St. Martin's, 1989.

Tat-siong Benny Liew

Q

Queer Readings

By 2007, according to the revised entry in the third edition of the *Oxford English Dictionary*, the adjective "queer" was commonly, if still not exclusively, associated with homosexuality, something even more true of the noun; this association had been a long one (for the adjective, the oldest citation in this sense is 1914; for the noun, 1894). That it remained an ambiguous association is borne out by the compilers' careful comment that "although originally chiefly derogatory (and still widely considered offensive, esp. when used by heterosexual people), from the late 1980s it began to be used as a neutral or positive term (originally of self-reference, by some homosexuals)." Some gay men and lesbians felt the need to replace not only the word "homosexual," compromised in their eyes by its historical association with a dominant medical, legal, and social discourse, but even the terms "gay" and "lesbian," which were proving inadequate to express the full range of nonconforming sexual desires and practices. Attempts were made to widen the scope of gay and lesbian by more inclusive labels such as LGBT (lesbian, gay, bisexual, and transgendered). The reclamation of the word "queer" from its use as an insult gained some popularity toward the end of the twentieth century—according to Michael Warner, writing in 1993, in "the last two or three years" (1993, p. xxvi). But it also brought about its own ambiguities. "Queer" came to be used in two different, though related, senses. First, it acted as shorthand, a loose umbrella term by which one could understand not only gay and lesbian but also bisexual, transgendered, transsexual, and any other minority that saw itself out of kilter with the sexually "normal." Secondly, "queer" began to be used as a self-referential identity tag, particularly by those involved in radical, anti-assimilationist sexual politics, of which the best-known example is Queer Nation (for details, see Jagose, 1996, pp. 107–109).

Queer Theory and Its Ambiguities. An added complication was the emergence in the 1990s of queer theory, a new academic approach to gender studies, which first came to public attention, according to Stephen Moore (2001, p. 12), at a 1990 conference on the subject at the University of California, Santa Cruz. With its origins in feminist and lesbian and gay studies, its early practitioners were academics in the fields of philosophy, culture, and literature. Defining queer theory in a sentence or two is notoriously difficult. Annamarie Jagose (1996, p. 1) comments that "part of queer's semantic clout, part of its political efficacy, depends on its resistance to definition, and the way it refuses to stake its claim." Further there is disagreement about its seminal thinkers. Arlene Stein and Ken Plummer single out Judith Butler and Eve Kosofsky Sedgwick (1996, pp. 13–14). Nicki Sullivan lists "Sedgwick, Butler, de Lauretis, Bersani, Califia, Warner, Watney, and so on" (2003, p. 66). Jagose (1996, p. 79), focusing on "the post-structuralist context in which queer emerges," adds to the names Althusser, Lacan, and Saussure that of Michel Foucault. Foucault (1990, pp. 42–43) famously argued that homosexuality was an invention of nineteenth-century psychiatrists and psychologists and what emerged at that time was the homosexual as a species. His social constructionist view of (homo)sexuality was developed by Judith Butler, especially in her *Gender Trouble* (1999) and *Bodies That Matter* (1993); she and Foucault together could be considered the most important contributors to the emergence of queer theory. She argued that the apparatus of "compulsory heterosexuality" (a key term in her work that is roughly equivalent to "heteronormativity") contrives to make (biological) sex, gender, and sexuality appear natural. As she put it: "Gender is the repeated stylization of the body, a set of repeated acts within a highly rigid regulatory frame that congeals over time to produce the appearance of substance, of a natural sort of being" (Butler, 1999, pp. 43–44).

Discourse, that is, the whole process whereby we communicate with each other, impels us from the moment of our birth on a life course of a "stylized repetition of acts" (Butler, 1999, p. 179), from which emerge our gender and our sexuality. It is significant that Butler calls this process "performativity," a term taken from linguistics. Our gender, and indeed our very identity, are molded through discourse. The subject is created by discourse, and not vice versa. Most queer theorists share this radical critique that puts into question the conceptual stability of both sexuality and gender itself. But their analysis may seem to undermine not only the beneficiaries of heteronormativity but also those who seek to challenge the power of those beneficiaries through identity politics—in particular feminists and lesbian and gay liberationists. If queer theory contests identity, it may well seem to be at odds with those who use queer as an identity tag or umbrella term. Indeed, Butler's own attitude to the possibility of resisting heteronormativity seems vague. She has suggested resistance through "practices of parody" (p. 179), which

led Martha Nussbaum to suggest that Butler had left women as "prisoners of the structures of power that have defined our identity," and that all "we can hope to do is to find spaces within the structures of power in which to parody them, to poke fun at them." Nussbaum concluded that the consequence was "a stance that looks very much like quietism and retreat" (Nussbaum, 1999, p. 38). This criticism is relevant to later reactions to queer theory, since in some critics' eyes it became an academic game, played particularly by gay men, and represented an erasure of feminist and lesbian concerns. (For further discussion, see Macwilliam, 2011, pp. 50–55.) Two comments are worth making here. One is a matter of fact: it is certainly the case that queer theory emerged not as a public political movement but as an academic critical tool that is concerned primarily with texts (including film, music, and television). Secondly, although it is true that queer theory questions identity and is especially suspicious of such binaries as male/female and gay/straight, it denies not so much their existence as their naturalness and their permanence, and is thus not necessarily at odds with identity politics, but merely emphasizes its historical contingency.

By 1994, Stephen Moore notes, interest in queer readings was fully engaged, at least as far as scholars of modern literature were concerned (2001, pp. 10–12; he lists twenty relevant papers given at the 1994 Modern Languages Association midwinter conference, along with twenty-seven books on the topic in the accompanying book exhibit). Biblical scholars and theologians in general lagged behind: ATLA Religion Database used "queer theology" as a subject for the first time in 1992, and by 1995 only six articles had been assigned that term; these articles, it should be added, ranged far beyond biblical studies. By 2000, however, queer theory was sufficiently important to have its own entry in the *Handbook of Postmodern Biblical Interpretation*. Laurel Schneider's useful essay (2000) was the first in a number of reflections on the nature and value of queer for biblical scholarship and theology. They range from the brief editorial by Stuart and Walton (2001, pp. 7–8), via Moore (2001, pp. 7–18) and Stone (2001, pp. 11–34), to the more recent and expansive Cornwall (2011, passim) and Macwilliam (2011, pp. 9–59). The editorial by Elizabeth Stuart and Heather Walton in a special issue of *Theology and Sexuality* featuring articles that had a "common engagement with queer theory" is doubly helpful not only in providing a brief summary of how "queer" can be used but also in alluding to ambiguity:

> The "essence" of queer theory…[is] that there is no essential sexuality or gender. "Queer" then is not actually another identity alongside lesbian and gay (although it is sometimes rather confusingly used to convey a radical coalition of lesbian, gay, bisexual, and transgendered persons) but a radical destabilizing of identities and resistance to the naturalizing of any identity. (Stuart and Walton, 2001, p. 8)

To some, then, queer is the rallying point for a realigned nonheterosexual identity, but to others it is not an identity so much as a stance or positionality, by means of which identity itself is subverted.

Queer and the Bible. This ambiguity is carried over into queer readings of the Bible, and in all three of the most prominent collections of essays on the topic that appeared between 2001 and 2011, both understandings of queer sit side by side within the same book covers. In his editorial introduction to the first collection of essays, *Queer Commentary and the Hebrew Bible*, Ken Stone discussed the existence of these two approaches. The first, using queer as an umbrella identity label, "places 'queer readings of the Bible' within the framework of conversations already taking place among biblical scholars about 'social location and biblical interpretation'" (Stone, 2001, p. 16). One might term this use of queer as an inward-looking use of queer. Stone links it to reception theory, so that in this understanding queer readings of the Bible are those that use the biblical text as a resource for a particular (loose) grouping within society. He cites as an example Mona West's paper in the collection; she suggests that the "poetry of Lamentations provides those in the Queer community who are in 'mute despair' words to order and articulate their experience of AIDS" (Stone, 2001, p. 141). Stone goes on to discuss what might be termed a more outward-looking use

of queer, one that looks beyond the ghetto in order to invest the insights of those on the margins with transformative value—as Schneider puts it, queer theory "is not just for or about so-called homosexuals" (2000, p. 206). Stone's other paper in *Queer Commentary and the Hebrew Bible* (Stone, 2001, pp. 116–139) is a good example of how queer theory can help us to question assumptions about gender. He reexamines the link between gender and food provision in Hosea 1—3; the literature on the topic, such as it is, is dominated by feminist interest in the relationship between food preparation and women. Using indicators of masculinity from cultural anthropology, Stone argues for a link between food provision and male honor, which allows him to reinterpret passages about food provision in Hosea 2 as articulating "a profound sense of anxiety about masculinity" (Stone, 2001, p. 135). The distinction between inward- and outward-looking uses of queer must not be pushed too far. Indeed, when one considers queer theory's suspicion of binaries, it would be ironic to entangle it in a new one. A suspicion that inward-looking uses of queer are merely a continuation of lesbian and gay treatments of the biblical texts may well be dispelled when the far wider range of minorities covered by the term "queer" is borne in mind; in this understanding heterosexual does not necessarily mean heteronormative, and what Robert E. Goss calls "gay normativity" (2002, p. 229) is at odds with queer. And for their part, queer theorists may well use gay or lesbian experiences/identities as a base for a new understanding of gender and sexuality. What is common to both approaches is that generally, in Stone's words, they shift "the focus away from the handful of texts that are endlessly analyzed in discussions of 'the Bible and homosexuality'" (2001, p. 18).

A further problem to consider before we explore more examples of queer readings is posed by Susannah Cornwall in the title of a chapter in her *Controversies in Queer Theology*. "Is the Bible Queer?," she asks, and expands on the question: "There is much debate, among queer scholars and others, about the extent to which biblical texts themselves are to be understood as promoting a particular heteronormative ideal, and the extent to which this sense has been read back into the Bible by its overwhelmingly heteronormative interpreters down the centuries" (Cornwall, 2011, p. 115). This question is important in that how one answers it dictates one's strategy of reading. To put the question another way, if heteronormativity is indeed promoted in the Bible, is it possible to find nonheteronormative traces lurking within the texts that one can latch on to? This is not a new question, of course. It has been asked in different ways by feminist and lesbian and gay scholars as well as liberation theologians. As far as queer theory is concerned, it may be relevant to recall Butler's concept of "necessary failures": "The injunction *to be* a given gender produces necessary failures, a variety of incoherent configurations that in their multiplicity exceed and defy the injunction by which they are generated" (Butler, 1999, p. 185)

Emboldened by this (admittedly rather vague) pronouncement, some biblical scholars have sought out slippages within the texts whereby the artificial nature of the gender process is revealed. These may be linguistic or structural flaws, or they may be previously unnoticed inversions of the "normal" gender pattern. Roland Boer (Guest et al., 2006, pp. 258–261), for example, has pointed out the oddity of applying the Hebrew verb *yld* (to give birth) to men, and Stuart Macwilliam has searched for both structural and linguistic slippages in the operation of the marriage metaphor in the Hebrew Bible prophets (see, for example, Macwilliam, 2011, pp. 84–96).

As already mentioned, Butler also suggested that parody might serve as resistance: "There is a subversive laughter in the pastiche-effect of parodic practice in which the original, the authentic, and the real are themselves constituted as effects" (Butler, 1999, pp. 186–187). This was interpreted by some as advocating drag performance, though Butler herself later questioned whether such parodying "of the dominant forms is enough to displace them" (Butler, 1993, p. 125). But certainly parody, and within this label one might include the reading of modern texts alongside or against the biblical, has been employed as a queer reading strategy. One might instance Stone's reading of the film *Paris Is Burning* against the struggle between Saul and David in 2 Samuel (Stone, 2011, pp. 75–98).

Some scholars have taken the very application of a (post)modern critique to an ancient text as in itself introducing something inappropriately alien. Sean Burke makes a robust response:

> I suspect that some will criticize the application of "queering" to biblical interpretation on the grounds that it is a strategy imported from outside the text. I argue, however, that the application of queering strategies developed *outside* the text enables a reader to see queering strategies already inscribed *inside* the text. (Hornsby and Stone, 2011, p. 186)

Queer Exemplars. This leads on to the wider question of how one goes about a queer reading. No single strategy predominates. Perhaps it can be maintained that older, established methods that cluster around an objective pursuit of historical reality do not feature greatly. Postmodern suspicion of the impartial scholar in pursuit of authorial intentionality has led to a favoring of literary approaches, though the use of methodologies drawn from psychology and the social sciences have by no means been abandoned. All this comes as no surprise when one bears in mind the similar sources used by, for example, Foucault, Sedgwick, and Butler. To obtain a flavor of the variety of strategies used, it may be helpful to make a selective tour of the major works published so far.

Take Back the Word. A good start could be made with *Take Back the Word* (Goss and West, 2000), a collection of essays that carries on the work of lesbian and gay biblical scholarship, but with differences hinted at by the phrase "queer reading" in the subtitle. It has an expanded scope that "engages the whole Bible and its message, not just selected texts and characters," and moreover takes into account "the multifaceted nature of our community as gay men, lesbians, transsexuals, and bisexuals from different ethnicities, socioeconomic standings, and religious communities" (p. 4). That queer is used as an identity label is evident from the frequent occurrence of "queer community," "queer readers," "queer people," and so on, though not all the contributors use such phrases. The methodology of most contributors is reader-response:

> These new voices have also produced a biblical hermeneutic that considers the particular social location of flesh-and-blood readers. Readers are members of specific communities, and their history with that community shapes the way they approach the biblical texts. (Goss and West, 2000, pp. 4–5)

Most of the contributors, then, give a response to particular texts from particular standpoints. Celia Duncan, for instance, reads "the story of Ruth as a bisexual midrash, making room for inclusive possibilities of alternative desires" (p. 92). Robert Goss, anticipating a significant strand in subsequent queer treatments of biblical texts, brings a passionately autobiographical element to his reading of the relationship between Jesus and the beloved disciple "to speak of the loss of his lover of sixteen years [to AIDS] and the ensuing grief" (p. 207). But amid all these voices, one or two hints of a radically new approach make a tentative appearance. It is true that in her foreword Mary Ann Tolbert does not give queer theory a warm welcome; she contrasts her earlier feminist optimism with "the increasingly powerful backlash against women, which has unfortunately even crept into some recent queer theory" (p. vii). But at least two of the contributors show some familiarity with the new arrival. Elizabeth Stuart argues, with a strong Butleresque echo, for a notion of queer "that challenges the understanding of the concept of the stable self and replaces it with an understanding of the self as unstable and constituted by 'performance' and improvisation within and in resistance to dominant discourses" (p. 31). Her paper anticipates another strand of queer treatments of biblical texts by using camp as a liberationist strategy. Ken Stone shows himself as an even greater enthusiast for queer theory. After a discussion of Wittig and Butler, he exposes incoherencies in the second creation account (Gen 2:4b–3:24) that lead him to argue not "that the Yahwist account is…a queer-positive text…[but that] the biblical contributions to the heterosexual contract, though clearly present and certainly visible in the Genesis

creation accounts, are less secure than many contemporary readers wish to admit" (p. 67).

Queer Commentary and the Hebrew Bible. *Queer Commentary and the Hebrew Bible* (Stone, 2001) makes an interesting contrast with *Take Back the Word*. It contains examples of both inward- and outward-looking uses of queer (Mona West's essay has already been cited as an outstanding example of the former). Indeed, in his introduction Stone clearly articulates queer's multivocal nature. But there is a shift in tone; this is not just because the contributions are fewer and longer and come almost exclusively from within the academic community. There is more frank and unapologetic avowal of the writer's own sexuality and the part it plays in exegesis. So Timothy Koch declares: "I am a gay man and therefore my own guiding sensibility is homoerotic; and I write from my experience" (p. 169). Koch rejects the usual critiques employed to deflect attacks upon those who are not heterosexual. He argues they grant "to the Bible the power to authenticate or authorize human beings," and he writes, "I name the locus of my authority as intrinsic" (p. 174). The result is an exegesis that has an air of parody, a defiant playfulness. He describes his strategy in gay terms as "Cruising the Scriptures," using "our own ways of knowing, our own desire for connection, our own savvy and instinct, our own response to what attracts us and repels us" (p. 175). This playfulness can segue into outrageousness, as in Boer's *Yahweh as Top: A Lost Targum*, which paints a picture of a psychoanalytic gathering on Mount Sinai, crammed with biblical characters (including Yahweh himself) in deviant disguise and all awash in camp and sadomasochism. Sadomasochism makes occasional appearances in queer writing. Lori Rowlett, for instance, explores its implications in her paper on Samson and Delilah in this volume (pp. 106–115), and aficionados of Foucault will recall that he described sadomasochism in terms of "desexualisation," which, according to David Halperin, should be thought of as a detachment of pleasure from the genitals (Halperin, 1995, pp. 85–91). This provocative style may be dismissed as self-indulgent or worse. One reviewer, for instance, found "Boer's contribution unnecessarily vulgar and over 'the top'"

(Brooke, 2002, p. 145). On the other hand, one could view Boer's tone as a deliberate rejection of the prevalent academic style of writing (sober, dispassionate, and making itself out to be authoritative), which symbolizes a larger rejection of heteronormativity itself. Interestingly, a perhaps more significant criticism emerges from one of the three "responses" that end the volume. Tat-siong Benny Liew argues that "queer theory, despite its emphasis on queering more than just the norm of heterosexuality, tends to inherit from lesbian and gay studies the centrality of sex and sexuality" (Stone, 2001, p. 186). The result is that race and ethnicity are pushed out. Liew calls for queer theory to "develop a multifocal reading that attends simultaneously to sexuality, gender, class as well as race and ethnicity" (p. 188).

The Queer Bible Commentary. In the most ambitious collection of queer readings to date, *The Queer Bible Commentary* (Guest et al., 2006) fills over 850 pages with 44 papers that cover all the biblical texts (with some books grouped together, notably the twelve minor prophets in one essay). It thus achieves a major success in getting away from those few texts that deal, or seem to deal, with same-sex desire. This is not to say that it sets out to be a verse-by-verse commentary. We learn from the brief preface (p. xiii) that, following the model set by *The Women's Bible Commentary* (Newsom and Ringe, 1992), this book focuses "specifically upon those portions of the scriptural text that have particular relevance for readers interested in lesbian, gay, bisexual and transgender issues"; that it sets out to demonstrate that the "mooring that the scriptures are thought to provide is not as unshakeable and secure as some might hope" and that the biblical texts "have the ever-surprising capacity to be disruptive, unsettling and unexpectedly but delightfully *queer*." Quite what is meant by queer and the method used to demonstrate that quality is left to the thirty-one contributors, and the result is a very wide variety of methodological approaches. Many contributors are inward-looking and may presuppose an LGBT audience or at least an audience with an interest in LGBT issues. Of these some

follow the familiar pattern of attempting to detoxify those biblical texts that have traditionally been cited as condemnatory of same-sex desire or practice. So David Tabb Stewart tackles Leviticus 18 and 20 (pp. 96–99). Others follow the equally familiar pattern of identifying characters in the texts that may exercise a special appeal to lesbians or gay men; so Mona West on Ruth and Robert Goss on the beloved disciple (pp. 190–194 and pp. 560–562, respectively). Other contributors use queer as an opportunity to critique the assumptions of a wider world. Some develop a trend that was noted as a feature of *Queer Commentary and the Hebrew Bible*, a parody of the biblical text that carries with it a queering of the normative practices of academic biblical scholarship. Jennifer Koosed is explicitly transgressive:

> As a queer commentary, my readings will be wayward, unmoored from standard academic forms and models, perhaps even drifting too far into uncharted territory. But new discoveries only come from such unruly explorations. (Guest et al., 2006, p. 339)

Koosed concludes, "In writing with a queer identity...I experience a perverse pleasure, gaiety if you will, in writing in ways a biblical scholar is not supposed to write" (p. 343). Roland Boer offers a parody of Chronicles that involves the use of a camp hermeneutic, "for it seems to me that the cultic gravity and over-the-top masculinity of the text gives out to the playful overindulgence of camp" (p. 267; another example of camp exegesis can be found in Macwilliam, 2011, pp. 167–206). Boer's remark is a reminder that when queer theory is added to a queer reading of a text, it is not only same-sex desire that comes under the spotlight; gender in general can be seen to be unstable, and the instability of masculinity, the top dog of heteronormativity, is an obvious and important target. This is the potential value of an outward-looking use of queer, one that Ken Stone, for one, fully recognizes in his study of David and the ideology of masculine power (Guest et al., 2006, pp. 195–221).

Bible Trouble. From its title, one would imagine that this collection of queer biblical writings represented the full acceptance of queer theory in biblical scholarship. Yet *Bible Trouble* (Hornsby and Stone, 2011—the reference is to Butler's *Gender Trouble*) maintains the practice of mixing inward- and outward-looking uses of queer, though it has to be said that the influence of queer theory upon its 16 papers is far more noticeable than in earlier collections. The most nuanced use of queer is that of Deryn Guest, who approaches queer theory with some caution as one of several "dialogue partners" to her lesbian-specific reading of Jael (p. 37). Some trends in previous queer readings of the biblical texts are more consciously articulated. If queer theory originally set out to subvert normative categories of sexuality and gender, its critique can be employed to besiege other normative strongholds. And here *Bible Trouble* makes a genuine effort to redress what critics have seen as a failing in earlier queer writings and to enact the program laid out in its preface: "Queer analysis today increasingly brings a critical lens to bear on the intersection of sexual dynamics with other dynamics such as race, class, nation, and culture" (p. ix). Among the several contributors who explore a queering of racial categories, Erin Runions reads Rahab as a queer borderline figure whose ethnicity is a major factor in her challenge to the genocidal ideology of the Deuteronomic Historian. Similarly, in dissecting the rivalry between the houses of Saul and David, Ken Stone sees the treatment by the biblical writer of Saul's Benjamite tribe as involving "something very close to ethnic slander" (p. 93).

Bible Trouble also continues the trend of subverting the norms of biblical scholarship itself: "Queer reading is characterized not simply by attention to diverse genders and sexualities but also by diversities of style, form, critical approach, and so forth" (Hornsby and Stone, 2011, p. x). Diversity of approach is certainly very much in evidence. To take a few examples, Runions combines, in an enticing strategical potpourri, an unfamiliar use of humor as an interruptive device with a more traditional deployment of redaction criticism to produce a new, if flawed, transgressive Rahab. Ken Stone reads 2 Samuel 3 alongside the film *Paris Is Burning*. Heidi Epstein extends the range of queer beyond gender

to find in Penderecki's *Canticum* (a musical realization of Song of Songs) "a loud hermeneutic of suspicion" (p. 119). Joseph Marchal reads two normative texts alongside each other—2 Corinthians on women prophets and a U.S. manual on mental health—in order to highlight the assumptions beneath the texts and how they can be challenged.

Finally, *Bible Trouble* continues the practice of *Queer Commentary and the Hebrew Bible* in containing a number of reflections on queer biblical readings. Perhaps the most heartfelt, and one from a confessional standpoint, comes from Sean Burke: "Are Christian communities today in need of ongoing conversion to a ministry of queering, in order that the Spirit might be poured out upon *all* flesh and *everyone* might be saved?" (Hornsby and Stone, 2011, p. 187).

A Queer Future? Of course such a missionary zeal is not typical of most queer readings. Yet there is a shared goal to unsettle the heteronormative assumptions that have been associated with the biblical texts by generations of Jewish and Christian readers and interpreters. Queer readings continue to debate the extent to which these assumptions (as well as queer counterreadings) are embedded in the texts or foisted upon them by their readers. In the pursuit of this shared goal, queer readings still demonstrate a concern about sexual orientation—although LGBT issues, to judge by the contributions to *Bible Trouble*, have been extended to include wider aspects of gender. Thus, masculinity has been a target of queer interest, for instance, in Stephen Moore's *God's Gym* (1996), one of the rare instances of single-author monographs of queer readings. In an awakening that has the capacity for further development, queer readings have begun to show a willingness to engage with issues of power and dominance beyond gender, particularly with regard to race, ethnicity, and social class. There is now an opportunity to respond to the charge of being "an elitist discourse" that was leveled at queer theory by Deryn Guest (2005, p. 51).

Less urgently, though still of significance to the academic world, queer readings share with many postmodern endeavors a concern for a new tone and stance when writing about biblical texts. Distrustful of the authenticity of traditional "dispassionate" scholarship, many writers have sought alternative strategies of honesty that underline the personal agendas with which all writers saddle their writings. Often self-disclosure and autobiography are integral to the readings (for an account of this, see Macwilliam, 2011, pp. 157–164) with the effect of adding entertainment to enlightenment. When the authorial veil is removed, as it is, to take an outstanding example, in Stephen Moore's *God's Beauty Parlor* (2001), the results can be dazzling.

[*See also* Gender; Heteronormativity/Heterosexism; Homosexuality/Queer; Intersectional Studies; *and* Queer Theory.]

BIBLIOGRAPHY

Brooke, George J. Review of *Queer Commentary and the Hebrew Bible*, edited by Ken Stone. *Journal for the Study of the Old Testament* 26, no. 5 (2002): 144–145.

Butler, Judith. *Bodies That Matter: On the Discursive Limits of "Sex."* New York: Routledge, 1993.

Butler, Judith. *Gender Trouble: Feminism and the Subversion of Identity.* New York: Routledge, 1999. Reprint of 1990 edition with revised preface.

Cornwall, Susannah. *Controversies in Queer Theology.* London: SCM, 2011.

Foucault, Michel. *The History of Sexuality.* Vol. 1, *An Introduction.* Translated by Robert Hurley. New York: Vintage, 1990. First published in French in 1976.

Goss, Robert E. *Queering Christ: Beyond Jesus Acted Up.* Cleveland, Ohio: Pilgrim, 2002.

Goss, Robert E., and Mona West, eds. *Take Back the Word: A Queer Reading of the Bible.* Cleveland, Ohio: Pilgrim, 2000.

Guest, Deryn. *When Deborah Met Jael: Lesbian Biblical Hermeneutics.* London: SCM, 2005.

Guest, Deryn, Robert E. Goss, Mona West, and Thomas Bohache, eds. *The Queer Bible Commentary.* London: SCM, 2006.

Halperin, David M. *Saint Foucault: Towards a Gay Hagiography.* New York: Oxford University Press, 1995.

Hornsby, Teresa J., and Ken Stone, eds. *Bible Trouble: Queer Reading at the Boundaries of Biblical Scholarship.* Atlanta: Society of Biblical Literature, 2011.

Jagose, Annamarie. *Queer Theory: An Introduction.* New York: New York University Press, 1996.

Macwilliam, Stuart. *Queer Theory and the Prophetic Marriage Metaphor in the Hebrew Bible.* Sheffield, U.K.: Equinox, 2011.

Moore, Stephen D. *God's Gym: Divine Male Bodies of the Bible.* New York: Routledge, 1996.

Moore, Stephen D. *God's Beauty Parlor: And Other Queer Spaces In and Around the Bible.* Stanford, Calif.: Stanford University Press, 2001.

Newsom, Carol A., and Sharon H. Ringe, eds. *The Women's Bible Commentary.* London: SPCK, 1992.

Nussbaum, Martha C. "The Professor of Parody: The Hip Defeatism of Judith Butler." *New Republic,* 22 February 1999, pp. 37–45.

Schneider, Laurel C. "Queer Theory." In *Handbook of Postmodern Biblical Interpretation,* edited by A. K. M. Adam, pp. 201–212. Saint Louis, Mo.: Chalice, 2000.

Stein, Arlene, and Ken Plummer. "'I Can't Even Think Straight': 'Queer' Theory and the Missing Sexual Revolution." In *Queer Theory/Sociology,* edited by Steven Seidman, pp. 129–144. Cambridge, Mass.: Blackwell, 1996.

Stone, Ken, ed. *Queer Commentary and the Hebrew Bible.* Cleveland, Ohio: Pilgrim, 2001.

Stuart, Elizabeth, and Heather Walton. "Editorial." *Theology and Sexuality* 8 (2001): 7–8.

Sullivan, Nikki. *A Critical Introduction to Queer Theory.* New York: New York University Press, 2003.

Warner, Michael, ed. *Fear of a Queer Planet: Queer Politics and Social Theory.* Minneapolis: University of Minnesota Press, 1993.

Stuart Macwilliam

QUEER THEORY

Queer theory emerged in the early 1990s from what was then the relatively new field of lesbian and gay studies, with significant influences from feminist and gender studies. Although the study of homosexuality plays an important role in queer theory, queer theory also analyzes the ways in which norms associated with sex and gender are created and reproduced, but also destabilized throughout society and culture, including within religious texts and practices. These norms include the privileging and naturalization of opposite-sex sexual relations; the organization of sexual and gendered meanings around stable, binary identities and fixed desires; and the valorization of reproductive kinship and monogamous marriage as primary goals for, and the foundation of, human society.

The term "queer theory" itself first appeared in a special issue of the feminist journal *differences*, which bore the title *Queer Theory: Lesbian and Gay Sexualities*. The editor of the volume, feminist film theorist Teresa de Lauretis, was one of two contributors to the volume who actually used the phrase (along with feminist film theorist Sue-Ellen Case), and she is often credited with coining it. The term "queer" was already being used at the time by activist groups, such as Queer Nation and ACT-UP, which had reclaimed the word "queer" from its former principal use as an insult and turned it into a rallying cry for political and social organizing. De Lauretis, however, combined the term "queer" with "theory" in an academic context as part of her project of interrogating the tendency to elide multiple differences in the study of lesbian and gay sexualities, including differences of gender, race, ethnicity, class, culture, geography, and generation. De Lauretis suggested that the "socio-cultural specificity" (1991, p. v) of such differences was too complex to be accounted for simply by substituting the phrase "lesbian and gay" in place of the older terms "gay" or "homosexual" as supposedly inclusive terms. Rather than being satisfied with unifying or inclusive narratives, the study of lesbian and gay sexualities needed to account for heterogeneities. By using what was then still a novel phrase, queer theory, de Lauretis attempted to bring a more differentiating lens to the study of sexuality, gender, and culture.

Only five years after the appearance of the collection edited by de Lauretis, New York University Press published a short volume by Annamarie Jagose titled *Queer Theory: An Introduction* (1996). The appearance of such a volume indicated that queer theory had already become an area of academic discourse sufficiently large and important to justify the publication of introductory summaries for those who were curious about the topic. By the time Jagose's introduction appeared, queer theory was associated closely with the writings of a number of influential scholars in the humanities, including Eve Kosofsky Sedgwick, Judith Butler, David Halperin, and Michael Warner. Most of these scholars were influenced in turn by various poststructuralist writings, especially the philosophical and historical work on sexuality, power, and discourse written by French philosopher Michel Foucault. Yet Jagose emphasized from the opening pages of her introduction that queer theory was difficult to define, suggesting that "its definitional indeterminacy, its elasticity, is one of its constituent characteristics" (Jagose, 1996, p. 1) and a source of much of its usefulness. This emphasis on "definitional indeterminacy" continues to be widespread in queer theory. A more recent introductory volume by Donald Hall, for example, which carries the title *Queer Theories* in the plural, argues explicitly that "there is no 'queer theory' in the singular, only many different voices and sometimes overlapping, sometimes divergent perspectives that can be loosely called 'queer theories'" (Hall, 2003, p. 5).

Given the resistance to definition and the emphasis on multiplicity and divergence in these and other discussions of queer theory, it might seem foolish to attempt to provide a summary of it for an encyclopedia. The attempt is necessary, however, since queer theories have provided some of the most widely discussed accounts of sex, gender, and sexuality in contemporary academic literature. These accounts have had significant, albeit varying, influence in numerous other academic disciplines, including biblical studies (see, e.g., Moore, 2001; Stone, 2005, 2013; Macwilliam, 2011; Hornsby and Stone, 2011; Guest, 2012).

Although the discussion that follows does not provide a simple definition for queer theory, it does identify several recurring themes or emphases that often characterize work associated with queer theory. No one of these themes or emphases automatically leads to the labeling of an academic piece as queer theory, and no academic piece associated with queer theory necessarily includes all of these themes or emphases. Taken together, however, they may be understood as coordinates to guide scholars who wish to explore issues or utilize analytical questions associated with queer theories for purposes of biblical interpretation. For convenience, these coordinates are organized here under the following categories: (1) radicalizing the study of sexual practice, (2) the critical analysis of categories of sexual identity,

(3) the critical analysis of sex/gender categories, (4) the critique of heteronormativity, and (5) other directions.

Radicalizing the Study of Sexual Practice. During the latter half of the twentieth century, sexuality increasingly came to be seen as a legitimate topic for academic research. The growth of academic studies of sexuality resulted from several intellectual developments, including feminist scholarship's arguments for analyzing relations formerly relegated to the "private" sphere. Within the broader category of sexual relations, queer theories tend to focus greater attention on forms of sexual practice and desire that contravene social norms for proper sexual behavior. Such attention necessarily includes within its purview homosexuality, which has often been outlawed, condemned, or otherwise stigmatized because it violates the assumption that sexual intercourse between a man and a woman is the only proper or natural form of sexual activity.

Queer theory builds on historical and social-scientific studies of same-sex relations from various times and places, from ancient Greece and Rome to Renaissance Europe to contemporary urban lesbian and gay communities. It also builds on studies of various types of same-sex relations, from rites of passage that involve oral insemination between young males in parts of Papua New Guinea to the "romantic friendships" between women in early modern Europe. For most queer theorists, however, such studies do not function simply as components of a comprehensive history or comparative analysis of a single object, "homosexuality." Rather, the varieties of same-sex sexual practices uncovered by historians and social scientists are used to raise critical questions about modern categories of sexual identity and desire (see the section "Critical Analysis of Categories of Sexual Identity").

In their examination of stigmatized forms of sexuality, moreover, queer theorists move beyond the history of same-sex relations to explore a wider range of nonnormative sexual practices. A significant influence in this regard is the anthropologist Gayle Rubin, who in 1984 published a groundbreaking article in the context of feminist debates over sexuality titled "Thinking Sex: Notes for a Radical Theory of the Politics of Sexuality." Rubin argued that scholarship on sexuality, including some feminist scholarship, has been unduly influenced by several "ideological formations" that distort perceptions of sexual practice. These formations include a "sex negativity," rooted in part in Christian tradition, that "always treats sex with suspicion" (Rubin, 2011, p. 148); a "fallacy of misplaced scale" that exaggerates the moral significance of sexual matters in comparison with other bodily matters, such as, for example, food and eating; and a "hierarchical system of sexual value" that evaluates sexual acts and the people who participate in them by comparing them to the standard of marital, reproductive heterosexuality (Rubin, 2011, p. 149). In place of such ideological formations, Rubin called for "a concept of benign variation" within the study of sexuality that accepts pluralism in sexual matters as in other matters of cultural practice. Significantly, Rubin extended this anthropological openness to sexual variation far beyond the mere tolerance for homosexuality. Her various writings include nonstigmatizing discussions of consensual sadomasochism, pornography, prostitution, cross-generational sex, and sex clubs.

Queer theory continues to build on Rubin's legacy by considering controversial sexual activities as legitimate objects for careful analysis and understanding rather than occasions for moral condemnation. Even forms of sexual interaction that are widely condemned in lesbian and gay communities may be interpreted sympathetically within queer theory. For example, one recent study by Tim Dean created academic controversy by combining empirical and theoretical tools to analyze in a nonstigmatizing way the reemergence in the United States of practices of "barebacking," or anal intercourse between men without the use of a condom, which had been generally disapproved by safer sex discourses in the wake of the AIDS crisis (Dean, 2009). Such studies are not written for shock value or to deny a role for sexual ethics. Rather, they attempt to explore the roles played by a range of sexual norms and practices in the creation of alternative communities, pleasures, and identities. Dean, for example, analyzed subcultural relations of intimacy and kinship that have been created among the men participating in bareback practices.

Although the study of radical sex practices might seem to have little relevance for biblical interpretation, queer theory points out that the boundaries between such practices and other phenomena that initially appear unconnected to them are less stable than is often assumed. For example, the dynamics of power, pleasure, bondage, and release associated with sadomasochism may also be at work in other contexts. Biblical scholars influenced by queer theory have therefore used studies of sadomasochism to analyze such biblical texts as the story of Samson and Delilah, the cycle of punishment and release that characterizes Judges and the Deuteronomistic History (Rowlett, 2001), and Jeremiah's poem (Jer 20:7–18) characterizing his experience of his prophetic relationship to God as a kind of sexual overpowering (Stone, 2007).

Critical Analysis of Categories of Sexual Identity. As noted above, queer theorists call attention to wide varieties of sexual practices and beliefs about sexual practices. One consequence of this attention is a critical perspective on modern Western categories of sexual identity, particularly the binary distinction between heterosexuality and homosexuality. In the modern West, the distinction between heterosexual and homosexual "sexual orientations" is premised on the belief that sexual desire for members of the opposite sex and sexual desire for members of one's own sex are mutually exclusive and, in most cases at least, unchanging dispositions that play a crucial role in individual identities. Indeed, the distinction between heterosexuality and homosexuality is discussed at times as if it corresponds to a distinction between two ontologically different types of people (e.g., heterosexuals and homosexuals or straights and gays) who might in principle be found anywhere. Yet research on same-sex desires and practices in other times and places indicates that the tendency to organize identity around the biological sex of one's preferred sexual objects may be quite recent and still somewhat restricted to industrial Western societies. Indeed, Foucault, in his influential *History of Sexuality,* Volume 1, argued that it was only in nineteenth-century Europe that homosexuality came to be understood "less as a habitual sin than as a singular nature….The sodomite had been a temporary aberration; the homosexual was now a species" (Foucault, 1978, p. 43). Foucault characterized this development as one of many effects of various productive mechanisms of power and knowledge that emerged around this time, such as observation, classification, comparison with norms, diagnosis, and the state management of populations. Although Foucault's periodization can be disputed, queer theory has generally followed his argument that the emergence of a specific sexual classification, "the homosexual," and its corresponding subjective self-understanding is a product of specific historical developments rather than a reflection of natural or transhistorical realities. Participants in same-sex sexual activities in other contexts do not necessarily understand themselves to belong to a distinct category of persons based on the gender of their preferred sexual object; and they do not necessarily understand their participation in same-sex relations to rule out sexual activity with members of the opposite sex.

Queer theorists such as Sedgwick have gone on to point out, however, that heterogeneities in sexual desire, practice, and identity do not simply result from historical change or cross-cultural difference. Even within specific contexts, individual lives, or cultural products, the desires, practices, and identities associated with sexuality may be, in Sedgwick's words, "unexpectedly plural, varied, and contradictory" (Sedgwick, 1990, p. 48). Thus, although queer theory builds on influential arguments for the "social construction" of sexuality and homosexuality (e.g., Weeks, 1985; Greenberg, 1988), many queer theorists take a deconstructive rather than a social-scientific approach to the fluidity and unpredictability of sexual desire, practice, and identification. A queer theoretical exploration of ancient texts, then, would not be satisfied with reconstructing ancient assumptions and norms about sexuality, using such assumptions and norms to reinterpret ancient texts, or noting the differences between those assumptions and norms and our own. Although each of these steps would be important, a reading of ancient texts informed by queer theory would also look for moments in those texts where the assumptions being made about sexual matters are potentially undermined or destabilized in the texts themselves.

Some lesbians and gay men have raised concerns about the possibility that queer theory's historicizing of the category of homosexuality, or its calling attention to instabilities in modern assumptions about fixed sexual desires and identities, might undermine the basis for political organizing on behalf of lesbians and gay men. Queer theorists do not call into question the empirical existence of same-sex desires or lesbian and gay communities, however, and they have generally been advocates for greater freedom for members of those communities, often belonging to such communities themselves. Several prominent queer theorists who challenge the fixed nature of modern sexual identity categories have published books that address queer politics explicitly (e.g., Sedgwick, 1993; Halperin, 1995). Thus, concerns about queer theory's potential negative consequences for lesbian and gay political organizing are probably misplaced.

Moreover, queer theory has consequences not only for our understanding of homosexuality but also for our understanding of heterosexuality. To conceptualize heterosexuality as a distinct phenomenon, one must distinguish it clearly from homosexuality. The identification of heterosexuality as a stable norm for sexual behavior depends upon its differentiation from homosexuality as heterosexuality's deviant other. If the binary distinction between heterosexuality and homosexuality is undermined, assumptions about fixed or consistent heterosexual identities and desires are as much at risk as assumptions about fixed or consistent homosexual identities and desires.

One implication of the critical analysis of modern identity categories for biblical scholarship is that scholars may need to be cautious about imposing such categories on biblical texts. The fact, for example, that biblical characters such as David or Ham have wives and sire children would not rule out the possibility of their participation in male-male sexual practices in the mind of an ancient audience.

Critical Analysis of Sex/Gender Categories. Queer theory does not simply raise critical questions about the binary distinction between heterosexuality and homosexuality. It also raises critical questions about binary distinctions between male and female sexes, binary distinctions between masculine and feminine genders, and the relationship between sex and gender itself.

The distinction between sex and gender has been a crucial tool for gender analysis. Users of the distinction generally assume that, although biological differences between male and female sexes are relatively obvious, cultures and societies construct and make use of those differences in a wide variety of ways. The term "gender" is therefore used most often to refer to the multiple ways in which biological sex is interpreted and organized. Rubin, in an influential discussion of this organization, refers to each society's "sex/gender system" as the "set of arrangements by which the biological raw material of human sex and procreation is shaped by human, social intervention and satisfied in a conventional manner, no matter how bizarre some of the conventions may be" (Rubin, 2011, p. 39). Other discussions of gender place more emphasis on differences between "masculine" and "feminine" psychological dispositions or bodily habits that may or may not correspond to an individual's biological sex. The distinction between sex and gender has been especially valuable for feminist efforts to combat the notion that women are, by virtue of being biological women, ill-suited for certain social roles, which in male-dominated societies often turn out to be exactly those roles that receive more power and prestige.

Queer theory makes several different moves with respect to this influential distinction between sex and gender. First, queer theory tends to emphasize even more heavily than many other gender analyses the wide scope of possibilities that exist for gendered behavior and identification. Consider for example "masculinity." Gender analyses of masculinity will often note the divergent conceptions of "masculine" behavior in different cultures. Some analyses also note that a male who fails to exhibit so-called masculine behaviors to the same degree as other males in the same society may for that reason receive less power or prestige than men who are supposed to be more "manly." Although such projects recognize the malleability of masculinity, they still tend to associate its various manifestations with male bodies. Queer theory might go further, however, and emphasize that there are many individuals with biologically male bodies who behave or self-identify in a range of ways that are considered "feminine"; and there are many individuals with biologically female bodies who behave or self-identify in a range of ways that are considered masculine. Thus queer theorists have explored such topics as the behaviors, identifications, and subcultural activity that Judith Halberstam refers to as "female masculinity" (Halberstam, 1998) or "feminine" identification and subcultural activity among gay men, especially in the practices associated with "camp" (Halperin, 2012). By making such moves, queer theory underscores how complicated the relationships between sexed bodies, on the one hand, and gendered behavior, dispositions, and identification, on the other hand, actually are.

Some queer theorists go further and emphasize not only the multiplicity and fluidity of gendered social roles, behaviors, and identifications, but also the instability of binary notions of biological sex that are widely assumed to underlie the sex/gender distinction. One critic of the biological categories "male" and "female," the French writer Monique Wittig, suggested that these categories are more political than natural. Although many differences among bodies obviously exist, the influence of binary categories of sex leads society, in Wittig's view, to "mark," socially and politically, exactly those parts of bodies that are most useful for sexual reproduction. Other social imperatives might well lead us to categorize bodies by marking other bodily features. Because binary categories of sex support the imperatives of heterosexual intercourse and reproduction, Wittig argued, "the category of sex is the political category that founds society as heterosexual" (1992, p. 5). Resisting this function of sex, Wittig tended to write in support of a utopia in which biological sex would no longer be granted significance.

Wittig's skeptical attitude toward the ontological significance of biological sex has had some influ-

ence on the work of the feminist philosopher Judith Butler. Although Butler takes some distance from Wittig's utopianism, she follows Wittig (as well as Foucault) in her interrogation of the assumption that binary biological sexes are a natural base or foundation on which cultural notions of gender are constructed. Could it not be the case, Butler asks, that binary notions of biological sex are themselves "the effect of the apparatus of cultural construction designated by *gender*" (Butler, 1999, p. 11)? In the course of exploring this question across several publications, Butler developed one of the most influential ideas to emerge from queer theory: a "performative" account of sex and gender.

Butler's performative theory attempts to displace the idea that either sex or gender is a "substance." Against such ideas, Butler suggests that gender has more to do with doing than with being. That is, "the substantive effect of gender is performatively produced and compelled by the regulatory practices of gender coherence" (1999, p. 33). As this reference to "regulatory practices" indicates, Butler does not believe that humans freely choose our genders, although her use of drag practices to illustrate some of her ideas has led to some misunderstanding about this point. We always act in relation to norms and social constraints that precede us. Over time, the repetition of ritualized practices that attempt to conform to gender norms produces the impression that stable, absolute distinctions can be made between male and female bodies and behaviors. We come to believe that our actions "express" an underlying gender identity. In Butler's view, however, coherent gender identities do not ground gender practices. Rather, repeated and "stylized" gender practices create gender identities. Gender identities are "a performative accomplishment which the mundane social audience, including the actors themselves, come to believe and to perform in the mode of belief" (Butler, 1999, p. 179).

Nevertheless, our repeated attempts to embody gender norms are never entirely successful. The contingency and instability of gender are exposed by the discontinuities that exist between gender norms and gender practices or between one gender practice and another. For Butler and other queer theorists, attention to such discontinuities is a potentially important political move. By recognizing or intensifying, rather than denying or outlawing, the differences that appear between one gender performance and another, we may destabilize what Butler calls "the compulsory order of sex/gender/desire" (Butler, 1999, p. 9), which assumes that a clear biological sex should be expressed in a coherent, "intelligible" gender (Butler, 1999, p. 23) that corresponds to a fixed, normally heterosexual, desire. The political hope is that such destabilization may make more room for the survival or flourishing of bodies and lives that stand in tension with what Butler calls "the imaginable domain of gender" (Butler, 1999, p. 13).

Although Butler's analyses are articulated in a theoretical language that is, at times, quite complex, she also does reference the treatment of those whose actual lives stand in tension with binary norms for sex and gender, including drag queens, transgender, and intersex persons (see, e.g., Butler, 2004, pp. 57–101). Transgender and intersex lives receive more attention from other scholars, however, who note that such lives not only expose the incoherence of binary notions of sex and gender but also challenge some assumptions prevalent among queer theorists themselves (e.g., Morland, 2009). The relevance for biblical interpretation of queer theory's interrogation of gender is perhaps more obvious than some other queer theoretical emphases. The Bible clearly refers to a binary distinction between male and female sexes and appeals to this distinction for purposes of heterosexual reproduction (e.g., Gen 1:27–28). Across biblical literature, characters are usually identified as belonging to one sex or the other and are represented as acting in relationship to ancient gender norms. The degree to which their actions conform to or transgress such norms is highly variable, however. By paying attention to such variability as it manifests in biblical texts, biblical scholars may help to undermine the assumption that gender is a coherent expression of two fixed, substantive biological sexes.

Critique of Heteronormativity. Queer theory suggests that assumptions about proper sexual practice (most often, heterosexual intercourse), fixed binary

sexual identities (heterosexual or homosexual), fixed binary sexes (male or female), and fixed binary genders (masculine or feminine) are articulated in ways that are mutually reinforcing in modern Western society. Together, such assumptions form part of a larger system of norms and institutions that is sometimes referred to critically as "heteronormativity." Heteronormativity, a term coined by Michael Warner (1993), often entails other assumptions as well, including a commitment to monogamous marriage as the foundation for society, a belief that sexual activity is most appropriately associated with romantic love and reproduction, and a valorization of successful child-rearing as the proper goal for a fulfilled life. A critique of heteronormative society's organization around the figure of the child and a good life defined by "reproductive futurity" has led to a lively debate among queer theorists about the dangers of subscribing to socially defined hopes for the future and whether hope for the future is itself compromised by heteronormativity (cf. Edelman, 2004; Muñoz, 2009). Matters less directly associated with sex, gender, and kinship can also be articulated to heteronormativity, including class-based assumptions about hard work, vocational commitment, and the appropriate display of bodily gesture and emotion. Rather than being restricted to matters of sex, gender, and sexual practice, then, heteronormativity is tied to larger "regimes of the normal" (Warner, 1993, p. xxxvi). It is reproduced across many spheres of modern life, including religious institutions, academic institutions, media, and other sites for popular culture.

If heteronormativity is understood to entail a wider field of norms and normalization and not simply the institutionalized preference for heterosexuality over homosexuality combined with a belief in fixed gender and sexual identities, then the aims of queer scholarship and activism are broadened in a corresponding way. As Warner argues, queer scholarship and activism "gets a critical edge by defining itself against the normal rather than the heterosexual, and normal includes normal business in the academy" (p. xxxvi). This way of understanding queer work helps to explain the indeterminacy of definitions of queer theory. Since "the normal" varies by time and place, queer opposition to it also takes on different forms. In Halperin's words, queer "acquires its meaning from its oppositional relation to the norm. Queer is by definition *whatever* is at odds with the normal, the legitimate, the dominant" (Halperin, 1995, p. 62).

One element of such opposition, however, is the recognition that heteronormativity is never as stable as its proponents claim. Like gender or sexual desire, heteronormativity is riven with contradictions and ambiguities. By calling attention to its incoherence, queer critics of heteronormativity attempt to make space for cultural forms and practices that provide alternatives to it.

Queer critiques of heteronormativity frequently note that individuals who might for certain purposes be considered queer—for example, some lesbians and gay men—may nonetheless subscribe to particular values associated with heteronormativity. Since the valorization of monogamous matrimony plays a key role in the cluster of assumptions associated with heteronormativity, some queer theorists have raised critical questions about the emphasis on marriage equality in lesbian and gay politics. Jasbir Puar has coined the term "homonormativity" to refer to the tendency of some lesbians and gay men to promote dominant or regressive norms. Puar notes, for example, that the push for gay marriage in parts of Europe and the United States is sometimes articulated with anti-Muslim rhetoric to reinforce a widespread binary opposition between "barbarism and civilization" (Puar, 2007, p. 20), which opposes Islam and terrorism to mainstream tolerance and gay marriage. Puar's arguments align her work with that of other queer theorists, discussed further below, who argue that the study of gender and sexuality must pay greater attention to the ways in which gender and sexuality relate to nationality, religion, race, and ethnicity.

Biblical scholars influenced by queer theory may wish to examine the many ways in which readings of biblical texts support or undermine contemporary heteronormativity. Moreover, if the queer critique of normativity extends to a critique of "normal business in the academy," as Warner (1993) suggests, then a biblical interpretation influenced by queer theory may put some distance between its own procedures and those of mainstream biblical studies. Rather than restricting itself to the application of conventional methods of biblical scholarship to new objects such as sexual practice and same-sex relations, queer biblical interpretation may experiment with new questions and new genres that displace or move beyond normative assumptions about proper academic method.

Other Directions. Although attention to sexual practice, sexual identities, gender, and heteronormativity have animated much work in queer theory, queer theorists in recent years have also moved in other directions. Like feminist theory, for example, and as evidenced in Puar's work noted above, queer theory has begun to take more seriously the inevitable entanglement of matters of sex, gender, and sexuality with matters of race, ethnicity, and nation. Discussions of "queer race" (e.g., Sullivan, 2003, p. 57–80) note that categories of race, like categories of gender and sexuality, are often taken to be natural and universal rather than historical and culturally specific. Yet modern notions about race are inextricably intertwined with notions about gender and sexuality that have too often been analyzed in isolation from racial dynamics. By taking up this set of issues, queer theory returns in some ways to the attention to multiple differences Teresa de Lauretis called for when she first coined the term "queer theory." Indeed, recognition of the "intersectionality" of sexuality and gender with race and culture returns queer theory to even earlier roots, since one of the first uses of the term "queer" in cultural theory was in Gloria Anzaldúa's *Borderlands/La Frontera*, one of several influential writings by radical women of color that emerged during the 1980s prior to queer theory (Anzaldúa, 1987). This strand of queer work has significant relevance for biblical interpretation, since matters of sexual practice and gender are related to matters of ethnicity and religion in numerous biblical texts including, for example, the story of Lot and his daughters that concludes the account of Sodom in Genesis 19 (Stone, 2013).

A number of queer theorists have also participated in a recent turn to "affect" as an important object for academic analysis. Such theorists point out that notions of the heteronormative "good life" are often entwined with notions about proper and positive feeling. Attention to more disturbing affects and experiences, such as shame or failure, may therefore be useful for the queer critique of heteronormative society (e.g., Halperin and Traub, 2009; Halberstam, 2011). An emerging interest in queer approaches to temporality has already been noted above. In fact, queer theorists have set out in so many new directions in recent years that some scholars have asked whether queer theory has now moved to a position "after sex" (Halley and Parker, 2011; cf. Hall and Jagose, 2013).

The relevance of some of these emerging queer questions for biblical interpretation is unclear. Nevertheless, biblical scholars have much to gain from greater attention to the rethinking of sex, gender, sexual practice, desire, and normativity that is still most closely associated with the term "queer theory."

[*See also* Heteronormativity/Heterosexism; Homosexual/Queer; Intersectional Studies; *and* Transgender/Third Gender/Transsexualism.]

BIBLIOGRAPHY

Anzaldúa, Gloria. *Borderlands/La Frontera*. San Francisco: Aunt Lute, 1987.

Butler, Judith. *Gender Trouble: Feminism and the Subversion of Identity*. 10th anniv. ed. New York: Routledge, 1999.

Butler, Judith. *Undoing Gender*. New York: Routledge, 2004.

Dean, Tim. *Unlimited Intimacy: Reflections on the Subculture of Barebacking*. Chicago: University of Chicago Press, 2009.

De Lauretis, Teresa. "Queer Theory: Lesbian and Gay Sexualities: An Introduction." In *Queer Theory: Lesbian and Gay Sexualities*, edited by Teresa de Lauretis. Special issue of *differences: A Journal of Feminist Cultural Studies* 3, no. 2 (1991): iii–xviii.

Edelman, Lee. *No Future: Queer Theory and the Death Drive*. Durham, N.C.: Duke University Press, 2004.

Foucault, Michel. *The History of Sexuality*. Vol. 1: *An Introduction*. Translated by Robert Hurley. New York: Random House, 1978.

Greenberg, David F. *The Construction of Homosexuality*. Chicago: University of Chicago Press, 1990.

Guest, Deryn. *Beyond Feminist Biblical Studies*. Sheffield, U.K.: Sheffield Phoenix, 2012.

Halberstam, Judith. *Female Masculinity*. Durham, N.C.: Duke University Press, 1998.

Halberstam, Judith. *The Queer Art of Failure*. Durham, N.C.: Duke University Press, 2011.

Hall, Donald E. *Queer Theories*. New York: Palgrave Macmillan, 2003.

Hall, Donald E., and Annamarie Jagose, eds. *The Routledge Queer Studies Reader*. New York: Routledge, 2013.

Halley, Janet, and Andrew Parker, eds. *After Sex? On Writing since Queer Theory*. Durham, N.C.: Duke University Press, 2011.

Halperin, David M. *Saint Foucault: Towards a Gay Hagiography*. New York: Oxford University Press, 1995.

Halperin, David M. *How to Be Gay*. Cambridge, Mass.: Harvard University Press, 2012.

Halperin, David M., and Valerie Traub, eds. *Gay Shame*. Chicago: University of Chicago Press, 2009.

Hornsby, Teresa, and Ken Stone, eds. *Bible Trouble: Queer Reading at the Boundaries of Biblical Scholarship*. Atlanta: Society of Biblical Literature, 2011.

Jagose, Annamarie. *Queer Theory: An Introduction*. New York: New York University Press, 1996.

Macwilliam, Stuart. *Queer Theory and the Prophetic Marriage Metaphor in the Hebrew Bible*. London: Equinox, 2011.

Moore, Stephen D. *God's Beauty Parlor: And Other Queer Spaces in and around the Bible*. Stanford, Calif.: Stanford University Press, 2001.

Morland, Iain. "What Can Queer Theory Do for Intersex?" In *The Routledge Queer Studies Reader*, edited by Donald E. Hall and Annamarie Jagose, pp. 445–463. New York: Routledge, 2013.

Muñoz, José Esteban. *Cruising Utopia: The Then and There of Queer Futurity*. New York: New York University Press, 2009.

Puar, Jasbir K. *Terrorist Assemblages: Homonationalism in Queer Times*. Durham, N.C.: Duke University Press, 2007.

Rowlett, Lori. "Violent Femmes and S/M: Queering Samson and Delilah." In *Queer Commentary and the Hebrew Bible*, edited by Ken Stone, pp. 106–115. Sheffield, U.K. Sheffield Academic Press, 2001.

Rubin, Gayle. *Deviations: A Gayle Rubin Reader*. Durham, N.C.: Duke University Press, 2011.

Sedgwick, Eve Kosofsky. *Epistemology of the Closet*. Berkeley: University of California Press, 1990.

Sedgwick, Eve Kosofsky. *Tendencies*. Durham, N.C.: Duke University Press, 1993.

Stone, Ken. *Practicing Safer Texts: Food, Sex and Bible in Queer Perspective*. London: T&T Clark, 2005.

Stone, Ken. "'You Seduced Me, You Overpowered Me, and You Prevailed': Religious Experience and Homoerotic Sadomasochism in Jeremiah." In *Patriarchs, Prophets and Other Villains*, edited by Lisa Isherwood, pp. 101–119. London: Equinox, 2007.

Stone, Ken. "Queer Criticism." In *New Meanings for Ancient Texts: Recent Approaches to Biblical Criticisms and Their Applications*, edited by Steven L. McKenzie and John Kaltner, pp. 155–176. Louisville, Ky.: Westminster John Knox, 2013.

Sullivan, Nikki. *A Critical Introduction to Queer Theory*. New York: New York University Press, 2003.

Warner, Michael. "Introduction." In *Fear of a Queer Planet: Queer Politics and Social Theory*, edited by Michael Warner, pp. vii–xxxi. Minneapolis: University of Minnesota Press, 1993.

Weeks, Jeffrey. *Sexuality and Its Discontents: Meanings, Myths and Modern Sexualities*. London: Routledge and Kegan Paul, 1985.

Wittig, Monique. *The Straight Mind: And Other Essays*. Boston: Beacon, 1992.

Ken Stone

R

RACE, CLASS, AND ETHNICITY

This entry contains six subentries: Hebrew Bible; Greek World; Roman World; New Testament; Early Judaism; *and* Early Church.

Ancient Near East

See Sexual Violence, *subentry* Ancient Near East.

Hebrew Bible

Biblical scholarship has not typically treated the ancient world in terms of race, class, or sexuality, partly because these ideas do not apply to biblical texts in any straightforward way. These are modern ideas, and their referents lie in the modern world. Moreover, their meanings vary; and this is a problem that vexes biblical scholars focused on pinning down such meanings for ancient texts. For example, on the one hand, historical anthropologists and cultural theorists may deploy these ideas in technical ways and derive meanings from their distinct and respective intellectual canons. On the other hand, public discourse may deploy them in less specific and even overlapping ways where people make everyday distinctions that appear to be readily apparent. Such was evident in the relationship between U.S. Jim Crow laws and those of the South African apartheid regime. The legal "racial" (as it was commonly called) discrimination that marked black life in the United States during the Jim Crow era did not apply equally to black South Africans visiting the United States because black South Africans were not considered "Negros" under U.S. law. The same held true for U.S.-born blacks visiting South Africa during the apartheid regime. These experiences are examples of legal structures apprehending ethnic or national distinctions for, in both instances, national origin mitigates so-called racial discrimination. Since the eighteenth-century European Enlightenment, Jewish, Chinese, Native American, and Arab peoples, among others, have been understood and constituted variously as races, ethnics, and nationalities.

Equally vexing is class. In both the modern world and the Hebrew Bible, terms for ethnic or racial differences easily become shortcuts to articulate socioeconomic class. For example, throughout twentieth-century U.S. social history, race/ethnicity frame class structures where terms such as "ghetto" and "barrio" simultaneously demarcate class and ethnic labels for Polish, Jewish, German, Latino, and African American groups. Although biblical scholars are more likely to use the term "class" than the terms "race" or "sexuality," its application has been particularly troubling because upward mobility was virtually impossible in agrarian societies (Lenski, 1984, p. 290). In the Hebrew Bible, *'am ha'arets* ("people of the land") may refer to Judahites who were not exiled in 587 B.C.E. and ascended to power and wealth in the absence of the exiled elite after the Babylonian devastation. The term, therefore, constructs an ethnic group based on class difference (Smith, 1989, pp. 179–197; Würthwein, 1950).

Like race and class, sexuality is also modern. It, too, forms a complex relation to race, ethnicity, and class where culture conscripts sexual-gender politics to construct racial/ethnic differences (Fausto-Sterling, 2000, p. 30). The sexual participates in meaning relations essential to racial/ethnic and class identity. For example, in the modern world, colonial regimes constructed the sexually "exotic" in ways that essentialized the alterity of the "native." In strategies of fetishization conquered peoples became the sexually signified perverse, dangerous, and erotic others that constituted the savage in distinction from the European civilized. Thus, sexuality entered into the construction of two racial/ethnic identities: the one, European and civilized and, by default, the other, the subaltern savage. The discussion below focuses on a similar strategy in the Priestly writers' imagination.

In the interpretation of the Hebrew Bible, scholars use the terms "race," "sexuality," and "class" heuristically to organize modern understandings of difference in the ancient world. As heuristics, rather than descriptions, these ideas help us see that the activity of distinguishing between groups of people by constructing identities from taken-for-granted differences is common to both moderns and ancients. The discussion below takes up the ways in which the intersection of ethnic identity and sexual-gender politics operates in strategies of differentiation in the Hebrew Bible. Three tropes are deployed for this purpose as examples: the other as uncircumcised, the other as sexually unclean, and the *issah zara* or "othered" (foreign) woman. These tropes correspond, by contrast, to three respective components of biblical Israel's default status, namely, circumcision, ritual cleanness in sexual practice, and endogamy.

Two matters require attention: First, the article focuses on the Priestly imagination since its cast shapes the final form of the Hebrew Bible. This approach, of course, vitiates what many scholars rightly recover as preceding voices, such as J, E, D, or Dtr., which in many cases possess ideologies at odds with P. Second, the article uses the adjective "biblical" to signify groups constructed by the Priestly imagination and "ancient"—as in ancient Israel—to signify the constructs of biblical scholarship (Davies, 1995). Moreover, terms for nations (e.g., "Egyptian," "Philistine," "Hivite," "Moabite," "Ammonite") also should be read as constructions of Priestly imagination unless the adjective, "ancient" appears before it.

Sexuality and Ethnicity: Constructing a Default Status. Circumcision, ritual cleanness in sexual practice, and endogamy all signify the sexual. In the Priestly imagination, they regulate male sexuality from its beginning to its "proper" actualization. Circumcision inscribes its discourse of differentiation upon the male sex organ as an initiatory rite, while ritual cleanness circumscribes ideal sexual practice until it realizes its fruition in endogamy and procreation with an Israelite woman. Ancient Israel, along with its neighbors in the ancient northeast African and ancient southwest Asian corridor (ancient Ammon, ancient Cush, ancient Edom, ancient Egypt, and ancient Moab), practiced circumcision as a gendered rite of inclusion into their respective cultic and other spaces, maintained certain ritual standards for sexual activity, and encouraged endogamy.

The Priestly material, however, takes the first, circumcision, and the third, endogamy, to construct an identity for biblical Israel beginning with its progenitor, Abraham. The second, ritual cleanness in sexual practice, becomes apparent only as the writers construct biblical Israel by contrasting it with the construction of an ethnic "other." Together, the three create a default status for Abraham's family and, by extension, for biblical Israel's ethnic identity.

The three components of this default status are multivalent insofar as each carries both apparent and idealized meanings. Circumcision's apparent marking is the clear physical difference between those who have and those who have not undergone the rite. Maintaining ritual cleanness in sexual practice and endogamous marriage's apparent dimensions are similarly self-evident. The three attach to the Priestly imagination's idealized meanings, namely, a covenant relationship with Yahweh and Yahweh's promise of perpetual tenure to the Levant.

First, circumcision, apparent and idealized, marks Abraham and all of his male descendants (Gen 17:10–11). They are a people whose covenant relationship with the deity entitles them to the land of Canaan. Joshua extends the practice. Immediately after crossing the Jordan, Joshua circumcises all males of the generation born in the Wilderness. In Joshua 5, the Deuteronomistic History (DH) places the rite among the other rituals that occur prior to taking the Land, which include erecting twelve stones of remembrance (4:1 ff.) and celebrating the Passover (5:10 ff.). In the story, the rite is mandatory; only after being circumcised can the Israelites possess Canaan. Second, the writers place Abraham and, by extension, the biblical Israelites in a world that was filled with the sexually unclean as constructed by the narratives. Despite their surroundings, Abraham and his family maintained ritual cleanness, the default status. In Leviticus 18:24 ff., the Priestly material articulates these sexual regulations and makes biblical Israel's tenure to land contingent upon adherence to them. Third, the endogamous marriages of Abraham, Isaac, and Jacob mark biblical Israel's origins (Gen 20:12; 24:3–4; 28:1–9) in accordance with the prohibition in Deuteronomy 7:1–6.

Sexuality and Ethnicity: Troping the Default Status. In three contrasting tropes on the default statuses, namely, the other as uncircumcised, the other as sexually unclean, and the *issah zara* or the "othered" (foreign) woman/wife, the Hebrew Bible takes up sexuality to construct ethnicity. Each trope bears an aberrant relationship to its concordant default and maps sexuality onto ethnicity in ways that construct identity.

Trope 1: The uncircumcised other. In Genesis 17, the same pericope where P introduces circumcision to Abraham, the writer articulates a basic negative implication:

Any uncircumcised male who is not circumcised in the flesh of his foreskin shall be cut off from his people; he has broken my covenant. (17:14)

The reference to ethnicity is oblique but stark; for to be "cut off," *věnikrětah*, is to be devoid of an *ethnos*. In Joshua 5, the DH signifies upon Egyptian ethnicity to convey a second meaning for the Israelites. Once the Israelites have healed from the rite of circumcision, Yahweh reveals to them, "Today I have rolled away from you the disgrace (*ḥerpāt*) of Egypt." The disgrace is their now-discarded foreskins, which is affirmed by Gilgal's etiological name, the hill of foreskins. The meaning of Israelite circumcision comes into relief only as something different from an imagined "other."

While Joshua 5:4–7 explains this "second" circumcision as applying only to the generation born after the Israelites had left Egypt, Sasson (1966) argues that Joshua's action had to do with the difference between Egyptian and Israelite forms of circumcision. His explanation more emphatically connects the rite to constructing difference. In other words, Sasson participates in the Priestly strategy of distinguishing biblical Israel from its neighbors in the Levant.

In Genesis 34, the Priestly material offers a provocative instance of the first trope. The writer deploys circumcision's meanings, both apparent and idealized, to signify ethnic difference and to construct identity for biblical Israel. The story foregrounds "foreigness." Jacob travels to a new region, Shechem, and purchases land from Hamor, who is both the city's father and the father of prince Shechem. Both Shechem and Hamor are "biblical" Hivites. They enter the narrative as "nobility," that is, a prince and his father, and so they are paradigmatic representatives of their people. In the horrific episode of the rape of Dinah that follows, P focuses on forced sexual intercourse by an uncircumcised "other" rather than the violent act *sui generis*. Hamor even offers to make recompense as provided in Deuteronomy 22:28. He proposes that his son Shechem marry Dinah and offers to compensate Jacob with an increased bride-price. But that is a remedy for

Israelites, not for "others." Dinah's brothers' response in Genesis 34:14 is telling: "We cannot do this thing, to give our sister to one who is uncircumcised, for that would be a disgrace (*ḥerpat*) to us." (Here P takes up the same language used by the DH.) The focus is on the sign of otherness and not only sexual violence.

The brothers' actions focus on otherness as well. They convince the entirety of the Hivite men to undergo circumcision. While the Hivites lie incapacitated, the brothers kill them along with Hamor and Shechem. First, the response not only punishes Hamor and Shechem (the actual rapist), but it takes Shechem up as synecdoche; he represents the entirety of Hivites, for in the Priestly imagination, the Hivites are a *people* who do this type of sexual thing. Second, the punishment reduces the source of Shechem's violent sexual act to the site of difference, namely, his foreskin. The writers treat Shechem's sexual-gender construction (male, uncircumcised, and rapist) and that of the Hivite people as both essential to and a signifier of Hivite "otherness." Ultimately, Dinah's brothers' violent act "erases" the sign of ethnic difference, for that is the thing that was "disgraceful."

Similar to P's portrayal of the Hivites in Genesis 34, the DH portrays the "biblical" Philistines as the paradigmatic other. They are biblical Israel's archenemy and competitor for land in Canaan. However, the DH reviles not simply the Philistines' rival claim for control of the land but the Philistines themselves, for the word translated as "uncircumcised" becomes a shortcut for Philistine (e.g., Judg 15:18; 1 Sam 14:6; 31:4). In other places, "Philistine" and "Philistines" appear with the adjective, "uncircumcised." This adds emphasis to their foreignness.

1 Samuel 18:17–27 narrates a similar instance of the taking of foreskins as the removal of an ethnic marker. Saul, who understands that David cannot afford the bride-price in shekels to marry Michal, sets the price at one hundred Philistine foreskins, which David triumphantly provides. If Genesis 34 expresses disavowal, then 1 Samuel 18:17–27 fetishizes the foreskin of the foreign "other."

Finally, Ezekiel takes up this trope with an emphatic tone. In Ezekiel 28, 31, and 32, the language

connects the uncircumcised with death twelve times (Ezek 28:10; 31:18; 32:19; 32:21; 32:24; 32:25; 32:26; 32:27; 32:28; 32:29; 32:30; 32:32). Only in two instances in Ezekiel 44, is the language not associated with death by the sword. In chapter 44 the phrase "uncircumcised in heart and flesh" takes on a more figurative meaning. In the other instances, the language of Ezekiel's couplets explicitly articulates the moral status of the uncircumcised, such as the Hivite in Genesis 34 and the Philistine in 1 Samuel. For Ezekiel, only death befits the uncircumcised "other."

Trope 2: The other as sexually unclean. The second trope, the sexually unclean, constructs "biblical" Egyptian, Moabite, Ammonite, and Canaanite ethnicity in Genesis 12, 20, and 26. In each episode, the writer projects a proclivity for aberrant sexual behavior onto the foreign king. Both Abraham and Isaac believe that the unnamed Pharaoh and King Abimelech will kill them and defile Sarah and Rebekah. Their concern is so grave that they both devise a ruse to circumvent the foreign king. Bailey terms the repeated plot the "jeopardizing the matriarch" motif. In each, a patriarch (Abraham twice and Isaac once) pawns off a matriarch (Sarah twice and Rebekah once) to foreign rulers (Egyptian and Canaanite). (Bailey, 1995; cf. Bailey, 2010) In each episode, a taken-for-granted presupposition about the foreigner's sexual practices motivates the decision (Gen 12:11–13; 20:11; 26:7). Although both narratives attempt to demonstrate what Israel is not, Bailey demonstrates the converse in the gaps of the text. He concludes by showing how the portrayal of the Egyptian and Canaanite defies the expectations of the patriarch's sexual imagination (Bailey, 1995).

The trope continues in Genesis 19:30 ff., where P inscribes sexual uncleanness upon the origins of Moab and Ammon in the Hebrew Bible. The two nations are the products of Lot's daughters engaging in sexual intercourse with their father. The daughters become impregnated and bear male offspring who are both nephew and half-brother to each of the sisters and son and grandson to Lot. The story further signifies sexual uncleanness upon the sons' origins with the names Moab, meaning "my father," and "Ben-Ammi," roughly translated as "son of my people," and inscribes the same upon their ethnicity. Their status attaches to their ethnicity as in Deuteronomy 23:3 (Bailey, 1995).

Throughout the narrative, the writers protect Lot, who is a member of Abraham's family, from culpability. He is too intoxicated to be aware of what his daughters do to him. In both instances (vv. 33, 35) of intercourse writers use *vattašqeynā*, the hiphil or causative stem of the verb. In other words, the daughters "made their father drink." Further, corresponding to each instance of intercourse, the writers twice assure the reader that Lot "did not know" (*vělō yāda*) when his daughters lay down or when they rose.

The peoples constructed by both tropes occupy the same moral status in the Priestly imagination and share similar fates in the text. P articulates the implications in a summary statement to the sexual prohibitions in Leviticus 18:

> But you shall keep my statutes and my ordinances and commit none of these abominations, either the citizen or the alien who resides among you (for the inhabitants of the land, who were before you, committed all of these abominations, and the land became defiled); otherwise the land will vomit you out for defiling it, as it vomited out the nation that was before you. For whoever commits any of these abominations shall be cut off from their people. (18:26–29)

In Genesis 34, Jacob's sons kill all of the Hivite men. In Joshua 3, the Hivites and the Canaanites are among the groups whom Yahweh commands Joshua and the Israelites to dispossess from the land. In Exodus 23:31, Yahweh promises the same regarding the land occupied by the Philistines. In Judges 3, Yahweh raises Ehud to kill 10,000 Moabites and subdue them for eighty years. Although the Ammonites were spared from a similar fate in Deuteronomy 2:19, both the Ammonites and the Moabites are excluded from biblical Israel's assembly in Deuteronomy 23.3, despite their shared kinship.

Trope 3: The issah zara or "othered" (foreign) woman. The third trope explicitly connects sexuality, gender, and ethnicity in the text and in the social world of ancient Israel. In the text, the problem of the *issah zara* appears as early as the patriarchal narratives and, in Genesis 26 and 36, differentiates Esau from his brother, Jacob. Perhaps because both the Edomites and the Israelites practiced circumcision, the writer uses the trope of the foreign wife rather than the first trope (the uncircumcised), as a strategy of differentiation. The trope appears again as the DH's first critique of both Solomon's and Ahab's reigns (1 Kgs 11:1–2; 16:31). Proverbs 1—8 contrasts the trope with Woman Wisdom (Camp, 1990; Yee, 1995; 2003). As a unit, the instructions bring together foreignness, femaleness, and sexuality and associate the amalgam of the three with death (Prov 2:16–19; 5:3–6; 7:22–27; see Marbury, 2007; Anderson, 2009).

The same amalgam works in dramatic fashion in the mass divorces in Ezra-Nehemiah where many scholars turn to explicate the social and political implications of exogamy for the Jerusalem community during Persian and Greek dominion. They show how an ideology of ethnicity regulates access to contested spaces of economic, political, and social power such as the Jerusalem cult (Smith-Christopher, 1994; Eskenazi and Judd, 1994; Hoglund, 1992; Dor, 2011; Southwood, 2011).

The Jerusalem community understood itself through its construction of the *'am ha'arets*, or people of the land, which signified both class difference and ethnic foreignness. Almost paralleling the presentation of the Philistines in the DH, the *'am ha'arets* contested with the *golah*, or returnees, for ascendancy, but this time under imperial rule. The literature chastises male members of the Second Temple community of Jerusalem who married these "foreign" women because the marriages expanded the circle of those who had access to power, resources, and influence over the *golah* community (Washington, 1995).

Under foreign dominion, taxes from temple communities flowed to provincial and other imperial treasuries. One source of local temple funding came from the tithes raised from its community's members. These tithes, which generally came in the form of in-kind tributes rather than coinage, depended upon the community's tenure to arable land. As men of the *golah* married foreign women, the question of their sons' loyalty to the Temple becomes an issue. In Nehemiah 11:3, Nehemiah laments when he sees that their offspring do not speak the language of Judah but that of their "foreign" mothers. If these offspring were to follow the customs of their mothers and no longer tithe from the land, the Second Temple's wealth and land base would erode. It would no longer be able to meet the imperial tax levy and would face retribution from the empire (Marbury, 2010; 2012).

Conclusion. Similar to modern strategies of differentiation, the Priestly imagination makes robust use of the sexual to construct ethnic identity. For the Jerusalem priesthood—the final group to shape the material—class, sexuality, and ethnicity intersect in identity formation. In the literature, three tropes—the uncircumcised, the sexually unclean other, and the *issah zara*, the "othered" woman—conscript sexuality to construct ethnicity for the Israelites in the Hebrew Bible and for the Second Temple community in the social world of ancient Judah. In these tropes, the biblical writers construct Israelite ethnicity through constructions of the "other." Ultimately, their strategies preserved power and wealth within the community while guarding its boundaries of inclusion.

[*See also* Imagery, Gendered, *subentries on* Deuteronomistic History, Priestly Material, *and* Wisdom Literature; Postcolonial Approaches; Sexual Transgression, *subentry* Hebrew Bible; *and* Sexual Violence, *subentry* Hebrew Bible.]

BIBLIOGRAPHY

Anderson, Cheryl B. "Reflections in an Interethnic/Racial Ear on Interethnic/Racial Marriage in Ezra." In *They Were All Together in One Place? Toward Minority Biblical Criticism*, edited by Randall C. Bailey, Tatsiong Benny Liew, and Fernando F. Segovia, pp. 47–64. Atlanta: Society of Biblical Literature, 2009.

Bailey, Randall C. "They're Nothing but Incestuous Bastards: The Polemical Use of Sex and Sexuality in Hebrew Canon Narratives." In *Reading from This Place: Social Location and Biblical Interpretation in the United States*, edited by Fernando F. Segovia and Mary Ann Tolbert, pp. 121–138. Minneapolis: Fortress, 1995.

Bailey, Randall C. "Why Do Readers Believe Lot? Genesis 19 Reconsidered." *Old Testament Essays* 23, no. 3 (2010): 519–548.

Camp, Claudia V. "The Female Sage in Ancient Israel and in the Biblical Wisdom Literature." In *The Sage in Israel and the Ancient near East*, edited by John G. Gammie and Leo G. Perdue, p. 187. Winona Lake, Ind.: Eisenbrauns, 1990.

Davies, Philip R. *In Search of "Ancient Israel."* Journal for the Study of the Old Testament Supplement Series 148. Sheffield, U.K.: Sheffield Academic Press, 1995.

Dor, Yonina. "The Rite of Separation of the Foreign Wives in Ezra-Nehemiah." In *Judah and Judeans in the Achaemenid Period*, edited by Oded Lipschits, Gary N. Knoppers, and Manfred Oeming, pp.173–188. Winona Lake, Ind.: Eisenbrauns, 2011.

Eskenazi, T. C., and Eleanore P. Judd. "Marriage to a Stranger in Ezra 9–10." In *Second Temple Studies II: Temple and Community in the Persian Period*, edited by T. C. Eskenazi and Kent H. Richards, pp. 266–285. Sheffield, U.K.: Sheffield Academic Press, 1994.

Fausto-Sterling, Anne. *Sexing the Body: Gender Politics and the Construction of Sexuality*. New York: Basic Books, 2000.

Hoglund, Kenneth. *Achaemenid Administration in Syria-Palestine and the Missions of Ezra and Nehemiah*. Society of Biblical Literature Dissertation Series 125. Atlanta: Scholars Press, 1992.

Lenski, G. E. *Power and Privilege: A Theory of Social Stratification*. Chapel Hill: University of North Carolina Press, 1984.

Marbury, Herbert Robinson. "The Strange Woman in Persian Yehud: A Reading of Proverbs 7." In *Approaching Yehud: New Approaches to the Persian Period*, edited by Jon L. Berquist, pp. 167–182. Atlanta: Society of Biblical Literature, 2007.

Marbury, Herbert Robinson. "Ezra-Nehemiah." In *The Cambridge Dictionary of Christianity*, edited by Daniel Patte, pp. 404–405. New York: Cambridge University Press, 2010.

Marbury, Herbert Robinson. *Imperial Dominion and Priestly Genius: Coercion, Accommodation, and Resistance in the Divorce Rhetoric of Ezra-Nehemiah*. Upland, Calif.: Sopher, 2012.

Sasson, Jack M. "Circumcision in the Ancient Near East." *Journal of Biblical Literature* 85 (1966): 473–476.

Smith, Daniel L. *The Religion of the Landless: A Social Context of the Babylonian Exile*. Bloomington, Ind.: Meyer-Stone, 1989.

Smith-Christopher, Daniel L. "The Mixed Marriage Crisis in Ezra 9–10 and Nehemiah 13: A Study of the Sociology of the Post-Exilic Judaean Community." In *Second Temple Studies 2: Temple and Community in the Persian Period*, edited by T. C. Eskenazi and Kent H. Richards, pp. 243–265. Sheffield, U.K.: Sheffield Academic Press, 1994.

Southwood, Katherine. "The Holy Seed: The Significance of Endogamous Boundaries." In *Judah and Judeans in the Achaemenid Period*, edited by Oded Lipschits, Gary N. Knoppers, and Manfred Oeming, pp. 189–224. Winona Lake, Ind.: Eisenbrauns, 2011.

Washington, Harold. "The Strange Woman (*Issah Zara/ Nokriyah*) of Proverbs 1–9." In *A Feminist Companion to Wisdom Literature*, edited by Athalya Brenner, pp. 157–185. Feminist Companion to the Bible 9. Sheffield, U.K.: Sheffield Academic Press, 1995.

Würthwein, Ernst. "Amos-Studien." *Zeitschrift für die Alttestamentliche Wissenschaft* 62, no. 1–2 (1950).

Yee, Gale A. "'I Have Perfumed My Bed with Myrrh': The Foreign Woman ('*Issa Zara*) in Proverbs 1–9." In *A Feminist Companion to Wisdom Literature*, edited by Athalya Brenner, pp. 110–126. Sheffield, U.K.: Sheffield Academic Press, 1995.

Yee, Gale A. *Poor Banished Children of Eve*. Minneapolis: Fortress, 2003.

Herbert Robinson Marbury

Greek World

Notions of race, class, gender, and legal status (i.e., slave versus free) profoundly informed ancient Greek ideas about sex and sexuality. Since surviving literary evidence mainly preserves what ancient writers *said* ancient Greeks and others did or should do sexually, it can be difficult to "check" the realities of sex in the Greek world against Greek ideology (one significant exception to this caveat is Egypt during the period of Greek rule). Similarly, we are limited by the fact that ancient literary evidence disproportionately preserves the experiences of certain sites, such as fifth- and fourth-century Athens, and the views of particular social groups, most notably the upper class.

While providing necessary background to various types of Greek thought and practice, the following discussion focuses on sexuality in the Greek world as it pertained to two intersecting categories of "other": slaves and foreigners.

Greeks and "Barbarians." Classical historians have demonstrated that there was an important transformation in the ways the ancient Greeks constructed their identity during the fifth century B.C.E. Although some Greeks had been in economic contact with other parts of the ancient Mediterranean since the Bronze Age (ca. 3000–1150 B.C.E.), the relationship between individual Greek city-states was generally much more salient during the early period of Greek history, so that identity for the Greeks was initially defined in relation to one's city-state or local community. It was only during the Persian wars (490–479 B.C.E.)—a dramatic series of encounters that united the separate Greek city-states against the powerful Persian Empire to their east—that a collective identification as "Greeks" ("Hellenes") forcefully emerged. The concept of the "barbarian" was likewise promoted during this time to articulate the qualities that ostensibly distinguished "Hellenes" from Persians (Hall, 1989; see also Thucydides, *History of the Peloponnesian War* 1.3.3). While the label "barbarian" was first applied to the Persians and varying groups within the Persian Empire, it extended over time to denote all non-Greeks. Despite the emergence of this categorical opposition, the distinction between Greek city-states continued nonetheless to hold meaning in many historical contexts; the Athenian definition of "foreigner," for example, could include anyone who was not an Athenian citizen, including residents in the city who had arrived from other Greek city-states.

The category of "Greek" widened considerably during the fourth century B.C.E., as Alexander the Great conducted his massive eastern campaigns (334–323 B.C.E.), introducing Greek culture and Greek administrative structures along the way. Even after the Romans conquered the Hellenistic kingdoms left in Alexander's wake, Greek culture—including the use of the Greek language itself—continued to distinguish these territories, and "Greek" itself remained a prominent term of identification.

Greek Slavery. The idea of the foreign "barbarian" infused Greek culture, yet many ancient Greeks had more regular and intimate encounters with "barbarians" through the institution of slavery. The Greek philosopher Aristotle (384–322 B.C.E.) famously elided the categories of slave and barbarian in his "natural theory" of slavery, arguing that barbarians, as opposed to Greeks, were naturally fitted to servitude (*Politics* 1252b). From the sixth century B.C.E. on, chattel slavery was the most prominent form of Greek slavery, and it usually derived from warfare or participation in various trade networks. Significantly, the geographic origins of Greek slaves were quite diverse. In early periods, Greek slaves seem to have come primarily from the north, with Thrace being especially well-attested as a source. Later, consonant with the dramatic conflicts of the fifth century, growing numbers of slaves would come from Asia Minor to the east, especially from Caria (Garlan, 1988, pp. 46–47). While there is continuing debate over the extent to which Greeks enslaved other Greeks, it is clear that victorious Greek city-states were quite willing to enslave Greek women and children following such conflicts (Rosivach, 1999, pp. 133–136).

There were publicly owned slaves in the Greek world, including those who labored in the brutal conditions of the Athenian silver mines. Privately owned slaves, on the other hand, were employed in both domestic and agricultural work, with some working in more specialized trades such as carpentry or commerce. Slaves also served in the sex trade, a phenomenon we will return to below.

Greek Conceptions of Sexuality. Modern scholars have often characterized ancient Athenian culture as supremely phallic, meaning that male sexual potency was treated as an important symbol of power and domination. A notorious fifth-century vase correspondingly portrays a Greek man preparing to rape a Persian man, graphically symbolizing the Greek victory over the Persians at the Eurymedon in 465 B.C.E. (Stewart, 1995, pp. 583–584).

In terms of Greek sexual practices, it is anachronistic to consider sexuality (e.g., homosexuality versus heterosexuality) a form of identification per se in ancient Greece. Rather, Greek thought classified sexual agents in terms of their modes of participation, drawing a prominent line between the active ("masculine") role of penetration and the passive ("feminine") one, a distinction that correlated closely with Greek views of gender. Even more, in classical Athens, civic status—and especially the crucial distinction between citizens and noncitizens—was central to attitudes and expectations about sex (Halperin, 1990b,

pp. 29–31). Thus, Greek male citizens were expected at all times to perform the penetrative role in sex, regardless of whether their partners were male or female. Conversely, adult Athenian men willing to assume the passive role were generally considered "effeminate" and a danger to the prevailing order (see, for example, Aeschines's *Against Timarchos*, dated to 346 B.C.E.).

Greek Marriage. Marriage was considered requisite for both Athenian men and women; unions among the upper class, in particular, allowed elite families to preserve their wealth and therefore reinforce class boundaries. Athenian women were expected to marry at a younger age than men, and the role of wife was conceived primarily around the production of children. While the sexual lives of Greek wives are generally overlooked in Greek sources (with the exception of fears concerning adultery), Aristophanes's comedy *Lysistrata* (411 B.C.E.) portrays Athenian women undertaking a sex strike to protest war, providing important insight into comic stereotypes of female sexuality. One of the many gaps in surviving Greek sources concerns female same-sex desires and acts, which are rarely acknowledged.

Social expectations, as well as stereotypes, ascribed to free lower-class women vis-à-vis sexuality are harder to glean from our sources. Still, in one suggestive passage from *Airs, Waters, Places* (a text from the Hippocratic corpus discussed at greater length below), the author seems to attribute an innate fertility to one group of lower-class women, asserting of serving women that "no sooner do they have intercourse with a man than they become pregnant, on account of their sturdy physique and their leanness of flesh" (ch. 21; trans. Chadwick and Mann in Lloyd, 1983).

During the fifth century, the Athenian state openly sought to regulate marriage practices, evidently seeking to stem a growing tide of Athenian upper-class men marrying foreign women. Attributed to the Athenian politician Pericles, a law passed in 451–450 B.C.E. stipulated that citizenship could only be passed down to children if both parents were Athenian citizens. Euripides's *Medea* (431 B.C.E.) seems to capture well the contemporary anxiety about such marriages. In less literary terms, we can see the consequences of such law in a legal proceeding dated to around 340 B.C.E., in which Neaira, a former prostitute from Corinth, was prosecuted for illegally passing her children off as Athenian citizens (Demosthenes 59). The speech against Neaira not only provides witness to the strict regulations guarding Athenian citizenship, but it also suggests some of the long-term challenges faced by a young woman born into the Greek sex trade. On the other hand, as has been much commented on, Pericles himself became involved with the foreign Aspasia, and eventually was able to get their child declared legitimate (Stewart, 1995, p. 590).

The social and political marginalization of children produced by "mixed" marriages remains the clear goal of Athenian legislation (for an overview of illegitimate children as a group, see Ogden, 1996). But whether the attempt to restrict citizenship also reflects an idealization of pure bloodlines or desire for "racial purity" in and of itself is a more difficult question. Modern debates often hinge on the emphasis that some Athenian writers give to the putative origins of the Athenians as an autochthonous group (Isaac, 2004, pp. 109–133).

Marriage in the Hellenistic era. The alleged virility of Alexander the Great clearly contributed to the mythic image of the young man already forming at the time of his death; still today, Alexander casts a formidable shadow over modern debates about ancient Greek sexuality. It seems clear that Alexander engaged in sexual relations with both men and women, and, far from prohibiting marriage with foreign women, Alexander used marriage as a means of consolidating his power and helping conciliate those he had defeated. In 324, for example, Alexander held a mass marriage ceremony, not only joining a large number of his officers to Persian brides but also marrying two Persian women himself. Roxane, a Bactrian woman Alexander had married in 327, gave birth to a son, Alexander IV, who was evidently perceived as a legitimate successor to Alexander and was murdered along with his mother in the power struggles that followed Alexander's death.

While literary evidence is the main source for reconstructing marriage and sexual mores in ancient Athens, documentary evidence from Egypt during the Greco-Roman period survives in rates unmatched anywhere else in the classical world. Such evidence—including letters, legal contracts, and census documents—attests that marriage between Greeks and Egyptians was not forbidden in Egypt under the Ptolemies, the Greek dynasty (305–30 B.C.E.) that had assumed control over Egypt after Alexander the Great's death. In fact, such "mixed marriages" increased over time during the Ptolemaic period. These marriages took place almost exclusively between Greek men and Egyptian women, presumably due at first to the military makeup of the Greek population, although this does not preclude the existence of social stigmas that might have prevented Greek women from marrying Egyptian men. The children of such marriages, significantly, seem to be treated as "Greek" in social and civic terms, a position of higher status than "Egyptian" in the Ptolemaic era.

Sex Outside Greek Marriage. Expectations of marriage did not preclude—for Greek men at least—a range of socially acceptable sexual outlets or relationships outside the marriage bond. Critical to such liaisons was the fundamental asymmetry of the prospective pairing, meaning that the sexual partners of male citizens were supposed to be "inferiors": "women, boys, foreigners, and slaves" (Halperin, 1990b, p. 30). Still, some limits were imposed. For example, a range of laws protected women related to Athenian citizens from sexual assault by other men (Halperin, 1990a, p. 92). One very particular Greek erotic relationship has been the subject of some controversy in the modern era: Greek pederasty, a term generally connoting sexual relations between younger boys and older men. Although the practice predates the fifth century, pederasty seems to have been assigned a distinct function by the upper class in Athens as a process of socialization. Acknowledged as potential objects of desire, boys of the citizen class were—like women of the same class—protected by laws prohibiting sexual assault as well as customs that dictated with whom (and how) affairs could take place (Halperin, 1990a, pp. 93–94).

The Greek sex trade. Given the endorsement of a range of sexual practices for Greek male citizens, prostitution was evidently an open feature of Athenian life, and was apparently viewed as quintessentially democratic—that is, as a sexual outlet that should be available to male citizens of any economic standing. In fact, Athenian prostitution seems to have been notoriously inexpensive (Halperin, 1990a, p. 101). Later legend had it that state support of brothels was initiated by Solon himself, the lawgiver credited with giving rise to Athenian democracy through his series of reforms (pp. 100–101). While the evidence is limited, modern scholars assume that foreign slaves (both male and female) provided most of the sex work in Athens, especially in brothels, although it seems likely that nonslave foreigners and resident aliens also worked in the Athenian sex trade as prostitutes, *hetairai*, and concubines, the last category denoting women engaged in longer-term sexual relationships with their owners (and possibly their owners' friends) in the case of slave women or "patrons" in the case of free women. Evidence from Ptolemaic Egypt suggests a similarly wide range of sex workers (with evidence for brothels coming mainly from urban centers), although the involvement of slave versus free women is difficult to calculate, as is the proportion of male to female prostitutes (Montserrat, 1996, pp. 107–109, 116–117).

The *hetaira* (often translated as "concubine" or "courtesan," although the word itself derives from the Greek term for "companion") is often given special attention in Greek sources. The *hetaira* is generally represented as having greater prestige and economic power than the "common" prostitute, and many *hetairai* were specifically trained in music and dance. *Hetairai* are strongly associated with the Greek symposium, a type of dinner party linked to male elite culture; in fact, Leslie Kurke has argued that cultural representations of the *hetaira* are pointedly used to signify the persistence of Greek aristocratic culture in the face of the growing public discourse of equality and democratization, the latter, as we have seen, represented by the more widely available prostitute (1997). Beginning at the end of the sixth century, *hetairai* are frequent subjects of Greek drinking vessels; many of these vases show *hetairai* pointedly adopting the sexually active role (Kurke, 1997, pp. 131ff.).

The Sexual Life of Slaves. In Aeschylus's *Agamemnon* (458 B.C.E.), the Greek queen Clytemnestra coldly positions Cassandra—once a Trojan princess and now a slave brought from Troy by Clytemnestra's husband, Agamemnon—as her sexual rival. Many such literary sources hint at the sexual abuse of Greek slaves, and historians generally assume it was a regular feature of all slaves' lives, not merely those in the sex trade (Wrenhaven, 2012, pp. 71–73). Documentary sources from Ptolemaic Egypt hint at the sexual prerogatives masters had with respect to slaves, and Montserrat even cites "the cruel mistress who bribes or forces her male slaves to have sex with her, usually with catastrophic results for the slave" as a "stock character in Greek literature from Egypt" (1996, p. 103). In terms of slaves' own desires, Attic comedy records the stereotype that slaves (like animals and "barbarians" more generally) lacked the ability to control their sexual urges, at times associating male slaves specifically with masturbation (Wrenhaven, 2012, p. 74). Further evidencing the anxiety surrounding male slaves as sexual agents, Plutarch (ca. 50–120 C.E.) cites a law from Solon that evidently forbade slaves from taking free boys as lovers (Plutarch, *Life of Solon* 1.6).

Xenophon's *Oeconomicus* (dated to ca. 362 B.C.E.), a Socratic dialogue about the appropriate methods for running a large estate, provides an invaluable resource for the study of Greek slavery. In the course of offering advice, one speaker suggests that slave accommodations in the Greek household were segregated by sex, proposing that slave masters restrict sexual relations between slaves and allow childbearing only for good slaves, who will then become more loyal to their masters (9.5). As Sarah Pomeroy notes in her commentary, while segregated housing leaves open the possibility of same-sex liaisons among slaves, nonreproductive relations between slaves remain generally unimagined in Greek sources (1994, p. 317). Later in the *Oeconomicus*, the speaker casually alludes to the sexual abuse of slaves, arguing that the sexual allure of wives is more appealing than that of slaves, given that slaves are forced to submit to their masters (10.12–13). Finally, in a section on the training of the estate's foreman (presumably a slave), the speaker declares that he avoids promoting any slave currently under the spell of passion for a young boy (12.14).

Texts like the *Oeconomicus* raise important questions about whether there existed in the Greek world a conscious strategy for using sexual reproduction as a means of acquiring new slaves. There is evidence for slaves "born in the house" in Ptolemaic Egypt, and the phenomenon is also attested elsewhere in the Greek world, although it does not seem overall to have been a major part of the Greek institution (Garlan, 1988, pp. 52–53; see also Pomeroy, 1994, pp. 298–300). Lacking legal rights to their own bodies, slaves were presumably not allowed to marry, but Laura Proffitt discusses the provocative presence of a slave character laying "claim to a family of sorts" in surviving fragments from one of the Greek comedies of Menander (ca. 342–289 B.C.E.) (2011, p. 152). Another intriguing text from the fourth century openly recognizes the existence of slave families, arguing (whether accurately or not) that even corrupt slave traffickers prefer to take a financial loss rather than break up slave families by selling their members separately.

Greek Ethnography and Sexuality. While the Greek treatment of slaves was determined in large part by their servile status, it is clear that the foreign origin of most slaves also contributed to the Greek perception of slaves, since they therefore fell into the broader category of "barbarian." So it is useful to consider briefly the role of sexuality in Greek ethnography, that is, in narratives that attempted to characterize a range of populations throughout the Greek world, including the Greeks themselves.

In his seminal work, the Greek historian Herodotus (born ca. 480 B.C.E.) points to the ways certain non-Greek populations allegedly had sexual intercourse outdoors, equating it with the behavior of animals (citations listed at Wrenhaven, 2012, p. 74). Generally speaking, however, gender is far more prominent than sexuality and sexual acts in delineating the differences between Greeks and "others"

in Greek thought and ethnographic writing. Thus, the "barbarian" is correlated again and again with a reprehensible femininity; in the case of the Persians this entails a long-standing association of Persians with decadence and luxury (Briant, 2002). So, too, the Amazons (a mythical tribe of women) played a continuing role in Greek self-definition, epitomizing the quintessential femininity of the external "other" and at times even standing in for the Persians themselves in Athenian art (Stewart, 1995).

One prominent theme related to sexuality in Greek ethnography, however, is fertility, a topic that overlaps with ancient medical writing; this intersection is especially evident in a text that is essential for reconstructing Greek views of identity and difference: the Hippocratic essay, *Airs, Waters, Places.*

Airs, Waters, Places. While the "Greek" and "barbarian" opposition occupied a major position in Greek thought, Greek views of human variation also relied on a related framework called the "ancient environmental theory," a theory proposing that differences between groups were produced by climate, meaning people in southern climates were thought to possess innately different physical and mental characteristics from those in northern ones. For the Greeks and later Romans, this meant they held a "natural" superiority because they occupied a "middle" position between the various geographic extremes, one that inherently endowed them with the most advantageous qualities (e.g., Aristotle, *Politics* 1327b).

The most extensive surviving elaboration of the ancient environmental theory comes from the Hippocratic *Airs, Waters, Places*, a treatise that has been loosely dated to the period of the Persian wars. While *Airs, Waters, Places* begins with a discussion of how certain factors like wind and water influence health, it takes a notably "ethnographic" turn in its second part as it outlines what it takes to be the fundamental differences between the peoples of Asia and Europe, linking each to their respective climates. In addition to other narrative strategies, *Airs, Waters, Places* at times seems to draw on a contrast that pervaded ancient medicine, namely, that of the "hot" and "dry" Libyans in the extreme south versus the "cold" and "wet" Scythians in the extreme north. The description of Libya is not itself preserved, but *Airs, Waters, Places* expressly links the cold climate of the Scythians to their poor physical health and general inability to reproduce prolifically, citing a lack of male sexual desire, a weak male performance in sex, and the "fatness" of Scythian women, which allegedly interfered with the entry of sperm into the womb (ch. 21).

Airs, Waters, Places also contrasts the Scythians with the Egyptians in passing (a group that often stood as the paradigmatic southern population instead of Libya). Although the section on Egypt is also missing from *Airs, Waters, Places*, this seems to hint at the long-standing Greek association of Egypt and the Nile itself with hyperfertility (Vasunia, 2001, pp. 45–47). We can find this ethnographic idea given more sinister interpretation by returning one final time to Greek literary sources, and more specifically Greek tragedy, where Egyptian men at times exemplify not the passivity that usually attends the effeminate barbarian but rather a "sexual aggressiveness" that pointedly both endangers and "repulses" Greek women (Vasunia, 2001, p. 47).

[*See also* Children, *subentry* Greek World; Legal Status, *subentry* Roman World; *and* Race, Class, and Ethnicity, *subentries on* Early Church, Early Judaism, New Testament, *and* Roman World.]

BIBLIOGRAPHY

Briant, Pierre. "History and Ideology: The Greeks and 'Persian Decadence.'" Translated by Antonia Nevill. In *Greeks and Barbarians*, edited by Thomas Harrison, pp. 193–210. New York: Routledge, 2002.

Garlan, Yvon. *Slavery in Ancient Greece*. Rev. ed. Translated by Janet Lloyd. Ithaca, N.Y.: Cornell University Press, 1988.

Hall, Edith. *Inventing the Barbarian: Greek Self-Definition through Tragedy*. Oxford: Clarendon, 1989.

Halperin, David. "The Democratic Body: Prostitution and Citizenship in Classical Athens." In *One Hundred Years of Homosexuality, and Other Essays on Greek Love*, pp. 88–112. New York: Routledge, 1990a.

Halperin, David. "One Hundred Years of Homosexuality." In *One Hundred Years of Homosexuality, and Other Essays on Greek Love*, pp. 15–40. New York: Routledge, 1990b.

Isaac, Benjamin. *The Invention of Racism in Classical Antiquity*. Princeton, N.J.: Princeton University Press, 2004.

Kurke, Leslie. "Inventing the *Hetaira*: Sex, Politics, and Discursive Conflict in Archaic Greece." *Classical Antiquity* 16, no. 1 (1997): 106–150.

Lloyd, G. E. R., ed. *Hippocratic Writings*. Translated by J. Chadwick and W. N. Mann. New York: Penguin, 1983.

Montserrat, Dominic. *Sex and Society in Græco-Roman Egypt*. London: Kegan Paul International, 1996.

Ogden, Daniel. *Greek Bastardy in the Classical and Hellenistic Periods*. Oxford: Clarendon, 1996.

Pomeroy, Sarah B. *Xenophon, "Oeconomicus": A Social and Historical Commentary*. Oxford: Clarendon, 1994.

Proffitt, Laura. "Family, Slavery, and Subversion in Menander's *Epitrepontes*." In *Reading Ancient Slavery*, edited by Richard Alston, Edith Hall, and Laura Proffitt, pp. 152–174. London: Bristol Classical Press, 2011.

Rosivach, Vincent J. "Enslaving *Barbaroi* and the Athenian Ideology of Slavery." *Historia* 48, no. 2 (1999): 129–157.

Stewart, Andrew. "Imag(in)ing the Other: Amazons and Ethnicity in Fifth-Century Athens." *Poetics Today* 16, no. 4 (1995): 571–597.

Vasunia, Phiroze. *The Gift of the Nile: Hellenizing Egypt from Aeschylus to Alexander*. Berkeley: University of California Press, 2001.

Wrenhaven, Kelly L. *Reconstructing the Slave: The Image of the Slave in Ancient Greece*. Bristol, U.K.: Bristol Classical Press, 2012.

Denise Eileen McCoskey

Roman World

The intersection of gender with the categories of race, class, and ethnicity is a complex and interesting one. Despite the dearth of women's voices in literature, elite male authors routinely use gender as a means to explore familial, social, and political issues. Similarly, concepts of race and ethnicity are used in order to express concerns about identity and ideology. In conjunction with the evidence from literature, archaeological and documentary materials often help to illuminate further our understanding of the role that all these categories played in ancient Rome.

Methodological Issues. To appreciate the full impact of race, ethnicity, and class with relation to gender in the Roman world, a few methodological problems should be noted. First, the expansive timescale: the "Roman world" spans from 753 B.C.E. to

476 C.E. (and arguably further), during which time attitudes cannot be deemed as constant. Second, race, ethnicity, and class are more complicated notions than they may initially appear because their functions in ancient Rome as categories to denote alterity worked very differently from our own. "Race" and "ethnicity" are both terms used to describe groups that can be identified as non-Roman; Romans freely gave citizenship rights to the peoples they conquered, even as they recognized that they belonged to different nations with different political institutions, religion, language, or somatic type. Class is also a problematic concept, since its traditional definition as a category describing people's relationship with means of labor and economic production does not adequately portray such distinctions in Rome. Roman society was a complex amalgam of elite senators and knights, freeborn men and women, freed slaves of low status but of significant wealth in many cases, and domestic and rural slaves, some of whom enjoyed better living conditions than free citizens.

The nature of our evidence also presents significant obstacles. Most of our information is from literary texts authored by elite males. Thus, we need to consider the context of the work in question: a satirist chastising women's laziness or men engaging in same-sex relations distorts reality to achieve specific narrative aims. Any perceived bias against such social groups cannot be taken at face value. Other evidence is even harder to contextualize and interpret: legal documents, inscriptions, graffiti, objects from the visual arts and material culture. Overall, our ability to reconstruct Roman reality with confidence is often hampered by insurmountable difficulties. For these reasons, this essay discusses the available evidence categorized by type of class and ethnicity and concludes with a discussion of race.

Roman Class Constructs. Greek influence in Roman literature and art is paramount. Roman ideas on gender and sexuality should be considered in view of Greek constructions of gender and sexuality and resulting hierarchies. The earliest surviving complete Roman texts are Plautus's comedies (ca. 250–184 B.C.E.), which are adaptations of Greek new comedy. Roman art was closely akin to late Hellenistic art and was often fashioned by Greek artists. Scholarship on Roman sexuality accepts Foucault's general schema, wherein sexual relations are primarily defined by the principles of dominance and submission. Within this framework, the male subject has the active role of penetrator and the female that of the passive recipient of the sexual act. During the republican period (200–31 B.C.E.), Roman law protected the male citizen body from sexual penetration, beating, and torture—but not that of freedmen or slaves. As a result, by being subject to penetration, freedmen and slaves were considered effeminate. For women, unmarried and married, virginity and chastity were prized qualities and safeguarded through legislation. *Stuprum*, a criminal sexual act, was a punishable offense. Women were also prohibited from engaging in behaviors that were thought of as conducive to adultery. For example, drinking wine was forbidden since the time of Romulus (753–716 B.C.E.; Virgil, *Aeneid* 1.737 and Servius's comment ad loc.).

All forms of same-sex intercourse were denigrated, and homoerotic behaviors became more acceptable after the upper classes began to adopt a Hellenized lifestyle (third century B.C.E.). Blame was only attached to the male who took the passive sexual role. The sex of the partner was immaterial, provided that the citizen male played the active role. Chastity of freeborn boys was a concern, with Roman jurists defining sexual intercourse with them as *stuprum* (same as unmarried women; Paulus, *Digest* 47.11.12; Skinner, 2014, p. 261). Social standing is so closely related to sexual privilege that writers regularly employ phallic imagery as a metaphor for power (e.g., Catullus 11.1–2; 28.9–10).

Marriage was a contract between the families of the bride and groom, ratified legally and ritually. Legally, there were two types of marriage: with *manus*, whereby the woman's fortune and all guardianship passed over from her father to her husband; or without *manus*, whereby the natal family kept all rights to her fortune and rights of guardianship (but not of her children—those remained under the control of her husband). Roman authors repeatedly refer to the ideal of *univira* (a "one-man woman"), although the extent of the actual practice remains doubtful for early Roman times and certainly defunct later. As the republic became more marred by civil wars (88–31 B.C.E.), resulting in the death of many citizen males, women increasingly married without *manus*, thus gaining more power over their own fortunes. They also routinely remarried after they were widowed or divorced. Elite Roman women at this time visibly act as patrons, investors, creditors, and benefactors, thus emerging as well integrated in the socioeconomic networks of Rome. Such visibility, however, fosters concerns about adultery, presenting some anxiety regarding the independence these women appear to enjoy. A classic example of such attitudes can be seen in the case of Claudia Metelli, who is viciously maligned by Cicero in his speech in defense of Caelius (Cicero, *On Behalf of Caelius* 31, 56 B.C.E.) as having provided a loan to young Caelius in exchange for sexual favors.

Whether responding to concerns regarding the stability of marriage during the times of civil war or by a genuine desire to reboot marital relations, Augustus (r. 31 B.C.E.–14 C.E.) launched new marriage legislation in 18 B.C.E. (Cassius Dio 54.16.1–2). The *Lex Iulia de maritandis ordinibus* regulated marriages among elite classes (senators and equestrians), and the *Lex Iulia de adulteriis coercendis* discouraged adultery. The former was supplemented in 9 C.E. by *Lex Papia Poppaea* and imposed legal disabilities on men and women who remained unmarried and rewarded parents of three or more children with benefits (*ius trium liberorum*). It also forbade senators to marry freedwomen but allowed freedwomen to marry freeborn men of the lower classes, provided those women were of good character. Under the new legislation adultery became a public crime, the offender tried before a criminal court. Jurisdiction is taken away from the wife's family and is transferred to the state. The adulterer was tried first, and, if he was convicted, the woman was tried next. Punishments were harsh and involved civil disabilities, such as the right to serve in the army for men and the right to remarry for women. A father who caught his daughter in the act could kill the adulterer; the husband could do the same only if the lover was of lower status (freedman,

gladiator, actor, or slave). Women exempt from this legislation included slaves, whores, madams, and foreigners not married to Roman citizens. Men could have sex with such women without committing *stuprum*. As a result, Augustus's marriage legislation created a new caste of sex workers. Prostitutes had to register as professionals with the authorities and could form a valid marriage only with freedmen (McGinn, 1998, pp. 194–199). Respectable and nonrespectable women were distinguished outwardly and legally (Skinner, 2014, p. 268).

Various early imperial literary texts betray anxiety over the integrity of male identity, sexual and otherwise. A prominent example can be seen in Roman elegy, a genre of love poetry that flourishes in this period. These poems depict reverse power dynamics between the poet-lover and his beloved (*puella*): the man is the slave (*servus amoris*), the woman his master (*domina*). Although the poems are mostly concerned with elite (married) women, courtesans also appear as objects of male desire within the same power configuration (e.g., Ovid, *Ars Amatoria* 1.31–34). Some have interpreted this gender dynamic as expressing a counterculture, while others see the poets using the beloved as an object manipulated by the poet, who ultimately holds all power. Whichever view one adopts, most scholars agree that Roman elegy's feminized, elite males reflect anxieties of the senatorial class over their gradual disempowerment in the new regime, where most power lies in the hands of the *princeps*.

During Augustus's reign, his sister Octavia and wife Livia rose in political significance. Livia's position is manifest in the city's architecture: a splendid portico was dedicated to her in 7 B.C.E. and became one of the most popular gathering places in the city. Augustus's failure to produce male heirs led him to adopt his stepson Tiberius to be the next Roman emperor in 4 C.E. Livia became the sole link between the Julian and Claudian clans. As such, she was included in the images commemorating the imperial family, setting a precedent for future empresses (Skinner 2014, p. 305).

During the early empire (14–117 C.E.), sources become extremely hostile toward the imperial family and imperial women in particular (e.g., Claudius's wife Messalina, Nero's mother Agrippina). The depraved empress becomes a trope, a woman without any moral constraints in the pursuit of power, a reflection of the regime in which she operates. This hostility may be interpreted as a result of the continued marginalization of the senatorial class and the growing popularity of the emperors.

The Foucaultian paradigm holds that sexual austerity emerges as an important value at this time. Philosophical movements (e.g., Stoicism) and medical writings express a shift in Roman ideas about marriage. While for freeborn lower classes marriage was hitherto not as important or desirable as for the elites, the emotional bond between the spouses now becomes significant, with Stoicism playing a key part in this change. Women's roles in marriage thus appear as more equivalent to the male roles. Sexual abstinence and virginity are now prized practices. The physician Galen offers a view of the human body as a fragile and complex mechanism with an inherent instability and in need of constant monitoring, while sexual activity is viewed as a possible source of disease. While not identical to early Christian sexual ethics, such ideas are linked to preexisting concerns about sexuality (Skinner, 2014, p. 318). Narratives disparaging women, however (e.g., Juvenal *Satire* 6), show that Roman attitudes to marriage have not radically changed at this time.

The literature of this period—particularly in the genre of satire—refers frequently to sexual categories such as *cinaedus* and *tribas*. *Cinaedus* describes a male who enjoys the passive sexual role, often positioned as the opposite of man (*vir*). A *cinaedus* is invariably effeminate and often described as addicted to being penetrated. According to physicians such as Caelius Aurelianus (fifth century C.E.), these men suffer from mental affliction (Skinner, 2014, p. 281). *Tribas* is the female equivalent of the *cinaedus*, a woman who plays the active role in sex acts. The startling function of a *tribas* as a penetrator renders her monstrous in many of the literary sources (e.g., Martial 1.90.8). Other nonliterary evidence (magic spells, medical texts, graffiti, etc.) attests to the fact that love between women was well known

in Rome. Furthermore, the poet Juvenal refers to what has been posited as a secret society of *cinaedi* (2.47). The historians Tacitus (ca. 56–after 117 C.E.) and Suetonius (ca. 69–122 C.E.) refer to the emperor Nero as having performed official wedding ceremonies between himself and other men (Tacitus, *Annals* 15.37; Suetonius, *Nero* 28–29). Based on this and other evidence, scholars have posited that perhaps a counterculture was operative in Rome during the first century C.E. and on (Richlin, 1993, pp. 542–593), while others consider the evidence scant and the question unanswerable (Skinner, 2014, p. 327).

By the time of the Second Sophistic (68–230 C.E.), a new model of heterosexual relationships emerges, whereby Eros is indispensable for the happiness of the couple and their emotional connection takes precedence over the wishes of the parents. Evidence for this is found in the new literary genre of the novel, which articulates a symmetry of genders. Herein we face a "new erotics," where virginity is prized as commensurate with love and marriage (Foucault, 1988, pp. 231–232; Skinner, 2014, p. 332). The Roman novel, however, presents a hero reared in an educational system that fails to prepare him for a role of leadership in public life. Quite the contrary, the hero ends up in the margins of society with his masculinity repeatedly in question and fortune playing a central role in determining his future. As a result, these male heroes, cast as victims of gender instability, express deeply rooted anxieties about disempowerment, social and otherwise.

Slaves, Freedmen, and Freedwomen. Roman slaves were usually people who had been seized as captives during war, were purchased in trade, or sold themselves into slavery to pay debts. Many slaves were foreigners (Greeks, Thracians, Germans, Carthaginians, Gauls, some Ethiopians, etc.), but many were native Italians, the result of the wars Romans waged in Italy. Offspring from slave unions were encouraged to propagate the slave population for any given household. Slaves (male or female) were the property of the master, who had the power of life or death over them and was free to engage in sexual activity with them—with or without their consent. Children born from such unions were also slaves. Slaves could own property, although it belonged to their master, and were allowed to use it. Skilled or educated slaves could earn their own money and save it to eventually buy their freedom.

Romans thought that slavery damaged slaves morally, some irreparably. Yet a slave could be morally rehabilitated through display of good behavior. Manumission could reward that gradual progress, placing the freed slave in a patron–client relationship in which the moral education could continue. Some scholars believe that the owner was still able to demand sexual services from freed slaves, which in they eyes of other Romans denied them full citizen status.

Ancient literary sources, especially during the empire, often caricature freedmen as usurping a status that does not belong to them. Satire is a source of biting criticism, placing freedmen in the same category as informants and criminals. Freedmen are also routinely stigmatized as effeminate. A good example is the portrait of Trimalchio in Petronius's *Satyrica* (75.10–76.2), where he is said to have used sex for advancement. Similarly maligned is his wife Fortunata, a former slave and chorus girl, who is described as greedy and sex crazed.

Nonliterary sources tell us that freedwomen in particular were able to own property and create their own wills, although sometimes with restrictions. For example, Acilia Plecusa, a freedwoman married to a Roman knight, had a son while a slave and a daughter while free. Her son was never promoted to full membership of the municipal council. As for herself, although we know that she commissioned inscriptions to commemorate her benefactions, we have no way of knowing whether she enjoyed social acceptance (Kleijwegt, 2012, p. 111). In a marriage between a freedwoman and her former owner, the husband's superiority was enhanced by the fact that he was also her patron. The emperor Claudius (r. 41–54 C.E.) introduced legislation wherein a freedwoman with four children qualified for benefits granted under the Augustan marriage legislation for Roman freeborn women with three or more children. The woman could thus be released from guardianship and would gain the right to dispose of her property

as she wished (Gaius, *Institutes* 3.44; Kleijwegt, 2012, p. 118). Roman and Latin freedwomen probably enjoyed greater freedoms than their counterparts of other ethnicities. According to Claudius's legislation, Latin freedwomen could obtain Roman citizenship, draw up a will, and dispose of their estate as they saw fit. Scholars conclude that the motivation behind Claudius's legislation was the existence of numerous wealthy freedwomen in Rome at the time (Kleijwegt, 2012, p. 118).

Roman comedies offer numerous examples of slave women who are eventually revealed to be freeborn noblewomen and are able to marry a nobleman. Yet those who remain slaves by the end of such plays never transcend their status by marrying a freeborn man. Similarly, freedwomen are never married to citizens in comedy. A century and a half later, the historian Livy presents in his narrative of the scandal of the Bacchanalia the former slave prostitute Faecenia Hispala as rewarded with full citizenship rights and married to an elite young man (39.19.5–7). Hispala is instrumental in saving the Roman state from a conspiracy that is described as "other" (i.e., foreign and sexually subversive). In Livy's idealized narrative, Hispala's upstanding morality transcends her status as slave and integrates her fully into the status of a Roman married woman (*matrona*).

Romanness and Ethnicity. Ethnicity may be broadly defined as a concept describing a particular group with a common ethnic name, along with shared history, language, religion, and culture. Yet this definition should not lead to a conflation of ancient Rome with the modern nation-state. Romanness (*Romanitas*) is rather complex and fluid, evolves differently in the various periods of Roman history, and is firmly embedded within Roman ideologies of masculinity and power. Citizenship and masculinity are virtually synonymous, with Romans generally described as possessing masculine qualities of strength, morality, and virtue, whereas foreigners are often cast in feminine terms, displaying moral and physical weakness, corruptibility, and fickleness.

Early in its history, Rome emerges as a mixed society, consisting of mostly Latin people but also Etruscans and Sabines, whose cultural influence on the new city was important. Scholars posit that ethnic mobility and cultural transmission at that time were based on horizontal social mobility. The Tarquin dynasty, for example, is seen as representative of a wider pattern of elite individuals and kinship groups moving across political and ethnic boundaries throughout central Italy (Lomas, 1997, p. 4). Although other Italian groups were distinct from the Romans in terms of language or other cultural aspects, Roman citizenship was granted to all Italians in 90/89 B.C.E., which demonstrates that for Romans, citizenship was not a matter of birth but of legal status.

Foreigners working and living in Rome did not have political rights, could not serve in the military, and could not make wills. They could inherit only if written into the will of a Roman soldier. Some had the right to marry, and others the right to engage in commerce. By the time of the late republic, legal distinctions between citizen and foreigner became more relaxed (Noy, 2000).

Romans often viewed various conquered peoples negatively, as they believed in their own superiority and in the inferiority of those subject to imperial rule. Romans theorized that they inhabited the center of the world, with Italy ideally situated in the middle between North and East (e.g., Pliny, *Natural History* 2.80.190; Vitruvius, *On Architecture* 6.1). Sources describe the Greeks as weak and effeminate, showing disdain for their conquered status (e.g., Cicero, *Letters to Quintus* 1.2.4). At the same time, however, Greek contributions in art and literature are ardently admired and zealously imitated (e.g., Horace, *Epistles* 2.1.156–157). Romans appear to share the Greek view that cultural and somatic differences were the product of environmental influence, not heredity (Pliny, *Natural History* 2.80.189). Negative sentiment is expressed on northern "paleness" and superior height (Caesar, *Gallic Wars* 2.30.4; 4.1.9). Peoples of the east (Trojans, Greeks, Persians, Egyptians, etc.) are associated with effeminacy and weakness, the result of excessive wealth and indulgence in luxurious life (e.g., Vergil, *Aeneid* 4.214–218).

Such views are complicated, however, by Roman incorporation of foreign deities and cults such as that of Cybele, Isis and Osiris, or Mithras. For instance, a famous temple dedicated to the goddess Cybele, whose priests were castrated males, was located on the Palatine Hill, the heart of Rome. Although a Roman citizen could not serve as her priest, the goddess's importance for Roman state religion cannot be disputed. Her arrival in the city of Rome from Asia Minor (204 B.C.E.) is firmly associated with Roman victory in the second Punic war and the defeat of Rome's fiercest enemy, Hannibal.

Another example of the complex contours of the intersection of ethnicity and gender in the Roman world can be seen in the case of the Egyptian queen Cleopatra (69–30 B.C.E.). Belonging to the royal family of the Ptolemies, themselves of Greek origin, Cleopatra embraced a hybrid Greek/Egyptian identity (McCoskey, 2012, pp. 11–23). Contemporary Roman sources, undoubtedly responding to Octavian's propaganda, utilize her status as a foreign woman to paint her as a threat to Roman masculinity: a power-hungry female who reduced Marc Antony to the status of an effeminate consort, desirous of imposing her degenerate morals on Rome (e.g., Propertius 3.11.29–46). Other sources, however, show respect for her intelligence, extensive education, and charisma (Plutarch, *Life of Antony* 25.5–28.1), although evidence for her actual physical appearance is scant (McCoskey, 2012, p. 18). A child, Caesarion, was allegedly born from a union with Julius Caesar, who never formally recognized him as his son. Still Octavian, Caesar's adoptive heir, perceived Caesarion as enough of a threat to have him killed. Augustan poets show admiration for Cleopatra's courage in death and her refusal to participate in Octavian's triumph after her defeat in the battle of Actium (31 B.C.E.; cf. Horace, *Odes* 1.37). Virgil's moving portrait of Carthaginian Dido in the *Aeneid*, a character purposefully recalling Cleopatra, shows an even greater complexity. Dido is an admirable model of leadership for Aeneas in his foundational quest; yet, even after her death, Dido remains a threat to Roman domination, poised to return in the form of Hannibal, her descendant (4.622–629).

Race and the Politics of Interpretation. The issue of race in ancient Rome remains hotly contested among scholars. A prevalent view, propounded by Snowden and Thompson, is that racism as discrimination based on difference in somatic type does not conform to modern ideas. In his study of Roman attitudes to blacks, Thompson (1989) argues that, although Romans show some prejudice against other somatic types, there is no consistent denigration of them or notion of permanent inferiority based on bodily features or skin color. He points out that blacks are slaves often but not always, belonged to different ethnicities, were dispersed in various localities, and were able to hold high-ranking posts. He presents evidence that ancestry and lineage were not considered permanently black, since offspring of mixed unions were considered white (e.g., Pliny, *Natural History* 7.51), and finally notes that manumission presented the option of transcendence of the status of the slave.

By contrast, Isaac (2004) argues for the existence of "proto-racism," that is, prejudices that can be construed as precursors of modern racist attitudes. For instance, Roman imperialism justifies conquest of other peoples based on Roman superiority; the assumption is thus that people with slave status deserve to be in that position. Isaac, however, has been criticized for not engaging with the practice of manumission or with instances where race is not associated with essentialized inferiority.

Ultimately, one must consider that scholars interpret texts through the lens of their own (often unintended) racial prejudices. This can be seen in various analyses of the portrait of Scybale in *Moretum* (31–35), an Augustan poem of unknown origin (Haley, 1993, pp. 30–31). Most recently, McCoskey (2012) tackles these issues from a more modern theoretical perspective, challenging the idea that race is a biological category and examining it as a social construct that justifies relations of power among groups. The issue of what constitutes race in Roman antiquity is still subject to debate, while the intersection of gender, race, class, and ethnicity emerges as a topic needing further inquiry.

[*See also* Children, *subentry* Roman World; Legal Status, *subentries on* New Testament *and* Roman World; Marriage and Divorce, *subentries on* New Testament *and* Roman World; *and* Race, Class, and Ethnicity, *subentries on* Greek World *and* New Testament.]

BIBLIOGRAPHY

Foucault, Michel. *The History of Sexuality.* Vol. 3: *The Care of the Self.* Translated by Robert Hurley. New York: Vintage, 1988.

Haley, Shelly P. "Black Feminist Thought and Classics: Remembering. Re-claiming, Re-empowering." In *Feminist Theory and the Classics*, edited by Nancy Rabinowitz and Amy Richlin, pp. 23–43. London: Routledge, 1993.

Isaac, Benjamin. *The Invention of Racism in Classical Antiquity.* Princeton, N.J.: Princeton University Press, 2004.

Kleijwegt, Marc. "Deciphering Freedwomen in the Roman Empire." In *Free at Last! The Impact of Freed Slaves on the Roman Empire*, edited by Sinclair Bell and Teresa Ramsby, pp. 110–129. London: Bristol Classical Press, 2012.

Lefkowitz, Mary R., and Maureen B. Fant. *Women's Life in Greece and Rome. A Source Book in Translation.* 3d ed. Baltimore: Johns Hopkins University Press, 2005.

Lomas, Kathryn, and Tim Cornell. *Gender and Ethnicity in Ancient Italy.* Accordia Specialist Studies on Italy 6. London: Accordia Research Institute, University of London, 1997.

McCoskey, Denise E. *Race: Antiquity and Its Legacy.* Ancients and Moderns. New York: Oxford University Press, 2012.

McGinn, Thomas A. J. *Prostitution, Sexuality and the Law in Ancient Rome.* New York: Oxford University Press, 1998.

Noy, David. *Foreigners at Rome: Citizens and Strangers.* London: Duckworth, 2000.

Richlin, Amy. "Not before Homosexuality: The Materiality of the *Cinaedus* and the Roman Law against Love between Men." *Journal of the History of Sexuality* 3 (1993): 523–573.

Skinner, Marilyn B. *Sexuality in Greek and Roman Culture.* 2d ed. Ancient Cultures. Malden, Mass.: Blackwell, 2014.

Snowden, Frank M., Jr. *Blacks in Antiquity: Ethiopians in the Greco-Roman Experience.* Cambridge, Mass.: Belknap, 1970.

Thompson, Lloyd A. *Romans and Blacks.* Norman: University of Oklahoma Press, 1989.

Vassiliki Panoussi

New Testament

The modern study of the New Testament in relationship to concepts and ideologies associated with race, class, and ethnicity is not without methodological difficulty, as these categories are not necessarily transparent, either in the texts or in the history of interpretation. It is also the case that scholarship concerning race, class, and ethnicity in the New Testament is heavily influenced by modern concepts and ideologies—that is, it is difficult to access the ancient world in an unmediated manner. Moreover, race, class, and ethnicity are inextricably bound up with gendered and sexualized discourses and identities, and serve as signifiers for difference, hierarchies, and power relations, both in the ancient world and modern scholarship. This essay attempts to chart the complexities of this topic, with reference to several key New Testament texts.

Modern Concepts of Race/Ethnicity and Class. Along with gender and sexuality, race, ethnicity, and class are social and ideological constructs formulated in the modern era that structure both individual identities and society as a whole by shaping how we see the world and influencing how we behave in the world. Hierarchical and intersectional, these cultural markers provide options and resources for some and restrict options and resources for others (Weber, 2010, pp. 23–24). The term "race" has no precise definition, but is described as a category of people who exhibit common biological traits, including physical characteristics such as skin color, hair texture, and the shape of eyes, nose, or head. Relatedly, "ethnicity" is described as nonbiological traits that provide members of a group with a sense of common identity and a shared culture based on, for instance, nationality, history, language, and religion (Newman, 2012, p. 32). Ethnicity is often placed within the context of race, particularly in the United States, since race has powerfully shaped the terrain on which ethnic groups have historically been viewed and treated. "Class" refers to the economic position in terms of the distribution of wealth and income, and in the distribution of power and authority in the workforce.

These identifiers function as interlocking social systems that are embedded in every social institution, operating concurrently in every social situation influencing social behavior and perception (Crenshaw, 1991). On an individual level, these cultural markers place a member of society in multiple locations simultaneously. For instance, she or he may be part of the dominant group in terms of race, yet also be part of a subordinate group, in terms of class, sexuality, and gender. Since these cultural identifiers are socially constructed and dependent on context, their meanings are fluid and can vary across different societies, regions, and also across time, and, therefore, their significance can change. However, it must be emphasized that these constructions only have meaning and significance when placed in binary oppositions and hierarchies that reflect social rankings and power relations (Newman, 2012, pp. 39–40).

The Conceptualization of Difference in the Greco-Roman World. Although there was no concept of nationalism in the modern sense in the first century C.E., the ancients did make note of difference in terms of physical characteristics, culture, and social standing. At the time of the writing of the New Testament texts, conceptualizations of difference formed the basis for the development of Roman imperial ideology. The Romans exhibited a range of prejudices, phobias, and hostilities toward certain groups based on physical characteristics (skin color, body shape, and body markings such as circumcision) and social status (Roman versus barbarian, imperial/senatorial classes versus freedpeople versus slaves). To a large degree, the Roman construction of difference can be traced to Hellenistic culture. The Greeks considered their culture superior and tended to despise foreigners (*barbaroi*). These attitudes were later inherited by the Romans and subsequently played a major role in shaping modern European and American prejudices against "non-Western" peoples (Coleman, 1997, p. 175).

Roman literature, medical treatises, and historical writings of the Augustan age provide ample evidence that Greco-Roman culture classified peoplehood based on color differences. *Albus, ater, candidus, fuscus*, and *niger* were the Latin terms used by authors to describe the skin color of the people with whom they came into contact; the term used in Greek to refer to black skin was *melas*. Scholars inhabit multiple positions regarding this categorization of skin hues. Modern scholars typically base these terms on the skin color charts of nineteenth-century lexicons, while some scholars prefer to understand the color ranges as degrees of brownness, arguing that the people who lived in the ancient Mediterranean world would not have had white skin (Thompson, 1989, pp. 10–11). The Ethiopian's dark skin color was used as the basis for the charting of color by the degree of melanin in the skin. The adjectives most used to describe the Ethiopian were *niger, ater*, and *fuscus*. Thus, black and the Ethiopian were used synonymously in the ancient world. As far as gradation is concerned, those south of the Ganges were dark or black. They were described as being browned by the sun, but not as dark as the Ethiopians, whereas peoples living north of the Ganges resembled Egyptians (Snowden, 1970, p. 3).

Roman authors borrowed from the Greeks the belief that physical differences were determined by the environment. According to this model, collective characteristics were the result of climate and geography. Scholars observe that the "environment theory" runs throughout Herodotus's *Histories* and is articulated as early as Hippocrates's *Airs, Waters and Places* (ca. fifth century B.C.E.), which had enormous influence on writers such as Plato, Aristotle, and Galen, as well as the early modern authors Montesquieu and David Hume (for a fuller reception history see Isaac, 2004, p. 60). Aristotle developed the idea politically by claiming that the Greeks were more capable of universal rule as a result of geographical region and environment. He held that the Greeks occupied the best environment between Europe (West) and Asia (East) and were therefore ideally capable of ruling others. The Greeks believed that the inhabitants of Persia were soft not only because of their climate and resources, but that Asian feebleness was also due to monarchic rule. Thus, Aristotle argued that the Persians were servile by nature and suited to Greek subjugation. Similarly, when the Romans gained control over the Mediterranean basin, Roman authors shifted the geographical center and portrayed

Rome as the navel of the universe. The works of Pliny the Elder, Cicero, and Seneca depict the Romans as the "superior" people in the north, and the Carthaginians, their major rival for power, who resided in the south, as "inferior."

Negative attitudes toward the *barbaroi* can help clarify for modern readers the underlying assumptions of Roman imperialism. Although there is a scholarly perception that the Romans never made a rigid distinction between themselves and the *barbaroi*, literary evidence suggests that the term was used to signify those peoples and tribes that had no Greek or Roman accomplishments (Isaac, 2004, pp. 169–223). The term was originally used by the Greeks to designate one who simply speaks a foreign language. Paul reflects this usage when he says: "If then I do not know the meaning of a sound, I will be a foreigner [*barbaros*] to the speaker and the speaker a foreigner [*barbaros*] to me" (1 Cor 14:11).

Greek and Roman authors used *barbaros* as a common rhetorical strategy to slander ethnic groups who were perceived as threats to power (Byron, 2002). Often, the portrayal of the barbarian or foreigner was of a sexually promiscuous female. The imperial court poets and authors of the early Roman Empire, intent on promoting the high moral agenda of Augustus, employed the image of the foreign woman as a seductress who needed to be controlled. Passion was a cultural stereotype projected onto Africans by Romans and Greeks (Haley, 2009, pp. 375–381). For instance, Livy writes of the danger of beautiful barbarian women, most notably the case of the Carthaginian princess Sophonisba, who drank poison to avoid appearing in a Roman triumph (*Ab urbe condita libri* 30.12.11–19). Through such characterizations, Augustan authors reinforced the perceived need for control of female sexuality, whether domestic or foreign, as well as projecting the other as dangerous and conniving (Haley, 2009).

Additionally, visual representation of the subjugated enemy as *barbaros* was integral to the formation of Roman imperial ideology. During the early Roman Empire, conquered barbarians were portrayed in various media, alone or with their conquerors, who were either discernible emperors or indiscernible representatives of the Roman army (Lopez, 2008, p. 31). Male barbarians were typically effeminized by being displayed in a subdued position with their hands bound behind their backs, while females were depicted in a mourning stance. Defeated enemies of Rome were often represented visually as degraded, physically abused, and humiliated females forced to their knees by the grip of the powerful, virile, male Roman emperor. These images served to legitimate the hierarchical relations of conquest and assimilation on patriarchal terms (Lopez, 2008).

Christian authors were quite aware of different "barbarian" groups within antiquity and, following the lead of dominant Greco-Roman cultural strategies, stereotyped the other in their writings. For instance, early Christian literature references to blackness, Egyptians, and Ethiopians were used as rhetorical devices or symbolic tropes that reflected ideological difference. The pejorative discourse was not necessarily directed specifically against Egyptians and Ethiopians, but symbolized those within the Christian communities whom the "orthodox" judged as heretics and thus were in disagreement with the dominant community (Byron, 2002).

Some scholars have maintained that Egyptians and Ethiopians were depicted positively in the ancient world. For example, Frank Snowden argued that there was an absence of color prejudice in antiquity by identifying many examples of Ethiopians as integrally involved in Greco-Roman life (1970). From his analysis of the Ethiopian eunuch (Acts 8:26–40), Snowden concludes that his race was not important, claiming that the early Christians used the Ethiopian as a motif in the language of conversion and as a means for emphasizing their conviction that Christianity was to include all humanity. However, there is evidence in the ancient Christian literature that contradicts this reading. The *Acts of Peter* (180–200 C.E.), for example, represents Ethiopians pejoratively, describing a female demon as "a most evil-looking woman, an *Aithiops* not *Aigyptios* but altogether *melas*" (*Acts Pet.* 22) (Byron, 2002).

The Greeks and Romans adhered to the idea that difference was a product of inherent acquired characteristics. Climate and geography were believed to

have had definite effects on all people living in a particular region, and these effects became permanent traits because of heredity. The ancient concept of autochthony approximates the concept of modern racism, for it established a hierarchy of peoplehood (Greek: *ethnē, laos*; Latin: *genus*) based on the fiction that some were of pure lineage while others were degenerated becuase of mixed descent. The notions of autochthony and pure lineage were major elements that legitimated the superiority of the Athenians over other groups (Plato, *Menexenus* 245c–d). Their myth of origin emphasized that the Athenians had lived in their own land from the beginnings of time without ever abandoning it and that they were of unmixed lineage. Considering themselves to be uncontaminated by other groups, they believed themselves to be superior. The Roman view of their own descent and lineage is quite different than that of the Greeks, indicated by the foundation myth of Romulus and Remus and the sojourn of Aeneas from Troy to Rome in Virgil's *Aeneid*. The idea of pure lineage did appeal to Roman authors when considering the other, although negatively. For example, the Romans looked down upon the Celtic tribes that had migrated into Galatia, claiming that these Gauls had degenerated due to: (1) emigrating from their homeland and (2) being contaminated by the blood of Asians as a result of mixed marriage. Also, connecting the Jewish way of life to the land of Judea was a critical component of the Roman rhetorical strategy to essentialize and stereotype the Jewish people (Wan, 2009, p. 136).

Ancient physiognomy—the stereotypical judging of the mental capacity and moral disposition of a people based on physical features was another way to describe differences in racial and ethnic terms. Hippocrates is often credited with being the first author to use the term *physiognōmoneō* in his medical treatise *Epidemics*, which contains several instances of such thinking as "those with a large head, large black eyes and a wide, snub nose are honest" (2.6.1). There is ample evidence in ancient medical treatises, rhetorical and physiognomic handbooks, and philosophical writings to conclude that, by the time of the Roman Empire, physiognomy was considered a quasi science. With this in view, Mikeal Parsons has proposed that in the Roman world the Ethiopian eunuch in Acts 8 would have been understood by Lucan audiences to be sexually ambiguous, socially ostracized, and morally corrupt based on the "principles" of ancient physiognomy. Yet the Lucan author subverts the prevalent Greco-Roman cultural ethos by illustrating with the eunuch's conversion to Christianity that all people are welcomed into the Kingdom (Parsons, 2006, p. 141). Denise Kimber Buell, on the other hand, uses the same evidence to suggest that early Christian texts did not subvert but followed the lead of the dominant Greco-Roman conceptualization of the other to shape a religious tradition that presented particular forms of Christianness as universal and authoritative. In this way early Christian authors mimicked the Roman imperial strategy of constructing difference. Similar to the Romans, early Christians did not consider descent a stumbling block to becoming Christian. However, like the Romans, they did "develop and ritually elaborate claims of primordial descent as a basis for defining Christian community" (Buell, 2005, p. 20). Clearly, there is no easy consensus among New Testament scholars regarding the relationship between the racial ideologies of these texts and those of their immediate sociocultural environment.

Social Class and Status in the Roman Empire. Roman society was hierarchical and extremely class-conscious. The emperor ruled the empire with the help of an elite social class that comprised approximately 2–3 percent of the population. This small, privileged group shaped the social ethos of the empire and controlled its wealth. There was no concept of a middle class in the ancient Roman world, and there was a large gulf between the minority elite and the majority nonelite of society.

The elite social classes consisted of a political senatorial class (*senatores*) that was rigidly defined and monopolized by families whose ancestors included at least one consul. A man could become a member of the equestrian class if he possessed property worth at least 400,000 sesterces. He did not have to be an Italian-born citizen. During the reign of Augustus, this class expanded and was allowed to occupy senior administrative positions. By the end of the first century,

they were recruited into the Senate. This led, over time, to the recruitment of the *barbaroi* into the senate class, and Rome did eventually have non-Italian emperors. Belonging to one of these elite classes guaranteed certain legal rights and imperial benefits.

The designation of women of the upper classes was more complex and problematic than men because women first belonged to the class of their fathers and then that of their husbands. The bond that kept the woman under the power of her father resulted in the woman being able to inherit her share of her father's wealth upon his death. Augustus saw fit to impose a law that prohibited female members of the senatorial class from entering a marriage contract with freedmen. The marriage law allowed the empire to maintain the strict class stratification of the elite and the nonelite classes. Elite Roman women had privilege, but no power, since they were prohibited from taking on an active role in public life. Their role was confined to the private sphere of the household. They were responsible for managing the daily activities of the house and expected to be the dignified wife and the good mother. However, they were resourceful and managed to exert considerable influence behind the scenes and through their patronage of men of a lower status.

There was more flexibility and movement in the ranks of the non-elite classes than among the elites. The lower classes included Roman citizens (*plebs*) and freedpeople (*liberti*), men and women who had been slaves but had either bought their freedom or had been manumitted. The children of freed slaves became full citizens and members of the lower class. The lowest class designation in the Roman world was that of a slave. The slave system in the Roman Empire differed from the modern system that enslaved Africans in that it was not structured around a particular race. Roman slaves comprised conquered people and the children of Roman citizens who had been sold into a life of slavery during difficult times. Some scholars argue that Roman slavery was not as harsh as modern slavery, basing their arguments on evidence suggesting that slaves could hold their masters' property as their own, that many were highly educated and performed administrative duties on behalf of their masters, and that many could buy their freedom. Just as former imperial slaves could gain access to power, the same is true in early Christianity. In 271 C.E., for example, the freedman Callistus became pope. Regardless, all slaves and their families were the property of their owners, who could do whatever they wanted to these enslaved bodies and face no punishment. Slavery was a dehumanizing and abusive system, both in the ancient world and in the modern era.

Roman society maintained a system of patronage wherein elite classes (*patroni*) offered protection to their *cliens*, who were mostly the plebians and freedpeople. Patronage might consist of legal help, food, or money. In return for their beneficence, the elite gained honor and procured political favors. Outside of Rome, Roman generals served as *patroni* to conquered peoples, and the Roman provinces would solicit influential men in Rome as their benefactors to lobby for their interests. The land of Judea during the time of the New Testament was in a *patroni-cliens* relationship with Rome. The Herodian family was appointed by the emperor as the local elites to administer Judea on behalf of Rome. However, because of constant unrest in the area, Roman governors were eventually assigned to the land.

The system of patronage further complicated sexual power, underscoring the point that Roman social and sexual hierarchies were interrelated. The patrons of freed slaves were their former slave owners. The freed slave was expected to provide part-time assistance to their former master or mistress and show continued dutifulness, even in matters of sexual activity (Skinner, 2005, p. 196). Sexual privilege was so interconnected to social status that writers used the phallus as a suitable symbol for the negotiation of power. For example, the poet Catullus, having served the governor of Bithynia in 57–56 B.C.E., says of his boss: "Memmius, while I lay on my back you slowly rammed me in the mouth with that whole beam of yours well and at length" (*Carmina* 28.9–10). In actuality, the governor did not have sex with Catullus, but had imposed restrictions on those in his employ to prevent them from financially exploiting other people (Skinner, 2005, p. 196).

Marilyn Skinner suggests that factors determining sexual deviance were not assigned the same degree of weight in the Greek polis as in the Roman Empire.

In the polis, adult manhood was the sole requirement for dominance over boys, women, and noncitizens. However, because Roman social stratification was far more complex, social standing was more decisive in sexual power relations than physiological manhood. The body of the Roman *vir*, the adult citizen male, was regarded as inviolable. They were thus legally protected from sexual penetration, beating, and torture, whereas slaves, freedpersons, and disreputable individuals did not enjoy the same protections. Roman males who did not have such bodily protection were effeminized. Although elite matrons were known to exploit their male slaves sexually, this was considered less acceptable than patrons exploiting female slaves. A matron who became pregnant by a slave disrupted the household, while the patron merely increased his property value (Skinner, 2005, p. 197).

Through a close reading of the New Testament texts, which were written during the development and modification of Roman imperial ideology, we can discern that the rhetorical strategies of the authors often serve to reinscribe a hierarchical social system that has racial, ethnic, and gendered overtones. For instance, the character Lydia in Acts 16 is considered by some to reflect the author's intention to illustrate that Christianity subverts the Roman social system. It is a woman and not a man who is the head of the household and who operates a business. However, it should be noted that a woman was able to own property and to run her own household in the Roman Empire under certain circumstances. Additionally, Lydia's control over the bodies in her household is insinuated when we read that all in her household were baptized.

Conclusion. Modern understanding of race, class, and ethnicity is ultimately anachronistic when located within the social and political milieus of the Greco-Roman world. Still, attention to the Greek and Roman contexts of the New Testament writings enables a somewhat more nuanced understanding of the texts as those that make use of rhetorical strategies that either subvert or reinforce the dominant racial, ethnic, and class categories of the time. While there may be no scholarly consensus on how to interpret the New Testament's racial, ethnic, and class-based textures, it is clear that these categories continue to serve as a site for the negotiation of hierarchies and power relationships.

[*See also* Intersectional Studies; Legal Status, *subentries on* New Testament *and* Roman World; Race, Class, and Ethnicity, *subentries on* Early Church *and* Roman World; *and* Womanist Criticism.]

BIBLIOGRAPHY

Buell, Denise Kimber. *Why This New Race: Ethnic Reasoning in Early Christianity.* New York: Columbia University Press, 2005.

Byron, Gay L. *Symbolic Blackness and Ethnic Difference in Early Christian Literature.* London: Routledge, 2002.

Coleman, John E. "Ancient Greek Ethnocentrism." In *Greeks and Barbarians: Essays on the Interactions between Greeks and Non-Greeks in Antiquity and the Consequences for Eurocentrism,* edited by John E. Coleman and Clark A. Walz, pp. 175–220. Bethesda: CDL, 1997.

Crenshaw, Kimberlé. "Mapping the Margins: Intersectionality, Identity Politics, and Violence against Women of Color." *Stanford Law Review* 43, no. 6 (1991): 1241–1299.

Glancy, Jennifer A. *Slavery in Early Christianity.* Minneapolis: Fortress, 2006.

Haley, Shelley P. "Be Not Afraid of the Dark: Critical Race Theory and Classical Studies." In *Prejudice and Christian Beginnings: Investigating Race, Gender, and Ethnicity in Early Christian Studies,* edited by Laura Nasrallah and Elisabeth Schüssler Fiorenza, pp. 27–50. Minneapolis: Fortress, 2009.

Isaac, Benjamin. *The Invention of Racism in Classical Antiquity.* Princeton, N.J.: Princeton University Press, 2004.

Lopez, Davina C. *Apostle to the Conquered: Reimagining Paul's Mission.* Paul in Critical Contexts. Minneapolis: Fortress, 2008.

Newman, David M. *Identities and Inequalities: Exploring the Intersections of Race, Class, Gender, and Sexuality.* 2d ed. New York: McGraw-Hill, 2012.

Parsons, Mikeal C. *Body and Character in Luke and Acts: The Subversion of Physiognomy in Early Christianity.* Grand Rapids, Mich.: Baker Academic Press, 2006.

Skinner, Marilyn B. *Sexuality in Greek and Roman Culture.* Malden, Mass.: Blackwell, 2005.

Snowden, Frank M., Jr. *Blacks in Antiquity: Ethiopians in the Greco-Roman Experience.* Cambridge, Mass.: Belknap, 1970.

Thompson, Lloyd A. *Romans and Blacks.* Norman: University of Oklahoma Press, 1989.

Wan, Sze-kar. "'To the Jew First and Also to the Greek': Reading Romans as Ethnic Construction." In *Prejudice and Christian Beginnings: Investigating Race, Gender, and Ethnicity in Early Christian Studies,* edited by Laura Nasrallah and Elisabeth Schüssler Fiorenza, pp. 129–158. Minneapolis: Fortress, 2009.

Weber, Lynn. *Understanding Race, Class, Gender, and Sexuality: A Conceptual Framework.* 2d ed. New York: Oxford University Press, 2010.

Lynne St. Clair Darden

Early Judaism

This entry first considers various dimensions of understanding "Jews" as an ethnic group and then turns to consider matters of sexuality and class.

Ethnicity and Identity. The title *Ioudaios* ("Judean"), attested both in Jewish writings and in non-Jewish documentary sources in antiquity, implies that Jews were classed as an ethnic group deriving from Judea. This designation has generated much debate about to what extent it indicates that Jews were recognized merely as sharing an ethno-geographical descent from Judea (e.g., Mason, 2007; cf. Cohen, 1999) or to what extent it encapsulates a lifestyle that could be denoted by our modern term "religion" (Schwartz, 2011). The rarity of any term that could be translated "Judaism" (Gk *Ioudaismos*) outside of the particular setting of 2 and 4 Maccabees might suggest there is no such notion. Within such an understanding, Jews were recognized as having an affiliation to their homeland and hence an ethnic or racial group; only the rise of Christianity and Christian attempts at their own self-definition prompted a category of religion (cf. Boyarin, 2004). It is possible, however, that a concept of religion can exist without a term for it, and certainly the category of an ethnic group in antiquity did not necessarily imply a shared geographical or blood descent. Rather the contingency of ethnic labels as forms of identity markers that could be called upon when needed entails no stable ethnic designation. *Ioudaios* ("Judean") carried more meanings than merely one of geographical descent and encapsulated elements that could be called Jewish.

The difficulty with the topic is that Jewish self-understanding would have changed over time, sometimes affected by historical events and sometimes determined by the context and purpose of any piece of writing. In similar fashion Greek ethnicity changed and manifested itself in different ways with the spread of Hellenism and interaction with other nations. That Jews could be termed "Judeans" in Hellenistic papyri alongside others bearing similar ethnic markers such as "Phrygian" or "Thracian" is an indicator that they were recognized as sharing an ethno-geographical descent from Judea. This recognition was continued by the Romans, who treated Jews as a group for tax purposes. However, those same papyri reveal the complexity of the issue. From early in the Ptolemaic period (mid-third century B.C.E.), many people whose names suggest they were Jews, as well as Egyptians, Persians, Thracians, and Arabs, are classed as Hellenes ("Greeks") (Clarysse and Thompson, 2006), an ethnic marker that clearly no longer denoted descent but instead participation in the Greek gymnasium and educational system. Here the ethnic term overlaps with class stratification; to go Greek was to move upward in society and gain such benefits as tax relief. Jewish intermarriage with local Egyptians can already be seen in the Elephantine papyri from Upper Egypt of the fifth century B.C.E., and the practice continues into the Ptolemaic period, judging by names found in Jewish Greek inscriptions. Therefore, pure descent was not a determinative factor in identifying one's ethnicity, and affiliation to social groups or practices was of equal importance. Indeed, in Egypt ethnic labels are more common in the third century B.C.E. than later, perhaps representing a greater sense of origins in the first generation of immigrants (Thompson, 2001). Such ethnic labels marked one's identity in contrast to being, for example, Egyptian or Greek, but over time this distinction became less important, especially when class or status might have exercised greater influence over one's position in society. Ethnicity, whether Judean or otherwise, was only one facet in complex social positioning where culture more than ethnicity defined one's identity.

There was nonetheless in antiquity an expectation that any particular ethnic group (an *ethnos*) displayed certain characteristics and that their behavioral patterns were determined by their *ethnos*. Thus, Herodotus established a tradition of ethnographic fascination (*Histories* II) that described the peculiar practices of different nations, and speculation over the Spartan way of life (Xenophon, *Constitution of the Lacedaemonians*) arose from belief that a distinct lifestyle defined that group. Medical treatises also supported the idea that the climate in which people lived defined their national habits (Hippocrates, *On Airs, Waters and Places*). Such associations between ethnicity and character traits explain how changing one's practice amounted to changing "nationality" and how ethnographic polemic against the barbarian outsider became a staple of Greek literature (see Hall, 1989). Ethnicity could be changed in as much as one's habits also changed.

Interpreting Ethnicity. To account for ancient Jewish ethnicity we may turn to modern studies of ethnicity, which posit that a number of facets combine to determine identity (see Hall, 2002, pp. 9–19). Identity is not static, however; at different times varying salient features will gain prominence. In particular, rather than a biological phenomenon, identity is recognized as a social manifestation in which criteria are constructed both through social relations and in the discourse generated by insiders and outsiders. Key to this understanding is that ethnicity is determined through opposition, in the same way that the Greeks constructed the barbarian as the opposite of themselves. Such oppositional identity is common throughout Jewish history. In the book Ezra-Nehemiah (late fifth century B.C.E.), there is an identity struggle for those re-establishing the political system in Judah after the exile. They seek to define their position as unsullied by intermarriage, accusing others of having mixed with pagan nations (Ezra 9; Nehemiah 13). However questionable the accusation and however "impure" the accusers were themselves, the accusations justify their claim to be the true ethnic group. Similar strategies operate in the time of the Maccabees (167–165 B.C.E.), when the victorious party (the Hasmoneans) at the end of the second century depict their opponents as religious renegades, covenant breakers (1 Macc 1:11–15), and even simply foreign (2 Macc 4). Here notably "Judaism" (*ioudaismos*) is defined as that opposed to anything foreign (both *hellēnismos*, "Greekness," and *allophulismos*, "foreignness"; 2 Macc

4:13). In reality the Hasmoneans behaved in the manner of Greek rulers and patronized Greek artists, but their ethnicity was defined through opposition to "Greeks."

In this understanding of ethnicity, religious, linguistic, or cultural phenomena are symbols that can be manipulated as part of the attempt at self-definition. Among Jews some issues were more prominent at times than others, Hellenistic Jews in particular downplaying legal and cultic identifiers (Collins, 2000). In their own writings Jews can be identified by shared traditions, despite the variety of modes of expression and cultural environments in which they lived. They self-identify through adherence to the Jerusalem Temple, to common myths of descent encapsulated in the Hebrew Bible, to observance of a shared legal tradition, and occasionally to a shared language of Hebrew, idealized if not spoken (Goodblatt, 2006). These markers were more prominent for some than for others, reflecting the fluid nature of ethnicity. They are incidental features used to demarcate Jews from others.

Conversion. Conversion presents a particular perspective on the issue of ethnicity. We know of individuals "converting" (*ioudaïzein*, "to act as a Judean"), especially in fictive tales, as seen in the case of Antiochus (2 Macc 9:12–17) and Achior the Ammonite (Judith 14:10). If those with other ethnic designations can take on the title *Ioudaios*, it implies that this ethnic term has as much elasticity as the label "Greek" (Cohen, 1990). In fiction, whole nations are said to have been circumcised and converted (Esther 8:17), and in reality other groups are converted as well: the Idumeans south of Judah (by John Hyrcanus, 129 B.C.E. or after; Josephus, *Ant.* 13.255–258) and the Itureans in the north (by Aristobulus, 104–103 B.C.E.; *Ant.* 13.318–319). These conversions may have been facilitated by some aspects of shared ancestry and the likelihood that these groups were already circumcised (Schwartz, 2001, pp. 36–38). The details of what conversion entailed are unclear but probably included adopting some practices and, for whole nations, loyalty and obedience. The Samaritans were in a peculiar position, deriving origins from within Jewish tradition and probably seen by many to be Jews but generating opposition on cultic terms (e.g.,

Sir 50:26); they were forced to submit to loyalty rather than joining by direct conversion (again under John Hyrcanus). In this sense they too became Judeans.

Sexuality and Ethnicity. It has been suggested that in antiquity sexuality, like ethnicity, was not a system that can be defined and categorized, which would imply a modern concept of sexuality as an understanding of the self (Foucault, 1976) or that classical writers abstracted sexual orientation from actual practices. Indeed, sexual practice was subsumed under wider cultural norms, especially that of power relations. Any particular sexual act was banned not because the act itself was seen as inappropriate but because it violated other governing principles of society. Sexual practice and norms are formed within a larger cultural system that defines proper practice, the acceptability of certain sexual acts, the divisions of class, age, and gender that can be transgressed, and the institutions that enforce such practices.

The study of sexuality in ancient Judaism has received far less attention than the role of women and gender, with the exceptions of Loader's broad surveys (e.g., Loader, 2011) and Satlow's (1995) analysis of the rabbis. The evidence we have for ancient Judaism is limited, largely dependent on literary sources that have their own biases and intentions, but much can be determined by comparison with the Greco-Roman world. Such comparison is afforded by the reality of direct contact the Jews had with Greeks and Romans and also by the comparability of social institutions (slavery being the most notable) even where contact cannot be proven.

It was inevitable that in trying to demarcate their own identity vis-à-vis others, Jews invoked sexual perversions to classify acceptable and unacceptable behavior. Groups or nations were dismissed as sexually deviant, in keeping with a wider ancient tradition of sexual polemic (Knust, 2006) or Jewish "rhetorics" (to use Satlow's term; 1995). Sexual practice was a cultural expression that helped to shape identity in that it was defined within the norms of social behavior established within Jewish society. Within the Bible itself there were demarcations and self-styled identity markers crafted in terms of sexuality and exclusion. Idolatry was cast as adultery and possibly cultic prostitution as early as the prophet Hosea (late eighth century). Sexual excess as a polemic against idolatry (e.g., Isa 57:3, 7–10) became a trope in the Hebrew Bible (Knust, 2006, pp. 7–8) and could be extended to polemic against nations that worship such idols (cf. *Sib. Or.* 3:8–45, on Rome). Idolatry in Judah and Israel during the divided monarchy could be portrayed as a form of prostitution (1 Kgs 14:24; 2 Kgs 23:7) and used in polemic against one's opponents (Jer 2:20; 3:6; cf. 2 Macc 6:4–5); in Numbers 25, often now deemed as reflecting postexilic concerns, Phineas's slaying of Zimri for sexual immorality occurred in the context of pagan sacrifice. The portrayal of the foreign woman recounted throughout Proverbs 1–9 (cf. Prov 23:7–8) may derive from similar social concepts. These biblical traditions provide the grounds for later Jewish polemic, though the later polemic is often shaped by Greco-Roman conventions. The danger associated with intermarriage is also a key biblical theme (Num 25; Ezra 9), leading to further castigation on sexual activities with those considered non-Jewish.

Sex and Class. As well as defining proper practice for Jews, sexual habits reflected class distinctions. Proper practice was less the determinant of class than the converse: class distinctions could be delineated through allowing certain sexual practices. Class within Judaism is ill-defined since much that is unspecified in biblical law is only partially clarified in later tradition and since nonliterary evidence is lacking. The one clear specification in the legal system is the identification of and special requirements for a priestly class, coupled with the distinction along gender lines between male and female. Purity laws served to distinguish between proper behavior distinct for priests or for women, and those transgressing the boundaries could be castigated (CD 5.6–7). We may note other class distinctions drawn, such as the typical distinction throughout antiquity between a slave and a freed person, and it can be presumed that economic distinctions, if varied, operated an effective distinction between groups. The little evidence we might derive for class as defined through sexuality functions in a way analogous to Jewish ethnic markers. Improper sexual behavior is attributed both to non-Jews and to those deemed as belonging to a lower class, as implied

by Rabbinic literature's suspicions of the sexual promiscuity of female slaves. Of key importance is the way in which the sexual act serves as a boundary to establish proper Jewish behavior.

Sex and Differentiation. It is striking that the majority of references to sexual practices are found in passages condemning such behavior. They form part of an oppositional identity whereby the authors present other nations as performing practices beyond acceptability. The roots of the topics chosen by Jewish writers lie in the biblical narratives, but the themes are often shaped more by concerns of the Greco-Roman world than by the biblical laws themselves.

Intermarriage. As noted, intermarriage was a concern in the Bible and continued in postbiblical Jewish literature. The book of Tobit (second century B.C.E.?), drawing particularly on Numbers 36, endorses endogamy (e.g., Tob 1:9; 4:12–13; 7:9–11) and especially the marrying of close family members. As a document that focuses on issues of diaspora living, the book seems to present this as a means of defining Jewish identity when among other nations. Exogamy or intermarriage is castigated as "prostitution" (*porneia*, Tob 4:12), implying that it is the equivalent of idolatry in biblical terms. The Greek Addition to Esther (C26–28; first century B.C.E.?) forbids marriage with any foreigner or even a proselyte, and Pseudo-Philo has Tamar declare she prefers incest to intermarriage (*Bib. Ant.* 9:5). It remains an enduring issue and can be found in many other texts from antiquity (e.g., *Testament of Levi, Jubilees*).

Rape. The act of raping an individual woman was seen as a typical act of the foreigner, such that the general Holofernes declares it would be deemed shameful of him if he did not rape Judith (Jdt 11:11–12). Rape is seen as a common practice of those from outside the norms of behavior (as the elders in *Susannah*) or as a form of condemnation of foreigners (e.g., *4 Ezra* 10.22; *2 Bar.* 21.11; 44.2; *T. Job* 39.1–2; Ps-Phoc. 198). The *Testament of Solomon* (first to second century C.E.) presents demonic behavior, combining pederasty, anal rape, and bestiality (*T. Sol.* 14:4). Rape as a form of marriage by capture was typified by the story of the rape of Dinah in Genesis 34. After Shechem captures and defiles Dinah, Shechem and his family are tricked into circumcision before being killed. The story leads to many variations on it, where the issue of purity of the Jews and some anti-Samaritan polemic intermingle (Jdt 9.2; Theod. 4.11; *Jos. Asen.* 23:14; Dem. 9).

Same-sex relations and bestiality. The one apparently explicit condemnation of male same-sex relations in the Bible is found in Leviticus 18:22 (cf. 20:13), a text open to a number of interpretations. Key to its understanding is the clear condemnation of the practice of men having sex "as with a woman," suggesting that it addresses the manner of sex, namely anal sex, rather than the act itself (cf. Boyarin, 1995). In this way, the Bible would conform to or be read subsequently as conforming to the Greek understanding of male same-sex acts: as famously understood by Dover (1978), Greek homosexuality was not an equal affair and was deemed acceptable only in the case of pederasty, when an adult male had sex with a younger boy (*pais*) in the submissive position. The act was permitted because the boy was in the junior position; it was an affront to social norms only if the senior took the submissive position, a situation that would then transcend social norms and class, since the man would be considered as taking on the role of the female or slave. The fact that the word *pais* can also denote a slave reinforces the submissive role of the receptive partner. While Jewish texts identify Jewish practice as abstaining from same-sex male relations, the practice of other nations is often condemned for transcending social norms and categories rather than for the male-male sexual act itself.

Frequent polemic in the *Sibylline Oracles* (of various dates) draws upon classical vocabulary to use descriptions of same-sex acts as terms of abuse and to distinguish the proper behavior of Jews from other nations. *Sibylline* 3.162–195 (second century B.C.E.) chastises a kingdom to come (probably Rome), specifically identifying same-sex male relations (*arsenikos*) and the setting up of boys (*pais*) in shameful houses. It appears that the sex here is between equals rather than with a junior, while male prostitution is condemned because it was seen as a violation of behavioral norms and perceived as effeminization of the person (Aeschines, *Against Timarchus* 185). The same *Sibylline* (3:394–600) describes in some detail

how the Jews surpass other nations by observing wedlock and abstaining from intercourse with male children (cf. *Sib. Or.* 4:31–33). The naming of many nations—Phoenicians, Egyptians, Romans, Greeks, Persians, Galatian, and all Asia—makes clear how the Judeans are their opposites. In similar fashion, *Sibylline* 5 (from the time of Hadrian) portrays Rome as effeminate (*thēludenēs*, 5:167), presumably implying she takes the female role in same-sex relations. It goes further and suggests Romans indulge in incest (so, too, *Pss. Sol.* 8:9) and bestiality (5:386–396). Although bestiality is a separate category, it reflects the transgression of categories in the same way as acts of improper male same-sex relations.

Androgyny. Comparable to the inappropriateness of homosexual role reversals where men appear to be women, the phenomenon of androgyny (one person combining male and female characteristics) also transcended such boundaries. Such gender mixing, presumably to be avoided in the light of the biblical injunction against cross-dressing (Deut 22:5), elicited fascination among Greeks. This is illustrated by the famous case in the Hippocratic corpus (mid-fourth century B.C.E.) of Phaethousa, who grew a beard and stopped menstruating when her husband was sent into exile (*Epidemics* 6.8.32). The Platonic myth of early humans originally being androgynous before being divided and hence being in perpetual search for their other half (*Symposium* 189e) was an idealized form of androgyny that found expression in classical art from the fourth century B.C.E. on, seen in depictions both of the god Hermaphroditus and of feminine expressions in male deities (Ajootian, 1999). By contrast, the actual identification of real-life human hermaphrodites led to condemnation and stereotyping.

An early indication of this condemnation in Jewish tradition is in the Septuagint translation of Proverbs (second century B.C.E.) where, in contrast to the quite different Hebrew text, the androgynous person will suffer as much as fools (Prov 18:8, "Fear casts down the hesitant, and the souls of the hermaphrodite will hunger"; cf. Prov 19:15). The hermaphrodite has already become an object of contempt or social outcast, a member of a lower class. The problem of the hermaphrodite becomes an issue in Jewish law where the ambiguity of the gender raises problems as to which laws apply—those for women or those for men (see *m. Bik.* 4; *t. Bik.* 2:3). This is to be seen as separate from the influence of the Platonic myth, which found its way into interpretations of Adam as a hermaphrodite in the first-century Jewish philosopher Philo (*Alleg. Interp.* 2, 4.12–13) and the Midrash (*Ber. Rab.* 8:1).

Role reversal. Role reversal whereby men take on women's characteristics or women take on male roles is an extended version of this confusion of male and female identities. Solomon's lack of control led to the shame of being dominated by a woman (Sir 47.19–21), a tendency of foolish men (1 Esdr 4:18–19; cf. *T. Jud.* 15.5–6). The portrayal of Holofernes in the book of Judith (second century B.C.E.), as Sisera before him (Judg 4; Ps-Philo, *Bib. Ant.* 31:3–7), is that of a military general overcome by the wiles of a woman. So, too, Samson (*Bib. Ant.* 43:5). Women meanwhile can take on male roles, as Judith does by defeating the enemy through sexual exploitation. That this was somehow inappropriate is seen in Pseudo-Philo's dismissal of Deborah's rule as punishment for Israel's men to be ruled by a woman (*Bib. Ant.* 30:2). Such female reversal of position, although enshrined in such biblical stories as that of Sisera, finds its greatest expression in Greek tragedy and comedy, as in Euripides's *Medea*, whose eponymous protagonist prefers to fight in battle line than to give birth (289–291; cf. Aristophanes's *Lysistrata; Assembly of Women*). In Jewish sources this is perhaps most explicit in 4 Maccabees from the second-century C.E., where the mother of the martyrs shows manly courage (14:11). Such role reversals transcend biological Greek understanding and the social segregation of gendered roles in Judaism.

Sex with slaves. Sex with slaves was a widespread activity in antiquity, reflecting the abuse of power through sexuality. It fits well into the social stratification of sexual acts, where male slaves are feminized through anal sex and thereby their lowly position objectified. The fact that male slaves worked in the household, the traditional domain for women, also emasculated them, placing them on an equal footing with women (who did not escape sexual abuse) and minors. That this was an issue in Judaism is shown by

Ben Sira (early second century B.C.E.), who rules against the sexual exploitation of slaves and forbids sex even with one's own maidservant (Sir 41:22). Philo recognizes but subverts the reality that slave owners treated their slaves like animals (*Spec. Laws* 2:83). The Mishnah (ca. 200 C.E.) also notes that the more female slaves an owner has, the more chances he has for unchastity (*m. 'Abot.* 2:7). Legal traditions accordingly developed around slaves (Hezser, 2005), especially concerning limitations on priests regarding marriage to a freed slave or proselyte; a female freed slave cannot marry a priest, even if a male freedman can marry a woman of priestly family (*m. Bik.* 1:5), since a female slave would be suspected of sexual promiscuity (*t. Hor.* 2:11).

The treatment of slaves typifies how sex can be used as a means of class distinctions, drawing upon Greco-Roman practice where the Bible is silent. The establishment of Augustan *mores* in the first century probably had some effect, but in similar fashion to Christian households we must assume a dual morality in which the exploitation of sex slaves contravened the ethics of the household (cf. Glancy, 2011, pp. 133–152). While accusations of pederasty and rape could be used as polemic against other nations as a mark of Jewish dissociation, they could also be used internally within Judaism as a mark of class distinction.

[*See also* Children, *subentry* Greek World; Gender Transgression, *subentries on* Early Judaism *and* Roman World; Race, Class, and Ethnicity, *subentries on* Greek World *and* Hebrew Bible; Same-Sex Relations, *subentry* Early Judaism; Sexual Transgression, *subentry* Early Judaism; *and* Sexual Violence, *subentries on* Early Judaism *and* Greek World.]

BIBLIOGRAPHY

Aileen Ajootian. "The Only Happy Couple: Hermaphrodites and Gender." In *Naked Truths: Women, Sexuality, and Gender in Classical Art and Archaeology*, edited by Olga Koloski-Ostrow and Claire L. Lyons, pp. 220–242. London: Routledge, 1999.

Boyarin, Daniel. "Are There Any Jews in 'The History of Sexuality'?" *Journal of the History of Sexuality* 5 (1995): 333–355.

Boyarin, Daniel. *Border Lines: The Partition of Judaeo-Christianity.* Philadelphia: University of Pennsylvania Press, 2004.

Brisson, Luc. *Sexual Ambivalence: Androgyny and Hermaphroditism in Graeco-Roman Antiquity.* Berkeley: University of California Press, 2002.

Clarysse, Willy, and Dorothy J. Thompson. *Counting the People in Hellenistic Egypt.* 2 vols. Cambridge, Mass.: Cambridge University Press, 2006.

Cohen, Shaye J. D. "Religion, Ethnicity and 'Hellenism' in the Emergence of Jewish Identity in Maccabean Palestine." In *Religion and Religious Practice in the Seleucid Kingdom,* edited by Pers Bilde et al., pp. 204–223. Aarhus, Denmark: Aarhus University Press, 1990.

Cohen, Shaye J. D. *The Beginnings of Jewishness: Boundaries, Varieties, Uncertainties.* Hellenistic Culture and Society 31. Berkeley: University of California Press, 1999.

Collins, John J. *Between Athens and Jerusalem: Jewish Identity in the Hellenistic Diaspora.* 2d ed. Grand Rapids, Mich.: Eerdmans, 2000.

Dover, Kenneth J. *Greek Homosexuality.* London: Duckworth, 1978.

Foucault, Michel. *The History of Sexuality.* Vol. 1: *An Introduction.* London: Allen Lane, 1976.

Glancy, Jennifer A. *Slavery as Moral Problem: In the Early Church and Today.* Minneapolis: Fortress, 2011.

Goodblatt, David. *Elements of Ancient Jewish Nationalism.* Cambridge, U.K.: Cambridge University Press, 2006.

Hall, Edith. *Inventing the Barbarian: Greek Self-Definition through Tragedy.* Oxford: Oxford University Press, 1989.

Hall, Jonathan M. *Hellenicity: Between Ethnicity and Culture.* Chicago: University of Chicago Press, 2002.

Hezser, Catherine. *Jewish Slavery in Antiquity.* Oxford: Oxford University Press, 2005.

Knust, Jennifer W. *Abandoned to Lust: Sexual Slander and Ancient Christianity.* New York: Columbia University Press, 2006.

Koltun-Fromm, Naomi. *Hermeneutics of Holiness: Ancient Jewish and Christian Notions of Sexuality and Religious Community.* Oxford: Oxford University Press, 2010.

Loader, William. *The Pseudepigrapha on Sexuality: Attitudes towards Sexuality in Apocalypses, Testaments, Legends, Wisdom, and Related Literature, with a Contribution by Ibolya Balla on Ben Sira/Sirach.* Grand Rapids, Mich.: Eerdmans, 2011.

Marchal, Joseph A. "The Usefulness of an Onesimus: The Sexual Use of Slaves and Paul's Letter to Philemon." *Journal of Biblical Literature* 130 (2011): 749–770.

Mason, Steve. "Jews, Judaeans, Judaizing, Judaism: Problems of Categorization in Ancient History." *Journal for the Study of Judaism* 38 (2007): 457–512.

Satlow, Michael. *Tasting the Dish: Rabbinic Rhetorics of Sexuality.* Brown Judaic Studies 303. Atlanta: Scholars Press, 1995.

Schwartz, Seth. *Imperialism and Jewish Society, 200 B.C.E. to 640 C.E.* Princeton, N.J.: Princeton University Press, 2001.

Schwartz, Seth. "How Many Judaisms Were There?" *Journal of Ancient Judaism* 2 (2011): 208–238.

Thompson, Dorothy J. "Hellenistic Hellenes: The Case of Ptolemaic Egypt." In *Ancient Perceptions of Greek Ethnicity,* edited by Irad Malkin, pp. 301–322. Center for Hellenic Studies Colloquia 5. Cambridge, Mass.: Harvard University Press, 2001.

James K. Aitken

Early Church

Early Christian writings are replete with examples of racial, ethnic, and class differences. These examples bear witness to the fact that the early church was composed of a wide variety of diversified communities geographically dispersed throughout lands situated along both the ancient Mediterranean Sea and the Red Sea. Scholarship on this topic has been generated along a number of trajectories that emphasize the rhetorical, theological, ideological, and ecclesial debates that are engendered as a result of the diverse composition of early Christian communities. For interpreters of the Bible and the early church, a good starting point for understanding race, ethnicity, and class is to clarify the ancient terminology and then to explore the different ways in which early Christian writers used this terminology and related conceptual categories to advance their arguments and understandings of the faith. Of equal importance is the need for interpreters to assess and understand the ways in which modern debates and the scholarship itself reflect racialized assumptions implicit in the conceptual and contextual worldviews of scholars dealing with this topic.

Race, ethnicity, and class also call attention to the power dynamics among early Christians and thus can be understood as social and political constructs for designating groups of people, as well as a rhetorical strategy for boundary making and self-definition. These social and political constructs are not isolated from the gendered realities that also existed in the early church. And thus, an intersectional interpretive framework that opens new possibilities for analyzing all of the constitutive elements of social relationships based on markers of difference is both recommended and necessary to uncover the interlocking systems of oppression implicit in writings that deal with race, ethnicity, and class (Crenshaw, 1995). In other words, it is impossible to discuss race, ethnicity, and class without also analyzing gender as a social construct and tool for political analysis (Scott, 1999).

Ethnicity. References to ethnicity (Gk *ethnos, ethnē, ethnikos*) are dispersed throughout biblical and non-biblical writings to indicate nations, groups of people, foreigners, gentiles, and "others." Ethnicity is generally defined in essentializing terms, which focus on what are considered fixed or observable qualities inherent in a particular ethnic group. In this way, ethnicity is understood as a biological feature of descent or ancestry referring to blood, seed, kinship, or genealogy. Cultural anthropologists and sociologists define ethnicity as a social construct subject to change depending on historical time and circumstances. Still others note that "ethnicity" is an "invented term," the product of modern scholarship (Sollers, 1989). Ethnicity is also closely related to race inasmuch as it is a social construct and, in this regard, terms such as *laos, phylon, genos, genus, natio,* and *syngeneia* are often interchangeably associated with ethnicity.

Among early Christians, ethnicity is generally connected with texts that attempt to demonstrate the universalizing and inclusive impulse of early Christianity, that is, that Christianity is to extend to the ends of the world (Acts 1:8c). This broad inclusivity is represented by the Ethiopian (*Aithiops*) eunuch, the ideal exemplar of conversion to Christianity (Acts 8:26–39). Ethnicity is also used to isolate some of the intra-Christian disputes in early Jewish-Christian communities, whereby differences between Jews (*Ioudaioi*) and gentiles (*ethnē*) become the hallmark for representing insiders and outsiders. It is this ethnic binary and other polarities of difference that Paul and his followers seek to overcome in their teachings (e.g., Gal 3:28, "There is no longer Jew or Greek, there is no longer slave or free, there is no

longer male and female; for all of you are one in Christ Jesus"; 1 Corinthians 12:13, "For in the one Spirit we were all baptized into one body—Jews or Greeks, slaves or free—and we were all made to drink of one Spirit"; Colossians 3:11, "there is no longer Greek and Jew, circumcised and uncircumcised, barbarian, Scythian, slave and free; but Christ is all and in all!"). Thus, the relativizing of ethnic (as well as gender and class) differences is one strategy for building a presumably universal and inclusive worldview among the early Christians.

Yet interpretations of ethnicity become more complicated when texts such as Acts 21:38 confuse Paul for "the Egyptian" (*hoi Aigyptios*) who was known for leading revolts among the early Jewish Christians in Jerusalem (Josephus, *Ant.* 169–172). In this case of mistaken identity (Acts 21:27–39), Luke strategically uses "the Egyptian" as a discursive device to disassociate Paul from those persons who would have been understood to have a more oppositional brand of Christianity. Among the Gospel writers, Jesus is depicted as one who associates with a Samaritan (John 4:1–42) and a Syrophoenician woman (Mark 7:24–30; cf. Matt 15:21–28), yet instructs his followers not to pray as the *ethnē* (Matt 6:32). When the writer of Titus refers to Cretans as "liars, vicious brutes, and lazy gluttons" (Tit 1:12–13), this is not simply directed at the Cretans, but rather at those who "must be silenced.… teaching for sordid gain what it is not right to teach" (Tit 1:11). In these examples, it is useful to examine the symbolic use of ethnicity through the lens of what is referred to as "ethnopolitical" rhetoric (Byron, 2002).

Ethnopolitical rhetoric, discursive elements in texts that refer to ethnic identities or geographical locations and function as political invective, is found not only in biblical writings, but also in patristic and monastic sources. For example, Tertullian says that "when God threatens Egypt and Ethiopia with extinction, he pronounces sentence on every sinful nation" (*Spect.* 3). Origen compared gentile converts to the black bride of Solomon; "though once blackened by their sin, they were now whitened by the grace of God" (*Hom. Cant.* 1.6). This argument was repeated by Jerome: "At one time we were *Ethiopians* in our vices and sins. How so? Because our sins had *blackened* us"

(*Homily 18 on Psalm 86*). According to Epiphanius, Origen's defense of the black bride in the Song of Solomon seems to have led him into a dilemma. The Roman authorities arrested him and offered him the following choice: either commit apostasy or have sexual intercourse with an *Ethiopian*:

> On account of his remarkable holiness and erudition he incurred the greatest jealousy and this stirred up even more those who were magistrates and prefects at that particular time. With devilish ingenuity the evil-doers contrived to bring disgrace upon the man and, what is more, to mark out this sort of vengeance: that they would procure an *Ethiopian* for the purpose of causing defilement to his body. In response to this, Origen, not tolerating that deceptive plan of the devil proclaimed that of the two propositions set before him he preferred to offer sacrifice.

It is not unusual to find references to ethnicity also intersecting with images of sexual encounters as in the foregoing example from Origen. Yet, this hyperbole about Ethiopian women is a recurring theme in late antique monastic writings such as the *Sayings of the Desert Fathers*:

> Twenty days passed when, suddenly, he saw the work of the devil appear before him, and it stood before him in the form of an *Ethiopian* woman, smelly and disgusting in appearance, so much so that he could not bear her smell. She then said to him, "I am she who appears sweet in the hearts of men, but because of your obedience and your labor, God does not permit me to seduce you, but I have let you know my foul odor." The Ethiopian woman left, and he thanked God. He came to his father and said: "Father, I no longer wish to go into the world, for I have seen the work of the devil and have smelled her foul odor." (Byron, 2002, p. 98)

The intersection of ethnicity and sexuality in this text is not necessarily concerned with the vivid encounter between the Ethiopian woman and the young man aspiring to become a monk. Rather, this story bears witness to the social relations, perceived threats, and other status disparities that existed in late antiquity.

Race. *Genos* ("race, family, or type") appears in the New Testament 20 times, in Matthew (Matt 13:47),

Mark (7:26; 9:29), Acts (4:6, 36; 7:13, 19; 13:26; 17:28, 29; 18:2, 24), 1 and 2 Corinthians (1 Cor 12:10, 28; 14:10; 2 Cor 11:26), Galatians (1:14), Philippians (3:5), 1 Peter (2:9), and Revelation (22:16). Paul explicitly refers to Judaism as a race in Galatians 1:14, and he implies that non-Christian Jews are a race in 2 Corinthians 11:26. Paul's reference to the "race of Israel" in Philippians 3:5 may refer to non-Christian Jews. In the works of the Apostolic Fathers and beyond, explicit reference to Christians as a race increases, to the point where it becomes a common phrase for referring to Christian worship in the third century. Clement of Alexandria, for example, quotes the *Preaching of Peter* where the author warns his readers against the worship of Greeks and Jews (*Strom.* 6.5.41) and calls his Christian addresses "ye who worship him anew as a third race (*tritō[i]) genei*)." The second-century text, *Epistle to Diognetus*, refers to Christians as a new race (*kainon touto genos*) in the context of describing the religion of the Christians. . . . and how they worship God (*Diogn.* 1.1). The *Martyrdom of Polycarp* likewise identifies Christians as the "godly, reverent, and righteous race" (*Mart. Pol.* 3.2; 14.1). Pseudo-Cyprian's *De Pascha*, written in the mid-third century, contains the expression, "We Christians are the third race."

The examples above are not to be associated uncritically with the modern understanding of race and racism, which is grounded in the nineteenth-century belief that a particular group of people is superior to another based on assumptions about social and moral traits predetermined by innate biological characteristics. In this regard, race is considered immutable, typically determined by skin color, and consists of a core inherited "essence." Although some scholars may easily use the terms "race" and "ethnicity" interchangeably, assuming that there is no easy way to distinguish the differences in modern parlance (Buell, 2005), it is not necessarily the case that the ancient writers were conceiving of race (*genos*) or ethnicity (*ethnos*) in the same way that these terms are used in contemporary discourses. The key interpretive distinction to make in reading for race in early Christian writings is the realization that our modern legacy of racial thinking very much informs and influences what is revealed or ignored in ancient writings. Indeed, attitudes about race and racism *in the present* affect how one interprets race and ethnicity *in the past.*

Modern Debates about Race and Ethnicity. Modern interpreters of race and ethnicity often find themselves weaving around a number of scholarly debates and self-understandings of identity. Although scholars across a wide range of disciplines might agree that racism is a modern construct and thus beyond the purview of ancient studies, biblical and early church scholarship is now understood as having deeply embedded "racializing" tendencies inherited from the intellectually dishonest historiography of the nineteenth-century philosophical movements in Germany that effectively erased Africa and Africans from the geographical landscape of antiquity (Kelley, 2002). The covert racism embedded in this interpretive tradition was inherited by biblical scholars in the United States and invariably led to racialized studies about the historical Jesus, the missionary activities of Paul, and many other aspects of the Bible, including the "myth of Ham" (Gen 9:18–25).

One of the most persuasive studies about racism or color prejudice in the classical world was provided by Snowden's (1970) landmark volume *Blacks in Antiquity,* wherein he collected a convincing set of representations of Ethiopians in the Greco-Roman world and concluded that there was no racism or color prejudice in antiquity. His study, however, emphasized a wide range of positive depictions of Ethiopians without likewise revealing the ubiquitous examples of pejorative depictions of Ethiopians in Greco-Roman writings. His research, conducted over a fifteen-year period and published on the heels of the tumultuous civil rights movement, not surprisingly offered a timely positive scholarly balm for the race question during his contemporary setting.

Although several scholars have noted limitations in Snowden's basic hypothesis regarding racism and racial prejudice in antiquity, generally his claims are regarded as the unrelenting benchmark upon which biblical scholars, church historians, and others exploring matters related to race in the ancient world begin and summarily end their research. His work, therefore, functions as a convenient justification for focusing on race as solely a product of modernity (Kelley, 2002). Such a focus invariably lets the classical writers and the classical world off the hook when it comes to exploring questions related to race in antiquity. Furthermore, some scholars appeal to Snowden's work as a way of absolving themselves of the responsibility of taking seriously the racialized attitudes that may have existed in the ancient world as well as their own subconscious racializing interpretive tendencies that continue to shape the hermeneutical assumptions and methods they employ. This, however, is not the final word. Many scholars are making great strides in raising awareness about racial ethnic interpretations of early Christian writings (e.g., Buell, 2005, Hodge, 2007, Nasrallah and Fiorenza, 2009, Sechrest, 2009). Yet there is still not a critical framework for analyzing the impact of white privilege in the interpretive process (McIntosh, 2010). Uncovering this "invisible" hermeneutic will lead to a wider range of exegetical, pedagogical, and curricular opportunities for theological educators and scholars of religion (Byron, 2012).

African American biblical interpreters have been on the forefront of addressing questions related to race in the Bible, initially during the 1970s and 1980s, through investigations of the "presence" of blacks in the Bible and, since the 1990s, through a variety of reconstructive cultural and historical interpretations and ideological readings of biblical and nonbiblical writings. Notably, Felder's (1989) conceptual framework for analyzing the "racial motifs in biblical narratives" stirred a new wave of scholarship dealing with racism in the Bible and contemporary biblical scholarship at the close of the twentieth century. Yet he, like others mentioned above, followed the assessments of Snowden and concluded, "We do not find any elaborate definitions or theories about race in antiquity" (Felder, 1989, p. 37).

During the first decade of the twenty-first century, a new wave of scholarship is demonstrating how racism was indeed "invented" in antiquity (Isaac, 2004) and furthermore holds "symbolic" significance for the authors of ancient texts (Byron, 2009). The categories of race and ethnicity are also being analyzed more critically as interchangeable social constructs, which enable interpreters to assess the identity-making strategies of the ancients. Isaac (2004) has identified what he calls "prototypes of racism" or "proto-racism" in Greco-Roman antiquity. Using a geographical approach, he examines specific groups (e.g., Syrians, Phoenicians, Egyptians, Parthians, Persians, Gauls, Germans, and Jews) for the purpose of isolating the effects of Greek and Roman imperialism as manifested in racial ethnic prejudice and stereotypes.

In addition to African American scholars, Latino/a and Asian American scholars are also providing many critical studies that deal with race, ethnicity, and class in the Bible and beyond. Indeed, the collaborative projects generated by "underrepresented" racial and ethnic interpreters identify convergences and differences in reading strategies among these different groups of interpreters and also highlight the challenging intersectionalities of race, gender, sex, and class that arise in the interpretive process (Bailey et al., 2009). Through this scholarship, an intentional turn to interdisciplinary methodologies and reading strategies leads to a broader palette of interpretive possibilities. As noted above, scholars who analyze race and ethnicity in some cases allude to the dynamics associated with class distinctions that are implicit in many of the texts. Yet for the most part, interpretations about class and social status are generally made in isolation of the racial and ethnic distinctions that existed in the Roman world among the early Christians. The following section is an effort to highlight some of the potential areas for further study vis-à-vis class analysis.

Class. Roman society was divided into distinct classes or "orders"—senatorial, equestrian, provincial decurian, freeborn and slave, patrician and plebeian, citizen and noncitizen (Rankin, 2004). Many of the writings in the New Testament indicate that class and status differences were a primary concern throughout the early Christian communities. In Corinth, for example, Paul is dealing with a stratified community that is composed of those who are wise, powerful, rich, honored, strong, and kingly (1 Cor 1:26–30; 4:8–10) as well as those who are "weak" or considered "fools for the sake of Christ" (1 Cor 4:10). Heads of house churches (*ekklesiai*), such as Gaius, Crispus, and Stephanas (1 Cor 1:14; 16:15–17; Rom 16:23; Acts 18:8), emerged as key players in the overall mission of Paul. In these early communities, women were also leaders in these assemblies, such as Chloe (1 Cor 1:11) and Prisca (Rom 16:3–4; or Priscilla as in Acts 18:2). In the letter of James, the author counsels against showing favoritism so that one who has gold rings and dresses in fine clothes is not privileged over a poor person (*ptōchos*) dressed in dirty clothes (Jas 2:1–4). Both are to be equally welcomed into the assembly. This preferential option for the poor is subsequently turned into a theological teaching (Jas 2:5): "Has not God chosen the poor in the world to be rich in faith and to be heirs of the kingdom that he has promised to those who love him?"

From these examples, we can see how early Christians were a type of kinship community that transcended fixed social categories and class boundaries. Male/female, slave/free, rich/poor, Jew/gentile, barbarian/Scythian, circumcised/uncircumcised—the list goes on—are to find equal footing in a new realm of community that transcends perceived and real notions of difference. Ultimately the *ekklesia* was to be a place for freedom: "for freedom Christ has set us free. Stand firm, therefore, and do not submit again to a yoke of slavery" (Gal 5:1); "where the Spirit of the Lord is, there is freedom" (2 Cor 3:17). Further, the ritual of baptism served as the rite of passage that erased ethnic, gender, and class distinctions: "as many of you as were baptized into Christ have clothed yourselves with Christ. There is no longer Jew or Greek, there is no longer slave or free, there is no longer male and female; for all of you are one in Christ Jesus" (Gal 3:27–28).

This idealist picture of the *ekklesia* takes a marked turn by the late first/early second century. Thus, by the writing of the deutero-Pauline epistles (Colossians, Ephesians, and 2 Thessalonians), the egalitarian house church becomes the patriarchal *Haustafeln*. And instead of shared leadership and free expression of spiritual gifts (1 Cor 12–14), hierarchies are established based on the male as head of the household (*paterfamilias*), and in turn women, slaves, and children are relegated to subordinate positions. The Household Codes (*Haustafeln*) become the source for competing and contrasting worldviews about ethnicity, race, and class (Eph 5:21—6:9 [cf. Col 3:18—4:1].

In particular, the Household Codes provide an opportunity to examine the prevalence of slavery in the Greco-Roman world.

Slaves were visible in every strata of society working in mines and the agricultural estates of the patricians. Slaves also worked in flour mills; constructed roads, aqueducts, and city buildings; and maintained public baths and temples. They replenished the supply of gladiators and prostitutes (*pornai*). In the domestic sphere, slaves worked as business managers, secretaries, merchants, nurses, tutors, pedagogues, barbers, butlers, laundrywomen, seamstresses, bath attendants, and wet nurses. Dancers and actors were also slaves (Martin, 2005). The teachings about slavery dispersed throughout the New Testament (Phlm; 1 Cor 7:17–24; Eph 6:5–6; Col 3:22) open the possibility for pursuing multilayered intersectional analysis that goes beyond strict binary assumptions about gender, ethnicity, class, and sexuality.

Interpretive Implications and Opportunities. By analyzing biblical and early church writings through the lens of race, ethnicity, and class, interpreters must address the hidden ideological assumptions that are implicit in ancient texts and complicit in the methods that are utilized to interpret the texts. Moreover, these categories call attention to the notion of intersectionality that is now a necessary theoretical framework for addressing the multiply marginalized subjectivities embedded in ancient writings and hovering in the scholarly legacy of feminist and antiracist work. In doing this work, sexuality becomes an explicit frame of reference and not hidden or embedded in predictable "gender" constructs. As much as the early Christians sought to neutralize or relativize ethnic, gender, and class differences (e.g., Gal 3:26–28), it is now generally accepted among scholars of ancient biblical and patristic literature that "difference matters" and indeed differences have much to teach us about the power dynamics within early Christian communities. The recognition of the multidimensional layers of reality among early Christians challenges interpreters to acknowledge the multiple sites (race, gender, class, and sexuality) that are continually being negotiated in contemporary interpretations of the Bible and the early church.

[*See also* Family Structures, *subentry* Early Church; Intersectional Studies; Legal Status, *subentries on* Early Church *and* Roman World; Mujerista Criticism; Race, Class, and Ethnicity, *subentries on* New Testament *and* Roman World; *and* Womanist Criticism.]

BIBLIOGRAPHY

Bailey, Randall C., Tat-siong Benny Liew, and Fernando F. Segovia, eds. *They Were All Together in One Place? Toward Minority Biblical Criticism.* Atlanta: Society of Biblical Literature, 2009.

Buell, Denise Kimber. *Why This New Race: Ethnic Reasoning in Early Christianity.* New York: Columbia University Press, 2005.

Byron, Gay L. "Ancient Ethiopia and the New Testament: Ethnic (Con)texts and Racialized (Sub)texts." In *They Were All Together in One Place? Toward Minority Biblical Criticism*, edited by Randall Bailey, Tat-siong Benny Liew, and Fernando Segovia, pp. 161–190. Atlanta: Society of Biblical Literature, 2009.

Byron, Gay L. "Race, Ethnicity, and the Bible: Pedagogical Challenges and Curricular Opportunities." *Teaching Theology and Religion* 15, no. 2 (2012): 105–124.

Byron, Gay L. *Symbolic Blackness and Ethnic Difference in Early Christian Literature.* New York and London: Routledge, 2002.

Crenshaw, Kimberlé Williams. "Mapping the Margins: Intersectionality, Identity Politics, and Violence against Women of Color." In *Critical Race Theory: The Key Writings That Formed the Movement*, edited by Kimberlé Crenshaw, Neil Gotanda, Gary Peller, and Kendall Thomas, pp. 357–383. New York: New Press, 1995.

Felder, Cain Hope. *Troubling Biblical Waters: Race, Class, and Family.* Maryknoll, N.Y.: Orbis, 1989.

Hodge, Caroline Johnson. *If Sons, Then Heirs: A Study of Kinship and Ethnicity in the Letters of Paul.* New York: Oxford University Press, 2007.

Isaac, Benjamin. *The Invention of Racism in Classical Antiquity.* Princeton, N.J.: Princeton University Press, 2004.

Kelley, Shawn. *Racializing Jesus: Race, Ideology and the Formation of Modern Biblical Scholarship.* London and New York: Routledge, 2002.

Martin, Clarice J. "The Eyes Have It: Slaves in the Communities of Christ-Believers." In *A People's History of Christianity.* Vol. 1: *Christian Origins*, edited by Richard Horsley, pp. 221–239. Minneapolis: Fortress, 2005.

McIntosh, Peggy. "White Privilege: Unpacking the Invisible Knapsack." In *Race, Class, and Gender in the United States*, 8th ed., edited by Paula S. Rothenberg, pp. 172–176. New York: Worth, 2010.

Nasrallah, Laura, and Elisabeth Schüssler Fiorenza, eds. *Prejudice and Christian Beginnings: Investigating Race, Gender, and Ethnicity in Early Christian Studies*. Minneapolis: Fortress, 2009.

Rankin, David. "Class Distinction as a Way of Doing Church: The Early Fathers and the Christian Plebs." *Vigiliae Christianae* 58 (2004): 298–315.

Scott, Joan Wallach. *Gender and the Politics of History*. Rev. ed. New York: Columbia University Press, 1999.

Sechrest, Love L. *A Former Jew: Paul and the Dialectics of Race*. New York: T&T Clark, 2009.

Snowden, Frank M., Jr. *Blacks in Antiquity: Ethiopians in the Greco-Roman Experience*. Cambridge, Mass.: Harvard University Press, 1970.

Sollers, Werner, ed. *The Invention of Ethnicity*. New York: Oxford University Press, 1989.

Gay L. Byron

READER-ORIENTED CRITICISM

"You Americans often have difficulty with Shakespeare. He was, after all, a very English poet and one can easily misinterpret the universal by misunderstanding the particular" (Bohannan, 1966, p. 1), said a British friend to Laura Bohannan, a North American anthropologist on her way to the Tiv of West Africa for fieldwork. Bohannan protested, insisting that "human nature is pretty much the same the whole world over; at least the general plot and motivation of the greater tragedies would always be clear everywhere although some details of custom might have to be explained" (p. 1). Failing to agree, her British friend gave her a copy of *Hamlet* for the journey, hoping that with prolonged meditation in the "African bush," Bohannan might "achieve the grace of correct interpretation" (p. 1), namely, the English one. Bohannan arrived at a season of heavy floods and hence spent most of her time reading *Hamlet* rather than doing anthropological fieldwork. As she writes, "before the end of the second month, grace descended on me. I was quite sure that *Hamlet* had one possible interpretation, and that one universally obvious" (p. 2).

When the Tiv invited Bohannan to tell them a story, it was *Hamlet* that she chose. Bohannan's choice was intentional as she thought to herself, "here was my

chance to prove *Hamlet* universally intelligible" (1966, p. 2). She found the opposite. The elders sitting and listening protested immediately about a dead king walking; for them, the word for scholar also meant a witch; a dead person could not walk, talk, or cast a shadow; Claudius's marriage to Gertrude the widow of the late king was culturally approved right away; that Hamlet scolded his mother and sought to kill his stepfather was shocking and unacceptable behavior; and they were convinced that Hamlet's madness could only be caused by witches who want to hurt him or creatures from the bush. Altogether, they stopped Bohannan nineteen times questioning, commenting, debating the story among themselves, disapproving, approving, and explaining the story the way it should go, according to their views, before they allowed Bohannan to continue with her narration. In the process the Tiv took *Hamlet* from Bohannan, retelling it, explaining it, and providing motivation behind the events in a fashion that took the story to a completely different direction. They were rewriting the story according to their worldviews and norms so much so that, as Bohannan notes, "*Hamlet* was again a good story to them, but it was no longer quite the same story to me" (p. 10). One of the key issues they wanted to know was whether the late king and Claudius were blood brothers. Bohannan soon realized that the story did not provide information about it. It was a gap.

When Bohannan became too upset with their numerous interruptions and decided to stop, they confidently urged her on, saying, "You tell the story well and we are listening. But it is clear that the elders of your country never told you what the story really means" (1966, p. 11). In so doing they, like Bohannan's English friend, believed that they had the correct meaning of *Hamlet*. Indeed at the very end they underlined their claim to correct interpretation, saying, "You must tell us some more stories of your country. We, who are elders, will instruct you in their true meaning, so that when you return to your own land your elders will see that you have not been sitting in the bush, but among those who know things and have taught you wisdom" (p. 12). Bohannan, obviously, could no longer hold on to the idea that the meaning of a story can "be clear everywhere" since people are the same everywhere.

The Tiv's extensive retelling (read rewriting) of the story was based, among other things, on two factors. First, they did not view a story and a storyteller (or author) as unchangeable authorities and entities. Rather, a storyteller provides data (or story) for an active communal participation in the co-telling of the story with the listeners. The moment of telling and hearing a narrative is also a moment of writing a new narrative with and through an old one. The African concept of active listeners can range from simply urging the storyteller to continue telling the story, to participants' occasional commentary on certain aspects, to the extreme of the audience taking the story from the teller and beginning to retell it to a different direction (Dube, 1999, pp. 145–150; 2001, pp. 6–26; 2001, pp. 26–49). *Hamlet* clearly was subjugated to the latter.

Second, the Tiv retold *Hamlet* according to their worldviews, norms, and experiences. The fact that *Hamlet* was a story that embodied different cultural norms invited an intense retelling according to their cultural worldviews and experiences.

But the rewriting was on both sides. Bohannan, too, began to tinker with the story in the face of her new audience. First, she started narrating *Hamlet* not according to its written opening but in what she terms a "proper style" of the Tiv, saying "Not yesterday, not yesterday, but long ago a thing occurred" (1966, p. 3). With the numerous interruptions from the Tiv, who protested certain perspectives as unacceptable, Bohanan began rewriting the story in anticipation of their response. She admittedly skipped culturally controversial aspects and at times asserted some points, although she was admittedly not quite sure about it. The fact of the matter is that Bohannan was seated among a group of elders who were authorities on cultural interpretation in their own setting, and she knew she could not win the debate.

Interpretation and meaning-making is a power struggle. Bohannan highlights for us how readers are shaped by the communities of interpreters and power relations within their work setting. She also demonstrates how readers can inhabit conflicting positions within various authoritative communities of interpretation. Here the British and the Tiv elders had firmly asserted themselves as the holders of correct interpretation of *Hamlet*. Yet, by asserting their own meanings as true, they brought Bohannan's claim for one self-evident universal meaning of a text to a rest.

Definitions of Reader-Oriented Criticism. Reader-oriented-Criticism is a cluster of perspectives that study readers, reading processes, the impact of interpretative communities, and how meaning is produced (Tompkins, 1980, p. ix; Bible and Culture Collective, 1995, pp. 24–26; McKnight 2004, pp. 179) . It is "a mode of literary criticism that prioritizes the role of the reader (rather than the author's intentions or the text's actual structure) in both establishing the meaning of the text and evaluating its critical worth" (Buchanan, 2010, p. 400). E. V. McKnight explains that, "this approach views literature in terms of its readers and their values, attitude, and responses, thus supplementing or displacing approaches to literature that focus on either the universe imitated in the work, the author, the original audience, or the works itself" (2004, p. 179).

In reader-response criticism, the identity of the reader is thus crucial in evaluating the meaning that is produced. Given that readers are not islands but are always located in particular contexts and social structures, reader-response criticism also studies the interpretative communities that define the parameters of legitimate interpretations and the social location of the reader (Segovia and Tolbert, 1995a, 1995b). Interpretative communities, a term that was developed by Stanley Fish "to explain how diverse readers consistently produce similar readings of certain types of texts" (Buchanan, 2010, p. 251), refers to the social or academic bodies that provide conventions of writing and reading texts. In biblical studies, interpretative communities, for example, include academic associations such as a Society of Biblical Literature, Society of New Testament Studies, and Society for Old Testament Studies. These academic associations provide acceptable standards of reading through the types of papers that are featured in their annual general meetings and published in their journals. Interpretative communities for biblical scholars also include faith-based institutions such as churches and synagogues. Yet for minority readers, such as women, black people, LGBT communities, and Two-Thirds World scholars, their interest-specific associations and movements constitute alternative interpretative communities. It follows that one reader can belong to several interpretative communities which are sometimes in conflict with each other on supposedly acceptable ways of reading and interpretation.

Theories of Reader Response in the Western Guild. In the western guild, reader-oriented criticism rose in opposition to the formalist ways of reading that dismissed the readers' role. In formalist theory, a literary text was supposedly self-contained and adequately equipped to communicate its meaning. The readers' responsibility was to correctly interpret the literary text without imposing their own background, interest, or emotions. The essay that is most-famed for articulating this position is Wimsatt and Beardsley's "The Affective Fallacy," which defined those who confuse the poem with its results (Tompkins, 1980, p. ix).

Several scholars from various perspectives, such as psychology (Norman N. Holland), phenomenology (Wolfgang Iser), deconstruction (Jonathan Culler), and feminism (Judith Fetterly), began to theorise the reader back into action (see Tompkins, 1980). Stanley Fish, for example, began to describe the reading process, highlighting that it is temporary rather than a spatial activity. In his famed article, "Is There a Text in This Class?," Fish began to take his theory of reading further, arguing that each reader is not limited by the text. He also coined the term "interpretative communities" to explain why different readers may end up with similar readings. Iser coined the idea of the implied reader, which is the reader a literary work appears to be written for (Buchanan, 2010, p. 246). Arguing that the reader encounters gaps that need to be filled to make sense of the text, Iser associated meaning with the active participation of both the reader and text.

In biblical studies, the above journey of the reader is also observable. Historical critical methods trained readers to be exegetes who bring out meaning from the text, instead of carrying out eisegesis, which is reading one's perspectives into the text. The historical critical scholar was thus expected to be objective and neutral toward the text in order to allow the text to communicate its original or intended meaning. The role of the reader began to slowly be accepted with the rise of narrative and rhetorical criticism. The latter presupposes that the authors composed their texts to persuade the targeted reader, basically to provoke the emotional involvement of the reader. The reader, therefore, was not supposed to be disinterested and neutral. Narrative criticism with its model of communication regarded the real reader and the real author to be outside the communication model of the text. Within the text, however, there was an internally built implied reader and implied author, who represented the ideal reader—namely, one who would understand the text as author "intended." Narrative and rhetorical criticism thus began to introduce the reader back into the picture. However, both methods held that meaning was in the text. The reader needed to master the devices of the text in order to understand the text correctly. These, in other words, were not much of a departure from historical criticism, since they were using different terms to search for the original or intended meaning in the text. The reader was still the servant of the text. Biblical scholars eventually accepted some of the above reader-response theories, but apparently only as historical critical readers in disguise (Moore, 1989, pp. 71–107; Bible and Culture Collective, 1995, pp. 20–37; Moore and Sherwood, 2011, pp. 99–114).

Questions of Reader-Response Criticism. The major questions of reader-response criticism can roughly be broken into three:

- Who is the reader?
- What are the social structures and interpretative communities that inform the reader?
- Where is meaning located: within the text, within the reader, or somewhere between the two?

These questions offer a range of practices, answers, and perspectives. Reader-response criticism thus constitutes a range of practices, depending on the amount of power one wishes to give to the reader, the text, and the interpretative communities they subscribe to.

Gender, and other social categories, such as race, ethnicity, class, sexuality, religiosity, etc., are central to reader-response criticism. Since gender is a culture- and time-specific social construction of men and women into socially prescribed roles (Tolbert, 2000, pp. 99–105), how readers respond to and interpret a text is affected by their gender, together with other social factors of their identity (Lozada, 2000, pp. 113–119). A black woman from a low-class, heterosexual orientation, for example, and a white man from a high-class homosexual orientation would give a different meaning to the same text, since they bring different experiences, questions, concerns, and communities of reading to it. Indeed, each reader is capable of generating different meanings of the same text, since the factors of their identities are multiple.

Given that each reader's identity is complex and fluid, reader-response criticism births multiple meanings of the text. The various interpretations raise critical questions concerning the location of meaning: Is meaning in the text or in the reader or somewhere between the two? Where one locates meaning, more often than not, reflects one's ideological views toward the text. The biblical text, in particular, is given authority as a scripture. It is thus affected by fierce interpretative communities and institutions who guard its authority through promoting certain ways of reading. Assigning meaning to readers, no doubt, seems to compromise its authority. Consequently, reader-response criticism has notably generated as many readers in biblical studies, reflecting the struggle between those who seek to locate meaning in the text and those who seek to locate it elsewhere. According to Stephen D. Moore:

> During this time the amazing reader had many aliases and roles, engaging the text or emerging from it in guises such as the Implied Reader, the Informed Reader, the Narratee, and the Model Reader. The carnival also featured the Reader in the Text and the Flesh-and-Blood Reader, the Competent Reader and the Literent, the Encoded or Inscribed Reader, the Subjective Reader, Superreader, the Newreaders, and the Wilful Misreader. (1989, p. 71)

Moore lists other readers, such as the "Unfeeling Reader" and "The Repressed Reader." These are academic biblical readers, who live in the shadow of the historical-critical reading conventions. The latter insist that the text should be honored far above the individual readers. Moore, who has closely analyzed reader-response critics in biblical studies, has consistently maintained that they are largely historical-critical scholars masquerading as reader-response critics (Moore, 1989, pp. 71–107; Moore and Sherwood, 2011, pp. 99–114).

Gender and Reader-Response Criticism. Feminist, womanist, LGBT, and other minority readers are highly diverse groups in and within themselves, and their reading practices differ widely; any generalizations here are dictated by constraints of space. Gender constructions both of texts and also their interpretative communities are central to the reading practices of these groups. Beginning with Elizabeth Cady Stanton's observation that the Bible is a male book, feminist and womanist readers come to the text with a hermeneutic of suspicion, treating the text as a site of crime (Schüssler Fiorenza, 1985, pp. 125–136). As a male book, the Bible excludes women's stories and presents women characters from a patriarchal perspective; it has been written, interpreted, and translated by men for centuries. The biblical interpretative communities and conventions are, in other words, thoroughly patriarchal. Although one cannot generalize the political practices of feminist and womanist readers, for neither is allegiance to the biblical text a given; the so-called original or intended meaning of the biblical text is not benign, or even available, to these readers, nor are the subsequent interpretations. Given that for centuries biblical interpretation in the academy and faith institutions was dominated and controlled by males, feminist and womanist readers find the interpretative communities and their conventions unsettling, exclusive, oppressive, and misogynist.

Women of color have particularly underlined that in addition to gender oppression, race/ethnicity, and social class must be treated with equal seriousness. Reading the story of Abraham, Sarah, and Hagar illustrates the point. Whereas early white feminists, who underlined patriarchal oppression, regarded both Sarah and Hagar as oppressed women, African American women have pointed out that Hagar is additionally oppressed because of her ethnicity as an Egyptian woman and because of her class as a slave. Moreover, Hagar is even oppressed by Sarah, a woman of higher class and privileged race (Williams, 1993, pp. 15–29).

Unless feminist readers pay attention to the link between gender, class, and race/ethnicity, their interpretations remain oppressive to women of color and hence only partially committed to justice. Similarly, a major contribution to the understanding of gender has been made by LGBT communities, who underline the social construction of sex and sexuality as well as promblematize heteronormativity (Hornsby and Stone, 2011; Moore, 2001). Just as women have highlighted that biblical books and their interpretative communities are male-centered, LGBT readers have highlighted that they are also heterosexually defined. Heterosexual readers construct other forms of sexuality as deviance, and LGBT readers thus problematize compulsory heterosexuality (Rich, 1986) as an ideology that legitimates the marginalization of people of other sexual orientations. Drawing upon their historical and contemporary experiences, women of color and LGBT communities have thus pushed the boundaries of feminist practice to consider gender, its intersectionality with race/ethnicity, class, sex, and sexuality, and constructions of these categories in biblical texts and the interpretative communities (Briggs, 1994, pp. 218–236; Spencer, 2004, pp. 264–273).

Cheryl Exum, writing from a feminist perspective, holds that:

> The starting point of feminist criticism of the Bible is *not the biblical texts in their own right but the concerns of feminism as a worldview and as a political enterprise.* Recognizing that in the history of civilization women have been marginalized by men and denied access to positions of authority and influence, feminist criticism seeks to expose the strategies by which men have justified their control over women. (1995, p. 65, emphasis added)

The quote underlines that feminist and womanist readers assign priority to their own agenda rather than to the biblical text and its male-dominated interpretative communities. Feminism, as a worldview and a political movement that seeks to promote the empow-erment of women, constitutes an interpretative community for feminist and womanist biblical readers. These readers are often in conflict with various other interpretative communities in biblical studies, who do not sympathize with the feminist movement and who seek to assign greater authority to the biblical text.

Feminist and womanist readers, therefore, do not have an easy relationship with biblical and other canonical texts. Neither do they have easy relations with traditional interpretative conventions and communities. By practice, feminist and womanist readers seek to resist the textual patriarchal constructions. They often seek to reread the available stories and to reimagine and re-member the excluded voices and histories of women, a process that gives the reader more freedom and power to re-create the text in attempt to include that which was left out. Although feminist and womanist readers are not identical, their reading agenda tends to swing toward the reader than the text in its creative reading.

Employing queer theory, which "seeks to disrupt modernist notions of fixed sexuality and gender" (Schneider, 2000 p. 206), LGBT readers "approach the Bible as a text to be interrogated for the ways in which it is read to support the heteronormative-regulating regime" (Kamionkowski, 2011, p. 132). LGBT reading of the biblical text seeks to highlight its queerness. These readings often demonstrate that while feminist readers are resisting readers, they are, more often than not, heteronormative. This is best illustrated in Averen Ipsen's (2009) study on *Sex Working and the Bible.* Ispen employs, among other theories of reading, Marcella Althaus-Reid's notion of decency-indecency to analyze feminist interpretations of biblical passages that feature sex workers. Consistently, feminist readers explain sex workers as either literary metaphors or patriarchal caricatures. In so doing feminist readers construct sex workers according to heterosexual norms of respectability rather than celebrate these varieties of sexual practices. Such readings silence the agency of sex workers and erase their historical presence from sacred texts. Applying queer theory, LGBT reader response seeks to highlight many queer places in the Bible, to problematize the masculinities and femininities prescribed by compulsory heterosexuality, and thus to chip away the claim of heterenormativity by highlighting that it is a social construction and not natural, divine, or unchangeable (Hornsby and Stone, 2011; Moore, 2001, pp. 1–18).

Oral Texts for Women and Marginalized Groups. The above opening story of reading, featuring the Tiv, seemingly blurs boundaries between reading written and oral texts. There are close relations between women, minority readers of canonical texts, and orality. First, orality intimates the best reader-response criticism, because it resists maintaining the object–subject dichotomy between the reader and the text. Contemporary reader-response critics often wrongly assume that the first biblical reader had a written copy of the biblical passages for reading. Original "readers," however, were not readers, but hearers of the biblical text. One copy of written gospel, epistle, or any part of what constitutes biblical literature was read aloud publicly to an audience, which listened to the reader. Moore (1989) thus points out that to carry out the minute analysis of the text-based Implied readers, Ideal readers, and Narratees, who are supposedly inherent within the written text, is to carry out an "analysis of a reading that in all probability never occurred" and "would seem the ultimate waste of time," since in an oral setting, "spoken words are events.…not things. They exist not in space but in time" (1989, p. 86). Yet given that reader response underlines reading as a temporal rather than spatial event, Moore holds that this interpretative method is nonetheless "more adequate to the oral-aural situations that would have formed the original" reading of the gospel than other most text-bound methods used in biblical studies (p. 88).

Because women and minority groups rarely participated in writing, choosing, interpreting, and translating canonical books, their experience, literature, and history remain largely oral. When women and minority groups are featured, their characterization reflects the perspective and prescriptions of those in power. A good example is Howard Thurman's African American "non-literate" grandmother, who had the Bible read to her by her grandson but refused to hear the Pauline letters (save for 1 Cor 13). When asked about her distaste for Paul, she answered,

"During the days of slavery," she said, "the master's minister would occasionally hold services for the slaves. Old man McGhee was so mean that he would not let a Negro minister preach to his slaves. Always the white minister used as his text something from Paul…'Slaves be obedient to them that are your master…., as unto Christ.' Then he would go on to show how it was God's will that we were slaves and how, if we were good and happy slaves, God would bless us. I promised my Maker that if ever I learned to read and if freedom ever came, I would not read that part of the Bible." (cited in Weems, 1991, pp. 61–63)

Thurman's grandmother used her experience as a former slave to respond to the biblical text critically, regarding issues of class and race. As an enslaved woman, who was fed with the master's religion and text, Thurman's grandmother realized that the Pauline text served the interests of her enslavers rather than her own. Although she chose to continue with the master's book and follow his religion, she did so on her own terms: she did not have the Pauline texts read to her. Instead she chose to hear such books as the Gospels. Her strategy may somewhat capture the posture of womanist readers, who also remain critically faithful to the biblical text and its institutions.

Many canonical books and scriptures do not represent the interests of women and the marginalized. Women's history and literature, therefore, tends to be oral, unrecorded. This state of affairs dictates particular styles of reading. A good illustration is Mark's account of the crucifixion of Jesus:

There were also women looking on from a distance, among them were Mary Magdelene, and Mary the mother of James the younger and of Joses, and Salome. These used to follow him and provided for him when he was in Galilee; and there were many other women who had come up with him to Jerusalem. (15:40–41)

Earlier in the Gospel, women have not been explicitly described as Jesus's disciples faithfully following him and providing for him. When Jesus hangs on the cross, the male disciples having fled, the narrator reveals that there were women who "used to follow him when he was in Galilee," and they "had come up with him to Jerusalem." The verse immediately causes female readers to realize that what they read throughout the Gospel is *not* a complete story. It is a story that mostly tells the experiences of male followers of Jesus. Women's history and experience thus remain in the periphery in oral form. Such verses force feminist and womanist readers to reread the Gospel to reclaim the suppressed stories of women and give voice to the silenced. They step back to reread the silences and reconstruct the unrecorded stories, experiences, and histories of women characters in the text. The verse also forces feminist and womanist readers to read the recorded stories with uneasy peace, treating the texts as a scene of crime, for both the violence of exclusion and the patriarchal prescription within the included stories (Exum, 1995; Capel Anderson, 1991, pp. 103–137). Moreover, it cements the feminist and womanist assumption that most canonized texts are male texts, which have also been read, interpreted, and translated within patriarchal perspectives that continue to marginalize women and minority groups.

The methodological practice of reading silences, giving voice to the voiceless, and rewriting texts and history indicates that womanist and feminist reading practices place more trust in the reader than in the text. Feminist and womanist reading processes are thus creative moments of rewriting the text to be more inclusive and justice loving. There are numerous examples to illustrate this practice. One is my reading of Ruth that focuses on the untold story of Orpah. She returns to her people and gods, as advised by Naomi, and the reader never hears what happened to her. The book tells us more about Ruth, the woman who forsook her land, gods, and people and followed Naomi, to become one of the key people in the genealogy of David. I chose to write "The Unpublished Letters of Orpah to Ruth" out of a postcolonial feminist agenda that celebrates one who returned to her gods and her land instead of embracing one who forsakes her own religion, culture, and lands (Dube, 1999, pp. 145–150; Donaldson, 1999, pp. 130–144). Similarly, in the article, "The Five Husbands at the Well of the Living Waters," I continue with a postcolonial feminist agenda to read the silences. In John 4:1–42, Jesus says to the Samaritan woman, "You have had five

husbands and the current one is not even yours." There is no further explanation as to whether she was widowed or divorced four times or had a mixture of both experiences. It is a major interpretative gap that has invited interpretations from various readers. In my article I seek to elaborate the identity of the five husbands and what they did to her, again, with an explicit postcolonial feminist agenda (Dube, 2001, pp. 6–26).

To a large extent African, Asian, and Latin American reader-response practices are also orally inflected. In these contexts, the Bible has come to co-exist with other indigenous texts that are either written, oral, or both. Two-Thirds World reader-response criticism is thus framed within and between various other texts, their cultural frameworks, and the political concerns of their communities. The Bible in the Two-Thirds World is fraught with colonial history. Given this background, chances are much higher for Two-Thirds World reader-hearers to privilege the reader than to remain faithful to a colonizing text.

Many Two-Thirds World titles tell the story of biblical characters who are dressed in African, Asian, Indian, or Buddhist colors. Jesus himself has enjoyed the most attention, as attested by such book titles as *The Many Faces of Jesus Christ, African Faces of Jesus*, and *Asian Faces of Jesus*, as well as by art where, for example, Jesus dons a Buddhist garb and strikes a Buddhist pose. Mercy Amba Oduyoye and Elizabeth Amoah's article, "The Christ for African Women," for example, employs not the male Jesus but a Ghanaian legendary woman as a Christ (1999, pp. 35–46), and Seratwa Ntloedibe-Kuswani's (2000) article, "Jesus as a Ngaka," reads Jesus as "witchdoctor," (to evoke the colonial stereotype. What is left of the character of the biblical Jesus thus becomes an interesting subject of debate.

These are stories of reader-response in the margins of Western scholarship. They are, in my view, so radical they are often not recognized as reader-response criticism. Their reader-response practice may not necessarily be plotted in the Western story of "from formalism to postructualism." Consequently they have been neatly quarantined as contextual, Asian, or African theology, while what passes as reader-response in mainstream biblical studies is, as Moore has said, "the Unfeeling" masquerading historical critic, who is mostly a white male. The trajectory of quarantining Two-Thirds World biblical readers is best represented by R. S. Sugirtharajah's *Voices from the Margin: Interpreting the Bible in the Third World*, which was reprinted three times between 1991 and 2006. In the last edition Sugirtharajah wrote an introduction entitled, "Still at the Margins," which was published as a separate book (2008). Why are Two-Thirds World biblical interpretations still at the margins? In my view, it is partly because their reader-response readings engage various other texts, norms, and philosophical frameworks that are outside the Western biblical thinking. As the opening story of the Tiv demonstrates, much reader response to classical texts is not necessarily driven by the popular Western theoretical giants such as Iser, Fish, and Culler. To their credit, The Bible and Culture Collective authors conclude their chapter on the state of reader-response criticism in biblical studies by applauding feminist, Two-Thirds World scholars, and deconstructionist readers (1992, pp. 60–67). This is reader response at the crossroad—in between boundaries and in resistance to various forms of oppression, including colonial domination.

[*See also* Canon/Canonicity/Canonization; Feminism, *subentry* Second-Wave Feminism; Historical-Critical Approaches; Intersectional Studies; Mujerista Criticism; Postcolonial Approaches; Queer Theory; *and* Womanist Criticism.]

BIBLIOGRAPHY

Althaus-Reid, Marcella. *Indecent Theology: Theological Perversions in Sex, Gender, and Politics.* London: Routledge, 2000.

Anderson, Janice C. "Matthew: Gender and Reading." In *A Feminist Companion to Matthew*, edited by Amy-Jill Levine, pp. 25–51. Cleveland, Ohio: Pilgrim, 2001.

Anderson, Janice C. "Feminist Criticism: The Dancing Daughter." In *Mark and Methods: New Approaches in Biblical Studies*, edited by Janice Capel Anderson and Stephen Moore, pp. 29–58. Minneapolis: Fortress, 2008.

The Bible and Culture Collective. "Feminist and Womanist Criticism." In *The Postmodern Bible*, pp. 225–271. New Haven, Conn.: Yale University Press, 1995.

Bible and Culture Collective. "Reader-Response Criticism." In *The Postmodern Bible*, pp. 20–69. New Haven, Conn.: Yale University Press, 1995.

Bohannan, Laura. "Shakespeare in the Bush." *Natural History* (August–September 1966): 1–12.

Briggs, Sheila. "Galatians." In *Searching the Scriptures*. Vol. 2: *A Feminist Commentary*, edited by Elisabeth Schüssler Fiorenza, pp. 218–236. New York: Crossroad, 1994.

Buchanan, Ian. *Oxford Dictionary of Critical Theory.* Oxford: Oxford University Press, 2010.

Donaldson, Laura. "The Sign of Orpah: Reading Ruth through Native Eyes." In *A Companion to the Book of Ruth and Esther*, edited by Athalya Brenner, pp. 130–144. Sheffield, U.K.: Sheffield University Press, 1999.

Dube, Musa W. "The Unpublished Letters of Orpah to Ruth." In *A Companion to the Book of Ruth and Esther*, edited by Athalya Brenner, pp. 145–150. Sheffield, U.K.: Sheffield University Press, 1999.

Dube, Musa W. "Fifty Years of Bleeding: A Storytelling Feminist Reading of Mark 5:24–35." In *Other Ways of Reading: African Women and the Bible*, edited by Musa W. Dube, pp. 26–49. Atlanta: Society of Biblical Literature, 2001.

Dube, Musa W. "Five Husbands at the Well of Living Waters." In *Talitha Cum! Theologies of African Women*, edited by Nyambura J. Njoroge and Musa W. Dube, pp. 6–26. Pietermaritzburg, South Africa: Cluster, 2001.

Exum, Cheryl. "Feminist Criticism: Whose Interests Are Served?" In *Judges and Methods: New Approaches in Biblical Studies*, edited by Gale A. Yee, pp. 65–90. Minneapolis: Fortress, 1995.

Fetterly, Judith. *The Resisting Reader: A Feminist Approach to American Fiction.* Bloomington: Indiana University Press, 1979.

Fish, Stanley. *Is There a Text in This Class? The Authority of Interpretative Communities.* Cambridge, Mass.: Havard University Press, 1980.

Fowler, Robert M. "Reader-Response Criticism: Figuring Mark's Reader." In *Mark and Methods: New Approaches in Biblical Studies*, edited by Janice Capel Anderson and Stephen Moore, pp. 50–88. Minneapolis: Fortress, 1992.

Hornsby, Teresa J., and Ken Stone, eds. *Bible Trouble: Queer Reading at the Boundaries of Biblical Scholarship.* Atlanta: Society of Biblical Literature, 2011.

Ipsen, Avaren. *Sex Working and the Bible.* London: Equinox, 2009.

Iser, Wolfgang. *The Implied Reader: Patterns of Communication in Prose Fiction from Bunyan to Beckett.* Baltimore: John Hopkins University Press, 1974.

Iser, Wolfgang. *The Act of Reading: A Theory of Asthetic Response.* Baltimore: John Hopkins University Press, 1978.

Kamionkowski, Tamar S. "Queer Theory and Histori-cal-Critical Exegesis: Queering Biblicists." In *Bible Trouble: Queer Reading at the Boundaries of Biblical Scholarship*, edited by Teresa Hornsby and Ken Stone, pp. 131–137. Atlanta: Society of Biblical Literature, 2011.

Küster, Volker. *The Many Faces of Jesus Christ*. Maryknoll, N.Y.: Orbis, 1999.

Lozada, Francisco, Jr. "Identity." In *Handbook of Post-modern Biblical Interpretation*, edited by A. K. M. Adam, pp. 113–119. Saint Louis, Mo.: Chalice, 2000.

McKnight, E. V. "Reader-Response Criticism." In *Methods of Biblical Interpretation*, edited by Douglas Knight, pp. 179–183. Nashville, Tenn.: Abingdon, 2004.

Moore, Stephen D. *Literary Criticism and the Gospel: The Theoretical Challenge*. New Haven, Conn.: Yale University Press, 1989.

Moore, Stephen D. *God's Beauty Parlor and Other Queer Spaces in and around the Bible*. Stanford, Calif.: Stanford University Press, 2001.

Moore, Stephen D., and Yvonne Sherwood. *The Invention of the Biblical Scholar: A Critical Manifesto*. Minneapolis: Fortress, 2011.

Ntloedibe-Kuswani, Seratwa. "Ngaka and Jesus as Liberators: A Comparative Reading." In *The Bible in Africa*, edited by Gerald West and Musa W. Dube, pp. 498–510. Leiden, The Netherlands: Brill, 2000.

Oduyoye, Mercy, and Elizabeth Amoah. "The Christ for African Women." In *With Passion and Compassion: Third World Women Doing Theology*, edited by Virginia Fabella and Mercy A. Oduyoye, pp. 35–46. New York: Orbis, 1990.

Rich, Adrienne. "Compulsory Heterosexuality and Lesbian Existence." In *Blood, Bread and Poetry: Selected Prose 1979–1985*. New York: Norton, 1986.

Schneider, Laurel L. "Queer Theory." In *Handbook of Postmodern Biblical Interpretation*, edited by A. K. M. Adam, pp. 206–212. Saint Louis, Mo.: Chalice, 2000.

Schreiter, Robert J., ed. *Faces of Jesus in Africa*. Maryknoll, N.Y.: Orbis, 1991.

Schüssler Fiorenza, Elisabeth. "The Will to Choose and to Reject: Continuing Our Critical Work." In *Feminist Interpretation of the Bible*, edited by Letty Russell, pp. 125–136. Philadelphia: Westminster, 1985.

Segovia, F. Fernando, and Mary Ann Tolbert, eds. *Reading from This Place*. Vol. 1: *Social Location and Biblical Interpretation in the United States*. Minneapolis: Fortress, 1995a.

Segovia, F. Fernando, and Mary Ann Tolbert, eds. *Reading from This Place*. Vol. 2: *Social Location and Biblical Interpretation in Global Perspective*. Minneapolis: Fortress, 1995b.

Spencer, Daniel T. "Lesbian and Gay Theologies." In *Handbook of U.S. Theologies of Liberation*, edited by Miguel A. De La Torre, pp. 264–273. Saint Louis, Mo.: Chalice, 2004.

Stone, Ken. "Sexuality." In *Handbook of Postmodern Biblical Interpretation*, edited by A. K. M. Adam, pp. 233–238. Saint Louis, Mo.: Chalice, 2000.

Sugirtharajah, R. S., ed. *Asian Faces of Jesus*. Maryknoll, N.Y.: Orbis, 1993.

Sugirtharajah, R. S., ed. *Voices from the Margin: Interpreting the Bible in Third World*. London: SPCK, 2006.

Sugirtharajah, R. S., ed. *Still at the Margins: Biblical Scholarship Fifteen Years after Voices from the Margin*. London: T&T Clark, 2008.

Thatcher, Tom, and Stephen D. Moore, eds. *Anatomies of Narrative Criticism: The Past, Present and the Futures of the Fourth Gospel as Literature*. Atlanta: Society of Biblical Literature, 2008.

Tolbert, Mary Ann. "Gender." In *Handbook of Postmodern Biblical Interpretation*, edited by A. K. M. Adam, pp. 99–105. St. Louis: Chalice, 2000.

Tompkins, Jane P., ed. *Reader-Response Criticism: From Formalist to Poststructuralism*. Baltimore: Johns Hopkins University Press, 1980.

Weems, Renita. "Reading Her Way through the Struggle: African American Women and the Bible." In *Stony the Road We Trod: African American Biblical Interpretation*, edited by Cain Hope Felder, pp. 57–77. Minneapolis: Fortress, 1991.

Williams, Delores S. *Sisters in the Wilderness: The Challenge of Womanist-Talk*. Maryknoll, N.Y.: Orbis, 1993.

Musa W. Dube

RELIGIOUS LEADERS

This entry contains nine subentries: Ancient Near East; Ancient Near Eastern Prophecy; Hebrew Bible; Greek World; Roman World; New Testament; Early Judaism; Early Church; *and* Late Antiquity.

Ancient Near East

The discussion of religious leaders in the ancient Near East is based on the combined evidence of a vast variety of documents: lexical and administrative texts, which give us information concerning ancient understanding of categorization and classification and mention numerous cult officials; temple hymns and descriptions of cultic rites, which grant us a glance into the performative activities of the religious personnel; and mythological compositions, which supply us with a key into the elaborate etiological explanatory system that surrounded ancient Near Eastern religious institutions. All these texts are usually found in palatial or temple archives and rarely even in private archives that belonged to families of nobilities. Last, but not least, archaeological remains of iconographic and artistic depictions of religious personnel and cultic scenes occasionally fill the gaps of topics left unaddressed by textual records.

Gender and Religious Leadership Roles. As a rule, the vast majority of high-ranking cultic personnel were men. On occasions, the king himself functioned as the highest religious authority, a situation that reflects an intertwining of the spheres of political administration and religion or cult. Two notable exceptions to this unbalanced androcentric division can nonetheless be noted: female high priestesses and gender ambiguous male cultic attendants. Together with male religious leaders, the two aforementioned categories are the focus of this article.

Male and Female Religious Leaders: High Priests and Priestesses. Several terms for priests, priestesses, and other cultic personnel in ancient Near Eastern sources are mentioned throughout this article. For additional such terms, the reader is referred to the bibliographical items listed below and most conveniently to the index found in Henshaw (1994, pp. 351–364).

The en/ēnu: High priest. One of the most significant figures in Mesopotamian cult organization was the *en*, a functionary already attested in some of the earliest cuneiform texts (ca. 3300–3100 B.C.E., usually termed "the archaic period") found in the Sumerian city of Uruk (biblical Erech, located in southern Iraq). The office held by this person may be defined as "priest-king," since his duties incorporated both religious and secular functions. As we will see, the intrusion of the political domain into the religious one was a frequently reoccurring phenomenon throughout the history of the ancient Near East. Indeed, the *en* acted as both the highest ruling authority of the city and its leading religious figure. He was perceived as a mediator between the populace of Uruk and its patron goddess, Inanna. As such, he was probably a charismatic figure, who gained power thanks to his abilities and personal qualities. As prime priest of the local deities, he handled both cultic and administrative activities of the temple and performed ceremonies and sacrifices for the gods. At the same time, he was in charge of daily life of the city, initiated building enterprises, and managed tax collection and its redistribution.

From the Early Dynastic period (beginning ca. 2900 B.C.E.), however, the political aspect of this office diminished until it was completely taken by other title holders: the *ensi* (a title usually translated as "governor") and the *lugal* (a title later on to designate "king"). The *en* continued, nonetheless, to perform his religious and cultic tasks, his role being equal to that of a high priest. Once the use of the Akkadian language became widespread at the expense of Sumerian, this title was loaned into Akkadian in the form of the term *ēnu*.

The nin-dingir(-ra)/ēntu: High priestess. The office of the *ēnu* had a female equivalent, known by the Akkadian designation *ēntu*. She was one of the most notable female cult attendants in Mesopotamia, frequently designated by the Sumerian title *nin-dingir(-ra)*. The terms *nin-dingir(-ra)/ēntu* are usually translated by modern scholars as "high priestess" and they are found as synonymous in various lexical lists. In some of these lists the *ēntu* was paralleled with several titles of female cultic personnel who were devotees of various deities and resided in cloisters, such as the *nadītu, qadištu, ugbabtu/gubabtu*, and *uppuštu*. These lexical equations, however, do not necessarily point to synonymy but more probably to similar semantics shared by these terms. Thus, all these titles were related to each other as denoting women who were engaged in cultic activities, but they stood for different professions.

The Sumerian term *nin-dingir(-ra)* appears in lexical lists already in the Fara period (ca. 2600 B.C.E.), whereas its Akkadian equivalent *ēntu* is attested from as early as the Old Akkadian period (2334–2154 B.C.E.). In Old Akkadian administrative texts we encounter various women who bore the title *ēntu* and were described as belonging to specific deities, such as Ninšubur and Enlil. Later on, in the Ur III period (2112–2004 B.C.E.), these priestesses were documented as servants of the deities Bau, Gatumdug, Hendursag, and Nindar. In the Old Babylonian period (ca. 2000–1600 B.C.E.) the attestations of the title become much more abundant and appear in various textual genres. After the end of this period, however, the title is scarcely attested, and the office probably almost ceased to exist, except for a brief recurrence at the end of the Neo-Babylonian period (625–539 B.C.E.), during Nabonidus's reign (556–539 B.C.E.). In many cases we note that the women chosen to fulfill this function came from the circles of the royal family and were either the king's daughters or sisters. This custom probably reflects the aspiration of secular rulers to strengthen their control over the sphere of religion and cult. The duties of the *ēntu* included the occasional commissioning of building enterprises, managing the estates of her cloister, and performing lustrations, prayers, and sacrifices for the gods. She also participated in the "sacred marriage" rite (see below).

Gender, sexuality, and high priesthood. The comparison between the *ēnu* and the *ēntu* is most revealing in regard to gender differences in Mesopotamian religion. The claim occasionally made by scholars that most *ēnu* priests served feminine deities whereas *ēntu* priestesses served male ones is inaccurate. Apparently, both officiants could serve deities of both sexes. As was noted, although the Sumerian term *nin-dingir(-ra)* is attested from early periods, the Akkadian term *ēntu*, and presumably the post of the high priestess it designated, only formed in Old Akkadian times. This may be viewed as evidence for the difference between the male and female offices of the high priesthood and testify to the fact that the female equivalent of an already well-established male office emerged at a later stage in history in the Semitic environment of the Old Akkadian empire. Caution is advised here, however, since the evidence in this regard is open for interpretation, and we are ignorant of the extent of activities and duties fulfilled by the *nin-dingir(-ra)* during the eras preceding Old Akkadian.

As for the range of their duties, as was specified above, both the *ēnu* and the *ēntu* were involved in a mixture of religious and secular activities. One major distinction between the *ēnu* and the *ēntu* lies in the aspect of sexuality incorporated in their performance. It has been argued that texts such as those describing the sacred marriage rite (see below) demonstrate that the role of the *ēntu* included sexual intercourse conducted as part of her cultic performance. Whether these descriptions were realistic or fictional, they clearly exhibit a social and cultural notion associating the role of the *ēntu* with sexuality. No parallel sexual aspect, however, appears to have accompanied the performance of the *ēnu*.

Gender ambiguity of male figures in Mesopotamia: The kalû. Although his role in cult was significant, the ritual lamenter known as *kalû* (Sumerian *gala*) seldom functioned as a high-ranking official. Rarely, however, he could gain significant power and esteem and hold the office of chief cultic lamenter, *kalamāhu* (Sumerian *gala.mah*). As such, he performed important administrative duties and could become a wealthy and powerful person. This male figure is one of the best documented cult personnel in Mesopotamia and, as explained below, the evidence suggests that although he was biologically male his gender may have been more aligned with femininity.

The earliest attestations of the *kalû* (under the Sumerian designation *gala*) appear in lists of persons dated to the Fara period. The role of the *kalû* as a professional lamenter in funerals is evident in texts from the Early Dynastic IIIb period (ca. 2500–2340 B.C.E.) and from Gudea's reign (2144–2124 B.C.E.). The documentation of the *kalû* in Ur III texts portrays a similar picture of a figure engaged in mourning rites.

The evidence seems to change from the Old Babylonian period onward. The duties and activities of the *kalû* evolved greatly and included music playing, singing, and chanting throughout the ceremonies of the goddess Inanna/Ištar. A corpus of proverbs dated to the Isin-Larsa period (ca. 2000–1900 B.C.E.) portrays the *kalû* as a ludicrous figure characterized as infertile. See for example the following: "A *gala* threw his son into the water, (saying:) 'May the city be built like me! May the country live like me!'" This proverb seems to present a humorous analogy between the barren *gala* (symbolized by throwing his son to the water) and the ominous future of the population, since for the inhabitants of the city and the country to be built and to live "like the *gala*" means to remain infertile.

In later periods, especially in the first millennium, the documentation of the *kalû* depicts him as a priest involved in various rites. In these rites he frequently used a Sumerian dialect known as *emesal*, sometimes translated by scholars as "women's language" but more probably meaning "thin/delicate speech." The use of this dialect by the *kalûs* has been the source of a wide debate among scholars, since apart from these cultic male lamenters only female figures used *emesal*. This may be suggestive with regard to the gender identity of the *kalû* and the association of this male figure with effeminacy.

Several mythological compositions attest to the relation between the *kalû* and the goddess Inanna/Ištar, most notably "Inanna's Descent to the Netherworld," "The Fashioning of the Gala," and "Inanna and Ebih." In these compositions the *kalû* is variously portrayed as a savior, soother, and votary of the goddess. According to documents dating from the Fara period to the end of Ur III (ca. 2600–2000 B.C.E.), he was a professional lamenter who performed funerary rites, with no evidence relating him to any cult. The earliest of these rites were exclusively performed by women; later, male *kalûs* and women performed them together; and eventually only *kalûs* were recorded as performing these rites. For this reason, the *kalûs* employed in their performance the *emesal* dialect, otherwise used by females alone. From the Old Babylonian period onward we find *kalûs* in contexts relating to Inanna/Ištar's cult. It is therefore possible to hypothesize that the initial affiliation of the *kalû* with femininity, as a lamenter who performed funerary rites characteristic of women, stood at the background of his gender ambiguity. Starting at the Old Babylonian period, he was no longer associated with funerary rites and seems to have become affiliated with Ištar, as he is mentioned in proverbs, mythological, and administrative texts with the goddess. The documentation of this figure is long-lasting

and continues even until the Hellenistic period. We notice in texts dating to these later periods that the role of the *kalû* remained virtually the same for many centuries.

As for the chief cultic lamenter, the *kalamāhu*, his title is attested from at least the Early Dynastic IIIb period. He was a high-ranking official and was in charge of various groups of workers, among them lower-rank *kalûs*. As a person who was originally *kalû* before becoming a chief-*kalû*, the *kalamāhu* likely possessed the traits of a feminine gender construct described above. However, scholars question whether the *kalamāhu* was indeed originally a *kalû* or merely fulfilled his role as a prebend holder. This doubt is probably unjustified, since although there is no evidence for the latter possibility we know for a fact that some *kalamāhu*s were previously *kalûs*, such as an Ur III period official named Dada. This person was recorded in various texts both as a *kalû* and as a *kalamāhu*, and since these texts are dated we can be certain that they document the very same person, who was originally a *kalû* and later on was promoted to the role of *kalamāhu*.

Known Individuals. Enheduanna, daughter of king Sargon of Akkad (2334–2279 B.C.E.), founder of the Old Akkadian empire, is the earliest *ēntu*-priestess at Ur known to us by name. Ancient traditions attribute to her the authorship of various literary compositions, most notably hymns exalting the patron goddess of the empire, Inanna/Ištar. Although the reliability of this attribution is now questioned by scholars, the very existence of this tradition exemplifies the importance Enheduanna enjoyed in later eras. Another known *ēntu* is Enannatumma, daughter of King Išme-Dagan of Isin (1953–1935 B.C.E.), who was also a high priestess and renovated two temples in the city of Ur.

A different high-ranking religious official discussed above, whom we occasionally know by name, is the *kalamāhu*. We have mentioned the *kalamāhu* Dada of the Ur III period and noted that much is known about the activities he performed along the years of his career. This person was a musical performer and an organizer of various ceremonies that took place in the court, which included singing and music playing. Thus he was in charge of other personnel, among them *kalûs*. Further, from an Old Babylonian private archive from the city of Sippar (southern Iraq) we learn that the owner of the archive was the *kalamāhu* Ur-Utu. He was in charge of the administration of the temple of Annunītum, a local goddess who was perceived as a manifestation of Inanna/Ištar. Ur-Utu was a wealthy and distinguished person, engaged in numerous business and religious activities. For example, he received payments for granting people the right to perform various cultic rites. We have abundant information documenting the lives and careers of these *kalamāhu*s, which grants us an acquaintance with them far more intimately than with the usual anonymous persons who held these offices.

The Royal Couple as Religious Leaders. We have some evidence from the history of the ancient Near East for kings and queens officiating religious roles as high priests. Mesopotamian rulers were usually considered their people's representatives before the gods, mediators between the celestial and the earthly worlds. In the Assyrian Empire specifically, the king was regarded as a high priest. As for their consorts, already in mid-third millennium B.C.E. certain wives of Sumerian city-governors (*ensi*) were involved in the arrangement of various cultic procedures. We thus know of Baranamtarra, wife of Lugalanda, Šagšag, wife of Urukagina (or Uruinimgina), and Dimtur, wife of Enentarzi, all from the city-state of Lagaš (southern Iraq), who organized ceremonies and cultic rites. In the second millennium B.C.E., Šibtu, wife of Zimri-Lim, king of Mari (1775–1762 B.C.E.) was in charge of the state affairs during her husband's frequent military campaigns. As such, she administered the ceremonial and cultic activities of the kingdom. Finally, in the first millennium B.C.E., a large number of documents attest to the involvement of Queen Naqi'a/Zakūtu, wife of Sennacherib, king of Assyria (705–681 B.C.E.), in the cult. One of these texts mentions the participation of both her and her husband in a ritual.

The best examples in this regard, however, come from the Hittite kingdom (ca. 1650–1200 B.C.E.), situated in the Anatolian plateau (modern Turkey). Hittite texts supply us with ample evidence for the function of the royal couple as religious leaders. In Hatti, the king assumed the role of the highest priest, venerating the prime deity of the Hittite pantheon, the Storm-god. The texts say explicitly that the land belongs to the Storm-god, under whose auspice the king rules. As such, the king acted as the leading celebrant of various cultic festivals throughout the year, especially during spring (the *purulli* and *antahsum* festivals) and autumn (the *nuntarriyashas* festival) time. These religious duties were of such high importance that occasionally a military campaign would be halted to allow the king to return to Hattusa, the royal capital (ca. 120 miles/200 kilometers east of Ankara, central Turkey), and celebrate an important festival.

His consort, the reigning queen (who assumed the title *Tawananna*), officiated similarly in the post of the highest priestess of the realm. We can therefore speak in this regard of gender as mirror image, the religious position of the reigning queen reflecting a female counterpart of the role assumed by the king. An excellent exemplification of this gender mirror image is found in nontextual evidence. A Hittite unfinished rock relief found in Fraktin, located in south-central Turkey, depicts the royal couple, King Hattusili III and Queen Puduhepa (1267–1237 B.C.E.), in an exact parallel: each one of them pours libation in front of the prime deity that corresponds to their sex, Tešub and Hepat. We see in this relief that the earthly royal couple venerates the celestial one, with the king and queen depicted alike. The posture and even size of Hattusili and Puduhepa are identical, thus insinuating equal cultic importance of the two. Naturally, the role of the Hittite king in the religious sphere was far greater than that of his consort; however, as his female mirror image, the queen enjoyed a highly distinguished religious rank herself.

Modern Debates. Questions about the role of sexuality and gender in the ancient religion and cult are highly complicated. As a result, their research is frequently controversial and highly contested. In what follows, I will mention a few of these controversies.

The sacred marriage ceremony. One of the heavily debated issues in the scholarship of ancient Near Eastern gender and religious studies involves the existence of the alleged institution of sacred marriage. This rite supposedly involved the engagement of the *ēntu* high priestess in sexual intercourse with the king, symbolizing the union between the celestial couple Dumuzi and Inanna. Scholars disagree whether the descriptions of this ceremony, the most notable of which is attributed to Iddin-Dagan king of Isin (1974–1954 B.C.E.), reflect true reality or are merely imaginary.

The kalû as homosexual or hermaphrodite. Various attempts have been made by modern scholars to relate possible etymologies of the Sumerian term *gala*, or Akkadian *kalû*, with traits of homosexuality or hermaphroditic qualities. For example, some suggest that the term *gala* may refer to homosexuality: the cuneiform signs "uš" and "ku" that make up *gala* can alternatively be read as "gìš" and "dúr": "penis" and "anus." Some suggest that the term *kalû* originated from the Semitic root *k-l-'*, conveying the meaning "both" or "two kinds" and thus indicating the hermaphroditic characteristics. These attempts remain conjectural.

Castration among cult attendants in Mesopotamia. Also debated is whether castration and self-emasculation account for the gender ambiguity among certain Mesopotamian male cult personnel. Because one of these figures, the *kurgarrû*, is frequently documented in myths and ritual texts as holding various weapons, probably cutting ones, certain scholars equate him with the *galli*, the first-millennium Anatolian priests of Attis and Cybele who later Roman sources describe as performing self-emasculation in reverence of their patron god Attis. The alleged parallel between the *kurgarrûs* and the *galli* has been taken even further to suggest that the gender ambiguity of other male figures in Mesopotamian cult such as the *kalû*, *assinnu*, and *pilpilû* should be explained in the same way. We must stress, however, that any resemblance between the Mesopotamian figures and the *galli* is unsubstantiated. No text documents the castration of any of these figures, and the only reason for the alleged comparison lies in the association of the *kurgarrû* with cutting weapons. This association received various alternative explanations, none of which related to corporal mutilation or castration.

[*See also* Deity, *subentry* Ancient Near East; Gender and Sexuality: Ancient Near East; *and* Religious Participation, *subentry* Sacred Prostitution.]

BIBLIOGRAPHY

Assante, Julia. "The kar.kid/*harimtu*, Prostitute or Single Woman? A Critical Review of the Evidence." *Ugarit-Forschungen* 30 (1998): 5–96.

Bryce, Trevor. *Life and Society in the Hittite World.* Oxford: Oxford University Press, 2002.

Cooper, Jerrold S. "Sacred Marriage and Popular Cult in Early Mesopotamia." In *Official Cult and Popular Religion in the Ancient Near East: Papers of the First Colloquium on the Ancient Near East "The City and Its Life," Held at the Middle Eastern Culture Center in Japan (Mitake, Tokyo), March 20–22, 1992*, edited by Eiko Matushima, pp. 81–96. Heidelberg, Germany: Universitätsverlag C. Winter, 1993.

Gabbay, Uri. "The Akkadian Word for 'Third Gender': The *kalû* (gala) Once Again." In *Proceedings of the 51st Rencontre Assyriologique Internationale*, edited by Robert D. Biggs, Jennie Myers, and Martha T. Roth, pp. 49–56. Chicago: University of Chicago Press, 2008.

Henshaw, Richard A. *Female and Male: The Cultic Personnel: The Bible and the Rest of the Ancient Near East.* Allison Park, Pa.: Pickwick, 1994.

Lambert, Wilfred G. "Prostitution." In *Aussenseiter und Randgruppen: Beiträge zu einer Sozialgeschichte des Alten Orients*, edited by Volkert Haas, pp. 127–157. Konstanz, Germany: Universitätsverlag Konstanz, 1992.

Marsman, Hennie J. *Women in Ugarit and Israel: Their Social and Religious Position in the Context of the Ancient Near East.* Leiden, The Netherlands: Brill, 2003.

Menzel, Brigitte. *Assyrische Tempel.* Vol. 1: *Untersuchungen zu Kult, Administration und Personal;* Vol. 2: *Anmerkungen, Textbuch, Tabellen und Indices.* Rome: Biblical Institute Press, 1981.

Peled, Ilan. "The Third Gender in the Ancient Near East: A Study of Institutionalized Gender Otherness." Ph.D. diss., Bar-Ilan University, 2012.

Renger, Johannes. "Untersuchungen zum Priestertum in der altbabylonischen Zeit." *Zeitschrift für Assyriologie und Vorderasiatische Archäologie* 58 (1967): 110–188; 59 (1969): 104–230.

Sallaberger, Walther. "Priester." *Reallexikon der Assyriologie und Vorderasiatischen Archäologie* 10 (2004): 617–648.

Watanabe, Kazuko, ed. *Priests and Officials in the Ancient Near East: Papers of the Second Colloquium on the Ancient Near East: "The City and Its Life," Held at the Middle Eastern Culture Center in Japan (Mitaka, Tokyo), March 22–24, 1996.* Heidelberg, Germany: Universitätsverlag C. Winter, 1999.

Westenholz, Joan G. "Enheduanna, En-Priestess, Hen of Nanna, Spouse of Nanna." In *DUMU-E2-DUB-BA-A:*

Studies in Honor of Åke W. Sjöberg, edited by Hermann Behrens, Darlene M. Loding, and Martha T. Roth, pp. 539–556. Philadelphia: University of Pennsylvania Museum, 1989.

Ilan Peled

Ancient Near Eastern Prophecy

Prophetic activity is known not only from the Hebrew Bible but also from a number of ancient Near Eastern (ANE) archives and inscriptions. The two main archives are the royal archives from Old Babylonian (OB) Mari (eighteenth century B.C.E.; Durand and Charpin, 1988) and the state archives of the Neo-Assyrian (NA) empire (seventh century B.C.E.; Parpola, 1997; Nissinen, 1998). There are also a small number of Transjordanian and Hittite inscriptions (Zakkur, Amman Citadel Inscription, Deir 'Allā, Tell Aḫmar) that attest to prophecy (translations of virtually all relevant texts can be found in Nissinen, 2003; for an overview of ANE prophecy see Stökl, 2012a, 2012b).

In both OB Mari and during the NA empire, prophets were part of the system of diviners, a kind of special advisory council to the king, providing them with the information they relied on for their decisions (Grabbe, 1995). This indicates that ANE prophets functioned as parts of the royal administration rather than being individual religious leaders who possessed the authority to challenge the king. This is partly due to the fact that the preserved ANE evidence for prophecy comes either from royal archives or royal inscriptions. Prophecy on behalf of rivals to the throne also existed, as is attested by a letter, SAA 16 59, which mentions that a female slave had been prophesying in favor of a rival to the throne.

It is striking that all terms used for prophets in the ANE are attested in both masculine and feminine forms. The professional titles which were used during the OB period are *āpilum / āpiltum*, and *raggimu / raggintu* during the NA; the term for (cult-)ecstatic *are mu/aḫḫû(m) / mu/aḫḫūtu(m)*. With regard to the function of the individual prophet, there does not appear to be any differentiation between male and female prophets. At Mari, however there is a distinc-

tion with regard to the distribution: there are many women among the lower-level *muḫḫû* and very few among the higher-level *āpilū* (Stökl, 2009). There may also be a difference with regard to the way that female prophets' oracles are treated and trusted (Hamori, 2012). No such differences can be seen in the NA empire, where the vast majority of attested prophets are women.

There is a popular theory that gender ambiguity is an intrinsic part of ANE prophecy (e.g., Huffmon, 1992; Nissinen, 2003, p. 200). In most texts the prophet's gender is indicated through the use of "gender determinatives." But there are some exceptions to this general rule. Additionally, the *assinnu*, whose role is often understood by modern scholars as performing gender ambiguously in late first-millennium texts, is connected to prophecy at Mari (early second millennium B.C.E.). Recently, Stökl (2013) and Zsolnay (2013) have questioned the interpretation of the data. Zsolnay points out that there is no indication that the Old Babylonian *assinnu* performed their gender ambiguously; instead their function appears to have been linked to the martial cult of the deity: Ishtar. At the same time, not a single *assinnu* is attested in connection with prophecy in the texts from the first millennium. Since the *assinnu* is attested relatively well in the first millennium and since there is evidence for prophecy in the first millennium, this absence is likely significant (Stökl, 2013; Zsolnay, 2013). The other three texts that are often taken as evidence for gender ambiguity in ANE prophecy are Neo-Assyrian and can be found on the same tablet, SAA 9 1, the first and largest of the collective tablets that preserve ten prophetic oracles to Esarhaddon (Parpola, 1997, pp. 4–11). Their significance lies in the fact that all three are contained on an otherwise well-written archival copy, which rules out the possibility that each case can be attributed to scribal idiosyncrasy.

The three cases are: (1) Ilūssa-āmur, (2) Bāia, and (3) Issār-lā-tašīaṭ. (1) The name of the female prophet Ilūssa-āmur is spelled with a female determinative in SAA 9 1.5: 5, but the gentilic in the following line is most probably masculine (*libbala[yya]*). The end of the word is broken away, and the grammatical gender has been restored by Parpola. Other restorations have been suggested, but in view of NA grammar and the attested forms of the gentilic, Parpola's restoration is reasonably certain. (2) The name of the female prophet Bāia is spelled with a female determinative in SAA 9 1.4: 40, where she is described as a "son of Arbela," i.e., a (male) person from Arbela. In SAA 9 2.2: 35, the prophet is described as a (male) "Arbelan" with a masculine gentilic. The identity of the prophet is uncertain as only parts of the last a-sign are visible. On the basis that the oracle in SAA 9 2.2 is similar to SAA 9 1.4, Parpola reconstructs the prophet's name as Bāia, but this is far from certain. (3) In the case of Issār-lā-tašīaṭ, the grammar of the name itself indicates that the prophet was male (Edzard, 1962) but the spelling of the gender determinative is unclear. According to Parpola, the scribe started writing the feminine gender determinative and then superimposed a masculine and a divine determinative, while Weippert (2002) sees a feminine and divine determinative. Since SAA 9 1 is an archival tablet from Nineveh, it is highly unlikely that the scribe saw the prophet's performance in Arbela. The scribe would therefore not have been able to detect any ambiguous gender performance.

[*See also* Gender and Sexuality: Ancient Near East.]

BIBLIOGRAPHY

Durand, Jean-Marie, and Dominic Charpin. *Archives épistolaires de Mari*. 2 vols. Archives royales de Mari 26. Paris: Editions Recherche sur les Civilisations, 1988.

Edzard, Dietz Otto. "ᵐNingal-gāmil, ˢIštar-damqat: Die Genuskongruenz im akkadischen theophoren Personennamen." *Zeitschrift für Assyriologie und Vorderasiatische Archäologie* 55 (1962): 113–130.

Grabbe, Lester L. *Priests, Prophets, Diviners, Sages: A Socio-Historical Study of Religious Specialists in Ancient Israel*. Valley Forge, Pa.: Trinity Press International, 1995.

Hamori, Esther J. "Verification of Prophecy at Mari." *Welt des Orients* 42 (2012): 1–22.

Huffmon, Herbert B. "Ancient Near Eastern Prophecy." In *Anchor Bible Dictionary*, Vol. 5, edited by Daniel N. Freedman, pp. 477–482. New York: Doubleday, 1992.

Nissinen, Martti. *References to Prophecy in Neo-Assyrian Sources*. State Archives of Assyria Studies. Helsinki: Neo-Assyrian Corpus Project, 1998.

Nissinen, Martti, with C. L. Seow and Robert K. Ritner. *Prophets and Prophecy in the Ancient Near East*.

Society of Biblical Literature; Writings of the Ancient World 12. Atlanta: Society of Biblical Literature, 2003.

Parpola, Simo. *Assyrian Prophecies*. State Archives of Assyria 9. Helsinki: Helsinki University Press, 1997.

Stökl, Jonathan. "Ištar's Women, YHWH's Men? A Curious Gender-Bias in Neo-Assyrian and Biblical Prophecy." *Zeitschrift für die Alttestamentliche Wissenschaft* 121 (2009): 87–100.

Stökl, Jonathan. "Ancient Near Eastern Prophecy." In *Dictionary of the Old Testament: Prophets*, edited by Mark J. Boda and J. Gordon McConville, pp. 16–24. Downers Grove, Ill.: InterVarsity, 2012.

Stökl, Jonathan. "Gender 'Ambiguity' in Ancient Near Eastern Prophecy? A Reassessment of the Data behind a Popular Theory." In *Prophets Male and Female: Gender and Prophecy in the Hebrew Bible, the Eastern Mediterranean and the Ancient Near Ea*st, edited by Jonathan Stökl and Corrine L. Carvalho, pp. 59–79. Atlanta: Society of Biblical Literature, 2013.

Weippert, Manfred. " 'König, fürchte dich nicht!' Assyrische Prophetie im 7. Jahrhundert v. Chr." *Orientalia* 71 (2002): 1–54.

Zsolnay, Ilona. "The Misconstrued Role of the *assinnu* in Ancient Near Eastern Prophecy." In *Prophets Male and Female: Gender and Prophecy in the Hebrew Bible, the Eastern Mediterranean and the Ancient Near East*, edited by Jonathan Stökl and Corrine L. Carvalho, pp. 81–99. Atlanta: Society of Biblical Literature, 2013.

Jonathan Stökl

Hebrew Bible

Religious leaders or religious specialists in the Hebrew Bible functioned as intermediaries between the worshipping community and its deity. Categories of religious leaders in the Hebrew Bible include priests, scribes, judges, and prophets. Religious leaders were both male and female, professional and lay. However, the preponderance of representation of religious leadership was male. This is in large part because the religious traditions represented as normative or orthodox in the Hebrew Bible provide us with the views of the male religious elites responsible for the texts. Women are associated more with the popular religious traditions that the writers considered heterodox, such as necromancy and wizardry. These different locations of power constructed through sexuality and gender in the Hebrew Bible are part of the focus of this entry.

Judges. The Hebrew noun *shophet* (judge) is a participial form of the verb *shaphat*, which means "decide," "rule," "govern" or "deliver." Judges were individuals either chosen for their moral character or endowed with God's spirit to inquire of God on behalf of the people, to settle disputations between parties, to teach the people God's statutes and instructions (Exod 18:13–20; Num 11:16–17; Judg 3:9–10), and to carry out punishment following judgments (Deut 19:16–19, 25:1–3). The average person likely associates the term in the Hebrew Bible with the charismatic figures who appear in the book of Judges. However, few of the "judges" in this period are represented as functioning in the judicial sense of the term. They function primarily as military leaders whom Yahweh raised up to deliver the Israelites from the hand of their enemies (Judg 2:16–19, 3:10), rulers of territory, and executors of justice (4:4, 16:31; 1 Sam 7:6).

Both laity and priests handled the administration of justice in ancient Israel (Deut 17:8–9, 19:17–18). However, the Hebrew Bible also depicts monarchs as administering justice, such as David (2 Sam 8:15), Absalom (15:2) and Solomon (1 Kgs 3:16–28). This conflicts with the responsibilities of the king as described in Deuteronomy 17:14–20, where the king is subject to the same authority as the people. Only one woman, Deborah in Judges, holds the office of judge in the Hebrew Bible. She is described as "judging" Israel in the forensic sense of deciding disputes (4:4–5). Most scholars take for granted that Deborah was a judge. However, each version of the origins of the judicial system in ancient Israel specifies that only men should hold this office. For example, the book of Exodus, which credits Moses's father-in-law, Jethro, with its institution, describes Jethro as instructing Moses to appoint upstanding men as officers to sit as judges for the people over minor cases, while Moses handled the major cases (18:13–27). A similar version in the book of Numbers depicts Yahweh commanding Moses to choose seventy elders to help him with judging the people (11:16–25). The Deuteronomic material conflates the two traditions, with Moses appointing tribal elders as military leaders and judges at his own initi-

ative to govern the people (Deut 1:9–17; cf. 16:18). This was a two-tiered system comprising tribal leaders in the local towns (16:18) and a council of Levitical priests and judges, who carried out judicial decisions too complicated for the local magistrates (17:8–12).

In contrast, 2 Chronicles 19:5–11 records that King Jehoshaphat instituted the judicial system in ancient Israel, appointing judges in each major fortified city of Judah, who were charged with simple cases. He appointed Levites and priests, followed by male heads of families as administrators over more difficult cases. This hierarchical structure depicts a centralized judicial system that invalidates the local tribal courts.

In each case mentioned, males are tasked with overseeing the judicial system in Israel. Deborah's depiction as both a prophet and judge (Judg 4:4) suggests that the writers wished to portray her in the tradition of Samuel, who is portrayed as both a prophet and judge, administering justice throughout Israel (1 Sam 7:15–17).

Priests. The priesthood in the Hebrew Bible has been defined in terms of its function as the institution for mediation (Vaux, 1997) and the administration of Yahweh's house (Leithart, 1999). The bulk of the information in the Hebrew Bible on the role and function of the *kohen* (priest) is found in the book of Leviticus. The priest's primary duties were related to table or altar service (Num 4:5–20). He was also responsible for presenting burnt sacrifices and offerings and overseeing the proper handling of offerings and declaring matters clean and unclean (Lev 1—7, 21—22), oracular consultation (Num 27:21; Judg 18:5), judging (Deut 17:8–13; 19:17), Torah instruction (Deut. 33:10; Hos 4:6; Mic 3:11), and guarding the sanctuary (Num 1:53; 3:28, 32).

Prior to the monarchy, male heads of households performed priestly duties. These were mostly rituals observed in the home, such as offering prayers and sacrifices on behalf of their families (Exod 12:1–13, 43–49). However, the book of Judges reports that a certain Micah built a shrine in his home and appointed his son to serve as priest at his sanctuary before replacing him with a Levite (Judg 17). Male heads of households also offered sacrifices at local shrines and high places (Gen 22, 31; Judg 13:19), as well as leading their families in worship during major festivals (Deut 16:16; 1 Sam 1:4).

The book of Exodus provides an account of the inauguration of the office of priesthood. According to Exodus 28—29, Yahweh instructed Moses at Mt. Sinai to construct the tabernacle and consecrate Aaron and his sons to serve Yahweh as priests for perpetuity. This command established a central dwelling place for encountering Yahweh and a permanent leadership for mediating between Yahweh and the people. It also officially established the male exclusivity of the priesthood in ancient Israel.

Women's primary relationship to the priesthood was by birth or marriage. Priests could marry only the virgin daughters of other priests (Lev 21:13). They were prohibited from marrying prostitutes or any other women who had been sexually defiled, including divorcees and widows (21:7, 13). If a priest's daughter married a nonpriest, she was cut off from a share of the sacred offerings. However, if she was widowed or divorced without offspring, she could return to her father's house and resume partaking of the offering (22:12–13).

Unlike the sons of Aaron, neither the daughters of Aaron nor any other Israelite women could be priests. Scholars have offered various reasons for the exclusion of women from the priesthood. One reason is the gender correspondence between deities and religious functionaries such as priests. For example, Jonathan Stökl (2009) argued that the scarcity of female prophets in the Hebrew Bible was likely a result of both monotheism and patriarchy. Stökl maintained that because Yahweh, Israel's deity, was male, the gender of the religious mediator must also be male. However, this does not account for the few Israelite female prophets in biblical Israel (see the section on prophets, below). Moreover, in Mesopotamia, where there were priests and priestesses, the gender of the cultic functionary was complementary to the gender of the deity, with male priests serving goddesses and female priestesses serving male gods.

Another reason cited for the exclusion of women is the physiological differences between females and males. According to this view, there was some doubt that females could perform the priestly role of animal sacrifice because of their limited physical strength. However, lifting heavy livestock such as a bull for sacrifice was the role of the worshipper, not the priest who sprinkled the blood of the animal on the altar (Lev 1:4–5, 3:2).

A woman's reproductive physiology is also cited as a reason. Ritual purity regulations defined menstruating women and women who have just given birth as ritually unclean and in need of purification (Lev 15:20–23; 12:2, 5). The discharge of blood during menstruation and childbirth required women to be secluded in order to avoid contamination. Anything that came into contact with a menstruating woman or her bed or seat was unclean. Therefore, she was denied participation in the cult during her time of impurity. For some, this explains why women are banned from the priesthood. However, men who had a sexual discharge were also made ceremonially unclean and excluded from cult participation until their purification by washing of clothes and bathing (Lev 15:3).

There were also distinctions made between Aaron's sons and non-Aaronite males. According to several texts, only Aaron's sons could be priests. All other males were excluded. However, this did not appear to apply to kings. Certain texts depict Israel's kings performing priestly duties. For example, King Saul offered sacrifices (1 Sam 13:8–9), although he might have viewed this as his role as the symbolic male head of the nation. Kings Jeroboam I and Ahaz are also depicted as presiding at the altar (1 Kgs 13:1–6; 2 Kgs 16:13). They are each condemned for sacrificing at unauthorized sites, but not for their sacrificial activity, implying that this was a normal function of the king. However, 2 Chronicles 26:16–21 is explicit in its condemnation of kings presiding as cultic functionaries.

The priestly texts made further distinctions between certain male members of Aaron's family. Male descendants with any physical defects, such as blindness, disability, skin disease, running sores, or damaged testicles were prohibited from performing certain priestly functions such as performing table service before the Lord: "He shall not come near to offer the food of his God" (Lev 21:18–21). They were also excluded from approaching the veil or the altar in order not to defile the Lord's sanctuary (21:23).

Levites. The priestly material distinguishes between the descendants of Aaron and descendants of Levi or Levites (*leviim*). Leviticus and Numbers depict the priests as the personal attendants of Yahweh in the house of Yahweh. By contrast, the Levites are described as lower clergy appointed by Yahweh to serve Aaron and his sons, overseeing the maintenance of the tabernacle and all its equipment, and setting up their tents around the sanctuary encamping the sanctuary to protect it from encroachment (Num 1:47–53, 3:5–39). The descendants of Levi's son Kohath ages twenty to fifty were set apart from Levi's other sons to set up and dismantle the tabernacle (Num 4:1–4, 15).

In contrast, the Deuteronomic material refers to the "Levitical priests," inferring that Levites and priests are one and the same (Deut 21:5, 31:9) and that table service was the Levites' prerogative (18:1–8). However, the postexilic texts reinscribe the distinctions between priests and Levites. For example, the books of Ezra and Nehemiah refer to the priests and Levites separately among the cultic personnel (Ezra 1:5; 2:36–63, 70; 6:18; Neh 7:39–60, 72).

Mourning Women. *Qonnanoth* (professional mourners) were among the few religious specialists in the Hebrew Bible that were almost exclusively female. Women skilled in mourning were called upon to sing dirges and lament on behalf of Zion in the book of Jeremiah (9:16–19; Heb 9:17–20). Jeremiah 9:20 implies that professional mourners trained their daughters or other women in the art of grieving. This same text gives the impression that they were older women known for their experience (9:17; Heb 9:16).

Other texts that associate wailing and chanting with women are 2 Samuel 1:24, where the daughters of Israel are summoned to weep for Saul and Jonathan, and Ezekiel 32:16–18, where Yahweh commands the women of the nations to chant a lamentation over Egypt and its hordes. Juliana Claassens (2010) has suggested that women may have belonged to guilds where they honed their craft. That these women are called upon to lead the community in public expressions of grief challenges the public/private dichotomy, which holds that women's work was restricted to the domestic realm.

Prophets. The term "prophet" (*nabi'*; fem. *nebi'ah*) in the Hebrew Bible is difficult to define because the term connotes different phenomena throughout the texts, therefore making it difficult for scholars to reach a consensus. This dilemma is complicated by the common understanding of the English term "prophet," from *prophetes*, the Greek translation of *nabi'*, as a "foreteller," one who predicts the future. Although biblical prophets might speak about future events, they are understood as "forthtellers," individuals who addressed the present while referring to Israel's past. Israelite prophets functioned at the most basic level as Yahweh's "mouthpieces" (Deut 18:18b), mediators between Yahweh and humans.

Prophecy is one among several forms of divine consultation that are sometimes referred to as "divination." The various terms for prophet in the Hebrew Bible are *ro'eh* and *chozeh* (seer or visionary), *ish ha-'elohim* (holy man or man of God), and *nabi'* (one who is called by Yahweh to speak on behalf of Yahweh). What is not as clear is the distinction between each type. For example, according to the Deuteronomic material, the figure now called a *nabi'* (prophet) in Israel was previously referred to as a *ro'eh* (seer; 1 Sam 9:9). Some scholars have argued that the *ro'eh* title reflects a nomadic setting, in contrast to the *nabi'* title, which emerged during the settlement period in ancient Palestine.

Other scholars, while in agreement that the use of the four different labels for prophet reflects linguistic usage in different times and places, contend that the variation is between the northern and southern kingdoms. For example, they maintain that the term *nabi'* may have been particularly prominent as a way of referring to prophets in Israel, while the *hozeh* label appears to have been particular to Judah.

Still another suggestion is that the different titles reflect different prophetic behavior. While there has been considerable debate whether Israelite prophets displayed ecstatic behavior or only spoke intelligibly, the *niphal* verb form of *naba'* (prophesy) in Hebrew means "to act as a *nabi'*," "to prophesy," or, in a derogatory sense, "to behave like a prophet" (Müller, 1998, p. 134). King Saul is described as having been possessed of the spirit of God and fallen into a prophetic frenzy, which caused him to prophesy with the prophets (1 Sam 10:5–6, 10–13). The prophets of Baal in 1 Kings

18:29 are said to have "raved until the time of the offer of the oblation" (NRSV). The word translated "raved" is literally "prophesied" and conveys the behavior of one crazed or in a frenzy.

Prophets also appear in the Torah, or Pentateuch. The first four books depict them as charismatic figures whose methods of divine revelations or disclosures to humanity were usually through visions and dreams (Num 12:6) and spirit possession (Num 11:16–17, 25). Only three figures are designated prophets: Abraham (Gen 20:7), Aaron (Exod 7:1), and Miriam (Exod 15:20). However, the text implies that other figures who received divine revelation through dreams and visions were prophetic figures, such as Jacob (Gen 28:11–12, 17–18; 31:4–16), Joseph (Gen 38:20–24), and Moses (Exod 3:4b).

The book of Deuteronomy presents Moses as the founder of the office of prophet in ancient Israel and the prophet par excellence, the model for all others who come after him (Num 12:6–8; Deut 13:1–5 [Heb 13:2–6], 34:10; cf. Hos 12:14). However, as David Petersen observes, according to Deuteronomy 34:10–12, there really is no prophet who is like Moses: "Whether as known by the deity face to face or as a performer of wonders, Moses had no competitors or imitators, either before him or after him" (2006, p. 317). Consequently, all other prophets are subordinate to Moses.

Unlike priests, prophets did not inherit their position. Rather, they were servants of Yahweh called by Yahweh. Therefore, the office of prophet is one of the few religious leadership positions that were open to individuals regardless of kinship or gender. For example, women could be prophets. There are four named women prophets in the Hebrew Bible: Miriam (Exod 15:20), Deborah (Judg 4:4), Huldah (2 Kgs 22:14; cf. 2 Chr 34:22), and Noadiah (Neh 6:14), as well as an unnamed woman (Isa 8:3). There are also women in Ezekiel 13:17 who are not identified as prophets but are accused of prophesying by unauthorized means. The text is ambiguous whether gender contributed to their being charged.

Scribes. The Hebrew word *sofer* (scribe) is a participle form of the root *safar*, which has a range of meaning from "to count (up)," "make a written record," "to count (out), or "to write." The role of the scribe changes over time in the Hebrew Bible. The first mention of a scribe in the Hebrew Bible was in the premonarchic period. The role of the scribe was to muster the tribes of Israel for battle (Judg 5:14). During the monarchic period scribes were officials affiliated with the Temple and the royal court who had administrative duties that were more reflective of the term's root. For example, Shaphan, a "scribe to the house of Yahweh" (2 Kgs 22:3) who served under King Josiah of Judah, was responsible for distributing Temple funds for Temple repair (22:5), as well as reading the "book of the Torah" to the king (22:8).

Scribes who served in the royal court include Seraiah, scribe to King David (2 Sam 8:17; variant spellings Sheva, 2 Sam 20:25; Shishah, 1 Kgs 4:3; Shavsha, 1 Chr 18:16); brothers Elihoreph and Ahijah, serving King Solomon (1 Kgs 4:3); and Elishama, a scribe in King Jehoiakim's house (Jer 36:12, 20–21). Jeremiah was placed under house arrest in the home of the scribe Jonathan (37:15, 20). Whether ancient Israel had scribal schools has yet to be determined by textual evidence. There is, however, a reference to a group of scribes who are accused of writing with a "false pen" (Jer 8:8).

By the postexilic period, the role of the scribes was to preserve and interpret the book of the Torah. For example, Ezra, who is described as both a priest and a scribe "skilled in the law of Moses" (Ezra 7:6), was responsible for reinstituting the worship of Yahweh in Judah for the returnees from Babylonia. This responsibility included reading the Torah for the people and interpreting it (Neh 8).

Although several scribes were Temple and government officials, scribes also served private individuals. For example, the scribe Baruch wrote down the words of the prophet Jeremiah (Jer 36:4, 17–18). He also read the scroll with the words dictated by Jeremiah in the house of Yahweh at Jeremiah's command (36:5–6, 8). Wealthy individuals and royalty were also trained in writing. Thus, Queen Jezebel wrote letters to the elders in the name of her husband, King Ahab (1 Kgs 21:8), and Queen Esther wrote letters confirming the institution of the feast of Purim (Esth 9:29).

The office of scribe does not appear to be a hereditary position. However, certain passages suggest that fathers (and at least one mother) may have trained their sons in the scribal tradition. For example, Shisha, a scribe in King David's administration (see above), was also the father of scribes Elihoreph and Ahijah. Jeremiah 36:10–12 infers that Shaphan's son Gemariah and grandson Micaiah may have been scribes. Ezra 2:55 lists the descendants of a female scribe, Hassophereth (lit. "female scribe"; the name appears as Sophereth in Nehemiah 7:57), who served under Solomon among the postexilic temple functionaries. She may have been the leader of a guild of scribes in monarchic Israel.

Final Thoughts. Religious leadership in the Hebrew Bible reflects the deployment of power through the social constructions of sexuality and gender. Who gets to represent Yahweh on behalf of the community is based not only on who is in power but also on the constructions of sexuality and gender. For example, the exclusion of males with crushed testicles or severed penises from performing certain priestly duties or participating in the assembly could have been based just as much on the sexual ambiguity of emasculated males as on their being seen as a source of defilement.

As mentioned above, there were different forms of divination. However, not all forms were acceptable. The biblical writers approved of noninductive forms such as prophecy and messages received through dreams, which did not require specific skills to perform. However, alternative forms of divination such as magic and necromancy (divination by inquiring of the dead), which may have required formal training, were considered heterodox. Yet priestly modes of divination that belonged to the latter, such as the Urim and Thummim (1 Sam 23:8–13) and the ephod (Exod 28; 39), were tolerated.

Women practiced both forms of divination. Although women could be prophets, the *eshet ba'alat-ob* (lit. "mistress of spirit" or medium) in 1 Samuel 28 (cf. Lev. 19:31), *mekash-shefah* (sorceress) and *yidde'oni* (lit. one with a spirit of divination or wizard) were denounced (Exod 22:18 [Heb 22:17]; Lev 19:31, 20:27). There is an imbalance between the penalties for female practitioners of forbidden forms of divination and those for male practitioners. For example, female sorcerers were sentenced to death (Exod 22:18 [Heb 22:17]). However, the fate of male sorcerers is not specified (Deut 18:10; Jer 27:9; Mal 3:5). Nevertheless, the fact that women practitioners are denounced suggests that there was a clientele for their arts despite the ban.

[*See also* Education, *subentry* Hebrew Bible; Imagery, Gendered, *subentry* Priestly Literature; *and* Popular Religion and Magic, *subentry* Hebrew Bible.]

BIBLIOGRAPHY

Botterweck, G. Johannes, Helmer Ringgren, and Heinz-Josef Fabry, eds. *Theological Dictionary of the Old Testament.* 9 vols. Translated by John T. Willis and David E. Green. Grand Rapids, Mich.: Eerdmans, 1974–1984.

Claassens, L. Juliana M. "Calling the Keeners: The Image of the Wailing Woman as Symbol of Survival in a Traumatized World." *Journal of Feminist Studies in Religion* 26, no. 1 (Spring 2010): 63–77.

Grabbe, Lester L. *Priests, Prophets, Diviners, Sages: A Socio-Historical Study of Religious Specialists in Ancient Israel.* Valley Forge, Pa.: Trinity Press International, 1995.

Lawrence, Beatrice. "Gender Analysis: Gender and Method in Biblical Studies." In *Method Matters: Essays on the Interpretation of the Hebrew Bible in Honor of David L. Petersen*, edited by Joel M. LeMon and Kent Harold Richards, pp. 333–348. Atlanta: Society of Biblical Literature, 2009.

Leithart, Peter J. "Attendants of Yahweh's House: Priesthood in the Old Testament." *Journal for the Study of the Old Testament* 24 (1999): 3–24.

Müller, H.-P. "נָבִיא *nāḇîʾ.*" In *Theological Dictionary of the Old Testament*, Vol. 9, edited by G. W. Botterweck, G. Johannes, Helmer Ringgren, and Heinz-Josef Fabry and translated by John T. Willis and David E. Green, pp. 129–150. Grand Rapids, Mich.: Eerdmans, 1998. German version of Vol. 9 was published in 1984–1986.

Nissinen, Martti. *Prophets and Prophecy in the Ancient Near East.* Edited by Peter Machinist. Atlanta: Society of Biblical Literature, 2003.

Petersen, David L. "The Ambiguous Role of Moses as Prophet." In *Israel's Prophets and Israel's Past: Essays on the Relationship of Prophetic Texts and Israelite History in Honor of John H. Hayes*, edited by Brad E. Kelle and Megan Bishop Moore, pp. 311–324. New York: T&T Clark, 2006.

Rooke, Deborah W., ed. *Embroidered Garments: Priests and Gender in Biblical Israel.* Sheffield, U.K.: Sheffield Phoenix, 2009.

Shectman, Sarah. "The Social Status of Priestly and Levite Women." In *Levites and Priests in Biblical History and Tradition*, edited by Mark A. Leuchter and Jeremy M.

Hutton, pp. 83–99. Ancient Israel and Its Literature 9. Atlanta: Society of Biblical Literature, 2011.

Stökl, Jonathan. "Ištar's Women, YHWH's Men? A Curious Gender-Bias in Neo-Assyrian and Biblical Prophecy." *Zeitschrift für die Alttestamentliche Wissenschaft* 121 (2009): 87–100.

Vaux, Roland de. *Ancient Israel: Its Life and Institutions.* Translated by John McHugh. Grand Rapids, Mich.: Eerdmans, 1997.

Zevit, Ziony. *The Religions of Ancient Israel: A Synthesis of Parallactic Approaches.* London: Continuum, 2001.

Vanessa L. Lovelace

Greek World

The great variety of Greek religious officials requires detailed examination of their functions, duties, and privileges. Officials were in charge of the rituals honoring the gods and served as mediators between gods and humans: the terms *hiereus* (priest) and *hiereia* (priestess) suggest a special relationship with the *hiera* (sacred). As a general rule, the gender of the official matches that of the deity. There are, however, many exceptions to this neat scheme of gendered relations to the gods, particularly in the cults of Apollo and Dionysus. Although priests and priestesses seem at first sight to have equal functions, the kind of influence they exerted on religious matters and their relationship to political authority depended on gendered legal status. A related issue concerns the authority of religious officials. They have long been considered as equivalent to civic magistrates, especially because they have been compared to Christian priests. Indeed, as studies show, Greek priesthoods were not necessarily intended for experts or for people having a vocation for religion. Moreover, the authority of priests was usually limited to the sphere of the sanctuary, dealing with its administration and ritual actions. While priests had no authority over the city, they served as mediators between the city and the gods, and the city participated actively in the regulation of cults and conduct of rituals.

Methodological Concerns. The position of ancient Greek women has been examined through a masculine and often fantasizing lens. Herein lies an array of ideological positions, from feminists' accusation of oppression to male anxiety about the feminine "otherness" and about women's violence toward men. Moreover, what we know about Greek women is written by men. Ancient authors had an interest in priestesses, but their works are lost. There was indeed a play by Aeschylus entitled *Hiereiai* and a comedy by Menander entitled *Hiereia*. Moreover, modern scholars have often compared information about ancient Greek women and information about women in modern Mediterranean societies: they were confined in the limits of the house, silent, powerless, and oppressed. While gender inequality clearly existed as a phenomenon, it is dangerous to generalize across the different city-states. For example, compared to the conservative Athenian society, Spartan women appear to have been trained and freely speaking. Women's roles in Greek religion must have varied significantly from city-state to city-state and region to region, as well as from one cult to another.

To speak generally, however, women have since antiquity been attributed a special relationship to the divine sphere because of their "irrational" nature. Therefore they have a special connection to the Dionysian cults and ecstatic, frenzied wanderings in the wild. However, their functions were far more varied and significant. A widely held view among twenty-first-century scholars is that Greek women were denied political citizenship but enjoyed religious citizenship. Nonetheless, priestesses, just as with priests, had to be descended from citizen families. They were *astai* (having only civic rights), sometimes for generations, as the priestess of Artemis Pergaia in Halicarnassus in the third century B.C.E. (Sokolowski, 1955, *Lois sacrées de l'Asie Mineure*, no. 73, l. 6–8). Furthermore, official positions in the service of the gods rendered them wholly visible in the public sphere. Not only were priestesses granted the right to attend events that were normally forbidden to women, as the priestess of Demeter Chamyne at Olympia who was permitted to watch the games (Pausanias, *Description of Greece* 6.20.9), they also had responsibilities and charges, such as for the possessions of the sanctuary, as shown by an Athenian inscription dating from the imperial period in which the priestess was accountable for the furniture (*IG* II² 1346, l. 5–7), and they were not excluded from participation in legal procedures, unlike ordinary women. Priestesses also had the power to appoint other religious officials (*IG* II² 1328, l. 16–17; Sokolowski, 1969, *Lois sacrées des cités grecques*, no. 166, l. 23–26). More significantly, they were able to bring to court cases of impiety and argue before the assembly, and therefore they would have had to deal with political bodies. In addition, they were eligible to receive honors usually reserved for men. Therefore priestesses were singled out not only from ordinary women but also from ordinary men.

Most of the evidence on prominent women representatives comes from Athens. In the following discussion I will present some examples from the Athenian evidence, complemented by some examples from elsewhere, showing the variety of practices depending on both the locale and the time period in question. One general trend is the increasing visibility of women in the public sphere, and with the coming of the Hellenistic age public honors were bestowed on benefactresses with more frequency. Priestesses are, however, the most prominent women of the classical period, having in the religious sphere a role equivalent to that of men.

The Priestesses of Athena Polias. Among the mostly highly ranked Athenian women, the priestesses of Athena Polias serving the city goddess are the most famous. We know of twenty-seven of them, which illustrates their exceptional position. Their mythic model is Praxithea, wife of Erechtheus, the king of Athens. She appears prominently in the lost play of Euripides entitled *Erechtheus*. In order to save the city and following the oracle of Delphi, she agreed to the sacrifice of their daughter. Erechtheus became a hero, the daughter was given divine status, and the goddess herself made Praxithea, whose name means "the one acting for the goddess," her first priestess.

The lifelong priesthood of Athena Polias was inherited by married women who were members of the *genos* of the Eteoboutadai, one of the most illustrious Athenian families that also provided the priest of Poseidon Erechtheus. The priestess was assisted in her service by other female attendants. She performed the preliminary sacrifices at the altar of Athena. She received barley, wheat, and an obol for each Athenian's

birth or death (Aristotle, *Oeconomica* 1347a). She also performed the *proteleia* (preliminary sacrifices) on weddings. Lycurgus's lost speech "On the Priestess" reports the administrative powers of the priestess of Athena Polias. By decree, she might add her seal to the register (frag. 6.4).

The first actual known priestess of Athena is Lysimache in the last quarter of the fifth century B.C.E. She was in office for over sixty years, and had had four children. The state honored her with a statue. Among the most honored priestesses was Chrysis. In 106/5 B.C.E., after having performed the Pythais, the official procession of the Athenians to Delphi, she was honored by the Delphians. She received the crown of Apollo and honors usually reserved for men. She and her descendants were bestowed the privileges of *proxenia* to Delphi (being special representatives), *promanteia* (priority in consulting the oracle), *prodikia* (priority of legal processes), *asylia* (inviolability), *ateleia* (freedom from taxes), *proedria* (a front seat) at competitions held by the city, and the right to own land and houses (*IG* II² 1136, l. 12–20). While honorary decrees were awarded to priests according to their own report, they were usually awarded to priestesses based on a report presented by their *kyrios* (guardian, usually their husband or father); this passage is lost in the decree for Chrysis.

Other priestesses of Athena Polias played an exceptional role because of their involvement in politics. One of them expelled the Spartan king Cleomenes from the Acropolis in 508 B.C.E. Indeed, he was trying to install the Athenian Isagoras as leader of an oligarchy, and the Spartans were planning to invade Athens (Herodotus, *Histories* 5.72). The same misadventure occurred to Cleomenes in Argos where the priestess of Hera refused him entry to the temple (6.81). In another critical situation, just before the battle of Salamis in 480 B.C.E., which impeded further Persian invasion, Themistocles was trying to lead the Athenians out of town. The Athenians were persuaded to leave the city when the priestess announced that the snake guarding the Acropolis had abandoned the place (Herodotus, *Histories* 7.142–144 and 8.41).

Priestesses of Demeter. The priestesses of another prominent cult, that of Demeter and Kore at Eleusis, were also descendants of a powerful family, appointed by lot among the members of the *genos* of the Philleidai. It is noteworthy that one of these acted against the hierophant Archias, the official in charge of showing the rituals to the initiates during the Eleusinian Mysteries. In the fourth century, Archias was found guilty of impiety (Demosthenes, *Against Neaira* 116–117). He was called to the law court because he had carried out an unlawful sacrifice during the festival of the Haloa for a *hetaira* named Sinope. His impiety was twofold: he had sacrificed in the courtyard of the sanctuary, which was illegal on that day, and had performed a sacrifice that was under the jurisdiction of the priestess.

Another Eleusinian priestess disobeyed civic authority. The Athenian politician Alcibiades was condemned to death for his involvement in the profanation of the Mysteries in 415 B.C.E. A decree stated that he was to be cursed by all priests and priestesses. A priestess of Demeter named Theano refused, stipulating that she was a praying, rather than a cursing, priestess (Plutarch, *Alcibiades* 22.5). The historical existence of Theano has been questioned. Theano is indeed the name of the only priestess mentioned in the *Iliad* (6.297–310), that of Athena in Troy. On behalf of the Trojans, she intervened by bringing a garment as an offering from the Trojan women who were asking for the help of the goddess. She thus appears as a model for priestesses. Whether or not Eleusinian Theano actually existed, it is noteworthy that seven years later, the hierophant Theodoros refused to rescind his curse against Alcibiades when the people favored his return (Plutarch, *Alcibiades* 33).

Priestesses of Demeter serving women-only festivals possess special authority. In the sanctuary of the Thesmophoroi in Piraeus in the fourth century B.C.E., no one was to free slaves, nor assemble *thiasoi*, nor make dedications or purifications or approach the altar and the buildings without the priestess (*IG* II² 1177, l. 3–7). The priestess therefore has control of what happens in her sanctuary, since her presence is required for a series of religious and civil actions. Yet the laws in case of transgression imply that the *demarch*, the magistrate presiding over the district, imposes a fine and takes the matter to a trial by jury.

Thus the priestess does not interact directly with the magistrates, but rather through an intervening entity in her transaction with the political body.

Other Prominent Female Officials. More prominent female officials, this time in oracular sanctuaries, served a male god. Euripides in his lost play the *Captive Melanippe* (frag. 494 Kn) shows the importance of women in ritual through the examples of the Pythia at Delphi and the priestess of Zeus at Dodona who both prophesy the gods' will. The oracles have a crucial role regarding religious as well as political issues. The oracular responses were preserved in the archives and produced when necessary.

The *pythia*, called a *mantis*, a *promantis* (diviner), and a *prophētis* (prophet), pronouncing the oracles of Apollo, had once been a young maiden, a status that changed because of a rape. Thereafter she had to be over fifty, still wearing a maiden's garment (Diodorus Siculus, *Bibliotheca historica* 16.26.6). She seems to have been chosen from among the local peasant women. Given the popularity of the oracle in the classical period, up to three *pythias* were prophesying by turns. The god was served by more priests and *prophētai* who assumed complementary tasks.

The *pythia*'s political authority has been both exaggerated and minimized in modern scholarship. The oracle was indeed consulted for state matters such as war or tyranny, and in most colonization expeditions. There are stories relating to manipulation, corruption, and blackmail of the *pythia* by politicians (Herodotus, *Histories* 5.63, 5.66, 5.90, 6.123; Aristotle, *The Constitution of the Athenians* 19.4; Jacoby, 1924–1958, vol. II A, p. 103, 70 frag. 206). Yet the presence of an uneducated woman at the center of the procedure would have limited the possibilities of influence. Even so, the Spartans claimed that the Delphic oracle gave them their constitution (Herodotus, *Histories* 1.65; Plutarch, *Lycurgus* 6). The Athenians consulted the *pythia* in 352 B.C.E. regarding the delimitation of the *hiera orgas* (sacred meadow) lying at the border of Megara to avoid a war. The *pythia* also participated in the appointment of the ten eponymous heroes of the tribes of Athens (Aristotle, *The Constitution of the Athenians* 21.6).

These stories relating the *pythia*'s authority form a clear picture of the influence exerted by the sanctuary of Delphi. Even if her personal relations to the politicians of the time were limited, she was pronouncing the will of the god and therefore influenced the outcome of most crises and expeditions.

More Female Attendants. Athenian girls, at least those descending from citizen families, had the occasion to officiate at festivals at various stages of their lives. Aristophanes's *Lysistrata* gives a much debated summary of these roles: a young girl at seven was an *arrēphoros* (carrier of things not to be spoken) serving Athena, then she was an *aletris* (flour grinder) for the founding goddess; at ten she would attend the Brauronia in honor of Artemis participating with the title of "bear" or, according to another interpretation, "playing the bear" in an initiation ritual. As a maiden, she would serve as a *kanēphoros* (basket bearer). All offices were filled by young girls or women, who were suitable since their families had the means to support them.

Once they became adults, women could inhabit a great variety of attendants' offices. Working along with the priestesses in charge, these lower officials had ritual and administrative functions that contributed to the management of the sanctuary. We know, for example, that a certain *trapezophoros* (one who bears, or takes care of, the offering table) and another one called *kosmō* (related to the adornment or furnishing) were collaborating with the priestess of Athena Polias, taking care of everything along with her (Lycurgus frag. 6.20). They were sometimes praised for their service, as was the *diakonos* (attendant) of the priestess of Athena Polias named Sueris in the third century B.C.E. (*IG* II² 3464). At times the name of their function was shaped after the title of male magistrates; the Thesmophoria, a women-only festival of Demeter, was administered in the Attic deme of Cholargos by two women called *archousai* after the Athenian chief magistrates (*IG* II² 1184, l. 3). Even though we know no more than their duties during the festival, other cult attendants did take initiatives on various levels. The *zakoros* (subordinate guardian) Timo, officiating in the sanctuary of Demeter on Paros, was accused of letting the Athenian general Miltiades get into the sanc-

tuary and do or see things that were forbidden to men (Herodotus, *Histories* 6.134–136). Miltiades was injured and died, and while the Parians accused Timo of betraying the city, the oracle of Delphi asserted that Timo was not responsible and only led Miltiades to meet his fate.

Other stories relate notable individual women even though they are not priestesses or cult officials. In the beginnings of the settlement of Thasos we find Cleoboia, who first brought the rites of Demeter from Paros (Pausanias, *Description of Greece* 10.28.3). The Ephesian colony of Massalia was likewise established under the presence of Aristarche, who introduced the cult of Artemis (Strabo, *Geography* 4.1.4). While we know very little about Cleoboia, Aristarche was a distinguished Ephesian instructed by the goddess to act as she did. She did what was necessary for the foundation of the colony and the new cult, and was appointed priestess as an honor.

Further Issues. Women had their own special position in the public sphere, especially when it came to religion. As worshippers, they attended sanctuaries and performed rituals. As officials of given cults they had specific duties overlapping with those of men. Priests and priestesses had equal functions, similar duties, and the same rules of appointment depending on status, wealth, and age. Indeed, procedures for appointment show that any citizen fulfilling specific requirements could become a priest, and, with the exception of hereditary priesthoods, any citizen could aspire to the priesthood. With sufficient financial means a priest was able to make the cult more impressive, as the honors occasioned by such generosity show. As to honors, females and males were praised in the same terms for the same services. Additionally, some female priesthoods had precise requirements for sexual status and conduct. Sometimes, priestesses enjoyed the same privileges as priests. The priestesses of Athena Polias had the privilege of cultic eponymy as well as the one of Demeter and Kore at Eleusis. Female priesthoods could also serve to date historical events, as happened with the dating of the beginning of Thucydides's *Peloponnesian War*, which uses the name of the priestess of Hera at Argos, Chrysis, along with the ephors of Sparta and the archon of

Athens (2.2.1). The names of the priestesses of Zeus at Dodona were also preserved (Herodotus, *Histories* 2.55.3).

It is not difficult to discern the significance of such female priesthoods. These women had exceptional positions and a strong sense of family pride. What, then, is the difference between priestesses and priests? Priesthood did not necessarily "convert a female to a male" as Susan Cole (2004, p. 122) has asserted. The phenomenon of female officials opposing political authority is indeed intriguing, as the possession of religious privileges is not equivalent to the possession of political rights. Priests collaborate with the demos (people), the magistrates, and other religious experts such as the *exēgētai* (expounders). Eventually the citizen body made decisions. Clearly, gender limited the independence of priestesses more often than not. An official, the *gynaikonomos* (supervisor of women), ensured that women were behaving properly. As a rule, female religious officials needed a *kyrios* to mediate the relationship with the political bodies. Here again, however, there are exceptions. An inscription dating from the fourth century B.C.E. from Arkesine on Amorgos shows a priestess of Demeter reporting directly to the *prytaneis* (members presiding at the council) and complaining about women's access to the sanctuary (*IG* XII 7, 4, l. 4–8). Another noticeable exception is reported in an inscription from Mylasa in Asia Minor, where "the women resolve[d]" issues in a cult of Demeter (Sokolowski, 1955, no. 61, l. 5), according to the expression that is usual for civic male magistrates making decisions. If women were able to adopt men's usage in their service, the differences were immediately recognizable. Iconographical evidence distinguishes priestesses with a key as wardens and priests with a knife as sacrificers. This, again, does not mean that women did not perform sacrifices, as modern scholars long conjectured, but they did perform them much less often than men.

Political power is as important for this issue as gender. Religious agents officiating in public cults on behalf of the political authority operate under its responsibility. Civic magistrates were also allowed to perform rituals. According to Aeschines (*Against Ctesiphon*

17–18), both priestesses and priests have to do with the public affairs (*ta koina*). According to law, they are accountable to the council and the people. Accountability does not involve only the individuals but also their families. Women's legal restrictions limit their acting capacity. Insofar as a priestess makes decisions and acts in her sanctuary, she behaves as her male counterparts do. But when she is to report before the assembly, her *kyrios* (guardian) speaks for her. The guardian may be necessary even to regulate sanctuary affairs, as is implied by a fourth-century B.C.E. inscription from Miletus where reports on those that did not give the priestess her perquisites were made by her guardian (Sokolowski, 1955, no. 45, l. 8–14).

Unlike priests, who have been compared to civic magistrates, female officials did not hold civic offices, at least not until the Hellenistic period. From the Hellenistic period on, and especially in Asia Minor, priests and priestesses officiate together in the same cults. Artemis Leucophryene in Magnesia is served by both a priest and a priestess (Sokolowski, 1955, no. 32, l. 15–16), as are Artemis Hymnia in Mantineia (Pausanias, *Description of Greece* 8.13.1) and the Corybants at Erythrai (Sokolowski, 1955, no. 23). Teams of male and female officials seem to be the rule for priesthoods of the imperial cult, at least in the first century C.E. Moreover, civic titles that had until then been reserved for men were bestowed on women.

Priests and priestesses often collaborated with civic magistrates in order to enforce rules and laws for orderly conduct of the rituals. While at times they were opposed to decisions made by state officials, they did not have the power to overcome their authority. Significantly, politicians had an active role in religious conduct and rituals, even in those held only by women. In fact, it is the demos that has the ultimate authority not only to enact regulations concerning priesthoods and fixing their payments but also to introduce new deities.

Even the most oppressed women in the classical period, the Athenians, acted as public religious officials. Although equality was impossible, given that women could not act alone in legal matters, priestesses and other female attendants were acting on behalf of the polis (Sourvinou-Inwood, 1995, p. 114). Order and good relation with the gods depended partly on women performing their own duties. Regarding religion, women were not exactly subordinated to men. They followed a different kind of hierarchy from which priests were excluded or in which they performed different functions. In this context, priestesses were acting in ways complementary to those of men, if often with more limited authority.

[*See also* Political Leadership, *subentry* Greek World; Religious Leaders, *subentries on* Early Church, New Testament, *and* Roman World; Religious Participation, *subentry* Greek World; *and* Social Interaction, *subentry* Greek and Roman Worlds.]

BIBLIOGRAPHY

Blok, Josine H., and Stephen D. Lambert, "The Appointment of Priests in Attic *Gene*." *Zeitschrift für Papyrologie und Epigraphik* 169 (2009): 95–121.

Chaniotis, Angelos. "Priests as Ritual Experts in the Greek World." In *Practitioners of the Divine: Greek Priests and Religious Officials from Homer to Heliodorus*, edited by Beate Dignas and Kai Trampedach, pp. 17–34. Cambridge, Mass.: Harvard University Press, 2008.

Cole, Susan Guettel. *Landscapes, Gender, and Ritual Space: The Ancient Greek Experience*. Berkeley: University of California Press, 2004.

Connelly, Joan Breton. *Portrait of a Priestess: Women and Ritual in Ancient Greece*. Princeton, N.J.: Princeton University Press, 2007.

Dillon, Matthew. *Girls and Women in Classical Greek Religion*. London: Routledge, 2002.

Garland, Robert. "Priests and Power in Classical Athens." In *Pagan Priests: Religion and Power in the Ancient World*, edited by Mary Beard and John North, pp. 73–91. London: Duckworth, 1990.

Graham, Alexander J. "Religion, Women, and Greek Colonization." In *Religione e Città nel Mondo Antico* 11 (1981–1982): 293–314.

Horster, Marietta. "Lysimache and the Others: Some Notes on the Position of Women in Athenian Religion." In *Studies in Greek Epigraphy and History in Honor of Stephen V. Tracy*, edited by Gary Reger, F. X. Ryan, and Timothy F. Winters, pp. 177–192. Etudes 26. Pessac, France: Ausonius, 2010.

Jacoby, Felix. *Die Fragmente der Griechischen Historiker*. Berlin: Weidmann, 1921.

Lambert, Stephen D. "The Social Construction of Priests and Priestesses in Athenian Honorific Decrees from the Fourth Century B.C. to the Augustan Period." In *Civic Priests: Cult Personnel in Athens from the Hellenistic Period to Late Antiquity*, edited by Marietta Horster and Anja Klöckner, pp. 67–133. Berlin: De Gruyter, 2012.

Maurizio, Lisa. "The Voice at the Center of the World: The Pythia's Ambiguity and Authority." In *Making Silence Speak: Women's Voices in Greek Literature and Society*, edited by André Lardinois and Laura McClure, pp. 38–54. Princeton, N.J.: Princeton University Press, 2001.

Osborne, Robin. "Women and Sacrifice in Classical Greece." *Classical Quarterly* 43, no. 2 (1993): 392–405.

Pirenne-Delforge, Vinciane. "Personnel de culte: Monde grec." In *Thesaurus cultus et rituum antiquorum (ThesCRA)*. Vol. 5: *Personnel of Cult, Cult Instruments*, pp. 1–31. Los Angeles: J. Paul Getty Museum, 2005.

Sokolowski, Franciszek. *Lois sacrées de l'Asie Mineure*, Paris: E. de Boccard, 1955.

Sokolowski, Franciszek. *Lois sacrées des cités grecques*, Paris: E. de Boccard, 1969.

Sourvinou-Inwood, Christiane. "Male and Female, Public and Private, Ancient and Modern." In *Pandora: Women in Classical Greece*, edited by Ellen D. Reeder, pp. 111–120. Princeton, N.J.: Princeton University Press, 1995.

Ioanna Patera

Roman World

When discussing the subject of religion, Roman writers rarely missed an opportunity to praise the antiquity of their religious traditions and their history of unwavering devotion to the gods. According to legend, Romulus founded Rome in 753 B.C.E. by performing a religious ritual designed to establish sacred space within the city's boundary (*pomerium*), whereas the next king, Numa (r. 715–673 B.C.E.), was credited with creating the organizational structure of Roman religion. These ancient roots were a source of pride for later Romans: not only did Cicero boast that the Romans "have excelled every race and nation in piety (*pietas*) [and]…religious matters (*religio*)," but also he and many of his contemporaries simply assumed that it was the people's adherence to their "ancestral customs" (*mos maiorum*) that ensured divine favor and Rome's place of primacy in the world (*On the Reply of the Haruspices* 19; *On the Nature of the Gods* 2.8–9; 3.5–6; Virgil, *Aeneid* 1.278–279).

Priestly Colleges and Public Cults. Because the performance of religious rites maintained the "peace of the gods" (*pax deorum*), religious symbols dominated the landscape: in the words of Livy, "There is no place in our city that is not filled with a sense of religion (*religiones*) and the gods" (5.52; see also 1.21.1). When shaping public policy, Roman politicians and generals ignored religious considerations at their own peril. Yet this does not mean that the religious practices of the state displayed a structural or doctrinal coherence. On the contrary, Roman reverence toward the divine was multifaceted and even inconsistent: instead of producing a systematic theology, the official cults were focused almost exclusively on public rituals and performances that ensured the health of the state (Cicero classifies religion under three categories: ritual, auspices [the observance of signs to ascertain the gods' will], and prophetic warnings through divine portents; *On the Nature of the Gods* 3.5). In this eclectic environment, the Romans relied upon various officially sanctioned religious functionaries (*sacerdotes*) who were charged with specific responsibilities in managing the state cults (*sacra publica*) and conducting other religiopolitical duties.

Rome's religious leaders were either members of an official priestly college or linked with less influential confraternities. The membership requirements and structure of the colleges were modified over the centuries, but by the end of the second century B.C.E. four major organizations achieve recognition as "most distinguished" (*amplissima*): the *pontifices*, the *augures*, the *quindecemviri*, and the *septemviri* (*Res. gest. divi. Aug.*, 9.1; cf. Cicero, *On the Laws* 2.20–21). Led by the *pontifex maximus*, the pontifical college regulated the religious life of the citizen body by controlling the religious calendar and sacred places, conducting public rituals (performed especially by priests known as the *flamines*), regulating burial sites, and formulating procedures for the introduction of new religious rites. As experts in Rome's religious heritage, they also functioned as an advisory body to the Senate and other political figures when the latter needed technical expertise and were even involved in more "political" affairs (e.g., publishing a record of the events of the state and adjudicating wills, inheritances, and adoptions). If the pontiffs provided a bridge between the individual and the state, the augurs were specialists in divination who acted as mediators between heaven and earth: they assigned sacred space and interpreted auspices to cultivate the benevolence of the gods. Magistrates could also call upon the college of the *quindecemviri* ("fifteen men") to interpret the meaning of portents, which they did by consulting the collection of oracles found in the ancient Sibylline books. Finally, the *septemviri* ("seven men") coordinated the sacrificial banquet dedicated to Jupiter, Juno, and Minerva during the Plebian Games. Aside from these major colleges, minor priestly groups were responsible for assessing prodigies, drafting declarations of war and peace, maintaining lesser festivals such as the Lupercalia, and, with the beginning of the empire, performing rituals associated with the emperor cult (Scheid, 2003, pp. 129–143).

Most of the *sacerdotes* of the major priestly colleges were men who, until the beginning of the third century B.C.E., came from the patrician class and held their (normally lifetime) appointments while simultaneously retaining membership in the Senate. Women's participation in this system was limited, but recent evaluations of the epigraphic material, combined with a re-examination of the literary sources, suggest that the opportunities for women to act as leaders were more varied than previously thought (Schultz, 2006). In the college of pontiffs, for example, the wives of the priests of Jupiter, Mars, and Quirinus were priestesses (*flaminicae*) bound by the same rules as their husbands and responsible for performing sacrifices. These women (and the *regina sacrorum*, the wife of the king of the sacred rites) were thus essential rather than ancillary members of the flaminate. Outside of the major colleges, it is clear that women could assume the office of the *piatrix, a* female interpreter of prodigies, whereas matrons participated in and even led ritual acts of supplication (*supplicatio*) on behalf of the state. In the Imperial period, women could also become priestesses in the cult of the emperor.

The cults of Ceres, Liber, and Juno Populona, which attest to the existence of priestesses (*sacerdotes*) and female magistrates (*magistrae*) and ministers (*ministrae*), provide additional evidence that Roman women assumed official leadership roles. More influential at a public level was the cult of the Vestal Virgins, an institution whose gender ambiguities and liminality contributed to its revered reputation and sacrality. Specifically, in this cult the priestesses were virgins who engaged in performances normally associated with married women: in a scene reminiscent of a *manus* marriage, they were taken away from their families by the *pontifex maximus*, who thereupon exercised authority over their behavior. They also wore clothing and hairstyles typical of brides or matrons and they presided over the Bona Dea festival, a celebration dedicated to women. At the same time, however, the Vestals enjoyed privileges characteristic of men, such as the power to provide legal testimony, draft a will, and manage their wealth while their father was still alive; as well as the accompaniment of an attendant (*lictor*) during public excursions. Further examination of their practices reveal similar aspects of ambivalence, such as performing private (i.e., feminine) duties (e.g., attention to the sacred hearth of Vesta and preparations of the salt and flour mixture [*mola salsa*] for sacrifice) in the Forum, the heart of public (i.e., masculine) space, and participating in rituals designed to promote fecundity. The link between private and public and purity and fertility suggests that the Romans connected the proper functioning of this cult with the maintenance of the "peace of the gods" and the health of the state (Beard et al., 1998, pp. 52–54; Kraemer, 1992, pp. 81–84).

Foreign cults. Rome's expansion in the later Republican period brought its citizens into contact with a number of foreign religions (*sacra peregrina*) from Asia Minor, Greece, and Egypt. The Senate was not adverse to introducing these cults into Roman society (they even sanctioned them to reestablish Rome's bond with the divine), and they became enormously popular avenues for both men and women who wanted to cultivate meaningful religious experiences—hope for a better life on earth and after death—that the state cults could not offer. Moreover, whereas the (mostly male) patricians and other Roman elites

controlled the state cults, the *sacra peregrina* were less restrictive with regard to class, ethnicity, and gender. Indeed, a full examination of the data (literature, epigraphy, and iconography) reveals that these cults drew their leaders from a broad spectrum of society, from the elites to slaves, Romans and non-Romans, and men and women. It should not be surprising, then, to discover that these cults articulate alternative models of leadership and social organization.

Magna Mater. In 205 B.C.E., the Senate authorized the importation of the cult of Cybele from Asia Minor. Taking the name Great Mother (Magna Mater), this goddess arrived with much pageantry, but legislation was passed early that prevented Roman citizens from joining the priesthood and participating in its processions (these restrictions were abolished under the empire). The anxiety provoked by this cult stemmed from its provocative expressions of gender ambiguity. Specifically, the cult leaders were priests (*galli*) who had castrated themselves in imitation of the god Attis, who performed this act upon himself after the Mother Goddess drove him mad and adopted women's dress and hairstyles. For the Roman mentality, which recognized the genitalia as a symbol of masculine power and virility and stereotyped femininity as derivative, soft, and weak, eunuchs were ambiguous "others" whose sexual identities subverted the "stable" categories of gender. Because castration made a man "unmanly," both physically and morally, it is thus understandable that Roman writers found the practice of the *galli* confusing and their behaviors objectionable (Catullus 63; Juvenal, *Sat.* 6.51–521; Julius Obsequens, *Book of Prodigies* 44a; see also Epictetus, *Discourses* 1.2.25–28). Women too were well represented as leaders—inscriptions reveal that about half of the cult officials were female—who presided over all aspects of the cult (e.g., caring for the shrine and statue of the deity, funding banquets, and celebrating the springtime mysteries by leading the procession with the high priest [*archigallus*]).

Dionysus. In these processions the priests would bear the image of the deity, accompanied by followers waving knives and playing music on cymbals, tambourines, and horns. This sort of activity was also characteristic of the devotees of Dionysus, the god of wine whose cult both literature and art connect with mysteries, secret initiations, and ritual license (see especially the frescoes found in the Villa of the Mysteries at Pompeii). Women also were at the heart of this cult as both participants and leaders. According to Euripides's *Bacchae*, a band of maenads (*thiasos*) accompanied the god wearing fawnskins, carrying wands (*thyrsoi*), handling snakes, playing flutes, and dancing wildly. Plutarch reports that women Dionysiac revelry dancing at the base of Mount Parnassus as early as the fifth century B.C.E., whereas literary and epigraphic sources attest to the existence of *thiasoi* in Greece and Asia Minor (Plutarch, *Mor.* 953D; Kraemer, 2004, pp. 16, 20–22). The duties of the female leaders remain frustratingly vague—inscriptions refer to them throwing raw meat (*omophagion*), carrying sacred objects, and leading ecstatic processions to the mountains and throughout the city—but they apparently oversaw the celebrations of both public and private celebrations of *thiasoi*, groups that could either be exclusively female or a mixture of men and women.

The cult of Dionysus appears on Italian soil by at least 400 B.C.E., the probable dating of a gold tablet found in a burial chamber at Hipponion that exhorts the deceased woman to drink from the waters of Remembrance to travel on the "sacred way which also other initiates (*mystai*) and *bacchoi* gloriously walk." Other scattered evidence from the fourth and third centuries B.C.E. reveal that Romans were familiar but not hostile to the traditions of Dionysus. This changed in the late second century, however. In 186 B.C.E., accusations against the cult in Rome placed Bacchants under official scrutiny. The investigation culminated in a senatorial decree (*Senatus Consultum de Bacchanalibus*) that banished men from holding the priesthood, dissolved the office of the magistrate, dismantled Bacchic cult sites, and placed severe restrictions on the cult's activity. During this reign of terror, around 7,000 people associated with the group were either imprisoned or killed.

Many questions about this event remain unanswered, but the senatorial decree offers important insight into the cult's religious leadership. Specifically, its restriction of the priesthood to women and its dissolution of the positions of *magister* and *promagister* imply that these positions had been open to both sexes. The specific actions against the men also cohere well with recent studies that argue the Senate's actions were designed to reassert authority over aristocrats from Etruria and Campania who had (supposedly) used the cult meetings as a forum for advancing their own political ambitions. Political considerations thus appear to have motivated the Senate rather than any general anxiety over female leadership or men and women worshipping together (points highlighted in Livy's account, 39.8.1–19.7). In this instance it appears that the historian is simply employing stereotypical gendered rhetoric that defined foreign cults as lascivious and female behaviors as deviant and corrupt (Schultz, 2006, pp. 82–92).

Isis. The suspicion that the Senate evinced for the cult of Dionysus was absent in the mystery religion of Isis. Indeed, this cult, which appeared in Italy at the end of the second century B.C.E., received official support from the beginning of the imperial period. In her Hellenistic incarnation, the Isis aretalogies speak of the goddess as the patron of women and routinely associate her with the principles of feminine domesticity (e.g., marriage, motherhood, fertility). Women no doubt came to the cult because of these associations, but her status as a savior who could alter a person's fate and ensure a better afterlife gave the cult broad appeal.

The two most important festivals dedicated to her were the *Isia*, which commemorated the death and resurrection of Osiris, and the Festival of the Ship of Isis (*Navigium Isidis*), which included the launching of a ship dedicated to Isis to mark the beginning of the navigational year. Evidence for these rites is rare and disputed, but if frescoes from Pompeii and Herculaneum do depict these ceremonies, then it is clear that women were central actors in these rites (see also Apuleius, *Metam.* 11). Still, even at the height of its popularity women appear to represent only a minority of cult leaders: in the last centuries of the republic the priesthood was originally restricted to men, with women only managing to hold lesser ministerial positions such as "basket-bearers" (*kane-phoroi*), attendants who opened the temples (*pas-tophoroi*), and stolists who dressed the statue of the goddess. In the imperial age, however, when the cult received support from emperors, over two dozen inscriptions refer to women with the titles *hiereia* or *sacerdos* and tombstone images, reliefs, and paintings portray women dressed in priestly clothes (i.e., linen garments and fringed mantles) and carrying distinctive cult objects such as the rattle (the *sistrum*). During the first centuries of the empire these priestesses could hold lifetime appointments (inscriptions refer to them as *hiereia dia biou* and *sacerdos perpetua*), yet there is no indication that they ever attained the highest echelons of the priesthood.

Mithras. The cult of Isis used initiations as the mechanism for bringing votaries into the various grades of priestly offices—Apuleius's *Metamorphoses*, for instance, details three separate initiations for Lucius, which culminate with him becoming a permanent attendant of the goddess (11.23–30). The cult of Mithras, a first-century C.E. Roman mystery religion that draws upon Persian traditions, utilized initiation ceremonies in a similar fashion to allow members to gain increasing rank and status. Because the literary evidence for this cult is almost completely lacking (and what does exist comes from nonmembers), scholars have had to rely on the (extensive) archaeological remains to determine how members organized their leadership. From this material it appears that Mithraic sanctuaries were modeled on the architecture of the universe. Astrological features were designed to mimic the cosmos and represent the stages in a votary's initiation: thus the floors in the Mithraea of Felicissimus at Ostia and St. Prisca in Rome consist of a mosaic of seven symbols corresponding to each of the seven planets: Raven (Mercury), Bridegroom (Venus), Soldier (Mars), Lion (Jupiter), Persian (Moon), Sun-Runner (Sun), and Father (Saturn).

The specific roles played by members of each rank are impossible to recover, but Porphyry speaks of three classes within these seven ranks, so that initiates of the first three categories (Raven to Soldier) were at the lowest level and those classed from Lion to Sun-Runner had received a complete initiation. Only those members of the highest order, Father, claimed the name "priest" (*sacerdos*) (*On Abstinence from Animal Food* 4.16). In the same passage, Porphyry also states that Mithraism termed women "hyenas," a designation that has almost universally been interpreted to mean that women were excluded from the cult, a conclusion seemingly in accord with the masculine imagery that dominates the material record. Yet the inclusion of the category "woman" in the Mithraic worldview suggests a place for the feminine in the ideological imagination of the cult, a position bolstered through the recognition of the feminine aspects of the Moon and Venus and, ironically, the omnipresent image of the sacrificed bull (Griffith, 2006).

Domestic Cult. In addition to the state cults and mystery religions, Romans also valued private cults (*sacra privata*), those practices centering upon the health of the family rather than the state (although even these rites tended to mirror official ritual practices). In this sphere, the male head of the household (*paterfamilias*) was responsible for executing sacrifices to the domestic gods (the Lares, protectors of the family, and the Penates, guardians of the storehouse) and performing rituals connected to the life cycle (e.g., birth, marriage, death) and ancestor worship.

Women too were active in attending to the religious life of the *domus*: they decorated the hearth with garlands, maintained the supplies of the storehouse (*penus*), prepared the materials used in ritual activities, and tended the hearth fire (responsibilities that mimicked those of the state's Vestal Virgins). There is also evidence of women joining their husbands in sacrifice during the Terminalia festival, and according to Plautus a young girl even substitutes for her wayward father by offering sacrifices at the family shrine of the Lares (*Pot of Gold*, 23–25). Other sources suggest that it was not unknown for women to perform without male supervision sacrifices of various kinds, even if it was more customary for men to act as officiants and the rest of the family as participants.

Judaism and Christianity. In the Roman imagination, both Judaism and Christianity fall under the category of foreign cults. Like many of these mystery religions, they exhibit significant breadth in their approaches to leadership. Israel's early authority figures are almost exclusively men whom God and the community invest with political, military, and religious power. Miriam, Deborah, and Huldah demonstrate, however, that Israel occasionally acknowledged women's prophetic and administrative activity (Exod 15:20; Judg 4:4; 2 Kgs 22:14). The Hebrew Bible also refers to the wife of the king as the "royal lady" (*gevira*), but it is unlikely that she had an official role in religious performances.

More evidence for women's involvement in leadership appears in the late Hellenistic period. References to "female elders" and "mothers" in Dead Sea Scrolls seem to indicate a formal office, whereas inscriptions from the empire confer upon women titles such as "ruler of the synagogue" (*archisynagōgos; archisynagōgissa*), "leader" (*archēgissa*), "elders" (*presbytera; presbyterēsa*), "mother of the synagogue" (*mētēr synagōgēs; mater synagogae*), and "priest" (*hiereia; hierissa*). When seen in the context of other Greco-Roman religious traditions, it is difficult to think that such terms were simply honorific titles. Rather, it is more plausible that these women, like their pagan counterparts, were active members of their communities as religious leaders, administrators, and benefactors (Brooten, 1982).

The expansion of leadership opportunities within the early Christian movement is equally apparent. Although the gospels' disciples and Paul continue the tradition of masculine authority figures, a variety of New Testament passages illustrate that other leadership configurations were possible. Some women, unattached to male partners, missionized and led communities: Paul, for instance, identifies Phoebe as a "deacon" (*diakonos*) and a "benefactor" (*prostatis*) and acknowledges four other women for their hard work in Christ (Rom 16:1–2, 6, 12). Missionary couples also were active, with Andronicus and Junia ("prominent among the apostles") and Prisca and Aquila receiving special attention (Rom 16:3, 7; cf. 1 Cor 16:19; Acts 18:8). The latter couple was also in charge of a house-church, a practice that quite likely put the women at the forefront of religious life (Rom 16:5; Phlm 2; Phil 4:2–3; Col 4:15). For Paul, then, there is nothing unusual

about women building, overseeing, and supporting Christian communities.

Those Christianities that sought to accommodate themselves to the patriarchal values of antiquity gradually restricted women's leadership roles. This development was neither linear nor uniform, but New Testament literature from the late first and early second centuries exhibits an androcentric turn. Authors instruct wives to be subordinate to their husbands and insist that women "learn in silence with full submission" (Col 3:18; Eph 5:22–24; 1 Tim 2:8–15; 1 Pet 3:1–7). Women's lives become subject to greater regulation as their work as teachers narrows to non-liturgical duties and the office of widows comes under tighter control (1 Tim 5:3–16; Tit 2:3–5). In this process, (male) bishops, presbyters, and deacons emerge as authorities responsible for disseminating the authentic teachings of the faith and shaping a (proto)-orthodox identity (1 Tim 1:3–4; 3:2; 4:11, 14; 5:17; 6:3; Tit 1:9; 2:1, 15). Christian texts from the second century continue to speak of women as prophets and teachers (e.g., the oracles of Priscilla and Maximilla from the New Prophecy, *The Acts of Thecla*, *The Gospel of Mary*), but those who value them come under increasingly hostile criticism. Employing the gendered rhetoric of the period, their opponents link women leaders with uncontrollable passions and irrationality, which signal a deviation from "truth" and unveil their heretical nature (Rev 2:20–23; Irenaeus, *Haer.* 1.13.5; 1.23.2; Epiphanius, *Medicine Chest* 79.3; Jerome, *Letter* 133.4).

[*See also* Popular Religion and Magic, *subentry* Roman World; Religious Leaders, *subentries on* Early Church *and* New Testament; *and* Religious Participation, *subentries on* Early Church, New Testament, *and* Roman World.]

BIBLIOGRAPHY

Beard, Mary. "Priesthood in the Roman Republic." In *Pagan Priests: Religion and Power in the Ancient World*, edited by Mary Beard and John North, pp. 19–48. Ithaca, N.Y.: Cornell University Press, 1990.

Beard, Mary, John North, and Simon Price. *Religions of Rome.* 2 vols. Cambridge, U.K.: Cambridge University Press, 1998.

Bowden, Hugh. *Mystery Cults of the Ancient World*. Princeton, N.J.: Princeton University Press, 2010.

Brooten, Bernadette J. *Women Leaders in the Ancient Synagogue: Inscriptional Evidence and Background Issues*. Chico, Calif.: Scholars Press, 1982.

Cohick, Lynn H. *Women in the World of the Earliest Christians: Illuminating Ancient Ways of Life*. Grand Rapids, Mich.: Baker Academic, 2009.

Griffith, Allison B. "Completing the Picture: Women and the Female Principle in the Mithraic Cult." *Numen* 53 (2006): 48–77.

Heyob, Sharon Kelly. *The Cult of Isis among Women in the Graeco-Roman World*. Leiden, The Netherlands: Brill, 1975.

Kraemer, Ross Shepard. *Her Share of the Blessings: Women's Religions among Pagans, Jews, and Christians in the Greco-Roman World*. New York: Oxford University Press, 1992.

Kraemer, Ross Shepard, ed. *Women's Religions in the Greco-Roman World: A Sourcebook*. New York: Oxford University Press, 2004.

Sawyer, Deborah F. *Women and Religion in the First Christian Centuries*. New York: Routledge, 1996.

Scheid, John. *An Introduction to Roman Religion*. Translated by Janet Lloyd. Bloomington: Indiana University Press, 2003.

Schultz, Celia E. *Women's Religious Activity in the Roman Republic*. Chapel Hill: University of North Carolina Press, 2006.

Schüssler Fiorenza, Elisabeth. "Word, Spirit and Power: Women in Early Christian Communities." In *Women of Spirit: Female Leadership in the Jewish and Christian Traditions*, edited by Rosemary Radford Ruether and Eleanor McLaughlin, pp. 30–70. New York: Simon & Schuster, 1979.

Warrior, Valerie M. *Roman Religion*. Cambridge, U.K.: Cambridge University Press, 2006.

David M. Reis

New Testament

Religious leaders in the New Testament are those individuals who sought to influence groups of people through various social processes to achieve specific goals. Of course, religious leaders during the New Testament period were also political leaders, and one cannot easily separate these two into discrete domains. Furthermore, leadership began within the context of the synagogue but also emerged within a network of house-churches, influenced by domestic discourses, with differing degrees of closeness to their original synagogal setting. This movement that found its source in Israel's messiah was navigating leadership amid competing non-Jewish movements as it expanded across the Mediterranean basin while still being led primarily, if not exclusively, by Jewish men (with some exceptions). In seeking to summarize the leadership structures that emerged from these intersecting influences, one must recognize the rhetorical nature of the extant texts. The occasional nature of Paul's letters, which serve as the earliest surviving evidence for religious leaders, should be taken into consideration when attempting to organize this material; since these letters are fragmentary and local, regional variation should be expected. Finally, although linguistic and social anachronism is a constant challenge when describing leadership practices in the first century C.E., this should not discourage interpreters from seeking to uncover key aspects of the roles, gender, and nature of leadership within the nascent movement(s). Although final answers are not attainable, what follows provides a general understanding of religious leaders in the New Testament; although much more could be said, the goal here is to provide a snapshot of what researchers within the field of gender and biblical studies have uncovered with regard to religious leaders in the New Testament.

Religious Leadership Roles. Religious leaders in the New Testament emerged within the cultural context of the Roman Empire and the Jewish Temple and synagogues as each negotiated differing models of gender. Roman religion was both a public and a private affair and thus officially designated leaders contributed to the formation of civic identity, while the head of the household ensured that everyday devotion to the family gods was enacted. Jewish religious leadership as well was socially constructed and reinforced gender hierarchies. Prior to 70 C.E., the Temple served as the primary focal point for Jewish religious life and only priests could officiate there; however, the synagogue allowed for a more diverse leadership group and after 70 C.E. became the center for Jewish life.

Religious roles in the New Testament may be divided into two categories: officially designated and charismatic. This division is an etic distinction brought in for heuristic purposes, recognizing, however, that institutionally ordered and charismatically recognized leaders interpenetrate one another in terms of social influence. Officially designated leaders include the disciples, apostles, prophets, elders, overseers, deacons, evangelists, and pastor-teachers. However, the use of the term "officially" raises an important issue concerning the nature of the Christ-movement at this early stage. The highly institutionalized nature of the movement is evident by the time of Irenaeus, but it does not follow that there was little to no institutional structure in place during the mid-first century. Clarke (2008) argues for an earlier construction of institutional roles undertaken by officially designated leaders. This view places the house-churches as the institutional setting for the majority of the movement, with each house-church led by an overseer and assisted by a deacon. Furthermore, if a region had several house-churches, then a council of elders met to provide further guidance to the movement, although the exercise of power was to be constrained by its leaders. This type of hierarchy is in opposition to the egalitarian impulse often discerned in the earliest Christ-movement that Clarke claims is the result of contemporary hermeneutical concerns. These same concerns may also construe religious leaders as exerting power in an undifferentiated way, and Ehrensperger (2009) has called this understanding into question. She rejects the idea that New Testament leaders led in a dominating manner and suggests that they relied instead on the transformative use of power. For both Clarke and Ehrensperger the roles of the religious leaders in the New Testament were constructed from kinship discourse (leading like a father but not the *paterfamilias*), educational discourse (teaching in ways associated with Jewish teaching and learning discourse), and empowerment discourse (building people up in ways that differed from imperial ideology).

Charismatic leadership is more challenging to discern in the sources because the movement, generally speaking, was charismatic and the role of prophets might be viewed in an ambiguous way since unofficial leaders could claim direct access to the divine and implicitly (or explicitly) challenge the leadership of the officially designated leaders. The idea that the earliest movement was led by prophets relies on the claim that overseers and deacons were a later development. The presence of charismatics in the earliest Christ-movement is undeniable but it does not follow that those same individuals had received special gifting to lead. First Corinthians 6:5 suggests that there was a distinction between administrative and nonleadership gifts. Although prophets and others with unique gifts would have contributed to leadership, this could occur alongside officially designated leaders such as overseers/bishops and deacons. For instance, Paul does not refer to elders in the Corinthian correspondence, but 1 Corinthians 16:15–16 directs the Corinthians to be subject to the household of Stephanus as well as to other co-workers and laborers among them. Thus, there is some level of asymmetry in the movement. Hierarchically ordered relationships existed, but leadership was also based on Paul's preeminence as the one who brought them the gospel and the trust that followed from that (2 Cor 10:14), rather than on some sort of institutional primacy or fixed ecclesial structure (Ehrensperger, 2009, p. 61). Religious roles in the New Testament developed as both officially designated and charismatic leaders interacted and together led local congregations; some of these major figures will now be highlighted.

Apostolic Leaders. Four major religious leaders emerge from the New Testament: Peter, James, John, and Paul. Peter is pictured in the Gospels as one of the Twelve disciples (Mark 3:16), a member of the inner circle (Mark 5:37), and the one who recognized Jesus as messiah (Mark 8:29). He became a central apostolic leader in the early days of the movement (Acts 1—5; Gal 1:18; 1 Pet 1:1) and participated in mission work primarily among the Jews (Gal 2:7–8). He was not the primary leader in Jerusalem; that was reserved for James, the brother of Jesus, who eventually took over the leadership in that city from the Twelve. He was one of the key early leaders within the movement and managed the Apostolic Council in Jerusalem as it sought to determine the way non-Jews should relate to Torah (Gal 2; Acts 15). John, one of the sons of Zebedee, was another early leader, one whom Paul described, along with Peter and James, as a pillar of the movement (Gal 2:9). He was a close associate of Peter and one of Jesus's inner circle (Luke 5:10; Mark 9:2). Paul's apostleship was not uncontested; his leadership position was weakened in that he had not seen Jesus in the flesh, nor had he been taught by Peter, James, and John, and he actually had persecuted the early Christ-movement (Gal 1:23). Thus, other leaders challenged the legitimacy of his apostleship, a challenge Paul met with his own recounting of his leadership autobiography (Gal 1—2). He argued that genuine leadership is shown in suffering and weakness (2 Cor 11:22–29; 12:7–10) and that although he had not seen Jesus in the flesh, he was nonetheless still a proper apostle, although "one untimely born" (1 Cor 15:8; see also Gal 1:1; 1 Cor 9:1).

Peter, James, John, and Paul were not the only ones to be described as apostolic leaders (i.e., those sent out by God with a message to proclaim). Mark 3:14–15 highlights the continuity between the Twelve disciples and the later apostles. The original commissioning of this group was "to the lost sheep of this house of Israel" (Matt 10:5–6), but later the mission was expanded to the nations (Matt 28:16–20). Thus, proclamation of a message is an early role for the apostolic leaders; however, the term "apostle" was not restricted to just the Twelve. Luke views Paul along with Barnabas as an apostle (Acts 14:14), whereas Paul intimates that James was an apostle (Gal 1:19; 1 Cor 9:5), that Paul, himself, also was one (1 Cor 9:1; 15:9), and he refers to Andronicus and Junia as apostles in Rome (Rom 16:7).

That there might be a woman among the apostles has led some interpreters to read the name as Junias, its male iteration, in line with the rest of those named. Epp (2005, pp. 68, 78), however, argues that Junia, the feminine name, is to be preferred to the otherwise unattested masculine name Junias and that the reading "outstanding among the apostles" fits the context better than "well-known to the apostles." The term "apostle" (*apostolos*) may be used in differentiated ways, and the rhetorical context must be brought into this discussion to determine the legitimacy and plausibility of the claim that Junia was an apostle (see Clarke, 2008, p. 91; Ehrensperger, 2009,

p. 54). Finally, although the term is not used for her, Mary Magdalene is often regarded as an apostle based on her witness to the resurrection and her missionary and proclamation activity (Brock, 2003; cf. Matt 28:10; John 20:16–18; 1 Cor 9:1). Apostleship and leadership are not interchangeable terms; there were leaders who were not considered apostles and those individuals will now be detailed.

Leaders and patrons. First Thessalonians 5:12 provides an apt starting point for understanding the nature of religious leadership from key passages and pertinent ancient vocabulary found in the New Testament. In this passage, the term "lead" (*proistēmi*) emphasizes "laboring" (*kopiaō*) and "admonishing/exhorting" (*noutheteō*) and describes religious leadership at the earliest stage we can access (Clarke, 2008, p. 71). Romans 12:8 notes that those who lead are particularly gifted for this purpose. The term as used in these two verses draws on household management discourse and suggests this context (along with the ancient system of patronage) as the proper locus for the emergence of leadership terminology. The patronage context is more explicit in Romans 16:1–2 where Phoebe is described as Paul's "patron" (*prostatis*), as well as the patron of others. Social relationships were structured around patronage and although it is not clear how this was transformed within the Christ-movement, some sort of reciprocity was central to the system. It is likely that, as Paul's patron, Phoebe provided material assistance to him and hospitality when needed. She would have been considered a leader in that she used existing social processes to influence a group of people to accomplish a certain goal. Williams (2006, pp. 38–41) has recognized the importance of the house, household, and patronage for understanding the overarching framework for leadership in the Christ-movement. For example, God is seen as the patron and the Christ-followers are seen as God's clients, with the leaders serving as brokers dispensing the patron's gifts. In this configuration, New Testament leadership is placed in its first-century Roman context, which highlights the complex interplay between social structures and religious experiences. Those tasked with mediating these experiences were defined as leaders. The New

Testament uses several key vocabulary words as labels to describe these individuals.

Overseers and stewards. Overseers (*episkopoi*) as leaders appear early in the Christ-movement and most likely reflected the general idea of "guardian," although the meaning of the term quickly shifted to something closer to "bishop." The more generic meaning of "overseer" is reflected in Acts 20:28, which further clarifies the nature of the "elders" in Ephesus (Acts 20:17). The elders were to be overseers of the flock given to them. A similar generic idea is evident in 1 Peter 5:1–2. There is a probable shift in meaning to bishop in Philippians 1:1, where Paul refers to "bishops" and "deacons." This represents a development from Acts and may serve as a midpoint to what is found in the Pastoral Epistles, when the office of bishop is more established (1 Tim 3:1). During this period, congregations received guidance concerning what types of persons were suitable for this position. They were to be effective organizers with culturally respected personal traits and domestic leadership skills since they were to function as examples (1 Tim 4:2; Titus 2:7; Heb 13:7). Goodrich (2013, p. 97) has contributed to the discussions concerning overseers and their role in leadership by emphasizing the importance of the stewardship metaphor seen in Titus 1:7. He understands there to be structural authority attached to the position and has brought into alignment the skills and ethical attributes expected for stewards in the Greek and Roman world and those of the overseer. In this configuration, Timothy and Titus, as regional leaders, were directed to identify individuals who had the attributes and the capabilities to run the household effectively and to place or appoint those individuals in positions of leadership in the household of God (1 Tim 3:1; Titus 1:5). The material in the Pastoral Epistles concerning elder qualifications (1 Tim 5:17–22; Tit 1:5–6) overlaps significantly with the qualifications for a bishop (1 Tim 3:2–7; Tit 1:7–9), although it is likely that the bishops were a subgroup identity appointed from among the elders (1 Tim 4:14). It cannot be ruled out, however, that these represent two names for the same leadership position. What is clear is that by the time of Ignatius these are two distinct church offices. There are no examples in the New Testament of women being referred to as overseers, although it should also be noted that the qualification lists result in the exclusion of many men as well.

Deacons and deaconesses. Deacons (*diakonoi*) as leaders in the Christ-movement are ubiquitous in the New Testament, although as in the case of the overseers, it is not clear when this term shifted in referent from a generic "servant" or "minister" to a "deacon." Mark 10:43 is a good example of the way remembrances of Jesus's teaching influenced the development of a leadership position with an emphasis on serving as a measure of greatness. The serving aspect is most clearly seen in Acts 6:2–3, where the "servant" is one who waits on tables; perhaps here the development of this leadership position from the earlier generic meaning begins. Paul refers to himself and Apollos as "servants" in 1 Corinthians 3:5 and to himself (and others) in 2 Corinthians 3:6 as "ministers of a new covenant." These may refer to a similar generic idea of servility but a shift occurs in Philippians 1:1, where he refers again to bishops and deacons who serve as an intermediate subgroup descriptor. By the time of the Pastoral Epistles, the term has further developed into an office since the congregation is given instructions concerning the way to identify those who qualify (1 Tim 3:8–13). As with overseers, these individuals are also to have strong organizational skills and to exhibit blameless moral character. The question asked about overseers concerning women is not as acute for deacons since Romans 16:1 refers to Phoebe as a "deacon" (*diakonos*) of the "congregation" (*ekklēsia*) in Cenchrea, a port city near Corinth. The question is: Does this signify a generic servile position or a later leadership office? It is unlikely that this refers to the generic category; rather, it refers to the middle use, similar to Philippians 1:1 (Matthew, 2013, p. 74). Although *diakonos* (and its associated word group) is used in the New Testament primarily in reference to males, deacons must have included mixed groups since at least in one case the word is used to refer to a woman and 1 Timothy 3:11 provides counsel to women who are associated with this leadership position (i.e., they are to model prototypical characteristics) (Witherington, 1990, p. 196). A further institutional development in the office of a deacon is noticeable in the third century (*Didascalia apostolorum 2.57.1–9*), where the office moves away from its New Testament descriptions.

Elders and presbyters. Elders were synonymous with overseers in some settings, but the New Testament also reflects some variation in practice. The approach of "elders" (*presbyteroi*) to leadership was developed from within existing Jewish practice (Campbell, 1994; Exod 19:7; Josh 20:4; 1 Macc 12:35; Mark 11:27). Elders are appointed in various congregations (Acts 14:23) and evident in Jerusalem (Acts 21:18); they led along with the apostles in the early Christ-movement (Acts 16:4). The Johannine epistles show evidence of an elder structure (2 John 1; 3 John 1) but transformed it into a single elder configuration, although what this position entailed is unclear. Outside of the Johannine literature, elders are given an explicit leadership position in 1 Timothy 5:7 and a ritual function in James 5:14.

All of these labels and key vocabulary terms, taken together, provide a general taxonomy for religious leaders in the New Testament. Other potential leadership labels and vocabulary that might be considered in a study of religious leaders in the New Testament but cannot be pursued here include pastor-teachers, evangelists, co-workers, widows, virgins, and prophets (see further Eisen, 2000; Zamfir, 2013). However, the social significance of these labels has been the source of several debates within New Testament studies. Three will be highlighted: the challenge of precept and practice, the interplay of domestic and congregational space, and Paul's gendered theology.

Modern Debates. Modern debates concerning gender and religious leadership revolve around the tension between the practices evident in the New Testament and certain precepts also found in the text (Alexander, 2013). Romans 16:1–16 highlights the religious leadership of several women within the Christ-movement and brings to the fore an ethos of mutuality (Matthew, 2013), whereas 1 Corinthians 11:2–16; 14:33b–36 and 1 Timothy 2:8–15 seem to offer blanket restrictions on practices most likely assumed in Romans 16. Alexander (2013, p. 21) makes sense of this seemingly contradictory evidence by noting the developing "anxieties" within the Christ-movement

with regard to "their precarious position in Roman society," but she also thinks these reflect the all too real challenges of living out "underlying theological principles" (e.g., Gal 3:28; 6:15–16; Phil 2:5).

Further, Økland (2004) has highlighted the leadership challenges associated with differing gender expectations when the "congregation" (*ekklēsia*) gathers in "household" (*oikos*) space, challenges evident in 1 Corinthians 11—14. She contends that Paul vacillates between differing gender models and this accounts for the rhetorical unsettledness in passages like 1 Corinthians 11:2–16 and 14:34–36. She recognizes in these texts a challenge to Roman imperial discourse by ideas of newness "in Christ" (Gal 3:28; 1 Cor 12:13; 2 Cor 5:17), provoking a debate over the nature of the household "in Christ": Had it been obliterated, transformed, or reprioritized (1 Cor 11:34; 14:35; 16:19; Rom 16:5)?

The influence of the restriction texts have led scholars to challenge the dominance of Paul's agency with regard to the construction of gender; some have suggested that he should be decentered and seen as only one among several voices in the formation of the early Christ-movement (Lopez, 2005). He also has been understood to be more complicit in reinforcing Roman imperial discourses than scholars like Ehrensperger and Clarke put forth (Vander Stichele and Penner, 2005). Both Penner and Lopez (2012) alert interpreters to the importance of recognizing the rhetorical nature of these texts; when interpreters study Paul and make claims about topics such as religious leadership and gender, they are at the same time studying and making claims about themselves.

[*See also* Family Structures, *subentries on* Early Church, New Testament, *and* Roman World; Paul; Religious Leaders, *subentry* Early Church; *and* Religious Participation, *subentries on* New Testament *and* Roman World.]

BIBLIOGRAPHY

Alexander, Loveday. "Women as Leaders in the New Testament." *Modern Believing* 54, no. 1 (2013): 14–22.

Brock, Ann Graham. *Mary Magdalene, the First Apostle: The Struggle for Authority.* Cambridge, Mass.: Harvard University Press, 2003.

Campbell, R Alastair. *The Elders: Seniority within Earliest Christianity*. London: T&T Clark, 1994.

Clarke, Andrew. *A Pauline Theology of Church Leadership*. Library of New Testament Studies 362. London: Bloomsbury T&T Clark, 2008.

Ehrensperger, Kathy. *Paul and the Dynamics of Power: Communication and Interaction in the Early Christ-Movement*. London: T&T Clark, 2009.

Eisen, Ute E. *Women Officeholders in Early Christianity: Epigraphical and Literary Studies*. Collegeville, Minn.: Liturgical Press, 2000.

Epp, Eldon Jay. *Junia: The First Woman Apostle*. Minneapolis: Fortress, 2005.

Goodrich, John K. "Overseers as Stewards and the Qualifications for Leadership in the Pastoral Epistles." *Zeitschrift für die Neutestamentliche Wissenschaft und die Kunde der Älteren Kirche* 104, no. 1 (2013): 77–97.

Lopez, Davina C. "Paul, Gentiles, and Gender Paradigms." *Union Seminary Quarterly Review* 59, nos. 3–4 (2005): 92–106.

Matthew, Susan. *Women in the Greeting of Romans 16.1–16: A Study of Mutuality and Women's Ministry in the Letter to the Romans*. Library of New Testament Studies 471. London: Bloomsbury, 2013.

Økland, Jorunn. *Women in Their Place: Paul and the Corinthian Discourse of Gender and Sanctuary Space*. Journal for the Study of the New Testament Supplement Series 269. New York: T&T Clark, 2004.

Penner, Todd, and Davina C. Lopez. "Rhetorical Approaches: Introducing the Art of Persuasion in Paul and Pauline Studies." In *Studying Paul's Letters: Contemporary Perspectives and Methods*, edited by Joseph A. Marchal, pp. 33–52. Minneapolis: Fortress, 2012.

Sawyer, Deborah F. *Women and Religion in the First Christian Centuries*. London: Routledge, 1996.

Vander Stichele, Caroline, and Todd Penner. "Paul and the Rhetoric of Gender." In *Her Master's Tools? Feminist and Postcolonial Engagements of Historical-Critical Discourse*, edited by Caroline Vander Stichele and Todd Penner, pp. 287–310. Leiden, The Netherlands: Brill, 2005.

Williams, Ritva H. *Stewards, Prophets, Keepers of the Word: Leadership in the Early Church*. Peabody, Mass.: Hendrickson, 2006.

Witherington, Ben. *Women and the Genesis of Christianity*. Cambridge, U.K.: Cambridge University Press, 1990.

Zamfir, Korinna. *Men and Women in the Household of God: A Contextual Approach to Roles and Ministries in the Pastoral Epistles*. Göttingen, Germany: Vandenhoeck & Ruprecht, 2013.

J. Brian Tucker

Early Judaism

When the Jews returned from the Babylonian captivity, sometime after 538 B.C.E., they were understood by the reigning Persian Empire as a religious more than an ethnic community. This is indicated by the fact that although at the opening stage of their return journey they were led by two men—one a scion of the secular royal House of David (Zerubbabel) and one an offspring of the religious priestly House of Zadok (Joshua son of Jehozadak) (Hag 1:1)—very soon the secular leader disappeared. For the next 360 years the high-priestly family that oversaw the return to Jerusalem continued to lead the Jews. This family functioned in the office of high priests in the newly built Temple in Jerusalem and conducted all negotiations, religious as well as secular, with the ruling power—even when in 332 B.C.E. it changed hands and the Greeks under Alexander the Great assumed power. After about 360 years, in 151 B.C.E., a high priest (Jonathan) from the Hasmonean family, which had just won a great military and victory over their Seleucid (Hellenistic) overlords and attained political independence, came to power, and religious and secular leadership were combined in a single same ruler.

Only under Roman occupation with the rise of a nonpriest to the kingship (Herod 40 B.C.E.–4 B.C.E.) did this personal union come to an end and the high priesthood returned to function on a purely religious basis. With the destruction of the Second Temple in 70 C.E., the priesthood lost its power base, and alternative religious Jewish manifestations came into existence—the study-house and the synagogue—with new forms of the leadership in the sage and the head of synagogue.

The following is a review of the role of gender in the developments described above.

The Priesthood. In biblical times we identify in Israel two forms of religious leadership. On the one hand, there was the priestly leadership that oversaw the Jewish sacrificial rituals, first all over the country and later in the Jerusalem Temple. This leadership claimed its descent from Aaron the brother of Moses and represented the religious establishment in Israel and then in Judah. The priests, according to the Bible, received their authority from their descent: one could not become but was born a priest. In the Bible, the priesthood is a male office, and the Temple was rarely visited by women. Whether this picture is strictly historical cannot be determined.

Some feminist scholars claim that biblical authors suppressed the reality of women's participation in the Jerusalemite or Israelite cult, but such a claim cannot be proven. In any case, the heritage received by postbiblical Judaism, based on its absolute dependence on the Torah, was one of an all-male priestly institution. During the entire Second Temple period only men ministered in the Temple, and women's participation was relegated to the woman's court. The women's court in the Second Temple was the largest court in the Temple, but although men and women mingled in it, women were not allowed beyond its boundaries; all meaningful ritual activity (except on specific occasions like Passover) was carried out in the inner courts such as the court of Israel (which was all male) or the court of the priests.

Prophecy. A second religious leader portrayed in the Bible is the prophet. This type of leader was chosen by God ad hoc to admonish the secular leadership and the people. In some cases, the prophet predicted the future. A true prophet was recognized by the verification of his or her predictions after the fact. Unlike the priest, who must be male and born into the priestly clan, the prophet could be anybody possessed by the spirit of God. A prophet could be male or female, and indeed the ultimate Deuteronomic prophet was a woman—Huldah (2 Kgs 22:14–20). She interpreted for King Josiah the meaning of the book of Torah he had just discovered and issued the Deuteronomic prediction of the end of the Kingdom of Judah based on the failure of its citizens to correctly observe its precepts.

The fate of prophecy in the Second Temple period is debated. Rabbinic Jewish tradition claims that the last of the prophets died with Malachi (ca. 400 B.C.E.), but Christians claim that Jesus was a prophet (e.g., Matt 13:57; 14:5). When the historian Josephus predicted to Vespasian that he would be the next emperor, he claimed to be a prophet (Josephus, *B.J.,*

3:8:9). It is quite possible that prophets were still active on the margins of society throughout the entire period. Evidence for their activity is scant but not completely absent. If the tradition of prophecy had not quite died out and traces remained in Second Temple Judaism, women may have been among the possible candidates for the title of prophet. Unlike the First Temple prophetesses, whose actions and words are recorded favorably, one prophetess mentioned in the postexilic book of Nehemiah (440s–30s B.C.E.) is treated negatively: Nehemiah does not like a certain Noadiah or appreciate her prophecies. In fact, he prays to God to punish her for joining his enemies (Neh 6:14), but he does designate her "prophetess" (*nevi'ah*) like her preexilic counterparts. Beyond this glimpse, the sources reveal no more of Noadiah's activities or influence.

The pseudo-epigraphic *Sybillan Oracles*, popular in the Jewish Diaspora (second century B.C.E. to second century C.E.), use the pagan Sybil to convey prophecies about Jewish history and fate. The blatant use of a female (albeit pagan) figure as prophetic in these texts may reflect the attitude to female prophecy in some Jewish circles. Prophetesses also appear in Christian documents, which may in turn reflect Jewish practices. Before Christianity became a separate religion, it was only one among many religious sects that dominated Second Temple Judaism. The four daughters of Philip the Evangelist, who are described at the end of the book of Acts as prophesying (Acts 21:9; 30s–40s C.E.), can easily be counted as Jewish women in a Jewish movement. In a movement that views its founding leader as a prophet, it is no surprise that prophecy held a prominent position and that prophetic movements (like Montanism) continued to emerge from it for many centuries and counted women among its prophets.

Jewish Sects. Christianity, or "the Jesus Movement," was one of several sects that dominated Jewish religious life in the Second Temple period. Sects like the Sadducees, the Pharisees, and the Dead Sea Sect were deeply involved in an ongoing debate on the very nature of Judaism—what was its law; what was its theology; how one worshiped as Jews; even what calendar a Jew should adopt. They were, however, marginal groups, only infrequently involved in established politics, and thus we find that they often tolerated women as hangers-on, supporters, and possibly also full members.

The question of women's leadership in these sects is not an idle one. There is little doubt, for example, that after the death of Jesus (33 C.E.), women, and especially Mary Magdalene, were very active in reviving the movement and keeping it alive (Matt 28; Mark 16:1–8; Luke 24:1–10; John 20:1–18). I have argued elsewhere that Mary Magdalene should be viewed as the true founder of Christianity because she is responsible for formulating the Christian doctrine on the empty tomb and the resurrection, both essential to Christianity.

Mary Magdalene's important leadership role in the foundation of Christianity was later suppressed, especially by Paul, who fails to mention her in his letters and does not include her among those who encountered the resurrected Christ (1 Cor 15:3–8). Nevertheless, Paul himself worked with Jewish women who preached early Christianity, such as Priscilla (Acts 18; Rom 16:3) and l Junia (Rom 16:7), who were known as apostles.

We know very little about the different sects of Second Temple Judaism, depending on the sources that have survived. The Pharisees, definitely a prominent Second Temple Sect, were probably the forerunners of the rabbinic movement, but most rabbinic documents were written many centuries after the Pharisees became the rabbis (Mishnah and Tosefta—third century C.E.; Palestinian Talmud—fourth century C.E.; Babylonian Talmud and haggadic Midrashim—sixth to seventh century C.E.); they do not necessarily reflect the exploits and activities of the historical Pharisees, both because of internal changes that occurred over time within the rabbinic movement itself and because the rabbis wished to disassociate themselves from their Pharisee forebears. The rabbis kept a scanty record about the leadership of their forerunners, and even the mythic Hillel and Shammai (30s B.C.E.) are never described as Pharisees. The one period during the Second Temple in which the Pharisees actively participated in the running of the Jewish state was during the reign of a Jewish

queen. In 76 B.C.E., Queen Shelamzion Alexandra (better known mistakenly as Salome Alexandra) was nominated to the throne by her Hasmonean husband, Alexander Jannaeus, on his deathbed; she reigned nine years, until 67 B.C.E. Like all others in his family before him, Jannaeus had been both king and high priest. Although Shelamzion could not serve in the traditional priestly function, which she relegated to her son, Hyrcanus II (see Josephus *B.J.* 1:5:1; *A.J.* 13:16:2), her alliance with the Pharisees placed her in a position to influence religious decisions and in effect made her a religious as well as a secular leader. The exact nature of her religious influence is unclear, but the rabbinic writings remember the queen as a ruler especially blessed by God (*Sifre Deut.* 42).

The sources regarding the Dead Sea Sect (third century B.C.E. to first century C.E.) provide testimony from within the sect itself. The documents known as the Rule of the Community, the Rule of the Congregation, and the Damascus Document give us a fair picture of the community organization and leadership. The sect was highly hierarchical and led by priests of the Zadokite family (e.g., CD IV, 1; 1QS V, 2; 1QSa I, 2). Documents describe the founder of the sect, the Teacher of Righteousness (e.g., CD XX, 32; 1QHab I, 13), and the Overseer of the camps (CD XIII, 16; 1QS VI, 12) and of elders (1QS VI, 8) along with other notables such as the fathers of the community (1QSa I, 16; 1QM III, 4). Because early scholars identified the Dead Sea Sect (following Sukenik, 1955) with the celibate male Essenes (*B.J.* 2:8:2) mentioned in Josephus, the field was slow to recognize that the sect certainly counted women among its number and that some texts describe women in leadership roles. In one document, certain women are given the role of overseers, whose job it is to determine whether certain girls are virgins at their entrance into marriage (4Q159; 4Q271). More important are women described as "mothers" (*amot*) of the community, alongside a group of men named "fathers" of the community (4Q270). This text is certainly hierarchical, distinguishing between the fathers who have something called *roqmah* and the mothers who lack it. But the existence of women leaders is clear. Women elders are apparently mentioned in a very fragmentary text

(4Q502). Because the male and female forms of "elder" in Hebrew (*zaqen; zeqenah*) are the same as "old man" or "old woman," this text was initially understood as referring simply to old men and women; Eileen Schuller (1993) has rightly argued, however, that had there only been male elders mentioned in this text, no one would have translated the word as old men.

Sages. With the destruction of the Temple (70 C.E.), traditional Jewish leadership ceased to exist, and also sectarian groups seem to have ended. A new movement came into existence and slowly rose to prominence, eventually even gaining the recognition of the Roman authorities—the rabbinic movement. The rabbis argued that their authority derived not from birth (as the priest) or from a direct instruction from God (like the prophet), but rather from the erudition in the holy law and scriptures. They argued, for example, that a scholar who is a bastard takes precedence, in the eyes of heaven, over a high priest who is an ignoramus (*m. Hor.* 3:8). One could, in theory, suppose that birth and gender not being a prerequisite, the scholars could count women among their number. In reality, however, to become a sage and join the leader ranks, one needed a long and thorough education in the holy scriptures.

Women were barred from this process at its very beginning, since educational institutions in Judaism, although relatively democratic, were purely male institutions. Rabbinic literature mentions literally hundreds of scholars, some of whom became prominent religious leaders. In this extensive literature, which covers many generations and many centuries, only one woman is possibly described as a sage—Beruriah (mid-second century C.E.). Although the Babylonian Talmud declares that Beruriah learned three hundred traditions each day from three hundred masters (*b. Pesaḥ. 62b*), this picture is not likely historically accurate. The later rabbis of the Babylonian Talmud did not know how she rose to prominence, because her teachings and their implication for her role as teacher and leader had been suppressed. A legend arose of a woman who was the daughter of a great sage and the wife of another, who mocked great sages, taught others, and learned more and better than any male sage. Her legend continued to develop until, in the Middle Ages, the great talmudic commentator, Rashi (to *b. ʿAbod. Zar. 18b*), chose to disgrace her memory rather than cherish it by arguing that she eventually succumbed to sexual temptation and then killed herself.

The Synagogue. The second institution that replaced the Temple was the synagogue. Synagogues existed before the Temple was destroyed in 70 C.E., especially in Jewish communities in the Diaspora. As a predestruction inscription from Jerusalem indicates, they were institutions of charity, hostels, community gatherings, and even study-houses. The function of a prayer house, which imitates the Temple ritual, only developed after the destruction of the Temple. Although there is little doubt that in the Middle Ages the synagogue and rabbinic society became interchangeable, scholars are now of the opinion that, during the early development of the two institutions (second to seventh century C.E.), they were separated one from the other and addressed different audiences.

Synagogues were not necessarily supervised by rabbis, and synagogue-goers were not necessarily guided religiously and spiritually by the rabbis. Synagogues hosted translators (who translated the Hebrew Bible mostly into Aramaic), preachers (who interpreted it for the listeners), and liturgists, known as *paytanim* (who wrote liturgical poems for the synagogue). These roles are evident from the rich literary heritage of the synagogue that has survived independently of rabbinic texts. Additional information about the synagogue and its leadership is available from inscriptional remains, which reveal more about the administrative organization of the synagogue. Synagogue inscriptions list the donors (including women) who assisted in the building of the structure, as well as various functionaries who ran the synagogue—the head of the synagogue (*archisynagogos*), members of the council of elders (the *gerousia*), the leader (*archon*), and the father of the synagogue and the scribe.

The same inscriptions reveal that women occupied many of these positions. Four inscriptions from late antiquity (second to fifth century C.E.) mention women *archisynagogoi*: one from Myndos (mentioning Thepompte), one from Smyrna (mentioning Rufina), one from Thebes (mentioning Peristeria), and one from Crete (mentioning Sophia). Two inscriptions, one from Briscea in Italy (a certain Caelia Paterna) and one from Rome (Sara Veturia Paucla; Marcella), mention women with the title "mother of the synagogue." Other inscriptions mention women who bear the title "elder": one from Greece (mentioning Rebecca), one from Malta (mentioning Eulogia), one from Rome (mentioning Sarra Uria), one from Venosa in Italy (mentioning Veronica, Mannine, and Faustina), one from Sevastopol in Asia (mentioning Sara), and one from Tripoli in Libya (mentioning Mauzazula). In one inscription from Byblos in Lebanon, a woman even bears the title of *archon* (Sambathi).

All these inscriptions indicate that leadership positions in the synagogues were not necessarily reserved for men alone. Of course, given that ancient Judaism was a thoroughly patriarchal society, more men than women bear these titles, but the evidence presented above lists a good number of women serving as functionaries in this institution. How women were able to fill these functions is not explained, but we may speculate that they were well-to-do members of the Jewish community and that the positions were voluntary. Well-to-do women may have volunteered and enjoyed the prestige and authority that went with these positions.

Another inscription may also reveal women's roles. A third-century C.E. inscription found in Aphrodisias in Asia Minor lists donors to a Jewish soup kitchen founded in that city. The founder, who heads the list of donors, is a woman—Yael—designated *prostates* (leader); she is the only woman in the list. Charity may have been a field in which Jewish women could lead and shine.

A note of caution may be in order. All the inscriptions that list women synagogue leaders originate from the Diaspora, and the only name recorded in the Jewish script is the woman *archon* from Lebanon's inscription. The other inscriptions are inscribed in Greek or Latin. Perhaps the Jews who produced these inscriptions, living in the Greco-Roman Diaspora, were influenced by the surrounding society in which they functioned, where women held religious functions in pagan and Christian religious institutions.

Or perhaps the male leadership tradition in Palestine was carried over from the Temple to the synagogue.

[*See also* Economics, *subentry* Early Judaism; Education, *subentry* Early Judaism; Imagery, Gendered, *subentry* Priestly Material; *and* Religious Leaders, *subentry* New Testament.]

BIBLIOGRAPHY

Ackerman, Susan. "Why Is Miriam also among the Prophets? (And Is Zipporah among the Priests?)." *Journal of Biblical Literature* 121, no. 1 (2002): 47–80.

Brooten, Bernadette J. "The Gender of Iael in the Jewish Inscription from Aphrodisias." In *Of Scribes and Scrolls: Studies in the Hebrew Bible, Intertestamental Judaism and Christian Origins Presented to John Strugnell on the Occasion of His Sixtieth Birthday*, edited by Harold W. Attridge, John J. Collins, and Thomas H. Tobin, pp. 163–173. Lanham, Md.: University Press of America, 1990.

Brooten, Bernadette J. *Women Leaders in the Ancient Synagogue*. Atlanta: Scholars Press, 1982.

Ilan, Tal. 1995. "The Attraction of Aristocratic Jewish Women to Pharisaism." *Harvard Theological Review* 88, no. 1 (1995): 1–33.

Ilan, Tal. "Beruriah Has Spoken Well: The Historical Beruriah and Her Transformation in the Rabbinic Corpora." In *Integrating Jewish Women into Second Temple History*, pp. 175–194. Tübingen, Germany: Mohr Siebeck 1999.

Ilan, Tal. "Huldah, the Deuteronomic Prophetess of the Book of Kings." *Lectio Difficilior* 11, no. 1 (2010). http://www.lectio.unibe.ch/10_1/ilan.html/ (accessed 30 September 2013).

Ilan, Tal. "In the Footsteps of Jesus: Jewish Women in a Jewish Movement." In *Transformative Encounters*, edited by Ingrid R. Kitzberg, pp. 115–136. Leiden, The Netherlands: Brill, 1999.

Ilan, Tal. "Once Again on Yael and the Aphrodisias Inscription." *Zutot* 4 (2004): 44–49.

Kraemer, Ross S. "A New Inscription from Malta and the Question of Women Elders in Diaspora Jewish Communities." *Harvard Theological Review* 78, no. 3–4 (1985): 431–438.

Rivkin, Ellis. "Defining the Pharisees: The Tannaitic Sources." *Hebrew Union College Annual* 40–41 (1970–1971): 205–249.

Schuller, Eileen. "Women in the Dead Sea Scrolls." In *Methods of Investigation of the Dead Sea Scrolls and the Khirbet of Qumran Site: Present Realities and Future Prospects*, edited by Michael O. Wise, Norman Golb,

John J. Collins, and Dennis G. Pardee, pp. 115–131. New York: New York Academy of Science, 1993.

Stoekel Ben Ezra, Daniel. "A Jewish Archontess: Remarks on an Epitaph from Byblos." *Zeitschrift für Papyrologie und Epigraphik* 169 (2009): 287–293.

Sukenik, Eliezer L. *The Dead Sea Scrolls of the Hebrew University*. Jerusalem: Magnes, 1955.

Tal Ilan

Early Church

While most early church leaders were men, Christianity was never an exclusively male movement. The earliest Christian sources, included in the New Testament corpus, attest to several influential women who share the same titles as their male co-workers (*diakonos, synergos, apostolos*). Early Christ-followers formed charismatically led house-based communities where women, along with men, exercised the gift of prophecy, and where women who hosted the assembly gatherings in their homes must have enjoyed an important position. Only gradually did the movement develop into a hierarchically structured organization with clerical offices. This entry considers what can be known about women holding these and other leadership positions in the early church. It is organized around different titles used for outstanding individuals, including officially designated roles such as bishop, presbyter, and deacon, as well as charismatic ones such as prophets, teachers, and the ascetic roles of virgins and widows.

Ancient sources seldom give direct answers to questions posed by present-day scholars. If sources refer to women at all, it is often in passing; much information must be inferred. As a rule, the sources are ambiguous and can be (and have been) interpreted in several ways. A basic ambiguity is rooted in the language itself. Greek and Latin (and several other ancient languages) are grammatically gendered and use the masculine plural not only for groups of men but also for groups of both men and women. When a text contains a noun in the masculine plural form, such as *diakonoi* or *apostoloi*, it is often impossible to know whether it has been used exclusively (for males) or inclusively (for males and females).

Another difficulty is the ideological thrust of the sources from this period, most of which betray an elite male point of view. They comprise theological treatises, letters, and homilies written by upper-class men to like-minded audiences and have no interest in describing reality as it was—but rather as it, in their view, ought to be. The same can be said of the so-called church orders, texts that claim to offer authentic apostolic teachings on church organization and other ecclesiastical matters. Such descriptions of clerical offices and women's roles in the church reveal more about the ideals of their authors than about the reality of early Christian communities. It is also noteworthy that during the first centuries there was no universal church legislation or unified practice; what was possible for women at one place and one time was forbidden at another place and another time. Another set of sources is provided by the apocryphal acts of apostles that include prominent female characters. These are fictional texts, which raises the question of whether they can be used to reconstruct the lives of real women.

Women's Leadership: Roles, Titles, Offices. When inquiring about leadership roles in early Christianity, an essential question is what precisely "leadership" signifies. Who would have been recognized as leaders, and how would one have been able to claim such power? Leadership can manifest itself in different forms; for example, a person who does not hold an officially designated position can nonetheless be acknowledged as a spiritual authority. In the New Testament writings, prominent individuals are called by such titles as *apostolos* (apostle), *episkopos* (overseer), *diakonos* (attendant or minister), and *presbyteros* (elder). In subsequent early Christian literature, the title "apostle" was reserved for Jesus's disciples and other great figures of the first generation, while the other three developed into clerical offices and are frequently translated as "bishop," "deacon," and "priest." However, especially in the last-mentioned case, this is anachronistic. There is another Greek word for priest, *hiereus*, but in early Christian parlance it is mostly used for Jewish and Greco-Roman priests.

The tasks and responsibilities of each of these offices and their interrelationship are not always easy to determine and probably varied locally. In several church orders, officeholders are listed in a hierarchically descending order. For example, in the *Apostolic Constitutions* (late fourth century C.E.), only bishops and presbyters are allowed to baptize, and deacons are instructed to assist them. Moreover, presbyters are forbidden to ordain deacons and other members of the lower clergy, for this right belongs to the bishop alone (*Apostolic Constitutions* 3.11). This places presbyters lower than bishops but higher than deacons. On the other hand, in the *Didascalia Apostolorum* (third century C.E.) bishops are compared to God, deacons to Christ, and deaconesses to the Holy Spirit. Presbyters are mentioned only after these and compared to the apostles (*Didascalia Apostolorum* 9; cf. *Apostolic Constitutions* 2.26).

Several other identifiable roles, such as teachers and prophets, were less closely tied with church organization. Would they have been counted among religious leaders? The answer depended on the one who gave it. Several sources describe power struggles between local church leaders and independent teachers. Some teachers, such as Justin Martyr in Rome or Clement in Alexandria, were settled and gathered a circle of disciples around them. Others were itinerant and spread their influence by moving from one community to another. Some were highly esteemed; others were rejected as "false teachers" and "pseudoprophets."

Additional official roles in the developing church included lectors, assistants, cantors, doorkeepers, widows, and virgins (*Apostolic Constitutions* 3.11, 15). From a gender-critical perspective, the most relevant of these are the ascetic roles of widows and virgins. Church orders list widows and virgins between clergy and laypeople, giving them only assisting roles and placing them in full submission to the local bishop. Thus, these are not leadership roles, strictly speaking. However, the precepts of the church orders and the writings of such male theologians as Tertullian, John Chrysostom, and Jerome—all of whom prohibit women from teaching—may reflect an attempt to restrict the activities of women who were deemed too independent. Moreover, in relation to the ordinary members of the community, those belonging to the "order" of widows and virgins enjoyed special status.

Female Bishops and Presbyters. The titles *episkopos* and *prebyteros* appear infrequently in the feminine forms *episkopa*, *presbytis*, and *presbytera*. Most of these, found in fragmentary epigraphic data, are difficult to decipher. According to traditional scholarly views, a feminine form does not refer to a female officeholder but to the wife of a male bishop or presbyter. This is possible, though it reflects the presupposition that women could not have held positions of authority in the early church—at least, not in any "genuine" Christian church, but only among groups that were condemned as heretics. The question of who represented orthodoxy and heresy, however, was far from settled in the first Christian centuries. There were several divergent groups that all thought they represented the original, apostolic teaching and practice while others deviated from "truth." Over the course of time, dominant forms of Christianity rejected women's leadership and applied this standard to earlier generations. Sometimes allowing women to hold prominent positions was the reason to label someone as heretical.

A case in point is Epiphanius of Salamis (late fourth century C.E.), who characterizes a Montanist Christian group whom he called Quintillianists as having "woman bishops, presbyters and the rest" (*Panarion* 49.2.5). Epiphanius does not question the doctrines of this group; it is their practice of letting women hold leadership roles that, in his view, shows that they have deserted the right faith (*Panarion* 49.3.1). It is not clear what Epiphanius means by "the rest." An obvious reference might be deacons; Epiphanius may have wanted to avoid mentioning them since there were female deacons in his church, something of which he approved (*Panarion* 79.3.6), as long as they did not perform liturgical functions.

Evidence concerning female presbyters tends to be unclear when the feminine form refers to an older woman, when to a wife of a male presbyter, and when possibly to a female officeholder. Again, the majority of these rare occurrences appear in epigraphic materials. Texts where the feminine *presbytis* is clearly used as an honorific title can be found in legendary narratives. In the *Acts of Philip*, the apostle raises a young man from the dead who describes the punishments he has seen in hell while dead. They include the torturing of a man and a woman who have slandered male presbyters (*presbyteroi*), female presbyters (*presbytides*), eunuchs, deacons, deaconesses, and virgins (*Acts of Philip* 1.12). In the *Martyrdom of Matthew*, the martyred apostle appears to the king who was responsible for his execution, but later converted, and appoints him presbyter (*presbyteros*), the king's wife presbyter (*presbytis*), the king's son deacon and the wife of the son deaconess. Although these are fictional stories, their matter-of-fact references to female officeholders seem to indicate that their authors knew of female presbyters and deacons.

Texts that deny female presbyters' presence in early Christianity offer another indication of their presence. Epiphanius claims that a woman has never acted as priest (*hierateuein*): had God intended women to be priests and perform baptisms, he would have made the mother of the Lord a priest and ordered her to baptize his son. Notably, Epiphanius knows of female presbyters (*presbytides*), but he explains that they are older widows. He further claims that female presbyters and female priests (*hierissai*) have never been assigned (*Panarion* 79.2–4). Another source that mentions female presbyters is Canon 11 of the Council of Laodicea (a regional synod probably held in the late fourth century C.E.) that prohibits appointing *presbytides* and female presiders (*prokathēmenai*). The terse formulation without any broader context makes it difficult to judge what the role and the tasks of these women were.

Some texts mention women who baptize without giving them any specific title. With the development of clerical offices, the right to baptize was invested in bishops and they could delegate it to presbyters (*Apostolic Constitutions* 3.16) and sometimes to deacons (Jerome, *Against the Luciferians* 9). Thus, texts that prohibit women from baptizing might indicate that in some communities, women functioned as presbyters. For example, the *Didascalia Apostolorum* disapproves of both women who baptize and those baptized by women, warning that this is a great danger for both parties (*Didascalia Apostolorum* 15). The author uses the same argument as Epiphanius: Christ was baptized by John, not by his mother. In other texts, the women who perform baptism seem to be itinerant teachers and prophets. Their baptizing activity is likewise condemned (Tertullian, *On Baptism* 17.4; Cyprian, *Letter* 75).

Deacons, Deaconesses, and Widows. The word *diakonos* has a wide range of meaning, from the person who serves food and drink at the table to a messenger or intermediary. The latter sense fits well with the usage of the word as an honorific title of Phoebe, the female *diakonos* of the church in Cenchrea (Rom 16:1–2). She comes to Rome as a representative of her community, perhaps carrying Paul's letter with her. Even though Phoebe's position is not explained in detail, it is unlikely that she has merely an assisting role in her church. Paul underlines her importance by calling her a *prostatis*, a benefactor or supporter of his ministry. It is also noteworthy that in the book of Acts, the tasks of the first *diakonoi* go beyond distribution of food and involve missionary activities (6—8). The reference to Phoebe proves that women as well as men bore the title of *diakonos* in the early church. Thus, when the word appears in plural (Phil 1:1; cf. 1 Tim 3:8–13), women cannot be automatically excluded. The earliest Latin reference to female deacons appears in Pliny's letter to the emperor Trajan (ca. 110 C.E.), where he mentions two female slaves called "deacons" (*ministrae*).

In later sources, a new office of deaconess appears, first in the East during the third century and later in the West. The earliest mention of a *diakonissa* occurs in the Latin translation of the *Didascalia Apostolorum*. It is unclear whether this is a later translation and what the Greek word used in the original might have been; a parallel passage in the later *Apostolic Constitutions*, preserved in Greek, uses the masculine form *diakonos* with a feminine article. In some instances, the variant *diakonē* is used (*Apostolic Constitutions* 8.13.14). Only after the office of deaconess became established was the masculine form reserved primarily for men.

With the rise and establishment of the female diaconate, the duties of this office were separated from those of their male counterparts. Deaconesses performed a special ministry for women; they assisted at the baptism of women and gave them religious instruction afterward. Moreover, they accompanied the bishop when he made pastoral visits to women's homes and were responsible for order among women at assembly gatherings (*Didascalia Apostolorum* 16; *Apostolic Constitutions* 3.16; 8.28). In several texts this is the only officially designated and approved role for women. Female officeholders were needed for the sake of decency, to help the male bishop with duties he could not perform without eroding propriety.

While deaconesses were deemed necessary in the church and were counted among the clergy, it is evident that their role was to assist the bishop, not to be leaders. Female deacons were not permitted any sacramental role, and in the church orders they are always listed after male deacons. The church orders also plainly state that deaconesses (as well as deacons) must fully submit to episcopal control and not act independently. However, paying pastoral visits and giving instruction to women on behalf of the bishop must have given deaconesses considerable authority among female community members.

Alongside higher and lower clerical positions, there were other designated groups that fell somewhere in between clergy and ordinary laity. In several texts widows, sometimes accompanied by virgins, appear as identifiable groups, though these were not considered church offices and involved no ordination. The order of widows is mentioned in 1 Timothy 5:3–16, where they appear both as objects of charity and as a group with specific duties and qualifications. Widows as an ecclesiastical institution are likewise mentioned in other early Christian texts (Ignatius, *Letter to the Philippians* 4; Tertullian, *On Monogamy* 11.1; *On Modesty* 13.7; *Didascalia Apostolorum* 15). Therein the tasks of widows included prayer, fasting, and private instruction of younger women. Widows are exhorted not to run around but to stay at home, as is proper for an "altar of God." They are strictly forbidden to teach without the bishop's permission, and even then their instruction should only concern basic issues. Should anyone inquire about more complicated matters, widows should lead the inquirer to the clerical officials. Such exclusion of women (and male laity) from

teaching and other leadership functions may imply that there were in fact widows who exercised these roles. Restrictions on women, especially widows, can be seen as a sign of a struggle for authority and power, where women who were too active must be put in their proper place.

Women as Teachers and Prophets. Not all religious authorities were bishops and other local church leaders. An important means of exercising leadership in the early Christian movement was through itinerant teachers, whose examples were the apostles whom Jesus had sent to spread the word. The title *apostolos* literally means "one sent forth"—thus, apostles were those commissioned to go and teach. In addition to Jesus's twelve disciples, the title was also used for first-generation heroes such as Paul and Barnabas. Occasionally, but infrequently, it was used for a woman (Rom 16:7). In subsequent early Christian literature Mary of Magdala and the other women at the tomb, who were first commissioned by an angel and then (according to Matt 27:57–66) by the risen Christ himself to tell the male disciples about the resurrection, were hailed with the title *apostola apostolorum*—"apostle to the apostles." In the *Acts of Philip*, she appears by the name Mariamne as a companion of Philip together with Bartholomew. Even though she is not explicitly called an apostle, the three main characters are collectively called *apostoloi* (*Acts Phil.* 13.1,5). Her duties include keeping a record of the places they visit, making preparations for the Eucharist, and baptizing women while Philip baptizes men (*Acts Phil.* 8.2; 14.9). Thus, while her role in this fictional story can be characterized as leadership, her leadership is subordinate to Philip's.

Thecla, the heroine of the apocryphal *Acts of Paul and Thecla* (ca. late second century C.E.), is another apostle figure. She hears Paul's preaching, converts to an ascetic form of Christianity, deserts her fiancé, commits herself to virginity, and becomes a follower of Paul. Even though she is not called an apostle, she is sent by Paul to "go and teach the Word of God" (*Acts Paul* 41). Thecla, who takes on masculine characteristics by cutting her hair and wearing her mantle in a manly fashion, begins to teach publicly, working independently of Paul or any other man, even though her missionary activities are reported very briefly.

While some scholars have argued that there was a real female teacher called Thecla, the majority view takes her story as fictional. Regardless, others maintain that the text was transmitted, perhaps even created, by independent ascetic women teachers who took Thecla as their role model. Yet others have been more cautious and claimed that the text does not offer a window into the lives of real Christian women. On the other hand, real women read, heard, and retold these stories—and were inspired by them. Tertullian (third century C.E.) condemns those who claim the example of Thecla for allowing women to teach and to baptize (*On Baptism* 17.4). Even though the *Acts of Paul and Thecla* only tells of Thecla's self-baptism, there might have circulated other stories of her baptizing activities. Yet, more than for her autonomy and authority, she was remembered as a martyr and especially as an ideal virgin, a perfect model to imitate.

Other female teachers appear only in passing in early Christian sources. One example is Graptē in the *Shepherd of Hermas*. The visionary Hermas is instructed to make two written copies of his visions and send one of them to Clement and the other to Graptē, who, for her part, is to recount them to the widows and orphans (Herm. *Vis.* 2.4.3). Graptē receives no title, which makes it difficult to deduce what her role was in the community—and it is impossible to know whether she was a historical figure or a fictional character. Be that as it may, the text shows that for its author, it was conceivable that women acted as overseers of widows and children. Origen (third century C.E.) lists several women teachers and their followers: Helena, Marcellina, Salome, Mariamne, and Martha (*Against Celsus* 5.62). While the three last-mentioned figures at least share the same name of Jesus's female followers and appear in some apocryphal texts, Origen tells nothing further of them.

While women are sometimes called "prophet" or "prophetess," the number of named female prophets is small. The New Testament mentions the aged Anna (Luke 2:36–38) and the four virgin daughters of Philip (Acts 21:9). These biblical figures appear frequently in later texts and are highly esteemed. On the contrary, several early Christian authors cast female prophets from their own period in a dubious light and see in women's authority a true sign of heresy. Most prophetesses are linked with the so-called Montanist movement, originally called the New Prophecy by its followers and often referred to as the Phrygian or Cataphrygian sect by their opponents. Two of its best-known prophets were women, Priscilla and Maximilla (Hippolytus, *Refutation of All Heresies* 8.19; Origen, *Commentary on 1 Corinthians*, fragm. 74). Epiphanius adds Quintilla as a third prophet (*Panarion* 48–49). According to Origen, the followers justify women's prophetic activity by invoking the example of biblical prophetesses. This, in Origen's view, is not a valid argument, for biblical women only prophesied in private, not in front of assemblies.

In the mid-third century C.E., Firmilian the bishop of Caesarea in Cappadocia wrote a letter to Cyprian, the bishop of Carthage, about baptism. He recounts an unnamed and otherwise unknown female prophet who performed miracles, celebrated the Eucharist, and baptized many (Cyprian, *Letter* 75.10). In Firmilian's judgment, she only pretended to be a prophet and was actually acting under demonic influence, but she seems to have been popular and performed the baptism according to the usual ecclesiastical practice. Even though Firmilian disapproves of the prophet and questions the validity of her baptizing, he condemns her because she lacks the Holy Spirit, not because of her gender. If this indicates that Firmilian did not oppose female prophets performing liturgical functions, then he differs in this respect from other writers, such as Tertullian (*On the Veiling of Virgins* 9.1) and Epiphanius (*Panarion* 79.3.4), who, to some extent, accepted female prophets but vehemently opposed their liturgical roles.

Women and Asceticism. Most, if not all, female teachers and prophets were celibate, either widows who refused to remarry or virgins who had never married. Virginity and asceticism belonged to Christian life from its beginnings, but voluntary continence instead of, during, or after marriage began to flourish in the fourth century C.E. Many ascetic women lived in urban settings in their family houses. For example, Macrina, the sister of Gregory of Nyssa and Basil the Great, of whom relatively much is known from her biography written by Gregory, lived with her mother and gathered a group of virgins to form an ascetic community in her house. Others followed her example. It is clear that these women held authoritative status in their own community, and their activities exceeded that. They played an influential role as friends and conversation partners of male theologians, as supporters of local churches, and as founders of monastic establishments. Yet, their influence was confined to private settings, in monasteries and within the family, for women's teaching in public was discouraged.

Other female ascetics practiced a solitary form of asceticism in the desert. Among the desert fathers whose teachings have been preserved in the *Apophthegmata Patrum*, there were "desert mothers," or *ammas*, such as Theodora, Sarah, and Syncletica. These singular figures, known for the rigor of their lifestyle, were highly esteemed. Pilgrims, both men and women, visited them frequently. They exercised great authority but their leadership was spiritual, not social or political.

Female leaders of ascetic communities—such as Macrina, Melania the Elder and her granddaughter Melania the Younger, Olympias, Paula and her daughter Eustochium—might have enjoyed great authority within and outside their communities, but spiritually they were under the pastoral control of the local bishop or another male member of the clergy. The influential women that we know by name belonged to the highest social stratum. As such, they were exceptional figures and enjoyed a position unavailable to women of lower classes. They formed an ascetic elite in two senses. First, they were members of the wealthy aristocracy who could take liberties that were unimaginable for most people. Second, celibacy and the monastic lifestyle became the "higher calling," in that those engaging in it were deemed superior to ordinary, married people.

Assessment. Christianity emerged in a male-dominated world where leadership roles were, as a rule, reserved for men. Ancient sources, however,

provide some indication that women had an active role in the Christian communities, sometimes even bearing clerical titles. Source materials are often fragmentary and ambiguous, which has led to differing scholarly stances, often based on either conscious or unconscious presuppositions. Those for whom any public position of authority for women in the church is unimaginable tend to take textual restrictions of women's rights to teach and baptize at face value, concluding that women have never functioned in leadership roles in the church. If there were women who received the title of a bishop or a presbyter, they belonged to heterodox groups. Those who are strongly in favor of women's active leadership in present-day religious communities deduce that women were equally active in shaping early Christianity and held leadership roles along with men. Gradually, a male-oriented hierarchy became dominant, and evidence of women's earlier leadership was suppressed.

Neither view is without problems. Claiming that the "true" church never allowed women's leadership and labeling those Christian groups who approved of it as heretical is not free from value judgment. Instead of "orthodoxy" and "heresy," it would be more accurate to speak about fundamental diversity during the first Christian centuries. Some Christian communities accepted women as leaders, others did not. Over time, those forms of Christianity that refused women's leadership gained power and were able to declare those groups where women's prominent roles were maintained as heretical. On the other hand, to state that there was an early egalitarian period in the church is equally generalizing and misleading. It often entails the biased idea that early Christianity adapted to the inferior, male-oriented order of Roman society and applied its gendered hierarchical models to developing ecclesiastical structures. Early Christian communities, however, were not disconnected from their wider cultural environment. Women in general were not more oppressed in the Greco-Roman or Jewish culture and society, and Christian women did not enjoy a more advanced position compared to other women of the time.

Women of sufficient social status could engage in civic leadership and exercise economic and political power in the Roman society. It was not different in early Christian communities. Most of the available sources originate from elite circles, and the women they describe are prominent members of the highest social classes. There might also have been other women who had considerable influence in their local communities, but their memory has not been preserved.

[*See also* Gender Transgression, *subentry* Early Church; Popular Religion and Magic, *subentry* Early Church; Religious Leaders, *subentries on* Late Antiquity, New Testament, *and* Roman World; *and* Religious Participation, *subentries on* Early Church *and* New Testament.]

BIBLIOGRAPHY

Castelli, Elizabeth A. "Virginity and Its Meaning to Women's Sexuality in Late Antiquity." In *A Feminist Companion to Patristic Literature* edited by Amy-Jill Levine and Maria Mayo Robbins, pp. 72–100. Feminist Companion to the New Testament and Early Christian Writings 12. London: T&T Clark, 2008.

Cooper, Kate. *The Band of Angels: The Forgotten World of Early Christian Women.* London: Atlantic Books, 2013.

Eisen, Ute. *Women Officeholders in Early Christianity: Epigraphical and Literary Studies.* Collegeville, Minn.: Liturgical Press, 2000.

Elm, Susanna. *"Virgins of God": The Making of Asceticism in Late Antiquity.* Oxford Classical Monographs. Oxford: Clarendon, 1994.

Lehtipuu, Outi. "The Example of Thecla and the Example(s) of Paul: Disputing Women's Role in Early Christianity." In *Women and Gender in Ancient Religions: Interdisciplinary Approaches*, edited by Stephen Ahearne-Kroll, Paul Holloway, and James Kelhoffer, pp. 338–367. Wissenschaftliche Untersuchungen zum Neuen Testament 263. Tübingen, Germany: Mohr Siebeck, 2010.

Madigan, Kevin, and Carolyn Osiek, eds. *Ordained Women in the Early Church: A Documentary History.* Baltimore: Johns Hopkins University Press, 2005.

Matthews, Shelly. "Thinking of Thecla: Issues in Feminist Historiography." *Journal of Feminist Studies in Religion* 17 (2001): 39–55.

Methuen, Charlotte. "Widows, Bishops and the Struggle for Authority in the *Didascalia Apostolorum.*" *Journal of Ecclesiastical History* 46 (1995): 107–213.

Miller, Patricia C., ed. *Women in Early Christianity: Translations from Greek Texts.* Washington, D.C.: Catholic University of America Press, 2005.

Osiek, Carolyn, and Margaret Y. MacDonald with Janet H. Tulloch. *A Woman's Place: House Churches in Earliest Christianity.* Minneapolis: Fortress, 2006.

Tabbernee, William. *Prophets and Gravestones: An Imaginative History of Montanists and Other Early Christians.* Peabody, Mass.: Hendrickson, 2009.

Torjesen, Karen J. *When Women Were Priests: Women's Leadership in the Early Church and the Scandal of Their Subordination in the Rise of Christianity.* San Francisco: HarperCollins, 1995.

Trevett, Christine. *Montanism: Gender, Authority and the New Prophecy.* Cambridge, U.K.: Cambridge University Press, 1996.

Outi Lehtipuu

Late Antiquity

Religious leadership in late antiquity, from the fourth to the sixth centuries, shows a variety of experience that may surprise modern readers who have become accustomed to the idea of male-dominated early Christian communities organized on the same lines as the patriarchal society of the Greco-Romans. For the first two centuries of its existence, Christianity was a religious movement practiced primarily in the private space of the household rather than the public space of the temple. In such domestic contexts, practical leadership by women seems to have been accepted. For example, in his Letter to the Romans the apostle Paul sent greetings to Junia, part of a husband and wife team whom he considered to be "eminent among the apostles" (Rom 16:7). As to whether she was an apostle herself or merely highly regarded by the apostles, the text is ambiguous. Another female disciple and colleague of Saint Paul, the virgin and martyr Thecla, became the subject of the apocryphal second-century work *Acts of Paul and Thecla* and the center of a widespread cult of women's piety in the fourth and fifth centuries.

Religious leadership roles in late antiquity were of two major types: those sanctioned by an official church order, increasingly institutionalized and hierarchical in nature, and the less constrained spiritual authority of those whose ascetic withdrawal from the life of the flesh was believed to allow them direct engagement with heavenly realities.

Gender and Church Orders. Gender roles in late antiquity were defined to some extent by social status, which was surprisingly fluid, as much linked to patronage networks as to wealth, as the newly Christian empire came under a series of external and internal pressures from the fourth century onward. This fluidity of roles and status existed as much in ecclesiastical and monastic secular spheres as it did in secular spheres. Bishops, whose original function was merely to oversee the community, gradually assumed the sole right to preach, while presbyters and deacons played important roles in administering the sacraments. With the responsibility of preaching came more episcopal power over the running of church affairs, including the appointment and discipline of a nearly all-male clergy. This was divided into two levels: minor orders such as porter, cantor, lector, and exorcist, and the major orders of priest, deacon, and bishop. However, women were not altogether excluded from offices of leadership in the newly organized church.

The diaconate was open to women who were virgins or formerly married, now widowed (*Constitutions of the Holy Apostles* 6). The same work (3.2.15, trans. Donaldson, 1885, p. 431) allows for women deacons "for the ministrations towards women," especially baptism. In the ecclesial typology of the east, the bishop was said to be in the image of God of Father; the deacon, of Christ; the deaconess, of the Holy Spirit; and the priests, of the apostles (*Didascalia apostolorum* 2.26.4). Female deacons continued to be ordained at least until the early medieval period. The Greek noblewoman Olympias is a well-known example of a Byzantine deaconess. A patron and friend of John Chrysostom while he was patriarch of Constantinople (398–403/4), Olympias ran a hospital and an orphanage, and provided hospitality for visiting monks out of her own pocket. There is inscriptional evidence for *presbytera, episkopa,* and *diakonissa,* the feminine forms of *presbyteros* (initially meaning "elder," later "priest"), *episkopos* ("overseer," later "bishop"), and *diakonos* ("steward" or "deacon"), although some scholars argue that these titles were reserved for wives and widows of the clergy, it being commonplace in both the eastern and western churches for lower clergy to marry. Nonetheless, the

Council of Laodicea in the late fourth century found it necessary to legislate against the appointment of female presbyters (Canon 11) and for the exclusion of women from the sanctuary (Canon 44).

The liturgy of the earliest church had in fact been antisacrificial, or at least spiritualized, the culmination of a trend beginning in the Hebrew scriptures, whereby sacrifice is removed from the domain of cultic ritual and becomes service, practical and ethical: acts of mercy, not sacrifice (cf. Hos 6:6 and Matt 9:13). Early Christians were often suspected of "atheism" precisely because they did not sacrifice as the pagans understood it. Sacrifice had been spiritualized and internalized so that we find, especially prominently in Paul's thought, the conviction that it is Christians themselves who constitute the new Temple. Early Christians eschewed cultic designations, as the titles given to leaders in the early church were initially secular. The bishop or *episkopos* was literally an overseer. The responsibilities of the *episkopos* were initially the same as, or at least modeled upon, the manager of a household, as 1 Timothy 3 suggests.

The sacralization of church leadership begins late in the in the third century with the identification of Christian ministry with the Levitical priesthood in the canons of the Council of Carthage, and it is with Cyprian of Carthage that we first find bishops and presbyters being called "priests" (*sacerdotes; Epistle* 63), although he was yet to associate their priestly function with the liturgy. When applied to the liturgy, the Levitical understanding of priesthood brought with it an increasing emphasis on notions of ritual purity, as can be seen in the canons of the Synod of Elvira (306), which enjoined celibacy for all ministers of the altar. Hence Pope Siricius (384–399) argued that since Christ came "not to destroy the law but to fulfill it" (Matt 5:17), "perfect sexual continence is now required of the priests who offer sacrifice on behalf of the Church" (Hunter, 2007, p. 215). The sacralization of church leadership and the exclusion of women from that leadership go hand in hand, as notions of ritual purity excluded women from the altar, given that they were polluted by menstruation, giving birth, and sexual activity, according to Levitical laws. The central Christian liturgy of the

Eucharist, which began as table fellowship in the woman-friendly space of house churches, evolved into a cultic practice that in anthropological terms was inimical to women.

By the late fourth century, the clerical orders, having been endowed with legal standing as servants of the empire, assumed a cultic function for the imperial church in the performance of a liturgical "sacrifice" that ensured the continuity and prosperity of the Roman Empire, whose leaders were now Christian, with the notable exception of Julian the Apostate (361–363). Post-Constantinian liturgies can be seen to mark the beginning of a process whereby Eucharistic language became specifically cultic in orientation (Daly, 1978, p. 138), with an increasing emphasis on the sacrifice of the Cross in Christian thought and practice. It is perhaps ironic that the main instigator of the official cult of the Cross was Helena, the mother of the first Christian emperor, Constantine the Great, who was credited after her death with having found the remnants of the True Cross at Golgotha in the course of her pilgrimage to Palestine in the 320s (Ambrose, *Funeral Oration for Emperor Theodosius*, 395 C.E.).

Mary Magdalene: The First Apostle? The figure of Mary Magdalene offers us an illuminating symbol of the diminishing role of women as leaders within the institutionalized church. Mary Magdalene exemplifies the manner in which women were gradually pushed from the center to the margins of Christianity. In the Synoptic Gospels, Simon Peter is always named first among the male disciples, while Mary Magdalene is given prominence among the female disciples, suggesting a primacy analogous to that of Peter (Maisch, 1998, pp. 9–11). In John's Gospel it is Mary Magdalene rather than Peter who is presented as the model for discipleship. In her witness to the disciples, Mary Magdalene uses the same apostolic formula, "I have seen the Lord," that Paul uses to legitimate his own apostolic authority (1 Cor 9:1; see Maisch, 1998, p. 12). It is only in John 21, considered by a large number of biblical scholars to be a later appendix, that Mary is displaced by Peter.

That Mary was chosen as the first witness was something that a number of church fathers felt needed explanation. Ambrose, for example, considers the event according to the typology of the "second Eve." As it was Eve who first brought the message of sin to Adam, it was appropriate that a woman (Mary) "should also have been the first to bring the message of the grace of the Lord" (Ambrose, *On the Holy Spirit* 3.11.74). Jerome considered that Christ first appeared to a woman in order to show his humility (*Letter* 12, "To Anthony"). Both Jerome and Augustine manage to turn Mary Magdalene's grace into a failure of faith in their consideration that Mary Magdalene was not allowed to touch his feet because she did not believe in his divinity (Jerome, *Letter* 59, "To Marcella"; Augustine, *Sermon* 244.2–3).

By the time of Gregory the Great (590–604), the figure of Mary Magdalene had undergone a transformation. She became a theological type of the church rather than a historical figure (Maisch, 1998, p. 31). The figure of Mary became conflated with Mary of Bethany, who anointed Jesus, along with the other anointing women, especially the sinful woman in Luke 7:36–49 (Johnson, 1998, pp. 146–150). Mary Magdalene was later dubbed "the apostle to the apostles" by the medieval philosopher Peter Abelard, but her apostolate was particular, being restricted to the twelve male apostles, whose apostolate by contrast was universal and ongoing. One might say that her apostolic authority was confined to the domestic rather than public sphere.

Female Asceticism. Women still exerted spiritual authority in ascetic contexts, whether as solitaries or as leaders and members of female communities. Ascetic leadership offered an alternative domain of spiritual authority to the ecclesial orders, and one that was at least theoretically more open to women. The consecration of male and female virgins in the fourth century was considered "white" martyrdom, compared to the "red martyrdom" of the second, third, and early fourth centuries. These were lay people who consecrated themselves to God's service through prayer, fasting, and chastity and remained living at home with their parents. They were often wealthy aristocratic women whose inherited wealth and property was left to the church.

Female communities of nuns were governed by an abbess, to whom absolute obedience was owed. In community this person had ultimate authority over every aspect of the lives of the women in her spiritual charge. In the 320s the Egyptian monk Pachomius set up chains of monasteries on military lines in Upper Egypt, where each monk had a cell and work to do for the community, for example making mats to sell, gardening, or pottery. Pachomius allowed for communities of women run along the same lines, but under his ultimate governorship.

The concept of gender goes further than "male" and "female" biological sex, and invites us to see masculinity and femininity as constructions of society, rather than biological necessities (James, 1997, p. xvii). Twenty-first-century thinking on the question of sex and gender sees biological sex as a given, albeit one that can be surgically changed, while gender slides along a spectrum that does not correlate with biological sex. The church fathers would have agreed that gender and sex need not correlate, but for them it was a matter of sublimating sexuality altogether in order to attain "perfect" male gender. For them, gender was a given; sex was mutable. Whereas bodies could change because they belonged to the transient realm of "becoming," gender as the social meaning attributed to the body was eternal, according to early Christian thinkers. To change one's gender status required transformation of the body, usually achieved through ascetic practices, thereby making themselves "eunuchs for the kingdom of God." Some ascetics took this ideal literally and resorted to self-castration, as in the case of Origen of Alexandria (d. ca. 254).

Some of the best examples of the sliding scale of gender are found in the sayings of the monks and nuns who inhabited the Egyptian desert from the end of the third century onward. These sayings have been preserved in several collections, including the *Apophthegmata*, preserved in Greek, Coptic, and Syriac versions and in a later Latin translation. They include the sayings of monks and nuns from the first desert father Anthony of Egypt (d. ca. 270) to the sixth-century Abba Phocas. Abbas Sarah and Syncletica were among the "desert mothers" whose sayings were included in the collection. The sayings attributed to the desert mothers were not necessarily ever uttered by historical women, but their inclusion in monastic literature for the edification of ascetic

men and women tells us much about how early Christians regarded the relationship between gender and spiritual authority.

As the inferior sex, women were seen as more subject to the weaknesses of the flesh than men. "Equality in late antiquity was a thoroughly androcentric concept that in effect required a renunciation of feminine specificity" (Casey, 2010, pp. 38–39). Thus the Egyptian desert mothers who triumphed over their inferior physical status in the solitary ascetic life could be seen as greater athletes than the men who achieved the same goal with fewer handicaps. The harsh conditions of desert life included lack of regular food and water and exposure to predations of wild beasts and to the elements, which together caused most of their outward female characteristics to fall away, such as the menstrual cycle; female ascetics' breasts shriveled; their hair fell out or was shaved off. In a typical example, Abba Bessarion and an old man came upon a brother in a cave, who was engaged in plaiting a rope. The brother ignored their presence and continued with his task. On their return journey they looked for him again and found him dead in the cave. Bessarion and the old man took the body to bury it and discovered to their astonishment that the "brother" was a woman (*Apophthegmata*, "Bessarion," in Ward, 1981, p. 41). Such female ascetics as the unnamed "brother" could be considered equal in spiritual terms to men, even excelling them in spiritual warfare, but at the cost of sacrificing their biological distinctiveness.

Charismatic Religious Leadership. A third kind of religious leadership in late antiquity was that based on the charismatic gifts of prophesy, preaching, speaking in tongues, or the interpretation of tongues. This kind of spiritual authority was much more accessible to women, and by its very nature less able to be co-opted by men. Several well-known female leaders emerged in the charismatic movement known as Montanism in the late second and third centuries, in Asia Minor and North Africa. They may have developed their own hierarchy of regional bishops, and they may have allowed female clergy, as Epiphanius of Salamis charged in 375 C.E. (*Panarion* 49.2.1–5). Epiphanius also objected to their conceptualization of the Holy Spirit in female form. The prophetess Priscilla reported that even Christ came to her "under the appearance of a woman" (*Panarion* 48.12; see Trevett, 1996, pp. 185–186). However, this movement did not survive the fifth century. In spite of powerful deaconesses like Olympias, and the flourishing cults of individual women such as Mary Magdalene and Saint Thecla, the leadership of women in both eastern and western churches never regained the acceptance that it had enjoyed in the earliest centuries of Christianity.

[*See also* Gender Transgression, *subentry* Early Church; Popular Religion and Magic, *subentry* Early Church; Religious Leaders, *subentries on* Early Church *and* New Testament; *and* Religious Participation, *subentry* Early Church.]

BIBLIOGRAPHY

Casey, D. *Flesh Made Word: Theology after Irigaray*. Saarbrücken, Germany: Lambert Academic Press, 2010.

Daly, Robert J. *The Origins of the Christian Doctrine of Sacrifice*. London: Darton, Longman & Todd, 1978.

Donaldson, James, trans. "*Constitutions of the Holy Apostles 6.*" In *The Ante-Nicene Fathers*. Vol. 7: *Fathers of the Third and Fourth Centuries*, edited by Philip Schaff, pp. 385–506. Edinburgh: T&T Clark, 1885.

Hunter, David G. *Marriage, Celibacy, and Heresy in Ancient Christianity: The Jovinianist Controversy*. Oxford: Oxford University Press, 2007.

James, Liz, ed. *Women, Men, and Eunuchs: Gender in Byzantium*. London: Routledge, 1997.

Jay, Nancy. *Throughout Your Generations Forever: Sacrifice, Religion, and Paternity*. Chicago: University of Chicago Press, 1992.

Johnson, Elizabeth A. *Friends of God and Prophets: A Feminist Theological Reading of the Communion of Saints*. New York: Continuum, 1998.

Maisch, Ingrid. *Between Contempt and Veneration...Mary Magdalene: The Image of a Woman through the Centuries*. Translated by Linda M. Maloney. Collegeville, Minn.: Liturgical Press, 1998.

Torjesen, Karen Jo. "Clergy and Laity." In *The Oxford Handbook of Early Christian Studies*, edited by Susan Ashbrook Harvey and David G. Hunter, pp. 389–405. Oxford: Oxford University Press, 2008.

Trevett, Christine. *Montanism: Gender, Authority, and the New Prophecy*. Cambridge, U.K.: Cambridge University Press, 1996.

Ward, Benedicta, trans. *The Sayings of the Desert Fathers: The Alphabetical Collection*. Rev ed. London: Mowbray, 1981.

Other primary sources from the first three Christian centuries are available online at Early Christian Writings, http://www.earlychristianwritings.com. Patristic sources are available in translation in Christian Classics Ethereal Library, http://www.ccel.org/ (both sites accessed 30 June 2013).

Bronwen Neil and Damien Casey

RELIGIOUS PARTICIPATION

This entry contains eight subentries: Ancient Near East; Sacred Prostitution; Hebrew Bible; Greek World; Roman World; New Testament; Early Judaism, *and* Early Church.

Ancient Near East

The stereotype of official state religion in stark contrast (if not open opposition) to popular religion and magic is not applicable to the ancient Near East. Instead, there was a symbiosis between public and private manifestations of commonly held beliefs. On the one hand, there was the official "religious" cult (*šangûtu*) performed by a professional priesthood and on the other what were often gender-specific popular rites performed either in public or in private but all designed to benefit the community as a whole.

The gods of polytheism were imagined as larger-and-longer-than-life-human beings. They slept in their houses (shrines/temples), got up in the morning, got dressed, ate two to four meals a day, took periodic baths, did their various jobs, got (re)married, partied on festival days, and went to bed. Some gods were dead and had to be brought up from the netherworld for their festivals. For all of these needs and wants, the gods were provided with servants, which is how the office of priest was understood.

The priesthood in Mesopotamia was a hereditary profession, with the exception of the very highest offices. In Assyria and Hatti, the king was also the high priest. In the early periods in Mesopotamia, in the Middle Babylonian period at Emar, and then again in the Neo-Babylonian period when revived under Nabonidus (555–539 B.C.E.), the major male divinities of the pantheon were served by lifelong-virgin chief priestesses (*entus*), considered the gods' human wives and the servants of their goddess-wives. The practice was still apparently alive in the time of Herodotus (Herodotus 1.199). Such women were highly educated, and one of them, Enḫeduanna (ca. 2300 B.C.E.), is the world's first known author.

In Mesopotamia, the *entu* priestesses were kings' daughters and represented the monarch before his god. At Emar, by contrast, the *entu* represented the community and was chosen by lot from among its membership, with every daughter eligible. Her marriage to the divinity was celebrated in a quasi-public festival with endless detours apparently to avoid offending Ḫebat, the Storm God's divine wife. Oil from the temple of Ninkur, the Emariot Hymen, was poured on the new *entu*'s head to consecrate her hair, which was then shaved off while her father held aloft the god's divine weapon. Afterward, in a wedding banquet in the temple the husband and wife feasted separately, each in their own quarters. More of Ninkur's oil went onto the *entu*'s head, and she was returned home by the *qidaši* men who acted as paranymphs in this ritual. Ninkur herself soon followed, taking up residence in the bride's house in a bed covered with a red linen cloth, a clear evocation of the bloody sheets expected of a virgin bride. In deference to Ḫebat, the honeymoon was to take place in the new bride's natal home and not in the temple she shared with her husband.

Now qualified to carry the divine weapon herself, the *entu* priestess was not allowed to (re)enter the Storm God's house until she had poured oil over Ḫebat's betyl (sacred stone). Another separate meal ensued, after which she was allowed to occupy her throne/chair and to don a red turban. She also received her dowry in the form of earrings and presents from her brothers. There was also a husband's gift of gold, and the elders of Emar contributed a silver necklace. Her brothers then lifted up her chair and carried her home in it followed by the divine ax, the Storm God's emblem. This was laid on top of Ninkur

in ritual enactment of the consummation of the marriage. It remained in place for seven days, the standard length for divine dalliance. A woman performed the ritual lamentation for Dumuzi, thus adding a touch of romance to the proceedings.

On the seventh day, two sheep were sacrificed to Ḫebat and a gold statue of the divine husband and wife was presented, after which before the *entu* priestess was allowed to dine. This meal was shared with seven and seven fifty-year-olds, doubtless reflecting the desire for a similarly long term in office for the *entu* priestess. The faithful *qidaši* men also dined with her, as did other high-ranking priestesses and several kings. Finally, the *entu* priestess was allowed to settle. She left her father's house for the last time, wrapping herself in the multicolored scarf of a new bride about to enter her husband's house. She was accompanied by two servant women and by Ninkur and her red linen cloth, which were returned to her temple, along with a thank-you offering of a lamb. One last banquet in the temple of the Storm God was attended by the elders, who presented the new bride with new clothes and furniture consisting of a chair with footrest and a bed with an Akkadian-style bedspread. She was serenaded with a *haleluyah* (joyful song) and presented with a table laden with cookies and wine, of which the table itself (minus the table cloth) went to one of the singers. Her sister washed the *entu*'s feet and received as her reward a silver ring placed in the washbasin, doubtless a good-luck charm for her own future marriage. Finally, everybody left and the *entu* went to bed.

Nadītus were the ancient Mesopotamian equivalent of nuns. They were married to a god and, in many cases, were literally cloistered, that is, confined to a courtyard building through whose exterior window grating they communicated with the outside world. Typically from priestly or royal families, they thought of themselves as praying statues working tirelessly to convey their families' needs to the gods. The uncloistered *nadītus* had important roles to play in supervising childbirth and funerals. Despite numerous parallels to modern Catholic praxis, this custom is known to have died out after the Old Babylonian period (second millennium B.C.E.).

Continuing into the Middle and Neo-Assyrian period was a variety of holy women, most prominently the *qadištu*. These were dedicated by their parents and, in addition to serving as midwifes' assistants and nursing contractors, they had an important part in the ritual of the god Adad. The *qadištu* women accompanied the god on his peregrinations. A male priest made the requisite offerings and purifications; their job was to perform an *inhu* song while the priest sat, and also to lift up the god. The *qadištu* women were adorned for the occasion in jewelry, which was removed after the god returned to his temple. For their services, the *qadištu* women were entitled to a share of the meat from the sacrificed sheep, the rest going to the gods, the priest, and temple officials. Apprentice *qadištu* women were expected to sing *zimru* songs.

The biblical *qedēšāh*, devoted to the West Semitic Hadad/Ba'al, had similar duties. According to a disapproving Hosea, these women used gold for Ba'al (Hosea 2:10), burned incense for Ba'al and, while decked out in jewelry (Hosea 2:15), invoked the name of Ba'al (Hosea 2:19). They further turned to gods other than Yahweh and ate raisin cakes (Hosea 3:1), drank wine (Hosea 4:11), practiced divination (Hosea 4:12), offered sacrifice on the mountaintops, and burned incense on the hills or in groves (Hosea 4:13). However, both *qedēšot* and their male counterparts, *qādēšim*, seem to have been legitimate devotees of Yahweh, and even had quarters within the Temple grounds where sacred hangings were woven for the Ašerah (2 Kgs 23:4–7). The male category is attested at Ugarit, where they appear singing songs in Ba'al festival context and at Emar in the installation of Ba'al's *entu* priestess.

The specific mention of *qedēšot* practicing divination is reminiscent of the equation in Ugaritic syllabaries of NU.GIG (*qadištu*) and NU.GIG.AN.NA (*ištarītu*) with SAG.KUD or KUD.DA and SAG.KUD.DA.A or KUD.DA.A, respectively. This would literally be "one who(se head) is slashed", that is, possibly a person who practices self-mutilation in order to induce an ecstatic trance. Bloody rites of this sort are mentioned by Hellenistic authors describing the cult of the Syrian Great Mother, and seem to go back to ancient times judging from such comments in Mesopotamian sources as "My brothers are drenched in their own blood like *mahhû* ecstatics" and the biblical story of Jezebel and the priests of Ba'al (1 Kgs 18:28–29).

These rites generally represent modified mourning rites designed to gain the sympathy and/or force the cooperation of the addressed divinity for some purpose (such as healing or bringing rain). In Mesopotamia, bloody rites may have been associated with prophecy, a self-declared profession engaged in by both men and women. Women seem to predominate, perhaps because they regularly slashed themselves when in mourning.

In addition to temple priests and holy women, there was also a small army of singers, weavers, launderers, butchers, cooks, courtyard sweepers, and even shepherds and farmers, all of whom were temple dependents. Described frequently in the late periods (Neo- and Late Babylonian), many of these functionaries were children dedicated to the temple by indigent parents or were slaves dedicated by owners no longer able to care for them. Both were housed and supported by the temple as a form of service to the community. Temples were also places of safe deposit for valuables, and they made low-interest microloans.

Staff payroll consisted of the leftovers of the sacrifices offered to the divinity or divinities living in the temple. The gods smelled the savor; the rest was consumed by human beings. Some of the lower-level staff of the large temples sold off their daily prebendiary's share of the sacrifice on the open market. The cooked or prepared items accruing to the owner or purchaser of such a prebend could be sold for profit, allowing the purchasers to eat finely prepared delicacies imbued with contact with the divinity.

More direct participation in the cult was possible on festival days when the gods came out of their temples and went in procession through the streets of the city. Probably the most spectacular example of such a festival was bonfire night, the "high festival" that is mentioned in Neo-Assyrian Astrolabe B and which was held in honor of the primordial god Anu on the 16th of Tebeṭu (approximately the winter solstice) at Uruk. In the evening watch in the room on the roof of the ziggurat of the temple Bit-Reš, a reed torch was lit with sulfur fire. This was carried down the steps of the ziggurat, around the temple, and out into the city. As it passed, the priests of temples, the night watchmen, and private citizens in their houses lit torches from the main torch and used them to light brush fires in every gate and doorway, every street and square. These brush fires were kept burning until the next day dawned, bathing the city in light. The "people of the land" also poured out libations to Anu, his wife Antu, and all the gods while reciting a special prayer.

Some festivals were the occasion for wrestling matches with silver rings for prizes. During festivals, special foods were prepared and distributed to the populace who were expected to provide a small counter gift to the temple as their contribution. For example, at Emar the participants in the *kissu* festival of Ninkur got a bite of what appears to be the ancestor of Moroccan *bisteeya*—a phyllo-dough pie stuffed with birds and dried fruit and nuts. Hittite festivals often had a *šalli ašeššar*, "great seating," apparently a communal banquet. Some texts also mention the participation of guest foreigners. In Assyria, even the more private parts of public rituals were meant to be observed by a small crowd admitted into the temple courtyard for this purpose.

Public festivals also received another form of popular participation in the guise of private rites timed specifically to coincide with them. So, for example, there was an annual ghost festival in Abu during which family ghosts paid a visit to their families, ghosts with no caretakers were fed, and all were then literally shipped home to the netherworld on miniature boats put into the river. This annual event marking the summer solstice was the occasion for a series of magical practices designed to send illness and bad luck back to the netherworld with the returning ghosts. The most complete example of this type of ritual is one directed against the demoness Lamaštu acting in concert with a family ghost to produce fever in an alcoholic patient. For the ritual compo-

nent of the treatment, a miniature cedar boat was manufactured and laden with richly outfitted figurines of Gilgamesh, Namtar, "Anything Evil," and a sorcerer and sorceress all packed into a human skull. The requisite sacrifices and the ritual "marriages" of the sorcerer and sorceress to "Anything Evil" and of "Anything Evil" to Lamaštu were performed. Prayers to Gilgamesh and the netherworld Anunnaki gods were recited, along with addresses to the family ghosts and strange ghosts for assistance. The ritual completed, the little boat was allowed to float down river, carrying off the patient's problem with it.

Calendric rites were performed by ordinary women who were not priestesses. In Assyria, after the annual harvest, a woman, carried on the heads, backs, and necks of other women, went out to scatter "as much seed grain as fits in their hands" in the just-harvested fields. Subsequently, the menfolk drew a magic circle, butchered sheep, and placed them on tables set up in open courtyards. The women removed internal organs from the freshly slaughtered sheep, allowing them to fall into their laps. The men presumably removed the carcasses, then put the detached organs back onto the table, where they were mixed with other ingredients before being put into dry wells. As we may gather from the ritual for the annual fall planting at Ugarit and from parallels with the festivals of Skira and Thesmophoria in classical Athens, the rotted organs, mixed with perfumed oil, spices, and honey, went into the ground along with the grain as a sort of fertilizer.

By means of this false planting, which could not and was never meant to grow and flourish, the last year's grain was made to pass on its powers of growth to next year's harvest. Similarly, the sheep of the Assyrian postharvest ritual gave their lives to fertilize next years' crops. If, despite all these noble sacrifices, the grain did not flourish, everybody in the society would die, and yet representatives of "official" religion barely participated in these rites.

Even more striking, an essential part of Dumuzi's (Tammuz's) resurrection and death festival, the annual summer "wailings" for Dumuzi, were rites performed by women in the privacy of their own homes with the assistance of their menfolk. To resurrect the god from his netherworld home, the women parched grain, producing clouds of smoke. They also soaked corn dollies in beer to make them float and sprout. Dumuzi remained dead, though present among the living and the ghosts visiting their former families. For the duration of the festival, Dumuzi was therefore localized in a model funeral bed where he was wailed over by the women and where both he and the family ghosts received funerary offerings. Dumuzi's particular share consisted of apples (a love charm for his lover Ištar) and special sweet cakes baked in ashes (*kaman tumri*) by the menfolk. Vessels used to make these offerings were smashed. The men perambulated the "sheepfold" (probably actually the city or town) playing flutes in honor of this god of shepherds. At the end of the festival, all festal items were discarded.

Another liminal festival provided the occasion for a private/public celebration engaged in by primarily men, with some assistance by women. At Emar, the month Marzaḫani was dedicated to a collective celebration of various *marzeaḥ* organizations (men's drinking clubs). In the middle of the month, there was a procession of the goddess Aštar-ṣarba, followed by a sheep and the divine ax, and first the women and then the men performed whirling dances in single-sex groups. The latter whirl dance was accompanied by a holocaust offering and ritual meals (*naptanu*) provided by the *marzeaḥ* organizations. The object of the exercise was to attract the "known gods" (family ghosts) who would have been released from the netherworld by the shifting of the seasons accompanied by the sirocco, a series of wind storms that the whirl dances were presumably meant to imitate.

At Ugarit, booths made of branches were set up on the roof, and the palace sponsored various offerings to visiting divinities including the Hurrian Ištar (Queen of Heaven) and the Star Gods, both of whom received their gifts in offering pits. A procession of children and a second procession of the entire community framed the festival. While in residence, the ghosts were rendered harmless by the men by drinking them-

selves into a stupor, as described in the literary composition known as "El on a Toot."

Neither Mesopotamia nor Israel had *marzeaḥ* organizations. Here, these popular rites of seasonal change were, once again, privately performed by women with male assistance and encouragement. According to the Mishnah (*Taʿan.* 4:8), the girls of Jerusalem went out on the tenth of Tishri in white garments to sing songs and to dance in the vineyards. Zephaniah 1:5 and Jeremiah 19:13 both mention incense offerings and libations made on rooftops of private houses to the hosts of heaven (the stars). In Jeremiah 44:15–19, the Israelites defend the practice on the grounds that it brought honor to the Queen of Heaven. They also mention the making of little cakes in her image. As we know further, it was the women who performed the rites, and the cakes (*kawânim*) in question were kneaded and shaped by women but baked in open fires by the men, and so are the exact equivalents of the Mesopotamian *kaman tumri*.

Comparison with rites known from the Sacrificial Tariff from Kition on Cyprus suggests that these Israelite women's rituals were timed to coincide with the festival of Sukkot. On Cyprus, the Holy Queen (that is, the goddess Ashtarte of Kition) was moved into a temporary dwelling (compare the "booth" of Sukkot) and received baskets of *hallot* (*ḥlt*) together with the *prmn* (= Greek *puramous*: "cakes of roasted wheat and honey") in a festival in the month of Etanim, the name given by the Phoenicians to the seventh month of the year. This "festival in the month of Ethanim" (1 Kgs 8:1–4) was chosen for Solomon's dedication of the Temple and by the returning exiles for the reintroduction of God into his land as described in Ezra 3. Such evidence points to women's private rites that directly coordinate with major calendric rituals.

In Mesopotamia, where grapes, raisins, and wine were imports, the only trace of this entire complex is a public whirl dance performed by women in honor of an alleged confrontation between Ištar and Ṣaltu as described in the literary composition "Ea and Ṣaltu": "Ṣaltu was created so that, like us, the people of future days might know. Let it be yearly. Let a whirl dance [*guštu*] be established among the rites [*parṣu*] of the year. Look [Ištar] at the people, all of them [f. pl.]!

Let them dance in the street. Hear their [f. pl.] shouting! Look, you, at the clever things they [f. pl.] do. Let their [f. pl.] mind be your mind."

Nonetheless, it is important not to downplay the significance of the contribution made by these ostensibly private rites, even in Israel. Their importance is reflected in the stinging rebuke delivered by the exiles to the prophet Jeremiah: "Ever since we stopped burning incense to the Queen of Heaven and pouring out drink offerings to her, we have had nothing and have been perishing by sword and famine!" (Jer 44:18): The Israelite Queen of Heaven is, of course, the Asherah whose intercession was essential to good relations between God and Israel and from which all benefits flowed.

[*See also* Popular Religion and Magic, *subentry* Ancient Near East; *and* Religious Leaders, *subentry* Ancient Near East.]

BIBLIOGRAPHY

Cohen, Mark E. *The Cultic Calendars of the Ancient Near East.* Bethesda, Md.: CDL, 1993.

Cohen, Mark E. "Observations on the Festivals and Rituals of Dumuzi/Tammuz." In *A Common Cultural Heritage: Studies on Mesopotamia and the Biblical World in Honor of Barry L. Eichler*, edited by Grant Frame, Erle Leichty, Karen Sonik et al., pp. 255–265. Bethesda, Md.: CDL, 2011.

Fleming, Daniel E. *Time at Emar: The Cultic Calendar and the Rituals from the Diviner's Archive.* Mesopotamian Civilizations 11. Winona Lake, Ind.: Eisenbrauns, 2000.

Foster, Benjamin. "Ea and Ṣaltu." In *Essays on the Ancient Near East in Memory of Jacob Joel Finkelstein*, edited by Maria de Jong Ellis, pp. 79–84. Hamden, Conn.: Archon, 1977.

de Moor, Johannes C. *The Seasonal Pattern in the Ugaritic Myth of Baʿlu.* Alter Orient und Altes Testament 16. Neukirchen-Vluyn, Germany: Neukirchener Verlag, 1971.

Parke, H. W. *Festivals of the Athenians.* Ithaca, N.Y.: Cornell University Press, 1977.

Peckham, Brian. "Notes on a Fifth-Century Phoenician Inscription from Kition, Cyprus (CIS 86)." *Orientalia*, n.s., 37 (1968): 304–324.

Scurlock, Jo-Ann. "Wailing for Dumuzi? A New Interpretation of K 164 (*BA* 2: 635)." *Revue d'Assyriologie* 86 (1992): 53–67.

Scurlock, Jo-Ann. "Animal Sacrifice in Ancient Mesopotamia." In *A History of the Animal World in the Ancient Near East*, edited by Billie Jean Collins, pp. 389–403. Leiden, The Netherlands: Brill, 2002.

Scurlock, Jo-Ann. "Popular Religion or Popular Participation in Public Rites at Ugarit, Emar, Judah, Mesopotamia, and Classical Greece?" In *Private and State: Proceedings of the 58th Rencontre Assyriologique Internationale*, Leiden, The Netherlands, 2012.

Scurlock, Jo-Ann. "Akkadian Medical Texts: Supernatural Causes: Lamaštu and Witchcraft; Rituals of the End of the Month Abu." In *Context of Scripture.* Vol. 4. Leiden, The Netherlands: Brill, forthcoming.

Scurlock, Jo-Ann. "Whirling (*Ṣâdu*) in the Month of Marzaḫani at Emar, or Why Did El Get, So to Speak, Drunk as a Lord in KTU 1.114." *Ugarit Forschungen* 44 (forthcoming).

Waerzeggers, Caroline. *The Ezida Temple of Borsippa: Priesthood, Cult, Archives.* Achaemenid History 15. Leiden, The Netherlands: Nederlands Instituut voor het Nabije Oosten, 2010.

Westenholz, Joan Goodnick. "Tamar, *Qĕdēšā, Qadištu*, and Sacred Prostitution in Mesopotamia." *Harvard Theological Review* 82, no. 3 (July 1989): 245–265.

Jo-Ann Scurlock

Sacred Prostitution

The theory of "sacred prostitution" originated in late nineteenth- and early twentieth-century romanticism which understood ancient religions as engaging in imitative magic designed to engineer the rejuvenation of nature in the spring, the growth of crops, and the fertility of humans and animals. Part of this fertility religion complex, it was argued, entailed sexual intercourse on temple grounds with the priestesses of the cult (sacred prostitution).

Often cited as evidence for sacred prostitution is a passage in Herodotus that details a Cypriote custom performed in honor of Mylitta (= Greek Hera and Roman Juno), the patroness of marriage (Herodotus 1.199). In 1861, J. J. Bachofen argued that, since marriage was an offense to Nature, the prospective bride in "primitive times" had to propitiate this divinity by engaging in premarital prostitution. As evidence, he described by Herodotus, however, this rite was not prostitution, sacred or otherwise, but instead a public defloration rite expected to terminate in marital fidelity. The source of this custom is likely a taboo in Cyprus on the husband shedding his wife's blood. By way of comparison, the Roman husband in a non-*manus* marriage was not supposed to kill a wife caught in adultery, and the Roman marriage ceremony required self-defloration by the bride by means of a stone phallus before first intercourse could commence (Kiefer, 1934).

No defloration rite would have been possible in either Mesopotamia or Israel, where a woman had to be a virgin on her first wedding night or face serious consequences. Indeed, Herodotus does not describe the intercourse as taking place in the temple itself; in the ancient Near East generally, sexual intercourse within the temple precincts brought impurity and the wrath of the gods.

Other "religious" dimensions of prostitution can be identified, however. In Mesopotamia, prostitutes working in tavern-brothels or walking the streets paid a tithe to the goddess Ištar, considered the patroness of their profession (Cooper, 2006). In one magical rite, sex with one of Ištar's *kezertu* women (ladies' maids) was understood to transfer divine anger from oneself to one more deserving of punishment. This rite was not related to official Mesopotamian religion and may not have been considered even a legitimate magical practice. Transfer rites are commonplace in ancient Mesopotamian magic, but deliberately passing one's problem on to another person was witchcraft, for which one could be executed.

Another passage in Herodotus often cited as evidence of cultic prostitution in ancient Mesopotamia (Herodotus 1.181) describes the highest class of Mesopotamian priestesses, the *ēntu*. In fact, these holy women were not prostitutes. Instead, they were understood as the wives of male divinities to whom they were dedicated, and they did not, as Herodotus himself notes, engage in sexual relations with mortal men. There were three classes of such holy women in Mesopotamia. At the top of the social hierarchy was the *ēntu* priestess who was married only to a god. As discerned from surviving marriage contracts involving these women, the *nadītu* was a god's second wife and could be a human's first wife. Finally, there was the *qadištu*, who could be a secondary wife to both gods and humans.

The name of this last holy woman corresponds to a class of male and female cult functionaries known from other West Semitic cultures, including ancient Israel. The common Semitic root related to *qadištu* means "pure" or "clean"—literally "holy woman" and "holy man," not, as usually translated, "prostitute" and "sodomite."

In the Hebrew Bible, the *qādēš* (male Canaanite cult functionaries) are mentioned in only seven passages, none of which give any hint of sexual activity (Gen 38:21–22, Hos 4:14, Deut 23:17, 1 Kgs 14:24, 1 Kgs 15:12, 1 Kgs 22:47, and 2 Kgs 23:7). The *qedēšah*, on the other hand, is mentioned in conjunction with actual prostitutes. In Genesis 38, Tamar is variously referred to as a *qedēšah* (= *qadištu*) and a prostitute (*zonah*) (Gen 38:15, 21–23). These female Canaanite cult functionaries receive condemnation in the laws (Deut 23:17), and Israelite men are separately forbidden from prostituting their daughters (Lev 19:29). Hosea gives us a description of these holy women's actual activities in the cult, not one of which has any demonstrable connection with sex (Hos 4:14).

To unpack prophetic objections to the *qedēšah*, we need to examine more closely the Mesopotamian *qadištu*, whose activities in the cult are strikingly similar. As we know from cuneiform laws and legal documents, the father who dedicated his daughter to a god as *qadištu* was supposed to give her a dowry, failing which she was entitled to one third share in the property of her father's house which she could hold for life. Legal documents show *qadištu*-women inheriting land and selling, purchasing, or renting houses and fields. The property in question did not in any sense belong to the husband that such a woman married. If her father made the proper arrangements, she was free to dispose of it wherever she wished; otherwise, she held it in trust for her brothers. The most common method chosen by *qadištus* to dispose of their personal wealth was to adopt other people's sons and daughters as their heirs. It is quite common to find contracts in which female cult functionaries appear as adopters of children. In none of the preserved examples is the holy woman's husband mentioned, and we may therefore presume that the children in question were not expected to inherit from him.

I suggest that these holy women's independence of action and absence of a male protector (or indeed the need for one) account for the ambiguous ways in which they are described in ancient Mesopotamian texts. In wisdom literature, female cult functionaries, slave girls, widows, and prostitutes are criticized for performing duties in public; engaging in unsupervised interaction with unrelated men; having children that were not their husband's; and earning their own living—activities that allowed them to function beyond their husband's control, sexual or otherwise. Acting outside gender norms, they were seen as both dangerous to and yet physically attractive to men.

This tolerated violation of gender boundaries and even inversion of gender roles by specific classes of women may be compared to "women without men" in modern North Africa and elsewhere in the Mediterranean world, whose reputations are similarly ambiguous. The same may be said for a less well studied but quite real category of "men without women," most notoriously the Omani *xanith* to whom the ancient Mesopotamian *kulu'u* may profitably be compared. These are men who dress and act like women, think of themselves as women, and prefer to congregate with "other" women.

[*See also* Deity, *subentries on* Hebrew Bible *and* Greek World; *and* Religious Leaders, *subentry* Ancient Near East.]

BIBLIOGRAPHY

Cooper, J. "Prostitution." In *Reallexikon der Assyriologie*, Vol. 11, edited by M. P. Streck, pp. 12–21. Berlin: Walter de Gruyter, 2006.

Harris, Rivkah. *Ancient Sippar: A Demographic Study of an Old-Babylonian City, 1894–1595 B.C.* Uitgaven van het Nederlands Historisch-Archaeologisch Instituut te Istanbul36. Leiden, The Netherlands: Nederlands Historisch-Archaeologisch Instituut te Istanbul, 1975.

Jansen, Willy. *Women without Men: Gender and Marginality in an Algerian Town.* Leiden, The Netherlands: Brill, 1987.

Kiefer, Otto. *Sexual Life in Ancient Rome.* London: Abbey Library, 1934.

Westenholz, Joan Goodnick. "Tamar, *Qĕdēšā, Qadištu,* and Sacred Prostitution in Mesopotamia." *Harvard Theological Review* 82, no. 3 (July 1989): 245–265.

Wikan, Unni. *Behind the Veil in Arabia: Women in Oman.* Baltimore: Johns Hopkins University Press, 1982.

Jo-Ann Scurlock

Hebrew Bible

Opportunities for women's and men's participation in ancient Israel's religious life can be assessed by considering the sacred spaces and the ritual calendar of the Iron Age and Second Temple periods. Purity status also affected ancient Israelites' ability to engage in their culture's religious traditions.

Sacred Space: The Iron Age. The religion of Iron Age Israel shared with other ancient Near Eastern religions the conviction that a nation's god lived among its people, in a "temple" (*hêkāl*) analogous to the "palace" (*hêkāl*) of the king. Like a king, moreover, a deity was attended by servitors who took responsibility for the god's well-being. Yet because in Israel, only male servitors—members of Israel's all-male priesthood—could minister to the deity's needs, women's opportunities to participate in the cult of the nation's god, Yahweh, were constrained.

Nevertheless, women were able to perform some acts of cultic service in the most renowned of Yahweh's divine dwelling places, the Jerusalem Temple complex of the southern kingdom of Judah. While our data are limited, extrapolation might suggest that some degree of women's participation was also possible at the northern kingdom's state temples in Bethel and Dan. Still, women could find more significant opportunities for exercising religious agency within household shrines and regional sanctuaries, where Yahweh was venerated yet not permanently resident.

The national temples of Jerusalem, Bethel, and Dan. Three biblical texts indicate women's ability to perform significant cult functions within the Jerusalem Temple (and perhaps, analogously, in the northern temples of Dan and Bethel). First Kings 15:13 describes

Maacah, the queen mother of Judah's King Asa, as having made an image for the Canaanite mother goddess Asherah, who arguably was worshipped in Maʿacah's day as Yahweh's consort. Maʿacah's Asherah image thus arguably stood within Yahweh's Jerusalem Temple compound, meaning Maʿacah can be said to have executed an important religious role by erecting a temple icon. Likewise, the women who are described in 2 Kings 23:7 as weaving garments for Asherah—that is, wraps that were somehow draped over the goddess's statue—can be said to have performed the important role of producing cult fabrics. Psalms 68:25–26 (in most English versions of the Bible 68:24–25) further suggests that women could serve as cult musicians, as it lists young women who play frame drums as participating in a procession into Yahweh's *qōdeš*, or sanctuary—probably the Temple precinct in Jerusalem.

Women also appear among the ritual community in texts that describe the tent of meeting, which biblical tradition construes as the Israelites' place of worship prior to the construction of the Jerusalem Temple. However, women in a state of impurity are forbidden to approach spaces like the tent of meeting and the Jerusalem Temple, where the presence of Yahweh, the "Holy God," is considered to be permanently manifest. To be sure, impure men are also forbidden access to Yahweh's holy spaces, but because Israelite women of childbearing age frequently experienced impurity—during their menses and during the fairly lengthy period of impurity that followed childbirth (forty days if the child was a boy; eighty days if a girl)—women seem to have been excluded from sanctified settings more often than men. Judith Romney Wegner (2003) has shown, moreover, that when women whose periods of impurity had ended bring the offerings required of them to the tent of meeting's entrance—and so, presumably, to an analogous space within the Jerusalem Temple—they are not said to bring their offerings "before Yahweh" (*lipnê yhwh*; Lev 12:6; 15:29): that is, they do not come into the presence of Yahweh at Yahweh's altar. Conversely, a man who has suffered a period of impurity is said to come *lipnê yhwh* when he presents his required offerings (Lev 15:14–15).

Regional sanctuaries. Even as Leviticus 12:6, 15:29, and related texts impose significant restrictions upon women's approaching the tent of meeting and Yahweh who is manifest within, Numbers 12:5 describes Miriam and her brother Aaron as standing at the entrance to the tent of meeting when Yahweh appears to them there. This very different sense of women's access to God's presence is possible because Numbers 12:5 (see also 27:2) stems from a strand in biblical thought that understands the tent of meeting *not* to be the place where Yahweh permanently resides, and where God's presence is permanently manifest, but rather a place where Yahweh can appear as needed. So too are Iron Age Israel's regional sanctuaries best understood as sites where Yahweh could be venerated, and where the deity might appear, but not where Yahweh permanently dwelt. These sanctuaries, which were scattered throughout ancient Israel and Judah at locations that were, say, within a 25–30 km radius of worshippers' homes, included the various "high places," or *bāmôt* shrines, that are referred to at several points in the biblical text (e.g., 2 Kgs 17:9). Other regional sanctuaries are known from archaeological data (e.g., the so-called Bull Site of the early twelfth century B.C.E.) or from a combination of archaeological and textual evidence (e.g., the premonarchic regional sanctuary of Shiloh).

From the preeminent biblical account about Shiloh (1 Sam 1:1—2:26), we learn, moreover, that on one occasion when this narrative's main characters—the family of Elkanah—came to Shiloh to worship, Elkanah's barren wife, Hannah, was able to engage in a remarkable constellation of ritual activities while beseeching Yahweh to give her a son (1 Sam 1:9–18). She prays (the only woman in the Hebrew Bible explicitly identified as doing so); she makes a vow (one of only three specific women in the Bible said to do this); she arguably takes on, until she gives birth to her miracle son, the commitments imposed on individuals known as Nazirites as part of their special dedication to God; and, arguably as well, she engages in a specific sequence of ritual actions—fasting, weeping, and approaching a sacred space—in an attempt to solicit Yahweh's divine oracle. All of this is furthermore undertaken "before Yahweh" (*lipnê yhwh*;

1 Sam 1:12, 15)—which is possible because Shiloh as a regional sanctuary is a place where Yahweh is only occasionally present and thus a place that need not safeguard the permanent presence of the "Holy God" by mandating that impurities, and especially the omnipresent threat of impurity associated with women of childbearing age, be zealously kept at bay.

Similarly, cultic service at Shiloh and other regional sanctuaries need not be zealously restricted to the purview of Yahweh's priestly ministers. Rather, 1 Samuel 1:1—2:26 depicts the worshippers who come to Shiloh—and not the priests resident there—as slaughtering sacrificial animals and then apportioning to Yahweh the share owed to the deity, while preparing the rest of the meat to be eaten in a communal meal (1 Sam 1:4–5, 24; 2:12–17). To be sure, 1 Samuel 1:1—2:26 indicates that it is specifically male worshippers, and more specifically still male heads of household, who perform these rites. Nevertheless, in 1 Samuel 1:25, Hannah is said to stand beside Elkanah when he slaughters a sacrificial bull (reading with the Septuagint [LXX]), and we might plausibly envision her as joining Elkanah as well when he approaches Yahweh's altar to offer up God's portion of the bull's flesh. Hannah, moreover, is said to take responsibility for bringing the bull to Shiloh, along with flour and wine that were also to be dedicated to Yahweh (1 Sam 1:24).

Household religion. The reason Hannah takes responsibility for bringing the various food offerings that were to be dedicated to Yahweh to Shiloh is that she, like women generally in ancient Israel, should be understood as the manager of her household's foodstuffs: that is, as the household member who oversees the processing and the distribution of a family's food resources, both the foodstuffs that were to be consumed by the household's residents on a day-to-day basis and the foodstuffs that were to be allocated to Yahweh (and/or some other god or gods). Moreover, not only did Israelite women undertake the obligation for distributing foodstuffs that were to be allocated to some god or gods at, say, Shiloh, women also had the responsibility for distributing foodstuffs that were to be dedicated to any deity or deities venerated within their homes. For example,

women produced raw ingredients, such as flour (Exod 11:5; Isa 47:2; Job 31:10), that other household members could use to prepare some cooked offering, such as bread cakes (Gen 19:3; Judg 6:19). Or, as in Jeremiah 7:16–20, women both prepared flour and used it to make bread cakes, which they would then arguably present to the deity to whom the cakes were dedicated—either by placing them in a small shrine niche that lay within their family home or in a dedicated shrine room that belonged to their extended family. Women also, according at least to Judges 17:1–5, could help appoint these sorts of dedicated shrine rooms—even, as in Judges 17:1–5, providing these household shrines with their most significant furnishing.

The Iron Age Ritual Calendar. As women were generally able to engage more productively in religious worship the more removed they were from temples where Yahweh was permanently resident, so too was it possible for women to engage more fully during set times of ritual observance if these occasions were divorced from major temple locations. This is true for the weekly observance of the sabbath, the monthly observance of the new moon, and the three annual pilgrimage feasts. The yearly clan festival and various life-cycle rituals were, however, something of an exception.

Sabbath. In ancient Israel, the weekly sabbath was, at least in part, the sort of temple-based observance during which women's participation, as we have seen, is constrained (see, e.g., Isa 1:13, which discusses the sabbath in conjunction with the bringing of offerings to Yahweh, presumably, given Isaiah's Jerusalem provenance, to Yahweh's Jerusalem Temple). Some rituals outside of temple purview, though, appear to have been a feature of the sabbath as well: namely, the cessation of certain customary labors. These include plowing and the reaping of grain (Exod 34:25; Deut 5:14); the gathering of wood and the kindling of fire (Exod 35:3; Num 15:32–36); and commercial activities (Amos 8:5). Yet none of these activities seem to be work in which women customarily engaged. Indeed, Exodus 12:16 may hint that on the sabbath, women were expected to *continue* their most customary work—food preparation—unabated.

However, in Exodus 31:5, 35:2; and Leviticus 23:3 (see also Exod 16:23), the sabbath is described using the phrase *šabbat šabbātôn*, usually translated as "a sabbath of solemn (or complete) rest." In the view of many commentators, this ups the ante, so to speak, so that under the terms of these texts, women may have had respite from all work, including food preparation. Second Kings 4:23 likewise might indicate that women could suspend their normal work on the sabbath in order to go to a local shrine to visit a "man of God" (in the case of 2 Kings 4:23, the prophet Elisha).

The new moon festival. Second Kings 4:23 suggests that another occasion on which women might journey to seek out a "man of God" is during the monthly celebration of the new moon. Nevertheless, the sort of temple setting that is less productive for women's exercise of religious agency is indicated for the new moon festival in Numbers 10:10, 28:11–15, 29:6; Isaiah 1:13–14; and Ezekiel 46:6. The setting of the new moon festival described in 1 Samuel 20—although not easy to determine—likewise seems to be a sanctuary complex, located within the enclave of King Saul at Gibeah. This royal sanctuary would likely have been governed by the same ideology that governed later national sanctuaries, whereby Yahweh was resident and perpetually present. As we have seen, this means certain standards regarding cultic purity and the sanctuary's holiness would have been in effect. Can it then be coincidental that no women are mentioned as joining Saul within his sanctuary complex to partake of the ritual meal that was part of the new moon celebration? As women were largely excluded from whatever temple rituals were associated with the sabbath, so too may purity concerns within royally sponsored temples have forced women to the periphery of those sanctuaries' new moon feasts.

The annual clan feast. Unlike the women of Saul's household, all Saul's male companions seem to have been expected to assemble for the new moon feast described in 1 Samuel 20. But one is absent: Saul's eventual successor, David, who is said have taken leave so that he could participate in an annual sacrificial ritual sponsored by his extended family or clan. The venue for such clan sacrifices was arguably some family sanctuary—perhaps, in David's case, the same shrine at which Samuel offered sacrifice when he came to David's hometown in 1 Samuel 16:5 to anoint him as Israel's future king.

Some scholars have suggested, moreover, that because in Israel "a 'household' is made up of the dead, the living, and the unborn" (Bergant, 1994, p. 50), a clan's annual sacrificial gathering invoked the presence of its deceased ancestors—or more specifically, as Karel van der Toorn has demonstrated through his work on the exclusively *male* kinship terminology used in Israelite personal names (1996, *Family Religion*, p. 229), its patrilineal ancestors. As with the dead, so too was it with the living; that because a clan's annual sacrificial feast was part of the male-dominated ancestor cult, even women who were resident in any given clan's households played little to no part? Van der Toorn (2003, p. 403) is definitive: "Women never participate." Ironically, therefore, a clan's annual sacrificial meal may not have been an occasion celebrated by the "family" writ large, as a clan's women members were not fully able to engage.

The pilgrimage festivals. Women's full engagement can likewise be compromised in the celebration of the three great pilgrimage festivals of the Israelite calendar. For example, according to Exodus 23:17, Exodus 34:23, and Deuteronomy 16:16, it is only "your males" who are required to journey to some sanctuary space to observe the feasts of (1) Maṣṣot, or the feast of Unleavened Bread and the associated celebration of Pesaḥ/Passover; (2) Harvest, also called Shavuʿot ("Weeks"); and (3) Ingathering/Sukkot. Still, Deuteronomy 16:11 and 14 require at least some women—a household's daughters, widows, and female slaves—to participate in the festivals of Shavuʿot and Sukkot, and Deuteronomy 31:10–13 more emphatically requires that every seven years at Sukkot, all "men, women, and children" must join in the celebration. Arguably, moreover, Sukkot is the occasion of the Shiloh ritual celebrations that are described in 1 Samuel 1:1—2:26, in which women readily engaged (Hannah, Elkanah's other wife, Peninnah, and possibly—according to the LXX—Peninnah's daughters).

However, Hannah is said to stay home from the Shiloh festival after she gives birth to Samuel and before he is weaned (a process that may have taken as long as three years; 2 Macc 7:27), and wives are not listed among the household women required by Deuteronomy 16:11 and 14 to observe the pilgrimages of Shavu'ot and Sukkot. This suggests that while wives may have been welcome to join in these pilgrimage celebrations, their participation was not necessarily required—when, for example, childrearing responsibilities made it unfeasible for them to journey away from home. Nowhere in Iron Age tradition, moreover, are women enjoined to make a pilgrimage journey at the time of Pesaḥ-Maṣṣot, and this may reflect a sensibility that this pilgrimage feast entailed both sanctuary- and domestically based observances. The former are undertaken by men, for whom sanctuary spaces are more religiously productive venues, whereas the domestic rituals of Pesaḥ-Maṣṣot—for example, the manufacture, for the festival's seven-day duration, of unleavened bread—may be more typically the province of women.

Life-cycle rituals. All life-cycle rituals, whether pertaining to men or women, aim to effect a transformation—the moving of an individual from one stage in life to another (from, say, "unmarried young maid" to "bride")—that necessarily disrupts what had previously been considered normative within that person's social group. This disruption, although its end—such as a marriage—is often considered a social good, nonetheless imperils what had been the group's fundamental constitution, and in response the group categorizes the individual or individuals undergoing life-changing transitions as dangerous. Indeed, so dangerous are the individuals going through life-cycle rituals that they must have whatever potential they possess for exerting agency constrained. For women, the result is ironic, for while life-cycle rituals are typically celebrated in the home, a venue that is generally conducive to women's exercise of religious power, the disempowering effect of life-cycle transitions results instead in women's disenfranchisement and their being rendered as marginal figures.

Moreover, because Israelite women—even within the home—were generally marginalized in relation to men, the marginalized position into which they are placed during life-cycle rituals is greater than that endured by their male counterparts. During the life-cycle ritual of birth, for example, a male infant is associated with only a forty-day period of maternal impurity, whereas the more marginalized female newborn renders her mother impure for twice as long. Similarly, the raucous feasts that celebrated the life-cycle ritual of marriage (Gen 29:22; Judg 14:10; Esth 2:18)—which involved drinking, gaming, and joyous music making (this is attested in Judg 14:10–18 and Isa 62:5, and by Greek and Roman materials)—seem to have been all-male affairs. The more marginalized bride and perhaps her women companions may have conversely marked the marriage by making music of a somber and even grievous nature. Life-cycle rituals associated with death also marginalize women in relation to men, as it is only men—as we have seen above—who are admitted into the company of the dead ancestors and are then subsequently invoked to join their living kin at an annual clan feast.

The Second Temple Period. The constraints imposed upon women during life-cycle rituals can also increase over time, so that an Iron Age woman's ability to bestow a name on her newborn during the life-cycle rituals associated with childbirth seems, by the Second Temple era, to have been increasingly claimed by—or at least shared with—men (Matt 1:25; Luke 1:59–63). Other opportunities for women to exercise religious agency were similarly curtailed during the Second Temple period. Most notably, the effort to dismantle all shrines and sanctuaries other than the Temple in Jerusalem—which had begun, according to 2 Kings 23:4–23, already in the late seventh century B.C.E.—came to fruition, meaning that the regional sanctuaries that seem to have served Iron Age women as productive fora for religious expression were no longer extant. Also worship at household shrines—if our fairly limited archaeological data are any guide—seems to have increasingly given way to worship centered at the Jerusalem Temple. To be sure, women were not excluded from Temple worship: in both Ezra 10:1 and Nehemiah 12:43, women are said to join in observances held there.

Still, by the late Second Temple period, the Jerusalem Temple had a special courtyard designated for women, which was positioned fifteen steps below the Temple and its main courts and further set apart by a wall. Women, that is, were apparently not allowed even to see the Temple's central area of assembly. Also in the Second Temple period, there were significant changes in the celebration of the pilgrimage festivals. Most notably, any sense that Pesaḥ-Maṣṣot entailed a component of domestic observance was lost, so that the entire seven-day festival was defined as a time of Temple celebration (Ezek 45:21; 2 Chr 8:12–13; 30:13, 21; 35:17; Ezra 6:22). Again, women were not excluded from these celebrations—note the women from the Galilee who accompanied Jesus on his Passover pilgrimage to Jerusalem (Matt 27:55; Mark 15:40; Luke 23:49)—but as we have just seen, these women's ability to access the Temple's main area of assembly may have been constrained. Moreover, their ability to contribute ritually to the festival's observance—such as by making cakes of unleavened bread—was not possible in the ways it had been when some aspects of Pesaḥ-Maṣṣot were observed in the home (see Luke 22:8, where two of Jesus's *male* disciples, not his women followers, prepare their company's Pesaḥ meal).

Issues concerning purity also constrained women's participation in the Temple-centered observance of Pesaḥ-Maṣṣot. Indeed, Numbers 9:6–13, which dates from the Second Temple period, establishes procedures for a second Pesaḥ to be observed a month after the first by those who were not in the proper ritual state to participate in the regular celebration of the holiday. Of course, impurity does not affect only women, but it does affect them disproportionately because of the recurrent impurities associated with menstruation and parturition. Again, then, women would have been disproportionately cut off from the primary Pesaḥ-Maṣṣot celebration once it became Temple-based.

Overall, the Second Temple period was marked by worship being centralized at the Jerusalem Temple, a venue where women's ability to engage religiously was limited. Only with the fall of the Temple in 70 C.E. did the possibility for more fulsome modes of religious expression reemerge.

[*See also* Popular Religion and Magic, *subentry* Hebrew Bible; *and* Religious Participation, *subentry* Early Judaism.]

BIBLIOGRAPHY

Ackerman, Susan. "Household Religion, Family Religion, and Women's Religion in Ancient Israel." In *Household and Family Religion in Antiquity: Contextual and Comparative Perspectives*, edited by John Bodel and Saul M. Olyan, pp. 127–158. Malden, Mass.: Blackwell, 2008.

Ackerman, Susan. "Who Is Sacrificing at Shiloh? The Priesthoods of Ancient Israel's Regional Sanctuaries." In *Levites and Priests in Biblical History and Tradition*, edited by Mark A. Leuchter and Jeremy M. Hutton, pp. 25–43. Ancient Israel and Its Literature 9. Atlanta: Society of Biblical Literature, 2011.

Albertz, Rainer, and Rüdiger Schmitt. *Family and Household Religion in Ancient Israel and the Levant*. Winona Lake, Ind.: Eisenbrauns, 2012.

Bergant, Dianne. "An Anthropological Approach to Biblical Interpretation: The Passover Supper in Exodus 12:1–20 as a Case Study." *Semeia* 67 (1994): 43–62.

Bird, Phyllis. "The Place of Women in the Israelite Cultus." In *Ancient Israelite Religion: Essays in Honor of Frank Moore Cross*, edited by Patrick D. Miller Jr., Paul D. Hanson, and S. Dean McBride, pp. 397–419. Philadelphia: Fortress, 1987.

Bynum, Caroline Walker. "Women's Stories, Women's Symbols: A Critique of Victor Turner's Theory of Liminality." In *Fragmentation and Redemption: Essays on Gender and the Human Body in Medieval Religion*, pp. 27–51. New York: Zone, 1991.

Cooper, Alan M., and Bernard R. Goldstein. "At the Entrance to the Tent: More Cultic Resonances in Biblical Narrative." *Journal of Biblical Literature* 116 (1997): 201–215.

Meyers, Carol. "Hannah and Her Sacrifice: Reclaiming Female Agency." In *A Feminist Companion to Samuel and Kings*, edited by Athalya Brenner, pp. 93–104. The Feminist Companion to the Bible 5. Sheffield, U.K.: Sheffield Academic Press, 1994.

Meyers, Carol. "Material Remains and Social Relations: Women's Culture in Agrarian Households of the Iron Age." In *Symbiosis, Symbolism, and the Power of the Past: Canaan, Ancient Israel, and Their Neighbors from the Late Bronze Age through Roman Palaestina*, edited by William G. Dever and Seymour Gitin, pp. 425–44. Winona Lake, Ind.: Eisenbrauns, 2003.

Meyers, Carol. *Households and Holiness: The Religious Culture of Israelite Women*. Minneapolis: Fortress, 2005.

Turner, Victor W. *The Ritual Process: Structure and Anti-Structure*. Chicago: Aldine, 1969.

van der Toorn, Karel. *Family Religion in Babylonia, Syria and Israel: Continuity and Change in the Forms of*

Religious Life. Studies in the History and Culture of the Ancient Near East 7. Leiden, The Netherlands: Brill, 1996.

van der Toorn, Karel. "Nine Months among the Peasants in the Palestinian Highlands: An Anthropological Perspective on Local Religion in the Early Iron Age." In *Symbiosis, Symbolism, and the Power of the Past: Canaan, Ancient Israel, and Their Neighbors from the Late Bronze Age through Roman Palaestina*, edited by William G. Dever and Seymour Gitin, pp. 393–410. Winona Lake, Ind.: Eisenbrauns, 2003.

Wegner, Judith Romney. "'*Coming Before the Lord*': The Exclusion of Women from the Public Domain of the Israelite Priestly Cult." In *The Book of Leviticus: Composition and Reception*, edited by Rolf Rendtorff and Robert A. Kugler, pp. 451–465. Supplements to Vetus Testamentum 93. Leiden, The Netherlands: Brill, 2003.

Susan Ackerman

Greek World

As a result of the conquests of Alexander the Great (b. 356 B.C.E., d. 323 B.C.E.) and his export of Greek culture and language into Asia, Persia, and Egypt, the "Greek world" in antiquity is far larger than Greece itself and was culturally dominant out of all proportion to the power of the Greek cities through most of its duration because of the "Hellenization" of the conquered regions. The "Greek world" includes the eastern provinces of the Roman Empire after their conquests in the region (Asia [the area of modern Turkey] after 190 B.C.E.; Greece after 146 B.C.E.; Syria after 64 B.C.E.; Egypt after 30 B.C.E.), which the Romans governed in Greek, since the Eastern Provinces were already Greek speaking. This variety of cultures brings with it a wide variety of religious and gender expectations. Gender is a concept that goes beyond the physical features determining an individual's sex, and ways of enacting gender go far beyond aspects of sexuality or gendered activities. For the Greek world in antiquity, our sources are fragmentary and rhetorical, and they often tell more about the construction of gender than of the lives of actual men and women.

Polytheism. The religions of the Greek and Greco-Roman worlds form a dynamic polytheistic network that was constantly evolving, with new gods or goddesses being discovered or transformed while old cults were never put aside, resulting in a very rich religious environment. The word "cult" has negative modern connotations, but it remains the best term to describe discrete ritual establishments. A cult is a particular liturgy devoted to the divinity that inheres in a particular object or place, and it may be practiced by one member or by thousands. For the most part, any participant in a particular cult may also participate in any number of others.

The gods, heroes, nymphs, or *daimones* of Greek and Greco-Roman polytheism may be thought of most usefully as amalgamating categories rather than as specific persons. "Artemis," for example, is a category name that included many different functions, such as guarding the young, protecting women in childbirth, sending plague or easy deaths, and protecting cities when Artemis is a tutelary goddess. But this category also includes different individuals, so to speak. Artemis of Ephesus, the great city protectress, is not the same individual as Artemis of Brauron, for whom little girls danced in saffron robes; Zeus Olympios, king of the gods, is not the same as the friendly serpent Zeus Meilichios, who protects the home. And yet at the same time, those two members of the Artemis family *are* the same, and those two members of the Zeus family are the same. As the centuries of cultural blending and transformation progressed, such overlapping identifications were nearly universal, if not universally popular. For example, the God of Israel, as the supreme god, could be identified with Zeus and therefore in some circles represented as a snake. Given the fluidity of these categories, it can sometimes seem as though there is one god and one goddess, each with a thousand names—and this perspective is sometimes expressed in philosophical writing. But for the general run of worshippers, the multiplicity was just that—many discrete powers with intricate relationships and long histories in which each worshipper plays several different parts, each with its own meaning and result.

Rhetoric, mythology, religion, and gender. Although the term "religion" in the modern sense is not meaningful for the ancient period, both individuals and governing bodies had strong ideas about tradition, blasphemy, atheism, and magic, and they used those concepts as part of rhetorical strategies against the introduction of frightening cults. This rhetoric often linked qualities of foreignness, danger, and unseemliness with qualities of femininity (or the absence of masculinity), sometimes by associating the cults with actual women or with a threat to women. The accuracy of these portrayals for the reconstruction of women's religious behavior has been increasingly called into question. The classic examples here concern the introduction of the worship of Dionysus into Greece, represented in Euripides's *Bacchae* (first performed 405 B.C.E.) and the Roman senatorial decree against the introduction of Bacchic rites into the city of Rome (186 B.C.E.).

The genders of gods as expressed through their adventures in mythology in epic and tragedy must be parsed very carefully for information about actual religious practice and gender expectations. Divine characters in tragedy and epic express how completely mortal life differs from the world of the divine, while mortal characters, almost by definition, appear because their actions are exceptional and beyond the norm. For the most part, the gender of a deity does not correspond to the gender of the majority of the worshippers or the priests or priestesses who officiated that cult (a notable exception to this is the cult of the god Mithras, which was male-only). Human female characters in epic, tragedy, and historiography often appear as the triggers for male action resulting from the woman's rape, murder, and/or suicide. Such myths often became linked to existing local worship around springs, groves, or ancient tombs; local cults of deceased virgins were extremely common throughout the Greek world (a biblical example of this is the tale of Jephthah's daughter, Judg 11:29–40).

Even if the representations in epic, tragedy, and historiography do not accurately portray the real lives of women or gendered roles in religious practice, they demonstrate the models of behavior that were internalized by both women and men. Masculinity was the model for good and righteous behavior toward which both men and women strove:

to be calm, measured, just; to live in accordance with the laws of gods and men; to benefit the family; and to be generous toward the city. In daily life, models of such behavior were encountered in the form of the inscriptions on bases of honorific statues that civic officials permitted to be erected in public spaces, and also on tombstones and monuments. These honorific statues praise both men and women for their public benefactions, but also for courage and for raising families. Both women and men could act as city benefactors, and were honored for their good works. Epigraphy generally expresses the ways individuals conformed to the highest traditional values, rather than celebrating their unique individuality.

Civic and Communal Worship. Collective forms of worship emphasize the relationship between a deity and a group, whether this group is a city, region, town, village, or tribe or family. Through shared consumption of the gifts of sacrifice, humans and gods were joined with strong bonds that were continually reinforced. Many older accounts of Greek and Greco-Roman religion tend to represent the public dimension of civic religion as empty spectacle devoid of meaning, which left desperate people hungry for "cults" (in the negative meaning of the term). In part, this trope dates back to Greek and Hellenistic philosophical writing and to the rhetoric of early Christian apologists and historians in late antiquity. It is not an accurate reflection of the enthusiasm, joy, and pride that accompanied civic forms of worship on the popular level, throughout many centuries.

Power and prestige in local society were greatly enhanced by public benefaction, which gave honor to the giver through the permission for the gift. People eagerly sought the right to give things to the city; to foot the bill for processions, sacrifices, or games; construct wings for temples; give statues or other gifts; and hold public office, either in government or in priesthoods. Roles played by individuals in the great celebrations of civic worship were affirmations of their status with respect both to men and the god in question. Greek cities and towns each had one or more tutelary or protective deities that represented the identity of that people and acted protectively on their behalf. Since civic religion celebrates and protects the stability and strength of the whole group, there were roles not only for both genders but for the married and the unmarried and sometimes for children, youths, and adults, and so forth, making these celebrations both gendered and inclusive, though not in the modern sense.

Temples and images. The focal points of worship were the objects and images of the gods and the holy buildings or precincts in which they were kept. The holy or the sacred had power that was both beneficial and dangerous, requiring careful ritual preparation for participants and for the images themselves.

The central image or object of a worship form is generally called the "cult statue." This term can include many different kinds of objects, from the black stone that represented Cybele in the sanctuary of Pessinus (later Rome), to the ancient wooden effigy of Athena Polias, to the carefully made image of Artemis of Ephesus, which was created for the goddess and in which she approvingly took up residence (despite the claim in Acts 19:35, Ephesians did not think their central cult statue had fallen from heaven). Sometimes cult statues are regarded as supernatural in origin, but this is not the norm. However they originated, they were regarded both as hosts of divinity and as divine objects in themselves, drawing power and blessing to the city.

A sacred precinct, or *temenos*, was marked by a boundary, within which special laws might apply; it was holy ground, a sacred space where events take on special significance, and therefore were carefully controlled. Plutarch relates that the priestess of Athena Polias once declined to give some delivery men a drink of water, in fear that this would become part of the ritual for the festival and thus need to be repeated every year (*Moralia* 534C). Most holy *temenoi* forbade birth and death within their precincts, and also barred people who were in a state of ritual impurity (most states of ritual impurity were easily rectified, but others such as homicide, were difficult). Pollution within the sanctuary angered the gods and could cause rejection of the offerings, placing everyone at risk. Collective observances emphasize the stability of the city or town and reassure all parties that things are as they always have been,

and for this reason innovation was usually not encouraged.

Procession and festival. Major civic observances usually involved a procession of the cult statue through the city, with stops along the way to mark events of significance to the history of the city or to honor the temples of other deities that had also been involved in the city's history or well-being. In the Athenian Panathenaic festival, the cult statue of Athena Polias was taken through the city at the head of a massive procession in which many ranks of the population appeared in specified roles: the young men of the city, young girls carrying implements for sacrifice, people transporting the new robe woven by girls of aristocratic families as a gift for the statue, priests and priestesses, citizens, residents, and others reinforced their social and gender roles as they led more than a hundred head of cattle for the sacrifice, which would be shared by the participants in a stratified, orderly way that reinforced tribe, class, and gender roles.

Festivals and sacrifices governed the local calendars and reflected the rhythm of the agricultural year; sowing, harvest, opening the new wine, and so forth, though local iterations of these are widely various. Most cities had some kind of civic festival for the married women of the city. In Athens this was dedicated to the goddess Demeter Thesmophorios and was a three-day observance that included both fasting and celebration and linked a celebration of justice, law, and civilization with the fertility of the earth and of human beings. The worship of Adonis was also women-only, and very widely observed. The festival marks the turn of summer through a ritual of mourning, linked to the planting of miniature gardens doomed to wilt in the hot sun. This practice is or eventually was linked to the mythological boy Adonis, who was beloved by various goddesses but died tragically young; after he was granted temporary apotheosis by Zeus his travels to and from the underworld mark the seasons of agricultural fertility.

Personal and Voluntary Observance. It is likely that most religious observances took place privately, in the home and in association with small domestic altars, hearths, and doorways, activities that leave little trace in archaeology, epigraphy, or literature. Families or individuals could create unique combinations of deities for personal worship, though usually the home altar would include the gods of the city, tribe, and family unit of the individual, as well as whatever other deities the person had encountered or heard of and wanted to include. The home setting is where rituals for birth and marriage would be performed, often with the fathers of the families acting in the role of priest. When a child was born, the family would announce its gender by what they hung on their doors. A girl was marked by a woolen fillet, an object associated both with weaving and with the worship of the gods, and a boy was marked by an olive wreath, linked perhaps to athletic victories. Rites of passage for both boys and girls were celebrated at different ages and in different ways throughout the Greek world. They often involved the initiation of the children into cohort groups apart from family, and could include athletic training and competition (for both genders) and often, for girls, beauty contests. Funerary ritual also took place mostly in the home, before the body was removed to the place of burial, usually outside of the city limits.

As noted earlier, most priesthoods were voluntary public benefactions taken up for a limited period of time, ordinarily a year. The Greek world had no class of professional clergy except for the individuals who actually performed sacrifices (since the sacrifice and butchering of large animals required both expertise and specialized equipment). The voluntary priests, however, were responsible for making sure that all of the steps and associated rituals for the sacrifices were properly carried out; in shrines too small for large animal sacrifice they would simply perform the vegetable or grain sacrifices themselves.

Voluntary worship could be as small and private as a leaf or flower placed on the domestic altar or a fleeting visit to the local shrine of a favorite or functionally relevant god or goddess, or as loud and splashy a spectacle as any of the civic processions. The terms "voluntary" or "optional" are difficult in that they may seem to imply that participation in city-wide or pan-Hellenic festivals was forced, or that the optional worship was not serious (or conversely that

it was the only meaningful form), two propositions that form part of modern or promonotheistic rhetoric that claims that ancient polytheism was meaningless ritual. In actuality, no one was capable of taking up all of the available religious options; those who tried could be ridiculed. People filled their lives with worship forms they chose depending on family and background, personal attraction, and also the needs of the day. For example, someone hoping for a child or worried about a child might direct more energy to Artemis or another of the child-protecting deities for that specific period of time, while someone with an illness might seek out Asklepios or one of many other healing gods, including the great goddess Isis. To later turn one's religious attention to other powers relating to other needs or ideas does not trivialize or invalidate the earlier devotion.

Initiations and "mysteries." Mystery religions or cults are voluntary observances that were joined through a ritual of initiation, the content of which was intended to remain a secret known only to other members of the group. Through keeping faith with the group and with the secret and performing the expected rituals or responsibilities, the initiate was promised an afterlife of happiness, feasting, or even a form of apotheosis. The fact of initiation itself was not a secret, nor was membership an exclusive religious option that closed off other choices. Initiates still participated in civic and family worship, and might be initiated into more than one mystery. Initiation also created the option of a new social network for the rest of one's life on earth, an important factor as people lived increasingly far from the land and from their homelands. There were many different mystery cults, some quite localized, others nearly worldwide.

The mysteries were centered on savior figures—divine beings who would offer the hope of a blessed afterlife to the human beings who sought it from them through initiation. Each mystery was centered upon a myth of origin that explained the painful events in the life of the divinity that caused her or him to establish the mystery and give this gift to humanity. Some saviors offered help directly in this world (Asklepios, Isis), but one did not need to be an initiate to partake in that benefit. Initiation, however, opened the gate to a blessed eternal life that only the initiates could reach. But within this club, salvation was extended to every member on an equal footing, and it is often argued that people were attracted into the mysteries in order to transcend social or gender constraints. Social mobility through post-initiation associations is increasingly important though the centuries of Roman rule, though their eternal life was not dependent on this, only upon initiation and maintaining its integrity.

The Eleusinian Mysteries of Demeter originated in remote antiquity and ended only with the forced closing of all non-Christian shrines by Theodosius in 392. Demeter and Persephone form the only "mother-daughter" pair of the much more common "goddess–consort" pattern of myths and religions of loss, rebirth and immortality that is linked to festivals of the seasons and of agriculture in many locations throughout the Mediterranean. In the Eleusinian myth, Demeter rests at the town of Eleusis while searching for her kidnapped daughter, is treated well there, and founds the mysteries as a gift for the region and for all of humanity. In historical times, the initiation took place over several days. Anyone was welcome to be initiated as long as they could speak Greek, had not killed anyone without purification, and had the cash needed to travel to Eleusis and purchase accommodation, robes, and sacrificial animals. The main initiation was led by a priest, but there was an important role for his priestess-wife, and other roles for officiants of both genders. Though various scholarly hypotheses exist about the content of the actual ritual, initiates were serious enough about protecting it that we do not in fact have definite knowledge of the full initiation. We do know that the ritual included things to be seen, things to be done, and things to be heard. As the "Greek world" expanded, so did the range of people who became initiates, though the requirement to speak or understand Greek remained in force.

Dionysus was the center of both public and civic worship in many cities, and a very widespread mystery initiation. The events in *The Bacchae* do not literally represent either the public or mystery acts of worship for Dionysus in historical times, but the joy and praise expressed in its choruses are good reflections of the emotional effect of the worship. The Dionysiac mysteries were able to take place anywhere that an authorized group was able to be formed and were not confined to any one particular language. The initiation promised eternal feasting and joy; images on inscribed tombstones sometimes represent the deceased reclining at a banquet while the living mourn. Both women and men could become initiates, but there is significant evidence that women often had leadership roles and were responsible for organizing new "branches" of the worship.

As the centuries progressed and Egypt became a more central part of the "Greek world," Isis became one of the most widely invoked and worshipped goddesses. Isis was a universal power, who functioned both as a this-world savior and as the center of an initiatory worship. In its Egyptian setting, the worship of Isis is both political and personal; she is the personification of rule; the wife of Osiris, the eternal ruler; and the mother of Horus, the visible ruler. All the members of this divine family are transposed into new keys in the Greco-Roman period, and are to be found in combination with almost every other deity, but of the three Isis was the most widely included in new religious settings. In its Greco-Roman articulation, the cult of Isis was served by both priestesses and priests, though it is the shaven-headed, linen-wearing priest that is more often represented in art and literature.

[*See also* Deity, *subentry* Greek World; Political Leadership, *subentry* Greek World; Popular Religion and Magic, *subentry* Greek World; Religious Leaders, *subentry* Greek World; *and* Social Interaction, *subentry* Greek and Roman Worlds.]

BIBLIOGRAPHY

Ahearne-Kroll, Stephen P., Paul A. Holloway, and James A. Kelhoffer, eds. *Women and Gender in Ancient Religions: Interdisciplinary Approaches.* Tübingen, Germany: Mohr Siebeck, 2010.

Beard, Mary, and John North. *Pagan Priests: Religion and Power in the Ancient World.* 2 vols. Ithaca, N.Y.: Cornell University Press, 1990.

Blundell, Sue, and Margaret Williamson, eds. *The Sacred and the Feminine in Ancient Greece.* New York: Routledge, 1998.

Dillon, Matthew. *Girls and Women in Classical Greek Religion.* New York: Routledge, 2001.

Dowden, Ken. *Death and the Maiden: Girls' Initiation Rites in Greek Mythology.* New York: Routledge, 1989.

Heyob, Sharon Kelly. *The Cult of Isis among Women in the Graeco-Roman World.* Leiden, The Netherlands: Brill, 1975.

Kraemer, Ross Shepard. *Her Share of the Blessings: Women's Religions among Pagans, Jews, and Christians in the Greco-Roman World.* New York: Oxford University Press, 1992.

Kraemer, Ross Shepard. *Unreliable Witnesses: Religion, Gender, and History in the Greco-Roman Mediterranean.* New York: Oxford University Press, 2011.

Kraemer, Ross Shepard, ed. *Women's Religions in the Greco-Roman World: A Sourcebook.* New York: Oxford University Press, 2004; revised edition of *Maenads, Martyrs, Matrons, Monastics: A Sourcebook on Women's Religions in the Greco-Roman World* (Philadelphia: Fortress, 1988).

Lefkowitz, Mary, and Maureen Fant. *Women's Life in Greece and Rome: A Source Book in Translation.* 3d ed. Baltimore: Johns Hopkins University Press, 2005.

Lidonnici, Lynn. "Women's Religions and Religious Lives in the Greco-Roman City." In *Women and Christian Origins*, edited by Ross Shepard Kraemer and Mary Rose D'Angelo, pp. 80–104. New York: Oxford University Press, 1999.

Penner, Todd, and Caroline Vander Stichele, eds. *Mapping Gender in Ancient Religious Discourses.* Biblical Interpretation 84. Leiden, The Netherlands: Brill, 2007.

Sissa, Giulia. *Greek Virginity.* Translated by Arthur Goldhammer. Cambridge, Mass.: Harvard University Press, 1990.

Winkler, John J. *The Constraints of Desire: The Anthropology of Sex and Gender in Ancient Greece.* New York: Routledge, 1990.

Lynn Lidonnici

Roman World

Women's religious participation in the Roman world varied according to social, sexual, and marital status. Different ritual roles were designed for married women (matrons, *matronae*), women in their first marriage (*univirae*), and girls (*virgines*). In Rome, in Italian towns, and in the Latin West, public festivals had been conferred to women to ensure the well-being of the civic community. These women's festivals varied from one town to another. Meeting annually to perform public rituals was an occasion for upper-class matrons to offer public sacrifices (on behalf of the civic community as a whole) and to participate in banquets. Sacrificing, banqueting, and dancing were the chief among women's ritual acts. Beside the public display of women's religious competences, these festivals provided the opportunity to form and strengthen the female networks.

Usually, public priests and priestesses as well as magistrates presided over public sacrifices. The hierarchically minor role of killing the animal was a task of sacrificial slaughterers (*popa, victimarius*; Schultz, 2006, p. 135). Men and women of all social strata participated in banquets of semipublic cultic associations and in the private cults. In these cults the most important symbolic role of a sacrificiant, who represented the community in whose name the sacrifice was accomplished, was confined mostly to men. Nevertheless, in women-only public festivals, women assumed the powerful role in the sacrifice; sometimes they presided over animal sacrifice, often over bloodless offerings.

Public Festivals of Women in the City of Rome. Wives, mothers, and daughters of senators and equestrians represented the women of the civic community in several public women's festivals.

Matronalia. Matrons gathered at the temple of the birth-goddess Juno Lucina on 1 March (the anniversary of the dedication of the temple). Ovid writes that the Roman matrons dedicated the temple to Juno on the Esquiline Hill themselves, stressing a capacity of matrons as a group to dedicate a public temple. At the Matronalia, with crowns of flowers on their heads, matrons prayed to the goddess to ensure an easy delivery and offered flowers to her (Ovid, *Fast.* 3.243–258). This festival was of importance for the *res publica* as a whole (Scheid, 1992, p. 386), since the reproduction of the community was one of its central concerns. During the Matronalia husbands prayed for their wives' health and conservation of the marriage. The husbands gave gifts to their wives and the matrons served a meal for their slaves at home, similarly as their husbands did at the festival of Saturnalia (Macrobius, *Sat.* 1.12.7). The cult of Juno celebrated the social role of the matrons as mothers and wives in Rome and, under different epithets, in many towns of Latium.

Matralia. The goddess Mater Matuta was a protector of children and a goddess of early light (*aurora*, Lucretius, *On the Nature of Things* 5.656–657). Mater Matuta was honored with the Matralia on 11 June (CIL I², 320), the anniversary of the foundation of the temple that the goddess inhabited together with the goddess Fortuna. According to the legend, Servius Tullius, the legendary sixth king of Rome, founded both temples in the Forum Boarium, which were devoted to women's concerns. Well-born married women gathered at the temple of Mater Matuta. They brought a female slave into the temple and then beat her and drove her out of the temple (Plutarch, *Mor.* 267D). The mothers offered honey-cakes (*liba*) to Mater Matuta (Ovid, *Fast.* 6.475–476); the aunts took their sisters' children in their arms and prayed to the goddess for their well-being (Ovid, *Fast.* 6.559–562; Plutarch, *Cam.* 5.2). This ritual celebrated the social roles of the maternal aunt (*matertera*: mother's sister) and mother. The maternal aunt was regarded as a second mother and helped with the education and further life of her sister's children. The statue of the Mater Matuta could have been approached only by matrons in their first marriage (*univirae*), like in women's cults of Fortuna Muliebris and Pudicitia, which stresses the importance of chastity of the worshippers. The private offerings to the goddess Mater Matuta reveal that not only female but also male worshipers dedicated objects to the goddess (for the cult of Mater Matuta at Satricum in southern Latium, see Schultz, 2006, p. 69); the cult concerned matters of both sexes. The goddess was worshiped all over central Italy.

Fortuna Muliebris. The Festival of Fortuna Muliebris ("Fortune of women"), the goddess of chance, prosperity, and favorable outcome, was celebrated on 6 July. Roman matrons went to her temple at the fourth milestone of the Via Latina to offer (probably) a blood sacrifice (Valerius Maximus 1.8.4; Dionysius of Halicarnassus, *Roman Antiquities* 8.55.3–4). Married women thanked her for helping with births and for surviving childbirth (Takács, 2008, p. 50). Fortuna was worshiped in many towns in central Italy under different epithets; in Praeneste as Fortuna Primigenia, here her statue represented a maternal deity nursing Jupiter and Juno as children (Cicero, *On Divination* 2.85–87).

Festival of Venus Verticordia and Fortuna Virilis. Women of Rome worshiped Venus under the epithet Verticordia ("turning the hearts [to chastity]") on 1 April. Women of all ranks wearing myrtle wreaths washed the statue of the goddess and bathed. At the same time, they burned incense to supplicate to the goddess Fortuna Virilis ("the Fortune of men") and drank the beverage of new brides, which was supposed to sedate them before the marriage was consummated. After the bath, the women decorated the statue of Venus with jewels and flowers (Ovid, *Fast.* 4.133–164). The women supplicated Venus Verticordia and Fortuna Virilis to protect the brides and to facilitate sexual union (Scheid, 1992, pp. 387–388; Staples, 1998, pp. 99–113). Venus's cult was common in Latium and in many towns of Italy, as well as on Sicily.

Secret ritual for Bona Dea. The nocturnal celebration of Bona Dea ("Good Goddess") in early December was celebrated in the house of a high magistrate (a consul or a praetor). The owner of the house and all men were excluded from the ritual (Cicero, *On the Response of the Haruspices* 37). Select upper-class matrons danced to the music and banqueted, and the banquet room was decorated with vines and various flowers. The Vestals sacrificed a sow to the goddess; the scarce sources do not tell anything about the role of the *damiatrix*, the priestess of Bona Dea (Paulus-Festus 60L). The women drank wine at the banquet, but referred to it as "milk" and to the vessel as "honey pot" (Macrobius, *Sat.* 1.12.25; Plutarch, *Mor.* 268D–E). These inversions and travesties have led some modern scholars to the interpretation that this festival was a reversal rite. Nevertheless, the deviations from the model of men's rituals in the public religion reveal a symbolic construction of gendered performance of public rituals. Women's festivals of Bona Dea and Ceres ritualized the dichotomy between men and women (Staples, 1998, p. 51; Šterbenc Erker, 2013, pp. 57–59). Male writers refer to the Bona Dea festival as secret, which reveals a male point of view. Sexual segregation was not an issue in a private cult of the goddess. Private offerings found in the deposit at the temple of Bona Dea on the Aventine were offered by both men and women, as the inscriptions show which mention the dedicants' gratefulness to the goddess for having healed their diseases (eyesight restored: *CIL* VI, 68; Brouwer, 1989, p. 44). Bona Dea was worshipped in central Italy, Aquilea, and Tarentum.

Secret ritual: *Sacrum anniversarium Cereris.*

At the end of June, the beginning of the harvest, Roman matrons celebrated the so-called Greek festival of the goddess Ceres (Paul-Festus 86L: *Graeca sacra*). Ancient authors mention the Greek origins of the festival and that priestesses from Greek towns of Italy came to Rome to perform the public rituals of Ceres (Cicero, *On Defense of Cornelius Balbus* 55; Valerius Maximus 1.1.1). As a preparation for the main ritual, the matrons abstained from sexual intercourse and fasted (i.e., they restrained from eating bread) to achieve symbolic purity; this purification rite was called *castus Cereris* (Festus 422L). The authors who refer to the omission of the women's festival of Ceres in 216 B.C.E. (after the Roman defeat at Cannae) mention only two details of ritual performance, a procession and a sacrifice (Livy 34.6.15), probably of a sow (Šterbenc Erker, 2013, pp. 105–106). Matrons did not use wine for libations at Ceres's altar (Dionysius of Halicarnassus, *Roman Antiquities* 1.33.1; contra Flemming, 2007, p. 99). In Ovid's depiction of a Ceres festival on Cyprus we find the features of the Roman ritual wherein matrons offer to the goddess crowns made of the first wheat (Ovid, *Metam.* 10.431–436). The matrons celebrated Ceres, the goddess of grain who invented agriculture, civilization, and forms of living in a civic community (especially marriage). In 191 B.C.E. a single holiday of "Ceres's fasting" (*ieiunium Cereris*), a purification ritual, was introduced to expiate the prodigies that had occurred in Italian towns (Livy 36.37.2–4).

Supplicationes.

In the republic, from the third century B.C.E. onward, women were involved in expiations of prodigies (portents recognized by the Senate as signs of divine anger that had to be appeased). *Supplicationes* were a form of expiation or thanksgiving ritual, performed all over the Roman world. The Senate ordered Roman citizens, men and women, to go to temples and supplicate the gods to help the city of Rome in moments of crisis. Men, matrons, and children wore wreaths (a sign that the ritual was performed in a "Greek" way, *Graeco ritu*), held olive branches in their hands, and visited the temples to pour wine on the altar and burn incense (Scheid, 1992, pp. 394–397; Schultz, 2006, pp. 28–33; 36–38; Šterbenc Erker, 2009, pp. 152–155). In some rituals of *supplicationes*, well-born matrons and girls took a prominent part along with the public priests. Livy mentions complex *supplicationes* of the year 207 B.C.E. According to Livy, a chorus of twenty-seven girls joined the public priests and matrons in a procession; the girls danced on the Forum and sang a hymn to appease the goddess Juno Regina. The public priests *decemviri* sacrificed two cows to Juno Regina and offered her two statues. Matrons who had collected money from their dowries offered a golden bowl to the goddess (Livy 27.37.7–15). By accomplishing supplications, an important ritual role of appeasing the gods and thus preserving the *res publica* was conferred to the matrons (Livy 10.23.1–2; 22.10.8; 27.51.8; 25.12.14; Schultz, 2006, p. 33). Literary representations of the republican *supplicationes* vary according to the degree of danger that menaced Rome. Livy (26.9.7–8) depicted very dramatically the *supplicationes* of the Roman matrons in 211 B.C.E. when Hannibal with his Punic troops drew close to Rome. One of the issues raised in Livy's history was that the Senate and public authorities could oblige men and women to take part in public rituals.

Under the empire, matrons performed *supplicationes* during Secular Games. During the festival in 17 B.C.E. the expected number of matrons (110) did not appear; therefore, the Senate obliged the matrons of Rome to finish their mourning in order to participate in the festival (CIL VI 32324, 112). During the Secular Games the matrons danced and held banquets with seats set out for the goddesses (*sellisternium*: a sacrificial banquet for the statues of goddesses put on the seats, *sellae*). The matrons banqueted together with the statues of the goddesses Juno, Diana, and Juno Regina and prayed to them to preserve and increase the *res publica* (Beard et al., 1998, pp. 201–206, 297). Apart from the matrons' involvement in Secular Games in 17 B.C.E. and 47, 88, and 204 C.E., matronal *supplicationes* declined under the empire.

Rituals of Public Female Priesthoods in Rome. The public rituals of several different female priesthoods are described in the extant literature.

Vestals. Vestal virgins tended the flame on the hearth of the temple of the goddess Vesta. Romans believed that their safety was in danger when the fire went out. The Vestals kindled a new fire on 1 March to symbolize the start of the New Year according to the religious calendar. The Vestals prepared the salted ground spelt (*mola salsa*), which was strewn on the victims at public sacrifices. The Vestals presided over animal sacrifices on several festivals (Fordicicia, Parilia, Consualia, and the December festival of Bona Dea), performed libations (a funeral libation, *parentatio*, at the tomb of the Roman heroine Tarpeia), and cleansed the temple of Vesta during the Vestalia on 9 June (Ovid, *Fast.* 6.249–304, 395–398). Augustus added to their traditional rituals annual sacrifices at the altar of Fortuna Redux on 12 October as well as at the Ara Pacis. Vestals were in charge of the cult of the deified Livia, Augustus's widow (Cassius Dio 60.5.2; Beard et al., 1998, p. 194). The six Vestal priestesses had a special sexual status; their dress and activities referred to the world of girls, brides, matrons, and men as well (Beard et al., 1998, pp. 51–54).

The flaminica Dialis and the regina sacrorum. The public priestesses *flaminica Dialis* (Jupiter's priestess) and *regina sacrorum* ("queen of rituals") sacrificed animals on festive days that marked the flow of time. On the Kalends (the first day of each month) the *regina sacrorum* offered a sow or a female lamb to Juno, the divine protector of the Kalends, in an an-cient king's palace on the forum, whereas her husband (*flamen Dialis*) sacrificed together with another priest (*pontifex minor*) to Juno (Macrobius, *Sat.* 1.15.19). The *flaminica Dialis* sacrificed a ram to the god Jupiter on every market day (*nundinae*) in the king's palace (Macrobius, *Sat.* 1.16.30), whereas her husband, the *flamen Dialis*, offered a sheep to Jupiter in his temple on the Capitoline hill on the Ides of every month. Both priesthoods were meant for a married couple, thus celebrating the ideal according to which a husband and a wife honored the gods by their respective rituals in a "complete" way (Scheid, 1992, pp. 384, 401–403).

Rituals of the empress. Livia followed the religious policy of her husband Augustus and had women's temples restored and dedicated them herself, the Bona Dea temple on the Aventine hill and the Fortuna Muliebris temple on the Via Latina. Livia was probably prominent in all matronal festivals, although the sources are silent on this point. After the death of Augustus in 14 C.E., she was bestowed the honorific title Julia Augusta and became a priestess of the deified Augustus (Ovid, *Letters from Pontus*, 4.9.107; Hemelrijk, 2007, p. 319). In this religious office she had a right to be accompanied by one lictor. Julia Augusta with her son, Emperor Tiberius, had the temple of her late husband built, as well as the temple of Concordia, and she organized games in his honor (Cassius Dio 56.46.1–3). Through these ritual roles Julia Augusta forged a model for priesthoods of the following widowed empresses (for Agrippina Minor as *flaminica Divi Claudii*; Tacitus, *Ann.* 13.2.15).

Semipublic and Private Rituals. In addition to the public rituals discussed above, other rituals are described as taking place in private and semipublic settings.

Cultic associations. Female worshippers and priestesses of Isis are known (CIL VI 512.2246; IX 1153; for a parody see Juvenal, *Sat.* 6.522–541); as initiates they had honorific titles, but the most important offices were reserved for men. In the Bacchus cult the female initiates held titles referring to their ritual competences (maenads, carriers of a basket or a box); their rituals differ from literary descriptions of wild maenads (Šterbenc Erker, 2013, pp. 217–230). Imperial freedwomen were priestesses in the "Phrygian" cult of Cybele/Mater Magna (Dionysius of Halicarnassus, *Roman Antiquities* 2.19.4–5; CIL VI 2260). Women were also among the adherents of Christianity. Upper-class writers portrayed women as liable to superstition and marginal religious activities (Scheid, 1992, pp. 397–400). Texts denigrating the cults of Isis, Bacchus, Cybele, and Christianity represent the worshippers of these cults stereotypically as female or effeminate (Beard et al., 1998, p. 297). Livy (39.15.9) refers to the stereotypes of bad influence of women in his account on the Bacchanalia scandal of 186 B.C.E. Such denigrations were commonplace in discourses on upper-class morals and norms of Roman gentlemen and cannot be taken at face value.

Family rituals. The maternal aunt supplicated for the newborn on *dies lustricus*, when the baby was named. At weddings, the bride offered wine and incense to the gods (Pseudo-Seneca, *Octavia* 699–702; Hersch, 2010, pp. 120–121); she anointed the doorposts of her new home and decorated them with *vitae* (woolen fillets, signs of chastity; Hersch, 2010, p. 178). Literary sources give a glimpse into idealized gendered tasks in Roman funeral rituals. Women were in closer contact with the dead, whereas men were kept at a distance from corpses. Women prepared the corpse for display; they washed, anointed, dressed, and covered it with a funeral cloth. It was a ritual obligation of women to mourn the dead by lamentation, singing dirges (*neniae*), and wailing out of sorrow (*ululare*). Women expressed their grief by scratching their cheeks and beating the chest in an "excessive" way, whereas men had to restrain their grief, mourning with dignity and self-discipline according to upper-class norms of behavior (Cicero, *Tusculan Disputations* 3.62; Seneca, *To Marcia* 7.3; *To Polybius* 6.2; Šterbenc Erker, 2011, pp. 45, 51). Men carried the bier, lit the funeral pyre, held funeral eulogies at the grave, presided over sacrifice in their family's name, and purified the participants of the funeral as well as the house of the dead (Šterbenc Erker, 2011, pp. 50–54). Women prolonged the mourning for a deceased father, husband, or child up to ten months after the funeral (Ovid, *Fast.* 1, 35–36; Seneca, *Letters to Lucilius* 63.13; Plutarch, *Num.* 12.3). During the festival Caristia (22 February), the family members (men and women) gathered at the family's tomb and offered incense to the dead of a clan ("Good gods," *di Manes*) and food to the Lares and banqueted (Ovid, *Fast.* 2.617–638).

Private religious specialists. A *Piatrix* specialized in expiations. Similar ritual techniques were probably used by female religious specialists called *saga* and *simpulatrix* (Paulus Festus 455L; Schultz, 2006, p. 133; Flemming, 2007, p. 106). Ovid describes a ritual of a female religious specialist at the festival of the dead (Feralia; 21 February). He mentions an old woman who performed rituals to Dea Tacita ("Silent goddess") to silence the evil tongues (*Fast.* 2.571–582). According to Ovid, the woman who poured a wine libation on a fish that she roasted on a grill usually drank the wine herself and got drunk. Takács (2008, p. 40) interprets this ritual as love magic. Ovid's humorous description offers a glimpse into private activities in which women helped with everyday concerns by performing rituals.

Italian Towns and the Latin West. In Italian towns and in the Latin West wives or daughters of the local elites held various public priesthoods and were involved in public sacrifices. On several funerary monuments priestesses in the towns of Italy were depicted in a moment of sacrifice of a sow at the altar (priestess of Ceres in Corfinium: *AE* 1900, 85: Helvia Pothine; *CIL* 10, 5073: Munnia, priestess of Ceres from Athina; *CIL* 9, 3089: Helvia Quarta a priestess of Ceres and Venus; Hemelrijk, 2009, p. 261). Inscriptions honor the public priestesses of Venus (Mamia from Pompei: *CIL* X 998; *CIL* X 816), Ceres (Pompei: *CIL* X 1074b; *CIL* X 812, *CIL* 1036), or public priestesses of Venus and Ceres (Surrentum: *CIL* X 688). In Greek colonies on Sicily, in Southern Italy, and in North Africa, the cult of Demeter/Ceres was important because the grain goddess Demeter was supposed to enable Greek colonizers to appropriate foreign land.

Provinces, colonies, and municipalities borrowed some rituals and priesthoods from the capital. As a mixture with previous local traditions, religious influences from the political center were taken up by the local elite to display their Romanization or loyalty to the emperor and his family. Julia Augusta, as priestess of her deified husband, provided a model for imperial *flaminicae* outside Rome (Hemelrijk, 2007). The *flaminicae* were public priestesses known from inscriptions from Gaul and North Africa (Hemelrijk, 2007; Witschel in Hemelrijk and Woolf, 2013). Especially in Romanized Africa, the flaminate was kept in the family—daughters inherited the religious office from their father or mother. As *flaminicae* of the imperial household, an empress, or the municipality or province, they executed their religious duties on behalf of the civic community (*CIL* II 114; *CIL* II 32; Takács, 2008, pp. 112–118). Priestesses of the imperial cult celebrated the birthdays of the members of the imperial family by performing offerings of wine and incense (*supplicatio*) and organizing games and banquets (*CIL* II, 1678). Thus, they probably presided over animal sacrifice (Rives in Hemelrijk and Woolf, 2013, p. 142) and distribution of food or money (Hemelrijk, 2007, p. 328). Women celebrated *taurobolium* ("bull-killing") in the cult of Cybele/Magna Mater for the health of the imperial household (*CIL* XIII, 1753–1754) in Gaul and Germania (*AE* 2004, 1015–1016; Spickermann in Woolf and Hemelrijk, 2013). Beside an active role in the imperial cult, imperial priestesses promoted themselves and their families in celebrations connected to other cults by dedicating sacral buildings, offering banquets to the elite and people, and financing games (Hemelrijk, 2007, p. 329, fn. 47). *Matres* (mothers) and *matronae* (married women) were honored in Gaul, Germania, and Northern Italy. The worship of *matres* and *matronae* celebrated the social role of mothers and wives and underlined the Romanization of the local elite. Women offered public sacrifices and dedicated temples, statues, and altars, but much less frequently than men (Hemelrijk, 2009, p. 267; on civic munificence of benefactresses: Hemelrijk in Woolf and Hemelrijk, 2013).

Historiography of Roman Religion. A revival of interest in women in Roman religion in the 1990s was permeated by the alleged marginality of their religious roles. Scheid (1992) argues in favor of women's unfitness for animal sacrifice, the central religious ritual. Referring to texts emphasizing that a man is an ideal sacrificiant, he understands the evidence for women's sacrificial competences as "exceptions to the rule." This structuralist interpretation was refuted by Schultz (2006, pp. 93, 131–137), who shows that Roman matrons participated in public sacrifices and offered private sacrifices in their own right (see Hemelrijk, 2009). Flemming (2007) draws attention to those texts, stressing the frequency of women's rituals in Rome. Takács (2008) overemphasizes the fertility aspect of women's rituals, but her historical contextualization of women's cults is useful. Such a range of interpretations of the evidence shows the contested nature of examining ancient gendered religious practices in the present.

[*See also* Popular Religion and Magic, *subentry* Roman World; Religious Leaders, *subentries on* New Testament *and* Roman World; Religious Participation, *subentries on* Early Church, Greek World, *and* New Testament; *and* Social Interaction, *subentry* Greek and Roman Worlds.]

BIBLIOGRAPHY

Beard, Mary, John North, and Simon Price. *Religions of Rome.* Vol. 1: *A History.* Cambridge, U.K.: Cambridge University Press, 1998.

Brouwer, Hendrik H. *Bona Dea: The Sources and a Description of the Cult.* Leiden, The Netherlands: Brill, 1989.

Flemming, Rebecca. "Festus and the Role of Women in Roman Religion." In *Verrius, Festus and Paul: Lexicography, Scholarship, and Society*, edited by Fay Glinister and Clare Woods, pp. 87–108. London: University of London, School of Advanced Study, Institute of Classical Studies, 2007.

Hemelrijk, Emily A. "Local Empresses: Priestesses of the Imperial Cult in the Cities of the Latin West." *Phoenix* 61, no. 3–4 (2007): 318–349.

Hemelrijk, Emily A. "Women and Sacrifice in the Roman Empire." In *Ritual Dynamics and Religious Change in the Roman Empire: Proceedings of the Eighth Workshop of the International Network Impact of Empire (Heidelberg, July 5–7, 2007)*, edited by Olivier Hekster, Sebastian Schmidt-Hofner, and Christian Witschel, pp. 253–267. Leiden, The Netherlands: Brill, 2009.

Hemelrijk, Emily, and Greg Woolf, eds. *Women and the Roman City in the Latin West*. Leiden, The Netherlands, and Boston: Brill, 2013.

Hersch, Karen K. *The Roman Wedding: Ritual and Meaning in Antiquity*. Cambridge, U.K.: Cambridge University Press, 2010.

Scheid, John. "The Religious Roles of Roman Women." In *A History of Women in the West*. Vol. 1: *From Ancient Goddesses to Christian Saints*, edited by Pauline Schmitt Pantel and translated by Arthur Goldhammer, pp. 377–408. Cambridge, Mass.: Belknap, 1992.

Schultz, Celia E. *Women's Religious Activity in the Roman Republic*. Chapel Hill: University of North Carolina Press, 2006.

Staples, Ariadne. *From Good Goddess to Vestal Virgins. Sex and Category in Roman Religion*. London and New York: Routledge, 1998.

Šterbenc Erker, Darja. "Women's Tears in Ancient Roman Ritual." In *Tears in the Graeco-Roman World*, edited by Thorsten Fögen, pp. 135–160. New York: de Gruyter, 2009.

Šterbenc Erker, Darja. "Gender and Roman Funeral Ritual." In *Memory and Mourning in Ancient Rome: Studies on Roman Death*, edited by Valerie M. Hope and Janet Huskinson, pp. 40–60. Oxford and Oakville, Conn.: Oxbow, 2011.

Šterbenc Erker, Darja. *Religiöse Rollen römischer Matronen in "griechischen" Ritualen*. Stuttgart: Steiner, 2013.

Takács, Sarolta A. *Vestal Virgins, Sibyls, and Matrons. Women in Roman Religion*. Austin: University of Texas Press, 2008.

Darja Šterbenc Erker

New Testament

The New Testament mentions a variety of rituals practiced and debated by early believers, including baptism, collective worship practices, circumcision, and Eucharist. Gender played a role, even if inexplicitly, in each of these acts. Yet religious participation also stretched beyond these rituals and into the everyday life of early believers. Rather than focusing on specific rituals alone, therefore, this entry will ex-amine religious participation in general among New Testament communities and how such participation was impacted by gender, especially in light of Greco-Roman androcentricism or, perhaps more precisely, phallologocentricism (that is, "interpreting the world according to a *logos* [logic] that is defined by the masculine"; Økland, 2004, p. 16).

Gospels and Acts. There are few, if any, passages in the Gospels and Acts that explicitly outline how gender impacts religious participation. The narratives, however, repeatedly present the effects of gender with variously gendered characters and their interactions with the divine and each other in public, private, and mixed settings.

The Gospels. The Gospels offer a number of portrayals of Jesus and his relationship with God as "Father" and "Spirit" as well as his teaching of the disciples, crowds, and conflicts with religious and political elites. Many (particularly feminist) interpreters have identified liberative examples of female participation in the Gospels, leading them to posit an egalitarian thread in the early Jesus movement (Schüssler Fiorenza, 1995). More recent trends, however, highlight the patriarchal perspective of these stories, suggesting they are perhaps not as inclusive as the first feminist studies hoped (Braun, 2003). For example, scholars have noted the Gospels' defenses of Jesus's masculinity as a means to claim legitimacy for both him and the movement he initiated (Moore and Anderson, 2003; Conway, 2008). The Gospels repeatedly highlight Jesus's ability to gain honor in winning challenge-riposte confrontations with religious and political leaders (Mark 12:1–37; Matt 27:11–14; Luke 6:1–11), his agency in choosing his death (Mark 8:31–33; Matt 26:36–56; John 10:1–18), his unique ability to rule God's kingdom and articulate the divine will (Luke 4:42–44; John 5:19–47), and his vindicating resurrection (Mark 16; Matthew 28; Luke 24; John 20—21). Further, those whom Jesus selects to follow him appear to be men of freeborn status (Mark 1:16–20; Luke 5:1–11; John 1:35–51), and whenever the "Twelve" are named, they are all men (Mark 3:13–19; Matt 10:1–4; Luke 6:12–15). Even though women also approached and followed Jesus (cf. Luke 8:1–3), they are not included in the first callings or listings of disciples. According to Conway, presenting Jesus as an ideal man (and one of miraculous origins in Matthew, Luke, and John) is part of their argument that Jesus is the most perfect reflection of the Divine (cf. John 1:14–16). Such an argument operates on the phallologocentric assumption that a man was necessarily closer to divinity or more godlike (Aristotle, *Generation of Animals* 732a7; Philo, *Questions and Answers on Exodus* 1.7–8; Conway, 2008, pp. 35–66; cf. Økland, 2004, p. 16 on *phallus*). Using this assumption helped Gospel writers communicate their Christologies, but it also communicates a sustained male-emphasis in early Jesus-believing communities.

Schüssler Fiorenza, however, rightly cautions against interpreting masculine language in the New Testament as excluding women from the Jesus movement (1995). Instead, Schüssler Fiorenza argues that the presence of women (and others) should be assumed in these instances, unless the text explicitly indicates otherwise. Osiek and MacDonald agree, noting that the presence of women, children, and slaves can be assumed in the background as they fulfill roles, such as meal preparation and serving, that are not of interest to ancient authors or audiences (2006, pp. 6–12, 246–248). Even when left unnamed, women and children participate in Jesus's ministry as members of the "crowds" (*oxloi, laos*) who surround him, although it is the "men" (*andres*) who dominate the scenes (cf. Mark 6:30–44; Matt 14:13–21; Luke 9:10–17; John 6:1–14). The Gospels also identify women and children as exemplars of faithfulness. The unnamed Syrophoenician woman wins healing for her daughter in a challenge-riposte with Jesus (Mark 7:25–30); Mary and Martha of Bethany serve, confess, and learn from Jesus (Luke 10:38–42; John 11:1—12:3); the Samaritan woman carries on an extended discourse with Jesus (John 4:1–30); children are blessed by Jesus (Mark 10:13–16; Matt 19:13–15; Luke 18:15–17); and Jesus imitates a slave by washing his disciples' feet in place of the "last supper" ritual in John 13. Scholars are torn, however, as to whether these nonmasculine presentations subvert or reinforce gender ideals. These narratives paved the way for at least some early believers to acknowledge the authority

of women disciples, such as Mary Magdalene and Martha (cf. Ernst, 2009). Yet it is also true that many of these nonmasculine images often reinforce socially expected roles. Even the shocking presentation of a foot-washing Jesus is a model to demonstrate the disciples' rightful position below him (13:12–16); just as Jesus obeys the will of the Father, so too should his disciples obey him. For this reason, some interpreters suggest that instead of undermining gender norms, these stories reinforce them as a means to highlight Jesus's masculinity and that of the followers who imitate him (Braun, 2003; Moore and Anderson, 2003).

Acts. Acts likewise communicates a degree of ambiguity toward gender and religious participation. As a volume offered to the elite man, Theophilus, his viewpoint, whether historical or otherwise, is the focus of the narrator (Acts 1:1–3; cf. Luke 1:1–4; D'Angelo, 2003, p. 285). Acts, however, also offers glimpses of inclusive gender participation among early believers such as that depicted in Peter's quotation of Joel 3:1–5, which includes all genders in the outpouring of God's spirit as a marker of the eschaton (2:17–21). Seemingly supporting such optimism is the later appearance of Priscilla instructing Apollos (18:26), Philip's four prophesying daughters (21:8), the woman "disciple" Tabitha (*mathētria*, 9:36–42), and women householders who host church gatherings in Jerusalem (12:12–17), Philippi (16:11–15, 40), and the "leading" women in Thessalonica (17:4). Nevertheless, interpreters have noted the consistent depiction of masculine control in Acts (D'Angelo, 2003; MacDonald, 2011). Only men are mentioned as possible candidates for Judas's replacement and deacons (1:15–26; 6:1–6); sustained attention in the narrative remains on men and their conflicts with other men; and few women speak in the narrative. For example, although described as having prophetic ability, Philip's daughters remain silent as the male prophet, Agabus, arrives to warn Paul (21:10–14). Stressing this masculine perspective further is the central debate over circumcision, a decidedly male marker, for full participation in the religious community (11:1–18; 15:1–29). For D'Angelo, (Luke-)Acts offers "praise for good women, albeit in proper relation to men"

(2003, p. 293). MacDonald notes, however, that this perspective does not diminish the fact that Acts offers "surprising insight into the lives of the marginalized," thereby acknowledging their participation in the Jesus movement (2011, p. 186).

Epistolary Literature. As documents often addressing practical concerns alongside pressing theological questions, New Testament letters contain a number of passages that directly address the current topic. These letters outline codes of conduct for worship communities and reflect idealized portraits of gendered participation as well as acknowledgements that expose more integrated realities.

The undisputed Pauline letters. The undisputed Pauline letters contain varied voices from Paul, shaped to address the particular circumstances of each community receiving his missives. Interpreters seeking a consistent theological perspective, including his thoughts on gender, have looked in vain (Økland 2004, pp. 20–30). Without space to analyze every significant passage, several key passages stand out for examination.

Galatians 3:28. Galatians 3:28 has often been used as proof of Paul's egalitarianism, alongside other passages that mention women leaders, householders, and patrons in the early believing communities (cf. Rom 16:1–16; Phil 4:2–3; 1 Cor 1:11; Col 4:15; Epp, 2005; Osiek and MacDonald, 2006, pp. 194–219). Paul's admonition to the Galatians that there is "no longer Jew or Greek, there is no longer slave or free, there is no longer male and female; for all of you are one in Christ Jesus" has been interpreted as an invitation to see past boundary distinctions, including gender, in Pauline communities. Such an interpretation is not without some merit, as this verse is located in the midst of a discussion concerning baptism, a rite in which all believers participate (3:21—4:7). Yet the larger context of Galatians, and indeed the language used to describe transformation into the family of God, remains rooted in masculinity. The conflict in Galatians centers on circumcision, as it does elsewhere in the nondisputed Pauline letters (and Acts), thus focusing the discussion on the inclusion of Jewish and non-Jewish *men* into the believing communities. Even if women are assumed to be included

in these conversations as ones attached to men, their participation is not of central concern. Instead, they are encouraged alongside the Galatian men with images of "sonship" so that, as legitimate males, they can "inherit" the blessing promised to the "sons of Abraham" rather than being "expelled" as the "son of the slave woman" (3:29; 4:30–31). However, the focus of Paul's instruction is that these male gentiles do not need circumcision to be "real men" and participate fully in the covenant. Instead, these men demonstrate their true "manhood" by remaining uncircumcised and thus free from the "guardianship" (*paidagōgos*) of the law rightly reserved for ruling over children and emasculated men (3:23—4:7; 5:12).

First Corinthians. First Corinthians is part of a larger set of letters called the Corinthian correspondence in which Paul calls the community toward unity and order (1:10–30). As a part of his instruction, he admonishes them concerning their sexual conduct and the roles of men and women in worship settings (11:2–16; 14:31–40). In chapters 5 through 7, Paul exposes the dangers of uncontrolled sexual exploits of (free) men in the community, which he terms *porneia* (5:1; 6:18; 7:2). To combat this unmanly lack of control, Paul makes concessions for men and women who should marry rather than "burn with passion," although he would prefer that all "remain unmarried" as he is (7:7–9). Most scholars understand 1 Corinthians 7 to point toward a growing ascetic movement among the Corinthians. That Paul agrees with the idea that sexual abstinence somehow enhances one's nearness to God is evidenced in his own preference for being unmarried and his call for couples to refrain from sex at times so they might pray (7:5). Such an idea was not uncommon in his milieu; ideal men exercised "self-control" (*sōphrosunē*) in all areas of their life, and some women could attain a more masculine status by showing similar control over their own passions as virgins or widows (Kraemer, 1988, pp. 211–214).

First Corinthians 11—14 centers on issues of community order during worship. Meeting in a household, early believers were at a crossroads of public and private space (Osiek and MacDonald, 2006, p. 4). Moreover, with gender-liminal women (perhaps inspired by the imminent eschatology of Paul described in 7:25–31) in the community, opportunities were rife for normal masculine protocols to be discarded or reshaped. Paul combats such tendencies by reinforcing patriarchal control through an interpretation of Genesis 2 in 1 Corinthians 11:2–16 that presents "man" as the "image of God" and "woman" as "the glory of man" (11:7). In order to avoid dishonoring their respective "heads" (*kephalē*; the "man" for women, and "Christ" for men), women are to pray and prophesy with heads covered and men with heads uncovered (11:4–5). Paul's instructions assume women's participation in worship, but within more culturally acceptable limits—Roman custom demanded the veiling of matrons in public (though see the discussion of "new women" in Winter, 2003). First Corinthians 14:34–36 follows with an explicit prohibition against women speaking in the assembly. Many scholars argue that verses 33b–36 are a non-Pauline interpolation reflecting later practice, because these verses potentially contradict the assumption of women speaking in 11:2–3 and disrupt the thought flow in 14:31–40 (Epp, 2005, pp. 15–20). Others suggest that 14:34–36 is a Corinthian assertion that Paul combats with incredulity, resting on the translation of *ē* in verse 36 as "What?!" rather than "Or." This interpretation prevents any contradiction, while demonstrating the adherence to social gender assumptions (perhaps especially Stoic thought) in the Corinthian community. In contrast, Økland argues that the prohibition was against women speaking *logos* (i.e., philosophical speech), which was gendered as masculine speech in the ancient world. Thus, while women can offer prayers or prophesy, they cannot, by their very nature, offer *logos* (pp. 206–208).

Philemon. In his letter to the slave-owner Philemon, Paul acts as patron and mediator for Onesimus, Philemon's slave whom Paul is returning to this former master (vv. 12–14). Establishing himself as both the patron of Onesimus *and* Philemon, Paul directs Philemon to accept Onesimus back "no longer as a slave but more than a slave, as a beloved brother" (vv. 15–17). While there is some debate over whether Paul is here insinuating that Philemon should free Onesimus, it is clear that Paul pictures some change in status for *this* slave even if he does not for slaves in general (Glancy, 2006, pp. 91–92). Glancy notes the availability of Roman slaves to their masters; as persons without honor, slaves were to submit to their masters' desires in all things, representing the most penetrable class and, therefore, the least manly (2006, pp. 12–29). If Onesimus is Philemon's "brother," however, then his body is not available for Philemon to punish in the same way. This transformation of status, while needing final sanction from Philemon, is rooted in Onesimus's conversion, indicating that gender transformation through religious participation is possible. Like the overlooked women in Galatia, Onesimus too can become a "man," a son, and heir to the promises of Christ. Being a believer makes one more manly—though how this identity manifested itself in day-to-day life is left unresolved (cf. Conway, 2008).

The disputed Pauline and Catholic letters. As later communications for believing communities, the disputed Pauline and Catholic letters demonstrate different sets of concerns. Yet consistent among them is a desire to assimilate with the larger Roman culture as much as possible without sacrificing loyalty to Christ. Of particular interest are the household codes found in three of these letters and the gender guidelines found in the Pastorals (1–2 Tim; Tit).

The Household Codes. The Household Codes are recorded in Ephesians 5:21–6:9, Colossians 3:18–4:1, and 1 Peter 2:18–3:7. Ephesians and Colossians are widely acknowledged as being literarily dependent, most scholars agreeing that Ephesians borrows and develops themes from Colossians. The letters encourage their audiences to persevere in the confidence of the reality of their salvation (Eph 2:1–22; Col 3:1–3). As a result of their redemption, they should live orderly and unified lives in the midst of the "gentile" debauchery that surrounds them. In light of cultural assumptions, it is not surprising that the authors use images of ideal masculinity to reinforce his notion of "order," instructing the audiences to control themselves and their households as "mature men" (Eph 3:16; Col 1:28). Playing their part in this order, wives, children, and slaves are told to submit. The household codes of Colossians and Ephesians are thus natural developments of the author's encouragement for spiritual order, made manifest in the daily lives of his readers. The agenda of 1 Peter is similar, though influenced as a response to external polemic and slander against his audience (4:12–19). Prefacing his discussion of slaves, wives, and children with an admonition for all to "honor the emperor" demonstrates the author's desire for the believers to mimic culture and thus appear nonthreatening to the imperial order (2:13–17). There is some debate as to whether these household codes were anything more than ideology reflecting well-known tropes from philosophical works (Osiek and MacDonald, 2006, pp. 132–136). That the authors felt compelled to create them, however, indicates at least some agreement with their presuppositions and some lack of congruence with these ideals in the communities.

The Pastorals. The Pastorals offer perhaps the most rigid adherence to expected gender roles in the New Testament. Drawing clear lines concerning gender in these communities, these letters adhere to early second-century ideals. Consistent throughout these letters is a desire for believers to give opponents no fodder for attacks against "the name and teaching of God" (1 Tim 6:1–2; cf. 5:14–15). Glancy and Conway suggest such language was in response to gendered attacks leveled against the believers, who perhaps had women and slaves in leadership positions (Conway, 2008, pp. 86–87; cf. Origen, *Against Celsus*). Replying to these threats, then, "Paul" reinforces gender norms and turns the gendered attacks against his opponents, charging them and their teachings with effeminacy. Such attacks are also reflected in his argument that "silly women" were more susceptible to vice and, therefore, to his opponents' teachings (1 Tim 5:11; 2 Tim 3:5–7). The opponents, like the weak-willed women they target, have fallen to false teachings and disorder. In contrast, the Pastorals identify the male householder in control of his house as the one fit for office, explicitly linking their households to the larger "household of God" (1 Tim 3:5, 12–15). Women, however, are to be silent in public

settings, adorned with "good works," and focused on childbearing and rearing (1 Tim 2:8–15; Titus 2:3–5); slaves are likewise to submit to their masters (1 Tim 6:1–2; Titus 2:9–10). The focus on marriage and children for women differs from Paul's preference for sexual asceticism in 1 Corinthians. Yet, even here, women are not entirely restricted from teaching roles; older women and "real" widows are to instruct younger women, and the influence of grandmothers and mothers over male relatives is demonstrated by "Paul's" praise of Lois and Eunice, Timothy's grandmother and mother, in 2 Timothy 1:5. Complicating the ideological construction further is the author's listing of Prisca's name before that of her husband, Aquila, in 2 Timothy 4:19, suggesting that even the rigid household instructions of the Pastorals had to make room for the realities and traditions of early communities (Osiek and MacDonald, 2006, pp. 29–35).

Revelation. Revelation makes use of stereotypical gendered language to communicate its message of God's victory through Christ. It is clear that men as well as women are included in the early movement, even if their roles were open to dispute. The woman characterized as "Jezebel" demonstrates the presence of female prophetesses and teachers. So persuasive is her message that she is threatened with (sexual?) violence and the destruction of her followers, stylized as her "children" (2:20–23; cf. Conway, 2008, p. 162). Other gendered images are used to symbolize participants in and opponents to God's agenda. As Collins notes, sexual purity is emphasized on the battlefield and temple, leading to the presentation of 144,000 male virgins who have "not defiled themselves with women" in 14:1–5 and the pure bride of Christ dressed for her wedding in 19:6–8 representing the new city of Jerusalem and her inhabitants (1984, p. 130). In contrast, the Whore of Babylon, the personification of Rome, drinks in her own destruction. Like "Jezebel" her sins are sexualized and her punishments are made to fit (17:1–19:2). The gendered language of Revelation has inspired a number of interpretations, ranging from those insisting the book resists imperial agendas (including gender ideals) to those who argue it offers a hypermasculinized (even beast-like) presentation of God and Jesus (Conway, 2008, pp. 159–72). The exaltation of sexual purity played into growing ascetic movements among early Jesus believers. The portrait of the 144,000 male virgins in particular resonates with metaphors of masculinity and gender transformation to describe salvation in other New Testament and nonbiblical works (see above; *Gospel of Thomas; Martyrdom of Perpetua and Felicitas; Acts of Paul and Thecla*).

Summary. In order to be persuasive for their audiences, New Testament authors were attendant to the sociocultural situations of their time, and thus they take advantage of common constructions of reality in order to communicate their messages in ways congruent with their contexts. These contexts assumed and reinforced the superiority of "real men," where manliness was determined by one's control of self and others (passions, body, and household). Yet the extent to which the New Testament endorses this ideology in the presentation of religious participation is a matter of some dispute. The New Testament reflects the participation of variously gendered believers, even though phallologocentric views dominate. The access of men is necessarily granted, but the presence of women, children, and slaves is also evident. They participate in baptism, attend worship, serve meals, prophesy, and pray; some act as householders, patrons, and leaders. Indeed, the influence of nonmasculine figures results in the management of their presence within larger cultural norms of propriety to protect the movement from slander. Further, New Testament authors use language of ideal masculinity to describe salvation and "perfection," resorting to well-established cultural images to explain the transformation accomplished through one's allegiance to Christ. Women, children, and slaves are welcome to participate in this transformation as well by becoming "sons," "heirs," and part of the "perfect man" (Luke 20:31–34; Gal 3:23–29; Eph 2:16). But in so doing, they are admonished to submit to "normal" masculine presuppositions that emphasize (self-) control and eventually come to reinforce general Greco-Roman expectations (Eph 5:21–6:9; 1 Tim 2:8–15).

[*See also* Imagery, Gendered, *subentry* Apocalyptic Literature; Jesus; Legal Status, *subentry* New Testament; Paul; Race, Class, and Ethnicity, *subentry* New Testament; *and* Religious Leaders, *subentries on* New Testament *and* Roman World.]

BIBLIOGRAPHY

Braun, Willi. "Fugitives from Femininity: Greco-Roman Gender Ideology and the Limits of Early Christian Women's Emancipation." In *Fabrics of Discourse: Essays in Honor of Vernon K. Robbins*, edited by David B. Growler, Gregory L. Bloomquist, and Duane F. Watson, pp. 317–332. Harrisburg, Pa.: Trinity International, 2003.

Collins, Adela Yarbro. *Crisis and Catharsis: The Power of the Apocalypse*. Louisville, Ky.: Westminster John Knox, 1984.

Conway, Colleen M. *Behold the Man: Jesus and Greco-Roman Masculinity*. Oxford: Oxford University Press, 2008.

D'Angelo, Mary Rose. " 'Knowing How to Preside over His Own Household': Imperial Masculinity and Christian Asceticism in the Pastorals, *Hermas*, and Luke–Acts." In *New Testament Masculinities*, edited by Stephen D. Moore and Janice Capel Anderson, pp. 265–296. Semeia Studies 45. Atlanta: Society of Biblical Literature, 2003.

Epp, Eldon Jay. *Junia: The First Woman Apostle*. Minneapolis: Fortress, 2005.

Ernst, Allie M. *Martha from the Margins: The Authority of Martha in Early Christian Tradition*. Supplements to Vigiliae Christianae 98. Leiden, The Netherlands: Brill, 2009.

Glancy, Jennifer A. *Slavery in Early Christianity*. Minneapolis: Fortress, 2006.

Kraemer, Ross Shepard, ed. *Maenads, Martyrs, Matrons, Monastics: A Sourcebook on Women's Religions in the Greco-Roman World*. Philadelphia: Fortress, 1988.

Kraemer, Ross Shepard, and Mary Rose D'Angelo, eds. *Women and Christian Origins*. New York: Oxford University Press, 1999.

MacDonald, Margaret Y. "The Women Householders of Acts in Light of Recent Research on Families." In *Finding a Woman's Place: Essays in Honor of Carolyn Osiek*, edited by David L. Balch and Jason T. Lamoreaux, pp. 171–188. Princeton Theological Monograph Series 150. Eugene, Ore.: Pickwick, 2011.

Moore, Stephen D., and Janice Capel Anderson, eds. *New Testament Masculinities*. Semeia Studies 45. Atlanta Society of Biblical Literature, 2003.

Økland, Jorunn. *Women in Their Place: Paul and the Corinthian Discourse of Gender and Sanctuary Space.* Journal for the Study of the New Testament Supplement Series 269. London: T&T Clark, 2004.

Osiek, Carolyn, and Margaret Y. MacDonald. *A Woman's Place: House Churches in Earliest Christianity.* Minneapolis: Fortress, 2006.

Schüssler Fiorenza, Elisabeth. *In Memory of Her: A Feminist Theological Reconstruction of Christian Origins.* 2d ed. London: SCM, 1995.

Winter, Bruce W. *Roman Wives, Roman Widows: The Appearance of New Women and the Pauline Communities.* Grand Rapids, Mich.: Eerdmans, 2003.

Alicia D. Myers

Early Judaism

Despite the unquestionable appeal of the concept of a singular Judaism, there are only ever persons and groups whose particular practices (including their ideas) have come to be seen both as related and as distinctive in various ways from those of other persons and groups. I share the reservations of Satlow (2006) about the existence, in antiquity or elsewhere, of a reified distinct and relatively coherent "religion" known as "Judaism," easily separable from the larger cultural practices of its adherents. Further, I generally share the position of Mason (2007) and others that the easy, automatic, and blanket designation of ancient persons as "Jews" foregrounds (intentionally or not) the so-called religious identification of such persons and obscures the ancient ethnic connotation of the term and its comparability with the terms (and categories) "Greek," "Roman," "Egyptian," "Germanic," "Celtic," "Nabatean," and "Persian." Thus I find it effective, if sometimes awkward, to regularly render the relevant Greek and Latin term by the English "Judean(s)," as the context seems to justify. This is true whether or not the idea of a distinct and monoform system, "Judaism," is a Christian ideological artifice constructed no earlier than the second century C.E. Since I have great reservations about when, where, and by whom a Judean biblical canon might have been effected, I have simply confined myself to evidence from the late fourth century B.C.E. (the beginning of Hellenistic culture in the far eastern Mediterranean) through the early seventh century C.E. (the beginnings of Islam).

Introduction. This entry poses two major questions: To what extent were Judean and/or Jewish religious practices differentiated by the sex of the performer, and to what extent did these practices themselves encode, authorize, and enforce gender difference and hierarchy? To ask these questions, though, regularly requires us to assess what we know about women's participation in such practices, since the vast majority of the evidence we have pertains to men's practices.

Ancient evidence for devotion to the God of Israel comes from diverse literary sources in Hebrew, Aramaic, Greek, and Latin, together with material remains including devotional and burial inscriptions, cult buildings, and artifacts ranging from synagogue furnishings to amulets to gold funerary glasses. Written largely by, and for the interests of, elite men, the literary sources only occasionally furnish accounts of women actors.

Rabbinic sources, compiled from the third century C.E. onward, pose their own special challenges. They authorize a set of practices mostly restricted to the rabbis and those who accepted their authority and represent women as minor and occasional actors of interest primarily to the degree that they enable or inhibit rabbinic performance of piety. It is unclear that they are reliable accounts even of women within rabbinic groups, let alone women outside rabbinic orbits. As four decades of scholarship has illuminated, literary accounts, including those of the rabbis, are never disinterested reports of women's practices. On the contrary, many are so deeply implicated in ancient representations and contestations of gender that their utility for historical reconstruction is severely compromised (Kraemer, 2011).

The evidence furnished by material remains might seem somewhat less compromised, but much of these data, particularly that of burial, donative, and honorary inscriptions, is still quite difficult to assess. Yet, to borrow from a rather vexed contemporary political analogy, we do our scholarship with the sources we have, not the sources we wish we had.

Women in the Temple Cult. As with other temples in the ancient Mediterranean, the primary (although by no means only) activity of the temple to the God of Israel in Jerusalem was the offering of gifts to the deity through the mediation of a professional priesthood. These offerings were typically either agricultural produce (oil, wine, grain, or grain products) or animal sacrifices (from small birds to large cattle). Some offerings took the form of thank-you presents, while others are envisioned as the consequences of unintentional violations of the deity's laws. In some instances, the size, scope, and perfection of the sacrifice correlates closely with the social status of the offerer. Gender permeates both these practices and their underlying cultural logic (according to which the most prestigious and expensive gifts are those of the most elite men, including kings and high priests).

The ancient Israelite priesthood was a hereditary male institution, passed from father to son. That women were not priests themselves goes without saying, although levitical regulations proscribe marriages between priests and certain women, and only marriage with a permitted wife could produce acceptable priestly sons. The female relatives of priests were permitted to eat certain special offerings given to priests. A tiny number of epitaphs refer to women as (female) priests, which are generally taken as references to female members of priestly families. One inscription dated to 27 B.C.E. (*JIGRE* 84) has given scholars a little more pause, since it is associated with a temple to the Judean deity in Leontopolis, Egypt, established by a disenfranchised high priest, Onias IV.

Biblical prescriptions do not specifically bar women from entrance in the Jerusalem Temple precincts, although the observation of biblical purity regulations, especially those regarding menstruation and childbirth, would have rendered women unable to enter the Temple complex on a regular basis. Both biblical codes and the first-century C.E. Judean author Flavius Josephus describe the Temple as divided into areas progressively restricted by both gender and ethnicity. According to *Against Apion* 2.102–104, the Herodian second Temple had an outermost courtyard open to all persons (except ritually impure women), a second courtyard limited to Judeans (again, excepting impure women), a third courtyard restricted to ritually pure Judean males, and a final courtyard restricted to ritually pure priests wearing appropriate clothing. In a more detailed account elsewhere (*War* 5.128–200), Josephus claims that there was a space set aside for Judean women's worship (*threskeia*), with its own gates, and that women were not allowed to use any other temple gates. This special space seems to be a Herodian innovation, related, perhaps, to the extensive public presence and activity of numerous Herodian women. How these divisions affected women's cult performance is uncertain.

Biblical prescriptions require women as well as men to bring certain sacrifices to the Temple. Although evidence for actual practice is scarce, women who lived within easy traveling distance could have brought such gifts on at least some occasions: others might, perhaps, have sent them. Some sacrificed animals were to be wholly burnt on the altar for the deity alone, but other sacrifices devote the inedible parts to the deity and prescribe the distribution of the edible meat to humans. The consumption of meat in ancient west Asia and the ancient Mediterranean itself appears to have been a major index of status, with elite males consuming the most and best meats with the most frequency, while free women, children, and enslaved persons consumed far less, including portions of sacrificial meat.

Some scholars (e.g., Jay, 1992) have suggested that the killing, cooking, and eating of sacrificial meat played a major role in the establishment and maintenance of gender hierarchy, but this remains disputed (Ullucci, 2012). At the same time, two things are noteworthy. Whatever role blood sacrifice played in these projects, ancient Israelite priestly geneaologies construct male lineages that effectively erase the actual reproductive roles of women. Priestly concerns for holiness and purity focus intently on the defiling nature of the blood women shed both in menstruation and childbirth, regularly rendering women unable to participate fully in Temple practice, if not also other cult devotions.

The destruction of the Temple in 70 C.E. largely ended both animal sacrifices and festival pilgrimage. Celebration of the festivals subsequently takes on other forms (which they may already have had for Judeans living far from Jerusalem, or within insufficient resources to do so). Rabbinic regulations envision that women will eat a portion of the Passover offering and focus on when ritually impure women may subsequently eat (*m. Pesaḥ.* 8.5), but accounts of rabbinic Seders generally seem to envision the Passover seder as restricted to males (Rosenblum, 2010). Some rabbinic regulations explicitly forbid women (as well as slaves and minors) to assemble on their own to celebrate the Passover (*m. Pesaḥ.* 8:7; *t. Pesaḥ.* 8:6). The rabbis expect that women as well as men will eat the obligatory unleavened bread during Pesach and fast (generally) on Yom Kippur, but they explicitly exempt women (as well as slaves, minors, and some other persons) from the requirement to "dwell" in a special booth (*sukkah*) during the festival of Sukkoth (*m. Sukkah* 2:8; *b. Sukkah 28a–b*). These differences are instances of a larger rabbinic framework in which men and women alike were all required to obey the so-called negative commandments, but women were exempted from certain positive commandments, particularly those which were time-bound, of which the requirement for all Israelite males, specifically, to appear before the Lord three times a year (Sukkoth, Pesach, and Shavuoth: Exod 23:14–17; Deut 16:16) is only one salient instance.

We know little about observance of these festivals in the later Roman period, apart from an occasional reference, such as John Chrysostom's invective about the wives of his Christian parishioners, whom he sought to prevent from attending synagogue services for the fall holiday cycle that included Rosh Hashanah, Yom Kippur, and Sukkoth (*Against Judaizing Christians* 2.3.4–6). Presumably, Jewish women were also attending. Pseudo-Philo's *Biblical Antiquities* explains the origins of a women's festival commemorating Jephthah's daughter, apart from which there is virtually no evidence for Jewish festivals observed only by women.

Women in Non-/Post-Temple Cult Observances. Despite the prominence of the Temple in the con-

ceptual framework of Judean religious practice, much devotion consisted of non-Temple activities, both before the destruction of the Temple and always for those persons who did not live in easy proximity to Jerusalem. Practices such as synagogue attendance, reading and study of Torah, prayer, sabbath, and festival observances and dietary regulations are perceptible in literary sources, while incantations and the making and fulfilling of vows are more visible in the inscriptions, amulets, and other cult objects. Life-cycle ceremonies such as birth and puberty rites, marriages, and funerals are surprisingly poorly documented. Tobit is a notable, but not necessarily reliable, account of such ceremonies. Rabbinic sources devote considerable attention to the legal processes of marriage and divorce but offer little instruction on how to celebrate a wedding or conduct a funeral. Many sources presume that such practices are common knowledge and offer only occasional indications of what women's practices might have entailed.

Synagogues (as buildings) appear to have played central roles in the lives of Judean communities long before the destruction of the second Temple, including in Jerusalem and Judea. Having no biblical authorization, synagogues also have no gender regulations licensed by biblical prescriptions. In Acts 12, 13, and 17, elite women are regularly among those in Greece and Asia Minor persuaded by Paul's preaching of Jesus, often apparently in synagogues; sometimes these women are cast as interested gentiles rather than Judeans, however, and one cannot assume the historical veracity of these accounts. The Gospels may also envision women as attending synagogue services in the Galilee on the sabbath, but this is at best ambiguous. As noted above, John Chrysostom excoriates Christian women for celebrating Jewish festivals, apparently including attending synagogues.

The most compelling evidence for women's involvement in ancient synagogues comes from inscriptions across the ancient Mediterranean, largely fourth century C.E. or later. Women donors are recognized in mosaic inscriptions at Apamea, Syria, and in various cities in Asia Minor. At Hamman Lif,

North Africa, the entire floor mosaic appears to have been the gift of a single woman, probably named Juliana. Burial inscriptions from Asia Minor, Crete, Malta, and elsewhere commemorate women with titles of synagogue office, including the title *archisynagogos* (head of the synagogue). Why such attestation is absent for the land of Israel is simply unclear; it may be a function of the random nature of archaeological finds or may reflect changes or differences in practices among various communities. Despite sporadic debate about whether these titles designate women with communal responsibilities, or only "honor" them for their familial and economic standing in their communities, most scholars now take these few epitaphs as evidence for the former, rather than the latter.

Comparative evidence from non-Judean associations and civic offices suggests that women were most likely to hold cult and civic offices when doing so was constructed as an appropriate gendered activity, for instance, as a kind of familial duty or piety, with women caring for larger groups as they would care for their smaller family units. Conversely, they were least likely to do so when holding office was seen as an exercise of inherently masculine authority over rightful subordinates.

While separate seating for women and men was common practice in public arenas and theaters, in some Christian churches, and for Jews in much later centuries, no archaeological evidence suggests such seating arrangements. No ancient synagogues have yet been found with upstairs balconies consistent with sex-segregated seating. Philo claims that when the Therapeutic monastics gathered on Shabbat, women and men sat separately, divided by a partial barrier (*On the Contemplative Life* 33). He also claims that at Shavuoth (probably), they ultimately sang as a unified choir reenacting the Israelites on the shore of the Reed Sea after the Exodus (*On the Contemplative Life* 85–88). Even if this is an accurate depiction of Therapeutae, there is no indication that such practices obtained in first-century synagogues, in Alexandria, or elsewhere.

Sabbath rest was a widespread, even defining practice, observed by women and men alike. Women commanding considerable slaves and servants might be able to set aside women's "work," especially child care and the provision (if not the actual preparation) of food. For others, rest would require gender-differentiated practices. Roman writers describe the windows of Jewish houses as smoky from sabbath lamps, while rabbis obligate women to light candles before the onset of Shabbat and to bake sabbath breads. In the canonical Gospels, Jesus's female followers refrain from attending to his tomb during the Sabbath. Rabbinic sources even contain the occasional tale about women attending synagogue on Shabbat. One late antique rabbinic collation, *Genesis Rabbah* (17:7), puts a particularly negative spin on women's sabbath obligations, not only claiming that women must light Shabbat candles as punishment for Eve's extinguishing of Adam's light but also warning that failure to do so would result in death in childbirth.

Numerous literary sources envision women praying to the God of Israel and narrate the contents of their prayers. In earlier biblical texts, women pray regularly for the birth of children, especially sons. In later writings, Judith prays for victory against the Assyrians and Sarah for divine protection from demons (in Tobit); Joseph's wife, Aseneth, prays for forgiveness from various errors and to serve Joseph as a slave, although the Jewish authorship of this text is uncertain (Kraemer, 1998b). While in the Hebrew Esther the protagonist never prays to the deity, in the expanded Greek retelling she prays repeatedly for divine support for her plans to protect her people. Numerous texts also depict women offering prayers of thanksgiving and praise. The rabbis obligate only men to pray daily and to wear special prayer garments including the fringed shawl known as a *talit* and special boxes wrapped around the head and hands known as *tefillin* (prayer objects). The rabbis require women to offer thanks after meals but nevertheless prohibit them from counting as part of a quorum of ten men required to recite "grace" after meals.

Like other people, Judeans had customary food practices, especially a refusal to eat pig meat. Rabbinic writings both presume and prescribe detailed regulations for food preparation and consumption, as well as for commensality (Rosenblum, 2010). They presume that men guarantee the kosher status of meat but hold women somewhat responsible for the purity of their pots and dishes and for the meals served to men. In both 2 Maccabees 7 and 4 Maccabees 14:11—18:24, a mother and her seven sons endure grievous torture and ultimately death rather than consume forbidden pig meat. Judith, who saves her people from the besieging "Assyrians," takes great care not to eat their polluting food, instead bringing her own special but otherwise unspecified foods into Holofernes's tent. While the Hebrew Esther entirely overlooks the likelihood that the queen might be consuming illicit food in the Persian court, the Greek character of Esther both acknowledges eating destestable gentile food, and claims that she does so only out of necessity (14:16–18).

Women and Devotional Study. Intellectual engagement with ancestral traditions in both oral and written form is often considered to have been a central devotional practice well before the destruction of the Temple. Scholars routinely assert that special Jewish education was widespread for boys, although we lack hard evidence that literacy rates among Jews would have been substantially different from the low rate of the general population, itself difficult to determine. In rabbinic sources, women virtually never engage in Torah study (with the prominent and problematic exception of a woman named Beruriah [Boyarin, 1993]). Some rabbinic authorities grant the possibility, while others see it as a profound transgression of the implicit positioning of Torah as female and Torah study as the quintessential act of masculinity (Satlow, 1996; Kraemer, 2011). Philo, on the other hand, depicts the study of philosophy, including Torah, as the primary activity of idealized celibate monastics, both women and men, called Therapeutae (on which see below). Late antique Christian authors make no specific mention of Jewish women's devotional intellectual work, while a small number of late antique epitaphs appear to commend women for piety that may have included study.

Other Instances of Women as Religious Agents and Actors. Surviving literary sources supply occasional representations of women as somewhat autonomous religious actors. The author of the Gospel of Luke (2:36–38) envisions a celibate widowed woman prophet (Anna) living in the Temple for many years, a representation difficult to reconcile both with biblical purity requirement, and with Josephus's accounts of purity and gender restrictions in the Temple. Juvenal offers a satirical depiction of a palsied Judean woman in Rome who interprets dreams for paltry sums (*Satire* 6). In the (perhaps Jewish) *Testament of Job*, three daughters born to Job after his desolation receive an inheritance of prophetic gifts, rather than earthly goods like their brothers. There is no evidence for demonstrably historical Judean women who function analogously to Judean male prophets. Glimpses of individual women's practices are occasional, such as Josephus's account of the Nazarite vows taken by Berenike, the granddaughter of Herod the Great, during the revolt against Rome (the same Berenike who became the consort of the Roman general and then Emperor Titus, under whom Jerusalem was destroyed).

Archaeological artifacts and occasional literary references demonstrate that Jewish women, like many if not most ancient persons, routinely employed incantations, amulets, and other practices often labeled as "magic" when seeking healing and divine aid for numerous endeavors. The name of the Judean God and those of his many agents seem to have been considered especially efficacious by non-Judeans and Judeans alike. In rabbinic sources, such practices are often commendable when performed by certain rabbis but condemned when performed by women.

Special Associations and Factions. Although Josephus, Philo, the Gospels, and the rabbis mention various Judean groups and associations (Essenes, Therapeutae, Pharisees, Sadduccees, Zealots) and various messianic movements, including those centered on John the Baptist, Jesus of Nazareth, Simon bar Giora, and Simon bar Kokhba, varying attention has been paid to questions of women's participation or affiliation with any of these. According to Josephus, early Pharisees had various women supporters, although he envisions Pharisees themselves as inherently male. The *Hypothetica*, attributed to Philo, claims that the Essenes were entirely male, while Josephus differentiates celibate male Essenes from those who married (while still presuming that Essenes themselves are men). Many of the Dead Sea Scrolls thought (with varying degrees of probability) to emanate from Essene authors envision a community of only men, although a few texts envision the group as possibly inclusive of women. Excavations of the cemetery next to the ruins at Qumran have yielded a small number of female skeletons that complicate but do not resolve any of these questions.

In a much-analyzed text already noted earlier, Philo asserts that women were full members of an association called the Therapeutae, whose most famous settlement was on the shores of the Mareotic Lake outside Alexandria. While some scholars take Philo's account to be historically reliable, at least with regard to the existence of monastic Judean women philosophers (Taylor, 2003), others have recently argued that the account of all the Therapeutae may constitute a kind of utopian exegetical exercise on Philo's part and that their historicity should not be presumed (Kraemer, 2011).

Although Esther and Judith are valorized as saviors of their imperiled people in specific historical circumstances, ancient accounts depict women only as supporters of messianic figures and not as themselves messianic candidates. Accounts of Jesus's life depict him with varying numbers of women supporters, while no individual women figure in the possible messianic movement around John the Baptizer. These differences may reflect more of the Gospels' attempt to subordinate John than actual demographic differences among their respective followers. Paul's undisputed letters demonstrate not only the interest of specific women in the Christ whom Paul preached but also their devotion to Paul himself as a charismatic freelance religious expert, a characteristic also reflected in Acts. Rarely noted is Josephus's brief but telling account of the importance of the wife of Simon bar Giora, a leader of the Judean revolt against Rome and a messianic candidate. Slim but tantalizing evidence hints at the roles of women in the second-century C.E. Bar Kohkba

revolt and the possibility that its messianic program included some elements of gender parity. There is insufficient evidence to gauge women's interest or participation in the North African revolt ca. 115–117 or the sporadic messianic movements in the late Roman period.

How Practices Authorize Gender (and Gender Authorizes Practices). As is generally true in the ancient Mediterranean and ancient west Asia, religious practices often differed for Judean women and men, differences that regularly effected the production of properly gendered persons. Further, the interpretations of shared practices regularly functioned to encode and authorize gender difference and hierarchy. This seems true even though the sources suggest that constructions of masculinity varied significantly. Judean men from the Maccabean fighters to the anti-Roman Sicarii seem to have privileged physical strength, athletic abilities, military prowess, and the selective use of violence. By contrast, early rabbis positioned their particular forms of Torah study as the ultimate act of masculine mastery over the self and subordinate others, as opposed to other Greek and Roman definitions that privileged deliberate, controlled exercise of physical power.

Correspondingly diverse constructions of femininity are less perceptible. The presumption that women (and gentiles) generally lacked masculine self-discipline and critical discernment undergirds rabbinic debates and positions about, among other things, whether women could or should study Torah or read Torah in public. Yet various Hellenistic stories suggest differing views about women's capacities, if not necessarily about the gendering of such capacities. The eponymous heroine (and chaste widow) Judith displays all the qualities of masculine self-discipline and self-mastery, putting to shame not only the men of her native Betulia but also the Assyrian general whom she easily assassinates (by playing, of course, to his sexual desires). The mother of the seven martyred sons exhibits both feminine modesty and masculine self-control when confronted with gruesome persecution. Further, the ability of some women to serve as officers in late antique diaspora synagogues suggests either that differing constructions of gender were operative, that such women were seen to be exceptional, or that the holding of such offices was not understood as an inappropriate exercise of masculine capacity and authority. The lack of corresponding literary evidence makes this impossible to assess.

So What? Scholarship as well as popular work on Jewish women has almost always been done for contemporary ideological purposes, whether those of self-identifying Jews or self-identifying Christians (these being the vast majority of those writing). These purposes have often had comparative aims: some Jewish positions/practices were better than other Jewish ones; Christian positions were better than Jewish ones; Jewish and Christian positions were better than Muslim positions, and so forth. Rarely has anyone approached these materials and questions from a larger religious studies vantage point to ask different (and perhaps better) questions. With what conditions (social, material, whatever) do these practices and positions correlate, and how are they related? What conditions correlate with strong gender asymmetry and which with less strong gender asymmetry? Are there any conditions that correlate with extensive gender parity? What we do with such data is a constructive exercise beyond the scope of this entry, but it is obviously the ultimate "So what?"—enabling us to better understand our own contemporary practices and values as well as the choices that may be available to us.

[*See also* Education, *subentry* Early Judaism; Paul; Popular Religion and Magic, *subentry* Early Judaism; Religious Leaders, *subentry* Early Judaism; *and* Religious Participation, *subentry* New Testament.]

BIBLIOGRAPHY

Boyarin, Daniel. *Carnal Israel: Reading Sex in Talmudic Culture.* Berkeley: University of California, 1993.

Brooten, Bernadette J. *Women Leaders in the Ancient Synagogue: Inscriptional Evidence and Background Issues.* Brown Judaic Studies 36. Chico, Calif.: Scholars Press, 1982.

Fonrobert, Charlotte. *Menstrual Purity: Rabbinic and Christian Reconstructions of Biblical Gender.* Stanford, Calif.: Stanford University Press, 2000.

Horbury, William. "Women in the Synagogue." In *The Cambridge History of Judaism*, Vol. 3, pp. 358–401. Cambridge, U.K.: Cambridge University Press, 1999.

Ilan, Tal. *Jewish Women in Greco-Roman Palestine: An Inquiry into Image and Status.* Texte und Studium zum Antike Judentum 44. Tübingen, Germany: Mohr Siebeck, 1995.

Ilan, Tal. *Mine and Yours Are Hers: Retrieving Women's History from Rabbinic Sources.* Arbeiten zur Geschichte des antiken Judentums und des Urchristentums 41. Leiden, The Netherlands: Brill, 1997a.

Ilan, Tal. "The Quest for the Historical Beruriah, Rachel, and Imma Shalom." *Association for Jewish Studies Review* 1 (1997b): 1–17.

Ilan, Tal. *Integrating Women into Second Temple History.* Texte und Studium zum Antike Judentum 76. Tübingen, Germany: Mohr Siebeck, 1999.

Jay, Nancy B. *Throughout Your Generations Forever: Sacrifice, Religion, and Paternity.* Chicago: University of Chicago Press, 1992.

Kraemer, Ross S. *Her Share of the Blessings: Women's Religions among Pagans, Jews and Christians in the Greco-Roman World.* New York: Oxford University Press, 1992.

Kraemer, Ross S. "Jewish Women in the Diaspora World of Late Antiquity." In *Jewish Women in Historical Perspective*, 2d ed., edited by J. Baskin, pp. 46–72. Detroit: Wayne State University Press, 1998a.

Kraemer, Ross S. *When Aseneth Met Joseph: A Late Antique Tale of the Biblical Patriarch and His Egyptian Wife, Revisited.* New York: Oxford University Press, 1998b.

Kraemer, Ross S. *Unreliable Witnesses: Religion, Gender and History in the Greco-Roman Mediterranean.* New York: Oxford University Press, 2011.

Kraemer, Ross S. "Gender." In *The Cambridge Companion to Ancient Mediterranean Religions*, edited by Barbette Stanley Saeth, pp. 281–308. Cambridge, U.K.: Cambridge University Press, 2013.

Levine, Lee I. "Women in the Synagogue." In *The Ancient Synagogue: The First Thousand Years*, pp. 471–490. New Haven, Conn.: Yale University Press, 2000.

Marks, Susan. "Women in Early Judaism: Twenty-five Years of Research and Reenvisioning." *Currents in Biblical Research* 6, no. 2 (2008): 290–320.

Mason, Steve. "Jews, Judeans, Judaizing, Judaism: Problems of Categorization in Ancient History." *Journal for the Study of Judaism* 38 (2007): 457–512.

Rosenblum, Jordan. *Food and Identity in Early Rabbinic Judaism.* Cambridge, U.K.: Cambridge, University Press, 2010.

Satlow, Michael L. "'Try to Be a Man': The Rabbinic Construction of Masculinity." *Harvard Theological Review* 89 (1996): 19–40.

Satlow, Michael L. *Creating Judaism: History, Tradition, Practice.* New York: Columbia University Press, 2006.

Taylor, Joan E. *Jewish Women Philosophers of First-Century Alexandria: Philo's "Therapeutae" Reconsidered.* Oxford: Oxford University Press, 2003.

Ullucci, Daniel. *The Christian Rejection of Animal Sacrifice.* New York: Oxford University Press, 2012.

Wassen, Cecilia. *Women in the Damascus Document.* Academia Biblica 21. Atlanta: Society of Biblical Literature, 2005.

Wegner, Judith. R. *Chattel or Person: The Status of Women in the Mishnah.* New York: Oxford University Press, 1988.

Ross S. Kraemer

Early Church

In the wake of feminist scholarship and interpretation (1970s to the present), scholars of early Christianity have looked not only behind, but also beyond canonical literature to examine women's leadership positions (as apostles, disciples, prophets, teachers, preachers, patrons, etc.); participation in rituals, festivals, and female somatic events (menstruation, childbirth, lactation, etc.); and their characterization in various roles (as mothers, daughters, wives, widows, virgins, and whores). Since the New Testament offers precious little information regarding women's involvement in these areas, noncanonical texts, with their rich narratives and female heroines, offer feminist biblical scholars more fertile ground to explore women's participation in and contribution to the development of nascent Christianity.

Many feminist scholars have placed high hopes on the New Testament Apocrypha, not only to illuminate the voices of real women, but also to liberate women from a church constructed and influenced by the pastoral letters (i.e., 1 and 2 Tim; Tit) and the writings of the church fathers (e.g., Tertullian of Carthage; c. 160 C.E.), who solidified the patriarchal hierarchy of Christian communities. Although this newfound interest in apocryphal literature indeed has revealed important insights into understanding the characterization of women in the ancient world and to the place of noncanonical literature in the history of biblical interpretation, recent critiques question whether these writings actually recover real women's voices (Vuong, 2013). A number of current studies focusing on apocryphal heroines in particular argue that such literature may tell us less about real women's voices than about the reflections of authors who used these narratives as a way to construct ideas about women, body, and gender in the Christian family, community, and broader society. Nevertheless, what remains true of these writings is their undeniable popularity and influence in shaping and constructing identity in antiquity; thus they can provide us a better understanding of women in the early church.

In what follows, I survey two popular and important noncanonical sources for understanding women's participation in the paradigmatic female somatic experience of menstruation, childbirth, and lactation in the early church. This examination, although not exhaustive, offers rather a general overview of two texts that are representative of their genre: the *Protevangelium of James* and the *Passio* or *Martyrdom of Perpetua and Felicitas.* In these gospel and martyrdom accounts, women are featured prominently, and female participation in gender-specific activities plays an important role in the women's characterization and the texts' rhetorical strategies. Whether these writings are the products of Christian imagination, their continued popularity not only among academic circles but also the general public has influenced and shaped ideas concerning attitudes toward women's autonomy and social and economic status, as well as social and religious roles of women in both private and public life. After a brief summary of the history of menstruation and childbirth in the early church, I will turn to these texts.

Menstruation and Childbirth in the Early Church. Early Christian writings about female bodily fluids (i.e., discharges from menses and lochia) are almost always connected to concerns about purity, specifically maintaining purity in sacred spaces. The incompatibility of menstrual blood and lochia with sacred spaces (i.e., Temple, altar, etc.) is widely attested in early Christian literature. The idea that menstruants and parturients should be kept from sacred spaces because they are impure is an interpretation that is often traced to Jewish ideas on purity, especially the laws found in Leviticus 12 (on parturients) and 15 (on menstruants). Although not identical, these impurities are related since both are understood as blood discharges from the womb; indeed, Levitical legislation specifies that the first stage of a parturient's discharge is like menstruation, thus she is impure like the menstruant (12:2; 12:5). Branham (1997) writes that the early Christian understanding of menstruants and parturients as impure is not surprising when considering early Christian reinterpretation and appropriation of Temple sacred space. As long as Christian rituals, institutions, and the clergy functioned as permanent replacements of the Jerusalem Temple, sacrificial blood (i.e., the Eucharist) would be considered incompatible with reproductive blood (i.e., menses and lochia) as menstruants and parturients were of the holy space of the Jerusalem Temple.

The early church fathers continued to attest to the incompatibility of women's fluids, especially menses, with sacred spaces and activities. Noteworthy, however, is the way in which their written discussions concerning menstruants as pollutants in particular are almost always interpreted or justified in light of the story of the hemorrhaging women found sandwiched within the Gospel narrative of the Jewish leader's daughter who is raised back to life (Mark 5:21–43; Luke 8:40–56; Matt 9:18–26). Problematic for this discussion, however, is the fact the woman with the twelve-year flow of blood is not a menstruant; her hemmorhage is pathological, placing her condition as a disease and therefore a more serious form of impurity. By the late fourth century C.E., Jerome (347–420) took this discussion to a new level. In his *Commentary on Zachariah*, Jerome goes beyond connecting the menstruant with a *zabah* (impurity caused by a serious form of illness or disease) and draws direct links between menstruation and sin: "Nothing is more filthy, unclean than a menstruant; whatever she will have touched, she makes it unclean, and still of whose filth is cleansed through the baptism of Christ, through the cleansing of sins" (III). Although Jerome may be alone in equating menstruation with sin, his view of menstrual blood

as reprehensible and shameful was influenced by earlier ideas concerning its polluting power. Third-century documents such as *Apostolic Tradition* of Hippolytus (Rome), the *Letter of Dionysius of Alexandria* (Alexandria), and the *Didascalia Apostolorum* (Syria) are three of our earliest Christian witnesses to the idea that menstrual blood is polluting and that menstruants should be isolated from religious participation.

In the *Apostolic Tradition*, Hippolytus of Rome (170–235 C.E.) appeals to apostolic authority for his understanding of the process for a person who has chosen to convert to Christianity. In discussing the qualifications of catechumens, he offers a list of candidates who should be excluded from receiving baptism on their appointed day, noting that if a female catechumen is menstruating on that day, another day will be set to perform the baptismal ceremony. Given that Hippolytus offers no explanation or justification for excluding menstruants from baptism, one might assume that he understands them to be impure and fears that they will defile the sanctuary (20.6). In the case of Dionysius's letter, written as a response to Bishop Basilides, Dionysius (d. 264/5 C.E.) addressees three categories in relation to sexual pollution: marital intercourse, nocturnal emissions, and menstruants. Of these, only menstruants are banned from entering "the house of God" or making contact with "the holy table," or the "body and blood of Christ" (*Patrologia Graeca* 10.1281–1282). Cohen (1991) argues that "the transference of temple terminology to the church is unmistakable" given that menstruants are restricted from participating in the sacrifice (i.e., communion) in the same way menstruants are restricted from offering sacrifices at the holy altar of the Temple (pp. 288–289). In the *Didascalia Apostolorum*, a case is made for the separation of menstruants not only from the Eucharist, but also from prayer and scriptural study, holy acts that should not be practiced when in a state of ritual impurity. What is fascinating about *Didascalia Apostolorum*, however, is the fact that the case made for the separation of menstruants from sacred places and activities was being made by the women themselves based on the belief that they were void of the Holy Spirit during this period. Having sketched this context, we now turn to our two noncanonical sources to examine the ways menstruation and childbirth are presented and to consider in what ways they are consistent or inconsistent with the evidence presented thus far.

The *Protevangelium of James*. The *Protevangelium of James* (*Prot. Jas.*) was an extremely popular and influential late-second- to early-third-century apocryphal narrative featuring Mary, the mother of Jesus. In no other extant text is Mary given as much prominence. Details about Mary's life as well her characterization as remarkably pure stand at the narrative's core—Mary is not simply a virgin; rather she is perpetually virginal (she remains a virgin before, during, and after childbirth), maintaining a sort of exceptional "sacred purity" that keeps her not only sexually pure, but also ritually and menstrually pure. Thus, virginity and purity are not temporary conditions, but are defining characteristics of her identity. Through the overarching theme of purity the narrative comments on important practices, rituals, and ceremonies in which women participated, including menstruation, childbirth, and breastfeeding: that is, the hallmarks of the female life cycle marking transitions from infancy to childhood, childhood to girlhood, and girlhood to womanhood.

Menstruation and impurity. The *Prot. Jas.*'s overarching interest in ritual purity is demonstrated by the consistent presentation of Mary as completely and remarkably free from all things profane and unclean and her parents' unfailing participation in offering Temple sacrifice. For example, the scene in which the priests ask Mary to leave the Temple (8:4) is striking since she had, even more remarkably, resided there from the age of three. Yet, upon turning twelve, Mary is asked to leave the Temple precinct because the priests fear that she may defile it. The type of pollution they fear has been overwhelmingly read as a sign of her impending menstruation although it is never stated in the narrative. However, Mary's age of twelve is mentioned twice at the moment the priests show concern, and her immediate removal is needed to ensure the Temple's continued purity. Although moral impurity in biblical litera-

ture is understood to be distinctly different from ritual impurity (i.e., menstrual impurity) since the latter is unavoidable and morally unproblematic, various early Christian texts attest to the blurring of such lines as our third-century sources indicate. Although the *Prot. Jas.* does not explicitly present Mary's possible menarche negatively—an important distinction from the harsh views discussed above—the text does attest to the separation of potential menstruants from holy places and spaces for fear of defilement, consistent with many biblical treatments and writings of the church fathers.

Childbirth, lactation, and impurity. Ideas concerning childbirth and breast feeding in early Christian writings are predictably linked to ideas concerning menstruation, the physical sign of female maturation and potential childbearing, and lactation, the bodily sign of new mothers. Impurity connected to menstrual blood with parturient blood is attested in Leviticus 12:5, which conflates purification rituals for childbirth and purification requirements of menstruants. More importantly, Luke 2:21–24 also offers a description of Mary waiting the prescribed days according to the Law before she is given entrance to the sacred space of the Temple because her postpartum state renders her ritually impure.

The *Prot. Jas.* offers two separate accounts involving childbirth and breast feeding. The first is Mary's birth itself by her mother Anna, who waited until the prescribed days were fulfilled before she "cleansed herself of the flow of blood, and gave her breast to the child, and called her name Mary" (5:9). Anna's decision to wait to breast feed her child attests to the concern for postpartum pollution and purification and their relationship to the female life cycle, impurity, and fertility. Although scholars including Cohen (1991), Klawans (2000), and Philip (2006) have noted that ritual pollution such as those produced by menstruants and parturients has no moral valence in biblical and early rabbinic practices, that ritual impurities should not be deemed shameful or denigrating are not as concrete in some early Christian writings as noted above. In this case, the *Prot. Jas.* identifies the postpartum state as an unavoidable impurity, incompatible with holy spaces in the same way menstrual blood defiles the sacred.

Noteworthy in the *Prot. Jas.*'s description of post-partum impurity is the connection it makes to breast feeding, not seen in any biblical laws or early Christian writings. Although a parturient's impurity may prevent her from coming into contact with holy things for a limited amount of time, there is no Levitical legislation or other orders that prevent new mothers from breast feeding children during this time period (cf. D, 4Q266 6 ii 11). Unlike other female fluids, milk—especially a new mother's milk—often connotes purity in early Christian literature because it was believed to have therapeutic powers. Although this detail may speak to the author's intention of presenting Mary as exceptionally pure and miraculously inclined (Mary consumes only two kinds of food throughout the entire narrative—milk and food from an angel's hand), it may also suggest the importance and popular use of wet nurses, especially among wealthy families in the ancient world, as well as the belief that if one could gain access to it, milk was ideal food especially for infants because of its purity.

The second account of a birth in the *Prot. Jas.* is that of Mary's birth of Jesus, which has some parallels to the infancy narratives of Matthew (1—2) and Luke (1—2). Although no description of the actual delivery is provided, the narrative does report that Mary breast fed her child immediately after birth (19:15–16). Mary's feeding of Jesus recalls Anna's feeding of Mary earlier in the narrative, but, of course, with one important difference: Anna waits until she is deemed no longer impure, whereas Mary does not. Mary's milk is deemed pure in a way that Anna's is not. Although consistent with the narrative's goal to present an exceptional Mary, Anna's decision to wait may be used to reinforce this ever-pure state, whereas Mary's decision to breast feed immediately may attest to the popular early Christian view of breast milk as not only pure and positive, but also holding healing powers.

Perpetua and Felicitas: Pregnancy, Childbirth, Lactation, and Martyrdom. The *Passio* of Perpetua and Felicitas is an early-third-century North African text that has gained much popularity among scholars of feminist and gender studies because it allegedly offers a firsthand account of a woman's and her female slave's experience of martyrdom. Possibly the earliest Christian text written by a woman with prominently featured female protagonists, this work is especially interesting because both martyrdoms are inextricably connected to each woman's experience of childbirth. Whereas the *Prot. Jas.* attests to the incompatibility between the blood of a menstruant or parturient with sacrificial blood (i.e., Temple altar), the *Passio* comments on the incompatibility of childbirth (postpartum blood) with martyrdom (martyr's blood). In his *Apology* (197 C.E.), Tertullian emphatically states that "the blood of the martyrs is the seed of the church" (50) and encouraged many to participate in this ultimate expression of devotion to God. It is perhaps to this calling that both Perpetua and Felicitas were moved, but in both cases their major obstacle to achieving this "glorious end" involved their recent participation in childbirth, thus transitioning from womanhood to motherhood, along with their rejection of motherhood for martyrdom.

Perpetua's experience. Perpetua's experience of martyrdom and childbirth may be linked to her status as a free, upper-class Roman citizen. Perpetua is married and after her arrest actually nurses her infant child during her sentencing. Although family worries concern Perpetua, the condition of her son functions as her greatest obstacle in achieving her goal and results in her ambivalent attitude toward motherhood and martyrdom. Specifically, Perpetua worries about being able to nurse her child when her father refuses to allow her baby to be with her in prison. This ambivalence and choice between motherhood and martyrdom perhaps attests to concerns specific to Christian martyrdoms not seen in earlier Jewish martyrdoms.

The Martyrdom of the Mother and her Seven Sons found in 4 Maccabees is perhaps one of our earliest examples of a martyrdom found in Jewish and Christian literature and is likely to have been known by the author of the *Passio*. In this popular narrative, a mother does not choose between martyrdom and motherhood, but engages completely in both experiences by being martyred along with her seven children. Probably composed in the first century C.E., the text carefully juxtaposes the maternal love she has for her sons with the consistent message of death for the sake of religion as noble and at times necessary. In this story, martyrdom and motherhood are clearly compatible. When the *Passio* makes clear that these two experiences are no longer compatible, the account may speak to the influence of the changing social structures that were developed and encouraged in the early church. Ideas of world renunciation, which included family, society, and social and traditional structures, heavily influenced the rhetoric of Christian martyrdom that repeatedly encouraged followers to take Christ's example and leave worldly concerns behind. That Perpetua breaks this important tie between father and daughter to achieve her goal of martyrdom only prepares her for choosing personal salvation over her role as mother.

Felicitas's experience. Much like her mistress, Felicitas's experience of martyrdom is also inexplicitly connected to pregnancy and childbirth. When introduced in the *Passio*, we are told that Felicitas is eight months pregnant, Perpetua's female slave, and the *conserva* of Revocatus (a fellow slave belonging to Perpetua's household). In her study on early Christian slavery, Glancy (2006) notes that despite the shared experience of pregnancy, childbirth, and lactation, social and symbolic meaning for free and slave women diverged significantly. Unlike elite women, a female slave's reproductive capacity made her markedly more valuable in the eyes of her owner. If Felicitas was perceived in this way, her experience of martyrdom may attest to gender-specific slaveholding patterns in the ancient world. Unlike her mistress, whose obstacle to martyrdom is being able to nurse her child, Felicitas's greatest worry is actually giving birth. Whereas Perpetua's expectation as an elite Roman mother involves nurturing her child to achieve martyrdom, Felicitas's successful martyrdom depends only on her giving birth to the child. No descriptions of nursing or motherly care are offered after the birth, as the narrative reports that the child is immediately given to one of the sisters,

who brought her up as her own (Musurillo, 1972, pp. 123, 125).

Feliticas's difficulty with achieving martyrdom is based on Roman law forbidding the execution of an expectant prisoner, since the slave-child was understood to be important property even if the slave herself was no longer valuable. Felicitas's pregnant state was deemed incompatible with a martyr's death since her death would mean the death of the child-property. Although Felicitas's eventual childbirth does allow her to participate in the arena, the description of her naked body so fresh from childbirth that it drips with milk alongside her mistress's young motherly body elicits a negative reaction from the crowd, which results in their being sent to be dressed in tunics. The crowd's reaction speaks to ancient understandings concerning the relationship between blood and milk, namely, that they should not occupy the same space at the same time. More specifically, menstruation, childbirth, and lactation were understood to represent three distinct stages of the same process in ancient conceptions of female physiology—thus, no more than one stage of this process should be participated in at any one time. In this context, then, Perpetua's and Felicitas's martyrdoms offer important ideas on women's roles in pregnancy, childbirth, and lactation in relationship to the Christian practice of martyrdom.

Assessment. Although female participation in menstruation and childbirth were deemed as ritual impurities in early Judaism, they were also female bodily experiences that were understood as unavoidable and even blessed (e.g., Gen 1:28). In other words, they rendered no moral or permanently negative connotation, although such a state would prevent women from access to holy things, places, and activities. Although early Christians seem to be influenced by such ideas of impurity in relation to female fluids, as evident by the continued practice of denying women entry to sacred spaces and activities under these conditions, the boundaries between minor ritual impurities (e.g., menstruation) and other more serious impurities (e.g., disease) and offenses (e.g., sin) are conflated. For many early church fathers, menstruation takes on a new connotation—it is not only an impurity, but also an illness. However, is this new interpretation of female bodily fluids consistent with all early Christian literature that speaks about women's experience of the body?

In focusing on the *Prot. Jas.* and the *Passio,* two non-canonical sources that feature women prominently and offer important ideas about women's experiences with menstruation, childbirth, and lactation, more nuanced understandings of ritual (im)purity and religious participation are possible. The *Prot. Jas.* attests to the removal of ritual impurities (even if they are only *potential* impurities) from sacred spaces, but seems to keep distinctions between ritual impurities like menstruation and childbirth and other more serious impurities intact. Ideas concerning lactation in this narrative connect mother's milk both to impurity (Anna) and purity (Mary).

In contradistinction, the *Passio* offers important ideas on childbirth and lactation that deal not with the incompatibility of these female bodily fluids with the sacred, but rather with the incompatibility of childbirth and lactation with the act of martyrdom. Evidence from these noncanonical sources thus provides critical understandings of the role gender played in defining and circumscribing women's ability to participate in church rituals and assemblies, specifically the natural and simultaneously impure construction placed on female menstruation, childbirth, and bodily fluids.

[*See also* Gender Transgression, *subentry* Early Church; Imagery, Gendered, *subentry* Priestly Material; Legal Status, *subentry* Early Church; Masculinity and Femininity, *subentry* Early Church; Religious Leaders, *subentry* Early Church; Religious Participation, *subentry* Early Judaism; *and* Social Interaction, *subentry* Early Church.]

BIBLIOGRAPHY

Branham, Joan. "Blood in Flux, Sanctity at Issue." *RES Anthropology and Aesthetics* 31 (1997): 53–70.

Castelli, Elizabeth. 'I Will Make Mary Male': Pieties of the Body and Gender Transformation of Christian Women in Late Antiquity." In *Body Guards: The Cultural Politics of Gender Ambiguity*, edited by Julia Epstein and Kristina Straub, pp. 29–50. New York: Routledge, 1991.

Cohen, Shaye. "Menstruants and the Sacred in Judaism and Christianity." In *Women's History and Ancient History*, edited by Sarah B. Pomeroy, pp. 273–299. Chapel Hill: University of North Carolina Press, 1991.

Cook, Leslie A. "Body Language: Women's Rituals of Purification in the Bible and Mishnah." In *Women and Water: Menstruation in Jewish Life and Law*, edited by Rahel R. Wasserfall, pp. 40–59. Waltham, Mass.: Brandeis University Press, 1999.

De Troyer, Kristin, et al., eds. *Wholly Woman, Holy Blood: A Feminist Critique of Purity and Impurity.* Studies in Antiquity and Christianity. Harrisburg, Pa.: Trinity Press International, 2003.

Glancy, Jennifer A. *Slavery in Early Christianity.* Minneapolis: Fortress, 2006.

Klawans, Jonathan. *Impurity and Sin in Ancient Israel.* New York: Oxford University Press, 2000.

Kramer, Ross Shepard, and Mary Rose D'Angelo, eds. *Women and Christian Origins.* New York: Oxford University Press, 1999.

Levine, Amy-Jill, ed. *A Feminist Companion to the New Testament Apocrypha.* Cleveland, Ohio: Pilgrim, 2006.

Meacham, Tirzah. "An Abbreviated History of the Development of Jewish Menstrual Laws." In *Women and Water: Menstruation in Jewish Life and Law*, edited by Rahel R. Wasserfall, pp. 23–39. Waltham, Mass.: Brandeis University Press, 1999.

Musurillo, Herbert, ed. and trans. *The Acts of the Christian Martyrs: Introduction, Texts, and Translations.* Oxford: Clarendon, 1972.

Philip, Tarja. *Menstruation and Childbirth in the Bible: Fertility and Impurity.* Studies in Biblical Literature 88. New York: Peter Lang, 2006.

Pomeroy, Sarah B. *Goddesses, Whores, Wives, and Slaves: Women in Classical Antiquity.* New York: Schocken, 1975.

Salisbury, Joyce E. *Perpetua's Passion: The Death and Memory of a Young Roman Woman.* New York: Routledge, 1997.

Vuong, Lily. *Gender and Purity in the Protevangelium of James.* Wissenschaftliche Untersuchungen zum Neuen Testament II. Tübingen, Germany: Mohr Siebeck, 2013.

Vuong, Lily. "The Impact of Social and Economic Status on the Experience of Martyrdom: A Case Study of Perpetua and Felicitas." In *Purity, Holiness, and Identity in Judaism and Christianity: Essays in Memory of Susan Haber*, edited by Carl S. Ehrlich, Anders Runesson, and Eileen Schuller, pp. 224–249. Wissenschaftliche

Untersuchungen zum Neuen Testament I. Tübingen, Germany: Mohr Siebeck, 2013.

Lily Vuong

Rhetorical-Hermeneutical Criticism

Hermeneutic-rhetorical criticism is a method of textual and cultural analysis that seeks to trace inscribed power structures of domination. In turn, feminist/feminism refers to a social movement and critical theory that asserts that wo/men ("wo/men" written with a slash includes marginalized men) are to be recognized as fully human with full citizen rights in society and religion. Feminist studies are not simply gender studies but are studies of pyramidal kyriarchal (derived from the Greek *kyrios* = Lord, master, father elite propertied male and *archein* = to rule) intersecting power structures such as gender, race, class, nationality, age, religion, or culture. This kyriarchal pyramid of domination is structured by the intersecting social systems of race, gender, sexuality, class, empire, age, and religion, which, taken together, can result in multiplicative effects of dehumanizing exploitation and subordination of the "other." Inspired by emerging literature on feminist rhetorics and discourse, I have developed a critical feminist rhetorical model of interpretation in concert with the emerging literature on the rhetoricality or rhetoricity and the discursive performativity of texts and knowledges.

Hermeneutic and Rhetoric. If a critical feminist hermeneutic-rhetorical analysis is primarily interested in emancipatory knowledge production, a traditional understanding of "hermeneutics" seems to be a mismatch for a method used to pursue such interests. Relying on a critical theory of language and the insights of liberation movements, a critical feminist hermeneutics is therefore best understood as a critical feminist rhetoric. Such a critical theory attempts to articulate rhetoric both as a complex process of reading and reconstruction and as a cultural-religious praxis of resistance and transformation. It moves from the traditional understanding of "hermeneutic," proposed by theorists such as Hans

Georg Gadamer, a German philosopher, to a form of interpretation that can best be described not as hermeneutic but as metic (Schüssler Fiorenza, 2011, pp. 55–78).

The terms "hermeneutic" and "metic" refer to two different ways of interpretation and understanding that are paradigmatically articulated in the mythical stories of the God Hermes and the Goddess Metis. Hermes is the messenger of the Olympian Gods who mediates divine revelation and knowledge to humans. According to Gadamer, hermeneutics has the task of translating meaning from one "world" into another (Bernstein, 1986, pp. 343–376). Like Hermes, the messenger of the Gods, hermeneutics not only communicates knowledge but also instructs, directs, enjoins, and, in its interpretation of signs and oracles as well as its revelatory power, has affinities to manticism and prophecy. It is a matter of practical understanding, which involves the Aristotelian virtue of phronesis—practical judgment and adjudication—which is secured only in the process of understanding.

The well-known "hermeneutical circle" claims that understanding can only take place if the parts of some larger reality are grasped in terms of the whole. In the "to and fro" of the hermeneutical circle or spiral, we can fuse or broaden our horizon with that which we seek to understand. However, whereas Gadamer understands the hermeneutical event as a fusion of horizons (*Horizontverschmelzung*) (Gadamer, 1997, p. 302), a critical feminist metic seeks to deconstruct the kyriarchal horizon of biblical texts and our own in order to change both horizons because the dominant cultural and religious horizon of the past and the present has been exclusive of wo/men as subjects of knowledge and understanding. Critical feminist theory agrees with Gadamer that people, both wo/men and men, are embedded in the history and culture that has shaped them, but adds that cultural and religious history has been distorted insofar as wo/men were not only excluded from the articulation and the production of knowledge in society and religion but were also written out of history and public consciousness in and through kyriocentric language and rhetoric.

It is not, therefore, the myth of Hermes but rather the myth of Metis that fully articulates the vision of a critical feminist hermeneutic and rhetoric, or, better, metic (Dolmage, 2009). Zeus, the father of the Gods, was in competition with the Goddess Metis. When she was pregnant with Athena, he feared that Metis would bear a child who would surpass him in wisdom and power. To avoid this, he transformed Metis into a fly and swallowed her wholesale in order to have her always with him and to benefit from her wise counsel as well as become pregnant with the child of Metis. According to Hesiod, Athena came fully grown and armored from the head of her father, Zeus. However, she only appears to be motherless; her mother is the Goddess Metis, the "most wise woman among Gods and humans" (Schüssler Fiorenza, 2011, pp. 55–80).

This myth of Metis and Zeus not only reveals the fear of the father of the Gods that the child of Wisdom would surpass him in knowledge, but it also lays open the conditions under which wo/men in kyriarchal cultures and religions are able to exercise wisdom and to produce knowledge. Read with a hermeneutics of suspicion, the myths of Metis and Athena illuminate that kyriarchal systems of knowledge and power are performative or rhetorical insofar as they objectify and swallow up wo/men in order to co-opt their wisdom and knowledge for their own interests of domination.

Critical hermeneutic-rhetorical-feminist studies are therefore best understood not simply as hermeneutics that understands texts but also as *metics*, as a critical discursive analysis that reveals the cultural and religious structures that disempower and marginalize wo/men and swallow up their wisdom and creativity. Critical feminist studies seek to make clear that knowledge and text are performative. Not only can liberating knowledges inscribed in cultural classics and religious scriptures be rediscovered and set free, but also structures of marginalization and dehumanization can be named and critically evaluated in and through a critical hermeneutic-rhetorical analysis.

The Renaissance of Rhetoric. It is significant that the decades in which feminist biblical hermeneutics has emerged and matured correspond to the intellectual renaissance of rhetoric. The confluence of both developments has enabled and shaped critical biblical studies as well. Critical feminist studies are an important area of scholarly research that seeks to produce knowledge in the interest of wo/men who, by law and custom, have been excluded from philosophy, theology, and biblical interpretation for centuries. Therefore, a critical feminist approach examines the intersecting structures of kyriarchal exclusion and domination that control the production of knowledge in a given discipline. Feminist biblical studies thus encompass both cultural and religious studies. Since the Bible continues to fuel cultural ideologies and stereotypes and to influence Western art, music, and literature, the criticism of the kyriachal elements of the biblical texts provided by a feminist critical-rhetorical analysis is not only religiously but also culturally significant.

Since the mid-twentieth century, a renaissance of rhetoric has taken place that has made it possible to focus anew on the discursivity and rhetoricality of science. Such a renaissance has significant connections to current efforts in the theory of science and the sociology of knowledge. This revitalization of rhetoric has thereby opened the doors for critical feminist work to be taken seriously, the flourishing of which is also closely connected to the development and spread of new media of communication. In the global communication society, rhetoric—or concern with the forms of public argumentation and persuasion—has attained a new significance.

Rhetoric is practiced today in four forms. *First*, as academic communication studies, it teaches the art of public speaking and debate. *Second*, the study of ancient rhetoric is devoted to the recovery of the classical handbooks and theories. *Third*, critical literary rhetorical studies seek to understand the arguments and persuasive power of texts in their contexts. *Fourth*, as the rhetoric of scholarship, it investigates the rhetoricity or rhetoricality of knowledge and its institutions. Insight into the constructedness of all knowledge, including scientific knowledge, shifts the question as to the criteria of scientific evidence from epistemology to the intersubjective ethical, social, and political realm. Contexts of communication and ultimately power relationships determine the validity of representation.

The Rhetoric of Science. This renaissance of rhetoric has received important impulses from feminist theory as well as from the debates on postmodernism. Its roots have to do with the linguistic-analytical turn in philosophy and its consequences for the theory of scientific knowledge, as well as with the rise of semiotics as the "logic of science." Most important are the insights and approaches of the sociology of science, or the so-called sciences of science (*Wissenschaftswissenschaften*). In different but generally complementary ways, the rhetorical character of scientific publication is both described and confirmed. The distinction between positivist interpretation and rhetorical interpretation is possible, but it is still important to avoid its positivistic-literalist antiquarian elements.

Critical hermeneutic-rhetorical-analysis emphasizes that, in the process of interpretation, texts and symbols are not simply understood or their true meaning grasped (hermeneutics). Rather, language is always already a construct, an exercise of power, and an action that either continues ideologies of domination or tries to interrupt them. Interpretation is not simply a one-way street, as in the positivist discovery of a single meaning of the text. It is a multivocal discourse that seeks by means of argumentation to persuade and to convince. This rhetorical nature of science comes to the fore in its language, its methods of interpretation, its sociohistorical models, its communicative situation, and the sociopolitical positioning and interests of interpreters. Interpretation is best understood not as reproduction but as creative action, since the interpretation of a text is always also a creative re-creation. A claim to objective, clear reproduction of an original meaning of the text or intention of the author abstracted from the person of the interpreter and her sociopolitical location is no longer scientifically possible.

Consequently, a critical-hermeneutic-rhetorical paradigm requires a scientific approach that articulates the scholar's social location, theoretical perspectives, and rhetorical situation as integral parts of the interpretive process. That requirement does not mean, however, that any and every interpretation of a text is acceptable. The text does indeed contain countless possible meanings, but it is best understood as a multivocal spectrum of meanings, each limited by a particular context. This multifaceted spectrum is differently activated in every particular act of interpretation, and depends on the ethical and sociopolitical standpoints not only of the interpreter but also of her recipients.

Nevertheless, academic and popular biblical interpretation continues to operate largely with a concept of scholarship that has long since been rendered outmoded. Many interpreters still make the claim that they can objectively find a single, objectively true meaning of a biblical text with scholarly-controlled methods, and thus discover its kernel of truth. But such a timeless, objectively discoverable truth cannot be filtered out of the text once and for all. Rather, the text must be understood in rhetorical terms as a speech act motivated by particular interests in specific sociopolitical and historical contexts. What is true on the level of the text applies also to the levels of interpretation and historical reconstruction. Only in this way can the multiple meanings of the textual signs and linguistic symbols be limited and the possible or probable field of meaning of a text be demarcated.

Contrary to historical-positivist analysis that tries to establish historical facts and as opposed to literary-critical interpretation that concentrates on the literary form and deep structure of a text, rhetorical analysis of discourse emphasizes the significance of the speech context, the inscribed power relationships, and the sociohistorical origin of the text to understand and evaluate the persuasive power of its argumentation. It asks, "What does the text do to those who subject themselves to its worldview?" A critical scientific rhetoric-analytic investigates the persuasive powers of a biblical text not only with regard to linguistic conventions, literary style, or the overall composition but also with regard to the interaction between author and addressees, or interpreters and reading public with a view to the socioreligious location and interests of the persuasive process inscribed in a text. Such a rhetorical biblical interpretation thus requires ethical evaluation.

In short, rhetoric as a communicative praxis that articulates interests, values, and visions is not simply another form of literary analysis (Brown, 1987, p. 85). Rather, critical-rhetorical analysis is a means of showing how biblical texts and their interpretations take part in creating and legitimating structures of oppression and dominance or in enacting ethical values, liberating visions, and sociopolitical acts of liberation. The reconceptualization of biblical scholarship as a critical rhetorical-ethical field of study and not simply as a positivist or hermeneutical praxis of interpretation makes available a framework for research that cultivates historical, archaeological, sociological, literary, theological, and other methods of reading but insists on sociopolitical and ethical questions of power as constitutive for the process of interpretation.

A Critical Feminist Hermeneutic-Rhetorical Analytic. A critical feminist rhetorical model of interpretation places wo/men as citizen-subjects, as the "*ekklēsia* of wo/men," into the hermeneutical center. Studies about "women" or "gender" in the Bible are not properly feminist unless they recognize wo/men in religion as historical, cultural, theological, and scientific subjects and agents. A critical feminist model presupposes that wo/men are producers of critical knowledge and thus requires a double paradigm shift in the ethos of biblical studies. It requires that a positivist, allegedly value-neutral objectivist ethos of scholarship and kyriocentric linguistically based cultural ethos be replaced with a feminist rhetorical paradigm of biblical studies.

Such a critical hermeneutic-rhetorical model of biblical studies is transdisciplinary. It seeks not only to integrate the insights of philology, classics, archaeology, sociology, anthropology, ethnography, epistemology, and historiography but also to recognize the fundamental feminist criticism of these academic disciplines and their feminist reconceptualizations. A critical feminist rhetorical analysis pays special attention to the corruption and ideologically alienating power of speech acts. Its fundamental methodological insight recognizes the andro/kyriocentric (male/lord-centered) functions of language as follows:

- Grammatically andro/kyriocentric language claims to be generic-inclusive language. It mentions wo/men only when they create difficulties, when they are the exception to the rule, or when they are occasionally referred to by name. At all other times, wo/men are subsumed under grammatically masculine expressions such as congressman, postman, chairman, or brother.

- Grammatically andro/kyriocentric language thus does not describe and reflect reality, but regulates and rhetorically constructs it. This function of andro-kyriocentric language has far-reaching consequences for the writing of history. Not only are wo/men historically marginalized or entirely written out of historical sources by androcentric texts, but they are also doubly marginalized by andro/kyriocentric models of reconstruction and eliminated from history altogether. Furthermore, andro-kyriocentric language is not reflective but active-performative. It simultaneously creates and shapes the symbolic worlds it pretends simply to represent.

- Andro/kyriocentric language is always already political and normative. It shapes and is shaped by existing concepts of reality and relations of domination. Andro-kyriocentric language serves hegemonic interests, and, in turn, hegemonic interests determine the content of andro-kyriocentric language. Hence an intra- and intertextual analysis of language and text is insufficient. It must be corrected by a critical, systematic analysis of religio-political structures of domination that perpetuate violence and exclusion.

- Andro-kyriocentric language and knowledge of the kyriarchal world are thus rhetorical. That is, they have been articulated by particular people for a particular group of readers, and they work with particular articulated or suppressed interests and goals. Since all the texts of the Bible and all knowledge of the world are both rhetorical and political, it is possible to change the cultural and religious frames of reference and constructs that are constantly reinscribed by such texts.

In light of this analysis, a critical feminist hermeneutic-rhetorical approach, therefore, must reject the linguistic immanentism of the New Criticism that emerged in biblical studies in the 1970s and the linguistic positivism of historical and theological criticism. Biblical criticism has remained in the captivity of empiricist-positivist science for far too long. Rhetorical criticism in biblical studies also shares in this captivity insofar as it has spent much of its energy in applying and reinscribing ancient rhetorical methods, disciplinary technology, terminological stylistics, and the scattered prescriptions of oratorical handbooks of antiquity into biblical texts. Most importantly, by reviving the technologies of ancient rhetoric, rhetorical biblical criticism has failed to develop a sociopolitical critical rhetoric of inquiry.

In contrast to these tendencies, Wayne Booth, in his work *The Rhetoric of Fiction* (1973), distinguishes between the actual author/reader and the implied author/reader and, in his later work, calls for a revived ethical and political criticism within literary criticism (Booth, 1982). The implied author is not the real author, but rather the image or picture that the reader will construct gradually in the process of reading the work. In other words, in the process of reading a biblical text the interpreter follows the directives of the inscribed author, who is not identical with the "real" author. These directives instruct the interpreter in understanding the original recipients' reactions to the writing. Since many things are presupposed, left out, or unexplained in a text, the audience must in the process of reading "supply" the missing information in line with the rhetorical directives of the speaker/writer. Historical critical scholars seek to "supply" such information generally in terms of the history of religions, including Judaism, while preachers and Bible-readers usually do so in terms of contemporary contexts, values, life, and psychology. For instance, readers obviously follow the directives of the implied author in understanding the Corinthian Christians as "others" of Paul or as his "opponents" when they characterize the Corinthians as foolish, immature, arrogant, divisive, libertine enthusiasts, or boasting spiritualists who misunderstood the preaching of Paul in terms of libertine enthusiasts or Gnostics.

To resist the rhetoric of the Pauline text, it becomes necessary to assess critically Paul's rhetoric in terms of its function for early Christian self-understanding and community by utilizing a four-stage critical rhetorical analysis (Schüssler Fiorenza, 2000). Such an analysis begins by identifying the rhetorical interests, interpretive models, and social locations of contemporary interpretation. Secondly, this rhetorical analysis delineates the rhetorical arrangement, interests, and modifications introduced by the author in order to elucidate them. Thirdly, it needs to establish the rhetorical situation of the text. Finally, it must reconstruct the possible historical situation and symbolic universe of the writer/speaker and the recipients/audience. Using such a critical rhetorical process of interpretation, the letter to the Corinthians is revealed not as the story of Paul but rather as the story of the Corinthian *ekklēsia* to which Paul's rhetoric is to be understood as an active response. The nature of rhetoric as political discourse therefore necessitates critical assessment and ethical evaluation.

The goal of critical feminist rhetorical biblical studies is to engender a paradigm shift that conceptualizes biblical studies as a rhetoric and ethics of inquiry intended to engender change and transformation. According to Thomas Kuhn, a new scientific paradigm can only rival the existing paradigms if it produces not only new knowledge but also new institutions (Kuhn, 1962). If the critical feminist paradigm of rhetorical biblical studies should gain sufficient strength to change the discourses of the discipline, then we will need to find ways to better institutionalize this emancipatory scholarship.

Feminist Hermeneutic-Rhetorical Criticism as Public Discourse. If biblical scholarship would abandon its centuries-old prejudice that regards rhetoric as "mere" rhetoric, as a technical means, style, or eloquence, and instead adopt an understanding of rhetoric as "the power to persuade and convince through argumentation," it would be able to analyze the process of communication anew as a powerful process of rhetorical action. Such an analysis could direct its attention, for example, to how a text constructs its arguments, to the power relationships in which a text attempts to intervene, and to the ways the interpretive discourse itself attempts to influence the social circumstances of which it is a part. A critical feminist rhetorical analysis not only aims to uncover the means by which authors and interpreters seek to convince and motivate their readers, but it also interrogates the structures of domination inscribed in the text and their functions in particular rhetorical situations and particular sociohistorical locations.

With reader-response criticism, a critical feminist-hermeneutic-rhetorical criticism agrees that none of the four text-immanent factors—author, addressee, rhetorical situation, and symbolic world—are identical with the actual, historically real author, addressee(s), rhetorical situation, or symbolic world of the text (Schüssler Fiorenza, 1999, pp. 105–128). However, neither are these elements to be understood as purely fictional. Rather, they must have a relationship to the reality about which the text speaks if communication should be successful and persuasive.

If someone presents a rhetorical discourse, according to classical rhetoric, s/he must not only decide what questions and themes s/he will address and what position s/he will take, but s/he must also establish the tenor and goal of her rhetorical intervention. This often requires a mixture of genres of discourse. According to classical rhetoric, the persuasive power of an argument is determined by its ethos, pathos, and logos. Ethos and pathos must be at work throughout the whole speech, but ethos is in play especially at the beginning of the discourse and pathos at the end.

Debates in public democratic gatherings, arguments in legal proceedings, and hymnal compositions celebrating heroes and heroines as well as Gods and Goddesses, are the originating locations of classical rhetoric and are shaped by the political-public pragmatic situations in which they arise. A critical

hermeneutic-rhetorical analytic seeks to discern not only the rhetorical stylistic means, but also especially the ideological practices and persuasive strategies of a text. It sees the text as a discursive interaction with its sociopolitical-religious locations, authors, hearers, and rhetorical situations. A critical hermeneutic-rhetorical analytic has its social location in communities of interpretation that critically investigate power relationships and seek to transform them.

Critical hermeneutic-rhetorical analysis understands the text neither as a window into reality nor as a double mirror for self-reflection, but rather as a political discourse that both reveals its perspective power and remains bound to the ideological functions embedded within its contexts. Unlike a formalistic and positivist scientific reading of the Bible, a critical-emancipatory rhetoric joins the theologies of liberation in insisting that the context is just as important as the text. What we see always depends on where we stand. The social location and context of the interpreter determine how s/he sees the world, perceives reality, or reads biblical texts. Therefore, the turn to ethics and ideology critique is of central importance for an emancipatory-rhetorical paradigm.

Contestations over the relationship between rhetoric and morality have occurred throughout the history of rhetoric. In the modern era, however, scholars have tended to adopt individualistic and privatized models of interpretation instead of creating a public space for a biblical rhetoric that articulates, applies, and enriches ethics and morality through public argument. A critical feminist hermeneutics that understands itself as a rhetorical-ethical discursive praxis therefore needs to replace objectivistic, positivistic, and apolitical methods of interpretation as still often practiced by dominant biblical scholarship with critical-rhetorical investigations. It needs to be interested in articulating a critical, historical-cultural, and religio-political scientific consciousness.

Language and Ideology. Hermeneutic-rhetorical analysis is thus best understood as an analysis and critique of language and ideology. Relationships of domination and power produce distorted forms of communication and result in the self-deception of scholars who are unaware of their own interests, needs, and perceptions of the social and religious worlds. Ideological-rhetorical criticism understands language as a means of inscribing forms of power in contexts of meaning and significance. Studying ideologies therefore does not mean merely analyzing a particular type of discourse but also means investigating methods of interpretation and bestowals of meaning that serve either to maintain kyriarchal relationships or to undermine them.

According to John B. Thompson, ideology works through three strategies or methods of operation (Thompson, 1984, p. 254). The first strategy explains the legitimacy of kyriarchy on the basis of tradition—for example the argument that Jesus and the apostles did not ordain any woman, although it is known that Jesus did not ordain anyone. The second strategy conceals kyriarchal relationships and keeps them from being known. It speaks of gender or femininity in dualistic terms but not of the multiplicative structures of kyriarchy, or argues that woman's natural way of being is that of selfless service and motherhood. This strategy prevents the foundations of society, religion, or scholarship from being critically analyzed and called into question. The third strategy in turn reifies and naturalizes social processes and attitudes.

Ideology creates the self-concept of oppressed people and intensifies it. It determines the consciousness of people who thereby internalize their subordinated position either as natural and inborn or as willed by God. An emancipatory rhetorical analysis of andro-kyriocentric biblical texts therefore demands not only cultural awareness and ideology critique but also a critical ethics of interpretation.

As a strategy for undermining oppressive ideologies, rhetoric as an intersubjective democratic process is ethical in a twofold sense. First, it opens up the author's range of realities and the methods she chooses for describing that reality. Second, it offers readers a choice in place of a total and necessary acceptance. Truth, when rhetorically established, presumes freedom of choice and the apprehension of alternative realities. An intersubjective democratic ethics understands "world, truth, and reality" as rhetorically-linguistically established and as the responsibility of those who act. Since the turn to ethics has made it clear that morality, truth, vision, and the knowledge of a good life are rhetorically-linguistically constructed and conveyed, biblical scholarship must develop both an ethics of life and an ethics of interpretation.

Ethics of Interpretation. An ethics of interpretation, which sees texts as rhetorical practices of communication, cannot confine itself to an exegesis of the text, but must also be critically responsible—ethically, politically, and theologically—for its own methods of interpretation, goals, and interests. Such an ethical-rhetorical paradigm of interpretation sees objectivity and method differently. In a scholarly-positivistic paradigm, methods are understood as techniques, rules, instructions, or prescriptions, while an ethical-rhetorical paradigm of interpretation sees them as questions to be asked or perspectives to be clarified.

Since biblical scholarship is at home in the kyriarchal institutions of academic and religious institutions, feminist biblical interpretation cannot simply assume that biblical research produces knowledge that liberates and transforms and serves the "good life" of wo/men. Instead, it must critically examine all claims of knowledge to see if they interrupt or further inscribe the interests of dominant powers. Therefore, an ethics of interpretation insists that all scientific methods, proposals, and results must be subjected to an ethical-rhetorical analysis and be examined to see how and whether they serve to continue discrimination or open up hermeneutical visions of a good life for all without exception.

Thus, an emancipatoryrhetorics and ethics of interpretation open up the possibility for, and points the way toward, a scientific interpretation that can take responsibility for the impact of the Bible on the well-being of the cosmopolis. As a result, ethics and political responsibility become integral components of textual interpretation and historical reconstruction. If biblical scholarship is understood as a rhetorical and communicative praxis, then its task is to analyze and demonstrate how biblical texts and their present-day interpretations are part of political and religious discourses that are always involved in power structures and thus require ethical and political critique. To enable such a democratic process of ethical adjudication and to protect the understanding of scripture from being coopted by fundamentalist literalism or academic positivism, it is necessary to articulate a radical democratic hermeneutic-rhetorical criticism that engenders such critical evaluations and adjudications.

This conceptualization of feminist hermeneutic-rhetorical criticism challenges biblical scholars to pay attention not only to the biblical text in its historical-cultural contexts but also to the cultural-political contexts in which it is interpreted today. Since biblical scholarship—feminist or not—has primarily focused on ancient texts and their sociocultural contexts, very little work has been done to analyze the effective power of biblical texts in contemporary situations (see Schüssler Fiorenza, 2001).

In contrast, feminist rhetorical criticism, situated in writing and composition departments, has not only explored archival and historical rhetoric but also the intersections of rhetorical practices, theories, and pedagogies in different cultural contexts today. Most likely due to the split between biblical studies and theological/religious studies that determines its socio-academic location, feminist biblical criticism has not sufficiently developed trans-disciplinary research and reading methods for contemporary interpretation. Nor have we developed a comparative scriptures criticism that would explore the articulation of a feminist critical hermeneutics in different religions. In addition, we lack critical ethnographic studies concerning how wo/men read and use the Bible or other sacred scriptures today. Consequently, much critical feminist work remains to be done in the future.

[See also Feminism, subentries on First-Wave Feminism, and Second-Wave Feminism; Gender; Historical-Critical Approaches; Intersectional Studies; Patriarchy/Kyriarchy; and Reader-Oriented Criticism.]

BIBLIOGRAPHY

Baron, Dennis. *Grammar and Gender*. New Haven, Conn.: Yale University Press, 1986.

Bernstein, Richard. "What Is the Difference that Makes a Difference? Gadamer, Habermas, and Rorty." In *Hermeneutics and Modern Philosophy*, edited by Brice R. Wachterhauser, pp. 343–376. Albany: State University of New York Press, 1986.

Booth, Wayne C. "Freedom of Interpretation: Bakhtin and the Challenge of Feminist Criticism." *Critical Inquiry* 9 (1982): 45–76.

Brown, Richard Harvey. *Society as Text: Essays on Rhetoric, Reason, and Reality*. Chicago: University of Chicago Press, 1987.

Code, Lorraine. *Rhetorical Spaces: Essays on Gendered Locations*. New York: Routledge, 1995.

Dolmage, Jay. "Metis, Mêtis, Mestiza, Medusa: Rhetorical Bodies across Rhetorical Traditions." *Rhetoric Review* 28, no. 1 (2009): 1–28.

Gadamer, Hans Georg. *Truth and Method*. New York: Continuum, 1993.

Hester Amador, J. David. *Academic Constraints in Rhetorical Criticism of the New Testament: An Introduction to a Rhetoric of Power*. Sheffield, U.K.: Sheffield Academic Press, 1999.

Johnson-DeBaufre, Melanie. "Texts and Readers, Rhetorics, and Ethics." In *Feminist Biblical Studies in the Twentieth Century: Scholarship and Movement*, edited by Elisabeth Schüssler Fiorenza, pp. 217–231. Atlanta: Society of Biblical Literature, 2014.

Kuhn, Thomas S. *The Structure of Scientific Revolutions*. Chicago: University of Chicago Press, 1962.

Lucaites, John Louis, Celeste Michelle Condit, and Sally Caudill, eds. *Contemporary Rhetorical Theory: A Reader*. New York: Guilford, 1999.

Martin, Troy W., ed. *Genealogies of New Testament Rhetorical Criticism*. Minneapolis: Fortress, forthcoming.

Nelson, John S., Allan Megill, and Donald N. McCloskey, eds. *The Rhetoric of the Human Sciences: Language and Argument in Scholarship and Public Affairs*. Madison: University of Wisconsin Press, 1987.

Penner, Todd, and Caroline Vander Stichele, eds. *Mapping Gender in Ancient Religious Discourses*. Biblical Interpretation 84. Leiden, The Netherlands: Brill, 2007.

Richards, Jennifer. *Rhetoric: The New Critical Idiom*. New York: Routledge, 2008.

Schell, Eileen E., and K. J. Rawson, eds. *Rhetorica in Motion: Feminist Rhetorical Methods and Methodologies.* Pittsburgh, Pa.: University of Pittsburgh Press, 2010.

Schüssler Fiorenza, Elisabeth. *In Memory of Her: A Feminist Theological Reconstruction of Christian Origins.* New York: Crossroad, 1983.

Schüssler Fiorenza, Elisabeth. *Rhetoric and Ethic: The Politics of Biblical Studies.* Minneapolis: Fortress, 1999.

Schüssler Fiorenza, Elisabeth. *Wisdom Ways: Introducing Feminist Biblical Interpretation.* Maryknoll, N.Y.: Orbis, 2001.

Schüssler Fiorenza, Elisabeth. *Transforming Vision: Explorations in Feminist Theology.* Minneapolis: Fortress, 2011.

Shapiro, Susan E. "Rhetoric as Ideology Critique: The Gadamer-Habermas Debate Reinvented." *Journal of the American Academy of Religion* 62, no. 1 (1994): 123–150.

Thompson, John B. *Studies in the Theory of Ideology.* Cambridge, U.K.: Polity, 1984.

Trible, Phyllis. *Rhetorical Criticism: Context, Method, and the Book of Jonah.* Minneapolis: Fortress, 1994.

Wire, Antoinette Clark. *The Corinthian Women Prophets: A Reconstruction through Paul's Rhetoric.* Minneapolis: Fortress, 1990.

Elisabeth Schüssler Fiorenza

S

SAME-SEX RELATIONS

This entry contains six subentries: Hebrew Bible; Greek World; Roman World; New Testament; Early Judaism; *and* Early Church.

Ancient Near East

See Gender and Sexuality: Ancient Near East.

Hebrew Bible

Same-sex relations existed in ancient Israel as attested by biblical laws that attempt to regulate and stories that seem to admit them. The homoerotic, however, often remains veiled because the text is not sexually explicit.

Affirmative Case for Same-Sex Relations. A biblical case affirming same-sex relations must examine creation and the putative "gender" of God. Although Hebrew grammar refers to God with masculine possessive suffixes, pronouns, and verb forms, the Bible hides God's genitals (Exod 33:18–23) and grammatical gender is not always used consistently. Sometimes God displays feminine attributes (Isa 66:13). In the first creation story God creates humanity in his image (Gen 1:27): "In the image of God he created

them [lit. him]; / male and female he created them." This poem places male *and* female in parallel with the image of God, suggesting divine gender is androgyne (male + female). Nevertheless, the hiddenness of God's genitals leaves indeterminate the question of gender. Thus, the four genders understood by early Rabbis (male, female, androgyne [*m. Bik.* 1:5], and indeterminate [not male, not female; *m. ʿArak.* 1:1]) are present in God. Any person of any gender stands in same-gendered (homophilic) and cross-gendered (heterophilic) relationship to the Deity who contains all genders and no gender. Might gendered human relations reflect the variety of divine-human relations?

Jay Michaelson (2011, p. 32) argues that same-sex sexual relations are part of creation. God "spread out the earth and what comes from it" (Isa 42:5), including numerous species that exhibit same-sex relations. Likewise, God creates the 1.7 percent of humans who are intersex (Mollenkott, 2001, p. 40), calling the whole of creation "very good" (Gen 1:31). The Deity gives life and breath and pours out God's "spirit upon *all* flesh" (Joel 2:28; 3:1 [Heb.], emphasis mine).

The Traditionalist Case against Same-Sex Relations. The traditionalist view is that same-sex relations are forbidden in the Hebrew Bible. The strongest evidence for this view is found in two legal prohibitions in Leviticus 18:22 and 20:13 and the "prime directive" of Genesis 1:22, 28, and 9:1, 7, "reproduce and multiply." Following Marvin Ellison (2004, pp. 67–72), several presuppositions undergird this view: (1) a binary biosex/gender framework where "opposites attract," which depends on (2a) gender hierarchy in a patriarchal society or (2b) gender complementarity where gendered roles are different but significant; (3a) that same-sex relations are gender nonconforming (where partners play "active" or "passive" roles contrary to gendered sexual norms) or (3b) perverse; and (4) a heterosexual/homosexual duality. The Hebrew Bible, when read closely and inductively, brings into question these presuppositions. The "prime directive," as affirmative law, does not exclude nonreproductive sexual relations. Indeed, the Song of Songs celebrates sex.

Sexual Landscapes. The biblical landscape of sex and sexuality differs from modern "Western" sensibilities. "Homo-" and "heterosexuality" are nineteenth-century coinages. The Hebrew Bible views sexual relations as behaviors ranged on a scale. At one end five behaviors—incest within certain relations, adultery, sex with menstruants, (metaphorical) sexual relations with divine beings, and bestiality—are forbidden. Of these, three behaviors draw the death penalty—adultery (Lev 20:10), four kinds of incest (Lev 20:11–14), and bestiality (Lev 20:15–16). At the opposite end, sexual relations in marriage are celebrated, including levirate "marriages" and polygamous relations. Between these two poles, sex with prostitutes, premarital heterosex, and sex by force are reprehended but not categorically forbidden; sex with slaves is implicitly permitted. Nearly all sexual relations cause temporary ritual impurity (Lev 15:2, 18). However, two nondischarging women after their period of "cleansing" (i.e., nonmenstruating, nonhypermenorrheic, or nonpostpartum) would be an exception. Sexual relations are also regulated by social class (Lev 21:7–15; Lev 19:20–22; Deut 21:10–16) and location (Deut 22:23–27).

Key Texts and Documents. Biblical narratives concerning same-sex relations include the Noah and Ham story (Gen 9:20–27) with its inner-biblical commentaries (Gen 19:30–38; Lev 18:3, 6–8; Hab 2:15; Lam 4:21); the incident at Sodom (Gen 19:1–11), its parallel story in Judges (Judg 19:15–25), and its inner-biblical exegesis (e.g., Isa 1:9–11, 3:8–9; Jer 23:14; Ezek 16:46–50; Job 31:31–32); Ehud and Eglon (Judg 3:12–30); Deborah and Jael/Yael (Judg 4—5); David, Jonathan, and Saul (1 Sam 18—2 Sam 1); Ruth and Naomi; Temple *qĕdēšîm* (1 Kgs 14:24, 15:12, 22:46 [v. 47 Heb.]; 2 Kgs 23:7); and the eunuchs in Esther (chs. 1–2, 4, 6–7) and Daniel (chs. 1 and 3). Key legal texts include Leviticus chapters 15, 18, and 20 (especially vv. 18:3, 6–8, 14, 22; 20:13) and Deuteronomy 23:10–15, 18–19; from ancient Near Eastern law: Hittite Law [HL] §§ 189–190 (ca. 1650–1180 B.C.E.) and Middle Assyrian Laws [MAL] A 19–20 (ca. 1076 B.C.E.). From biblical poetry, key texts include the "sex-positive" Song of Songs.

Homoeroticism in the Biblical World. The Hebrew Bible gives little attention to homoeroticism. Possible texts include the story of Sodom in Genesis 19, alleged prohibitions of homosexual relations at Leviticus 18:22 and 20:13, "cross-dressing" at Deuteronomy 22:5, the seduction between Ehud and Eglon (Judg 3:12–30), and passages thought to address ritual male prostitution (1 Kgs 14:24, 15:12, 22:46 [v. 47 Heb.]; 2 Kgs 23:7). The translation of *qĕdēšîm* as "male prostitutes" is unsustainable (Stone, 2006, pp. 234–235). Although it is difficult to read "silence" or sexual innuendo, the fact that biblical texts only explicitly treat cases at behavioral boundaries (rape, relations in the royal court, incests) suggests the central issue of permission is not in question.

Lesbian, gay, bisexual, and transgender and queer biblical interpreters have advanced alternative interpretations for the passages above and offered homoerotic readings of David and Jonathan and lesbian readings of Ruth and Naomi. If one construes the relative silence of the Hebrew Bible to mean that same-sex relations were not the most important matter or not aberrant except in boundary cases, then "traditionalists" are too exuberant in their readings. Paradoxically, they also fail to recognize all the prohibitive texts (Lev 18:6–7, 14).

First boundary case—rape. The "parade" boundary case is the story of Sodom in Genesis 19:1–11. Although within the story the men of Sodom want to rape Lot's male visitors (v. 3), the hearer or reader knows the visitors are angels. The reader who imagines the men of Sodom inviting the visitors for sex play misses the horror of male-on-male rape and angel rape, which inverts the hospitality of Abraham and Lot. Hospitality may also motivate the Ephraimite in Gibeah, who takes in the Levite and his second-rank wife (Judg 19:15–21). In this parallel story, the men of Gibeah demand the Levite for sex, but are satisfied when he pushes his secondary wife outside. These men rape her all night. The "outrage at Gibeah" is a partial commentary on Genesis 19, stressing the woman's rape and not the male object of initial desire (vv. 22–25). One might say, from a modern perspective, that the rapists of Gibeah were "bisexual" if crimes of violence were about sex. Inner-biblical readers of Genesis 19 stress quite different matters from contemporary readers. When Isaiah alludes to Sodom, he sees hypocrisy (1:9) and public avowal of sin (3:9); Jeremiah, adultery and false-dealing (23:14); and Ezekiel, the Sodomites' offense against hospitality as arrogant neglect of the poor and needy (16:49).

Genesis 19, as a story of an attempt to rape angels, resonates with the picture of "sons of god" cohabiting with "daughters of men" (Gen 6:1–4), the prohibitions of metaphorical "whoring" after ghosts and spirits in Leviticus 20:6, and the sexual innuendos associated with passing "seed" to Molekh (Lev 18:21 with v. 20). Concern about divine-human sex appears elsewhere in the ancient Near East: Gilgamesh is the fruit of sexual congress between a human and a goddess, but spurns relations when propositioned by the goddess Ishtar to focus on his intimate male friend, Enkidu.

Second boundary case—royal court. Setting aside the encounter of Eglon with Ehud (Guest, 2006, pp. 162–174; Judg 3:12–30), Jonathan and David provide the parade example of male homophilic or erotic relations in the royal court. Anthony Heacock (2011, pp. 35–39) argues that readers of this story fall into three main camps. (1) The political-theological reader stresses Jonathan's and David's "covenant love" that allows for a transfer of Jonathan's royal inheritance to David. Jonathan subordinates himself to David and so moves along the narrative of David's rise to kingship. (2) The homoerotic interpretation stresses eight texts: 1 Samuel 16:12 (David is handsome); 1 Samuel 18:1–4 (Jonathan loves and covenants with David);

1 Samuel 19:1 (Jonathan delights in David); 1 Samuel 20:17 (Jonathan loves David); 1 Samuel 20:30 (Saul accuses Jonathan of a treacherous relationship with David); 1 Samuel 20:41–42 (the pair kiss and weep with each other); 1 Samuel 23:18 (the two mutually covenant); and 2 Samuel 1:26 (David laments Jonathan's death while praising his love). (3) The homosocial interpretation suggests that "warrior-buddy" friendship stands in the foreground but the texts are ambiguous about a homoerotic dimension. Heacock argues that whether there was "homogenitalic" contact remains unknowable because the text is not explicit. Indeed, Heacock notes that any love relationship between Jonathan and David is weakly evidenced by David. Heacock labels it a "one-sided affair" on Jonathan's part. But Stone (2006, p. 208) contrasts David's and Jonathan's declarations of love with the "heterosexual" acts found in 2 Samuel, all corrupted by power politics.

Ken Stone (2011) suggests that "few parts of the Bible are more beholden to notions of virile manhood than the David narratives" because of their focus on "military valor and traffic in women" (p. 94). At ancient Sparta warrior eroticism was part of the militaristic mix—so possibly here (Stone, 2006, p. 207). Those who read this way often assign Jonathan a passive or feminized role. Tempting as it is to read passive/active sexual roles into the Bible, are they really indigenous to Israel or the ancient Near East? The Middle Assyrian Laws (ca. 1076 B.C.E.) require, "If a man sodomizes [lit. 'fornicates with'] his comrade and they prove the charges against him and find him guilty, they shall sodomize him and they shall turn him into a eunuch" (Roth, 1997, p. 160; Mal A20). Here the "comrade" is a social equal (not a slave or half-free) and implicitly is raped (cf. Mal A19). The punishment includes a "measure for measure" component—to be sodomized—plus castration. The punishment itself shows that male same-sex relations are not automatically forbidden. What is at question here may be a violent crime or a violation of social class rather than someone accepting a passive sexual role. But what is at question for Jonathan and David?

Saul (who also loves David, 1 Sam 16:21) suspects something is amiss when he accuses Jonathan at

1 Samuel 20:30. The phrase attributed to Saul, "the shame of your mother's nakedness," recalls the tradition of Leviticus 18:6–16. "Uncovering nakedness" is technical language for incest and menstrual sex—not all sex—and implies that Jonathan literally or metaphorically commits incest with his brother-in-law David and, by extension, exposes his father and mother.

Third boundary case—incest. There are six major competing interpretations of Leviticus 18:22 and 20:13: (1) These verses condemn all forms of homosexuality for all people, as in, "Do not practice homosexuality" (New Living Translation); (2) they condemn only male homosexuality: "You shall not lie with a male as with a woman"; (3) they condemn only male-male anal intercourse (Boyarin, 1995); (4) they condemn males in the sexually passive role but not males in the active role (Olyan, 1994; cf. Mal A19); (5) they condemn male-on-male incest (Aaron ben-Elijah, 1972; Stewart, 2006); and (6) they apply only to those who live in the Land of Israel because sexual sins pollute the Land—a locational view (Milgrom, 2000; Lev 18:25–28).

Leviticus 18:22 and 20:13 do *not* refer to female same-sex relations. If this is not apparent to the reader from the male-focused context of the text, it should be from the direct object phrase that starts the verse: *wĕʾet-zākār* (with respect to a male). The New Living Translation above overlooks this.

Interpretations of Leviticus 18:22 and 20:13 are troubled by grammatical anomalies in the Hebrew original—by the absence of an "as" (Heb., *k-*) and the disconcerting plural, "lyings of a woman" (*miškĕbê ʾiššâ*), that Ibn Ezra called "the whole interpretive problem." Rashi, in his comment on Leviticus 20:13, emphasizes the shared element that allows an analogy: "penetrating, as one sticks a brush in the tube of paint." But the translators' use of "as" disguises the technical nature of the phrase "lyings of a woman."

That "lyings of a woman" is technical language becomes clear in two ways: first, the singular, "lying of a male," refers to male-female copulation and specifically defloration (e.g., Num 31:17). The similar phrase in the plural, the "lyings of your father," refers to Reuben's lying with his stepmother Bilhah (i.e., male-

female incest [Gen 49:4]). These two phrases refer to male-female sexual relations *from the male perspective*. It is the male who is the sexual subject, including the father whose bed is defiled, although "women's lyings" are mentioned.

This technical argument about the Hebrew phrasing can be coupled with a contextual argument. Leviticus 20:13 nests within a section that requires death for certain incests: verses 11–12, stepmother and daughter-in-law incest; verse 14 taking both mother and daughter sexually. Analogously, verse 13 should be about incest with father, son, and son-in-law, giving us a possible translation for "lyings of a woman" as "male-male incest analogous to male-female incest." As a solution to the grammatical anomaly, the fourteenth-century Karaite, Aaron ben-Elijah offered "incest" (*The Crown of Torah*, 1972).

The problem of reading Leviticus 20:13 as a prooftext in isolation from context is compounded when done with Leviticus 18:22. Its immediate context places it fourth in a summary list of forbidden practices: menstrual sex (v. 19); adultery (v. 20); "seed to [the god] Molekh" (v. 21), and a prohibition of male and female initiated bestiality (v. 23). The earlier part of the chapter consists of incest prohibitions (vv. 6–18) primarily focused on women victimized by males. However, verse 14 specifically forbids incest by the male persona, to whom the commands are addressed, with his paternal uncle. Verse 7 also appears to equate the son's incest of his mother with incest of the father. Verse 6, when read with Leviticus 21:1–3 listing one's near kin, prohibits father-son and brother-brother incest (as well as mother-son, father-daughter, and brother with virgin sister). After this extensive incest list—the largest extant in the ancient world—one expects that in the summative list of sexual sins that follows (i.e., vv. 19–23), incest should also find a place.

Although the diagnostic term *tôʿēbâ* (abhorrence) shows up in verse 22, it also appears in the rhetorical close of the chapter in verses 26, 27, and 29, making it clear that all the sexual behaviors of the chapter are abhorrent. They form a frame with verse 3 that prohibits Israelites repeating the practices of Egypt and Canaan. In Egypt adultery was the "great sin" and brother-sister marriage a common Pharaonic practice. *Tôʿēbâ* can semantically "diagnose" other domains (e.g., idolatry [Deut 13:14–15] and unjust weights and measures [Deut 25:15–16]). However, if *tôʿēbâ* diagnoses all the sexual behaviors of Leviticus 18, why is it repeated in verse 22? Within its ancient (patriarchal) context the key violative relationship is between father and son (Lev 18:6–7). From this all other incests are permutations. Thus, verse 22 recollects and stresses male-male incest.

The reference to Egypt and Canaan signals us to return to their first mention in Genesis 9:22 and 10:6 as sons of Ham and grandsons of Noah. When Noah becomes drunk and passes out, Ham sees his father's nakedness. When Noah awakes and "knew what his youngest son had done to him" (v. 24), he curses his grandson Canaan. The biblical editor places a veil over the scene. But something sexual has happened—something more than a casual view by Ham of Noah's nakedness. He mocks, or gazes too long, or castrates—as suggested by early commentators. Or possibly he has sex with his father or mother. Later we see Lot's daughters incesting their father when he is drunk (Gen 19:30–38). Habbakuk decries getting one's fellow drunk to gaze at him naked (2:15). This very phrase "nakedness of his father" (*ʿerwat-ʾābîw*, Gen 19:22) is echoed by "nakedness of your father" at Leviticus 18:7 (*ʿerwat-ʾābîkâ*) and the repeated use of *ʿerwat* with a kin term for incest throughout verses 7–16. The curse seems out of place—and disproportionate—unless "something was done," as Genesis 9:27 implies. Leviticus 18, with its reference to Ham's son Canaan and reuse of the nakedness language, seems to expand upon a concern about incest in the Noah/Ham story.

The concern for male-male incest also shows up in the only other attested list of forbidden incestuous relationships in ancient Near Eastern law. Hittite Law 189 reads, "If a man sins (sexually) with (his) son, it is an unpermitted sexual pairing [*ḫurkil*]" (lit.). Like Leviticus 18, the list also forbids son-mother, father-daughter, and, at HL 190, son-stepmother incest. Like Leviticus 18:22, it adds a diagnostic term—*ḫurkil*—the Hittite equivalent of *tôʿēbâ*.

Same-sex relations among women. If a veil is drawn over what happens between Noah and Ham or David

and Jonathan, the more so for women. Monique Wittig (1992, p. 32) argues that "it would be incorrect to say that lesbians…live with women, for woman has meaning only in heterosexual systems of thought." Thus a "lesbian-identified hermeneutic…operates from…hetero-suspicion in order to counter the general erasure of women's interests" (Guest, 2006, p. 178), including homoerotic relations. One lesbian response to why women's same-sex relations are not covered in Leviticus is that they have been erased—or that interpretations erase them.

In Judges Deborah and Yael act as subjects. Guest points out that Deborah and Yael meet in a Midrash-like retelling of the story by Sara Maitland. Maitland's women write the "Song of Deborah" for women to sing together when they work, exulting in women's triumphs (p. 180). We need such new Midrashim because what we have in Judges is what "men thought about women rather than a representation of women's authentic lives" (p. 178).

Thus we are left to our imaginations to reconstruct such lives. Did purity restrictions surrounding women's discharges foster relationships when prevented from general social intercourse? Did matriarchs in polygamous households act in solidarity? When women shared work—as in the weaver's workshop (Lev 13:47–58)—was there also intimacy?

The parade example of an intimate women's world is what West calls "the closest physical relationship between women expressed anywhere in the Bible" (2006, p. 191). Ruth pledges to Naomi, "where you lodge, I will lodge; your people shall be my people, and your God my God. Where you die, I will die—there will I be buried" (Ruth 1:16b–17a). Ruth certifies this with an oath: "May the Lord do thus and so to me, and more as well, if even death parts me from you!" (v. 17b). This pledge and oath are richer than those of Jonathan and David (cf. 1 Sam 20:42; 23:18). Ruth names her relationship and stays with Naomi. Naomi takes on the role of mentor, showing Ruth how they should survive and suggesting strategy that provokes Boaz to act as levir. The three form a family. When Ruth has her first child, Naomi becomes co-mother. "A son has been born to Naomi," neighbor women declare when she takes him to her breast (Ruth 4:16–17). Ruth loves Naomi and makes this happen (Ruth 4:15).

Women's same-sex relations are not legally symmetrical with men's. Male sexual discharge (Lev 15:2–18) pollutes on every occasion, including relations with a wife (Lev 15:18). But only *some* vaginal discharges (lochial, menstrual, and dysmenorrheal) ritually pollute. Thus it is possible for women to have sexual relations together when pollution from discharges is not an issue; men cannot. This is one possible reason women's same-sex relations are not included in Leviticus 18:22 and 20:13 when these verses are understood according to their linguistic sense. Boyarin (1995, p. 339) notes the lack of interest by the Babylonian Talmud in female same-sex relations except when it might stimulate women to illicit sex with men (*b. Yebam. 76a; b. Šabb. 65a–b*).

Same-sex relations among eunuchs. The Hebrew Bible and rabbinic literature recognize several categories of individuals that might loosely fall under modern categories of "transgender," "intersexual," or "asexual": eunuchs made or born so, celibates by God's demand (Jer 16:1–2), women or men with incomplete or disabled genitals (Num 5:27; Lev 21:20; Deut 23:1; v. 2 [Heb]), androgynes (ha-Adam), and persons with indeterminate gender (Stewart, 2011, pp. 78–81). Some scholars argue for eunuchs as a "third gender" (West, 2006, p. 280). In Esther and Daniel, communities of eunuchs act in coordination (Esth 1–2; 4; 6–7; Dan 1; 3); thus one could presuppose homosocial relations. Although homoerotic relations are possible for eunuchs, the Bible remains silent about them.

Summary and Conclusion. Within the Hebrew Bible same-sex relations are a bounded practice. They are not permitted as rape or incest, nor are they permitted with numinous beings or beasts. The key forbidden homoerotic relationship is between father and son. Parties to two representative same-sex relationships, whether sexually active or not, make pledges and use "love" to describe how one feels for another: Jonathan for David; David for Jonathan after death; Ruth for Naomi. Although Malachi 2:14 refers to a covenant of marriage, no different-sex characters are shown making similar covenants and pledges

except "Solomon" and the Shulamite in the Song of Songs. The Hebrew Bible tends to draw a veil over homoerotic details, leaving only sexual innuendo or symbolic traces to hint at something more. The boundary cases suggest that same-sex practices were permitted or overlooked in the biblical eras. In the history of reception of the Bible, further controls are put in place.

[*See also* Creation; Gay Liberation; Gender Transgression, *subentry* Hebrew Bible; Male-Female Sexuality, *subentry* Hebrew Bible; Queer Readings; *and* Sexual Transgression, *subentry* Hebrew Bible.]

BIBLIOGRAPHY

Aaron ben Elijah. *Keter torah: Sefer vayikra* (The Crown of Torah: The Book of Leviticus). Ramleh, Israel: Hayyim ben Yitshaq ha-Levi, 1972. [Hebrew].

Boyarin, Daniel. "Are There Any Jews in 'The History of Sexuality'?" *Journal of the History of Sexuality* 5, no. 3 (1995): 333–355.

Ellison, Marvin M. *Same-Sex Marriage? A Christian Ethical Analysis.* Cleveland, Ohio: Pilgrim, 2004.

Guest, Deryn. "Judges." In *The Queer Bible Commentary*, edited by Deryn Guest, Robert E. Goss, Mona West, and Thomas Bohache, pp. 167–189. London: SCM Press, 2006.

Heacock, Anthony. *Jonathan Loved David: Manly Love in the Bible and the Hermeneutics of Sex.* Sheffield, U.K.: Sheffield Phoenix, 2011.

Michaelson, Jay. *God vs. Gay? The Religious Case for Equality.* Queer Action/Queer Ideas. Boston: Beacon, 2011.

Milgrom, Jacob. *Leviticus 17–22.* Anchor Bible 3A. New York: Doubleday, 2000.

Mollenkott, Virginia Ramey. *Omnigender: A Trans-religious Approach.* Cleveland, Ohio: Pilgrim, 2001.

Nissinen, Marti. *Homoeroticism in the Biblical World: A Historical Perspective.* Minneapolis: Fortress, 1998.

Olyan, Saul M. "'And with a Male You Shall Not Lie the Lying Down of a Woman': On the Meaning and Significance of Leviticus 18:22 and 20:13." *Journal of the History of Sexuality* 5, no. 2 (1994): 179–206.

Roth, Martha T. *Law Collections from Mesopotamia and Asia Minor.* Atlanta: Scholars Press, 1997.

Stewart, David Tabb. "Leviticus." In *The Queer Bible Commentary*, edited by Deryn Guest, Robert E. Goss, Mona West, and Thomas Bohache, pp. 77–104. London: SCM Press, 2006.

Stewart, David Tabb. "Sexual Disabilities in the Hebrew Bible." In *Disability Studies and Biblical Literature,* edited by Candida R. Moss and Jeremy Schipper, pp. 67–87. New York: Palgrave Macmillan, 2011.

Stone, Ken. "Queer Reading between Bible and Film: *Paris Is Burning* and the 'Legendary Houses' of David and Saul." In *Bible Trouble: Queer Readings and the Boundaries of Biblical Scholarship,* edited by Teresa Hornsby and Ken Stone, pp. 75–98. Semeia Studies 67. Atlanta: Society of Biblical Literature, 2011.

Stone, Ken. "1 and 2 Samuel" and "1 and 2 Kings." In *The Queer Bible Commentary,* edited by Deryn Guest, Robert E. Goss, Mona West, and Thomas Bohache, pp. 195–250. London: SCM Press, 2006.

West, Mona. "Ruth" and "Esther." In *The Queer Bible Commentary,* edited by Deryn Guest, Robert E. Goss, Mona West, and Thomas Bohache, pp. 190–194, 278–285. London: SCM Press, 2006.

Wittig, Monique. *The Straight Mind and Other Essays.* New York: Harvester Wheatsheaf, 1992.

David Tabb Stewart

Greek World

Greece of the archaic, classical, and Hellenistic periods featured a widespread, but not universally practiced culture of same-sex love and sexuality.

Varieties. The Greek language had no one term corresponding to the modern "homosexuality" (Halperin, 1990, pp. 15–53). What we would now cover with that designation comprised at least three separately constructed but in some respects parallel sets of behavior: (1) pederasty, referring to transitional relationships usually between young men prior to the age of marriage and adolescent boys; (2) age-equal relationships either among adolescents or, less commonly, among adult men; and (3) lesbian relations either between adult women (as seen on several vase paintings) or between a mature woman and an adolescent girl prior to marriage (as implied in the poetry of Sappho). Most of our literary sources, which are written from the standpoint of elite adult men, emphasize pederasty, but the age boundaries at which one ceased to be the younger "beloved" (*erōmenos*) and became a more assertive "lover" (*erastēs*) are not clearly defined: beard growth marked the end of physical attractiveness for many poetic sources, but we also know cases of men who shaved their beards to remain youthful looking (Agathon, Alcibiades), and vase painting frequently shows unbearded youths actively courting either a younger adolescent or another youth at approximately the same stage of physical development. Relationships between adult men are far less common in the visual record, but a number of literary texts suggest that some adult men did enjoy adopting the passive sexual position relative to another adult man (Ps.-Aristotle, *Problems* 4.16; Caelius Aurelianus, *Chronic Disorders* 4.9). Perhaps the most famous example of such a relationship is that between the Iliadic heroes Achilles and Patroclus, which came to be interpreted as homosexual in fifth-century B.C.E. and later sources (Aeschylus, *Myrmidons*; Plato, *Symposium* 179e–180b); such a lifelong relationship also appears to have bound together the historical Pausanias and Agathon, who appear together as a couple in both Plato's *Protagoras* (dramatic date of 431 B.C.E.) and *Symposium* (416 B.C.E.), and left Athens together after 411 (Aelian, *VH* 2.21).

Origins and Social Contexts. Some scholars trace the origins of pederasty back to Indo-European or Minoan origins, based on anthropological constructions of pederasty as an initiatory rite or form of bonding between experienced and neophyte warriors (see Hubbard, 2003, pp. 14–15, 58). The relative paucity of evidence among other early Indo-European cultures weakens the Indo-European genealogy; however, the seventh-century B.C.E. bronze figurines of ithyphallic warriors holding hands, one of visibly shorter stature than the other, does lend some support to those who claim an early Cretan origin. Aristotle (*Politics* 2.10; in support of his view, see Percy, 1996, pp. 59–72) also suggests the practice originated in Crete as a measure for controlling overpopulation, possibly by facilitating a delayed age of marriage for males. This localization of the origin in Crete may be mistaken, but behind it is perhaps a more profound insight about Greece as a whole: poor fertility of the land did impose certain limits on the carrying capacity of the environment, encouraging an adaptive cultural strategy of lower population growth through delayed age of marriage and, in turn, the evolution of alternative sexual outlets for young men and adolescents. In a classic 1907 article, Erich Bethe suggested that it was the highly militarized culture of Sparta, dependent upon strong bonds of mutual support among an elite warrior group, that was the formative influence, and that the early Cretan manifestations of pederasty were derivative of a broader diffusion of Dorian military practice in the southernmost parts of Greece. It should be noted that the earliest datable written evidence for pederasty is found in graffiti carved into a rock face on the island of Thera (Hubbard, 2003, pp. 82–83), which was settled by the Spartans.

It should be noted, however, that both the Kato Syme figurines and the Thera graffiti were not found in archaeological locations that had any particular military significance but near sacred precincts of Hermes (a god of transitions), Aphrodite, and Apollo (associated with male adolescence). Sappho's poetry, also from the seventh century B.C.E., suggests some connection with the cult of the love goddess Aphrodite on the island of Lesbos (see especially frags. 1, 2, 94.21–22, 96.26–30 V); other poems emphasize themes of marriage or loss of formerly beloved girls to marriage, as if the homoerotic liaisons in Sappho's circle fulfilled a social function of educating girls into a romantic and musical sophistication that would make them attractive as future brides. Some critics have proposed a similar scenario behind the equally archaic *Maidens' Song* of Alcman (frag. 1 PMG), a long lyrical narrative and encomium performed by a chorus of Spartan girls as part of a ceremony worshipping the goddess Dawn (also invested with erotic powers in Greek mythology), but there is much about this complex and fragmentary poem that remains disputed. At the very least, the poem, including allusions to the girls' mutual attractions, seems designed to showcase their beauty before an appreciative public that might include male suitors and their families.

The growing institutionalization of athletics in the seventh and sixth centuries should be viewed as a corresponding opportunity for displaying the physical excellence and erotic appeal of boys and young men (see Scanlon, 2002). Athletic nudity and the addition of a special division of competition for boys both date to this period. One of the original uses of commemorative statuary in the archaic period was to preserve for eternity the idealized nude form of a victorious athlete in his physical prime. Vase painting also featured young athletes as a favored theme, sometimes accompanied by either age-equal or clearly older male admirers; some vases suggest that athletic trainers had an erotic interest in their pupils, raising the possibility that pederastic motives may have led some to sponsor the training and travel of talented young athletes whose families were not wealthy enough to pay for it (Hubbard, 2005). Other vases suggest that the gym was a place where pederasts might encounter and court youths they fancied. Graffiti written by the lovers of competing athletes decorated a tunnel leading into the stadium at Nemea, the site of one of the four major pan-Hellenic athletic festivals (Hubbard, 2003, p. 84).

The drinking party, or symposium, was another context of male socialization that facilitated erotic bonds between older and younger men. Only here the qualities that made a youth desirable extended beyond the merely physical to include musical and verbal aptitude, as well as the self-confidence and poise to consort on an equal footing with men of more experience and wisdom. The rather substantial collection of wisdom poetry attributed to the sixth-century Megarian aristocrat Theognis consists of political and social advice directed by the poet to his sometimes unfaithful beloved Cyrnus; these poems, like most Greek elegy and monodic lyric, were intended for performance and re-performance at elite symposia. Fifth-century vase painting often shows men and youths reclining together comfortably on a single banqueting couch. Such sympotic scenes also reveal the presence of much younger, even preadolescent boys as naked servants serving the men wine or wiping them with sponges; the boys' nudity and the evident attention that the men pay them suggest that the symposium could also play host to a less pedagogical and more hedonistic flirtation with slave boys, as also documented in the famous anecdote about the tragic poet Sophocles kissing the wine boys of Ion of Chios (Athenaeus 603d–604f).

Evaluation and Social Criticism. Some critics (e.g., Halperin, 1990, pp. 15–53, basing his views on the earlier work of Foucault [1985]) have viewed pederasty through the same lens as male-female and master-slave relationships, that is, as an unequal pairing between a privileged citizen male (in the active, penetrative position) and a social inferior at his disposal (in a passive, penetrated position). However, this view may be too much influenced by negative modern constructions of child sexual abuse. It is best to evaluate the institution of pederasty within the terms and constructs that ancient sources themselves set up for its description. Pederastic verse describes the pursuing lover as the one who is "yoked" (Theognis 1357–1358), "dragged" (Theognis 371–372), or "burned" (Theognis 1359–1360) by passion. Vase painting never shows boys engaging in oral sex, shows anal sex only among age equals, but more often depicts men looking at boys' genitals or fondling them, as if to suggest that their chief interest was in appreciating boys' growing masculinity. The most intimate acts that we find in clearly pederastic scenes are kissing and intercrural intercourse, in which the man bends himself rather awkwardly to rub between a boy's thighs (see Lear and Cantarella, 2008, pp. 106–138); these scenes contrast markedly with depictions of heterosexual coitus, which place the man in a much more dominant posture.

Literary sources ranging from the elegies of Theognis to Plato's *Symposium* suggest a pedagogical function for pederastic relationships of the best type, although acknowledging that not all pederasty conformed to this ideal. The most common gifts that we see on courtship vases are consistent with a pedagogical intention: lyres (for encouraging musical pursuits), crowns (rewarding athletic or musical talent), fighting cocks (to promote a spirit of unsentimental competition), and wild game (suggesting a shared interest in hunting, culturally coded as an important rite of passage for adolescent males). More broadly, the principal social benefit of pederasty appears to be the assimilation of male adolescents, especially those of elite class, into the pursuits of young gentle-men: masculine activities like hunting, athletics, even gambling and drinking. It should be noted that demographers estimate as many as a third to a half of Athenian boys would have lost their own fathers by the age of eighteen, especially during and after times of war. Pederasty may thus have offered many boys and youths older role models who could, in lieu of a father, oversee and facilitate their entry into the adult community.

This is not to say that pederasty was either practiced or approved universally among the Greeks of the classical period. Plato's *Phaedrus* attributes to the orator Lysias a speech intended to persuade a youth to avoid the company of lovers, who can be so possessive as to manipulate a beloved into dependency or so jealous as to keep him away from the company of other good men. The two literary genres that can be said to appeal most directly to the prejudices of the common man were comedy and forensic oratory: both depict pederasty with suspicion and ridicule, implying its association with prostitution, effeminacy, overindulgence, and upper-class privilege (Hubbard, 1998). Behind both genres lurks the nested premise that all pederasty, inasmuch as it involved giving lavish gifts, was a form of prostitution, thus training boys in the arts of manipulation and bribery.

The orator Aeschines prosecuted his political rival Timarchus in 346 B.C.E. based on what he claims to be a law of Solonic origin barring former male prostitutes from political participation. It is unlikely that the premonetized economy of Solon's period had any clear concept of "male prostitution" in contradistinction to the traditional gift giving that was typical in artistic depictions on black-figured vases of the sixth century, and in 399 B.C.E. the earlier orator Andocides (1.100–101) briefly mentions this law without identifying it as Solonic, suggesting that he did not regard the law as archaic, but of more recent origin. Our first reference to use of such a law comes in a comic allusion to the demagogue Cleon's erasure of one Grypus/Gryttus from the citizen rolls based on these grounds (Aristophanes, *Knights* 875–880, dated to 424 B.C.E.). The law likely emerged in the context of Athens's attempts in the mid-fifth century to redefine eligibility for citizenship; being a prostitute, male or female, would be classed as more befitting the status of a metic (a migrant to Attica, holding no citizen rights). Aeschines's apparently successful prosecution of Timarchus produced no clear evidence of actual prostitution, but inferred it merely from his having consorted with multiple men of varied backgrounds when he was young. That a majority of the large Athenian jury would find this convincing evidence of guilt itself reveals the degree to which negative popular attitudes toward pederasty had developed by this point in Athens's democratic development.

Our literary record of both comedy and forensic oratory begins in the last decades of the fifth-century B.C.E. Interestingly, red-figured vases ceased showing explicit scenes of pederastic courtship (and heterosexual pornography as well) around 460 B.C.E. (Shapiro, 1981), possibly due to the moralizing influence of the austere, personally aloof democratic leader Pericles, who dissociated himself from the city's sympotic culture completely (Plutarch, *Pericles* 7.4–5). Scholars have argued (Hubbard, forthcoming) that Pericles's policy of aggressive expansion of Athens's overseas empire both gave more political influence to the lower classes (who were needed to row the ships) and encouraged a growing birthrate among fully Athenian families (whose children would be needed in loyal service to the Athenian state's increased manpower needs). As we have seen before, postponement of male marriage age was a response to pressures of overpopulation; underpopulation would encourage the opposite move. We do have some evidence of much earlier male marriage ages during the late fifth century (Xenophon, *Symposium* 2.3). Subtle social pressures against sexual alternatives to marital intercourse and procreation would tend to develop in such a demographic and political environment. These could range from a general caution in artistic representations to political attacks on opponents because of wild or self-indulgent sexual behavior when young.

Platonic Love. The examination of pederasty in philosophical literature of the fourth century B.C.E. should be interpreted within the context of the increasingly hostile social and political environment of the time. The trial and death of Socrates in 399 B.C.E., allegedly for "corrupting the youth" (in a nonsexual sense), piqued philosophical discourse about the proper relations between a master and student as well as the legitimacy of pederasty more generally. The setting of early works like Plato's *Lysis* and *Charmides* in private wrestling schools, where men and adolescent boys gathered for intellectual conversation as well as naked exercise, foregrounds the audience of philosophy as exactly the sort of elite young men and boys who traditionally formed pederastic attachments. The ubiquity of male love among this social circle is colorfully portrayed in the opening of the *Charmides*, where the title character's adolescent charm and beauty causes everyone in the room to fall in love with him, including his age-mates, younger boys, and even the elderly Socrates himself, who "catches on fire" when Charmides sits next to him such that he can see into the boy's cloak (155c–e). Although Socrates is constantly surrounded by attractive young males and enjoys their company, he is completely continent with regard to any overt physical act, chiding one of his students for kissing another (Xenophon, *Memorabilia* 1.3.8–14) and refraining from the slightest caress when the brilliant young Alcibiades sleeps with him during a military encampment (Plato, *Symposium* 219b–d).

Plato's *Symposium* is a dialogue in which several characters present their views of love at a dinner party hosted by the tragic poet Agathon to celebrate his first tragic victory in 416 B.C.E. Agathon's lover Pausanias introduces the influential distinction between what he calls a "heavenly [Uranian] Love" and the "common [pandemic] love." The latter is purely physical and can be directed toward either boys or women, whereas the former is a loftier love of character, aiming at improvement and personal growth of the beloved; Pausanias says that this love is best directed toward older boys or young men, who are capable of philosophical education. Critics have sometimes made the mistake of identifying Pausanias's views with mainstream Athenian protocols of behavior, but in fact his view of love, like those of the other characters, is idiosyncratic, reflecting his own love of the now adult but still youthful-looking Agathon, which he defends as based on character and philosophical understanding rather than pure lust. It finds later confirmation in the view of some Stoics, who taught that it was proper to love a youth up to the age of twenty-eight (Athenaeus 13.563e).

Socrates's speech develops Pausanias's dyadic understanding of love into a multitiered philosophical conception, encapsulated in the metaphor of the "ladder" (*Symposium* 211c): love of a person's beautiful body is but the lowest step on the ladder, while love of two or more bodies is the next step, because it allows the mind to conceptualize physical beauty more generally. Yet another step higher is the love of beautiful character (i.e., Pausanias's Uranian love), which at a more general level becomes a technology of producing beautiful characters in many men through education, lawgiving, art, or music, what we might consider sublimation of the erotic instinct. The highest step on the ladder is an appreciation of all forms of beauty, such that one can develop a philosophical understanding of Beauty itself. Erotic love of individual persons is thus useful only inasmuch as it can lead toward a depersonalized philosophical comprehension of the transcendental Idea of Beauty.

Plato's *Phaedrus*, which is generally assumed to be a bit later than the *Symposium*, develops this framework further by postulating love as a remembrance of the soul's prebirth glimpse of transcendental Beauty. Seeing and falling in love with a beautiful boy sparks this long-buried memory of union with the Ideal; souls are imagined as chariots drawn by two horses, one that aims to pull the soul upward toward reunion with this primeval ideal of Beauty and Goodness, and another intemperate horse that merely lunges toward the physical object that awakens our remembrance of Beauty. The skilled charioteer must learn to balance and control these two independent forces. The *Phaedrus* also marks an advance upon the *Symposium* by explaining the reciprocal love that the younger partner bears toward his lover as a mirroring of the lover's excitement (*Phaedrus* 255b–e).

Despite the common usage of "Platonic love" in modern parlance as an expression for a purely nonphysical bond, physical attraction to beauty was certainly the starting point of love in these dialogues, even if its ultimate trajectory is to surpass the attachment to any one human body by engendering contemplation of Beauty at the most generalized level possible. As such, it reflects the protreptic intent of Plato's exoteric writings generally: an inducement to the educated young to pursue the quest for philosophical understanding. In this way, Plato's discussions of male love aim to recuperate the social prestige that pederasty had enjoyed in the archaic and early classical periods by appropriating it for goals of a higher pedagogy.

Homosexuality and "Nature." One of Plato's latest works, the *Laws*, presents the Athenian Stranger voicing a less benign view of pederasty as an act *para physin* (not so much "against Nature," as it is usually translated, but "to the side of Nature," that is, off the road of Nature); he also proposes that it has no role in the ideal state that this dialogue aims to construct (636b–d, 835e–842a). Some critics have seen this view as a shift of attitude toward physical sexuality in Plato's old age; others have suggested that physical consummation of sexual desire with other males was already implicitly censured in the earlier dialogues. However, the Athenian Stranger does not translate the unmediated voice of Plato any more than other characters in his dialogues; his views may rather reflect what Plato saw as the typically "Athenian" judgment of his time, in contrast with the more tolerant approach of the Spartan and Cretan interlocutors, who praised their institutions of male commensality and fraternity. This text nevertheless represents the origin of a negative interpretation of homosexuality as a violation of the natural order, a view that becomes influential on Stoicism of the Roman period and in the writings of Saint Paul.

The "unnatural" character of homosexuality was by no means universally accepted: the pseudo-Aristotelian *Problems* 4.16 proposes that some men enjoy the passive position in anal intercourse because their anatomy is deformed in such a way as to make the anus a seat of pleasure (see also Aristotle, *Nicomachean Ethics* 7.5.3–5). The late Roman medical writer Caelius Aurelianus (*Chronic Disorders* 4.9.134–135) attributes to the pre-Socratic philosopher

Parmenides the explanation that such sexual and gender disorders stem from a failure of the male and female seed to blend properly at the moment of conception (see Hippocrates, *On Regimen* 1.28–29 for a slightly different genetic explanation). The speech of the comic poet Aristophanes in Plato's *Symposium* parodies these medical theories with a colorful myth of sexual preference predetermined at birth, depending upon our genetic descent from primeval ancestors who were double-sexed (male-male, female-female, or male-female). Cumulatively, these texts show that there was a substantial body of opinion that same-sex attraction was a quality endowed to some individuals by natural processes composing our genetic makeup; the same texts, however, consider it a deviation from the normal path of development.

An alternate strategy adopted by some defenders of pederasty was to concede the point that it was not practiced by animals and therefore was not grounded in Nature, but to make a virtue of it by arguing that pederasty was a mark of advanced civilization, a superior invention to improve upon the bare requirements of human subsistence (Lucian, *Erotes* 33–36).

[*See also* Education, *subentry* Greek World; *and* Social Interaction, *subentry* Greek and Roman Worlds.]

BIBLIOGRAPHY

Bethe, Erich. "Die dorische Knabenliebe: Ihre Ethik und ihre Idee." *Rheinisches Museum für Philologie*, n.s., 62 (1907): 438–475.

Brooten, Bernadette J. *Love Between Women: Early Christian Responses to Female Homoeroticism.* Chicago: University of Chicago Press, 1996.

Dover, K. J. *Greek Homosexuality.* Cambridge, Mass.: Harvard University Press, 1978.

Foucault, Michel. *The History of Sexuality.* Vol. 2: *The Use of Pleasure.* Translated by R. Hurley. New York: Pantheon, 1985. English translation of *L'Usage des plaisirs*, first published in 1984.

Halperin, David M. *One Hundred Years of Homosexuality: And Other Essays on Greek Love.* New York: Routledge, 1990.

Hubbard, Thomas K. "Popular Perceptions of Elite Homosexuality in Classical Athens." *Arion*, 3d ser., 6, no. 1 (1998): 48–78.

Hubbard, Thomas K., ed. *Homosexuality in Greece and Rome: A Sourcebook of Basic Documents.* Berkeley: University of California Press, 2003.

Hubbard, Thomas K. "Pindar's *Tenth Olympian* and Athlete-Trainer Pederasty." In *Same-Sex Desire and Love in Greco-Roman Antiquity and in the Classical Tradition of the West*, edited by Beert C. Verstraete and Vernon Provencal, pp. 137–171. Binghamton, N.Y.: Harrington Park, 2005. Part of a special double-issue of the *Journal of Homosexuality* 49, nos. 3–4 (2005).

Hubbard, Thomas K. "Diachronic Parameters of Athenian Pederasty." In *Diachrony: Diachronic Aspects of Ancient Greek Literature and Culture*, edited by José González. Berlin: Walter de Gruyter, forthcoming.

Lear, Andrew, and Eva Cantarella. *Images of Ancient Greek Pederasty: Boys Were Their Gods.* London: Routledge, 2008.

Percy, William Armstrong, III. *Pederasty and Pedagogy in Archaic Greece.* Urbana: University of Illinois Press, 1996.

Rabinowitz, Nancy Sorkin, and Lisa Auanger, eds. *Among Women: From the Homosocial to the Homoerotic in the Ancient World.* Austin: University of Texas Press, 2002.

Scanlon, Thomas F. *Eros and Greek Athletics.* New York: Oxford University Press, 2002.

Shapiro, H. A. "Courtship Scenes in Attic Vase-Painting." *American Journal of Archaeology* 85 (1981): 133–143.

Thomas K. Hubbard

Roman World

Extant sources for same-sex relations, also known as homoerotic activity, in Roman culture are largely produced by and for a small elite of male citizens, and this limited perspective may account for the monolithic view of sexuality preserved both in artistic representations and in an array of legal, scientific, philosophical, and literary texts. As a result, it is difficult to determine the extent to which this perspective represents that of the population as a whole, much less the range of sexual activity that would have taken place in private.

Active versus Passive. In ancient Rome this dominant elite paradigm conceived of erotic attraction and sexual activity as determined less by the biological sex of the object of desire than by the relative social status of each participant. In recent decades, scholars have appealed to a so-called penetration model to explain Roman sexual dynamics: according to this model, every sexual pairing, whether same-sex or opposite-sex, and whether oral, anal, or vaginal, involves partners with diametrically opposed and noninterchangeable roles, one active and insertive, the other passive and receptive. According to this model, the division between insertive and receptive roles tends to be rigid—the ability to penetrate assists in defining the identity of the insertive partner, and vice versa—and the sex of the receptive partners is largely irrelevant. As a result of these key distinctions, modern notions of "homosexuality" or "heterosexuality" become inadequate to describe Roman sexual practice, since these terms presuppose that the biological sex of the actors serves as a defining characteristic of each actor's identity.

The literary persona of the god Priapus has provided scholars with a fitting paradigm for this sexual dynamic. The god's prominent erection underscores the fascination with large penises evidenced elsewhere in the material and textual sources, a fascination that also distinguishes Roman views from Greek, where small penises represent the aesthetic ideal of tender youth, with large penises and erections characterizing the inhuman sexuality of beasts such as satyrs. Roman versions of Priapus employ the phallus to threaten penetration in the vagina, anus, or mouth for those who interlope on his territory. Regardless of the sex of the persons performing the receptive role, they are identified with a subservient status that contributes to their identity in the larger society. Priapus's ithyphallicism has further figurative meaning in the arts as indicating potency of the male not only in the realm of sex, but in those of politics and business as well. To demonstrate a less than masculine attitude in one area invites accusations of a general lack of virility in others. This is the situation to which the first-century B.C.E. poet Catullus responds in one of his more abusive works. The gentle nature of his verse—presumably his famous love poetry to his mistress, Lesbia—has led his friends Furius and Aurelius to accuse the poet himself of having "insufficient sexual integrity" (16.4: *parum pudicum*), as any man who expresses himself so delicately in his verse as Catullus does must be the type who prefers to serve as the penetrated rather than

as the penetrator. Catullus defends himself by asserting verbally his sexual dominance over these two friends: "I will fuck your anuses and fuck your faces, you *pathicus* Aurelius and *cinaedus* Furius" (16.1–2). The active force of the verbs describing Catullus's actions, combined with the passive associations of the words describing his friends, mirror the active/passive dichotomy that pervades mentions of sexual activity in Latin texts. Catullus, as both the grammatical and physical subject of the verbs meaning, respectively, to insert a penis into another's mouth and anus (*irrumare, pedicare*), transforms his friends into the sexual deviants. Furthermore, Aurelius's epithet *pathicus* underscores his receptive role in sex, while *cinaedus* is the common noun used in Latin to describe a man who enjoys being penetrated by other men.

Extensive discussion of how sexuality is perceived in medical literature is restricted to one Latin text, Caelius Aurelianus's *De morbis chronicis* (On Chronic Diseases, fifth century C.E.?). Adhering to the dominant paradigm, Caelius diagnoses the adult man who wishes to be penetrated (and, in passing, women who have intercourse with women) as having a mental imbalance that drives him to pursue sexual pleasure in all ways possible (4.9). This diagnosis of general sexual wantonness irrespective of the sex of one's partner demonstrates once again that same-sex relations among men and women do not resemble modern conceptions of the "homosexual."

Female-Female Sexual Activity. The overarching conception of sexual intercourse as an insertive act informs literary representations of female-female homoerotic activity as well. From the earliest extant allusion in a play of Plautus in the early second century B.C.E. on through to the end of the classical era, the language and imagery for sexual activity between women necessitates that one of the participants adopt a male, insertive, role in intercourse. Indeed, what may seem a literary trope used by the poet Ovid well reflects the nonliterary record. The young girl Iphis dismisses her love for another girl by using examples from nature to "prove" that such a conception is unnatural and impossible; as a result, the only solution to her erotic dilemma is for the goddess

Isis to transform Iphis into a man, thereby retaining the natural dichotomy of the sexes (*Metamorphoses* 9.666–797).

The common designation of the insertive woman by the noun *tribas*, from the Greek verb meaning "to rub," echoes her anatomical role. The *tribas* appears most frequently in the satiric texts of Juvenal and Martial, where the presumed impossibility of a distinct female-female sex act informs the humor. In these portrayals, verisimilitude dictates that sex change must occur figuratively to the *tribas* through the use of a phallus substitute, either a dildo or an enlarged clitoris. The conception becomes particularly clear in a legal declamation from the Augustan era preserved by Seneca the Elder concerning a husband who caught his wife in bed with another woman. The orator quotes the husband's imagined reaction: "I first looked at the man, to see whether he was natural or sewn on" (*Controversies* 1.2.23; all Greek and Latin translations by author). It is important to note the double standard: although playing the insertive role in intercourse, the dominant woman in same-sex relationships does not, like the man, deserve respect but rather prompts shock, disapproval, and disgust.

The paucity of source material makes it impossible to decide the degree to which this consistent bias in the literary evidence echoes any real experience of female homoeroticism, since none of the women mentioned are attested as historical. There is also no unambiguous mention in legal texts, while astrological texts chiefly allude to the various planetary alignments under which the *tribas*, like the *cinaedus*, could be born. In his *Interpretation of Dreams* Artemidorus classifies dreams of women having sex with one another as dreams of unnatural acts, but it is difficult to ascertain whether Artemidorus imagines any real-world correspondence, since other dreams in this section include having sex with a god or a corpse (1.80). The sparse visual record offers only unverifiable hints; worth mentioning is an Augustan-era funerary relief of two women joining hands in a gesture that, in male-female contexts, normally signifies marriage.

Objects of Desire. A description of the restrictions that delimit a free man's sexual practices occurs early in the literary record of the Romans, and its strictures continued to be valid throughout the classical period. In the early second century B.C.E., a slave character in a comedy of Plautus offers to his young master the following piece of romantic advice: "Nobody stops any man from going on a public road. As long as you don't make your way through a fenced-in area, keeping away from brides, widows, and virgins, young men and free boys, you may love anything you want" (*Curculio* 35–38). The distinctions made by the slave would have been familiar to the Roman audience hearing his words. His listing underscores an important point in Roman sexuality: social and civic status plays a greater role in the choice of a sexual partner than biological sex.

Slaves and freedmen. The category of sex partners that the slave characterizes as "anything you want" encompasses slaves and freed slaves (freedmen). Plautus's own comedies contain many jokes that rest on the assumption that no legal or ethical barriers prevented a master from using a slave sexually, provided that the master plays the insertive role. Moreover, there is no indication that the sex of the receptive partner reflects negatively on the master's masculinity. For sons of the master, the existence in households of a *concubinus*, a young male slave that the boy retains as lover and companion, ideally until marriage, appears to have been widespread. Several examples also survive of men retaining *concubini* even after marriage. The treatment of slaves as property to be exploited at will extends throughout the classical period and explains why law prohibits the sexual use of another's slave without the owner's permission, since this would constitute improper use of another citizen's private possession. Indeed, occasional visits to prostitutes—typically slaves—are condoned in the sources, since they allow release for young men of the elite, and prevent them from pursuing those people on Plautus's taboo list. The sex of the prostitute is unimportant; the only provisos are that the free citizen must take the active role in any encounter and that he not overindulge emotionally, physically, or financially.

The most celebrated male-male couple from Roman antiquity that has firm historical support fits into this pattern, but only to an extent. The emperor Hadrian had a celebrated relationship with the young boy Antinous, who died mysteriously at the age of twenty (130 C.E.). While a Greek-style pederastic relationship would certainly be in line with Hadrian's well-known philhellenism, it seems more likely that the relationship follows the distinctly Roman model and that Antinous was a social inferior—not only younger, but presumably a former slave. When Roman sources criticize this bond, it is on account of Hadrian's reaction to the loss of his beloved. In addition to grieving in a manner characterized as excessive, Hadrian marked his love as special by honoring Antinous after death with numerous statues and shrines, eventually deifying him. The unemotional use of pretty male slaves as prepubescent sex objects (*deliciae*) was ubiquitous in Roman society; through his actions, Hadrian takes the unusual step of sublimating this practice into an affective relationship between men.

Freeborn women, boys, and men. Approximately two centuries after the proclamation of Plautus's slave, the elder Seneca preserves in pithier form an analogous sentiment from the late first-century B.C.E.: "The sacrifice of sexual integrity (*impudicitia*) is a crime for the freeborn, a necessity for the slave, and a duty for the freedman" (*Controversiae* 4, preface 10). The term *impudicitia* recalls the charge of "insufficient sexual integrity" (*parum pudicum*) that caused the poet Catullus to assert his masculinity by threatening to rape his male friends. The epigram in Seneca shows that, while sexual subservience is expected of slaves and freedmen, such a situation threatens the freeborn status of a Roman male. Catullus was defending more than just his sexual identity. This distinction separates most clearly Roman sexuality from the Greek practice of pederasty, by which both the older and younger lovers had free status. At Rome, a sexual relationship between freeborn males was not only deemed inappropriate, but was subject to legal penalties throughout the Roman period (see below).

By silently including slaves, both male and female, along with freedmen under the category "anything you want," Plautus's slave implies that these two

groups are accessible to the freeborn male without distinction regarding their sex. The truth of this implication is confirmed by abundant testimony that it was normal to view women, girls, and young boys as equally valid receptive partners for the insertive male. Remarks about men indiscriminately penetrating boys and females occur across the range of textual sources, from graffiti, to oratorical invective, to staged comedies, to satirical poetry, to serious works of history. Craig Williams succinctly describes the underlying assumption: "Men's desires are normally aroused by boys and women, who function simultaneously as stimulant, object, and receptacle" (2010, p. 27).

Amid this apparent lack of discrimination, the male slave or freedman who is an adult stands out as distinct from boys and women. This contrast emerges most tellingly in the shadowy figure of the *exoletus*. Textual evidence makes clear that relations among free adult males, while not infrequently attested, always retain charges of being nonnormative, if not deviant (Seneca, *Natural Questions* 1.16.1–3; Suetonius, *Galba* 22). As a result, those desires are often met by a category of nonfree men, including slaves, freedmen, and paid prostitutes, deemed *exoleti*. This group of postadolescent males pleasured other adult men by adopting both the insertive and the receptive positions in intercourse. Meaning literally "outgrown," the very word *exoletus* attests that he acts outside the aesthetic norm.

Law. References in legal texts reinforce the two principal biases emphasized thus far: that homoerotic activity between males was conceived of as nonreciprocal and that social status played a key role in determining legality. Same-sex activity among females nowhere receives explicit mention.

The concept of *stuprum* underlies the legal status of same-sex relations among men. The term *stuprum* can apply to the sexual violation by an adult male of either another freeborn male or of an unmarried female. None of the many sources citing this charge imply that one type of rape was different from the other. The violation committed is not, however, dependent upon the use of force—consent on the part of each actor can still constitute *stuprum*—but upon whether the receptive partner possesses freeborn status. If the receptive partner is a freeborn male, the violator could receive the death penalty. The earliest evidence for legal intervention in male-male sexual relationships dates to sometime in the mid-second century B.C.E. with passage of the Lex Scantinia, a law still enforced during Domitian's reign in the late first century C.E. The precise application and penalties of the law remain unclear, but it is generally agreed to have made sexual activity between two male freeborn persons a crime. Despite the paucity of evidence, analogous texts from the classical period make it likely that punishment would have been meted out only to the receptive partner (e.g., Valerius Maximus 6.1.5; Paulus, *Opinions* 2.26.13). The Augustan adultery law of 17 B.C.E. adds to the law by punishing anyone who allows his house to be used for an assignation between two adult men (Papinianus, *Digest* 48.5.9[8]).

A legal principle dating at least to the early empire, and probably earlier, groups with pimps, disgraced soldiers, and assorted persons deemed disreputable by the state any freeborn man who "has played a woman's role with his body," that is, who has played the receptive role in male-male intercourse, regardless of whether the act involved payment or not (Ulpian, *Digest* 3.1.1.5–6). Such men received severe restrictions to their civic rights but were not, it should be stressed, hunted down for punishment or considered criminals if penalized. It is apparently only in 559 C.E. that Christian principles contribute to the establishment of the death penalty for any male involved in same-sex relations, regardless of whether he played the insertive or the receptive role (Justinian, *Novels* 141).

For every law there are always exceptions, and in Roman history that would normally be the emperor. Allegations of emperors sexually violating freeborn boys or men with impunity proliferate in historical and biographical sources, with especially opprobrious remarks concerning Tiberius, Caligula, and Nero.

Marriage. The earliest unambiguous allusion to marriage between men occurs in a context of oratorical invective. In his *Second Philippic*, Cicero remarks that a male lover had rescued the young Marc Antony from a career as a female prostitute and placed him in a "stable marriage" (44). Although the remark is intended to be amusingly hyperbolic, the way in which Cicero imagines the relationship reflects a trend also attested to in the early empire. As the satirist Juvenal narrates in elaborate detail (2.117–142), and as epigrams of Martial confirm (1.24, 12.42), an all-male marriage is conceivable only if one of the men is figured as "bride." Just as the logic of Roman sexuality must supply one phallic partner to create a relationship between women, conversely an all-male marriage necessitates that one man play the woman's part. This metaphorical bride thereby ineluctably occupies the receptive, female, role in sexual activity.

It is difficult to assess the truth behind Juvenal and Martial's poetic attacks. Historical texts, however, offer details that seem derived from actual events. Once again, it is the emperors who possess the ability to transcend cultural strictures, although in this instance they are still constrained by the notion that the marital union of members of one sex necessitates the creation of two opposing genders. Two marriages with men involved Nero (who was during his life married to three women). In one of these he played only the man's role, using a castrated boy "as a wife in all things" (Dio 62.28.2–3). In the second, our sources make explicit that Nero was the designated female: he wore the characteristic bridal veil, supplied a dowry, and even, according to one source, imitated on his wedding night the wailings of a woman being penetrated (Tacitus, *Annals* 15.37.4; Suetonius, *Nero* 29). A similar portrayal characterized the wedding of the emperor Elagabalus (*Augustan History* 17.10.5, 17.11.7). Each of these weddings appears to have been publicly celebrated, and is unlikely to have been solely the product of a hostile tradition.

Lower down the social ladder, no publicly celebrated male-male marriages are attested, although artistic evidence provides intriguing possibilities (Haeckl, 2001). It is unclear whether a law from 342 C.E. preserved in the Theodosian Code punishing by death "a man marrying as a woman" refers to actual marriage—and thereby implies that such marriages did occur—or whether the phrase simply offers a metaphor for sexual relations (9.7.3).

Art. To attempt to reconstruct popular attitudes, written texts need to be read through for biases. A perspective less restricted by class boundaries lies in material remains, but their inherent silence and often unclear context offer their own interpretive challenges. Generally, art seems to support text. In depictions of male-male sex, the receptive partner is nearly always a boy, visibly younger than his lover, and details often indicate servile status. Moreover, the vast majority of poses depicted have close analogues in depictions of male-female lovemaking (and not infrequently on the same work of art), with the boy and woman exchanging roles. Visual equivalence of boy and woman seems to reflect the same ideological perspective on the receptive partner that occurs in the textual evidence.

At other times, art provides a perspective that is rare or unknown in the written record. A particularly provocative wall painting from a tavern in Pompeii, depicted with captions, appears to show two men in effeminate clothing (perhaps *cinaedi*?) ordering drinks from an aggressive barmaid, but uncertainty of text and image makes firm conclusions impossible (Clarke, 2005). Two other painted scenes, from Pompeii's Suburban Baths, depict sex acts unparalleled elsewhere: an adult male being anally penetrated while simultaneously penetrating a woman. In one case the woman's penetration is vaginal from the rear; in the second it is oral (a woman, in turn, performs cunnilingus on her). This appearance of man as both penetrator and penetrated challenges the model for Roman masculinity that dominates written texts. Similarly surprising—and unique—is a panel that depicts a fully clothed man (who wears a toga, confirming his status as a citizen) performing cunnilingus on a woman. The subservient position of the man—like a fellator, a male cunnilinctor is universally reviled—would have been intolerable by the code one can construct from elite texts.

Similar uncertainty over interpretation prevails over the well-known Warren Cup, an exquisite silver goblet from the early first century C.E. adorned with two scenes of male-male anal penetration. One side offers little controversy: a young slave boy is anally penetrated by an older freeborn youth (social status is clear from hairstyles). On the opposite side, however, is depicted anal intercourse between two men of different ages, but clearly adult and freeborn. Agreement over why this representation differs from expectations presented in the written record has not yet been reached—is the younger man a prostitute? does the image satirize Roman moral legislation? or is this a rare instance of the acceptable display of lovemaking between two adult males?

The Real Story. Despite the full variety of references to same-sex relations, no source reveals what went on in the privacy of the bedroom. Although even nonliterary sources, such as graffiti and material evidence, seem to confirm the prevailing view that male-male intercourse was limited concerning who could act as penetrator and who as penetrated, hints at an active subculture of *cinaedi* occur in several sources. These hints have prompted some scholars to argue that there were indeed adult men in Rome who actively sought to be penetrated by other men, and that perhaps even reciprocal relationships occurred in ways akin to modern conceptions of homosexuality. The possibility continues to provoke heated debate (Richlin, 1993, and Taylor, 1997, vs. Williams, 2010, pp. 209–224).

[*See also* Homosexual/Queer; Legal Status, *subentry* Roman World; Male-Female Sexuality, *subentry* Roman World; Marriage and Divorce, *subentry* Roman World; *and* Sexual Transgression, *subentry* Roman World.]

BIBLIOGRAPHY

Brooten, Bernadette J. *Love Between Women: Early Christian Responses to Female Homoeroticism.* Chicago: University of Chicago Press, 1996.

Butrica, James L. "Some Myths and Anomalies in the Study of Roman Sexuality." *Journal of Homosexuality* 49, nos. 3/4 (2005): 209–269.

Clarke, John R. *Looking at Lovemaking: Constructions of Sexuality in Roman Art, 100 B.C.–A.D. 250.* Berkeley: University of California Press, 1998.

Clarke, John R. "Representations of the *Cinaedus* in Roman Art: Evidence of 'Gay' Subculture?" *Journal of Homosexuality* 49, no. 3/4 (2005): 271–298.

Dalla, Danilo. *Ubi Venus mutatur: Omosessualità e diritto nel mondo romano.* Milan: Giuffrè, 1987.

Haeckl, Anne E. "Brothers or Lovers? A New Reading of the 'Tondo of the Two Brothers.'" *Bulletin of the American Society of Papyrologists* 38, nos. 1–4 (2001): 63–78.

Hallett, Judith P., and Marilyn B. Skinner, eds. *Roman Sexualities.* Princeton, N.J.: Princeton University Press, 1997.

Hubbard, Thomas K., ed. *Homosexuality in Greece and Rome: A Sourcebook of Basic Documents.* Berkeley: University of California Press, 2003.

Richlin, Amy. *The Garden of Priapus: Sexuality and Aggression in Roman Humor.* Rev. ed. Oxford: Oxford University Press, 1992.

Richlin, Amy. "Not before Homosexuality: The Materiality of the *Cinaedus* and the Roman Law against Love between Men." *Journal of the History of Sexuality* 3, no. 4 (1993): 523–573.

Skinner, Marilyn B. *Sexuality in Greek and Roman Culture.* 2d ed. Malden, Mass.: Wiley-Blackwell, 2013.

Taylor, Rabun. "Two Pathic Subcultures in Ancient Rome." *Journal of the History of Sexuality* 7, no. 3 (1997): 319–371.

Williams, Craig A. *Roman Homosexuality.* 2d ed. Oxford: Oxford University Press, 2010.

Anthony Corbeill

New Testament

New Testament references to same-sex relations are scattered and elusive, since modern categories and perspectives on sexuality are not easily mapped onto ancient terminology, practices, and attitudes. Still, it is possible to identify two broad categories of references to same-sex relations in the New Testament: general references to same-sex activities and specific references to characters that might be interpreted as participants in same-sex relations. The former have received a great deal of scholarly and popular attention as a result of contemporary debates about homosexuality. This attention revolves around the question of whether these references can or should be read as injunctions against homosexuality.

Ancient Homoeroticism. Current scholarship on ancient sexual practices and attitudes toward same-sex relations emphasizes that perspectives on socially acceptable sexual activities and partners are historically determined. Modern categories of "homosexuality" and "heterosexuality" are problematic for describing ancient attitudes and practices, since sexual practices and preferences in ancient Greek and Roman contexts typically were not categorized in terms of the participants' sex. Sexual activity between two people of the same sex was not considered significantly different than between two people of differing sexes, and the social appropriateness of particular sexual activities and relations was gauged primarily by social and political concerns (Williams, 1999). The modern idea of "sexual identity," moreover, is problematic for understanding ancient individuals or groups, as the idea reflects the modern tendency to define individual identity in relation to sexual relations and to imagine "sexuality" as a domain distinct from one's social and political identity. David M. Halperin suggests that modern scholars should "de-center *sexuality* from the focus of cultural interpretation of sexual experience" (1989, p. 271).

In Greek and Roman contexts, sexual activity in general was understood as involving an active (penetrating) participant and a passive (penetrated) participant. The social understanding of who should inhabit these roles was not determined primarily by the individuals' sex. Instead, the division into active and passive roles reflected political and social distinctions related to citizenship, status as slave or free, and age. Still, ancient Greek and Roman perspectives on sex were phallocentric, privileging sexual activity that required the insertion of a penis into a vagina, anus, or mouth; thus it was assumed that females were biologically, socially, and politically, more suited for the passive sexual role. However, possession of a penis did not ensure one's status as "active," since certain groups of biological males (e.g., male slaves) were understood as naturally passive (Parker, 1997).

Male homoeroticism. In classical Greece, pederastic relations between freeborn males played a significant cultural role, introducing freeborn males into the social and political realm. Participants included an adult male lover (*erastēs*) and a youth or boy (*pais*), sometimes described as the beloved (*erōmenos*), reflecting a distinction between social superior and inferior. These relationships were warranted only among free male citizens, solidifying this group's bond and distinguishing them as social superiors over others, including women and foreigners (Halperin, 1989). Pederastic relationships in classical Greece were associated with the *gymnasion*, where male youths trained and exercised in the nude. Even after the classical period, Roman authors who disapproved of the Greek acceptance of same-sex relationships with citizen boys associated the *gymnasion* with pederasty (Williams, 1999). Pederastic relationships were understood differently than same-sex relations with male prostitutes. Both were socially acceptable, as long as the freeborn male remained the active partner; however, a citizen boy risked losing his honor if perceived as a prostitute (Nissinen, 1998).

For Romans male same-sex relationships were socially acceptable only between citizen men and male prostitutes, male slaves, and noncitizen boys, as long as the citizen male was (or was perceived as) the active partner. Citizen boys and men were generally off-limits as passive sexual partners to freeborn males, although there were exceptions in practice. The first-century B.C.E. poet Catullus, for example, expressed love for the freeborn Juventius in his verses. The Roman poets in general reveal that same-sex desire between men was considered natural, although there existed some limits regarding how one acted upon this desire.

While many scholars discussing ancient same-sex relations resist the notion that there was an ancient sexual identity, Amy Richlin (1993) maintains that references to certain men who liked to be penetrated (*kinaedi*) implies that ancients did identify homosexuality as a category. Negative appellations such as *pullus* ("chick"), *effeminatus* ("effeminate"), or *mollis* ("soft") used for adult men who inhabited the passive sexual role reflect the Roman assumption that appropriate masculine behavior was marked by exercising power over another and not vice versa. To be the passive partner in any sexual relationship signaled inferiority and a lack of honor vis-à-vis one's partner. In this way, Roman gender hierarchy, which associated masculinity with power, dictated perspectives on appropriate sexual practices and partners.

Like Greeks and Romans, ancient Jews did not distinguish between homo- and heterosexuality. Daniel Boyarin (1995) suggests that this allows for a range of male-male intimacy, including physical contact between males. However, the rabbis typically spoke against male-male anal intercourse, affirming the prohibition in Leviticus. However, according to Boyarin, this reflected a concern with hybridity and the possibility of a man being treated as a woman. Michael Satlow (1994) adds that some among the ancient rabbis understood male-male intercourse as an act of arrogance (using something that does not belong to one) and excessiveness. The association between same-sex acts and excessiveness appears throughout Second Temple Jewish descriptions of gentiles.

Female homoeroticism. Less scholarly work has been done on female same-sex relationships in the ancient world, although Bernadette Brooten's *Love Between Women* (1996) makes a substantial contribution to the field, drawing upon references to lesbianism in Greek and Latin literature, postbiblical Jewish traditions, ancient art, love spells, and ancient astrological texts. Still, ancient women's own perspectives on same-sex relations are difficult to find, although there are a few fragmented evidences, including the suggestive lines by the Greek poet Sappho (seventh–sixth centuries B.C.E.) of Lesbos, providing the term "lesbian."

Since sexual relations were imagined as including active and passive roles, same-sex relations between women were assumed to include an active and penetrating partner (*tribas*) along with a passive partner. (Passive partners were not identified through particular nomenclature, because they were understood as acting as "women.") A woman who adopted the active or categorically masculine role, the *tribas*, violated traditional gender categories. At times this social deviance was imagined as having anatomical effects, as the *tribas* was occasionally described as penetrating her partner with an enlarged, penis-like clitoris. According to Diane Swancutt (2007), the image of the *tribas* was deployed mainly by elite Roman males anxious about the changing social landscape of the empire including the growing political influence of Roman matrons. In addition to *tribas*, other terms for female homoeroticism include *frictrix/fricatrix* and *Lesbia* (Brooten, 1996). It is possible that *tribas* and *frictrix* derive from verbs meaning "to rub," reflecting ancient male assumptions about the mechanics of female homoeroticism. This linguistic possibility underscores that most ancient descriptions of women in same-sex relations reflect the assumptions of men.

General References to Same-Sex Practices. Among the texts possibly referring to same-sex practices in the New Testament are three general references situated within the Pauline and deutero-Pauline writings. These instances appear in contexts in which the primary topic is not homoerotic activities, and therefore the implications of these texts are hotly debated.

Romans 1:26–27. Scholarly conversation around Romans 1:26–27 tends to break down into debates about whether these verses describe same-sex practices or not. For some, the text describes unambiguously Paul's belief in God's condemnation of homosexual activity, female and male, linking same-sex eroticism to humanity's "fall" (Hays, 1986). Other interpreters highlight the uncertainty about the text's meaning and raise the question of whether these verses, embedded within a larger argument about gentile sinfulness, should be taken as Paul's teaching about same-sex eroticism.

Discussions of Romans 1:26–27 often revolve around the meanings of "natural" or "nature" and "unnatural," as Paul describes women "exchanging natural intercourse for unnatural intercourse" in v. 26. Some interpreters suggest that "unnatural" intercourse or, more literally, "beyond nature" (*para physin*) could include any number of sexual practices that would have been considered unnatural for women in the ancient context, including women allowing themselves to be anally penetrated by men (e.g., Thomas Hanks, "Romans," in Guest et al., 2006). Despite this, since v. 27 compares women's unnatural intercourse with men who have passion for one another, most scholars read v. 26 as a reference to homoeroticism as well. As Brooten (1996) observes, Paul's negative characterization of women's homoeroticism reflects the assumptions of his historical context, which understood female same-sex relations as necessarily transgressing natural gender roles.

In v. 27 Paul describes men who give up what is natural, presumably using females (*thyleias*) for sex, and who burn with passion with one another, implying some type of male homoeroticism and associating this with shamefulness and error. The question is whether or not Paul understands all examples of male same-sex practices as shameful or only particular acts or participants. John Boswell (1980) famously argued that Paul's description of those engaging in "unnatural" intercourse precluded those for whom same-sex eroticism was natural, namely homosexuals. In other words, Paul describes heterosexuals participating in same-sex acts. While some interpreters have found this persuasive, Boswell's view assumes a modern view of sexual identity that cannot be easily mapped onto these verses.

Still, other scholars note that Romans 1:26–27 does not offer a condemnation of same-sex desire per se, for in the ancient context there is no distinction between same-sex and other-sex desire. Dale B. Martin suggests that these contested verses reflect Paul's belief in the "corruption inherent in sexual passion itself" (1995, p. 348). In other words, these verses can be understood as similar to ancient Jewish traditions that cast gentiles as excessive, especially in sexual matters, characterizing this excessiveness especially in terms of same-sex eroticism. This, Martin suggests, is implied in Paul's use of the phrase *para physin*, or "beyond nature."

1 Corinthians 6:9–10 and 1 Timothy 1:9–10. Both of these texts offer vice lists including terms traditionally translated as forms of male homoeroticism, *arsenokoitēs* and *malakos*. The former, *arsenokoitēs*, appears in both 1 Corinthians and 1 Timothy, but it is an uncommon term attested mainly in texts influenced by New Testament traditions. Given its rarity the term's translation is uncertain, and consequently it has been translated variously as "abuser of themselves with mankind" (KJV), "sodomite" (NAB; NRSV), and "homosexual offender" (NIV). Each of these translations draws upon the fact that the term seemingly combines *arsen* (male, man) and *koitē* (bed). However, scholars are unclear as to how these components relate, whether the term refers to a male prostitute who might be "bedded" by males or females or a man who has sex exclusively with men (Nissinen, 1998). Martin argues that "the etymology of a word is its history, not its meaning" and prompts interpreters to determine the word's meaning within its literary context (2006, p. 39). Doing so reveals that *arsenokoitēs* is typically grouped with economic sins, implying that part of its connotation is economic. Martin concludes that the term's precise meaning cannot be determined and, consequently, it should not be read through a modern heterosexist lens that presumes a reference to male homoeroticism.

In addition to *arsenokoitēs*, Paul includes *malakoi* (which precedes *arsenokoitēs*) in his list of those who will not "inherit the kingdom of God," along with fornicators, idolaters, adulterers, thieves, and the like (1 Cor 6:9–10). This term, which has been translated as "effeminate" (KJV; NAS), "male prostitutes" (NIV; NRSV), and "homosexuals" (NKJV), is well attested in comparison to *arsenokoitēs*. Despite the varied translations into English, contemporary scholars highlight that the term literally refers to softness and was used metaphorically to describe men who acted effeminately. This might include allowing oneself to be penetrated by another male, although not necessarily. Thus, while some modern interpretations explicitly link this term to prostitution or same-sex relations, it is better understood as a reference to those who do not conform to ancient gender expectations.

Same-Sex Characters and Pairs. Given the differences between ancient and modern perspectives on same-sex relations and practices, it is difficult to make definitive statements about whether a particular same-sex dyad in the New Testament can or should be understood as a possible same-sex kinship pair (i.e., sisters) or same-sex erotic pair. Traditionally, male-male and female-female pairings in the New Testament have been interpreted through the lenses of heterosexual norms. As a result, female pairs might be described as sisters (e.g., Tryphaena and Tryphosa) and males as master and slave or father and son (e.g., the Roman centurion and his *pais*). In light of this, a number of scholars have begun to

revisit references to same-sex dyads in the New Testament, asking whether or not these can be understood in terms of same-sex relations and activities.

Romans 16:12 and Philippians 4:2–3. In a 1990 article Mary Rose D'Angelo suggests that the female pairs Tryphaena and Tryphosa and Evodia and Syntyche referenced by Paul in Romans 16:12 and Philippians 4:2, respectively, should be understood not only as female missionary pairs but as possible kinship pairs and even, perhaps, erotic partnerships. She raises this possibility in light of a Roman funerary relief in the British Museum depicting two freedwomen grasping hands (*dextrarum inuctio*) in a way indicative of marriage portraits.

Tryphaena and Tryphosa, described as those who "labor in the Lord," are mentioned by Paul in an extended greeting at the conclusion of Romans. The similarity of this pair's names suggests some relationship between the two, although it remains unclear whether they are biological sisters, freed slaves from the same *familia* who have been given similar names, or women who have adopted similar names signaling a personal bond. D'Angelo notes that the greeting includes a number of male-female missionary pairs, including husband and wife partners. Thus, she maintains that scholars should not preclude the possibility that these two might have a similar type of relationship.

Evodia and Syntyche are mentioned in Paul's letter to the Philippians, in which he calls the women to be of the same mind in the LORD (4:2). Interpreters traditionally assume that the two women are quarreling and in need of some reconciliation between them. However, the text is not clear, and some suggest Paul perhaps calls the women to share the same mind with him. In 4:3 the two women are depicted as a pair, in fact, who struggle and work alongside Paul and others. The fact that they are described as a pair raises the possibility for D'Angelo that Evodia and Syntyche should be understood as co-missionaries and as existing in a same-sex relationship. While the text only offers a brief glimpse into the lives of these two women, the nature of their relationship should not be circumscribed by heteronormative assumptions.

Philemon. Paul's letter to Philemon, concerning Onesimus, a slave of unclear status (perhaps runaway or manumitted), has not traditionally been read in terms of homoeroticism. However, Joseph A. Marchal (2011) makes a case for reading the letter in light of ancient assumptions about the sexual use (*chrēsis*) of slaves by masters and masters' family and friends. Marchal points out that the language of "use," employed in reference to Onesimus, as a term for sexual intercourse is assumed in Romans 1:26–27. Read in light of historical assumptions about sexual desire and protocols about appropriate sexual partners, the letter to Philemon raises the possibility of a homoerotic relationship between Paul and Onesimus, as well as Philemon and Onesimus.

Matthew 8:5–13. This healing story revolves around a Roman centurion's request that Jesus heal his "boy" (*pais*). In making his request, the centurion suggests that Jesus perform the miracle from a distance, claiming that he is not worthy to have Jesus enter his home. Although in Greek traditions *pais* is often understood as the younger partner in a male homoerotic pair, in this story it has traditionally been translated as "servant" (KJV; NIV; NRSV) in alignment with Luke's version of the story (7:1–10), which uses the term *doulos*, "servant." Recognizing that *pais* does not necessarily mean "servant" and that Matthew typically uses *doulos* to refer to servants, some scholars suggest it be understood as the centurion's son. In a cowritten article, Theodore W. Jennings and Tat-siong Benny Liew, however, argue that the *pais* should be understood as the centurion's favorite "boy," suggesting that this story includes a homoerotic relationship (2004). The centurion's request that Jesus heal the *pais* from a distance reveals, according to Jennings and Liew, the centurion's anxiety about Jesus as a competitor for the boy's affections. If Jesus were to heal the boy, the centurion would be indebted to him as a client, and, if Jesus demanded, the centurion would then have to allow Jesus to have a sexual relationship with the *pais*. Finally, reading this text in terms of same-sex relations does not preclude a slave and master relationship, given the assumption that slaves are available for their masters' sexual use.

The beloved disciple. In contrast to many other same-sex pairings in the New Testament, the relationship between the "beloved disciple" and Jesus, referenced in the Gospel of John (13:21–26; 19:25–27; 20:1–10; 21:20–24), has received attention in the interpretive tradition. Although not necessarily imagined as a sexual relationship, the relationship between the beloved disciple, assumed to be John, and Jesus was understood in terms of John's virginal devotion to his master, teacher, and friend in medieval Christian tradition. Robert E. Goss explains, "For nearly two millennia, men attracted to the same sex have intuited a homoerotic relationship between Jesus and the Beloved Disciple" ("John," in Guest et al., 2006, p. 560).

Although the beloved disciple is not explicitly identified by name in the text, many scholars connect him to John the son of Zebedee. This traditional association persists, even though scholars have suggested that the beloved disciple might be Thomas, Lazarus, or even Mary Magdalene (although references to the beloved disciple and Mary together preclude such an identification). Whoever the beloved disciple might be, the relationship between him and Jesus is characterized in terms of intimacy, including physical closeness. During a meal that Jesus shares with his disciples, the disciple reclines next to Jesus (13:23), resting in his bosom or lap. While reclining to eat was traditional within the historical context, the emphasis on the physical closeness between the disciple and Jesus and the reference to this event at the end of the Gospel (21:20) highlights the importance of this moment and the uniqueness of this relationship, according to Jennings (2009). The imagery of two men reclining in a meal setting, moreover, evokes classical Greek and Etruscan depictions of the symposium, where a beloved (*erōmenos*) male youth sits against the chest of his older male lover (*erastēs*).

The fact that the beloved disciple is singled out by Jesus from the cross, when Mary and the disciple are told, respectively, "Woman behold your son" and "Behold your mother," similarly underscores the privileged relationship between Jesus and John (19:26–27). Although it has not traditionally been read as such, the text can be read as an adoptive relationship between the beloved and Jesus's mother—the beloved as the adoptive son taking care of his "mother-in-law" in her time of grief (Jennings, 2009).

Mark 14:50–52. Mark's account of Jesus's arrest includes a cryptic reference to "a certain young man" wearing only a linen cloth, who runs off naked after someone pulls off his cloth. Some interpreters read this as a reference to a possible same-sex encounter, given the use of a term suggesting the male's youth (*neaniskos*) and the reference to his nakedness (*gymnos*). Jennings (2009) suggests that these references would communicate to a gentile audience that the character is an object of desire, while a conservative Jewish audience might be scandalized by the reference to the youth's nudity, a symbol of the decadence associated with Hellenistic practices, including pederasty.

Assessment. In a response to Nissinen (1998), Stone (2001) suggests that the impulse to identify and explain references to "homosexuality" in the biblical world perpetuates the problematic notion that there is an ancient understanding of this modern category. Such investigations assume that modern interpreters can identify ancient eroticism and that genders referenced in texts align with the genders of historical characters. While the interrogation of New Testament passages that might refer to homoeroticism continues to be necessary since they carry weight in contemporary discussions, biblical scholars engaged in questions related to same-sex relations and homoeroticism are moving away from focusing primarily on "what the Bible says about homosexuality" and beginning to explore the various ways that biblical texts reflect the concerns and perspectives of same-sex-oriented persons and communities.

[*See also* Gay Liberation; Homosexual/Queer; Queer Readings; *and* Same-Sex Relations, *subentries on* Greek World *and* Roman World.]

BIBLIOGRAPHY

Boswell, John. *Christianity, Social Tolerance, and Homosexuality: Gay People in Western Europe from the Beginning of the Christian Era to the Fourteenth Century.* Chicago, University of Chicago Press, 1980.

Boyarin, Daniel. "Are There Any Jews in 'The History of Sexuality'?" *Journal of the History of Sexuality* 5, no. 3 (January 1995): 333–355.

Brooten, Bernadette J. *Love Between Women: Early Christian Responses to Female Homoeroticism.* Chicago: University of Chicago Press, 1996.

D'Angelo, Mary Rose. "Women Partners in the New Testament." *Journal of Feminist Studies in Religion* 6, no. 1 (Spring 1990): 65–86.

Guest, Deryn, Robert E. Goss, Mona West, and Thomas Bohache, eds. *The Queer Bible Commentary.* London: SMC, 2006.

Halperin, David M. "Is There a History of Sexuality?" *History and Theory* 28, no. 3 (October 1989): 257–274.

Hays, Richard B. "Relations Natural and Unnatural: A Response to John Boswell's Exegesis of Romans 1." *Journal of Religious Ethics* 14, no. 1 (Spring 1986): 184–215.

Jennings, Theodore W., Jr. *The Man Jesus Loved: Homoerotic Narratives from the New Testament.* Cleveland, Ohio: Pilgrim, 2009.

Jennings, Theodore W., Jr., and Tat-siong Benny Liew. "Mistaken Identities but Model Faith: Rereading the Centurion, the Chap, and the Christ in Matthew 8:5–13." *Journal of Biblical Literature* 123, no. 3 (Fall 2004): 467–494.

Marchal, Joseph A. "The Usefulness of an Onesimus: The Sexual Use of Slaves and Paul's Letter to Philemon." *Journal of Biblical Literature* 130, no. 4 (Winter 2011): 749–770.

Martin, Dale B. "Heterosexism and the Interpretation of Romans 1:18–32." *Biblical Interpretation* 3, no. 3 (1995): 332–355.

Martin, Dale B. "*Arsenokoitês* and *Malakos*: Meanings and Consequences." In *Sex and the Single Savior: Gender and Sexuality in Biblical Interpretation*, pp. 37–50. Louisville, Ky.: Westminster John Knox, 2006.

Nissinen, Martti. *Homoeroticism in the Biblical World: A Historical Perspective.* Translated by Kirsi Stjerna. Minneapolis: Fortress, 1998.

Parker, Holt N. "The Teratogenic Grid." In *Roman Sexualities*, edited by Judith P. Hallett and Marilyn B. Skinner, pp. 47–65. Princeton, N.J.: Princeton University Press, 1997.

Richlin, Amy. "Not Before Homosexuality: The Materiality of the *Cinaedus* and the Roman Law against Love between Men." *Journal of the History of Sexuality* 3, no. 4 (April 1993): 523–573.

Satlow, Michael L. "'They Abused Him Like a Woman': Homoeroticism, Gender Blurring, and the Rabbis in

Late Antiquity." *Journal of the History of Sexuality* 5, no. 1 (July 1994): 1–25.

Stone, Ken. "Homosexuality and the Bible or Queer Reading? A Response to Martti Nissinen." *Theology and Sexuality* 7, no. 14 (March 2001): 107–118.

Swancutt, Diana M. "*Still* Before Sexuality: 'Greek' Androgyny, the Roman Imperial Politics of Masculinity, and the Roman Invention of the *Tribas*." In *Mapping Gender in Ancient Religious Discourses*, edited by Todd Penner and Caroline Vander Stichele, pp. 11–61. Biblical Interpretation 84. Leiden, The Netherlands: Brill, 2007.

Williams, Craig A. *Roman Homosexuality: Ideologies of Masculinity in Classical Antiquity*. New York: Oxford University Press, 1999.

Lynn R. Huber

Early Judaism

Neither the Hebrew Bible nor any of the texts of the Rabbinic Period (the first seven centuries of the Common Era) make any mention of sexual orientation or identity, although they mention opposite-sex and same-sex sexual activity. In fact, until the Medieval Period, anal intercourse was the only male same-sex interaction that was prohibited, and female same-sex intercourse was not considered sex, let alone prohibited.

Male Same-Sex Relations. Leviticus 18 and 20, which are part of the Holiness Code, contain the only exhortation against same-sex intercourse in the Hebrew Bible. Leviticus 18:22 states, "Do not lie with a man the 'lyings' of women; it is an abhorrence (*to'evah*)." Along with the other sexual prohibitions in Leviticus 18, this prohibition is reiterated in Leviticus 20: "If a man lies with a male the 'lyings' of women, the two of them have done an abhorrent thing; they shall both be put to death—their bloodguilt is upon them" (Lev 20:13). This prohibition has often been mischaracterized as a blanket prohibition against "homosexuality." Yet the subject of this verse is clearly not *female* homosexuality, and it likely is not even male "homosexuality." Instead, Leviticus 18:22 and 20:13 seem to be prohibiting some specific form of male same-sex intercourse.

No evidence exists that the rabbis of the Rabbinic Period read the Torah as prohibiting any form of sexual or sensual interaction between men other than anal intercourse, nor is there any evidence that they chose to outlaw other forms of same-sex sexual or sensual interactions as a "fence" around this Torah prohibition. On the contrary, rabbinic sources imply that no such prohibition existed during the Rabbinic Period. That the rabbis prohibited male same-sex anal penetration but no other same-sex sexual or sensual interactions corresponds with the cultural mores of the Rabbinic Period, which evince a strong reaction to male-male sexual penetration but little concern for other intimate contact between men. In fact, until Maimonides's innovation in the twelfth century of distinguishing between sensual contact with and without desire, prohibiting same-sex contact would have been impractical to implement.

Rabbinic vilification of anal intercourse between men. The rabbis felt extreme opprobrium for the act of anal intercourse between men and for those who engaged in such acts. Because men who engage in anal intercourse with other men willingly violate a law so serious that it carries the death penalty (Lev 20:13), the rabbis assumed that they would also commit murder, idolatry, and other immoral acts (e.g., *y. Sanh. 23b–c* [6:6]).

What lies behind the rabbis' opprobrium for same-sex anal intercourse? In Genesis Rabbah (63:10), the Jewish people cry out before God, "Master of the Universe, it is not fair that we should be subjugated to the seventy nations [of the world], but certainly not to this one [Rome] which is penetrated like women." In this passage, the penetrated male is likened to a woman and viewed as inferior by virtue of his sexual position. The one who is penetrated is not fit to rule, and it is a disgrace to be ruled by someone who has been so subjugated (see also *y. Qidd. 61a* [1:7]). For the author, being penetrated by other men makes Roman men "like women." If penetration is a form of "conquest" of the Other, then to be conquered by men who have been penetrated is like being conquered by those who themselves have been subjugated.

Ironically, this rabbinic disdain for Romans is itself closely related to Roman attitudes. In Roman culture it was deemed appropriate for adult male citizens to penetrate their social inferiors—women and male slaves—but penetrating their equals or their superiors was considered to be a disgrace to the one penetrated, and to be ruled by one who himself was penetrated was an added humiliation. According to the Babylonian Talmud (*b. Sanh. 73a*), from one perspective, for a male to be raped is worse than for a female, since it is "not his normal way." Rashi (ad loc.) explains that it is not a man's way to be penetrated, and therefore there is a great disgrace involved in having been penetrated. This explains why the rabbis felt a need particularly to prohibit anal intercourse between men. While the rabbis may not have approved of two men being amorous with one another, if such activity did not include anal intercourse it did not violate the rabbinic sensibility that an adult Jewish male (the rabbinic analog to the Roman male citizen) must never be sexually penetrated.

The rabbis were reluctant to mete out the death penalty, however, which led them to restrict the biblical prohibition to its most narrow interpretation. Whenever the Torah called for the death penalty, the rabbis read the Torah prohibition (*de-oraita*) in its most limited sense. Often they would then add a rabbinic prohibition (*de-rabbanan*) or use more minor prohibitions in the Torah (which did not result in the death penalty) to cover the broader scope of the prohibition. As with the other sexual transgressions in Leviticus 18 and 20 (incest, adultery, and bestiality), the rabbis read Leviticus 18:22 and 20:13 as limited to the act of penetration itself.

Because they assumed that the Bible could only be prohibiting anal penetration, they were puzzled by the purpose of the additional phrase in the verses: "the lyings of women." Once the Bible stated that it is forbidden for a man to lie with a man, it was obvious to the rabbis that the only form of penetration between men could be anal penetration. Therefore, the Bible had no need to add the extra phrase "the lyings of women." The rabbis interpreted the plural "lyings of women" to mean that when a man has sexual intercourse with a woman who is prohibited to him, both vaginal and anal intercourse are prohibited; and each carries the same penalty.

Thus, the Babylonian Talmud (*b. Sanh. 54a–b*) quotes the *Sifra* (*Qod.* 10:11): "'The lyings of women'—the verse teaches you that there are two forms of sex with a woman [i.e., vaginal and anal]. R. Ishmael said, 'Behold this came to teach [about men] and it turned out to have already been taught.'" This phrase "it came to teach [about X] but turned out to have already been taught" appears a number of times in rabbinic literature, always meaning that the point the analogy has been brought to make has already been made or is intuitively obvious. Since the assumption is that the Bible would not make an analogy unnecessarily, if the analogy between heterosexual and homosexual sexual acts sheds no light on the latter, it must have been brought to shed light on the former. The plural "*lyings* of women" (*mishkevei ishah*) is not needed to teach about male-male sex since there is only one form of sex between men: men have only one orifice that falls under this prohibition. Rather, it comes to teach that women have two orifices the penetration of which count as sex: one (the anus), which they have in common with men, and the other (the vagina), which they do not (thus Rashi on *Sanh. 54a*, s.v. *harei zeh ba lelamed*).

A rabbinic fence around the Torah? Did the rabbis add a rabbinic extension to the prohibition against male-male anal intercourse to cover other forms of sexual/sensual interaction? While it is widely assumed that they did, there is no evidence of such an extension to the prohibition. On the contrary, several passages demonstrate that the biblical prohibition was not extended for same-sex male interactions.

In the Babylonian Talmud (*b. Ber. 24a*), Rabbi Isaac states that for a man to see merely "a handbreadth of a woman['s body] is *'ervah* [nakedness/sexual sin]," broadening the heterosexual prohibition beyond the scope of the Torah prohibition. The Palestinian Talmud similarly extends the heterosexual prohibition to include looking at a woman's body: "One who looks at the heel/rump of a woman is like one who looks at her vagina, and one who looks at her vagina, is as if he has sex with her" (*y. Ḥal. 58c*). In contrast, when it comes to same-sex interactions, we find countless examples of rabbis naked with one another in the bathhouse without any concern that the Torah prohibition against men having anal intercourse with other men may have been extended to include men looking at other men's bodies (e.g., *y. 'Abod. Zar. 42b* [3:1] and *Sem.* 12:12).

Numerous stories exist in rabbinic texts of rabbis kissing other rabbis (albeit in a show of platonic love). The rabbis were so comfortable with the notion of two men having intimate contact that they interpreted the "thigh" under which Abraham had his slave put his hand to swear an oath as Abraham's penis. According to one rabbinic reading of Genesis 24, Abraham had his slave hold his (Abraham's) penis in his hand and swear by it (Gen R. 59:8 on Gen 24:2; see also Rashi on Gen 24:2). Even though the rabbis did not read anything sexual into this interaction, their comfort with two men having physical contact with one another's genitalia stands in stark contrast to their prohibition against men and women having far less physical contact with one another. This contrast demonstrates that the fence they extended around the heterosexual prohibition was explicitly rejected for same-sex interactions. It reveals that the rabbis did not prohibit men from contact with one another, not even genital contact.

The reason for their different treatment of same-sex and opposite-sex nonpenetrative physical interactions can best be understood from the Talmud's explanation of why the sages permitted men to be alone with one another. While a man and a woman are forbidden from being in seclusion with one another, two men are permitted to be alone together (*m. Qidd.* 4:12). The Babylonian Talmud (*b. Qidd. 82a*) explains that Jewish men are not suspected of same-sex anal intercourse, and with that statement it dispels any suspicion that it was going to extend the fence around the Torah to other same-sex interactions. Since the rabbis of the Talmudic period understood any extension of the prohibition as applying to all men or to no men, they chose not to extend it.

Of course, the rabbis' restraint from adding a rabbinic fence around this law was not so that men could have non-anal sex with one another. Rather, their reason was practical: if the rabbinic decree

were extended for men with men, as it had been for heterosexual prohibitions, men would lead utterly isolated lives. They could not touch or be alone with anyone, man or woman. Additionally, the rabbis would have to explain why it was that previous sages had violated this rule, as rabbinic literature is replete with stories of men hugging and kissing and going to the bathhouse. Since the rabbis did not have a notion of homosexuality per se, they did not distinguish between homosexuals and heterosexuals, assuming that all Jews are disinclined to male-male anal intercourse. The Babylonian Talmud (*b. Qidd. 82a*) concludes, therefore, that no rabbinic fence around the *de-oraita* decree was needed. This left no sexual or sensual interactions between men prohibited (*de-oraita* or *de-rabbanan*) except for anal intercourse.

With Maimonides (1135–1204), however, the picture changes entirely. Maimonides distinguished between nonpenetrative sexual/sensual activities (e.g., kissing and hugging) with and without desire (*Issurei Bi'ah* 21:1 and 21:6). For Maimonides, only engaging in such activity with desire is technically forbidden. With this innovation, Maimonides could extend the prohibition to include sensual contact without casting aspersions on prior rabbis known to have kissed or hugged other rabbis and without having to stop men from all interactions with all other men.

Clearly, the rabbis of the Rabbinic Period understood the Torah prohibition of male-male sexual activity to be limited to anal intercourse. There is no evidence that they instituted a rabbinic decree to expand the Torah prohibition. Indeed, the evidence shows that they explicitly chose not to add a rabbinic decree. It was not until Maimonides, many centuries later, that this ruling was changed.

Female Same-Sex Relations. No prohibition of female same-sex intercourse exists in the Hebrew Bible, and, as we might expect from the rabbinic focus on penetration (especially of men), the rabbinic opprobrium for male same-sex anal intercourse does not extend to female same-sex sexual activity. In fact, rabbinic discussions of female same-sex sexual activity barely exist. The *Sifra* (a third-century Midrashic commentary on the book of Leviticus) does connect women marrying other women with the actions of the Egyptians proscribed in Leviticus 18:3, but this is the only clear piece of evidence of rabbis in the Rabbinic Period showing marked disfavor for such female-female marriage and, by extension, perhaps for female same-sex sexual activity. The Talmudic discussion of whether female same-sex sexual activity bars a woman from marrying a priest may seem at first sight like evidence of rabbinic disfavor for the activity. Nevertheless, the discussion really centers on whether such "sex" is deemed to be sex, enough to qualify those who engage in the activity as promiscuous (and therefore "whores") and thereby disqualify them from marrying into the priesthood. The discussion barely touches upon the rabbis' attitudes toward the activity, although the description of the activity as lewd may go beyond the legal implications for which it is invoked and thus speak to the rabbinic attitude toward the activity and those who engage in it.

The Babylonian Talmud (*b. Yebam. 76a*) states:

Rava said, "The law follows neither the son [Rabbah son of Rav Huna] nor the father [Rav Huna]. Regarding the son, as we have said [in the previous statement]. Regarding the father, for Rav Huna said, 'Women who rub against one another are disqualified [from marrying] into the priesthood.' And, even according to Rabbi Eleazar who said, 'an unmarried man who has sex with an unmarried woman not for marital purposes, makes her a whore/promiscuous [and thereby disqualified from marrying a priest],' that is in the case of a man [who has sex with her], but with a woman, it is merely lewdness [*pritzuta be-'alma*]."

With this statement, the Talmud makes clear that it does not consider women "rubbing" with women (the verb it uses for female same-sex sexual activity) to be forbidden or to change their status, declaring the act to be "merely lewdness."

On the other hand, the *Sifra* (*Ahare Mot* 9:8 on Lev 18:3) prohibits women from marrying other women, stating:

Like the actions of the land of Egypt…you shall not do, nor like the actions of the land of Canaan…shall you do" (Lev 18:3). I might have thought [that this implies] that we may not build buildings nor plant saplings like they did [since these were among the activities of these peoples], the Torah teaches, "nor shall you walk in their laws" (ibid., loc. cit.). This means their laws which have been engraved to them and to their fathers and to their fathers' fathers [and not other practices]. And what would they do? A man would marry a man, and *a woman [would marry] a woman*, a man would marry a woman and her daughter, and a woman would marry two men. Therefore, it is said, "nor shall you walk in their laws."

The *Sifra*, however, only explicitly prohibits same-sex marriage and not same-sex sexual activity or even same-sex relationships, although perhaps it ought to be understood as implying a prohibition against the sexual activity as well. If the *Sifra* read Leviticus 18:3 as prohibiting female same-sex sexual activity and not just female same-sex marriage, then it presumably should also be reading Leviticus 18:3 as prohibiting male same-sex sexual intercourse as well as sexual intercourse with a woman and her daughter. These other activities, however, are forbidden by other verses, resulting in a redundancy in the Bible, a hermeneutical problem for the *Sifra*, given its hermeneutical rules that two verses cannot come to teach the same law. The fact that the *Sifra* never addresses female same-sex relations implies that it reads Leviticus 18:3 as forbidding marriage alone. Nevertheless, since other biblical verses prohibit sexual intercourse between the parties of the other marriages mentioned in the passage, it is possible that the *Sifra* understands female same-sex sexual activity as forbidden from another verse as well. That verse is never mentioned, however, leaving it likely that the *Sifra* considers marriage to be the only thing prohibited between women. While this may seem odd, the fact that the rabbis generally consider penetration to be the only sexual act prohibited by the Torah fits with our findings that the rabbis never treat the nonpenetrative sexual actions between women as prohibited, even if this text prohibits them from marrying one another.

The question remains whether the Babylonian Talmud was aware of this passage in the *Sifra* when it declared female same-sex activity to be merely lewdness and what this declaration would have meant. Men of the priestly class are forbidden to marry women who have fallen into the category of *zenut* (whoredom/promiscuity). The debate would seem to be whether same-sex activity puts the women in this category as heterosexual sex does. According to the Palestinian Talmud (*y. Giṭ. 49c* [8:10]), the school of Hillel, which the law follows, held that same-sex activity did not prevent them from marrying men of the priestly class (implying that it does not qualify as "sex"). Likewise, the Babylonian Talmud rejects Rav Huna's position, declaring that such activity is "merely lewdness" and does not affect their status.

How should we understand this in light of the *Sifra*? Scholars have long noted that the Babylonian Talmud had a different version of the *Sifra* from the Palestinian version that has survived to today, often lacking passages found in the one we have. In this case, not only does the Babylonian Talmud never quote or refer to this passage from our *Sifra*, it fails to mention the passage in at least two relevant places. The first is in *Yebamot 76a* (above), and the second is in *Hullin 92a–b*, in which the Talmud states that gentile men never married other men. Had it known this passage from the *Sifra*, the Talmud should have quoted it as contradicting that fact, if only to go on to solve the contradiction by means of a limiting of one or the other statement.

Furthermore, we can determine from *b. Shabbat 65a–b* that female same-sex sexual activity was not understood to be forbidden in the Babylonian Talmud. In *b. Shabbat 65a–b* we learn that Samuel's father did not allow his daughters to sleep with one another. Initially, the stam (the anonymous portion of the Talmud) suggests that this practice supports Rav Huna's position (which was rejected in *b. Yebam. 76a*) that women who "rub" with one another are forbidden to marry into the priesthood (and that this was Samuel's father's concern). The stam concludes, however, that his concern was that his daughters should become accustomed to sleeping with others, presumably because they then might end up sleeping with men (thus Rashi). If the stam understood female same-sex sexual activity to be forbidden, even by

rabbinic prohibition, then it should have and would have factored that in to this discussion.

The stam in *b. Shabbat 65a–b* knew that Rav Huna's position had been rejected by Rava. They needed to explain why Samuel's father was known for this practice in spite of the fact that it does not disqualify women from marrying a priest. If the stam in *b. Shabbat 65a–b* had held that women were forbidden to have sex with one another, they would have had no need to resort to the flimsy excuse that Samuel's father did not want his daughters to become accustomed to sleeping with other bodies. They could have stated that the reason he did not allow them to sleep together was because having sex with one another is itself an infraction. Thus, whether the redactors of the Babylonian Talmud knew of the *Sifra*'s prohibition of same-sex marriage or not (and all evidence suggests that they did not), we can conclude that they did not consider women "rubbing" with one another to be prohibited though they did consider it to be "lewd."

In the twelfth century, however, Maimonides elided these distinct texts/issues with one another, stating:

> Women who rub one another (*b. Yebam. 76a*), it is forbidden. And this is of the actions of the Egyptians that we were warned against, as it is said, "like the actions of the land of Egypt you shall not do" (Lev 18:3). The sages said, "What would they do? A man would marry a man, and a woman would marry a woman, and a woman would marry two men." (*Sifra, Ahare Mot 9:8*)—*Issurei Bi'ah*, 21:8

Maimonides reverses the Talmud's ruling, prohibiting women from "rubbing" on the basis of Leviticus 18:3. From this point on, the Talmudic passage would never fully be read independently of the *Sifra*, and female same-sex intercourse would be seen as associated with the Levitical prohibition.

Conclusion. In the Rabbinic Period, the *Sifra* outlawed same-sex marriages, though it is not clear whether its authors considered female same-sex sexual intercourse to be prohibited as well. In the Babylonian Talmud, female same-sex sexual activity is not considered under the category of sex and is therefore not considered to be forbidden. Rather, it is considered to be "merely lewd." In the Medieval Period, Maimonides combined the Talmudic passage with the *Sifra*, extending the issue far past that of lewdness, declaring female same-sex sexual activity forbidden and connecting it to Leviticus 18:3.

[*See also* Male-Female Sexuality, *subentry* Early Judaism; Marriage and Divorce, *subentry* Early Judaism; Masculinity and Femininity, *subentry* Roman world; Same-Sex Relations, *subentries on* Hebrew Bible *and* Roman World; *and* Sexual Transgression, *subentries on* Early Judaism *and* Roman World.]

BIBLIOGRAPHY

Boyarin, Daniel. *Carnal Israel: Reading Sex in Talmudic Culture.* Berkeley: University of California Press, 1993.

Boyarin, Daniel. "Are There Any Jews in 'the History of Sexuality'?" *Journal of the History of Sexuality* 5 (1995): 333–355.

Brodsky, David. "Sex in the Talmud: How to Understand Leviticus 18 and 20: *Parashat Kedoshim* (Leviticus 19:1–20:27)." In *Torah Queeries: Weekly Commentaries on the Hebrew Bible*, edited by D. Shneer, J. Lesser, and G. Drinkwater, pp. 157–169. New York: New York University Press, 2009.

Cantarella, Eva. *Bisexuality in the Ancient World.* Translated by Cormac Ó Cuilleanáin. New Haven, Conn.: Yale University Press, 1992.

Chapnik, Elaine. "'Women Known for These Acts' through the Rabbinic Lens: A Study of Hilkhot Lesbiut." In *Keep Your Wives Away from Them: Orthodox Women, Unorthodox Desires*, edited by Miryam Kabakov, pp. 78–98. Berkeley, Calif.: North Atlantic Books, 2010.

Dorff, Elliot N. "Biblical Law and Rabbinic Precedent in Hard Cases: The Example of Homosexual Relations in Conservative/Masorti Halakhah." *Jewish Law Association Studies* 22 (2012): 44–59.

Foucault, Michel. *The History of Sexuality.* 3 vols. Translated by Robert Hurley. New York: Pantheon, 1985.

Greenberg, Steven. *Wrestling with God and Men: Homosexuality in the Jewish Tradition.* Madison: University of Wisconsin Press, 2004.

Halperin, David M. *One Hundred Years of Homosexuality, and Other Essays on Greek Love.* New York: Routledge, 1990.

Halperin, David M. "Is There a History of Sexuality?" In *The Lesbian and Gay Studies Reader*, edited by Henry Abelove, Michele Aina Barale, and David M. Halperin, pp. 416–431. New York: Routledge, 1993.

Halperin, David M. *How to Do the History of Homosexuality.* Chicago: University of Chicago Press, 2002.

Kosman, Admiel. "'Two Women Who Were Sporting with Each Other': A Reexamination of the Halakhic Approaches to Lesbianism as a Touchstone for Homosexuality in General." *Hebrew Union College Annual* 75 (2004): 37–73.

Olyan, Saul M. "'And with a Male You Shall Not Lie the Lying Down of a Woman': On the Meaning and Significance of Leviticus 18:22 and 20:13." *Journal of the History of Sexuality* 5 (1994): 179–206.

Parker, Holt N. "The Teratogenic Grid." In *Roman Sexualities*, edited by Judith P. Hallett and Marilyn B. Skinner, pp. 47–65. Princeton, N.J.: Princeton University Press, 1997.

Rapoport, Chaim. *Judaism and Homosexuality: An Authentic Orthodox View.* London: Vallentine Mitchell, 2004.

Richlin, Amy. *Garden of Priapus: Sexuality and Aggression in Roman Humor.* Rev. ed. New York: Oxford University Press, 1992.

Roth, Joel. "Homosexuality Revisited." http://www.rabbinicalassembly.org/sites/default/files/public/halakhah/teshuvot/20052010/roth_revisited.pdf.

Sarah, Elizabeth. "Judaism and Lesbianism: A Tale of Life on the Margins of the Text." *Jewish Quarterly* 40 (1993): 20–23.

Satlow, Michael. "They Abused Him Like a Woman: Homoeroticism, Gender Blurring, and the Rabbis in Late Antiquity." *Journal of the History of Sexuality* 5 (1994): 1–25.

Satlow, Michael. *Tasting the Dish: Rabbinic Rhetorics of Sexuality.* Atlanta: Scholars Press, 1995.

Walters, Jonathan. "Invading the Roman Body: Manliness and Impenetrability in Roman Thought." In *Roman Sexualities*, edited by Judith P. Hallett and Marilyn B. Skinner, pp. 29–43. Princeton, N.J.: Princeton University Press, 1997.

David Brodsky

Early Church

The practice of and attitudes toward intimate relationships between persons of the same sex in the early church are best understood in the context of Greco-Roman antiquity, in which relationship mores in general, as well as social conditions and practices, were defined by slavery, social stratification, subsistence living in an agrarian economy, imperialism, and communal values. These conditions are generally in contrast to modern Western values, so any study of ancient same-sex liaisons must take these into consideration.

Scholarship has established that the majority of people in the Roman Imperial period (approximately first century B.C.E. through the early fourth century C.E.) lived at subsistence level, and many were in fact slaves, totally dependent for at least part of their lives on owners and patrons. With virtually no control over their own bodies, they were subject to regular abuse and exploitation (Dynes, 1990, p. 1121; Dynes, 1992, pp. xiii–xiv; Martin, 2005, pp. 221–228). Members of the elite strata of society, especially men, controlled most social situations, including interpersonal and sexual relationships, and most of the literature that has survived antiquity was written by such men. Underlying philosophies and traditions, such as active and passive roles, the patronage system, and honor and shame (Brooten, 1996, pp. 208–212), all of which may be unfamiliar to modern people, further defined same-sex relationships in the early church. These differences require careful examination of the evidence but can shed new light on same-sex liaisons between both men and women and help move the current discussion forward in important ways.

Evidence for Same-Sex Relationships in Greco-Roman Antiquity. It is fairly common knowledge that elite men of antiquity had relationships with boys and young men, both free and slaves (Boswell, 1994, pp. 54–55), and that this behavior was not necessarily viewed as unethical, exploitative, or unnatural. There is also general knowledge about the poet Sappho of the island of Lesbos, her circle of girls, and their types of relationships, although she lived much earlier (at the end of the seventh and the beginning of the sixth centuries B.C.E.) and much of what is known is in fact legend (Reynolds, 2001, passim).

More recent scholarship, using literary and archaeological evidence—including inscriptions, papyri, architectural remains, burials, and works of art—has definitively established that people in Greco-Roman antiquity did engage in what we would today call consensual, adult same-sex relationships. While much of the evidence on such liaisons may be negative, it serves to demonstrate the very existence of same-sex

couples and the lives they lived despite cultural disapproval or, in some cases, with the approval of the early church.

There is textual evidence for both deep affection among same-sex couples and cohabitation. Several Greek erotic spells from Egypt, dating from the second through fourth centuries C.E., depict the attempt of one woman to become attracted to another (Brooten, 1996, pp. 73–113). Dozens of astrological texts cited by such ancient writers as Dorotheos of Sidon (ca. 25–75 C.E.), Manetho (probably first century C.E.), the astronomer and mathematician Claudius Ptolemy (second century C.E.), and Ptolemy's contemporary Vettius Valens of Antioch (Brooten, 1996, pp. 115–130), in generally condemning homosexual pairings, prove their very existence throughout the early Christian era. In the ancient literature of the time one can find many examples of same-sex unions. Some prominent male pairs contemporary with the first Christians included the emperor Hadrian and Antinoüs, Catiline and his lover mentioned by Cicero, and the protagonists of Petronius Arbiter's *Satyricon* (Boswell, 1994, pp. 58–68). The emperor Nero, who ruled 54–68 C.E., married a man, Sporus, in public and "lived with him as a spouse," and the poet Martial in the second century penned verse about the "bearded Callistratus [marrying] the rugged Afer / Under the same law by which a woman takes a husband" (Boswell, 1994, pp. 80–81). Lucian in *Dialogues of the Courtesans* (5.3) has a woman depict herself as being married to a woman for many years, and a novelist contemporary with Lucian describes the marriage between Berenice, the daughter of the king of Egypt, to Mesopotamia (Boswell, 1994, p. 82).

Homosexual pairings can also be seen in various art forms. Greek vase paintings from earlier antiquity provide proof that female and male couples existed prior to the Roman Imperial period and thus might well have been known to early Christians. (Brooten, 1996, pp. 57–59, provides five probable examples of female pairs in erotic poses dating from 650 to 350 B.C.E.) "Many hundreds of Greek vase-paintings" also show male couples, usually older, bearded men conversing with younger men or boys (Dover, 1978, pp. 4–9). In the early Christian era, a funerary relief from the Augustan era (27 B.C.E.—14 C.E.) shows two women clasping their right hands; this posture was generally used to portray a heterosexual union, but the inscription below the relief demonstrates that this was a union between two freedwomen, Fonteia Eleusis and Fonteia Helena (D'Angelo, 1990, pp. 65–72; Brooten, 1996, p. 59). In addition, a wall painting from Pompeii depicts two women having oral sex (Brooten, 1996, p. 60).

Evidence for same-sex relationships in the New Testament. The New Testament features several same-sex pairs in a relatively positive light. The letters of Saint Paul reflect the earliest stages of Christian development, since they date to the 50s C.E. While we know little about the pairs to whom he refers—Evodia and Syntyche (Phil 4:2–3) and Tryphaena and Tryphosa (Rom 16:3–4)—it is fairly certain that they were not fictitious. Mary Rose D'Angelo argues, "Evodia and Syntyche can be seen as a missionary couple, partners in the mission, rather than as individual members of Paul's missionary team. They may in fact have been independent of Paul....Second,...the 'religious conflict' [mentioned in Phil 4:2] is a dispute not between Evodia and Syntyche but between Paul on the one hand and the two women missionaries on the other" (D'Angelo, 1990, p. 76). In essence, Evodia and Syntyche and Tryphaena and Tryphosa were on a par with the heterosexual missionary pairs of Prisca/Priscilla and Aquila (1 Cor 16:19; also in 2 Tim 4:19), and of Andronicus and Junia, Philologus and Julia, and Nereas and his "sister," all mentioned in Romans 16. While some scholars have argued that Evodia and Syntyche were fictitious or were real but in conflict with one another, D'Angelo's conclusions support the other evidence discussed above that they were an example of a same-sex pair in antiquity.

The Gospels were composed and began circulating in the mid-60s through the early second century C.E., long after the death of Jesus; thus some characters portrayed by the evangelists may not have been historical. The same-sex pairs depicted in the Gospels, especially Mary and Martha and Philip and Bartholomew, nevertheless reflect the values of the fledgling church and were acknowledged in the first Christian centuries as important in spreading the Good News.

Mary and Martha, although widely interpreted as biological sisters in the Gospel accounts, lived together in Bethany with or without their brother Lazarus (depending on the Gospel). In later legend, the women traveled (or at least finished their lives) together, preaching the Christian message and winning converts. It is possible that, if they were real-life women at the time of Jesus, they were a nonrelated couple committed to both God and one another, with the designation of "sister" being an early title reflecting nonrelational companionship that only later came to be translated in the biological sense (D'Angelo, 1990, pp. 77–81; Boswell, 1994, pp. 67–71). (Lazarus, similarly, could be a "brother" in the sense of a brother in the faith.) In two translations of the *Epistula Apostolorum* of the second century, Martha and Mary are mentioned together. The Ethiopic text of the work refers to "Sarah, Martha, and Mary Magdalene" caring for Jesus's body, while the Coptic reads, "There went to that place <three> women: Mary, she who belonged to Martha, and Mary <Magd> alene" (Duensing, 1963, p. 195). "She who belonged to Martha" suggests companionship rather than kinship.

While it is possible that these women were products of evangelistic imagination and legend, the pairing of Mary and Martha still demonstrates the power of a female pair by merely surviving in the literature. As in the case of Saints Perpetua and Felicity, martyred together in Carthage around 203 C.E., the Martha-Mary stories inspired devotion for centuries in places as distant as France and Spain. Boswell notes that "the precise nature of the relationship between [Perpetua and Felicity] is not clear," in that it is not known for sure whether they shared a household; their husbands were not mentioned in the official martyrologies; and they kissed each other before they were killed. It was the "paired femaleness" of this couple that seemed to appeal most to Christians who heard their story (Boswell, 1994, pp. 139–141). Mary and Martha share the same traits: they are supposedly widowed; they may have a brother; and they live together. Mary and Martha constituted a popular and compelling pair in early Christianity and won converts to the faith.

The apostles Philip and Bartholomew are mentioned more or less together in the Synoptic Gospels and apocryphal literature and appear in later same-sex liturgies. In those liturgies, with the exception of Saints Sergei and Bacchus (discussed below), it is Philip and Bartholomew for whom there is the most evidence of pairing. There is little about these two men in the New Testament, however, which raises the question as to where the tradition of them as a couple originated. In John 1:43–51, Jesus calls Philip to be his disciple. Philip in turn finds Nathanael, and a dialogue ensues that could be one not just between two casual friends but between two people in a committed relationship. Thus Nathanael and Bartholomew are one and the same person. Among the arguments to support this is the mention of Philip with Nathanael in John 1:45–46 and with Bartholomew in lists of the Twelve (Matt 10:3, Mark 3:18, Luke 6:14, Acts 1:13).

Evidence for same-sex relationships in other early Christian literature. As Christianity grew, stories developed and circulated about New Testament figures and others to promote the faith. Philip and Bartholomew became quite popular both as paired missionaries and as models of love and fidelity (Boswell, 1994, p. 160 and passim). In the *Epistula Apostolorum* they are mentioned together in a list of disciples (Duensing, 1963, p. 192). In the apocryphal *Acts of Philip*, Bartholomew accompanies Philip to Hierapolis and Lyconia, along with Mariamne (Santos Otero, 1992, p. 469). The two apostles converse with Jesus in various Gnostic discourses, including *Sophia Jesu Christi* and *Pistis Sophia* (Trevijano, 1992a, p. 112). In *The Two Books of Jeu*, the text reads, "All the apostles…answered with one voice, Matthew and John, Philip and Bartholomew and James, saying: Lord Jesus, thou living one…" (Puech, 1963, p. 262). In the second treatise of the Codex Askewianus, in which portions of *Pistis Sophia* are found, the text reads, "But…while Jesus was saying this,…Philip and Bartholomew were in the south (with their faces) turned towards the north" (Puech, 1963, p. 258).

Sergei and Bacchus were another pair that grew considerably in popularity and influence. Roman soldiers of high social status who lived in the late third and early fourth centuries, the two men were Christians, devoted to the faith and to each other. What ultimately led to their martyrdom was not their affection for each other but their loyalty to Christ (Boswell, 1994, pp. 147–148). Over time, they came to be seen as "the quintessential 'paired' military saints, usually referred to and often pictorially depicted together (sometimes rubbing halos together and with their horses' noses touching)." A monastery was dedicated to them in Euphratesia and they became the special saints of the Byzantine army (Boswell, 1994, pp. 153–154).

The significance of Orthodox and Roman Catholic liturgies celebrating same-sex "marriages," including documents from the Vatican and Mount Athos, cannot be underestimated (Boswell, 1994, passim). While most of the examples come from the tenth through fourteenth centuries, the fact that they exist and were obviously utilized under church auspices is irrefutable proof that same-sex pairs were approved by the church, at least in certain locales (Boswell, 1994, pp. 283–344). Given other evidence from Greco-Roman antiquity, the liturgies also demonstrate a trajectory of practice from the early church into later times. Same-sex burials in later antiquity provide further evidence for this lifestyle and its approval by the church (Abrahamsen, 1997, pp. 33–56; Boswell, 1994, p. 88; cf. Brooten, 1996, p. 351n205).

Attitudes toward Same-Sex Relationships in Antiquity. Opinions on same-sex relationships in antiquity varied, as did the reasons for those opinions. While Sergei and Bacchus, for instance, were proof that there was "a widespread and ancient Hellenistic connection between homoeroticism and the military" (Boswell, 1994, p. 145; see also pp. 61–65), long-standing social mores dictated that male and female same-sex pairings be viewed negatively. These negative views are, in part, what contribute to pejorative opinions in the modern West.

In antiquity, gender roles were highly circumscribed. Men were expected to be active, strong, and honorable, while women were expected to be passive, compliant, weak, and devoted to the men of their families and to their children. Deviations from these roles were viewed as unnatural, undermining of the social fabric, dangerous, shameful, and sometimes evil. A man who took on the passive role of a same-sex pair was viewed as overly feminine, while women who bonded with one another were criticized for not fulfilling their passive, natural, familial roles. Since society at large and the patriarchal church approved only of marriages between elite men and women, other types of consensual, adult relationships were often seen as deviant (Dynes, 1990, pp. 1121–1122; Brooten, 1996, pp. 53–57 and 144–146).

Ancient authors, mostly male, made different arguments against male and female homosexuality. Some authors focused on tribades, for instance—women who actively sought sexual relations with or penetrated other women. The term comes from the Greek verb *tribein*, to rub or wear down (Hallett, 1992, p. 183; Brooten, 1996, p. 126). A number of ancient medical texts depicted such women as mentally ill and needing to be treated with mind control or even clitoridectomy (Brooten, 1996, pp. 143–173). The astrological texts condemned homosexual behavior based upon the "gender" of the planets and how they are aligned: "Opposite positions of the stars can cause female masculinization and male feminization" (Brooten, 1996, p. 129 and passim).

It is such perspectives that provide the context for New Testament passages that devalue the same-sex lifestyle: Romans 1:18–32, 1 Corinthians 6:9–10, 1 Timothy 1:10, and Jude 7—8. In 1 Corinthians 6:9–10, Paul condemns "homosexuals" using the Greek word *malakoi*, which can be translated as "men who assume a passive sexual role with other men" (Brooten, 1996, p. 260). Romans 1:18–32 is one of the most influential Pauline texts on sexual behavior, with verses 26 and 27 cited as proof that God condemns homosexuality. Men who are attracted to and have sexual relations with other men, and women similarly, are seen to be "unnatural" and "dishonorable."

Both 1 Timothy 1:10 and Jude 7—8 were written after Paul's death and reiterate condemnation of sexual perversion and unnatural lust. In a culture that was so defined by the communal values of honor and shame, early Christians who defied traditional mores were viewed as dishonoring not only themselves but also the nascent community, a minority group struggling for survival and identity. The "deviant" individual brought shame upon himself or herself and, even more importantly, on the group.

Modern Debates and Legacy. In the modern West, especially since the 1970s, the issue of same-sex relationships has been both divisive and unifying. On the negative side, scriptural passages have served to condemn same-sex pairings and the homosexual lifestyle. Gay, lesbian, and transgender youth are still thrown out of their homes by parents who do not approve of them, suicide remains high among this population, and so-called queer people are still at risk of assault and murder. Sermons preached in many churches continue to berate people who live the same-sex lifestyle, and the polity of many established, mainstream denominations forbids same-sex unions and the ordination of openly gay persons to the priesthood.

However, scholarship has demonstrated that the ancient context is in many ways vastly different than the modern one, which requires new ways of thinking about social issues. Western culture is significantly more individualistic than the culture out of which early Christianity emerged; self-actualization is now generally perceived as more important than cultural values such as honor and shame. Gender roles, for the most part, are significantly less stratified than they were in antiquity; modern Western women have become much more active, strong, powerful, and in the public eye, while men are less stigmatized for being sensitive and nurturing. Therefore, the ancient arguments against female action and initiative and against male passivity and gentleness hold considerably less sway.

Significantly, however, scholarship has also shown that the general social mores and perspectives against homosexuality in antiquity were not monolithically negative. As noted above, the ancient world did in fact paint positive pictures of male and female couples, and the early church in a number of significant ways celebrated their lives and contributions.

In the early twenty-first century, whether by court order or the enacting of legislation, several states across the United States allow same-sex unions and marriage. In many communities same-sex couples are almost completely integrated into the social fabric, raising children, owning homes, assuming leadership roles, holding public office, and generally living normal middle-class lives. The positive examples of same-sex couples in early Christianity support this development. The evidence gleaned from recent scholarship can enable the Western Christian to see that our ancestors in the faith valued the contributions of same-sex pairs, not only allowing them to be married and buried together but building churches and monasteries in their honor, depicting them in art, and placing them on their calendar of saints. Whether the argument for equality hinges on current values such as individuality and civil rights or on evidence from ancient cultures, including Christianity, the trend is toward the acceptance, approval, and celebration of loving same-sex relationships between consenting adults.

[*See also* Gender Transgression, *subentries on* Early Church, New Testament; *and* Same-Sex Relations, *subentries on* Greek World, New Testament, *and* Roman World.]

BIBLIOGRAPHY

Abrahamsen, Valerie. "Burials in Greek Macedonia: Possible Evidence for Same-Sex Committed Relationships in Early Christianity." *Journal of Higher Criticism* 4, no. 2 (1997): 33–56.

Boswell, John. *Same-Sex Unions in Premodern Europe.* New York: Villard, 1994.

Brooten, Bernadette J. *Love Between Women: Early Christian Responses to Female Homoeroticism.* Chicago: University of Chicago Press, 1996.

D'Angelo, Mary Rose. "Women Partners in the New Testament." *Journal of Feminist Studies in Religion* 6 (1990): 65–86.

Dover, K. J. *Greek Homosexuality.* Cambridge, Mass.: Harvard University Press, 1978.

Duensing, Hugo. "Epistula Apostolorum." In *New Testament Apocrypha*, edited by Wilhelm Schneemelcher, vol. 1, pp. 189–227. Translated by A. J. B. Higgins et al. English translation edited by R. McL. Wilson. Philadelphia: Westminster, 1963; original German edition 1959.

Dynes, Wayne R. "Rome, Ancient." In *Encyclopedia of Homosexuality*, edited by Wayne R. Dynes, vol. 2, pp. 1119–1126. New York: Garland, 1990.

Dynes, Wayne R., and Stephen Donaldson, eds. *Homosexuality in the Ancient World.* New York and London: Garland, 1992.

Hallett, Judith P. "Female Homoeroticism and the Denial of Roman Reality in Latin Literature." In *Homosexuality in the Ancient World*, edited by Wayne R. Dynes and Stephen Donaldson, pp. 179–197. New York: Garland, 1992.

Martin, Clarice. "The Eyes Have It: Slaves in the Communities of Christ-Believers." In *Christian Origins*, edited by Richard A. Horsley, pp. 221–239. People's History of Christianity 1. Minneapolis: Fortress, 2005.

Puech, Henri-Charles. "Gnostic Gospels and Related Documents." In *New Testament Apocrypha*, edited by Wilhelm Schneemelcher, vol. 1, pp. 231–362. Translated by A. J. B. Higgins et al. English translation edited by R. McL. Wilson. Philadelphia: Westminster, 1963; original German edition 1959.

Reynolds, Margaret. *The Sappho Companion.* New York: Palgrave, 2001.

Santos Otero, Aurelio de. "Later Acts of Apostles." In *New Testament Apocrypha*. Vol. 2: *Writings Relating to the Apostles: Apocalypses and Related Subjects*, rev. ed., edited by Wilhelm Schneemelcher, pp. 426–482. Translated by R. McL. Wilson. Cambridge, U.K.: James Clark, 1992.

Trevijano, R. "Bartholomew." In *Encyclopedia of the Early Church*, edited by Angelo Di Berardino, Vol. 1, p. 112. Translated by Adrian Walford. Cambridge, U.K.: James Clark, 1992a.

Trevijano, R. "Philip." In *Encyclopedia of the Early Church*, edited by Angelo Di Berardino, Vol. 2, p. 680. Translated by Adrian Walford. Cambridge, U.K.: James Clark, 1992b.

Valerie Abrahamsen

SEXUALITY

Sexuality is the broad term that refers to categories of sexual desire. Although heterosexuality is considered by most the "normal" and "natural" sexuality and all other sexualities are unnatural and deviant, sexual desire manifests itself in a variety of ways. In the history of scholarship regarding sexuality, much attention has been given to the subject of what determines or creates one's sexual desires. In its most simplified form, it is referred to the "nature vs. nurture" debate. On the one hand, does sexual desire occur naturally, that is, is it a part of the genetic and biological makeup of each of us? On the other hand, later thinkers asked, is there such a thing as sexuality at all? Or, as they propose, do we have pleasures that have been socially organized into a discipline that we call "sexual?"

Sexology. With the rise of scientific method in the late 1800s and early 1900s came the sexologists: biologically trained scientists who studied human sexuality. The sexologists maintained that sexuality is a natural human drive, as essential and amoral as the need for food, water, sleep, or self-preservation. They assumed that males and females are naturally attracted to one another and aimed to prove that sex between men and women is healthy and normal. Sexology, like most scientific research, was driven by ideological concerns. For example, the assertion that a good and robust sex life within a marriage strengthens that relationship is still a strong and central claim found within contemporary writers who use the content, if not the data, of the early sexologists. The underlying mission in the valorization of sex between married couples is ostensibly to bolster the institution of marriage itself.

The claim that sex is normal and natural was extended in the twentieth century to include homosexual couples as well. A few sexologists were able to use their work to argue against civil rights offenses against homosexuals. Karl Heinrich Ulrichs and Havelock Ellis, for example, worked toward a decriminalization of homosexuality by arguing that it is a naturally occurring condition.

The most notable theorist coming out of the field of sexology was, of course, Sigmund Freud. Freud practiced in Vienna with the notable sexologist Richard von Krafft-Ebing, but later departed from Krafft-Ebing and formed his own practical theories. Although Freud remained tied to the notion that sex is biological and occurs naturally in humans, his work proved to be groundbreaking and opened the doors to the complexity of human psychosexual development.

Sigmund Freud. Freud was the first to formulate a psychosexual theory of human development. Freud's theories, although androcentric, heterosexist, and biologically based, laid the foundation of sexual theory to which countless others later responded. To his credit, Freud recognized the complexities of all sexualities, that one's environment can influence one's sexuality, and posited that every single person's sexuality has a myriad of sexual objects and desires at varying degrees.

Freud lays the groundwork for human psychosexual development in "Three Essays on Sexuality." In his conception of sexuality, one could say that Freud had a Darwinian approach: he begins with the notion of "normality" and seeks to explain anomalies, or deviations from that norm. However, although Freud is heavily criticized for his focus on normal sexual development, Freud adamantly and frequently stresses the idea that whatever sexual aberrations one might conceive of, every perversion, every deviance, is present in every individual's sexual development. In other words, although Freud uses the word "normal" frequently, he includes "perversions" under the umbrella of normal sexuality, that the sexual life of normal adults is beset with perversion. Still, the definition of normal sex for Freud is genital-centered, heterosexual intercourse with a monogamous, romantic partner.

For Freud, sexuality has two main components: (a) the sexual objects onto which we (b) direct our desires. In its most basic form, sexuality seeks pleasure (not reproduction, as the sexologists argued), and that pleasure seeking begins when we are born. As an infant develops, it (or we) goes through a series of phases in which the foci of desires, and the desires themselves, evolve. First there is the oral phase, in which the center and fulfillment of all sexual desire emanates from oral contact with the mother's breast. With the pleasure that comes from lips-to-nipple contact, we at first connect erotic pleasure with nourishment. Then we learn that we can "invert" this pleasure, that is, we can fulfill our own sexual desires by sucking our thumbs, and at that point, pleasure becomes a distinct sensation no longer connected to necessity or to another person. Our first sensations of erotic pleasure, Freud notes, are ones without an object.

After experiencing pleasure via our mouths, we next discover the anal erogenous zone at the approximate age of two to four years old. The locus of pleasure is the stimulation of the mucus membrane (through defecation mainly) and the control and release of the sphincter muscle. Pleasure is both passive and active (or sadistic and masochistic). Again,

Freud sees this phase as an inversion—there is no "other" object of our desire. The pleasure derived from defecation is connected to the pleasure of creating something unique—a pleasure that Freud asserts that normal women would transfer to child bearing in later development.

At around the age of four to seven, we enter the "phallic" phase. The pleasure within this stage is first experienced through the necessary act of urination, but that pleasure is also traumatic as the subject (imagined as male by Freud) begins to notice that not everyone has a penis and develops a fear of being castrated. The fear of castration results, in part, from being reprimanded for touching our genitals or for masturbating. In this phase, according to Freud, we begin to understand that we cannot be sexually satisfied by our mother because of the incest taboo, and we begin the process of resolving the "Oedipus complex," Freud's famous dilemma which posits that we go through a phase in which we seek to kill our father so that we can acquire our mother. We resent our father because he stands between the subject and the object of desire, and "his" prohibitions (against incest and murder) take the form of a fear of castration—the father will castrate the son to guard the sexuality of the mother. Women experience this as well—girls desire the mother and envy their father's penis (which represents access to the mother). Girls feel inferior because of their lack of a penis and set about to acquire one, or rather to acquire the privilege that comes with a penis.

The Oedipus complex must be resolved in a way that orients the girl and the boy toward a socially acceptable (i.e., not incestuous) heterosexual desire. Women resolve the Oedipus (Electra) complex by earning the phallic social privilege by giving birth. Boys resolve their fear of castration by turning their desire away from their mother and onto appropriate female bodies.

The genitals are easily and often aroused and remain, in normal maturity, the source of pleasure. After a latent phase (between the ages of seven and fourteen) in which we learn to let go of the mother as object of desire and to reconcile with the father, we enter the final genital phase.

Freud sees perversion (and specifically "inversion," or homosexuality) as the product of being stalled (unable to resolve the Oedipus complex) in one of these nongenital phases or a *regression* back to those phases in later life. Inversion in women (lesbianism), according to Freud, is the result of never successfully navigating through the oral phase or reverting back to it and consequentially never shifting the object of desire from the mother to the father. For homosexual men, Freud posits that infantile sexual development is delayed by never fully moving through the anal stage and from shifting the desire from the mother onto the father.

For Freud, "abnormal" sexuality is a result of not being able to negotiate the balance between one's own pursuit of sexual pleasure and the social acceptance of such. If one is overly focused on the pursuit of erotic pleasure, the result is perversion and social deviance. If one restricts or represses erotic pleasure, the results are equally perverse. Although Freud continuously and emphatically stresses that all perversions are present in some degree in each and every individual, it is impossible not to see the development of sexuality as a heterosexual, androcentric, and triumphalist narrative in Freud's work.

To his credit, Freud's theories of sexual development are the foundation for every important work on sexuality thereafter: Freud believed that pleasure, not reproduction, is the primary sexual drive; he understood that the development of sexuality is social (although sex itself, according to Freud, is a biologically based drive); and Freud maintained that sex is not only a physical sensation but also one that is simultaneously a product of the mind and body. And the mind is, of course, culturally influenced.

Jacques Lacan. Where Freud placed so much emphasis on the body and on physicality in psychosexual development, Lacan's emphasis resides firmly upon language. Freud saw sexual development as a natural and thus normal process that culminated (in the healthy and normal person) into a properly constructed (and normal) heterosexuality. Lacan, on the other hand, understood this development entirely within a linguistic, culturally constructed realm (following mainly the work of Ferdinand de Saussure, a

French semiotician). Our sexual desire, according to Lacan, is dependent on others—we learn who and what to desire based on culturally generated cues. Lacan theorized ideological structures that allow every individual to understand his or her relationship to both the self and others. Lacan posits that there is a "real" existence to which, once we acquire language, we forever lose access and expressibility.

The way in which we develop as we lose access to "the Real" closely resembles Freud's stages of development. Lacan divides the formative years into three groups: the Real, the Imaginary, and the Symbolic. We begin with no delineation between ourselves and others. We are a part of our mother's body, still joined to her primarily with mouth to nipple, with the beginnings of the fragmentation of our body into pleasure areas: the vagina, the penis, the anus, because of the focus of attention to those areas. Lacan sees this as a shift from the Real into "the Imaginary"—as specific parts of our body begin to feel pleasure, we begin to associate that pleasure with something *outside* of ourselves; desire has a source and an object: the mother's nipple, her gaze, the sound of her voice. In this phase, famously known as the mirror phase, we see a reflection of our self; we know that we are both self and other. We are beginning to move away from a sense of wholeness, from a self-identity whose desires are fundamental and somewhat simple.

Our self in the mirror is "other" in that it is "me" over there. Yet, it is a perfect image, one that we despise because it is better, but one that we love and desire because we want to be it. The image in the mirror is uncomplicated, light, and joyful, not full of the complexities and psychic disturbances we feel as we progress toward acquiring language and forever rupturing the connection to our self. The locus of desire and sexual fulfillment has moved from a place within us, from a site of comfort and recognition. At once internal and external, the mirror image becomes the object of desire; it is an object that is no longer real, is constructed and imagined as perfection, and is simultaneously in and out of our control. But the crucial distinction between this stage and the Real is that the object of desire (the I/other in the mirror) has become

unobtainable. And at the same time, we begin to realize that all objects of our desire are unobtainable, beyond our realm of influence, and, most important, are a product of the world around us.

At this point language erupts and displaces reality. Everything finds its definition only in relation to an other—language (as it represents the real) is only intelligible through an internal logic of its own that plays out in a dualistic system and only makes sense in relation to another word: mother/father, I/other, or male/female. And because all language is symbolic (hence this phase's designation as "the Symbolic"), these words represent (or are signifiers of) categories of the Real. For example, the phallus is not the penis (as Freud would assume); for Lacan, the phallus represents the arenas of power bestowed upon the phallic sign.

In the same sense, "I" is no longer a "real I," but an I that is defined only over and against something else. That entrance into the Symbolic is, as Lacan remarks, a traumatic event; I is an empty signifier. We forever lose access to and comprehension of the Real. We cannot know a real I, merely an I that is externally determined. Likewise, the Lacanian theories of psychosexual development reinterpreted Freud's Oedipal crisis as a relative signifier as well.

Freud described the Oedipal complex, as explained above, as a crisis generated toward an actual father. For Lacan, the "phallus" and the "father" are symbols; the phallus symbolizes all of the knowledge and power that is lost from the move from the Real to the Symbolic; it is all of the socially constructed power that accompanies the penis. The father signifies the external, cultural locus for all of the power, sanctions, and control that culture places upon the subject.

In his turn from Freudian biology to Saussurian linguistics, Lacan creates what has become the bedrock of poststructuralist theory on the social construction of sexuality: although he never explicitly asserts that all sexualities have the same beginnings, are culturally driven, and could, all things being equal, be equally valued, his work implies all of this as it locates the development of sexuality within the interaction of the subject with the society. Lacan's theories of psychosexual development have been the impetus for all poststructuralist thought concerning the formation of sexuality.

In addition to shifting from a biologically based theory of sexuality, Lacan diverges from Freud by saying that women's sexuality develops differently from that of men. Freud claims that women and men develop in a similar way in that the clitoris (in psychosexual development) is a small penis, so that women also develop a castration complex, which manifests as "penis envy." Lacan, on the other hand, saw women as having, simultaneously, a sense of "lack" (*manqué*) and a sense of joy (*jouissance*). The sense of lack comes twofold: for (1) not having a penis, which precludes having access to power (as it is manifested in the symbolic) and (2) forever losing identity, or one's being. Joy comes about in the absence of not having a penis to lose (no castration complex). Lacan's theories of psychosexual development, as were Freud's, are not entirely satisfactory for women either. Following closely and building upon Lacan is Julia Kristeva.

Julia Kristeva. Whereas Lacan explained Freud in terms of "the signified," Kristeva introduced "the abject" into the mix. "The abject" is Kristeva's term for those things that cannot be completely subsumed into the Lacanian "symbolic order." The abject (blood, pus, and other corporeal oozings) exists in the subject prior to its acquisition of language, sometimes at the end of one's life, and within those persons who experience certain psychotic breaks (for example, certain types of schizophrenia) that render them external to the symbolic order. The crucial detail that Kristeva brings to the table here is that the body—although its articulation, and thus its reception, is shaped by society—maintains an essence that erupts and interrupts its own linguistic rendering.

The abject (horror) occurs at the time that we begin to leave Lacan's Real and enter into the Symbolic; it is a mirror of Lacan's mirror. The psychic panic that erupts when we are faced with losing the distinction self and other, or subject and object, becomes one of horror. There are, as Kristeva argues, corporeal realities that cannot be wholly subsumed by language, such as vomit, shit, or a dead body.

Kristeva's work reflects one offshoot of sexual theory that struggles to hold on to a "real," or essential body; she and others posit that traces of bodies destabilize order and resist complete linguistic erasure. It is in contrast to this notion that we see the most notable thinkers regarding the construction of sexuality: Michel Foucault and Judith Butler.

Michel Foucault. In all of the early work on sexuality, there is an assumption that sex and sexuality are real things, that is, that every human being has desires that are uniquely sexual in nature and that certain pleasures can be perceived as purely sexual. The sexologists and Freud saw sexuality as biologically and genetically determined, basic to us and necessary for survival. Freud created a space within that domain that took into consideration the effects that family dynamics, communal perceptions, and other organizational systems have on psychosexual development. Lacanian expansions to Freud's ideas produced a barrage of critique in the mid- to late twentieth century that questioned the "essential" nature (i.e., one that has an a priori existence, uncreated) of sexuality. The fallout from the Lacanian poststructuralist examination of sexuality was multidisciplinary and global. Jeffery Weeks, a British sociologist, and the American sociologists John Gagnon and William Simon argued that categories of sexuality are created; they are not naturally occurring entities, but rather, distinct categories of sexuality that are produced and maintained by cultural mechanisms. More, Gagnon and Simon questioned whether there are actually distinct feelings, desires, or touches that are *sexual*. In other words, how do we determine what counts as sexual? With its origins in Lacanian psychoanalysis and its continued examinations in the field of sociology, the idea that *sexuality* and *sex* are culturally produced is initially, and most clearly and brilliantly, articulated in Michel Foucault's *A History of Sexuality*.

Foucault's thesis is simple: we learn to be sexual beings. And we learn sexuality primarily through social institutions: the religious, the political, the juridical, the medical, the pedagogical, the economic, and the psychiatric. Each discipline articulates, defines, codifies, regulates, polices, and thus maintains and sustains sexuality. The feelings and desires do exist in our bodies prior to social articulation, but social forces organize all the various, disparate, and complex impulses into sexualities. The physical experiences are classified as sexual, and those sexualities are regulated and hierarchized, made moral or immoral, normal or perverse.

Foucault begins by examining the Victorian age, when, according to Foucault, the production of sexuality began. Foucault writes that the claim that the Victorians were sexually repressed is bogus, that everyone, everywhere talked about sex. From the innovation of the confessional in Catholicism to the detailed courtroom confessions and the sexologists, sexuality went from acceptable sexuality (what two monogamous, married heterosexuals did) and everything else to a plurality of sexualities. The myth of sexual repression was propagated and reiterated, according to Foucault, because that which is forbidden is desirable. By keeping sex repressed, liberation and transgression can then be linked to pleasure. Most importantly, sex becomes connected to truth, revolution, utopia, and happiness. All the world's functions (politics, economics, cultural rules) are founded on the "myth of sexual repression" and are mutually reinforcing. The illusion that sex can and must be controlled set into motion all of these modern disciplinary social organizations with the single motive of keeping the uncontrollable (sex) controlled. Foucault (1986) writes,

> At issue is not a movement bent on pushing rude sex back into some obscure and inaccessible region, but on the contrary, a process that spreads it over the surface of things and bodies, arouses it, draws it out and bids it speak, implants it in reality and enjoins it to tell the truth: an entire glittering sexual array, reflected in a myriad of discourses, the obstination of powers, and the interplay of knowledge and pleasure. (p. 72)

Thus, according to Foucault, humans are sexual, humans have somatically based desires, but the labels of sexuality (heterosexuality, homosexuality, cisexuality, bisexuality, asexuality, etc.) and the identification of sex and sexuality as a category are socially produced inventions. And what Foucault offers is

that "sexualities" have been produced en masse; from the simple Victorian categories of "good" sexuality (married, monogamous heterosexuality) and "bad" sexuality (everything else), the nineteenth century and beyond has seen an explosion in the production of sexualities. Foucault's point is this: the production of sexualities is to give the centers of control (the religious, the political, the economic, etc.) a reason to exist. As populations moved to urban centers and the industrial age required that people be literate for states to maintain economic prosperity, there needed to be, according to Foucault, greater and more rigorous control over bodies. Bodies had to be disciplined, and the way to control bodies is to control sexuality; if the body can be regulated, social forces can monitor whole populations. Thus, for Foucault, the production of sexualities is the way that contemporary societies control the masses.

Judith Butler. Judith Butler begins with Foucault but shifts her focus from the production of sexuality to the production and maintenance of gender and sex itself. Whereas most theorists have uncritically accepted that there are *naturally* two opposing and genitally determined sexes, Butler maintains that gender regulation actually produces the sexes—that all of the social control that Foucault imagines to be at the base of the production, discipline, and maintenance of sex is aimed at gender. These social processes are ubiquitous and pervasive, yet invisible. The mechanisms that construct gender depend on the invisibility of the process to create the illusion that masculinity and femininity occur naturally. Butler recognizes that when sex is accepted as occurring naturally, apart from cultural processes, and that men and women are seen as sexually complementary, heterosexuality is recognized as the only appropriate and normal expression of sexuality.

Butler argues that we perform gender and that cultural forces dictate how, as women and as men, we are supposed to act. And when we step outside those tightly drawn gender roles and act in a way that would be inappropriate to our assigned gender, society punishes us. The disciplinary measures come in various forms: economic losses (limited or no employment options, housing restrictions, diminished opportunities for market interaction), a loss of civil rights, and often physical violence. Thus, although gender is a performative process, albeit an unstable one, one's gender identity is not optional; society puts enormous pressures on each of us to conduct ourselves only in socially acceptable ways: gender-appropriate clothing, hair, mannerisms, colors of toys, language, employment, sexual partner, etc. The list of ways in which a culture requires its participants to conform to gender norms is literally endless and so comprehensive that it is uncritically accepted as natural.

Gender regulation, according to Butler, is the foundation and impetus for the creation of two sexes. Butler shows that sex (the cultural iteration of physical genitalia) is as unstable and no less culturally produced as gender. The very fact that some genitals are surgically altered to fit into the "either/or" of male/female indicates that sex cannot be reduced to a simple binary. The point is this: social structure (Foucault's power) rests entirely on the organization of gender into two opposing and complementary binaries. To give the illusion that gender and all of its apparatuses are natural occurrences, gender is presumed to be an essential, biological expression of a body that is sexed either as male or as female, when in reality the body is shaped to fit a predetermined gender.

Biblical Studies in the Production of Sexuality. Modern biblical studies became a discipline around the same time as the sexologists (and all the other disciplines) were producing sexuality (according to Foucault). Therefore, much of what Bible scholars have been doing is reproducing modes of "acceptable" sexuality, which is, of course, heterosexuality. Although the Bible (the Hebrew Bible more specifically) has countless examples of nonmonogamous heterosexuality, the prevailing narrative that has been delivered to twenty-first-century believers is that God has ordained (most notably in the creation story of Genesis 2—3, which features Eve and Adam) that one man and one woman should be joined together sexually with the sole purpose of reproduction.

The Bible interpreters' understanding of sexuality has been much in line with the apostle Paul's understanding of sexuality (and gender), in that gender and sexuality are naturally occurring, that God made male and female only, and that those two sexes are opposite and complementary with sexual desire only for one another in the intention of producing offspring. All other sexualities are deemed "unnatural."

Biblical references to nonheterosexuality are sparse. The only sexuality *explicitly* presented in the Bible is heterosexuality. Except for a few brief prohibitions, the Levitical laws are concerned only with the details of heterosexual couplings. And the primary metaphors of the relationship between the deity and believers are of heterosexual couplings (husband and wife, man and prostitute, man and wanton woman, father and daughter, and bride and groom). Although there have been musings about the possible bisexuality of King David, or possibly Joseph, and some speculation about whether eunuchs would have been asexual or possibly homosexual, the Bible does not offer direct evidence, in its law, poetry, histories, or metaphors, of nonheterosexuality.

The fact that sex between two men warranted an explicit prohibition (Lev 18:22; 20:13) suggests that men did indeed have sex with one another. Likewise, Paul's comments in Romans 1:26–27 suggest that women had sexual desire for other women, as did men for other men. As Bernadette Brooten has shown with her extensive research on female homoeroticism in the ancient world (specifically male attitudes toward female homoeroticism), Paul's understanding of gender and sexuality was right in line with that of his contemporaries: because of the "naturalness" of the active male and the passive female, sex between women is unnatural because, Paul and his contemporaries assumed, one of the females would have to take on the active male role. Yet, these brief references in Leviticus and in Romans do not constitute our modern notion of sexuality. That we classify whole persons as *being* heterosexual, or *being* homosexual, or *being* any sexuality is a recent (since the nineteenth century) phenomenon.

In short, there is no discussion or understanding of sexuality in the Bible. There are simply appropriate and inappropriate sexual acts, and the degree of propriety or impropriety depends upon the prevailing social attitudes. The notion of sexuality has been inserted into the text. For example, modern translators and interpreters have understood Genesis 19 (the story of the destruction of Sodom) to be a condemnation of male homosexuality, but a close study of that text and its references in Isaiah 3:9, Jeremiah 23:14, and Ezekiel 16:49 does not support that reading. Likewise, sex between certain classes of males (between an older man and a boy or between an elite male and a slave, for example) was an acceptable practice for Greek and Roman males from at least the sixth century B.C.E. Yet, again, this would not be understood as a sexuality in the way that we understand the term today.

Another example of a misapplication of a biblical text to address sexuality is the use of 1 Corinthians 6:9, Paul's exclusion of men who are *arsenokoites* and *malakos* from the kingdom of heaven. This text has been used to say that homosexuals are condemned to hell. Again, a thorough linguistic exploration, as Dale Martin makes in his article "*Arsenokoites* and *Malakos*: Meanings and Consequences," of these two Greek words which are commonly translated to mean homosexuals, suggests that whatever Paul means (and no one is quite sure), he does not have a whole class of people in mind. Rather, Paul, as did those who crafted the Levitical codes, condemned (presumed) specific sexual acts. As Martin argues, no one is quite sure what *arsenokoites* means, and even if the word has sexual connotations, it seems to be a condemnation of an economically based sexual injustice or exploitation. The second word, *malakos*, is used often by Paul's contemporaries to refer to "effeminate" behaviors in males. Being effeminate, that is, behaving in a way that does not conform to what the prevailing society perceives as masculine, is not interchangeable with a modernist understanding of homosexuality.

A historical-critical approach to "sexuality studies" by bible studies scholars is an anachronistic misnomer. The various historical-critical methods, methods of biblical study given an inordinate amount of credibility and authority by general readers, have been understood as a discovering or an uncovering of sexuality in the ancient world. Rather, the biblical critical methods produce and reproduce sexuality for and with the modern reader. There is no concept of sexuality to be discovered in the Bible; we can only know how the Bible has been used in the production and maintenance of modern sexualities.

[*See also* Creation; Gender; Paul; Queer Theory; *and* Sexual Transgression: Overview.]

BIBLIOGRAPHY

Brooten, Bernadette. *Love Between Women: Early Christian Responses to Female Homoeroticism.* Chicago: University of Chicago Press, 1993.

Butler, Judith. *Gender Trouble: Feminism and the Subversion of Identity.* New York: Routledge, 1990.

Butler, Judith. *Bodies That Matter: On the Discursive Limits of Sex.* New York: Routledge, 1993.

Foucault, Michel. *A History of Sexuality,* Vol. 1. Translated by Robert Hurley. New York: Vintage, 1986.

Gagnon, John, and William Simon. *Sexual Conduct: The Social Sources of Human Sexuality.* Chicago: Aldine, 1973.

Gay, Peter, ed. *The Freud Reader.* New York: Norton, 1989.

Hornsby, Teresa J. *Sex Texts and the Bible.* New York: Skylight Paths, 2007.

Martin, Dale. *Sex and the Single Savior: Gender and Sexuality in Biblical Interpretation.* Louisville, Ky.: Westminster John Knox, 2006.

Rubin, Gayle. "Thinking Sex: Notes for a Radical Theory of the Politics of Sexuality." In *Pleasure and Danger,* edited by Carol Vance, pp. 143–178. New York: Routledge & Kegan Paul, 1984.

Weeks, Jeffrey. *Sex, Politics, and Society: The Regulation of Sexuality since 1800.* London: Longman, 1981.

Teresa J. Hornsby

SEXUAL TRANSGRESSION

This entry contains seven subentries: Overview; Hebrew Bible; Greek World; Roman World; New Testament; Early Judaism; *and* Early Church.

Overview

"Sexual transgression" is not ontologically real. The phrase is a power-laden "seeming": it functions as a sociolinguistic sleight-of-hand in a cross-cultural card game pointing ideologically, and so quite significantly, to the power a given group or culture bequeaths to its dominant definitions of "normalcy," broadly understood. "Normalcy" is the effort to create a stable, cultural (and often legal) set of givens for human in-group interaction, typically in order to sustain a set of "elites" most able to effect "normalcy" and thereby to retain the moral, sociopolitical, and economic cache typically given the "normal." These givens can acquire over time the sensibility of "naturalness," "ubiquity," and "universality," but they are, in actuality, agentially chosen "truths" set by empowered players within these specific cultural systems. Said more simply, understanding "transgression" and "sexual transgression" in the periods in which the biblical narratives were produced requires us to understand the distinct efforts of different groups—Judeans, Greeks, Romans, and that liminal tribe called the Christians—to define themselves as peoples and in particular the manner in which they defined themselves over against other peoples by setting gendered sexual "norms" of acceptability and deploying the slander of sexual deviancy against others. It also, simultaneously, requires us to understand how moderns are describing them.

Theoretical and Cultural Starting Points in the Study of Sexual Transgression. Since the 1970s, scholarly moves in the study of "sexual transgression" of the ancient Mediterranean have undergone several major shifts. In the late 1970s and early 1980s, classicists and historians like K. J. Dover and John Boswell deployed a historical positivism and an essentialist understanding of "sex" and "sexuality" in the study of *Greek Homosexuality* (1978, 1989) and *Christianity, Social Tolerance and Homosexuality* (1981), producing important monographs that assumed the security of "history" and the historical study of a factual, singular "past" to highlight the transtemporal historical presence of one group of modern Western "sexual transgressors" (namely, male homosexuals) in the vibrant life of ancient Athens, Rome, and emergent Christianity. It made for luscious reading, not to mention an imagistic admiration of our very self, almost as if a time portal had opened and we could

see our gay selves supping at symposia. During the same time period, feminist scholars such as Phyllis Trible (1984), Elisabeth Schüssler Fiorenza (1984), and Carol Meyers (1988), who were rightly concerned with the seeming silence of women's voices in the Bible, famously highlighted the "texts of terror" in the biblical corpus; they sought to "reveal," through eloquently "suspicious" studies below or behind the textual surface, the discovery, disappearance, dismemberment, and/or memorialization of "women" (as modern Westerners understood the term). Note that for these early feminist biblical scholars, "sexuality" had far less to do with sex acts than with biological sex or gender; "transgression" was the presence of the sexed/gendered subject herself, an irony not lost on the scholarly interlocutors who sought to rediscover their ancient counterparts.

The scholarly politics of sexual transgression—"we've always been here, get used to it"—embedded in this kind of essentialist positivist historicism gave way in the early 1990s to the impact of cultural criticism and poststructuralist thought. Linguistic moves prefigured by Saussure and Gadamer found their home in the twistily exultant *Dissemination* of Derrida (1981): tracing his finger upon Plato's *pharmakon*, he wrote of *Logos*:

The truth of writing, that is, as we shall see, (the) non-truth, cannot be discovered in ourselves by ourselves. And it is not the object of a science, only of a history that is recited, a fable that is repeated. The link between writing and myth becomes clearer, as does its opposition to knowledge, notably the knowledge one seeks in oneself, by oneself. And at the same time, through writing or through myth, the genealogical break and the estrangement from the origin are sounded. One should note most especially that what writing will later be accused of—repeating without knowing—here defines the very approach that leads to the statement and determination of its status. One thus begins by repeating without knowing—through a myth—the definition of writing—which is to repeat without knowing. This kinship of writing and myth, both of them distinguished from *logos* and dialectics, will only become more precise as the text concludes. (pp. 74–75)

In 1978, Hayden White in *Tropics of Discourse* had deployed a newly emerging cultural criticism to compatible effect, underscoring the instability of "history"—the illusion of it as an orderly science of the past—much as Derrida sought to undercut the stability of "the word," instead penning an ever-moving, disseminating *logos*. Both were strongly impacted by Michel Foucault's insistence on the empowered, cultural bases for language—that words have no set referents in transcultural reality but are rather figurative and thus mythic, culturally specific "strategies that sanction conceptualizing rituals" (White, 1978, pp. 231–232)—rituals, that is, like the study of history and science and sexual activity. As Foucault's own genealogy, *The History of Sexuality*, articulated, sexual identity and homosexuality were nineteenth-century cultural inventions (1976, p. 43).

These linguistic-cultural challenges to structuralism and historical positivism found receptive ears among scholars of sex and Bible. I will focus on the work of one of them: Dale B. Martin. In a series of outstanding articles now collected in the volume *Sex and the Single Savior* (2006), Martin integrated and deployed insights from White, Derrida, and Foucault in seismic, cultural-critical, and ideological-critical genealogies of "sexual transgression" as it was being debated by Paul scholars. In "Heterosexism and the Interpretation of Romans 1:18–32" (1995), for example, he eschewed the approach of scholars who were treating Romans 1 as the (homo)sexual transgression passage par excellence in favor of uncovering the modern, heterosexist ideological assumptions (about nature and homosexuality) that regulated their cultural overdetermination of the text's "acts." In "*Arsenokoites* and *Malakos*: Meanings and Consequences" (1996), he took a compatible but distinct tack; offering a genealogy of translation, he identified the cultural constraints on the translation of the terms in different time periods in order to demonstrate, definitively, that *arsenokoites* and *malakos* have not until the present period been conjoined to carry the modern weight of meaning (homo-)sexuality. Instead, he showed precisely what we do not know about these terms for a Paul who never used them elsewhere and, in 1 Corinthians 6:9, stuck them

in a vice list riddled with primarily *economic* signifiers. As he says in "The Myth of Textual Agency," the Bible does not speak; we are always already the agents of its interpretation. Martin's cultural critical and ideological genealogies of scholars' inculcation of modern standards of "normalcy" into ancient texts on "transgression" have been challenged, but never bested.

Genealogy also bred gendered and (gender?-) queer turns in the study of ancient sex. The most significant were born from the unexpectedly sinuous slow dance of Judith Butler's *Gender Trouble: Feminism and the Subversion of Identity* and David Halperin's *One Hundred Years of Homosexuality*, authored in the same year (1990). In *Gender Trouble*, Butler argued definitively that, like language itself, gender and human subjects are culturally constructed and performative. We are made and constantly in the making; we are what we do to and with our bodies. Launching a full-frontal assault on essentialist (white) feminists' love of "woman," Butler argued that the category is as fraught as it is definitionally squishy—fraught by what we may now call "intersections" with sexual desire, class, and race too-often erased from its meaning and fraught by the false dualism between gender, understood as enculturated, and biological sex, treated as a fixed, "natural" ontology. (The distinction had worked, for a time, in white feminists' efforts to break "the glass ceiling," but for Butler it had lost its mystique.) So Butler offered the first well-known feminist gender challenge to the solidity of biological "sex," one that has subsequently been refined by such scholars as Thomas Laqueur (1990), Alice Domurat Dreger (1998), and Anne Fausto-Sterling (2000, 2012). Such researchers showed that biological "sex" has been culturally created by modern medicine as dual and "naturally" stable, as "male" and "female." But Butler argues that supposedly naturally "sexed" bodies are defined at several incompletely overlapping levels at once (phenotypically, genotypically, hormonally) and, further, that they only signify their "sex" through gendered displays, one of which was sexual performance. Domurat Dreger builds on this picture, detailing the intentional ideological erasure of third-gender/sexed bodies by twentieth-century physicians so alarmed by the number of non–dually sexed bodies discovered in physical exams that they *worked* to entrench culturally the "natural" truth that there exist but two sexes: "male" and "female." Finally, Laqueur adds the backstory to Butler's critique of "sex": that physicians into the 1900s understood "female" bodies not as a separate sex but, like ancient doctors, as a physical inversion or deformity of the masculine form—woman was incomplete man, the vagina was an undescended penis, and sexual gender deviance was attached to the figures of the *tribas* (sexually dominant woman) and the *mollis* (male softie). In short, "from the Greeks to Freud," male writers and doctors in the West assumed ideologically the "natural" existence of a hierarchical, gendered body continuum grounded in the theoretical perfection of physical masculinity.

But Butler's more famous argument is that "heterosexuality" is constructed normatively to attach desire, as a "natural" orientation, to a particular "biological sex"; persons are "driven" to desire members of the same or opposite sex. Further, because biological sex is gendered dualistically as either male or female, the category of "(hetero)sexuality" requires the presence of its abject opposite, "homosexuality," to remain stable. After all, one can only be "driven" to desire the same or "opposite" sex—as opposed, say, to desiring muscles, soft skin, a strong back, chocolate, or some other luscious object—in a *dually* sexed/gendered sexuality system fixated on "orientation." In other words, the assumptions about sex, gender, and sexuality regnant in 1990—that there are two sexes, two genders, and two sexualities that, when performing "normally" and "naturally," overlap to create a biologically driven heteronormativity—are a triadic modern gender construction, sex-gender-sexuality, each element of which requires the other two lest the three-legged stool of modern sex/uality split in half. Thus, Butler famously concluded, feminist political praxis should focus not on "woman" but on making gender trouble; rather than exalting "woman" they should queer the heteronormative triad, especially in the "gender-sexual" sphere, by troubling seemingly set gender assumptions about dress, walk, talk, and sexual touch.

Butler's jaw-droppingly important book made David Halperin's *One Hundred Years of Homosexuality* on the profound difference between "homosexuality" and ancient male sexual performance an easy swallow. Halperin did not know the work of Butler (or that of Laqueur, for that matter). But after demonstrating that the word "homosexuality" did not make it into the *Oxford English Dictionary* until 1892, Halperin showed that throughout the nineteenth century the modern organization of sexual preference around object choice (i.e., for a person of same or different sex) "was not clearly distinguished from other sorts of non-conformity to one's culturally defined sex-role: deviant object-choice was merely one of a number of pathological symptoms exhibited by those who reversed, or 'inverted,' their proper sex-roles by adopting a masculine or feminine style at variance with what was deemed natural and appropriate to their anatomical sex" (pp. 15–16). It wasn't until Freud that "sexuality" was given a biological base (and an orientational "drive" train). Put another way, before the rise of "sexuality" as a cultural construct, Westerners typically treated "normalcy" in gendered terms and assimilated sexual behaviors, "normal" and "abnormal," to gendered standards of conduct.

Halperin showed that ancient Greeks likewise defined what we moderns might call male "homoeroticism" in fundamentally gendered terms. "Masculinity" of sex role was aligned with penetration and other markers of social dominance, high status, and hierarchical superiority, while femininity (in anatomical "women" and "men") was aligned with sexual receptivity and inferiority. In this elite Greek economy of sex, "sexual transgression" was marked by opposition to these standards: for women, it was to be insertive, dominating, to become *tribades*. For adult males, it was to choose to take the position of women, the receptive, penetrated position. Doing so, Halperin accurately implied, threatened elite Greek men with effeminizing "sexual transgression"—they could become diseased, prefer the feminine position in sex, and potentially transform into girlish softies (*molles, malthakoi*), a malady Caelius says he observed more often as men aged (1990, pp. 22–23). Critically, the gendered nature of "sex" and "sexual transgression" in Halperin's portrait of Athenian male sex play extended well beyond the strictly "sexual" sphere.

> Sexual activity is thematized as domination…between social superior and social inferior. "Active" and "passive" sexual roles were therefore necessarily isomorphic with superordinate and subordinate social status; hence an adult, male citizen of Athens can have legitimate sexual relations only with statutory minors (his inferiors not in age but in social and political status): the proper targets of his sexual desire include, specifically, women, boys, foreigners, and slaves—all of them persons who do not enjoy the same legal and political rights [*sic*] and privileges that he does (p. 30).

In other words, not only did Greek elites fundamentally gender sex acts and sexual actors and assume the existence of a plurality of gendered actors, they also regulated "sexual transgression" based on gendered notions of status difference, social power, and politics.

In 1991, Halperin followed up this watershed work with *Before Sexuality*. Coedited by John Winkler and Froma Zeitlin, *Before Sexuality* is a *tour de force* that demonstrated and expanded Halperin's thesis in exquisite detail. As a whole, the research of this group of scholars revealed that ancient Mediterranean peoples lived (emphatically) *before sexuality*, in performatively gendered worlds of sexual deviance and display. In these worlds "women" were thought fundamentally wet, dirty, and wild; astronomy and swaddling were body-molding acts; physiognomy could tell you the "make" of a man; and men could, by failing to work their gender daily (sexually and in several other ways), become women or, worse, something(s) in-between, the androgyne or *mollis*. If acknowledged, the extent of the difference between a world in which "sexual transgression" was materially gendered and ours, of the imagined (hetero)normative, would require modern scholars of sex to reposition studies of ancient "sexual deviance" not *just* within specific socio-historical contexts that admitted the centrality of gender performativity and plurality but *also* within multi-axial fields of knowing that included (the gendering of and intersections of gender with) politics, ethnicity, empire, status, rhetoric, and sexual slander.

Quarter Turn: Doing Sex "History" Differently after Halperin. Emphasizing that Halperin and others developed these critical insights about the gendered nature of ancient sex at the end of the twentieth century is required because scholars of ancient sex are still wrapping our collective head around the diverse implications of these insights. Together with *Gender Trouble, One Hundred Years of Homosexuality* and *Before Sexuality* marked the end of the reign of "essentialist" treatments of sex and "sexual deviance" in the ancient world. After Foucault, Halperin, and Butler, even scholars of Paul could not, with a modicum of scholarly integrity, continue to say that Paul (or Jesus) *ever* discussed "sexuality" (much less "transgression" of that sexuality). But Halperin's *Before Sexuality* also functioned as something of a gauntlet thrown. It marked the beginning of a still-current split between scholars who acknowledge Halperin and speak of sex and sexual deviance as fundamentally gendered acts and those who highlight gender but still use the language of "homo-" (and presumably hetero-) "eroticism," as well as those who embrace plurality but keep the concept of sexualit(ies) and insist on the existence of ancient "sexualities" that are simply different from our own.

Among those scholars who have heeded Halperin's (and Foucault's and Butler's) fundamental warning that "sexuality" is modern, some have tenaciously stuck to the language of "sexuality" in their depictions of ancients' sexual conceptions, perhaps despite knowing better, and quite possibly because publishers told them that entitling their studies "Roman gender deviance is sexy" wouldn't sell books (Williams, 1999). The unfortunate consequence of the refusal of the modern in this otherwise excellent book is the confusion of the fundamental difference between "our" orientational systemic of sex categories and ancient one(s) that Williams himself knows were built on gender performativity. For a modern audience, it is an ideological intercalation that confuses far more than it illuminates. It arguably hands over to moderns the power of forgetting contexts—cross-cultural difference as well as multi-ethnic pluralities of approaches to sex and transgression as gendered ancient realities—so that we may again name those realities in our own image.

Others uncomfortable with the language of sexuality have acknowledged the ancient foundational focus on gender performance, shifting their descriptions of "sexual deviance" to "homoeroticism," but the ideological effect of naming "deviance" primarily as "homo-" anything is an unwitting replication of modern assumptions that there are but two sexes and that sexual orientation is transculturally "real." Martti Nissinen's *Homoeroticism in the Biblical World: A Historical Perspective* (2004) and Bernadette Brooten's flawlessly researched *Love Between Women* (1996) exhibit this tension between the gendered character of ancient sexual self-definition (quite apart from object choice) and that of modern Westerners. An extraordinary scholar, Brooten repeatedly brings life to the gendering of ancient denunciations of certain sex acts by women, but her study is skewed by the belief, or perhaps the hope, that like women-loving women today, *real* "women who loved women" existed behind ancients gender-typing.

Still other scholars have acknowledged the "turn to gender" not by turning to gender but by turning from the singular "sexuality" to the plural, "sexualities" (Hallett and Skinner, 1997; Hubbard, 2014). As a political strategy, embracing the plural does work to distribute and decenter the power of a centralized singular, and much scholarship on sex in modernity has therefore shifted to embrace this language (e.g., the excellent journal *Sexualities*; for the pluralization of gender study, see, e.g., Ramet, 1996). But there are real troubles for this move as a schematization of ancient sex. For one, some scholars, like Thomas Hubbard, would (I believe) like to use it to return to the age of Dover and Boswell (2003). Second, as I argued in "*Still* Before Sexuality" (2007), supposed terms denoting different Roman "sexualities" are all gendered passive and active, indicating that the masculo-penetrative gender binary articulated by Halperin is the culturally regulatory force for "normalcy" in Greece and Rome (pp. 13–21). But the biggest problem with this naming practice is that introducing "sexualities" reasserts (however subliminally) the dominant symbolic of "orientation" in a way that hides not only the centrality of gender to ancient "sex" but also the various "extra-sexual" cultural dy-

namics that contributed to ancients' understanding of sex *as* gendered (again: rhetoric, slander, politics, interethnic strife, imperialism, and ethnic difference). The reason for this failure of insight is, I believe, that we "moderns" have worked so often and so hard to hide from ourselves the ideological impact of these mechanisms in the construction of "sexual orientation"— and perhaps because we really do want sexual orientation to exist before it did.

The obverse of this rusty coin is that with the erasure of a regnant, transcultural "sexuality," a door has been opened wide to the robust, multi-axial gender analysis of sexual normalcy and sexual deviance in the ancient Mediterranean. Scholars who walked through that door have indeed begun in earnest to engage gender pluralities, gender reversals, and gender cultures and the rhetoric, slander, politics, interethnic strife, imperialism, and ethnic difference that gave them all meaning.

This emerging body of literature is large, and I can only gesture here to some of its directions and the underlying refinements to method and gender theory that these works reflect. First and foremost is the openness to plurality in sex stories and practices and the consequent recognition that biblical texts, like the multiple intersecting worlds they reflect, never had just one pattern for acceptable or unacceptable sexual relations (Knust, 2011). Second, growing awareness of the distinct ethnic contexts of biblical texts facilitates a much deeper understanding of the role of sex, desire, and sexual deviance in group definition and intergroup relations. For instance, Craig Williams (1999) highlights important distinctions between Greek and Roman elite standards for masculinity: for example, Halperin's treatment of the gendered "penetrator-penetrated" frame was critical for understanding a dominant Greek ideology of sex, but while some elite Greeks idealized *eros* between the adult *erastes* and young *eromenos* as education, for Romans the penetration of future *viri* was prohibited because of the imperial fear of effemination. Similarly, I argued in "Sexy Stoics" (2004) and "Disease of Effemination" (2003) that Judean treatments of sexual "transgression" are differently pointed but, for the same reason, imperialism. Paul, Josephus, and Philo of Alexandria all insisted vehemently that Judeans did not engage in sexual license "like the nations" did; Philo went so far as to say that "androgynes" who practiced effeminating intercourse should perish unavenged (*On the Special Laws* 3.37–39). In other words, it was *far too* effeminating for an already-effeminated subject group like Judeans to be associated with "sexual transgression." As "*Still Before Sexuality*" shows, imperialism even lies at the root of Roman gendered charges of sexual deviance against fellow Romans. Fearing penetration of the Roman "body" by conquest, Roman men responded to their gendered paranoia of "Greek invasion" by stereotyping their "proximate others" (elite Roman women) as sexually luxuriant, andrygynous *tribades* unduly influenced by their imperial other (Greeks). In *Abandoned to Lust* (2006), Jennifer Wright Knust extends the study of interethnic and politicized sexual slander, arguing convincingly that such stereotyped accusations of sexual license and depravity—slander of various kinds from adultery to incest to bestiality—were leveled, with searing specificity, by Romans against Greeks, Greeks against Romans, Romans against Christians, Jews against "the nations," and Christian Jews like Paul against nonbelieving "nations" and even believers, when they were "the nations." As Knust details, "accusations of sexual licentiousness…depended upon and reinforced cultural codes about the characteristics" appropriate to the elite, and by slandering others, 'elites' were able to self-define as powerful and virtuous" (2006, p. 47). She rightly states that the ancient categories of "man" and "woman" (and, I would add, "androgyne" and "eunuch," among others) were defined in no small part by such slander. In short, specific ethnic, imperial, and political groups' gender definition depended, in part, on leveling the charge of sexual transgressions against equally specific "others." Dominant groups, like the Romans, slandered subject peoples sexually for social control, and subject groups (like Jews and Christians) slandered both other subject groups (Greeks) and dominant groups sexually to retain their ideological power or to regain a sense of control over others. Sexual slander serviced the masculine phallus of cultural control.

In addition to the studies of the *tribas*, the androgyne, and the *malakos*, research of other gender-ambiguous categories of person like slaves and eunuchs has also contributed insights to the study of ancient gender, especially as a tool of and response to empire. For instance, Matthew Keufler argues in *The Manly Eunuch* (2001) that dominant masculinities (e.g., of Roman elites) exist in a dialectical relationship with the peoples they have dominated. Taking cues from postcolonial theorists like Homi Bhabha and Gayatri Spivak, Keufler and others have recognized that the dominated can create new masculine ideals for themselves through mimickry, hybridity, or "postcolonial" inversion of dominant goods. As Eric Thurman showed in "Looking for a Few Good Men: Mark and Masculinity" (2003), the gendered logic of colonial mimickry is precisely what enabled early Christians to stake claim to the august title "Son of God" in order to revirilize—however ambiguously—a Judean Christ crucified and effeminated by the Romans. It is quite possibly why Matthew cited Jesus as embracing the gender-deviant "eunuch for the kingdom of heaven" as the exception to the rule against divorce (19:12). (On this and other transgressive readings of the Jesus Movement, see Moxnes, 2003.) Kuefler argues that such revirilization is the reason that late antique period Christians, in a time of reduced Roman power, inverted the Roman masculine ideal of the "perfect male-penetrator" and redeployed early Christian traditions of acceptable gender-ambiguity to assert a "new masculine ideal" for Christians—as "eunuchs for the kingdom of heaven." The gender-ambiguous, even (or perhaps especially) in their "sexual transgressiveness," can empower disempowered peoples; gender ambiguity was a counter-imperial power play.

This is but one reason why, in the study of "sexual transgression," recognizing the role of status, especially of slave and free, is so critical. As Keith Bradley (1998), Jennifer Glancy (2006, 2011), Clarice Martin (2006), and other scholars of slavery have shown, slaves hardly counted as human in the Roman hierarchy of persons. As "talking tools" they did not have gender, were defined as the sexual property of their masters, were consequently called "boys" when adult, and yet had a "social currency" as slaves, both in economic and sexual terms and, because of their "deviance" from Roman standards of selfhood, required their own rules for sexual "propriety." Both Roman and Christian household codes (from Ephesians to 1 Peter) demonstrate how central slaves were to "normal" domestic economies and, indeed, how dangerous they were if they ever climbed above their "place" (Dixon, 1992; Osiek and Balch, 1997); early Christians exhibited the contradictions of gender power inherent in the category of "the slave" by at once bowing as slaves before a crucified *kyrios* or "master" (Rom 1:1; Phil 1:1) and mimicking Roman household codes in an effort to best their Roman counterparts at "the perfect normal." Slaves of Christ themselves, Christians enslaved fellow Christians and simultaneously used slaves' enslavement to protect their communities, through assimilation to a Roman domestic norm based on top-down patronal rule, from harm or death at Roman hands. It was a most ironic form of Christian "masculinity" (that is, community-resistance to imperial control).

From slander to enslavement, empire to effeminacy, multi-axial study of sexualized gender transgressions demonstrate the value of poststructuralist gender theories and interdisciplinary research (e.g., ethnicity studies, postcolonial studies). They produce richly diverse ancient narratives of "sexual transgression" that are as genuinely reflective of the intersecting cultures that produced them as we can offer. "Sexual transgression" has never been a singular reality. But the study of it, which is necessarily both modern and ancient, teaches us about the ancient and modern worlds, what is at stake for us in naming the "sexual transgressive" in the past, and consequently informs the manner in which we use gendered conceptions of sexual propriety to sustain ourselves and our societies' sense of stability—quite often at the expense of others.

Let Us Conclude with Those Who Went "Queer"... Whether They Actually Did or Did Not. The language of things "queer" exploded in biblical studies (and elsewhere) after Judith Butler troubled gender. Suddenly, it seemed, everyone was writing "queer" theologies and books about the queer Bible. But for the most part they were just a little bit too much like the gay and lesbian "Love Boat." And so, with the caveat that I have great respect for the brave, real-world leadership of such people as Robert Goss, biblical studies was nevertheless "blessed" with *Take Back the Word: A Queer Reading of the Bible* (2000) and *Queering Christ: Beyond Jesus Acted Up* (2007). Such books and their descendants, which continue to populate the publishing market, are efforts to make Jesus and the Bible open and affirming for non–straight-identifying people—whether gay, lesbian, straight, bisexual, or transgender—by making Jesus and the Bible, well, just fabulously gay. And yet they do not destabilize the sexed *or* gendered identities that "queer" theorists showed to have sustained "heteronormalcy" and its stable, abhorrently "transgressive" homosexual other. This work is vinegar in a holey wineskin masked as "old vine" wine.

In fact, most biblical studies that go under the title "queer" deal with issues facing the identity groups named above (although trans folks are really just beginning to find a serious hand hold in biblical scholarship; see Swancutt, 2006; Leone, 2013; Nyland, 2007). Unlike the work of Goss, several are indeed rigorous in their efforts to approach biblical texts, both as ancient texts and, because of the Bible's iconic power, as culturally and politically dynamic spaces in which peoples determine "who shall live and who shall die." Works in this genre include two books authored or edited by Ken Stone (2001, 2005). Always careful, in his introduction to *Queer Commentary* Stone recognizes the potential problems of identity politics for this kind of "queer biblical engagement" but argues nevertheless for a reader-centered approach. While highlighting critiques of the work that occur even within the pages of the book—for example, that biblical narratives of domination remain even as the aberrancy of homosexual "transgression" is being decentered, Stone argues that such queer commentaries are nevertheless a powerful enterprise. They undermine heteronormativity (per se) "in" the ancient and modern spaces of scripture by highlighting the Bible's life-giving resonances for sexually "transgressive" biblical readers (e.g., God as Top; God as Lover; the deep joys of food and sex) (2001, pp. 20–34).

There are a few notably delicious exceptions to the rule of "queer" as an umbrella term meant to appeal to modern "sexually transgressive" readers: Stephen Moore's *God's Beauty Parlor and Other Queer Spaces In and Around the Bible* (2001) is a masterful poststructuralist romp through the gender-ambiguous masculinity of historical Jesus and Paul studies. In the 2010s, outstanding contributors put current queer theories to the test in Ken Stones's *Bible Trouble: Queer Reading at the Boundaries of Biblical Scholarship*, co-edited with Teresa Hornsby (2011). Similarly, Sean Burke's *Queering the Ethiopian Eunuch* (2013) offers a lovely refusal to resolve the ambiguities of Luke's narrative about the eunuch's geographic, ethnic, colonial, and gender transgressiveness, arguing—with a bit of theoretical slippage about authorial intent—that "Luke" upholds the eunuch's gender and ethno-political ambiguity as a symbolic pointer to the direction the Christian mission was to take in Acts. Finally, Dale Martin's "The Queer History of Galatians 3:28" argues vigorously against a modern "egalitarian" understanding of the text in its first historical contexts, correctly recognizing the central (andrygynous) masculinity of the figure of Christ there, and yet it wonderfully refuses the "original" masculine as the solution to the text's meaning, pushing against the hegemony of historical criticism for a plurality of viable bottom-up possibilities, as well as a variety of (sexed, raced, and gendered) mixing of kinds that refuses modern dualities. This is queer history and ethical thinking at its best (2006, p. 89).

Finally, apt critiques that "queer" scholarship aimed at sexually transgressive readers too often fails to account for the needs of nonwhite readers or to destabilize sexuality itself as a cultural construct have also been met by queer theologians like Patrick Cheng (2013). Cheng seeks to be inclusive of persons experiencing oppressions based on their sexual or gendered "transgression" of heteronormativity while at the same time challenging the theological, sexual, political, and identity boundaries and binaries (between gay and straight, male and female, god and human, and East and West) that sustain it. Especially helpful is Cheng's deployment, upon the problematics of "the intersectional transgressive," of Homi Bhabha's notion of colonial hybridity (1994): that the developed cultural identities of colonized subjects create an ambivalence and anxiety in colonial "masters" (understood by Cheng in geopolitical, racial, and sexual terms) and, as a consequence, decenter their power over those they have colonized. Embracing "the Christian transgressive" as hybrid, Cheng argues that sex- and gender-queers and "the Christ" may together experience their lives as love incarnate—as erotic, out, liberative, transgressive, and hybrid—rather than as "sin," the cultural symbolic of the heteronormative colonizer. That is indeed good news.

[*See also* Gay Liberation; Gender; Homosexual/Queer; Intersectional Studies; Masculinity and Femininity, *subentries on* Greek World *and* Roman World; Queer Readings; Race, Class, and Ethnicity, *subentries on* Early Judaism, New Testament, *and* Roman World; Sexuality; *and* Sexual Transgression, *subentries on* Roman World *and* Early Judaism.]

BIBLIOGRAPHY

Bhabha, H. *The Location of Culture.* New York: Routledge, 1994.

Boswell, J. *Christianity, Social Tolerance and Homosexuality.* Chicago: University of Chicago Press, 1981.

Bradley, K. *Slavery and Society at Rome.* Cambridge, U.K.: Cambridge University Press, 1998.

Brooten, B. *Love Between Women: Early Christian Responses to Female Homoeroticism.* Chicago: University of Chicago, 1998.

Burke, S. *Queering the Ethiopian Eunuch.* Minneapolis: Fortress, 2013.

Butler, J. *Gender Trouble: Feminism and the Subversion of Identity.* New York: Routledge, 1990.

Cheng, P. *Radical Love: Introduction to Queer Theology.* New York: Seabury, 2011.

Cheng, P. *From Sin to Amazing Grace: Discovering the Queer Christ.* New York: Seabury, 2012.

Cheng, P. *Rainbow Theology: Bridging Race Sexuality and Spirit.* New York: Seabury, 2013.

Derrida, J. *Dissemination.* Chicago: University of Chicago Press, 1981.

Dixon, S. *The Roman Family.* Baltimore: Johns Hopkins University Press, 1992.

Domurat Dreger, A. *Hermaphrodites and the Medical Invention of Sex.* Cambridge Mass.: Harvard University Press, 1998.

Dover, K. J. *Greek Homosexuality*. Cambridge, Mass.: Harvard University Press 1978.

Fausto-Sterling, A. *Sexing the Body: Gender Politics and the Construction of Sexuality*. New York: Basic Books, 2000.

Fausto-Sterling, A. *Sex/Gender: Biology in a Social World*. New York: Routledge, 2012.

Foucault, M. *The History of Sexuality: An Introduction*. New York: Vintage, 1976.

Gadamer, H.-G. *Truth and Method*. London: Bloomsbury Academic Press, 2004.

Goss, R. *Queering Christ: Beyond Jesus Acted Up*. Eugene, Ore.: Wipf and Stock, 2007.

Goss, R., and M. West. *Take Back the Word: A Queer Reading of the Bible*. Cleveland, Ohio: Pilgrim, 2000.

Glancy, J. *Slavery in Early Christianity*. Minneapolis: Fortress, 2002.

Glancy, J. *Slavery as Moral Problem: In the Early Church and Today*. Minneapolis: Fortress, 2011.

Hallett, J., and M. Skinner, eds. *Roman Sexualities*. Princeton, N.J.: Princeton University Press, 1997.

Halperin, D. *One Hundred Years of Homosexuality and Other Essays on Greek Love*. New York: Routledge, 1990.

Halperin, D., J. Winkler, and F. Zeitlin, eds. *Before Sexuality: The Construction of Erotic Experience in the Ancient Greek World*. Princeton, N.J.: Princeton University Press, 1991.

Harper, K. *From Shame to Sin: the Christian Transformation of Sexual Morality in Late Antiquity*. Cambridge, Mass.: Harvard University Press, 2013.

Hornsby, T. J., and K. Stone, eds. *Bible Trouble: Queer Reading at the Boundaries of Biblical Scholarship*. Atlanta: Society of Biblical Literature, 2011.

Hubbard, T. *Homosexuality in Greece and Rome: A Sourcebook of Basic Documents*. Berkeley: University of California Press, 2003.

Hubbard, T. *A Companion to Greek and Roman Sexualities*. Malden, Mass.: Wiley-Blackwell, 2014.

Knust, J. Wright. *Abandoned to Lust: Sexual Slander and Ancient Christianity*. New York: Columbia University Press, 2006.

Knust, J. Wright. *Unprotected Texts: The Bible's Surprising Contradictions and Sex and Desire*. New York: HarperOne, 2011.

Kuefler, M. *The Manly Eunuch: Masculinity, Gender Ambiguity, and Christian Ideology in Late Antiquity*. Chicago: University of Chicago Press, 2001.

Laqueur, T. *Making Sex: Body and Gender from the Greeks to Freud*. Cambridge, Mass.: Harvard University Press, 1990.

Leone, K. *The Transsexual and the Cross: Disproving the Myth That Transsexuality Is a Sin*. K.T. Leone, 2013.

Macwilliam, S. *Queer Theory and the Prophetic Marriage Metaphor in the Hebrew World*. Sheffield, U.K.: Equinox, 2011.

Martin, C. "The Eyes Have It: Slaves in the Communities of Christ-Believers." *In Christian Origins*, Vol. 1, *People's History of Christianity*, edited by T. A. Horsley, pp. 221–239. Minneapolis: Fortress, 2006.

Martin, D. B. *Sex and the Single Savior*. Louisville, Ky.: Westminster John Knox, 2006.

Meyers, C. *Discovering Eve: Ancient Israelite Women in Context*. Oxford: Oxford University Press, 1988.

Moore, S. *God's Beauty Parlor and Other Queer Spaces in and Around the Bible*. Stanford, Calif.: Stanford University Press, 2001.

Moxnes, H. *Putting Jesus in His Place: A Radical Vision of Household and Kingdom*. Louisville, Ky.: Westminster John Knox, 2003.

Nissinen, M. *Homoeroticism in the Biblical World: A Historical Perspective*. Minneapolis: Fortress, 2004.

Nyland, A. *Study New Testament for Lesbians, Gays, Bi, and Transgender: With Extensive Notes on Greek Word Meaning and Context*. Uralla, Australia: Smith and Stirling, 2007.

Osiek, C., and B. Balch. *Families in the New Testament World: Households and Housechurches*. Louisville, Ky.: Westminster John Knox, 1997.

Phillips, K., and B. Reay. *Sex Before Sexuality: A Premodern History*. London: Polity, 2011.

Ramet, S. *Gender Reversals and Gender Cultures: Anthropological and Historical Perspectives*. New York: Routledge, 1996.

Saussure, F. de. *Course in General Linguistics*. Chicago: Open Court, 1998.

Sheridan, V. *Crossing Over: Liberating the Transgendered Christian*. Cleveland, Ohio: Pilgrim, 2001.

Stone, K. *Practicing Safer Texts: Food, Sex and Bible in Queer Perspective*. London: T&T Clark, 2005.

Stone, K., ed. *Queer Commentary and the Hebrew Bible*. Cleveland, Ohio: Pilgrim, 2001.

Swancutt, D. M. "'The Disease of Effemination': The Charge of Effeminacy and the Verdict of God (Romans 1:18–2:16)." In *New Testament Masculinities*, edited by S. D. Moore and J. Capel Anderson, pp. 193–233. Atlanta: Brill and the Society of Biblical Literature, 2003.

Swancutt, D. M. "Sexy Stoics and the Rereading of Romans 1.18–2.16." In *The Feminist Companion to Paul*, edited by A.-J. Levine with M. Blinckenstaff, pp. 42–73. Feminist Companion to the Bible Series. London: T&T Clark, 2004.

Swancutt, D. M. "Sexing the Pauline Body of Christ: Scriptural 'Sex' in the Context of the American Christian Culture War." In *Toward a Theology of Eros:*

Transfiguring Passion at the Limits of Discipline, edited by V. Burrus and C. Keller, pp. 65–98. New York: Fordham University Press, 2006.

Swancutt, D. M. "*Still* Before Sexuality: 'Greek' Androgyny, the Roman Imperial Politics of Masculinity, and the Roman Invention of the Tribas." In *Mapping Gender in Ancient Religious Discourses*, edited by T. Penner and C. Vander Stichele, pp. 11–61. Leiden, The Netherlands: Brill, 2007.

Schüssler Fiorenza, E. *In Memory of Her: A Feminist Theological Reconstruction of Christian Origins*. New York: Crossroad, 1984.

Thurman, E. "Looking for a Few Good Men: Mark and Masculinity." In *New Testament Masculinities*, edited by S. D. Moore and J. Capel Anderson, pp. 137–161. Semeia Studies 45. Atlanta: Society of Biblical Literature, 2003.

Trible, P. *Texts of Terror: Literary-Feminist Readings of Biblical Narratives*. Minneapolis: Fortress, 1984.

White, H. *Tropics of Discourse*. Baltimore: Johns Hopkins University Press, 1978.

Williams, C. *Roman Homosexuality: Ideologies of Masculinity in Classical Antiquity*. New York: Oxford University Press, 1999.

Diana M. Swancutt

Ancient Near East

See Gender and Sexuality: Ancient Near East.

Hebrew Bible

In the Hebrew Bible, sexuality itself is good, and sometimes even celebrated. Sex between a husband and wife is built into creation, part of the natural, divinely ordained order of things. Yet sexuality is also viewed as potentially dangerous when it varies from forms of expression that are considered part of the order of the world.

Because of this potential danger, the Hebrew Bible is filled with attempts to control and regulate forms of sexual expression and choices of sexual partner. Often the texts that attempt to regulate sexual behavior are found in legal collections, which also present the consequences of engaging in these forbidden sexual acts as severe, involving both individual pun-

ishment and putting the entire community at risk of exile from the land.

Yet the legal collections are in part a delineation of ideals of behavior, a reflection of how certain individuals felt members of society ought to act, rather than a reflection of actual societal norms. While some of the laws, commands, decrees, and prohibitions in the legal collections probably reflected mainstream mores, others likely did not. If one considers texts from other genres, one sometimes gets a different picture regarding societal values, norms, and mores regarding sexuality. Sometimes sexual acts that are prohibited and punished in the legal collections are depicted negatively in other biblical genres, and sometimes they are not. Therefore one must consider texts from all genres, not just the prescriptive texts, to get a fuller idea of what might have been the reality of the culture that produced these texts.

The forms of sexual expression identified as sexual transgressions in one or more prescriptive texts include male-male sexual relations, rape, incest, bestiality, adultery, sexual promiscuity, sex with a menstruant, and possibly autoeroticism. Male-male sexual relations and rape are discussed in other entries. Other acts are discussed below, with particular attention paid to how much evidence from other genres corroborates the condemnation of these acts in prescriptive texts. Sometimes the narrative and poetic texts confirm the belief that a certain sexual behavior or choice of sexual partner is illicit, and other times they show a glimpse of alternative views about these sexual behaviors and choice of partners, revealing that perhaps the society that produced the Hebrew Bible was more diverse than may first appear.

Incest. Incest, the violation of prohibitions against sexual relations, cohabitation, or marriage between close relatives, is treated as a sexual transgression in four texts in the legal collections. In all cases, the restrictions against sex with close relatives are addressed exclusively to males and concern which female relatives, including both blood kin and kin through marriage, are sexually off-limits. No distinction is made between consensual and nonconsensual sexual relations.

Leviticus 18:6–18, which provides the most detailed guidelines, opens in verse 6 with a general statement prohibiting sexual contact with *šĕ'ēr bĕśārô*, "close kin" (author's translation). Verses 7–18 follow with prohibitions against sexual contact or marriage with twelve categories of female kin, starting with those closest: mother, father's wife, sister (full or half), granddaughter, stepsister who is part of one's father's clan, paternal and maternal blood aunts, (paternal) blood uncle's wife, daughter-in-law, brother's wife, both a woman and her daughter or granddaughter (labeled as *zimâ*, depravity, because, as the author specifies, they are kin) and both a woman and her sister (while the former is alive). Noticeably absent is a prohibition against sex with one's own daughter. A possible explanation (originally proposed by Rattray, 1987, p. 542) is that the daughter does not need to be stated in verses 7–18 because *šĕ'ēr bĕśārô*, close kin, in Leviticus 18:6 includes the daughter (as well as two other female kin: the mother and sister).

Leviticus 20:11–12, 14, 17, and 19–21 includes seven categories of female kin in its restrictions: father's wife, daughter-in-law (labeled as *tebel*, illicit mixing), marriage with both a woman and her mother (labeled as *zimâ*, depravity), sister (both full and half), maternal and paternal blood aunt, uncle's wife, and brother's wife. Penalties range from death to *karet* (likely the cutting off of one's family line through a combination of premature deaths and infertility), childlessness, and "bearing one's sin," an unspecified punishment by divine agency.

Deuteronomy 23:1 (22:30 in NRSV) is a prohibition against marrying one's father's wife. Since polyandry was not practiced, the prohibition refers to marriage to one's father's former wife. The purpose of this law may have been to stop the practice of sons laying claim to their father's wives after they died (see 1 Kgs 2:13–25). In Deuteronomy 27:20, 22–23, sex with three categories of female kin (father's wife, sister or half-sister, and mother-in-law) are part of the list of sins that often escape detection that, if committed, result in a self-imposed curse in the communal self-imprecations of Deuteronomy 27:14–26.

Ezekiel 22:10–11 is the one prophetic text to address forbidden incestuous relations, grouping sexual re-

lations with one's father's wife, daughter-in-law, or half-sister with other transgressions, both sexual and nonsexual, committed by leaders of the people (Ezek 22:9–12) that God will punish with exile (Ezek 22:13–16). As in Deuteronomy 27, these female kin may have been singled out because sex with them was considered likely to escape detection.

There are several narrative texts that describe sexual relations between relatives that are deemed incestuous in one or more of the legal collections. Sometimes the narrative texts and the legal collection both depict a sexual act between relatives as illicit. At other times, relationships categorized as incestuous in legal collections are not presented as problematic in narrative texts. Abraham is married to his paternal half-sister, Sarah (Gen 20:12). Jacob marries two sisters, Leah and Rachel (Gen 29:21–30). Moses and Aaron are sons of Amram and his aunt Jochebed (Exod 6:20). Judah has sex with his daughter-in-law Tamar (Gen 38:18). In 2 Samuel 13:1–14, Tamar tells her half-brother Amnon that David would not deny him her hand in marriage. While this may have been a lie on Tamar's part in order to attempt to escape a rape, it seems unlikely. When Amnon casts her out afterward, Tamar accuses him of committing an even greater wrong than the rape, reflecting her expectation that he should do the right thing and marry her.

The sometimes contradictory understandings of incest that we find among the biblical texts can be explained several different ways. One possibility is that what relationships between kin were considered incestuous varied over time: indeed, all of the examples noted above predate the giving of the Torah and the prohibitions on incest it contains (other than Amnon/Tamar). Another possibility is that the restrictions in legal collections were an attempt to impose stricter regulations on which kin one could marry or engage in sex. A final, and perhaps most likely, possibility is that sexual and marital relationships in the narrative texts reflect exceptional cases. Royalty is often not subject to the same mores that apply to the rest of society, which could explain Tamar's belief that she could marry Amnon. Other relationships in question come from folk traditions and legends about patriarchs, who were part of Israel's mythic history, which is not necessarily reliable evidence of social conditions and sexual mores of an earlier period, or any period.

Lastly, there is the issue of Levirate marriage. Leviticus 20:21 states that if a man marries his brother's wife, it is *nidâ*, impurity, and they will remain childless. This law makes levirate marriage illicit, punished by God with childlessness. But according to Deuteronomy 25:5–10 and Genesis 38, it is a man's duty to marry his deceased brother's wife if she is childless, to produce offspring for his brother. There are a few possible explanations. Levirate marriage perhaps was seen as an exception to the law against marrying one's sister-in-law, and it was understood that such behavior was forbidden otherwise. Another possibility is that attitudes toward the practice evolved over time. Lastly, Leviticus 20:21 could have been an innovation intended to eliminate a practice that up to that point was acceptable.

Bestiality. Bestiality, sexual relations between a person and an animal, is categorized as a transgression in several legal collections. Exodus 22:18 states that anyone who lies with an animal will be put to death. In Deuteronomy 27:21, lying with an animal is part of the list of sins that, if committed, result in a self-imposed curse in the communal self-imprecations of Deuteronomy 27:14–26. Leviticus 18:23 prohibits both men and women from having sex with animals, labeling such behavior *tebel*, illicit mixing. Leviticus 20:15–16, the only text that specifies that the animal is also punished, sentences both the man or woman and the animal to death and adds that both have incurred bloodguilt.

One narrative text may imply acts of bestiality. Genesis 2:18–22 explains that a woman was created after Adam failed to find a suitable helpmate among the animals. While it is not explicit in the text, perhaps the way Adam tested helpmates was through attempts at sexual intercourse. If this is the case, then it is implicit in Genesis that sex between humans and animals is not considered part of the order of things, since Adam found the animals unacceptable as partners.

It is difficult to draw general conclusions about the mores of Israelite society as a whole based on the limited available evidence. However, given that bestiality is presented as a transgression in three different biblical legal collections and the only other possible reference presents sex with animals as unnatural, bestiality likely was generally viewed as unacceptable.

Adultery. Adultery (often, but not always, denoted by the root *n'p* and its nominal derivatives) is understood in the Hebrew Bible as consensual intercourse between a married or betrothed woman and a man other than her husband, whose own marital status is immaterial. It is the one sexual act prohibited in the Decalogue (Exod 20:14; Deut 5:12). Leviticus 18:20 also prohibits adultery, while both Leviticus 20:10 and Deuteronomy 22:22 sentence a couple who commits adultery to death. In Deuteronomy 22:23–24, a betrothed woman (legally bound to her husband) and a man caught having what is assumed to be consensual sex within the town are sentenced to stoning. The one case in the legal collections where the stated punishment for adultery is not death for both parties is Numbers 5:13–30, in which a wife suspected of adultery but never caught must drink the "water of bitterness." The way her body responds will prove her guilt or innocence.

The narrative texts present more variety in terms of who is punished and how they are punished. Pharaoh and his household suffer plagues for his inadvertent commission of adultery (Gen 12:10–20). Judah sentences Tamar, found to be pregnant while awaiting levirate marriage, to be burned, though the sentence is not carried out (Gen 38:24–36). Reuben loses his birthright (Gen 49:3–4). God punishes David with the death of the child from his adulterous sex with Bathsheba (2 Sam 11–12). While Absalom is not punished directly for adultery, his death is the result of his rebellion against his father, to which his adulterous act is integrally related (2 Sam 16:21–23; 20.3).

Proverbs 2:16–19; 5:1–23; 6:20–35, and 7:1–27 warn young men to avoid the adulterous "strange woman," whose charms cost too high a price. The author focuses on the negative consequences of adultery for the man, which is described as a path to ultimate self-destruction (elaborated upon in Prov 6:27–35 as including disgrace within the community and suffering the wrath of the cuckolded husband). The consequences for the woman were not the author's concern.

In prophetic texts such as Hosea 4:1–3 and Jeremiah 7:9; 23:10, 14, adultery is grouped with other sins that the people are guilty of committing, and for which the people may they suffer God's wrath. Additionally, some of the prophets (e.g., Hos 4:1–3; Jer 3:6–10; and Ezek 16 and 23) use adultery as a metaphor for Judah and Israel's religious and/or political infidelity to God. In these metaphors, only the woman is depicted as guilty of adultery, only she is punished, and it is her husband (God) who punishes her with divorce and, in some texts, sexual humiliation. However, prophetic metaphors are likely not a reliable source for drawing conclusions about actual practice.

While all of these texts consider adultery to be a serious transgression, there is quite a bit of variety regarding who was considered guilty, who was punished, what the punishment was, and who delivers the punishment. It is probable, given the biblical evidence, that a variety of sanctions, both formal and informal, were employed against adultery in order to discourage members of society from engaging in it.

Sexual Promiscuity. When a woman engages in sexual activity that is considered a violation of the rights or honor of a male who has authority over her, whether husband or father, it is labeled as sexual promiscuity (*znh*) in biblical texts. As Phyllis Bird has demonstrated, the basic meaning of the root *znh* is "to engage in sexual relations outside of or apart from marriage" (1989, pp. 75–80). Thus *znh* covers all instances of sexual intercourse in which there is an absence of a marriage bond between otherwise acceptable partners, including adultery, premarital sex, and the licit sexual activities of a prostitute. It is used both literally and figuratively. When used literally, the subject is always female. When used figuratively, the subject is those (usually men) who engage in religious infidelity, acting promiscuously with other gods.

The *qal* feminine participle form of *znh*, *zônâ*, when used as a noun, denotes a prostitute. The biblical texts that mention prostitutes reflect a society in which prostitution is licit and tolerated. Women who work as prostitutes appear to be without husbands or male guardians, and thus are not violating the rights or honor of any male by having sexual relations outside of marriage. In contrast, adultery and premarital sex are considered illicit.

Since adultery is discussed above, this section considers texts in which a woman who is still under the authority of her parents engages in behavior labeled as *znh*, sexual promiscuity. Three texts, Leviticus 19:29, Leviticus 21:9, and Deuteronomy 22:20–21, treat such behavior as a grave matter with severe consequences. Leviticus 19:29 warns each man not to desecrate his daughter by making her a prostitute or allowing her to be sexually promiscuous, depending on how one interprets the *hip'il* of *znh*, lest the land become promiscuous and filled with depravity (*zimâ*). Leviticus 21:9 states that when a priest's daughter desecrates herself through sexual promiscuity, she is sentenced to death by burning, because her illicit behavior also desecrates her father. Deuteronomy 22:20–21 states that if a husband's accusation that his bride was not a virgin when she married is found to be true, she should be stoned to death in front of her father's house because she committed an outrage (*něbālâ*) against Israel by acting promiscuously while living in her father's house. The woman is guilty of both premarital sexual promiscuity and marrying under false pretenses, by claiming to be a virgin.

There is a question as to whether these texts are representative of attitudes toward young women's sexuality as a whole in ancient Israel, since there are other biblical texts in which young women who engage in sex out of wedlock while living under their father's authority are not treated as harshly. In Exodus 22:15–16, no blame appears to be placed on the young woman who is seduced. Rather, her seducer must pay a bride price and, if her father chooses, marry her. In Deuteronomy 22:13–19 (to which verses 20–21 were likely added later, changing the meaning of the passage as a whole), it appears that the only punishment a woman and her family would suffer if her husband was successful in his accusation that she wasn't a virgin when she married is divorce, returning the bride price, and, likely, humiliation.

While none of the texts present daughterly premarital sexual activity in a positive light, they do provide evidence that there was some variation in how seriously the matter was viewed.

Sex with a Menstruant. In four biblical texts, sex with a woman who is menstruating is designated as a sexual transgression. Leviticus 18:19 prohibits males from approaching a woman sexually during her time of menstrual impurity. Leviticus 20:18 states that if a man has sex with a menstruant (expressed as *'iššâ dābâ*, a woman in her [menstrual] infirmity), they will both be subject to *karet*. Ezekiel 18:6 groups sex with a menstruant with other sexual sins that the righteous avoid, while Ezekiel 22:10 groups sex with menstruating women with other transgressions, both sexual and nonsexual, committed by leaders of the people (Ezek 22:9–12) that God will punish with exile (Ezek 22:13–16).

However, there is one text in which sex with a menstruating woman is treated differently. Leviticus 15:24 states that if a man lies with a woman during her menstrual impurity, he will take on her impurity and be ritually impure seven days. In this case, sexual relations with a menstruating woman are treated as a source of ritual impurity, but not as a serious sexual transgression. The sexual act is neither prohibited nor punished. After seven days the period of ritual impurity is over, and the man can go back to life as usual, just as a woman can after her seven day period of ritual menstrual impurity.

There are several possible explanations for the difference between Leviticus 15 and the other texts. The first is that the Priestly text, Leviticus 15:24, and the Holiness texts, Leviticus 18:19 and 20:18, reflect different concerns. The Priestly law focuses solely on the incurring of ritual impurity, while the Holiness laws focus on the incurring of moral impurity and its consequences. If this is the case, there is no innate contradiction between them, and sexual relations with a menstruant would result in both (temporary) ritual defilement and *karet* for both parties. Another possibility is that Leviticus 15 concerns inadvertent sexual relations with a menstruant—the woman's menstruation began during intercourse, and thus neither party was aware of the impurity risk. However,

Leviticus 15:24 gives no indication that this is the case. The last possibility is that the Priestly source did not consider sex with a menstruant to be problematic, as long as neither party approached the sanctuary during their period of ritual impurity. If this is the case, then the Holiness source collection took an innovative step and made a sexual act that was previously not considered a sexual transgression of any severity into a serious sexual transgression.

Autoeroticism. There are some possible biblical references to autoeroticism, generating sexual arousal and/or achieving sexual gratification through physical or mental self-stimulation without the participation of another person or creature. While masturbation is the most recognized form, erotic daydreams and nighttime dreams are also forms of autoeroticism.

There are no clear references to masturbation in the Hebrew Bible. While Genesis 38:8–10 is sometimes interpreted as a condemnation of masturbation, there Onan practices a form of coitus interruptus (withdrawing penis from vagina before ejaculation) to prevent the impregnation of his sister-in-law Tamar. Two other texts might refer to masturbatory behavior. Ezekiel 16:17 describes God's metaphoric bride Jerusalem melting down gold and silver jewels he gave her and using them to make herself male images, with which she behaves promiscuously. Similarly, in Ezekiel 23:7, Yahweh's metaphoric wife Oholah (sexually) "defiles" herself with idols.

Since erotic dreams and daydreams are forms of autoeroticism, two other texts should be considered. Leviticus 15:16–17 states that if a man has an emission of semen, he will be impure until evening. The circumstances behind the emission are not mentioned. The emission is treated as a natural and normal phenomenon, as defiling as ejaculation during intercourse, which is treated separately in the next verse. Deuteronomy 23:10–11 states that if a man has a nocturnal seminal emission in the camp during a military campaign, he becomes impure until evening and must remain outside the camp until his period of impurity is over. While there may have been a distinction between masturbation and unintentional forms of autoeroticism, such as erotic dreams, in ancient Israel, there isn't enough evidence to draw a definitive conclusion.

Illicit Sex and Biblical Worldview. The Hebrew Bible often reflects a belief that cosmic order hinges on maintaining clear distinctions between certain categories, such as sacred and profane, clean and unclean, humans and animals, and male and female. Keeping things in proper categories maintains the stability of the world by upholding the proper order of the universe. At the same time, there is great concern with upholding societal order by maintaining harmonious relations between members of society and between members of each household. Each of the acts identified by one or more biblical texts as a sexual transgression was believed by someone to have posed a threat to either the cosmic or societal order, or both.

On a societal level, incestuous acts were problematic because they blurred family lines, which could pose a threat to the stability of family structure. Since marriage within the extended family was encouraged and even viewed as desirable, it was necessary to clarify which matches with kin were permissible and which were not to maintain peaceful relations within the household. The understanding of adultery and sexual promiscuity in biblical texts revolves around female sexuality, since the concern is with protecting the sexual property of the husband. Of central importance was a man's knowing that his wife's or future wife's offspring, who would inherit his property and continue his name and line, were in fact his own. Adultery and premarital promiscuity threatened the stability of family and society, since such behavior raised questions about paternity and wreaked havoc on relationships between members of the community.

On a cosmic level, both bestiality and sex between a man and his daughter-in-law are labeled *tebel*, illicit mixing (Lev 18:23 and 20:12). In both instances, the illicit mixtures involve semen. In the case of bestiality this likely reflects a concern with the blurring of borders between the categories of animal and human; sex with animals results in a forbidden mixing of the species. In the case of a man having sex with his son's wife, the issue may be the intermixing of father's and son's semen in the same woman. Leviticus 20:18 explains that the man who has sex with a menstruating woman has uncovered the source of her (blood) flow. It was perhaps direct contact with this source of ritual impurity, the woman's menstrual fluid, that was problematic, though it could also be that a man who had sex with a menstruant intentionally brought upon himself relatively long-lasting impurity (seven days) that was easily avoidable. Intentionally taking on ritual impurity put the whole community at risk.

In the end, each of these sexual transgressions was viewed as putting the entire community at risk, creating danger at a familial, societal, and/or cosmic level. For this reason, they had to be strictly controlled and regulated and, ideally, eliminated entirely, lest the community and the cosmos devolve into chaos.

[*See also* Legal Status, *subentry* Hebrew Bible; *and* Marriage and Divorce, *subentry* Hebrew Bible.]

BIBLIOGRAPHY

Bigger, Stephen F. "The Family Laws of Leviticus 18 in Their Setting." *Journal of Biblical Literature* 98 (1979): 187–203.

Bird, Phyllis. "To Play the Harlot: An Inquiry into an Old Testament Metaphor." In *Gender and Difference in Ancient Israel*, edited by Peggy L. Day, pp. 75–94. Minneapolis: Fortress, 1989.

Brenner, Athalya. *The Intercourse of Knowledge: On Gendering Desire and 'Sexuality' in the Hebrew Bible*. Biblical Interpretation 26. Leiden, The Netherlands: Brill, 1997.

Coogan, Michael. *God and Sex: What the Bible Really Says*. New York: Twelve, 2010.

Ellens, Deborah L. *Women in the Sex Texts of Leviticus and Deuteronomy: A Comparative Conceptual Analysis*. Library of Hebrew Bible/Old Testament Studies 458. New York: T&T Clark, 2008.

Ellens, J. Harold. *Sex in the Bible: A New Consideration*. Westport, Conn.: Praeger, 2006.

Frymer-Kensky, Tikva. "Pollution, Purification, and Purgation in Biblical Israel." In *The Word of the Lord Shall Go Forth: Essays in Honor of David Noel Freedman in Celebration of His Sixtieth Birthday*, edited by Carol L. Myers and M. O'Connor, pp. 399–414. Winona Lake, Ind.: Eisenbrauns, 1983.

Frymer-Kensky, Tikva. "Law and Philosophy: The Case of Sex in the Bible." *Semeia* 45 (1989): 89–102.

Levine, Baruch A. *Leviticus*. JPS Torah Commentary. Philadelphia: Jewish Publication Society, 1989.

Lipka, Hilary B. *Sexual Transgression in the Hebrew Bible.* Hebrew Bible Monographs 7. Sheffield, U.K.: Sheffield Phoenix, 2006.

Milgrom, Jacob. *Leviticus 17–22: A New Translation with Introduction and Commentary.* Anchor Bible 3A. New York: Doubleday, 2000.

Pressler, Carolyn. *The View of Women Found in the Deuteronomic Family Laws.* Beihefte zur Zeitschrift für die alttestamentliche Wissenschaft 216. Berlin: Walter de Gruyter, 1993.

Rashkow, Ilona N. *Taboo or Not Taboo: Sexuality and Family in the Hebrew Bible.* Minneapolis: Fortress, 2000.

Rattray, Susan "Marriage Rules, Kinship Terms, and Family Structure in the Bible." *Society of Biblical Literature, Seminar Papers* 26 (1987): 537–544.

Hilary Lipka

Greek World

Sex in the ancient Greek world was not itself transgressive. For the classical period, sex is primarily associated on a divine level with the goddess Aphrodite and her son Eros (also the Greek word for "desire"). It is, however, also associated with the god Dionysus, and its outcome, in the form of childbirth, is associated with Hera, Artemis, and a series of lesser deities. "The works of Aphrodite" (or of Dionysus), associated with pleasure and procreation, carried a divine sanction, making sexual abstinence a more problematic mode of life. That said, sexual activity, through its association with bodily fluids, most crucially female bodily fluids (because of associations with menstruation), was regarded as polluting; brief periods of sexual abstinence were held to be essential for the purity required to undertake certain religious rituals. But prolonged abstinence (despite its own divine instantiation in figures such as Artemis and Athena) was subversive and transgressive, resonating as a rejection of the social and therefore quintessentially human role.

Thus, sex was regarded as an essential part of human life, valued both as the fundamental catalyst of procreation and as vital and pleasurable recreation. This is not to suggest, however, that sex for the ancient Greeks was valued in an uncomplicated or purely positive way: just as in religious terms sex is both sacred and polluting, so generally it was both an accepted and highly valued element of human existence and, at the same time, a source of conflict, tension, transgression, and shame. The source of these more negative associations of sex serves as a microcosm of certain attitudes to the divine and mortal spheres of life framing much of the ancient Greek attitudes to sex and sexuality.

For the ancient Greeks, rules of human social or sexual engagement do not emerge from the divine world. Divine interest in mortal affairs is partial, tangential, and generally impossible to predict. A small number of highly generalized prohibitions may be guaranteed by divine backing, but usually by a deity in a particular cult persona, which may have only limited purchase on their more usual role (such as the role of Zeus Hiketesios as the protector and guarantor of suppliants). However, the transformation of these general rules into complex systems for human interaction and regulation operates entirely on the human plane. As for other spheres of human life, such as warfare, justice, and recreation, so also for the rules framing acceptable and transgressive acts of sex.

Incest. As in most ancient societies, the Greeks regarded incest as abhorrent and wrong, that is, as a human sexual transgression, although it must be noted that it occurs frequently in relations between gods. Thus Zeus and Hera are husband and wife, but also sister and brother (and also children and, in some versions, grandchildren of a similarly incestuous union); the gods of ancient Greece are not models or moral arbiters for the mortals who worship them. Although not emanating from the gods in any straightforward way, prohibitions against incest are explored in literary contexts reflecting the Greeks' sense of their own origins and a previous world where gods and mortals interacted more freely and directly, that is, in myth and tragedy.

The most obvious example of the Greeks' relationship to incest is its exploration in the Oedipus myth, the most full version of which is Sophocles's play *Oedipus Tyrannus* (fifth century B.C.E.). The play opens with the citizens of Thebes going to their king, Oedipus, to ask him for help with a terrible pestilence that has afflicted their city, blighting their crops and all the fertility of land, animals, and human beings. They have good reason for believing that their revered king may be able to help them in this crisis because he had previously saved the city, arriving as a stranger, but becoming their king (after the mysterious disappearance of their former ruler) when he solved the riddle posed by the monstrous Sphinx ravaging their land. Oedipus believes that just as he had used his human powers of deduction and intelligence to save the city then, so he can now. When the message comes back from the oracle of Apollo that to save the land they must find the accursed killer of Thebes's former king, Laius, Oedipus sets to it. He is initially unsuccessful and ends up in a heated exchange with the prophet Teiresias who, goaded by a furious Oedipus, tells him that he himself is the cursed killer. Oedipus is further enraged and complains bitterly to his wife Jocasta, who tells him that prophetic speech carries no weight: she is proof of this, since she and her former husband, Laius, were given the prophecy that their son would kill his father and marry his mother, but they exposed the infant and thus avoided the terrible fate. Of course, the audience already knows the story and knows that Oedipus's hunt will turn out to be for himself: that he is the accursed killer and incestuous husband to his own mother and that the children he has fathered are his brothers and sisters.

Freud's infamous use of the Oedipus myth as the central symbol for his belief in the infant's sexual obsession with their opposite-sex parent has almost overshadowed the original play, and thus exploring incest in its ancient context is revealing. Without doubt the incest in *Oedipus Tyrranus* is regarded as sexually transgressive. Although some might call the play "a sexual tragedy" (Sissa, 2008, p. 123), it is also a tragedy of human knowledge and attempts to order the world. Oedipus and those around him believe in the human ability to understand and make better the world in which they live, but those attempts are proven to be in this instance (and in all instances potentially) futile. Incest, although signifying sexual horror, is also a moment of the failure of categories and the failure of human attempts to order and police those categories. Jocasta should have been one of

the few women in the world Oedipus could *not* marry and have sexual congress with (given that the story mentions no other close relations for Oedipus, perhaps the *only* woman on whom this prohibition should have fallen). Humans must order the world—since such order will not emanate from the gods—but human understanding is flawed and partial, so mistakes of judgment get tragically made. Sex is a moment highly fraught with such dangers for three main reasons: it is a moment of mixture (e.g., heterosexual sex between two fundamentally mismatched beings, male and female); it has such profound consequences in childbirth and the continuance of the human species into the next generation; and, finally, its vital relationship with pleasure and passion means that it can be a moment of loss of rational control. Incest, especially as it is represented in this tragedy, is transgressive because it speaks of humans' failure to see what needs to be seen and make the right critical decisions to order their world correctly.

As in many ancient societies, the Greeks regarded parent-child sexual relations as incestuous. However, it is interesting to examine the perspective on consanguineous marriage and sex from a different source, fifth- and fourth-century Athenian law. If tragedy reflects the fifth-century Athenian context from which it emerges, it does so by projecting backward onto a mythic and Panhellenic world. But the Athens we can glimpse through legal speeches is a different entity. Herein we have an Athens that is not historically "real" in any provable sense because we have no way of checking the "facts" of the cases presented or how much editing went on subsequently or even, with some speeches, whether they were rhetorical exercises never intended for delivery in court at all but which represent the ways Athenians thought they should represent themselves to their fellow citizens. They may not reflect what actually happened, but they do show us what individual Athenians wanted others to believe of them or expected their peers to find believable.

In this world, incest as such is never mentioned, but consanguineous marriage is. The marriage of an uncle and niece would seem to be reasonably common (Lysias 32; cf. Menander *Aspis*), and indeed in many ways is seen as an ideal marriage, especially with a paternal uncle, allowing the property of the two brothers to be divided as little as possible (particularly favored if one brother dies leaving his daughter to inherit: her marriage to her paternal uncle allows the two brothers' inheritances to be united into one line of male inheritance, effectively from grandfather to grandson). It is even the case that half-sibling marriage was acceptable in Athens *as long as the siblings did not share the same mother*. Such disregard for paternal consanguinity seems strange to us, but from the point of view of inheritance, this is an idealized match: paternal property remains intact, with no dowry alienated, and indeed the property added to by the addition of the dowries of the two mothers. How regular an occurrence such a marriage would be is impossible to tell.

This is an interesting companion piece to the depiction of consanguineous relations in the *Oedipus Tyrannus*. The sexual transgression of incest excited horror in Athens and Greece more widely, but certain consanguineous relations appear to have been positively valued. Where the boundaries of appropriateness and transgression were placed in relation to sexual and marital relations is perhaps not quite where we would expect. Clearly parent-child relations were highly transgressive, but other very close, transgenerational relations were not. Full siblings were clearly prevented from marriage, but extend that even as far as half-siblings and we begin to find the prohibition weakening, if not indeed disappearing altogether.

Law and Politics. For fifth- and fourth-century Athens, much of the picture we can construct about intimate domestic details such as sex and marriage comes from legal sources. A vital preoccupation of this period, and particularly in this genre of texts, is the civic life of the democratic city. The democratic rule of law, its equality for all (male) citizens, regulation of public and private life in accordance with it, form one of the most significant ordering systems for this period. Thus transgression—and for this topic, sexual transgression—is played out in these terms.

From an ancient Greek legal and political perspective, then, what would count as sexual trans-

gression? There are three parallel issues at work here. The first is that for heterosexual encounters, the Athenian legal system treats as acceptable sex that which is sanctioned by the *kurios* (legal guardian) of the woman involved. Sex that occurs without his consent (regardless of the consent of the woman in question) is transgressive and, in certain terms, illegal. Second, the legal system seeks to ensure the legitimate and appropriate inheritance of property, the equally valuable cultural capital of citizenship, and importantly (but sometimes difficult to locate in the sources) the religious duties of family cult. The third factor is the ideological division of the category of heterosexual encounters into "procreative sex" and "recreative sex." Although we should note that this division is by no means total (for instance, the procreative, imagined as just as much the "realm of Aphrodite" as the recreative, is expected to be pleasurable, often for both male and female—in some medical versions, indeed, the female orgasm is held to be essential for conception), there are other ways in which the boundary between the two is ideologically highly impermeable. For example, the birth of legitimate heirs is the goal of procreative sex, but entirely inappropriate to recreative sex.

In these terms, then, sexual transgression is sex that inappropriately breaks this boundary or that confuses issues of legitimacy and inheritance and the *kurios*'s control of sexual access to his female dependents. Adultery would be very high on such a list because it takes the object of legitimate procreative sex with one man and makes her the partner of another for illicit recreative sex. Such an act transgresses in this way, but also in terms of the *kurios*'s control and the integrity of inheritance. Adultery is a punishable crime in Athens. We also have a long and fascinating legal case traditionally ascribed to the fourth-century orator Demosthenes, which details the case again a woman called Neaira ([Dem.] 59 *Against Neaira*). By the latter half of the fourth century B.C.E. it is no longer merely that the children of a union between an Athenian citizen and a non-Athenian would not be able to inherit citizenship: at this point such unions are themselves illegal. The speaker is prosecuting Neaira (although the attack is aimed primarily at her partner Stephanus) on the grounds that they have lived in marriage although Neaira is not an Athenian. In the course of the speech the speaker effectively has to demonstrate what sexual activity counts as legitimate procreative, marital sex and what does not through painting Neaira as a nonrespectable, non-Athenian woman who has engaged in sexual activity with multiple partners—in one incident on the same occasion at a drinking party, including, while her main partner was asleep and she was drunk, with the host's serving men. This is presented as a sexual transgression, although not in and of itself: the speaker states that if Neaira's status is as he claims (a foreign, slave-born, prostitute), the sex detailed in this account is not transgressive, but if her status is as she and Stephanus are claiming (that is, that she is capable of being an Athenian wife and engaging in procreative sex), then it is hugely so.

A famous line toward the end of the speech has the speaker claim that in Athens "we have *hetairai* (courtesans/prostitutes) for the sake of pleasure, *pallakai* (concubines) for the day-to-day care of our bodies and wives for the procreation of legitimate children, and as careful guardians of our domestic concerns." Of course such a claim comes at a highly rhetorical moment in a speech where a specific argument is being made about the role or rather roles of women, but it is still valuable to note that the speaker's sense of outrage here is expressed in terms of the transgression of these demarcated boundaries of sex and its female personnel.

Homosexuality. The French philosopher and cultural critic Michel Foucault famously and controversially declared that there was no such thing as homosexuality in the ancient world (1980). Rather than a denial of ancient homoerotic practices, his claim is that structuring sexual identity around the genders of the desiring partner and the desired object (e.g., homosexual, heterosexual, and bisexual) does not work for the ancient world. Although many of Foucault's ideas have been challenged and even rejected by later scholars, these claims have had a profound impact on the study of ancient sexuality. What has emerged is a sense that ancient Greek sexuali-

ties were conceptualized not by object choice, but by sexual role. So there was an active, desiring, pursuing, initiative-taking, penetrating, getting-sexual-pleasure sexual role, coded as "adult male," and a passive, desired, pursued, penetrated, giving-sexual-pleasure role that was coded as "not adult male." In heterosexual relations, the not adult male role falls uncontroversially to the female, but how does this work in relations between, for instance, two men?

There is widespread evidence in the ancient Greek world that male-male sexual encounters and relationships were relatively common and regarded in a positive light and that the expectation was that an adult male would engage in both homosexual and heterosexual behaviors. Although it is hard to quantify exactly how prevalent such practices were and some scholars would argue that it was a behavior linked only with specific echelons of society (i.e., the elite), there is certainly a wealth of evidence to support the existence and acceptance of such practices. Vase paintings, homoerotic love poetry, a court case, and a philosophical text discussing the nature of eros ("love/desire") focused not exclusively but primarily on male-male relations all point in that direction.

Claims about ancient Greek sexual identities notwithstanding, it would seem that a strict etiquette governed expectations of male-male contact, and relationships that did not conform to this etiquette were regarded as transgressive. Thus the males involved in a relationship needed to be clearly identifiable as performing the roles of *erastes* and *eromenos*. The *erastes*, the active and pursuing sexual role, was suitable to the adult male or the male in the socially superior position (a "master"), whereas the *eromenos* role ("beloved") was suitable to a younger, adolescent male or one in a socially inferior position (e.g., a slave). Sexual relationships between same-status males were regarded as abhorrent. So the standard, idealized homoerotic relationship is between an adult male (who is also married, thus appropriately involved in procreative heterosexual activity, and perfectly likely to engage in other recreative heterosexual encounters) and a young male of similar social class, but inferior standing because of his youth. The prime time of an adolescent's sexual attractiveness to adult males is "between puberty and the growth of the first beard" (i.e., roughly mid to late teens). Sexual activity is acceptable between such parties, but should result from a prolonged phase of courtship where the elder male displays to the younger (and the group at large) his erotic devotion to the younger male, but also his credentials as a male mentor to the younger, concerned for his acculturation into proper modes of male behavior such as military courage and other male social virtues. In this idealized scenario, after this courtship phase, sexual contact is acceptable and the younger male accepts the sexual advances of the elder, including sexual penetration. In the most highly idealized situation, this would be intercrural (between the legs). Anal penetration, although legitimately desired by the elder, would be resisted or granted only very privately and sparingly by the younger male. The younger male's body, although in his youthfulness a legitimate object of the sexual advances of the elder male, still needs to be treated as the future body of an adult male, that is, as a body that will be impenetrable. Excessive habituation to more extreme forms of sexual penetration at this youthful stage can put that future impenetrability in jeopardy. Oral penetration is never acceptable for a nobly born youth.

Bestiality. In myth, the god Zeus takes on the form of a swan to enjoy sexual congress with Leda and the form of a bull to snatch away Europa (ancient depictions of the latter scene focus always on the moment of carrying off, not sexual relations). Zeus also turns Io into a heifer in an attempt to hide his sexual interest in her from his jealous wife Hera. In the eventual union of Zeus and Io (from which the demigod Epaphus is born) it is unclear whether she is restored to her human form before or by the transforming act of sex.

As a curse on Minos, the king of Crete who has offended the gods, his wife Pasiphae is caused to fall violently in love with a bull. She persuades (or in some versions, forces) the master craftsman Daedalus to make her a hollowed-out simulation of a cow, into which she can climb for her to consummate her passion. From this union, the monstrous Minotaur is born.

Dionysus is also a god associated with sex, but primarily with the ecstatic release found in the sexual act, just as with the ecstatic release of (excessive) alcohol, religious frenzy, or the experience of alternative realities allowed by these or by the assumption of different identities in drama. Dionysus is associated with excessiveness, with what allows individuals to exist and experience the world outside themselves, with the mixing and crossing of boundaries—but then using the insight gained from such transgressions as a way of returning to one's normal, nonecstatic role with better understanding. One could say Dionysius is a god of (controlled) transgression.

Traditionally and mythically Dionysius's followers are Maenads (women in ecstatic religious frenzy, able and willing to transgress all normal female boundaries) and satyrs. These creatures are half man and half goat and represented as interested in excessive production and consumption of alcohol and transgressive sex. Generally depicted as ithyphallic, with highly erect and often enormously enlarged penises, they are often shown in vase paintings, on drinking cups, and on other vessels associated with alcohol as engaged in excessive sex of all kinds: exaggeratedly penetrative homo- and heterosexual activity, bestiality, autoeroticism, and other sexual encounters that can be interpreted as aggressive or even violent.

Excess and Order. For the ancient Greeks, a vital human need is to create order in a world that is chaotic, unknowable, and highly complex and over which humans have important but only limited power. Patterns dictated by unchangeable fate and divine exhortation or prohibition are fragmentary and, at best, can only be guessed in advance. Sex was a moment of danger and potential transgression because it is a moment when the delicate but profoundly important hierarchies of order and control are acted out (by proper sex conforming to expected norms) or are put under threat or even destroyed (by transgressive sex). Sexual transgression is therefore defined as actions that break the boundaries humans have created to try to make their world an ordered place: but even these transgressions are ultimately divinely sanctioned by figures such as Aphrodite and especially Dionysus, so humans "can never win."

[*See also* Legal Status, *subentry* Greek World; Male-Female Sexuality, *subentry* Greek World; Same-Sex Relations, *subentry* Greek World; Sexuality; *and* Sexual Transgression, *subentries on* New Testament *and* Roman World.]

BIBLIOGRAPHY

Davidson, James. *Courtesans and Fishcakes: The Consuming Passions of Classical Athens*. New York: St. Martin's, 1998.

Dover, Kenneth J. *Greek Homosexuality*. Cambridge, Mass.: Harvard University Press, 1978.

Golden, Mark, and Peter Toohey, eds. *Sex and Difference in Ancient Greece and Rome*. Edinburgh: Edinburgh University Press, 2003.

Goldhill, Simon. *Foucault's Virginity: Ancient Erotic Fiction and the History of Sexuality*. Stanford Memorial Lectures. New York: Cambridge University Press, 1995.

Halperin, David, John Winkler, and Froma Zeitlin, eds. *Before Sexuality: The Construction of Erotic Experience in the Ancient Greek World*. Princeton, N.J.: Princeton University Press, 1990.

Henderson, Jeffrey. *The Maculate Muse: Obscene Language in Attic Comedy*. New York: Oxford University Press, 1991.

Hunter, Virginia J. *Policing Athens: Social Control in the Attic Lawsuits, 420–320 B.C.* Princeton, N.J.: Princeton University Press, 1994.

Keuls, Eva C. *The Reign of the Phallus: Sexual Politics in Ancient Athens*. Berkeley: University of California Press, 1993.

Omitowoju, Rosanna S. *Rape and the Politics of Consent in Classical Athens*. Cambridge Classical Studies. New York: Cambridge University Press, 2002.

Sissa, Giulia. *Sex and Sensuality in the Ancient World*. Translated by George Staunton. New Haven, Conn.: Yale University Press, 2008.

Winkler, John J. *The Constraints of Desire: The Anthropology of Sex and Gender in Ancient Greece*. New Ancient World. New York: Routledge, 1990.

Rosanna S. Omitowoju

Roman World

Inherent in the notion of transgression is the existence of a stable and in some sense monolithic normativity, one that is clearly demarcated without appreciable interstitial space between what is permissible and not. Yet, in the realm of sexuality, the location and nature of boundaries are often unclear. What is strictly legal in practice may nonetheless be culturally or socially illicit within the whole, or within a particular subset of the culture. The multiculturalism of the ancient Roman world further complicates any attempts to generalize across, or even within, the temporal and geographical space one might call "the Roman world," as even a cursory overview of sexuality in the first century demonstrates. A discussion of "sexual transgression," therefore, must accommodate a multiplicity of norms—whether real or idealized—and/or must reconfigure binary notions of transgression as it considers the texts, authors, and historical circumstances under which transgressive acts entered public dialogue.

Active/Passive Inversions. Scholars of ancient sexuality have tended to agree that acts were generally categorized according to rigid dichotomies of active versus passive (or insertive versus receptive), masculine versus feminine, social superior versus social inferior (e.g., Halperin, 1990; Winkler, 1990; Parker, 1997). Generally speaking, the active/passive paradigm configures normative sexual practices as those that preserved the integrity of the citizen's body and protected the citizen's legitimate lines of succession, reinforcing the role of the male citizen as the penetrator in the sex act rather than penetrated, and positing self-control as an ideal of male Roman temperament and behavior. "Normal" female sexuality, conversely, was passive and penetrated. Sexual practices wherein these polarities were reversed, or wherein the sexual appetites were fulfilled in an immoderate manner, potentially not only transgressed cultural ideals or notions of propriety but, importantly, transgressed political ideals, since the integrity of the state depended upon the maintenance of hereditary lines and political legacies.

An understanding of the close relationship between the individual body and the body politic may also shed light on the highly pejorative contexts in which we find references to transgressive persons: *cinaedi* and *pathici* (anally passive males), *tribades* (active females/"lesbians"), *fellatori* (givers of fellatio), *cunnilincti* (givers of cunnilingus), and others that occur with frequency in epigram and satire. The same focus on citizenship and the state also explains, at least partially, the lack of censure implied in certain visual representations of the same acts, such as in the well-known frescoes of Pompeian brothels or the molded images on terracotta oil lamps. In short, it is not that the acts are transgressive per se, but rather that transgression depends upon the social and political position of the actors.

The penetrated male: **cinaedus** *or* **pathicus.** The *vox propria* for the passive partner in anal sex, *cinaedus*, like its less common synonyms *pathicus* and *catamitus*, is of Greek origin and occurs most commonly in coarse joking contexts in epigram, satire, and other invective verse, as well as in Plautine New Comedy. Together the three epithets occur 10 times in Plautus, thrice in Lucilius, 11 times in Catullus, 7 in the *Carmina Priapea*, 23 in Martial, and 7 in Juvenal. This distribution is not insignificant, indicating that the words are primarily pejorative rather than purely descriptive. Because the male citizen who is anally penetrated allows his status to be compromised, it comes as no surprise that the epithets (particularly *cinaedus*) are often joined with other kinds of personal and political ridicule (e.g., Catullus 10, 16, 29; Martial 2.28, 4.43; Juvenal 4.105–106; and Gellius, *N.A.* 6.12.5.17).

Cinaedus and its synonyms belong to a broad semantic domain, connoting more than mere sexual passivity. The terms are associated with a wide variety of general character traits and physical features that the Romans identified with "softness" (Lat *mollitia*) or lack of masculinity, such that the identity of the *cinaedus* was communicated visibly in his dress and manner, and on his body (Williams, 2010). At the heart of the various characteristics associated with *mollitia*, there lies one primary feature—the loss of self-control or abandonment to physical pleasure viewed as anathema to notions of the idealized Roman male (cf. Catullus 25, 29; Juvenal 2, esp. lines 88–120). Hence we find colorful literary representations wherein the dangers of immoderation are displaced onto the anus itself, and it becomes "voracious," "capacious," and "swollen," a metaphorical representation of the *cinaedus* as a whole (Catullus 33.3; Martial 6.37; Juvenal 2.1–4).

Passivity and Political Invective. Even when there were no outright charges of sexual passivity, suspicions of *mollitia* carried a particular stigma. In the waning days of the republic and throughout the Principate, a high threshold of manliness was applied to public figures, and allegations of effeminacy proved to be an effective form of political slander, not merely because the caesar's physical appearance served as an embodiment of the state, but also because *mollitia*, and its concomitant lack of self-control, may have indicated a predilection for other vices including violence. Among the various signs of "softness," depilation of the legs, face, or buttocks was often singled out as a particularly telling offense. Neither Julius Caesar nor Augustus were exempt from such allegations (Suetonius, *Julius* 45.2; *Augustus* 68.1), and by the end of the Julio-Claudian period, slander against smooth-skinned politicians had reached campy extremes, particularly in the case of the emperor Otho, whose penchant for depilation was accompanied by a love of facial cosmetics and the wearing of a toupee to cover his baldness (Suetonius, *Otho* 12; cf. Tacitus, *Hist.* 1.22; Juvenal 2.99–116).

The penetrating female: **tribas.** All but invisible in the Roman world, lesbianism in its few literary appearances is derided as transgression against the traditional active/passive dichotomy and/or as transgression "against nature" (Brooten, 1996, pp. 235–241; Hallett, 1997; Parker, 1997; for a contrary view, Butrica, 2005). The paradox of the Roman "lesbian," or Latin *tribas*, however, is that the action denoted by the noun itself, namely, "rubbing," from the Greek *tribein*, is not the transgressive activity; rather, transgression often arises from a form of penetration accompanying the act. Strangely, nowhere in the literature is the "rubbing" itself criticized. Three of Martial's epigrams and a letter of Seneca the Younger raise the specter of the lesbian as a pseudophallic monster whose genital deformity, an enlarged clitoris, allows her to usurp the role of male penetrator (Martial 1.90, 7.67, 7.70; Seneca, *Ep.* 95.20–21). For the first-century fabulist Phaedrus, too, the "anomaly" of the *tribas* was thought to be the possession of an actual penis (Phaedrus 4.16). In Juvenal's sixth satire, the lesbian transgression is also one of penetration, although this time via streams of urine rather than the clitoris (6.306–313; see also the story in Seneca the Elder where the woman in question is called a *phēlarrena moichon*, a pretend-man or fake-male adulterer; *Controv.* 1.2.23). The crime of the *tribas*, however, cannot be reduced simply to the penetrative act. Even as the *cinaedus* transgresses social order and proper gender roles with his "softness," so too the *tribas* transgresses not merely because of the usurpation of the phallic act but also because of her assumption of masculine behaviors and activities, such as wrestling or drinking (e.g., Martial 7.67). In at least one literary example, the masculine behaviors of the *tribas* extend to the realm of pederasty. The Roman version of Sappho, the quintessential lesbian, is transformed into a man in pursuit of a beloved boy in Ovid's *Heroides* 15. Sappho's beloved boy is entreated to return to his lover as the submissive partner using language typical of pederastic courting. Not only is the example of female pederasty unparalleled in literature of the classical period, but the assumption of this male role suggests that the *tribas* has the power to subvert the social order at multiple levels simultaneously.

Bestiality. The scarcity of serious prose accounts of bestiality in the Roman world is paradoxically matched by a plethora of sexual motifs involving animals in literature and in art.

In literature. Broadly construed, cross-species encounters—whether divine and human, divine and animal, or a combination thereof—lie at the heart of some of the most popular myths, in ancient as well as in modern times. Even Rome's foundation story of Romulus and Remus suckled by a she-wolf suggests a kind of primal fantasy involving the interrelationship between the animal and human realms. That the founding twins were born to a vestal virgin impregnated by the god Mars adds another dimension to the romance of cross-species encounters. The bestial motif is not unique to the indigenous Roman tradition; bestial encounters occur with the same frequency in the inherited Greek tradition as well. Such tales, then, suggest a certain confluence of the animal and divine realms, and may imply that the human/nonhuman encounter addresses fundamental questions about the nature of humanity. Among the few

literary examples of bestiality outside the Greco-Roman mythological canon, Apuleius, the second-century Latin novelist, provides the most extended narrative (*Met.* 10.19–22) in a scene in which Lucius, the protagonist who has been transformed into an ass, enjoys a fantastical tryst with a woman who is enamored of all his bestial qualities and proportions. This episode stands out both for its detailed description of the coital act as well as for its overwhelmingly positive portrayal of bestiality outside the standard exempla from the Greco-Roman mythical corpus. Other references to bestiality in literature tend to occur in isolated satirical references, such as Juvenal, *Sat.* 6.331–334, wherein the act is meant to ridicule the wanton sexual behavior of matrons.

In art. Intercourse between human and beast, whether merely implied by the image of hybrid offspring or whether described in flagrante delicto, is visible in several aspects of material culture. The images of satyrs, centaurs, and hermaphrodites that abound in painting, sculpture, and other media all suggest a fascination with hybridity and suggest that "bestiality" in some form was ever present to the eyes and the imaginations of the Romans. Even explicit encounters between humans and animals are frequent in some aspects of material culture, such as in terracotta oil lamps of the first–third centuries C.E. Like the literary references to bestiality or near bestiality, on lamps the human figure is almost invariably female whereas the animal is male. Such a rigid gender typology may suggest that transcendence of existential categories achieved in these encounters is primarily accessible to males, and only vicariously or passively accessible to females. Under this interpretation, the bestial encounter ultimately reinforces rather than subverts hierarchies of power. Alternatively, the levity of the images and in some cases the gynocentric focus (e.g., London, British Museum 1865.11-18.249 [Q900], see below) may suggest precisely the opposite: that the beneficiary of temporary transcendence is the woman. Representations of the myth of Leda both on oil lamps and especially on Roman sarcophagi (London, British Museum 1865.11-18.250A [Q871], ca. 40–70 C.E., and

1814.7-4.51 [Q1359], ca. 175–225 C.E.; Athens, American School of Classical Studies in Athens Agora excavations L519) may also suggest that the bestial motif essentially represents an exploration of the nature of the human, animal, and divine.

1814.7-4.51 [Q1359], ca. 175–225 C.E.; Athens, American School of Classical Studies in Athens Agora excavations L519) may also suggest that the bestial motif essentially represents an exploration of the nature of the human, animal, and divine.

However one interprets the iconography, the motif is most apparent on oil lamps, which feature human/bestial intercourse in several subject types: (1) an African or Ethiopian woman (caricaturized) with a crocodile (London, British Museum 1865.11-18.249 [Q900] and 1836.2-24.480A [Q1004], both first century C.E.); (2) a woman with a horse or donkey (e.g., London, British Museum 1917.4-26.30 [Q3271], late third century C.E., on which see Clarke, 2007, pp. 226–227); (3) a woman with a monkey (e.g., London, British Museum 1814.7-4.53 [Q1356], 1814.7-4.54 [Q1355], 1756.1-1.648 [Q1403], 1836.2-24.479 [Q1405], all ca. 175–225 C.E.). Similarly, a number of oil lamps also feature interspecies coitus, but without humans (e.g., a donkey mating with a lion, London, British Museum 1756.1-1.270 [Q758], late first century B.C.E.–early first century C.E.). Such interspecial examples would seem to belong to a similar aesthetic.

Cross-Dressing. Since Roman dress was an external advertisement of one's class and citizen status, cross-dressing, regardless of the motive, was a transgression that posed special dangers. The social importance of Roman dress is nowhere clearer than in the case of prostitutes and adulteresses, who were required to wear the toga, the customary male dress. For the male citizen the toga bespoke social privilege; for women the donning of the toga indicated precisely the opposite—a lack or loss of status and a marginalized place in society (McGinn, 1998, pp. 156–171, and see below). Whereas in the modern world dress often reflects identity, whether permanent or temporary, in the Roman world dress and identity were contiguous, such that cross-dressing arguably betrayed a bona fide transgression of the social order, not merely a pretended or temporary one.

In history. The republican period features a notorious example in the incident of 4 December 62 B.C.E., when a young politician, P. Clodius Pulcher, disguised himself to infiltrate the festival of the Bona Dea, the "Good Goddess," whose celebrations were restricted to women (Plutarch, *Cic.* 28, *Caes.* 9–10; Cicero, *Har.* 37). The outrage was compounded by Clodius's motive, a desire for a sexual liaison with Pompeia, Julius Caesar's wife. The event became a paradigmatic cautionary tale against the profanation of religion, the family, and state.

For those in the public spotlight, even the slightest hint of effeminacy in dress was noted with disdain. For Julius Caesar, the mere addition of long fringed sleeves to his tunic was enough to arouse suspicion (Suetonius, *Iul.* 45). Under the Principate, tales of cross-dressing public figures reached new heights, and in each case, the act of cross-dressing is connected with a real or imagined change in status. Among the vices of the emperor Caligula, dressing in the guise of both gods and goddesses earns special censure (Cassius Dio 59.26.6–8). If Caligula's dress revealed aspirations to a higher status, Nero's cross-dressing revealed quite the opposite. Several sources report that he not only dressed in women's attire, he also crossed gender boundaries in a more outrageous manner by marrying a freedman named Pythagoras to play the role of his husband (i.e., the penetrator), as well a certain Sporus, whom he had castrated and renamed to play the role of his wife (Suetonius, *Nero* 28; Cassius Dio 62.13.1, 62.28.3). In the third century, Elagabalus, another imperial libertine, married his male lover as well (*S.H.A.*, Elagabalus 10.5), an instance that might represent a genuine transgendered orientation, for according to the source, this emperor not only wore makeup and worked with wool (Cassius Dio 80.14.3–4), he also desired to become a woman insofar as was possible and even consulted a surgeon about the possibility of fashioning a vagina in his body (Cassius Dio 80.16.7).

In literature. For all the social anxiety that attached to gender-ambiguous behaviors in real society, in mythical and religious traditions, cross-dressing was sometimes severed from social taboos. Thus, Hercules, the icon of Roman masculinity, dressed as a woman while enslaved to the Lydian queen Omphale. Although Ovid's treatment of this episode in the *Heroides* (*Her.* 9.53–118) implies that the hero's dress is to be regarded as a symbol of his sexual submission to the Queen, there is little sense of stigma in Ovid's portrayal (cf. *Fasti* 2.305–330). First-century works of art including statuary, fresco painting, and Arretine ceramics also tend to confirm that this aspect of the Hercules myth was an object of celebration and positive interest.

Incest. *Incestum* (also *incestus, -ūs*), literally meaning "an unchaste or impure act" was the term Romans originally applied to violations of the chastity of vestal virgins (Cicero, *Inv.* 1.73; Livy 2.42.11; Seneca the Elder, *Controv.* exc. 6.5), but *incestum* extended also to marriage between ascendant or descendant kin of either consanguinate or affinate relationship (Gaius, *Inst.* 1.59–64; Paulus, *Dig.* 23.3.39.1; Marcian, *Dig.* 23.2.39.1, 48.18.5; Tacitus, *Ann.* 12.5–6). In contrast to the Greek traditions of endogamous marriage, Roman marriage was exclusively exogamous, both by law and custom, and hence violations were regarded as crimes against natural law (*ius gentium*), as well as civil law (*ius civile*) (Paulus, *Dig.* 23.2.68). Although legal commentaries list prohibited marital relationships in detail, the precise application of specific laws is not altogether clear. In general, charges levied against the defendant depended on the marital status of the female: *adulterium* (adultery) if married and *stuprum* (illicit fornication) if unmarried (Papinian, *Dig.* 48.5.39).

That the concept of incest was intrinsically bound to the concept of marriage in the Roman world may suggest that the element of societal taboo was in some sense secondary to material concerns about inheritance and property; the jurists of the Severan period, however, maintain that incest is both a violation of law and pollution of blood ties (Papinian, *Dig.* 48.5.39), and the scandalous allegations of incest made against Christians (Minucius Felix, *Oct.* 31; Tertullian, *Ad Scap.* 4.4.7; Theophilus, *Autol.* 3.4; and elsewhere) also suggest that the behavior was a taboo associated with ethnic minorities, foreigners, and others whom the Romans considered "inferior."

Historical exempla. Allegations of incest are commonly levied against political figures and others in the public limelight. Cicero, for example, accused

his enemy P. Clodius Pulcher of having an affair with his sister Clodia (Cicero, *Pro Cael.* 13.32; *Att.* 2.1.5). And against emperors, such allegations were nearly ubiquitous: Gaius Caligula was accused of incest with his sisters (Suetonius, *Cal.* 24, 36); Nero, with his mother, Agrippina the Younger (Suetonius, *Ner.* 28; Tacitus, *Ann.* 14.2); Titus, with his sister-in-law (Suetonius, *Tit.* 10); Domitian, with his niece (Suetonius, *Dom.* 22), and so on. When levied as political slander, allegations of incest are often tied closely with other forms of illicit sexual activity.

Incest in myth. Cautionary tales about the dangers of incest are common in literature, such as the nonextant but influential *Zmyrna* of Cinna, describing the illicit love between Myrrha and her father, Cinyras, and later versions of the same tale, such as Ovid's (*Met.* 10.311–502), as well as the myths of Byblis and her brother Caunus (Ovid, *Met.* 9.450–665) and Canace and Macareus (Ovid, *Her.* 11). Even in the case of affinate kin, the consequences for incest are dire (Seneca, *Thy.* 220–244; Ovid, *Met.* 6.424–674).

Masturbation. In his book on the interpretation of dreams, Artimedorus, a second-century writer of the second sophistic, categorizes masturbation among the practices regarded "natural, legal, and customary" (*kata physin kai nomon kai ethos*). Indeed, the act appears seldom in Roman art and literature, and when it does is unremarkable per se; rather, the censure attaches merely to the motivation or need for the practice (cf. Ovid, *Fasti* 1.423–438; Martial, *Ep.* 2.43, 9.41, 11.46, 11.73, 14.203; Juvenal, *Sat.* 6.237–238, 10.204–206). In the Christianized empire, however, stigma against masturbation increases. Prohibitions against masturbation are often associated first with Saint Thomas Aquinas (*Summ. Theol.* 2a2ae; *Quaest.* 154.1–12), but fleshly lust, even in marriage, is condemned as early as Augustine (*Civ. Dei* 14.13). The first (nearly) explicit prohibition against the practice is found in Augustine's contemporary John Cassianus, one of the desert fathers, who regarded masturbation as a type of fornication (*Coll.* 5.11.4).

Oral Sex: The *Os Impurum*. The Romans, unlike the Greeks, held the penetrated mouth as an object of derision, and according to the first-century rhetorician Quintilian, the oral penetration of a citizen was regarded a crime (*Inst.* 11.1.84). In ancient literature, oral sex is often imagined as a forced activity (Catullus 16, 21; *Priap.* 28, 35; Apuleius, *Met.* 8.29), and the mouth performing this act becomes "impure" or "polluted" (*S.H.A.* 1.7, 5.11; Gellius, *N.A.* 1.5.1; Artemidorus, *Interpretation of Dreams* 79.13–14). Because of the taboo attached to oral sex, it is one of the most frequently attested allegations against political figures, such as Catullus's invective against Julius Caesar and his chief engineer (*praefectus fabrum*) in Gaul in Poem 57. The emperors Tiberius, Nero, and Commodus were all alleged to have been devotees of various oral perversions.

Pederasty. Although the practice was not celebrated in Rome as it was in Greece, pederasty (same-sex or non-same-sex) was nonetheless tolerated under specific circumstances. Sex with a freeborn boy was forbidden as *stuprum*, illicit sexual activity, and was covered by the republican-era *lex Scantinia*, with the same legal strictures that applied to sex with an unmarried freeborn woman or girl, or with a widow (Quintilian, *Sent.* 5.4.14; cf. Modestinus, *Dig.* 48.5.35; Papinian, *Dig.* 48.5.6 and 48.5.9). The exact nature and purview of the *lex Scantinia*, however, has been the subject of much debate (see Robinson, 1995, pp. 58, 70–71). Further, not all slaves were considered fair game, only those belonging to the suitor, and violations against slaves of others were prosecutable as property offenses similar to theft (*Dig.* 47.10.25, 48.5.6 pr.). In like manner, forced pederasty or rape was more easily prosecutable since it was covered under the broader provisions of laws on violence (e.g., *lex Julia de vi publica*, Ulpian, *Dig.* 48.6.3.4). Although none of the applicable laws mention the age of the boy/girl affected, we may surmise that sex with very young children or infants was also taboo (Artemidorus, *Interpretation of Dreams* 79.13).

Summary. Several conclusions emerge from the survey of transgressive activities above. First, most sexual transgressions in the Roman world were only covered by law in the broadest of senses. Prosecutable offenses were generally classified under the categories of adultery (*adulterium*), illicit fornication (*stuprum*), and/or incest (*incestum*); in other regards, Roman law was silent. The dialogue surrounding marginalized sexual practices thus occurred more commonly outside the courtroom—for ridicule and/or humor in genres such as satire, epigram, graffiti, and comedy; for political purposes in oratory, history, and imperial biographies; and in myths and other fanciful literary tales, sometimes with an admonitory tone, but often without any pejorative sense. In art, too, sexual transgression enjoyed a similar license of fiction, since the acts depicted were not connected with the body of a particular Roman citizen and thereby with the body of the state.

[*See also* Children, *subentry* Roman World; Gender Transgression, *subentry* Roman World; Legal Status, *subentry* Roman World; Masculinity and Femininity, *subentry* Roman World; Race, Class, and Ethnicity, *subentry* Roman World; *and* Same-Sex Relations, *subentry* Roman World.]

BIBLIOGRAPHY

Brooten, Bernadette J. *Love Between Women: Early Christian Responses to Female Homoeroticism.* Chicago: University of Chicago Press, 1996.

Butrica, James. "Some Myths and Anomalies in the Study of Roman Sexuality." In *Same-Sex Desire and Love in Greco-Roman Antiquity and in the Classical Tradition of the West*, edited by Beert C. Verstraete and Vernon Provencal, pp. 209–269. New York: Harrington Park, 2005. Published simultaneously as *Journal of Homosexuality* 49, nos. 3–4 (2005).

Clarke, John R. *Looking at Laughter: Humor, Power, and Transgression in Roman Visual Culture, 100 B.C.–A.D. 250.* Berkeley: University of California Press, 2007.

Hallett, Judith P. "Female Homoeroticism and the Denial of Roman Reality in Latin Literature." In *Roman Sexualities*, edited by Judith P. Hallett and Marilyn B. Skinner, pp. 255–273. Princeton, N.J.: Princeton University Press, 1997. Originally published in *Yale Journal of Criticism* 3, no. 1 (1989): 209–227.

Halperin, David M. *One Hundred Years of Homosexuality: And Other Essays on Greek Love.* New York: Routledge, 1990.

Johns, Catherine. *Sex or Symbol: Erotic Images of Greece and Rome.* Austin: University of Texas Press, 1982.

McGinn, Thomas A. J. *Prostitution, Sexuality, and the Law in Ancient Rome.* New York: Oxford University Press, 1998.

Parker, Holt N. "The Teratogenic Grid." In *Roman Sexualities*, edited by Judith P. Hallett and Marilyn B. Skinner, pp. 47–65. Princeton, N.J.: Princeton University Press, 1997.

Puliatti, Salvatore. *Incesti Crimina: Regime giuridico da Augusto a Giustiniano*. Milan: A. Giuffrè, 2001.

Richlin, Amy. *The Garden of Priapus: Sexuality and Aggression in Roman Humor*. Rev. ed. New York: Oxford University Press, 1992.

Robinson, O. F. *The Criminal Law of Ancient Rome*. Baltimore: Johns Hopkins University Press, 1995.

Skinner, Marilyn B. *Sexuality in Greek and Roman Culture*. Ancient Cultures. Malden, Mass.: Blackwell, 2005.

Williams, Craig A. *Roman Homosexuality*. 2d ed. Oxford: Oxford University Press, 2010.

Winkler, John J. *The Constraints of Desire: The Anthropology of Sex and Gender in Ancient Greece*. New York: Routledge, 1990.

Heather Vincent

New Testament

The authors of the New Testament texts penned their own reflections on the nature of sexual transgression from within the cultural matrix of the Roman world and hence were in large part dependent on its terms. Hence, discussion begins with Roman understandings of sexual transgression before moving to the New Testament itself.

Sexual Transgression in the Roman World. Notions of sexual transgression in the early Roman Empire were fundamentally inseparable from concerns about gender and status. As much scholarship has demonstrated, ancient Romans tended to conceive of sexed bodies using the logic of a pyramid or a hierarchically organized spectrum. At the top were to be found free adult men (i.e., citizens) of elite social standing. Below were lesser men, men of ambivalent or imperiled masculinity, and various degrees of nonmen: women, children, slaves, effeminate men, and eunuchs, to name a few (Walters, 1997; Moore, 2001). This framework has also been deemed a "one-sex" model insofar as women were considered lesser versions of men (Laqueur, 1990). Working from within this conceptual apparatus—a sliding scale of status variables oriented toward perfect masculinity—and attuned to its attendant anxieties, Roman writers articulated a set of normative claims regarding inappropriate, illicit, or even monstrous possibilities for the sexual interaction of bodies.

Since these writers were generally themselves elite Roman males, the perspective they put forward was an idealized and ideological one, not necessarily reflective of the sexual experiences of others "on the ground." Yet theirs is the dominant (and remarkably uniform) viewpoint that the preponderance of our surviving sources presents.

One significant consequence of this gendered worldview was an acute concern with so-called active and passive roles in sexual relations. Free adult men confirmed and maintained their masculinity by always taking (or being thought to take) the penetrative/insertive role (Williams, 1999), whereas females, boys, and slaves of both sexes were supposed to play the receptive role. (Here freeborn males not yet fully grown occupied an especially ambivalent position insofar as they were Roman citizen "men-to-be" and thus needed to protect themselves and/or be protected from the "unmanliness" of penetration; Walters, 1997, p. 33.) Depending on the bodily orifices available in any given sexual encounter, the receptive role could include vaginal, oral, and/or anal penetration—none of which would constitute transgressive sexual behavior on the part of penetrator or penetrated as long as the proper hierarchical roles were maintained.

Not surprisingly, then, Roman reflections on sexual transgression tended to cluster around bodily practices that threatened or subverted this economy of gender and status. Sex acts improperly or "unnaturally" engaged in could undermine a man's true manliness, causing him to fall precipitously down the "gradient of relative masculinities" (Burrus, 2007, p. 4). Consequently, Roman writers predictably represented adult citizen males who allowed themselves to be penetrated—or, even worse, enjoyed or desired such penetration—as aberrant, diseased, and depraved. Male prostitution was explicitly linked to such pathetic behavior and derided accordingly as soft, effeminate, and slavish. By way of contrast, free Roman men understood themselves to have a certain jurisdiction over their own bodies, and therefore the right to protect those bodies from the invasions and intrusions of penetrative touch. But this prerogative extended to them alone. Women who usurped the masculine sexual role, acting as unpenetrated penetrators rather than passive recipients (usually, in the Roman male imagination, by means of a dildo or enlarged clitoris), were generally regarded as monstrous (Brooten 1996; Swancutt, 2004).

A related concern had to do with the question of excess. In keeping with the ancient Roman penchant for a loosely Stoicizing approach to ethics and bodily practice, Greco-Roman moralists emphasized the importance of self-mastery (*enkrateia*) and moderation (*sōphrosynē*). Such an emphasis proved consonant with the dominant perspectives found in ancient medical literature, perspectives that were themselves influenced by philosophical understandings of human physiology. Ancient medical writers such as Galen (129–ca. 199 C.E.) conceived of bodily health in terms of balance and equilibrium. In male bodies, this balance skewed in the direction of dryness, solidity, and vital heat, while in female bodies moisture, coldness, and permeability predominated. But regardless, because many medical writers believed that both male and female bodies produced seminal fluid that could be discharged—thereby changing the balance of the body—they saw the need for limiting and regulating sexual activity. Overindulgence in sex could be dangerous and lead to illness, but so too could total abstinence, especially if undertaken too quickly and without the proper preparation. The key, rather, was to achieve the correct and moderate balance (Rousselle, 1988; Laqueur, 1990; Martin, 1995).

Thus while it was legal and indeed expected for male citizens to enjoy the services of prostitutes, to do so in an extravagant or uncontrolled way was roundly condemned—and often associated with the softness of "Greek" and other foreign ways (Knust, 2006). Similarly, Roman moralists understood the desire for too much sex as problematic, regardless of whether opposite-sex or same-sex pairings were in view. Indeed, as Roman moralists puzzled over the origin of "unnatural" sexual practices (such as men desiring to be penetrated or desiring to penetrate a person who was inappropriate or off-limits), some came to the conclusion that the problem was one of inordinate desire: not desire fundamentally disordered in its kind, but rather gone off the rails in its degree of excess. Ancient concerns about immoderate masturbation or Roman women experimenting with bestiality also fell under this same logic (Martin, 2006).

For elite women specifically, this ideal of moderation was construed in terms of chastity (understood as faithfulness to one's husband), modesty in adornment, and devotion to household tasks. Meanwhile, anxieties about "wild" women proliferated, and in the early empire, any extramarital sex on the part of free Roman women was criminalized under the emperor Augustus (r. 27 B.C.E–14 C.E.). Here a gendered double standard should be noted. Either sex could commit the crimes of adultery (Greek *moicheia*, Latin *adulterium*) and fornication/sexual immorality (Greek *porneia*, Latin *stuprum*), but for women, these terms signified sex with any man other than one's husband. In the case of elite men, by contrast, sexual activity with women of lesser (i.e., noncitizen) status, prostitutes, or one's own slaves of either sex continued to be acceptable, even within the bounds of marriage. The charge of *stuprum* or *adulterium* applied to men who had sexual relations with a person who was socially off-limits, such as a married citizen woman or a freeborn boy (i.e., a future adult citizen). In this way, such a double standard in the Roman legal system served to underscore and reinforce the ways in which the irreducibly interrelated norms of gender and status governed the cultural evaluation of sex acts as described above (Knust, 2006).

The New Testament. The authors of the New Testament texts were influenced by both the Roman matrix and Israel's sacred scriptures (as mediated through both Hebrew and Greek traditions). The sexual prohibitions of the Torah focus primarily on issues of purity, interwoven in some cases with concerns about property law. Emissions from sexual organs are carefully regulated for both sexes, but the texts tend toward a broadly androcentric perspective insofar as they especially highlight concerns regarding the polluting capacity of women's bodies. Bestiality (Exod 22:19; Lev 18:23; 20:15–16), varieties of incest (Lev 18:6–18), cross-dressing (Deut 22:5), and some form of sexual interaction between men (Lev 18:22; Lev 20:13) are all unequivocally proscribed, but in the case of this last item, it is by no means clear exactly what sexual act (anal intercourse?) is being forbidden.

Alongside this array of sexual practices, adultery—here construed as illicit sex between a man and a woman married, betrothed, or otherwise belonging to another man (i.e., through slavery or concubinage)—is treated as both a purity concern and as a property offense. Prohibitions on prostitution seem in context to be concerned primarily with temple prostitution and thus ritual purity. Autoeroticism and sexual acts between women are not mentioned (Countryman, 2007). While this scriptural background needs to be considered when interpreting the sexual prohibitions of the New Testament, the degree to which New Testament authors had the proscriptions of the Torah and other parts of the Jewish scriptures in view (and/or their elaboration in later extracanonical Jewish writings) continues to be a matter of scholarly debate.

The Gospels and Acts. The New Testament gospels offer remarkably little direct discussion about the specifics of sexual transgression. What discussion we do find centers on the issues of adultery (*moicheia*), sexual immorality broadly construed (*porneia*), and desire/lust (*epithymia*). (Of these terms, *porneia* has an especially broad semantic range; in some contexts its connotations can include prostitution.) In the synoptic tradition, *porneia* and *moicheia* are figured in purity terms as transgressions that originate from the heart and lead to defilement (Matt 15:18–20; Mark 7:21–23). The Sermon on the Mount intensifies this emphasis on purity of heart by recasting *moicheia* as most fundamentally an issue of internal disposition: "But I say to you that everyone who looks at a woman with lust (*epithymēsai*) has already committed adultery with her in his heart" (Matt 5:28; see Loader, 2005). Here Matthew's Jesus may be linking adultery to the Decalogue's prohibition on coveting property (including a wife) that belongs to another (Exod 20:17). Or he may in fact be making a much more rigorous statement about the problematic and transgressive nature of

sexual desire in general, even when experienced involuntarily (Martin, 2006; Countryman, 2007).

The Gospels' further exploration of these issues takes place in the context of reflections on divorce. All three of the Synoptics connect divorce and remarriage to *moicheia* (Matt 5:32, 19:9; Mark 10:11–12; Luke 16:18). Matthew and Mark justify this connection by appeal to marriage as a divinely wrought state of becoming "one flesh," thereby using the Genesis creation narrative to trump the Torah's apparent acceptance of divorce (Matt 19:3–8; Mark 10:2–9; cf. Deut 24:1–4). In Matthew, both references to divorce modify synoptic parallels (as found in Mark and Q) by adding the so-called exception clause: divorce leads to adultery except in the case of *porneia*. The precise meaning of this ambiguous exception has been much debated, but scholars have overwhelmingly interpreted it as a partial mitigation of the divorce prohibition's stringency as seen in Mark and Q. It has also been suggested that the exception clause does not attenuate the prohibition on divorce (which, on this reading, Jesus forbids in any and every case; see Matt 19:6), but instead applies to remarriage—here figured as a kind of second offense except in cases where the original divorce took place because of *porneia*. This reading has the advantage of being consistent with Matthew's eschatologically oriented asceticism and his tendency to render certain Torah regulations more rigorous rather than less (Martin, 2006).

At the same time, the general ethos of all four Gospels is not one of intense anxiety regarding matters of sexual transgression. In Matthew, female prostitutes (*pornai*) are singled out alongside tax collectors (and without condemnation) as being those who are entering the kingdom of God ahead of the chief priests and the elders (Matt 21:31–32). Similarly, in John, while Jesus by no means endorses the various marital and extramarital liaisons of the Samaritan woman at the well, neither does he explicitly condemn them or her (John 4:16–26). The famous pericope of the woman caught in adultery (John 7:53—8:11), while probably not original to John's Gospel, shows a corresponding lack of concern with specifically condemning the sexual transgression in view. On the whole, the eschatological outlook of the Gospels shifts the emphasis away from the centrality of household and family, and with them the complications of sexual relationships. This perspective can be seen in an especially pointed way in the exhortation of Luke's Jesus to "hate" one's familial connections for the sake of discipleship (Luke 14:26), an orientation that also extends in a more muted way through the book of Acts and the modes of Christian community imagined therein (Countryman, 2007).

The Pauline epistles. Several of the New Testament writings written by (or attributed to) the apostle Paul, however, show significantly greater interest in matters of sexual transgression. Paul repeatedly exhorted followers of Jesus to avoid *porneia*, associating it with licentiousness (*aselgeia*) and the problem of individual and collective impurity (2 Cor 12:21; Gal 5:19–21; 1 Thess 4:3–7). The condemnation of *porneia* and its association with gentile depravity was a common trope in Jewish writings of the Second Temple period, and Paul freely harnessed it to do the work of communal self-definition. Combining this familiar theme of gentile sexual degeneracy with biblical polemics drawn from the Septuagint and common Greco-Roman rhetorical devices such as virtue and vice lists, the apostle put forward a particular form of argument that would go on to become extremely prominent in early Christian discourse—one wherein the boundaries between chosen insiders and "gentile" outsiders that defined the community of those "in Christ" were negotiated in sexual terms (Knust, 2006).

In 1 Corinthians 5–7, Paul offers an extended reflection on a variety of sexual offenses, linked conceptually by concerns about pollution and the dangers of desire. The apostle attacks the incestuous relationship of a man and his stepmother, calling for the offending man's expulsion from the community (1 Cor 5:1–13). Here his primary concern does not seem to be the man's ultimate fate but rather the health of the Corinthian Christian community as a whole. Insofar as the communal "body" of Christ is dangerously permeable, the polluting offender must be violently expelled, destroying the fleshly contam-

inant (*sarx*) for the sake of the health of the spirit (*pneuma*). In this context, the individual, social, and cosmic resonances of the *pneuma/sarx* opposition would all seem to be fundamentally interconnected in Paul's logic. The apostle then goes on in 1 Corinthians 6:12–20 to probe further this problem of the body's boundaries, exploring the dangerous and even unthinkable pollution that might defile the pneumatic body of Christ by means of a Christian body engaging in sexual intercourse with a prostitute (Martin, 1995). Finally, in 1 Corinthians 7, he rounds out his discussion of the problems of *porneia* with a strikingly negative appraisal of the desire that animates them. Here, in a marked contrast to modern Christian readings that have attempted to enlist him as a champion of sexual expression within heterosexual marriage, Paul does not in fact discriminate between legitimate and illegitimate forms of erotic passion. Instead he outlines a radical eschatological program for the eradication of all sexual desire—one that shows no concern whatsoever for Christian procreation and that treats sexual relations between married men and women as a somewhat lamentable concession, a prophylaxis for the weak along the road to extinguishing desire entirely (Martin, 1995; 2006).

Discussion of Pauline or pseudo-Pauline views on sexual transgression with members of the same sex has primarily centered on the interpretation of three passages: the vice list in 1 Corinthians 6:9, the somewhat similar list in 1 Timothy 1:9–10 (considered by the vast majority of critical scholars to be pseudonymous), and the more extended discussion in Romans 1:18–32. In 1 Corinthians 6:9, Paul puts forward a list of different kinds of transgressors who will not inherit the kingdom of God. With respect to sexual transgression, this list includes not only men who practice sexual immorality generally (*pornoi*) and adulterers (*moichoi*) but also *malakoi* (NRSV translation: "male prostitutes") and *arsenokoitai* (NRSV translation: "sodomites"; cf. also 1 Tim 1:10). The translation and interpretation of the latter two terms is contested in the scholarly literature. Most basically, *malakos* signifies softness or effeminacy. In the case of male-male sexual interaction, it could sometimes (but need not necessarily) indicate the penetrated partner in anal sex—but even then always with a view primarily to the broader charge of effeminacy rather than the specific sex act. (*Malakos* could, for example, often refer to nonsexual behavior or to other kinds of sexual behavior deemed potentially effeminate, e.g., masturbation; see Martin, 2006.) The translation of *arsenokoitēs* as "sodomite" or "homosexual" is derived from combining the term's two parts: "male"/*arsēn* and "(marriage) bed"/*koitē*. This is a neologism on Paul's part as far as we know, and some scholars have proposed that the apostle derived the term from the Septuagint form of the prohibition on "lying with a male" in Leviticus (20:13), though in that case the Greek text does not combine the two words (*arsēn, koitē*) into a single term; it does, however, place forms of them next to each other (Scroggs, 1983; Hays, 1996). Others have argued that this approach is linguistically problematic and that the meaning of *arsenokoitēs* is basically unknown. It has been suggested, given the other contexts in which the term later appears, that it may refer to some sort of sexual-economic (though not necessarily same-sex) exploitation (Martin, 2006).

Romans 1:18–32 was traditionally considered (even in modern scholarship) a more or less timeless and effectively acultural censure of all forms of homoerotic practice, male and female. More recently, the text has become the subject of significant scholarly controversy. While certain scholars continue to maintain some version of this position (Hays, 1996; Gagnon, 2001), numerous additional arguments and interpretive frameworks have been proposed for understanding what Paul is up to in these verses. These include working out worries about purity, offering a critique of Roman pederastic relationships, deploying the phrase "unnatural" (*para physin*) in the sense of "contrary to custom," condemning only truly heterosexual persons for engaging in same-sex acts, and/or providing a time-bound illustration whose real point is about idolatry (see Martin, 2006, pp. 18–35, for a thorough overview plus references). Perhaps most compelling is the work of scholars such as Bernadette Brooten and Dale Martin who draw attention to the ways in which Paul's argument in Romans 1 remains fully bound up in the Roman economy of gender and status hierarchies described above (Brooten, 1996; Martin, 2006). As Brooten shows, most fundamentally at issue in the passage is a notion of "natural" and "unnatural" sex acts whose conceptual basis is inseparable from this ancient gender hierarchy: men as active and penetrative, women as passive and penetrated. Sex acts between two persons of the same sex, at least as imagined by ancient thinkers, disrupt and threaten this hierarchy. Thus Stephen Moore summarizes: "Sex in this symbolic economy is nothing other—*can* be nothing other—than eroticized inequality" (Moore, 2001, p. 153). Accordingly, Martin and others argue for a greater recognition (in both scholarship and theological debate) of how profoundly and radically divergent are the "logics of sexuality" that underpin Romans 1 in its ancient context and contemporary discussions of homosexuality, respectively (Martin, 2006, p. 60).

General epistles and Revelation. The remaining books of the New Testament touch on a number of the themes already examined. Concerns with purity and pollution appear (Heb 13:4, Jas 1:27), but at the same time, the sexual transgressions of a specific character held up for approbation—in this case, Rahab the prostitute (*pornē*)—are not explicitly condemned (Heb 11:31; Jas 2:25). Accusations of sexual sin and enslavement to desire are mobilized rhetorically to condemn both Christian insiders/rival teachers (2 Pet 2:1–3, 12–14; Jude 16–19) and depraved outsiders, as represented by Rome, the "mother of whores" (Rev 17:5, NRSV). (See discussion in Knust, 2006.) Jude 7 makes a cryptic reference to the Sodom and Gomorrah narrative that has clear sexual overtones but no unambiguous censure of any specifically homoerotic element in the story. Rather, the issue seems to be one of sexual defilement with respect to the proper ordering of angels and human beings in the cosmic hierarchy (Countryman, 2007).

Modern Categories and Debates. In addition to the points of scholarly disagreement already discussed, numerous other debates continue to animate the field. For example, in what ways did the growing prominence of Christianity (and with it the New Testament texts) change the ways that acts related to sex (quotidian, transgressive, renunciatiory) were imagined and practiced in the ancient world vis-à-vis self-formation? (Foucault, 2005). Did something like the conceptual category of "sexuality"—in the sense of a subjective disposition or fixed orientation toward a particular sexual object choice—exist in the ancient world or not? What are the implications either way for interpreting New Testament and other ancient texts? (Brooten, 1996; see critique in Halperin, 2002) How should contemporary theological interpreters make sense of the sheer difference of history that the New Testament texts confront us with? Strategies in these theological conversations include ignoring or attempting to mitigate this difference, calling for certain biblical passages to no longer be considered authoritative (Brooten, 1996), rereading the scriptures to recover suppressed exemplars of alternative sexualities (Jennings, 2003), probing the internal and unresolved *aporias* of early Christian reflections on sexualized bodies as a potential theological resource (Dunning, 2011), and/or abandoning "the hegemony of historical criticism" entirely in favor of self-reflexively queer reading practices (Martin, 2006, pp. 88–90). These remain debates that are far from settled.

[*See also* Gender Transgression, *subentries on* New Testament *and* Roman World; Legal Status, *subentry* Roman World; Marriage and Divorce, *subentry* New Testament; Paul; Same-Sex Relations, *subentry* New Testament; *and* Sexual Transgression, *subentry* Roman World.]

BIBLIOGRAPHY

Brooten, Bernadette J. *Love Between Women: Early Christian Responses to Female Homoeroticism.* Chicago: University of Chicago Press, 1996.

Burrus, Virginia. "Mapping as Metamorphosis: Initial Reflections on Gender and Ancient Religious Discourses." In *Mapping Gender in Ancient Religious Discourses*, edited by Todd Penner and Caroline Vander Stichele, pp. 1–10. Leiden, The Netherlands: Brill, 2007.

Countryman, L. William. *Dirt, Greed, and Sex: Sexual Ethics in the New Testament and Their Implications for Today.* Rev. ed. Minneapolis: Fortress, 2007.

Dunning, Benjamin H. *Specters of Paul: Sexual Difference in Early Christian Thought.* Philadelphia: University of Pennsylvania Press, 2011.

Foucault, Michel. *The Hermeneutics of the Subject: Lectures at the Collège de France, 1981–1982.* Edited by Frédéric Gros. Translated by Graham Burchell. New York: Palgrave Macmillan, 2005. English translation of *L'herméneutique du sujet*, first published in 2001.

Gagnon, Robert A. J. *The Bible and Homosexual Practice: Texts and Hermeneutics.* Nashville, Tenn.: Abingdon, 2001.

Halperin, David M. *How to Do the History of Homosexuality.* Chicago: University of Chicago Press, 2002.

Hays, Richard B. *The Moral Vision of the New Testament: Community, Cross, New Creation; A Contemporary Introduction to New Testament Ethics.* San Francisco: HarperSanFrancisco, 1996.

Jennings, Theodore W., Jr. *The Man Jesus Loved: Homoerotic Narratives from the New Testament.* Cleveland, Ohio: Pilgrim, 2003.

Knust, Jennifer Wright. *Abandoned to Lust: Sexual Slander and Ancient Christianity.* New York: Columbia University Press, 2006.

Laqueur, Thomas. *Making Sex: Body and Gender from the Greeks to Freud.* Cambridge, Mass.: Harvard University Press, 1990.

Loader, William. *Sexuality and the Jesus Tradition.* Grand Rapids, Mich.: Eerdmans, 2005.

Martin, Dale B. *The Corinthian Body.* New Haven, Conn.: Yale University Press, 1995.

Martin, Dale B. *Sex and the Single Savior: Gender and Sexuality in Biblical Interpretation.* Louisville, Ky.: Westminster John Knox, 2006.

Moore, Stephen D. *God's Beauty Parlor and Other Queer Spaces In and Around the Bible.* Stanford, Calif.: Stanford University Press, 2001.

Rousselle, Aline. *Porneia: On Desire and the Body in Antiquity.* Translated by Felicia Pheasant. Oxford: Blackwell, 1988. First published in French in 1983.

Scroggs, Robin. *The New Testament and Homosexuality: Contextual Background for Contemporary Debate.* Philadelphia: Fortress, 1983.

Swancutt, Diana M. "Sexy Stoics and the Rereading of Romans 1.18–2.16." In *A Feminist Companion to Paul*, edited by Amy-Jill Levine with Marianne Blickenstaff, pp. 42–73. London: T&T Clark, 2004.

Walters, Jonathan. "Invading the Roman Body: Manliness and Impenetrability in Roman Thought." In *Roman Sexualities*, edited by Judith P. Hallett and Marilyn B. Skinner, pp. 29–43. Princeton, N.J.: Princeton University Press, 1997.

Williams, Craig A. *Roman Homosexuality: Ideologies of Masculinity in Classical Antiquity.* New York: Oxford University Press, 1999.

Benjamin H. Dunning

Early Judaism

Understandings of and responses to sexual transgression underwent significant change in early Judaism. Through exegetical (Midrashic) interpretation, early legal statements (e.g., Mishnaic or Toseftan, redacted ca. 200 C.E.) and talmudic discourse, rules related to sexual transgressions were developed, elaborated, minimized, and innovated. Rabbinic traditions were diverse and differed between individual sages, between historical periods—tannaitic (ending ca. 200–250 C.E.), amoraic (ending ca. 500 C.E.), and the later redactorial periods (Babylonian Talmud ca. 500–650 C.E. and prior to ca. 425 C.E. for the Palestinian Talmud)—and geographically between Palestinian and Babylonian traditions.

Nonetheless, notable trends may be identified in the area of sexual transgression. In the absence of a Temple cult (postdestruction from 70 C.E.), rabbinic law and culture adapted to the impossibility of Temple-contingent rituals and laws, such as sacrificial atonement for transgression, ritual purity, and the bitter waters of the Sotah. The construction and regulation of sexual transgression was influenced by asceticism, perhaps variously under Greco-Roman and Persian-Zoroastrian influence. This included notions of male and female sexuality as difficult to control and the development of negative attitudes toward sanctioned sexual activity and sexual thoughts. There is also a tendency toward the creation of legal "fences," where formerly permitted sexual activity becomes prohibited in an attempt to prevent more serious transgressions. The association of formerly permitted acts with highly transgressive acts further allowed for the inclusion of the nontransgressive within a more problematic framework. Sexual transgression also forms part of the negative construction of the Other, as some rabbinic traditions attribute prohibited or nonnormative sexuality to nonrabbis (especially the *am ha'aretz*) and gentiles. This coexists, however, with a portrayal of male sexuality (and the evil inclination or *yester harah*) in the Babylonian Talmud as extremely powerful, putting even the greatest sages at constant risk of sexual transgression (Rosen-Zvi, 2011). In a number of areas, such as the laws of *niddah*, male sexuality, sex segregation, *Sotah*, and male masturbation, the latest layers of the Babylonian Talmud are characterized by increasing stringency and extremely negative attitudes.

Nonreproductive Sexual Activity. Early Jewish literature addresses various forms of nonreproductive sexual activity.

Autoeroticism. There is no explicit biblical ban on masturbation. Most tannaitic and amoraic sources appear to oppose male self-arousal on an ascetic basis as part of a broader privileging of sexual self-control and a negative attitude toward sexual thoughts, even in the absence of any action (*hirhur aveirah*). Male masturbation might also be avoided on the grounds that it could lead to a slippery slope of forbidden acts, such as violation of the *arayot* (the sexual transgressions of Lev 18 and 20) or idolatry. One early text that is sometimes understood as a negative stance on male masturbation is *m. Niddah* 2:1, which encourages women to "check" for menstrual blood, whereas the man is discouraged from checking and states his hand should be cut off (see Satlow, 1995b, pp. 153–167).

Discussion of female masturbation is extremely limited. This silence may be the result of a general lack of consideration of female sexual activity in the absence of males, which is common to both biblical and rabbinic sources. The nonprocreative emission of what was believed to be female seed does not seem to have been a matter of concern. Elsewhere, it is suggested that women are encouraged to check frequently for menstrual bleeding because they do not have feeling and so presumably would not become sexually aroused (*b. Nid. 13a*). Brief mentions of female self-arousal, however, include an idol designed as a dildo for female masturbation (*b. 'Abod. Zar. 44a* in reference to 2 Chr 15:16) and a possible description of female and male masturbation as sexual display (*b. Meg. 12a–b*).

Nonprocreative seminal emission. Despite the common assumption that nonprocreative male seminal emission is prohibited in Judaism, such is not the case. A broad rabbinic principle holds that a man may engage in any sexual activity with his wife (this may at times ignore the preferences of the wife; see *b. Ned. 20b*). Apart from later layers of the Babylonian Talmud, most sources appear to share Greco-Roman notions of male and female seed, including that the male seed is not precious in and of itself. Michael Satlow has argued that the prohibition of nonprocreative seminal emission primarily appears within the latest layers of the Babylonian Talmud and within the antecedent sources of the *sugyot* (Talmudic sections or topical discussions); the *sugyot* themselves do not appear to have shared such a concern (Satlow, 1995b; *b. Nid. 13a–b*).

Levirate marriage. The concern regarding wasted seed is at times connected to the act of Onan (hence onanism) who in Genesis 38 refused to fulfill his levirate obligation to produce offspring in the name of his dead brother. Earlier, and especially Palestinian, sources often interpret the nature of his transgression not as masturbation but as a denial of duty, hedonism, lust, and selfishness (see, for example, *Gen. Rab.* 85:5). Rabbinic tradition is deeply ambivalent regarding levirate marriage, which is a violation of Leviticus 18:6 and 20:21 (see, for example, *b. Ketub. 2b*), going so far as to state that a levirate union where the levir engaged in procreative intercourse for any reason other than fulfilling his duty produces offspring that are close to being *mamzer*s (*b. Yebam. 39b*).

Anal sex. Anal sex (heterosexual, performed upon the woman) is exegetically connected to the phrase *mishkevei ishah* or "lyings of a woman" (Lev 18:22; 20:13). The biblical use of the plural is used to understand more than one way of a male lying with a woman (*Sifra* a.k.a. Torat Kohanim *Kedoshim* Pereq 9:14, *92b*). These two ways are sometimes termed *shekedarkah* and *lo shekedarkah*, "according to its way" and "not according to its way," which may suggest vaginal and anal/oral sexual connection (Satlow, 1995a, pp. 238–242; *b. Ned. 20b; b. Sanh. 58b*).

Male homosexual/sex. *Mishkevei ishah* is constructed as normative and permitted, in sharp contrast to *mishkav zakhur* (lying of a man), which is prohibited and subject to capital punishment (Lev 18:22). The nature of the specific homosexual act,

which is prohibited, is a matter of debate among scholars. It is frequently noted that the biblical text has no notion of a sexual orientation per se, but only of a sexual act.

The same may be true of rabbinic sources. Rabbinic sources, however, do construct sex acts between males as atypical of Jewish men, whereas gentile men are suspected of such acts.

Female homosexual/sex. Same-sex sexual activity between women is not mentioned in biblical law, but marriage between women (as well as between men) is prohibited by *Sifra*, an early Midrash to Leviticus. *Sifra* expands the levitical *arayot* (prohibited relationships) of Leviticus 18 and 20 (specifically the ban against the statutes of the Egyptians) to include a ban on female-female marriage and a woman marrying two men (*Sifra Aharei Mot* 9:8, Weiss edition, *85a–b*). The Babylonian Talmud only briefly mentions sexual acts between women, first in a discussion as to whether such sexual activity has the ability to effect female status change by rendering a woman unfit to marry into the priesthood (*b. Yebam. 76a*) and second in a discussion which suggests that Jewish women may not be suspected of such behavior (*b. Šabb. 65a*). This lack of interest is likely caused by a general lack of concern regarding female sexual activity when it does not involve men (see, however, Maimonides Mishneh Torah *Issurei Bi'ah* 21:8).

Bestiality. Bestiality is prohibited for both men and women following Leviticus 18:23 and 20:15–16, but was constructed as an act of which Jews are not suspect and came to be attributed to gentiles. In contrast, see *b. Qiddushin 81b* where sages avoid being in the presence of animals for fear of engaging in bestiality. This concern regarding the sexual temptation posed by animals is likely part of a late Babylonian rabbinic discourse, which emphasizes the power of male sexuality and the difficulty of controlling it (the so-called evil inclination, *yester harah*; see Rosen-Zvi, 2011).

Expanding the Levitical *Arayot.* Rabbinic literature expands the list of prohibited relationships (*arayot*) provided in Leviticus 18 and 20 and creates a category of *sheniyot* or secondary rabbinic prohibitions, which prohibit a wider range of familial relations and create a hierarchical gradation of prohibited relations (*b. Yebam.* 21a, *m. Yebam.* 2:3–4). In *Sifra Aharei Mot* (Parashah 9 and Pereq 13, *85c–86d*), Leviticus's references to the acts of the Egyptians and Canaanites are expanded to include prohibitions of female-female marriage and polyandry, as well as a general prohibition of intermarriage. None of these rulings, however, holds a central place in rabbinic legal tradition.

Incest. Certain close familial relations not prohibited by Leviticus 18 and 20 continue to be permitted and even highly preferred in rabbinic tradition, namely uncle-niece marriages (aunt-nephew is biblically prohibited, see however CD 5:7–10 where both of these couplings are forbidden) and cousin marriages (Satlow, 2001).

Niddah. Sexual relations with a woman in the state of *niddah* (menstrual impurity) are prohibited (Lev 18:19) and biblically punishable by excision (Lev 20:18). These prohibitions can be seen as more punitive than earlier parts of Leviticus: the laws of Leviticus 15 on the *zav* ("male with an emission") and *niddah* ("menstruant") prescribe only procedures for purification (Meacham, 1999). Even within the Bible, the term *niddah*, like *zonah/zenut* ("harlot"), came to be associated with sexual transgression and idolatry. Rabbinic literature expanded the laws of *niddah* significantly, emphasizing the severity of sexual relations with a *niddah* and extending this description to most forms of contact between husband and wife, while subsuming the period of biblical *niddah* within the more stringent framework of *zivah* (irregular menstrual bleeding); it also created the rabbinic category of "minor *zavah*," which resulted in an extended period of each menstrual cycle when sexual relations and physical contact came to be prohibited, possibly under ascetic considerations (Meacham, 1999). A notable exception to this pattern of rabbinic stringency is the status of the offspring of sexual relations with a *niddah*, which, unlike the offspring of the other *arayot*, is not deemed a *mamzer* (*b. Yebam.* 49a–b). It should be noted that although biblical law is unclear as to whether the state of *niddah* affects all women, in rabbinic law gentile women are not deemed to be subject to menstrual impurity, just as gentile male emissions likewise do not transmit impurity (for the special case of *niddah* and Samaritan women, see *m. Nid.* 4:1).

Molekh ritual. In rabbinic sources, the *molekh* ritual is exegetically conflated with the deuteronomic passing of the child through the fire (a joined description is already found in 2 Kings 23:10). The dominant interpretive tradition is that it consists of a ritual of child sacrifice to an idol. A minority tradition developed that the *molekh* ritual is in fact marriage or sexual relations with a gentile woman, either for the purposes of idolatry or resulting in the production of idolatrous offspring (see *Tg. Ps.-J.* to Lev 18:21 and *Tg. Neof.* marginalia to Lev 20:2). This tradition was banned in *m. Megillah* 4:9 and rejected by *Sifra Qodashim* Parashah 10:3, but transmitted by *y. Megillah* 4:10, *75c* as an early exegesis of Leviticus 18:21. Following this targumic and exegetical tradition, intermarriage or sexual relations between Jews and gentiles were understood as a capital crime (Clenman, 2013).

Boel aramit. The *molekh* tradition is at times linked to the *boel aramit* (one who has sexual relations with an Aramean woman; read gentile). The *boel aramit* is subject to deadly attack by zealots (see *m. Sanh.* 9:6). In both the Babylonian and the Palestinian Talmuds, the *boel aramit* is connected to Numbers 25, where Zimri is understood to have had sexual connection with the Midianite woman Kozbi, for which transgression both of them are summarily speared to death by Pinchas, who in turn receives divine approval for his killing. *m. Sanhedrin* 9:6 is classed as authoritative in both Talmuds (*b. Sanh. 82a*, *y. Sanh. 27b*). Both Talmuds, however, betray some ambivalence toward this zealot killing of the *boel aramit*, given its unclear connection to rabbinic legal jurisdiction and due process; *y. Sanhedrin 27b* forcefully rejects Pinchas's actions (Clenman, 2013). The Babylonian Talmud rules that should the zealots fail to kill him, the *boel aramit* is to be punished by excision (*karet*; see *b. Sanh. 81b–82a*).

Intermarriage with gentiles. The Pentateuch provides specific prohibitions of intermarriage, which the rabbis did not understand to amount to a general prohibition of intermarriage, aside from a minority tradition of exegesis to Deuteronomy 7:3–4 (see Hayes, 2002). The laws regulating entry to the congregation in Deuteronomy 23 were understood as marital and sexual laws in rabbinic tradition. Exegesis allowed the rabbis to permit marriages with Moabite and Ammonite women, perhaps motivated by the Moabite and Ammonite female ancestry in the royal messianic lines, despite the ban in Deuteronomy 23:4–7 (*Sifre* Devarim Pisqa 249, *m. Yebam.* 8:3). Some early sources argue further for an abandonment of the nation-specific marriage laws of Deuteronomy 23 in view of the impossibility of identifying biblical identities subsequent to historical population displacements and the ubiquity of intermarriage (see, for example, *t. Qidd.* 5:4). Talmudic historical constructions attribute general prohibitions of intermarriage and sex between Jews and gentile to the court of Shem (*b. ʿAbod. Zar. 36b*) and the Hasmonean court (*b. Sanh. 82a*).

Sexual Exclusivity and Access. Various rabbinic texts limit sexual access, both within and beyond the bounds of marriage.

Adultery. Adultery in both biblical and rabbinic law is understood as the violation of the exclusive sexual access of a man to his wife (Lev 18:20; Deut 22:22; Exod 20:14). A sexual act between a man and a married woman is thus adulterous and, likewise, a married woman with any man other than her husband is deemed adulterous, whereas a married man with a single woman (or married to more than one woman) is not considered adulterous (nor is a male homosexual or female homosexual act). The biblical law regarding false virginity claims (Deut 22:13–21) appears to defy other deuteronomic laws, which call for the death penalty when a bride is found not to be a virgin. The paradox is that any relations would have occurred prior to marriage and hence would have been nonadulterous. Rabbinic sources solve this problem by concluding that the bride engaged in relations between bethrothal (*kiddushin* or *erusin*) and marriage (*nisuin*), which would be adulterous and hence a capital crime (note that the same solution is used for the burning of the daughter of a priest in Lev 21:9).

Sotah. The biblical *Sotah* ritual was contingent upon a specific priestly ritual held at the temple, to be enacted in a case where the husband suspects that his wife may have been adulterous (Num 5:11–31). The ritual of humiliation and the drinking of the bitter waters appears to be meant to resolve this suspicion. The case of the *Sotah* must be distinguished from the transgression of adultery, which is a capital crime and must be proven according to rabbinic due process. The treatment of the *Sotah* is much expanded in talmudic sources, rendered even more explicit, punitive, and legally problematic than the biblical description despite the impossibility of the ritual in a post-Temple context (Rosen-Zvi, 2012). A new rabbinic legal status of the doubtful *Sotah (safeq sotah)* became a means for further formalizing anxiety regarding female sexuality, as the Palestinian Talmud puts it, "so that the daughters of Israel will not explode in carnality (*zimah*)" (*y. Ketub. 1:1 25a*). Most significant for the situation of the rabbinic *Sotah* is that she is immediately and permanently forbidden to her husband, so that sexual relations between husband and wife are rendered transgressive and the couple must divorce. This stringency is a sort of compensation for the fact that she cannot drink the bitter waters, rendering any resolution impossible. Upon divorce, the husband would normally be required to grant his wife the *ketubah* payment, a financial surety and protection. The *Sotah*, however, is denied her *ketubah* payment. This obviously inequitable situation resulted in some rabbinic concern regarding the ease with which a man may dispatch his wife and divest his wife of her *ketubah* by simply expressing suspicion regarding her sexual activity or questioning her virginal status (see *b. Ketub. 10a–b*).

Zonah. The status of *zonah* ("prostitute/harlot") and the notion of *zenut* ("prostitution/whoredom") in biblical literature do not appear to be transgressive per se aside from the rule against prostituting one's daughter (Lev 19:29). Nonetheless, a priest was not allowed to marry *a zonah* (Lev 21:7), and for the daughter of a priest to be a *zonah* was a capital crime (Lev 21:9), though in this context, the term may be understood as referring to any of a variety of categories of woman deemed unfit to marry a priest (*b. Yebam.*

61b). Moreover, *zonah* and *zenut* are used generally as negative terms for female sexuality (as in Genesis 34:31) and especially as a metaphor for the betrayal of the divine and the following of idols (sometimes both metaphorical and literal, perhaps, as in Numbers 25:1–3). The meaning of the term *zonah* in biblical and rabbinic literature is both specific, as in a harlot or prostitute, and general, as in sexually active (see Kriger, 2011). In early Judaism, some women are automatically considered to have the status of a *zonah*, including gentile females older than three years and a day and Jewish women over that age who have been taken captive. The former may be connected to a disputed tradition that gentile women are sexually available to all (*hefqer*) and have no notion of marriage (*b. Sanh.* 82a). This debate may be contextualized within a broader tendency to construct the Other (gentile, *am ha'arets*) as sexually problematic. For a male to have relations with a *zonah* is generally undesirable, perhaps for ascetic considerations, yet some traditions permit relations with a prostitute (see, for example, *t. Tem.* 4:2). For a prohibition of relations between a nonpriest and a *zonah*, see the discussion of the *qedesah*, below. In contrast, for a woman to be a *zonah* (whether by default or profession) is a matter of status change, rendering her prohibited in marriage to the priest. Precisely which type of sexual relations rendered a woman a *zonah* was a matter of some debate (*m. Yebam.* 6:5, *b. Yebam.* 61b). Sex between a man and a single woman appears to be permissible following biblical law but becomes problematic in rabbinic tradition, which developed rules even against seclusion (*yichud*) of men and women to avoid any sexual contact (*m. Qidd.* 4:11; 12 in some editions). *B. Avodah Zarah* 36b constructs a history of prohibition of various sexual transgressions, especially between Jews and gentiles, culminating in decrees against seclusion with gentile women and Jewish women.

Qadesh and qadeshah. The term *qadesh* (m.) or *qadeshah* (f.) suggests a man or woman dedicated to a temple and its deity, which is biblically banned (Deut 23:18). This prohibition has often been interpreted as a ban against Temple prostitution (perhaps not unlike the *molekh* ritual as a sexual act for idolatrous ends), although it has been recently argued that sacred prostitution did not exist in antiquity. Not unlike the case of the *molekh* ritual, the meaning of the term *qadesh/ah* and the nature of the activity that is prohibited remain unclear. The prohibition is understood in two ways in early rabbinic literature and the targumim: as a ban on prostitution and relations with prostitutes (*Neof.* and *Ps.-J.* to Deut 23:18) or as a ban against sexual relations (or marriage) with slaves (*Tg. Onq.* to Deut 23:18). Diane Kriger notes that Josephus banned marriage between free men and slaves as well as marriage between free men and prostitutes (*Ant.* 4:8:23; Kriger, 2011, p. 325). The notion of *qadesh/ah* as a slave is not far from its most basic meaning, namely a person belonging to another entity, here a temple/deity. *Qadesh/ah* is also sometimes connected with the *zonah*, as in *b. Sanhedrin* 82a, which exegetically links idolatry, intermarriage, and male homosexuality to Malachi 2:12.

Sexual assault. Biblical law imposes upon the rapist a fine and forced marriage to the victim with no option of divorce (see Deuteronomy 22:23–29). Rabbinic law allows the father and the minor daughter the option of refusing the marriage (*b. Ketub.* 39b). It likewise calls for additional payment of damages due to the father relative to his means and circumstances, as compensation for humiliation and other losses for the rape of his daughter, whether a minor or age of majority (*b. Ketub.* 42a–43b). A woman who has been sexually assaulted is considered exempt from the death penalty for adultery if married (for a prohibition of rape within marriage see *b. Eruv.* 100b), and she is permitted sexually to her husband (unless he is a priest, *b. Yebam.* 56b). A minor is generally considered unable to consent (see *b. Yebam.* 33b and 61b, *y. Soṭah* 1:2). However, according to some sources the father's will may represent the minor daughter's (see *b. Qidd.* 5a and commentaries there) or if a father contracts his minor daughter in marriage, he may give her over to sexual intercourse (*biah*) to the groom against her will, for the purposes of contracting the marriage (*b. Qidd.* 3b, *Tosafot s.v. ha'av zakai* and *y. Ketub.* 4:6).

The beautiful captive. The *yefat toar*, known as the "law of the beautiful captive," is a military law that allows for a man on the battlefield to take as his wife a captive woman whom he finds attractive (Deut 21:10–14). Following her capture, she undergoes a sort of protoconversion. If he subsequently does not desire her, he may send her away but is forbidden from selling her or otherwise treating her as a slave. The primary problem in a rabbinic context becomes whether the soldier may have sexual relations with her prior to her protoconversion (e.g., on the battlefield). Some argue yes, but only once; others argue that he may not and must wait until following her protoconversion, reflecting negative ascetic attitude toward the entire practice (see Sifrei Deut Pisqa 218, b. Qidd. 21a, b. Sanh. 21a–22a, Elman, 1997; Stern, 1998).

[*See also* Imagery, Gendered, *subentry* Priestly Material; Male-Female Sexuality, *subentry* Early Judaism; Marriage and Divorce, *subentry* Early Judaism; Race, Class, and Ethnicity, *subentry* Early Judaism; *and* Sexual Violence, *subentry* Early Judaism.]

BIBLIOGRAPHY

Biale, David. *Eros and the Jews: From Biblical Israel to Contemporary America*. New York: Basic Books, 1992.

Boyarin, Daniel. *Carnal Israel: Reading Sex in Talmudic Culture*. Berkeley: University of California Press, 1993.

Clenman, Laliv. "The Faceless Idol and Images of Terror in Rabbinic Tradition on Molekh." In *The Image and Its Prohibition in Jewish Antiquity*, edited by Sarah Pearce. Oxford: Journal of Jewish Studies, 2013.

Cohen, Shaye. *Beginnings of Jewishness: Boundaries, Varieties, Uncertainties*. Berkeley: University of California Press, 1999.

Diamond, Eliezer. *Hunger Artists: Fasting and Asceticism in Rabbinic Culture*. Oxford: Oxford University Press, 2004.

Eilberg-Schwartz, Howard. *God's Phallus and Other Problems for Men and Monotheism*. Boston: Beacon, 1994.

Elman, Pearl. "Deuteronomy 21:10-14: The Beautiful Captive Woman." *Women in Judaism* 1, no. 1 (1997). https://jps.library .utoronto.ca/index.php/wjudaism/article/view/166.

Fonrobert, Elisheva Charlotte. *Menstrual Purity: Rabbinic and Christian Reconstructions of Biblical Gender*. Stanford, Calif.: Stanford University Press, 2000.

Hayes, Christine. *Gentile Impurities and Jewish Identities: Intermarriage and Conversion from the Bible to the Talmud*. Oxford: Oxford University Press, 2002.

Kriger, Diane. *Sex Rewarded, Sex Punished: A Study of the Status "Female Slave" in Early Jewish Law*. Edited by Tirzah Meacham (leBeit Yoreh). Boston: Academic Studies Press, 2011.

Meacham, Tirzah (leBeit Yoreh). "An Abbreviated History of the Development of the Jewish Menstrual Laws." In *Women and Water: Menstruation in Jewish Life and Law*, edited by Rahel R. Wasserfall, pp. 23–39. Hanover, N.H.: Brandeis University Press, 1999.

Meacham, Tirzah (leBeit Yoreh). "Sotah." In *Jewish Women: A Comprehensive Historical Encyclopedia*. http://jwa .org/encyclopedia/article/legal-religious-status-of-suspected-adulteress-sotah.

Rosen-Zvi, Ishay. *Demonic Desires: "Yetser Hara" and the Problem of Evil in Late Antiquity*. Philadelphia: University of Pennsylvania Press, 2011.

Rosen-Zvi, Ishay. *The Mishnaic Sotah Ritual: Temple, Gender and Midrash*. Leiden, The Netherlands: Brill, 2012.

Satlow, Michael. *Tasting the Dish: Rabbinic Rhetorics of Sexuality*. Atlanta: Scholars Press, 1995a.

Satlow, Michael. "Wasted Seed: The History of a Rabbinic Idea." *Hebrew Union College Annual* 65 (1995b): 137–175.

Satlow, Michael. "Texts of Terror: Rabbinic Texts, Speech Acts, and the Control of Mores." *Association for Jewish Studies Review* 21, no. 2 (1996): 273–297.

Satlow, Michael. *Jewish Marriage in Antiquity*. Princeton, N.J.: Princeton University Press, 2001.

Stern, David. "The Captive Woman: Hellenization, Greco-Roman Erotic Narrative, and Rabbinic Literature." *Poetics Today* 19, no. 1 (1998): 91–127.

Laliv Clenman

Early Church

Early Christian reflection on sexual transgression focuses on adultery (*moicheia*), fornication (*porneia*), and pederasty (*paidophtheria*) (*Didache* 2.2, 5.1; *Epistle of Barnabas* 10.6, 19.4, 20.1; cf. Hermas, *Mandates* 8.38.3). However, early Christians did not always agree on the definitions of these terms or the scope of sexual transgression. Celibate marriages, marriage to non-Christians, and second marriages were particularly controversial practices.

As a product of classical culture, early Christian treatment of sexual transgression is deeply intertwined with gender slippage and social hierarchy. Rules governing adultery focused on the status of the woman, and prohibitions of same-sex intercourse were rooted in social norms for the respectable behavior of men and women.

During this period, early Christian thinking also sees a transition from forbidden and permitted acts to forbidden and permitted desires. Sexual transgression becomes something that takes place primarily in the heart. As a solution to desire, some Christians see sexual renunciation as the only option, while others imagine procreative sexual intercourse without desire. Sexual renunciation generally occupies the pinnacle of the ideal sexual life, at one end of a scale descending downward into certain kinds of acceptable marriage, followed by a host of possible transgressions.

Christian Morality in the Greek and Roman World. Early Christians disapprove of *porneia* and pederasty, sexual acts generally accepted by their Greek and Roman peers. The third-century North African apologist Tertullian contrasts Christian chastity with the sexual decadence of Greeks and Romans (*Apology* 39.11–13; all translated titles by author). Athenagoras (ca. 177) complains, "The adulterers and pederasts defame the eunuchs and the once-married [Christians]" (*Plea* 34.3; all translations by author). This kind of sexual slander functions as boundary-drawing rhetoric, but also reveals the acceptable sexual practices for those making them.

While earlier generations of scholars emphasized the moral gap between Christianity and "paganism," others have challenged the trend by arguing that there is great continuity. Michel Foucault, for instance, emphasizes continuity between Christian regulation of sexual morality and its Greek and Roman context. He locates the Christian rupture, however, in the hermeneutics of the self and discernment of desires (Foucault, 1986). In contrast, Kathy Gaca emphasizes that sexual renunciation in early Christianity breaks with and misinterprets Stoic philosophy (Gaca, 2003). However, Giulia Sissa argues that the contribution that even Foucault sees Christianity making is just as central to non-Christian thinking (Sissa, 2008).

Focusing on material transitions, Kyle Harper argues that the real Christian change to Greek and Roman sexual morality does not arrive until the legal changes banning forced prostitution and same-sex intercourse in the fifth century (Harper, 2013). The question of continuity is always selective, as

Bernadette Brooten shows that "a focus on female homoeroticism makes this continuity clearer than would a focus on male homoeroticism" (Brooten, 1996, pp. 2–3). Brooten's argument suggests that, depending on the specific issue, the case for "continuity" between early Christian and Greek and Roman sexual morality may be stronger or weaker.

Marriage and Celibacy. The Pastoral Epistles warn against those who advocated abstaining from marriage (1 Tim 4:3), insisting that women's salvation depends on bearing children (1 Tim 2:15). This view won little support, however, and the view that celibacy was greater than marriage went almost unchallenged through the end of the fourth century. The apostle Paul had set the moral framework for early Christian sexuality (1 Cor 7).

Even within marriage, sexual transgression from desire remains a risk. Ignatius of Antioch (ca. 111) advises that bishops should exercise oversight of those seeking to get married to ensure "that their marriage may be for the Lord and not desire" (*To Polycarp* 5.2). Tertullian explains that marriage is not forbidden, but that this does not make it good (*To His Wife* 1.3). Marriage is only acceptable as a means of avoiding sexual temptation (*To His Wife* 1.4–5; cf. *Exhortation to Chastity* 12). He praises those "who have preferred to marry God" and live in continence (*Exhortation to Chastity* 13.4). However, Tertullian objects to those who forbid marriage entirely, maintaining only that the Lord prefers continence (*On Monogamy* 3.1).

Some practices of sexual renunciation included "spiritual marriages" in which a couple either never has intercourse or renounces intercourse after a period of time (Tertullian, *Exhortation to Chastity* 12). There was always suspicion about such arrangements. Irenaeus of Lyons (180s) accuses his "gnostic" opponents of fraudulently living as "brother and sister," only to be exposed when the woman becomes pregnant (*Against Heresies* 1.6.3). These practices are often condemned and even forbidden by some later church councils (Eusebius, *Ecclesiastical History* 7.30.12–13; Council of Elvira [306], canon 27; Council of Nicaea [325], canon 3; Cyprian, *Epistle* 62.2; Jerome, *Epistle* 22).

Fornication and Adultery. Early Christians taught that marriage was the only acceptable sexual relationship.

Adultery is defined as sex with an honorable woman—generally, a woman who is married. The transgression injures both her honor and her husband's. Fornication is sex with a dishonorable woman who lacks the social status of a household; this includes public prostitutes. The marital status of the male is not relevant to the definition of adultery or fornication.

Early Christian sexual ethics prohibit fornication (*Epistle of Barnabas* 19.4; *Didache* 2.2). Paul condemns sex with prostitutes, believing that it pollutes the body of Christ, not the marriage bed (1 Cor 6:12–20). Clement of Alexandria (late second century) laments the prostitution of both boys and girls. He warns that such acts lead to unforeseen consequences, such as a man unknowingly engaging in sex with a child of his that was a product of sex with prostitutes (*The Instructor* 3.3.21; cf. Tertullian, *To the Nations* 1.16.14–20). He is also critical of slave owners who profit by selling the flesh of women and boys (*The Instructor* 3.3.22). Athenagoras and Justin, too, bemoan the marketplace of fornication and pleasures through prostitution (*Plea* 34.3; *1 Apology* 1.14.2).

Early Christians considered some marriages to be sinful. Clement advocates that Christians must only marry other Christians (*Miscellanies* 3.73.3, 97.3, 107.1). Tertullian warns, "Believers contracting marriages with gentiles are established guilty of sexual crime [*stuprum*], and are to be excluded from all communication with the brotherhood" (*To His Wife* 3.1). Those who were married before their conversion were exempt.

While adultery is strictly prohibited, the consequences were not always clear. Early Christians typically allow divorce in the case of adultery (Matt 5:32, 19:9). The lived reality was more complex. The *Shepherd of Hermas* (early second century) asks, what if a wife commits adultery and the husband continues having intercourse with her? If he is ignorant, he does not sin, but if he knows about it he has become a partner in her immorality. They should divorce unless the adulterous spouse has repented.

Forgiveness for adultery is controversial. In *Hermas*, adultery may be forgiven only once (2.4.1–11, 8.3). In contrast, Tertullian argues that adultery is an irre-

missible sin (*On Modesty* 2, 4, 22). Origen (early third century) too argues that adultery and fornication cannot be forgiven (*On Prayer* 18). A third-century bishop, Cyprian of Carthage, reports that bishops disagreed on whether adultery was forgivable, using their own discretion (*Epistles* 51.21). Some Christians suggested the custom was that only the husband should be forgiven for adultery, but the wife should not be (Basil, *Epistle* 188.9, 199.21).

Second Marriages. Early Christians frequently oppose remarriage after divorce or widowhood. Justin Martyr warns that the "twice married are sinners" (*1 Apology* 15). Second marriages are considered adultery because a married couple becomes "one flesh" (Matt 19:9; cf. Athenagoras, *Plea* 33). Others cite the Pastoral Epistles' rules about bishops being married only once (1 Tim 3:1–7; Tit 1:6–9; cf. Tertullian, *On Monogamy* 12).

Tertullian warns, "Second marriage will have to be termed no other than a species of sexual crime [*stuprum*]" (*Exhortation to Chastity* 9.1). Though he acknowledges that second marriages are not absolutely forbidden, Tertullian writes his treatise *To His Wife* to persuade his wife to not remarry if he dies first (see also *On Exhortation to Chastity*). He sets up a hierarchy where chastity is the greatest good, then marriage, then second marriage as it descends further and further from the ideal (*Exhortation to Chastity* 9–11). Tertullian insists, "We admit one marriage, just as we do one God" (*On Monogamy* 1.4).

Sex as Transgression. The practice of celibacy is diffuse, not limited to any one variety of Christianity, time period, or region. Tatian (second century) condemns sexual relations and is often identified with the Encratite movement (from Greek *enkrateia*, meaning continence or self-control). He warns that any sexual activity is a state of uncontrolled desire, fornication, and bondage to Satan (Clement, *Miscellanies* 3.12.81). The slogan "Marriage is *porneia*" was a powerful rhetorical weapon (Clement, *Miscellanies* 3.12.89).

The second-century *Acts of Paul and Thecla* similarly praises sexual renunciation. Paul's beatitudes extol continence, virginity, and celibate marriage (1.12–22). Thecla is praised and blessed by God for calling off her wedding, refusing all suitors, and living a life of virginity. Many of the so-called Apocryphal Acts feature females persuaded by the message of chastity.

Early Christians appeal to various typologies to explain sexual renunciation. The *Acts of Judas Thomas* envisions the lack of sexual activity as a return to primordial purity (12–14). Julius Cassianus, reportedly a former Valentinian, advocates sexual renunciation on the belief that sexual difference would be abolished, and taught, "Let no one say that because we have these parts, that the female body is shaped this way and the male that way, the one to receive, the other to give seed, sexual intercourse is allowed by God" (Clement, *Miscellanies* 3.13.91). Marcion renounces sexual intercourse and procreation to oppose the creator of the material world (Clement, *Stromateis* 3.3.12). Others teach that God created the human body above the navel, while the half below the navel was created by the devil (*Miscellanies* 3.4.34). In the *Testimony of Truth*, sexual intercourse is connected to the Law and as such must be opposed (29.26–30.17). The anonymous author of the *Treatise on the Resurrection*, attributed to Justin Martyr, argues the coming resurrection, the virgin birth, and Christ's own ascetic example have abolished desire and marriage (*Treatise on the Resurrection* 3–5). Others teach that Mary was a virgin both before and after the birth of Jesus, miraculously maintaining her purity in parturition (*Protoevangelium of James* 19.3).

Some portions of the New Prophesy movement may favor sexual renunciation and oppose marriage, connecting sexual purity to receiving spiritual gifts (Epiphanius, *Panarion* 48.9.7). However, there was likely diversity of opinion among those influenced by this movement. Tertullian's later writings show his affinity to the New Prophesy, and though he preferred celibacy, he does not forbid marriage.

Sex for Procreation. For many early Christians, the purpose of marriage is not a safeguard against excessive desire (as Paul had described it), but only to produce children. Athenagoras emphasizes, "Each of us thinks of his wife whom he has married according to the laws laid down by us, and that only for the purpose of procreation" (*Plea* 33.1). Justin Martyr lays out two paths that Christians follow, marriage for the purpose of having children or a life of sexual continence (*1 Apology* 29).

Clement of Alexandria most thoroughly explains a procreationist perspective, seeking to eliminate sexual desire from procreation entirely. Clement argues that sexual desire is always sinful, but that it is possible to engage in sexual intercourse without desire. Married Christians should avoid any activity that might arouse desire, including kissing, dancing, and singing (*The Instructor* 3.11.80–82). He prohibits all unproductive sexual intercourse, including during menstruation, pregnancy, and nursing, and likely masturbation (*Miscellanies* 2.23.143; *The Instructor* 2.10.83, 91). Citing Matthew 5:28, for Clement all sexual desires, even with a spouse, are adultery (*Exhortation to the Greeks* 108.5). Christians must experience a transformation to practice passionless sexual acts (*Miscellanies* 3.7.58, 10.69, 12.82).

Sexual Communalism. Practices of sexual communalism in early Christianity are difficult to reconstruct. Irenaeus reports vaguely on the sexual license of several groups (*Against Heresies* 1.23, 25, 26, 28). He accuses Marcus of practicing a secretive "bridal chamber" rite that consisted of ritual sex (*Against Heresies* 1.13.4, 21.3). Irenaeus also tells of two women who escaped and reportedly exposed the sexual license of these groups (*Against Heresies* 1.6.3). According to Clement, the Antitactae resist the Creator by opposing his commandments, including the interdiction against adultery and sex with boys (*Stromateis* 3.34–36). These reports, however, rest primarily on rumor and slander.

In one case, Clement mentions Nicolaus, who sought to fulfill the command "Treat the flesh with contempt" by offering his wife to the apostles (*Miscellanies* 3.4.25–26). While Clement redeems Nicolaus and his family from the charges of indecency, Irenaeus connects him to fornication (*Against Heresies* 1.26.3). By the time of the fourth century, the legends of Nicolaus's sins multiply under Epiphanius, who accuses him of daily intercourse, eating semen and menstrual blood, consuming aborted fetuses, and spawning several imitators in licentiousness (*Panarion* 25.2.1, 26.1.1–3, 26.3.3).

There may be one genuine case of Christian sexual communalism. Epiphanes was the author of the treatise *On Righteousness*, which has been preserved only in a citation by Clement (*Miscellanies* 3.2.5–8).

Epiphanes, who may have been the son or student of the teacher Carpocrates, taught what has been pilloried as "libertinism," although this perspective misrepresents the philosophical and theological motivations informing these sexual practices. Epiphanes draws on Plato's recommendation in *Republic* 5 of sexual communalism, including the sharing of women and children. Epiphanes's vision of sexual communalism has roots in early Christian communalism such as that depicted in Acts 4:32—5:11: "They held everything in common." God created sexual desires, and acting on them in moderation is appropriate for his creation, grounding Epiphanes's sexual ethics in the goodness of the created order.

Castration/Eunuchs. Early Christians debated the meaning of the saying of Jesus: "There are eunuchs who have made themselves eunuchs for the sake of the kingdom of heaven" (Matt 19:12); and further, when advising against lust, "It will do you less harm to lose one part of you than to have your whole body thrown into hell" (Matt 5:29). The interpretations conflict regarding whether the saying is taken literally as in self-castration or metaphorically as in celibacy.

Eunuchs enjoy prestige in the eyes of many Christians. Marcion reportedly admires eunuchs (Tertullian, *Against Marcion* 1.29). Justin Martyr approvingly cites the example of an Alexandrian who had asked a surgeon to make him a eunuch (*1 Apology* 29). Eusebius praises Origen's castration (*Ecclesiastical History* 6.8). There are legitimate questions about the reliability of Eusebius's account, but either way it reveals some early Christian attitudes toward castration.

Opponents of castration in early Christianity decry the gender ambiguity it created and challenge its necessity. Tertullian laments that the castrated male is "a third sex, suited to male and female, joining male and female qualities" (*To the Nations* 1.20.4). The third-century *Acts of John* depicts John condemning a young man who castrated himself to avoid temptation (53–54). The Council of Nicaea officially bans willful castration for clerics, but not for laypeople (Canon 1).

Same-Sex Intercourse. For men, same-sex intercourse includes sex with adult males, perhaps slaves or prostitutes, as well as with young boys. Early Christians condemn such sexual relationships. Christian apologists frequently contrast male-male sex among non-Christian Greeks and Romans with their own restrained sexual practices (Justin Martyr, *1 Apology* 29; Athenagoras, *Plea* 34; Tertullian, *To the Nations* 1.16.14–20).

Early Christians condemn same-sex relations because of concerns about gender slippage that extended even to those of lower status, believing that it is shameful for any male to behave as a woman. Clement condemns sex with young boys "as though they were girls" (*The Instructor* 2.10.90). The boys, too, who engage in these types of activities, even as slaves under duress, ought to choose death rather than "renounce their own natures and play the role of women" (*The Instructor* 3.3.21). He is nostalgic for the old Roman laws that prohibited males using their bodies in the "feminine role contrary to the law of nature" (*The Instructor* 3.3.23).

Clement also opposes anal intercourse because of his view that sex is for procreation alone. He notes that nature has made the passage at the end of the intestines for expelling excrement alone and that no animals, not even hypersexual hyenas, engage in anal sex. Hyenas, both male and female, he argues, have a separate orifice between the tail and anus which leads neither to the womb nor intestines. When male hyenas lie with other males or pregnant females, they use this other orifice instead of the anus (*The Instructor* 2.10.85).

Early Christians also oppose female-female sexual relations. Clement condemns women who switch roles and act as the penetrator of both men and women, and he laments that women are "given in marriage and marry [other women]" (*The Instructor* 3.3.21). Clement's procreationist ideology again controls his view on proper sexual conduct, along with his view that women's usurpation of a male's penetrative role constituted a dangerous blurring of gender divisions. Tertullian too bemoans *frictrices*, or women who have sex with women (*On the Philosophers Cloak* 4.9; cf. *On the Resurrection of the Flesh* 16.6).

Early Christian apocalyptic texts frequently imagine the divine punishments for those who betray their gender by engaging in same-sex acts. The *Apocalypse of Peter* describes a scene in hell where men "who defile their bodies, behaving like women," and women "who have sex with one another as a man with a woman" must repeatedly leap from a high cliff (17). The *Acts of Thomas* is similarly concerned with those who "exchanged the intercourse of man and woman," again revealing that the problem with such acts was the supposed reversal of sexual roles of men and women (6.51–61). The third-century *Apocalypse of Paul* depicts a group of men and women in a burning pit. The angel explains, "They are those who have committed the iniquity of Sodom and Gomorrah, men with men. Therefore they pay the penalty unceasingly" (39).

Oral Sex. There are few references to such specific sexual acts in early Christian texts. In one case, the *Epistle of Barnabas* allegorically interprets the prohibitions of eating certain animals in the Law as referring to certain vices. The author explains that it is forbidden to eat the weasel, believing that it conceives with its mouth. Consequently, the male reader is advised not to "perform a lawless act in the mouth…nor cling to unclean women who perform the lawless act in their mouth" (10.8).

Desire as Transgression. *Epithumia*, variously translated as desire, lust, or passion, occupies a central place in early Christian thought. The *Didache* warns: "Do not be filled with *epithumia*, for *epithumia* leads to *porneia*" (3.3). The *Shepherd of Hermas* adds that a thought in one's heart about *porneia* constituted a sin, "but if you always keep thinking about your own wife you will never sin" (2.4.1–2). Here, desire is a step toward sin, but in some cases desire was the sin.

Early Christians renouncing desire drew from Jesus's warning that a man desiring a woman had committed adultery already in his heart (Matt 5:28). Justin Martyr reaffirms this teaching, noting that God judges not only acts but also thoughts (*1 Apology* 15).

The Christian problematization of sexual desire drew upon Platonic and Stoic ideas of controlling the passions, but frequently exceeded them in the degree to which desire must be mastered. Clement of Alexandria explains that the idea of continence, "set forth by Greek philosophers, teaches that one should fight desire.…But our ideal is not to experience desire at all. Our aim is not that while a man feels desires he should get the better of, but that he should be continent even respecting desire itself" (*Miscellanies* 3.7.57). Clement puts forward the idea that sexual intercourse without desire is possible for the purpose of procreation.

Legacy. Christianity in the fourth and fifth centuries follows the trajectories laid out by earlier Christians as it coalesces around orthodox teachings and structures. Adultery, fornication, and same-sex intercourse are forbidden. Celibacy and sexual renunciation remain ideal choices for clerical and monastic life, and the ascetic urge becomes more popularly practiced. Marriage and procreation are permitted and defended against those who would forbid them altogether, but are still considered inferior to celibacy—despite Jovinian's challenge to this framework in the 390s. Control of desires is increasingly theorized in monastic contexts, with the ideal of even eliminating involuntary desires and nocturnal emissions. Legal regulation of prostitution and criminalization of same-sex relations characterize this period of Christianization of sexual morality. Christian concern for sexuality focuses on the purity not only of the individual or the church but also of the city and the cosmos.

[*See also* Gender Transgression, *subentry* Early Church; Marriage and Divorce, *subentry* Early Church; Paul; Same-Sex Relations, *subentry* Early Church; Sexuality; *and* Sexual Transgression, *subentries on* Roman World *and* New Testament.]

BIBLIOGRAPHY

Boyarin, Daniel, and Elizabeth A. Castelli. "Introduction: Foucault's *The History of Sexuality*: The Fourth Volume, or, a Field Left Fallow for Others to Till." *Journal of the History of Sexuality* 10, nos. 3/4 (2001): 357–374.

Brooten, Bernadette J. *Love Between Women: Early Christian Responses to Female Homoeroticism*. Chicago: University of Chicago Press, 1996.

Brown, Peter. *The Body and Society: Men, Women, and Sexual Renunciation in Early Christianity*. New York: Columbia University Press, 1988.

Clark, Elizabeth A. *Reading Renunciation: Asceticism and Scripture in Early Christianity*. Princeton, N.J.: Princeton University Press, 1999.

Foucault, Michel. *The Care of the Self.* Vol. 3: *The History of Sexuality.* Translated by Robert Hurley. London: Penguin, 1986.

Gaca, Kathy L. *The Making of Fornication: Eros, Ethics, and Political Reform in Greek Philosophy and Early Christianity.* Berkeley: University of California Press, 2003.

Harper, Kyle. *From Shame to Sin: The Christian Transformation of Sexual Morality in Late Antiquity.* Cambridge, Mass.: Harvard University Press, 2013.

Hunter, David G. *Marriage, Celibacy, and Heresy in Ancient Christianity: The Jovinianist Controversy.* Oxford: Oxford University Press, 2007.

Hunter, David G., trans. and ed. *Marriage in the Early Church.* Minneapolis: Fortress, 1992.

Knust, Jennifer Wright. *Abandoned to Lust: Sexual Slander and Ancient Christianity.* New York: Columbia University Press, 2006.

Martin, Dale B. *Sex and the Single Savior: Gender and Sexuality in Biblical Interpretation.* Louisville, Ky.: Westminster John Knox, 2006.

Pagels, Elaine H. *Adam, Eve, and the Serpent.* New York: Random House, 1988.

Rousselle, Aline. *Porneia: On Desire and the Body in Antiquity.* Translated by Felicia Pheasant. Oxford: Blackwell, 1988.

Sissa, Giulia. *Sex and Sensuality in the Ancient World.* Translated by George Staunton. New Haven, Conn.: Yale University Press, 2008.

Taylor G. Petrey

SEXUAL VIOLENCE

This entry contains seven subentries: Ancient Near East; Hebrew Bible; Greek World; Roman World; New Testament; Early Judaism; *and* Early Church.

Ancient Near East

Enough evidence has been preserved for us to conclude that ancient Near Eastern cultures had a conception of sexual violence that in some ways overlaps with our own but was in some ways very different. In the discussion below, we will consider how various forms of sexual violence are treated in ancient Near Eastern sources and consider what conclusions can be drawn about the attitude of these cultures toward such behaviors.

Due to the fragmentary nature of the evidence, we cannot compose a complete picture of attitudes toward sexual violence in the ancient Near East. We can, however, create a rough, tentative sketch, keeping in mind that some cultures and time periods are better represented by the preserved evidence than others. The sources are diverse, including legal collections, court records, myths, and (in the case of sexual violence used as a strategy of war and in controlling subject populations) royal inscriptions, engravings on victory steles, and reliefs on palace gates and walls. While the legal collections provide a valuable glimpse into the sexual norms and mores of these societies, they were not intended as literal guidelines for actual court proceedings. Because many legal documents and records related to legal proceedings have been preserved from these cultures, we know that there is often little correspondence between the provisions stated in the legal collections and contemporary legal practice. Rather than reflections of normative juridical decisions, the legal collections were often expressions of principles or ideals. The other evidence must also be approached with caution. Myths about the gods often had little to do with the reality of daily life or the norms associated with it. Depictions and descriptions of war in royal inscriptions, on victory steles, and on palace wall and gate engravings primarily served a propagandistic function, with the intent of either scaring those who viewed them into submission or convincing the gods that the king was worthy of their support.

The Nature of Sexual Violence. Sexual violence refers to the forcing, coercing, or manipulation of an individual into unwanted, nonconsensual sexual activity. Contemporary Western society includes in this category rape (for the purposes of this article defined as vaginal or anal sexual intercourse with another person without his or her consent), attempted rape, and other forms of sexual assault such as forced or coerced contact between the mouth and penis, vagina, or anus; nonconsensual penetration of the anus or vagina by a hand, finger, or other object; sexual relations with those considered too young or incapable for other reasons of giving consent (such as intoxication); and unwanted sexual contact (such as touching or kissing). In addition, forced stripping and/or exposure of the genitalia, sexual mutilation, exposure to threats of a sexual nature, involuntary prostitution, and being subject to other forms of coercive sexual exploitation are considered forms of sexual violence. According to the contemporary understandings, survivors of such acts often experience sexual, physical, and/or psychological trauma. The psychological consequences can be both short term and long term, including feelings of depression, guilt, shame, anger, fear, and other symptoms associated with posttraumatic stress disorder.

Certain sexual acts that are now considered under the umbrella of sexual violence have not historically been considered as such. Marital rape is a relatively new concept and still is not accepted in much of the world. The idea that a slave can be raped by an owner is another relatively new concept, since historically slaves have been viewed as the sexual property of their owners and thus without personal agency or autonomy. The idea of a woman's rape as primarily an offense against the woman instead of an offense against the males of her household (her husband, if she is married, and father and/or brothers, if she is not) is also a relatively new concept. A recent development is the idea that bestiality, which encompasses vaginal or anal intercourse with an animal and oral-genital contact between humans and animals, is a form of sexual violence given that the animal is incapable of giving consent.

Forms of sexual violence attested in ancient Near East sources include rape, unwanted sexual contact, sexual relations with those considered too young or incapable for other reasons of giving consent, forced stripping and/or exposure of the genitalia, sexual mutilation, and exposure to threats of a sexual nature. The rest of this article will examine how these categories of sexual violence are treated in ancient Near Eastern sources. Additionally, we will consider whether there is any evidence that these cultures had a conception of coercive sex within marriage, sex with one's slaves, and/or bestiality as acts of sexual violence. Lastly, we will consider whether these cultures understood these acts the same way that we do in contemporary society in terms of being a violation of personal sexual integrity and resulting in trauma on the part of survivors. Before we can do this, however, we must consider how we can identify a sexual act as falling under the category of sexual violence in these sources by examining how ancient Near Eastern sources indicated that a sexual act was nonconsensual.

The Language of Sexual Violence in Ancient Near Eastern Texts. Because this overview addresses issues of vocabulary, it is divided into the various languages attested.

Sumerian language sources. There is no term for rape in Sumerian, nor is there a combination of terms or a way of describing the sexual act that consistently indicates that an act is one of sexual assault. While it has been suggested that the Sumerian term *niĝaĝarše*, which occurs in the Laws of Ur-Nammu (UN) 6 and 8, denotes the use of force or violence in sexual contexts, the term seems to more likely refer either to violating or usurping the rights of the legal guardian of the woman or using guile or deception to gain sexual access to the woman. The term **dab** (written usually as **dab** or **dab₅**), which most commonly means seize, take, or hold, depending on the context, is often (but not always) used in contexts in which people, land, and/or objects are seized by force; yet it does not necessarily indicate coercion in the few sexual situations in which it is used. Since **dab** is equated in several lexical texts with Akkadian *ṣabātu*, which is used in both coercive and noncoercive sexual contexts, it seems highly unlikely that its usage in sexual contexts can definitively identify a sexual act as coercive. Thus, in Sumerian texts, the only way to determine whether a sexual act is consensual or not is to consider the larger context, including the description of circumstances and/or verbal exchanges leading up to the sexual act and the consequences of the sexual act.

Akkadian language sources. One term in Akkadian, *mazû*, seems to specifically denote rape when used in the D stem, where it means literally "press down." However, since this usage of *mazû* only occurs three times and one of the contexts is highly fragmentary and thus unclear, the conclusion that the D stem of *mazû* denotes rape is somewhat tentative. Additionally, all three texts in which *mazû* is used in this way date from the Middle to Late Assyrian period, so the term might have also been limited to a specific geographical area within a limited time period. It also has been suggested that *naqābu* sometimes denotes rape. However, the term actually denotes the taking of a woman's virginity in both consensual and nonconsensual sexual situations. Several terms denote illicit sex, such as *nâku*, but they are not consistently used in the context of nonconsensual sex and in fact are more often used in cases of illicit consensual sex. In the two times the adjective *nīku* (fem. *nīktu*) is used (both times in the Middle Assyrian Laws), the context indicates that it refers to a raped woman. Whether these few occurrences provide enough evidence that *nīku* means "raped" is unclear.

Nonconsensual sex is denoted in Akkadian texts in other ways as well. The use of a term of force, such as the verb *emūqu* ("to force") or the derived adverb *emūqa* ("by force"), combined with a term for sex denotes nonconsensual sex. Both *emūqu* and *emūqa* are sometimes used in combination with *ṣabātu* in sexual contexts, in which case the combination can be translated as "seize by force." The combination of *ṣabātu* with the noun *daʾānu* is also used in sexual contexts to denote nonconsensual sex and can be translated as "seize by force." In one law in the Code of Hammurabi (LH), *kubbulu* ("to make immobile, hold or pin down") is used in combination with a term for sexual relations to denote coercive sex. The combination of a term for "seize" such as *ṣabātu* along with a term describing a sexual act is used in cases of both nonconsensual and consensual sex. For example, in the myth of Nergal and Ereškigal, Nergal seizes (*ṣabātu*) Ereškigal in his arms and kisses her before having rough, but consensual, sex with her. Given this usage, one must rely on the larger context, such as the description of the interaction between the individuals before the sexual encounter and/or the consequences after, to determine whether the sex is considered consensual or not.

Hittite language sources. No term in Hittite specifically denotes nonconsensual sex. The term *ēp* ("to seize") is used twice in sexual contexts, both in the same law (Hittite Laws [HL] 197)—once in a case of nonconsensual sex and once in a case of consensual

sex. In nonsexual contexts the verb *salik* has various meanings, including to touch, approach, invade, penetrate, and enter (usually in an unwelcome or polluting manner). When used in sexual contexts *salik* appears to denote illicit but not necessarily coercive sex. It is used several times in HL 195 to denote various prohibited incestuous sexual relations, and it also is used in the Zalpa Legend in the context of prohibited incestuous sexual relations (in this case, between brothers and sisters). Given the evidence, there is no reason to think that *salik* in sexual contexts denotes coercive sex. Rather, it seems to denote illicit sex, perhaps specifically in the form of incest. Similarly, the terms *wen* and *wasta* when used in the context of sexual acts appear to denote various degrees of illicit sex but not necessarily coercive sex. Thus, with Hittite texts as with Sumerian texts one must always rely on the larger context to determine whether a sexual act was considered consensual or not.

Sexual Violence against Women. The form of sexual violence against women referred to most frequently in ancient Near Eastern sources is sexual assault in the form of rape. Other forms include unwanted physical contact in the form of groping (possibly) or kissing. Incidents of sexual assault are attested in the legal collections and some myths. In the legal collections that address cases of sexual assault of women, the status of the woman (whether she is a free married, betrothed, or single [unmarried and not betrothed] woman or a slave) determines the severity of the crime and the outcome. With one exception, the only preserved sources that address cases of sexual assault against married women are the legal collections; in these works, a married woman is considered to be the sexual property of her husband, and the crime in such cases is treated as a case of adultery (sexual relations with a married woman) in which the woman is considered innocent of any wrongdoing.

Only one text in the Sumerian legal collections (UN 6) addresses sexual assault of a married woman (in this case the wife of another man who is still a virgin). The terminology used to describe the sexual encounter does not in itself give any indication that the sex was nonconsensual (see *niĝaĝarše*), but the absence of punishment for the woman is an indication that the sex was viewed as coerced. Moreover, the law immediately following UN 6 deals with the same circumstances in which the woman is described as initiating the sexual encounter; here, the woman is put to death and the man is not punished. The author perhaps assumes that since the woman is the initiator of the sexual encounter, the man may not have known she was married and is thus not considered culpable for adultery.

LH 130 states that if a man pins down and has sexual relations with (*ukabbilšima ina sūniša ittatīlma*) the wife of another man (specified as a virgin still living at her father's house) and is caught in the act, the man will be put to death and the woman will go free. The use of the D stem of *kabalu* in this context denotes that the man has used force. The fact that the author specifies that while the man is put to death the woman goes free also indicates that this is treated as a case of sexual assault.

The Middle Assyrian Laws (MAL) address three different scenarios that involve the rape of a married woman. MAL A 12 is a clear case of sexual assault, given that the woman is described as refusing the man's sexual proposition and as trying to defend herself. The man is described as taking or seizing her by force and as having sex with her (*emûqamma iṣṣabassi ittiakšši*). The man is sentenced to death, and no blame is attached to the woman. MAL A 16 presents two different circumstances: consensual sex between a married woman and a man and nonconsensual sex between the pair. In the case of consensual sex, the man goes free and the punishment of the woman is left up to the husband. In the case of rape (denoted by *emūqamma ittiakši*), the author states that the man will receive the same punishment as the wife. This leads to some ambiguity: Is the woman punished if she has been found to be a victim of sexual assault? This ambiguity arises because the law combines two different cases. Most likely what is intended is that the husband in a case of rape gets to choose the punishment of the man who raped his wife, but the punishment should be the same as he would give his wife if it had been a case of consensual sex.

MAL A 23 presents three different circumstances for a the scenario in which a married woman invited to the house of another woman is given by the hostess to another man for sexual purposes. In the first case, the sex seems to be consensual; in this case, the woman's husband has the authority to penalize her in any way he sees fit, and the hostess and the other man are punished the same way. The other two scenarios seem to both involve nonconsensual sex. If as soon as she leaves the house the wife declares that she was victimized, saying that she did not know what the other woman intended and that the hostess brought a man to her by trickery and he had sex with her (*kî pīge aʾīla ana muḫḫiša tultērib u ittiakši*), it is taken as a case of nonconsensual sex: the wife is considered innocent of any wrongdoing and the other parties receive the death penalty. In the third scenario, the woman does not declare her innocence, even though the circumstances appear to be the same; in this case, the husband may punish his wife as he sees fit, and the other woman and the man are put to death.

In HL 197, whether a sexual act (presumably between a man and a free married woman, given that a husband is mentioned in the final part of the law) is deemed consensual is based solely on where it took place. If the location was an uninhabited area (in this case, in the mountains), it is assumed to have been a case of sexual assault, since presumably no one would have heard the woman scream and been available to help; in this case, the man is put to death. If the sexual act took place in a house (implied to be in a city), it is assumed to have been consensual, since otherwise someone would have heard her scream for help; in this case, the woman will be killed, though the text does not specify if the man will also suffer punishment. If her husband catches the two having sex (presumably under the second set of circumstances), he may kill both with impunity.

While there is no evidence of a concept of marital rape, a married woman is given the right under certain circumstances to refuse her husband sexual access, suggesting some degree of personal sexual autonomy. LH 142–143 states that if a woman refuses to have sex with her husband and the court determines that she has kept chaste and behaved in an upright manner, and her husband has been going out (*waṣu*, which implies carousing with other women) and thus belittled her, the woman can take her dowry and go to her father's house without any punishment. However, if the woman has been going out (*waṣu*), thus belittling her husband, she is to be cast into the water (meaning to be executed by drowning). The legal collections do not indicate whether a husband forcing his wife to have sex in a situation in which she had the right to refuse was considered rape. Such a determination is unlikely, given that marital rape is a relatively modern concept.

MAL A 9 also addresses another form of sexual assault. The first part states that a man who is convicted of raising his hand against (*qāta* used with *abālu*) a married woman (treating her "like a child," the text adds) will have his finger cut off. The second part states that if the man kisses her, his lower lip will be cut off. If one interprets the first half of the case in light of the second, then "raising the hand" may imply some kind of sexual contact, especially since the woman's marital status should not matter in a case of regular assault. Since only punishment of the man is mentioned for the kiss, it could be that the situation involved nonconsensual touching or kissing of another man's wife.

The one nonlegal text that includes an account of sexual violence against married women is the Epic of Gilgamesh, in which Gilgamesh insists on deflowering all of the brides of Uruk under the right of *droit de seigneur*. Since there is no corroborating evidence that any ancient Near Eastern ruler ever insisted on taking such privileges, it seems more likely that Gilgamesh's actions are simply a narrative element to illustrate why the people of Uruk felt the need to ask the gods for intervention to protect them from their king (and thus introduce Enkidu to the story) and not a reflection of any sort of reality.

The only reference to sexual assault against a betrothed woman occurs in one text from the legal collections, Laws of Ešnunna (LE) 26, which states that a man who abducts and takes the virginity of a woman who is betrothed to another man without the permission of her father or mother will be put to death. No

punishment is stated for the woman, apparently indicating that she was considered an innocent victim, abducted against her will. This law gives the impression that the authors of this legal collection viewed sexual assault against betrothed women in the same way as sexual assault against married women. Once the bride-price is paid, the woman is considered legally to be the sexual property of her husband-to-be, even though she is still living with her family. The offender in such cases is sentenced to death.

Situations in which a single (unmarried, nonbetrothed) woman is sexually assaulted appear in one text in the legal collections and a few Sumerian mythological texts. MAL A 55 presents the case of the rape of a young woman who is still a virgin and still living with her parents. The description of the sexual encounter—"if he seized a young woman by force and pressed her down" (*kî daʾāne batulta iṣbatma umanziʾši*)—indicates that it is a case of nonconsensual sex. The consequences vary depending on whether the rapist is married. If he is married, the father may rape the wife of his daughter's rapist and keep possession of her in his household (as a form of *talion*), and he may give his daughter to the man as a wife. If he is not married, the rapist shall give an extra third in silver to her father over and above the regular bride-price of a virgin, and the father can decide whether to marry his daughter to the rapist, who will not have the option of ever divorcing her. The father is also given the option, whether the man is married or not, of accepting the money and marrying his daughter to whomever he wishes.

The young woman who was raped is given no voice in the matter, though the option of marrying her rapist without giving him the option of divorce is intended for her benefit: it will provide for her welfare, assuming that her chances of finding a suitable husband are now greatly reduced. The option given to the father to rape the assailant's wife indicates that the welfare of women was not the primary concern of the authors of this law. Needless to say, the innocent wife of the perpetrator has no recourse if the father chooses to commit an act of legally sanctioned sexual violence against her as compensation. Even if the option of raping the assailant's wife is only intended as a scare tactic, it still demonstrates that women were viewed as property with no legal sexual autonomy. It is primarily the father whose rights are viewed as violated and the father who can choose how he is compensated. In the law immediately following, a young single woman loses her virginity to a man in a case of consensual sex. In that instance, the father is compensated for his lost bride price the same as he is in the case of rape, though the rest of the consequences are different. The father can choose to punish his daughter any way he sees fit, but he cannot force the man to marry his daughter and no harm is to come to the man's wife.

Three Sumerian myths depict cases of sexual violence against unmarried, nonbetrothed females. In the myth of Enlil and Ninlil, Ninlil explicitly rejects Enlil's sexual advances, explaining that she is too young for sexual relations with men and concerned about getting into trouble with her parents (and possibly her girlfriends [the text is fragmentary]). Enlil responds by ignoring her objections, instead focusing on gaining physical access to her, seizing her, and having sex with her. The sexual act itself is not described in terms associated specifically with rape, since the language of seizing or grabbing a woman in the context of sex is also used in ancient Near Eastern descriptions of consensual sex; however, the larger context, namely Ninlil's elaborate refusal of Enlil's advances and his decision to have sexual relations with her without further attempts to persuade her, seems to indicate that this was a case of nonconsensual sex. This conclusion is confirmed by the consequences of his act. Enlil is condemned by the assembly of gods and banished. Ninlil's pursuit of Enlil after the sexual encounter does not indicate her consent to the encounter but rather her desire for him to marry her, especially since she knew she was pregnant from the encounter.

Two other Sumerian myths also depict rape. In each case, the larger context of the account rather than specific language indicates the nonconsensual nature of the sex. In the myth of Enki and Ninḫursaĝ (also discussed below), Enki gets Uttu drunk on beer and then takes advantage of the situation to gain sexual access to her. As a result of the act, Enki is cursed by Ninḫursaĝ, Uttu's great-great-grandmother. In the myth of Inana and Šukaletuda, the sleeping goddess Inana is raped by the gardener Šukaletuda, who comes upon her on his plot of land. When Inana wakes up and realizes what happened, she is furious. When she finally catches the gardener she sentences him to death. Here it is very clear that the act of rape itself is considered a crime; Inana tells Enki at one point that she demands compensation for what was done to her, and her rapist is harshly punished.

Three texts, one legal record and two from the legal collections, address taking the virginity of a slave woman. The Sumerian text *A Trial at Nippur* refers to a case in which a man seized another man's female slave, brought her into a building, and deflowered her. As noted above, since terms for seizing or grabbing hold of a woman are also used in ancient Near Eastern texts in cases of consensual sex, there is no way to determine with certitude whether the sex in this case is considered consensual. The consequences in this particular case—the woman's owner brought charges, produced witnesses, and the guilty party had to pay him compensation—would be the same whether the sex was consensual or not. The same is true of the defloration of a slave woman addressed in another Sumerian text, UN 8, since the punishment described would be the same for consensual or nonconsensual sex. In this case, the guilty man pays the owner five shekels of silver. In LE 31, a man who deflowers the female slave of another man must pay her owner one third of a mina of silver as compensation. The text specifies that the slave remains with her owner. As in the previous two cases, there is no way to tell from the wording whether the sex is consensual or not.

In each of these cases involving the defloration of a slave, the person who receives compensation is the woman's owner, since legally the slave is his property and her defloration is a property crime. The crime is the same whether the sex was consensual or not, since the slave, as his property, has no legal autonomy and thus legally cannot give consent. Since consent is immaterial to the outcome of the case, the authors do not include this information, and thus there is no way for us to determine whether or not any of these cases involved rape. Of course, since the female slave was the sexual property of her owner, he could use her any way he wanted sexually, and legally it was not considered rape.

Sexual Assault against Men. Two texts in the legal collections, both in the MAL, address sexual violence against men. MAL 20 appears to involve male-male rape. The law states that if a man has sex with another man of the same status (*tappāšu inīk*) and the judges prove the charges against him and find him guilty, they shall have sex with him and turn him into a eunuch (*inikkūš ana ša rēšēn utarrūš*). The description of the sexual act itself gives no indication that the sex act is nonconsensual, but the consequences suggest it is a case of male rape: the man found guilty of the charges is punished with what appears to be communal rape followed by castration, and the other man is neither charged with a crime nor punished. If this ruling was aimed against consensual homosexuality, both parties would presumably be punished. Instead, the punishment is based on the principle of *talion*. The aggressor will be raped just as he raped another; just as he forced the other man into a feminine role by making him be a passive sexual partner, the passive role is permanently imposed on him (castrating him also has preventive value, since he will never be able to commit the same crime again). Since the text specifies that the victim was a *tappā'u*, a man of equal social status, one wonders if the rape of a man of a lower social status would be considered a criminal offense.

MAL A 8 mentions another form of sexual violence against men, the mutilation of a man's testes. The law states that a woman who crushes the testicle of a man in a fight will have her finger cut off. If the other testicle becomes infected by the first or is also crushed, her eyes will be gouged out.

Incest as a Form of Sexual Violence. Two of the legal collections address cases of incest. While it can be taken for granted that incest between a father and daughter or other substantially younger family member living within his household is nonconsensual sex and thus can be considered rape, in the ancient Near Eastern legal collections incest is treated distinctly from rape. While no legal text explicitly describes a sexual act as both incestuous and as coerced, it is evident within some of the legal texts that certain cases of incest were also considered to involve rape.

LH addresses several cases in which the sex is treated as both incestuous and nonconsensual. LH 154 states that if a man has sex with his daughter, they shall make him leave the city. Since the incest occurred while the daughter was presumably still living with her parents and under her father's authority, it does not violate the rights of another man and thus it is not a capital crime. The father, in fact, has sexual control over his daughter and thus technically has the right to do with her sexuality as he sees fit. However, given the severity of the punishment the authors must have viewed the situation as problematic. Banishment involves the loss of one's family, possessions, societal connections, and citizenship. The fact that no punishment is mentioned for the daughter implies that she is not considered guilty of any crime, indicating that the case is considered one of nonconsensual sex and incestuous rape.

LH 155 and 156 both address a case in which a man chooses a wife for his son and has sex with her himself. In LH 155, the man's son has already had sex with the woman, and in punishment the father is bound and thrown into the water (to drown). Since the future father-in-law is given the death penalty and no mention is made of punishment for his son's future wife, she apparently was considered an innocent victim and the case is one of nonconsensual incest and rape. In LH 156, the son has not yet had sexual relations with the woman. In that case, the father-in-law compensates her with one half mina of silver in addition to giving her back whatever she brought from her father's house so that she can marry whoever she chooses. Given that the woman is not penalized in any way but instead receives generous compensation, this also appears to be understood as a case of rape. It is noteworthy that the woman alone is compensated, rather than her family or the man's son.

HL 189, 190, and 195 appear in a group of Hittite Laws that attempt to define the parameters of incest. Each of these laws designates certain sexual pairings

as incestuous. While none of the pairings are described according to consent, likely a case of a man
having sexual relations with his daughter (189), stepdaughter (195), or son (189) was not consensual on
the part of the younger partner. Sexual pairings considered to be incestuous are labeled *hurkel*, an illicit
or prohibited sexual act. While no punishment is
cited for any of the prohibited incestuous pairings, it
is possible that the punishment was the same as for
acts of bestiality that were labeled *hurkel*.

Incest is also an element in the Sumerian myth of
Enki and Ninḫursaĝ. Enki has sex with and impreg-
nates his daughter and then continues to do the same
to additional generations of the daughters born of
his daughters, all of whom are identified as young.
The description of his sexual relations with his first
three daughters gives no indication that the sex is
nonconsensual, even though sexual relations between
a father and his young daughters can generally be
assumed to be nonconsensual on the child's part. In
the myth, Enki's behavior with these daughters is
not problematized as rape or incest. Only when one
of his daughters, Uttu, attempts to resist him is his
behavior described as having negative consequences
for him. Since the gods are depicted as living in a world
where they are not constrained by human norms,
mores, and laws, the treatment of incest in this myth
does not indicate that incest was in any way condoned
among humans.

Bestiality as a Form of Sexual Violence. There is
very little evidence for ancient Near Eastern attitudes towards bestiality. Sex with certain animals is
addressed in a few cases in the Hittite Laws (187, 188,
199, and 200). In some cases, humans are the initiator of the sexual encounter, and in some cases animals are. HL 187 and 188 state that a man who has
sexual relations with a cow or a sheep has committed *hurkel*, an illicit or prohibited sexual act, and
he will be sentenced to death. In both cases, the man
will be brought to the king's court, and the king can
either have the man killed or spare his life (in which
case, he may have been banished); it is specified,
however, that he will not appear before the king in
person, likely because he was viewed as having incurred pollution. The killing of the animal is not
indicated, but given that HL 199 specifies that in the

case of a man who has sex with a pig or a dog the
animal and human will suffer the same fate (death
or being spared by the king), it could be that in the
case of the cow or sheep the animal is not harmed.

Contemporary animal advocates have contended
that because animals are unable to consent these
sex acts should be considered nonconsensual. The
second part of HL 199, however, suggests that the
animal could be the sexual aggressor. If an ox is the
sexual aggressor, the ox is put to death and the man
will be spared. A sheep will be substituted for the
man and put to death, which seems to indicate that
in such cases both the human and the animal incur
pollution. If a pig is the sexual aggressor, it is not
considered *hurkel* and apparently the pig goes un-
punished. This law indicates that animals might
have been viewed as having sexual agency.

HL 199 states that if a man has sex with a horse or
a mule, it is not *hurkel* but he shall not approach the
king or become a priest; it seems he is still polluted
by his act but perhaps to a lesser degree than if he
had sex with a cow, sheep, pig, or dog. In all these
cases, sex with animals appears to be viewed primarily as a matter of pollution. A man who engages in
these sexual relations, whether consensually or not,
is polluted. It is not clear why sex acts with cows,
sheep, pigs, and dogs are considered *hurkel* and punished with death, while sex with horses or mules is
not, or why a sexually aggressive pig is spared punishment but not a sexually aggressive ox.

**Sexual Violence as a Strategy of War and Foreign
Policy.** The last category of sexual violence addressed
is the use of sexual abuse and sexual humiliation as a
strategy of war and foreign policy. The purpose of
sexual violence as a strategy of war is evident: it
traumatizes the enemy. Sexual violence is a very effective means to degrade, intimidate, and humiliate
prisoners of war and subject populations. Such acts
utterly demoralize the victim by causing both physical and psychological harm.

As early as the beginning of the third millennium
B.C.E., enemy soldiers are depicted naked. Not only
were dead and captured soldiers depicted naked,
but in several reliefs from the third millennium
B.C.E. so are enemy soldiers in the midst of battle.
Clearly the point was not to provide an accurate

historical record of what the battle scene looked like but to make a statement. Nakedness was associated with defeat and death. The viewer of these steles knew that the naked soldiers were on the losing side, very likely destined for death. Nakedness was also associated with helplessness, vulnerability, and a loss of social identity. Stripping the enemy was a way of dehumanizing and depersonalizing him. Clothing was associated with being civilized, so being naked also meant being deprived of the accoutrements of civilization. The stripping of the enemy soldiers symbolizes stripping them of everything they have and everything they are. Their only identity becomes corpse or prisoner.

Evidence for the use of sexual assault and sexual humiliation as a strategy of war and foreign policy in the ancient Near East proliferates in the first millennium B.C.E., when the Neo-Assyrian kings started to describe and depict the torture of enemy soldiers in great detail in royal inscriptions, steles, and engravings on palace walls and gates. The reliefs that lined the walls of several royal palaces from this period show explicit scenes of the torture of prisoners of war, recording in detail acts of violence against the people the Neo-Assyrians fought and subjected. The reliefs also show the corpses of the enemy often beheaded or impaled and sometimes dismembered. In the scenes of torture of the enemy and of the enemy dead, the enemy soldiers are often depicted naked, as are male captives. Chapman's *The Gendered Language of Warfare in the Israelite-Assyrian Encounter* (2004, pp. 160–163) contends that the nakedness of the male enemy soldiers is sometimes combined with images of penetration via the placement and the aim of battering rams, the drawn bows of Assyrian soldiers, and through images of impaled naked males. Such images would indicate that sometimes the nakedness of the defeated enemy in the Neo-Assyrian depictions of battle and siege signifies a sexual vulnerability absent in earlier iconography of war. Castration of enemy soldiers is not widely attested, but in one text (where he describes the siege and capture of Babylon after it rebelled against the Assyrians) Sennacherib says he removed the testicles of enemy soldiers (*Annals of Sennacherib* 46, lines 10–13).

These depictions of warfare in the royal inscriptions, steles, and the palace reliefs should not be taken as objective historical documents. They were intended first and foremost as works of political propaganda aimed at instilling fear and discouraging rebellion against the Assyrian kings. The wall sculptures of Neo-Assyrian kings such as Aššurnaṣirpal II took this propagandistic idea even further. Visiting kings and dignitaries would see huge representations of the Assyrians always victorious and the enemy always defeated, usually naked and dead, sometimes tortured. Members of the royal court would also be reminded of the power of the king and be encouraged through fear to remain loyal to him.

In contrast to the male captives and prisoners of war, the women captives who first appear in the first millennium B.C.E. in Assyrian wall reliefs are always clothed (though not always fully clothed). The women are usually depicted being led away in a group from their destroyed cities, often with children and sometimes even with some possessions in tow. Apart from one possible exception (a relief of Aššurbanipal that appears to depict the sexual assault of a foreign queen), captive women are usually not depicted as subject to sexual abuse; however, in one relief, the Balawat palace gate (constructed during the reign of Ashurnaṣirpal II), a group of women appears with exposed breasts and another with their skirts slightly hiked up, exposing the ankles, and, in some cases, the knees, perhaps indicating some type of sexual exposure with the intent to humiliate and perhaps express sexual availability. Generally, though, the women in these scenes are fully clothed and appear to be left unmolested. There are also no descriptions of sexual assault of women in any of the Neo-Assyrian royal inscriptions.

This does not mean that women captives escaped sexual abuse. In the Neo-Assyrian vassal treaties, the curses often threaten that if the vassal king violated the treaty his wives and the wives of his nobles would be forcibly stripped and/or raped by an enemy. Another theme in the treaty curses is the sexual humiliation of men: "may your soldiers become women"; "may your king and soldiers become prostitutes in the city square." This language suggests that while sexual abuse of prisoners of war and subject peoples was not described or depicted, it very likely occurred.

Conceptualizing Sexual Violence: The Ancient Near East versus Today. Ancient Near Eastern cultures had a conception of sexual violence that at least in some ways resembles our own. Both women and men were understood as able to be coerced into sex and subject to other forms of sexual assault, abuse, and humiliation. However, these cultures did not presume that slaves could be raped by their owners or likely that a wife could be raped by her husband. A conception of rape and other forms of sexual assault as violations of personal sexual integrity is not well reflected in ancient Near Eastern sources. In the legal collections, the rape of women is usually treated primarily as an offense against their husbands or fathers, with the woman often receiving no compensation. In a few cases, though, women are given compensation, and in LH 156 the woman alone receives compensation, indicating some acknowledgment that the act of sexual assault was a violation against her personally. Little explicit evidence suggests an understanding of the trauma experienced by those who are survivors of rape and other forms of sexual assault. The effectiveness of the propaganda strategies employed by the Neo-Assyrian kings to keep their subjects in line, however, may provide indirect evidence: only if stripping, sexual mutilation, and sexual humiliation were deeply traumatizing would such images be effective.

[*See also* Children, *subentry* Ancient Near East; Deity, *subentry* Ancient Near East; Family Structures, *subentry* Ancient Near East; Gender and Sexuality: Ancient Near East; Legal Status, *subentry* Ancient Near East; *and* Marriage and Divorce, *subentry* Ancient Near East.]

BIBLIOGRAPHY

Bahrani, Zainab. *Women of Babylon: Gender and Representation in Mesopotamia.* London: Routledge, 2001.

Chapman, Cynthia. *The Gendered Language of Warfare in the Israelite-Assyrian Encounter.* Winona Lake, Ind.: Eisenbrauns, 2004.

Cifarelli, Megan. "Gesture and Alterity in the Art of Assurnasipal II of Assyria." *Art Bulletin* 80 (1998): 210–228.

Cooper, J. S. "Virginity in Ancient Mesopotamia." In *Sex and Gender in the Ancient Near East, Proceedings of the 47th Rencontre Assyriologique Internationale, Helsinki,* *July 2–6, 2001, Part I*, edited by S. Parpola and R. M. Whiting, pp. 91–112. Helsinki: Neo-Assyrian Text Corpus Project, 2002.

Finkelstein, J. J. "Sex Offenses in Sumerian Laws." *Journal of the American Oriental Society* 86 (1966): 355–372.

Gadotti, Alhena. "Why It Was Rape: The Conceptualization of Rape in Sumerian Literature." *Journal of American Oriental Society* 129 (2009): 73–82.

Hoffner, Harry A. "Incest, Sodomy and Bestiality in the Ancient Near East." In *Orient and Occident: Essays Presented to Cyrus H. Gordon on the Occasion of His Sixty-fifth Birthday*, edited by Harry A. Hoffner, pp. 81–90. Neukirchen-Vluyn, Germany: Neukirchener Verlag, 1973.

Lafont, Sophie. *Femmes, Droit et Justice dans l'Antiquité orientale: Contribution à l'étude du droit pénal au Proche-Orient ancient.* Göttingen, Germany: Vandenhoeck & Ruprecht, 1999.

Lieck, Gwendolyn. *Sex and Eroticism in Mesopotamian Literature.* London: Routledge, 1994.

Nissinen, Martti. *Homoeroticism in the Biblical World: A Historical Perspective.* Translated by Kirsi Stjerna. Minneapolis: Fortress, 1998.

Peled, Ilan. "Amore, more, ore, re…Sexual Terminology and Hittite Law." In *Pax Hethictica: Studies on the Hittites and Their Neighbors in Honour of Itamar Singer*, edited by Yoram Cohen, Amir Gilan, and Jared L. Miller, pp. 247–260. Wiesbaden, Germany: Harrassowitz, 2010.

Roth, Martha T. *Law Collections from Mesopotamia and Asia Minor.* Atlanta: Scholars Press, 1995.

Scholz, Susanne. "'Back Then It Was Legal': The Epistemological Imbalance in Readings of Biblical and Ancient Near Eastern Rape Legislation." *Journal of Religion and Abuse* 7 (2005): 5–35.

Scurlock, J. A. "But Was She Raped? A Verdict through Comparison." *NIN* 4 (2003): 61–103.

Hilary Lipka

Hebrew Bible

Social scientists find that the incidence of sexual violence varies dramatically among cultures, historically and in the present. A continuum runs from those rare cultures where sexual violence is practically absent to the most "rape-prone" societies. Like most ancient Near Eastern cultures, ancient Israel tends toward the violent range of this continuum. Gender and sexuality are conceived in such a way that sexual coercion is not necessarily recognized as violence. Forced sex might be regarded as an economic offense rather than an assault. A notion of "sexual violence," therefore, does not exist in biblical antiquity.

Biblical Terminology for Acts of Sexual Violence. Biblical Hebrew has no term corresponding to the word "rape," although most readers will recognize many accounts of the crime in the Hebrew Bible. The chief expressions for sexual intercourse in the Hebrew Bible are "to go into, penetrate," (e.g., Gen 16:2) and "to lie, sleep with" (e.g., Lev 15:18; cf. English "go to bed with"). The grammatical subject of these verbs is uniformly masculine, with two exceptions: Lot's daughters, who "lie with" their father (Gen 19:32–35), and Tamar, under imperative from Amnon: "Come, lie with me" (2 Sam 13:11).

The central Hebrew term related to sexual violence is the verb *'anâ*. Concretely the word signifies a state of being bent over, crouched, or bowed down. Figuratively, the verb conveys being weak, subjected, degraded, humiliated, and oppressed. Thirteen times a transitive form of this verb, *'innâ*, occurs with a woman as the object: Genesis 16:6, 9; 31:50; 34:2; Deuteronomy 21:14; 22:24, 29; Judges 19:24, 25; and 2 Samuel 23:12, 14, 22, 32. Euphemistic translations such as "to humble, dishonor," etc., obscure the fact that *'innâ* typically refers to sexual coercion or violence and, in at least one instance, resistance (Tamar, 2 Sam 23).

The term *'ālal* in its intensive forms denotes severe mistreatment, often sexual abuse (Exod 10:2; Num 22:29; Judg 19:25; Jer 38:19; 1 Chr 10:4). The verb *ṭāḥan*, "to grind," is a graphic term for receptive intercourse, in the attested usage always coerced sex; for example: "[if I have sinned], then let my wife grind for another, and let other men kneel over her" (Job 31:9–10; cf. Isa 47:2; Lam 5:13; Judg 16:21). The verb *šāgal*, of obscure origin, evokes so stark a picture of sexual violence that the Masoretes consistently replace the word with the less disturbing term *šākab*, "to sleep with." The word refers to the rape of women by conquering armies (Isa 13:16; Zech 14:2; see also Deut 28:30) and in Jeremiah 3:2 to a sexual act regarded as especially obscene (Gravett, 2004).

Legal Provisions. The sanctions of Deuteronomy 22:22–29 regulate male-to-female sexual assault, but only in a circumscribed and tendentious way. Although the measures are sometimes referred to as "rape laws," they are not intended to protect persons against sexual violence. Rather, the motivation of the laws is to secure men's exclusive ownership of sexual access to women. The three cases presented in verses 23–24, 25–27, and 28–29 are best understood as a subset of the general law of adultery preceding them in verse 22, although the selection of cases seems haphazard. The laws sometimes acknowledge factors such as coercion, consent, or resistance, but the cases do not necessarily hinge on these aspects.

The first measure, regarding adultery, addresses the general situation in which "a man is caught lying with the wife of another man" (v. 22). The purpose of the law is simply to establish that a man's possession of a woman by marriage is inviolate. In this case there is no consideration of the possibility that the woman might have been coerced or that she called for help or resisted, although these factors pertain in the subsequent cases (vv. 23–29). In such a case of adultery, the man and the woman alike are subject to the capital penalty.

In the case of the "engaged virgin," where the sex occurs within the confines of a town, the woman is deemed presumptively guilty for failing to cry out to the townspeople for help (a gross presumption, vv. 23–24). She is summarily condemned along with the man. In the third case, an engaged woman, "seized" by a man in the open country, is exonerated because she "may have cried for help." In this instance only the attacker is executed (vv. 25–27).

The fourth case exposes the rationale of the previous sanctions. Properly, when a woman is transferred from one household to another, money changes hands. If no man other than the father already "owns" a woman who is raped, a financial transaction makes the offended household whole (but not the woman). The assailant is obligated to pay to the woman's father a bride-price of 50 shekels of silver and perhaps an additional sum as a fine. Additionally, the attacker must take the woman as wife, with no possibility of divorce (cf. Exod 22:16–17). This is a grim irony: a solution for sexual assault is the victim's marriage to the attacker into perpetuity (22:28–29).

Deuteronomic law governs warfare, including the capture of women in battle. Many commentators regard these laws as humane measures intended to mitigate the brutality of warfare. The Israelites, for example, are to offer terms of peace before attacking a city, and they are not to destroy fruit-bearing trees (Deut 20:10, 19–20). Certain exemptions are granted to those who might be called up for battle. Thus, a man who has planted a vineyard but not yet enjoyed its fruit should return home, "or he might die in the battle and another be first to enjoy its fruit" (Deut 20:6). Similar leave is given to a man who has built a house but not dedicated it or engaged a woman but not married her (Deut 20:5, 7).

Some interpreters also regard the law governing the capture of women in warfare as generous (Deut 21:10–14). The law provides that the combatant must marry the captured woman and afford her a full month period of mourning before initiating sex with her. Additionally, she is not to be sold as a slave. This law, some assert, precludes rape on the battlefield. Yet others maintain that the law simply regulates sexual coercion in the aftermath of war. A "full month" is not an ordinary interval for mourning. It may be that the man refrains from intercourse for a month to ensure that the woman's menstrual cycle is completed, assuring his paternity of any children resulting from intercourse with her. In this light, the man's treatment of the woman appears manipulative and coercive, not generous. It is striking that the reason for the sanction against selling the woman into slavery is that the man has "abused her" (Deut 21:14).

Biblical Accounts of Sexual Violence. Two instances of sexual coercion frame the great flood narrative of Genesis chapters 6–8. First the "sons of God" (lesser divine beings who attend the heavenly court; cf. 1 Kgs 33:19; Job 1:6), "see" the women on earth and "take" for themselves all whom they wish (the collocation of the verbs, "to see" and "to take," appears also in Shechem's assault of Dinah; Gen 34:2). Second, after the flood, Noah falls asleep drunk in his tent and his son Ham "sees the nakedness" of his father (Gen 9:22). To "see the nakedness of" signifies incest in Leviticus 20:17, and "to uncover the nakedness of" is a generic term for intercourse (Lev 18:6; 20:18). Ham, therefore, has molested his father, Noah. Consequently, Ham's son Canaan and his descendants are condemned to slavery (Gen 9:25–27).

In Genesis 19 two divine messengers, after receiving lavish attention from Sarah and Abraham, approach Lot's city, Sodom. The men of the city demand that Lot turn over the visitors so that they may "know them" (v. 5). The context makes clear that sexual assault is their aim. Lot offers the men his two virgin daughters instead, but the men persist. Consequently, the messengers blast the attackers with blindness and destroy the city. Although this narrative eventually gave rise to the terms "sodomy" and "sodomite" with reference to male-to-male sex, the sex of the assailants' would-be victims is not the decisive factor in Genesis 19. Elsewhere in the Hebrew Bible, Sodom is notorious for the general cruelty of its inhabitants and their arrogance and unwillingness to protect the vulnerable (Ezek 16:49; Isa 1:10–17; Amos 4:11; cf. Matt 10:15; Luke 10:12). Emphasis on sexual misdeeds at Sodom comes to the fore only in the latest biblical tradition and the Pseudepigrapha (e.g., 2 Pet 2:4–8; Jude 6–7; 2 En 10:4).

The story of Sarah's slave Hagar certainly relates an instance of sexual coercion, if not sexual assault (Gen 16). Sarah, having no children, directs Abraham to "go into" Hagar so that Sarah might acquire a child (v. 2). When Hagar conceives, Sarah treats her abusively. Eventually Hagar escapes to the wilderness, where an angel of the Lord promises her a great progeny. Surrogate motherhood in the manner of Sarah and Hagar appears to have been an accepted practice in the ancient Near East. Nonetheless, many contemporary interpreters view the treatment of Hagar as domestic violence or sexual abuse.

The narrative of a Levite and his secondary wife in Judges 19 is a reflex of the Genesis 19 story, but with a gruesome outcome. When the woman escapes the Levite's possession and returns to her father's house in Bethlehem, the Levite retrieves her and travels north to Gibeah, where they lodge for the night. As at Sodom, the men of the town demand that the sojourner be put out of the house so they can rape him. This time the woman is released to the attackers. She endures a vicious overnight gang rape and dies at daybreak. The Levite dismembers the dead woman and sends the 12 pieces of her body throughout all Israel, issuing a call to war against Gibeah. The contrast of the two narratives—Lot being spared in the Genesis story, but the woman in Judges 19 murdered—perhaps illustrates women's vulnerability in contrast to men's relative safety from sexual violence.

Scholars debate whether Dinah, in Genesis 34, is the object of rape. Some maintain that Dinah's fate is "appropriate" to the ancient Near Eastern group-oriented cultural context of the story. It is anachronistic, they assert, to impose upon the narrative a present-day concept of rape. This line of interpretation emphasizes the larger social transaction between Jacob and Hamor's respective kinship groups. The bond between Shechem and Dinah creates, by proxy, a bond between the two social groups, although the bond is dissolved by the Israelites' eventual massacre of the other group (Gen 34:25–31; Bechtel, 1994).

Others assert that it is necessary—ethically—to apply a present-day concept of rape to Dinah's story precisely because there is no problematized notion of violence against women in biblical antiquity. In the biblical story Shechem assaults Dinah when she has gone out "to visit the women of the region" (v. 1). He sees her, takes her, penetrates, and humiliates her (v. 2; the final verb is *innâ*). Many present-day readers have little difficulty recognizing that Shechem rapes Dinah.

Royal Intrigue and Politics. Sexual coercion and subterfuge frequently appear in biblical stories from the royal courts of the Ancient Near East. Joseph, for example, rises to the position of steward in the household of Potiphar, Pharaoh's commander of the royal guard (Gen 39). Potiphar's wife enjoins Joseph: "Lie with me" (v. 7). When Joseph resists, Potiphar's wife frames him with a charge of assault, landing Joseph in the royal prison.

At the beginning of the book of Esther, the drunken King Ahasuerus demands that his queen Vashti display her beauty to his banquet guests (Esth 1:11). She is to appear before the king wearing the royal crown (likely only the crown, according to traditional readings). When Vashti refuses to be exposed, the enraged king banishes her, issuing an edict that all women in the kingdom must submit to their husbands' authority. Exposure of women here is a ruthless means of subjugation. Judith, the hero of the book that bears her name, fights back against male domination. She gains access to the enemy commander Holofernes by deceit and the promise of sex. Inside the general's tent, she waits until he falls into a drunken sleep and carries out a spectacular assassination.

The story of King David's rise to power depicts a series of exchanges in which men obliquely consolidate their prestige by assaulting women who belong to their rivals. Abner's intercourse with Saul's concubine Rizpah, for example, exposes Ishbaal's weakness in his inability to control sexual access to the women of his household (2 Sam 3:6–11). Likewise, Amnon's rape of Tamar undermines Absalom and David's honor (2 Sam 13:1–39). Adonijah, having lost the struggle for the throne, tries in vain to rehabilitate his standing by asking for David's concubine Abishag (1 Kgs 2; Stone, 1996).

Warfare. The ancient Near Eastern sources indicate that sexual assault was a common instrument of war. In the Hebrew Bible, for example, King Saul, pinned down in battle by Philistine archers, chooses death rather than risk abuse by enemy fighters. Saul says to his armor-bearer, "Draw your sword and thrust me through with it, so that these uncircumcised may not come and thrust me through, and make sport of me" (2 Sam 30:4). The latter two verbs signify sexual assault. Facing the fall of Jerusalem, King Zedekiah dreads the same fate: "I am afraid of the Judeans who have deserted to the Chaldeans, for I might be handed over to them and they would abuse me" (Jer 38:19). Lamentations decries sexual attacks upon women and men in the fallen city: "Women are raped in Zion, virgins in the towns of Judah ... young men are compelled to grind, and boys stagger under loads of wood" (Lam 5:11, 13; cf. Job 30:11 for the sense of "grind."). A taunt from the prophet Nahum alludes to the rape of defeated Assyrian soldiers: "Look at your troops; they are women in your midst!" (Nah 3:13);

likewise Jeremiah: "The warriors of Babylon…have become women!" (Jer 51:30).

Several times the Hebrew Bible depicts large-scale, indiscriminate seizure of women by Israelite groups (Num 31:9–35; Judg 21:12–24). In these passages the Deuteronomic law of the war-captive woman does not appear to apply (Deut 24:1–10). In the scholarly literature on these texts, commentators variously refer to the capture of the women as "wife stealing," "redistributing limited goods," "forced marriage," and "mass rape." Interpreters disagree as to which of these terms are appropriate to the material.

In the Numbers 31 account, 32,000 captive women "who had not known a man by sleeping with him" are cataloged as plunder, along with the 675,000 sheep, 72,000 oxen, and 61,000 donkeys captured by the Israelites (Num 31:32–35). From a certain matter-of-fact vantage point, this is a commonplace example of ancient Near Eastern practices necessary to sustain a population. Other interpreters insist that these women are chattel, destined inevitably to endure sexual violence.

Daughter Zion: The Raped City. In the Hebrew Bible, as in other ancient Near Eastern literatures, cities are frequently conceived in the figure of a woman: mother (Isa 66:8–13), queen (Isa 62:3), or virgin daughter (Isa 37:22), a woman married (Isa 62:5), widowed (Isa 47:8, 9; 54:4; Lam 1:1), and, not infrequently, a woman raped (Jer 6:1–8; 13:22; Isa 47:1–4; Nah 3:5–6). In the poetic language of the prophets, military invasions figure as sexual assaults, and God appears as a vengeful rapist. These texts are graphic; at times they reveal more about sexual violence in ancient Israel than do the prose texts surveyed above (Weems, 1995).

Jeremiah, envisioning an attack on Jerusalem by armies from the north, commingles the language of military siege and sexual assault. The invaders of the city "go into her," crying out, "prepare war against her" (6:3–4). God berates Jerusalem:

> It is for the greatness of your iniquity that your skirts
>   are lifted up,
> and you are violated…
> I myself will lift up your skirts over your face,
> and your shame will be seen.
>
> (Jer 13:22, 26)

Nahum addresses the city of Nineveh in like terms:

> I am against you, says the Lord of hosts,
>   and I will lift up your skirts over your face;
>   and I will let nations look on your nakedness and
>   kingdoms on your shame.
> I will throw filth at you and treat you with contempt
>   and make you a spectacle.
>
> (Nah 3:5–6)

Isaiah directs similar abuse to Babylon:

> Come down and sit in the dust, maiden daughter Babylon!
> Sit on the ground without a throne, daughter Chaldea!
> For you shall no more be called tender and delicate.
> Take the millstones and grind meal, remove your veil,
>   strip off your robe, uncover your legs, pass through
>   the rivers.
> Your nakedness shall be uncovered, and your shame
>   shall be seen.
> I will take vengeance, and I will spare no one.
>
> (Isa 47:1–3)

Standard translations do not convey the raw quality of these passages. They portray degrading treatment, forceful stripping of women, rape, and murder. Numerous interpreters have described the material as "prophetic pornography" (e.g., Exum, 1996). Jeremiah 4:30–31, for example, focalizes the woman's "beauty" along with the lethal impulses of those who punish her:

> And you, O desolate one, what do you mean that you
>   dress in crimson,
>   that you deck yourself with ornaments of gold,
>   that you enlarge your eyes with paint?
> In vain you beautify yourself.
> Your lovers despise you; they seek your life.
>
> (Jer 4:30)

Lamentations displays daughter Zion as a "mockery" (1:8; the Hebrew term evokes the word "unclean," thus, menstruating):

> Her uncleanness was in her skirts; she took no
>   thought of her future;
> her downfall was appalling, with none to comfort her.
>
> (Lam 1:9)

Groaning, exposed, and abandoned, Daughter Zion laments that her attackers have prevailed over her.

The language evokes a picture of the woman as not only ritually unclean, but also bleeding from the assault.

Ezekiel chapters 16 and 23 develop these motifs in vivid detail. God's tirades, laced with lurid sexual imagery, hurl disgust upon the cities of Jerusalem and Samaria. The violence includes child abuse, the murder of children, destruction of homes, stripping, gang rape, mutilation of women, and stoning. There is little comfort in the momentary cessation of this violence: "So I will satisfy my fury on you, and my jealousy shall turn away from you; I will be calm, and will be angry no more" (6:42). It is an eerie quiet, certain to be shattered by more spasms of violence, as the following chapters of the book bear out.

Hosea and Gomer. The book of Hosea derives from northern traditions, not attached to the southern capital city of Jerusalem. In place of a city personified as a woman, Hosea's "wife of whoredom," Gomer, represents the land of Israel (1:2). The names of Gomer's children, Lo-ruhamah ("No pity," 1:6), and Lo-ammi ("Not my people," 1:9), signify God's rejection of the Israelite people. Hosea commands the children: "Plead with your mother… that she put away her whoring from her face, and her adultery from between her breasts" (2:2). He threatens to "strip her naked… expose her as in the day she was born… and kill her with thirst" (2:3). God will hedge in the woman and build a wall to contain her, strip the woman naked and devastate her (2:6, 9–12). The children receive no mercy. This picture coincides with the abuse detailed in Isaiah, Jeremiah, and Ezekiel: summary condemnation of the woman, sexual denigration, the hapless fate of the children, stripping and exposure, and murderous threats.

In the book of Hosea God's disposition abruptly reverses: "Therefore I will now allure her, and bring her into the wilderness, and speak tenderly to her… there she shall respond as in the days of her youth" (2:14–15). The vocabulary here is telling: the term translated "allure" is usually rendered "seduce," "entice," or "deceive," indicating sexual misuse. The phrase "speak tenderly to" (literally, "speak to the heart of") is referred to two other women in the Hebrew Bible: Dinah, when she is raped by Shechem (Gen 34:3), and the Levite's concubine (Judg 19:3).

It would be misleading to suggest that the sexual violence in these texts is only figurative. Although outside the prophetic literature there is scant biblical attestation of public stripping, exposure, and sexual assault of women, there is little doubt that these practices were well known in ancient Israel. The force of the prophets' rhetoric derives from the audience's familiarity with such scenes. These manifestations of violence against women are well attested in other ancient Near Eastern literatures. In some traditional societies they can be observed still in the early twenty-first century.

[*See also* Family Structures, *subentry* Hebrew Bible; Imagery, Gendered, *subentries on* Deuteronomistic History *and* Prophetic Literature; *and* Legal status, *subentry on* Hebrew Bible.]

BIBLIOGRAPHY

Abasili, Alexander I. "Was It Rape? The David and Bathsheba Pericope Re-examined." V*etus Testamentum* 61, no. 1 (2011): 1–15.

Anderson, Cheryl B. *Women, Ideology, and Violence: Critical Theory and the Construction of Gender in the Book of the Covenant and the Deuteronomic Law.* London and New York: Continuum, 2004.

Bal, Mieke. *Murder and Difference: Gender, Genre, and Scholarship on Sisera's Death.* Bloomington: Indiana University Press, 1988.

Bechtel, Lyn M. "What if Dinah Is Not Raped? (Genesis 34)." *Journal for the Study of the Old Testament*, 19, no. 62 (1994): 19–36.

Blyth, Caroline. *The Narrative of Rape in Genesis 34: Interpreting Dinah's Silence.* Oxford: Oxford University Press, 2010.

Exum, J. Cheryl. "Prophetic Pornography." In *Plotted, Shot, and Painted: Cultural Representations of Biblical Women*, pp. 101–128. London and New York: Continuum, 1996.

Fewell, Danna Nolan, and David M. Gunn. "Tipping the Balance: Sternberg's Reader and the Rape of Dinah." *Journal of Biblical Literature* 110, no. 2 (1991): 193–211.

Gravett, Sandie. "Reading 'Rape' in the Hebrew Bible: A Consideration of Language." *Journal for the Study of the Old Testament* 28, no. 3 (2004): 279–299.

Keefe, Alice A. "Rapes of Women, Wars of Men," *Semeia* 61 (1993): 79–97.

Niditch, Susan. "Eroticism and Death in the Tale of Jael." In *Gender and Difference in Ancient Israel*, edited by Peggy Day, pp. 43–57. Minneapolis: Fortress, 1989.

Pressler, Carolyn. "Sexual Violence and Deuteronomic Law." In *A Feminist Companion to Exodus and Deuteronomy,* edited by Athalya Brenner, pp. 102–112. Sheffield, U.K.: Sheffield Academic Press, 1994.

Scholz, Suzanne. *Sacred Witness: Rape in the Hebrew Bible.* Minneapolis: Fortress, 2008.

Stone, Ken. *Sex, Honor, and Power in the Deuteronomistic History.* Sheffield, U.K.: Sheffield Academic Press, 1996.

Thistlethwaite, Susan Brooks. "'You May Enjoy the Spoil of Your Enemies': Rape as a Biblical Metaphor for War." *Semeia* 61 (1993): 59–75.

Washington, Harold C. "Violence and the Construction of Gender in the Hebrew Bible: A New Historicist Approach." *Biblical Interpretation* 5, no. 4 (1997): 324–363.

Weems, Renita. *Battered Love: Marriage, Sex, and Violence in the Hebrew Prophets.* Philadelphia: Fortress, 1995.

van Wolde, Ellen. "Does *ʿINNÂ* Denote Rape? A Semantic Analysis of a Controversial Word." *Vetus Testamentum* 52, no. 4 (2002): 528–544.

Harold C. Washington

Greek World

There has been an escalation in scholarly interest in sexual violence in ancient Greece since the late twentieth century, especially acts committed by males against females. According to Nancy Sorkin Rabinowitz (2011) interest in this topic was inspired by the attention given to rape by twentieth-century feminism. This interest led to scholarly debates on whether something similar to modern concepts of rape existed in antiquity, the extent to which the victim's consent was a significant factor, the role of sexual violence within marriage, whether a female voice can be located in representations of sexual encounters, and whether sexual violence is a motivating factor for warfare. Many of the attempts to recover societal perceptions have focused on the interpretation of the relevant laws, particularly those of Athens. Other areas of focus include representations in art, myth, historiography, and drama, notably Menandrian comedy. Less attention has been paid to sexual violence against males, for which there are also fewer ancient sources.

The Concept of Rape. It is clear from legal and literary evidence that there was a concept of sexual violence in antiquity, but it is far from clear whether this concept matched modern definitions of rape. There is no Greek word that corresponds directly with our term "rape," and it has been proposed that looking for a concept of rape in antiquity risks anachronism and distortion of the evidence (Harris, 2004). While it is easy to find depictions of acts that we today might regard as rape, not least the array of mythological encounters between gods and young females, it is difficult to determine whether the ancient Greeks would have interpreted them as such. The Greek terms that are most often used in circumstances that from a modern perspective look like rape are *bia* and *hybris,* but these words have a wider semantic range, and any sexual connotation needs to be inferred from context (Rabinowitz, 2011). *Bia* covers physical violence and strength as well as sexual violence. *Hybris* denotes an act intended to dishonor another, typically but not invariably including violence (Harris, 2004). A sexual act that is an act of *hybris* is one that attacks the sexual honor of the victim, but it can include consensual sex such as adultery, which is conceived of as degrading to a woman's husband (Cohen, 1991). Omitowoju (2002) has shown that the Athenian emphasis on male control over female kin rather than on female consent makes sexual violence in Athenian law significantly different from modern, consent-focused concepts.

Violent Responses to Sexual Offenses. Lysias 1 ("On the Murder of Eratosthenes"), an oration dating to the early part of the fourth century B.C.E., has been used as key evidence for Athenian legal views of sexual violence and sexual behavior more broadly. Having recounted that he caught Eratosthenes in the act of having sex with his wife, the speaker, Euphiletus, claims that his decision to kill him on the spot was his legal and civic duty. The law of justifiable homicide upon which Euphiletus bases his defense exonerated a man who killed someone taken in intercourse with his wife, mother, sister, daughter, or concubine (Demosthenes 23.53; cf. Lysias 1.30). Although the homicide law does not differentiate between a violent or nonviolent sexual encounter, Euphiletus makes the case that seduction is more severe than coercion (Lysias 1.32–33). How to interpret this evidence has provoked a substantial debate over whether rape was perceived by the classical Athenians as a more or less serious offense than seduction. Edward Harris (1990) argues that Euphiletus misrepresents the laws in his own favor by suppressing certain details, such as the existence of alternative methods of dealing with an adulterer, including legal remedies, public humiliation, and fines. Yet he notes that, irrespective of the legal position, the sentiment regarding seduction being worse than coercion probably rang true for the Athenians of the jury. Christopher Carey (1995) and Daniel Ogden (1997) emphasize that sex through seduction would have been perceived as more serious because of the importance placed on protecting bloodlines by Athenian men. If a woman were raped she might be likely to denounce her attacker; if seduced she would be more likely to try to pass off any child as her husband's with the result that an adulterine bastard might be introduced into the household.

The fear of infidelity by women of the household appears to have been a major preoccupation for Greek men, and in myth fierce responses typically follow any attempt at seducing a man's female kin. The Homeric epics revolve around violent responses to the seduction of wives. *The Odyssey* culminates in the slaughter of the suitors who are wooing Penelope by Odysseus upon his return home. *The Iliad* portrays an army of Greek warriors intent on destroying the entire city of Troy in revenge for the abduction of one of their leader's wives. In each of these plots it is apparent that the men concerned view the seduction of their wives as an offense to their honor that must be avenged. Women are constructed as passive figures fought over by proprietorial men. Assaults against women are interesting insofar as they are offenses against their male kin (McHardy, 2008). These myths go some way toward explaining why Euphiletus elected to kill his wife's lover on the spot rather than taking him to court (McHardy, 2008).

Marital Rape. As he was the "tyrant" in the house, a citizen man's sexual access to his wife and slaves appears to have been largely unquestioned—or, at least, it is unlikely that domestic violence or violent sex with a man's own wife or slaves would have resulted in legal action. Greek women were given in arranged marriages by their fathers or brothers, and a woman's only recourse to action would have been through these male relatives. There was no legal concept of marital rape and perhaps no concept of marital rape per se. According to Jeffrey Henderson (1996), it is unlikely that forced sex with a wife would have been conceived of as rape, since sex within marriage would have been part of a wife's duties and her obedience to her husband would have been expected. Lloyd Llewellyn-Jones (2011) suggests that the comic playwright Aristophanes alludes to the escalation of force and violence employed by a husband who wishes to assert his authority over his wife in his play *Lysistrata* (ca. 411 B.C.E.). In this play the women of Athens and Sparta undertake a sex strike in order to persuade their warring husbands to make peace. When the lead character Lysistrata proposes this plan to the other women, they express anxiety that their husbands will beat then and force them to have sex or will divorce them (*Lysistrata* 158–162). Lysistrata responds that men do not take pleasure out of forced sex (162–166). The power relations between men and women are reversed in this play, and men are shown capitulating to women because of their overwhelming desire for sex with their wives. The play makes use of the perceived sexual power of women over men to suggest that they have authority within marriage, but it is hinted that because this is the topsy-turvy world of comedy, control in marriage would actually have been the domain of Athenian husbands (Sommerstein, 1998).

Links between Rape and Marriage. The concept that sexual violence and marriage are closely linked has been explored in various categories of evidence. Greek art at times uses imagery of sexual violence to depict marriage. Connections between rape and marriage are made by the female chorus of Aeschylus's *Suppliants* (ca. 460s B.C.E.). In the play the daughters of Danaus have run away from home, seeking protection from forced marriage to their cousins. While the men consistently refer to their desire for marriage, the frightened women express their fear of male violence and force. Similarly, the author of the Homeric

Hymn to Demeter (possibly composed in the seventh century B.C.E.) portrays the abduction and forced marriage of Persephone—arranged by her father and uncle—as marriage from a male perspective, but rape from a female perspective. Rabinowitz (2011) has argued that the association of rape and marriage in Greek literary sources points to women's lack of autonomy in their choices in life.

In Menandrian comedy, which was written and originally performed in the latter part of the fourth century B.C.E., sexual violence against a young woman leads to marriage so often as to amount to a cliché. Scholars are divided over how to interpret the prevalence of this particular plotline. Some have suggested that the plots are based on comic conventions and do not reflect real life in Athens. Others believe that an understanding of Athenian attitudes to sex can help explain what happens in the plays. David Cohen (1993) has suggested that sex between young unmarried couples in the plays is passed off as forced so that the reputation of the girl involved is not ruined. Alan Sommerstein (1998) contends that the plots may reflect a strategy drawn from real life where young couples can choose their own marriage partners rather than being given in arranged marriages. Susan Lape (2001) has claimed that the level of intoxication of the young men gives them an excuse for their behavior. Harris (2004) has suggested that to reach a satisfactory explanation it is necessary to reexamine the concept of sexual violence. In his view, the plays reveal that Athenians would have been sympathetic to a young man who sexually assaulted a young unmarried woman, provided that he was willing to make amends by marrying her. This is because the concern around sexual violence was not about the consent of the woman but about her prospects as a wife and mother. So while there were circumstances in which sexual attacks could precipitate extreme violent responses (for example having sex with another man's wife), in other circumstances sexual violence would not have provoked outrage. For example, mythic attacks by gods that lead to pregnancy and the birth of heroes appear acceptable, as the sexual violence could be seen to have served a useful purpose.

Warfare. Sexual violence has often been regarded as ancillary to warfare. However, some studies have explored the possibility that a key motivating factor was the enslaving of enemy women and their subsequent concubinage. According to Kathy Gaca (2011) sexual violence was an objective of a range of warfare types, notably predatory warfare, such as raids and hunting; parasitic warfare, where men take over the woman's homeland (e.g., via colonization); and punitive warfare, such as that following the breaking of a truce. In all these types of warfare women are captured and used for labor and for reproduction. Fiona McHardy (2008) has used evolutionary approaches to argue that underlying Greek epic tales of wars over women, such as the Trojan War, which is said to be fought over the theft of Helen from Menelaus, is a competitive drive in men to secure female reproductive resources.

In *The Iliad* the warriors besieging Troy kill male combatants and seize their female relatives. Competition over these females is so intense that it precipitates a major quarrel between Achilles and Agamemnon over who should take possession of Briseis, the female "prize" won by Achilles's spear, causing Achilles to withdraw from fighting and the Greek war effort to be threatened. This epic and tragedies about the Trojan War, such as Euripides's *Hecuba* (ca. 424 B.C.E.) and *Trojan Women* (415 B.C.E.), depict elite women captured in war becoming concubines of the men who have slaughtered their husbands and fathers. They would then be expected to have children with these men, as happens in Euripides's *Andromache* (ca. 428–425 B.C.E.) and Sophocles's *Ajax* (ca. 450–430 B.C.E.). In *Seven against Thebes* the women of Thebes, fearing defeat in war, speak of their fear of being captured, enslaved, and sexually conquered by the invading enemy. They equate this enslavement and sexual conquest to marriage through their use of vocabulary used in relation to Greek weddings. The blurring in these stories of enforced captivity and marriage parallels the blurring around sexual violence and marriage discussed in feminist critiques (Rabinowitz, 2011).

Women's Experiences. For some scholars, the numerous mythological encounters between gods and young females constitute an extreme manifestation of the unpleasantness of women's lives in the patriarchal world of ancient Greece. James Robson (1997) has pointed to the humiliation of girls violated by gods disguised as beasts and has noted that many elect to commit suicide—an indication of despair at what they have suffered. For others, the evidence demonstrates that women could be understood to consent to, and even experience desire in, encounters that, from a modern perspective, look solely coercive. According to Mary Lefkowitz (1993), mythological encounters between gods and young females depict seduction rather than rape, because the gods sought to make the experiences pleasurable for their partners.

Some studies have argued that it is impossible to recover what ancient Greek women might actually have experienced in encounters that now appear violent and coercive. The goal, according to these scholars, should be to locate constructions of female desire in particular genres rather than to attempt to determine whether the sources can be taken as evidence of what women felt about coercive sex. Rabinowitz (2011) has argued (contra Lefkowitz, 1993) that the ambiguity in Euripides's *Ion* (ca. 414–412 B.C.E.) between sexual violence and desire comes out of a cultural construction of female sexuality where coerced sex is represented as a female desire. Deacy (2013) has also explored interplays of desire/coercion and victimage/agency in mythological women's narrations of encounters with gods, including Persephone's account of her violent abduction by Hades in the Hymn to Demeter. She concludes that the desire and eroticism experienced by the girls in the flowery meadows from which they are "plucked" is not generated by the male gods who seize them but by themselves.

Sexual Violence against Men. Evidence for sexual violence perpetrated by females upon males has been less studied, reflecting the limited evidence for sexually coercive females. The dawn goddess Eos was credited with an insatiable desire for sex (Apollodorus 1.4.4) that caused her to abduct young mortal males. Robin Osborne (1996) has argued that visual depictions of Eos's abductions subverted the conventions of sexual relationships and inverted concepts of female desire to enable an exploration of female behavior that was inconceivable in everyday society. Lefkowitz (2002) has suggested that these scenes do not refer to anxieties around the dangers of female sexuality or reflect attitudes toward human sexual behavior, but instead depict the power of the immortals.

Male-on-male sexual violence is not overtly discussed by ancient authors, but could be used as a metaphor for military defeat. Cohen (1991, 1993) has discussed how the laws on *hybris* could have been used to prosecute cases of male rape; he sees this law as a possible recourse for those wishing to pursue men involved in cases of sex with minors in the absence of laws regarding statutory rape. While scholars have typically seen pederastic relationships in ancient Greece as ones in which boys are seduced through gifts and courtship rather than being forced, it is possible that young boys might have been more vulnerable to suffering sexual violence than young girls or have been expected to experience it as part of the transition from boyhood to maturity. Ephorus (mid-fourth century B.C.E.) refers to ritualized pederastic rape on Crete (Strabo, *Geography* 10.21.4). The exemplary pederastic relationship in Greek myth between Zeus and Ganymede comes about following the forcible abduction of the youth by the god (Apollodorus 3.12.2). Diverse feelings about homosexual rape are revealed in the sources on the forcible rape by Laius of Pelops's son Chrysippus. Laius's behavior was apparently considered understandable because of the exceptional beauty of his victim (Apollodorus 3.5.5). However, the boy's father did not condone the action and reacted violently in response (Hyginus, *Fabulae* 85), and Hera's fury at the Thebans' toleration of Laius's actions caused her to send the sphinx to ravage Thebes (schol. Eur. Phoen. 1760). As in cases of sexual violence against females, the sources focus on the power of the gods and of adult males in intimate relationships and reveal a significant degree of ambiguity concerning attitudes to sexual violence.

[*See also* Children, *subentry* Greek World; Legal Status, *subentries on* Greek World *and* Roman World; *and* Sexual Violence, *subentries on* Hebrew Bible, New Testament, *and* Roman World.]

BIBLIOGRAPHY

Carey, Christopher. "Rape and Adultery in Athenian Law." *Classical Quarterly*, n.s., 45 (1995): 407–417.

Cohen, David. "Sexuality, Violence, and the Athenian Law of *Hubris*." *Greece and Rome*, 2d ser., 38 (1991): 171–188.

Cohen, David. "Consent and Sexual Relations in Classical Athens." In *Consent and Coercion to Sex and Marriage in Ancient and Medieval Societies*, edited by Angeliki E. Laiou, pp. 5–16. Washington, D.C.: Dumbarton Oaks Research Library and Collection, 1993.

Deacy, Susan. "From 'Flowery Tales' to 'Heroic Rapes': Virginal Subjectivity in the Mythological Meadow." *Arethusa* 46 (2013): 395–413.

Deacy, Susan, and Karen F. Pierce, eds. *Rape in Antiquity: Sexual Violence in the Greek and Roman Worlds*. London: Duckworth, 1997.

Gaca, Kathy L. "Girls, Women, and the Significance of Sexual Violence in Ancient Warfare." In *Sexual Violence in Conflict Zones: From the Ancient World to the Era of Human Rights*, edited by Elizabeth D. Heineman, pp. 73–88. Philadelphia: University of Pennsylvania Press, 2011.

Harris, Edward. M. "Did the Athenians Regard Seduction as a Worse Crime than Rape?" *Classical Quarterly*, n.s., 40 (1990): 370–377.

Harris, Edward. M. "Did Rape Exist in Classical Athens?: Further Reflections on the Laws about Sexual Violence." *Dike* 7 (2004): 41–83.

Henderson, Jeffrey, trans. and ed. *Staging Women: Three Plays by Aristophanes*. London: Routledge, 1996.

Lape, Susan. "Democratic Ideology and the Poetics of Rape in Menandrian Comedy." *Classical Antiquity* 20 (2001): 79–119.

Lefkowitz, Mary R. "Seduction and Rape in Greek Myth." *Consent and Coercion to Sex and Marriage in Ancient and Medieval Societies*, edited by Angeliki E. Laiou, pp. 17–37. Washington, D.C.: Dumbarton Oaks Research Library and Collection, 1993.

Lefkowitz, Mary R. "'Predatory' Goddesses." *Hesperia* 71 (2002): 325–344.

Llewellyn-Jones, Lloyd. "Domestic Abuse and Violence against Women in Ancient Greece." In *Sociable Man: Essays on Ancient Greek Social Behaviour in Honour of Nick Fisher*, edited by S. D. Lambert, pp. 231–266. Swansea: Classical Press of Wales, 2011.

McHardy, Fiona. *Revenge in Athenian Culture*. London: Duckworth, 2008.

Ogden, Daniel, "Rape, Adultery and Protection of Bloodlines in Classical Athens." In *Rape in Antiquity: Sexual Violence in the Greek and Roman Worlds*, edited by Susan Deacy and Karen F. Pierce, pp. 25–41. London: Duckworth, 1997.

Omitowoju, Rosanna. *Rape and the Politics of Consent in Classical Athens*. Cambridge, U.K.: Cambridge University Press, 2002.

Osborne, Robin. "Desiring Women on Athenian Pottery." In *Sexuality in Ancient Art: Near East, Egypt, Greece, and Italy*, edited by Natalie Boymel Kampen, pp. 65–80. Cambridge, U.K.: Cambridge University Press: 1996.

Rabinowitz, Nancy Sorkin. "Greek Tragedy: A Rape Culture?" *EuGeStA: Journal on Gender Studies in Antiquity* 1 (2011): 1–21.

Robson, James. "Bestiality and Bestial Rape in Greek Myth." In *Rape in Antiquity: Sexual Violence in the Greek and Roman Worlds*, edited by Susan Deacy and Karen F. Pierce, pp. 65–96. London: Duckworth: 1997.

Sommerstein, Alan H. "Rape and Young Manhood in Athenian Comedy." In *Thinking Men: Masculinity and Its Self-Representation in the Classical Tradition*, edited by Lin Foxhall and John Salmon, pp. 100–114. London: Routledge, 1998.

Susan Deacy and Fiona McHardy

Roman World

In the ancient world, sexual violence was in large measure normalized and naturalized. It was condemned only when instances of sexual violence contravened other codes of value, such as honor associated with status and class. Thus, defining what constitutes sexual violence in the ancient world is not a question that can be solved by adopting an ancient definition. No such definition exists that corresponds to twenty-first-century understandings of sexual violence. The Latin verb *stupro* is variously translated as "rape," "dishonor," "defile," "disgrace," "ravish," etc. The root of the English rape, namely *rapere*, connotes violent seizure of property, and although it may, within that connotation, indicate sexual violence, *stupro* is more common. Likewise, the Greek terms such as *atimia* and *hybris* set honor and dishonor as the primary continuum of virtue within which sexual activity has its moral valence.

Modern definitions of sexual violence such as that of the World Health Organization envision a social landscape different from that of Roman antiquity. As a definition of sexual violence, the World Health Organization offers "any sexual act, attempt to obtain a sexual act, unwanted sexual comments or advances, or acts to traffic, or otherwise directed, against a person's sexuality using coercion, by any person regardless of their relationship to the victim, in any setting, including but not limited to home and work" (Krug, 2002, p. 149). To expand the scope of the present inquiry to comments in antiquity is not practicable. The modern focus in the use of the term "sexual violence" highlights a dignity that attaches to humanness itself, regardless of class, status, gender, or ethnicity, whereas the ancient terms described above have their function within a highly differentiated valuation of humans along axes of class, status, gender, and ethnicity. The focus in this essay is coercive sexual acts and coercive acts against a person's sexuality or sexual functionality. Admittedly, this too amounts to organizing an account of the ancient world by means of a modern concept.

Within the Roman conception of sexual activity primarily understood as a hierarchical structure of penetrator and penetrated, three qualities are prominent: phallocentrism, aggression, and utility. "Phallocentrism" gestures to excessive representations of the penis in Roman art, sculpture, and vocabulary. The figure of Priapus—a minor fertility god sporting an enormous erection—adorned Roman houses and figured prominently in Roman comedy. The vast number of terms for the penis in Latin literature, in one account 120 distinct terms (Mattingly, 2010, p. 106), witnesses to the disproportionate focus on male genitalia, most often as an image of power, in Roman literature. The character of these representations is most often violent, with metaphors of weapons representing the penis (Mattingly, 2010, p. 106). In parallel, "metaphors of sexual intercourse are predominantly ones of striking, cutting, wounding, penetrating, digging, triumphing—typical soldiers' work" (Mattingly, 2010, p. 106). Sex without aggression was nearly inconceivable. Finally, "utility" gestures to the basic verb of sexual intercourse: for a dominant partner to "use" a subordinate partner (Brooten, 1998, p. 245; Marchal, 2011, pp. 753–754).

When Paul writes that it is the will of God "that each one of you know how to take [*ktasthai*] a thing [*skeuos*] for himself in holiness and honor" (1 Thess 4.4 lit.), the verb and the noun are as vague in Greek as in English. *Skeuos* indicates an item possessed for use value and *ktasthai* [from *ktaomai*] procuring or

gaining from use. Whether Paul is referring to a person or masturbation is unclear, but the instrumental vision of sexual activity is plainly evident. Such utilitarian understanding of sexual activity abets the integration of sex and violence in Roman society. Romans and Greeks characteristically envisioned sexual activity as occurring in relationships of differential power. Conversely, power relations were also envisioned in sexual terms. Thus violence in the exercise of power was frequently sexual.

Maiming and Disfigurement. To return to the World Health Organization's definition, acts directed against a person's sexuality and sexual function are instances of sexual violence. Forcible mutilation, modification, or maiming of the genitals of individuals in the ancient world clearly constitutes sexual violation. It seems likely that male slaves and subalterns were more susceptible than females to sexual maiming for three reasons: (1) the externality of male primary sexual organs, (2) the desirability, or even fungibility, of sexually unmaimed female slaves and subalterns in a "market" where wealthy males formed the primary source of demand, and (3) the anxiety of elite males over the sexual potential of their slaves and subalterns.

Male slaves were subject to the possibility of penile infibulation or castration. Penile infibulation involved stretching and piercing the foreskin of an uncircumsised penis and then employing a connector, in the form of thread, leather, or metal—a *fibula*—to prevent, or make excruciating, an erection. The purpose of this procedure was a regime of control, domination, and in some cases punishment of enslaved males. Aulus Cornelius Celsus narrates the procedure of infibulation:

The foreskin covering the glans is stretched forwards and the point for perforation marked on each side with ink. Then the foreskin is let go. If the marks are drawn back over the glans too much has been included, and the marks should be placed further forward. If the glans is clear of them, their position is suitable for the pinning. Then the foreskin is transfixed at the marks by a threaded needle, and the ends so this thread are knotted together. Each day the thread is moved until the edges of the perforations have cicatrized. When this is assured the thread is withdrawn and a fibula inserted, and the lighter this is the better. (Celsus, *De Medicina* 7.25)

Martial and Juvenal frequently allude to infibulated slaves. There are no witnesses to voluntary infibulation by elite Roman males. Figures with an infibulated penis are also depicted in several extant ancient sculptures directly or in renaissance reproductions of no-longer-surviving originals.

Castration represents a more extreme position on the bodily modification continuum—ranging from hair cutting through tattooing to castration—to which male slaves, as the *property* of their owners, were subject. The procedure was intended to ensure docility, not only by physical means, but also by enacting permanently and crucially the prerogative of ownership (Joshel, 2010, pp. 40, 71, 97–98). The presence of eunuchs in Roman society—viewed by elites as a disturbing ambiguity—witnesses to the practice of castration and its enactment on those without the power to refuse it (Kuefler, 2001, p. 32). Martial's epigram on the punishment of a slave for adultery gives a glimpse into the performance of castration within unequal power relationships:

You have relations, boy Hyllus, with the wife of an armed tribune, and all the time are dreading only a boy's punishment. Alas for you! in the midst of your enjoyments you will be gelded [*castrabere*]. You will reply "This is not permitted." Well? Is what you are doing, Hyllus, permitted? (Martial, *Epigr.* 2.60)

The circumstance Martial describes shows the conflation of status and sexual violence. Although the horror of castration is assumed to be forbidden by Roman law, the proscription has no force when a mere boy (*puer*, often indicating slave) offends a tribune. Having penetrated illegitimately the property (i.e., wife) of a citizen, the "boy" will be punished by a castration that would be illegitimate to practice on a citizen male. It was also practiced on slaves to increase their value for some tasks (Herodotus, *Hist.* 8.105). A passage in Herodotus also treats castration as punishment, narrating a scene in which a father and sons are forced to castrate each other (*Hist.* 8.104–106). Such abuse combines its effect on the individual

with violence to the family lineage in terms of honor and physical person. The medical account of castration given in Paulus's *Epitomae medicae* indicates that although the operation is in some ways improper, it is necessary for a surgeon to understand its correct practice because the powerful often forced surgeons to perform the operation (Brooten, 1998, p. 171n71). That the patient was at least equally under duress is a reasonable assumption.

Female genital mutilation seems less common although not unknown. It did not add value to slaves nor was it as technically feasible as the mutilation of males. Nevertheless, accounts of clitoridectomy survive in medical texts from the high empire. Soranos's *Gynaikeia* gives instruction on a partial surgical removal of an excessively large clitoris (Brooten, 1998, pp. 162–169). Brooten has demonstrated that this is not a case of ritual clitoridectomy, but of a medicalized response to disposition and behavior transgressing social norms, preeminently in the usurpation of male sexual activeness that Romans understood as essential to female same-sex desire and practice. Fainter traces of clitoridectomy appear in Philoumenos and Strabo (*Geogr.* 17.2.5, 16.4.9; Brooten, 1998, pp. 169–173).

Women were also subject to maiming punishment, such as that described in Herodotus's *Histories* 4.202 wherein the women of Barke had their breasts cut off in response to the death of Arkesilaos. Elsewhere Herodotus narrates another instance of this punishment on an individual level (*Hist.* 9.112). Such extremity of violence contravened Greek (and later Roman) ideals of elite self-mastery, but it is necessary to understand that the ideals of self-mastery were necessary, at least in part a result of the extremities of power that permitted horrific violence. Moreover, ideals of self-mastery held the most force in conditioning the public image of elite males in his dealings under the gaze of fellow citizens. The provinces, the front in war, and the privacy of the house offered fewer disincentives to extremes of violence. Maiming ranged the political scene of violence down to the domestic sphere where its prerogative was widely deployed, sometimes to permanent effect. Augustine recounts his mother's attitude to a husband's authority to beat to the point of disfigurement. She blamed the wife.

As a result, while many matrons whose husbands were more gentle than hers bore the marks of blows on their disfigured faces, and would in private talk blame the behavior of their husbands, she would blame their tongues, admonishing them seriously—though in a jesting manner—that from the hour they heard what are called the matrimonial tablets read to them, they should think of them as instruments by which they were made servants. (*Conf.* 9.19.9)

Christian views on spousal abuse evinced little if any difference from non-Christian attitudes.

Christian texts also participated in a worldview in which sexual maiming was normalized. In Paul's discussion of circumcision in Galatians 5:12, he makes clear his wish that "those who unsettle you would castrate [*apokopsontai*] themselves." Genital mutilation is Paul's response in this case to disagreements among followers of Jesus. Similarly, his pun in Philippians 3:2–3 on "those who mutilate the flesh [*katatomê*]" and "we" who are the "circumcision" [*peritomê*] is difficult to set into compact English, but a close and brief rendering might be "beware of those who cut off, we are those who cut around." Female sexual maiming is less common in Christian texts, but the story that inaugurates the *Acts of Peter* gives some sense of the way in which Christian values of sexual asceticism did not fully transform the idea of the female body as the instrumental property of the authoritative male. Peter's daughter is paralyzed on one side, and he is challenged that, despite his miraculous healing powers, he has neglected his own daughter. Peter responds by healing her and inspiring the crowd to further praise of God, and then he revokes the healing and returns her to her infirmity. His explanation to the outraged crowd is that God warned him in a vision that she would be a great temptation to men should she remain healthy. The purpose of the infirmity is to make her unmarriageable. A fragmentary seduction story begins in the manuscript and makes it clear that sexual attractiveness and function is the matter at stake (*Acts Pet.* 1.128–135).

Sexual maiming was acceptable within the Roman world as long as the maimed party was other to the elite male: some combination of female, enslaved, or barbarian.

Coerced Sexual Action. The habit of envisioning power relationships in sexual terms had effects in every sphere of human life, from politics on the widest scale down to acts of private imagination. Interpreting a scene on the Greek Eurymedon vase (R1155) that depicts a naked and erect Greek warrior approaching from behind a bent-over Persian archer, K. J. Dover (1978) reads the scene as saying, "We've buggered the Persians" (p. 105). From foreign war through domestic slavery to marriage or erotic lust, power was expressed through sexual coercion.

David Mattingly (2010) observes that "the psychological taint of sexual humiliation and degradation has been a powerful tool for sustaining social difference between rulers and ruled in many colonial societies" (p. 95). In the implementation of victory, entire cities were given over to soldiers to plunder. Rape of defeated populations was part of the likely condition of defeat. Literature occasionally records the rape of elite women, but seldom of nonelites (Livy 38.24.1–11). In the case of Boudicca, Queen of the Iceni, the rape of her daughters as reported by Tacitus was an enactment of sexual violence to put a subject population in its place by sexually dominating its elite women (*Annals* 14.31–35). Defeated soldiers were also subject to sexual violence. The phenomenon that the Eurymedon vase illustrates is demonstrated in Justinian's *Digest* in a section recording legislation from the high Roman Empire that lists persons unable to bring accusations in court (3.1.1.5). Among them are disreputable men who willingly have sex in a womanish way, that is, who are the receivers of penetration. An exception, however, is made for men who are raped [*stupratus*] by robbers or enemies. The assumption of the passage is clear: losing combatants (and those unfortunate enough to fall into the hands of highwaymen) will routinely be the recipients of sexual violence (*Digest* 3.1.1.6). On a larger scale, conquest itself was portrayed visually in terms of sexual violence. In the Sebasteion of Aphrodisias, Claudius's conquest of Britain and Nero's of Armenia are depicted as a muscular military man—the emperor idealized and personifying the empire—physically dominating a naked or seminaked woman cast as the personification of the defeated nation (on this trope, see Lopez, 2008, pp. 43–45). "Phallic aggression" was the way in which Romans conceived the extension of their political hegemony. It was also the practical consequence of Roman victory at the local level of defeated populations, but in the *longue durée* the practice of enslavement subjected people to more enduring sexual violence.

Varro's description of the slave as "a speaking tool" seems intended to encapsulate the contradiction of slavery: human and chattel (*Agriculture* 1.17.1). This contradiction is the factor that normalized the sexual use of slaves in the Roman Empire. Edmonson (2010) notes "it was simply taken for granted that part of the degradation of being a slave involved gratifying the sexual urges of one's master" (p. 352). Artemidorus's manual of dreams offers an interpretation of sex with one's slave: the gender of the participants is not important, but who penetrates whom is. To dream of penetrating one's slave indicates a dreamer in proper possession of his household. To dream of being penetrated by one's slave indicates improper submission to a slave, just as one would be sexually violated by an enemy (*Oneirocritica* 88.5–12; see Richlin, 2006, p. 340). The sexual acts are not criticized; only the position of the dreamer within the implied hierarchy is significant. Prostitution as well was an industry that depended overwhelmingly on slave and subaltern labor. From the entourage that followed the Roman legions to the workers of the urban brothels, prostitution was never outlawed. Paul's condemnation of having sexual relations with a prostitute in 1 Corinthians 6:15–16 criticizes the pollution to the client, not the morality of the endeavor. The sexual coercion endemic to prostitution was not the subject of moral critique in Paul's time. Such sexual coercion was basic to the status of slave (Richlin, 2006, p. 349).

Christian admonitions to slaves cannot be taken apart from this context: witness the second-century command in Peter's name: "Slaves, be submissive in all fear to your masters, not only to the kind and gentle but also to the crooked or perverted" (1 Pet 2:18 lit.). This advice could not function without reference to the practice of masters making sexual use of slaves. Likewise, the situation of Onesimus inferred from the letter to Philemon must include the master's prerogative of the sexual use of slaves. Marchal (2011) has argued that the usefulness of Onesimus would include a "good for intercourse" (Phlm 26, 27 lit.) dimension that most interpretations of Philemon occlude (p. 761). To be a slave was to be socially dishonored, socially alienated, and fungible in every way (Stewart, 2012, pp. 50–53). Amy Richlin's translation of a passage from the Petronius's *Satyricon* highlights the condition of the slave: Trimalchio proclaims, "I was my master's sex toy (*ad delicias*) for fourteen years. What the master orders is not shameful. I also serviced the mistress" (75.11). The last sentence, concerning the slave and the mistress, twists the knife in the sexual anxieties of the elite Roman male.

Christian texts advocating sexual renunciation do not fully escape this morality of sexual activity governed primarily by positions of class and power. The *Acts of Andrew* depict the struggles of the new Christian Maximilla to keep herself pure from the sexual advances of her non-Christian husband Aegeates. The sexual usability of slaves is the key to Maximilla's strategy. Maximilla dresses her slave Eucleia as a dissimulating substitute for herself in sexual relations with her husband, the proconsul Aegeates. It is only Eucleia's boasting among other slaves that eventually lets the truth of the matter out. As a result, Aegeates mutilates Eucleia, starves her, and has other slaves who know of his dishonor crucified. Maximilla's deception has run its course, but there is no hint in the text that Maximilla's treatment of slaves as sexual tools (speaking or unspeaking) should be criticized. The plot of this Christian narrative is built on the absolute normalcy of slaves as sexual objects deployed equally on behalf of the purposes of Christian or non-Christian owners (*Acts Andr.* 4.339–341).

The nonelite imagination of sexual relations is difficult to access, but Greek and Coptic magical papyri offer some view. In one example, a spirit is commissioned to fetch for a man a sexual partner. She is to be deprived of all abilities to eat, sleep, or concentrate until she comes to the client of the spell and fulfills his wishes; until that point the spirit is to "burn her guts, her breast, her liver, her breath, her bones, her marrow" (PGM IV.1496–1595). In the words of another magical spell, the desired disposition is that the fetched lover be "submissive" (*hypotassomenên*; PGM VII.593–619). Christian erotic spells work within the same understanding of love and sex. ACM 73 (Heidelberg Kopt 684) is set in the mouth of the famous North African bishop Cyprian. His spell curses its female object with the desire, agitation, and sleeplessness so common in Greco-Roman erotic spells and adds alienation from the father, son, and Holy Spirit. The spell adjures the Angel Gabriel (who is elsewhere put into this role for his success in getting Mary and Joseph together) to "hang her by the hair of her head and the lashes of her eyes. Bring her to him N son of N, in longing and desire, and she remains in them forever as you [Gabriel] brought the good news of the father to the pure virgin Mary as a true and actual message, so may the good news be come true and actual for me." The second good news is a desirable woman brought to submission through every manner of agony.

At the extremity of Christian and Jewish imagination, the beginnings and the ends of the world, sexual coercion remained. In narratives of the beginnings of the world, the transgression of the watchers in Genesis and *1 Enoch* set sexual violence at the origin of evil (Gen 6:1–4; *1 En.* 6.1–9.11). Similarly, texts of demiurgical speculation such as the *Apocryphon of John, Hypostasis of the Archons,* and *On the Origin of the World* depict scenes of the rape of Eve or of Sophia to narrate the confusion of essences in the nature of humans and the dreadful transgression at the foundation of the human world. Eschatological texts such as Revelation deploy images of sexual violence to condemn its opponents and to communicate the judgment of the world (Marshall, 2010). Apocalypses attributed to Peter and Paul, as well as the *Acts of Thomas,* depict punishments corresponding to sexually unacceptable practices in their tours of hell (Brooten, 1998, pp. 303–314).

Assessment. The Roman world was characterized by frequent and largely accepted sexual violence. Christianity showed at best a very limited power to modify these conditions. In many ways it reinforced them

through the sacralization of codes of gender hierarchy and obedience in marriage. Although Christians self-consciously cultivated sexual virtue, Peter Brown (1988) notes that "clergy showed themselves as little prepared as the philosophers had been to overturn the institution of household slavery. By their hesitation on that issue, they doomed themselves from the outset to an honorable ineffectiveness on the issue of marital fidelity. Most infidelity took the form of sleeping with one's own slaves: it was simply one assertion, among so many others, of the master's power over the bodies of his dependents" (p. 23). The power dynamic to which Brown refers underwrote a wider scope of sexual violence than the particular coercion of sex with one's own slaves. In its foundations, it was not substantially challenged or changed by Christianity in the Roman Empire.

[*See also* Legal Status, *subentries on* New Testament *and* Roman World; Paul; Political Leadership, *subentry* Roman World; Sexual Transgression, *subentries on* Early Church *and* Roman World; *and* Sexual Violence, *subentries on* Early Church *and* New Testament.]

BIBLIOGRAPHY

Brooten, Bernadette J. *Love Between Women: Early Christian Responses to Female Homoeroticism.* Chicago: University of Chicago Press, 1998.

Brown, Peter. *The Body and Society: Men, Women, and Sexual Renunciation in Early Christianity.* New York: Columbia University Press, 1988.

Dover, K. J. *Greek Homosexuality.* London: Duckworth, 1978.

Edmondson, Jonathan. "Slavery and the Roman Family." In *The Cambridge World History of Slavery,* Vol. 1, *The Ancient Mediterranean World,* edited by Keith Bradley and Paul Cartledge, pp. 337–361. New York: Cambridge University Press, 2010.

Joshel, Sandra R. *Slavery in the Roman World.* New York: Cambridge University Press, 2010.

Krug, Etienne G., ed. *World Report on Violence and Health.* Geneva: World Health Organization, 2002.

Kuefler, Matthew. *The Manly Eunuch: Masculinity, Gender Ambiguity, and Christian Ideology in Late Antiquity.* Chicago: University of Chicago Press, 2001.

Lopez, Davina C. *Apostle to the Conquered: Reimagining Paul's Mission.* Paul in Critical Contexts. Minneapolis: Fortress, 2008.

Marchal, Joseph A. "The Usefulness of an Onesimus: The Sexual Use of Slaves and Paul's Letter to Philemon." *Journal of Biblical Literature* 130, no. 4 (2011): 749–770.

Marshall, John W. "Gender and Empire: Sexualized Violence in John's Anti-Imperial Apocalypse." In *Feminist Companion to the Apocalypse of John*, edited by Amy-Jill Levine with Maria Mayo Robbins, pp. 17–32. New York: T&T Clark, 2010.

Mattingly, David J. *Imperialism, Power, and Identity: Experiencing the Roman Empire*. Princeton, N.J.: Princeton University Press, 2010.

Richlin, Amy. "Sexuality in the Roman Empire." In *A Companion to the Roman Empire*, edited by David S. Potter, pp. 327–353. Malden, Mass.: Blackwell, 2006.

Stewart, Roberta. *Plautus and Roman Slavery*. Malden, Mass.: Blackwell, 2012.

John W. Marshall

New Testament

In the New Testament, sexual violence is not overt but implied. Such violence is treated metaphorically (as in the subjection and burning of the "Whore of Babylon"; see Rev 18:9–19), or the possibility of such violence is revealed indirectly through models of submission to authority and the valorization of suffering with Christ (as in the household codes; see Eph 5:21–6:9 and 1 Peter 2:18–21). Thus, discussion about sexual violence in the New Testament requires interpreting texts within the sociohistorical context of the patriarchal culture of the first-century Roman Empire and applying modern sociological inquiries about sexual abuse and domestic violence in texts about adultery, divorce, prostitution, marriage, celibacy, and implications of pederasty.

In Roman antiquity, the male head of house had absolute authority (*patria potestas*) over the bodies of the members of his household, which included his wife, children, and slaves. Though Jewish culture also was based on a patriarchal model, Jewish constructions of fatherhood and sexual relationships did not emphasize complete dominance and entitlement. Within this context of often-conflicting gentile and Jewish values, the New Testament's attitude toward sexuality and gender roles is, at times, ambiguous. Throughout the New Testament, the power dynamics of gender and sexuality fluctuate from idealizations of social equality to the re-inscription of traditional hierarchies of subservience, particularly for women and slaves, in a context of potential violence.

Patriarchal Society and Domestic Violence. In Roman antiquity, one of the expressions of elite males' social and economic power was sexual dominance. That the ancient construction of sexuality perceived the male as "penetrator" and the female as "penetrated" reveals active and passive roles conducive to male control over females (or over subordinate males who took the passive role of a female). Males could exercise their dominance and sexual entitlement by means of force, which by modern sensibilities would be considered sexual abuse or rape; in ancient times, however, such force was merely a dominant male's prerogative.

The New Testament was written by and for people of a subordinate social and religious group (primarily Jewish) in the context of the imperial power of Hellenistic Rome. The nascent church frequently had to struggle with pressures to conform to both Jewish and gentile cultural ideals. The contextual ambiguity can be seen in several examples. On the one hand, Jesus included women among his followers and modeled a life of celibacy, adoptive kinship, and nonviolence, and the apostle Paul set forth an ideal of sexual mutuality (1 Cor 7), with gender equality in Christ (Gal 3:28). Paul also named women among apostles and his co-workers (e.g., Rom 16:1, 3, 6–7, 12, 15; Phil 4:2–3), and he used the metaphor of slavery as a model for all Christians to follow, while proclaiming master-slave equality in Christ (Gal 3:28; Phlm). (Such notions of equality were already present in some strands of nascent Judaism and in Greek philosophies.) On the other hand, Jesus's inner circle of twelve disciples was all male, and Paul exhorted his congregations to follow some of the dominant culture's gendered conventions of female subordination (1 Cor 11:3–16; 14:34–36). The deutero-Pauline and Catholic Epistles depict an even more hierarchical relationship between men, women, children, and slaves than do the undisputed letters of Paul.

That Paul apparently followed some of the hierarchical gender roles of his time, despite his exhortations to mutuality in marriage and his inclusion of women as church leaders, can be seen in his injunction that women wear head coverings in worship "because of the angels" (1 Cor 11:3–10). The meaning of this instruction has been much disputed: perhaps the sight of uncovered women was an offense to the angelic host believed to be present in worship (illustrated in the Qumran text *Songs of the Sabbath Sacrifice*). Alternatively, uncovered women might be sexually tempting to these angels, prompting sexual violation (see Gen 6:1–4; 1 Enoch 6–7). Women's sexuality seems to have been perceived as dangerous and provocative, something to be hidden from males and controlled by males (so that males would not lose control).

The household codes. The *haustafeln* or "household rules" (Eph 5:22–6:9; Col 3:18–4:1; 1 Pet 2:11–3:12; see also 1 Cor 11:3, 11–12) define Christian domestic ideals that closely follow patriarchal Roman household mores, in which a wife, biological offspring, adoptees, and slaves are under the control of the male head of house. While there is evidence that a woman could be the matriarch of a household (Lydia in Acts 16:14–15), far more typical was the patriarch. In the era of the New Testament, the Roman emperor Augustus bore the title *Pater Patriae* (Father of the nation), an authoritative model for all socially and economically dominant men; in effect, each head of house was emperor of his domain. The *paterfamilias* had the authority, if he so desired, to use violence against members of his household. The first-century Roman moralist Valerius Maximus cites several illustrative stories of husbands' violent punishment of their wives for various infractions, including drunkenness (*Memorable Deeds and Sayings* 6.3.9–12).

The hierarchy established by the dominant culture, mirrored in the household codes, provided opportunity for clandestine abuse. The ideals of the New Testament household codes are meant to guard against such abuse, because they call for mutual respect and love between husband and wife, benevolence to children and slaves, with the male head of house exhorted to mimic Christ in his self-giving love for the church. However, the language of headship gives the husband/father the sort of authority that can result in abuse, including sexual violence, toward women, children, and slaves. Because the

New Testament tells wives to submit to their husbands, modern pastors and social workers counsel many battered women who refuse to leave abusive relationships. And, because of the idealistic situation portrayed by the New Testament household codes, many churches tend to overlook or blatantly ignore signs of sexual and domestic abuse.

Slaves. The household codes also include injunctions aimed at slaves, exhorting them to be obedient and submissive to their masters. In a particularly difficult text, 1 Peter 2:18–21 says that slaves will receive credit for submitting to harsh masters, because when they endure unjust beatings, they are suffering in emulation of Christ. Feminist scholars have argued that the model of emulating the suffering of Christ justifies the violent abuse of those who take a subordinate role.

The household codes reflect the low social status of slaves, who are at the bottom of the Roman hierarchy. Slaves had neither personal rights nor ownership of their own bodies, and so were in a particularly vulnerable position physically as well as socially. In Roman culture, the head of household had sexual access to his slaves, both male and female. Modern readers would consider this sort of sexual dominance rape, but in the ancient world a slave did not have any personal rights and must obey his/her master or mistress in all things. A slave's body was considered the master's property, to be bought, sold, loaned, and used in whatever way the master saw fit.

Slaves could receive violent retribution for disobedience (which could include resisting sexual advances). Roman literature provides examples of the violent punishment of slaves for disobedience. In some cases, punishment involved impalement and crucifixion, so that the male prerogative to show dominance through penetration was translated metaphorically to piercing the flesh (impalement or crucifixion) in the slave's execution.

Adultery and Divorce. In the year 18 B.C.E., Octavian (Augustus) passed a law (*lex Julia*), which allowed fathers to kill their own daughters and their lovers caught in adultery, and under some circumstances, allowed husbands to kill their wives' adulterous partners. The law was modified in 9 C.E. by the passage of the *lex Papia Poppaea*, yet it provides a clear iteration of the patriarch's and husband's power to arbitrate marital infractions and mete out punishment for sexual violations, a right that was not granted to women.

Jewish law had always forbidden adultery (Exod 20:14). The New Testament story of Joseph deciding to divorce Mary quietly, without public disgrace, when he believed she was guilty of adultery (Matt 1:19) demonstrates the possibility of nonviolent separation. The story of Jesus forgiving the adulterous woman (John 7:53–8:11) also provides an example of mercy and forgiveness, while illustrating a case of inequality of retribution against the male and female partners, as the story makes no mention of the man involved. (However, we do not know from this isolated example if the situation was normative.) In the context of the New Testament, both the Matthean and Johannine stories of suspected adultery illustrate that judgment and punishment were mainly a male prerogative. The same was true in Roman law and custom. A wife could not accuse her husband of adultery, but a husband or father could punish his wife or daughter, sometimes violently, for acts of adultery.

A common result of adultery was divorce. In past generations of New Testament scholarship, divorce was portrayed as an act of violence against women: they were cast out to live in destitution, sometimes having to resort to prostitution. Recent scholarship has shown this scenario to be false. Jewish women had marriage contracts (*ketuboth*) that gave them legal rights to whatever money or goods they brought to the marriage. In the New Testament period, Roman women also had legal access to portions of the household wealth and could divorce their husbands. Thus, when Jesus forbids divorce (Mark 10:2–9; Matt 19:3–9), he is not setting a new liberating standard for helpless women. Rather, he is reinforcing a much older value (Gen 2:24). In modern times, the New Testament injunction against divorce sometimes proves to be nonliberative and conducive to ongoing violence, when couples stay in abusive relationships.

Prostitution and Pornography. The New Testament indicates the low social ranking of prostitutes, who were among the "sinners" and tax collectors, and other outcasts (Matt 21:31–32; Luke 15:30), although the prostitute Rahab is twice mentioned as a model of faith (Heb 11:31; Jas 2:25). It is a common misconception then and now that prostitutes choose to be prostitutes; the majority of women (or men) who turn to prostitution do so as a last resort when they cannot otherwise make a living. Except for an elite few, the typical prostitute has a very low income, poor healthcare, and suffers abuse from handlers and clients.

The Whore of Babylon. The New Testament inherits the Old Testament attitude toward "whoredom" as the moral equivalent to adultery (e.g., Ezek 16; Hos 2), particularly in the book of Revelation. The Jewish-Christian author of Revelation compares the city of Rome to Babylon (a reference to the Babylonian destruction of Jerusalem in 587/86 B.C.E.), and describes Babylon as a "whore" (*pornē*). Rome, pictured as "the great whore" (*tēs pornēs tēs megalēs*) is a grotesque, lascivious, obscenely wealthy, and powerful woman who persecutes the saints (Rev 17:1–6). The writer of Revelation hopes for the destruction of the whore (Rome) and the victory of Christ; but his vision for this victory includes the sexually violent destruction of this female figure, who is stripped naked and burned with fire (Rev 17:16; 18:8–10; 19:3).

Artistic portrayals of the Whore of Babylon through the ages have accentuated her provocative sexual demeanor as she straddles a "beast" and raises her goblet of the saints' blood. Some of the portrayals verge on the pornographic (the term "pornography" comes from the Greek word *pornē*, for prostitute, and *porneia*, for illicit sexual acts). Revelation's description of her violent destruction is a spectacle that vindicates the bloody martyrdoms of Christians who have died under the Romans, but the fact that the violent imagery is directed at a highly sexualized female image reinscribes cultural assumptions that tolerate abuse of women, often based on misconceptions about the uncontrolled, dangerous sexuality of women. The violent abuse committed by God as jealous husband toward Israel as metaphorical wife who has prostituted herself or "whored" after other gods (Ezek 16) is echoed in the violent destruction of the Whore of Babylon, who is a symbol of idolatry. Within the context of patriarchal power, such exultation in the destruction of a woman (even a metaphorical one), by the authority of God, is dangerous to real women.

Jezebel. The book of Revelation also resorts to language of sexual violence in the treatment of Jezebel, a woman prophet from Thyatira (Rev. 2:20–23). Her real name is unknown, but she is called Jezebel to conjure the image of the idolatrous queen who opposed Elijah (1 Kgs 19:1–3; 21:23), and who, after painting her eyes, was thrown from a window, trampled, and eaten by dogs (2 Kgs 9:30–37). Revelation says the false prophetess Jezebel will be thrown, not out a window but onto a bed (an insinuation of rape), and her children will be murdered (Rev 2:22–23). While violent ends await other false prophets (Rev 19:2–21), only the two female opponents receive sexualized violent retribution.

Woman clothed with the sun. A third female character, "the woman clothed with the sun" (who seems to be a symbol of the mother of Jesus), suffers sexual violence when she is pursued by a dragon while she is in labor (Rev 12:1–6). The imagery is symbolic of Rome's threat to the church, but the woman's vulnerability is couched in terms of sexual violence: a woman giving birth attracts pursuit and destruction. The dragon threatens to consume her child while she is in a most vulnerable situation and unable to flee; paradoxically, it is also a consummate moment of female sexuality, while she is giving life. Although she and her child are rescued, she must flee into the wilderness without her child (Rev 12:5–6).

The virgin church. The book of Revelation associates life in the age to come, symbolized by the New Jerusalem, with the virginal purity of both men and women. The 144,000 virgin men who have not defiled themselves with women (Rev 14:3–4) and the bride of the Lamb (Rev 19:7; 21:2,9–10) are virginal metaphors for the church. As the book of Revelation dispatches Jezebel and the Whore of Babylon in the context of implied rape, pornographic violence, and burning, it upholds a standard of virginity or sexual purity for those who are worthy to enter the wedding feast of the Lamb and the New Jerusalem. Thus, Revelation depicts female sexuality in terms of graphic violence or idealized purity, even as it depicts the triumphant church as the 144,000 virgin males entering the bride, which is, in itself, an implied sexual act. The Christian tradition of the perpetual virginity of the mother of Jesus (based on Matt 1; Luke 1) and Paul's commendation of those who remain virgins (1 Cor 7) also contributes to the idealization of virginity.

Pederasty, Eunuchs, and Celibacy. Pederasty was a common practice in the Greco-Roman world, except among Jews. An adult male might establish a patron-relationship with a youth. Part of this relationship was sexual. In modern times, such a relationship would be considered abusive and illegal, but in gentile Greco-Roman culture, it was common and accepted. However, Jewish culture perceived pederasty as sexual violence. Jesus advises his listeners that it is better to cut off an offending hand or foot or pluck out an eye than cause any of the "little ones" to stumble (Mark 9:42–48). While this saying can be interpreted metaphorically in reference to causing an innocent to sin, some scholars have suggested that it is a reference to pederasty. The punishment of cutting off "hand" or "foot" may then be regarded as euphemisms for genitalia. The harshness of the penalty infers the severity of the crime.

Jesus's instruction to "become eunuchs for the kingdom of heaven" (Matt 19:12) refers to celibacy, rather than actual castration, and the saying does not involve sexual violence, self-inflicted or otherwise (although the third-century church father Origen apparently took the injunction literally). That the saying about becoming a eunuch is closely followed by Jesus's instruction to become "like children" (Matt 19:13–15) reinforces the Matthean ideal of the formation of a nonreproductive "fictive" or theological family headed by God the Father. As Joseph adopts the infant Jesus into his family (Matt 1:20–21; 2:14, 20–21), and as the disciples are enjoined to call no one "father" but the Father in Heaven (Matt 23:9), the gospel suggests that adoptive—rather than biological—fatherhood is the new ideal in the Kingdom of Heaven. This policy of adoptive kinship under the fatherhood of God potentially undermines constructs of the *patria potestas* in favor of a more egalitarian community unburdened by concerns for keeping wealth in a biological family line, and without male notions of entitlement to sexual dominance and its related violence.

When the apostle Paul writes to the church at Corinth about matters of marriage and sexuality, he wishes they could all be as he is, most likely a reference to his being unmarried and celibate (1 Cor 7:7). Renunciation of marriage and family for the sake of a higher calling was already an ideal practiced by adherents of some Greek philosophies and some members of ascetic Jewish sects, such as the Essenes. Celibacy may have been a deterrent to sexual violence in some cases, but just as the high ideals of Christian marriage under the headship of Christ do not always deter domestic abuse, celibate communities can be a context for violence. The Roman Catholic church has had to admit that some celibate priests have committed acts of sexual abuse.

The New Testament and Implications of Sexual Violence for Today. Although modern attitudes toward sexuality and gender equality have changed to some extent, and more women function as the head of house and as professional and lay leaders in the church, Christian culture remains predominantly patriarchal, and biblical authority is a means of enforcing this worldview. Domestic violence, sexual violence toward women and children, abuse of prostitutes, and pornography that depicts violence against both males and females remain common phenomena in today's society.

The New Testament does not condone domestic violence or sexual abuse, but the authority of the church and the domestic hierarchy promoted in many New Testament texts causes some victims of sexual violence to be silent about their abusers, especially when those abusers are husbands, pastors, or priests. Because of its injunctions for women to be subordinate and not to divorce, domestic abuse and sexual violence occur in Christian congregations and families, despite the church's high ideals

and best intentions. The New Testament's lascivious depictions of Jezebel and the Whore of Babylon contribute to disparagement of prostitutes and toleration of violence against women. In addition, children, women, and men are victims of a worldwide black-market trade in sex slaves that thrives, largely without intervention from the church.

[*See also* Family Structures, *subentries on* New Testament *and* Roman World; Imagery, Gendered, *subentry* Apocalyptic Literature; Marriage and Divorce, *subentries on* Early Judaism *and* New Testament; Paul; *and* Race, Class, and Ethnicity, *subentry* New Testament.]

BIBLIOGRAPHY

Blickenstaff, Marianne. *While the Bridegroom Is with Them: Marriage, Family, Gender, and Violence in the Gospel of Matthew.* Journal for the Study of the New Testament: Supplement Series 292. London: T&T Clark, 2005.

Cohen, Shaye J. D., ed. *The Jewish Family in Antiquity.* Brown Judaic Studies. Atlanta: Scholars Press, 1993.

Glancy, Jennifer A. *Slavery in Early Christianity.* Oxford: Oxford University Press, 2002; Minneapolis: Fortress, 2006.

Kroeger, Catherine Clark, and Nancy Nason-Clark. *No Place for Abuse: Biblical and Practical Resources to Counteract Domestic Violence.* 2d ed. Downers Grove, Ill.: InterVarsity, 2010.

Lefkowitz, Mary R., and Maureen B. Fant. *Women's Life in Greece and Rome: A Source Book in Translation.* 2d ed. Baltimore: Johns Hopkins University Press, 1992.

Levine, Amy-Jill, ed. *A Feminist Companion to the Apocalypse of John.* London: T&T Clark, 2009.

Loader, William. *The New Testament on Sexuality.* Grand Rapids, Mich.: Eerdmans, 2012.

Matthews, Shelly, and E. Leigh Gibson, eds. *Violence in the New Testament.* New York and London: T&T Clark, 2005.

Neufeld, Thomas R. Yoder. *Killing Enmity: Violence and the New Testament.* Grand Rapids, Mich.: Baker, 2011.

Osiek, Carolyn, and Margaret Y. MacDonald. *A Woman's Place: House Churches in Earliest Christianity.* Minneapolis: Fortress, 2006.

Pippin, Tina. *Death and Desire: The Rhetoric of Gender in the Apocalypse of John.* Louisville, Ky.: Westminster John Knox, 1992.

Pomeroy, Sarah B., ed. *Plutarch's Advice to the Bride and Groom and A Consolation to His Wife.* Oxford: Oxford University Press, 1999.

Selvidge, Marla J. "Reflections on Violence and Pornography: Misogyny in the Apocalypse and Ancient Hebrew Prophecy." In *A Feminist Companion to the Hebrew Bible in the New Testament,* edited by Athalya Brenner, pp. 274–285. Sheffield, U.K.: Sheffield Academic Press, 1996.

Streete, Gail Corrington. *The Strange Woman: Power and Sex in the Bible.* Louisville, Ky.: Westminster John Knox, 1997.

Tracy, Steven R. "Patriarchy and Domestic Violence: Challenging Common Misconceptions," *Journal of the Evangelical Theological Society* 50, no. 3 (September 2007): 573–594.

Treggiari, Susan. *Roman Marriage: "Iusti Coniuges" from the Time of Cicero to the Time of Ulpian.* Oxford: Clarendon, 1991.

Marianne Blickenstaff

Early Judaism

Postexilic Jewish texts from the Apocrypha through rabbinic literature adhere to the biblical precedent of viewing sexual violence through the perspective of a female's primary male kin, whether her father, husband, or fiancé. In Jewish apocryphal, apocalyptic, and sectarian texts from Qumran, sexual violence becomes increasingly framed in terms of intermarriage and national interests. In late antique legal writings, sexual violence is discussed primarily in terms of the resultant economic damage to the father (the default custodian of a female until she is married), as well as in contexts relating to the validity of marriage initiated by rape or abduction rather than by negotiated contract. The rabbinic sages follow the deuteronomic trend of shifting legal authority over adjudicating sexual offenses from fathers, fiancés, and husbands to civil authorities like themselves.

Key Vocabulary. Biblical Hebrew lacks a word that signifies rape. *Innâ*, meaning to degrade, disgrace, or abuse, is the word that comes closest. *Innâ* is used in descriptions of Sarai's treatment of the concubine Hagar (Gen 16:6), Dinah's experience at the hands of Shechem (Gen 34:2), and Amnon's rape of his sister Tamar (2 Sam 13:12–14). The Damascus document (4Q270 Fragment 4, line 3b; ca. second century B.C.E.) is the earliest text to employ the verbal form in Aramaic to denote specifically the act of raping a female. This connotation of the verb, confined to the Hebrew use, becomes common in rabbinic literature (Talshir, 2003, p. 217).

Key Texts. Apart from the ancient legal sources that rewrite or synthesize biblical law, early Jewish interpretive literature and legal writings have occasion to discuss sexual violence only indirectly. Various early Jewish texts like Judith, Jubilees, Maccabees, the Testament of Levi, and Josephus rewrite and recount the biblical narrative of Shechem's rape of Dinah (Gen 34). The story enabled ancient interpreters to discuss their perceptions of sexual transgression and its consequences. Most of them placed Simeon's and Levi's violent response to the rape of their sister in terms of an injustice inflicted on Israel as a whole. Subsequent Jewish legal material is concerned with determining the obligations falling on the perpetrators who forced sex upon women.

Historical Background. Sexual violence is taken for granted in societies where only a minority is afforded the privileges of self-determination. This complicates the analysis of sexual violence, especially because extant texts are written from the perspective of those least likely to suffer it. The perspective of victims of sexual violence is absent from early Jewish sources. While it is likely that males and females suffered from sexual violence in antiquity, early Jewish sources attest only to its occurrence against minor males and females of all ages.

As Tal Ilan points out, one of the implicit assumptions in androcentric societies, including rabbinic Jewish society, is that "women who are raped begin by resisting the attacker but eventually even they enjoy the act" (Ilan, 2006, p. 185; cf. *y. Soṭah* 4:5, *19d*). In the Tosefta (roughly contemporaneous with the Mishnah, ca. 200 C.E.), a brief statement captures the rabbis pondering this matter: "the one who rapes and the one who seduces—What is the difference between rape and seduction? In rape he pays damages for pain, in seduction he does not pay damages for pain; Rabbi Shimon said neither [the rapist nor the seducer] pay damages for pain because it [the pain of intercourse] is inevitable. They said to him, there is no comparison between one who is taken willingly and one who is taken against her will" (*t. Ketub.* 3:8 lit.).

Second Temple Period Texts. The Temple Scroll (150–125 B.C.E.), recovered from the library of the sectarian community in Qumran, is the earliest legal document that records rulings on sexual violence and its repercussions (Temple Scroll, 11Q19, column LXVI [= fragment 15–20], line 8). Synthesizing the laws on seducing a virgin from Exodus 22:15–16 and the laws on raping a virgin from Deuteronomy 22:23–29, the Temple Scroll states: "If a man violates a young virgin who is not betrothed, and she suits him according to the Law and he lies with her and they are discovered, the man who lay with her will give the girl's father fifty silver shekels and she will be his wife, since (he raped her), and he cannot dismiss her all her life" (Martinez and Tigchelaar, 2000, p. 1052). The legal materials would leave the impression that rape is only an issue that affects marriageable young females, and, in particular, their fathers.

Michael Satlow has suggested that seduction and rape were alternative social institutions in the honor/shame based society of ancient Israel that allowed couples to marry against their parents' wishes without causing family rupture and allowing the parents to maintain a sense of family honor (2001, p. 124–132). So, if a father forbade a couple to marry, then a young woman could claim to have been seduced or raped and thus contract marriage without the father's permission.

Perhaps the earliest mention of sexual violence in a literary context is in the apocryphal book of Judith (200–100 B.C.E.). The protagonist declares she is a descendant of the tribe of Simeon and proudly invokes her ancestor's response to the perpetrators of the rape of Dinah, here understood as all the townsmen of Shechem. "Judith cried out to the Lord with a loud voice, and said: 'O Lord God of my ancestor Simeon, to whom You gave a sword to take revenge on those strangers who had torn off a virgin's clothing to defile her, and exposed her thighs to put her to shame, and polluted her womb to disgrace her; for you said, 'It shall not be done'—yet they did it" (Jdt 9:1–2). According to this tradition, the entire town participated in the rape of Dinah. This explains the collective punishment of Shechem, which merited the punishment of death on the basis of gentiles ("strangers") who threatened the integrity of Israel. Israel is threatened in precisely this way in the book of Judith. The antagonist Holofernes voices the intent to rape Judith. "For it would be a disgrace if we let such a woman go without having intercourse with her. If we do not seduce her, she will laugh at us" (Jdt 12:12).

In the Testament of Levi, Levi explains that he was zealous to kill the Shechemites not only because Shechem had violated his sister but also because the whole city was guilty of attempted rape throughout the generations. "[The townspeople] wanted to do the same thing to Sarah and Rebecca that they did to Dinah our sister" and "this is how they treated the nomadic people, seizing their wives and murdering them" (*Testament of Levi* 6:8–9, 10–11; trans. Charlesworth, 1983, vol. 1, p. 790). Again the threat of rape is magnified to an existential threat to Israel.

The *Book of Jubilees* (125–100 B.C.E.) makes this perspective on rape most explicit as it describes the rape of Dinah, recounts Simeon's and Levi's revenge, and ends with an exhortation about intermarriage: "And you, Moses, command the children of Israel and exhort them not to give any of their daughters to the gentiles and not to take for their sons any of the daughters of the gentiles because that is contemptible before the Lord" (*Jubilees* 30:11–12; trans. Charlesworth, 1983, vol. 2, p. 113).

In his retelling of the biblical account, the Jewish historian Josephus (first century C.E.), also discusses the rape of Dinah in terms of marital relations with foreigners (Josephus, *Jewish Antiquities* 1:337–338).

Translations of the Hebrew Bible into Aramaic for recitation in synagogues in Palestine also stressed the ethnic dimension of the rape of Dinah: "…it is fitting that they should say in the congregations of Israel and in their schoolhouse: 'Uncircumcised were slain on account of a virgin and servers of idols because they defiled Dinah, the daughter of Jacob…'" (*Targum Neophyti Genesis* 34:31; McNamara, 1992, p. 164).

What is notable about all of these rewritten biblical stories from the Second Temple period is that Dinah's experience of sexual violence is not the authors' concern; rather the implications of such a marital relationship for the Jewish people as a whole is foregrounded.

Because intermarriage was such a widely deplored transgression, later Jewish interpreters like the rabbis struggled to explain Esther's marriage to the Persian king Ahasuerus (Esth 3:17). The section of the Babylonian Talmud tractate Megillah known as the Esther Midrash (10b–17a) asserts that Esther was married to Mordecai and that Esther's sexual relations with the king were not consensual. Further exonerating her, the sage Abaye is quoted as saying that she was "like natural ground," i.e., utterly passive (*b. Sanh. 74b*).

The brief biblical account about Reuben and Jacob's concubine Bilhah becomes a story of sexual violence in later Jewish interpretation as well. In the *Book of Jubilees* (33:1–20) Reuben violates Bilhah while she sleeps. However, the author of Jubilees explicitly frames the crime as that of incest alone—the crime of a son illicitly engaging in sexual relations with his father's concubine. The text warns future generations of Jews that this crime is punishable by death to both parties. The sexual assault of a lower-status woman is not the text's concern.

Similarly, the *Testament of Reuben*, which shares source material with the *Book of Jubilees*, retells this episode (chs. 3–4) but casts it as an example of the general evils of women. The testament shifts some of the blame to Bilhah herself who, according to this version, was drunk and sleeping naked when Reuben came upon her, thus inviting the male gaze that led to sexual relations (Rosen-Zvi, 2006).

Likewise, Pseudo-Philo's *Biblical Antiquities* (also known as *Liber Antiquitatum Biblicarum*) recounts the gruesome gang rape and death of the Levite's concubine at Gibeah (Judg 19:1–30). It blames the victim for her end, stating that she had previously engaged in sexual relations with the Amalekites (*LAB* 45:3). Attention thus shifts from sexual violence to the crimes of idolatry and intermarriage.

In contrast, the historian Josephus was embarrassed by the brutality of the biblical story and made great effort to smooth out its rough edges (*Antiquities* 5.136). In his version, the concubine is the wife of the Levite. She dies of her own shame, expecting that her husband will hold her responsible for the sexual violence she endured.

The translation into Greek of the Book of Daniel for the Hellenistic Jewish communities of the Eastern Mediterranean prompted a few additions to the original text, including the story of Susanna, a pious Jewess, threatened with rape who manages to escape the sexual advances of two esteemed men in her community (Bar Ilan, 1998).

Texts after the Jewish Revolt and Early Legal Writings. Pseudepigraphic texts written in the aftermath of the second Jewish revolt (66–70 C.E.) make mention of rape of virgins and wives as part of the devastation of war. So 4 Ezra: "For you see that our sanctuary has been laid waste....our free men have suffered abuse, our priests have been burned to death, our Levites have gone into captivity, our virgins have been defiled, and our wives have been ravished…" (4 Ezra 10:22–23; trans. Charlesworth, 1983, vol. 1, pp. 546–547). Here, as elsewhere, rape is only conceived as a crime against virgins or wives.

Two Baruch (early second century C.E.), in its list of twelve calamities that will befall Israel before the coming of the messiah, names the tenth as the time of "rape and much violence" (2 Bar 27:11; trans. Charlesworth, 1983, vol. 1, p. 630).

A tradition preserved in the legal code of the Mishnah (ca. 200 C.E.) may reflect the historical experience of Jews living in wartorn Palestine between the first revolt in 66 C.E. and the second Jewish revolt in 132 C.E.: "If gentiles said to many women, 'give us one from among you that we may defile her, and if not we will defile you all', let them defile them all, but let them not betray to them one soul from Israel" (*m. Ter.* 8.12, trans. Danby, 1938). Whereas some have seen in this statement an allusion to Roman persecution of the Jews during their revolts, David Daube (1965) argues that such a scenario would be unbecoming of the disciplined Roman army and more likely reflects the criminal attitude of men operating outside the law. The legal background informing the Mishnah's position on handing over a woman to gentiles probably derives from Deuteronomy 24:7, the prohibition on selling a fellow Israelite to others.

In the Mishnah's tractate on marriage contracts (*Ketubbot*), girls and women remain akin to property of fathers, brothers, and husbands, and their word regarding their own sexual experience is still considered suspect. Here the Mishnah distinguishes between seduced females who are of a certain status due to their presumed virginity and those women of marginal status (the female proselyte, captive, or redeemed bondwoman) whose lack of virginity is relatively certain and thus are not protected from sexual coercion by the threat of a fine (*Ketub.* 3:2). This section of the Mishnah also fills in a lacuna left by Leviticus 18:6–20 and 20:10–21—the lists of people forbidden from sexual relations—which strikingly omits daughters (Wegner, 1988).

In its legal discussions of seduction and rape, the Mishnah enumerates four legal categories for females: 1) those under the age of three (until which age the rabbis believed a ruptured hymen could regrow), 2) minors between the age of three and nine and a day, 3) a girl between nine and a day and twelve and a half, and 4) beyond girlhood after the age of twelve and a half. The Mishnah also distinguishes the types of compensation a father of a seduced or raped girl receives. For rape, they uphold the biblically prescribed fine as well as adding compensation for indignity, blemish, and pain. If the rape and the resultant legal process take place after a female reaches maturity, she receives the compensation (*m. Ketub.* 4:1).

Elsewhere the Mishnah states that "it is all one whether a man violated or seduced a woman from among the greatest of the priestly stock or the least in Israel: he must pay fifty *selas*; but compensation for indignity and for blemish is in accordance with [the condition of life of] him that inflicts the indignity and her that suffers the indignity" (*m. 'Arak.* 3:4). In *Chattel or Person? The Status of Women in the Mishnah*, Judith Romney Wegner (1988) highlights the equivalent fines assessed of men who rape or seduce virgins. She explains that for the rabbis the loss of a women's virginity under whatever circumstance is perceived solely as an economic disadvantage to the father of the victim. In their legal rulings on this topic, she notes that the rabbis were somewhat limited by explicit biblical prescriptions that left no room for maneuver (unlike dowries, which could go to the woman herself by the time of the composition of the Mishnah). Still, Wegner asserts that the "perception of the violated girl as damaged goods takes no account of her as a person. Above all it ignores the greater heinousness of rape as compared with seduction; the suffering of the victim does not affect the criminal penalty" (Wegner, 1988, p. 24).

Talmudic Texts (Fourth–Sixth Century c.e.). In their interpretations of the biblical laws on rape and seductions in the volumes of the Talmud, the sages introduce legislation that marginally improves women's status in cases of rape (e.g., their legal rulings sometimes confirm that victims of sexual violence merit monetary compensation themselves; see *Ketub. 42a–43b*), but most of their discussions of cases of abduction and rape center on the nature of the established marital bonds (i.e., the obligations now resting on the new male owner of the woman) and the legal implications for divorce should it arise. The biblical presumption was that sex, even coerced, created a marital bond. Where the biblical law constrained the seducer or rapist of an Israelite virgin to pay the full bride price for her and marry her without the possibility of divorce, the rabbis added the caveat that the rapist could not marry her against her or father's will (see *b. Qidd. 44a*; *Yebam. 19b*).

Michael Satlow argues, "Rabbinic law makes the cryptic biblical laws workable: it gives the father the same power of veto over the marriage of his raped or seduced minor daughter; it limits marriages based on seduction or rape to those whom the rabbis deem to be legally capable of marriage to each other; it takes into account relative social standing for the payment of torts: and it assumes that the father will approve, and that a man will marry the girl he raped" (2001, p. 128).

Yifat Monnickendam (2011) has collected and analyzed the sources on rape and marriage customs in

Palestinian and Babylonian sources and concluded that rabbinic authorities strove whenever possible to invalidate rape and abduction of virgins as means for contracting marriage, consolidating marital law as an area of rabbinic jurisdiction.

The rabbis also address the issue of coerced sex in marriage. Wives are obligated to have intercourse with their husbands, and though a husband may force his wife to submit to sexual relations, most rabbis advise against it (*b. ʿErub. 100b*).

Some versions of *Toledot Yeshu*, an early medieval satire of Jesus's life, include descriptions of how his mother Mary conceived him. The narrators generally chose to exonerate Mary of any wrongdoing by describing her as a pious Jewess, unmarried or betrothed, who is raped and becomes pregnant with Jesus. Aside from Bilhah in Jubilees, it is the only Jewish document that includes a woman's poignant protestations against the experience of rape (Gager and Ahuvia, 2013). Of course, these detailed descriptions have more to do with ridiculing the Christians' foundational event than presenting a woman's perspective on coerced sex or sexual violence.

The potential for sexual violence by men against boys is mentioned in the Talmud but is apparently without legal repercussions if the boy is below the age of three or nine, depending on which authority is cited (*b. Sanh. 54b*).

Modern Debates Regarding the Materials and Categories. The concept of sexual violence is problematic for antiquity. Where most people were powerless, compulsion and its attendant violence permeated society in a way that is difficult for people in the modern West to comprehend. As Rachel Adler points out, "what modern Jews consider heinous sexual crimes carried no criminal penalties in these earlier Judaisms" (1998, p. 130). Summing up the cognitive dissonance between present and past, she writes that in "social contexts where women are regarded more as people than as commodities, rape is defined by the experience of the victim. Hence, contemporary thinking about rape emphasizes the terror, violation, and degradation experienced by its victims. But where all sexual intercourse is viewed [by men] as an expression of dominance and submission, rape seems

more normal; it is simply an improper method of acquisition" (p. 130). This interpretation is in line with Monnickendam's observations that the rabbis sought to annul actions that would circumvent their own legal guidelines for marriage (2011).

Thus, sexual violence and its legal consequences are only discussed for a narrow subsection of the population. Against minor boys, captive women, and slaves it was taken for granted.

Jacob Neusner (1998) and Judith Hauptman (1998) emphasize the improvements of rabbinic law over biblical law in the handling of sexual violence and in the treatment of women in particular. As Hauptman writes, in the Mishnah the rabbis place sexual violence in the realm of civil misdemeanors, thus making them more progressive than earlier biblical law that punished rapists with marriage to the victim. Others, like Wegner (1988), conclude that Jewish legal materials on sexual violence reflect a reality where females were treated like chattel, not full human beings.

As mentioned above, Satlow hypothesizes that rape was an alternative social institution that allowed couples to create their own bonds without shaming their parents. Historian Tal Ilan calls this theory "male fantasy that completely ignores the real dangers of rape and the extremely traumatic character of biblical and postbiblical rape laws primarily for the raped woman—who is now compelled to marry the rapist" (2004, p. 356).

Overall, early Jewish sources do not permit access to victims' experiences of sexual violence. They reveal what men in certain contexts thought, composed, and transmitted, but not a revealing portrait of individuals' experiences.

[*See also* Legal Status, *subentry* Early Judaism; *and* Male-Female Sexuality, *subentry* Early Judaism; *and* Marriage and Divorce, *subentry* Early Judaism.]

BIBLIOGRAPHY

Adler, Rachel. *Engendering Judaism: An Inclusive Theology and Ethics.* Philadelphia: Jewish Publication Society, 1998.

Bar Ilan, Meir. *Some Jewish Women in Antiquity*. Atlanta: Scholars Press, 1998.

Berlin, Adele. "Sex and the Single Girl in Deuteronomy 22." In *Mishneh Todah: Studies in Deuteronomy and Its Cultural Environment in Honor of Jeffrey H. Tigay*, edited by N. Sacher Fox, D. A. Glatt-Gilad, and M. J. Williams, pp. 95–112. Winona Lake, Ind.: Eisenbrauns, 2009.

Biale, Rachel. *Women and Jewish Law: The Essential Texts, Their History, and Their Relevance for Today*. New York: Schocken, 1984.

Charlesworth, James H. *The Old Testament Pseudepigrapha*. 2 vols. Garden City, N.Y.: Doubleday, 1983.

Danby, Herbert, trans. *The Mishnah*. London: Oxford University Press, 1938; repr. 2008.

Daube, David. *Collaboration with Tyranny in Rabbinic Law*. New York: Oxford University Press, 1965.

Feldman, Louis H. "Josephus' Portrayal (*Antiquities* 5.136–174) of the Benjaminite Affair of the Concubine and Its Repercussions (Judges 19–21)." *Jewish Quarterly Review* 90, nos. 3–4 (2000): 255–292.

Frymer-Kensky, Tikvah. "Virginity in the Bible." In *Gender and Law in the Hebrew Bible and the Ancient Near East*, pp. 79–96. Journal for the Study of the Old Testament: Supplement Series 262. Sheffield, U.K.: Sheffield Academic Press, 1998.

Gager, Johnn, and Mika Ahuvia. "Some Notes on Jesus and His Parents: From the New Testament Gospels to the Toledot Yeshu." In *Envisioning Judaism: Studies in Honor of Peter Schäfer on the Occasion of His Seventieth Birthday*, pp. 997–1019. Tübingen, Germany: Mohr Siebeck, 2013.

Hauptman, Judith. *Rereading the Rabbis: A Woman's Voice*. Boulder, Colo.: Westview, 1998.

Ilan, Tal. "Jewish Marriage in Antiquity by Michael Satlow." *AJS Review* 28, no. 2 (2004): 354–356.

Ilan, Tal. *Silencing the Queen: The Literary Histories of Shelamzion and Other Jewish Women*. Tübingen, Germany: Mohr Siebeck, 2006.

Kugel, James. *Traditions of the Bible: A Guide to the Bible as It Was at the Start of the Common Era*. Cambridge, Mass.: Harvard University Press, 1998.

Loader, William. *The Pseudepigrapha on Sexuality: Attitudes towards Sexuality in Apocalypses, Testaments, Legends, Wisdom, and Related Literature*. Grand Rapids, Mich.: Eerdmans, 2011.

Martinez, Florentino Garcia, and Eibert J. C. Tigchelaar, eds. *Dead Sea Scrolls*. Leiden, The Netherlands: Brill, 2000.

McNamara, Martin, ed. and trans. *Targum Neofiti 1, Genesis. Translated with Apparatus and Notes*. Collegeville, Minn.: Liturgical Press, 1992.

Monnickendam, Yifat. "Halakhic Issues in the Writings of the Syriac Church Fathers Ephrem and Aphrahat, Talmud." Ph.D. diss, Bar Ilan University, 2011.

Neusner, Jacob. *How the Rabbis Liberated Women*. Atlanta: Scholars Press, 1998.

Rosen-Zvi, Ishay. "Bilhah the Temptress: The Testament of Reuben and 'The Birth of Sexuality.'" *Jewish Quarterly Review* 96, no. 1 (Winter 2006) 65–94.

Satlow, Michael L. *Jewish Marriage in Antiquity*. Princeton, N.J.: Princeton University Press, 2001.

Segal, Eliezer. *The Babylonian Esther Midrash: A Critical Commentary*. 3 vols. Atlanta: Scholars Press, 1994.

Talshir, David. "On the Use of אנס in Aramaic and in Hebrew." *Meghillot: Studies in the Dead Sea Scrolls* 3 (2003): 205–229 [Hebrew].

Wegner, Judith Romney. *Chattel or Person? The Status of Women in the Mishnah*. New York: Oxford University Press, 1988.

Mika Ahuvia

Early Church

Christian communities developed within cultures that held long-standing views about sexual violence. Forcible intercourse with a woman was viewed primarily as a crime against her father or husband. Often there was no legal distinction between consensual and forced sexual relations. Unmarried female victims frequently had to marry their rapists. Male victims of homosexual rape could be deprived of the right to participate in civic life. Human trafficking, prostitution, sexual exploitation of male and female slaves, and the abuse of prisoners were tolerated.

For Christians and non-Christians alike, the honor of a woman and her family was assessed in terms of her chastity and modesty. A respectable woman was expected to have *pudor*, Latin for "modesty" and "shame." Sexually available women such as female slaves, prostitutes, and musicians were viewed as lacking *pudor*. A woman from an upstanding family was expected to be a virgin prior to marriage and sexually faithful to her husband within marriage. Sexual contact—or the suspicion of sexual contact—threatened her honor, even if she did not consent. In a well-known Roman story, the matron Lucretia was sexually assaulted by Sextus Tarquinius (sixth century B.C.E.) and restored her honor by committing suicide.

Christian experiences of sexual violence during persecution, martyrdom, and warfare caused some authors to challenge traditional beliefs about victims' dishonor, arguing that victims retained their innocence and honor. Others believed it was virtually impossible for heterosexual rape to occur without victims provoking it, consenting to it, enjoying it, or sinning in some way.

Ancient Laws and Terminology. Studying sexual violence in antiquity is complicated by differences between ancient and modern understandings about sexual abuse. Reliance on translations of ancient texts, especially outdated translations, can compound the confusion. In Roman law, *stuprum* ("disgrace," "defilement") referred to unlawful sexual relations outside marriage, particularly fornication. The Greek equivalent of *stuprum* was *phthora* ("corruption"). *Stuprum* was usually not used for a man's sexual use of his own slave, a lower-status concubine, or a prostitute. The Latin term closest in meaning to modern concepts of "rape" (defined herein as forcible vaginal, anal, or oral sexual penetration) is *per vim stuprum*, "defilement by force." Sometimes *violare* ("to violate") was used to refer to forcible intercourse, but it could also denote illicit sexual relations without coercion or force. Laws varied at different times and places, but, depending on the victim's social standing, *per vim stuprum* could be punished by execution, exile, fines paid to the victim's family, or forfeiture of property. Frequently, to salvage family honor, an unmarried victim's parents chose to marry her to her rapist rather than prosecuting him.

Raptus, the Latin cognate of the English word "rape," means theft of property or abduction of a person. The Greek equivalent was *harpagē*. Whether or not sexual assault occurred, abducted women usually experienced dishonor and social shame. Frequently men abducted and raped prospective brides to force families to consent to the marriage. *Raptus* also referred to cases where a woman left with another person voluntarily, without the consent of her father or guardian. A man who eloped with a woman without her father's consent was guilty of *raptus*. Thus it is difficult for modern historians to accurately distinguish between consensual and nonconsensual cases of *raptus*.

Civil law imposed harsh penalties for abductors and sometimes for victims as well. In *Codex Theodosianus* 9.24.1, a law enacted in 326 C.E., Emperor Constantine decreed capital punishment for both perpetrators and victims, stating that the women were to blame for venturing outdoors. The law asserted that even if the abductor broke down the door and seized a woman who was inside her home, she could have prevented abduction by physical resistance or screaming for help. In cases of forcible abduction, this law allowed for a lesser penalty for victims, who were deprived of inheritances rather than executed. Later laws, more sympathetic toward victims, awarded women the property of their abductors, who were executed.

One of the Novels ("new laws") of Emperor Justinian (ca. 483–565 C.E.) dealt with abduction of nuns, deaconesses, and other female ascetics. According to Novel 123.43, a man who seduced, forcibly abducted, or raped such a woman was to be executed. The law did not distinguish between consensual and nonconsensual cases. The victim was confined to a female monastery where she could be guarded. Her property was confiscated and given to her monastic community, probably to prevent situations in which women were abducted for marriage and, by extension, for their property. The rapist or seducer's property was also confiscated and turned over to the woman's monastery.

Unwanted sexual advances could be prosecuted as *iniuria* ("injury"), a legal category that included physical violence as well as verbal offenses to one's dignity, such as slander or insult. A man could be charged with *iniuria* for accosting a virgin, married woman, or widow unless he could persuade the court she had been dressed as a prostitute or other sexually available woman. Homosexual rape of an upstanding male citizen was a capital offense. A legal guardian who had sexual intercourse with his female ward could be deported and his property seized. In the fourth century C.E., sexual abuse of a preadolescent girl was punished by exile. Forcible intercourse with someone else's slave normally resulted in a fine paid to the owner. When a freeborn woman had sexual relations with her male slave, the slave was presumed to have consented, resulting in both parties being subject to execution.

If she were subjected to marital rape or battering, a woman's best recourse was the intervention of her birth family, which could put social or political pressure on husbands. In the case of divorce, the woman's dowry had to be returned, so there were financial incentives to treat one's wife well. However, if a birth family refused to intervene or a woman's social status was lower than her husband's, she had few options for protection.

Sexual Abuse of Martyrs. Numerous ancient sources deal with sexual violence inflicted upon Christians persecuted for their faith. Some documents may reflect historical events, but most writings are embellished literary accounts emphasizing God's miraculous protection of women threatened with rape. In the Greco-Roman world, male and female prisoners were often assaulted by sexually abusive guards. Persecuted Christians could experience rape, public nudity, sexual mutilation, or forced prostitution. Sometimes the rape of female prisoners and castration of male prisoners were enacted in arenas and amphitheaters for public entertainment. The First Letter of Clement to the Corinthians, by Clement of Rome (d. ca. 99 C.E.), mentioned Christian women abused as "Danaids," a reference to the daughters of the Greek god Daneus, who were given as prizes to winners of a footrace.

In *Apology* 50.12, Tertullian (ca. 160–225 C.E.), writing in North Africa, reported that a Christian woman had been condemned to prostitution in a brothel. It is not known how frequently this form of punishment occurred, but Christians popularized stories of God protecting virgin martyrs such as Agnes of Rome (early fourth century C.E.) from sexual assault by brothel patrons.

In some literary accounts, women threatened with sexual violence insisted that their bodies and souls would not be "polluted" even if they were raped. Other stories suggested that rape subjects women to spiritual danger. In a Syriac narrative, characters

expressed concern that women raped by Roman soldiers would "lose the reward of their ascetic life" (Brock and Harvey, 1987, p. 158). Some early Christians praised women who committed suicide rather than endure rape, though later theologians expressed discomfort with this.

Most "passions" (accounts of suffering and martyrdom) were written decades after periods of persecution, to emphasize God's power, commend celibacy, and encourage readers to resist sexual temptation. The female martyr, usually a virgin, was Christ's faithful bride, whose divine bridegroom protected her from rape. For instance, Lucia of Sicily (d. ca. 303 C.E.) was condemned to die by collective rape ("gang rape"), but the men were unable to abuse her because her body remained immoveable. Such accounts conveyed moral lessons: if the virgin martyr retained her virginity despite being captured by armed guards, then the reader should be able to remain chaste when faced with less overwhelming forces.

Forced nudity of martyrs as sexual abuse. Male athletes regularly competed unclothed, but public nudity was considered shameful for women. Passion narratives told about women martyrs stripped and compelled to "compete" in arenas against dangerous animals. Persecutors intended forced nudity as sexual violence and sexual shaming, but some Christian writers encouraged readers to resist this cultural understanding. In Syriac accounts, authors insisted that women martyrs stripped and exposed to public view were not shamed, since God had created female bodies and the women would have retained their modesty if possible (Brock and Harvey, 1987, pp. 76, 110, 165). Other Christians shared the societal view that female nudity was shameful but claimed that God shielded women from view with clouds of fire or struck the eyes of lustful voyeurs with lightning.

Sexual mutilation of Christian martyrs. Historical accounts mention sexual mutilation of male and female martyrs. In *Apology* 15.4–5, Tertullian said he personally witnessed the public castration of a man forced to play the role of a eunuch attendant of the goddess Cybele. Christian literature contains graphic accounts of the mutilation and amputation of women's breasts. These stories' sexually sadistic elements have caused modern interpreters to characterize this literature as pornography for the titillation of male audiences.

Sexual Violence in the Apocryphal Acts. Beginning in the second century, "acts" of the various apostles became popular. Reminiscent of the New Testament Acts of the Apostles, but filled with more adventure, intrigue, and convoluted plots, these non-canonical accounts of apostles' lives and deaths are called the Apocryphal Acts. Most scholars agree that they were inspired by Hellenistic novels featuring abductions, pirate attacks, and threats of rape. In the second-century *Acts of Paul and Thecla*, Thecla fights off a sexual attack by a prominent citizen of Antioch. In later additions to the legend, Thecla, now an elderly woman living in a remote cave, escapes from a gang of rapists by disappearing into a miraculous opening in a rock. Though most Christian narratives emphasized the youth and beauty of women threatened by rape, this account recognizes the reality that older women, too, were at risk for sexual violence.

Marital rape in the Apocryphal Acts. The Apocryphal Acts promoted marital celibacy as the Christian ideal. A typical character is the fiancée or wife who becomes Christian and then refuses to have sexual relations with her pagan husband. Though these are fictional accounts filled with miraculous rescues, they may reflect a social situation in which Christian women desiring celibacy faced the threat of marital rape. In the *Acts of Thomas* 9.98, a husband tried to rape his wife, who ran away naked and slept in her female servant's room. The *Acts of Andrew* 24 relates a story in which a man did not dare to force his wife, since her status was higher than his, and he feared her family's retaliation. In the *Acts of John* 63, a woman named Drusiana became committed to celibacy; in response, her husband locked her up, threatening to kill her. Eventually he converted and agreed to celibacy. Since, in these Acts, the ideal male convert respects his wife's wishes, the stories probably were used to instruct Christian husbands not to harass or force their wives. The audience may have included women who themselves were subjected to marital rape, so the words of a female protagonist in

the *Acts of Thomas* 13.152 perhaps brought comfort: "You have power over my body; do to it as you please, but my soul I will not destroy with you" (Elliott, p. 503). Christian literature tended not to condemn marital rape per se, but instead rebuked husbands' attempts to force wives who had made a commitment to celibacy.

Church Regulations and Responses to Sexual Violence. Though sexual violence perpetrated by Christians was often ignored or tolerated, church leaders responded in unofficial ways, through sermons and moral exhortation, and in official ways, through church discipline. Many canons (church rules) prescribed set amounts of time that offenders were excluded from receiving communion. Sometimes bishops intervened in situations to prevent or punish sexual abuse.

Abduction marriage and rape. In the Mediterranean region, many marriages began with abduction and sexual assault. Basil the Great (ca. 330–379 C.E.), the bishop of Caesarea, wrote harshly about a man who had abducted a young woman and detained her against her family's will. Basil excommunicated the man's family and ordered his village to return the girl to her father (Letter 270). According to Basil's brother Gregory of Nyssa (ca. 330–395 C.E.), their own mother, Emmelia, had been in danger of abduction when orphaned at a young age. Basil's Canon 22 (Letter 199) ordered men who abducted women to return them to their families. An engaged woman was to be offered to her original fiancé, who could receive her in marriage or, under the circumstances, decline to wed her. If the woman was not previously betrothed, the family could permit her to marry her abductor. A widow who had been abducted could choose whether to remain with her captor. Basil's canons punished fornicators with four years of excommunication, but Canon 49 made clear that women violated by force were guiltless and not subject to punishment.

Sexual abuse of slaves. Some early Christians recognized the vulnerability of slaves. The *Apostolic Tradition* (ca. 215 C.E.), attributed to Hippolytus of Rome, declared that a slave who was her master's concubine could be admitted for baptism if she remained monogamous and raised her children. This requirement of monogamy, however, would preclude her entry into a consensual relationship with another partner. Canon 49 of Basil of Caesarea said that slave women violated by their masters were not subject to church discipline. However, amid numerous rules regarding sexual behavior, Basil mentions no punishment for male masters who sexually abused their female slaves.

The *Acts of Andrew* 17–22 tells the story of a Christian woman who, wishing to be celibate, enlisted her "comely, exceedingly wanton" female slave to take her place in the marital bed. It is not known whether this strategy was commonly employed by Christian women, whose commitment to celibacy could have increased the sexual exploitation of slaves. Sermons repeatedly condemned men's sexual use of slave women, but preachers tended to be concerned with husbands' marital fidelity, not the rights and dignity of victimized slaves. Homilies on the story of Abraham and Hagar (Gen 16) urged men not to make sexual use of their female slaves, who could become presumptuous like Hagar. Though sermons criticized women who physically punished female slaves, little is known about women's sexual abuse of female slaves. Fourth-century regulations attempted to prevent owners from forcing Christian slaves into prostitution.

Sexual abuse of children. Church regulations spoke harshly about sexual contact with children. Since the Greek word for child (*pais*) could refer to a boy, youth, or a child of either gender, one cannot be certain whether specific rules concerned the abuse of minors or homosexual relations with young men. The *Didache*, a first-century Greek document with instructions regarding church practice, condemned those who had sexual relations with children or boys. Canon 71 from the Synod of Elvira (ca. 306 C.E.), in southern Spain, ordered that men who sexually abused boys were to be denied communion, even on their deathbeds.

Clergy sexual abuse. Letters and historical chronicles occasionally mention cases of church officials harassing, seducing, or sexually assaulting nuns and female parishioners. In *Ecclesiastical History* 7.16, the fifth-century historian Sozomen reports that a noblewoman was raped by a deacon when she was praying in a church in Constantinople. The bishop deposed the offending deacon and decreed that clergy should not supervise private penitential prayers inside church buildings, where they would have access to parishioners. Modern studies of clergy sexual abuse point to the power differential between clergy and laity, but ancient cases of abuse, if they were addressed at all, were probably treated as instances of sexual immorality rather than violence or abuse of power.

Biblical Interpretation. Most biblical commentators in the early church used the story of Dinah (Gen 34), who was abducted outdoors when going out to see the women of the region, as a cautionary tale to admonish virgins to stay indoors. Others used Dinah's example as a moral lesson, instructing listeners to stay within the "tents" of the church and orthodox doctrine rather than "departing" to listen to heretics. Dinah was usually viewed as responsible for her assault. Amnon's rape of his sister, Tamar (2 Sam 13), was, ironically, used to stress the moral dangers of unrelated men and women dwelling together. The story of the Levite's concubine, who was gang raped in place of her master (Judg 19) and the parallel story of Lot offering his virgin daughters to be raped by the men of Sodom (Gen 19) were employed to argue that homosexual rape, a "sin against nature," was more severe than the more "natural" vaginal rape of a woman. Instructions regarding sexual use of captive women after shaving their heads (Deut 21) were treated as allegories about employing pagan literature after shearing it of its immoral excesses. There was relatively little recognition of the sexual vulnerability of Bathsheba (2 Sam 11) or servants and slaves such as Hagar, Bilhah, and Zilpah (Gen 16 and 30).

The Rape of Eve in Gnostic Literature. A cache of documents discovered in 1945 in Nag Hammadi, Egypt, contains three treatises that retell Genesis 1—3 in terms of sexual assault upon Eve. These fourth-century documents, preserved in the Coptic language, reflect the Gnostic tradition that asserted that the material, visible world was created by some lesser being and should be rejected in favor of a spiritual reality. In *The Nature of the Rulers* (also translated as *The Hypostasis of the Archons*) and *On the Origin of the World*, evil "rulers," or powers, who subjugate the material world attempt to rape a female spiritual being in the garden. Her spirit escapes into a tree. She leaves a material copy of herself, Adam's wife, whom the rulers rape orally, vaginally, and perhaps anally. This echoes the Greek account of Daphne, who transformed into a tree to escape Apollo's rape attempt. In a reinterpretation of Genesis 6, Eve's daughters are in constant danger of sexual assault from the rulers. An enlightened woman, Norea, is also preyed upon by the rulers who are unable to rape her. Another version of this story is told in *The Secret Book of John*. The brutal sexual violence in these narratives emphasizes the evil nature of the material world's rulers, as well as the flawed origins of most of Eve's children, conceived through ongoing sexual assaults by the rulers.

Augustine's Theological Reflections on Rape. Rape was used as a strategy of war, to assert dominance over the enemy, subjugate conquered peoples, and shame male and female war captives. A wartime rape occasioned the most sustained early Christian discussion of sexual violence, found in *The City of God* 1.16–29, by Augustine of Hippo (354–430 C.E.). Augustine began this work shortly after the sack of Rome (410 C.E.), when the invading Visigoth army looted Rome for three days, sexually assaulting many inhabitants, including virgins publically committed to celibacy. Augustine reports that non-Christians used these rapes as an excuse to mock Christians, since God apparently failed to protect them. Endeavoring to console rape victims, Augustine assured them that if men gratified their lust on women's bodies, women nevertheless retained their chastity in soul, mind, and body, even if (as he thought might happen) their rebellious bodies experienced sexual arousal during the attack.

Augustine criticizes non-Christians for their admiration of Lucretia, who committed suicide after being raped. If Lucretia was truly innocent of the rape, she was guilty of self-murder. He suggests that she had perhaps internally consented to the attack or was overly interested in the outward appearance of honor.

Augustine endeavored to explain how a benevolent God could permit rape. He suggested that some Roman Christian women had been too proud of their chastity. God used the sexual assaults to remove the "tumor" of pride while it was still small, before it developed into a more deadly sin. Though he addresses only female rape victims in *The City of God*, Augustine discusses homosexual rape—something he considers particularly heinous—in his treatise *On Lying* 10–17.

Modern Perspectives on Early Christian Writings about Sexual Violence. Virtually all ancient texts dealing with sexual violence were authored by men, who speculated about how sexual violence affected—or ought to affect—victims. Despite some authors' pastoral attention to victims' psychological and spiritual well-being, there was little recognition of their possible physical trauma. Many church regulations seemed more concerned with enforcing celibacy and marital fidelity than with preventing or punishing sexual violence. Attempts to curb rape focused on regulating female behavior rather than that of rapists. Abuse was certainly underreported, especially clergy sexual abuse, pedophilia, and same-sex violence. Despite several studies about sexual violence and ancient Christianity, the topic remains underexamined in modern scholarship.

[*See also* Legal Status, *subentry* Early Church; Marriage and Divorce, *subentry* Early Church; Same-Sex Relations, *subentry* Roman World; *and* Sexual Violence, *subentries on* Greek World, Hebrew Bible, New Testament, *and* Roman World.]

BIBLIOGRAPHY

Arjava, Antti. *Women and Law in Late Antiquity.* New York: Oxford University Press, 1996.

Brock, Sebastian P., and Susan Ashbrook Harvey, trans. *Holy Women of the Syrian Orient.* Berkeley: University of California Press, 1987.

Clark, Gillian. *Women in Late Antiquity: Pagan and Christian Lifestyles.* New York: Oxford University Press, 1993.

Elliott, J. K., ed. *The Apocryphal New Testament: A Collection of Apocryphal Christian Literature in an English Translation.* Oxford: Clarendon, 1993.

Grubbs, Judith Evans. "Abduction Marriage in Antiquity: A Law of Constantine (*CTh* IX 24.1) and Its Social Context." *Journal of Roman Studies* 79 (1989): 59–83.

Grubbs, Judith Evans. *Law and Family in Late Antiquity: The Emperor Constantine's Marriage Legislation.* New York: Oxford University Press, 1995.

Laeuchli, Samuel. *Power and Sexuality: The Emergence of Canon Law at the Synod of Elvira.* Philadelphia: Temple University Press, 1972.

Laiou, Angeliki E., ed. *Consent and Coercion to Sex and Marriage in Ancient and Medieval Societies.* Washington, D.C.: Dumbarton Oaks Research Library and Collection, 1993.

Robinson, O. F. *The Criminal Law of Ancient Rome.* Baltimore: Johns Hopkins University Press, 1995.

Schroeder, Joy A. *Dinah's Lament: The Biblical Legacy of Sexual Violence in Christian Interpretation.* Minneapolis: Fortress, 2007.

Thompson, Jennifer J. "'Accept This Twofold Consolation, You Faint-Hearted Creatures': St. Augustine and Contemporary Definitions of Rape." *Studies in Media and Information Literacy Education* 4, no. 3 (2004): 1–17.

Thompson, John L. *Writing the Wrongs: Women of the Old Testament among Biblical Commentators from Philo through the Reformation.* New York: Oxford University Press, 2001.

Joy A. Schroeder

SOCIAL INTERACTION

This entry contains five subentries: Ancient Near East; Greek and Roman Worlds; New Testament; Early Judaism; *and* Early Church.

Ancient Near East

Our primary sources for social interaction in the ancient Near East in the first millennium B.C.E. are extensive. However, they are overwhelmingly the product of one area—Mesopotamia—and of one social group—the male scribes trained in the writing of cuneiform texts, mainly on the extremely durable medium of clay. Nevertheless, although partial, they provide a rich source for the social links—both peaceful and otherwise—between the men and women of an ancient society and their reflections upon them.

The "Military–Agricultural Complex." Unlike the modern West, ancient people's lives were much more conditioned by how basic food production and defense were organized. Few of us in the modern world feed ourselves from our own fields or expect to fight in our countries' wars. Yet such of course was the norm for much of an ancient population. Moreover, those who could avoid such tribulations were directly dependent on how much surplus they could extract from the primary producers and how much of those producers' time could be spared from this effort for military undertakings instead. Moreover, membership of the extractive class was not guaranteed and those at the lower end of the scale usually sought some kind of collective way of maintaining their free status. Our best attested case studies from the first millennium ancient Near East—Assyria and Babylonia—utilized a labor tax on land to either supply the bulk of their army or fund the hiring of more professional troops. A significant portion of the free male population in both areas leveraged their ability as scribes to secure their economic well-being through collective endeavors: either the royal administration that supported their armies or the temples that fed and clothed their gods.

The limited complexity of ancient Near East societies means that these choices had a profound effect on all other aspects of social interaction. Craft production was heavily structured by these institutional arrangements. Military service fell mainly on primary producers lacking influence within the palace and temple organizations and who were therefore at the mercy of economic forces unless dependent on elite patrons. At least in the case of Babylonia, issues of purity and pollution inherent in priestly membership had a major influence on relationships with fellow citizens.

Warfare. According to our earliest records, Mesopotamian city-states used a corvée to maintain the irrigation system on which their agriculture depended. This levy, which was coordinated by the king, could also function as a militia. In first-millennium B.C.E. Mesopotamia, we see two distinct responses to the contrasting demands of food supply and defense—one in Assyria and one in Babylonia.

Assyria of the late second millennium and early first millennium B.C.E. was basically an inflated version of the original city-state of Aššur. The king was the high priest of the national god (also called Aššur). As such, he took direct responsibility for supplying the temple of the god. Beginning in the latter half of the second millennium B.C.E., the Assyrians began to create a unified territorial state across the whole of northern Mesopotamia. After conquest, Assyrian governors were increasingly imposed rather than native rulers being left in place as client kings. The conquered population were "counted as Assyrians," meaning that they had to supply offerings to the temple of Aššur and they were liable to be called up for *ilku* (militia/corvée service). Provincial governors augmented their levies with ethnic groups specializing in particular types of warfare, such as the Ituaen archers and the Qurraean spearmen. This basic force was augmented with a smaller elite unit, the "Royal Cohort" (*kiṣir šarrūti*), which seems to have been a standing force under the direct command of the king or members of the royal family. During the early first millennium B.C.E., the Assyrians conquered the lowland Near East and much of the surrounding highlands. Babylonia was a frequent victim of Assyrian aggression and conquest, although never integrated into Assyria proper. Assyria was eventually destroyed as both a political entity and a major cuneiform culture in the late seventh century. (In contrast, the conquered Babylonia maintained a vibrant cuneiform tradition until the beginning of the common era.) Much of the Assyrian Empire was absorbed into a short-lived Neo-Babylonian Empire. This in turn was conquered by the Persian Empire.

Compared to Assyria, Babylonia was more of a federation of cities than a single enlarged city-state. Each city had its own temples with its respective high priest. The gods were supplied mainly from the temples' own landholdings, although these lands were often granted by the king. It is not entirely clear whether there was a general obligation to serve in the levy incumbent on all land holdings. More certainly, however, kings granted land to both individuals and temples with specific military obligations: bow-fiefs, horse-fiefs, and chariot-fiefs. These also seem to have been referred to as *ilku.*

One text links the holding of a bow-fief to the status of free citizen; it could be a source of income and status as well as a burden. Fines were payable if the *ilku* service was not met. The large estates granted to members of the royal family and high officials carried with them the obligation to provide military units. Even urban houses may have carried an obligation to serve. Bow-fiefs came with civic as well as military obligations. The system reached deep into society with the obligated population being divided into decuries (*eširtu*) based on everyday professions. Even where a fief-holder sent his dependents to perform service obligations, he may still have had to accompany them as their supervisor.

Mesopotamian women neither fought in wars nor commanded armies. Poorer women would bear the burden of running a household in the absence of conscripted males. All women were subject to the privations of war, and some were reserved for victorious kings and their favorites. Many more constituted the plunder of individual soldiers, usually to be sold on for profit to slave dealers. Most characteristic of Neo-Assyrian and Neo-Babylonian warfare was the deportation of entire segments of a population. This practice reflected the underlying underutilization of land and the need for labor and defense. Depictions of such deportees on Neo-Assyrian reliefs focus on displaced mothers caring for their children, a perhaps subconscious recognition that the "military–agricultural complex" relied ultimately on the mutual reproductive capacity of men and women together.

In Mesopotamia, the quintessential weapon was the bow; the majority of armies consisted of lightly armed archers augmented with equally lightly armed spearmen. Elite troops were cavalry and chariotry. Both functioned mainly as platforms for mounted bowmen, although they would also charge light-armed infantry where the latter had lost cohesion.

They were ineffective, however, against more heavily armored and disciplined troops such as a phalanx of Greek Hoplites or Macedonian pikemen. Hence, although Mesopotamia remained an economic power beyond the mid-first millennium B.C.E., its military was unable to produce enough cavalry to match Iranian powers or support heavy infantry to match Mediterranean ones (Barjamovic, 2013; Fuchs, 2011; Garfinkle, 2013; Jursa, 2010; Kuhrt, 2001; Macginnis, 2010; Driel, 2002).

Organization of Manufacturing. The structures that emerged to coordinate the competing needs of agricultural productivity and military preparedness deeply affected the organization of the rest of the economy. In Assyria, the economy was dominated by the provincial system that funneled resources to the Aššur temple and underpinned the national army. The government adapted the military hierarchy to organize large numbers of civilian workers. From the time of Tiglath-Pileser III, professions were organized in cohorts.

Babylonia too had a provincial system, but our source material far better attests to the role of the major temples of the individual cities in economic activity. The basic role of a temple was to be a house for a deity. Just as a human householder required food, drink, clothing, and household items, so did the divine one; it was the human duty to provide these goods. Our earliest records describe both male and female temple priesthoods as making offerings to the gods. In the early first millennium, however, the old priestly titles disappear from our records of temple practice and are subsumed under the designation "enterers of the shrine" (*ērib bīti*), now almost exclusively male. Moreover, the organization of priesthoods begins to reflect the supply and production of cultic items. Moreover, those responsible—for the provision and processing of materials, also exclusively male—are accorded priestly status. Apart from some deliberate archaizing such as King Nabonidus reviving the ancient title of *en*-priestess of Nanna at Ur for his daughter Erišti-Sin, women are virtually invisible in cultic roles in first-millennium B.C.E. Babylonia.

The provision of cultic goods was organized on a prebendary system in which the citizen-cum-priest would receive an income for the carrying out of a commission. These commissions to provide particular items (the prebend) in each temple were divided (and subdivided) into rotating time slots. Using the resources of its extensive landholdings, the temple would grow the food or buy the raw material necessary for each prebend. The prebend holder would take the raw materials and process them into the required items; he would gain profit from direct payment, the overprovision of raw materials, or rights to shares of offerings after they had been presented to the gods. As such, prebends were sources of income like any other and could be traded as any other commodity. Women could hold prebends, but until the Seleucid period they could not buy and sell them, receiving them passively through inheritance or endowment by relative. Because they could not be consecrated as priests, female prebend holders subcontracted prebendary tasks to males.

The focus on the activities of priests in Mespotamian documents leads to a severe underestimation of women's roles in manufacturing. The numerous classes of temple dependents (*širku*) included women as well as men. Although they are virtually invisible in our sources, traditionally female undertakings such as weaving and milling must have been important in actuality. Furthermore, although our sources originate in the temples, they do provide hints that central and provincial palaces—whose own records we lack—continued their traditional practice of devoting large numbers of women to the production of textiles.

Effectively, the prebend system divided the temple community into a number of subunits focused on the production of particular products such as food, beer, or pottery. Some priests specialized in specific subunits; others would be members of multiple subunits. Priests could also be holders of prebends in more than one temple, and there were injunctions against them using the resources of one temple for a prebend in another. Despite this, the professional subunits had a fair degree of separate identity. Within the temple precinct, they exercised control over their own rosters, the admittance of new colleagues, and their workspaces within the temple precinct. The members of each subunit had various links with each other beyond the common task of provisioning the deity. The prebend system basically extended its influence over all craft activity in a city. Prebend holders would subcontract their work to nonconsecrated craftsmen, while also undertaking private work on the side. The recurring nature of priestly prebends allowed priests time for other economic pursuits while still circumscribing their freedom of movement. Priestly artisans therefore probably purveyed their skills to private clients as well.

The intersection of religion and production provided a powerful template for structuring social relations. Greater access to the gods and dependency on others for fulfilling one's role were equated with greater purity, so at the top of the social hierarchy were those priests who took the works of others and physically presented them to the gods. Below them were those who were allowed to present their goods to the enterers of the shrine in the main courtyard of the temple. Finally, there were the priests who were allowed no farther than the numerous workshops and storage areas of the temple precinct. Priests were drawn from the wider class of free citizens (*mār banî*). Beyond them lay the dependents and slaves. The various classes were recognizable by onomastic differences. Free male citizens had family names recognizing either ancestors or the profession in which consecrated family members traditionally held their prebend. Female members of such families, however, were designated by their relationship to individual males as wives or daughters. Dependents had only patronymics, whereas slaves were identified by their masters' names (Bongenaar, 1997; Joannès, 2013; Jursa, 2010; Nielsen, 2010; Postgate, 1987; Waerzeggers, 2010).

Growth of Patronage. In first-millennium B.C.E. Babylonia, the agrarian landscape consisted of a variety of fields that owed to the king one or more of the three kinds of military service—bow, horse, or chariot. The actual ownership could be in the hands of major officials, members of the royal family, temples, or small landowners. Except in the last case, the actual farming was always done by dependent laborers, on whom also fell the pertinent service obligation. Often this service was commuted into a payment. When it was not, farmers on corvée service needed money to purchase equipment and to compensate them for loss of time while fulfilling their military or civil duties. Neither palace, estate, nor temple bureaucracies were actually set up to collect such payments nor were the farmers often able to pay. This led to the emergence of a class of urban entrepreneurs such as the Murašu family of Nippur who specialized in covering these various expenses of the farmers in return for marketing their crops to their own advantage. Often these patronage relations were couched in terms of adoption, with the farmer adopting the patron. In such cases, it was crucial that the adopter remain on the land to do the actual work.

Such a system had some obvious advantages in terms of efficiency and indicates that the institutional bureaucracies of palace and temple were less extensive in their reach than sometimes assumed. A reform of the last Neo-Babylonian king Nabonidus granted large amounts of temple land as a concession to entrepreneurs in return for supplying the manpower obligated. This situation also suggests that soldiers granted fields for their upkeep were likely to fall inexorably into debt, resulting in the decline in levels of equipment, training, and morale (Macginnis, 2010; Driel, 2002).

Conceptions of City Life. For most men in the ancient Near East, a typical career path involved first aiding and then succeeding one's father in his sustenance activities. For the majority of men, these activities were intimately connected to plots of land, either owned directly or worked through some institutional arrangement. Technically, daughters with brothers did not inherit, but they were entitled to a dowry out of the family patrimony. Opportunities for significantly increasing a family's wealth were in most cases probably limited, so that a woman's guaranteed share came at the price of very close male supervision by her father, brothers, husband, or sons. Although they faced such legal hindrances as not being fully allowed to witness contracts, women nonetheless could conduct business on their own behalf.

The relationship between priesthood and scribal status in first-millennium B.C.E. Babylonia affects the literary representation of social interaction. For example, the extensive compilation of omens called *Šumma Alu* highlights various aspects of public and private city life and valorizes them as presaging either good or bad fortune. The omens suggest, for example, that family life was hierarchical, that there was an ethos of secrecy and suspicion in dealings with fellow citizens, and that there was a negative view of city life in general.

Thus *Šumma Alu* frames the interests of husband and wife as diametrically opposed:

> If the threshold of the house is high with respect to the courtyard, the owner of the house will be placed above the lady of the house. If the threshold of the courtyard is high with respect to the house, the lady of the house will be placed above the owner of the house. (Freedman, 1998)

Scholars have long debated whether the position of women deteriorated over the millennia in ancient Mesopotamia. The sacralization of much of the free male population of urban Babylonia may well have exacerbated this development. At a most obvious level, women holding priestly office almost disappear from our records. More insidiously, the purity requirements for priestly succession placed an emphasis on the virginity of brides.

The ethos of male social interaction exhibited in *Šumma Alu* is one of secrecy and suspicion. Babylonian houses were built for privacy. They had high walls with little access to the street. When focusing beyond domestic walls, *Šumma Alu* betrays a deep suspicion of human engagement. The omens treat secrecy as a great virtue and consider ambitions hidden to be more likely of success.

The values implied by these omens involve the subversion of common literary tropes. For example, elsewhere in Mesopotamian literature elevation is seen as positive and lowness as negative. In *Šumma Alu*, however, the adjective "high" is equated with the lips and hence dissimulation, whereas "low" is equated with the truth that is in one's heart. The need to keep your true plans and ambitions secret is highlighted by *Šumma Alu*'s insistence that casual mannerisms and minor public accidents have an underlying significance. Similarly, although temple organization imbued social life with an innate hierarchy, the outlook of *Šumma Alu* is one of competition. Two of the Middle Assyrian laws from the previous millennium had both affirmed the social primacy of the sexually potent male citizen and implied the concomitant threat to social order that the misuse of such power could bring:

> If a man furtively spreads rumors about his comrade, saying, "Everyone sodomizes him," or in a quarrel in public says to him, "Everyone sodomizes you," and further, "I can prove the charges against you," but he is unable to prove the charges and does not prove the charges, they shall strike that man 50 blows with rods; he shall perform the king's service for one full month; they shall cut off his hair; moreover, he shall pay 3,600 shekels of lead.
>
> If a man sodomizes his comrade and they prove the charges against him and find him guilty, they shall sodomize him and they shall turn him into a eunuch. (Roth et al., 1997, pp. 159–160)

In contrast, *Šumma Alu* uses a similar context to subvert any sense of social solidarity among citizens:

> If a man has sex per anum with his social peer, that man will become foremost among his brothers and colleagues. (Guinan, 1997)

In *Šumma Alu*, engagement with public institutions is also frowned upon. Houses smelling of the ingredients ritually added to the bricks of palaces are sure signs of bad luck. Similarly, a seemingly positive approbation of a city—elevation—takes on a negative connotation in the first line of the composition:

> If a City is set on a height, living in that city will not be good. (Freedman, 1998, p. 19)

Because Mesopotamian cities of any longevity would gradually increase their elevation as they were continually rebuilt on top of generations of ever-increasing detritus, the omen therefore casts all city life in a negative light.

Assessment. In our best attested example of social interaction in first millennium B.C.E., Mesopotamia, much that initially seems strange to us can be attributed to the particular nature of the collective measures that the less wealthy members of the free male population took to avoid economic oblivion. By utilizing their scribal skills within the great institutions, these males had a profound effect on craft production, the quality of recruits for the army, and interaction with their fellow city-dwellers, both male and female.

[*See also* Economics, *subentry* Ancient Near East; Gender and Sexuality: Ancient Near East; Religious Leaders, *subentry* Ancient Near East; *and* Religious Participation, *subentry* Ancient Near East.]

BIBLIOGRAPHY

Baker, Heather D. "Urban Form in the First Millennium BC." In *The Babylonian World*, edited by Gwendolyn Leick, pp. 66–77. New York: Routledge, 2007.

Barjamovic, Gojko. "Mesopotamian Empires." *Oxford Handbooks Online*, 2013. http://www.oxfordhandbooks.com/view/10.1093/oxfordhb/9780195188318.001.0001/oxfordhb-9780195188318-e-5.

Bongenaar, A. C. V. M. *The Neo-Babylonian Ebabbar Temple at Sippar: Its Administration and its Prosopography*. Istanbul: Nederlands Historisch-Archeologisch Instituut te Istanbul, 1997.

Freedman, Sally M. *"If a City Is Set on a Height": The Akkadian Omen Series Šumma Alu Ina Melê Šakin*. Vol. 1: *Tablets 1–21*. Philadelphia: Occasional Publications of the Samuel Noah Kramer Fund 17, 1998.

Fuchs, Andreas. "Assyria at War: Strategy and Conduct." *Oxford Handbooks Online*, 2011. http://www.oxfordhandbooks.com/view/10.1093/oxfordhb/9780199557301.001.0001/oxfordhb-9780199557301-e-18.

Garfinkle, Steven J. "Ancient Near Eastern City-States." *Oxford Handbooks Online*, 2013. http://www.oxfordhandbooks.com/view/10.1093/oxfordhb/9780195188318.001.0001/oxfordhb-9780195188318-e-4 (accessed 27 January 2014).

Geller, M. J. *Evil Demons: Canonical Utukkū Lemnūtu Incantations*. State Archives of Assyria Cuneiform Texts. Helsinki: Neo-Assyrian Text Corpus Project, 2007.

Guinan, Ann. "Auguries of Hegemony: The Sex Omens of Mesopotamia." *Gender & History* 9, no. 3 (1997): 462–479.

Guinan, Ann. "The Perils of High Living: Divinatory Rhetoric in Šumma Alu." In *DUMU-E₂-DUB-BA-A: Studies in Honor of Ake W. Sjöberg*, edited by Hermann Behrens, Darlene Loding, and Martha Tobi Roth, pp. 227–235. Philadelphia: Samuel Noah Kramer Fund, University Museum, 1989.

Guinan, Ann. "Social Constructions and Private Designs: The House Omens of *šumma ālu*." In *Houses and Households in Ancient Mesopotamia: Papers Read at the 40th Rencontre Assyriologique Internationale, Leiden, July 5–8, 1993*, edited by K. R. Veenhof, pp. 61–68. Publications de l'Institut historique-archéologique néerlandais de Stamboul 78. Leiden, The Netherlands: Nederlands Historisch-Archeologisch Instituut te Istanbul, 1996.

Joannès, F. "The Economic Role of Women in Neo-Babylonian Temples." *Carnet de REFEMA*, 2013. http://refema.hypotheses.org/745.

Jursa, M. *Aspects of the Economic History of Babylonia in the First Millennium B.C.: Economic Geography, Economic Mentalities, Agriculture, the Use of Money and the Problem of Economic Growth* (with contributions by J. Hackl, B. Janković, K. Kleber, E. E. Payne, C. Waerzeggers, and M. Weszeli). Alter Orient und Altes Testament 377. Münster, Germany: Ugarit-Verlag, 2010.

Kuhrt, Amélie. "Women and War." *NIN: Journal of Gender Studies in Antiquity* 2, no. 1 (2001): 1–25.

MacGinnis, John. "Mobilisation and Militarisation in the Neo-Babylonian Empire." In *Studies on War in the Ancient Near East. Collected Essays on Military History.* Alter Orient und Altes Testament 372, edited by Jordi Vidal, pp. 153–164. Münster, Germany: Ugarit-Verlag, 2010.

Nielsen, John P. *Sons and Descendants: A Social History of Kin Groups and Family Names in the Early Neo-Babylonian Period, 747–626 B.C.* Leiden, The Netherlands: Brill, 2010.

Postgate, J. N. "The Assyrian Army in Zamua." *Iraq* 62 (2000): 89–108.

Postgate, J. N. "Employer, Employee and Employment in the Neo-Assyrian Empire." In *Labor in the Ancient Near East*, edited by Marvin A. Powell, pp. 257–270. American Oriental Series. New Haven, Conn.: American Oriental Society, 1987.

Roth, Martha Tobi, Harry A. Hoffner, and Piotr Michalowski. *Law Collections from Mesopotamia and Asia Minor*. Atlanta: Scholars Press, 1997.

Steele, Laura D. "Women and Gender in Babylonia." In *The Babylonian World*, edited by Gwendolyn Leick, pp. 299–316. New York: Routledge, 2007.

van de Mieroop, Marc. *The Ancient Mesopotamian City.* Oxford: Oxford University Press, 1997.

van Driel, G. *Elusive Silver: In Search of a Role for a Market in an Agrarian Environment; Aspects of Mesopotamia's Society.* Leiden, The Netherlands: Nederlands Instituut voor het Nabije Oosten, 2002.

Waerzeggers, C. A. H. "The Babylonian Priesthood in the Long Sixth Century B.C." *Bulletin of the Institute of Classical Studies* 54, no. 2 (2011): 59–70.

Waerzeggers, C. A. H. *The Ezida Temple of Borsippa: Priesthood, Cult, Archives.* Leiden: Nederlands Instituut voor het Nabije Oosten, 2010.

Philip Jones

Hebrew Bible

See Social Interaction, *subentry* Early Judaism.

Greek and Roman Worlds

A variety of societal structures and organizations provided a range of mediums for interaction outside of the religious realm for persons living in the Greco-Roman world. The study of social interaction in the ancient world has been greatly enhanced by recent emphases on "social history" as a historiographical lens through which to analyze the ways in which social relations and movements (particularly those extending beyond the purview of societal and political elites) functioned within history. Drawing from broader trends in the field of both history and sociology, then, within the study of the ancient world, the work of Moses Finley (1953) and Ramsay MacMullen (1974) represents signal contributions. Such work on social history has expanded the possibilities for connections to the study of gender and sexuality in the ancient world by acknowledging the ways in which social interaction within and between different groups impacted social and political developments. Additionally, such emphases have been bolstered by work specifically aimed at uncovering women's (elite and nonelite) social history and contributions to these worlds (e.g., Pomeroy, 1975; Fantham et al., 1994); and studies of slavery, prostitution, and sexuality have all contributed to a more general understanding of how persons and groups interacted in the classical world (e.g., Hopkins, 1978; Glazebrook and Henry, 2011).

Broadly speaking, sources regarding social interaction in ancient Greece and Rome are pieced together from a combination of literary texts, inscriptions, and archaeological remains (from types of buildings to the contents remaining within). In the literary realm, descriptions of day-to-day processes—and the social interactions involved therein—are typically incidental to the actual topic of any given text; for instance, the contents of a philosophical discourse are the main focus of Plato's *Symposium*, but from the description of the banquet embedded in this discussion, it is possible to glean some details about the social nature of Greek *symposia* more generally. Thus, scholars interested in studying such interactions must draw from a multitude of different texts, and still, the vantage point pieced together from such a study is often unlikely to present a comprehensive picture. Furthermore, the majority of the literature from the Greco-Roman world was written from the perspective of male elites, thus favoring and privileging their concerns and perhaps accidentally representing others. One cannot assume that these sources, therefore, represent the experiences of the majority of persons who lived and interacted in these worlds (and even when women, slaves, or others are "given voice" in these texts, their words are still penned and imagined by male authors). This does not mean that *no* relevant information about general social interactions can be found in the literary evidence, but its perspectival nature must be accounted for, especially when considering the gendered and sexual natures of social interaction.

Despite the more elite nature of literary texts, it is also possible to look to archaeological remains for at least some evidence for the kinds of social interactions more widely experienced in day-to-day Greco-Roman life. Inscriptions—such as those for membership lists for associations, funerary inscriptions and tombstones, or graffiti—regularly give glimpses into some of the mundane aspects of Greco-Roman social life, giving particular emphasis to the types of activities that were deemed important to publicly record or memorialize. Likewise, analyzing the remnants of buildings, from private residences to places of business and public amenities, allows scholars to investigate the ways in which these buildings were structured for social purposes and to speculate about the ways in which buildings or rooms were used. Further aiding such investigations are the artifacts contained in or around these buildings, which enable the identification of different spaces (and their usage) and give clues about how different persons might have moved and interacted within these areas.

Archaeological remnants have particular impact on the study of gender and sexuality and their relationship to social interaction. Although such concerns may be ancillary or (more often) absent from literary texts, these remains often attest to the presence of women and others who are rendered invisible in literary production/study: "*wo/men were there*" (Johnson-DeBaufre, 2010, p. 73). Thus, women's presence has been confirmed by various archaeological remains, and such remains have been used to provide support for and problematize assumptions about the gendered nature of space in ancient Greece and Rome. These remains can also provide insight into sexualized spaces (such as brothels) and about the sexual use of various spaces (e.g., imagery on vases). Drawing from all of these sources and from the scholarly conversations surrounding them, this essay will analyze the gendered and sexual natures of social interaction in several specific realms of the Greco-Roman world.

Public and Private Space. In what kinds of spaces did social interaction occur, and how were such spaces marked in terms of gender and sexuality? The delineation between public space (such as that of politics) and private space (particularly that of the *oikos* or *domus*) has traditionally been important for distinguishing the gendered dimensions of social interaction in the Greco-Roman worlds. Typically, the private space of the house has been cast as the realm of women, whereas the public sphere is that of men. From the outset, however, it must be noted that such a statement reflects an ideal, representing the

opinions and descriptions found in literary sources written almost exclusively by elite (free) men. Although such descriptions of the ideal may reflect elite male experience of social interaction between gendered bodies, it does not represent the experiences of most wo/men (inclusive of all women and men not represented by elite male voices), particularly those of lower social status.

This gendered distinction of public and private space has been offered as an explanation for women's invisibility in the public realm (an invisibility that is then replicated in scholarship). Pomeroy (1975) summarizes these effects when she concludes, "the reward of the 'good' woman in Rome was likely to be praise in stereotyped phrases; in Athens she won oblivion" (p. 229). Particularly from a literary perspective, the ideal for (elite) classical women was that they rarely strayed from the *oikos* or *domus* and their realm was within the household, generally meaning bearing and raising children. To live up to such an ideal meant to act in such a way that would not bear significant mention in classical Greek texts; Roman women were more likely to receive public praise in such roles (although often such praise was posthumous). However, such an ideal has not fully erased the evidence of the daily lives of Greek and Roman women, both those who stayed in the private realm of the house and those who did conduct their lives or businesses in the public sphere.

In classical Athens in particular (fifth and fourth centuries B.C.E.), both literary and archaeological evidence supports the division of the household into gendered quarters, specifically the *andrōn* as the male quarters (also important to the Greek symposium) and the most interior space (and thus the most private/secluded) as the female quarters. Although these female quarters were spatially the most secluded, this did not mean that the women who inhabited them were kept from interacting with other women. Images found on vases that depict women together in the house suggest that these quarters were frequently a space for female social interaction in classical Greece. Additionally, in larger elite households, there is evidence that these quarters were often inhabited by many women (of varying degrees of status/position), creating a space within the home for a variety of social interactions. However, women were rarely completely secluded in such spaces: as one example, vase paintings depict going in groups ("chatting animatedly") to collect water from public fountain houses. In addition, women of lower status would not have been afforded the luxury of their own homes or private quarters for working and interacting, and they often worked together in more public places outside of the home (Fantham et al., 1994, pp. 101–109).

By the height of the Roman Empire (ca. second century C.E.), this public-private distinction, although still remaining mostly in place, became more blurred as it became more acceptable (at least within the discourse) for women to be publicly acclaimed. Such a portrayal can in part be attributed to the portrayal of the most elite women of the imperial family and court as playing some role in imperial politics. Although, as in the case of classical Greece, most elite women (especially those who were Roman citizens) were primarily responsible for the maintenance of (or overseeing) the household and child rearing, social interaction with women of similar status—for entertainment, gossip, and well-being—was typical both for amusement and as part of one's societal duties (D'Ambra, 2007, pp. 128–129). Again, the lower one's status in society, the more likely one would be to inhabit workspaces and interact more broadly with others in public venues, whether these interactions are service/work-oriented or more social in nature.

Symposia. The Greek *symposion*, described most famously by Plato, was a space for social interaction in the form of a dinner party, usually geared toward elite and often philosophically minded men. As described by James Davidson (1997), it was "a highly ritualized occasion and an important crucible for the forging of friendships, alliances and community in ancient Greece, an almost perfect example in fact of the anthropologists' commensal model of drinking in which socializing is paramount" (p. 43). At symposia, men would gather to dine, drink, and discuss relevant political and philosophical topics; according to Plato, such discussion took the form of a friendly

competition, wherein each participant would give a speech on a chosen topic with the goal of having one's speech declared the best. Using the symposium space as a venue for philosophical dialogue, treatises such as Plato's (or Xenophon's) were constructed by their author to advance his own perspective; however, such depictions of these social gatherings still give scholars a glimpse into the types of interactions expected in a typical symposium.

The traditional location for symposia was in the home, most often in the *andrōn* ("men's quarters"), which marked the space as decidedly male centered and oriented. The activities of the symposium, whether eating, drinking, pleasure, or discussion, were designed for the entertainment of the male participants. Although the topic under discussion may involve women or sexuality more broadly, as in the case of Plato, where the topic is *erōs* ("sexual desire"), the perspectives and interests in the conversation represent the concerns of men. In Plato, although a woman's voice (Diotima) is brought into the dialogue via Socrates's speech, her voice (and thus her perspective) is filtered through and projected entirely by men. Thus, as David Halperin (1990) has suggested, gender only enters into such dialogue to institutionalize the normative project of (male) philosophy (p. 150). Additionally, the symposium and its location in the *andrōn* have been analyzed in terms of its relationship to the city/*polis*. For example, Leslie Kurke (1999) has suggested that the sympotic space represents an "anti-city," which valued elite friendships and networks that were cultivated in the private home as opposed to in public, under the authority of the *polis* (p. 17–18).

Although the formal participants in symposia were exclusively male, sources attest to the presence of women at these dinner parties, although these women were rarely, if ever, members of the upper social classes. Women's presence at symposia was oriented toward the entertainment and service of the elite male attendees; the most prominently discussed female presence were the *hetairai*, who entertained elite men by providing sexual favors. Traditionally, the figure of the *hetaira* ("courtesan") is contrasted with the *pornē* ("prostitute") as a woman who provided sexual favors and company to men. What traditionally distinguishes *hetairai* is that they typically provided their services to a single elite patron in exchange for lavish payment, gifts, or treatment; thus, this figure was treated with an air of greater sophistication because her lot was quite different from that of the more typical brothel slave. From literary descriptions to vase paintings depicting men receiving various forms of sexual gratification from women, it is clear that sexual pleasure was frequently included as part of the symposium's social nature and jovial atmosphere.

The forms of sexuality found in the Greek symposium were not limited to the heterosexual interaction between the male participants and the female *hetairai*. Pederasty is another common feature often discussed in the context of the philosophical symposium. The topic is discussed in the course of Plato's sympotic discourse, and it appears that the symposium gained a reputation for such sexual activity; Philo of Alexandria specifically condemns such settings in contrast to the ascetic Therapeutae (*On the Comtemplative Life*, §48–63). Such practices in the context of the symposium have typically been connected with Greek education (*paideia*) and assumed to be part of youth philosophical training. However, since the penetration of freeborn adult males was generally forbidden, the penetration of freeborn youth was less commonly accepted than intercourse between elite men and male slaves/prostitutes. Even in Plato's *Symposium*, as Halperin (1990) argues, Socrates's and Diotima's discussion of *erōs* (which is declared to be the best of the speeches) subtly discourages pederastic relations by exhibiting a preference for sexual relations between women and men (pp. 142–147).

Associations. Outside of the home, one mode through which social interaction occurred was through the formation of "voluntary associations" (also referred to as "guilds" or, in Latin, *collegia*). These associations, often organized around a specific trade or craft, allowed persons to assemble for both professional and social purposes. Additionally, associations were formed to create social networks among members based upon geographic/ethnic identity, by neighborhood, by common ritual/cult participation, or from familial or household networks (Harland, 2003, p. 19). Information about the nature and organization of these associations comes mostly from archaeological remains, particularly in the forms of dedicatory inscriptions (e.g., public notices honoring a patron) or funerary inscriptions; tombstones frequently identified members of an association since participation usually included a guarantee of proper burial. Membership in an association was generally formal, as in belonging to a professional society, in that dues were required to enter and remain in the organization. As the label "voluntary" implies, membership was not required of practitioners of a specific trade and craft, but opting not to join (or the refusal of membership) likely had social and occupational consequences. Alongside such dues, then, were both formal benefits, such as provisions for burial and a professional network, and informal benefits, including social and political opportunities. Associations were primarily local, so as to formally and physically connect persons with similar trades and crafts in the same general area, thus simplifying meeting and networking.

Although associations were often professionally inclined, the exact nature of their professional business is largely unknown because most of the remnants of these groups take the form of public displays, inscriptions, or membership lists. Records of association meetings have not been found or were not kept, possibly because—depending on the political nature of the meetings and the association—public record of activities was not prudent. From the evidence, it does appear that one social purpose of these organizations was to establish systems of patronage for various trades and crafts, thus increasing the social status and influence of the members of an association. As such, associations often provide an example of and concrete evidence for social interaction among persons less stratified in the Roman social hierarchy.

There is no evidence that membership in associations was restricted based on gender, but the majority of available data attest to male participation. Among the collected primary sources/inscriptions, there are membership lists that include women's names and evidence of some women's associations, such as a first-century C.E. statuary dedication by a women's synod (*synodos*) in Alexandria (Ascough et al., 2013). Other remnants attest to familial language used by Roman *collegia*, which specifically identified certain members as *matres* ("mothers"). These references could refer to female members wanting to increase their social rank in the organizations. Although these references are fewer in number, the lack of specific mention of women's participation does not mean that women were not present or included, formally or informally, in the business or social life of voluntary associations.

The Military. Gender and sexuality played a role in certain aspects of military organizations and campaigns in the Greco-Roman world. One of the most famous examples of female military might in ancient Greece comes from Greek descriptions of the Amazons, a society consisting of female warriors depicted with considerable strength. Tales (especially of mythic Greek victory over them) and artistic depictions of the Amazons in their military garb abounded in classical Athenian society and beyond; however, these descriptions come solely from a Greek perspective and are highly idealized and mythologized. Thus, Greek representations of Amazons as hostile to men and marriage and as inverting social gender hierarchies should be interpreted in light of Greek stereotypes against foreigners ("barbarians"), and depictions of Amazonian strength (and their eventual defeat) were in part constructed to reinforce the normalcy of male warriors and patriarchal social structures. Behind such mythical descriptions, however, there is archaeological evidence from Scythia supporting the presence of women who fought in wars. Ultimately, the literary and pictorial evidence of the Amazonian warriors gestures toward the probability that ancient militaries were not exclusively male spaces even as they point to the gendered anxieties Greeks projected onto foreign societies and their armies (Fantham et al., 1994, pp. 128–135).

In the advent of Roman conquest and Rome's transition from republic to empire (especially from the second century B.C.E. onward), the role and structure of its military proved critical to its territorial expansion and the maintenance of the empire. A highly professionalized, trained, and bureaucratic organization (originally consisting solely of citizens but then expanding into lower classes as the need for more soldiers arose), members of the Roman army were separated and distinguished from civilians during their service. Prior to the reign of Augustus, the Roman army was primarily a vehicle for this conquest; in the period following Augustus's reign, the army began to transition into structure more suited to occupying conquered territories and maintaining peace and loyalty to the empire within them. As such, the various legions of the army tended to develop individual identities and characteristics based upon their regional locations.

Although soldiers in the Roman army consisted entirely of men, women were present both in and around Roman military spaces (e.g., camps or forts). Some women would travel with or alongside the army, as evidence attests to their presence through the settlements that would emerge in the immediate vicinity of the military camps (D'Ambra, 2007, p. 131). Although women traveled with and visited Roman military camps, sexuality in the army was regulated, in particular by a ban on marriage for all Roman soldiers that was initiated by Augustus and lasted through 197 C.E. during the reign of Septimius Severus. Although legal and archaeological evidence attests to the fact that male soldiers still maintained long-term relationships with women, such relationships would not have been recognized as legitimate by the empire (thus permitting the legal and social benefits of marriage) until after a soldier's retirement; such legislation impacted the social lives of soldiers and their partners, often meaning that soldiers married and procreated at a later age. Although soldiers still engaged in sexual relations with women (in long-term relationships as well as sex with slaves and prostitutes or by rape), the effect of the ban had its greatest effect on any offspring resulting from such encounters. Even for citizen women, children fathered by a soldier were considered illegitimate and would not qualify for citizen status (when a child was born of a slave/prostitute or from rape, s/he was already considered illegitimate by wider society). There is evidence that soldiers cared for their children, although it is possible that some chose to expose female offspring (Phang, 2001, pp. 296–322).

Male soldiers likely engaged in sexual intercourse with other men, although the evidence for such interaction is less definitive. During the Roman Republic period of the second century B.C.E., sources (e.g., Polybius) appear to record punishments (often death) for soldiers who engaged in intercourse with other men, although the exact acts alluded to in such references remain ambiguous. Most likely, as was the typical Greco-Roman attitude to value the male penetrative role for freeborn/citizen men, only soldiers who allowed themselves to be penetrated (and those who penetrated another soldier) faced negative repercussions, particularly in light of a desire to preserve the "impenetrability" of the Roman soldier and army; intercourse with male slaves and prostitutes as the passive partner appears to be as common and acceptable for soldiers as it was for the typical male citizen. There is no direct evidence of less hierarchical sexual relations between male soldiers; there is only evidence of the prosecution of male soldiers taking a passive sexual role (and officers who forced others to do so) during the middle Republic. As the structure and composition of the army changed under the empire, it is possible that these attitudes toward (or at least regulation of) such situations relaxed (Phang, 2001, pp. 262–295).

Athletics. Athletics, via organized sport and the *gymnasium*, offered another venue for interaction in the Greco-Roman world. Especially given the focus placed upon the (usually nude) athletic body, social interaction in this realm was marked by issues of gender and sexuality. Athletics provided a competitive space in which physical strength and the body were put on display for the public, including the Olympic Games, other athletic festivals (often related to funerary rituals or in honor of a specific god/dess), and training in the *gymnasia*. As was often the case within broader social hierarchies, the competitive nature in the athletic sphere has been described as a "zero-sum" game: one person's victory (and the honor associated with it) necessarily came at the defeat of another (Scanlon, 2002, p. 11).

Imagery, in terms of both literary description and visual representation, further points to the ways in which the body was eroticized in the athletic event; in fact, certain athletic festivals were celebrated in connection with Eros, the god of sexual desire. In the case of vase depictions, it is not uncommon to find men in a gymnasium or athletic context engaging in sexualized activities with prostitutes (*hetairai*) or other men, usually of differing ages (adult-youth). In terms of actual erotic interaction in the athletic sphere, athletic training (a form of *paideia*) appears to have included pederastic "initiation" for young boys. According to Thomas Scanlon (2002), such practices originated in the athletic customs outside of Athens, in Crete and Sparta; by the sixth century B.C.E., pederasty was a commonly accepted and expected feature of the Greek gymnasium (pp. 64–97, 199–273).

Most athletic events and activities were limited to male participants, and women were actually prohibited from attending events such as the Olympic Games. There is evidence of women victors, such as Kyniska of Sparta, in the Olympic horse races (*hippikos agōn*), but she would not actually have been present in the competition because the victor in these race was the horse's owner, not the male rider. However, women did compete in their own (separate) competitions at times. The most extensive evidence of female athletic participation comes from Sparta, but women's athletic events are also attested across the Greek world, most notably in the *Heraia* in Olympia, an athletic race/festival in honor of the goddess Hera. Spartan women's athletics were particularly notable in ancient sources because the participants would often compete in the nude or seminude, which was unheard of in classical Athens. Such notability is confirmed in the findings of archaic statues of women in "racing costume," seminude (compared to contemporaneous depictions of women) yet not eroticized (Fantham et al., 1994, pp. 59–60). In addition, the athletic training for these women seems to have included some amount of education (including literacy) for younger women.

Slaves and Others on the Margins. Because of the nature of the literary and archaeological remnants, most of the solid evidence regarding social interaction in the Greek and Roman worlds attests to the activities of elite men and, at least occasionally, women; however, the majority of wo/men did not live such lives or have the ability to participate in these activities. Although sources attest to the presence of slaves and other lower-class workers, there is little evidence reflecting the realities of their social lives. Enslavement in the Greco-Roman world was widespread and often harsh; most accounts of slavery—and interactions between masters and slaves—give only an idealized perspective of these interactions from the elite/master's view. Slaves likely formed informal social networks as well as romantic relationships and families; however, Roman law did not validate slave relationships and families. In particular, children of slaves (whether fathered by another slave, their master, or another) remained slaves and could be sold or employed at their masters' discretion.

The lives of prostitutes in the Greco-Roman world are the most obvious example of the ways in which the lives of those on society's margin were gendered and sexualized. Although the roles of the *hetairai* ("courtesans") as sympotic prostitutes have been discussed above, the figure and ideal of the *hetaira*, certainly by Roman times and even in the classical period, was primarily a literary construct. The far more common lot of prostitutes (both female and male) was to be enslaved in a brothel context as a *pornē*, having little control of their bodies or the profit made from their sale. Although there is evidence that prostitutes were marginalized because of their slave status and by some level of moral disdain, physical evidence for prostitution (brothels, graffiti, etc., as found particularly in Pompeii) indicates that spaces of/for prostitution were integrated into the Greco-Roman city without a sense of moral zoning (Peachin, 2011, p. 648). Although no account exists of the daily interactions among prostitutes or between prostitutes and other persons, the lack of evidence that prostitutes were separated from the rest of the city/society suggests that their participation in the social lives of the average city-dweller would not have differed drastically from any other of the enslaved/poorer classes.

Assessment. There were many vehicles, both formal and informal, for social relationships and networking in the Greek and Roman worlds. Generally speaking, the evidence for such interaction increases in proportional relationship to participants' social status, but, clearly, this does not mean that nothing can be said about "the others" in the Greco-Roman world. Furthermore, in almost any arena for social interaction, issues of gender and sexuality can be identified, whether because of the persons who were included/excluded, the types of activities in which participants engaged, or the nature by which the interactions were described and depicted.

[*See also* Economics, *subentry* Roman World; Education, *subentries on* Greek World *and* Roman World; Family Structures, *subentries on* Greek World *and* Roman World; *and* Legal Status, *subentry* Roman World.]

BIBLIOGRAPHY

Ascough, Richard A., Philip A. Harland, and John S. Kloppenborg. *Associations in the Greco-Roman World: A Companion to the Sourcebook*, 2013. http://www.philipharland.com/greco-roman-associations/ (accessed 19 December 2013).

D'Ambra, Eve. *Roman Women*. Cambridge, U.K.: Cambridge University, 2007.

Davidson, James. *Courtesans and Fishcakes: The Consuming Passions of Classical Athens*. New York: St. Martin's, 1997.

Fantham, Elaine, Helene Peet Foley, Natalie Boymel Kampen, Sarah B. Pomeroy, and H. Alan Shapiro. *Women in the Classical World: Image and Text*. New York: Oxford University Press, 1994.

Finley, Moses I. *Economy and Society in Ancient Greece*. New York: Viking, 1953; repr. 1981.

Glazebrook, Allison, and Madeleine M. Henry, eds. *Greek Prostitutes in the Ancient Mediterranean, 800 B.C.E–200 C.E.* Madison: University of Wisconsin Press, 2011.

Halperin, David M. *One Hundred Years of Homosexuality: And Other Essays on Greek Love*. New York: Routledge, 1990.

Harland, Philip A. *Associations, Synagogues, and Congregations: Claiming a Place in Ancient Mediterranean Society*. Minneapolis: Fortress, 2003.

Hopkins, Keith. *Conquerors and Slaves: Sociological Studies in Roman History*. Vol. 1. Cambridge, U.K.: Cambridge University Press, 1978.

Johnson-DeBaufre, Melanie. "'Gazing upon the Invisible': Archaeology, Historiography, and the Elusive Wo/men of 1 Thessalonians." In *From Roman to Early Christian Thessalonikē: Studies in Religion and Archaeology*, edited by Laura Nasrallah, Charalambos Bakirtzis, and Steven J. Friesen, pp. 73–108. Harvard Theological Studies 64. Cambridge, Mass.: Harvard University Press, 2010.

Kurke, Leslie. *Coins, Bodies, Games, and Gold: The Politics of Meaning in Archaic Greece*. Princeton, N.J.: Princeton University Press, 1999.

MacMullen, Ramsay. *Roman Social Relations: 50 B.C. to A.D. 284*. New Haven, Conn.: Yale University Press, 1974.

Miller, Stephen G. *Ancient Greek Athletics*. New Haven, Conn.: Yale University Press, 2004.

Peachin, Michael, ed. *The Oxford Handbook of Social Relations in the Roman World*. Oxford: Oxford University Press, 2011.

Phang, Sara Elise. *The Marriage of Roman Soldiers (13 235): Law and Family in the Imperial Army*. Leiden, The Netherlands: Brill, 2001.

Pomeroy, Sarah B. *Goddesses, Whores, Wives, and Slaves: Women in Classical Antiquity*. New York: Schocken, 1975.

Scanlon, Thomas F. *Eros and Greek Athletics*. Oxford: Oxford University Press, 2002.

James N. Hoke

New Testament

The New Testament provides a diverse collection of the ways in which early Christians sought to navigate their relationship to and interaction with one another and broader society. The social interactions depicted traverse the fine line between rhetoric and historicity, the ideal and the actual. As such, these interactions provide partial glimpses of the lives of early Christians filtered through particular, often patriarchal, authorial lenses. The renewed interest in social-scientific criticism (sometimes called social-historical criticism), along with attention to social history that arose in the latter half of the twentieth century, helped to place the social relations of early Christianity and the lens through which they were imaged in relation to, not in isolation from, the broader civic, political, religious, and cultural frameworks operating within Greco-Roman society. Using the social sciences, these biblical scholars began to explore not only the historical contexts of texts but also how the social contexts and cultural patterns of Mediterranean society might be expressed, implied, or reenvisioned in biblical texts. Judge, Malina, Neyrey, Meeks, and others engaged in interdisciplinary approaches that utilized sociological-anthropological models and theories in addition to cross-cultural comparative studies to suggest fuller depictions of the lives of the early Christians.

In the same period, feminist and liberationist scholars brought attention to the women and other marginalized groups often overlooked or neglected in these traditional treatments. Schüssler Fiorenza (1983) signaled the rise in attention to "women's history," which sought to reconstruct the lives and contribution of women within the history of early Christianity. In her work Schüssler Fiorenza, along with others such as Margaret MacDonald (1999) and Ross Shepard Kraemer (1992), have helped to challenge traditional understandings of the role of women in early Christianity by recognizing how the texts and traditional interpretations were products of patriarchal cultures imbued with androcentric perspectives. Additionally, feminists showed that the invisibility of women in the public sphere and in accounts of social interactions presented a conceptual idealization of society rather than the actual lived experience of women (Osiek and MacDonald, 2006, p. 3). Epigraphic and other archeological materials further aided in supporting such claims by showing instances of women taking part in a range of professional and social aspects of public life.

Illuminating women's history and the histories of other marginalized persons such as slaves and prostitutes has helped to disrupt the often rigidly erected binaries thought to govern the Greco-Roman world, especially with regard to gender. These histories demonstrate that social interactions rarely were determined on the basis of one aspect of identity. Instead, factors of class, ethnicity, geographic location, level of Romanization, and status as free/d or slave shaped the nature of and accessibility to certain social interactions. For example, an elite woman would have much more freedom in the public sphere than was previously assumed when strict public/private distinctions were upheld on the basis of gender. Finally, it should be understood that the social experimentation or conservatism present in New Testament texts with regard to gender and social interactions provides points of comparison with the ever-evolving social dynamics found within Greco-Roman society.

Honor and Shame. The values of honor and shame played fundamental roles in shaping the social interactions of the Mediterranean world. Constructions of honor and shame took diverse forms depending on factors such as geographic location, cultural expectations, and level of Roman enculturation. Despite these variations, the concepts of honor and shame contained gendered assumptions that are particularly relevant to examining the social interactions depicted in the New Testament. In general, honor related to one's esteem or reputation within the eyes of a community. It was a masculine value either established through genealogy or acquired through competition and the virtue of one's daily living (Rohrbaugh, 2010, p. 118). Shame, on the other hand, was characterized as a feminine attribute. Shame was conceived of in both positive and negative senses. The negative understanding of shame was associated with loss of reputation, which could be a result of factors such as one's chosen profession (e.g., prostitute or tax collector). In the positive sense, shame was constructed as a concern for one's honor. This applied most readily to women and a concern for the proper control of their sexuality. Thus, masculine honor and feminine shame were intertwined by the need for the man to preserve his honor through the protection of his female kin's

sexual chastity as well as through his own self-mastery.

Concern about shame and honor did not escape the consciousness of the early Christian communities. Language and constructions of shame and honor are prevalent throughout New Testament texts, helping to define and regulate the community's social interactions and how they are perceived by broader society. At times, the New Testament conceptualization challenges dominant ideologies by ascribing honor to those considered low, weak, and shameful by society (1 Cor 12:22–24 NRSV) while assigning shame to the powerful and prestigious (Matt 23). Yet with regard to sexuality, the traditional societal values of female sexual virtue and passive submission focused on male desire and self-control remained largely unaffected (Rom 1:24–32; 1 Cor 7:36–38; Gal 5:19–26; 1 Tim 2:9–15). Thus, female sexuality existing outside what was deemed virtuous became an area of concern for the early Christian assemblies (*ekklēsia*) as seen in the desire to remarry young widows (1 Tim 5:11–14) or to avoid lying with prostitutes for fear of communal pollution (1 Cor 6:15–16). The collectivism found within Mediterranean culture carried the implication that the actions of one member carried implications for the reputations of all with whom the individual was formally associated. Thus, concern about honor and shame influenced social interactions on individual and communal levels.

Patronage, Friendship, and Hospitality. The social relationships formed through the practices associated with patronage, friendship, and hospitality display the negotiations of power, honor, and responsibility that took place within Mediterranean culture. Although the duration, purpose, and social expectations of each relationship differed, they collectively highlight the ways in which multiple aspects of identity must be considered when constructing the range of social relationships in which an individual could engage.

Patronage. The patronage system of the Greco-Roman world functioned as a reciprocal exchange of goods, services, or resource between two parties in an unequal relationship. In such relationships, the client, whether an individual or a group, received resources with the expectation that loyalty and public support would be reciprocated from the patron. The patronage system provided opportunities for both men and women because both could function as patrons or clients. For women, this carried particular benefits in the political realm. Although women were unable to vote or hold elected office, patronage provided an avenue to influence political matters and other negotiations from which their gender formally excluded them. Although this level of power was normally associated with elite women, epigraphic evidence shows that women of lower status who had acquired modest resources through business or trade also served as patrons (Osiek and MacDonald, 2006, pp. 201–203).

Aspects of the patronage system present themselves in a number of places throughout the New Testament. It appears that a number of men and women served as patrons providing for the needs of the early Christian assemblies. Women and men such as Mary the mother of John Mark, Lydia, Gaius, and Nympha demonstrated patronage to a group by opening their homes to the early Christian assemblies (Acts 12:12, 16:14–15; Rom 16:23; Col 4:15). Likewise, care for widows, often performed by other widows with financial means, demonstrated how personal resources could be used to benefit the assembly through the reduction of financial strain on the collective whole (Acts 9:36–42; 1 Tim 5:9–10). Personal patronage also took place in the early assemblies as witnessed in the relationship of Phoebe and Paul in Romans 16:1–2. Paul describes Phoebe as a benefactor (*prostatis*) of many, including the apostle himself. Although the motives for Paul's specific naming of Phoebe as a benefactor are debated, what remains clear is the influential role that Phoebe held with Paul and the wider assembly (MacDonald, 1999, pp. 207–209).

These examples of the patronage system within the early Christian assemblies provide glimpses of how women and men with resources could gain the ability to exercise power and acquire honor not traditionally afforded them by society. It remains disputed, however, whether such displays of wealth served to bolster the early Christian assemblies or perpetuated further inequalities to the detriment of the assemblies (Tamez, 2007, pp. 7–14).

Friendship. Friendship in the ancient world was traditionally framed as a relationship between two men of equal or nearly equal status. The bond of friendship often superseded that of the marital relationship as a space where men mutually developed aspects of their political and spiritual lives and provided mutual assistance to one another. Within the gospel of John, Jesus's relationship with the beloved disciple may be viewed to reflect such intimacy (John 13:23, 19:26–27, 21:20–23). Additionally, at John 15:12–15, Jesus names his disciples as his friends (*philos*), closing the gap of inequality between them by no longer calling them slaves. Although Jesus shows love toward women as well, such as Mary and Martha (John 11:5), the most explicit outward expressions of friendship tend to focus on male relationships.

The language of friendship is sparse within the New Testament, particularly in the letters of Paul. One reason for this may be that during the early Roman Empire the language of friendship became intertwined with the patronage system. Although friendship in the traditional sense was assumed to be among equals, it also could represent varied degrees of asymmetrical relationships such as those found within the patronage system (*amici minors, amici paupers, amici inferiors*; Osiek and MacDonald, 2006, pp. 196–197). The possibility for blurring the distinctions between friendship and patronage may explain Paul's apparent preference for using the language of kinship over that of friendship.

Hospitality. As within broader Mediterranean culture, hospitality (*philoxenia*) was a valued practice of early Christianity. Early Christians were called to extend hospitality, which generally included providing food, lodging, provisions, and protection to guests and travelers. The resources and social networks offered as part of hospitality proved vital for the spread of Christianity as they sustained the ministry of Jesus, his disciples, and later itinerant missionaries. As the organizational structure of the assemblies developed, hospitality became a characteristic expected of the overseer or bishop (*episkopos*) of the assembly (1 Tim 3:2; Tit 1:8). Despite general exhortations to show hospitality (Rom 12:13; Heb 13:2), the practice came to define community boundaries, with those outside the confines of the group excluded from receiving the welcoming embrace of the community (2 John 9–11; 3 John 9–10).

Hospitality carried with it certain gendered assumptions. For example, it was customary for the male head of the household to formally extend the offer of hospitality. Some scholars read Jesus's exchange with the Samaritan woman at the well in John 4 as following the customary protocols of hospitality (Arterbury, 2005, pp. 113–118). The New Testament also demonstrates that female patrons and heads of households, along with couples such as Aquila and Priscilla, also extended hospitality to the assemblies and itinerants like Paul. Regardless of who offered the hospitality, the actual work of providing for guests often fell to women. Whether directly involved in providing the services or overseeing the actions of the household, women served as the embodiments of hospitality. This is perhaps best seen in the Pastoral Epistles, where one of the "good works" necessary for a widow to be officially placed on the list of widows was to have shown hospitality (1 Tim 5:10).

Voluntary Associations. The legitimacy of comparing Christian assemblies to voluntary associations (*collegia*) and their organizational structures remains debated among biblical scholars. As with other comparative projects executed within social scientific criticism, however, the aim of such scholarly endeavors is not to identify a direct genealogy between the groups but rather to explore the similarities and differences found within the language, structuring principles, actions, and makeup of these organizations. Hence, similar to comparative studies of early Christian assemblies and synagogues, placing assemblies and voluntary associations in conversation can open up greater understanding of the social interactions of the early Christian communities.

Greco-Roman voluntary associations afforded individuals the opportunity to gather on the basis of a shared trade, cult, familial network, geographic location, etc. These associations provided social, professional, and political benefits to their members such as shared meals, funerary and burial practices, and patronage benefits. The makeup of associations varied depending on the nature of the association. Although men comprised the majority of professional associations, there is evidence of all-female and mixed-gender groups composed especially in religious associations. Membership lists and other epigraphic sources indicate not only participation but also the leadership of women and other marginalized persons in some mixed-gender associations. Richard Ascough (2003) posits that associations afforded such individuals "a location in which they could participate more fully in collective life than was usually allowed them in the Greek and Roman cities and villages" (p. 58).

The early Christian assemblies may have appeared to broader society as similar to voluntary associations in existence at that time. Members of Christian assemblies may have also belonged to other associations related to their occupation, household, or neighborhood. Comparative work with voluntary associations has helped to highlight that Christian assemblies were not homogenous in their use of language or organizational structure. Many appear to be of mixed gender, given that many of Paul's letters acknowledge female leaders and patrons within the community. For example, in Philippi, Euodia and Syntyche, two women with no male counterpart, are named among those who struggled with Paul "in the work of the gospel," likely serving as leaders in the community (Phil 4:2). Even in texts such as 1 Thessalonians that contain no explicit reference to or instruction for women, Melanie Johnson-DeBaufre (2010) argues that women's presence in the community must be taken seriously despite their seeming textual invisibility (pp. 92–102).

As with voluntary associations, the Christian assemblies also held the potential for social experimentation in roles defined by gender, class, or status. For example, experimentation with regard to gender and sexual norms seems to have taken place within the meals of the Corinthian assemblies. Paul's (or a later author's) exhortation for the silencing of women in the assembly suggests that such actions carried implications not only for the assembly but also within broader society (Taussig, 2009, pp. 158–161).

The Military. The Roman imperial system was undergirded by a highly gendered ideology of conquest and domination. Within this ideological framework, Roman military victory is imaged as invulnerable and impenetrable masculinity that conquers penetrable and controllable femininity. Triumph imagery such as found on victory monuments and coins graphically depicts this ideology with the feminized conquered nation in a place of submission to a Roman solider, emperor, or the hypermasculine, militarized Roma (for example, Judea Capta coins, Claudius and Britannia at Aphrodisias; Lopez, 2008). The entirely male Roman military and governing structures served as physical embodiments of this ideology that maintained control over Rome's ever-increasing colonial expansion. Tactics of fear and intimidation such as public executions, torture, and rape were used to shame, feminize, and subdue occupied peoples and to quell possible rebellion. The trial and crucifixion of Jesus displays the traditional reenactment and enforcement of Roman domination. Jesus as a social deviant is physically tortured, verbally mocked, and sexually humiliated (Mark 15:16–20 and parallels). As David Tombs (1999) suggests, the possibility of sexual assault also existed in the hypersexualized environment of torture and crucifixion (pp. 100–107). Thus, Jesus's trial and public crucifixion functions on several levels to shape the interactions between the general public and the Roman military. It is a public display of imperial power enforced by military might to engender terror and submission. The act is meant not only to shame and feminize Jesus as an individual, but also to bring shame on all those who associate with him.

The response to Jesus's crucifixion event displays the complex ways in which early Christianity sought to negotiate broader social interactions within an environment imprinted with Jesus's Roman imperial ideology. Subverting the dominate culture by bestowing honor and glory on the one society deemed a criminal (1 Cor 1:18–25), the cross that was deemed shameful by society became a site dominant for the early Christians (Gal 6:14).

This inversion of values, however, did not preclude Christians from occasionally employing highly masculinized military rhetoric and imagery to frame their interactions with the broader society (Hobbs, 1995, pp. 266–268). Missionaries become fellow soldiers (Phil 2:25; Phlm 2), and metaphors of military warfare are employed to describe Christian life and discipleship (2 Cor 10:1–5; 1 Tim 1:18; 2 Tim 2:3–4). The use of military imagery also plays a prominent role in depictions of Christians engaging in spiritual warfare (Eph 6:11–18) as well as in apocalyptic visions, particularly in the book of Revelation. The hypermasculinized battles and judgment of Revelation that includes the brutal, fiery death of the feminized Rome in the figure of the Great Whore Babylon (Rev 17) leaves an unsettling image of how the gendered elements of victory and conquest continue to perform in the visions of John of Patmos and other faithful Christian soldiers.

Contribution. Attention to the social interactions depicted in the texts of the New Testament illuminates the diverse ways in which early Christian communities navigated life in community and society. Comparative studies engaging contemporaneous cultural systems open spaces to explore how the early Christian assemblies negotiated issues of power, honor, and identity formation. Recognizing that the texts provide limited vantage points through which to view the social relations of early Christianity, continued attention to gender, as well as race and ethnicity, class, and status as free/d or slave, will aid with continued efforts to more fully acknowledge the diverse social locations, privileges, and oppressions experienced by the members of early Christian assemblies.

[*See also* Economics, *subentry* New Testament; Imagery, Gendered, *subentry* Pauline Literature; Religious Participation, *subentry* New Testament; Social Interaction, *subentries on* Early Church, Early Judaism, *and* Greek and Roman Worlds; *and* Social-Scientific Approaches.]

BIBLIOGRAPHY

Arterbury, Andrew. *Entertaining Angels: Early Christian Hospitality in Its Mediterranean Setting*. Sheffield, U.K.: Sheffield Phoenix, 2005.

Ascough, Richard S. *Paul's Macedonian Associations: The Social Context of Philippians and 1 Thessalonians.* Tübingen, Germany: Mohr Siebeck, 2003.

Hobbs, Raymond. "The Language of Warfare in the New Testament." In *Modelling Early Christianity: Social-Scientific Studies of the New Testament in Its Context,* edited by Philip F. Esler, pp. 259–273. London: Routledge, 1995.

Johnson-DeBaufre, Melanie. "'Gazing upon the Invisible': Archaeology, Historiography, and the Elusive Wo/men of 1 Thessalonians." In *From Roman to Early Christian Thessalonikē: Studies in Religion and Archaeology,* edited by Laura Nasrallah, Charalambos Bakirtzis, and Steven J. Friesen, pp. 73–108. Cambridge, Mass.: Harvard University Press, 2010.

Kraemer, Ross Shepard. *Her Share of the Blessings: Women's Religions among Pagans, Jews, and Christians in the Greco-Roman World.* New York: Oxford University Press, 1992.

MacDonald, Margaret Y. "Reading Real Women through the Undisputed Letters of Paul." In *Women and Christian Origins,* edited by Ross Shepard Kraemer and Mary Rose D'Angelo, pp. 199–220. New York: Oxford University Press, 1999.

Osiek, Carolyn, and David L. Balch. *Families in the New Testament World: Households and House Churches.* Louisville, Ky.: Westminster John Knox, 1997.

Osiek, Carolyn, and Margaret MacDonald, with Janet H. Tulloch. *A Woman's Place: House Churches in Earliest Christianity.* Minneapolis: Fortress, 2006.

Rohrbaugh, Richard L. "Honor: Core Value in the Biblical World." In *Understanding the Social World of the New Testament,* edited by Dietmar Neufeld and Richard E. DeMaris, pp. 109–125. London: Routledge, 2010.

Schüssler Fiorenza, Elisabeth. *In Memory of Her: A Feminist Theological Reconstruction of Christian Origins.* New York: Crossroad, 1983.

Tamez, Elsa. *Struggles for Power in Early Christianity: A Study in the First Letter to Timothy.* Maryknoll, N.Y.: Orbis, 2007.

Taussig, Hal. *In the Beginning Was the Meal: Social Experimentation and Early Christian Identity.* Minneapolis: Fortress, 2009.

Tombs, David. "Crucifixion, State Terror, and Sexual Abuse." *Union Seminary Quarterly Review* 53, nos. 1–2 (1999): 89–109.

Karri L. Whipple

Early Judaism

Within the period of early Judaism (500 B.C.E.–500 C.E.), Jews engaged in a variety of social interactions both with other Jews and with non-Jews. These interactions helped to cement relationships among individuals, families, and communities, contributed to the material well-being of Jewish communities, and expanded the range of social, cultural, and economic opportunities for Jews. Social interactions in early Judaism were often informed by the practices and ideas already established in the biblical texts and thus carry with them a religious dimension. An examination of social interactions, however, focuses more on how Jews experienced their daily lives not only as Jews but also within the broader social and cultural milieus in which they lived. These interactions developed not only from biblical traditions but also from the adaptation of new ideas spurred on by the engagement with other cultures, particularly Hellenistic and Roman. The available sources, primarily textual (e.g., Josephus, Philo, rabbinic texts) and epigraphic, provide a wide range of attitudes and aspirations but offer only fleeting glimpses in the actual practices of Jews, and even fewer regarding women, in this period.

Social Interactions among Jews. Perhaps the most common if not the most important social interaction was that of marriage. Marriages created new social units that not only served as the legitimate venue for the production of children and the perpetuation of family lines but also became an important center of economic production. Various biblical traditions (Exod 21:10–11; 22:16–17; Deut 24:1–4; 25:5–10) present basic rules that regulated the formation and dissolution of a marriage, along with appropriate conduct expected of husbands and wives, including the disposition of economic assets during marriage and after death through inheritance. Marriages were most typically established through the offering of a *mohar* (bride price), in which the husband or his family would present a sum of money to the bride's father. Ancient Israel was a polygynous society, permitting a man to marry multiple wives while a woman was permitted to be married to only one man at a time. Husbands were obligated to provide food, clothing, and marital rights (*onah*). Wives, at least according to one perspective, were expected to fear God, garner respect from the community, and make important contributions to the household's economic productivity (Prov 31). If the husband predeceased his wife before the birth of children, the husband's brother was expected to take his sister-in-law as a wife and enable her to bear a child that would be recognized as the issue of the deceased man (Gen 38:8; Deut 25:5–6).

In early Judaism marriage continued to be a critical element of social relations. The rabbis expressed this understanding in particularly enthusiastic statement, "Whoever has no wife is in a situation lacking in goodness, without help, without joy, without blessing, without atonement, even without peace, without life, nor his he a complete person" (*b. Qidd. 29b*). Several epitaphs lament those who died before marriage (e.g., *CIJ* 1509, 1512). While marriage remained an integral part of Jewish life, the practices that defined and regulated marital unions underwent significant transformation. Polygyny remained an accepted practice (*m. Yebam.* 16.1; *m. Ketub* 10.1; *m. Qidd.* 3.6), although some Jews objected to or discouraged a man from taking multiple wives (CD 4.20–21; ARNB 2). Instead of the bride price, it became customary for women to bring wealth into the marriage in the form of a dowry (*T. Jud.* 13.4; *T. Jos.* 18.3; Ps.-Phoc. 199–200; Philo *Fug.* 29; *Spec.* 2.125) and, at least in rabbinic discussions, to retain ownership of the principle, which could then be bequeathed to her children. Marriage documents, sometimes referred to as a *ketubah*, specified the responsibilities a husband had for his wife, such as the provision of food and clothing, and also stipulated a sum that the husband would owe his wife upon the dissolution of the marriage, either through divorce or death (*m. Ketub.* 1.2; 5.1). Many traditions also identify the expectations for women in marriage, such as submission to their husbands, and the performance of certain tasks, particularly those concerned with child rearing, food preparation, and clothing production (*Spec.* 1.138; *Ag. Ap.* 2.201; *m. Qidd.* 5.5). While many traditions from the Bible to the rabbis (Deut 24:1; *Ant.* 15.259–260; *m. Yebam.* 14.1) vest men only with the ability to effect divorce, there is some suggestion that in practice wives could initiate the process.

Two other important developments in marriage played a vital role in defining Jewish identity. Whereas biblical traditions understand that the transmission of ethnic identity passes through the father, the early rabbis adopted the principle of matrilineal descent in which personal identity was determined by the mother (*m. Qidd.* 3.12). A second marital practice that greatly defined Jewish identity during this period is the widespread practice of endogamy. Biblical traditions (Exod 34:11–16; Deut 7:1–4) enjoined the Israelites not to marry among the seven nations that inhabited the land that Israel possessed. During the Persian period and later, the targeted restrictions became a generalized prohibition against marriages with all non-Jews. Throughout the period endogamy remained widely accepted (Ezra 9:11–12; Tob 4.12; *Jub.* 30.7; Add Esth C26; *Jos. Asen.* 8.5–7) and practiced (Tacitus *Hist.* 5.5.2). Beginning with biblical traditions and continuing throughout antiquity, various groups of elite Jews, such as priests and later rabbis, also expressed a preference for marriages between members of their own social group, and disparaged marriages with socially undesirable persons, such as a prostitute, *mamzer*, or *am ha-aretz* (Lev 21:7, 13–15; 22:12; *Ant.* 4.244–245; 14.403; *Sifra Qed.* 7; *b. Pesaḥ.* 49a–b; *b. Qidd.* 69a–74a).

The family and its household was also an important center of economic activity, both production and sale. The book of Proverbs extols men who engage in honest, hard work (Prov 12:9; 16:11; 18:9). Women, too, were expected to contribute to the material well-being of the family. Proverbs 31 describes a woman of valor as one who "seeks wool and flax and works with willing hands" and "considers a field and buys it." In the book of Tobit, Anna keeps the family alive through her work (Tob 2.11–12). The rabbis maintain the importance of economic self-sufficiency. They require that a father teach his son a trade; although certain trades, including those associated with women, were strongly discouraged (*b. Qidd. 29a, 82a*). The rabbis also acknowledged the significant economic role played by women. They identify several forms of household labor as the responsibility of women (*m. Ketub.* 5.5). Most of these tasks, such as food preparation and serving (Gen 18:6) and textile production (Prov 31:22), have clear biblical antecedents. Women also frequently engaged in income-producing occupations, sometimes alongside men, particularly the production and sale of textiles and foodstuffs, but also as innkeepers, hairdressers, midwives, and professional mourners (*m. Roš. Haš.* 2.5; *m. Ketub.* 4.4; 9.4; *m. B. Qam.* 10.9; 11.7; *m. Hal.* 2.7; *m. Kelim* 15.3; *t. Demai* 4.32; *t. B. Qam.* 11.7; *t. Qidd.* 5.14). In contrast to the financial autonomy assumed by women in Proverbs 31, however, the rabbis grant husbands economic control of their wives' income (*m. Ketub.* 6.1).

Another common social interaction was that between master and slave. The Bible depicts slavery as an appropriate social practice and slaves, both male and female and both Israelites and foreigners, as a regular presence in Israelite society. Prominent biblical figures, both men and women, owned slaves and transmitted them to their children, particularly as a gift or inheritance (Gen 16:1; 29:29; 2 Sam 6:20–22; 1 Kgs 9:22). Legal materials prescribe the appropriate treatment of slaves (Exod 21:2–9, 20–21, 26; Lev 25:39–46). Throughout the Hellenistic and Roman periods, Jews continued to see slavery as a necessary, even proper, part of the social order (Tob 10.10; Jdt 8.7; Sus 15; Philo *Spec.* 2.123; Josephus *Life* 429; *t. Soṭah* 2.9; *Sifrei Deut* 188; *Cod. theod.* 16.9.4), The rabbis, a few of whom were slave owners themselves (*m. Ber.* 2.7; *y. Giṭ.* 4.6 [*46a*]; *y. Ketub.* 5.5 [*30a*]), frequently discuss issues surrounding the acquisition, status, treatment, and manumission of slaves (*m. Ketub. 8.5; b. Yebam. 45a–48b; b. Giṭ. 37b–45a; b. Qidd. 14b–24b*). Slaves performed a variety of tasks within homes and on large estates, including food and clothing production, cleaning, washing, the care and education of children, assistance with business transactions, and afforded their masters an enhanced social status.

Jews were not only slave owners but also slaves themselves, owned by masters who were both Jews and non-Jews. Jewish enslavement came about in part because of economic indebtedness (2 Kgs 4:1; Philo *Spec.* 2.122; *Sifre Deut* 26), although the practice was subject to criticism (Lev 25:39; Jer 34:9–22; Amos 2:6; Neh 5:1–5), and its effects mitigated, in theory if not also in practice, through the requirement that Israelite slaves be freed in the sabbatical year (Exod 21:2; Deut 15:12; Jer 34:14; Philo *Spec.* 2.84–85; *m. Qidd.* 1.2). More frequently, Jews became slaves as the result of military conquest, particularly in the two revolts against Rome (*J.W.* 1.180; 2.68; 3.303, 539; *Ant.* 12.144). Enslavement for Jews was particularly problematic, not only because of the humiliation and physical hardship involved, but also because sale to a non-Jewish owner could result in Jewish slaves being exposed to idolatry and having to abandon their Jewish life and identity (*m. Giṭ.* 4.4–6; *t. ʿAbot. Zar.* 3.16–18). For this reason, some Jews considered the prospect of enslavement unbearable. Josephus dramatically recounts a story of how almost a thousand Jews who had fled to Masada during the First Revolt made the decision to die as free persons rather than be captured by the Romans and sold into slavery (*J.W.* 7.323–336, 382, 386). Clearly, however, not all Jews would have approved such drastic decisions (e.g., Esth 7:4; Jdt 7.26–27).

Jews also interacted with one another through the practice of benefaction. Numerous inscriptions record the names of persons, both men and women, who donated funds toward the construction, maintenance, and operation of synagogues, which served not only as houses of worship but also community centers. While a single individual occasionally functioned in this role, more commonly these projects were the result of a collective effort undertaken by multiple persons and sometimes the community as a whole. The rabbis went so far as to permit a community to obligate its members to support such projects (*t. B. Meṣiʿa* 11.23).

Jewish social interactions extended not only to institutional needs but also to the care and well-being of poor and disadvantaged members of the community. Deuteronomy commands Israelites to give gladly and generously to the poor (Deut 15:7–11), and specifies certain categories of people, the orphan, the widow, and the sojourner, who deserve special protection and consideration (Deut 10:18; 14:29; 15; 16:11, 14; 24:17; 27:19). Biblical traditions exhibit a particular interest in ensuring an adequate supply of food. The rules for agricultural practices mandated that a portion of the crop be set aside for such persons (Deut 24:19–21). Prophetic writers advocated for the charitable provision of food. Isaiah announces that God desires people to share their bread with the hungry, and Ezekiel identifies the giving of food to the hungry as a mark of righteousness (Isa 58:7; Ezek 18:7, 16). Nehemiah reported how he responded to the cry of the destitute in Jerusalem by loaning them money and grain and by calling upon the wealthy and powerful to return the property and a portion of the goods exacted from them (Neh 5:1–13). Tobit informs his son that he should concern himself with the poor since charity both delivers a person from death and serves as an excellent offering to God (Tob 4.1–11). Sirach expresses similar sentiments as well, and connects assisting the poor with observing the commandments (Sir 4.1–6, 8; 10.22; 29.9). The community at Qumran also demonstrated a concern for the poor through moral suasion and a charitable program that required its members to contribute the equivalent of two days' wages every month for aiding the poor, needy, and other individuals without means of support (CD 6.16, 21; 14.12–15; 1QS 6.19–20). In Rome, a Jewish man earned praise for having been a "lover of the poor" (*CIJ* 203). The rabbis also placed considerable emphasis on the value of charity, describing it as an act of righteousness, a form of expiation from sin, a religious duty greater than all sacrifices (*b. Sukkah 49a*; *ARNA* 4), equal to all other commandments (*y. Pe'ah* 1.1 [*15b–c*]; *b. B. Bat. 9a*), an antidote to death (*y. Pe'ah* 1.1 [*15b*]; *b. Roš. Haš. 18a*; *b. Sanh. 156b*; *b. B. Bat. 10a*; *ARNA* 3), and capable of bringing redemption nearer (*b. B. Bat. 10a*). The rabbis also prescribed that communities should establish regular programs or institutions, such as the *tamhui*, to provide sustenance for the poor.

Social Interactions between Jews and Non-Jews. Jews interacted socially not only with each other, but also with non-Jews. Such interactions were quite varied and complex and often governed by religious commitments and values. By requiring Jews to worship only the God of Israel (Exod 20:3), and to refrain from the practices of the nations (Lev 18:3, 24–26; 20:23; Deut 12:30; 18:9), biblical traditions inhibited Jews from engaging fully in social relations with non-Jews. In later periods, Jews continued to deny the reality of other deities, to ridicule those who worshipped them, and in certain circumstances to refrain from associating too closely with their non-Jewish neighbors (Isa 44:6–20; *Jub.* 11–12; 20; 22; Aris. Ex. 134–138; *Sib. Or.* 3.29–53; Wis 13–15; Philo, *Dec.* 52–81). Specific beliefs and practices greatly restricted certain types of interactions. The principle of endogamy made marriages between Jews and non-Jews a rarity. Dietary laws (e.g., Lev 11) made it difficult for Jews to dine with non-Jews (*Jub.* 22.16–17; Jdt 12.1–2; Aris. Ex. 139–142; *t. 'Abot. Zar.* 4.6; *b. 'Abot. Zar. 8a*; Tacitus *Hist.* 5.5.2). Refusals by Jews to marry non-Jews and share meals with them prompted some non-Jews to describe Jews as hostile and misanthropic (e.g., *Ag. Ap.* 1.309; 2.121, 258; Tacitus *Hist.* 5.5.1; Philostratus *Vit. Apol.* 5.33). On occasion, these attitudes translated into acts of violence against Jews and their communities, such as the destructive anti-Jewish riots of Alexandria in 38 C.E.

Despite these attitudes and practices, Jews developed a more tolerant if not sometimes appreciative attitude toward gentiles and their cultural practices and institutions. In certain respects, these attitudes have their foundation in the biblical traditions that implore Israelites to treat others who lived among them (i.e., sojourners) with respect and justice (Exod 22:20; 23:9; Lev 19:33–34; 24:22; Num 9:14; 15:15–16; Deut 1:16; 10:19; 24:17). The Septuagint takes this idea a step further by expressing a more accepting attitude toward pagan worship as it translates the injunction "You shall not revile God" as "You shall not revile gods" (Exod 22:27). And despite the antipathy toward pagan worship in general, Jews often recognized that individual non-Jews could be considered righteous (*t. 'Abot. Zar.* 9.4; *t. Sanh.* 13.2), and even worthy of assistance, as seen in the rabbinic mandate that care for the poor be extended to gentiles as well as Jews (*m. Giṭ.* 5.8; *t. Giṭ.* 3.13; *y. Demai* 4.6 [*24a*]; *y. 'Abot. Zar.* 1.3 [*39c*]). Jews not only developed a more accepting attitude toward non-Jews but also willingly accommodated themselves to the urban culture in which they lived. The story of Gamliel and the bath of Aphrodite exemplifies this attitude.

A philosopher finds the great sage bathing in the bathhouse of Aphrodite and points out that Jewish law forbids the rabbi from such activities (Deut 13:8). The rabbi responds, "They do not say, 'Let us make a bathhouse as an ornament to Aphrodite,' but they say, 'Let us make Aphrodite as an ornament to the bathhouse'" (*m. ʿAbot. Zar.* 3.4). Gamliel's clever riposte reflects widespread thinking not only among rabbis but among Jews in general, who, by differentiating between the ritual and the aesthetic, were able to participate in activities that might otherwise be perceived as a violation of Jewish principles.

Jews lived and worked alongside non-Jews in numerous contexts. Jews often served in the armies of the Hellenistic monarchs and Roman Empire. Many Jews, both men and women, frequented bathhouses (*t. Soṭah* 5.9; *t. Qidd.* 7.6–7), and many men partook of the education and socializing offered through the gymnasium (e.g., *CPJ* 2.151), two of the most important civic institutions of the time. Jews attended venues of entertainment, such as theaters, odea, stadia, hippodromes, and amphitheaters, and joined non-Jews in a wide array of public events such as plays, athletic and musical competitions, and, in the Roman period, chariot racing and gladiatorial combats. Philo was a regular attendee of theatrical performances, as were Jews in Miletus, Aphrodisias, and possibly Sicily, where seats were specifically designated for their use. Not all Jews approved of such entertainments. The rabbis in particular expressed an aversion to such activities and the places of their performance (*b. ʿAbot. Zar. 18b*) and used the biblical injunction against following the practices of the nations (Lev 18:3) to justify their position (e.g., *Sifra Aharei Mot 13*). A few Jews led a life as men of public letters, such as philosopher, sophist, rhetor, or poet. The most famous example is the philosopher Philo of Alexandria, who melded his understanding of Jewish texts, ideas, and practices with his knowledge of Greek philosophy to produce a complex presentation of Judaism as an expression of universal truth.

Jews also assumed a variety of administrative titles and responsibilities in municipal governments and the Roman imperial bureaucracy. In the Hellenistic period Jews functioned as police officers, secretaries, and possibly advisors of the Ptolemaic kings, all positions part of the state apparatus (*CPJ* 1.17–19, 25, 194–226, 137; *CIJ* 1443; 2 Macc 1.10; *Ag. Ap.* 2.64; *J.W.* 1.175; *b. Sanh. 25b*). In the late Ptolemaic period, one Onias served as secretary or scribe in the royal court (*CPJ* 137). In Alexandria, Alexander, the brother of Philo, and Demetrius served as *alabarch* or customs superintendent (*Ant.* 19.276; 20.100, 147), while other Jews served as river guardians (*Ag. Ap.* 2.64; *J.W.* 1.175; *b. Sanh. 25b*). In first century Cyrene C.E., Eleazar, the son of Jason, was one of the city's *nomophulakes*, and thus among those responsible for the recording and proper administration of the laws (Lüderitz 8). In the imperial period we have several more examples of Jews who assumed civic posts. In the mid-third century C.E. a Jew served as *praepositus stationis*, an official in charge of a custom's post, in Pannonia (*CIJ* 677=*IJudO* Pan3). Jews served as *archiatros*, official municipal doctors, one in second-century Ephesus and another in fifth-century Venosa (*CIJ* 745=*IJudO* 2.32; *CIJ* 600=*JIWE* 1.76). In the first half of the third century, two persons from the Phrygian city of Akmonia assumed various magistracies, including the *agoranomia* (oversight of the market), *sitonia* (supervision of the grain supply), and *strategia* (civic administrator); the titles place them among the city's elite (*CIJ* 760=*IJudO* 2.173, *CIJ* 770=*IJudO* 2.172). In the fifth century two Jews of Side in the south-central region of Asia Minor known as Pamphylia held the post of *zugostates* and so were responsible for ensuring the value of the coinage used there. By the third century Jews served in leading municipal positions, including *bouleutes* or city councillor (*CIJ* 770=*IJudO* 2.172, *CIJ* 788=*IJudO* 2.236). The mosaics from the impressive synagogue in Sardis record the names of nine Jews who held this office. For at least some Jews, assumption of civic office was understood as part of, rather than a deviation from, Jewish life. In the third century Tiberius Claudius Polycharmus prided himself on having performed political functions for the city of Stobi. He did so not only as a citizen of the city but, as he himself noted, in accordance with Judaism (*CIJ* 694=*IJudO* Mac1).

Around this same time Jews also assumed important positions in the administration of the Roman Empire. A Jew in Sardis served as assistant in the imperial archives (*IJudO* 2.76). A few Jews held the posts of *comes* and *palatinus*, titles designating important positions in the imperial court and in provincial administration of the late empire. Certainly the most famous Jew to rise to the office of prefect was Tiberius Julius Alexander, who served as prefect of both Judea and Egypt. By the time he assumed these posts, however, Alexander had renounced his association with the Jewish community.

Participation in civic life, however, had its limitations. While Jews contributed frequently to their own communal institutions, such as the synagogue, they very rarely acted as benefactors of civic buildings or programs. One of the few example comes from the second century B.C.E., when Niketas from Jerusalem donated one hundred drachmas toward the festival of Dionysus in his adopted home of Iasos in Asia Minor (*CIJ* 749=*IJudO* 2.21). Jews also refrained from involvement in the rituals of pagan cults. There are, however, some possible exceptions. Some Jews may have participated in Dionysiac cults (3 Macc 2.25–33), others invoked the gods Zeus, Ge, and Helios in manumission texts from the Bosporus, still others used the Latin expression *dis manibus* on epitaphs, and a few offered praise to god in the temple of Pan Euodos in Egypt (*CIJ* 6*, 60*, 63*, 71*, 464, 678; 690, 711b, 749; 1537–1538; *JIGRE* 121; 122). In each case, however, it is not clear whether these Jews acted so because that is what was expected of them or because it reflects their deep-seated recognition of the reality and power of other gods. Regardless, Jewish participation in pagan religious life remained exceptional.

Social interactions existed not only with Jews participating in civic life but also with non-Jews participating in Jewish communal life. The best documented examples of these interactions are those non-Jews, often referred to as God-fearers, who adopted Jewish observances and participated in the synagogue (*J.W.* 7.45; *Ant.* 14.110; *Ag. Ap.* 1.166–167; 2.82; Acts 10.2). Non-Jews also functioned as benefactors of the Jewish community through their contributions to the Temple in Jerusalem (*Ant.* 14.110) and to synagogues (e.g., *CIJ* 766=*IJudO* 2.168).

An inscription from the city of Aphrodisias provides a fascinating example of the interactions between Jews and non-Jews in late antiquity (*IJudO* 2.14). One side of a square pillar records the names of persons belonging to a group that called itself *dekania* and their donations toward the construction of a memorial. At the head of the list stands a woman, Yael, who is identified as the *prostates* (president) of the organization. This mention and scattered references particularly in the epigraphic record (e.g., Veturia Paula in Rome, *CIJ* 523=*JIWE* 2.577) indicate that women frequently assumed positions of leadership in the Jewish community. The other side contains the names of fifty-five men, most if not all of whom can be identified as Jews. After a brief gap the lower register lists the names of fifty-two men, almost certainly non-Jews, classified according to the inscription as *theosebeis*, generally translated as God-fearers. At the head of the latter group stand nine local magistrates. The inscription, written most likely sometime in the fourth or possibly early fifth century C.E., reflects very close interactions between Jews and non-Jews in Aphrodisias. Remarkably, five of the eighteen persons belonging to this Jewish organization were not born as Jews, including three proselytes, that is, non-Jews who joined the Jewish community as converts, and two *theosebeis* or God-fearers. Despite many uncertainties in the interpretation of this text, it appears that the Jewish community established an alimentary program that provided food relief to the residents of the city and that many non-Jews joined them in making financial contributions to this program. It is impossible to know how common such cooperative interactions were in antiquity, but this one instance offers a glimpse into what social interactions were possible between Jews and non-Jews.

[*See also* Economics, *subentry* Early Judaism; Family Structures, *subentry* Early Judaism; Marriage and Divorce, *subentry* Early Judaism; Race, Class, and Ethnicity, *subentry* Early Judaism; *and* Religious Participation, *subentry* Early Judaism.]

BIBLIOGRAPHY

Barclay, John. *Jews in the Mediterranean Diaspora: From Alexander to Trajan (323 BCE–117 C.E.)*. Berkeley: University of California Press, 1999.

Cohen, Shaye J. D. *The Beginnings of Jewishness: Boundaries, Varieties, Uncertainties.* Berkeley: University of California Press, 2001.

Feldman, Louis H. *Jew and Gentile in the Ancient World.* Princeton, N.J.: Princeton University Press, 1993.

Goldenberg, Robert. *The Nations that Know Thee Not.* New York: New York University Press, 1998.

Goodman, Martin. *Rome and Jerusalem.* New York: Vintage, 2008.

Gruen, Eric. *Diaspora: Jews amidst Greeks and Romans.* Cambridge, Mass.: Harvard University Press, 2004.

Hamel, Gildas. *Poverty and Charity in Roman Palestine First Three Centuries C.E.* Berkeley: University of California Press, 1990.

Hezser, Catherine. *Jewish Slavery in Antiquity.* Oxford: Oxford University Press, 2005.

Ilan, Tal. *Jewish Women in Greco-Roman Palestine.* Tübingen, Germany: J. C. B. Mohr, 1995.

Lieu, Judith, John North, and Tessa Rajak, eds. *The Jews among Pagans and Christians in the Roman Empire.* London: Routledge, 1994.

Peskowitz, Miriam. *Spinning Fantasies: Rabbis, Gender, and History.* Berkeley: University of California Press, 1997.

Satlow, Michael. *Jewish Marriage in Antiquity.* Princeton, N.J.: Princeton University Press, 2001.

Gary Gilbert

Early Church

This entry focuses on the ways in which gender and sex functioned in the social realm of the early Christians, outside of the realm that is normally designated "religious." To be sure, there is necessary overlap between the New Testament, Early Judaism, and Greco-Roman topics, but this entry will focus primarily on the texts and evidence from the early Christians, as well as the theoretical issue of whether/how to distinguish between early Christians and others in the same milieux.

The earliest contemporary studies of women and gender in early Christianity focused primarily on religious roles, especially the ordination of women, along with women ascetics, the role of Mary, and gendered God-language. In such studies, the modern concerns are clear: feminist scholars wanted to find a "useable past" in order to find historical precedent for women who want to be ordained today. Focusing on social interactions, then, represents a shift away from exclusively religious roles. This entry will focus on a few different social arenas: the household, meals, the military, patronage systems, associations, and schools.

Household and Family Relations. Aristotle divides the household into three primary relationships or roles: marriage, the parent/child relationship, and the master/slave relationship (see *Politics* 1253b–1254b). As scholars of the New Testament *Haustafeln* have emphasized, a threefold description is somewhat misleading. Because the *paterfamilias* is the dominant person in each of the relationships that his subordinates (wife, children, slaves) have with him, a pyramid, with the *paterfamilias* at the top, might be a more accurate image. Even with these limitations, Aristotle's delineation is helpful for understanding some of the constituent parts of the early Christian household or family. The gendered dimensions of the household in the early church will thus be discussed using Aristotle's three relationships.

Marital relations. The marital relationship receives much attention in a variety of early Christian texts: Pauline epistles focus on husbands and wives (see, e.g., 1 Cor 7; Col 3:18–19; Eph 5:22–33), as do Tertullian (e.g., *To My Wife; On Monogamy*) and Augustine (e.g., *On the Good of Marriage*). The *topos* of rejecting one's family ties, including one's spouse, has roots in the canon; in Luke's gospel, Jesus says, "Whoever comes to me and does not hate father and mother, wife and children, brothers and sisters, yes, and even life itself, cannot be my disciple" (14:26; par. Matt 10:37; *Thomas* 55, 101) and is an important theme in later texts about martyrdom and asceticism (e.g., the *Apocryphal Acts of the Apostles*, the *Passion of Perpetua and Felicitas, Life of Antony, Life of Mary of Egypt*; see also Justin Martyr's *Second Apology* 2). Moreover, many early Christian texts advocate chastity as the ideal and, regardless, see self-control within marriage as necessary (see Tertullian's *Exhortation to Chastity*, Methodius's *Symposium*, Gregory of Nyssa's and John Chrysostom's *On Virginity*, Clement's *Paedagogus* 2.10 and *Stromateis* 3.6). The Greek words for husband

and wife are instructive, while also ambiguous, for modern interpreters: *gunē* can mean wife or woman, and *anēr* can mean husband or man.

Parents and children. A prominent question for scholars of childhood in early Christianity is whether "Christianity made a difference" in the lives of ancient children, who are typically viewed as vulnerable and marginalized. This question is raised with respect to a number of other topics, like marriage, slavery, and so on, but seems especially pressing for scholars of childhood. This may be because of the famous scenes of Jesus blessing children and/or because of a powerful desire to see Jesus and the early church as welcoming to children.

Some early Christian writers proscribe exposure, the sexual use of children, and abortion/contraception (e.g., *Didache* 2.2; *Epistle to Diognetus* 5.6), which has typically been used as proof that the early church bettered the lives of children in antiquity. This is evidence, however, that can be read both ways: if the church leaders have to warn against it, then perhaps their congregants are, in fact, doing the things they tell them not to do. Moreover, the reasons these things are prohibited are not always exactly what modern readers might hope for: for example, Justin and Clement warn against exposing an infant, because an exposed infant could be raised as an enslaved prostitute and the father might accidentally commit incest with her when she is older (Clement, *Paedagogus* 3.3.21; Justin, *First Apology* 27).

Masters and slaves. The traditional picture of slavery in the Greco-Roman world has emphasized its benign character, especially in comparison with the chattel slave societies in the sixteenth- to nineteenth-century Americas. This has been done with reference to certain peculiar features of ancient slavery, like the practices of frequent manumission and self-sale. More recent scholarship, especially following Orlando Patterson's *Slavery and Social Death* (1982), has emphasized the cruel realities of ancient slavery: slaves were considered "talking tools" (Varro, *Res Rustica* 1.17) and the slave's body was completely subject to the use and abuse of his or her master (in fact, the Greek *soma*, "body," was frequently used to refer to slaves; see Rev 18:13). Although traditional scholarship often saw the early church making an already-benign institution into a relatively benevolent relationship, eventually crediting Christianity with slavery's demise in the ancient world, recent scholarship has seen the early Christians as, at best, adhering "to the most humane thinking of their day with regard to how unwise it was to abuse slaves" (Osiek and MacDonald, 2006, pp. 116–17).

Scholars in feminist and gender studies have emphasized the difference between sex and gender; in the Greco-Roman slave system, slaves have sex (and are either *doulos* or *doulē*), but not gender. Likewise, a slave might age but would not normally attain the same status as a free adult (the Greek *pais* and the Latin *homo* or *puer* might be used to refer to an enslaved adult male, which is not equivalent to *anēr* [Greek] or *vir* [Latin]). Thus, the desire to see some kind of solidarity between female slaves and their female masters is probably misguided: they are separated by a chasm of class difference. Slaves, both male and female, adult and children, were at the disposal of their masters; they were available to be sexually used by their masters. A wife who had sex with a slave could have been charged with adultery, while her husband was permitted to have sex with his slaves. Certain slave children were called *delicium*, that is, "pets." Slave marriages and families were not recognized, so couples and families could be separated by their masters.

Communal Meals. The practices related to food preparation, dietary taboos, and meal etiquette often indicate a culture's larger values and social structures. This is certainly the case with the ancient world, in general, and the early church in particular. Meals, banquets, and symposia were formalized and ritualized parts of the ancient Greco-Roman world. One of the distinctive features of the early church was regular participation in communal meals, which comes to be part of early Christian self-definition. In this way, however, members of the early church were not unlike other Greco-Roman people: meal practices were part of weddings, funerals, religious and social groups, and general social interactions. The Eucharist or agape feast was just one kind of meal practice in the larger, common meal tradition in the Greco-Roman world (Smith and Taussig, 2012; Corley, 2010).

Studies of ancient Greco-Roman meal practices have emphasized the importance of symposia and other highly ritualized meals; the gendered dimensions of these practices have not been overlooked. Ancient banquets were (ideally) segregated by gender and status, especially related to the arrangement of the participants during the meal and festivities: traditionally, only free adult males could recline, while women, children, and slaves were expected to sit. Some meals seem to have been either exclusively male, segregated by gender, or only inclusive of female slaves and female performers. Certain earlier approaches to the study of Christian meal practices focused on the apparent inclusivity of the early church, as women, children, and slaves were present at community meals. This was, in fact, one of the slanders apparently leveled against early Christians: that people of both sexes and all ages ate together (see Minucius Felix, *Octavius* 8.4–12.5). Recent work on meal practices has shown that women participated in many Greco-Roman meals in greater numbers in the late Republican era; the participation of women in the early church's meals, then, is not at all unique, though it may have been notable.

One of the distinctive features of an ancient Greco-Roman meal was the position, and therefore status, of the participants: some philosophical texts assert that women are ideally included in meals as only either entertainment or slaves. Textual evidence points to women's participation in other ways, however. For example, in the Gospel of Thomas, Salome is portrayed as present and reclining on a couch with Jesus; she scolds him: "Who are you, sir? You have climbed onto my couch and eaten from my table as if you are from someone" (61:2). In the Gospels of Mark and Matthew, an anonymous woman anoints Jesus's head while he is reclining; the challenge directed against her is not about her gender, but about the money spent on oil (Mark 14:3–9; Matt 26:6–13; cf. Luke 7:36–50 and John 12:1–8). Although both of these texts involve Jesus, much recent work on the gospels (both canonical and noncanonical) has emphasized the need to read this literature for the ways in which it reflects the interests of the communities that produced them and not necessarily that of Jesus's own time. Clement of Alexandria discusses the participation of women in banquets at the end of the second century C.E. When he does so, he wishes to circumscribe their participation and encourage them to be well clothed and well mannered (and he advises young people, especially young women, to avoid them altogether; see *Paedagogus* 2.7). Moreover, the proposition from many feminist biblical scholars that we should assume the presence of women until proven otherwise is relevant here: just because women are not explicitly mentioned in a text does not mean that women did not participate in the meals of the community that produced the text.

Military Culture. As with many topics in the early church, the evidence for Christians in the military in the Roman Empire is sparse. Before the late second century C.E., sources are silent on Christians serving in the military. For some interpreters, this is clear evidence that early Christians did not serve in the military (either because it required killing or because it required idolatry or both); for others, this silence is indication that it would not have been viewed as problematic. While this early silence on Christians serving in the military is open to interpretation, there are other bits of evidence that could be relevant: for example, John the Baptist's admonition to soldiers in Luke 3:14 ("Do not extort money from anyone by threats or false accusation, and be satisfied with your wages") or the portrayal of a gendered holy war in Revelation, as well as, more generally, the metaphorical use of war and military terms (e.g., Eph 6:10–18; *1 Clement* 37:1–4). The impact of war more generally on both civilian and noncivilian life is clear in texts like Josephus's *Jewish War*, where women and children are presented as objects of *pathos* ("suffering"; see, e.g., *Jewish War* 6.201–213).

The most explicit evidence comes from a later period. The early church fathers and church orders address the question of whether Christians can serve in the military. For example, in the second half of the second century C.E., Athenagoras (*Plea for the Christians* 35) stated that Christians cannot endure killing anyone and Origen argued that the "Christian Lawgiver....nowhere teaches that it is right for his own disciples to offer violence to any one, however wicked" (*Contra Celsum* 3.8). Tertullian likewise argues that military life is incompatible with Christian devotion: although he references the existence of Christians in the military ("We have filled every place among you—cities, islands....the very camp!" in *Apology* 37), he argues that a soul cannot serve "the standard of Christ and the standard of the devil, the camp of light and the camp of darkness.... [the Lord] in disarming Peter, unbelted every soldier" (*On Idolatry* 19.2). Some authors reference John the Baptist's words in Luke 3 as an intermediate ethic: Christians can be soldiers but should not take advantage of their position.

Criminals and prisoners of war were publicly executed as *noxii* in Roman spectacles, which were both public demonstrations of the empire's power and dominance as well as entertainment for the masses; some martyr narratives place the drama of the martyrology in the context of these public executions. At Dura Europos, a Roman garrison located on the Euphrates, archaeologists have excavated the earliest known house church, which dates to the early third century C.E.; evidence from this site could be instructive for scholars inquiring after early Christian involvement in the Roman military.

Patronage Systems. Greco-Roman social relations were governed by notions of reciprocity, mutual exchange, friendship, and dependence, which were represented in systems of patronage. The patron–client relationship was normally one between two individuals who were of unequal social rank, in which the higher status individual gained honor for herself or himself by providing food, loans, invitations to dine, advice, professional recommendations, and the like in exchange for loyalty, public praise, and votes from the lower status individual. This relationship might be extended to the public practice of euergetism (from the Greek *euergetēs*, "benefactor"), in which a wealthy benefactor might sponsor a group's activities, build a bath or fountain, or hold a civic banquet in exchange for similar honors: an inscription, public positions, an honorable seat at the banquet, and so on.

Certain early Christian traditions figure God as the ultimate patron (as does Josephus in his *Antiquities*) and Jesus as the broker of divine benefits, although Jesus and the twelve are presented as having female patrons in Luke 8:1–3. Paul's letters give evidence of him presenting himself as both patron and client. Texts that mention a woman and her household probably indicate a patron who hosts a house-church (e.g., Tavia in Ignatius's *Letter to the Smyrneans* 13.2, Mary in Acts 12, perhaps Chloe's people in 1 Corinthians 1:11).

Family language was sometimes used in patronage systems; for example, among Augustus's titles was *pater patriae* ("father of the country"), and later empresses, like Julia Domna, were called *mater castrorum et senatus et patriae* ("mother of the army, senate, and country"). In this context, familial language in early Christianity might be understood as referencing systems of patronage, as well as the household, discussed above.

Voluntary Associations. Early Christian congregations share many traits with ancient Jewish synagogues and Greco-Roman guilds or associations (referred to as *collegia, thiasoi, hetaeria, synergasia,* among others), so much so that recent scholarship has emphasized seeing them as various forms of the same system rather than as insulated from each other (Harland, 2013). These associations could be established related to a trade (e.g., a guild of bakers or goldsmiths), ethnic or immigrant groups (e.g., Judeans or Alexandrians), or devotion to a deity (e.g., Dionysus or Demeter worshippers). Groups had patron deities, shared meals, officers, rituals, and membership dues, as well as funerals for their members. Family language was common here, too, as a leader of a group might be called "mother" or "father," and members sometimes referred to each other as "brothers" ("sisters" is less frequently attested in the inscriptions and monuments that are the sources for associations). Some groups were apparently segregated by gender, with attested male-only groups outnumbering female-only groups, but women are named in lists of members and/or patrons of predominantly male associations.

Education and Schools. Formal education in the Greco-Roman world included primary education, perhaps for boys and girls; secondary school, almost exclusively for boys, taught by the *grammaticus*; and higher education in rhetoric, medicine, and philosophy. Education was not inclusive or public but was mainly for elite boys and was paid for privately, either by hiring a tutor or sending children to a local schoolteacher. Some wealthy girls seem to have been educated too, though to what degree and for how long is unknown; for example, the nobly born Perpetua is described as "well-educated" (*liberaliter instituta; Passion of Perpetua and Felicitas* 2.1), but that is the only brief reference to her schooling. Informal education would have taken place in the home or shop, training girls as household managers (including weaving, cooking, etc.) and boys as artisans, builders, etc. Formal *paideia* included literacy, arithmetic, moral training, physical health, and so on.

Most *paedagogoi*, the slaves who supervised the education of owner's children, were male, though a few female pedagogues are attested. Slaves were sometimes literate, but their training seems to have been of a different variety: they were not educated to become virtuous senators, citizens, etc., but to serve their owners and to fetch a higher price in the slave market.

Some Christian authors warn against the dangers of participation in schools, which would have included offerings and teaching literature about the Greek and Roman deities (see Tertullian *De Idolatria* 10). In general, there is no evidence that Christians formed their own schools; certain famous schools that developed later, such as Justin's school in Rome, the Catechetical School of Alexandria, and Origen's school in Caesarea, seem to have been informal study circles. Some scholars suggest that both Christian *ekklesiae* and Jewish synagogues had something in common with philosophical/rhetorical school.

Theoretical Considerations. A few theoretical concerns are important for interpreting this material. Though more could be mentioned; four will be noted here: class/status issues, the relationship between the evidence (material or textual) and lived reality, the purported difference between early Christians and their contemporaries, and the categories

of "religious" and "nonreligious." First, it has become commonplace to note that elites are much easier to find (both in textual and material evidence), so scholars of early Christianity wrestle with how representative the evidence is when trying to discuss members of lower classes, including slaves, poor women, and children, etc. The second issue is related: if the evidence is fragmentary, haphazard, and more representative of upper-class existence, scholars encounter the problem of accounting for lived reality. Moreover, Gillian Clark (1993), Elizabeth Clark (2004), Kate Cooper (1996), and others have argued that the rhetorical nature of the evidence precludes scholars from accessing the lived experience of ancient people.

The final two theoretical concerns are both category problems: the difference (or lack thereof) between Christians and non-Christians in antiquity and the modern categories of "religious" and "nonreligious." As mentioned in the introduction, it is not always easy to find evidence for Christians in the earliest centuries C.E.; in some ways, they were indistinguishable from their contemporary Romans, Jews, and others. And finally, modern Westerners distinguish between "sacred" and "secular" realms in ways that may not have made sense to the ancients. For example, the social banquet that included eating, drinking, socializing, and philosophizing also included elements that modern interpreters might label "religious." Likewise, participation in the military included a religious oath. Focusing on the social interactions of ancient Christians, then, necessarily includes attention to religious matters.

[*See also* Children, *subentry* Early Church; Economics, *subentry* Early Church; Education, *subentry* Early Church; Family Structures, *subentry* Early Church; Male-Female Sexuality, *subentry* Early Church; Marriage and Divorce, *subentry* Early Church; Race, Class, and Ethnicity, *subentry* Early Church; Religious Participation, *subentry* Early Church; *and* Social Interaction, *subentries on* Greek and Roman Worlds *and* New Testament.]

BIBLIOGRAPHY

Bakke, O. M. *When Children Became People: The Birth of Childhood in Early Christianity*. Minneapolis: Fortress, 2005.

Clark, Elizabeth A. *History, Theory, Text: Historians and the Linguistic Turn.* Cambridge, Mass.: Harvard University Press, 2004.

Clark, Gillian. *Women in Late Antiquity: Pagan and Christian Lifestyles.* New York: Oxford University Press, 1993.

Cooper, Kate. *The Virgin and the Bride: Idealized Womanhood in Late Antiquity.* Cambridge, Mass.: Harvard University Press, 1996.

Corley, Kathleen E. *Maranatha: Women's Funerary Rituals and Christian Origins.* Minneapolis: Fortress, 2010.

Glancy, Jennifer A. *Slavery in Early Christianity.* New York: Oxford University Press, 2002.

Harland, Philip. *Associations, Synagogues, and Congregations: Claiming a Place in Ancient Mediterranean Society.* 2d ed. Kitchener, Ont.: Philip A. Harland, 2013.

Horn, Cornelia B., and John W. Martens. *"Let the Little Children Come to Me": Childhood and Children in Early Christianity.* Washington, D.C.: Catholic University of America Press, 2009.

Kraemer, Ross, and Mary Rose D'Angelo, eds. *Women and Christian Origins.* New York: Oxford University Press, 1999.

Osiek, Carolyn, and Margaret Y. MacDonald. *A Woman's Place: House Churches in Earliest Christianity.* Minneapolis: Fortress, 2006.

Patterson, Orlando. *Slavery and Social Death: A Comparative Study.* Cambridge, Mass.: Harvard University Press, 1982.

Smith, Dennis E., and Hal Taussig, eds. *Meals in the Early Christian World: Social Formation, Experimentation, and Conflict at the Table.* New York: Palgrave Macmillan, 2012.

Wheatley, Alan B. *Patronage in Early Christianity: Its Use and Transformation from Jesus to Paul of Samosata.* Eugene, Ore.: Pickwick, 2011.

Kathleen Gallagher Elkins

SOCIAL-SCIENTIFIC APPROACHES

"Social sciences" is the very broad label for the diverse academic disciplines that seek to investigate human social structures, interrelations, and behaviors extending from relationships between human individuals to interactions between groups within large-scale complex societies. These social disciplines use a range of methodologies that are to some extent empirical and, thereby, in some way analogous with methodologies applied in the natural (or hard) sciences. These methodologies, however, are variegated, ranging from quantitative and positivist approaches, characterized by accepting as authoritative only information derived from either sensory experience or logical (such as mathematical) treatments (e.g., statistical surveys), to qualitative and interpretivist approaches, such as ethnography. Among the social sciences are social (or cultural) anthropology, archaeology, political science, sociology, psychology, economics, social history, and cultural studies—a list that is far from exhaustive. Reflecting the field's tendency to inter- and multidisciplinarity, new subdisciplines (e.g., neuropsychology and sociobiology) continue to emerge.

While social sciences began to form during the period of intellectual ferment known as the Enlightenment (seventeenth and eighteenth centuries), they acquired more firmly defined contours in the early twentieth century. Towering intellectual giants such as Karl Marx (1818–1883), Émile Durkheim (1858–1917), and Max Weber (1864–1920) shaped the social sciences. Marx influenced profoundly the disciplines now known as economics and political science, while Durkheim and Weber are widely regarded as the founders of sociology. Also deeply influential for the social sciences and roughly contemporaneous are Claude Lévi-Strauss (1908–2009), a pioneering figure in anthropology, and Sigmund Freud (1856–1939), the father of psychoanalysis. By now, social sciences are firmly embedded in academic consciousness and institutions (as well as beyond them).

Social-scientific criticism has also infused biblical studies. This takes a variety of forms and often merges traditional approaches (e.g., theological, philological, or historical-critical approaches) with newer approaches such as feminist, ideological-critical, womanist, and queer approaches. Sometimes the social-scientific turn takes the form of applying a heuristic model or positivist data developed in the context of one or other of the social sciences to biblical texts, but more frequently the process is less formal and more experimental, reflecting biblical studies' susceptibility to ideas, concepts, vocabulary, and ways of thinking emerging from the social sciences. Importantly, social-scientific methods focus more on the world *behind* the text than the world *in* the text. They often challenge the notion that the text is reliable for historical reconstruction, probing the social factors unmentioned in and even deliberately elided by biblical accounts—for example, the voices of the nonliterate and members of low socioeconomic classes. Social-scientific readings of biblical texts tend to emphasize the human origins and contexts of biblical texts and thereby challenge theological claims and assumptions of historicity. Towards this endeavor, findings from archaeology have been particularly significant.

The quest for reconstructing the social world in the background of biblical texts can be traced back to the late nineteenth and early twentieth centuries. Examples are the formulations of the documentary hypothesis by Julius Wellhausen (1844–1918), theologian William Robertson Smith's (1846–1894) foregrounding of comparative study, Sigmund Mowinckel's (1884–1965) location of psalms in the cultic context of a New Year festival, theologian Johannes Pedersen's (1883–1977) attention to social contexts, and the biblical archaeology of William Foxwell Albright (1891–1971). But it has only been since the 1960s and particularly the 1970s that a more self-conscious absorption of theoretical concepts from the social sciences has transpired in a critical reaction to these earlier figures. Central to this have been, among others, George Mendenhall's essay "The Hebrew Conquest of Palestine" (1962), social anthropologist Mary Douglas's foray into biblical purity laws in *Purity and Danger* (1966), John Rogerson's *Anthropology and the Old Testament* (1978), and Norman Gottwald's material-sociological volume *The Tribes of Yahweh* (1979).

Liberation theology, associated particularly with Gustavo Gutiérrez (1974) and the context of Latin America, emerged concurrently with the critical application of social-scientific methods to biblical texts. Rogerson (2006, pp. 18–19) may well be correct in recognizing the impact of contemporaneous social justice movements (such as the U.S. civil rights movements of the 1960s and the 1968 student uprisings in Europe) in the new attentiveness to matters of class in biblical texts. Moreover, with the force of second-wave feminism in this same era came a new emphasis on social constructions pertaining to gender, particularly on the roles and oppressions of women. This then influenced various strains of ideological criticism and also gave rise to explorations of masculinities. The notion that meaning is subjective as well as constructed by social forces has continued to inspire new readings shaped by social sciences, such as postcolonial, queer, and womanist readings. As part of this the social world not just *behind* but also *in front of* the text has come to the fore.

In what follows, I offer examples of social-scientific approaches to biblical texts that apply methods, studies, data, or ideas from social anthropology, psychology/psychoanalysis, archaeology, and gender and cultural studies. These serve to provide a sample of how social-scientific approaches to the Bible have intersected with gender studies.

Social Anthropology. Social anthropology has been particularly influential in social-scientific studies of gender in biblical texts. The distinctive methodology of this social science is variously called fieldwork, participant observation, or ethnography: the practice of gathering information firsthand by observing human subjects as well as closely interacting with them over an extended period. Emerging in the nineteenth century in a context of colonialism and influenced by sociocultural variants of the currents of thought that precipitated Darwin's theory of evolution, early social anthropologists attempted to discern "elementary" forms of human institutions by studying mostly numerically small, face-to-face, non-Western communities. Over time there have been profound shifts in the discipline. One has been a shift from its tendency to consider itself primarily scientific and objective toward more interpretative and humanistic approaches. Another has been a shift in focus from so-called (and misnamed) elementary (or traditional or primitive) societies toward a broader array of human communities, including those of modern, Western settings. Social anthropology, however, has retained its emphasis on ethnography and remained multidisciplinary in that most practitioners are anthropologists *of something* in particular and *somewhere* in particular (e.g., marriage rituals among the Bedouin of Algeria) with some specialized background in the history, previous ethnographic investigation, and languages of their chosen region.

Due to a notion that ethnographic research in small-scale, face-to-face societies captures values akin to the societies reflected in ancient texts, social anthropological studies have had a considerable impact on both classical and biblical studies. Biblical archaeologist Jennie Ebeling's research on women in antiquity, for instance, draws heavily on the fieldwork of anthropologist Hilma Granqvist, who documented the lives of the villagers of Artas, a small settlement near Bethlehem, in the first half of the twentieth century. Ebeling argues that for all the many differences that exist between Iron Age I (beginning ca. 1300 B.C.E. and the putative context of many biblical narratives, e.g., Judges) and life in Artas in the 1920s and 1930s, these small-scale, rural communities and the similarities of climatic and terrestrial conditions lend themselves to comparison and analogy.

Hebrew Bible and New Testament studies have enthusiastically embraced the ethnographic studies conducted mainly in circum-Mediterranean countries espousing honor and shame as pivotal or core social values. According to these studies—a sample of which is contained in a volume edited by J. G. Peristiany and assertively titled *Honour and Shame: The Values of Mediterranean Society* (1965)—men and women who are not closely related either by blood (consanguines) or marriage (affines) lead separated lives. Ties of kinship are strong, and individuals' moral obligations are primarily concentrated on maintaining or advancing the honor of the family. Men do so by means of their public standing or publicly acknowledged reputation, which is derived first through antecedence (hence, a good reputation, or name, is to some degree inherited) and second through prowess. While the societies described in these studies are hierarchical and while it is honorable to submit to someone with more honor, among relative equals, men are expected to contest

for and defend their honor through prowess in zero-sum competitions.

Women's honor, meanwhile, is called shame—in the positive sense. Positive shame determines women's reputation, claim to pride, and stature in both the family and the wider community. Unlike men's honor, it is a passive value and associated above all with women's sexuality. It is determined above all by virginity before marriage and continence thereafter. Shame exercises constraint on women's behavior and creates an acute sensitivity to public opinion, so that even any suggestion or implication of sexual misconduct must be avoided. Different from men, who are expected to be competitive, the qualities conferring women's honor (i.e., positive shame) include shyness and emotional restraint. But there is also a negative meaning of "shame," expressing the diametric opposite of honor: namely, profound indignity or humiliation incurred when honor is diminished or destroyed. Claudia Camp helpfully refers to "the shame-by-which-one-must-be-bound in order to avoid the shame-that-destroys" (1991, p. 5). The most damaging source of this negative shame is the sexual misconduct of women. If a woman's positive shame is lost, it can never be recovered. This shame, moreover, is so powerfully defiling that it contaminates not only a woman herself but also her kin. Because a man's honor is so inextricably tied up with the sexual purity of his female relatives (rather than with his own), women's lives in honor-shame societies tend to be circumscribed.

Johannes Pedersen (1926) identified honor and shame as interactive and social core values of the Bible long before the emergence of the anthropological studies of Peristiany and others but did not emphasize the gender dimension. Instead—and indicative of the theologically informed nature of his approach—Pedersen aligned honor with the heaviness of the soul that receives divine blessing and shame with an absence of blessing—an empty soul and diminished social status. He acknowledged a progression from an earlier, agonistic warrior type of honor (e.g., of such men as Jephthah, who fight for and gain honor and of women such as Abigail who exercise wit and initiative to achieve their ends) to a later type, where honorable men are motivated by social harmony and obtaining property, whereas women are reduced to little more than their father's or husband's possession.

Over time, however, the gender-dimension of honor-shame so dominant in the ethnographic studies began to exert an effect on biblical studies. Hence, anthropologist Julian Pitt-Rivers (1977) examined narratives of the Bible in the light of ethnographic observations in the Mediterranean region. He considered the story of Shechem and Dinah (Genesis 34) a turning point in the Israelites' adoption of the honor-shame value system. Not too long after this, biblical scholars, too, embraced the honor-shame model. Camp (1991) applied the model to account for the preoccupation, bordering on neurosis, concerning daughters' capacity to stain male honor, evident in the apocryphal book of Ben Sira. Ken Stone (1996) illuminated how male-male competition for honor utilizes females as conduits in the Deuteronomistic History.

The popularity of the honor-shame model in biblical studies reached its height in the 1990s. Hence, J. H. Neyrey (1991) enthusiastically claimed that "It is truly an understatement to say that the whole of Luke's Gospel, almost every piece of social interaction, should be viewed through the lens of honor and shame," and "seeing [Jesus's] life through the lens of honor and shame, we begin to view it from the native's perspective and to appreciate the social dynamic as natives see it" (p. 64). There was even a special volume of the journal *Semeia* titled *Honor and Shame in the World of the Bible* (1996). By this time, however, there were also voices of caution from within the discipline of social anthropology itself, pointing out that the meanings of "honor" and "shame" vary considerably from cultural context to cultural context (Herzfeld, 1980) and that often exist considerable discrepancies between, on the one hand, observable behavior, and, on the other, what people (and, by extension, texts) claim (Wikan, 1984).

The subject of shame has also been approached in contradistinction to guilt, rather than honor. Shame-cultures (wherein people are particularly

sensitized to *external* sanctions, such as the disapproval of other community members) contrasted with guilt-cultures (wherein people respond to *internalized* sanctions) have been analyzed in social anthropological studies, such as those by Ruth Benedict and Margaret Mead. These designations have been absorbed into biblical studies (e.g., Daube 1969)—though with much less alacrity than have the honor-shame studies.

Psychology and Psychoanalysis. Most shame-guilt discussion in biblical studies draws on the social sciences of psychology and psychoanalysis rather than social anthropology. Psychology, using empirical methods, aims to discern mental and behavioral traits of human activity, including pathological forms, with a view to assessing and, if pertinent, treating them. Consequently, psychologists are scientific investigators and sometimes also mental health experts that address social, behavioral, and cognitive manifestations.

Psychoanalysis, on the other hand, is the investigation of particular psychological pathologies. While Freud's methods and theories have been much reformed (notably by Jacques Lacan [1901–1981]), psychoanalysis continues to expound the following key claims: (1) events in early childhood have a particularly formative effect on subsequent mental and behavioral development; (2) the unconscious has a profound influence on mental well-being; (3) conflicts between the conscious and unconscious can result in mental and emotional disturbance; and (4) by bringing early influential (and often traumatic) experiences from the unconscious into the conscious (through such methods as dream analysis and free association), such conflicts can, with the guidance of trained therapists, be resolved.

Psychoanalytic approaches tend to begin with close investigation of an individual's (often aberrant) behavior and then map this onto more generalized psychic phenomena. Hence, Freud identified the Oedipus complex—that is, a stage of psychosexual development in boys typically occurring around the age of three to six years, when a boy's repressed unconscious drives supposedly revolve around a desire sexually to possess his mother—as a universal phenomenon in young boys, which could explain more widely observed developmental behaviorisms. In more recent times both the Western-centric assumptions of Freud's claims and his primary focus on males, often to the exclusion or misrepresentation of female experience, have been widely critiqued. Psychoanalysis is even widely designated a pseudoscience, or as neither scientific nor social-scientific. Nevertheless, psychoanalysis remains influential—including in biblical studies. Just as social anthropologist Pitt-Rivers used the Bible in order to retroject his observations onto antiquity, so Freud also turned to biblical narratives in order to construct the case that his ideas concerning, for example, conscious-unconscious intrapsychic conflict, have wide, even universal application over a considerable passage of time—most famously and extensively so in his final monograph, *Moses and Monotheism* (1939).

The topics of guilt and shame prevalent in Freud's writings continue to be discussed in psychological and psychoanalytic interpretations of the Bible. In such examinations, internal versus external sanctions (the juxtaposition central to the anthropological studies) are important, yet shame is associated more closely with very early childhood and the emergence of the ego, whereas guilt is associated with the later developmental stage of the superego when the desires and values of the parents are internalized. The first mention of shame is in Genesis 2:25 in the story of Adam and Eve. Freud himself (surprisingly perhaps) published nothing on this text.

In more recent times, however, it has become a popular focus for psychoanalytic interpretation. One example is Lyn M. Bechtel's (1995) discussion depicting this first instance of shame as describing the psychic development of moving from childhood to self-aware adulthood. For Bechtel (as for Freud) the particular (i.e., an account of the first human couple) has wider application (i.e., it describes larger patterns of psychic growth). Anna Piskorowski's (1992) feminist-Lacanian and Ilona Rashkow's (2000) feminist-Freudian readings introduce feminist criticism into psychoanalytic exegesis. Piskorowski's interpretation argues that Genesis is a tale that inculcates social and family norms. Rashkow identifies a dysfunctional family where the authoritarian father (God) displaces his own sexual longings on to his daughter (Eve) and where paternal jealousy regarding his children's (Adam and Eve's) love for their mother transpires in the repression of the mother, with only the presence of the tree and the serpent hinting at her once powerful presence as a fertility nature goddess.

Feminist Archaeology. Feminist archaeology offers another example of how social sciences have been absorbed into biblical studies. Just as the feminist psychoanalysis of Rashkow adapts Freudian ideas in order to acknowledge and depict women's perspectives and experiences, so feminist sensibilities have also influenced biblical archaeology. This is represented most notably by Carol L. Meyers. In some respects, Meyers's *Discovering Eve* (1988) fits into broader patterns and trends in biblical archaeology: first, it moves away from an earlier aim of biblical archaeology to affirm depictions in the biblical text and instead lets the archaeological witness speak for itself; and second, it focuses less on the "celebrities" of antiquity and more on the lives of regular people.

Both of these trends are evident in the work of other biblical archaeologists, such as William G. Dever. Hence, the title of his textbook *The Lives of Ordinary People* (2011) makes the point explicitly. Dever states unequivocally at the outset that "the archaeological data, not the textual data, will be the primary source initially. To be sure, the textual data will be considered....But the biblical texts will be subsidiary and will often prove to be of minimal importance" (Dever, 2011, pp. vi–vii). Dever discusses women's lives most fully in a section titled "A Theoretical Rural House," which refers to "recent studies by women biblicists and archaeologists" (p. 164) and to domestic tasks such as bread making, domestic pottery, and weaving (pp. 159–169). Meyers's book, however, is much more squarely focused on women's roles, and her methodology combines close and critical analysis of biblical texts with sociological and archaeological findings. Like the feminist-psychoanalysts discussed above, Meyers is drawn to the story of Adam and Eve in Genesis 2—3 and focuses on this narrative in order to illustrate how the paradigms for female roles in biblical texts reflect the perspectives and concerns of urban elite males. Like Dever, Meyers argues that the biblical witness is not accurate, particularly when it comes to the lives and concerns of nonelites. Drawing instead on archaeological evidence of rural life in antiquity, Meyers argues for a much less marginal presence of women than the biblical text might suggest. Consequently, her investigation makes the case for a wide range of women's household functions (some of them very significant) as well as for women's roles beyond the domestic sphere, such as economic and jural-legal roles.

In her later work, Meyers (2009) challenges the notion that the societies behind the biblical texts constitute patriarchies, in which women are (only) subordinated. Instead, she advocates a more nuanced heuristic model, which she calls "heterarchy," which recognizes the possibility of "multiple systems and multiple loci of power, with women as well as men shaping society" (p. 98). Meyers has been joined by other feminist archaeologists, among them Susan Ackerman (2003), Eleanor Ferris Beach (2005), and Jennie Ebeling (2010). In *The Jezebel Letters*, Beach not only uses evidence from archaeology to reconstruct women's lives, but also supplements this with extensive fictional reconstructions.

The practice of naming women characters unnamed in biblical texts or of imaginatively reconstructing biblical women's lives with recourse to scholarship is well established in feminist biblical criticism and represents another trend in biblical gender studies. One well-known example is Anita Diamant's 1997 novel *The Red Tent*, which retells some of the patriarchal narratives of Genesis from the perspective of Jacob's daughter Dinah. The aim of this practice is to draw attention to the suppression of women and their experiences and to resist this suppression actively and dynamically.

Gender and Cultural Studies. In the area of cultural studies, notions of the social construction of gender and sexuality are increasingly prominent,

largely thanks to Michel Foucault's three-volume *The History of Sexuality*. This seminal work was profoundly shaped by the social sciences and argues, for example, that Western sexuality was socially constructed by such forces as capitalism.

Influenced by second-wave feminism, the predominant gender emphasis in 1970s and 1980s biblical criticism was on feminine figures. This period was marked by the polarization between feminist interpretations that emphasize positive depictions of feminine figures, such as Phyllis Trible's essays on Eve and Ruth in her significant text, *God and the Rhetoric of Sexuality* (1978), and feminist interpretations pointing out how biblical texts marginalize and oppress women characters, such as Trible's essays in *Texts of Terror* (1984). The latter tendency has been particularly influential, seeking to demonstrate not only how biblical texts such as Judges 11 and 19, or Hosea 1—3 and such examples of the prophetic woman metaphor as Ezekiel 16 and 23, harm both the women *in texts* and also the *actual* women *in front of* the text. Two representative samples appear in *A Feminist Companion to the Latter Prophets* (1995). The first is Fokkelien van Dijk-Hemmes's (1995) examination of Ezekiel 23. Here she advocates an F-reading—that is, a reading focalized by a feminine reader—which forcefully discloses the abusive nature of the woman metaphor in this chapter, in that it characterizes the sexual abuse of girls as their own fault (Ezek 23:3). The second is Naomi Graetz's (1995) analysis of the punishment of Hosea's wife, which Graetz associates with domestic abuse and battered wife syndrome, consequently deeming this metaphor acutely toxic to actual women. There has been some disagreement among feminist biblical scholars as to whether metaphor ought to be read (too?) literally. Christl Maier, for example, emphasizes that the prophetic woman metaphors pertain to "fictional, female character[s] in a fictional relationship with God" (2008, p. 112).

Over time, and particularly since the 1990s, there have been three more interesting developments within the intersection between biblical studies and gender. First, feminist criticism has been called to account by womanist African American women theologians. Womanist criticism identifies and resists the tendency in second-wave feminism to treat as normative, or absolute, the perspectives of middle-class white Western women. Subsequently, this approach has developed (and been injected by postcolonial criticism) into readings distinctive to *mujeristas* (Central and Latin American women) and readings by Asian and African women theologians. All these interpretations acknowledge and advocate perspectives of nonwhites and emphasize class/economic hierarchy as a significant interpretational category alongside female gender. Second, in response to the feminist push for acknowledging that women's experiences are more variegated and complex than just "other" vis-à-vis men's experiences, more attention has come to be focused, too, on variegated (including nonhegemonic) masculinities and men's experiences. Third, in what Marie-Theres Wacker calls a "deconstructive turn in feminism" (2006, p. 642), postfeminism has absorbed also lesbian, gay, and queer (that is gender-confusing readings resisting gender bifurcation) interpretations of the Bible.

The term "womanism" was first used by author Alice Walker. With reference to biblical criticism and gender, it is an approach drawing on both feminist criticism and black theology that seeks to empower and liberate women of color. It does so by identifying either positive but neglected constructions of women of color in the biblical text or racially discriminating passages. These passages are then critically examined, challenged, and sometimes reconstructed and revised. Womanist criticism first grew to prominence among African American scholars in the United States, notably, Renita Weems. Weems's *Just a Sister Away* (1988) brings race in power relations that concern women (such as those between Sarah and Hagar in Genesis 16 and 20) to the fore and also motivates contemporary readers of the biblical texts to recognize and redress social injustice. Since then womanism has come to embrace also other women of color, based both in the United States and beyond. Womanist criticism has reexamined feminist interpretations and often cast a critical light. Hence, the many positive feminist

evaluations of Ruth, for instance, such as the aforementioned by Trible, have come to be challenged. African American biblical scholar Wil Gafney (2009), for example, notes particularly Ruth's Moabite ethnicity and builds a strong case that Ruth is abducted in rape marriage and sexually exploited. In the course of her argument Gafney brings in parallels of "forced exogamous procreation and unwelcome conjugal unions" from modern-day Rwanda, Sudan, and Ethiopia (2009, p. 33). Somewhat similarly, Asian American scholar Gale Yee (2009) notes affinities between the stereotypes associated with Asian women and the idealized depiction of Ruth. Both, Yee argues, are depicted as model minorities. Far from regarding this as desirable, Yee points out the dangers and reification of such depictions. Both Gafney and Yee are sensitized by their own social location, and both refer to social scientific observation and data from contemporary times and apply this critically to the biblical text. In doing so, both navigate between the world *behind* and *in front of* the biblical text. Such methods appear also in New Testament studies and outside of the United States. One example is the work of Musa Dube (1992), a biblical scholar based in Botswana, whose analysis and retelling of the story of Jesus's encounter with the Samaritan woman at the well (John 4) is transformed by bringing it into dialogue with traditional African storytelling and by addressing the story particularly to women of southern Africa.

In recent times there has also been a marked interest in masculinities. The idea that masculinity and femininity are not integral or fixed but shaped by social forces is evident already in the work of Stone on honor and shame (1996); hence, Stone describes how in Judges 19 a male in a homosexual act is perceived as assuming a position that is, according to the cultural values reflected in the text, allotted only to females (i.e., of penetrated sexual object rather than penetrating sexual subject). As Stone goes on to say, such a man, in effect, becomes "feminized" (or "demasculinized") and, consequently, dishonored—the reason being that masculinity is, by implication, not only different from but also superior to femininity (1996, pp. 79–81). Two more explorations of masculinity in biblical texts are David J. A. Clines's "David the Man: The Construction of Masculinity in the Hebrew Bible" (1995), contrasting contemporary ideals of masculinity with those implied in the David story and drawing attention to how this can subvert the reading process, and Stephen D. Moore's *God's Gym* (1996), navigating both Hebrew Bible and New Testament alongside the modern preoccupation with the male body image. The idea originating in feminism that women are not "other" (i.e., more than "not men") but subjects in their own right with their own rights, speaking with diverse voices, has, therefore, led to a similar movement with regard to masculine identities.

Further examples of gendered identities appear in queer studies. Queer studies emerged from LGBT (lesbian, gay, bisexual, transgender) studies and again emphasizes the social and cultural construction of both gender and sexuality. Rather than interpreting gender and sexuality in terms of a masculinity/femininity duality, however, queer studies problematizes and sometimes destabilizes the topic yet further. Hence Deborah Rooke (2009), for instance, proposes also the idea of intersex. In her article on the incest laws of Leviticus, consequently, she accounts for men's avoidance of certain female family members by suggesting that such women, having had sex with a male relative of the man addressed, in these laws effectively become masculinized and thereby intersex and, hence, taboo. Queer readings are often highly experimental and among the most creative in contemporary biblical criticism. One example demonstrating this is the collection of essays in *Bible Trouble* (2011).

Finally, some social-scientific approaches to the Bible bring into dialogue biblical texts and images and popular culture. This has again yielded highly creative interpretations pertaining to gender. Examples include Roland Boer's interpretations in *Knockin' on Heaven's Door* (1999), where he considers Song of Songs alongside pornography, Ezekiel alongside heavy metal music, and the biblical David alongside the roles of actor Keanu Reeves. A further example is Katie Edwards's examination of Genesis

2–3 alongside depictions of Adam and Eve in advertising.

Conclusion. As this impressionistic sample has demonstrated, social-scientific approaches, particularly from the 1960s and 1970s onward, have applied and adapted models, constructs, ideas, and vocabulary from a range of social sciences in often highly creative and experimental ways. Models and methods from social anthropology and political science were applied in biblical studies early on, with social justice movements of the 1960s bringing a focus on class and social hierarchy. Also emphasizing social justice, second-wave feminism was forceful in injecting both psychoanalytical approaches and biblical archaeology, casting a critical focus on women's lives and roles. Over time, scholarship has incorporated critical sensitivity to divergent masculinities, sexualities, and the perspectives of women of color. Alongside this, not only the social world behind but also in front of the text has come into play. Social-scientific approaches, consequently, are among the most multifarious and multidisciplinary in terms of critical examinations of gender and the Bible.

[*See also* Economics, *subentry* Hebrew Bible; Feminism, *subentry* Second-Wave Feminism; Imagery, Gendered, *subentry* Prophetic Literature; Masculinity Studies; Mujerista Criticism; Patriarchy/Kyriarchy; Queer Theory; Reader-Oriented Criticism; Sexuality; *and* Womanist Criticism.]

BIBLIOGRAPHY

Ackerman, Susan. "Digging Up Deborah: Recent Hebrew Bible Scholarship on Gender and the Contribution of Archaeology." *Near Eastern Archaeology* 66, no. 4 (2003): 172–184.

Beach, Eleanor Ferris. *The Jezebel Letters: Religion and Politics in Ninth-Century Israel.* Minneapolis: Fortress, 2005.

Bechtel, Lyn M. "Genesis 2.4b–3.24: A Myth about Human Maturation." *Journal for the Study of the Old Testament* 67 (1995): 3–26.

Boer, Roland. *Knockin' on Heaven's Door: The Bible and Popular Culture.* London: Routledge, 1999.

Camp, Claudia. "Understanding a Patriarchy: Women in Second Century Jerusalem through the Eyes of Ben Sira." In *"Women Like This": New Perspectives on Jewish*

Women in the Greco-Roman World, edited by Amy-Jill Levine, pp. 1–39. Atlanta: Scholars Press, 1991.

Chalcraft, David J., ed. *Social-Scientific Old Testament Criticism: A Sheffield Reader*. Sheffield, U.K.: Sheffield Academic Press, 1997.

Clines, David J. A. "David the Man: The Construction of Masculinity in the Hebrew Bible." In *Interested Parties: The Ideology of Writers and Readers of the Hebrew Bible*, pp. 212–241. Journal for the Study of the Old Testament Supplement Series 205. Sheffield, U.K.: Sheffield Academic Press, 1995.

Daube, David. "The Culture in Deuteronomy." *Orita* 3 (1969): 27–52.

Dever, William G. *The Lives of Ordinary People: What the Bible and Archaeology Tell Us about Everyday Life in Ancient Israel*. Grand Rapids, Mich.: Eerdmans, 2011.

Douglas, Mary. *Purity and Danger: An Analysis of Concepts of Pollution and Taboo*. London: Routledge and Kegan Paul, 1966.

Dube, Musa W. "Jesus and the Samaritan Woman: A Botswana Feminist Theological Reflection on Women and Social Transformation." *Boleswa Journal of Occasional Theological Papers* 1, no. 4 (1992): 5–9.

Ebeling, Jennie R. *Women's Lives in Biblical Times*. London: T&T Clark, 2010.

Edwards, Katie B. *Admen and Eve: The Bible in Contemporary Advertising*. Sheffield, U.K.: Sheffield Phoenix, 2012.

Gafney, Wilda C. "Mother Knows Best: Messianic Surrogacy and Sexploitation in Ruth." In *Mother Goose, Mother Jones, Mommie Dearest: Biblical Mothers and Their Children*, edited by Cheryl A. Kirk-Duggan and Tina Pippin, pp. 23–36. Atlanta: Society of Biblical Literature, 2009.

Gottwald, Norman K. *The Tribes of Yahweh: A Sociology of the Religion of Liberated Israel, 1250–1050 B.C.E.* Maryknoll, N.Y.: Orbis, 1979.

Graetz, Naomi. "God Is to Israel as Husband Is to Wife: The Metaphoric Battering of Hosea's Wife." In *A Feminist Companion to the Latter Prophets*, edited by Athalya Brenner, pp. 126–145. The Feminist Companion to the Bible 8. Sheffield, U.K.: Sheffield Academic Press, 1995.

Gutiérrez, Gustavo. *A Theology of Liberation*. London: SCM Press, 1974.

Herzfeld, Michael. "Honor and Shame: Problems in the Comparative Analysis of Moral Systems." *Man* 15 (1980): 339–351.

Hornsby, Teresa J., and Ken Stone, eds. *Bible Trouble: Queer Reading at the Boundaries of Biblical Scholarship*. Atlanta: Society of Biblical Literature, 2011.

Maier, Christl M. *Daughter Zion, Mother Zion: Gender, Space, and the Sacred in Ancient Israel*. Minneapolis: Fortress, 2008.

Matthews, Victor H., and Don C. Benjamin, eds. *Honor and Shame in the World of the Bible*. Semeia 68. Atlanta: Scholars Press, 1994.

Mendenhall, George E. "The Hebrew Conquest of Palestine." *Biblical Archaeologist* 25, no. 3 (1962): 66–87.

Meyers, Carol L. *Discovering Eve: Ancient Israelite Women in Context*. New York: Oxford University Press, 1988.

Meyers, Carol L. "Contesting the Notion of Patriarchy: Anthropology and the Theorizing of Gender in Ancient Israel." In *A Question of Sex? Gender and Difference in the Hebrew Bible and Beyond*, edited by Deborah W. Rooke, pp. 84–105. Hebrew Bible Monographs 14. Sheffield, U.K.: Sheffield Phoenix, 2009.

Moore, Stephen. *God's Gym: Divine Male Bodies of the Bible*. New York and London: Routledge, 1996.

Neyrey, J. H. *The Social World of Luke-Acts*. Peabody, Mass.: Hendrickson, 1991.

Pedersen, Johannes. *Israel: Its Life and Culture*. London: Oxford University Press, 1926.

Peristiany, J. G., ed. *Honor and Shame: The Values of Mediterranean Society*. London: Weidenfeld & Nicolson, 1965.

Piskorowski, Anna. "In Search of Her Father: A Lacanian Approach to Genesis 2–3." In *A Walk in the Garden: Biblical, Iconographical and Literary Images of Eden*. edited by Paul Morris and Deborah Sawyer, pp. 310–318. Journal for the Study of the Old Testament Supplement Series 136. Sheffield, U.K.: Sheffield Academic Press, 1992.

Pitt-Rivers, Julian. *The Fate of Shechem or the Politics of Sex: Essays in the Anthropology of the Mediterranean*. Cambridge, U.K.: Cambridge University Press, 1977.

Rashkow, Ilona. *Taboo or not Taboo: Sexuality and Family in the Hebrew Bible*. Minneapolis: Fortress, 2000.

Rogerson, J. W. *Anthropology and the Old Testament*. Oxford: Blackwell, 1978.

Rogerson, J. W., and Judith M. Lieu, eds. *The Oxford Handbook of Biblical Studies*. Oxford: Oxford University Press, 2006.

Rooke, Deborah W. "The Bare Facts: Gender and Nakedness in Leviticus 18." In *A Question of Sex? Gender and Difference in the Hebrew Bible and Beyond*, edited by Deborah Rooke, pp. 20–38. Hebrew Bible Monographs 14. Sheffield, U.K.: Sheffield Phoenix, 2009.

Stiebert, Johanna. *The Construction of Shame in the Hebrew Bible: The Prophetic Contribution*. Journal for the Study of the Old Testament: Supplement Series 346. Sheffield, U.K.: Sheffield Academic Press, 2002.

Stone, Ken. *Sex, Honor, and Power in the Deuteronomistic History*. Journal for the Study of the Old Testament Supplement Series 234. Sheffield, U.K.: Sheffield Academic Press, 1996.

Trible, Phyllis. *God and the Rhetoric of Sexuality*. Overtures to Biblical Theology. Minneapolis: Fortress, 1978.

Trible, Phyllis. *Texts of Terror: Literary-Feminist Readings of Biblical Narratives.* Overtures to Biblical Theology. Minneapolis: Fortress, 1984.

van Dijk-Hemmes, Fokkelien. "The Metaphorization of Woman in Prophetic Speech: An Analysis of Ezekiel 23." In *A Feminist Companion to the Latter Prophets*, edited by Athalya Brenner, pp. 244–255. The Feminist Companion to the Bible 8. Sheffield, U.K.: Sheffield Academic Press, 1995.

Wacker, Marie-Theres. "Feminist Criticism and Related Aspects." In *The Oxford Handbook of Biblical Studies*, edited by J. W. Rogerson and Judith M. Lieu, pp. 634–654. Oxford: Oxford University Press, 2006.

Weems, Renita J. *Just a Sister Away: A Womanist Vision of Women's Relationships in the Bible.* San Diego, Calif.: LuriaMedia, 1988.

Whitelam, Keith W. "The Social World of the Bible." In *The Cambridge Companion to Biblical Interpretation*, edited by John Barton, pp. 35–49. Cambridge, U.K.: Cambridge University Press, 1998.

Wikan, Unni. "Shame and Honor: A Contestable Pair." *Man* 19 (1984): 635–652.

Yee, Gale A. "'She Stood in Tears amid the Alien Corn': Ruth, the Perpetual Foreigner and Model Minority." In *They Were All Together in One Place? Toward Minority Biblical Criticism*, edited by Randall C. Bailey, Tat-siong Benny Liew, and Fernando F. Segovia, pp. 119–140. Atlanta: Society of Biblical Literature, 2009.

Johanna Stiebert

TRANSGENDER/THIRD GENDER/ TRANSSEXUALISM

"We are a movement of masculine females and feminine males, cross-dressers, transsexual men and women, intersexuals born on the anatomical sweep between female and male, gender-blenders, many other sex and gender-variant people, and our significant others. All told, we expand understanding of how many ways there are to be a human being." (Feinberg, 1998, p. 5)

These words, written by prominent transgender activist and writer Leslie Feinberg, mark a significant moment in the history both of the word "transgender" and the movement for and about which it speaks. Susan Stryker, a transgender scholar, filmmaker, and activist, attributes the origin of the use of "transgender" as an umbrella term to Feinberg's 1992 pamphlet, *Transgender Liberation: A Movement Whose Time Has Come.* Stryker writes,

"Transgender, in this sense, was a 'pangender' umbrella term for an imagined community encompassing transsexuals, drag queens, butches, hermaphrodites, cross-dressers, masculine women, effeminate men, sissies, tomboys, and anybody else willing to be interpolated by the term, who felt compelled to answer the call to mobilization." (2006, p. 4)

Stryker also forges a link between Feinberg's 1992 pamphlet and Sandy Stone's watershed article "The

Empire Strikes Back: A Posttranssexual Manifesto," published in 1991, writing, "To a significant degree, Feinberg's 'transgender' came to name the ensemble of critical practices called for by Stone's 'posttranssexual manifesto'" (2006, p. 4).

Prior to this time, the word "transgender" had been used to refer to individuals whose identities fell somewhere on a spectrum between "transvestite" and "transsexual." Stryker explains, "If a *transvestite* was somebody who episodically changed into the clothes of the so-called 'other sex,' and a *transsexual* was somebody who permanently changed genitals in order to claim membership in a gender other than the one assigned at birth, then a *transgender* was somebody who permanently changed social gender through the public presentation of self, without recourse to genital transformation" (2006, p. 4). David Valentine, author of *Imagining Transgender: An Ethnography of a Category,* writes that "the idea of transgender as a radical alternative or as a 'third way' between transexuality and transvestism, both of which developed through the previous two decades, was quickly overtaken in the early 1990s by a third usage of transgender as a *collective* (often spoken of as a *spectrum* or *umbrella*), inclusive of all and any gender variance" (2007, p. 33). Valentine also casts Feinberg's 1992 pamphlet as "among the first published uses of the collective form of transgender which explicitly politicized transgender identification beyond individual radical acts and called for a social movement organized around its terms" (2007, p. 33).

The publication of Feinberg's and Stone's pieces, then, help to establish the early 1990s as an important moment for the mobilization of the term "transgender." In tandem with these publications, grassroots activism and transgender politics were also taking hold. For example, in 1991, debates about transgender inclusion occurred in the wake of the Michigan Womyn's Music Festival's exclusion of a postoperative transsexual woman from participation in the yearly event.

Transgender Nation, an offshoot of the San Francisco chapter of Queer Nation, began in 1992; part of their early work included organizing against the inclusion of "gender identity disorder" in the American Psychiatric Association's *Diagnostic and Statistical Manual* (see Stryker, 1994, and Spade, 2006). In Nebraska in 1993, Brandon Teena was brutally raped and murdered for transgressing gender boundaries. Kate Bornstein, a transgender performance artist, activist, and author was also active during the early 1990s, and her book, *Gender Outlaw: On Men, Women and the Rest of Us*, was published in 1994. These are some of the events of the early 1990s that, along with Feinberg's and Stone's published pieces, helped shape and organize transgender politics and establish transgender studies.

By the mid-1990s, the growing use of the word "transgender" as a preferred umbrella term to classify numerous identities had been established. Susan Stryker reflects, "Perhaps the most surprising aspect of the whole transgender thing back in the 1990s was the startling rapidity with which the term itself took root, and was applied to (if not always welcomed by) the sociocultural and critical-intellectual formations that were caught up in, or suddenly crystallized by, its wake" (2006, p. 2). She writes that "transgender" has become the term of choice "for a wide range of phenomena that call attention to the fact that 'gender,' as it is lived, embodied, experienced, performed, and encountered, is more complex and varied than can be accounted for by the currently dominant binary sex/gender ideology of Eurocentric modernity" (2006, p. 3). Valentine similarly

points out that "particularly in the mid-1990s, 'transgender' has become ubiquitous in progressive community-based organizations, identity-based political movements, popular media accounts, international human rights discourses, academic debates, anthropological descriptions of gender variance cross-culturally, and, astonishingly, it is even finding its way into the medical establishment, the very institution to which transgender was originally opposed" (2007, pp. 33–34). Significantly, Valentine notes that many of the participants in his study did not identify themselves as transgender (2007, p. 3). The self-appellation of the term "transgender" was, and remains, uneven by those often categorized as "transgender" by others.

Although there is widespread agreement that the term "transgender" rose to prominence in the early and mid-1990s, definitions of the term—articulations of who exactly falls under such an "umbrella"— demonstrate some significant variations. Valentine writes, "The very flexibility of transgender, its strength as a tool of political organizing, thus makes it possible to use without specifying who is being invoked in particular instances" (2007, p. 39). Viviane K. Namaste writes, "A variety of different identities are included within the 'transgender' label: cross-dressers, or individuals who wear the clothes associated with the 'opposite' sex, often for erotic gratification; drag queens, or men who usually live and identify as gay men, but who perform as female impersonators in gay male bars and leisure spaces; and transsexuals, or individuals who take hormones and who may undergo surgery to align their biological sexes with their genders" (2000, p. 273). Joanne Meyerowitz (2002) provides a different listing, writing, "'Transgendered' includes, among others, some people who identify as 'butch' or masculine lesbians, as 'fairies,' 'queens,' or feminine gay men, and as heterosexual cross-dressers as well as those who identify as transsexual." She continues to point out, "The categories are not hermetically sealed, and to a certain extent the boundaries are permeable" (2002, p. 10). Although there is a degree of variation in the lists by Namaste and Meyerowitz, and indeed others, Valentine points out that the minimal definition includes transsexuals and, usually, (male) transvestites (2007, p. 39). He also writes that the flexibility of the term "transgender" "enables one group—frequently transsexuals—to stand in for others while giving the impression of collectivity" (2007, p. 40). Despite these remarks, which posit a close connection, at times to the point of slippage, between the categories of "transgender" and "transsexual," the relationship between the two is far more fraught.

In fact, whether or not transsexuals are included or choose to include themselves in the category is a point of debate and contention. Stryker, in her introductory article to the *GLQ* Transgender Issue, writes, "In this introduction, I use transgender not to refer to one particular identity or way of being embodied but rather as an umbrella term for a wide variety of bodily effects that disrupt or denaturalize heteronormatively constructed linkages between an individual's anatomy at birth, a nonconsensually assigned gender category, psychical identifications with sexed body images and/or gendered subject positions, and the performance of specifically gendered social, sexual, or kinship functions" (1998, p. 149). She continues, "I realize that in doing so, and by including transsexuality…within the transgender rubric, I am already taking a position in the debate about how these terms interrelate" (1998, p. 149).

Vivian K. Namaste, Jay Prosser, and Henry Rubin are some of the most prominent scholars to address tensions between the categories of "transgender" and "transsexual." All of these authors call attention to a consistent erasure of transsexuals in many discussions about and uses of the term "transgender." They also critique the hierarchy that is often established—both implicitly and explicitly—by some feminist and queer theorists and theories where transgender is a privileged site of queerness over and against transsexuals' lives, bodies, specificity, and subjectivity. In *Invisible Lives: The Erasure of Transsexual and Transgendered People*, Namaste writes, "While the term 'transgender' has entered into public discourse within certain Anglo-American academic and activist contexts, its use is challenged by transsexuals" (2000, p. 61). Citing works by Margaret Deirdre O'Hartigan (1997), Max Valerio (1997), and Mirha

Soleil-Ross (1997), Namaste writes that "these writers ask important questions about the use and definition of the term 'transgender,' inquiring about the extent to which it erases transsexual specificity" (2000, p. 62). She continues, "It is especially important to cite transsexuals (and transsexuals who refuse to call themselves 'transgendered') given that the objections they raise rarely circulate within established lesbian and gay communities" (2000, p. 62). In *Sex Change/Social Change*, Namaste writes,

"Yes, we can state that we are not men and not women when all is well in the world. But would someone please tell me how to get an apartment when one is neither a man nor a woman? Where does one find a physician to treat neither men nor women? And an employer? My point is that this *transgendered* discourse is utopic, and one profoundly informed by privilege: it assumes that one already has a job, housing, and access to health care." (2005, p. 22 [emphasis added])

Henry Rubin points out that "transsexuals thus often continue to be disparaged even while *transgenders*—an umbrella term meant to represent a range of queer genders such as drag queens, cross-dressers, butches, and trannies who do not pursue all or any of the surgical/hormonal options—are celebrated" (1998, p. 276). Jay Prosser succinctly writes, "There is much about transsexuality that must remain irreconcilable to queer" (1998, p. 59). He elaborates, "the specificity of transsexual experience; the importance of the flesh to self; the difference between sex and gender identity; the desire to pass as 'real-ly-gendered' in the world without trouble" (1998, p. 59).

As the passages quoted above begin to demonstrate, the at-times-fraught relations between "transgender" and "transsexual" is part of another set of tensions between "transgender/transsexual" and "queer," as the latter is deployed in queer theory and politics. The relationships between and interconnectedness of the categories "transsexual," "transgender," and "queer" are not always clear and are themselves sometimes as contingent, flexible, and amorphous as the categories and real lives they are deployed to contain. Sometimes "transgender" and "transsexual" may be used as synonyms in opposition to "queer," but sometimes "transgender" and "queer" are aligned in opposition to "transsexual" (see Halberstam, 1998, p. 291, and Stryker, 1998, p. 149). The alignment between "queer" and "transgender" is open to substantial critique, according to Namaste, Prosser, and Rubin, as well as others, when it results in the privileging of transgender subjects and bodies over and against transsexual ones. In such instances, transsexuals are not erased but dismissed and characterized as "gender conservatives" (Elliot, 2010, p. 37). Rubin notes,

> "At the same time that 'queer' signifies one condition for articulating a radical trans agenda, it also represents an opportunity for the appropriation of transsexuals by nontranssexual queers. Trans phenomena are the new queer chic; our lives have been appropriated to demonstrate the theories of gender performativity, but only to the extent that they fail to reproduce the normative correspondence between body morphology and gender identity assumed as a matter of course by nontranssexuals." (1998, pp. 275–276)

He further writes, "Queer appropriations and the new movement among some transgenders to resignify themselves in a queer register carry an implicit critique of transsexuals who choose not to queer their identities. These more traditional transsexuals (is that an oxymoron?) choose to 'play it straight'—to pass, to assimilate" (1998, p. 276).

In *Debates in Transgender, Queer, and Feminist Theory: Contested Sites*, Patricia Elliot (2010) provides a useful survey and engaging analysis of the debates about the accuracy of a transgender rubric that professes to include transsexuals. In her section titled "The Transgender/Queer Perspective," Elliot identifies some of the key figures of this debate as "radical transsexuals Sandy Stone, Kate Bornstein, and Riki Wilchins, as well as transgender theorist Judith Halberstam and non-trans queer theorist Judith Butler" (2010, p. 41). Riki Wilchins is the author of *Read My Lips: Sexual Subversion and the End of Gender* (1997) and co-editor, along with Joan Nestle and Claire Howell, of *Gender Queer: Voices beyond the Sexual Binary* (2002); she is also a founding member of Camp Trans, the Transsexual Menace, and the Gender Policy Action Committee (GenderPAC). Halberstam's work on the "border wars" between (transgender)

butch and FTM identities includes "F2M: The Making of Female Masculinity" (1994) and *Female Masculinity* (1998). Butler's influential works include *Gender Trouble: Feminism and the Subversion of Identity* (1990), *Bodies That Matter: On the Discursive Limits of "Sex"* (1993), and *Undoing Gender*, particularly the chapter "Undiagnosing Gender" (2004).

Susan Stryker in her 1998 article also sees the possibility of a successful alliance among transgender, transsexual, and queer categories, writing, "I want to suggest in this essay that *transgender* can in fact be read as a heterodox interpretation of *queer*.... Transsexuality, by extension, can also be queer" (1998, p. 149). However, some years later, she seems less optimistic. Writing "I wanted to help define 'queer' as a family to which transsexuals belonged," here she characterizes this aspiration as a largely unfulfilled vision that nevertheless still takes her breath away (2004, p. 213). She further writes,

> "Queer theory has become an entrenched, though generally progressive, presence in higher education, but it has not realized the (admittedly utopian) potential I (perhaps naively) sensed there for a radical restructuring of our understanding of gender, particularly of minoritized and marginalized manifestations of gender, such as transsexuality. While queer studies remains the most hospitable place to undertake transgender work, all too often queer remains a codeword for 'gay' or 'lesbian,' and all too often transgender phenomena are misapprehended through a lens that privileges sexual orientation and sexual identity as the primary means of differing from heteronormativity." (2004, pp. 213–214)

Stryker writes that "the field of transgender studies has taken shape in the shadow of queer theory." She points out, however, that "transgender studies is following its own trajectory and has the potential to address emerging problems in the critical study of gender and sexuality, identity, embodiment, and desire in ways that gay, lesbian, and queer studies have not always successfully managed" (2004, p. 215). In this article, Stryker refers to transgender studies as queer theory's "evil twin," and we do well to remember their coterminous conceptions and births. To consider trans phenomena "the new queer chic," as seen in the passage by Rubin quoted above, demonstrates the failure to recognize and take seriously that both terms, "queer" and "transgender," were deployed in the early 1990s (Stryker, 2006, p. 7; Valentine, 2007, p. 24). The reasons behind the relative success, establishment, institutionalization, and entrenchment of queer theory and queer studies relative to the "newness" of transgender theory and transgender studies in academic settings need to be interrogated.

Transgender Studies. The publication of *The Transgender Studies Reader*, edited by Susan Stryker and Stephen Whittle, in 2006 marks an important step toward the establishment and institutionalization of transgender studies in academic settings. The compilation's chronological scope reaches back to the nineteenth century, with the inclusion of a selection from Richard von Krafft-Ebing's *Psychopathia Sexualis* (1877); the book also contains selections from Magnus Hirschfeld's *The Transvestites* (1910) and David Cauldwell's *Psychopathia Transexualis* (1949). In the prefatory remarks to Cauldwell's selection, Whittle and Stryker make note of a historical shift in "transgender phenomena," writing that "Prior to the spectacular publicity given to male-to-female transgender Christine Jorgensen in 1952, most medical and media attention was focused on female-to-male individuals" (2006, p. 40). *The Transgender Studies Reader* also includes the mid-twentieth-century publications of Harry Benjamin, Robert Stoller, and Harold Garfinkel. By incorporating such works at the outset, *The Transgender Studies Reader* successfully charts the shift, encapsulating the evolution from the study of "transgender phenomena" or "studies of transgenderism" to transgender studies. In the former, "transgenderism" is spoken about or studied from a nontransgender, presumably "normative," position. In the latter, positions of "normativity" are themselves brought into question and critiqued, and transgender/transsexual people speak from their positions as knowing subjects. Stryker writes, "Transgender Studies begins with performatively authorized transgender speaking and subject positions, in dialog with other voices" (2011, p. 13).

In her introductory article to *The Transgender Studies Reader*, Stryker defines transgender studies, writing, "Transgender studies, as we understand it, is the academic field that claims as its purview transsexuality and cross-dressing, some aspects of intersexuality and homosexuality, cross-cultural and historical investigations of human gender diversity, myriad subcultural expressions of 'gender atypicality,' theories of sexed embodiment and subjective gender identity development, law and public policy related to the regulation of gender expression, and many other similar issues" (2006, p. 3). She writes,

> "Most broadly conceived, the field of transgender studies is concerned with anything that disrupts, denaturalizes, rearticulates, and makes visible the normative linkages we generally assume to exist between the biological specificity of the sexually differentiated human body, the social roles and statuses that a particular form of body is expected to occupy, the subjectively experienced relationship between a gendered sense of self and social expectations of gender-role performance, and the cultural mechanisms that work to sustain or thwart specific configurations of gendered personhood." (2006, p. 3)

And finally,

> "Transgender studies, at its best, is like other socially engaged interdisciplinary academic fields such as disability studies or critical race theory that investigate questions of embodied difference, and analyze how such differences are transformed into social hierarchies—without ever losing sight of the fact that 'difference' and 'hierarchy' are never mere abstractions; they are systems of power that operate on actual bodies, capable of producing pain and pleasure, health and sickness, punishment and reward, life and death." (2006, p. 3)

The Transgender Studies Reader is divided into subsections, and these sections work to map the terrain of the field during its formation as articulated from the 1990s to the mid-2000s. Following the first section on "Sex, Gender, and Science," which contains the early articles on the study of "transgenderism" mentioned above, the next section is titled "Feminist Investments." This section includes the early "feminist" critique and derision of transsexuals in an excerpt from Janice Raymond's infamous *The Transsexual Empire: The Making of the She-Male* (1979). Yet this excerpt is contextualized by the editors' inclusion of Carol

Riddell's pamphlet Divided Sisterhood: A Critical Review of Janice Raymond's *The Transsexual Empire*, published within a year of the book, as well as Sandy Stone's "The Empire Strikes Back: A Posttranssexual Manifesto." Stryker and Whittle write in their preface to Raymond's excerpt, "Paradoxically, because it provoked such an outraged, anguished, and deeply motivated counter-response from transgender people, it also did more than any other work to elicit the new lines of critique that coalesced into transgender studies." They further write, "As will be seen throughout some of the articles in this anthology, Raymond provided the impetus for many transsexuals to begin theorizing their own lives, and asking whether they could ever claim the name 'feminist'" (2006, p. 131).

The Transgender Studies Reader then proceeds to present sections on "Queering Gender," wherein some of the investigations into the "transsexual/transgender" rift discussed above are included; the volume continues with other sections on "Selves: Identity and Community," "Transgender Masculinities," "Embodiment: Ethics in Time and Space," and finally "Multiple Crossings: Gender, Nationality, Race." This last section includes articles that critically examine U.S.- and Euro-centric assumptions in transgender theorizing, question the applicability of the categories of "transgender" and "transsexual" in cross-cultural (non-Western) settings, and challenge pervasive racism and ethnocentrism in the field. Thus, Katrina Roen, in her piece "Transgender Theory and Embodiment: The Risk of Racial Marginalization," asks, "Where are people of racial 'minorities' situated in queer and transgender theories? Despite the claims of inclusiveness of both transgender and queer writings, do perspectives of whiteness continue to resonate, largely unacknowledged, through transgender and queer theorising?" (Roen, 2006, p. 656). She also asks, "How might investing in aspects of current transgender discourse amount to complicity with the colonising culture of which medical discourses are only a small part? How can transgender theorising be critical of its own racialised politics in a way that is productive for those who place race first and gender second?" (Roen, 2006, p. 664). In their article "Romancing the Transgender

Native: Rethinking the Use of the 'Third Gender' Concept," Evan B. Towle and Lynn M. Morgan write, "Despite our commitment to the value of ethnographic comparison, we are skeptical of the utility of the generic transgender native in the popular literature. Understanding of other cultures is not enhanced by broad, decontextualized transcultural surveys or by accounts that encourage readers to take cultural features out of context" (Towle and Morgan, 2006, p. 668). They quote David Valentine: "If... 'transgender' has a specific history and set of meanings which implicitly mark it in terms of its difference from USAmerican understandings of 'gay,' then labeling *bantut* [Philippines] or *travesti* [Brazil] as 'transgender' is just as problematic" (Towle and Morgan, 2006, p. 669). In Emi Koyama's article, "Whose Feminism Is It Anyway? The Unspoken Racism of the Trans Inclusion Debate," Koyama writes about the debates surrounding the Michigan Womyn's Music Festival, "I have become increasingly alarmed in the recent months by the pattern of 'debate' between white middle-class women who run 'women's communities' and white middle-class trans activists who run trans movement. It is about time someone challenged the unspoken racism, which this whole discourse is founded upon" (Koyama, 2006, pp. 698–699). Helen Hok-Sze Leung, in "Unsung Heroes: Reading Transgender Subjectivities in Hong Kong Action Cinema," writes, "More recently, there is increasing recognition that more research on transgender phenomena outside of the Euro-American context is needed. This is the result of an anxiety in the field that the notion of 'transgender' itself may be in danger of reifying into an exclusionary narrative that is rooted only in the experiences of Europeans and North Americans" (Leung, 2006, p. 686). Such concerns are also raised in Stryker's introductory article, where she succinctly writes, "It is far too easy to assimilate non-Western configurations of personhood into Western constructs of sexuality and gender in a manner that recapitulates the power structures of colonialism. 'Transgender' is, without a doubt, a category of First World origin that is currently being exported for Third World consumption" (Stryker and Whittle, 2006, p. 14).

Other edited volumes that explore transgender in cross-cultural perspective include *Female Desires: Same-Sex Relations and Transgender Practices Across Cultures*, edited by Evelyn Blackwood and Saskia Wieringa; *Third Sex, Third Gender: Beyond Sexual Dimorphism in Culture and History*, edited by Gilbert Herdt; *Gender Reversals and Gender Cultures: Anthropological and Historical Perspectives*, edited by Sabrina Ramet; and *Body Guards: The Cultural Politics of Gender Ambiguity*, edited by Julia Epstein and Kristina Straub. The cross-cultural and historical applicability of the terms "transgender" and "transsexual" remains a subject of debate. Some—for example, Kate Bornstein in *Gender Outlaws* (1994, p. 143) and Leslie Feinberg in *Transgender Warriors* (1997)—claim "transcestors" reaching far back through history. There is undeniable power in the assertion of historical precedent and presence: if other cultures at other historical or contemporary moments have valued more flexible conceptions of genders, gender identities, and gender expressions, then there is hope that gender can be thought—imagined and inhabited—differently. However, in addition to the criticisms of this admittedly appealing and powerful strategy articulated by Towle and Morgan (2006), others would question this endeavor on social constructionist grounds. As Valentine writes, "From this [social constructionist] viewpoint, to imagine historical subjects as 'gay,' 'lesbian,' or as 'transgender' ignores the radically different understandings of self and the contexts that underpinned the practices and lives of historical subjects" (2007, p. 30). Thus the debates over essentialist versus constructionist approaches seen previously in the context of both gender (male/female) and sexuality (gay/straight) binaries exist in the context of transgender historicizing as well.

New Terminologies. In a review of *The Transgender Studies Reader*, Brice Smith observes that in Whittle's foreword he "never uses the word 'transgender,' opting instead for 'trans'" (2008, p. 318). Smith continues, "Whittle's preference for 'trans' suggests that 'transgender' is already dated and anticipates an evolution in transgender studies" (2008, p. 318). It is hard not to see some of the motivation behind this more recent shift from "transgender" to "trans" as a way to mitigate the erasure of transsexuals that often accompanied the use of the term "transgender" discussed above. Whittle writes, "The word 'trans,' referring to a 'trans woman' or 'trans man' (of whatever subtype of trans identity) is a very recent take on the umbrella term 'transgender'" (p. xi). He continues, "'Trans' as a stand-alone term did not come into formal usage until it was coined by a parliamentary discussion group in London in 1998, with the deliberate intention of being as inclusive as possible when negotiating equality legislation" (p. xi). And Whittle points out, "We see new language being developed constantly; for example 'per' as a pronoun was developed by U.K. community members with nonexistent gender identities, and similarly the U.S. term 'hir' for those who have both" (pp. xi–xii). In the United States one might also find "ze" or "zie" as an alternative to he or she as well as "hir" as an alternative to his or her. More recently, "trans*" is being used to signal this term's openness and inclusion and differentiate it from "trans," which is now more often used for trans men and trans women. Transgendered, with the appended "ed," is considered offensive to many trans and transgender people. Along with "trans," "transsexual," and "transgender," one will also encounter "cis," "cissexual," and "cisgender." "Cis-" is derived from the Latin prefix *cis-*, which means "on this side of," in contrast with *trans*, connoting "on the other side of." Cissexual and cisgender are at times being used instead of "nontrans." Emi Koyama explains that the terms originate from trans activists "who wanted to turn the table and define the words that describe nontranssexuals and non-transgenders rather than always being defined and described by them" (2013; see also Serano, 2007, and Enke, 2013).

Future Directions. Just two years after Whittle's foreword to *The Transgender Studies Reader*, *Women's Studies Quarterly* published its 2008 issue with the title "Trans-." Susan Stryker, Paisley Currah, and Lisa Jean Moore's introductory essay "Introduction: Trans-, Trans, or Transgender?" reflects on these different terms, ultimately opting for the less nominalistic and more relational term "trans-" to further open the field of transgender studies and expand its horizons.

Instead of thinking of the "trans" in transgender as a horizontal movement between two fixed gendered spaces, "man" and "woman," Stryker, Currah, and Moore propose thinking instead of "'trans-' along a vertical axis, one that moves between the concrete biomateriality of individual living bodies and the biopolitical realm of aggregate populations that serve as resource for sovereign power.... 'Trans-' thus becomes the capillary space of connection and circulation between the macro- and micro-political registers through which the lives of bodies become enmeshed in the lives of nations, states, and capital-formations, while '-gender' becomes one of several sets of variable techniques or temporal practices (such as race or class) through which bodies are made to live" (Stryker et al., 2008, pp. 13–14). The authors also write, "Those of us schooled in the humanities and social sciences have become familiar, over the past twenty years or so, with queering things: how might we likewise begin to critically trans- our world?" (2008, p. 13). "Transing" is then described by the authors as "a practice that assembles gender into contingent structures of association with other attributes of bodily being, and that allows for their reassembly" (2008, p. 13). In this "Trans-" volume of *Women's Studies Quarterly*, Stryker, Currah, and Moore assemble "work that situates 'trans-' in relation to transgender yet moves beyond the narrow politics of gender identity" (2008, p. 15).

The recently published *Transgender Studies Reader 2* (2013) forefronts this broader conception of trans (gender) work. Along with sections on "Transfeminism" and "Timely Matters: Temporality and Trans-Historicity," both themes that have related sections in the earlier *Transgender Studies Reader*, one finds sections on "Making Trans-Culture(s): Texts, Performances, Artifacts," "Radical Political Economy," and "Transsexing Humanimality." There is an increased focus on trans critiques of biopolitics, surveillance, neoliberal economies, and social policies. There is a broader geographic range covered as "the field of transgender studies is moving strongly in transnational directions" (Stryker and Aizura, 2013, p. 8). Editors Susan Stryker and Aren Z. Aizura write, "The field of transgender studies has grown with unexpected speed to unanticipated dimensions over the past few years; if the near future resembles the recent past, we can scarcely imagine what a *Transgender Studies Reader 3* might look like" (2013, p. 12). Readers interested in transgender studies and its future manifestations, while looking forward to the publication of a third reader, are now able to learn about, and participate in, such work in the academic journal *TSQ: The Transgender Quarterly*, published by Duke University Press as of May 2014.

[*See also* Gender; Intersectional Studies; *and* Queer Theory.]

BIBLIOGRAPHY

Bornstein, Kate. *Gender Outlaw: On Men, Women, and the Rest of Us*. New York: Vintage, 1995.

Butler, Judith. *Gender Trouble: Feminism and the Subversion of Identity*. New York, Routledge, 1990.

Butler, Judith. *Undoing Gender*. New York: Routledge, 2004.

Elliot, Patricia. *Debates in Transgender, Queer, and Feminist Theory: Contested Sites*. Aldershot, U.K.: Ashgate, 2010.

Enke, A. Finn. "The Education of Little Cis: Cisgender and the Discipline of Opposing Bodies." In *The Transgender Studies Reader 2*, edited by Susan Stryker and Aren Z. Aizura, pp. 234–247. New York: Routledge, 2013.

Feinberg, Leslie. *TransLiberation: Beyond Pink or Blue*. Boston: Beacon, 1998.

Halberstam, Judith. "F2M: The Making of Female Masculinity." In *The Lesbian Postmodern*, edited by L. Doan, pp. 210–228. New York: Columbia University Press, 1994.

Halberstam, Judith. *Female Masculinity*. Durham, N.C.: Duke University Press, 1998.

Koyama, Emi. "Whose Feminism Is It Anyway? The Unspoken Racism of the Trans Inclusion Debate." In *The Transgender Studies Reader*, edited by Susan Stryker and Stephen Whittle, pp. 698–705. New York: Routledge, 2006.

Koyama, Emi. "'Cis' Is Real—Even if It Is Carelessly Articulated." http://eminism.org/blog/entry/399 (accessed 30 October 2013).

Leung, Helen Hok-Sze. "Unsung Heroes: Reading Transgender Subjectivities in Hong Kong Action Cinema." In *The Transgender Studies Reader*, edited by Susan Stryker and Stephen Whittle, pp. 685–697. New York: Routledge, 2006.

Meyerowitz, Joanne. *How Sex Changed: A History of Transsexuality in the United States.* Cambridge, Mass.: Harvard University Press, 2002.

Namaste, Viviane K. *Invisible Lives: The Erasure of Transsexual and Transgendered People.* Chicago: University of Chicago Press, 2000.

Prosser, Jay. *Second Skins: The Body Narratives of Transsexuality.* New York: Columbia University Press, 1998.

Roen, Katrina. "Transgender Theory and Embodiment: The Risk of Racial Marginalization." In *The Transgender Studies Reader,* edited by Susan Stryker and Stephen Whittle, pp. 656–665. New York: Routledge, 2006.

Rubin, Henry S. "Phenomenology as Method in Trans Studies." *GLQ: A Journal of Lesbian and Gay Studies* 4, no. 2 (2998): 263–281.

Serano, Julia. *Whipping Girl: A Transsexual Woman on Sexism and the Scapegoating of Femininity.* Emeryville, Calif.: Seal, 2007.

Smith, Brice. "Susan Stryker and Stephen Whittle's *The Transgender Studies Reader.*" *Women's Studies Quarterly* 36, no. 3–4 (2008): 318–320.

Spade, Dean. "Mutilating Gender." In *The Transgender Studies Reader,* edited by Susan Stryker and Stephen Whittle, pp. 315–332. New York: Routledge, 2006.

Stone, Sandy. "The Empire Strikes Back: A Posttranssexual Manifesto." In *Body Guards: The Cultural Politics of Gender Ambiguity,* edited by Julia Epstein and Kristina Straub, pp. 280–304. New York: Routledge, 1991.

Stryker, Susan. "My Words to Victor Frankenstein above the Village of Chamounix: Performing Transgender Rage." *GLQ: A Journal of Lesbian and Gay Studies* 1, no. 3 (1994): 237–254.

Stryker, Susan. "The Transgender Issue: Introduction." *GLQ: A Journal of Lesbian and Gay Studies* 4, no. 2 (1998): 145–158.

Stryker, Susan. "Transgender Theory: Queer Theory's Evil Twin." *GLQ: A Journal of Lesbian and Gay Studies* 10, no. 2 (2004): 212–215.

Stryker, Susan. "(De)Subjugated Knowledges: An Introduction to Transgender Studies." In *The Transgender Studies Reader,* edited by Susan Stryker and Stephen Whittle, pp. 1–17. New York and London: Routledge, 2006.

Stryker, Susan, and Stephen Whittle, eds. *The Transgender Studies Reader.* New York and London: Routledge, 2006.

Stryker, Susan. "Transgender Studies 2.0." http://koensforskning.ku.dk/trans/stryker.pdf/2011 (accessed 23 October 2013).

Stryker, Susan, Paisley Currah, and Lisa Jean Moore. "Introduction: Trans-, Trans, or Transgender?" *Women's Studies Quarterly* 36, no. 3–4 (2008): 11–22.

Stryker, Susan, and Aren Z. Aizura, eds. *The Transgender Studies Reader 2.* New York and London: Routledge, 2013.

Towne, Evan B., and Lynn M. Morgan. "Romancing the Transgender Native: Rethinking the Use of the 'Third Gender' Concept." In *The Transgender Studies Reader,* edited by Susan Stryker and Stephen Whittle, pp. 666–685. New York and London: Routledge, 2006.

Valentine, David. *Imagining Transgender: An Ethnography of a Category.* Durham, N.C.: Duke University Press, 2007.

Gwynn Kessler

WOMANIST CRITICISM

The challenges of writing about womanist biblical criticism are as varied as scholars who claim this moniker. Even though this approach took root in the biblical academy nearly three decades ago, it continues to emerge. At this writing, there is no womanist reader or collection of womanist biblical criticism. There have been several offerings to describe womanist readings/interpretations and how they function in biblical criticism discourse, however, and by looking over those offerings one may get a clear sense of the expansiveness and multiplicity of methods, strategies, and resources used. A quick overview will display, however, a consistency in the diversity: womanists begin at the nexus of texts and real human bodies, especially poor black women and girls.

Early on, womanist biblical scholars were deeply concerned about building a heuristic model and taxonomy for their work. The work of Renita Weems, the first African American woman to receive a degree in Hebrew Bible in the United States, was included in the edited volume *Black Theology* in 1993. Having understood that womanist thought had changed black theology, the editors Gayraud S. Wilmore and James H. Cone included Weems's article along with one by New Testament scholar Clarice J. Martin, along with a full section on womanist theology, which included nine

essays. Weems reflected on the womanist biblical enterprise, especially working through the confluence and conflicts of interpretation among feminists and black (male) liberationists. She did not lay out a roadmap for the process, but she clarified what is at stake for womanist criticism, particularly the role of power.

Martin's essay in the volume (1990; reprinted in Wilmore and Cone, 1993) was in fact a "quest." She hunted for a model to employ the categories of "race," "gender," and "class" beyond mere reporting to a consideration of realities not easily separated as a way of approaching texts. Both Weems and Martin disabused themselves of a mythic objectivity and claimed subjectivity as subjects and as a stance.

Hebrew Bible/Old Testament scholar Wil Gafney conjoined the feminist-womanist project in her 2006 essay. Self-identifying as "hybrid," Gafney consciously uses both terms, and yet her essay spends a great deal of time describing and making room for a womanist biblical criticism. The same year, Old Testament scholar Nyasha Junior's work was included in an edited volume (2006). My own work as a biblical scholar has sought to build a womanist biblical criticism as a gateway to interpretation for the practical field of preaching, as best evidenced in my chapter on preaching (Bridgeman, 2013). Also published in 2013 were two entries by New Testament scholar Mitzi Smith.

Origins/Beginnings. Womanist biblical criticism emerged in the context of a burgeoning womanist discourse located initially in literary circles. Alice Walker first used the term "womanist" in a short story, "Coming Apart," in 1979, in which she described the black wife's character as a womanist, or, as she noted "a feminist, only more common." At the beginning of her 1983 volume of essays, she elaborated on her now iconic definition. For Walker, the word "womanist" deepened the work of feminism, taking into account not only sexism but also racism. Though today many womanists separate womanism from feminism, Walker originally linked the two.

An outgrowth of womanist religious discourse begun by ethicists and theologians, womanist work began as a protest to the realities that North American feminism did not attend to issues of race and class and that North American liberation theologies (especially done by black men) did not attend to gender. In this "in-between" space, womanist thought arose and found its voice.

Like all ideological strategies, womanist criticism admits that it is an "interested" enterprise. Womanists reject notions of unbiased objectivity; they are consciously biased but, as I have noted elsewhere, not bigoted. "This bias is the preferential reading through a stated, uncovered, made-known lens, i.e., the life of poor black women, especially, but really the particularities of black lives in general" (Bridgeman, 2013).

Womanist criticism began, also, with a concern for the black church rather than the academy. For this reason, its critics have often deemed it "not rigorous." However, womanist biblical scholars—and ethicists and theologians attending to biblical work—have sought to make the work they do simple and free of academic jargon in order to be in full conversation with the church. Because many of the first womanists were Christians—most of whom were also ordained clergy—womanist biblical scholars have sought to bring the art of critical questioning to pulpits and bible studies in local churches. This enterprise makes it very different from the work of the guild. Womanist interpreters, more often than some of their white/feminist counterparts, are trying to remain in pulpits or women's conference circles in—at this point—predominantly conservative churches, especially if they do not feel their contributions are valued in the biblical guild. Womanist work seeks the survival and flourishing for black women, with the notion that if black women thrive, a culture will be created in which all persons may thrive.

A History of Womanist Biblical Criticism. Two biblical scholars often mentioned as progenitors of the womanist biblical criticism/interpretation field are Weems and Martin. Weems's 1989 Princeton dissertation became her 1995 book, which examines the marriage metaphor in the Hebrew Prophets. Her 1988 trade book was written with African American women in mind, "out of disgust," tired of seeing the reality of women of color cited as a postscript. While the book interprets biblical texts, it was not written for the academy but with religious churchgoing black women in mind. She reissued the book as a self-published volume in 2005, with some edits and additional chapters and a title no longer including the word "womanist." In her work, Weems explains that womanist biblical scholarship often seems homiletical and folksy because its practitioners often write with "the whole folk" in mind, i.e., the unschooled or unlearned religious reader. In order not to cave in to temerity in the church and to withstand micro-aggressions in the biblical guild, she claims that womanists must develop an audacious sensibility.

In her 2007 volume, Rev. Dr. Elaine Flake interpreted biblical texts for preaching from a womanist perspective. A friend and colleague of Weems in the African Methodist Episcopal Church, Flake used what she calls a "hermeneutic of healing," calling readers to dismantle anti-female attitudes "even those perpetuated in scripture." Flake writes that the preacher-exegete must affirm the positive role of women; show sensitivity, especially toward maligned biblical women; preach against the evils of racial and gender discrimination; acknowledge African ancestry in the text and in the preaching moment; and present Jesus as an advocate for women.

Biblical scholar Koala Jones-Warsaw provided one of the first womanist biblical readings, an interpretation of Judges 19–21, presented at the Society of Biblical Literature in 1992 and published a year later (1993). She took exception to Phyllis Trible's (1984) reading offered on behalf of the woman alone and sought instead to read for the whole folk. Jones-Warsaw called critics to "walk around in the text," standing in the place of all the characters, taking into account not only gender but also ethnicity, class, and race. Her work did not delve deeply enough into the text and was unnecessarily dismissive of Trible's reading, but, alongside Weems, she hinted at a trail for other womanist biblical critics to follow.

Weems's role within Old Testament womanist scholarship is paralleled by Martin's in the New Testament. The first self-identified womanist biblical scholar in the United States, Martin's expertise and field of research includes language, hermeneutics, history of exegesis, womanist thought, and African American religion. She reads the New Testament believing that translation and interpretation history opens a way to redeem the Bible as scripture while resisting texts considered oppressive. Martin delves into the thorniness of translation in a quest for liberative interpretations.

Michael Joseph Brown's analyses of some womanist biblical scholarship (2004, pp. 89–119) pay particular attention to Weems, Martin, Cheryl Kirk-Duggan, and Wilma Bailey. Brown notes that Weems and Kirk-Duggan, both working with mostly Old Testament texts, are willing to argue that biblical texts are complicated and complicit in African American (women's) oppression. Old Testament scholar Bailey's work is examined because she is African American rather than explicitly womanist, but her work follows womanist trends by focusing on Hagar (1994), a biblical character frequently addressed in womanist writings. Primarily an ethicist trained also in biblical texts, Kirk-Duggan is concerned with violence in biblical texts, but as a womanist she also brings womanist critical attention to texts that are fruitfully engaged via race, gender, and class. Trained as a classical singer, Kirk-Duggan also interprets texts using black musicology.

Brown rightly notes that the interpretative work of all these scholars serves to advocate. Appropriating and resisting texts in varying degrees, they each pull on extrabiblical and modern and postmodern cultural knowledge passed on through and by African American women as sources: autobiographies, songs, sermons all aid in the interpretive womanist work.

The Conflict/Differences with Feminism. In the introduction to her collected volume (2006), Layli Phillips distinguishes womanism from black feminism and (nonblack) feminism. She calls womanists and black feminists "sisters," able to support one another but not identical. She describes womanism as committed to holistic liberation and given to the use of intersectionality for thriving. She also notes that though Walker was the first to use the term "womanist" in print, she was heir to the work of "birthmothers" to the movement, Chikwenye Okonjo Ogunyemi and Clenora Hudson-Weems. While the collection of essays crosses several disciplines and fields of study as well as racial/ethnic backgrounds and includes a brief section of womanist theology, no biblical critics/scholars are included. Nyasha Junior's observation (2006) that few womanist biblical readings appear in feminist readers assumes that womanist biblical work is a subset of feminism; Phillips ably demonstrates that it is not, even if it began in that vein. Womanist work is cousin to feminist work, but not especially beholden to it.

In the 1980s and 1990s, womanist scholars (followed by women from other cultures—mujeristas, Asian, postcolonial, etc.) challenged then-majority feminists for their expressly North American, middle-class, "white woman" analyses that could not appreciate their own privilege. Budding womanist scholars often felt marginalized in feminist circles and ostracized in black (male) liberationist circles.

In the mid-1990s and beyond, feminists took seriously womanists' critiques and incorporated them into their work (especially class and race). Womanist scholars saw these efforts as white feminists co-opting their critical and epistemological work. Womanists claimed co-optation was at the center of what some white feminists had always done, maintain power over other women critics by muting their voices, subsuming their work under the term "feminist," policing publishing doors, and telling other women's stories, if they were told at all. In the economy of ideas, womanists insist that our critical work is important to the multiplicity of tactical strategies against oppression, often quoting Audre Lorde that "the master's tools will not dismantle the master's house." While most womanist critics bring the history of scholarship to a text, they also insist that already accepted critical analyses are not needed to legitimate womanist criticism.

Accusations of "essentialism" have stalked womanist work in other disciplines and may be one of the reasons womanist scholarship has been less prolific in biblical studies. Steeped in modernist historical-critical training and methodology, womanist biblical scholars have been reticent to break past those boundaries and often rely on historical-critical methodologies, as evidenced, for example, in Martin's work. And yet, all criticism has at its core assumptions, presumptions, and communities that oversee the interpreter. Resisting the (particularly white) accusation that they are not being "scholarly," womanist biblical critics include conversational partners and co-interpreters in their work (especially other liberationists/ideological critics) before finally turning to dominating/traditional scholarship. The womanist interpreter, however, undertakes her own work before consulting others in order to resist colonizing thought and the suppression of one's own hermeneutics of challenge and suspicion. A womanist biblical scholar does not need (white) feminists, (male) liberation theologians, or any other critics to legitimate her or his work. Just as feminism was allowed to stand on its own as a field of criticism, womanism deserves the same respect.

Various Womanist Strategies. Most womanist interpretive strategies are undergirded by Walker's definition: a womanist is an African American woman or a woman of color who subscribes to a code that is committed to asking hard, even unanswerable questions. A womanist cares about injustices and pain in the world. Committed to woman-culture only as the first task, the womanist is "committed to survival and wholeness of entire people, male *and* female" (Walker, 1983). This commitment is manifested in her love of the earthy, aesthetic, and unex-

plainable: as reflected in a love of art and movement, the earth and cosmos, food and community, revolutionary struggle, and loving "the folk," and especially herself. Self-love—as precursor to communal love—fuels womanist work.

Womanists look to a proverbial and particularly African way of being, i.e., observation ("go watch the ant") and hospitality ("come to the feast"). These ways do not differ per se from other liberationist/ideological forms of criticism, but they are particular. Herein is womanist criticism's strength and weakness: not all critics have come from the social location of the subject whose questions are presumed central, i.e., poor black women.

Yvonne Chireau in her 2003 monograph notes that womanist interpretation puts black women's lives "at the center of inquiry" as a first pillar of its criticism. Moving (black) women from margin/edge to center de-centers power brokers and forces us to look at who is at stake in the text. Sometimes this "center" is embodied in the critic herself, but self-reflection is never sufficient. Cultural criticism and a broad interdisciplinary reading strategy help critics bring poor, black women to the text. A significant task of African American biblical interpretation and womanist criticisms in particular is to see the black body/culture as locus of knowledge and interpretation.

New Testament womanist scholar Mitzi Smith demonstrates such a centering as she reads the lives of two nineteenth-century black women preachers in her 2011 article. She describes how black women preachers use Pauline texts to build a powerful political discourse for freedom, activism, and advocacy. In addition, Smith depends on a personal criticism, i.e., "personal testimony," as a black woman who works as a womanist biblical scholar. In her 2013 essay on the feeding miracle in the Gospel of Matthew, she recounts her family's begging for bread and its impact on reading the very texts she now interprets. Smith understands "scraps" and "crumbs" as means to survival because she saw her mother dignify the gifts that came to help her feed her children.

Womanist biblical critics look for the underside of questions within the biblical text and its contemporary and intertextual conversation partners, with an a priori assumption that biblical inquiry wields its best fruits when critics look for the vantage point of the marginalized, the oppressed, the silenced, or the voiceless in current society and in ancient texts. The womanist critic names herself an expert of the questions that plague her. If the text cannot answer a particular question—either because of its genre or its apparent "intentions"—her question does not become invalid.

One goal of the womanist critic is to expose power and identify whether power is used for dominating or liberating purposes by narrators, texts, and readers. To shed light on how power functions in texts and their interpretations, the critic asks such questions as: Who is in danger because of who wields power? What happens when/if power is left unchecked? What would freedom look like in the text? What would wholeness for the whole community be? What is the cost of "orthodox" readings, and is there liberating room for heterodoxy? and Where and how is a deity present in the text for the oppressed (or oppressor)? This unmasking/exposing of people, texts, scholarship, and reading strategies is directed at the ancient texts/worlds as well as contemporaneous ones.

Womanists employ some of the same tools that feminists and other liberationists/ideological critics do, including critical gender studies, Marxist/class analyses, postcolonial criticism, literary and rhetorical criticisms, and critical race theory. Literary and cultural criticisms (especially infused with critical race theory) are perhaps the most persistent strategies to which womanists turn in their "by any means necessary" approach to wresting first understandings then meanings from texts. But womanists also take seriously alternative interpretations that reveal the silencing of the margins. Thus, though womanists wield historical-critical tools, they are not at all beholden to them.

Womanist biblical criticism is grounded epistemologically in (black) women's ways of knowing. We supplement our inquiries with experience and intuition. As Christian womanist ethicist Emilie Townes writes, "What arrogance we commit when we allow the inadequacies of our training to determine what we can come to know and how. When any of us who do intellectual work are candid, we know that there are wide gaps and large chasms in the methodologies we have been trained to use in our disciplines" (2006, pp. 244–245).

Gafney, mentioned above, addresses the issue of biblical translation as a way to be what she calls a "fem/womanist hermeneut." In her foundational essay posted online in the Society for Biblical Literature Forum (2006), Gafney lays out several principles for translation, all intended to undermine and disrupt normative translation processes and to unmask the ways in which translation may obscure meanings and interpretations. She calls critics to:

1. "Take the bible seriously in all its plurality," which requires a respect for the looser canons of the biblical texts, not merely the accepted canon of a particular communion.
2. Translate for hearers. If the text is alliterative, then the translation ought also be alliterative.
3. Use comparative philology and semantic range to determine meaning.
4. Track what Gafney calls "God-girl talk"—instances in the text where second person feminine form endings are used to describe deity or people—and to make these endings plain in translation.
5. Recover and reclaim the Afro-Asian continental context of the scriptures.
6. "Recover women obscured by masculine grammar." She presumes, for example, that all plural forms of the word "prophet" include women and men unless "there is specific language limiting the group."
7. End the privilege of German scholarship and translation, "abandoning Germanic norms in translation means abandoning the anti-Semitism and anti-Judaism inherited by the Western biblical critical enterprise."

As noted above, New Testament scholar Martin also concerns herself with translation issues. In her first three publications (1989, 1990, 1991), she demonstrates how a womanist interpretation, reflecting the quarto-centric interests of gender, race, class and language issues, allows for a reading freeing for all people, and especially for black women.

For New Testament womanist critics, Jesus becomes a lens into the texts. Jesus becomes a "sister" to womanist interpreters, living in the interstices of society among women, befriending them, holding theological conversations with them, touching and healing them. He suffers because he confronts evil and powers that be. This stance is clear in Raquel St. Clair's work (2007, 2008). Resisting the notion that black peoples (women in particular) should suffer as a part of their Christian identity, St. Clair argues that suffering is not a necessary part of discipleship but rather the consequence Jesus suffered because of evil. Pursuing a "hermeneutic of wholeness," St. Clair calls biblical interpretation to go beyond recovery to a rethinking of categories such as "servant" and "suffering."

Like most womanist biblical scholars, St. Clair is indebted to the work of theologians and ethicists such as Jacqueline Grant, Katie G. Cannon, Delores Williams, Emilie Townes, Toinette Eugene, JoAnne Marie Terrell, Shawn Copeland, and Kelly Brown Douglas. Grant's 1989 work was one of the first monographs to delineate how Jesus functions in many black religious environs; as an African Methodist Episcopal minister, she challenged the sexist and androcentric claims of black church leaders and laity. Similarly, Douglas challenged a Christianity that did not take seriously the lives and exigencies of real black people, asserting that Christ symbolically is a black woman and thus is partner in the struggle to survive and flourish (1989). Douglas also challenged the church's notions of sex and sexuality in her 1999 volume, her enduring contribution to womanist readings of biblical texts about sex and sexuality.

Roman Catholic womanist pastoral theologian Toinette Eugene also ties her work to interpreting texts. Her 1987 essay claims that womanist biblical work is not limited to those trained in Bible. As stressed throughout this entry, womanists are deeply concerned that their work speak to black churchgoers—for whom the biblical has primacy—a reality that leads womanist scholars of every discipline to address directly biblical texts.

No longer content only to reclaim an African past from the text and lift up the marginalized in the text, modern womanist work considers how texts make plain and obscure meanings, the intersectionality of oppressions, and how claims are made on communities in the texts and beyond. They seek to address a community beyond the scholarly ones. Because readings "count" as people resonate with them, an interpreter must be persuasive in her reading of texts, making her case to a community of readers so that her interpretation takes its place among "possible meanings."

My Work. Caught between a hard-core historical critical training and an entrenched fascination with reader response and ideological criticisms, especially womanist thought beyond the academy, my own work has been varied. Were I to rewrite my 2002 dissertation (one of the first dissertations to use the term "womanist" in its title), I would take more care with power analyses, the role of class in the book, and in ecological theology. I would take more care to provide taxonomy and a closer reading of the text itself. Such observations, of course, come after years of attending academic conferences in which womanist theologians and ethicists have built taxonomies and heuristic paradigms by which to do their work.

As an ordained minister, translating the critical work of the academy into pulpits I regularly fill—first as a pastor for more than twenty-five years and later as a visiting scholar-preacher—I believe my work to be at the core a womanist enterprise, an attempt to discover some liberative word between texts and peoples, a "loving the whole folk" and saving all who will be saved. As such, I am centering black women's concerns even if I never explicitly say or write this phrase.

There is no reason, in my mind, to privilege the academy's definition of biblical scholar, especially since womanist scholars and scholarship deliberately seeks to be "in the pews." Womanist scholars remember that the church has prepared us for this work and we owe it to that audience to be faithful readers, critics, and interpreters, even when it chaffs the church. The guild, in this way, is secondary.

The Future of Womanist Biblical Scholarship. As more women claim the moniker "womanists," the fields of meaning will clarify and broaden at the same time. Several African American women have now written dissertations that claim the term "womanist," but to date there is only one monograph (St. Claire, 2008) that explicitly uses the term (self-described womanist Cheryl Anderson's 2009 monograph uses the term "inclusive interpretation"). The pressures of new interpretative resources, such as postcolonial, queer theory, and (dis)ability studies, are forcing womanist scholars to revisit the intersectionality of their work.

Womanist biblical critics are still in the stage of knowledge production. In this stage, womanists are called to several tasks:

1. They must mine the mother lode of Africana histories, cultures, stories, and artifacts, in the Americas as well as in the African diaspora throughout the world. These histories are critical to forming questions for interrogating biblical texts since several scholars have convincingly demonstrated that African and Asian worldviews are deeply embedded in biblical texts, especially the Hebrew Bible. Womanist critics must undo the way that dominating scholarship has obscured black presence and black worldview while critiquing the oppressive and liberative impulses in the biblical text itself. In the near future, womanist biblical scholars must publish more and in concentrated ways, first as monographs but also in the communal commitments womanist work expects—in collected and edited volumes.

2. Their work must continue to balance a rigorous scholarship that can be translated beyond the academy. Womanist biblical critics must make plain the work its field of study already has uncovered.

3. Womanist biblical exegetes must continue the linguistic and translation work reflected in Martin's and Gafney's work. Marginal readings must be given serious weight in order for readers to see beyond the dominating impulses of a text.

4. Womanist biblical critics must continue to employ suspicion and resistance as a method to question motives and motivations within texts, histories of interpretations, and interpreters, including the ones embedded within the text. They must always seek the dignity of the most marginalized and question any "givens" within texts and interpretations that continue to imbue the powerful with more power.

5. Womanist critics must ask alongside and on behalf of persons on the margins. When reading with outsiders, womanist scholars must also interrogate their own points of privilege, considering what people outside of "legitimate" constructs must do to survive and seek to uncover survivalist strategies within texts and communities.

6. Since agency is at the root of radical subjectivity, womanist biblical scholars also must look for agency and willfulness (womanish ways) in the text: where it is, who takes it for themselves and from others, and who has freedom—the ability to choose and act for one's own in freedom and dignity.

If done with care and rigor, the womanist critic will come away from the texts with new insight and fuse the world of the text with the world of the reader. Womanist critics maintain that they do their work for "the whole folk," and therefore reading the ancient texts embraced by present people requires an imaginative interpretation that benefits whole communities, not just poor black women.

This work must be done with an audacious humility, a bold provisionality. We see from our vantage point alone, but we sit in a circle of learners, questions, and critics; we offer interpretations in order to illumine the multivalent possibilities in every biblical text. This acknowledgment that no reading represents every story or all knowledge is essential so that womanist biblical critics may resist essentializing and universalizing their readings.

In the end, womanist biblical critics are charged with making their interpretative voices clear and prophetic in the cacophony of rivers of voices. We are called to explore our understanding of the Divine as we seek to comprehend the texts. We also are called to hold accountable our religious institutions until we all experience health, wholeness, and liberation. I argue for a hermeneutic of struggle in which we wrestle with the deity and the texts, reading against the texts and against traditions (2006). By making the margins visible, we make the center whole.

[*See also* Historical-Critical Approaches; Intersectional Studies; Mujerista Criticism; *and* Race, Class, and Ethnicity, *subentry* Hebrew Bible.]

BIBLIOGRAPHY

Anderson, Cheryl. *Ancient Laws and Contemporary Controversies: The Need for Inclusive Biblical Interpretation.* New York: Oxford University Press, 2009.

Bailey, Wilma Ann. "Hagar: A Model for an Anabaptist Feminist?" *Mennonite Quarterly Review* 68, no. 2 (1994): 219–228.

Bridgeman, Valerie J. "Retribution as First Response: Did God Punish New Orleans?" In *The Sky Is Crying: Race, Class, and Natural Disaster*, edited by Cheryl A. Kirk-Duggan, pp. 3–12. Nashville, Tenn.: Abingdon, 2006.

Bridgeman, Valerie. "'It Ain't Necessarily So.' Resistance Preaching and Womanist Thought." In *Preaching and the Personal*, edited by Dwayne Howell, pp. 71–79. Eugene, Ore.: Pickwick, 2013.

Brown, Michael Joseph. "The Womanization of Blackness." In *Blackening of the Bible: The Aims of African American Biblical Scholarship*, pp. 89–119. London: T&T Clark, 2004.

Byron, Gay L. *Symbolic Blackness and Ethnic Difference in Early Christian Literature.* New York: Routledge, 2002.

Byron, Gay L. "Ancient Ethiopia and the New Testament: Ethnic (Con)texts and Racialized (Sub)texts." In *They Were All Together in One Place: Toward Minority Biblical Criticism*, edited by Randall. C. Bailey, Tat-Siong Benny Liew, and Fernando F. Segovia, pp. 161–190. Atlanta: Society for Biblical Literature, 2009.

Cannon, Katie G. *Katie's Canon: Womanism and the Soul of the Black Community.* New York: Continuum, 1995.

Chireau, Yvonne P. *Black Magic: Religion and the African American Conjuring Tradition.* Berkeley: University of California Press, 2003.

Douglas, Kelly Brown. "God Is as Christ Does: Toward a Womanist Theology." *Journal of Religious Thought* 46, no. 1 (1989): 7–16.

Douglas, Kelly Brown. *Sexuality and the Black Church: A Womanist Perspective.* Maryknoll, N.Y.: Orbis, 1999.

Eugene, Toinette M. "A Hermeneutical Challenge for Womanists: The Interrelation between the Text and Our Experience." In *Perspectives on Feminist Hermeneutics*, edited by Gayle Gerber Koontz and Williard Swartley, p. 26. Occasional Papers no. 10. Elkhart, Ind.: Institute of Mennonite Studies, 1987.

Flake, Elaine. *God in Her Midst: Preaching Healing to Wounded Women.* Valley Forge, Pa.: Judson, 2007.

Gafney, Wil. "Translation Matters: A Fem/Womanist Exploration of Translation Theory and Practice for Proclamation in Worship." *SBL Forum* [cited March 2006]. http://sbl-site.org/Article.aspx?ArticleID=509 (accessed 21 October 2013).

Gafney, Wilda C. M. "A Black Feminist Approach to Biblical Studies." *Encounter-Indianapolis* 67, no. 4 (2006): 391–403.

Grant, Jacqueline. *White Women's Christ and Black Women's Jesus: Feminist Christology and Womanist Response.* Atlanta: Scholars Press, 1989.

Jones-Warsaw, Koala. "Toward a Womanist Hermeneutic: A Reading of Judges 19–21." In *A Feminist Companion to Judges*, Vol. 4, edited by Athalya Brenner, pp. 172–186. New York: Continuum, 1993.

Junior, Nyasha. "Womanist Biblical Interpretation." In *Engaging the Bible in a Gendered World: An Introduction to Feminist Biblical Interpretation in Honor of Katharine Doob Sakenfield*, edited by Linda M. Day and Carolyn Pressler, pp. 57–46. Louisville, Ky.: Westminster John Knox, 2006.

Kirk-Duggan, Cheryl A. "Let My People Go! Threads of Exodus in African American Narratives." In *Yet with a Steady Beat: Contemporary U.S. Afrocentric Biblical Interpretation*, edited by Randall C. Bailey, pp. 123–143. Atlanta: Society of Biblical Literature, 2003.

Kirk-Duggan, Cheryl A. *The Sky Is Crying: Race, Class, and Natural Disaster.* Nashville, Tenn.: Abingdon, 2006.

Kirk-Duggan, Cheryl A., and Tina Pippin, eds. *Mother Goose, Mother Jones, Mommie Dearest: Biblical Mothers and Their Children.* Semeia Studies 61. Atlanta: Society of Biblical Literature, 2009.

Lawrence-Lightfoot, Sara. "Katie Cannon: The Fruit of My Labor." In *I've Known Rivers: Lives of Loss and Liberation*, pp. 15–107. Reading, Mass.: Addison-Wesley, 1994.

Martin, Clarice J. "Womanist Interpretations of the New Testament: The Quest for Holistic and Inclusive Translation and Interpretation." *Journal of Feminist Studies in Religion* 6, no. 2 (1990): 41–61.

Martin, Clarice J. "The Haustafeln (Household Codes) in African American Biblical Interpretation: 'Free Slaves' and 'Subordinate Women'." In *Stony the Road We Trod: African American Biblical Interpretation*, edited by Cain Hope Felder, pp. 206–231. Minneapolis: Fortress, 1991.

Martin, Clarice J. "Womanist Biblical Interpretation." In *Dictionary of Biblical Interpretation*, Vol. 2, edited by John H. Hayes, pp. 655–658. Nashville, Tenn.: Abingdon, 1999.

Page, Hugh, ed. *The Africana Bible: Reading Israel's Scriptures from Africa and the African Diaspora*. Minneapolis: Fortress, 2009.

Phillips, Layli, ed. *The Womanist Reader: The First Quarter Century of Womanist Thought*. New York: Routledge, 2006.

Smith, Mitzi J. "'Unbossed and Unbought': Zilpha Elaw and Old Elizabeth and a Political Discourse of Origins." *Black Theology: An International Journal* 9, no. 3 (2011): 287–311.

Smith, Mitzi J. "'Give Them What You Have': A Womanist Reading of the Matthean Feeding Miracle (Matt 14:13–21)." *Journal of the Bible and Human Transformation* 3/1 (September 2013). http://www.bibleandtransformation.com/JBHT/Volume_3_(2013)_files/JBHT%203%201%20Smith.pdf (accessed 14 October, 2013).

Smith, Mitzi J., and Lalitha Jayachitra, eds. *Teaching All Nations: Interrogating the Great Commission*. Minneapolis: Fortress, 2014.

St. Clair, Raquel A. "Womanist Biblical Interpretation." In *True to Our Native Land: An African American New Testament Commentary*, edited by Brian K. Blount pp. 54–62. Minneapolis: Fortress, 2007.

St. Clair, Raquel A. *Call and Consequences: A Womanist Reading of Mark*. Minneapolis: Fortress, 2008.

Townes, Emilie M. "The Womanist Dancing Mind: Speaking to the Expansiveness of Womanist Discourse." In *Deeper Shades of Purple: Womanism in Religion and Society*, edited by Stacey M. Floyd-Thomas, pp. 236–247. New York: New York University Press, 2006.

Travis, Irene S. "Love Your Mother: A Lesbian Womanist Reading of Scripture." In *Take Back the Word: A Queer Reading of the Bible*, edited by Robert E. Goss and Mona West, pp. 35–42. Cleveland, Ohio: Pilgrim, 2000.

Trible, Phyllis. *Texts of Terror: Literary-Feminist Readings of Biblical Narratives (Overtures to Biblical Theology)*. Philadelphia: Fortress, 1984.

Walker, Alice. *In Search of Our Mothers' Gardens: Womanist Prose*. San Diego, Calif.: Harcourt Brace Jovanovich, 1983.

Weems, Renita J. *Just a Sister Away: A Womanist Vision of Women's Relationships in the Bible*. San Diego, Calif.: LuraMedia, 1988.

Weems, Renita J. "Reading Her Way through the Struggle: African American Women and the Bible." In *Stony the Road We Trod: African American Biblical Interpretation*, edited by Cain Hope Felder, pp. 57–77. Minneapolis: Fortress, 1991.

Weems, Renita J. "Womanist Reflections on Biblical Hermeneutics." In *Black Theology: A Documentary History*, Vol. 2: *1980–1992*, edited by James H. Cone and Gayraud S. Wilmore, pp. 216–224. Maryknoll, N.Y.: Orbis, 1993.

Weems, Renita J. *Battered Love: Marriage, Sex, and Violence in the Hebrew Prophets*. Minneapolis: Fortress, 1995.

Weems, Renita J. *Just a Sister Away: Understanding the Timeless Connection between Women of Today and Women of the Bible*. West Bloomfield, Mich.: Walk Worthy, 2005.

Valerie Bridgeman

Topical Outline of Contents

Entries in the body of *The Oxford Encyclopedia of the Bible and Gender Studies* are organized alphabetically. This outline provides an overview of the conceptual scheme of the *Encyclopedia*. Entries and subentries are arranged according to the following topical headings:

Gender Theory
History and Method
Across the Biblical Canon
Social World

GENDER THEORY

Gender
Heteronormativity/Heterosexism
Homosexual/Queer
Patriarchy/Kyriarchy

Queer Theory
Sexuality
Sexual Transgression
Transgender/Third Gender/Transsexualism

HISTORY AND METHOD

Asian/Asian American Interpretation
Disability Studies
Feminism
   First-Wave Feminism
   Second-Wave Feminism
   Third-Wave Feminism
Gay Liberation
Historical-Critical Approaches
Intersectional Studies

Linguistic Turn Approaches
Masculinity Studies
Mujerista Criticism
Postcolonial Approaches
Queer Readings
Reader-Oriented Criticism
Rhetorical-Hermeneutical Criticism
Social-Scientific Approaches
Womanist Criticism

ACROSS THE BIBLICAL CANON

Authors of Biblical Books
Canon/Canonicity/
   Canonization
Creation
Imagery, Gendered
   Priestly Material
   Deuteronomistic History

Prophetic Literature
Wisdom Literature
Apocalyptic Literature
Gospels
Pauline Literature
Jesus
Paul

SOCIAL WORLD

Directory of Contributors

Valerie Abrahamsen

Independent Scholar

Same-Sex Relations: Early Church

Susan Ackerman

Dartmouth College

Religious Participation: Hebrew Bible

Mika Ahuvia

Princeton University

Popular Religion and Magic: Early Judaism
Sexual Violence: Early Judaism

James K. Aitken

Faculty of Divinity, University of Cambridge

Race, Class, and Ethnicity: Early Judaism

Annalisa Azzoni

Vanderbilt University

Marriage and Divorce: Hebrew Bible

Jon L. Berquist

Disciples Seminary Foundation, Claremont School of Theology

Family Structures: Hebrew Bible

Julye Bidmead

Chapman University

Legal Status: Ancient Near East

Marianne Blickenstaff

Westminster John Knox Press

Sexual Violence: New Testament

Valerie Bridgeman

Methodist Theological School of Ohio

Womanist Criticism

David Brodsky

Brooklyn College

Same-Sex Relations: Early Judaism

Pierre Brulé

University of Rennes 2, France, Emeritus

Children: Greek World

Sean D. Burke

Religion Department, Luther College

Gender Transgression: New Testament

Gay L. Byron

Howard University School of Divinity

Race, Class, and Ethnicity: Early Church

Jared C. Calaway

University of Mississippi

Popular Religion and Magic: New Testament

Lauren Caldwell

Wesleyan University

Legal Status: Roman World

Eva Cantarella

University of Milan

Marriage and Divorce: Greek World

Greg Carey

Lancaster Theological Seminary

Imagery, Gendered: Apocalyptic Literature

Damien Casey

Australian Catholic University

Religious Leaders: Late Antiquity

Agnes Choi

Department of Religion, Pacific Lutheran University Washington

Economics: Early Church

Jin Young Choi

Colgate Rochester Crozer Divinity School

Asian/Asian American Interpretation

Laliv Clenman

Leo Baeck College, U.K.; Department of Theology and Religious Studies, King, College London

Sexual Transgression: Early Judaism

L. Stephanie Cobb

Department of Religious Studies, University of Richmond

Masculinity and Femininity: Early Church

Anthony Corbeill

University of Kansas

Same-Sex Relations: Roman World

Kathleen E. Corley

Department of Religious Studies and Anthropology, University of Wisconsin–Oshkosh

Jesus

Mary Rose D'Angelo

Notre Dame University

Marriage and Divorce: New Testament

Lynne St. Clair Darden

The Interdenominational Theological Center

Race, Class, and Ethnicity: New Testament

Steed Vernyl Davidson

Pacific Lutheran Theological Seminary; Church Divinity School of the Pacific

Authors of Biblical Books

Peggy L. Day

University of Winnipeg

Deity: Hebrew Bible

Susan Deacy

Department of Humanities, University of Roehampton, U.K.

Sexual Violence: Greek World

Michal Beth Dinkler

Yale Divinity School

Imagery, Gendered: Gospels

Musa W. Dube

Department of Theology and Religious Studies, University of Botswana

Reader-Oriented Criticism

Carrie Elaine Duncan

Department of Religious Studies, University of Missouri–Columbia

Economics: Early Judaism

Benjamin H. Dunning

Fordham University

Sexual Transgression: New Testament

Susan Grove Eastman

Duke University Divinity School

Imagery, Gendered: Pauline Literature

Kathy Ehrensperger

University of Wales, Trinity Saint David

Paul

Neil Elliott

Fortress Press

Economics: New Testament

Erin E. Fleming

Department of Near Eastern Studies, Johns Hopkins University

Children: Ancient Near East
Creation
Education: Ancient Near East

Carole R. Fontaine

Department of Bible and Proclamation, Andover Newton Theological School

Imagery, Gendered: Wisdom Literature

Chris Frilingos

Department of Religious Studies, Michigan State University

Children: New Testament

Kathy L. Gaca

Department of Classical Studies, Vanderbilt University

Male-Female Sexuality: Early Church

Kathleen Gallagher Elkins

Department of Religious Studies, St. Norbert College

Social Interaction: Early Church

Gary Gilbert

Claremont McKenna College

Social Interaction: Early Judaism

Anne Goddeeris

Katholieke Universiteit Leuven, Belgium

Economics: Ancient Near East

Elizabeth W. Goldstein

Department of Religious Studies, Gonzaga University

Imagery, Gendered: Priestly Material

Deirdre Good

General Theological Seminary

Deity: New Testament

Rhiannon Graybill

Department of Religious Studies, Rhodes College

Male-Female Sexuality: Hebrew Bible

Leticia Guardiola-Saenz

Seattle University

Mujerista Criticism

Deryn Guest

University of Birmingham

Gender Transgression: Hebrew Bible

Susan E. Haddox

University of Mount Union

Masculinity and Femininity: Hebrew Bible

Judith P. Hallett

Department of Classics, University of Maryland

Family Structures: Roman World

Pauline Hanesworth

Higher Education Academy, Scotland

Popular Religion and Magic: Greek World

Judith Hauptman

Jewish Theological Seminary

Legal Status: Early Judaism

Rachel Havrelock

Department of English, University of Illinois at Chicago

Political Leadership: Hebrew Bible

Richard Hawley

Department of Classics, Royal Holloway, University of London

Family Structures: Greek World

Karina Martin Hogan

Department of Theology, Fordham University

Children: Early Judaism

James N. Hoke

Drew University

Social Interaction: Greek and Roman Worlds

Teresa J. Hornsby

Drury University

Heteronormativity/Heterosexism Sexuality

Thomas K. Hubbard

University of Texas, Austin

Same-Sex Relations: Greek World

Lynn R. Huber

Department of Religious Studies, Elon University

Same-Sex Relations: New Testament

Susan E. Hylen

Emory University

Political Leadership: New Testament

Tal Ilan

Freie Universität Berlin

Religious Leaders: Early Judaism

Ann Jeffers

Department of Theology, Heythrop College, University of London

Popular Religion and Magic: Hebrew Bible

Marguerite Johnson

University of Newcastle, Australia

Masculinity and Femininity: Roman World

Philip Jones

University of Pennsylvania

Social Interaction: Ancient Near East

Marianne Bjelland Kartzow

University of Oslo

Intersectional Studies

Sarit Kattan Gribetz

Fordham University

Education: Early Judaism

Michele Kennerly

Department of Communication Arts & Sciences, Penn State University

Education: Roman World

Gwynn Kessler

Department of Religion, Swarthmore College

Transgender/Third Gender/Transsexualism

Bradford A. Kirkegaard

San Diego State University

Male-Female Sexuality: Roman World

Jennifer L. Koosed

Religious Studies Department, Albright College

Children: Hebrew Bible

Ross S. Kraemer

Department of Religious Studies and Program in Judaic Studies, Brown University

Religious Participation: Early Judaism

Christian Laes

Universiteit Antwerpen

Children: Roman World

Julie Langford

University of South Florida

Marriage and Divorce: Roman World

Joshua L. Langseth

Coe College

Deity: Roman World

Lillian I. Larsen

Department of Religious Studies, University of Redlands

Education: Early Church

Justin Marc Lasser

Manchester University, Indiana

Popular Religion and Magic: Early Church

Outi Lehtipuu

University of Helsinki

Religious Leaders: Early Church

Sarra Lev

Reconstructionist Rabbinical College

Gender Transgression: Early Judaism

Nicola Denzey Lewis

Department of Religious Studies, Brown University

Popular Religion and Magic: Roman World

Lynn Lidonnici

Department of Religion, Vassar College

Religious Participation: Greek World

Tat-siong Benny Liew

Department of Religious Studies, College of the Holy Cross

Postcolonial Approaches

Yii-Jan Lin

Pacific School of Religion

Male-Female Sexuality: New Testament

Hilary Lipka

University of New Mexico

Sexual Transgression: Hebrew Bible
Sexual Violence: Ancient Near East

B. Diane Lipsett

Salem College

Marriage and Divorce: Early Church

Davina C. Lopez

Eckerd College

Historical-Critical Approaches

Vanessa L. Lovelace

The Interdenominational Theological Center

Religious Leaders: Hebrew Bible

Stuart Macwilliam

University of Exeter, U.K.

Queer Readings

F. Rachel Magdalene

Institut für Alttestamentliche Wissenschaft, University of Leipzig

Legal Status: Hebrew Bible

Herbert Robinson Marbury

Vanderbilt Divinity School

Race, Class, and Ethnicity: Hebrew Bible

Joseph A. Marchal

Ball State University

Homosexual/Queer

John W. Marshall

University of Toronto

Sexual Violence: Roman World

John W. Martens

Department of Theology, University of St. Thomas

Children: Early Church

Denise Eileen McCoskey

University of Miami

Race, Class, and Ethnicity: Greek World

Fiona McHardy

Department of Humanities, University of Roehampton

Sexual Violence: Greek World

Tirzah Meacham (leBeit Yoreh)

University of Toronto

Male-Female Sexuality: Early Judaism

Melvin G. Miller

New Testament and Early Christian Studies, University of South Africa

Children: Early Church

Kristina Milnor

Department of Classics and Ancient Studies, Barnard College

Political Leadership: Roman World

Stephen D. Moore

The Theological School, Drew University

Masculinity Studies

Melissa Mueller

Department of Classics, University of Massachusetts Amherst

Economics: Greek World

Susan E. Myers

University of St. Thomas

Deity: Early Church

Alicia D. Myers

United Theological Seminary

Religious Participation: New Testament

Bronwen Neil

Australian Catholic University

Religious Leaders: Late Antiquity

Surekha Nelavala

Lutheran Theological Seminary at Gettysburg

Feminism: Third-Wave Feminism

Julia M. O'Brien

Lancaster Theological Seminary

Imagery, Gendered: Prophetic Literature

Jorunn Økland

University of Oslo

Canon/Canonicity/Canonization

Rosanna S. Omitowoju

University of Cambridge

Sexual Transgression: Greek World

Vassiliki Panoussi

College of William & Mary

Race, Class, and Ethnicity: Roman World

Heather D. D. Parker

Department of Near Eastern Studies, Johns Hopkins University

Education: Ancient Near East

Ioanna Patera

Harvard University

Religious Leaders: Greek World

Laurie E. Pearce

University of California, Berkeley

Family Structures: Ancient Near East

Heike Peckruhn

Iliff School of Theology, Contingent Faculty

Disability Studies

Ilan Peled

The Hebrew University of Jerusalem

Religious Leaders: Ancient Near East

Todd Penner

Austin College

Historical-Critical Approaches

Walter D. Penrose Jr.

San Diego State University

Gender Transgression: Greek World

Pheme Perkins

Boston College

Education: New Testament

Matthew J. Perry

John Jay College of Criminal Justice

Economics: Roman World

Taylor G. Petrey

Kalamazoo College

Sexual Transgression: Early Church

Christina Petterson

University of Newcastle, Australia

Linguistic Turn Approaches

Daniele Pevarello

Trinity College Dublin

Education: Greek World

Gillian Ramsey

University of Toronto

Political Leadership: Greek World

David M. Reis

Department of Religious Studies, University of Oregon

Legal Status: Early Church
Religious Leaders: Roman World

Helen Rhee

Department of Religious Studies, Westmont College

Family Structures: Early Church

Lynn E. Roller

University of California, Davis

Deity: Greek World

Deborah W. Rooke

University of Oxford

Patriarchy/Kyriarchy

Robert M. Royalty Jr.

Department of Religion, Wabash College

Political Leadership: Early Church

Timothy J. Sandoval

Brite Divinity School, Texas Christian University

Education: Hebrew Bible

Deborah F. Sawyer

Independent Scholar

Gender

Susanne Scholz

Southern Methodist University

Feminism: Second-Wave Feminism

Joy A. Schroeder

Trinity Lutheran Seminary, Capital University

Sexual Violence: Early Church

Elisabeth Schüssler Fiorenza

Harvard Divinity School

Rhetorical-Hermeneutical Criticism

Jo-Ann Scurlock

Department of History, Elmhurst College

Popular Religion and Magic: Ancient Near East
Religious Participation: Ancient Near East
Religious Participation: Sacred Prostitution

Robert Seesengood

Albright College

Masculinity and Femininity: New Testament

Claudia Setzer

Manhattan College

Feminism: First-Wave Feminism

Cynthia Shafer-Elliott

William Jessup University

Economics: Hebrew Bible

Katherine A. Shaner

*Wake Forest University School
of Divinity*

Family Structures: New Testament

Sarah Shectman

Independent Scholar

Marriage and Divorce: Ancient Near East

Robert E. Shore-Goss

MCC in the Valley

Gay Liberation

Giulia Sissa

University of California, Los Angeles

Male-Female Sexuality: Greek World

Robert N. Stegmann

*Department of Theology and Christian
Ministry, Cornerstone Institute; Department
of Old and New Testament, Stellenbosch
University, South Africa*

Legal Status: New Testament

Darja Šterbenc Erker

Humboldt-Universität zu Berlin

Religious Participation: Roman World

David Tabb Stewart

*Department of Religious Studies, California State
University, Long Beach*

Same-Sex Relations: Hebrew Bible

Johanna Stiebert

Theology and Religious Studies, University of Leeds, U.K.

Social-Scientific Approaches

Jonathan Stökl

*Department of Theology and Religious Studies,
King's College London*

Religious Leaders: Ancient Near Eastern Prophecy

Ken Stone

Chicago Theological Seminary

Imagery, Gendered: Deuteronomistic History
Queer Theory

Terje Stordalen

University of Oslo

Canon/Canonicity/Canonization

Saana Svärd

University of Helsinki

Political Leadership: Ancient Near East

Diana M. Swancutt

*School of Theology, Boston University; Boston Poverty
Consortium*

Sexual Transgression: Overview

Eric Thurman

Sewanee: The University of the South

Gender Transgression: Roman World

J. Brian Tucker

Bible Department, Moody Theological Seminary

Religious Leaders: New Testament

Kristi Upson-Saia

Occidental College

Gender Transgression: Early Church

Shulamit Valler

Department of Jewish History, University of Haifa, Israel, Emeritus

Family Structures: Early Judaism
Marriage and Divorce: Early Judaism

Heather Vincent

Department of Classics, Eckerd College

Sexual Transgression: Roman World

Lily Vuong

Valdosta State University

Religious Participation: Early Church

Harold C. Washington

Saint Paul School of Theology

Sexual Violence: Hebrew Bible

Annette Weissenrieder

San Francisco Theological Seminary; Graduate Theological Union

Masculinity and Femininity: Greek World

Karri L. Whipple

Graduate Division of Religion, Drew University

Social Interaction: New Testament

Ilona Zsolnay

Babylonian Section, University of Pennsylvania Museum

Deity: Ancient Near East
Gender and Sexuality: Ancient Near East

INDEX

Page numbers in boldface refer to the main entry on the subject. Page numbers in italics refer to illustrations and tables.

in ancient Near East, **1:25–31**, 196
  as purpose of marriage, **1:**481
dedicated to temple service, **2:**206
in early church, **1:55–60; 2:**407
in early Judaism, **1:49–55**
  desire for male children, **1:**471
economic value of, **1:**123–124
in Greek world, **1:35–40**
  illegitimate in Athens, **1:**489
  legitimacy, **1:**208
Hebrew Bible on, **1:31–35**
as investment in antiquity, **1:**219
monetary value of vows related to, **1:**122–123, *122*
New Testament on, **1:44–49**
obligations in early Christian families, **1:**229–230
in Roman world, **1:40–44**
  expectation for, **1:**133
  paterfamilias, **1:**131, 212
  remaining with father after divorce, **1:**418, 494
  understood as being irrational and wild, **1:**231
sexual abuse of
  early Christian writers on, **2:**407
  early church and, **2:**380
socialization of, **1:**120
  patriarchy and, **2:**5–6
China
  ancestor worship in, **1:**4
  influence on biblical interpretation, **1:**1–2
Chireau, Yvonne, **2:**434
Chloe, **2:**47
  leadership by, **2:**150
Christ and the Homosexual (Wood), **1:**257
"Christ for African Women, The" (Oduyoye and Amoah), **2:**158
Christian community imagery
  familial images, **1:**375
  gendered imagery for, **1:**375–377
  national-religious images, **1:**376
  pastoral images, **1:**375–376
Christianity, early. *See* early Christianity
Christianity, Social Tolerance, and Homosexuality (Boswell), **1:**47, 257, 258; **2:**298
Christians, early
  development of masculine gendered identities, **1:**434

executions in Roman Empire, **1:**432–433
failure to achieve masculine status according to Romans, **1:**432
as new race, **2:**148
objections to same-sex relations and prostitution, **1:**43
opposition to *paidophthoreō*, **1:**46
Christologies
  in Asian/Asian American interpretation, **1:**6
  identifying Jesus with Wisdom, **1:**97
Christ the Educator (Clement of Alexandria), **1:**434
Chronicles
  exclusion and repression of the maternal body, **1:**440
  on judges, **2:**168
  reference to Asherah in, **1:**78
Chrysis, **2:**174
Church and the Homosexual, The (McNeill), **1:**257
church as bride of Christ, **1:**375
Chuza, **2:**42
Cicero
  on adultery, **2:**130
  on decline of rhetoric, **1:**173
  definition of *virtus*, **1:**523
  on education, **1:**172
  on funerary rituals, **2:**68–69
  on incest, **2:**322
  on religion, **2:**67–68, 178, 179
  on same-sex marriage, **2:**272, 286
  on self-mastery, **1:**300
  on superiority of Romans, **2:**136, 178
  on *vir* and *virtus*, **1:**535
  on women in political leadership, **2:**34
cinaedus, **1:**294–295, 303; **2:**318
  for male recipient of a sexual act, **1:**534
Cincinnatus as citizen-farmer, **1:**170
Cinna, **2:**322
circumcision, **1:**26
  as bodily sign of covenant, **1:**447
  defect and, **1:**106
  ethnicity/identity based on, **2:**118–121
  in Galatians
    conflict over, **1:**307; **2:**230
    as reconception of Israel, **1:**542–543
  as genital mutilation in Greco-Roman culture, **1:**307